Disrupting the British World, 1600-1980

Richard Brown

Published by Authoring History

http://richardjohnbr1066.wordpress.com/
https://sites.google.com/site/lookingathistory/

Resistance and Rebellion in the British Empire 1600-1980, (Clio Publishing), 2013.
ISBN-10 0955698383
ISBN-13: 978-0-9556983-8-5

Resistance and Rebellion in the British Empire 1600-1980, (Authoring History), 2013.
ASIN: B00EQFE538

Disrupting the British World 1600-1980, Second edition, (Authoring History), 2017.
ISBN-10: 1541336283
ISBN-13: 978-1541336285

Cover: 'A Rebel Negro armed & on his guard', Stedman, John Gabriel, *Narrative of a Five Years Expedition against the Revolted Negroes of Surinam between French Guiana and Guyana from the year 1772 to 1777,* 2 Vols. (J. Johnson), 1813, Vol. 2, p. 90.

The Rebellion Quartet

Three Rebellions: Canada, South Wales and Australia, Second edition, (Authoring History), 2016

Famine, Fenians and Freedom, 1830-1882, Second edition, (Authoring History), 2017

Disrupting the British World 1600-1980, Second edition, (Authoring History), 2017

Ireland, Revolution and Diaspora 1882-1923, (Authoring History), 2018

An empire founded by war has to maintain itself by war.

Charles de Montesquieu, *Considerations on the Causes of the Romans' Greatness and Decline*, 1734

For Margaret

Without whom none of this would have been possible and now a silent voice

Contents

Acknowledgements

This, the final volume of my *Rebellion Trilogy* on colonial rebellion and in its revised version the third volume of *Rebellion Quartet*, was initially researched and written after I retired from full-time teaching in 2006. Much of the writing took place in 2009 and 2010 and during the early months of 2011 though the first edition was not published until 2013. It owes much to numerous people whose ideas I have warrened for information and insights into this complex and contentious subject. As with the other books in the series, I must register my thanks to friends and colleagues for their support and forbearance in taking their work and moulding it to my own purposes. Writing a book that attempts to look at global issues would not have been possible without their pioneering work. Doing research and writing can be an isolating experience but for the comments of others and the sense of security you get from knowing that you are not alone in what you do.

Perhaps I was lucky to teach in a succession of schools where students were interested in learning and thinking about the past but I have always found them to be positive and disciplined in their approaches to study and responsive to both the story of the past and the different ways in which it can be viewed. I have nothing but good memories of the thousands of students I taught and tutored. Being a teacher remains one of the most fulfilling of the professions and, despite the vagaries of government initiatives (more in my thirty-four years in the classroom than I care to remember) and the increasingly target-oriented focus of learning, there is nothing more enjoyable than observing students learning to become critical in their approach to life at whatever academic level.

My greatest debt as always, however, is to my late wife Margaret who lived with my work all our married life. Without her whole-hearted support over these many long years I could never have carried out this project, let alone the others that I have undertaken, through to fruition. Dedicating this volume to her is so little when she gave me so much. Having support where it matters most has always been an essential part of the process of research and writing. It is easy to forget just what a sacrifice producing a book is for your partner when you are ensconced with your books and ideas pondering your next paragraph. Her kindly voice is now silent.

Abbreviations

ADB: *Australian Dictionary of Biography*, 18 Vols. (Melbourne University Press), 1966-.

Brown, Richard, *Famine, Fenians and Freedom*: Brown Richard, *Famine, Fenians and Freedom, 1840-1882*, (Clio Publishing), 2011; *Famine, Fenians and Freedom, 1830-1882*, (Authoring History), Second edition, 2017. References are to the second edition unless stated otherwise.

Brown, Richard, *Three Rebellions*: Brown, Richard, *Three Rebellions: Canada 1837-1838, South Wales 1839 and Victoria, Australia 1854*, (Clio Publishing), 2010; *Three Rebellions: Canada, South Wales and Australia*, second edition, (Authoring History), 2016. References are to the second edition unless stated otherwise.

CHR: *Canadian Historical Review*

DCB: *Canadian Dictionary of Biography*, 22 Vols. (University of Toronto-Université Laval), 1966-2014.

HRA, *Historical Records of Australia*, Series I, Governors' despatches to and from England, 1788-1848, 26 Vols. (Government Printer), 1914-1925, also available as a searchable CD, (Archive CD Books Australia), 2009. No Series II. Series III: *Historical Records of Australia*, Series III, Despatches and papers relating to the settlement of the states, 6 Vols. (Government Printer), 1921-1923, also available as a searchable CD, (Archive CD Books Australia), 2012. Series IV: *Historical Records of Australia*, Series IV, Legal papers, 1 Vol. (Government Printer), 1922.

HRA, Resumed Series III: *Historical Records of Australia*, Resumed Series III, 3 Vols. (Melbourne University Press), 1997-

HRNSW: *Historical Records of New South Wales*, 7 Vols. (Charles Potter, Government Printer), 1892-1901, also available as a searchable CD, (Archive CD Books Australia), 2010.

HRNZ: *Historical Records of New Zealand*, 2 Vols. (J. Mackay, Govt. Printer), 1908-1914.

NSW: New South Wales.

NZ: New Zealand.

OHBE: Louis, Wm. Roger, (General Editor), *Oxford History of the British Empire*, 5 Vols. (Oxford University Press), 1998-1999.

VDL: Van Diemen's Land.

WA: Western Australia.

Preface

Although I was not aware of it at the time, I grew up with stories of colonial rebellion. Looking at grainy photographs of the Pyramids, I did not realise that they and the stories about Egypt originated during the Suez crisis of 1956 or that tales about almond trees and the Troodos Mountains were memories of Cyprus in 1958 during the EOKA campaign that officially claimed the lives of over a hundred British military personnel. It was only later when I watched events unfold in Prague in August 1968 that I began to understand both the nature of colonial rebellion and imperial repression, for that is what the 'Prague Spring' undoubtedly was. Colonial rule, however benign, always becomes unbearable and provokes resistance and, unless the issues of those suffering colonial oppression are recognised, understood and addressed, rebellion.

Before and after 1800, slaves, transported convicts, native peoples and settlers were, perhaps inevitably, antagonised by the increasingly intrusive British colonial administration. There was an unrelenting series of military and naval interventions touching every part of the globe to increase the scale of Empire, to defend Britain's national interests and to combat resistance and rebellion. Although English liberties were transplanted to Britain's colonies, whether of a settler or non-settler character, that transplantation was rarely uncontested as those with political power or wealth argued that the process should be slowed until colonies were 'sufficiently mature' to benefit from English legal principles while some individuals and groups were deliberately excluded from this constitutional largesse.[1] Commerce, Christianity and Civilisation threatened peoples who already had their own versions of trade, religion and culture but who were regarded by white settlers and officials as racially, morally and politically inferior. Where peoples were deprived of their freedom, stripped of their rights, exploited for their labour and resources and excluded from colonial political and institutional processes, colonial oppression provided the grounds in which resistance and rebellion took root and flowered. Those who took part in rebellions sought to change intolerable and unacceptable socio-economic and cultural systems by force rather than by reform or passive resistance. That resistance was frequently contained and rebellion eventually crushed, reflected the realities of colonial rule, the dominance and discipline of British armed force. Hilaire Belloc put it with brutal simplicity:

Whatever happens we have got
The Maxim Gun, and they have not.[2]

To Edgar Wallace's fictional Sanders of the River, the Maxim guns rattled out the signature tune of Empire: 'Ha-ha-ha-ha-ha-ha-ha-ha!' as they taught

---

[1] On the question of exclusion see, Greene, Jack, P., (ed.), *Exclusionary Empire: English Liberties Overseas 1600-1900*, (Cambridge University Press), 2009.

[2] Belloc, Hilaire, *The Modern Traveller*, (Edward Arnold), 1898, p. 41. See also the discussion of the Maxim gun in MacDonald, Robert, H., *The Language of Empire: myths and metaphors in popular imperialism, 1880-1918*, (Manchester University Press), 1994, pp. 25-26

Sanders' Africans another lesson.[3] Rebellion, even if it led to a temporary reverse in Britain's military might, was followed by repression as any surviving leaders were tried and punished but in their deaths or exile provided a legacy of colonial resistance that was taken up by subsequent generations.[4]

My two previous books on colonial rebellions have concentrated on developments in Britain, Canada and Australia between the 1830s and 1880s.[5] This volume explores anti-colonial rebellions within the British Empire in a broader chronological and geographical perspective using examples from the seventeenth through to the twentieth century. In addition, 'rebellion' is a broad concept encompassing resistance to the authorities as well as direct action. The opening chapter examines the development and nature of Britain's burgeoning Empire from its origins in the seventeenth century, how it was peopled and governed. Chapter 2 considers the ways in which colonial authorities treated native peoples in Virginia, Australia and New Zealand in their quest for greater access to land and why that treatment, whether legalised by treaty or purchase or by brutal expropriation led to resistance and rebellion. Chapter 3 looks at the question of slavery in the British Empire and the nature of slave resistance and rebellion especially, in Africa and the 'middle passage', in the American colonies, the West Indies and in Mauritius. Although the slave trade was abolished in the British Empire in 1807 and slaves were emancipated after 1833, the results of slavery continued to be a problem and a cause of discontent and disturbance as can be seen in the Morant Bay rebellion in Jamaica in 1865.

Chapter 4 explores the question of convict labour. New South Wales and Van Diemen's Land were the only parts of the British Empire that was specifically founded as penal colonies, something later extended to Western Australia. Convicts proved to be a volatile group whose ability to resist colonial authorities was considerable and who in 1804 rose in rebellion in NSW. However, transportation of convicts was also an important feature of Britain's Empire before the establishment of NSW in 1788 and was used in other parts of the Empire especially in the nineteenth century. Their use in Singapore and the Andaman Islands is examined. Slaves and convicts satisfied the needs of the Empire for workers but indentured labour enjoyed a revival in the decades after 1834 as Asian and Pacific workers especially migrated to areas where there remained a need for cheap labour. Although there was less resistance among

---

[3] Wallace, Edgar, *Sanders of the River*, (Ward Lock), 1911, p. 164. The use of the Maxim gun as a signature tune is also evident in his *Sanders*, (Hodder & Stoughton), 1926, pp. 129, 138.

[4] For the development and methodology of global history, see Crossley, Pamela Kyle, *What is Global History?*, (Polity Press), 2008, Bayly, Christopher, 'History and World History', in Rublack, Ulinka, (ed.), *A Concise Companion to History*, (Oxford University Press), 2011, pp. 3-26, and Osterhammel, Jürgen, 'World History', in Schneider, Axel, and Woolf, Daniel, (eds.), *The Oxford History of Historical Writing, Volume 5: Historical Writing since 1945*, (Oxford University Press), 2011, pp. 93-112. Bentley, Jerry H., (ed.), *The Oxford Handbook of World History*, (Oxford University Press), 2011, provides a synthesis of current thinking.

[5] Brown, Richard, *Three Rebellions: Canada 1837-1838, South Wales 1839 and Victoria, Australia 1854*, (Clio Publishing), 2010, and *Famine, Fenians and Freedom 1840-1882*, (Clio Publishing), 2011.

these workers than among slaves and convicts, disruption was not uncommon when the terms of indentures were breached or workers were unjustifiably exploited. Increasingly, however, there was resistance among white settlers to these 'economic migrants' that led to the emergence of racist policies to restrict both the number of migrants and especially their rights, issues discussed in Chapter 5.

Chapters 6-8 examine rebellions that had specific causes though underlying them all was a growing contempt for colonial rule. Taxing goods, such as tea or property or land have historically been the ways by which the state raised revenue. Taxation is never popular but its ability to magnify grievances was especially evident in Britain's colonies where its arbitrary nature and frequently inept implementation led to rebellion and, in the case of the American colonies, to revolution. In the context of the British Empire, taxation was frequently seen by those affected as unfair and exploitative. The consequences of this were seen across the Empire in the American colonies and in Africa and are examined in greater detail in Chapter 6. The inexorable pressure of Empire and the loss of hope especially among native peoples created an environment where millenarian movements, which sought to transform the world and liberate people from colonial oppression, could thrive. For the Xhosa in South Africa, the Māori and the Métis in Canada, the belief in the imminence of a divine kingdom and the importance of prophets led to resistance to imperial rule and is considered in Chapter 7. The role of nationality and nationalism in challenging the hegemony of colonial power and calls for independence from imperial authority in Cyprus, Kenya and Southern Rhodesia forms the basis of Chapter 8. Ultimately, the most successful form of resistance since it contributed to the collapse of Britain's imperial ambitions, nationalist movements drew on ethnic or tribal identity and an often imprecise and ambiguous concept of 'nationhood'. Yet the 'armed struggle' often proved far less effective or significant in achieving independence than the subsequent rhetoric and emerging mythologies of liberation movements suggest. Decolonisation was the result less of military resistance than political negotiation between British governments that were prepared to agree to independence and nationalist politicians who were eager to take the reins of power in post-colonial constitutions.

The final rebellion, if that is what it was, occurred in NSW in early 1808 when Governor William Bligh was arrested and removed from power by a combination of military and settler action is examined in Chapter 9. It expressed the Lockean right of resistance to tyrannical authority and was, in many respects, a rebellion within the colony's governing élite. Its epithet, the 'Rum' Rebellion, was not given until almost half a century later but, as historians later argued, it had nothing to do with rum and could hardly be called a rebellion. Unlike the other rebellions explored in this volume, it was neither populist nor violent; it was a very British coup. The last chapter draws together the discussion of different types of colonial resistance and rebellion and provides an explanation of how they can be explained in terms of institutional structures, relationships between colonists and colonised and motives and opportunities and reconsiders the place of 'borderlands' in explaining the incidence of resistance and rebellion.

Preface: Second Edition

The first edition of ***Resistance and Rebellion*** was completed in 2011 and finally published early in 2013. In the intervening years, I have continued to grapple with the issues raised in the original volume publishing more detailed discussion of rebellion in Britain, Canada and Australia. Unlike the other two volumes in the original *Trilogy*, I have made few changes to the structure of the original text other than removing the section on Eureka Stockade in Victoria from the chapter on tax rebellions because I have written about this extensively in subsequent work.[1] Preparing this second edition for publication has given me the opportunity to revisit the original material and take account of the most recent research and publications. I have delved further into newspapers from Britain and Ireland and Australia and New Zealand and have added further references to them. The British provincial press had often detailed coverage of colonial issues–generally based on reports from national newspapers–indicating that there was a nationwide awareness of current colonial issues. Unless stated otherwise, all footnotes that cite *Three Rebellions* or *Famine, Fenians and Freedom* refer to their second editions.

I have, however, changed its title to *Disrupting the British World 1600-1980*. For two decades, the notion of the 'British World' has played a significant role in helping define and refine the postcolonial view of the formal British Empire as an empire of exploitation, slavery, racism and cultural annihilation. Yet it could also be an empire of conscience that recognised the folly of the slave trade that it had done so much to develop and then made its end a central tenet of policy. It has taken the debate beyond the physical confines of those regions of the map coloured red through the broad themes of diaspora, culture and identity has led to a variety of interpretations about how that 'world' was imagined. This opening-up of a postcolonial narrative focuses on the shifting patterns of connection and interdependence and aspirations and emotions of ordinary people caught up in the oft-tragic emergence of modernity and the suffering spread in the inexorable if 'jittery' development of the imperial project. This book emphases the centrality of the marginal, the exploited and the working-classes as a disruptive force in shaping the 'British World', to conjure up new visions of society, articulate their aspirations and be active participants in changing society. This reflects the need to look beyond political and economic élites and explore the aspirations of those caught up in imperial modernity and the ways in which their view 'from below' contributed to the making of modernity, capitalism and globalisation.

---

[1] Of importance, has been my discussion of Eureka in my *Settler Australia, 1780-1880, Volume 2: Eureka and Democracy*, (Authoring History), 2013 and *Three Rebellions*, second edition.

Chapter 1 Forging and losing an Empire

To found a great Empire for the sole purpose of raising up a people of customers, may at first sight appear a project fit only for a nation of shopkeepers. It is, however, a project altogether unfit for a nation of shopkeepers; but extremely fit for a nation that is governed by shopkeepers.[1]

The British Empire, like all empires, was born in violence and sustained by it.[2] Death was an ever-present theme across the centuries from the settlers who succumbed to tropical diseases, the natives with no immunity to imported diseases such as smallpox and influenza, the convicts and slaves whose blooded backs bore the burden of economic expansion to the indentured workers transported half way around the globe to labour or die in foreign climes. Resistance and rebellion and death were also endemic features of empire as convicts, slaves, nationalists and religious zealots sought to end the exploitation and expropriation of the imperial system. Whatever the benefits that empire brought, they were bought with the blood of the unfree, the oppressed, the racially degraded and those who fought for freedom from the shackles of imperial rule. No empire is benign and the British Empire from the seventeenth century through to its final implosion in the aftermath of the Second World War—an expansion characterised by its 'jerkiness', the spasmodic upheavals of settler energy--was no exception. But it was also an empire of movement as individuals and families, despite the physical perils, left Britain's shores temporarily or permanently escaping from the oppression, persecution and poverty of home to seek salvation, economic prosperity and political freedom in the 'new worlds' creating in its wake what had been called the 'British World'.[3]

---

[1] Smith, Adam, *An Inquiry into the Nature and Causes of the Wealth of Nations*, 2 Vols. (W. Strahan and T. Cadell), 1778, Vol. 2, p. 223.

[2] Burbank, Jane, and Cooper, Frederick, *Empire in World History Power and the Politics of Difference*, (Princeton University Press), 2010, Parsons, Timothy H., *The Rule of Empires: Those who built them, those who endured them, and why they always fall*, (Oxford University Press), 2010, Darwin, John, *After Tamberlane: The Global History of Empire*, (Allen Lane), 2007, and Morris, Ian, *Why the West Rules for Now: The patterns of history and what they reveal about the future*, (Profile Books), 2010, provide contrasting perspectives on the nature of empire.

[3] Louis, Wm. Roger, (General Editor), *Oxford History of the British Empire,* 5 Vols. (Oxford University Press), 1998-1999, and Marshall, P. J., (ed.), *Cambridge Illustrated History of the British Empire*, (Cambridge University Press), 1996, provide good overviews of Britain's imperial expansion and implosion. See also, Darwin, John, *The Empire Project: The Rise and Fall of the British World-System, 1830-1970*, (Cambridge University Press), 2009, Darwin, John. *Unfinished Empire: The Global; Expansion of Britain*, (Allen Lane), 2012, Ferguson, Niall, *Empire: The Rise and Demise of the British World Order and the Lessons for Global Power*, (Allen Lane), 2002, James, Lawrence, *The Rise and Fall of the British Empire*, (St Martin's Griffin), 1997, and Judd, Denis, *Empire: The British Imperial Experience, From 1765 to the Present*, (Harper Collins), 1996.

An empire of place

From its genesis to its eventual demise, the British Empire lasted over three hundred years and at its peak, included parts of every continent from small Caribbean colonies to the immensities of India, Australia and Canada; an empire on which the sun truly never set. Imperial aspirations were nothing new. England had been at the centre of the Norman Empire between 1106 and 1204 and its imperial ambitions had played a major part in its expansion and then defence of its French possessions during the Hundred Years War (1337-1453). In April 1533, in the Act in Restraint of Appeals that outlawed appeals from English courts to courts beyond the realm, Henry VIII had proclaimed the Crown of England to be 'Imperial' and the realm of England to be 'an Empire'.[4] Although regarded by some as an early expression of 'national sovereignty', 'empire' was used in its medieval sense of a territory that accepted no earthly authority superior to the Crown, including the Papacy and the Act declared England an independent country in every respect. Wales was integrated into this imperial polity in legislation passed in 1536 and 1542 when Ireland was also declared a kingdom and 'united and knit' to the 'Imperial Crown of the Realm of England'.[5] Later this came to be regarded as that of Great Britain with Scottish Union in 1707, then of the United Kingdom after Irish Union in 1801 and finally, the British Empire 'girding the globe'.

An English empire, 1600-1700

In the sixteenth century, the Crown had few resources to devote to overseas ventures.[6] England's imperial ambitions were largely internal with the incorporation of Wales and the union of the Protestant kingdoms of Scotland and England with the accession of James VI to the English throne on the death of Elizabeth I in 1603 and the eventual Act of Union in 1707. Catholic Ireland posed a different problem with its predominantly Roman Catholic population.[7] The solution was the attempted colonisation of the country by the 'plantation' of Protestant settlers from England, Scotland and Wales. Up to 100,000 people moved across the Irish Sea by 1641 to enhance agricultural production but also to civilise the backward Irish through religious conversion. English institutions were largely replicated in Ireland but its Parliament was reserved for Protestants. Irish Catholics became an important source of labour, but they were also a source of unrest and rebellion and, in alliance with Catholic France, a potential

[4] See, Koebner, Richard, 'The Imperial Crown of the Realm': Henry VIII, Constantine the Great and Polydore Vergil', *Historical Research*, Vol. 26, (1953), pp. 29-52.

[5] Although often called Acts of Union, the real engine of unification lay in Edward I's Statute of Rhuddlan of 1284 by which Wales was annexed to England.

[6] Armitage, David, *The Ideological Origins of the British Empire*, (Cambridge University Press), 2000, pp. 24-60.

[7] Ohlmeyer, Jane H., ''Civilizinge of those rude parts': Colonization within Britain and Ireland, 1580s-1640s', and Barnard, T. C., 'New Opportunities for British Settlement: Ireland, 1650-1700', *OHBE,* Vol. 1, pp. 124-147, 309-327.

threat to England's internal security.[8] Britain as an internal empire under English hegemony was of critical importance to the subsequent course of overseas empire building. Not only were significant sections of the Irish and Scottish aristocracy recruited to the ranks of Britain's imperial élite but Ireland served as a laboratory for the development of imperial strategies in areas such as the military, land administration and finance. It was merchants and chartered companies, sponsored and often partially financed by the Crown, that were at the forefront of developing trade links with Russia, the eastern Mediterranean and central Asia. From the outset, the Crown was an active participant rather than passive enabler in overseas trade and exploration. It acted in its imperial capacity; it took the position that it had:

> ...a legal, sovereign, prerogative, and imperial obligation to authorize, supervise, protect, and proclaim its overseas holdings, particularly when faced with challenges from other European colonising monarchs.[9]

The company model of empire with government charters defining monopolies and legitimising the private exercise of governmental functions played a major role in developing Britain's imperial ambitions.[10] The Levant Company, founded in 1581, established commercial links with the Ottoman Empire establishing an important Protestant-Muslim alliance against Catholic Europe.[11] India was colonised by a private company, the British East India Company founded in 1599 and which did not belong to the Crown until 1858.[12] The Company offered the Mughal Empire, a largely land-based power, direct links to important European markets from its fortified trading posts or 'factories' in Calcutta, Bombay and Madras. This enabled 'company men' to infiltrate Asian trading networks that proved highly lucrative. The ships of the East India

---

[8] Canny, Nicholas, 'Irish Resistance to Empire? 1641, 1690 and 1798', in Stone, Lawrence, (ed.), *An Imperial State at War: Britain from 1689 to 1815*, (Routledge), 1994, pp. 288-321.

[9] Macmillan, Ken, *Sovereignty and Possession in the English New World: The Legal Foundations of Empire, 1576-1640*, (Cambridge University Press), 2006, p. 6.

[10] Bown, Stephen R., *Merchant Kings: When Companies Ruled the World, 1600-1900*, (Thomas Dunne Books), 2010, pp. 1-6, 103-148, 193-290, examines the East India, Hudson's Bay and British South Africa Companies.

[11] Zahedieh, Nuala, 'Overseas Expansion and Trade in the Seventeeth Century', *OHBE*, Vol. 1, pp. 398-422, provides a general overview. Epstein, M., *The Early History of the Levant Company*, (Routledge), 1908, and Wood, A. C., *A History of the Levant Company*, (Oxford University Press), 1935, pp. 1-59.

[12] Lawson, Philip, *The East India Company*, (Longman), 1993, and Wild, Antony, *The East India Company: Trade and Conquest from 1600*, (Lyons Press), 2000, are good short studies. Chaudhuri, K. N., *The Trading World of Asia and the English East India Company, 1660-1760*, (Cambridge University Press), 2006, and Bowen, H. V., *The Business of Empire: The East India Company and Imperial Britain, 1756-1833*, (Cambridge University Press), 2006, provide greater detail. Stern, Philip J., *The Company-State: Corporate Sovereignty and the Early Modern Foundations of the British Empire in India*, (Oxford University Press), 2011, revises the standard narrative of the Company's history, that it was a commercial body to trade with Asia, that accidentally became a territorial state and empire in the mid-eighteenth century.

Company fleet traded mainly in bullion, textiles and tea with Bengal. It was not until the mid-eighteenth century that it challenged Mughal sovereignty and its coercive, administrative and financial processes resembled the power exercised by empires elsewhere. The Royal Africa Company, established in 1663, developed 'factories' in Africa and financed the development of the British slave trade with British colonies in the Caribbean supplying the slave labour necessary for the tobacco, rice and sugar plantations. Its monopoly was short-lived and in 1698 the Crown concluded that the interests of the plantation system were better served by allowing competition in supplying slaves.[13]

After 1606, the Virginia Company provided the capital that launched the settlement of North America. The Crown did not initiate this settlement but sought to control the process by limiting the company's role to possessing territory rather than the right to rule it.[14] The North American plantations were slow to develop and vulnerable. It was only after the company was wound up in 1625 that Virginia began to show a profit largely through the cultivation and export of tobacco. Critical in Britain's success in North America was the influx of immigrants on a larger scale than that by Spain to Spanish America: by 1700, some 250,000 people of European descent in British North America compared to 150,000 spread across the broader area of Spanish settlement.[15] Unlike the dramatic conquests of imperial Spain, British settlement was more gradual and less confrontational accepting that land had to be purchased from the Indians. In 1670, the Hudson's Bay Company was established by royal charter granting it a monopoly over the Indian trade especially in furs. It held some 1.5 million acres of land as Rupert's Land in northern Canada until it relinquished its ownership in 1868, two years before the company was finally abolished.[16] By 1686, these colonies shipped goods worth over £1 million to London. Exports to the colonies consisted mainly of woollen textiles; imports included sugar, tobacco and other tropical groceries for which there was growing consumer demand. In the Caribbean, Britain acquired Barbados in 1625 and Jamaica thirty years later. The islands were transformed by the development of sugar plantations and by the massive import of African slaves.[17]

Both proprietary and chartered colonies were methods of indirect rule by the Crown that gained the benefits of revenue through trade and taxation without

---

[13] Collins, E. D., *The Royal African Company: A Study of the English Trade to Western Africa under Chartered Companies from 1585 to 1750*, (Yale University Press), 1899, and Davies, K. G., *The Royal African Company*, (Longman, Green), 1957.

[14] See, ibid, Macmillan, Ken, *Sovereignty and Possession in the English New World: The Legal Foundations of Empire, 1576-1640*, pp. 6, 13. The Crown was 'especially concerned to ensure that its imperium, or independent and absolute sovereignty, and its dominium, or right to possess and rule territory under its jurisdiction, were fully and legally expressed'.

[15] Elliott, J. H., *Empires of the Atlantic World: Britain and Spain in America, 1492-1830*, (Yale University Press), 2006, provides a valuable comparative study.

[16] Willson, Beckles, *The Great Company (1667-1871): A History of the Honourable Company of Merchants-Adventurers Trading into Hudson's Bay*, (Smith, Elder and Company), 1900, and MacKay, D., *The Honourable Company: A History of the Hudson's Bay Company*, (Musson Book Co.), 1936.

[17] Beckles, Hilary McD., ''The Hub of Empire': The Caribbean and Britain in the Seventeenth Century', *OHBE,* Vol. 1, pp. 218-240, provides a succinct discussion.

the expense of direct administration. However, the Royal Charter identified the boundaries of companies' territory or influence and laid down their rights and responsibilities. Since charters were granted for a specific period before they had to be renewed, the Crown exerted considerable influence over companies' activities and, in the seventeenth and eighteenth centuries both proprietary and chartered colonies were converted into Royal colonies governed by officials appointed by the Crown rather than by private individuals or corporations. Apart from Connecticut and Rhode Island which maintained their chartered status until 1776, Virginia, the Carolinas, New Hampshire, New York, New Jersey and Georgia were brought under royal control. Although this occurred in Virginia in 1624, the movement against the chartered and proprietary colonies began in the 1670s under Charles II and lasted to 1729 when the Carolinas became royal provinces. Massachusetts was the first to fall a victim to this new policy, losing its original charter in 1684. New York followed in 1686, New Jersey in 1702 and the Carolinas passed into royal hands and the governments of Pennsylvania and Maryland were each taken from their respective proprietors for a short time. Georgia, founded in 1733, flourished as a proprietary colony for nineteen years and was then following the terms of its charter transferred to the Crown.[18]

This network of trading settlements provided the British state with the means to transform itself into what has been called a 'fiscal-military' polity.[19] It focussed on protecting sea-routes with high levels of taxation and strong banking institutions that financed large-scale spending by both public and private institutions.[20] English government sought to establish an institutional framework of governors, courts and a Board of Trade and Plantations to oversee trade but attempts by the Crown to tighten its control over the North American and Caribbean colonies in the 1670s and 1680s created tension over questions such as the right to set taxes that was to explode a century later. This fiscal-military state played no direct role in overseas trade but, through regulatory legislation ensured that the diverse elements of the nascent empire were linked directly to England. Navigation Acts in the 1650s and 1660s banned the import of Asian, African and American goods to Britain in foreign ships so that the country could benefit from the profits of the re-export trade.[21] This protectionism was linked to the gradual abandonment of state monopolies and their replacement with

[18] Nellis, Eric, *An Empire of Regions: A Brief History of Colonial British America*, (University of Toronto Press), 2010, provides an accessible articulate introduction. See also, Foster, Stephen, (ed.), *British North America in the Seventeeth and Eighteenth Centuries*, (Oxford University Press), 2013. Canny, Nicholas, and Morgan, Philip, (eds.), *The Oxford Handbook of the Atlantic World*, (Oxford University Press), 2011, Coffman, D'Maris, Leonard, Adrian and O'Reilly, William, (eds.), *The Atlantic World*, (Routledge), 2015, and Miller, Joseph, (ed.), *The Princeton Companion to Atlantic History*, (Princeton University Press), 2015, provide a comprehensive overview of Atlantic history.

[19] On the 'fiscal-military state', Brewer, John, *The Sinews of Power: War, Money and the English State, 1688-1783*, (Knopf), 1989, and the discussion in ibid, Stone, Lawrence, (ed.), *An Imperial State at War: Britain from 1689 to 1815*, pp. 1-32.

[20] Wennerlind, Carl, *Casualties of Credit: The English Financial Revolution, 1620-1720*, (Harvard University Press), 2011, pp. 17-44, 161-196.

[21] Wallerstein, I., *Mercantilism and the Consolidation of the European World-economy, 1600-1750*, (Academic Press), 1980, places English policy in its global context.

commercial competition. Although it regulated and taxed them, a less intrusive state had much to offer merchants and settlers and provided the financial and investment engines for economic growth during the eighteenth and early-nineteenth centuries. Imperial expansion in the sixteenth and seventeenth centuries gave far greater autonomy to settlers than did Britain's imperial rivals.

A global power, 1700-1815

Britain rose to a dominant commercial and military position among European trading empires during the long eighteenth century achieving maritime hegemony and economic dominance. Britain achieved this largely because of its relatively rapid rate of growth in per capita income and of international trade supported by a structural shift from agriculture to manufacturing.[22] By 1800, Britain was the world's richest economy and this combined with its military and especially naval dominance and its fiscal ability to fund conflict gave it a global geo-political hegemony that persisted until the outbreak of war in 1914. What made Britain different from its European rivals was not its extensive regulation of foreign trade, shipping and colonial economic activity, since mercantilist policies were pursued by most European nations. British mercantilism existed within a domestic framework of free market competition and private enterprise without parallels in Europe and had adopted a strategy on colonisation less dependent on direct governmental investment and administration in establishing and sustaining settler economies abroad.[23]

The need to provide centralised governance and supervision of established colonies was evident from the early-seventeenth century. The Virginia Charter in 1606 contemplated a separate Privy Council for colonial affairs though special commissioners were not appointed until 1634. For the remainder of the century, colonial affairs were managed by a succession of committees or Councils of State of the Privy Council.[24] In May 1696, a Board of Trade was established to manage colonial affairs and trade policy and from the early eighteenth century the Secretary of State for the Southern Department dealt with the colonies. In 1768, a Secretary of State for the American Department was appointed and, until the post and the Board of Trade were abolished in 1782 following the loss of the American colonies, dealt with colonial developments in British North America. Colonial affairs were briefly transferred to the Home Office but in 1786 the Privy Council for Trade and Plantations was re-established. In 1794, the new Secretary of War was also nominally Secretary for the Colonies though the departments were not united until 1801 by which time the Committee for Trade and the Plantations had ceased to exist.[25]

The form of government in royal, chartered and proprietary colonies was strikingly uniform with three institutions corresponding to the King and the two Houses of Parliament.[26] The Governor or Lieutenant-Governor was appointed

---

[22] On maritime history and empire, see O'Hara, Glenn, *Britain and the Sea since 1600*, (Palgrave Macmillan), 2010.

[23] O'Brien, Patrick, 'Inseparable Connections: Trade, Economy, Fiscal State and the Expansion of Empire 1688-1815', *OHBE*, Vol. 2, pp. 53-77.

[24] There were two Secretaries of State during the seventeenth century but there does not appear to have been the regular allocation of the work associated with the colonies to one of them.

[25] Steele, Ian K., 'The Anointed, the Appointed and the Elected: Governance of the British Empire, 1689-1784', *OHBE*, Vol. 2, pp. 105-127.

[26] Although the term 'Crown Colony' was not widely used until the nineteenth century to describe colonies ruled by a governor appointed by the Crown, the directly ruled colonies of the seventeenth and eighteenth centuries were, in practice, equivalent to the later Crown colonies.

by the Crown or by the proprietor or proprietors. He was supported by an Executive Council, also appointed by the Crown; and a Legislative Assembly of representatives elected by the people. The Governor directly represented the Crown or the proprietor but he also owed a duty to the people over whom he was placed and when the interests of the two were conflict placed the Governor in an invidious position.[27] Gubernatorial powers were extensive.[28] Governors convened, prorogued or dissolved the legislature and could veto any of its laws. They commanded the militia and appointed many officials, such as judges, magistrates and sheriffs, through their powers of patronage and, especially in the early period, had industrial, commercial, and ecclesiastical as well as political duties.[29] Governors had no power over the public purse and this was an restraint on their power. In the American colonies, the Executive Council usually consisted of twelve men, though in Massachusetts there were twenty-eight, and in early Maryland only three. They had to be residents of the colony in which they served, and were usually men of wealth and generally sided with the Governor in disagreements with the Assembly. The functions of the Council were threefold: it advised the Governor; was the Upper House of the legislature; and, it was frequently the highest court of the colony. The Assembly or Lower House of the legislature, elected largely by property-owners, represented the people and was the chief legislative power though its acts could be vetoed by the Council in its role as the upper house, by the Governor or be set aside by the Crown within a certain time after their passage.[30] The legislature in every American colony was bicameral, except in Pennsylvania and Georgia where it consisted of a single house. Assemblies had the sole power for taxation, a right they maintained with tenacity. It was widely believed that colonial liberties were secure so long as assemblies retained this sole right for taxation.[31] On many occasions assemblies refused to grant governors their salaries until certain laws they had passed had been approved.[32] Assemblies also often meddled in purely executive affairs, such

---

[27] In Connecticut and Rhode Island and in Massachusetts before 1684, the people elected the governor.

[28] On the role of the colonial governor see, for instance, Abbot, W. W., *Royal Governors of Georgia 1754-1775*, (University of North Carolina Press), 1959, and Batinski, Michael C., *Jonathan Belcher, Colonial Governor*, (University of Kentucky Press), 1996.

[29] Magistrates or Justices of the Peace, appointed by the Governor, stood at the base of the judicial system and tried petty civil cases only. County courts tried civil cases involving sums to a certain amount and criminal cases not involving capital punishment. The highest colonial court was usually composed of the Governor and the Council although in some colonies, the Governor appointed a body of judges for this function, while he and the Council acted as a Court of Appeals. In certain cases, a further appeal could be made to the Privy Council in England.

[30] On electoral system see, Bishop, Cortlandt F., *History of Elections in the American Colonies*, (B. Franklin), 1893, provides a detailed account of assembly and local elections. Dinkin, Robert J., *Voting in Provincial America: A Study of Elections in the Thirteen Colonies, 1689-1776*, (Greenwood Press), 1977, adopts a rather broader approach.

[31] Rabushka, Alvin, *Taxation in Colonial America*, (Princeton University Press), 2008, is a monumental study of the issue.

[32] Beeman, Richard R., *The Varieties of Political Experience in Eighteenth-Century America*, (University of Pennsylvania Press), 2006, examines the nature of political organisation and process across the colonies.

as military matters and the appointment of officials because of their control over taxation.

After the Royal African Company's monopoly was withdrawn in 1698, British traders became the largest and most efficient carriers of slaves to the New World. Private merchant houses provided the capital for this business activity and Jamaica, the largest British slave colony, was the wealthiest colony in the British Empire. Despite these developments, Britain's overseas colonies and trade was still vulnerable to the military and naval power and commercial and imperial aspirations of France and the Netherlands, as well as Spain and Portugal. The apotheosis of Britain's imperial expansion in the eighteenth century occurred after its victories in the Seven Years War (1756-1763).[33] British troops defeated the French at Quebec in 1759 and the East India Company defeated local Indian rulers supported by French advisers at Plassey in 1757. The British Empire was now a global empire based on trade and military and naval power and ranged from colonies of European settlement in North America and the slave-based plantation economies of the West Indies to Britain's growing territorial power and influence in Bengal through the East India Company.[34] By 1775, Britain possessed far more land and people in the Americas than either the Dutch or the French, her main northern European rivals for international power and prestige.

Trade and colonisation proceeded apace. In 1700, most foreign commerce, by volume and value, was still conducted with Europe, but during the eighteenth century British overseas trade became 'Americanised'.[35] An integrated Atlantic economy came into being after 1750, in which merchants in British, American, West Indian and Iberian ports established firm commercial ties and a modern, enterprising outlook about making money through imperial trade. Rapid population growth in North America provided an expanding market for British exports. By 1797-1798, North America and the West Indies received 57 per cent of British exports and supplied 32 per cent of imports. Commerce with colonies stimulated merchants to provide ships, as well as goods for expanding settler societies. The slave trade also became a vehicle for establishing an empire of slavery in the Caribbean and southern American colonies, and emigrants

---

[33] Anderson, F., *Crucible of War: The Seven Years' War and the Fate of Empire in British North America, 1754-1766*, (Vintage), 2001. See also, Lenman, Bruce P., 'Colonial Wars and Imperial Instability, 1688-1793', *OHBE*, Vol. 2, pp. 151-168. Baugh, Daniel A., *The Global Seven Years War 1754-1763: Britain and France in a Great Power Contest*, (Routledge), 2011, and Dziembowski, Edmond, *La guerre de Sept Ans (1756-1783)*, (Perrin), 2015, take a broader view.

[34] Simms, Brendan, *Three Victories and a Defeat: The Rise and Fall of the First British Empire, 1714-1783*, (Allen Lane), 2007, gives an interesting slant on decline and fall but Marshall, P. J., *The Making and Unmaking of Empires: Britain, India and America c.1750-1783*, (Oxford University Press), 2005, provides the best analysis of this transition.

[35] See, Nash, R. C., 'The organization of trade and finance in the British-Atlantic economy, 1600-1830', in Coclanis, Peter A., (ed.), *The Atlantic economy during the seventeenth and eighteenth centuries: organization, operation, practice, and personnel*, (University of South Carolina Press), 2005, pp. 95-151.

sailed to the colonies in search of better material conditions. Colonies became linked to the metropolis by complex shipping routes.[36]

The American colonies proved to be highly productive and lucrative in terms of agricultural staples, initially sugar and tobacco and later grains, coffee and cotton. The growing crisis in the thirteen American colonies in the early 1770s and their subsequent rebellion clarified the limits of British imperial power. The debate between colonists and the imperial parliament and within parliament itself concentrated on where authority lay in the colonies. At the heart of the problem was whether colonists, who were not represented in the imperial parliament, should be subject to its taxation.[37] The loss of the thirteen American colonies in the War of Independence (1775-1783) was a major blow to British imperial prestige while the impeachment of Warren Hastings, Governor-General of Bengal four years later reflected an anxiety that imperial corruption would strangle British liberties.[38] Whether this represented the end of the 'First British Empire' is questionable since Britain recovered swiftly from this disaster and normal, if on occasions bellicose, relations were soon restored between the American states and British merchants.[39] What is clear is that the loss of the American colonies led to a refining of Britain's imperial ambitions and geo-political position. The disruption of the British Empire in the American Revolution marked the beginning of the self-critique of empires, as certain Enlightenment figures in the metropole and in the colonies challenged the legitimacy of the imperial project.

There has also long been debate about the economic impact of British imperialism on India dating back to the late-eighteenth century when Edmund Burke called in parliament for an end to corruption in the regions then controlled by the East India Company.[40] This described the new economy as a form of 'plunder' and a catastrophe for the traditional economy of Mughal India blaming the British for the depletion of food and money stocks and the high level of taxation that caused the great famine of 1770 that carried off one-third of the population of Bengal.[41] However, Marshall has questioned the received view

---

[36] Price, Jacob M., 'The Imperial Economy, 1700-1776', *OHBE*, Vol. 2, pp. 78-104.

[37] Gould, E. H., *The Persistence of Empire: British Political Culture in the Age of the American Revolution*, (University of North Carolina Press), 2000, pp. 106-147.

[38] Marshall, P. J., *The impeachment of Warren Hastings*, (Oxford University Press), 1965, Carnall, G. and Nicholson, C., (eds.), *The Impeachment of Warren Hastings: Papers from a Bicentennial Celebration*, (Edinburgh University Press), 1989, and Dirks, Nicholas B., *The Scandal of Empire: India and the Creation of Imperial Britain*, (Belknap Press), 2006, a rather one-dimensional book, consider this issue. Bowen, H. V., *The business of empire; the East India Company and imperial Britain, 1756-1833*, (Cambridge University Press), 2006, examines the transition from trade to dominion.

[39] Harlow, Vincent T., *The Founding of the Second British Empire 1763-1793, Vol. II: New Continents and Changing Values*, (Longmans), 1964, remains the classic statement. See also, Bayly, C. A., *Imperial meridian: the British Empire and the world*, (Longman), 1989, a more revisionist study.

[40] Peers, Douglas M., and Gooptu, Nandini, *India and the British Empire*, (Oxford University Press), 2012, provides a valuable summary of new ways of thinking about the imperial impact on India.

[41] Ray, Rajat Kanta 'Indian Society and the Establishment of British Supremacy 1765-1818', *OHBE,* Vol. 2, pp. 508-529.

that the prosperity of the formerly benign Mughal rule gave way to poverty and anarchy.[42] Rather than marking a sudden disruption, the British takeover did not represent a sharp break with Indian patterns of rule. British control was delegated largely through regional Mughal rulers and was sustained by a buoyant Indian economy in certain regions and sectors for the rest of the eighteenth century. The British took Indian bankers into partnership and raised revenue through local tax administrators, maintaining existing Mughal rates of taxation. Ray observed that the East India Company inherited an onerous taxation system that took one-third of the produce of Indian cultivators. Instead of the nationalist account of the British as alien aggressors, seizing power by brute force and impoverishing the areas under their control, Marshall offers a story in which the British were actors in what was essentially an Indian drama and in which their rise to power depended upon a high level of cooperation with Indian élites.

The extent to which British hegemony in empire, trade and industry was based on the growth of imperial commerce has been hotly debated.[43] Some argue that growth in manufacturing production owed more to domestic than to overseas demand stressing the importance of agricultural productivity and other supply-side factors as the vital components of British economic growth.[44] By contrast, others maintain that British manufacturing production received the additional stimulus of a large overseas trading empire and this induced producers to increase productivity and introduce new technologies to meet this additional demand. The economic impact of slavery on British economic development is also contested.[45] Negative assessments emphasise that the profits of slavery and the slave trade were modest and that the contribution of slavery and the slave trade to national income was at best marginal. However, revenue from slavery

---

[42] Marshall, P. J., 'The British in Asia: Trade to Dominion 1700-1765', *OHBE*, pp. 487-507, especially, 495-501.

[43] Daunton, M. J., *Progress and Poverty: An Economic and Social History of Britain 1700-1850*, (Oxford University Press), 1995, Mokyr, Joel, *The Enlightened Economy: An Economic History of Britain 1700-1850*, (Yale University Press), 2009, Allen, Robert C., *The British Industrial Revolution in Global Perspective*, (Cambridge University Press), 2009, and Floud, Roderick, Humphries, Jane, and Johnson, Paul, (eds.), *The Cambridge Economic History of Modern Britain. Volume 1: 1700-1870*, (Cambridge University Press), 2014, are the most up-to-date studies. Griffin, Emma, *A Short History of the British Industrial Revolution*, (Palgrave), 2010, pp. 126-143, considers the global context of industrialisation.

[44] On the problems of measuring growth see, Berg, M., and Hudson, P., 'Rehabilitating the industrial revolution', *Economic History Review*, Vol. 45, (1992), pp. 24-50, Crafts, N. F. R., 'British economic growth 1700-1831: a review of the evidence', *Economic History Review*, Vol. 36, (1983), pp. 177-199, Crafts, N. F. R., and Harley, C. K., 'Output growth and the British industrial revolution: a restatement of the Crafts-Harley view', *Economic History Review*, Vol. 45, (1992), pp. 703-730, Jackson, R. V., 'Rates of industrial growth during the industrial revolution', *Economic History Review*, Vol. 45, (1992), pp. 1-23, and Crafts, N. F. R., 'Productivity Growth in the Industrial Revolution: A New Growth Accounting Perspective', *Journal of Economic History*, Vol. 64, (2004), pp. 521-535.

[45] Morgan, Kenneth, *Slavery and the British Empire: From Africa to America*, (Oxford University Press), 2007, provides a good synopsis of current thinking. See also, Richardson, David, 'The British Empire and the Atlantic Slave Trade, 1660-1807', *OHBE*, Vol. 2, pp. 440-464.

and the slave trade filtered back into the British economy in indirect ways, with bankers, insurance specialists and country gentlemen all participating as active investors. Some historians think that the profits of slavery and the slave trade, as a proportion of national income, were impressive. Finally, there is debate over the economic impact of colonies on Britain's wealth. Some historians suggest that the protectionist trade network led to the Caribbean colonies becoming a burden on the mother country, once defence and administration costs are considered and that trade with India, with an imbalance between imports and exports, was a similar drain on British capital. Modern studies show that the net drain on the British economy from protecting the British Caribbean colonies or from participating in the East India trade has been exaggerated. There can be little doubt that trade and empire gave a significant boost to the proliferation and sophistication of financial services and that this was of considerable benefit to the long-term development of the British economy.[46]

No historian would argue that trade and empire had a minimal impact on emerging British industrialisation; the important question is exactly what its impact was.[47] The current consensus is that trade and empire were significant for British economic growth in the late-eighteenth and early-nineteenth centuries, even if not decisively so. British hegemony in empire and trade by 1815 was such that Britannia did rule the waves; but this would not have been achieved without the strong support provided by the 'military-fiscal' state and the Royal Navy.[48] The ability of the British government to raise taxes and loans to support aggressive military policies and the superiority of the Royal Navy over other European navies played a significant part in creating the conditions through which trade and empire could flourish.

The problem of incorporating foreign conquests presented by the acquisition of French Canada in 1763 was not unique but gave rise to an increasing concentration of control and authority in London. After 1763, the only area where the Empire gained new territory by settlement rather than conquest was in Australia in 1788, but because of its penal nature it was initially given autocratic military government. War veterans found New South Wales an

---

[46] Goldstone, Jack A., *Why Europe? The Rise of the West in World History 1500-1850*, (McGraw-Hill), 2008, and Goldstone, Jack A., 'Engineering Culture, Innovation and Modern Wealth Creation', in Karlsson, C., Johansson, B., and Stough R. R., (eds.), *Entrepreneurship and Innovations in Functional Regions*, (Edward Elgar), 2008, pp. 23-49.

[47] On the nature of the 'industrial revolution', see, More, Charles, *Understanding the Industrial Revolution*, (Routledge), 2000, King, Steven and Timmins, Geoffrey, *Making sense of the Industrial Revolution: English economy and society 1700-1850*, (Manchester University Press), 2001. See also, Berg, Maxine and Hudson, Pat, 'Rehabilitating the Industrial Revolution', *Economic History Review*, Vol. 45, (1), (1992), pp. 24-50, and Temin, Peter, 'Two Views of the British Industrial Revolution', *Journal of Economic History*, Vol. 57, (1), (1997), pp. 63-82.

[48] On Britain's development into a maritime and mercantile state see, Scott, Jonathan, *When the Waves Ruled Britannia: Geography and Political Identities, 1500-1800*, (Cambridge University Press), 2011. Morriss, Roger, *The Foundations of British Maritime Ascendancy: Resources, Logistics and the State, 1755-1815*, (Cambridge University Press), 2010, examines the organisation vitality of the fiscal-military state in naval matters.

ideal destination after 1815: it was opening up for free emigrants, British army officers could obtain land grants and they could obtain cheap convict labour to work the land.[49] They had a profound impact on NSW, VDL and South Australia at a time of expanded growth with their skills in medicine, surveying, mapmaking and engineering and formed the nucleus of colonial power structures. Also, in the aftermath of the loss of the American colonies, imperial authority began taking a more interventionist role in the oldest parts of the Empire that had previously enjoyed a considerable degree of self-government. In the West Indies for instance, the abuse of self-government by the white population saw growing intervention by London to protect native and slave populations. This represented a significant shift from the mid-eighteenth century position that every British colony should have a government modelled on Britain's constitutional structures. No British colony was given representative institutions after the beginning of the war with France in 1793 but when peace was finally secured in 1814-1815, there was little indication that the British Government had any intention of returning to the older representative system. Direct rule by the Crown was justified where a colonial society was divided by race, nationality or wealth to such an extent that no single group can provide good governance in the interests of the whole population. This position reflected contemporary fears of colonial instability caused by the misrule of powerful minorities but also concerns about the appropriateness of British institutions in conquered territories where a minority of British settlers was dwarfed by the native population.

An 'Anglo-world', 1815-1914

As the leading force in finance and manufacturing and the dominant European naval and military power, Britain had every reason to expand across the globe and few could prevent it doing so. During the nineteenth century, it acquired 10 million square miles–a territory that included 400 million people, making it the largest of Europe's imperial powers. The development of an institutional structure providing direction from London was an important part of that process. In 1801, the War Office was renamed War and Colonial Office reflecting the growing importance of colonial issues.[50] The institutional solution was the Colonial Office that began to take shape after 1812 and was well formed by the mid-1820s when a new post of Permanent Under-Secretary for the Colonies was created. In 1854, the War and Colonial Office was divided and a new Colonial

---

[49] Wright, Christine, *Wellington's Men in Australia: Peninsular War Veterans and the Making of Empire c. 1820-40*, (Palgrave Macmillan), 2011.

[50] The evolution of the colonial service is traced in: Hall, Henry L. *The Colonial Office: A History*, (Longman, Green and Co.), 1937, Jeffries, Charles, *The Colonial Office*, (Allen & Unwin), 1956, and Pugh, R. B., 'The Colonial Office, 1801-1925' in Benians, E. A., Butler, James and Carrington, C. E., (eds.), *Cambridge History of the British Empire*, *Vol. 3: The Empire-Commonwealth*, (Cambridge University Press), 1959, pp. 711-768. Young, D. M., *The Colonial Office in the early nineteenth century*, (Longman), 1961, and Blakeley, Brian L., *The Colonial Office, 1868-1892*, (Duke University Press), 1972. See also, Hamilton, C. I., *The Making of the Modern Admiralty: British Naval Policy-Making 1805-1927*, (Cambridge University Press), 2011, for background on the role and administration of the Royal Navy.

Office was created to deal specifically with the needs of the colonies and assigned to the Secretary of State for the Colonies. The division of the office into geographical departments was continued, general business being entrusted to the chief clerk. In 1870, a General Department took some of the work of the chief clerk, an Accounts Branch was set up in 1869 and there was a separate Emigration Department from 1878 to 1894.

By the mid-nineteenth century, the British Empire provided an imperial structure that was a focus for allegiance and economic expansion but more importantly it was also a heterogeneous plurality of peoples of different origins, beliefs, political ideas and aspiration.[51] It was an empire of conquest, occupation and settler colonialism[52] in which there were different 'histories'. In some instances, there was a 'formal' transfer of sovereignty and the imposition of direct administrative control. In others, the situation was more 'informal', the product of trade, investment and diplomacy often combined with one-sided treaties and occasional armed intervention.[53] In both cases, expansionism was less the product of an imperial plan than the result of strategic considerations determined by circumstances. The result was what historians have recently called the 'British' or 'Anglo-world'. What Britain exported to the world was not 'civilisation', as many thought at the time, but modernisation. British imperialism injected many of the institutions of modernisation, especially its systems of finance, transportation and manufacturing into the territories it controlled.

Imperial government increasingly accepted that some form of responsive, representative and eventually responsible self-government was necessary at least in the white-settler colonies. The alternative was the possibility of American type 'revolutions' where colonies broke away from Britain. In those countries where British culture and legal systems already existed and where there was a dominance of British immigrants, such as Canada, New Zealand and Australia, modernisation was a comparatively painless process. Britain did not repeat the mistakes of the 1770s and allowed these colonies to move slowly towards responsible government within the empire. All the colonies of British North America became self-governing between 1848 and 1855, except the colony of Vancouver Island. Nova Scotia achieved responsible government in January-February 1848 followed by the Province of Canada later that year. They were followed by Prince Edward Island in 1851 and Newfoundland and New Brunswick in 1855. The Canadian colonies were federated as a Dominion in 1867, except for Newfoundland that remained a separate self-governing colony, a separate Dominion between 1907 and 1934, reverted to being a Crown Colony in 1934 and finally joined Canada in 1949. Colonies in Australia received responsible government from the 1850s and formed a federation in 1901. New

[51] Cell, John, *British Colonial Administration in the Mid-Nineteenth Century: the Policy-Making Process*, (Yale University Press), 1970.
[52] Morgan, Cecilia, *Building Better Britains? Settler Societies in the British World, 1783-1920*, (University of Toronto Press), 2017. See also, Veracini, Lorenzo, ''Settler Colonialism': Career of a Concept', *Journal of Imperial and Commonwealth History*, Vol. 41, (2), (2013), pp. 313-333, for the historiographical development of the concept.
[53] See, Darwin, John, 'Imperialism and the Victorians: The Dynamics of Territorial Expansion', *English Historical Review*, Vol. 112, (1997), pp. 614-642.

Zealand remained a Crown Colony until 1907, when it too became a Dominion.[54]

In other areas, such as India and Asia generally and in the Middle East, the political, cultural and legal systems remained less pervious to British influence. These countries had their own internal structures governing the direction and the pace of their evolution that were less susceptible to Western brands of social engineering.[55] However, while imperialism might not have dramatically transformed their cultures, it could and frequently did lead to the modernisation of their financial and technological infrastructures. For instance, even before the British takeover in 1882, British investment incorporated Egypt into the global economy, producing the modernisation, diversification and industrial growth that made the country a major international supplier of raw materials, especially cotton. While in India, investments made by British financiers in railways, ports and factories gave Indian products world markets, led to long-term economic growth and some short-term economic booms after 1860 and augmented the resources of the unmodernised agrarian sector of the economy.[56]

Why British imperial possessions increased dramatically in the nineteenth century has long been a matter of debate. 'The Imperialism of Free Trade' is perhaps the most cited article in the historiography of British imperialism.[57] Robinson and Gallagher saw the empire as an iceberg with only the formal empire visible while hidden was a much larger empire of informal trade and influence. Central to British interests were keeping tariffs low and ensuring that British merchants had access to markets and Britain accomplished this without conquest or annexation. Successive British governments preferred this approach because it was cost-effective and convenient: it did not require the panoply and expense of administrative imperialism and may also have reflected their recognition of the limits of British power. Long before the 1880s and the scramble for Africa and the Middle East, British free trade had established a global empire of dependency and influence. Robinson and Gallagher shifted the debate about the economic results of imperialism to a global level persuading many people that a country did not have to be conquered militarily to lose its independence. The same could happen through trade and investment from a more powerful economy. This informal approach was only abandoned in favour of direct intervention or annexation where 'national' interests were in question and was strongly influenced by the importance attached to British supremacy of the Indian sub-continent. It suggests that empire-building after 1880 was reactive

---

[54] Burroughs, Peter, 'Imperial Institutions and the Government of Empire', *OHBE*, Vol. 3, pp. 170-197.

[55] Hopkins, A. G., 'Development and the Utopian Ideal 1960-1999', *OHBE,* Vol. 5, pp. 635-652.

[56] Lalvani, Kartar, and English, Peter, *The Making of India: A Story of British Enterprise,* (Whittles Publishing), 2011, assesses Britain's contribution to the development of India's institutional; and physical infrastructure.

[57] Robinson, Ronald, and Gallagher, John, 'The Imperialism of Free Trade', *Economic History Review*, second series, Vol. 6, (1953), pp. 1-15. See also, MacDonagh, Oliver, 'The Anti-Imperialism of Free Trade', *Economic History Review,* Vol.14, (1962), pp. 489-501.

or defensive and aimed at maintaining existing zones of influence from the intrusion of other powers rather than seeking new ones.

Historians have questioned the 'informal empire' thesis and found that Robinson and Gallagher underestimated the political and economic obstacles to effective domination.[58] In South America, it was only in Brazil that the British found malleable political collaborators.[59] In the United States after 1776, Britain exerted no direct political influence, although its population, long accustomed to British goods, paid for them through large exports of primary produce such as cotton and tobacco. In Asia, most existing political systems were largely beyond the reach of British diplomatic influence or even the threat of British warships and Indian troops, while intercontinental trade had little influence on most Asian economies.

> Concepts of informal empire are even more difficult to apply to Asia, outside the Indian subcontinent, or to Africa, than they are to the Americas.[60]

The idea of 'informal empire' exaggerates both the British government's willingness to intervene overseas before the 1880s and its success in establishing more than a superficial paramountcy over parts of the wider world.[61] In reality, influence was more ambiguous and fluid and was not simply from Britain to the outside world but rather a mutually beneficial process.

> Britain established a commercial or financial presence in a region did not mean, necessarily, that she gained either economic or political paramountcy over it. Only at the highest level of abstraction can Latin America, China, Ottoman Turkey, and Africa in the mid-nineteenth century be described as parts of a British informal empire.[62]

'Gentlemanly capitalism', an essentially commercial ethos combined with the gentlemanly values of a rentier class resident chiefly in southern England, was also important.[63] Economic imperialism was a vehicle of commercial and financial expansion that persisted well into the twentieth century.[64] The problem

---

[58] See, for instance, Marshall, P. J., 'Britain without America: A Second Empire?', *OHBE,* Vol. 2, pp. 577-595, and especially Cain, P., and Hopkins, A. G., *British Imperialism: Innovation and Expansion, 1688-1914*, (Longman), 1993.
[59] Miller, R., *Britain and Latin America in the Nineteenth and Twentieth Centuries*, (Longman), 1993, and Platt, D. C. M., *Business Imperialism 1840-1930: An Inquiry Based on British Experience in Latin America*, (Oxford University Press), 1970. See also, Bulmer-Thomas, V., *The Economic History of Latin America since Independence*, (Cambridge University Press), 2003, pp. 31-38, 72-81, 101-107,
[60] Marshall, P. J., 'Introduction', *OHBE,* Vol. 2, p. 25.
[61] Lynn, Martin, 'British Policy, Trade and Informal Empire in the Mid-Nineteenth Century', *OHBE,* Vol. 3, pp. 101-121.
[62] Ibid, Lynn, Martin, 'British Policy, Trade and Informal Empire in the Mid-Nineteenth Century', p. 120.
[63] Ibid, Cain, P., and Hopkins, A. G., *British Imperialism: Innovation and Expansion, 1688-1914*, pp. 45-46.
[64] Ibid, Cain, P., and Hopkins, A. G., *British Imperialism: Innovation and Expansion, 1688-1914*, pp. 471-474.

is that there is no single explanation for Britain's imperial expansion and it is often unclear how far Britain's intervention was driven by policy-makers in Whitehall, pressure groups motivated by defending and enhancing Britain's 'national interests', by gentleman capitalists or by local officials responding to local circumstances or by geo-politics.

During the 1830s and 1840s, British colonial policy was often hesitant. In China, for instance, Palmerston decided to intervene in 1839 because of the threatened destruction of British opium trade at Canton, not because of a planned decision or the strong pressure for direct actions from British officials and merchants. Although Britain was successful in the two Opium Wars (1839-1842 and 1855-1860) in using military force to ensure that China engaged in the opium trade it did not want, the advance of Russian power in the North and growing French and American commercial interests ruled out unilateral action in China and the need for cooperative policies by the great powers.[65] Britain's attitude reflected its awareness of the limitation of its power in China and recognised that a shift from informal to formal empire was only possible where there were no potential European or American rivals. Policy towards NZ and South Africa in the 1830s was equally opposed to annexation. It was only when the New Zealand Company decided to colonise parts of NZ and there was revived French 'interest' in the islands that British policy moved towards annexation leading to the ambiguous Treaty of Waitangi in 1840. In South Africa, the annexation of Queen Adelaide's Land in 1836 was rejected by the Colonial Office but eight years later it annexed Natal and in 1848, British rule was extended to include the Boers beyond the Orange River. Increasing Boer resistance and the disastrous eighth Kaffir War led to the 'conventions' policy that gave the Boers in the Transvaal and Orange Free State their independence in 1852 and 1854.[66] The revival of the expansion of the eastern frontier in the late 1870s led to the disastrous decision to annex the Transvaal culminating in the First Boer War and the catastrophic defeat of British troops at Majuba Hill in 1881. For the second time, at least temporarily Britain withdrew from involvement in the interior. In both NZ and South Africa, British attitudes to expansionism fluctuated between aggressive territorial advances and often disillusioned retreats. Colonial policy may have been flexible and opportunistic but it was certainly not coherent. There was a lack of direction and control by the Colonial Office in areas where Britain's national interest was neither clear nor

---

[65] Costin, W. C., *Great Britain and China, 1833-1860*, (Oxford University Press), 1937, remains the classic account. Van Dyke, Paul A., *The Canton trade: life and enterprise on the China coast, 1700-1845*, (Hong Kong University Press), 2005, examines the early trade between China and the West. See also, Bickers, Robert, *The Scramble for China: Foreign Devils in the Qing Empire, 1832-1914*, (Allen Lane), 2011, and Fairbank, John K., *Trade and diplomacy on the China coast: the opening of the treaty ports, 1842-1854*, (Stanford University Press), 1969.

[66] De Kiewiet, C. W., *British Colonial Policy and the South African Republics, 1848-1872*, (Longman, Green and Co.), 1929, and Galbraith, J. S., *Reluctant Empire: British Policy on the South African Frontier, 1834-1854*, (University of California Press), 1963. See also, Hamilton, Carolyn, Mbenga, Bernard K., and Ross, Roibert, (eds.), *The Cambridge History of South Africa*, 2 Vols. (Cambridge University Press), 2010, 2011, Vol. 1, pp. 253-391, Vol. 2, pp. 102-210.

threatened. The determinant of British action was often local circumstances and the more interventionist attitudes of local officials, merchants, missionaries and settlers.

India was central to imperial thinking despite being ruled by the East India Company before 1857.[67] This was ironic since initially India was not regarded as having any particular strategic value and its commercial potential was limited until the Indian hinterland was opened by massive railway construction in the 1860s and 1870s that offered major benefits to trade and yet it proved the key for Britain's late-nineteenth century expansion east and south of Suez.[68] The reason why imperial expansion in India proved so dynamic had little to do with policy-makers in London who sought as far as possible to check Anglo-Indian ambitions but were frequently thwarted by the powerful East India lobby in the Commons. Despite the threat of dismissal, successive governor-generals extended the Company's territorial control and in the early 1840s, Sind and the Punjab were annexed against London's wishes.[69]

There were also several factors that were unique in India that made expansion beneficial. Pre-conquest India had already begun its commercial revolution leading to wealth and power moving from the inland empire to the coast opening the subcontinent's economy to foreign traders far more than in China.[70] Company men quickly insinuated themselves into Indian society and economy and became a pressure group with the initiative and belligerence to dominate the coastal economy. Their inheritance of the established taxation systems in Bengal and elsewhere provided the revenue necessary to fund their territorial ambitions and, when necessary, to pay for military assistance from London.[71] In addition, the Company exploited existing administrative structures for 'colonial purposes' as well as the endemic rivalries between the different Indian principalities through their military, financial and diplomatic expertise. India was also, from the 1750s through to the 1820s, a major arena in the global struggles for imperial dominance between Britain and France. The need to keep French interests at bay meant that the expansionist attitudes of the Company proceeded largely unchecked by parliamentary or governmental veto. India became the 'jewel in the Crown' almost by default since the Colonial Office

[67] The literature on India is immense but Peers, Douglas M., *India under Colonial Rule 1700-1885*, (Longman), 2006, and Copland, Ian, *India 1885-1947*, (Longman), 2001, provide a succinct narrative and commentary. Bates, Crispin, *Subalterns and Raj: South Asia since 1600*, (Routledge), 2007, pp. 22-92, is a detailed analysis. See also, Parsons, Timothy H., *The Rule of Empires: Those who built them, those who endured them, and why they always fall*, pp. 168-230, and Washbrook, D. A., 'India, 1818-1860: The Two Faces of Imperialism', *OHBE*, Vol. 3, pp. 395-422.

[68] On the economic significance of India see, Charlesworth, Neil, *British Rule and the Indian Economy, 1800-1914*, (Macmillan), 1982, for a summary of the historiography to 1980.

[69] Bearce, G. D., *British Attitudes towards India, 1784-1858*, (Oxford University Press), 1961, is the classic liberal interpretation of British intentions in India.

[70] Chaudhuri, K. N., *Trade and Civilisation in the Indian Ocean: An Economic Analysis from the rise of Islam to 1750*, (Cambridge University Press), 1985, pp. 34-62, 80-97, provides the context for this development.

[71] Marshall, P. J., *Bengal: The British Bridgehead, Eastern India 1740-1828*, (Cambridge University Press), 1988, examines developments that yielded Bengal to the British.

exerted little coherent control over developments and expansion, a situation given administrative credence in 1858, after the Mutiny, when India finally came fully under the jurisdiction of the British state with the creation of the India Office as a separate government department.[72] In 1876, Queen Victoria took the title of empress of India, the first time the British monarch was formally identified as the ruler of an empire.

The Colonial Office did not have responsibility for all British possessions overseas since, from 1858, British possessions in India and certain other nearby areas passed from the East India Company and the Indian Board of Control to the India Office and certain informal protectorates and other areas, particularly Egypt were under the authority of the Foreign Office.[73] The India Office was responsible for the direct administration of British India and Burma but also other areas at different times.[74] The Secretary of State for India was assisted by a statutory body of advisers, the Council of India, and headed a staff of civil servants organised into a system of departments largely taken over from the East India Company and Board of Control establishments, and housed in a new India Office building in Whitehall. The Secretary of State for India inherited all the executive functions previously carried out by the Company, and all the powers of 'superintendence, direction and control' over the British Government in South Asia previously exercised by the Board of Control.

During the decades after the Mutiny in 1857, India was ruled with greater care.[75] Land taxes were reduced and controls were introduced over the alienation of land. The creation of a British-built rail network brought India together increasing the ability of middle-class Indians to travel rapidly over great distances. India was being shaped into a coherent entity and Indian political activists increasingly began to claim that space as their own. The unification of the territory was accompanied by internal differentiation of its people. The British saw India as a series of 'communities' divided along caste and religious lines establishing boundaries between Hindus, Muslims, Sikhs and Parses that had previously been less clear-cut. For Indian intellectuals and activists, their vision of 'Bharat Mata' or 'Mother India' was juxtaposed with British notions of the Raj, emphasised Hindu traditions and history downplaying the large presence of Muslims including their connection to the Mughal Empire.[76] Parallel to the political critique of the Raj for failing to live up to its previous liberal value was an economic analysis of the fruits of Indian labour being funnelled to Britain, what Indian intellectuals called 'the drain'. Indian critics argued that the economy was manipulated to serve British rather than Indian interests, made it vulnerable to fluctuations in global markets and emphasised exports even when drought conditions threated famine. For Indians, British rule produced little economic

---

[72] This follows ibid, Darwin, John, 'Imperialism and the Victorians: The Dynamics of Territorial Expansion', pp. 626-627.

[73] Seton, Malcolm, *The India Office*, (Putnam's Sons Ltd.), 1926, is a lucid if dated account by its Deputy Under-Secretary.

[74] These included Afghanistan, Russian and Chinese Central Asia, Tibet, Nepal, Bhutan and Sikkim to 1947 and Malaysia and South-East Asia to the late 1860s.

[75] Moore, Robin J., 'Imperial India, 1858-1914', *OHBE*, Vol. 3, pp. 423-446.

[76] On the development of Indian thinking, see Bayly, C. A., *Recovering Liberties: Indian Thought in the Age of Liberalism and Empire*, (Cambridge University Press), 2012.

growth and only small improvements in gross domestic product. Inadequate political representation, discrimination, drain of wealth and the inequities of the land revenue system provided the grievances that the Indian National Congress, formed in 1885, was to build on.

Britain's view of its national interest was central to the development of its empire after 1850. Expanding commercial activities was beneficial and desirable and was reinforced from the late 1840s with the final replacement of free trade for protectionism.[77] Colonisation by British migrants enjoyed widespread support among politicians and religious and commercial organisations. In neither area did the state play a central role reflecting the emergence of Gladstonian finance in the 1850s based on the need to reduce the costs of government. However, much government wanted not to intervene across the globe, it found itself buffeted by the unpredictability of public opinion, by threatened commercial interests and powerful lobbies and by the need to maintain support in the House of Commons. Political expediency and fickle patriotism frequently undermined the imperial objectives of the Colonial Office. Gladstone found to his cost in the early 1880s when he refused to act to support General Gordon in the Sudan. He was subjected to a vehement campaign vilifying his inaction and then found it too late to prevent Gordon's death in Khartoum in early 1885. From the 'Grand Old Man', he became the 'Murderer of Gordon'.[78]

By the 1870s, British policy shifted away from informal influence towards a more formal approach to empire largely because it took military intervention to adapt African and Asian economies to the requirements of British commerce and investment. This process was aided by shifting social attitudes that made conquering and ruling non-European peoples more acceptable. The impact of Social Darwinism was central to this process with its view that non-European peoples were incapable of modernity or of recognising Britain's superior culture because they were at a lower level of evolution, were 'inferior' and so unqualified to govern themselves.[79] Events such as the 1857 Indian Mutiny and the Morant Bay rising in Jamaica in 1865 confirmed an increasingly flagrant racism to create a 'new imperialism' and was reinforced by military power though it was easier to defeat non-European enemies in open warfare than to maintain that dominance through costly military occupation.[80]

---

[77] See, Howe, Anthony, *Free Trade and Liberal England, 1846-1946*, (Oxford University Press), 1997, pp. 1-69, and Trentmann, Frank, *Free Trade Nation: Commerce, Consumption and Civil Society in Modern Britain*, (Oxford University Press), 2008, pp. 134-187. See also, Tomlinson, B. R., 'Economics and Empire: The Periphery and the Imperial Economy', *OHBE*, Vol. 3, pp. 53-74.

[78] For the imperial myth-making potential of his death, see Johnson, Douglas, 'The death of Gordon: a Victorian myth', *Journal of Imperial and Commonwealth History*, Vol. 10, (1982), pp. 185-210, and Judd, Denis, 'Gordon of Khartoum: the making of an imperial martyr', *History Today*, Vol. 35, (1), (1985), pp. 19-25.

[79] Hawkins, Mike, *Social Darwinism in European and American Thought, 1860-1945: nature as model and nature as threat*, (Cambridge University Press), 1997, and Bannister, Robert C., *Social Darwinism: Science and Myth in Anglo-American Thought*, (Temple University Press), 1989.

[80] Schwarz, Bill, *Memories of Empire: Volume 1, The White Man's World*, (Oxford University Press), 2011, pp. 55-106, provides an elegant discussion of this issue. See also

The nineteenth century territorial expansion in British presence in Africa was immense but, with the exception of Cape Colony and the mineral resources of Transvaal, it was economically insignificant.[81] Britain took an active part in the European partition of Africa in the 1880s triggered by King Leopold of Belgium's claim to the Congo in 1879 and the British occupation of Egypt three years later.[82] Each new imperial acquisition was apt to provoke new efforts on the part of imperial competitors. For instance, Bechuanaland, located north of the Orange River became the object of dispute between the Germans to the west, the Boers to the east, and the British in the Cape Colony to the south. Although Bechuanaland had almost no economic value, the 'Missionaries Road' passed through it toward territory further north. After the Germans annexed Damaraland and Namaqualand (modern Namibia) in 1884, the British annexed Bechuanaland in 1885. In North Africa, colonial expansion was linked to the fortunes of the declining Ottoman Empire. Frightened by the Russian threat to their lands, the Ottoman Empire agreed to hand over the administration of Cyprus to Britain in 1878 in return for British support while Britain in turn agreed to allow France a free hand in Tunisia.[83] Britain expanded its coastal holdings in West Africa but also gained control of Egypt, Sudan and British Somaliland in Northeast Africa; Zanzibar, Uganda and what later became Kenya in East Africa;[84] Nyasaland, Northern Rhodesia and Southern Rhodesia in central Africa; and Swaziland, Basutoland and Bechuanaland in southern Africa though to took three years of war against the Boer republics between 1899 and 1902 to consolidate British rule over South Africa.[85] British action was in part motivated by strategic rivalry with other European powers. Britain also strengthened the frontiers of India by finally annexing Burma in 1886, acquired sovereignty over most of the states in the Malay Peninsula in 1896 and occupied numerous islands in the South Pacific between 1874 and 1900. The Persian Gulf states were incorporated into the British sphere of influence and she gained influence in the Yangtze River valley as part of the European scramble for

---

Mantena, Karuna, *Alibis of Empire: Henry Maine and the Ends of Liberal Imperialism*, (Princeton University Press), 2010, pp. 21-55, 179-188.

[81] Pakenham, Thomas, *The Scramble for Africa: White Man's Conquest of the Dark Continent from 1876 to 1912*, (Avon Books), 1991, provides the best narrative. See also, Newbury, Colin, 'Great Britain and the Partition of Africa, 1870-1914', *OHBE*, Vol. 3, pp. 624-650.

[82] Alaf Lutfi al-Dayyid-Marsot, 'The British Occupation of Egypt from 1882', *OHBE*, Vol. 3, pp. 644-689.

[83] For the centrality of the Mediterranean to nineteenth British power overseas see the extended argument in Holland, Robert, *Blue-Water Empire: The British in the Mediterranean since 1800*, (Allen Lane), 2012, pp. 7-148.

[84] Gjersø, Jonas Fossli, 'The Scramble for East Africa: British Motives Reconsidered, 1884-95', *Journal of Imperial and Commonwealth History*, Vol. 43, (5), (2015), pp. 821-860.

[85] Trapido, Stanley, 'Imperialism, settler identities, and colonial capitalism: the hundred year origins of the 1899 South African War', in ibid, Ross, Robert, Mager, Anne and Nasson, Bill, *The Cambridge History of South Africa*, *Volume 2, 1885-1994*, pp. 66-101, and Saunders, Christopher, and Smith, Iain R., 'Southern Africa 1795-1910', *OHBE*, Vol. 3, pp. 597-623.

concessions in China in 1897.[86] The empire expanded faster than previously, quadrupling in size in the last thirty years of the century.

Britain's empire in the long nineteenth century was far from a coherent whole but by 1914, the system was far from being in disarray.[87] There was an extraordinary range of constitutional, political, economic and cultural relationships contained within Britain's multiple imperial connections.[88] Within the empire were dominions, 'dependencies' and the informal empire of influence rather than direct rule. This seemingly chaotic configuration bears no relation to any suggestion of a systematic empire built to a blueprint. There was no imperial project but a 'Greater Britain', a decentralised amalgam of coercion, control, devolution, paternalism, racism and networks that spanned the globe but whose only common point of reference was collaboration with British imperial authority; an empire in name but little else.[89]

An empire in decline, 1914-1980

The principal cause of the decline in Britain's imperial power was identified by historian A. J. P. Taylor:

> Though the object of being a Great Power is to be able to fight a great war, the only way of remaining a Great Power is not to fight one. This was the secret of Great Britain's greatness so long as she stuck to naval warfare and did not try to become a military power on the continental pattern.[90]

Britain had already fought and won an unsatisfactory colonial war against the Boers between 1899 and 1902 that caused something resembling a crisis of confidence in the superiority of British civilisation.[91] What happened between

[86] Crump, Thomas, *Asia-Pacific: A History of Empire and Conflict*, (Hambledon Continuum), 2007, pp. 1-23, examines the situation at the turn of the century.

[87] Offer, Avner, 'Costs and Benefits, Prosperity and Security, 1870-1914', *OHBE*, Vol. 3, pp. 690-711.

[88] British and Irish efforts to forge a Christian empire through missions to the settlement colonies played a major role in the development of empire. There was no incompatibility between commerce and Christianity. See, Carey, Hilary M., *God's Empire: Religion and Colonisation in the British World, c.1801-1908*, (Cambridge University Press), 2011, and Carré, J., (ed.), *Le monde britannique: Religion et cultures (1815-1931)*, 2nd ed., (Sedes), 2009, pp. 141-156.

[89] On 'Greater Britain', see Bell, Duncan, *The Idea of Greater Britain: Empire and the Future of World Order, 1860-1900*, (Princeton University Press), 2007, Bell, Duncan, *Reordering the World. Essays on Liberalism and Empire*, (Princeton University Press), 2016, pp. 91-117, 166-181, and Koditschek, Theodore, *Liberalism, Imperialism and the Historical Imagination: Nineteenth Century Visions of a Greater Britain*, (Cambridge University Press), 2011, that explores the symbiotic relationship between the writing of history and developing imperial agendas.

[90] Taylor, A. J. P., *The Origins of the Second World War*, (Hamilton Hamish), 1961, p. 284.

[91] The military setbacks of the early period of the war, the cost, together with the revelations of the physical unfitness of volunteer recruits gave new urgency and new sources of support to fears of relative national decline. See Searle, G. R., '"National efficiency" and the "lessons" of the war', in Omissi, David Enrico, and Thompson,

1914 and 1918 was a world war of imperial powers and four did not survive.[92] The German, Austro-Hungarian and Ottoman empires were dismembered creating, especially in Europe unstable nascent democracies that failed to keep totalitarian tendencies at bay and succumbed over the next twenty years to authoritarian governments or fascism in one form or another. The Tsarist Empire, weakened by defeats and slaughter, was destroyed in the revolutions of 1917 leading to the formation of the Communist Soviet state with its messianic internationalism that threatened liberal democratic ideas. Britain fought the war as an imperial power and troops from across the Empire fought and died in their thousands alongside Britain's eventual conscript army in different theatres of war.[93] Although the war had a catastrophic impact on Britain's population with over 900,000 dead, on its manufacturing economy, already in relative decline by 1914, and especially its global financial supremacy, it gained further colonial possessions from Germany in Africa and elsewhere and mandates in the Middle East from the League of Nations. British debt was fourteen times what it had been in 1914 and this would affect the post-war defence spending required to defend Britain's huge overseas commitments.[94] But the main losses to Britain were moral. How could the British and Europeans spend four years butchering each other and then assert their right to govern other peoples wisely? Britain's growing domestic weakness, the impact of global depression in the 1930s, the emergence of aggressive Nazism, itself a consequence of the punitive nature of the Treaty of Versailles in 1919 and Britain's support for its appeasement meant that when a Second World War broke out in 1939, Britain further squandered the resources of empire and by 1945 she was bleeding, bankrupt and exhausted.[95] The Indian subcontinent gained independence and division into Pakistan and India in 1947, Britain's global prestige was irreparably damaged by the Suez fiasco in 1956 and as the 'winds of change' swept across Africa, the apparatus of empire was finally dismantled and colonies were given their independence. Sir Roy Denman, a Labour Party elder statesman summed up this process:

Andrew Stuart, (eds.), *The Impact of the South African War*, (Palgrave), 2002, pp. 194-211, and more generally in Searle, G. R., *The quest for national efficiency: a study in British politics and political thought, 1899-1914*, (Oxford University Press), 1971.

92 Holland, Robert, 'The British Empire and the Great War, 1914-1918', *OHBE*, Vol. 4, pp. 114-137.

93 On the role of imperial troops see, for instance, Pati, Budheswar, *India and the First World War*, (Atlantic Publishers), 1996, pp. 7-64, Smith, Richard, *Jamaican Volunteers in the First World War: Race, masculinity and the development of national consciousness*, (Manchester University Press), 2004, Winegard, Timothy C., *Indigenous Peoples of the British Dominions and the First World War*, (Cambridge University Press), 2011, and Grey, Jeffrey, *A Military History of Australia*, 3rd ed., (Cambridge University Press), 2008, pp. 80-118.

94 Turner, John, (ed.), *Britain and the First World War*, (Allen & Unwin), 1988, remains a good collection of essays.

95 Thompson, Andrew, (ed.), *Britain's Experience of Empire in the Twentieth Century*, (Oxford University Press), 2011, provides a valuable overview of Britain as a global power in the twentieth century,

> At the beginning of the twentieth century, Britain, as the centre of the biggest empire in the world, was at the zenith of her power and glory. Britain approaches the end as a minor power, bereft of her empire...Britain will end the century little more than Switzerland. It will have been the biggest secular decline in power and influence since seventeenth-century Spain.[96]

In retrospect, the beginnings of imperial decline originated before the outbreak of war in 1914. British policy was seen increasingly as reacting to situations in non-European regions instead of creating them as was previously the case. Revolutions in Persia in 1906 and China in 1912 narrowed Britain's room for manoeuvre and indigenous politics emerged in some colonies such as India, Egypt, Ceylon, the Gold Coast and Rhodesia though these developments did not yet impinge on British politics. The non-settler colonies had little political leverage but it became increasingly evident that the political liberties given to the settler colonies could not long be delayed elsewhere in the empire.[97]

Despite the cost of the First World War in human and financial terms, Britain was still an extremely wealthy country at the heart of a global system of production in 1918 and, despite the domestic effects of slump in the 1930s, this remained the case in 1939 Although Britain obtained new colonial possessions in Africa and in the Pacific, largely from Germany, it was in the Middle East, especially oil-rich Persia where the most important gains were made at the expense of the dismembered Ottoman Empire.[98] Most British politicians still believed that India's security lay in controlling territories beyond the frontiers of the Raj. The problem was that this strategy left Britain over-extended since most of the new possessions needed expensive direct rule to maintain their stability and security and 'the future was to lie with the expansion of influence not the expansion of rule.'[99] This was evident in the policies of Conservative and Labour governments during the 1920s. Politicians were determined to avoid another war and willingly used the League of Nations and disarmament talks as the medium through which to achieve this. This façade of internationalism hid a limited commitment by British governments whose concerns were focused on domestic considerations, a consequence of growing economic weakness.[100] This increased rather than reduced the importance of empire since colonial development was

[96] Cit, Buchanan, Patrick J., *Churchill, Hitler and the Unnecessary War: How Britain Lost Its Empire and the West Lost the World*, (Crown Publishers), 2008, p. xvi.
[97] Hyam, Ronald, 'The British Empire in the Edwardian Era', *OHBE*, Vol. 4, pp. 47-63.
[98] On Britain in the Middle East see, Fieldhouse, David, *Western Imperialism in the Middle East, 1914-1958*, (Oxford University Press), 2006, and Levey, Zach, and Podeh, Elie, (eds.), *Britain and the Middle East: From Imperial power to junior partner*, (Sussex Academic Press), 2008, for broader studies Detailed discussion can be found in, Sluglett, Peter, *Britain in Iraq: Contriving King and Country, 1914-1932*, (Columbia University Press), 2007, and Miller, Rory, (ed.), *Britain, Palestine and Empire: The Mandate Years*, (Ashgate), 2010.
[99] Gallagher, John, edited by Anil Seal, *The Decline, Revival and Fall of the British Empire: The Ford Lectures and other essays*, (Cambridge University Press), 1982, p. 90.
[100] On international Inter-War politics see, Steiner, Zara, *The Lights That Failed: European International History 1918-1933*, (Oxford University Press), 2005, and *The Triumph of the Dark: European International History, 1933-1939*, (Oxford University Press), 2011, for a monumental study of developments.

regarded as critical in reviving Britain's economy. There were important changes in the institutions that governed the Empire. In 1907, the Dominion Division of the Colonial Office had been created and from 1925 separate Secretaries of State for Dominion Affairs were responsible for British relations with the Dominions: Canada, Australia, New Zealand, South Africa, Newfoundland and the Irish Free State, as well as the self-governing colony of Southern Rhodesia.[101] The remaining departments were grouped in a Crown Colonies Division. The territories mandated to Britain following the First World War were also managed by the Colonial Office. These changes demonstrated that it was necessary to maintain Britain's global interests but equally it was essential to reduce the imperial burden on British tax-payers and to accommodate demands emerging from colonial politics.[102]

One possible solution was to follow the nineteenth and early-twentieth century experience of Canada, Australia, New Zealand and South Africa and give additional colonies dominion status. This would reduce imperial costs by giving colonies devolved powers to administer local issues while retaining influence over imperial matters. It provided one way of resolving the status of India but following the collapse of Gandhi's non-cooperation campaign in 1922 there was a hiatus in Indian politics for the rest of the decade. There was talk of dominion status in 1929 but it went no further.[103] Britain could detach itself from the direction of territories and simply defend essential British interests. For instance, when London recognised the independence of Egypt in 1922, it retained control over the security of the Suez Canal, defence, protection of foreign interests and the integrity of the Sudan.[104] A third approach was to reduce British control in favour of a strong ruler who, though rarely ideal, could at least provide stability. This explains why Britain agreed to the rule of Mustafa Kemal Ataturk in Turkey, of Amanullah in Afghanistan and Reza Khan (later Shah) in Persia. An alternative was to remain in the country and rely on collaborators as in Iraq and Palestine. In Iraq, it worked within limits until an army *putsch* in 1936 but in Palestine it did not work at all prompting politicians to discuss whether to leave or stay as early as 1921. Jews were prepared to collaborate while Arabs, who were seen as incapable of running an administration, would not. This rag-bag of alternatives reflected the managerial priorities of civil servants in the Colonial Office and the vagaries of party politics in the 1920s but its openness to ideas of reform and adaptation left the empire vulnerable to nationalist challenges and critiques.[105]

---

[101] Garner, J., *The Commonwealth Office, 1925-68*, (Heinemann), 1978, pp. 3-14.

[102] Holland, R. F., *Britain and the Commonwealth Alliance, 1918-1939*, (Macmillan), 1981, and Constantine, Stephen, *The Making of British Colonial Development Policy*, (F. Cass), 1984. See also, *Imperial Policy and Colonial Practice 1925-1945*, (HMSO), 1996, for valuable sources.

[103] Owen, Nicholas J., *The British Left and India: Metropolitan Anti-imperialism, 1885-*1947, (Oxford University Press), 2007, pp. 136-196, examines developments in the 1920s.

[104] On the British occupation of Egypt, see Thompson, Jason, *A History of Egypt*, (American University in Cairo Press), 2008, pp. 252-272, and Petry, Carl F., and Daly, M. W., (eds.), *The Cambridge History of Egypt*, 2 Vols. (Cambridge University Press), 1998, Vol. 2, pp. 285-333.

[105] Cell, John, 'Colonial Rule', *OHBE*, Vol. 4, pp. 232-254.

During the 1930s, domestic constraints caused by the global slump and growing international pressures were of such magnitude that earlier suggestions of further colonial development evaporated.[106] Declining world trade in 1932 led Britain to abandon free trade outside the Empire though not within it. At the Ottawa Conference Britain wanted free trade with the Dominions and India but they insisted on keeping some tariffs and a system of imperial preferences was instead adopted. These helped the Dominions but worsened Britain's balance of payments since the Dominions exported more to Britain after 1932 while Britain's imports to them fell. In addition, the broad imperial consensus among the British political parties broke down especially after the formation of the National government in 1931 and factions emerged within those parties over the future direction of the Empire. Winston Churchill, for instance, unsuccessfully directed the campaign to defeat new plans for constitutional reform in India in 1934 and 1935. The Government of India Act 1935 gave provincial self-government but left the Viceroy in control of important issues such as foreign policy.[107] Although rebellions and political demands in the Empire were largely contained in the 1920s and early 1930s, protests, strikes, riots and political activism such as the wave of strikes in the British West India between 1935 and 1938 and the resurgence of the Indian National Congress were not just local events but signaled empire-wide problems. Challenges to white authority steadily grew in the late 1930s throughout Africa especially in mining communities between 1935 and 1940. These were exacerbated by the outbreak of war in 1939.

From 1940, war reduced the size of Britain's empire.[108] In the Far East, Singapore, Malaya and Burma fell to the Japanese in 1942 demonstrating the vulnerability of the old imperial system to concerted military assault. Colonial troops played an important role in the conflict. Native African soldiers from East and West Africa though not from South Africa, for instance, served overseas in Palestine, Ceylon, India and Burma.[109] Just how far this shaped their post-war attitudes to empire is debatable, since nationalist demands pre-dated 1939, but evidence of ex-servicemen in Ghana's nationalist struggle suggests that soldiers returned to the rural areas where they were enlisted and became involved in local rather than territorial politics.[110] Although their involvement reflected a sense of imperial patriotism, there were also more parochial concerns. Many 'volunteers' had been forced to enlist by local tribal chiefs and in fighting their allegiance was less to 'king and country' than 'tribe and chief'. Britain needed Indian support

---

[106] Stevenson, John, and Cook, Chris, *Britain in the Depression: Society and Politics, 1929-1939*, (Longman), 1994, and Rothermund, Dietmar, *The Global Impact of the Great Depression, 1929-1939*, (Routledge), 1996, examine the impact of the depression from national and international perspectives.

[107] Muldoon, Andrew, *Empire, Politics and the Creation of the 1935 India Act: Last Act of the Raj*, (Ashgate), 2009.

[108] Jackson, Ashley, *The British Empire and the Second World War*, (Continuum), 2006, considers the impact of the war on the empire; see especially, pp. 21-40, 525-534. See also, Jeffery, Keith, 'The Second World War', *OHBE*, Vol. 4, pp. 306-328.

[109] On this issue, see Killingray, David, *Fighting for Britain: African Soldiers in the Second World War*, (James Currey), 2010.

[110] Ibid, Killingray, David, *Fighting for Britain*, pp. 214-220.

but the offer of Dominion status once the war was ended made in the aftermath of the fall of France in 1940 and again in 1942 was rejected by the Indian Congress; nothing short of independence would satisfy Indian politicians. The following year a calamitous famine in Bengal left three million people dead but London's response to this disaster was indifferent and reinforced Indian views on the necessity of independence.[111] Subhas Chandra Bose, disagreed with Gandhi's non-violent resistance and led a breakaway Indian National Army in armed struggle fighting with the Japanese against the British in Burma establishing a free Indian Government in Singapore. The war ended with Indians united that the Raj must end but divided over what should succeed it with growing tensions between the Muslim League and the multi-religious but Hindu-dominated Congress. In cultivating the development of the League during the war, Britain had laid the seeds for partition.[112]

The Second World War was a watershed that marked a reordering of the world, seeing the decline of the old European colonial powers left financially-crippled by the conflict and struggling to find relevancy in the emerging bi-polar international system of the Cold War. The end of Empire, and Britain's effective subordination to the United States, were made inescapable by the enormous costs of defeating Germany and Japan. Britain did not 'win' the war; it merely, and barely, survived it. In the aftermath of victory, there was growing pressure for retaining the economic independence many colonies had enjoyed for six years and growing support in Britain for the end of British imperialism.[113] The empire may have been relatively insignificant in metropolitan life but its impact on Britain remained important. Food imports from Canada, Australia and NZ helped relieve the stark realities of austerity and Afro-Caribbean and Asian immigrants helped fill crucial gaps in the labour market, despite deep-rooted racist anxieties that led to riots notably in Nottingham and Notting Hill in 1958 and formed the core of new diasporic communities. The Labour victory in the 1945 General Election did not result in decolonisation since many Labour politicians, especially those in the Cabinet, were committed to empire. Attempts to make colonies more economically efficient through a policy of 'new imperialism' were designed to improve the import of cheap food and export earnings.[114] The critical word was 'development' as Britain abandoned the old

---

[111] Collingham, Lizzie, *The Taste of War: World War Two and the Battle for Food*, (Allen Lane), 2011, pp. 141-153, considers the Bengal famine in the context of Britain's mobilisation of the Empire to supply food.

[112] Pandey, Bishwa Mohan, *Historiography of Indian's Partition: An Analysis of Imperialist Writings*, (Atlantic Publishers), 2003, pp. 1-21, 130-156, places partition in its historiographical context.

[113] General studies of decolonisation include, Darwin, John, *Britain and Decolonisation: The Retreat from Empire in the Post-War World*, (Macmillan), 1988, Boyce, D. G., *Decolonisation and the British Empire, 1775-1997*, (Macmillan), 1999, and Hyam, Ronald, *Britain's Declining Empire: The Road to Decolonisation 1918-1968*, (Cambridge University Press), 2006. See also Louis, Wm Roger, 'The Dissolution of the British Empire', *OHBE*, Vol. 4, pp. 328-356.

[114] Heinlein, Frank, *British Government Policy and Decolonisation, 1945-1963: Scrutinizing the Official Mind*, (Routledge), 2002, pp. 11-86, considers the Attlee governments.

colonial doctrine that colonies should pay for themselves with metropolitan investment in communications, transport, housing, schools and health facilities as well as agricultural and farming projects. The aim was to raise standards of living for colonised people and establish a structure in which long-term improvements in productivity could be achieved. Development promised to make the Empire richer and more politically legitimate. After Suez, this proved to be an untenable position since the march of democracy was regarded as incompatible with imperialism and pragmatically the universal welfare state meant that the empire had to be sacrifice to finance it. Britain also faced opposition to the continuance of empire from the United States that wanted a global system of free trade and disliked Britain's maintenance of imperial preferences. America's malevolent view of the British Empire doomed it. A principled anti-imperialism, at least as much as self-interest, drove the American policy that many in Britain saw as little better than a stab in the back. Neither Britain nor the United States wanted decolonisation to lead to communist expansion and there was little pressure to decolonise where it was likely to lead to communists gaining power.[115]

British decolonisation occurred first 'East of Suez', in Asia, in India and Burma and then Malaya.[116] In India, the issue was not independence itself but what form that independence would take. The Labour government initially sought to establish a unitary state under Congress leadership but this and a federal settlement were intolerable to the Muslim League.[117] Lord Mountbatten, the last Viceroy was instructed by the Labour government to achieve Britain's withdrawal by June 1948. The result was the partition of the subcontinent into India and Pakistan in August 1947, a process accompanied by inter-communal violence especially in areas with mixed religious populations. The speed of Britain's withdrawal has been blamed for deaths of over a million people and the displacement of a further 13 million but others maintain that swift withdrawal saved lives. In fact, the violence predated the decision to partition as communities became increasingly insecure and turned in on themselves. There was little opposition in Britain largely because India had ceased to be an imperial asset. It had already declined as a market for British exports, a situation worsened by the boycotting of British goods in the 1930s and Britain's key interest was no longer manufacturing but finance that operated whether there was an imperial structure or not. There was no longer any imperial logic for the continuance of the Raj.

---

[115] Lynn, Martin, (ed.), *The British Empire in the 1950s: Retreat or Revival?* (Palgrave), 2005, concludes that the 1950s were a messy passage in the empire's transformation.

[116] Grob-Fitzgibbon, Benjamin, *Imperial Endgame: Britain's Dirty Wars and the End of Empire*, (Palgrave Macmillan), 2011, argues that between 1945 and 1960 the British government developed a successful imperial strategy based on devolving power to indigenous peoples to keep these soon-to-be former colonies within the British and Western spheres of influence during the Cold War.

[117] On the independence of India and Pakistan see, Moore, R. J., *Escape from Empire: The Attlee Government and the Indian Problem*, (Oxford University Press), 1983, Tunzelmann, Alex von, *Indian Summer: The Secret History of the End of an Empire*, (Simon & Schuster), 2007, and Clarke, Peter, *The Last Thousand Days of the British Empire*, (Allen Lane), 2007.

Decolonisation in Malaya was a more measured process.[118] Malaya was an ethnically divided society consisting of a Chinese community that was slightly larger than the Malay and a smaller Indian community. Opposition to the Japanese occupation had been headed by the Malaysian Peoples' Anti-Japanese Army, a Chinese and communist-dominated organisation that was in a strong position in 1945 but disarmed when Britain promised equal rights for the Chinese community. Decolonisation was complicated by the importance of Malayan tin and rubber exports in paying off Britain's war debts and the nature of Britain's imperial involvement in the Malayan archipelago. There were Crown Colonies such as Singapore that were directly administered from London and the Malay States, protectorates where local sultans worked in close collaboration with imperial Commissioners and whose powers were preserved in a federal constitution in 1946. A further problem was the formation of the United Malays' National Organisation in 1946 that successfully prevented the British from applying their promise of equal rights for Chinese and Indians.

This resulted in a communist insurgency as angry young Chinese volunteered for the communist guerrilla training camps in the jungles, the so-called 'liberated areas'. Malayan communists failed to recognise Britain's unwillingness to decolonise if it allowed a communist take-over. In June 1948, martial law was introduced but there were insufficient troops or police to defeat the insurgency militarily. A change of policy established resettlement communities that eventually held a quarter of the Chinese community and in 1952, an anti-insurgency campaign gave guerrillas amnesty if they agreed to be re-educated and the insurgency petered out. The Chinese community was divided on class lines over communism and business people, who opposed it, formed the Malayan Chinese Association. The communist threat made ethnic cooperation necessary and it formed links with the United Malays' National Organisation and in 1953, the two parties formed an alliance with the Malayan Indian Congress. This coalition won the 1955 elections and formed the first government of the newly independent Malay Federation. Multi-ethnic cooperation proved short-lived and, with the decline of the communist threat, in 1963, a new, expanded state of Malaysia was established in which Malay dominance was reasserted with British agreement. But protecting the new federation of Malaysia against Indonesian aggression became increasingly expensive and in late 1967, following the devaluation of the pound, the decision was made to withdraw Britain's military presence east of Suez, a process completed by the early 1970s.[119]

Britain's strategic defence against the new Soviet threat required air bases from which to bomb Southern Russia, the Soviet Union's industrial heartland. That meant remaining in the Middle East even after the collapse of British control in Palestine and its hasty evacuation in 1948 and maintaining their bases

[118] Harper, T. N., *The End of Empire and the Making of Malaya*, (Cambridge University Press), 1999, and Hack, Karl, *Defence and Decolonisation in Southeast Asia: Britain, Malaya and Singapore, 1941-1968*, (Routledge), 2001. See also, Stockwell, A. J., 'Imperialism and Nationalism in South-East Asia', *OHBE*, Vol. 4, pp. 465-489, and Sutton, Alex, *British Imperialism and the Political Economy of Malaysian Independence'*, *Journal of Imperial and Commonwealth History*, Vol. 44, (3), (2016), pp. 470-491.
[119] Pham, P. L., *Ending 'East of Suez': The British Decision of Withdraw from Malaysia and Singapore 1964-1968*, (Oxford University Press), 2010.

in Egypt, Iraq, Jordan and the Gulf. This led to the confrontation with President Nasser in Egypt over the vast Suez Canal zone and the disastrous decision to seek his overthrow by force in collusion with Israel. Prime Minister Anthony Eden's aggressive stance during the Suez crisis in 1956 savagely exposed Britain's financial and military weakness and destroyed much of what remained of Britain's influence in the Middle East and its global prestige.[120] Britain's claim on American support, as the crisis amply demonstrated, could no longer be taken for granted and her position as the third great power was threatened by a resurgent France and West Germany who presided over the new European Economic Community that twice rejected Britain's entry. British politicians believed that Britain would remain at the 'top table' of world power especially as it had the nuclear deterrent and had maintained influence over its post-colonial territories through the Commonwealth that most had joined. But this was a chimera, reinforced by the continuing crises in the British economy.

The problem with the political dimension of Britain's 'new imperialism' was that, although its aim was to be Africans acquiring power at the centre of each colony, the timetable for achieving this was imprecise.[121] Britain wanted each colony to develop in its own way and at its own pace. Initially, it attempted to persuade African activists to participate in 'local councils' that would slowly modify traditional rule into something more progressive. This decentralised solution quickly failed as political parties in the colonies demanded full participation in each territory's legislative and executive institutions, while social movements demanded better wages, fairer crop prices and more educational facilities. Political mobilisation within the different colonies was largely peaceful though this was not always the case as the Mau Mau Emergency in Kenya in the early 1950s indicates. By the late 1950s, the Colonial Office had concluded that, though it was unclear whether most colonial people were ready for their freedom, cultivating friendly post-colonial relations with independent states was more cost-effective than trying to hang on to the colonies.[122]

By February 1960, when Harold Macmillan gave his 'winds of change' speech in South Africa, the decolonisation of British Africa had already begun.[123] Ghana (Gold Coast) gained its independence in 1957 followed by Nigeria and Somalia (British and Italian Somaliland) in 1960, Tanzania (Tanganyika) and

---

[120] Kyle, Keith, *Suez: Britain's End of Empire in the Middle East*, (Weidenfeld & Nicolson), 1991, (I. B. Tauris), 2011, remains the most valuable discussion of this imperial debacle. See also, Smith, Simon C., (ed.), *Reassessing Suez 1956: Perspectives on the Crisis and its Aftermath*, (Ashgate), 2008, and Tunzelman, Alex von, *Blood and Sand: Suez, Hungary and The Crisis that Shook the World*, (Simon & Schuster), 2016. See also, Smith, Simon C., 'Britain's Decision to Withdraw from the Persian Gulf: A Pettern not a Puzzle', *Journal of Imperial and Commonswealth History*, Vol. 44, (2), (2016), pp. 328-351.

[121] See, for instance, Schuknecht, R., *British Colonial Development Policy after the Second World War: The Case of Sukumaland, Tanganyika*, (LIT Verlag Munster), 2010, an excellent case-study.

[122] Hargreaves, John, *Decolonization in Africa*, 2nd ed., (Longman), 1996. See also, Falola, Toyin, and Roberts, A. D., 'West Africa', and Lonsdale, John, 'East Africa', *OHBE*, Vol. 4, pp. 515-544.

[123] Ibid, Heinlein, Frank, *British Government Policy and Decolonisation, 1945-1963: Scrutinizing the Official Mind*, pp. 217-290, examines policy between 1959 and 1963.

Sierra Leone the following year, Uganda (British East Africa) in 1962 and Kenya (British East Africa) and Zanzibar in 1963, Zambia (Northern Rhodesia) and Malawi (Nyasaland) in 1964, Gambia in 1965, Botswana (Bechuanaland) and Lesotho (Basutoland) in 1966 and finally Swaziland and Mauritius in 1968. Why this occurred so quickly is a matter of some debate. For some, decolonisation is evidence of the economics of decline as the value of goods produced fell largely because of American competition. Others suggest that colonial economies expanded after 1945 and that decolonisation was 'a revolution in rising expectations'. Iain Macleod, the Colonial Secretary from 1959 to 1961, believed that unless the speed of decolonisation was increased, there would be widespread unrest and bloodshed that British military forces would have been unable to contain. Macmillan accepted these political arguments and his position was strengthened by the political and personal support of President John F. Kennedy who also favoured decolonisation in Africa.

The independence of growing numbers of colonies in the post-war period and the termination of mandates led to a decrease in the responsibilities of the Colonial Office. After the independence of India in 1947 and Burma the following year, the Dominion Office was merged with the India and Burma Office to form the Commonwealth Relations Office responsible for Britain's relationship with its former colonies. In July 1961, responsibilities for overseas aid and development formerly borne by the Colonial Office were transferred to the new Department of Technical Co-operation and several technical advisers were transferred with them. In March 1962, relations with Northern Rhodesia and Nyasaland were transferred to the Central African Office that was under the personal control of the Home Secretary. In 1966, the Commonwealth Relations Office merged with the Colonial Office to form the Commonwealth Office. Two years later, this department was finally merged into the Foreign Office, establishing the modern Foreign and Commonwealth Office.

This institutional change marked a major turning point in Britain's relations with its Pacific Islands. In place of long-nurtured traditions of trusteeship for indigenous populations that had evolved in the Colonial Office, the new Foreign & Commonwealth Office concentrated on fostering British interests that meant reducing distant commitments and focussing on the Atlantic world and Europe. In the aftermath of the Second World War, Britain had announced that the Pacific Islands were so small, remote and with limited resources that they could never become independent states. The tenacity of Pacific Islanders in maintaining their cultures contrasted with the more strident Afro-Asia nationalisms. Anti-imperialist pressure in the United Nations had a major role in this change in policy, as did the pioneering examples marked by the release of Western Samoa by New Zealand in 1962 and Nauru by Australia in 1968. The result, between 1970 and 1980, was independence for six new states--Tonga, Fiji, Solomon Islands, Tuvalu, Kiribati, and Vanuatu.[124]

[124] McIntyre, W. David, *Winding up the British Empire in the Pacific Islands*, (Oxford University Press), 2014.

Decolonisation in the West Indies occurred between 1962 and 1983 and was less problematic than in Africa or Asia.[125] Attempts in 1958 to establish a Federation of the West Indies as a political unit that would become independent of Britain as a single state and create a strong trading partner for Britain faltered within four years resulting in the independence of Jamaica, Trinidad and Barbados by 1966. Although the Caribbean states retained close links with Britain, they looked increasingly to the United States for support especially against Cuban supported communist agitation. Cyprus proved an obdurate problem for British decolonisation with its population divided into Greeks and a minority of Turks. After a bloody and extended rebellion against British rule by those in favour of union with Greece (*Enosis*), the island was given its independence in August 1960. This failed to resolve unrest and the threat of civil war led to United Nations intervention in 1963. After a coup in 1974 by pro-Enosis elements in the military, Turkish forces invaded Northern Cyprus and a separate state was proclaimed there in 1983. Although Britain retains two military bases in Cyprus—the Sovereign Base Areas of Akrotiri and Dhekelia--the problem of policing the partitioned state passed out of British hands and the 'green line' between Turkish and Greek Cyprus is controlled by the United Nations.

When Britain finally entered the European Community in 1973, the line had been drawn under Britain's imperial age. But the ending of an empire is rarely a tidy affair. The Southern Rhodesian rebellion lasted until the formation of Zimbabwe in 1980, Britain fought a war to retain the Falkland Islands in 1982 and Hong Kong continued, with Chinese agreement, as a British dependency until 1997. Fourteen former Crown colonies, such as the British Antarctic Territory, the Falklands, Gibraltar and the British Virgin Islands remain as British Overseas Territories that have yet to gain independence or have voted to remain British territories.[126] American Secretary of State Dean Acheson's much cited comment in a speech at West Point in 1962 that 'Great Britain has lost an Empire and has not yet found a role' was both poignant and, in the aftermath of decision of the referendum on 23 June 2016 to leave the EU, true.

An empire of movement

The British Empire was not only an empire of place, it was also an empire of movement.[127] From the early-seventeenth century, emigrants left British Isles and

---

[125] Rothermund, Dietmar, *The Routledge Companion to Decolonization*, (Routledge), 2006, pp. 210-221, provides a good summary of developments in the West Indies. See also, Johnson, Howard, 'The British Caribbean from Demobilization to Constitutional Decolonization', *OHBE*, Vol. 4, pp. 597-622.

[126] The term 'British Overseas Territory' was introduced by the British Overseas Territories Act 2002, and replaced the name 'British Dependent Territory' introduced in the British Nationality Act 1981. Collectively they cover an approximate land area of 667,000 square miles with a population of just over a quarter of a million people.

[127] See, Bade, Klaus J., Emmer, Pieter C., Lucassen, Leo and Oltmer, Jochen, (eds.), *The Encyclopedia of European Migration and Minorities from the Seventeenth Century to the Present*, (Cambridge University Press), 2011. Richards, Eric, *Britannia's Children: Emigration from England, Scotland, Wales and Ireland since 1600*, (Hambledon Continuum), 2004, and Murdoch, Alexander, *British Emigration, 1603-1914*, (Palgrave),

sought new opportunities first in the burgeoning colonies in North America and, especially during the nineteenth century in the newly independent United States and across the British Empire from Canada to New Zealand and Australia to South Africa and India. It is a process that continues especially within the unrestricted labour markets of the European Union. Where these emigrants came from within the British Isles, their religion, when and why they left the country, what they took with them in the form of skills and capital and where they settled really did matter. Poverty, persecution, famine, all provided justification for emigration.[128] In 1783, at the end of the American War of Independence, up to 100,000 Loyalists were evacuated from the fledgling United States, in which their futures were bleak, and sailed for Britain, Canada, Jamaica and the Bahamas in search of a fresh beginning.[129] Opportunities could be immense for pioneer settlers when opening up parts of Canada and Australia or more limited for those who arrived as convicts in the American colonies or Australia or in the established communities of east-coast towns and cities of what became the United States, with little but physical labour to offer the labour market. Emigration figures show that between 1821 and 1915 some 10 million people left Great Britain and a further 6 million left Ireland for non-European destinations. More than half went to the USA and a further fifth to Australasia. Emigration was far more important for Irish and Scottish populations than it was for England: between 1853 and 1900, net emigration represented 9 per cent of natural increase in England and Wales but 25 per cent in Scotland. It is also important to note that of the 4¾ million who left England and Wales, only about 2¼ million were permanent migrants.

Emigration, whether forced in the case of convict labour or by choice, was a risky process for those involved. In addition to uncertainty about opportunities in new lands, there were the dangers of the voyage itself. Once aboard ship, there was no place to escape from disease. Even among regular sailors, usually selected from among fit men, there were often epidemics or other unexpected dangers to health lurking at overseas ports, or else unhygienic supplies to contend with during any voyage. Things might be worse for civilian passengers. Convicts and emigrants were generally from among 'the labouring poor' in Britain. Furthermore, there were usually women and children on ships bound for on the long voyage to Australia whose physical condition often meant that they were in an even weaker state. Ships with convicts or emigrants might accommodate a variety of social classes compared with a naval man-of-war. Indeed, they carried microcosms of British society.[130]

2004, provide an overview. Belich, James, *Replenishing the Earth. The Settler Revolution and the Rise of the Anglo-World, 1783-1939*, (Oxford University Press), 2009, Harper, Marjorie, and Constantine, Stephen, *Migration and Empire*, (Oxford University Press), 2010, and Bickers, Robert, (ed.), *Settlers and Expatriates*, (Oxford University Press), 2010, focus on the nineteenth and twentieth centuries.

[128] I have explored the issue of the Irish diaspora in considerable detail in my *Famine, Fenians and Freedom, 1830-1882*, pp. 10-92.

[129] Jasanoff, Maya, *Liberty's Exiles: The Loss of America and the Remaking of the British Empire*, (Harper Press), 2011, pp. 351-358, seeks to measure this exodus.

[130] Foxhall, Katherine, *Health, Medicine and the Sea: Australian Voyages, c1815-1860*, (Manchester University Press), 2012.

The experiences and attitudes of emigrants were different in and across time. Treating the global British as if they all belonged to a single movement or that their experiences in one destination were representative of their experiences elsewhere impoverishes their rich and complex history. There were other peoples who moved within Britain's empire but far less freely. Slaves were taken from West Africa across the Atlantic to the American and Caribbean colonies and indentured labourers, free unlike slaves but equally restrained, crossed the oceans to labour in the plantations of the empire before and especially after slavery was abolished in 1833. Although the experiences of these economic migrants varied, underpinning them all was a brutal system of labour exploitation maintained by the culture of the whip. Whether Ferguson is right that the British Empire 'made' the modern world is questionable, but there is no doubting the lasting impact of migration within that empire. The unlocking of natural resources, the development of international trade and the spread of English language and culture were the result of the movement of the British overseas. Many emigrants saw themselves not as migrants but as participants in a project of 'overseas settlement': migration was simply the movement to foreign lands while settlement meant populating a wider *British* world

Adult migration

Migration was an integral part of the political process through which British identity, the British state and the British Empire were constructed. Although the notion of an imperial Britain may not have been well received in Scotland, Wales and Ireland in the seventeenth and eighteenth centuries, there was greater common ground in the idea of imperial Britain existing overseas. British settlement in the American colonies became the basis for Britain's notion of empire and emigration and, at least until the late-eighteenth century, was an expression of the movement of British energies from east to west, first in Ireland and then further west to the American colonies.[131] Attitudes to emigration were, however, ambivalent and in 1719 Parliament banned the emigration of artisans who were central to Britain's economic expansion. Adam Smith suggested that colonial wealth could impoverish countries rather than enrich them and implied that emigration reduced the energies of the country when population was needed for the transformation of Britain itself.[132] Colonies could be populated by slaves and by Protestants from northern Europe rather than British emigrants and Britain could still expand its empire.

During the nineteenth century, retaining Britain's population was increasingly viewed not as the basis for economic and commercial growth but as a cancer that endangered British society. Emigration provided a solution that allowed the poor to escape from the impoverished rural and urban slums to the expanding colonies, themselves a source of wealth for Britain's continuing prosperity and greatness. Emigration to the British colonies in the nineteenth and twentieth centuries was openly encouraged by the government and charities

[131] Horn, James, 'British Diaspora: Emigration from Britain, 1680-1815', *OHBE,* Vol. 2, pp. 28-52.

[132] For his discussion on colonies see, Smith Adam, *The Works of Adam Smith, Vol. 3, The Nature and Causes of the Wealth of Nations*, (T. Cadell), 1811, pp. 343-399.

and by individuals and parishes. Whether this was the British state 'shovelling out the poor' as some colonial commentators believed, its aim was to populate the empire with British citizens as well as alleviating social distress in Britain and Ireland.[133] Rising levels of literacy meant that pamphlets calling for emigration proved popular among working- and middle-class audiences.[134] For instance, John A. Etzler published *Emigration to the tropical world for the melioration of all classes of the people of all nations* in 1844, while J. Boyd wrote *State directed emigration* in 1883 and P. J. Andrews *The coming race?: some reflections on the inherent dangers of mass civilisation in Britain and the opportunities for balanced spiritual development by peopling the dominions* in 1929. The Empire Parliamentary Association issued pamphlets on emigration to Canada and Australia and the Salvation Army *Organised Empire migration and settlement* in 1930. There were also publications from other organisations such as the Imperial Immigration League, the Landholders and Commercial Association of British India, the Clerkenwell Emigration Society, the Fund for Promoting Female Emancipation and the London Compositors' Emigration Aid Society. Books, children's literature, souvenirs, paintings, public monuments and lectures all transmitted narratives of martial heroism from the mid-nineteenth century reinforcing the notion that emigration was not only practical but also, in some ways, heroic.[135] Foreign missionary representatives canvassed working-class Sunday schools and chapels and middle-class philanthropists for subscriptions but the missionary presence at local level extended far beyond this.[136] Missionary organisations was so effective that contemporaries claimed, 'many a small tradesman or rustic knows more of African or Polynesian life than London journalists'.[137] Popular culture was saturated by imperial images from sauce bottles and biscuit tins to plays and in due course films, all of which amounted to populist propaganda on an industrial scale.[138]

---

[133] See, for instance, Moran, Gerard. ''Shovelling out the poor': assisted emigration from Ireland from the great famine to the fall of Parnell', in ibid, Duffy, Patrick J., and Moran, Gerard, (eds.), *To and from Ireland: planned migration schemes c.1600-2000*, (Geography Publications), 2004, pp. 137-154.

[134] Piesse, Jude, *British Settler Emigration in Print, 1832-1877*, (Oxford University Press), 2016, considers the importance of metropolitan periodical print culture.

[135] MacKenzie, J. M., 'Heroic myths of empire,' in MacKenzie, J. M., (ed.), *Popular Imperialism and the Military*, (Manchester University Press), 1992, pp. 10-38, considers the heroic reputation of Henry Haverlock, David Livingstone, Charles Gordon and T. E. Lawrence.

[136] Thorne, Susan, ''The Conversion of Englishmen and the Conversion of the World Inseparable': Missionary Imperialism and the Language of Class in Early Industrial Britain', in Cooper, Frederick, and Stoler, Laura Ann, (eds.), *Tensions of Empire: Colonial Cultures in a Bourgeois World*, (University of California Press), 1997, pp. 238-262.

[137] 'Christian Missions and the Westminster Review', *London Quarterly Review*, Vol. 7, (1857), pp. 209-261, at p. 239.

[138] Porter, Bernard, *The Absent-Minded Imperialists: Empire, Society and Culture in Britain*, (Oxford University Press), 2004, despite overwhelming evidence to the contrary, insists that popular culture promoting the imperial ideal had no effect on the public.

Scottish and especially Irish[139] emigration were far greater than that of the English in proportion to the size of their respective populations. Emigration from Scotland proved particularly successful.[140] Sir Charles Dilke, writing in 1869, remarked:

> In British settlements, from Canada to Ceylon, from Dunedin to Bombay, for every Englishman that you meet who has worked himself up to wealth from small beginnings without external aid, you find ten Scotchmen.[141]

The Scots grasped the opportunities afforded by union in 1707 and there were large outflows of men and women looking for a new life and a new beginning, initially in North America. Between 1763 and 1777, 50,000 Scots largely from the west of Scotland settled in North America.[142] They quickly dominated the tobacco trade and other areas of economic life, such as fur-trapping in Canada. Education and religion were other areas of cultural life where the Scottish influence was dominant. Such was the strength of the Scottish presence in America that 19 of the 56 delegates who signed the Declaration of Independence came from Scotland or Ulster. The Scottish presence was also strongly present in India.[143] Henry Dundas became President of the Board of Control in 1784 and with his support Scots came to dominate the activities of the East India Company. By 1792, they made up one in nine Company officials, one in eleven common soldiers and one in three officers. Scottish scholars and scientists made important contributions to Indian culture and society: for instance, Colin Campbell completed the first geographical survey of India; Alexander Kydd created the Botanic gardens in Calcutta while others developed the infrastructure of India. Even after the dissolution of the East India Company in 1857 and the introduction of competitive entry into the British administration, they still played an important part in the running of India. Scots were important to the development of the Empire in diverse ways: as businessmen, as educators, as missionaries, as imperial administrators and soldiers.[144] Whether this made

---

139 Reid, Richard, *Aspects of Irish assisted Emigration to New South Wales 1848-1870*, Ph.D., Thesis, Australian National University, 2012.

140 Gray, M., 'The Course of Scottish Emigration, 1750-1914: Enduring Influences and Changing Circumstances', in Devine, T. M., (ed.), *Scottish Emigration and Scottish Society*, (John Donald), 1992, pp. 16-36, provides a good summary. See also, Mackenzie, John M., and Devine, T. M., (eds.), *Scotland and the British Empire*, (Oxford University Press), 2011, and Devine, T. M., *To the Ends of the Earth: Scotland's Global Diaspora, 1750-2010*, (Allen Lane), 2011.

141 Dilke, Charles W., *Greater Britain: A record of travel in English-speaking countries during 1866 and 1867,* (Harper & Brothers), 1969, p. 511.

142 Dobson, D., *Scottish Emigration to Colonial America, 1607-1785*, (University of Georgia Press), 2004, and Landsman, Ned C., 'Nation, Migration and the Province in the First British Empire: Scotland and the Americas 1600-1800', *American Historical Review*, Vol. 104, (1999), pp. 463-475.

143 Bryant, G. J., 'Scots in India in the Eighteenth Century', *Scottish Historical Review*, Vol. 64, (1985), pp. 22-41, provides a good overview.

144 MacKenzie, John M., and Dalziel, Nigel R., *The Scots in South Africa: Ethnicity, Gender and Race, 1772-1914*, (Manchester University Press), 2007, Szasz, F. M., *Scots in the North American West, 1790-1917*, (University of Oklahoma Press), 2000, pp. 21-48,

the empire a 'Scottish empire', as some historians have argued is debatable.[145] Whatever the importance of Scots as emigrants or administrators of empire, decisions about the direction of empire and the policies through which it was ruled were made in London. It was the British state that dominated the empire.

As concerns over 'surplus population' grew, there was an increase in landless peasants from the Highlands and unemployed craftsmen, labourers and small farmers from the Lowlands willing to emigrate. Most were aged between 16 and 29 and men rather than women. Whatever the cause, Scotland lost between 10 and 47 per cent of its natural population increase every decade between 1830 and 1940; a rate exceeded only in Ireland and Norway. Even these countries were dwarfed by emigration from Scotland in the years 1904-1913 and again in 1921-1930, when over half a million people emigrated exceeding the entire natural increase and constituted one-fifth of the total working population.[146] Until about 1855, a number of the emigrants from the Highlands were actually forced to leave the land because of mass evictions.[147] The Emigration Act in 1851 made emigration more freely available to the poorest with the Highlands and Islands Emigration Society established to manage the process of resettlement. Under the scheme a landlord could secure a passage to Australia for a nominee at the cost of £1 and between 1846 and 1857, over 16,000 people, largely poor young men, were assisted to emigrate. Many settled in Canada in places such as Ontario and Nova Scotia, where they could continue to farm and maintain their style of life and ethnic identity. In Nova Scotia in the first half of the nineteenth century, 59 per cent of settlers from Britain were Scots-born. In the Lowlands, the decision to move abroad was nearly always the outcome of the desire to improve living standards because they experienced low wages, poor housing conditions and unemployment and, unlike in the Highlands, was voluntary. Emigration was seen by trades unions and other voluntary groups as a practical solution to unemployment and economic depression. The high points in emigration corresponded with years of severe economic depression in the late 1840s and early 1850s, the mid-1880s and between 1906 and 1913. Emigration was heavy in the period 1871-1931 but it was more than offset the increase in the population due to new births. This trend was brought to a halt in the 1930s as the global depression saw emigrants

---

151-194, and Hamilton, Douglas J., *Scotland, the Caribbean and the Atlantic World 1750-1820*, (Manchester University Press), 2005, discuss the range of Scottish imperial involvement.

[145] On this issue see, Devine, T. M., *Scotland's Empire*, (Penguin), 2003, and Fry, M, *The Scottish Empire*, (Tuckwell Press), 2001.

[146] Richards, E., 'Varieties of Scottish emigration in the nineteenth century, *Australian Historical Studies*, Vol. 21, (1985), pp. 473-494. See also, McCarthy, Angela, 'Scottish Migrant Ethnic Identities in the British Empire since the nineteenth century', in ibid, Mackenzie, John M., and Devine, T. M., *Scotland and the British Empire*, pp. 118-146.

[147] Richards, Eric, *A History of the Highland Clearances: Agrarian Transformation and the Evictions 1746-1886*, (Croom Helm), 1982, provides the context while *A History of the Highland Clearances, Volume 2: Emigration, Protest, Reasons*, (Croom Helm), 1985, pp. 179-285, examines emigration.

returning home and the numbers leaving Scotland were at their lowest for a century.[148]

Canada was the most important destination of emigrants during the first half of the nineteenth century and between 1825 and 1835, over 70 per cent of emigrants from Scotland settled there.[149] This changed substantially after 1860 and especially 1900 as skilled urban workers became the most important emigrants. In 1912 and 1913, 47 per cent of adult male emigrants from Scotland described themselves as skilled, compared with 36 per cent of those from England and Wales. Only 29 per cent classed themselves as labourers. In the late-nineteenth century, individuals' social class frequently determined the country where they settled. Unskilled labourers tended to opt for Canada and Australia, while skilled workers preferred South Africa and the USA.[150] The middle-classes strongly preferred South Africa. Emigration acted as a safety valve for modern Scotland and although the British Empire was the main beneficiary of this process, the former also benefited in terms of wealth and profit. The great commercial Palladian mansions of Edinburgh and Glasgow were built from the profits of the colonial trade. In addition, substantial areas of employment were dependent on Empire providing the economic mortar that held the Union together. The collapse of the Empire after 1945 forced Scotland to make a painful transition from an economy based on heavy industry to one dependent on services and electronics. It also led to a redrawing of the political map as the Unionist vote evaporated. In 1955, Scottish Conservative Party took 50.1 per cent of the popular vote and held half of Scotland's 72 parliamentary seats. This high-point was followed by a gradual decline from 1964 until in 1997, with 17.5 per cent of the popular vote, it took no seats at all and only one seat in the 2001, 2005, 2010 and 2015 General Elections.[151]

---

[148] Harper, M, *Emigration from Scotland between the wars: opportunity or exile?* (Manchester University Press), 1998.

[149] Calder, Jenni, *Scots in Canada*, (Dundurn Press), 2003, is a good introduction. Ibid, Jasanoff, Maya, *Liberty's Exiles: The Loss of America and the Remaking of the British Empire*, pp. 147-213, looks at the Loyalist exodus to Canada in the 1780s and 1790s. Hornsby, Stephen J., 'Patterns of Scottish emigration to Canada, 1750-1870', *Journal of Historical Geography*, Vol. 18, (1992), pp. 397-416. See also, Campey, Lucille H., *The Scottish Pioneers of Upper Canada, 1784-1855: Glengarry and beyond*, (Dundurn Press), 2005, *After The Hector: The Scottish Pioneers of Nova Scotia and Cape Breton 1773-1852*, (Dundurn Press), 2004, and *An Unstoppable Force: The Scottish Exodus to Canada*, (Dundurn Press), 2008. On Canadian immigration policy, see Kelley, Ninette, and Trebilcock, M. J., *The Making of the Mosaic: A History of Canadian Immigration Policy*, (University of Toronto Press), 1999.

[150] Macmillan, D. S., *Scotland and Australia, 1788-1850: emigration, commerce and investment*, (Oxford University Press), 1967, 'The Scots', in Jupp, James, (ed.), *The Australian people: an Encyclopedia of the Nation, Its People and Their Origins*, (Cambridge University Press), 2001, pp. 644-665, and Prentice, Malcolm D., *The Scots in Australia: A Study of New South Wales, Victoria and Queensland 1788-1900*, (University of Sydney Press), 1983, provide the context.

[151] Devine, T. M., 'The Break-up of Britain?: Scotland and the end of Empire: The Prothero Lecture', *Transactions of the Royal Historical Society*, sixth series, Vol. 16, (2006), pp. 163-180.

The adult experience of emigration in England and Wales paralleled that in Scotland.[152] The bulk of the migrant population went to the United States in the eighteenth century, although Canada and Australia were popular destinations after 1815. America fell behind Canada and Australia in attracting large groups of emigrants after 1900 and South Africa was beginning to attract emigrant in significant numbers. In 1911, of the more than 450,000 Britons who left the United Kingdom, almost half settled in Canada, nearly a quarter in Australia and approximately one tenth in South Africa. Subsidised emigration made it possible for the poor to be sent abroad, in the main to North America and Australia. The Poor Law Amendment Act 1834 secured the passage of more than 25,000 'paupers' by 1860 and the Colonial Land and Emigration Commissioners helped 370,000 people move to Australia between 1840 and 1869.[153] Young men made up most migrants though couples and family units were also prominent. Migrants came from many different types of occupations. Most Welsh emigrants were miners or worked in the iron, steel, copper and tin industries. However, general labourers and workers from the building trades and textile workers, engineers, farmers, clerical and commercial workers were also represented. In the 1880s, when emigration had reached massive proportions, the most important group among the immigrants was urban unskilled workers. This suggests that, by the 1880s, the occupations of British emigrants reflected closely those of Britain's population.[154]

Adult emigration, whatever its motivation in Britain, was determined by the economic needs of the colonies that were different at different times. Most of New Zealand's English, at least until 1920, were largely from the rural, working-class. Unlike the United States, which attracted unskilled labourers and industrial workers, New Zealand recruited agricultural labourers and pre-industrial craftsmen among the men and domestic servants among the women. It needed labourers and tradesmen for its farms, ports, mines and towns and artisans to meet the needs of its growing population. Builders were in especial demand and emigrated in large numbers helped by the introduction of assisted migration in 1871. Migration from England tailed off in the late-1880s and 1890s because of depression in the New Zealand economy.[155] This also corresponded with a change the regional origins and occupations of the English arrivals. The numbers

---

[152] For Wales see Bowen, H. C., (ed.), *Wales and the British Overseas Empire: Interactions and Influences, 1650-1830*, (Manchester University Press), 2011. For England see, Bueltmann, Tanja, Gleeson, David T., and Macraild, Donald M., (eds.), *Locating the English Diaspora, 1500-2010*, (Manchester University Press), 2014.

[153] Richards, Eric, 'How Did Poor People Emigrate from the British Isles to Australia in the Nineteenth Century?' *Journal of British Studies*, Vol. 32, (1993), pp. 250-279, and Beever, A., 'From a Place of 'Horrible Destitution' to a Paradise of the Working class: The Transformation of British Working class Attitudes to Australia 1841-1851', *Labour History*, no. 40, (1981), pp. 1-15.

[154] Erickson, Charlotte, *Leaving England: Essays on British Emigration in the Nineteenth Century*, (Cornell University Press), 1994, and Baines, Dudley, *Migration in a Mature Economy: Emigration and Internal Migration in England and Wales 1861-1900*, (Cambridge University Press), 1985.

[155] Simpson, Tony, *The immigrants: the great migration from Britain to New Zealand, 1830-1890*, (Godwit), 1997.

engaged in agricultural work declined, while those working in industry and mining increased. These trends continued in the twentieth century and became even more marked after 1945. The post-1900 development of coal mining in New Zealand was aided by the arrival of miners from northern England. Industry expanded with the influx of skilled industrial workers from Yorkshire and Lancashire. The rapid growth of trade unions after 1890 was associated with the migration of English workers in the textile, clothing, footwear, mining and marine transport industries. Over 80,000 assisted British migrants arrived in New Zealand between 1947 and 1975, selected for the contribution that they could make to industry, education and health.[156] As New Zealand became less focused on England and ended all forms of assisted migration, and as England turned its attention to Europe rather than to the Commonwealth, so the appeal of migrating to New Zealand began to fade.[157]

Child and youth migration

Child migration played an important role in emigration as early as 1617 when the Virginia Company considered sending 'vagrant' children to the Americas. Although a hundred children were sent from Liverpool and London in 1618 and 1619, question about its legality were not resolved until early 1620 when the Privy Council authorised child migration.[158] Throughout the seventeenth century, children were sent to the American and Caribbean colonies in increasing numbers but this failed to meet the perennial labour shortage and in 1645 kidnapping or 'spiriting' children had grown to such an extent that Parliament made it a felony. This did not prevent the practice and in the 1740s, over 500 children were kidnapped for the colonies in Aberdeen and its surrounding area though it declined with the loss of the American colonies after 1775.

By the early-nineteenth century, there were increasing concerns about the numbers of children and young people especially, though not exclusively in urban areas, regarded as 'outcasts' with few prospects and a tendency to become involved in criminal activity. Some historians argue that this represented an 'invention' of juvenile crime but there was not so much an 'invention' as a 'reconceptualisation' of the juvenile offender during the nineteenth century.[159]

---

[156] Hutching, Megan, *Long Journey for Sevenpence: Assisted Immigration to New Zealand from the United Kingdom, 1947-1975*, (Victoria University Press), 1999.

[157] Phillips, Jock, & Hearn, Terry, *Settlers: New Zealand Immigrants from England, Ireland & Scotland 1800-1945*, (Auckland University Press), 2008: see http://www.nzhistory.net.nz/culture/home-away-from-home/sources

[158] Johnson, Robert C., 'The Transportation of Vagrant Children from London to Virginia, 1618-1622', in Reinmuth, H. S., (ed.), *Early Stuart Studies: Essays in Honor of David Harris Wilson*, (University of Minnesota Press), 1970, pp. 137-151.

[159] Shore, Heather, *Artful Dodgers: Youth and crime in early nineteenth-century London*, (Royal Historical Society), 1999, Duckworth, Jeannie, *Fagin's Children: Criminal Children in Victorian England*, (Hambledon), 2002, and Abbott, Jane, 'The press and the public visibility of nineteenth-century criminal children', in Rowbotham, Judith and Stevenson, Kim, (eds.), *Criminal conversations: Victorian crimes, social panic, and moral outrage*, (Ohio State University Press), 2005, pp. 23-39. See also, Carpenter, Mary, *Reformatory schools for the children of the perishing and dangerous classes and for juvenile offenders*, (C. Gilpin), 1851, and Adshead, Joseph, 'On juvenile criminals,

Contemporary reports commented on the swarms of ragged children infesting the metropolis and investigations by social and penal reformers were heavily influenced by a hard-core of juvenile offenders. People's awareness of juvenile crime was raised by the publication of *Oliver Twist* in 1837. Dickens shocked people with his description of the Artful Dodger and Fagin's trained gang of metropolitan pickpockets. His story may have been fiction but it was successful in getting people thinking about child crime and how to deal with it. Discussion of juvenile offenders occurred in other parts of the country but it was rarely as influential as the metropolitan perspective.[160]

There was an explosion of voluntary organisations, strongly motivated by evangelical zeal, and some state involvement in sponsoring migration as a means of improving the life chances of children. Although this was not a new solution to child poverty--pauper children had been sent to the Cape Colony, Western Australia and Canada from at least the late-eighteenth century--the enthusiastic adoption of the practice by all the main child rescue agencies from the late 1860s meant that many thousands of children were uprooted and sent abroad.[161] The underlying philosophy stressed the importance of separating child and parent in some circumstances and also pervaded those parts of the world to which the children were sent. It was absorbed in the colonial situation, in often brutal ways, when Indigenous Australians and First Nations children in Australia and Canada were forcibly removed from their homes. In 1830, the Children's Friend Society, which aimed to reform outcast children, was formed and during the 1830s sent between 700 and 800 boys as child migrants to the Cape Colony and a smaller number to Toronto in Upper Canada. In 1849, Ragged Schools, a movement founded five years earlier, received £1,500 to send 150 children to New South Wales. The following year, Parliament enabled Poor Law Guardians with the consent of the Poor Law Board to fund the emigration of any child in their care. This led to some child migration as, for instance, the St Pancras Poor Law Guardians sent a small number of children to British colonies in the Caribbean. In 1875, John Doyle, Poor Law Inspector was highly critical of some aspects of child migration to Canada and this led to a decline the number of children being sent abroad by workhouses, industrial schools and reformatories. Most child migrants now came from private care institutions.

The main pressure for child rescue and the religious impulses which powered it can be laid at the door of four men, Thomas Barnardo, Thomas Bowman Stephenson, Edward de Mountjoie Rudolf and Benjamin Waugh, the founders of Dr Barnardo's Homes, National Children's Homes, the Church of England Central Homes for Waifs and Strays and the National Society for the Prevention of Cruelty to Children. Their success in attracting financial and other support for their work owed much to their ability to tailor their publicity to contemporary ideas about childhood, the threats posed to it by urban life and the negligence of poor parents. Their publications also included skilfully chosen

---

reformatories, and the means of rendering the perishing and dangerous classes serviceable to the state', *Transactions of the Manchester Statistical Society*, (1855-6), pp. 67-122.

160 Ibid, Harper, Marjorie, and Constantine, Stephen, *Migration and Empire*, pp. 247-276, provides an up-to-date analysis of child migration.

161 Boucher, Ellen, *Empire's Children: Child Emigration, Welfare and the Decline of the British World, 1869-1967*. (Cambridge University Press), 2014, pp. 23-92.

illustrations and photographs in case mere words failed to convey the message. Removing children from poor and inadequate homes was a Christian duty and in the best interests of the child. Not only did their rescuers consider that the children's expectations of a better life would be enhanced if they were removed from failing parents, they believed themselves to be called to a higher and more important mission, the salvation of those children's souls.

The initial focus for migration was Canada.[162] Scottish-born evangelist, Annie Macpherson opened her House of Industry in Spitalfields in 1869 to encourage emigration from the deprived East End of London.[163] The following year, she escorted her first party of 100 children to a receiving centre at Belleville in Ontario. In 1872, she opened two further Canadian receiving homes at Galt in Ontario and Knowlton in Quebec arranging emigration parties from Barnardo's, the Orphan Homes of Scotland (founded by William Quarrier) and the Smyly homes of Dublin as well as her own London Homes of Industry.[164] In this she received growing support from Thomas Barnardo who had begun his own work with the poor in London and who, by 1881, had embraced child migration enthusiastically.[165] The Custody of Children Act 1891, largely the work of Barnardo, legalised the work of private emigration societies in what had previously been a grey legal area.

Maria Rye, described in 1869 as 'the most successful of the priestesses of emigration',[166] founded the Female Middle-Class Emigration Society in 1861, and was responsible for escorting parties of young women to Australia, Canada and New Zealand.[167] From 1869, she also assisted young girls from workhouses, aged between 5-12 years. In September 1869, she sent her first party of 76 children--including many from Liverpool workhouse schools--to Canada. In the Annual Report of 1874, she said that the 'expense of taking a child out of the gutters in London, and placing it in Canada...may be roughly reckoned at £15

---

[162] Bagnell, Kenneth, *The Little Immigrants: The orphans who came to Canada*, (Macmillan), 1980, and Parr, Joy, *Labouring Children: British immigrant apprentices to Canada, 1869-1924*, (Croom Helm), 1980, provide a sound history of the Canadian migrations. See also, Dorbett, Gail H., *Nation Builders: Barnardo Children in Canada*, (Dundurn Press), 2002, pp. 11-64, and Parker, Roy, *Uprooted: The Shipment of Poor Children to Canada, 1867-1917*, (The Policy Press), 2010.

[163] Lowe, Clara, M. S., *God's Answers: A Record of Miss Annie Macpherson's Work at the Home of Industry, Spitalfields, London and in Canada*, (Nisbet and Co.), 1882.

[164] Macpherson, Annie, *Canadian Homes for London Wanderers*, (Morgan, Chase & Scott), 1870, and *Summer in Canada*, (Morgan & Scott), 1872, furnish Macpherson's views on child migration while, Christopher, Alfred, M. W., *Visits to Miss Macpherson's three homes for boys and girls in Canada*, 1872, provides supportive comment.

[165] Wagner, G. M. M., *Barnardo*, (Weidenfeld & Nicolson), 1979, and Williams, A. E., *Barnardo of Stepney: the father of nobody's children*, (Allen and Unwin), 1966.

[166] *The Times*, 29 October 1869, p. 7.

[167] Rye, M. S., *Emigration of Educated Women*, (Emily Faithfull & Co.), 1862, Rye, M. S., *What the People Say About the Children and What the Children Say About Canada*, (James Wade), 1871, Alcock, Rutherford, *Miss Rye and the Disposal of Our Pauper Children*, 1879, Marquess of Lorne, 'Miss Rye's Girls Homes', *Girls Own Paper*, May 1884. Parr, Joy, Maria Susan Rye', *DCB*, Vol. 13, and Diamond, Marion, *Emigration and Empire: The Life of Maria S. Rye*, (Garland Publishing), 1999, provide biographical details.

per head'.[168] Her main home in England was in Peckham, opened in 1872. Most girls spent up to a year there before they were sent to Canada via Liverpool and Quebec, from where they would travel by train to the reception home at Niagara, called 'Our Western Home'. In 1874, the Local Government Board asked Andrew Doyle, one of its senior inspectors, to report on the schemes for emigration of workhouse children to Canada, following concern expressed about the schemes operated by Maria Rye and Annie MacPherson. He also noted that children of all kinds, including 'street arabs', juvenile delinquents and respectable orphans were thrown together in an unsatisfactory manner. Doyle's report concluded that more discrimination and greater supervision was required in the selection of placements for the children. Although young children were frequently adopted, and generally well placed and treated with kindness and affection, most older children were placed in farm service and many of them suffered hardship, ill-treatment and deprivation. He thought that safeguards must be put in place to provide for their protection by suggesting the local government in Canada provide a system for visiting and supervising children. Local committees could be established and visits made by school inspectors. He found that many children had not been visited for two to three years, and many others had been lost altogether. He recommended that girls should not be sent to Canada after the age of about 7 to 8 years. as older girls tended to suffer more than younger children from homesickness.

Doyle was highly critical of the work of Rye and Macpherson, noting that children experienced poor travelling conditions, lack of training prior to emigration and little supervision on placement. Macpherson responded positively to Doyle's report, accepting some of the criticisms and making changes, but Rye was very hostile, partly because Doyle was a Roman Catholic, and corresponded with him to defend her position.[169] Her activities continued much as they had before. Following Doyle's report, the Local Government Board stopped the emigration of children from workhouses in March 1875, a decision that forced Maria Rye to suspend sending out more children for two years. On her retirement in 1896–she died in 1903--the management of her organisation passed to the Church of England Waifs and Strays Society (later the Children's Society) that sent out approximately 3,940 children to Canada, Australia and Southern Rhodesia between 1883 and 1995.

The Roman Catholic Church was also involved in child migration that was pioneered by the 'Crusade of Rescue' in London from 1859 and by Father Nugent in Liverpool from 1870.[170] His was the first of the Catholic organisations to send children to Canada working with with local parish priests who placed the

---

[168] Liverpool University, Special Collections and Archives, GB 0141 D630 1/1.

[169] Andrew Doyle's charges, and Rye's response to them, were published in pamphlet form and in 'Pauper Children (Canada)', *Parliamentary Papers*, House of Commons, 1875, 63, no.9: pp. 255-298, *Copy "of a report to the right honourable the president of the Local Government Board, by Andrew Doyle, esquire, local government inspector, as to the emigration of pauper children to Canada"*, pp. 277, 284, 286.

[170] Furnival, John, *Children of the Second Spring. Father James Nugent and the Work of Child Care in Liverpool*, (Gracewing Publications), 2005, pp. 167-275, and Bennett, Canon J. O., *Fether Nugent of Liverpool*, (Liverpool Catholic Children's Protection Society), 1949, (Birkenhead Press), 1993.

children with local families in Quebec and Ontario. In 1870 a small party of 24 children and Father Nugent set sail for Canada where he became a pioneer in finding new homes, new lives and new opportunities for destitute children. On their arrival, he embarked on a nine-month lecture tour of Canada and America, pleading the case for 'Nobody's Children'. His argument was that 'poverty is no crime, but a misfortune'. Activities were centralised by the Archdiocese of Westminster from 1903 with the formation of the Catholic Emigration Association that conducted the emigration of all Catholic children of 18 years and under from the British Isles to Canada.[171]

The rhetoric of child migration changed in the early-twentieth century and became less religious and more imperial in tone. The National Waifs Association published *Emigration schemes for poor law children* by Thomas Barnado in 1905 and Thomas Sedgwick wrote *Lads for the Empire* in 1914. Mrs Elinor Close adopted a new approach when, in 1903, she called for the training of workhouse children in Canadian farm schools before their placement with Canadian farmers. Kingsley Fairbridge popularised the farm school movement with the support of the Oxford-based Child Emigration Society and the offer of land near Perth by the WA government.[172] From 1911 to 1939, the Dreadnought Trust subsidised youth migration to Australia, largely to New South Wales, with some government assistance. Fairbridge established the first home at Pinjarra, some thirty miles south-east of Perth.[173] The outbreak of war in 1914 ended all emigration from Great Britain but the tentative approaches to child migration since 1900 laid the foundations for post-war developments.[174]

British care societies resumed sending children to Canada in 1920 though on a smaller scale than before the war and increasingly the focus lay in Australia. The Empire Settlement Act in 1923 provided money from central government to assist emigration including child and youth migration. The first Barnardo child migrants arrived in New South Wales and Kingsley Fairbridge received substantial support from the Overseas Settlement Board in London for his farm school in Pinjarra in 1923 and although he died the following year, his farm school movement was accepted as a superior approach to child migration. In 1924, Sir Richard Linton founded the Big Brother Movement in Sydney to encourage youth migration on a large scale. Child migration to Canada was ended during the global slump in the 1930s and there was also a significant reduction in the numbers of children going to Australia. Catholic leaders in Australia were also involved in child migration planning a farm school at Tardun

---

171 'The Catholic Emigration Association. Its Work in Canada', *The Tablet*, 7 October 1905, p. 28.

172 See, Fairbridge, Kingsley, 'Child Emigration to British Colonies', *The Child*, Vol. 1, (1910), pp. 251-254, and Crane, Denis, *John Bull's Surplus Children: A Plea for Giving Them a Fairer Chance*, (Horce Marshall), 1915.

173 Sherrington, Geoffrey, and Jeffery, Chris, *Fairbridge: Empire and Child Migration*, (Woburn Press), 1998, 2013, examines the creation of the Fairbridge child migration scheme and its history in Canada and Australia.

174 Swain, Shurlee, and Hillel, Margot, *Child, Nation, Race and Empire: Child Rescue Discourse, England, Canada and Australia, 1850-1915*, (Manchester University Press), 2010, scrutinices the promotional materials produced by the societies to publicise their work and the children's literature that accompanied it.

that was staffed by the Christian Brothers in the mid-1920s but it was not until 1938 that the first 114 child migrants under Catholic auspices arrived in WA.[175]

The outbreak of war in Europe in 1939 led to the suspension of child and youth migration. The publication of the Curtis Committee Report in 1944 heralded a change in child care principles. Social change meant that few British children were available for child migration and youth migration to Australia was far more popular. In 1952, John Moss, a retired Home Office inspector and member of the Curtis Committee toured Australian child care institutions and his report was sympathetic to child migration for some deprived British citizens.[176] However, a Home Office committee that visited Australia four years later was more critical in its analysis. Its confidential report was highly critical of some Australian care institutions and far less sympathetic to the whole idea of child migration.[177] Child migration had not resumed to Australia until 1947 with most migrants placed in Western Australian institutions and about half of the migrants were from Catholic families. The Big Brother Movement in NSW and Tasmania renewed its youth migration to Australia and during the 1950s brought 400 young men a year. Overall, some 12,500 teenagers came to Australia under the scheme since its inception in 1925 and 1983, when it ceased to sponsor youth migrants. British Catholic care organisations ended child migration in 1956. In 1967, the final nine child migrants came to Australia with the Barnardo organisation. In all, 7,000 child migrants came to Australia between 1947 and 1973 and 1,300 to New Zealand, Rhodesia and Canada. Child migrants were used as cheap labour on Canada's farms, as a means of boosting Australia's post-war population and to preserve white, managerial élite in Rhodesia. One of the earlier motives of the schemes had been to maintain the racial unity of Britain's Empire and certain groups of children were excluded as countries would not accept physically handicapped or black children.[178]

From the mid-1980s, there had been an intense controversy over child migration and especially the physical and sexual abuse migrants suffered. In 1986, the Child Migrant Trust was established to assist former child migrants find their relatives and reunited them with their families. The publication of *Lost Children of the Empire* in 1989 publicised child migration and encouraged popular and academic interest in the issue.[179] This was followed by the formation of organisations in Britain and Australia, government enquiries into child migration and legal action for compensation by former residents of Christian Brothers Boys Homes in Western Australia. An association of former child migrants called Home Children Canada--the term by which child migrants were

[175] Coldrey, D. M., *Child Migration, the Australian Government and the Catholic Church, 1926-1966,* (Tamanarick Publishing), 1992, remains an important study. See also, Gill, A., *Orphans of the Empire: The Shocking Story of Child Migration to Australia*, (Random House), 1997.

[176] Moss, John, *Child Migration to Australia*, (HMSO), 1953.

[177] *Child migration to Australia: Report of a Fact-Finding Mission*, (HMSO), 1956.

[178] On post-war migration see, Paul, Kathleen, 'Changing Childhoods: Child Emigration since 1945', in Lawrence, Jon, and Starkey, Pat., (eds.), *Child Welfare and Social Action in the Nineteenth and Twentieth Centuries: International Perspectives*, (Liverpool University Press), 2001, pp. 121-143.

[179] Bean, Philip, and Melville, Joy, *Lost Children of the Empire*, (Unwin Hyman), 1989.

known--estimates that two-thirds of the children sent to Canada were abused though this is not supported by Canadian officials. In August 1998, the Western Australia Legislative Assembly passed a motion apologising to former child migrants for any abuse they had suffered in the state's institutions during their childhood and In November 2009, Kevin Rudd the Australian Prime Minister apologised to the 500,000 'forgotten Australian' who were abused or neglected in orphanages and children's homes from 1930 to 1970 and those child migrants taken from Britain to Australia after the war often without their parents' consent.[180] In February 2010, Prime Minister Gordon Brown apologised for the United Kingdom's 'shameful' role in sending more than 130,000 children to former colonies where many suffered abuse.[181]

Exporting Britishness

'Britishness' is a recent cultural phenomenon originating in the eighteenth-century expansion of the British Empire into North America, India and the Caribbean and in the consolidation of earlier expansion and conquest in Ireland, Scotland and in the border regions of the British Isles. This internal colonialism, accompanied by economic revolution was just as critical to the creation of the British state and to the identity of 'Britons' during the eighteenth and early-nineteenth centuries. Linda Colley presented Britishness as an over-arching identity 'superimposed' over a series of older attachments and loyalties such as to a region or religious denomination. Her main argument was that British national identity was created during the prolonged wars fought with the French Catholic 'other'.[182] Another important factor that brought peoples in England, Wales and Scotland together was their common Protestantism as differences between Anglicanism and Dissent lost their fissile character when confronted by aggressive Catholicism. By contrast, Robbins suggested that British national identity was formed in the nineteenth century from what he called the 'blending' of English, Scottish and Welsh culture because their geographical proximity had meant that there has always been a great deal of interaction and exchange between them.[183] For Robbins, Britishness was a compound created from the interaction of these various cultures.

Colley's explanation for the emergence of British national identity in the eighteenth century is less persuasive for the nineteenth. The *Pax Britannica* in Europe after 1815 meant that there was no external 'other' against which the British could coalesce and the religious divisions with Protestantism between Nonconformists and Anglicans militated against the creation of a broad

---

[180] Pierce, Peter, *The Country of Lost Children: An Australian Anxiety*, (Cambridge University Press), 1999, traces the ambivalent and disturbing history of the figure of the lost child.

[181] 'Gordon Brown sorry for 'shameful' colonial child resettlement programme', *The Times*, 25 February 2010.

[182] Colley, Linda, *Britons: Forging the Nation 1707-1837*, (Yale University Press), 1992, revised edition with new introductory essay, (Yale University Press), 2009, pp. xi-xxxi.

[183] Robbins, Keith, *Nineteenth-century Britain: Integration and Diversity*, (Oxford University Press), 1989.

Protestant culture.[184] For the majority of the peoples of the British Isles what was striking about the mid-nineteenth century is how weak British national identity was.[185] Different groups attached different meanings to concepts such as 'Britishness' and 'British national identity'. In general, feelings of Englishness, Scottishness and Welshness continued to be stronger than any overarching sense of British national identity. What united the Scots, Welsh, English, and to a lesser extent, the Irish was a common political culture based not only on loyalty to the Crown, but also the recognition that the imperial parliament was sovereign.

Britishness was recreated in and by white-settler societies and meant more overseas than it did in Britain itself but the critical question is what variants of Britishness were exported to the colonies? Nineteenth century colonists tended to refer to themselves as 'British' rather than as 'English', 'Scottish', or 'Welsh' yet proportionally Scottish and especially Irish emigration remained larger than that from England.[186] Despite this, what is striking is how far the four ethnic groups that made up the United Kingdom retained their own cultural identities and institutions.[187] There were Caledonian, Hibernian and Welsh societies, newspapers, churches and eisteddfods across the empire through which people expressed their own nationality. Beginning in the eighteenth century, when English institutions echoed other ethnic organisations by providing sociability and charity to fellow nationals. For instance, organisations such as the St George's societies and the Sons of England contributed to the evolving character of English identity across North America, Africa, Southeast Asia and the Antipodes gave these associations new meaning in the late-nineteenth and early-twentieth centuries. Competitive ethnicity prompted English immigrants to form such societies and how both Irish Catholic hostility in America and Canada and Boer opposition in South Africa challenged the English to assert a more robust ethnic identity

Advances in communications reduced the time letters took to reach the colonies and from the 1850s the creation of global telegraphy enhanced this further. Instead of it taking perhaps six months for letters to reach New South Wales, by 1850 this had been reduced by half with the introduction of steam ships and to a matter of hours once the oceanic telegraph cables reached Australia in 1872.[188] Britishness may have been inclusive, an expression of the

---

[184] Figes, Orlando, *Crimea: The Last Crusade*, (Allen Lane), 2010, makes a strong case for the religious origins of the war that became a crucial part of late-Victorian patriotic mythology contributing to a new ethos of muscular Christianity.

[185] Brockliss, Laurence, and Eastwood, David, (eds.), *A Union of multiple identities: the British Isles, c.1750-c.1850*, (Manchester University Press), 1997.

[186] Meaney, Neville, 'Britishness and Australia: some reflections', *Journal of Imperial and Commonwealth History*, Vol. 31, (2003), pp. 121-135.

[187] See, for instance, Mackenzie, John, and Dalziel, Nigel R., *The Scots in South Africa: ethnicity, identity, gender and race, 1772-1914*, (Manchester University Press), 2008, Buettner, Elizabeth, 'Haggis in the Raj: private and public celebrations of Scottishness in late imperial India', *Scottish Historical Review*, Vol. 81, (2002), pp. 212-239, and Jones, Aled, and Jones, Bill, 'The Welsh world and the British empire, c. 1851-1939: an exploration', *Journal of Imperial and Commonwealth History*, Vol. 31, (2003), pp. 57-81.

[188] Wenzlhuemer, Roland, *Connecting the Nineteenth-Century World: The Telegraph and Globalisation*, (Cambridge University Press), 2014, pp. 77-84, considers the question of

realities of imperial rule by the British rather than merely the English. But it was increasingly a diverse idea, mediated and diluted through the developing experiences of different colonies in which the proportion of people with direct British ancestry declined and settler communities steadily diverged from each other because of the working of responsible government increasingly reflected parochial concerns.

Local crises may have caused appeals for British support but generally there was a widespread awareness within colonial society that it had ceased to be unequivocally British but without any real sense that something different had taken its place. White settlers were already seen as 'colonials' as opposed to 'Englishmen' from the 'Mother' country and a snobbish air of cultural and social superiority continued among the British élite in their attitudes to 'colonials' well into the twentieth century. White colonial references to Britain as the 'Mother country' reinforced conceptions of Britain and British culture as superior to derivative white colonial cultures. What remained by 1914 was sentimental, if ill-defined, identity with the mother country.[189]

What gave white-settler society communal solidarity was not a sense of nationality but its white Anglo-Celtic racial ties? If Britishness was defined in relation to 'others', then its sense of racial superiority provided the confidence that the Empire was grounded in a common racial citizenship. Some late-eighteenth-century liberal thinkers were critical of European imperial expansion not only for its devastating domestic consequences but also for its moral hypocrisy and the misery it wreaked on its conquered subjects.[190] This liberal assessment was anchored in a positive view of the capacities of non-Europeans and a 'moral respect' for cultural difference, autonomy and self-determination.[191] For instance, Burke's critique of colonies came not from a conservative instinct to protect traditional societies, but from a liberal commitment to the moral equality of all human beings and a rejection of the 'arbitrary and unaccountable power' colonisers had over their subjects.[192] The eighteenth century view that the hierarchy of societies resulted on cultural not racial differences was abandoned in favour of permanent racial divisions and the limits they set to cultural change.

By the 1830s, however, this scepticism toward empire gave way to a more imperialist variant of liberalism that was driven by a profound sense of national self-confidence and European cultural superiority. This marked the beginning of the 'turn to empire' as the ideological voice moved away from the position of Smith, Burke and Bentham towards making a critical distinction between colonies of largely white settlement and colonies of conquest with subject peoples

---

telegraphy as a 'tool of empire'. See also, Hugill, Peter J., *Global Communications since 1844: Geopolitics and Technology*, (John Hopkins University Press), 1999, pp. 25-52.

[189] Young, Robert J. C., *The Idea of English Ethnicity*, (Blackwell Publishing), 2008, pp. 196-230, provides a succinct discussion of Dilke, Seeley and Froude on imperial English ethnicity.

[190] This is explored in Pitts, Jennifer, *A Turn to Empire: The Rise of Imperial Liberalism in Britain and France*, (Princeton University Press), 2005, pp. 25-122.

[191] Mehta, Uday Singh, *Liberalism and Empire: a study in nineteenth-century British liberal thought*, (University of Chicago Press), 1999, by contrast, takes the view that imperialism was essential to the liberal project.

[192] Ibid, Pitts, Jennifer, *A Turn to Empire*, p. 63.

and, as a result, in developing an 'empire of race' where there is little toleration of the culture of native populations.[193] The emergence of Social Darwinism and the growing stereotyping of racial differences reinforced this view and led to changes in the ways colonies were administered. In white-settler colonies, it led to the emergence of exclusionary policies that sought to maintain white dominance over the labour process, something that had widespread support among trade unions and working men. In India, the tolerant social relations between Indians and Europeans that characterised the eighteenth and early-nineteenth century were replaced by a growing reluctance to involve local people in colonial government and increasing discrimination. Colonial peoples were expected to adapt their own needs and aspirations to British rule. But identities were fluid. People may have identified themselves as British but their sense of place was unequivocally Australia or Canada or Natal. Local patriotism did not compete with settlers' allegiance to the Crown but rather gave voice to it.

In late-nineteenth and early-twentieth century Canada, ideal citizens were those who were born into the British race. They spoke English, proclaimed a Protestant faith, were middle-class and had white skin and lived in specific ways characterised by 'self-control, self-discipline, self-determination...self-mastery'.[194] They embraced 'property ownership, rootedness and an orderly family life'.[195] They were 'well-to-do; Church-going; English speaking'.[196] Languages spoken, faiths professed and the daily ways of living of some groups of people were targeted for replacement by British, Protestant and middle-class ways of living marked by temperance, sexual restraint and other forms of self-control. Nineteenth century colonials and the policies, laws and institutions they produced, were inherently white, patriarchal and *bourgeois* in nature. It appears that in Canada, this sense of moral responsibility justified efforts within colonial institutional structures that included education, the penal system, the health and mental health system, the immigration system and Christian churches to protect Canadian citizens from the threat of degeneracy said to be posed by other racial groups. The 'Anglo-Australian race' was regarded as the product of the multiplying British stock and it was this racialist concern that led to the so-called White Australia Policy, sanctioned in the Immigration Restriction Bill in 1901, unambiguously seeking to preserve the 'British character' of Australian society. This bill prohibited the immigration into Australia by 'non-Europeans' or 'the coloured races'. The fact that this bill was the first major legislative issue dealt with by the parliament of the newly-created Commonwealth of Australia, suggests the importance of 'racial purity' as the symbolic cement for the imagined

---

[193] Ward, Stuart, 'Imperial Identities Abroad', Stockwell, Sarah (ed.), *The British Empire: Themes and perspectives*, (Blackwell Publishing), 2008, pp. 219-243.

[194] Stoler, A. L., *Race and the education of desire: Foucault's history of sexuality and the colonial order of things*, (Duke University Press), 1995, p. 8.

[195] Ibid, Stoler, A. L., *Race and the education of desire*, p. 128.

[196] Anderson, J. T. M., *The education of the new-Canadian: A treatise on Canada's greatest educational problem*, (J. M. Dent & Sons), 1918, p. 27.

community of the fledgling nation.[197] What it meant to be British became increasingly racially and imperially circumscribed.

The unapologetic racism of British settler colonialism was much more than a self-legitimating myth. The commonplace belief in a global continuum of British peoples brought real material consequences and this settler diaspora was integral to the emerging dynamics of a modern global economy. The ideas and assumptions associated with 'Greater Britain' were instrumental in forging economic and commercial structures and networks. The revolution in transport and communications from the 1860s occasioned by steam power and telegraphy brought new potential for wider and more integrated networks of global economic activity. Settler communities recognised their capacity to exploit their own racially exclusive self-image for commercial and financial ends but the boundaries were never stable and always ambiguous. Inter-racial sex was unexceptional; 'poor whites' were everywhere; distance from inferiors was only intermittently maintained. In India, the categories heaved at the seams between British, 'domiciled European', 'poor white', 'Anglo-Indian', 'Eurasian' and 'native'.

The British state was a global state and Britishness, as opposed to being English, Welsh, Scottish or Irish, was integral to that imperial state. British patriotism was transformed into an imperial patriotism. Empire Day was widely celebrated especially in schools before the 1950s. Britishness was an imperial identity and the loss of Empire eroded that identity abroad as well as at home. This can be illustrated by the post-war experience of Australia. Although lessons might have been drawn from Britain's failure in the Pacific War, its resistance to Australia's war-time demands and the military-industrial success of the United States, reactivating the British connection after 1945 was a primary aim of both major Australian political parties. British sentiment suffered little damage during the war and may even have been strengthened. The continuing importance of Britishness to Australia can be seen in the launch of the mass immigration programme in 1946-1947.[198] Although this policy would eventually change Australia into a multi-ethnic society, that was not its aim; in fact, the reverse. Its purpose was to preserve and build a stronger, white British Australia and Immigration Minister Arthur Calwell assured Australians that all migrants would be 'Caucasian' and 'nine out of ten would be British'.

The norms of 'White Australia' and the assimilation into a 'British' society for increasing numbers of non-British immigrants remained largely intact until the early 1970s.[199] The notion of 'independent Australian Britons', a phrase

[197] Jupp, James, *From White Australia to Woomera: The Story of Australian Immigration*, (Cambridge University Press), 2007, pp. 6-18, provides a succinct account of White Australia policy.

[198] Hammerton, A. James, and Thomson, Alistair, *'Ten Pound Poms': Australia's Invisible Migrants*, (Manchester University Press), 2005, is a valuable study of post-war emigration.

[199] On the imperial legacy and the importance of Britishness in Australian history, Gare, Deborah, 'Britishness in recent Australian historiography', *Historical Journal*, Vol. 43, (2000), pp. 1145-1155, and Meaney, Neville, 'Britishness and Australia: some reflections', *Journal of Imperial and Commonwealth History*, Vol. 31, (2003), pp. 121-135.

those went back to the turn of the century, remained a fairly accurate description of how Australians viewed themselves.[200] This is hardly surprising since the development of 'Britishness' as part of late-Victorian imperial ideology coincided with the debates over Australian federation and its future constitutional status between 1880 and 1900.[201] During the Royal Tour of Australia in 1954, the *Sydney Morning Herald* commented:

> Australia is still and always will be a British nation whose greatest strength lies in the tradition she has inherited from England.[202]

Today, explicit references to Britishness are rare[203] and Britishness as a distinctive site of symbolic value had become largely irrelevant to contemporary Australian culture. Much of this was caused by Britain's withdrawal from its former imperial zones of influence east of Suez between 1967 and 1973 and with a new self-awareness and assertion of independence in Australia. Of crushing importance was Britain's decision to join the European Economic Community in 1961, though only after two refusals in 1963 and 1967, did this finally occur in 1973. Britain, it now appeared, was determined to pursue a new relationship with Western Europe that could no longer be reconciled with the idea of a worldwide community of British people. Australia was, in effect, cast aside and this rendered the symbolic power of Britishness obsolete. The 'new nationalism' that was evident in Australia from the 1970s was one response to this as Australian society sought a new role in an 'imperial-less' world. The 1999 referendum against constitutional change to an Australian republic is often cited as evidence of the continuance of 'British' sentiments. This had less to do with continuing cultural ties with Britain than with an unpopular republican model. Australians have been loath to change their constitution: there were 42 referendums between 1901 and 1999 and on only eight occasions have Australians voted in favour of change. Australians felt comfortable in voting 'no' because a republic made little constitutional difference because Australia was already independent.[204] It already has its own distinctive cultural institutions, styles and occasions and their originality is not incompatible with resemblances to British and American cultures. Britishness remains, though much diminished and still diminishing, to be adapted, borrowed and refashioned but in a distinctly Australian context.

The impact of rapid decolonisation and of mass non-white immigration from the former Empire in the late 1950s and 1960s precipitated a crisis of Britishness and the emergence of far-right racist political groups in Britain. The question of immigration policy became an issue though rarely a dominant one in

---

[200] See, for instance, its use in Hancock, W. K., *Australia*, (Ernest Benn), 1930, p. 50.
[201] See, Ward, Stuart, 'Transcending the Nation: A Global Imperial History', in Burton, Antoinette, (ed.), *After the Imperial Turn: Thinking with and through the Nation*, (Duke University Press), 2003, p. 45.
[202] 'The Queen and the Commonwealth', *Sydney Morning Herald*, 3 February 1954, p. 2.
[203] On this change see, Ward, Stuart, *Australia and the British Embrace: The Demise of the Imperial Ideal*, (Melbourne University Press), 2001.
[204] Jones, Kerry, 'Why Australians Voted No in the 1999 Republican Referendum', in Warhurst, John, and Mackerras, Malcolm, (eds.), *Constitutional Politics: The Republican Referendum and the Future*, (University of Queensland Press), 2002, pp. 41-48.

British politics. The problem was that the inexorable link between concerns about immigration and charges that these were 'racist' meant that the mainstream political parties adopted a largely neutral stance on the subject leaving the field to the far-right. This may have been a teneable position in the 1960s and 1970s but with the assertive rhetoric of the European Union over its four 'freedoms'—that included free movement in the EU—and its physical expansion with the accession of eastern European countries, there was no longer any possibility of 'controlling' the level of labour immigration from the EU. By 2000, what 'Britishness' was was becoming increasingly unclear. This was exacerbated from the late 1990s with the introduction of devolved government encouraging the rise of nationalism and separatism in Scotland and Wales. The threat to the United Kingdom this posed and especially the emergence of a multi-ethnic society in which the consensus over agreed values appears to have broken down precipitated an incomplete debate over what Britishness means today.[205] The referendum on 23 June 2016 with the victory of those calling for Brexit reflected a call for 'control' over how the United Kingdom was governed and marked the rejection of a stuttering European federalist project in favour of a looser relationship with the Continent. It was a reassertion of 'Britishness' but without any real conclusions about what Britishness is.

Conclusions

There were four main elements in the British Empire. The white-settler colonies of Australia, New Zealand and Canada were largely the consequence of seventeenth and eighteenth century colonisation but experienced a considerable influx of new immigrants in the nineteenth and twentieth centuries. They had a particularly important place for emigrants, investors and imperial advocates and when Sir Charles Dilke spoke of a Greater Britain he highlighted their importance as centres of 'Britishness'. In these colonies, the native population was subjected to expropriation by settlers but also to the ineffectiveness of the Colonial Office that sought to mediate between the increasingly majority settlers and the original inhabitants. By contrast, in the British territories in the Caribbean and South Africa, white settlers were in a minority but had an entrenched economic and political position from which they demanded the same rights as settlers elsewhere. The native majorities claimed the same political and legal rights as settlers resulting, in South Africa, in moves toward racial segregation that inaugurated the struggles against apartheid that persisted with growing ferocity into the 1990s.

The British were in a massive minority in India but ruled the subcontinent until independence and partition in 1947. This was not because they were innately superior as many in the nineteenth century believed or because of superior technology and organisation because, at least until the mid-nineteenth century their Indian opponents were often as well-armed and showed considerable organisational ability. Success in India was a combination of adapting to Indian conditions, something evident from the outset by the East India Company, raising Indian armies, funded by Indian revenue with the

[205] See, Ward, Paul, *Britishness since 1870s*, (Routledge), 2004, and Weight, R., *Patriots: National Identity in Britain, 1939-2000*, (Macmillan), 2002, explore this debate.

support of Indian allies and single-mindedness in pursuit of their common interests. Also, important especially after the Mutiny in 1857, was the abandoning of rapid Westernising reform and transformation for a more conservative ethos mediated through native princes and large landowners. The result was the development of indirect rule and some two-thirds of India was administered by local rulers, whose authority had been left largely intact and local people retained institutions and practices with which they were already familiar. This proved a popular, cheap and pragmatic solution to the problem of British minority rule in India (but also in West Africa and Malaysia) though the distinction between indirect and direct rule was often blurred and local rulers had little choice but to accept British 'advice'.

There were also colonies acquired by conquest especially in Africa in the two decades before 1900. Land was seized from native rulers and the bulk of the population were easily distinguishable from their rulers by race, religion, language and what the Victorians saw as their state of civilisation. These colonies appeared to offer little economic opportunities in terms of raw materials or potential markets and, until the 1920s, investment on infrastructure and personnel was limited. The cost of maintaining military control over these colonies was significant resulting in the introduction of local taxes such as the Hut Tax that exacerbated already significant levels of native resistance and the development of a cash economy to make the colonies self-supporting. It was in these colonies that the brutal and savage nature of colonial warfare was most evident and weapons such as dum-dum bullets, whose use was restricted in Europe, were widely employed. Finally, there were those territories within Britain's informal empire where the level of intervention varied. In China, for instance, economic imperialism was enabled by force as British military and naval forces opened Chinese markets to British imports including opium from India. In Latin America and Siam, British intervention was subtler relying in British commercial and political influence to gain economic advantages in domestic markets.

Sir John Seeley memorably remarked that 'we seem, as it were, to have conquered and people half the world in a fit of absence of mind.'[206] Imperial expansion and Seeley was writing at the height of the 'scramble for Africa', was not the consequence of the deliberate imperial design of politicians. Whether there was coherent colonial policy in the seventeenth, eighteenth and early-nineteenth centuries is a matter of conjecture. Harlow argued that there was a preference for 'trade rather than dominion' in the late-eighteenth century and it proved easier for successive British governments to maintain a coherent trading policy than one grounded in the aggressive enlargement of empire. There was an absence of concerted political pressure for imperial expansion; for instance, there was no major debate on an Indian question in the House of Commons between 1793 and 1803 and when ministers in London became concerned at the pace of expansionism in India, Lord Cornwallis was dispatched as Governor-General to halt further expansion of British territories. Early analysis of colonial policy suggests that Britain had blundered into 'the best places of the earth and

[206] Seeley, John, *The Expansion of England: Two Courses of Lectures*, (Macmillan), 1883, p. 10.

means to keep them'.[207] The dramatic expansion of imperial acquisitions in the 40 years after the loss of the American colonies continues to be treated almost as aberrations of war. Imperial warfare and the extension of empire resulted in an enlarged sense of national identity, the beginnings of the notion of a 'British world' in which 'Britishness' was exported to newly acquired lands. Until the development of reliable electric telegraphy, policy made in London took weeks or on occasion months to reach the colonial officials.[208] This made planned 'policy' extremely difficult. Britain seized territories to appropriate their revenues to finance imperial 'garrison states', chiefly in Asia but also in Australia and the Cape and imperial policy was driven by the imperatives of local finance and by the tensions and resistance this provoked in native societies.[209]

Increasingly, during the nineteenth century, the diversity of activities resulted in policy being characterised by pragmatism and expediency rather than principles and long-term planning. The British government never had an 'Imperial Department' and the Colonial Office, Foreign Office, India Office, War Office and Admiralty and the Board of Trade shared responsibility for managing the empire. In white-settler colonies after being given devolved powers, the Colonial Office relaxed its supervision over colonial law-making while the Crown Colonies used Orders-in-Council based on the advice of Crown Law Officers in London rather than on consultation with local opinion. There was considerable criticism of the Colonial Office from white-settler colonies that led to the development of Colonial and Imperial Conferences from 1887 and the creation of a Dominion Division separate from those governing Crown Colonies twenty years later. This reflected administrative rationalisation but also reinforced white settlers' sense of racial superiority over non-white dependent peoples. Policy towards native peoples was grounded in a limited understanding of local cultures and societies, focused on revenue, security and prestige and was frequently administered with insensitivity and oppression leading to protest, resistance and rebellion.[210] The nineteenth century approach to administering the empire remained largely unaltered after 1918 reflecting the continuance of the 'official mind' in determining policy and the politically pragmatic approach to colonial affairs generally. Colonial policy in the inter-war years was dominated by how imperial exports could help revive an ailing British economy while, at least until 1932, protecting colonial economies through imperial preferences. The Second World War finally shattered this economic relationship and although the post-war Attlee government sought to revive it through its policy of 'new imperialism', it proved too late. Anti-colonialism expressed through native nationalism and the untenable military and administrative cost of maintaining

---

[207] Egerton, Hugh E., *A Short History of British Colonial Policy*, (Methuen), 1897, pp. vii-viii.

[208] Nickles, David P., *Under the Wire: How Telegraphy changed Diplomacy*, (Harvard University Press), 2003, pp. 1-14, 79-133. See also, Fahie, John J., *A History of Wireless Telegraphy, 1838-1899*, (William Blackwood and Sons), 1899, and Beauchamp, K. G., *History of Telegraphy*, (IET), 2001, pp. 94-99, 102-133, and 162-177.

[209] See, Bayly, C. A., 'The First Age of Global Imperialism, c. 1760-1830', in Burroughs, Peter and Stockwell, A. J., (eds.), *Managing the Business of Empire: Essays in honour of David Fieldhouse*, (Frank Cass & Co. Ltd.), 1998, pp. 28-47.

[210] Porter, Andrew, 'Introduction', *OHBE*, Vol. 3, pp. 15-19.

empire led increasingly to a policy of decolonisation as the former colonies were granted their independence. The Commonwealth may have survived but by 1980 only the rump of empire remained.

The British Empire took nearly three hundred years to develop but only decades to decline and fall. It was a complex phenomenon in which the four ethnic groups that made-up Britain and Ireland interacted with empire and with its native peoples in different ways.[211] Like previous empires, it was fatally weakened from without and lost confidence from within. Benjamin Disraeli had memorably described colonies as 'millstones around our necks' in a letter to Lord Malmesbury on 13 August 1852 whose costs outweighed their benefits.[212] His conclusion may have been premature but proved, a century later, to be right. When Britain was the dynamo of the global economy, empire provided the markets and resources essential to maintain its global hegemony. Imperial troops fought in Britain's wars and colonial governments were prepared to tolerate Britain's colonial policies. The Second World War ended the illusion of Britain as a great power, though it still maintained the charade, while the Suez crisis showed just how far its power and influence had been diminished. Within a generation, most of the empire disappeared as colonies were granted their independence by successive British government no longer able to afford the panoply of imperial power before they took it themselves. Britain's territories may have been a fraction of what they were in the hey-day of empire but its financial and commercial institutions, so crucial to the success of empire, allowed it to remain a global player until the global slump after 2008 called this into question. The much-esteemed 'special relationship' with the United States was dealt a body-blow by public reaction to Britain's involvement in the Iraq war and its bloody aftermath and Britain's long-term relationship with Europe was regarded by many with hostility and was undecided until the EU referendum on 23 June 2016. The sudden end of empire meant that Britain lacked global direction, something that successive governments have failed to correct. British politicians may still like to think of Britain as the 'policeman of the world' but the gunboats have gone and pretence is only possible under the umbrella of the European Union, NATO or the United Nations as part of multi-national forces. What Britain's future role is remains undecided and unclear and in 2017 distinctly so. Acheson's comment remains as true now as when he said it in 1962.

---

[211] MacKenzie, John M., 'Irish, Scottish, Welsh and English Worlds? A Four-Nation Approach to the History of the British Empire', *History Compass*, Vol. 6, (5), (2008), pp. 1244-1263, explores the ways in which the four nations had separate and different relationships with empire.

[212] His view of colonies had changed by the time he gave his celebrated speech at the Crystal Palace on 24 June 1872 when he made a profession of faith in the Empire.

Chapter 2 Native rebellion and land hunger

Unhappy People! to have lived in such Times, and by such Neighbours! - We have seen, that they would have been safer among the ancient Heathens, with whom the Rites of Hospitality were sacred. - They would have been considered as Guests of the Publick, and the Religion of the Country would have operated in their Favour. But our Frontier People call themselves Christians![1]

In December 1763, the massacre of Native Americans in Lancaster County, Pennsylvania, by the Paxton Boys--a vigilante group formed to retaliate against local American Indians in the aftermath of the French and Indian War and Pontiac's Rebellion--was not a tale of instant retaliation for killings and scalpings by Indians but a relatively well-planned slaughter.[2] In mid-December, up to 60 men attacked the Conestoga Indiantown and killed six Indians in their homes. The other 14 members of this settlement were not at home during the killings and took refuge in Lancaster workhouse, ten or so miles away. A fortnight later, two days after Christmas, a similar sized group rode into town, broke into the workhouse and killed everyone inside including eight children. There followed a few weeks of rumour and terror in Philadelphia as the Paxton Boys were said to be coming to the state capital to kill Moravian Native Americans sheltered there by the city authorities. Although the panic passed, the Paxton Boys claimed the 500 acres granted to the Conestoga Indians by 'right of conquest' but were driven off by provincial militia and their settlement burned but the legal authorities never brought the Paxton Boys to justice although the identity of their leaders was well-known. Seizing land unlawfully was one thing, but the murder of peaceful and defenceless Indians another. The limits of law enforcement were clearly demonstrated.[3]

In 1838, at Myall Creek in NSW, a group of 11 stockmen murdered no less than 28 Indigenous Australian men, woman and children.[4] The men roped

---

[1] Franklin, Benjamin, *A Narrative of the Late Massacres, in Lancaster County*, (Anthony Armbruster), 1764, p. 26.

[2] Presbyterian Scots-Irish frontiersmen from central Pennsylvania, centred in Paxton Township along the Susquehanna River, formed a vigilante group in response to fear of American Indian caused largely by the French and Indian War and exacerbated by Pontiac's Rebellion. The Paxton Boys also felt that the government of colonial Pennsylvania was negligent in using tax money to provide subsistence to the Indians living among them. See, Engels, Jeremy, ''Equipped for Murder': The Paxton Boys and 'The Spirit of Killing All Indians' in Pennsylvania, 1763-1764', *Rhetoric & Public Affairs*, Vol. 8, (2005), pp. 355-382.

[3] Kenny, Kevin, *Peaceable Kingdom Lost: The Paxton Boys and the Destruction of William Penn's Holy Experiment*, (Oxford University Press), 2009, is the most recent study of these events. See also Merrell, James, *Into the American Woods: Negotiators on the Pennsylvania Frontier*, (W. W. Norton), 1999, Griffin, Patrick, *American Leviathan: Empire, Nation and Revolutionary Frontier*, (Hill and Wang), 2007, Spero, Patrick, *Frontier Country: The Politics of War in Early Pennsylvania*, (University of Pennsylvania Press), 2016, and Dunbar, John, (ed.), *The Paxton Papers*, (Nijhoff), 1957.

[4] Milliss, Roger, *Waterloo Creek: the Australia Day Massacre of 1838, George Gipps and the British Conquest of New South Wales*, (McPhee Gribble), 1992, describes the Waterloo Creek and Myall Creek massacre. See also Blanch, Russell, *Massacre: Myall Creek revisited*, (Grah Jean Books), 2000, Stewart, Peter, *Demons at Dusk: Massacre at*

their victims together, and then hacked, shot and beheaded them. The next day the killers left but returned two days later, burned the bodies and then set off in pursuit of ten Indigenous Australian men who were working on a neighbouring property at the time of the first massacre. The stockmen hunted them down and murdered most of them. Almost three weeks later the atrocity was reported to police in Sydney in the absence of the local police magistrate. Governor George Gipps ordered an investigation that opened on 28 July 1838. Eventually, ten suspects were identified and taken to Sydney for trial but their leader, John Fleming, escaped. Given the accepted opinion about Indigenous Australian people among settlers, public opinion soon supported the accused and a prominent landholder offered to finance their defence. The *Sydney Herald*, for instance, portrayed a society in which there was desperate settler isolation, victimisation and abandonment in which morally superior settlers were contrasted with their oft-demonised, alternately degenerate or effeminate 'others' and that contributed to the formation of a distinct colonial identity, no longer fully British but not yet fully Australian.[5] A juror commented:

> I look on the blacks as a set of monkeys, and the earlier they are exterminated from the face of the earth the better ... I would never see a white man hanged for killing a black.[6]

The first trial in November 1838 was based on limited evidence since no-one, apart from the killers, had witnessed the massacre and they had removed all bodies before they could be recovered as evidence. The accused pleaded not guilty and in the absence of any corpse, the jury took only fifteen minutes to pronounce the accused not guilty to the cheering of the crowd in the court. But Attorney-General James Plunkett asked for, and was granted another indictment. The second trial, ten days later, accused only seven of the original ten men and focused on the killing of just one Indigenous Australian child. In the end the jury found them guilty of the murder of the child, and on 18 December 1838, the seven stockmen were hanged. Whilst this outcome was the first time in Australian history that white settlers were punished for murder of Indigenous Australian people, the colonial authorities' commitment to justice for Indigenous Australian people soon waned and the involvement of the three other men in the massacre was never investigated. Settler attacks continued well into the twentieth century.

Unlike other colonies in the British Empire where the extraction of resources—sugar, cotton, minerals or diplomatic and military considerations--were the main reason for Britain's presence, settler societies were established through the creation of 'new homes' for British migrants combined with the dispersal, dispossession and often destruction of indigenous peoples and the acquisition of indigenous labour. Colonial frontiers were ambiguous places, comprising official

---

Myall Creek, (Temple House), 2007, and Tedeschi, Mark, *Murder at Myall Creek*, (Simon & Schuster), 2016.

5 Wood, Rebecca, 'Frontier violence and the bush legend: The *Sydney Herald*'s response to the Myall Creek massacre trials and the creation of colonial identity', *History Australia*, Vol. 6, (3), (2009), pp. 1-19.

6 'Local News', *The Australian*, 18 December 1838, p. 2. See also 'The Blacks', *Sydney Herald*, 5 October 1838, p. 3: 'The whole gang of black animals are not worth the money the colonists will have to pay for printing the silly [court] documents.'

borders, and areas allocated for settlement that marked the advancing limits of colonial authority.[7] They were not static, changing to accommodate new settlers as successive administrators explored new possibilities for development. There were also unofficial frontiers, borderlands that extended beyond the reach of government scrutiny, inhabited by settlers who did not wish to be restricted by intrusive legislation and competition and by those who wished to escape the law. On the other side of these frontiers were the indigenous people occupying the borderlands, who were often unable to distinguish between official and unofficial conduct nor grasp the enormity and speed of the changes thrust upon them. It is not surprising that the frontiers were often places of conflict.[8]

Resistance to colonial rule was largely a consequence of the indistinct links between the colonial authorities and settlers and native peoples who formed far from homogenous groups with a range of social, economic, political, ideological and cultural structures as well as a wide range of languages. Indigenous communities created their own oral histories--passed down from generation to generation--about what their encounters with colonists meant. While the relationship between colonial government and colonists was based broadly on the Lockean principle of consent, that with native peoples was based more on the need to impose order on what was regarded as a chaotic Hobbesian state of nature.[9] Idealistic schemes to establish orderly communities, secure an unlimited market in land and economic independence collapsed and were replaced by a pragmatic vision of a nation founded on the State imposing order on a disorganised world. The inevitable clash of cultures pitted settlers and pastoralists, who believed in the right to own and use the land against warrior hunter-gatherers who were connected spiritually and economically to the land itself.[10]

Land hunger, Native resistance, Settler rebellion

Indigenous resistance was closely linked with the ever-expanding nature of the colonial frontier.[11] Once a colony was successfully established, there was an influx of new settlers motivated by the promise of land and opportunities for economic

---

[7] Ibid, Morgan, Cecilia, *Building Better Britains? Settler Societies in the British World, 1783-1920*, chapter 1. See also, Veracini, Lorenzo, ''Settler Colonialism': Career of a Concept', *Journal of Imperial and Commonwealth History*, Vol. 41, (2), pp. 313-333, for the historiographical development of the concept.

[8] Benton, Lauren, and Ford, Lisa, *Rage for Order. The British Empire and the Origins of International Law, 1800-1850*, (Havard University Press), 2016.

[9] For the problematic status of native peoples and the legitimacy of settler actions see Karsten, Peter, *Between Law and Custom: "High" and "Low" Legal Cultures in the Lands of the British Diaspora: The United States, Canada, Australia and New Zealand, 1600-1900*, (Cambridge University Press), 2002, pp. 23-118, Benton, Lauren, *Law and Colonial Cultures: Legal Regimes in World History, 1400-1900*, (Cambridge University Press), 2002, pp. 1-30, 167-209, and Benton, Lauren, *A Search for Sovereignty: Law and Geography in European Empire, 1400-1900*, (Cambridge University Press), 2010, pp. 162-221.

[10] Ford, Lisa, and Rowse, Tim, (eds.), *Between Indigenous and Settler Governance*, (Routledge), 2013.

[11] Saul, Scott Weiden, *The First Frontier: The Forgotten History of the Struggle, Savagery & Endurance in Early America*, (Houghton Mifflin Harcourt), 2012, examines the first clashes between European settlers and Native Americans on the East Coast.

enrichment and this placed pressure on available resources and increasingly on the frontier between 'the colony' and 'the native'.[12] The authorities, especially in the American colonies, sought to reduce tensions between Native Americans and colonists by negotiating treaties with Indian tribes to cede land for settlement. For instance, in July 1652 the tribe signed a treaty with Richard Bennett, then Governor of Virginia, ceding land on the western side of Chesapeake Bay. This did not prevent conflict since aggressive settlers frequently ignored treaty obligations. But there were also pressures within 'the colony' between the colonial élite that monopolised political office and the best land and smaller freeholders who sought greater access to land. This was particularly evident in the American colonies in the seventeenth and eighteenth centuries.[13]

Between the early 1640s and mid-1670s, Sir William Berkeley was the dominant figure in the political and economic development of Virginia and was Governor between 1642 and 1652 and 1660 and 1677. Berkeley's main initiative when he first became Governor was to encourage diversification of Virginia's agricultural economy. Tobacco was the staple cash crop but, on his plantation at Green Spring, Berkeley experimented with alternative exports such as flax, fruits, potash, rice, silk, and spirits.[14] He regarded diversification in the economy based on free trade as central to Virginia's prosperity, but also supported by a close-knit colonial society and autonomy from London. In this policy, he was supported by the colony's elected General Assembly that passed the legislation vital to Berkeley's success. However, during the 1660s, economic diversification resulted in increased taxation and resistance to his leadership increased.[15] Loss of the Dutch trade during the Second and Third Anglo-Dutch Wars (1664-1667 and 1672-1674) and over-production lessened the value of tobacco, conflict broke out with Native Americans and the revival of proprietary land grants compounded Berkeley's troubles.[16] By the early 1670s, Berkeley's administration was detested by small farmers and frontiersmen.[17] Increasingly divorced from their concerns,

---

[12] Horn, James, 'The Conquest of Eden: Possession and Dominion in Early Virginia', in Appelbaum, Robert, and Sweet, John Wood, (eds.), *Envisioning an English Empire: Jamestown and the Making of the North Atlantic World*, (University of Pennsylvania Press), 2005, pp. 25-48, examines the movement towards more belligerent Anglo-native relationships.

[13] Beverley, Robert, *The History and Present State of Virginia*, A New Edition with an introduction by Susan Scott Parrish, (University of North Carolina), 2013, Campbell, Charles, *History of the Colony and Ancient Dominion of Virginia*, (J. B. Lippincott and Co.), 1860, pp. 271-326, on the Bacon rebellion.

[14] On the development of the Virginian tobacco industry see Walton, Gary M., and Shepherd, James F., *The Economic Rise of Early America*, (Cambridge University Press), 1979, pp. 37-44,

[15] Billings, W. M., *'Virginia's Deploured Condition', 1660-1676: The Coming of Bacon's Rebellion*, (Northern Illinois University Press), 1968, provides a valuable context. See also Yirush, Craig, *Settlers, Liberty and Empire: The Roots of Early American Political Theory, 1675-1775*, (Cambridge University Press), 2011.

[16] Wertenbaker, Thomas J., *The Planters of Colonial Virginia*, (Genealogical Publishing Co.), 1922, pp. 84-100, examines developments in the tobacco industry in the 1660s and 1670s.

[17] Berkeley, Sir William, *A Discourse and View of Virginia*, London, 1663, Smith, William H., (ed.), 1914, and 'Enquiries to the Governor of Virginia, submitted by the

he relied on a small coterie of wealthy planters who Bacon later referred to as 'unworthy favourites and juggling parasites'. His style of leadership contributed to political discord because he would not check the misrule of his subordinates. Restrictions were placed on the right to vote with the introduction of new land ownership requirements in 1670, and Berkeley co-opted the Council and avoided calling for new elections to replace the Assembly chosen in 1662.

With a compliant legislature, Berkeley could levy taxes, despite restrictions on his power to do so without the will of the Burgesses, and did so not by taxing land but through the increasingly unpopular of a poll tax. Taxation continued to increase while tobacco prices fell. Tobacco prices were depressed when colonists were forbidden to sell to French customers and Dutch ships were blocked from trading with Virginia. Virginia's House of Burgesses established perpetual slavery for blacks, but costs of growing tobacco was still higher than other crops. Maryland and the Carolinas were competing commercially against Virginia, the English market was constricting, and finished goods from England were rising in price. There was increasing resistance to the actions of the colonial élite, especially lack of protection against native attacks. Berkeley had worked to establish peace with the tribes and successfully negotiated a settlement in which lands east of the Blue Ridge Mountains were reserved for the white settlers. However, during the 1660s and early 1670s, the mushrooming population began to spill over into Native American lands west of the mountains in violation of treaty obligations and led to escalating clashes between the races.[18] Many Virginians, including unemployed former indentured servants, thought the Governor stood in the way of further economic development in the colony.[19]

Bacon confronts Native Americans

Bacon's Rebellion[20] in 1675-1676 is a complicated case of economic confusion, anti-authoritarian attitudes amongst colonists, serious errors made by Virginia's

---

lords commissioners of foreign plantations, with the governor's answers to each distinct head', printed in Hening, W. W., (ed.), *The Statues at Large; Being a Collection of All the Laws of Virginia, From the First Session of the Legislature, in 1619*, 13 Vols. (R. & W. & G. Bartrow), 1823, Vol. 2, pp. 511-518, provide valuable information on Virginia in the 1660s and early 1670s. For Berkeley see Billings, Warren M., *Sir William Berkeley and the Forging of Colonial Virginia*, (Louisiana State University Press), 2010.

[18] Virginia's colonial population had grown during Berkeley's tenure from 8,000 in 1642 to 40,000 by 1677.

[19] Anon, 'A Narrative of the Indian and Civil Wars in Virginia, In the Years 1675 and 1676', *Collections of the Massachusetts Historical Society*, 2nd series, Vol. 1, (1814), pp. 6-8, examines attempts to contain the Indian threat.

[20] Important contemporary accounts can be found in Cotton, Ann Mrs, *An Account of our Late Troubles in Virginia, Written in 1686*, published from the original manuscript in the Richmond (Virginia) *Enquirer*, 12 September 1804, and in *Tracts and Other Papers, Relating Principally to the Origin, Settlement, and Progress of the Colonies in North America, from the Discovery of the Country to the Year 1776, Collected by Peter Force*, Vol. 1, (Peter Force, Washington), 1835, pp. 81-91. See also 'Papers relating to Bacon's Rebellion, in ibid, Hening, W. W., (ed.), *The Statues at Large; Being a Collection of All the Laws of Virginia, From the First Session of the Legislature, in 1619*, Vol. 2, pp. 543-560, ibid, Anon, 'A Narrative of the Indian and Civil Wars in Virginia, 76', pp. 3-47, and [Thomas Mathew] T. M., a Planter from Northumberland and an Assembly Member, 'The

Governor, and resentment of and by Native Americans.[21] It also reflected mounting anxieties among settlers that Indian unrest in Maryland and along the Delaware River would spill over into Virginia, a growing hysteria reinforced by false or exaggerated reports of Indian attacks. Despite rising levels of frustration, Berkeley remained popular with King Charles II for evicting non-conformist Puritans and defeating the Dutch at Wilmington, Delaware. He had also granted the Powhatan Indians rights to land near the York River. This diplomacy brought peace, but at a price. Europeans, arriving in Virginia hoping to find cheap land, were upset to find the most prized land off limits. In July 1675, several Doeg Indians raided Thomas Matthews' plantation in the Northern Neck of Virginia near the Potomac River; supposedly he had not paid for something he had obtained from the tribe. His herdsmen, Robert Hen and a Doeg were killed.[22] In retaliation, colonists struck back and Colonels Giles Brent and George Mason with a force of militia gave chase to the murderers across the Potomac River into Maryland. Although the king of the Doegs was killed, this punitive raid brought Virginia into direct conflict with the Susquehanock who had previously been at peace with the settlers. With murders now committed on both sides of the Potomac, Maryland and Virginia raised a force of a thousand men that laid siege to the Susquehanock stronghold in Maryland. During the siege, five 'great men' who had been sent from the fort to treat for peace were killed and after seven weeks in which 50 besiegers were killed, the Susquehanock quietly escaped from their fort at night.

At the beginning of 1676, the Susquehanock struck back, killing 36 colonists in a sudden revenge raid on the plantations of the Potomac and Rappahannock Rivers.[23] Berkeley condemned the situation, recognising a

---

Beginning, Progress, and Conclusion of Bacon's Rebellion in Virginia, In the Years 1675 and 1676', in ibid, *Tracts and Other Papers, Relating Principally to the Origin, Settlement, and Progress of the Colonies in North America, from the Discovery of the Country to the Year 1776, Collected by Peter Force*, Vol. I, pp. 59-78. Oberg, Michael L., (ed.), *Samuel Wiseman's Book of Record: The Official Account of Bacon's Rebellion in Virginia, 1676-1677*, (Lexington Books), 2005, provides an official account of the rebellion by Samuel Wiseman, Charles II's scribe assigned to the rebellion's investigation, while Andrew, Charles M., (ed.), *Narratives of the Insurrections, 1675-1690*, (C. Scribner's Sons), 1915, pp. 9-142, prints several contemporary accounts.

[21] For modern studies see Wertenbaker, Thomas J., *Virginia Under the Stuarts*, (Princeton University Press), 1914, pp. 62-111, Washburn, W. E., *The Governor and the Rebel: A History of Bacon's Rebellion in Virginia*, (University of North Carolina Press), 1957, Webb, Stephen S., *1676: The End of American Independence*, (Alfred A. Knopp), 1984, pp. 3-166, Thompson, Peter, *Bacon's Rebellion: Empire and the Making of Virginia*, (Oxford University Press), 2006, Rice, James D., *Tales from a Revolution: Bacon's Rebellion and the Transformation of Early America*, (Oxford University Press), 2012, and ibid, Billings, Warren M., *Sir William Berkeley and the Forging of Colonial Virginia*, pp. 210-266.

[22] For Matthews' account of this incident written thirty years later, see above T. M., a Planter from Northumberland and an Assembly Member, pp. 60-61.

[23] Ragan, Edward DuBois, ''Scatter'd upon the English Seats': Indian Identity and Land Occupancy in the Rappahannock River Valley', in Bradburn, Douglas, and Coombs, John C., (eds.), *Early Modern Virginia: Reconsidering the Old Dominian*, (University of Virginia Press), 2011, pp. 207-238.

dangerous escalation of tensions.[24] He immediately investigated the Doeg and Susquehannock attacks, hoping to preserve peace with the tribes while also pacifying the settlers. He called a court and placed a force to march against the Native Americans under command of Sir Henry Chicheley and some other gentlemen of Rappahannock County but when the party was ready to set out, Berkeley changed his mind, withdrew the commission and ordered the men to be disbanded and no steps were taken for the defence of the colony. Turning to the second problem of pacifying the colonists, Berkeley called a 'Long Assembly' in March 1676. The assembly declared war on the 'bad' Native Americans and created a defensive zone around the settlements at the heads of the rivers and on the frontiers with a military chain of command with heavy taxes introduced to build and maintain them. These fortifications afforded no real defence, as their garrisons could not fire on Indians without permission from the Governor.[25] The Long Assembly tightened controls over trade favouring traders who supported the Governor preventing independent traders, who had close and long-established links with the Native Americans, from continuing their commercial activities. A commission was created to oversee trade and ensure the Indians did not receive arms and ammunition. Nathaniel Bacon was not one of the favoured traders, and he was also angry that the Governor had denied him a commission in the local militia.

Berkeley's failure to address the problem of Indian raids led to the formation of a small army of volunteers in Charles City County that was prepared to take unauthorised action to protect their communities. Bacon emerged as their natural leader accepting an unofficial appointment as 'General'.

> ...the Indians...commit abundance of ungarded and unrevenged mirthers; by which meanes a grate many of the outward plantations were disarted; the doeing whereof did not onely terefye the wholl colony, but subplanted those esteemes the people had formerly for Sr. W. B. whom they judged too remise in applying meanes to stop the fewrye of the Heathen; and to settle their affections, and expectations, upon one Esqr. Bacon...[26]

Nathaniel Bacon, born in Suffolk in 1647 and seen as a troublemaker, was sent to the colonies by his father in the early 1670s. His father's support enabled him to purchase two estates on the James River and he settled at Curles, in Henrico County. Intelligent and eloquent, Bacon was popular, but reportedly had little taste for labour. He was also related to Berkeley through the marriage of his cousin Frances Culpeper, Lady Berkeley. Outraged by Bacon's actions, Berkeley rode into the latter's homestead with a militia force of 300 men. Bacon, wisely, fled into the forest with some 200 volunteers, perhaps searching for a more secure meeting place. Frustrated, on 10 May the Governor declared Nathaniel Bacon a rebel but offered to pardon the volunteer Indian fighters if they returned home peacefully. Bacon would be given a fair trial for his disobedience, Berkeley stated, but would certainly be relieved of his Council seat. Bacon's response was

---

[24] Ibid, Anon, 'A Narrative of the Indian and Civil Wars in Virginia, pp. 9-10.

[25] Berkeley appears to have ignored a petition sent from 'your poor distressed subjects in the upper parts of the James River…', *Calendar of State Papers, Colonial Papers,* Vol. 9, p. 392, dated May 1676 that contributed to the beginnings of Bacon's rebellion.

[26] Ibid, Cotton, An. Mrs, *An Account of our Late Troubles in Virginia,* p. 84.

to attack an encampment of Occaneechi Indians on the Roanoke River between Virginia and North Carolina. Bacon now found himself in dispute with both the Indians and the Crown.

On 29 May 1676, Berkeley declared that everyone who failed to return would be termed rebels and many of Bacon's men--landowners whose property could be confiscated--heeded the declaration and disbanded. Bacon, left with just 57 loyalists, continued up-river.[27] With their provisions nearly exhausted, the band stumbled into the Occaneechi tribe led by Persicles in its fort on an island in the north branch of the James River. Persicles had accepted the Susquehanock when they arrived from the north, but they 'being exercised in warr for many years with the Senecaes...endeavoured to beat the Ockanagees of their own Island.' Persicles was conferring with conquered Mannakin and Annelecton tribes people to surprise and cut off the Susquehanock when Bacon appeared at the island fortress. Bacon tried to buy provisions, but the tribe put them off for days. Persicles insisted the English execute his Susquehanock prisoners, which Bacon refused to do. As the last of the food gave out, Bacon's men waded across a branch of the river to the fort and one of his men was shot. Suspecting the tribe of collusion with Berkeley, the rebels stormed the fortification, blew up the Indians' supply of guns and powder and killed 150 people, many of them defenceless men, women and children. The dead included Persicles, his wife and children. Eleven of Bacon's party were also killed in the two-day fight before the small band returned to their homes.[28]

News of the victory was enthusiastically received in the frontier counties and there were growing protests at the costly and ineffective forts. Berkeley was increasingly losing control of the situation and to appease the people not only had the forts dismantled but on 18 May dissolved the legislature and called free elections for a new Assembly. Bacon was soon elected one of the burgesses of Henrico County in defiance of Berkeley's proclamations. Going down river to Jamestown to take his seat in the Assembly, Bacon wisely was accompanied by a friendly escort. Above the town, Bacon sent ahead to learn whether he would be allowed to take his seat. In reply, the Governor opened fire on the sloop from the fort's guns. Bacon sailed back upriver to the home of Richard Lawrence, a sympathiser where he, Lawrence and William Drummond conferred for hours. Returning to his boat, Bacon was discovered, alarms were sounded and several boats with armed men chased after Bacon's little sloop until it was driven aground by the *Adam and Eve* and Bacon was forced to surrender. Although his supporters were kept in irons, Berkeley freed Bacon after he had given his parole as a gentleman. In fact, Bacon's growing popularity across the colony gave Berkeley no other choice.[29]

---

[27] Ibid, T. M., a Planter from Northumberland and an Assembly Member, pp. 63-64.
[28] See William Sherwood to Secretary Sir Joseph Williamson, 1 June 1676, *Calendar of State Paper, Colonial Papers,* Vol. 9, p. 399, and Phillip Ludwell to Williamson, 28 June 1676, *Calendar of State Papers, Colonial Papers,* Vol. 9, pp. 414-415.
[29] Ibid, Anon, 'A Narrative of the Indian and Civil Wars in Virginia, pp. 11-12.

Crisis in Jamestown

Members of the new Assembly including Nathaniel Bacon gathered in Jamestown on 5 June and listened to Governor Berkeley report about the Indian massacres.[30] Bacon was then compelled to kneel in front of the burgesses and confess his offense, and to beg the pardon of God, the King and the Governor. Berkeley then pardoned Bacon and his supporters restoring his seat in the Assembly and promising him a commission to go out against the Indians to be delivered in three days. The commission did not arrive, possibly because the Assembly was confronting other matters. Berkeley, believing all was quiet and that his pardon was not binding, issued secret warrants to seize Bacon. Whether Bacon felt his work was done, he left Jamestown unaccompanied. His old comrades in arms welcomed him home in Henrico County, believing he was commissioned officially to defend their territory and homes. When they learned he was once more a fugitive, they 'sett their throats in one common key of Oathes and curses and cried aloud, that they would either have a Commission...or else they would pull downe the Towne.'

Rumours reached Jamestown on 22 June that Bacon was approaching at the head of 500 enraged men. His army was made up of frontiersmen, planters deeply in debt, and freedmen whose release from indentured bondage brought little relief. There was no moderation and little reason in the mass of rebels. Berkeley summoned the York train bands to defend Jamestown against Bacon's presumed attack. Only 100 showed up but many were rebel sympathisers. Four guns were dragged to Sandy Bay to cover the narrow neck of land connecting the peninsula to the left bank of the river. Messengers rushed to Jamestown, advising of Bacon's army's approach and in the face of this apparently overwhelming threat, Berkeley dismounted the guns, withdrew the soldiers and retired to the State House.

Four days later around 2.00 p.m., Bacon and his men, now numbering 600 on foot and horseback entered the city without resistance. A file of fusiliers arrayed themselves on the green before the State House. Half an hour later, a customary drum tattoo called the Assembly to order. Two Council members demanded to know what Bacon wanted.[31] Bacon answered that he had come for a commission as General of Volunteers enrolled against the Indians and that his men would refuse to pay levies for new forces. Angrily, Berkeley signed a commission and presented it. Bacon read it to his soldiers and declared that the powers were insufficient. Bacon drew up a new paper, indicating his loyalty to the King and the legality of his past actions and appointing himself General of all the

[30] For the twenty pieces of legislation passed in early June, sometimes referred to as 'Bacon's Laws', see ibid, Hening, W. W., (ed.), *The Statues at Large; Being a Collection of All the Laws of Virginia, From the First Session of the Legislature, in 1619*, Vol. 2, pp. 341-365. While Bacon was entitled to participate in the Assembly of June 1676, he probably conducted no other business at that time. Later, he was mistakenly credited with populist reforms in the colony's regulations allowing freemen to vote and creating term limits of certain offices, but most of the bills had been written and were awaiting legislative approval.

[31] Ibid, T. M., a Planter from Northumberland and an Assembly Member, pp. 68-70.

forces in Virginia used against the Native Americans.[32] Berkeley refused to sign it and, with his Council members withdrew to his private apartment at the other end of the State House. But faced with the overwhelming force, Berkeley was compelled to concede and an hour later, Bacon entered the Assembly chamber and received the commission authorising him to march against the Native Americans. The following day, Bacon returned to the House of Burgesses with an armed guard, demanding that certain persons obeying the Governor's orders be removed from office and that letters to the King denouncing Bacon as a rebel be publicly contradicted. Berkeley swore he would rather be killed than submit but the Burgesses advised him to grant Bacon whatever he wanted. Shortly, a letter was written to the King and signed by Berkeley and the Burgesses, attesting to Bacon's loyalty and justifying his actions. Several of Berkeley's supporters were assigned to prison and blank commissions were written for officers to command under Bacon. Everything Bacon wanted was granted 'as long as they concerned not life and limb'.

Berkeley's capitulation allowed Bacon to fight the Native Americans without interference. With this, Berkeley lost all claim to authority and Bacon's rebellion was in full force. Leading 1,000 men, Bacon marched against the Pamunkies, killing many and destroying their camps. Meanwhile, loyal colonists in Gloucester, disarmed earlier by Governor Berkeley, petitioned for protection. Berkeley responded with animation, hurrying to the town again proclaiming Bacon a rebel and a traitor.

> It vext him [Bacon] to the heart to thinke that while he was hunting Wolves, tigers and bears, which daly destroyd our harmless and innosscent Lambs, that hee and those with him, should be persewed in the reare with a full cry, as more savage beasts.[33]

Berkeley summoned militia from throughout that county and Middlesex, some 1,200 men, proposing that they pursue Bacon and arrest him. The men greeted the Governor with shouts of 'Bacon! Bacon!', and they withdrew from the field, leaving the humiliated Governor to ponder the chasm separating the people and their government.[34] Bacon, nearing the York River, heard of the situation and marched back to Gloucester on 29 July. Berkeley, knowing he had been abandoned, escaped with a few friends across the Chesapeake Bay to John Custis' house in Accomack County on the Eastern Shore, safe because Bacon had no boats to follow him.

During this pause in the confrontation, Bacon was faced with a quandary. He could fight, knowing the terrain and new methods of unorthodox fighting would make 500 Virginians the equal of 2,000 regular troops. He could also appeal to the Dutch or French for assistance. But the people would *not* openly reject their ties of blood, religion and language to England. He had to deceive the people with pretence of loyalty, take an oath of allegiance and demand it of his followers, arguing that it was in the Crown's interest to disobey a King's order,

---

[32] On the militia and its effectiveness see Risdale, D. A., and Barnes, Don W., *Soldiers of the Virginia Colony, 1607-1699*, (Dietz), 2000, and Shea, William L., *The Virginia Militia in the Seventeenth Century*, (Louisiana State University Press), 1983.
[33] Ibid, Cotton, An. Mrs, *An Account of our Late Troubles in Virginia,* p. 85.
[34] Ibid, T. M., a Planter from Northumberland and an Assembly Member, p. 72.

arrest his Governor and fight his troops. To succeed he knew he had to seduce the wealthy planters, and so called at least 69 influential plantation owners to his home at Middle Plantation on 3 August 1676.[35] Bacon persuaded them to sign three oaths: to assist him in fighting the Indian war, to resist all attempts of the Governor to raise troops against him, and to resist His Majesty's troops until Bacon could bring his cause to the attention of King Charles II. As 'General by Consent of the People', Bacon issued his Declaration of the People the next day. Seen by some as foreshadowing the Declaration of Independence a century later, Bacon wrote it without consulting anyone, but central to the document was his attack on Berkeley's policy towards the Indians and the willingness of traders to sell them weapons.[36] Bacon also undertook civil administration at this time on the ground that Berkeley had 'absented himself from the Government'. With four members of the Council, he ordered the election of a new Assembly on 4 September in Jamestown.[37] Uppermost in his mind was the fight on two fronts. His men seized the English ship lying in the James River, impressing Captain Larrimore and her crew. This vessel, along with a sloop and a bark with four guns, were placed under the command of Captain William Carver and Giles Bland to patrol the Western shore.

Attacks on two fronts

Bacon simultaneously turned to renew his attack against the Occaneechi and Susquehanock. For some reason, however, his attention was turned to the Pamunkeys. Crossing the James to the York River, he met with Colonel Giles Brent with reinforcements from plantations on the Potomac and Rappahannock. The small army was fired upon by the Pamunkeys, who then fled into the swamps, except for one woman and her child. An elderly nurse of the Pamunkey queen was found and she was forced by Bacon's men to be their guide. Unwilling to betray her people she led them far astray. Angry at being taken miles from their quarry, Bacon ordered that the old woman be knocked in the head and killed. The army then wandered randomly, following one lead and then turning to another, all the time realising the Assembly would meet shortly in Jamestown. A tired and discouraged army begged Bacon to take them home, but he resolved that he would rather die in the woods, living on chinquapins and horse flesh, than betray the confidence placed in him. As the army split, half to remain and half to return home, Bacon's group floundered into the main camp of the Pamunkeys. The enemy was surrounded by swamp on three sides, but fled as the English charged in. Securing his plunder and captives, Bacon and his men turned back to the plantations.

Disgruntled, Governor Berkeley remained at his home at Green Spring trying to ignore the problem Bacon presented. But, by September, he had regained his spirit. Captain Carver had arrived at the coast of Accomack and went ashore under a flag of truce. Bland and his men remained on board to guard the

---

35 *Calendar of State Papers, Colonial Papers,* Vol. 9, p. 438.

36 Ibid, Anon, 'A Narrative of the Indian and Civil Wars in Virginia, pp. 15-18, provides a cogent discussion of Bacon's Declaration.

37 Proclamation, 11 August 1676, *Calendar of State Papers, Colonial Papers,* Vol. 9, p. 441.

ships and Larrimore's sailors. Larrimore somehow managed to get a message to the Governor, urgently requesting rescue. Berkeley sent 26 men under Colonel Philip Ludwell out to Larrimore in two small boats. Ludwell's men entered Larrimore's boat through an open gun port and quickly arrested Bland. Captain Larrimore and his crew grabbed spikes to help and the rebels surrendered immediately. Carver returned unsuspecting, and was immediately tried for treason, condemned and hanged. Berkeley now felt strong enough to retake Jamestown and fortify it. The Indian fighting continued and Bacon was nowhere in sight as the date of the Assembly approached. Bacon's friends had left Jamestown and it was occupied now by the Governor's sympathisers. Berkeley arrived on 7 September on Captain Larrimore's ship, with the *Adam and Eve* and 16 or 17 sloops.[38]

Bacon and his army, crossing the James River at his own house at Curles, surprised a band of Appomattox Indians who lived on both sides of the river. The militia killed many people, scattered the rest and burned the village. Moving southward, he then destroyed tribal towns on the banks of the Nottoway, Meherrin and Roanoke. Native Americans fled in advance, often without food. Having exhausted their own provisions, Bacon dismissed a large part of his forces but having learned of the Governor's return to Jamestown, he collected a force, estimated variously as 150, 300 or 800 from New Kent and Henrico, and informing them of the situation quickly marched them and the Indian captives to Jamestown.[39]

Jamestown had been fortified with a palisade 'ten paces in width, running across the neck of the peninsula', and defended with three large guns.[40] The ships had been laid broadside, bringing their guns to bear on the probable attack. In town, Berkeley's forces numbered 1,000 men, three times the force Bacon could bring. Jamestown contained a church and some 16 or 18 brick houses. The population had been reduced to about a dozen families. Within the besieged town, the Governor hoped Bacon's troops would run out of food and force the rebels to retire from the field. For his part, Berkeley had supplied his troops from his home three miles distant. In this tense standoff, Bacon captured the wives of several loyalists and threatened to use them as shields if the governor attacked. He was busy having his men build earthworks around the Governor's fortification. On 16 September, a lookout standing on a rooftop announced the rebels were going attack. Six or seven hundred English troops were ordered to storm Bacon's redoubt, but many were there by compulsion with no heart for fighting. Bacon rode along his hastily constructed breastwork, reconnoitring the Governor's position. Dismounting, he addressed his men to advance, had a trumpet sound the attack and ordered them to fire. With the first volleys from the rebels, Berkeley's troops turned and fled. Only twelve men were killed in the attack but Berkeley's humiliation was incalculable and realising the enormity of

[38] Ibid, T. M., a Planter from Northumberland and an Assembly Member, pp. 73-75.

[39] On the events in Jamestown see above Cotton, An. Mrs, *An Account of our Late Troubles in Virginia,* pp. 86-89.

[40] Ibid, Anon, 'A Narrative of the Indian and Civil Wars in Virginia, pp. 24-25, contains a contemporary description of Jamestown.

his defeat, he stole away in the night with his sympathisers after nailing up the guns and leaving the houses empty.

Bacon stormed Jamestown on 19 September but news also arrived that his former ally Colonel Brent had collected troops in the counties bordering the Potomac and would march with 1,000 men to assist Berkeley. If this happened, and supported by the fleet, Bacon would be cut off in Jamestown. In his anger, he determined to burn Jamestown, saying there would be no more sanctuary there. His leaders agreed. Richard Lawrence and William Drummond, who owned two of the best houses, each set fire to their own homes as examples. The soldiers fired the rest of the community, including the church and statehouse. Bacon's forces marched to the York River, crossing at Tindall's Point (Gloucester) to confront Colonel Brent. Many of the Virginian soldiers, sympathising with Bacon's success, deserted. Bacon stopped and set up a headquarters at Colonel Augustine Warner II's homestead where he called a convention in Gloucester. Here he administered his oath of allegiance to the people of the county and began planning another expedition either against the Indians or the Governor's troops in Accomack.[41]

Restoring order

Bacon found himself in an increasingly desperate position. The influential plantation owners withdrew their support and the king's troops would shortly arrive in Virginia. With no navy and no army Bacon was doomed. During this Bacon fell ill with dysentery and died on 26 October aged twenty-nine. His body was never found. He was briefly succeeded by his Lieutenant General, Joseph Ingram--a dandy, a fool, and a man of low birth--though he showed military skill against the Governor. After Bacon's death, the rebellion collapsed and Berkeley regained control over the government of the colony.[42]

Once reports of the rebellion reached London, the Crown sent 1,000 troops, ships, and a commission to crush Bacon and inquire into the reasons for the tumult.[43] The Crown needed an orderly Virginia especially as the customs revenues collected on Virginian tobacco provided the margin of royal independence from Parliament.[44] Bacon's rebellion disrupted that conduit and was a significant blow to this model of government.[45] The king ordered an armed force of 1,300 men to be raised and immediately sent to Virginia. The troops sailed on 24 November 1676 with the remainder of the fleet following in early December. *The Bristol,* under Admiral Sir John Berry and Francis Moryson,

---

[41] Ibid, Anon, 'A Narrative of the Indian and Civil Wars in Virginia, pp. 34-26, provides a detailed account of the siege and burning of Jamestown.

[42] Ibid, Anon, 'A Narrative of the Indian and Civil Wars in Virginia, pp. 31-47, narrates events after Bacon's death.

[43] Ibid, T. M., a Planter from Northumberland and an Assembly Member, pp. 75-76, considers the aftermath of the rebellion.

[44] Giles Brand to Secretary Sir Joseph Williamson, 28 April 1676, in *Calendar of State Papers, Colonial Papers,* Vol. 9, pp. 385-386, suggested that 'the yearly revenue of more than 100,000l, which Virginia yearly afford to his Majesty will be much abated…'

[45] *Calendar of State Papers, Colonial Papers,* Vol. 9, pp. 459-460, established a commission of inquiry on 3 October 1676. See also pp. 460-463, 476-477, on preparations for the expedition from England.

sailed up the James River on 29 January 1677, with the other forces arriving between 1 and 14 February.[46] Berkeley used these forces in exacting revenge. Among his first acts was to hang leaders of the rebellion, some 23 men.[47] He seized rebel property without benefit of trial. Finally, an outraged Assembly insisted that the executions and reprisals stop.[48] Colonel Herbert Jeffreys, one of the commissioners, had orders to replace Berkeley and he and Sir John Barry and Colonel Francis Moryson, his fellow commissioners soon quarrelled with Berkeley, who was reluctant to give up the government.[49] Finally, on 5 May 1677, Berkeley left for England to clear his name but died on 9 July before he had the opportunity of doing so. The Treaty of Middle Plantation, the formal peace treaty between the Native Americans and the colonists, was signed on 29 May 1677, and after Berkeley returned to England. Jeffreys' internal reforms erased much of the political autonomy built during Berkeley's regime and reasserted imperial control over Virginia.[50] In the aftermath of the rebellion, the Crown was determined to crush both Berkeley's misgovernment and the rebels and replace them with direct royal rule.

What was Bacon's rebellion?

Bacon's Rebellion has been interpreted as an attempt at political reform directed against the allegedly oppressive rule of the Governor and represented a prologue to the American Revolution.[51] Late-twentieth century historians, however, have questioned this thesis and emphasised controversy over Indian policy and class divisions within the colony as fundamental causes of the rebellion. Berkeley and his provincial élite were opposed by substantial planters who were excluded from the advantages of patronage and were denied access to land.[52] According to Alan

[46] *Calendar of State Papers, Colonial Papers,* Vol. 10, pp. 11-12.

[47] On those executed see Berkeley, Sir William, 'A List of Those That Have Been Executed for the Late Rebellion in Virginia', in ibid, *Tracts and Other Papers, Relating Principally to the Origin, Settlement, and Progress of the Colonies in North America, from the Discovery of the Country to the Year 1776, Collected by Peter Force*, Vol. I, pp. 93-96. For negative reactions to the executions see above Cotton, Ann Mrs, *An Account of our Late Troubles in Virginia,* pp. 89-90.

[48] On 25 September 1676, Charles II had issued a warrant authorising Berkeley to pardon all persons except for Bacon, *Calendar of State Papers, Colonial Papers,* Vol. 9, pp. 456-457. Berkeley issued the proclamation on 10 February 1677: *Calendar of State Papers, Colonial Papers,* Vol. 10, p. 19.

[49] Secretary Sir Henry Coventry to the Attorney-General, 16 September 1676, *Calendar of State Papers, Colonial Papers,* Vol. 9, p. 449, suggests that the decision had already been made in London to replace Berkeley but that he should be allowed to retired gracefully and retain the 'title and dignity of Governor'; he died the following year. A letter of recall was issued on 5 November 1676, *Calendar of State Papers, Colonial Papers,* Vol. 9, p. 483.

[50] *Calendar of State Papers, Colonial Papers,* Vol. 10, p. 97.

[51] On this issue see Frantz, John B., (ed.), *Bacon's Rebellion: prologue to the Revolution?* (Heath), 1969, and ibid, Webb, Stephen S., *1676, The End of American Independence*, pp. 409-416.

[52] Bailyn, Bernard, 'Politics and Social Structure in Virginia', in Katz, Stanley N., Murrin, John M., and Greenberg, Douglas, (eds.), *Colonial America: Essays in Politics and Social Development*, (McGraw-Hill), 1993, pp. 17-41.

Taylor, 'the Chesapeake's leading men lacked the mystique of a traditional ruling class.'[53] Newcomers, such as Bacon and Giles Bland had a higher social status in England than many planters in Virginia. They found upward mobility blocked by the Governor and his circle. In this scenario, Bacon was not a democrat but elitist, his ambitions thwarted by an ossified colonial political and social system whose legitimacy to rule he rejected. The volatility in Virginia in the 1670s was caused by the existence of a divided élite in an unstable and expanding society. It proved to be a rebellion with many causes but one which produced no real programme of reform or revolutionary manifesto. Bacon had probably never intended to turn protest into rebellion.

The ensuing civil war exposed deep social rifts between the poor whites and the Anglo-American élites of the Chesapeake region and many servants and slaves rallied round Bacon's flag.[54] After 1660, the exploitation of planters made it increasingly difficult for ex-servants to find land suitable for tobacco production. The best land adjacent to the rivers had already been allocated and former servants faced the option of either moving further west where marginal land was made even less appealing by the Native American attacks or sinking back into being tenants on unfavourable terms. As poor whites made their way to the frontier to establish farms of their own, they encountered various Native American groups, some friendly others hostile. Berkeley's policy was to keep the Native Americans divided, maintaining good relations with friendly Native Americans that also supplied him with valuable trade in deerskin. On the frontier, however, settlers made no distinctions between Native Americans and killed them indiscriminately following minor skirmishes and escalating tensions. For Morgan, the consequence of Bacon's rebellion was the rapid move in the last quarter of the seventeenth century to replace unpredictable indentured labour with the extensive use of African slaves on tobacco plantations. Native Americans and Africans were increasingly lumped together in a single pariah class while small and large planters with their common interest in profit and land came together in a single master class.

Bacon was articulate, charismatic and well-educated and gathered a small army of disenchanted farmers and poor whites calling for change in Crown policy. After Berkeley and the House of Burgesses refused to declare war against the frontier Indians, Bacon and his followers took matters into their own hands and attacked Native American settlements, killing friendly and hostile natives. The rebellion was also an attack on those planters whose fortunes were amassed over years of hard work and shrewd business ventures. These men comprised the 'favourites' Bacon referred to, tied to the royal Governor and his policies that included a monopoly on the deerskin trade. In his 'Declaration of the People', Bacon listed the grievances leading to the uprising including charges of unjust taxes, the monopoly of beaver and deerskins, and frontier Indian policies. Bacon also attracted fugitive slaves to his cause. The rebellion was both anti-elitist and

[53] Taylor, Alan, *American Colonies: The Settling of North America*, (Penguin Books), 2001, p. 139.

[54] This is discussed in Morgan, Edmund S., *American Slavery, American Freedom: the Ordeal of Colonial Virginia*, (Norton), 1995, pp. 250-270, and Parent, Anthony S., *Foul Means: the Formation of a Slave Society in Virginia, 1660-1740*, (University of North Carolina Press), 2003, pp. 135-172.

anti-Indian but, although there is evidence of class conflict in Virginia, it is doubtful whether Bacon, from a privileged background, saw rebellion in terms of social revolution. It is more likely that Bacon was merely using popular anger over hated policies to gather a following in order to achieve his own, personal elitist agenda by helping himself to loyalist property. The little we know about Bacon from the fragments about him that remain have been pliant enough to shape him as the patriot who struck the first blow for American independence or an Indian-hating opportunist who ruined the reputation of a popular Governor.[55]

Although Bacon's rebellion was a confused affair and revealed the mixed motivations and tangled outcomes of warfare in colonial America, access to land lay at its core. It began as a crusade against the Native Americans and ended as a series of plundering forays against those who still supported Berkeley. The rebellion changed little within the colony for gentlemen continued to monopolise the best land, the highest offices and most slaves. The Native Americans suffered most; those within the colony lost population and land, and the Susquehanock to the north were decimated by Iroquois warriors, who seized the opportunity to attack. By the 1680s, they existed only as Iroquois dependents and the Iroquois were free to sell their lands to colonial planters. For the next two hundred years, in colonial and then republican America the position of the Native Americans and their ownership of land was constantly disputed formally and informally. The consensus that emerged on the frontier in the aftermath of the American Revolution rested on shared interests between the authorities and settlers in physical safety, economic opportunity, and racial solidarity. The resulting state more closely resembled Hobbes' pragmatic concerns with order and security than either the Commonwealth men's idealist republic or John Locke's optimistic liberalism. Indian-hating became the foundation of a racialised national identity that offered membership in the community to all men who had white skin.[56] Settlers and élites united around the idea of their shared whiteness and the commitment of the government to promote the interests of whites at the expense of native peoples. The politicisation of the people during the Revolution was accompanied by the spread and acceptance of a racialised national identity that overcame and muted class differences.

Expanding the frontier in Australia

While access to native lands in North American colonies was achieved by a combination of agreement, purchase, guile and force, when the British occupied Sydney Cove in 1788 the colonial government in Australia claimed all lands for the Crown from its formal declaration of annexation on 7 February 1788.[57] The

---

[55] Billings, Warren M., Selby, John E., and Tate, Thad W., *Colonial Virginia: a History*, (KTO Press), 1986, p. 85.

[56] See, for instance, Knouff, Gregory, *A Soldiers' Revolution: Pennsylvanians in Arms and the Forging of Early American Identity*, (Pennsylvania State University Press), 2004, pp. 155-194.

[57] The principle of British sovereignty over Australia was asserted on four occasions, in 1788, 1824, 1829 and 1879. See, Connor, Michael, *The Invention of Terra Nullius: Historical and Legal Fictions on the Foundation of Australia*, (Macleay Press), 2005, a contentious study.

notion that Australia was *terra nullius*,[58] unowned land was used as justification for it being settled not invaded and that the Indigenous Australian population had no territorial rights over it.[59] Rather than implying mere emptiness or land being 'substantially uninhabited', *terra nullius* was broadly construed as an absence of civilised society and English common law allowed for legal settlement of 'uninhabited or barbarous country'. Although Australia was clearly not empty land, the presence of scattered and Indigenous Australian groups would have been widely perceived, through contemporary European eyes, as evidence of a barbarous country and consequently no legal impediment to occupying the land and colonial settlement. For Indigenous Australians, the arrival of an entirely alien culture represented disaster. Transformed from custodians of their ancestral lands, enjoying a rich material and spiritual culture to dispossessed 'savages', their world was indeed turned upside down.[60]

Testing terra nullius

Terra nullius rested on several empirical assertions about Indigenous Australian life: that Indigenous Australians were few, that they roamed throughout the land without a sense of boundaries and that they claimed no particular territories as their own. In fact, early settlers quickly learned that the Indigenous Australians did not lack property, divided land among individuals and passed property rights down from one generation to the next. This resulted in growing uncertainty as to the validity of *terra nullius* among colonial officials in NSW and in London. Both Governor King and Macquarie felt some unease about the appropriation of lands from Indigenous Australians. By the early 1820s, there was a growing belief in Britain and Australia especially by missionaries and church organisations that

---

[58] *Terra nullius*—an expression from Roman law meaning 'nobody's land'--is used to describe territory which has never been subject to the sovereignty of any state or over which any prior sovereign has expressly or implicitly relinquished sovereignty. Sovereignty over territory which is *terra nullius* may be acquired through occupation, though in some cases doing so would violate an international law or treaty

[59] See Reynolds, Henry, *Aboriginal sovereignty: reflections on race, state, and nation*, (Allen & Unwin), 1996, pp. 1-15, 86-107, and especially Attwood, Bain, *Possession: Batman's Treaty and the Matter of History*, (Melbourne University Press), 2009, and Ford, Lisa, *Settler Sovereignty: Jurisdiction and Indigenous People in America and Australia 1788-1836*, (Harvard University Press), 2010, pp. 158-182.

[60] Indigenous Australian readers are advised that this section contains the names of deceased persons. The question of whether we should use 'Indigenous Australians' or 'Aborigines' or 'Aboriginal people' is not simply a semantic one but reflects a view that Indigenous Australians feel it is inappropriate. Many Indigenous Australian people dislike the term 'Aborigines' because it has been imposed on them during colonisation. Some also dislike 'Aboriginal', although it is widely used though preferably as an adjective, as in 'Aboriginal peoples'. There has therefore been a widespread adoption in many parts of Australia of alternative words, usually the word for 'person' from a local indigenous language. For instance, the word *koori*i is used extensively across south eastern Australia. In other regions, different words have been adopted: *Murri* over most of south and central Queensland, *Bama* in north Queensland, *Nunga* in southern South Australia, *Noongar* (Nyoongah) around Perth, *Wongi* in the Kalgoorlie region, *Yolngu* in Arnhem Land, *Anangu* in central Australia, *Yuin* on the south coast of New South Wales and *Palawa* in Tasmania.

terra nullius was an injustice towards Indigenous Australians and by the 1830s, criticism of *terra nullius* was widely expressed in the Colonial Office and in Parliament.

The increasingly ambivalent attitude towards the notion of *terra nullius* was reflected in a series of contradictory legal judgements in the late-1820s and 1830s.[61] The first test of *terra nullius* in Australia occurred with the decision of *R v Tommy* indicating that the native inhabitants were only subject to English law where the incident concerned both Indigenous Australians and settlers and not where the case concerned only natives.[62] The rationale was that Indigenous Australian tribal groups already operated under their own legal systems, a position supported by the decision in *R v Ballard.* Chief Justice Forbes stated:

> I believe it has been the practice of the Courts of this country, since the Colony was settled, never to interfere with or enter into the quarrels that have taken place between or amongst the natives themselves. This I look to as matter of history, for I believe no instance is to be found on record in which the acts of conduct of the Aboriginals amongst themselves have been submitted to the consideration of our Courts of Justice. It has been the policy of the Judges, & I assume of the Government, in like manner with other Colonies, not to enter into or interfere with any cause of dispute or quarrel between the aboriginal natives. In all transactions between the British Settlers & the natives, the laws of the mother country have been carried into execution.[63] Aggressions by British subjects, upon the natives, as well as those committed by the latter upon the former, have been punished by the laws of England where the execution of those laws have been found practicable. This has been found expedient for the mutual protection of both sorts of people; but I am not aware that British laws have been applied to the aboriginal natives in transactions solely between themselves, whether of contract, tort, or crime.[64]

This position was reversed in *R v Murrell* in which Justice Burton concluded that Indigenous Australians had not attained sufficient numbers and civilisation as to be recognised as sovereign states governed by their own laws, and that the land was unappropriated by anyone at the time it was taken into actual possession of the King. Burton's judgement was an explicit statement of a *terra nullius* theory.[65] He also concluded that Indigenous Australians would have been

---

[61] Finnane, Mark, 'The Limits of Jurisdiction: Law, Governance and Indigenous Peoples in Colonized Australia', in Dorsett, Shaunnagh, and Hunter, Ian, (eds.), *Law and Politics in British Colonial Thought: Transpositions of Empire*, (Palgrave Macmillan), 2010, pp. 149-168, and Kercher, Bruce, 'The Recognition of Aboriginal Status and Laws in the Supreme Court of New South Wales under Forbes, CJ, 1824-1836', in Buck, A. R., McLaren, John, and Wright, Nancy E., (eds.), *Land and Freedom: Law, Property Rights and the British Diaspora*, (Ashgate), 2001, pp. 83-102, provide a succinct overview of the issues.

[62] 'Domestic Intelligence: Supreme Court', *Monitor*, 26 November 1827, p. 7, 'Editorial', *Monitor*, 29 November 1827, p. 6.

[63] The court had already decided that Indigenous Australians were subject to its jurisdiction when they conflicted with the Europeans who had come to occupy their lands. This was fully argued and decided in *R v Lowe*, 1827. See 'Criminal Court', *Australian*, 23 May 1827, pp. 3-4, for discussion of this precedent.

[64] 'Supreme Court', *Sydney Gazette,* 23 April 1829, p. 2.

[65] 'Supreme Court', *Sydney Gazette*, 23 February 1836, p. 3, and 'Supreme Court', *Sydney Gazette*, 12 April 1836, p. 3.

liable for murdering one another whether they were aliens or British subjects, a subtle way around the argument that they were subject only to their own customs and usages. Yet, five years later in *R v Bonjon*, Justice Willis held that a single judge of the Supreme Court of NSW was not bound by the decision in *Murrell* and that it had no jurisdiction over crimes committed by Indigenous Australians against one another.[66] They were not amenable to English law, except in cases of conflict with the British since express enactment or treaty made them subject to English law.[67] Indigenous Australians were distinct though dependent allies, not British subjects. They had not consented to British occupation or sovereignty and were entitled to exercise their own usages and laws.[68] The strongly contrasting judgments in *Ballard* and *Bonjon* were more consistent with the writings of Vattel on the rights of nomadic peoples and, as the judgment in *Bonjon* showed, also because they were more consistent with the treatment of native peoples in other jurisdictions.[69]

In 1835, John Batman, one of the founding pioneers of Victoria, first settled at Port Phillip and tried to buy the land from the Indigenous Australians through a 'treaty'.[70] His treaty was signed on the banks of a creek on 16 June 1835 and was an agreement with eight Indigenous Australian leaders to transfer 100,000 acres of prime farming land in the Port Phillip area to Batman. However, the transaction was not as straightforward as it appeared. Batman's claim to this territory was based on the European idea of land ownership and legal contracts, a concept that was completely foreign to the native people of Victoria. For them land was not about possession, but belonging. Territories may belong to different groups, but land cannot be bought or sold. Batman also claimed that he had negotiated with Indigenous Australian 'chiefs' who oversaw this land. But he was negotiating with tribal elders who were not in a position to sell their people's land, even if they had wanted to, and it is probable that none of the 'signatories' thought that this was what they were doing. The local Indigenous Australians were as unable to comprehend the idea of selling their land as Batman was of appreciating the value it held for them. The exchange that took place that day, and the 'treaty' that marked it, was at best the result of a cultural

---

66 Davies, Susanne, 'Aboriginals, Murder, and the Criminal Law in Early Port Phillip, 1841-1851', *Historical Studies*, Vol. 22, (1987), pp. 313-335.

67 See Wilson, Alan, 'John Walpole Willis', *DCB*, Vol. 10, pp. 704-707, for his period in Canada that may have influenced his judgement, and Behan, H. F., *Mr. Justice J. W. Willis: with Particular Reference to his Period as First Resident Judge in Port Phillip 1841-1843*, (Glen Iris), 1979, and Barry, John V., 'Willis, John Walpole (1793-1877)', *ADB*, Vol. 2, pp. 602-604.

68 'Supreme Court', *Port Phillip Patriot*, 20 September 1841, p. 1.

69 Vattel, Emeric de, *Droit des gens; ou, Principes de la loi naturelle appliqués à la conduite et aux affaires des nations et des souverains*, 2 Vols. (Abraham Droz), 1758, *The Law of Nations or the Principles of Natural Law Applied to the Conduct and to the Affairs of Nations and of Sovereigns*, (T. & J. W. Johnson), 1853, pp. 98-109.

70 Brown, P. L., 'Batman, John (1801-1839)', *ADB*, Vol. 1, pp. 67-71. See also Bonwick, John, *John Batman, the founder of Victoria*, (Fergusson and Moore), 1868, pp. 66-83, and Boyce, James, *1835: The Founding of Melbourne & The Conquest of Australia*, (Black Inc), 2013.

misunderstanding by both sides.[71] Inconsistencies in Batman's accounts of how the 'treaty' was signed throw his claims of legitimate purchase into doubt. The story of the treaty deeds differs from the story in Batman's journal and his report to Sir George Arthur, the VDL Lieutenant-Governor. Attwood concluded:

> We will never really know how much of the [Port Phillip] Association's narrative was true because of the paucity of contemporary sources. Indeed, all we have are the few accounts created by these colonisers. In respect of the famous treaty-making, we cannot even be sure it took place. Arguably, it might simply be an imaginary event that never happened. In the end, it probably doesn't matter very much whether it occurred or not. (I assume that some parts of the treaty-making did take place.) What is more important historically are the stories that have been told about it. [72]

Historians now question whether the eight Indigenous Australian chiefs signed their 'marks' on the contract, a theory arguably substantiated by Batman's own journal, in which he described how he had made the chiefs' 'signatures' on the deeds. While radicals have largely dismissed Batman's dealings as a shameful example of colonial self-interest and perfidy, Indigenous Australians, however, have cast Batman as a 'kind and just' man who established mutual understanding with their forebears and recognised their ownership of the land. In the 1930s and 1960s, the Australian Aboriginals' League and the Aboriginals Advancement League invoked his name in campaigning for Aboriginal rights.[73]

Both the transfer to a person rather than the Crown and its implicit recognition of native ownership and occupation of the land prompted Bourke to act. He effectively quashed the treaty with his Proclamation on 26 August 1835[74] and its re-publication on 3 May 1836 restating the doctrine of *terra nullius* upon which British settlement was based, reinforcing the notion that the land belonged to no one prior the British Crown taking possession of it in 1788:

> Whereas, it has been represented to me, that divers of His Majesty's Subjects have taken possession of vacant lands of the Crown, within the limits of this Colony, under the pretence of a treaty, bargain, or contract, for the purchase thereof, with the Aboriginal Natives; Now therefore, I, the Governor, in virtue and in exercise of the power and authority in me vested do hereby proclaim and notify to all His Majesty's Subjects, and others whom it may concern, that every such treaty, bargain, and contract with the Aboriginal Natives, as aforesaid, for the possession, title, or claim to any lands lying and being within the limits of the Government of the Colony of New South Wales...and including also Norfolk Island, is void and of no effect against the rights of the Crown; and that all persons who shall be found in possession of any such Lands as aforesaid, without the license or authority of His Majesty's Government, for such purpose first had and

[71] Kenny, Robert, 'Tricks or treats? A case for Kulin knowing in Batman's treaty', *History Australia*, Vol. 5, (2), (2008), pp. 1-38.

[72] Doyle, Helen, *Possession: Batman's treaty and the matter of history*, (Melbourne University Press), 2009, p. 47.

[73] For the subsequent histories of the treaties, see Attwood, Bain, with Doyle, Helen, *Possession: Batman's treaty and the matter of history*, (Melbourne University Press), 2009.

[74] 'Annoyances in some cases Distress of respectable Emigrants', *Sydney Monitor*, 2 September 1835, p. 2, for comment.

obtained, will be considered as trespassers, and liable to be dealt with in like manner as other intruders upon the vacant lands of the Crown within the said Colony. [75]

Its publication in the colony meant that people found in possession of land without the authority of the government would be considered trespassers.[76] Although some contemporaries recognised that the Indigenous Australian occupants had rights in the lands, something confirmed in a House of Commons report on Indigenous Australian relations in 1837, the law followed and almost always applied the principles expressed in Bourke's Proclamation. Glenelg supported Bourke's position completely rejecting the view that Indigenous Australian had any rights to dispose of their land.[77] Any recognition of Batman's treaty would have had a catastrophic effect on Australian land policy virtually amounting to recognition that Australia was not the property of the Crown but of its native population. It would have been an admission that since 1788 the British had been freely disposing of land that did not belong to them. In 1847, the Supreme Court of NSW affirmed that all un-granted land in Australia belonged to the Crown: *terra nullius* had proved impossible to dislodge.[78]

The existence of *terra nullius* in Australia is something of a puzzle especially as imperial policy in North America had already turned away from the principle. There is no reason to assume that the British government could not have established treaty arrangements with Indigenous Australians as it did later in NZ and elsewhere had it recognised native 'ownership' of the land. The critical distinction, which originated with James Cook in 1770, was that consent to the British taking possession was unnecessary since the land seemed 'waste' and unowned. In the late-eighteenth century, many believed that a society without agriculture was consequentially a society without property rights in land. The implication was that since the Indigenous Australian people were not farmers, they were not sovereign owners to be offered treaties. The eighteenth century jurist William Blackstone, who was regarded as authoritative on the matter in subsequent cases in several countries with legal systems based on English common law, drew a clear distinction between colonies won by conquest or treaty and those where 'lands are claimed by right of occupancy only, by finding them desert and uncultivated' (though he was unclear on whether they were

[75] National Archives: CO 201/247, ff 411, published in the *New South Wales Government Gazette*, 2 September 1835.

[76] In practice, although Bourke's action had voided any 'treaty' that was made, it did not prevent significant movement of settlers of the Port Phillip Association from VDL and from other parts of NSW into the Port Phillip District from late 1835 onwards. In his despatch of 10 October 1835, Bourke recommended that the settlement should be recognised and, though initially the Colonial Office had doubts about doing so, Lord Glenelg supported Bourke's recommendations and on 9 September 1836 a notice recognised the existence of a settlement that had already existed for a year.

[77] *Report from the Select Committee on Aboriginals (British Settlements): with the minutes of evidence*, appendix and index, 1837, pp. 10-15.

[78] Boucher, Leigh, and Russell, Lynette, (eds.), *Settler Colonial Governance in Nineteenth-Century Victoria*, (ANU Press and Aboriginal History Inc.), 2015, especially pp. 1-26.

uninhabited), and peopling them from the mother countries.[79] This ambiguity enabled later commentators to argue that only cultivated land was in actual possession and that in colonies of settlement English law was 'immediately there in force' on the assumption that no prior legal code and no land tenure had ever existed: it was *terra nullius.*

The words of the Privy Council in *Vajesingji v Secretary of State for India* in 1924 are among many other pronouncements that defined the concept of *terra nullius* unambiguously: 'territory hitherto not occupied by a recognised ruler'.[80] New Holland was considered a paradigm case of *terra nullius* because the British could identify no territorial units with a recognisable form of government, not because there had been no Indigenous Australian inhabitants.[81] It is the High Court that was mistaken in accepting that British explorers, Whitehall officials or Australian colonists held the false belief that Australia was uninhabited or nearly so. The consistent legal doctrine from 1788 was that the original British claim of sovereignty extinguished all prior rights to property and that after 1788, 'all titles, rights, and interests whatever in land which existed' were the 'direct consequence of some grant from the Crown', and people given these grants acquired property rights through mixing their labour with the soil. Despite the growing unease about the doctrine and suggestions in the 1830s and 1840s that land policy in Australia should be changed, once established as the basis for land ownership, it would have been extremely difficult to reverse. Some of the early British perceptions that the number of Indigenous Australian were few and lacked a conception of property were erroneous. Other arguments were also employed such as they were not farmers and would not offer as much military resistance as other native peoples the British had encountered. Although the first may have been broadly correct, the extent of Indigenous Australian resistance was greater than anticipated. Had the British known more about the Indigenous Australians from the start, they might have recognised their property rights. But once *terra nullius* had been implemented, it could not be reversed, even when British opinion about Indigenous Australians began to change. This state of affairs did not fundamentally alter until the Australian High Court's decision in the Mabo Case in 1992 that reconceptualised the modern basis of land law in Australia.[82] However, despite the decision, two established features from the early colonial period were not altered. The first principle is the power of the Crown as sovereign to grant land in fee simple and to extinguish other proprietary rights inconsistent with the grant. *Mabo* reaffirmed that the doctrine of tenure is the

---

[79] Prest, W., 'Law for Historians: William Blackstone on women, colonies and slaves', *Legal History*, Vol. 11, (2007), pp. 105-115, especially pp. 109-111.

[80] *Law Report*, 51 Ind. App. (1924) at 360, cit, Dawson J., in *107 Australian Law Report*, 1, p. 94.

[81] See Walters, Mark, 'Towards a 'Taxonomy' for the Common Law: Legal History and the Recognition of Aboriginal Customary Law', in Kirkby, Diane, and Coleborne, Catherine, (eds.), *Law, History, Colonialism: The Reach of Empire*, (Manchester University Press), 2001, pp. 125-139.

[82] The *Mabo* case radically altered this position and increasingly historians see Australian colonisation as 'conquest' rather than 'settlement'. Stephenson, M. A., and Ratnapala, Suri, (eds.), *Mabo: A Judicial Revolution, The Aboriginal Land Rights Decision and its impact on Australian Law*, (University of Queensland Press), 1993.

origin of land-holding in Australia establishing the Crown as sovereign owner and entitled to grant land to private individuals on whatever conditions necessary to serve the Crown's objectives. This was evident in the instructions given to successive colonial governors before being established as a statutory power in the Imperial Land Act 1831.

Reacting to invasion

Any analysis of the Indigenous Australian response to invasion before the 1960s tended to be hindered by the deliberate concealing of the levels of brutality between settlers and Indigenous Australians. European brutality was minimised and the Indigenous Australian response was peaceful; they were described as 'passive victims'. In addition to this, Indigenous Australian culture was 'rigid and unchanging ... unable to cope'.[83] From the 1960s onwards, historical analysis tended to over-compensate in an attempt to right previous wrongs. Many argued that Europeans were invaders, had brutally taken the land and by doing so had destroyed the hunter-gatherer lifestyle of the native people.[84] Indigenous Australians resisted but were completely overwhelmed, eventually forced to rely on whites for their existence whilst picking up the pieces of what was left of their culture. Notwithstanding, this view fails to emphasise the multi-faceted Indigenous Australian response to colonisation. Reynolds, nevertheless, has argued: 'Black response to invaders was more complex and more varied than has been described before'.[85]

Captain James Cook made three voyages to the South Pacific between 1768 and 1779 and on each occasion carried 'Secret Instructions' from the British Admiralty. These contained an outline of the route of the voyage, described the activities he and his men were to undertake, and how he was to report his progress. The instructions were secret in that they held the real intentions and plans for the voyage, whilst other papers issued would be made available on demand to demonstrate Cook's authority for his command and the enterprise. On his first voyage, Cook sailed in the *Endeavour* to Tahiti so as to assist in the scientific observation of the transit of the planet Venus, and then sailed south in search of the fabled 'Great Southern Continent'.[86]

---

[83] Reynolds, H., *The Other side of the Frontier: Aboriginal resistance to the European invasion of Australia*, (Penguin Books), 1995, p. 2.

[84] On the question of conquest see, Atkinson, Alan, 'Conquest', in Schreuder, Deryck M., and Ward, Stuart, (eds.), *Australia's Empire*, (Oxford University Press), 2008, pp. 33-53, and Day, David, *Claiming a Continentt: A New History of Australia*, (Harper Collins), 2005, pp. 27-115.

[85] Ibid, Reynolds, H., *The Other side of the Frontier*, p. 2.

[86] Beaglehole, J. C., *The Life of Captain James Cook*, (Stanford University Press), 1974, and his editions of Cook's journals, *The Journals of Captain James Cook: the Voyage of the Endeavour,1768-1771*, (Cambridge University Press), 1955, *The Journals of Captain James Cook: the Voyage of the Resolution and Adventure, 1772-1775*, (Cambridge University Press), 1961, and *The Journals of Captain James Cook: the Voyage of the Resolution and Discovery, 1776-1780*, 2 Vols. (Cambridge University Press), 1967, are the standard works. Edwards, Philip, (ed.), *James Cook: The Journals*, (Penguin Books), 2003, is an abridged version.

The 'Secret Instructions', dated 30 July 1768 authorised Cook to take possession of 'a Continent or Land of great extent', thought to exist in southern latitudes and instructed him 'with the Consent of the Natives to take possession of Convenient Situations in the Country in the Name of the King of Great Britain'.[87] These provided that should he find the Continent, he should chart its coasts, obtain information about its people, cultivate their friendship and annex any convenient trading posts for the Crown. Cook followed the coast of NZ and then turned west, reaching the southern coast of NSW on 20 April 1770.[88] He sailed north, landing at Botany Bay one week later, before continuing to chart the Australian coast all the way north to the tip of Queensland.[89] There, just before sunset on 22 August 1770, on Possession Island, he declared the coast a British possession.

> Notwithstand[ing] I had in the Name of His Majesty taken possession of several places upon this coast, I now once more hoisted English Coulers and in the Name of His Majesty King George the Third took possession of the whole Eastern Coast . . . by the name New South Wales, together with all the Bays, Harbours Rivers and Islands situate upon the said coast, after which we fired three Volleys of small Arms which were Answerd by the like number from the Ship.[90]

Over eight days and nights in late April 1770, Captain Cook and the men of the *Endeavour* made their first extended landfall on the east coast of New Holland. Cook had recorded signs that the coast was inhabited during the voyage north noting as he returned to the ship the large number of fires on all the land and islands about them, 'a certain sign they are Inhabited'. Both Cook and Joseph Banks wrote accounts of the attempts to 'form a connection with the natives', but this was downplayed by later historians that a common misconception is that there was no interaction with the locals or so little that it was not worthy of sustained comment.[91] The problem, as Nugent clearly demonstrates, was how both sides read the encounter. For instance, what might have appeared as potentially aggressive behaviour to Cook, especially weapon waving, loud shouting and body decoration, was in fact a description of customary behaviour when local Indigenous Australian groups encountered strangers, whether they were native peoples or explorers. Cook then sailed through Torres Strait, returning to England in May 1771. Cook's 'Secret Instructions' represented the first official expressions of British interest in Australia combining the pursuit of scientific discovery with the desire to find exploitable natural resources and to expand Britain's control of strategic trading posts around the globe and assumed

---

[87] This Letterbook contains the only surviving set of Cook's original Secret Instructions. See *HRNSW*, Vol. 1, (1), pp. 398-402, for the secret instructions for Cook's third voyage.
[88] Ibid, Edwards, Philip, (ed.), *James Cook: The Journals*, pp. 120-121.
[89] Ibid, Edwards, Philip, (ed.), *James Cook: The Journals*, pp. 122-123.
[90] Ibid, Edwards, Philip, (ed.), *James Cook: The Journals*, pp. 170-171.
[91] Unlike Cook's interaction with other peoples in the Pacific and New Zealand, his contacts with the peoples in Australia have been relegated to a footnote in history perhaps because they were so brief. Nugent, Maria, *Captain Cook was here*, (Cambridge University Press), 2009, provides a narrative and critique of the interactions between the explorers and the native inhabitants.

that these varied interests could be made compatible with a respect for the native populations in those countries. Cook's observations along the NSW coastline on his first voyage formed the foundation for Britain's decision to establish the colony at Botany Bay in 1788.[92]

Governor Arthur Phillip arrived in NSW in early 1788 with instructions by the British government to 'conciliate' the indigenous people, '...and if any of our subjects should wantonly destroy them...', then punishment would follow.[93] The Indigenous Australians' lives and livelihoods were to be protected and friendly relations with them encouraged, but the 'Instructions' make no mention of protecting or even recognising their lands. It was hoped that the land would be seized without bloodshed and with the cooperation of the native people. This proved impossible to achieve and Broome argued that 'Contradiction lay at the heart of British policy', and conciliation was doomed from the beginning.[94] The land was simply seized and Indigenous Australians immediately lost any rights without being compensated. This was reinforced after Phillip began to issue grants of land to officers and freed convicts who warned the Indigenous Australians to stay off 'their land'.[95] The early British residents showed far greater contempt for the Indigenous Australians than British colonists presented toward native peoples in other places. Settlers in North America made their share of disparaging remarks about Indians, but they also praised Indian technology, social life and political organisation. Comments on Indigenous Australians by contrast, were mainly variations on a single theme. They were not regarded as human equals and any interaction between them was tainted by this misconception. Although Indigenous Australians had their own moral code and customary law, for the early convicts and free settlers in NSW they were regarded as 'savages'. For Phillip and a few of his officers, there was an acceptance of the Romantic notion of the 'noble savage', but this idea soon faded with the realities of contact. By 1809, the naturalist George Caley, sent to NSW by Sir Joseph Banks to gather botanical specimens, summed up two decades of British observations. He told Banks, 'I believe it is universally said that the natives of New South Wales are the most idle, wretched and miserable beings in the world.'[96]

The colony was founded as a penal settlement and most of the initial inhabitants were hardened men who were insensitive to the complexities and nuances of Indigenous Australian cultures. Phillip hoped for 'conciliation' but the

---

[92] *HRNSW*, Vol. 1, (1), contains extracts from Cook's private log and the log book of the *Endeavour*. However, the volume is perhaps most valuable for the journals of officers, pp. 175-298.

[93] Gumbert, M., *Neither Justice Nor Reason*, (University of Queensland Press), 1984, p. 11. Phillip was given two commissions before he left England: *HRA*, Series I: Vol. 1, pp. 1-9. It was the second commission, dated 25 April 1787 that provided Phillips with instructions on the Aboriginal question.

[94] Broome, R., *Aboriginal Australians: a history since 1788*, 4th ed., (Allen & Unwin), 2010, p. 22.

[95] Phillip's instructions on land grants, 22 August 1789: *HRA*, Series I: Vol. 1, pp. 124-128.

[96] George Caley to Joseph Banks, 16 February 1809, in Currey, J. E. B., (ed.), George Caley, *Reflections on the Colony of New South Wales*, (Lansdowne Press), 1966, pp. 177-178.

struggle over the land and cultural differences was destined to be bloody.[97] For the first two years of conciliation the Gamaraigal tried to avoid the invaders, were terrified of the strange white people and perplexed as to why they were there. Blainey argues that initially Indigenous Australians acted with 'calm apathy' towards the invaders, because they were only able to comprehend their own world. Even Captain Tench and Governor Phillip noticed the 'blacks' had relatively ignored their attempts at friendly interaction. In contrast Reynolds argues that Indigenous Australians were not 'passive and incurious people' and in fact responded with curiosity at initial contact with the Europeans.[98] Indigenous Australians often scoured newcomers' camps for goods Europeans had abandoned and put them to their own uses. It was social protocol for some Indigenous Australian groups to ignore visitors when they first arrived for to be overly inquisitive was considered bad manners.[99] Yet, instead of acting indifferently to the settlers, they broke tradition and responded with great interest. For instance, when Phillip and some officers were eating a meal on Sydney Harbour, a group of heavily armed Indigenous Australians approached. Fearing a violent confrontation Phillip was surprised that so intrigued were they with the dining proceedings that his officers grew annoyed with the intrusion. Phillip eventually drew a circle around the dining party to eat his meal in peace.[100]

Indigenous Australians went to great lengths to incorporate the settlers within their traditional framework adapting their traditional beliefs to understand the European invasion on their own terms. They comprehended only the world they existed in and believed that all people must have a spiritual bond with the land and the people.[101] For Indigenous Australians the whiteness of the colonists' skin signified death and many communities accepted the Europeans as dead ancestors who had returned to their land. This view was widespread. For instance, Buckley reported that the Port Phillip Indigenous Australians recognised whites as having 'returned to life in a different colour', while around Sydney Indigenous Australians frequently referred to the invaders as 'ghosts'.[102] The belief that colonists were returned dead ancestors had a huge effect on the way Indigenous Australians responded to initial contact with Europeans. It determined the fate of the invaders. If people were seen as strangers their fate was possibly death, but if people were familiar then this could mean acceptance rather than retaliation. Consequently, settlers sought to maintain these misconceptions in the hope that the Indigenous Australians would be pacified, and this response to the colonists enabled the growth of the settlement without incurring the full wrath of the native

---

[97] Ibid, Broome, R., *Aboriginal Australians*, pp. 18-29. See also Perry, T. M., *Australia's First Frontier: the Spread of Settlement in New South Wales 1788-1829*, (Melbourne University Press), 1963, Turbet, Peter, *First Frontier: the Occupation of the Sydney Region 1788 to 1816*, (Rosenberg Publishing), 2011, and Roberts, Stephen, *History of Australian Land Settlement 1788-1920*, (Melbourne University Press), 1924.

[98] Ibid, Reynolds, H., *The Other side of the Frontier*, p. 25.

[99] Ibid, Reynolds, H., *The Other side of the Frontier*, p. 29.

[100] Turnbull, L., *Sydney: biography of a city*, (Random House), 1999, p. 31.

[101] Berndt, R., & C., *The World of the First Australians: Aboriginal Traditional Life: Past and Present*, (Aboriginals Studies Press), 1999, p. 492.

[102] Ibid, Reynolds, H., *The Other side of the Frontier*, p. 30.

peoples.[103] Once they were aware that the colonists were not dead ancestors, some native people nonetheless accepted them into a kinship system. This had benefits for both parties enabling Indigenous Australians to classify appropriate behaviour towards the invaders and accept appropriate behaviour from the invaders. Kinship systems encouraged reciprocity where sharing of the land, gifts and women were expected. Indigenous Australians were surprised by the amount of possessions that settlers had and were confused by their reluctance to share them. For instance, the Bangerang and Ngooraialum accepted European names in the hope of encouraging a reciprocal relationship with the settlers. However, cultural misunderstandings soon arose when settlers did not reciprocate and many Indigenous Australians responded with violence.[104] Indigenous Australian resistance was met with even greater levels of settler violence in which their warriors' skill with spears was outmatched by the blunt force of settlers' rifles.

The major arena for cultural confusion was over land and there is disagreement about how Indigenous Australians saw the land. For some commentators, their resistance to settler expansion assumes that there was a clear sense of land ownership and that boundaries were rigidly defined. When settlers entered their land, Indigenous Australians regarded it as trespass and warned them to leave. The second view suggests that the tribal boundaries were far less defined. Tribes shared certain sacred sites. Neighbouring clans mingled and hunted and foraged on each other's land. Accustomed to people foraging on their land, Indigenous Australians initially did not see the white presence as an intrusion and had no idea that settlers were going to stay and 'own' the land. Conflict over women was another recurring theme in frontier areas. The pioneer population of NSW was largely womanless and this resulted in the ceremonial exchange of women and the offer of sexual favours as a means of hospitality or method of diplomacy. Conflict arose when European men refused to bring offerings to tribes that had granted them access to their women.

Indigenous Australian culture endorsed the idea of 'revenge killings'. If harm had been done to the group or individual, it was accepted that they could retaliate with equal harm on those who had inflicted the injury. Deaths caused by settlers often led to retribution--only occasionally did Indigenous Australians attack settlers in general. Not without criticism, Reynolds drew attention to evidence that Indigenous Australians intended 'to attack and kill whites whenever they met any' to gain vengeance.[105] As a result, he concluded that Indigenous Australians intended mass and indiscriminate revenge because of the very presence of the colonists, irrespective of specific actions.[106] retaliation may have led to a brutal response:

---

[103] Ibid, Reynolds, H., *The Other side of the Frontier*, p. 39.

[104] McBryde, I., 'Exchange in south-eastern Australia: an ethno-historical perspective', in Chapman, V., and Read, P., (eds.), *Terrible Hard Biscuits*, (Allen & Unwin), 1996, pp. 54-59.

[105] He cited among others B. Doyle in Maitland in 1842, J. D. MacTaggart in NSW in 1858, the magistrates of Upper Dawson in 1857 and Frederick Walker in Queensland in 1861.

[106] Ibid, Reynolds, H., *The Other side of the Frontier*, p. 78.

> With their poor technology, simple weapons, and elementary notions of both strategy and tactics, the Aboriginals were no match for the invaders in any clash of interest between them.[107]

But what was not so widely known or appreciated until recently is just how effective their resistance was to the original stages of invasion.

Most Indigenous Australians reacted to European violence according to custom. Those who had committed offences were targeted for retaliation with the expectation that settlers would also conform to this tradition. Soon Indigenous Australians realised that revenge killing was not being honoured as many innocent Indigenous Australians were killed. Traditional battle formations were also ineffective because they were extremely vulnerable to modern weapons. Alternatively, some Indigenous Australian groups resorted to sorcery or withdrew from confrontation altogether. Others broke from tradition and decided that all whites should be held accountable for their actions. Small raiding parties became the most effective method of fighting and proved efficient in isolated settlements where settlers were vulnerable. Initially, Indigenous Australian tactics were superior when their bush-craft, local knowledge and effective weapons matched military firepower and speed of horses.[108] Some Indigenous Australians quickly realised the value of guns and used them against settlers. There are reports of this occurring in Tasmania in the 1820s, Victoria in the 1840s, and in Cape York in the 1880s and 1890s. Some settlements were so terrorised and almost completely destroyed that Governor Hunter wrote in 1800 that Aboriginals: '...might spread desolation over our cultivated lands and reduce us to extreme distress...'[109] By 1816, the efficiency of guerrilla warfare drove Governor Macquarie to disarm Indigenous Australians around towns in NSW and to ban groups of six or more in an attempt to control violence.[110] Yet, disarming Indigenous Australian and providing settlers with more military power only hindered the ability of the native people to defend themselves. Indigenous Australians started to 'come in' to settlements because of the effects of violence, disease and starvation.

Indigenous Australians also adapted to their new environment, successfully cooperating with settlers, and were not simply 'passive victims'. Native people demonstrated innovation by trading items such as fish for European food and wares such as glass, iron and clothing. By 1791, trade had flourished between the settlers and Indigenous Australians around Sydney.[111] As trade across traditional routes developed, European merchandise became highly prized to replace traditional materials in tool kits:

> European goods like steel axes and knives, pieces of iron, tins, cloth and glass were all eagerly sought and used by Aboriginal tribes even before contact had been made with

[107] Ibid, Berndt, R., & C., *The World of the First Australians: Aboriginal Traditional Life: Past and Present*, p. 492.
[108] Ibid, Reynolds, H., *The Other side of the Frontier*, p. 103.
[109] Hunter to Portland, 2 January 1800, *HRA*, Series I: Vol. 2, p. 403.
[110] Macquarie to Bathurst, 8 June 1816, *HRA*, Series I: Vol. 9, pp. 141-145 prints his proclamation.
[111] Ibid, Turnbull, L., *Sydney: biography of a city*, p. 35.

settlers on the advancing frontier. Western food, tobacco and alcohol also exerted a tremendous attraction.[112]

Indigenous Australians adapted traditional cooking methods to cook a variety of new foods such as rabbit, cattle and flour for damper. They also started to store and preserve food, something many had never needed to do before. Reynolds cited evidence from Normanton and other Queensland towns of Indigenous Australians employed as houseboys, firewood cutters, stable hands, yard cleaners, nurse girls, washerwomen, charwomen and gardeners, some of whom bargained for wages. There was considerable opposition by artisans to the entry of Indigenous Australians into their trades because wages and conditions would suffer. There was in addition, much evidence of less constructive Indigenous Australian accommodations, such as prostitution, begging and pilfering. Sharing or prostitution of their women by Indigenous Australian males occurred almost as soon as whites appeared. Sometimes Indigenous Australians expected such offers would strengthen amity and respect as well as elicit major material reciprocity, but the objective effect was to reduce respect for Indigenous Australian culture, even among those very willing to take advantage of the opportunities for sex made available.

Indigenous Australian culture was also influenced by European concepts. Images of people, ships and events were incorporated in traditional art throughout Australia. For instance, in the Darling Downs, a detailed painting of a ship was found on a tree. Keen observation of European culture led some Indigenous Australians to incorporate new dances and songs at traditional corroborees. There are many accounts of different dances such as the 'cattle dance' performed by Queensland communities, where Indigenous Australians exactly imitated the cattle's characteristics. Also, traditional songs now included events, domestic animals or European songs and hymns. The historical record clearly shows that Indigenous Australians were not 'passive victims' nor was their culture 'unchanging and fragile', crumbling under the impact of invasion. Despite the pressures of dispossession, they displayed cultural innovation and adaptation while maintaining their resilient cultural traditions.

Contesting grounds

The Indian 'Mutiny' and the 'Māori Wars' shows how the settlers understood and justified their treatment of indigenous people in the light of interracial conflicts in other parts of the Empire. Violent British reprisals against the Sepoys in India could be used to justify the settlers' own reprisals against Indigenous Australians and the re-assertion of imperial control on the sub-continent with colonists asserting that their right to govern the Australian continent could be interpreted as legitimising their own dispossession of indigenous people. Frontier conflict proved an inescapable feature of Australian life for six generations.[113] It

---

[112] Ibid, Reynolds, H., *The Other side of the Frontier*, p. 39.

[113] Reynolds, H., 'Violence in Australian History', in Chappell, D., Grabonsky, P., and Strang, H., (eds.), *Australian Violence: Contemporary Perspectives*, (Australian Institute of Criminology), 1991, pp. 13-23, at p. 15. See also Connor, John, *The Australian Frontier Wars 1788-1838*, (University of New South Wales Press), 2002, Moses, A. Dirk,

was a silent resistance and a largely silent war. Violence was accepted as a necessary consequence of colonial progress and was widely reported in the colonial press though it was never sanctioned or officially recognised by the colonial authorities. Attacks on Indigenous Australians were supported by public opinion, especially in rural areas and tacitly assented to by governments. The resulting brutalisation of public opinion was noted by many who visited the colonies. In 1883, Sir Arthur Gordon, the South Pacific Commissioner, wrote to his friend Prime Minister William Gladstone:

> ...men of culture and refinement, of the greatest humanity and kindness to their fellow whites, and who when you meet them at home you would pronounce to being capable of such deeds, talk, not only of the wholesale butchery...but of the individual murder of natives, exactly as they would talk of a day's sport, or of having had to kill some trouble-some animal.[114]

Guns were an accepted presence in frontier life and private individuals were frequently involved in skirmishing with resident clans. Community complicity included both the local magistracy and police who generally favoured settlers even if the evidence indicated otherwise protecting those who were 'hard on the blacks'. Those who spoke out against the slaughter were reviled and threatened with violence. Indigenous Australian resistance was largely anonymous involving unnamed individuals or groups of warriors. Some resistance leaders were known only by nicknames such as Brian Boru, Boney, Blucher, Pompey and Musquito, who was a war leader of the Dharruk people in the Hawkesbury and Broken Bay areas. Others such as Pemulwuy, Windradyne, Calyute and Yagan and Weeip who were allies against the colonial forces in WA, Dundalli, in the Brisbane area and Jundamurra in the West Kimberley were known by their Indigenous Australian names. Frontier violence first occurred in NSW and VDL and spread as the continent was colonised to WA, Victoria, Queensland and to the Northern Territory, lasting until the Coniston massacre in 1928 and further reprisal expeditions in the Northern Territory in 1932 and 1933.

New South Wales 1788-1829

Before the colony was six weeks old, relations between the Europeans and Indigenous Australians had already deteriorated into what Captain Watkin Tench called 'this state of petty warfare.'[115] In December 1790, John McIntyre, Governor Phillip's gamekeeper who was believed to have killed Indigenous

---

(ed.), *Genocide and Settler Society: Frontier Violence and Stolen Indigenous Children in Australian History*, (Berghahn Books), 2012, and Kiernan, Brian, *Blood and Soil: a World History of Genocide and Extermination from Sparta to Darfur*, (Yale University Press), 2007, pp. 249-309.

[114] Cit, Knaplund, A., 'Sir Arthur Gordon on the New Guinea Question, 1883', *Historical Studies*, Vol. 15, (1955-1957), pp. 330-331.

[115] See Tench, W., *Sydney's First Four Years*, (Angus & Robertson), 1961, p. 137. Borch, M. F., *Conciliation, Compulsion, Conversion: British attitudes towards indigenous peoples, 1763-1814*, (Rodopi), 2004, pp. 73-120, and ibid, Turbet, Peter, *First Frontier: The Occupation of the Sydney Region*, pp. 17-62, examines the relationships between the two societies in those early years of the colony.

Australian people, was speared by Pemulwuy and four other Indigenous Australians and died the following month. A military expedition of 50 men under Captain Watkin Tench, was despatched to make 'a severe example' of the suspected clan. Six men were to be captured of whom two were to be hanged and four sent to Norfolk Island. If they could not be taken alive they were to be shot and decapitated.[116] This expedition proved fruitless largely because of the soldiers' inability at navigating through the bush.

Punitive expeditions became the common reponse of governments threatened by Indigenous Australian resistance and the prospect of settlers abandoning their farms and stations. Military parties were despatched to the Hawkesbury in the 1790s and the 1800s and deployed around the fringes of European settlement on the Cumberland Plain in 1814 and 1816, at Bathurst in 1824, and along the Hunter Valley two years later.[117] They were used in similar ways in both VDL and WA in the 1820s and 1830s. As the frontier expanded, private punitive expeditions became a common feature of colonial life, while in 1848 the NSW government established the paramilitary Native Mounted Police. Enthusiastically adopted by the new Queensland government in 1859, the force patrolled the vast northern frontier until the first decade of the twentieth century. It reached a peak of 250 men in the 1870s and then slowly declined. Throughout its history, the force was officially instructed to 'disperse' any large gatherings of Indigenous Australians in order to prepare the way for the advancing wave of settlement.

Pemulwuy, (also spelt Pemulwoy, Pemulwy, Pemulwei) led the first Indigenous Australian resistance against the British at Sydney for twelve years.[118] He was probably the leader of the Bidjigal people and lived near Botany Bay. From 1790 to 1802, he used guerrilla tactics against soldiers and settlers and gained legendary status among his people, who believed that he could not be killed. Pemulwuy persuaded the Eora, Dharug and Tharawal people to join his campaign against the newcomers and from 1792, led a series of raids on settlers at Prospect, Toongabbie, Georges River, Parramatta, Brickfield Hill and the Hawkesbury River. In 1797, Pemulwuy led 100 fighters, including some escaped Irish convicts into 'the Battle of Parramatta' and confronted the British troops near the river. He also led several attacks directly on the NSW Corps including the sacking of the Lane Cove settlement and the capture of Parramatta. His coordinated raids were primarily against farms to weaken the newly established colony that was dependent on crops of wheat and maize and their limited livestock. Because such resources were desperately needed by the colony, historians have posited the attacks were calculated war strategies devised by Pemulwuy to weaken his enemy. In the late 1790s, emancipist John Wilson was adopted into a tribe on the Hawkesbury River, where he was later joined by

[116] Ibid, Tench, W., *Sydney's First Four Years*, pp. 205-213.

[117] Ibid, Connor, John, *The Australian Frontier Wars 1788-1838*, pp. 35-68, considers Aboriginal resistance in the Hawkesbury-Nepean River between 1795 and 1816 and in the Bathurst and Hunter Valley districts in the 1820s.

[118] Kohen, J. L., 'Pemulwuy (c. 1750-1802)', *ADB*, Supplementary Volume, pp. 318-319. See also, ibid, Turbet, Peter, *First Frontier: The Occupation of the Sydney Region*, pp. 53-58, 122-126.

another ex-convict, William Knight.[119] The two were believed to be assisting Indigenous Australians in fighting colonial forces and by the late 1790s there were at least seven or eight other convict runaways operating in the bush. By November 1801, two of them, William Knight and Thomas Thrush, were believed to have allied themselves with Pemulwuy.

On 1 May 1801, Governor King issued a government and general order that Indigenous Australians near Parramatta, Georges River and Prospect could be shot on sight, and on 22 November a general order outlawed Pemulwuy offering a reward for his death or capture. In mid-1802, he was finally hunted down and shot dead. His head was hacked off, preserved and sent to England.[120] There is some disagreement about whether Pemulwuy was concerned about the presence of colonists or whether his actions reflected breaches in Bidjigal law. When Pemulwuy speared McIntyre, there had been no settlement in Bidjigal land and little contact with the Bidjigal at all. As a gamekeeper, McIntyre probably ventured into Bidjigal territory and was disliked by Indigenous Australians because of his aggressive conduct. His spearing may have been punishment for breaking laws. Also, it was almost eleven years between McIntyre's death and the date Pemulwuy was outlawed. If Governors saw him as a guerrilla leader, then he could have been outlawed far earlier. It is difficult to estimate whether they regarded his actions as typical of hunter gatherer people or as retaliation against poor behaviour by settlers.

Conflict began once more when the British expanded into inland NSW.[121] The settlers who crossed the Blue Mountains were harassed by Wiradjuri warriors, who killed or wounded stock-keepers and stock and were subjected to retaliatory killings. Windradyne, belonged to the northern Wiradjuri clan who occupied the land on which Bathurst was later built.[122] Aggression towards Indigenous Australians increased month-by-month as more settlers arrived. Many settlers gave them food laced with poison or blatantly shot to kill whenever individuals or groups were sighted. Windradyne, their young leader, was captured in 1822 while attempting to rescue a small group of his people and when he was finally released, he quickly organised and led a group of his men in a retaliatory raid. They planned to attack a group of whites who were meeting one night at a place known as the 'Murdering hut', so called because many of Windradyne's people had been taken there on previous occasions, subjected to all sorts of indecencies then murdered. Windradyne's raid was successful and seven stockmen were killed. Following this daring incident, official reprisals were swift and draconian. Martial Law was declared on 14 August 1824 and local soldiers, police and settlers were given official permission to administer summary justice.[123] Many of the local men quickly began their brutal campaign and a reward was

---

119 Wilson was outlawed by General Order, dated 13 May 1797: *HRA*, Series I: Vol. 2, p. 79.

120 King to Lord Hobart, 30 October 1802, *HRA*, Series I: pp. 582-583, details the attacks by Pemulway.

121 Ibid, Turbet, Peter, *First Frontier: The Occupation of the Sydney Region*, pp. 183-188, 191-217.

122 Roberts, D. A., 'Windradyne (c.1800-1829)', *ADB*, Supplementary Volume, pp. 408-409; see also above Connor, John, *The Australian Frontier Wars 1788-1838*, pp. 56-61.

123 *HRA*, Series I: Vol. 11, p. 410.

offered for the recapture of Windradyne. The crisis subsided quickly, although the failure to capture Windradyne delayed the repeal of martial law until 11 December. Two weeks later he and a large number of his people crossed the mountains to Parramatta to attend an annual feast where he was formally pardoned by Governor Brisbane. Windradyne then returned to Bathurst and in later years was intermittently reported as being involved in raids on maize crops or in clashes with settlers around Lake George. In 1828, an Indigenous Australian being led to his execution for the murder of a stockman at Georges Plains attempted vainly to pin the crime on Windradyne. Mortally wounded in a tribal fight on the Macquarie River, Windradyne died on 21 March 1829 at Bathurst hospital, and was buried at Bathurst.[124]

Western Australia 1826-1834

The first British settlement in WA was established by the British Army at Albany in 1826 where relations between the garrison and the local Minang people were generally good. Open conflict between Noongar and European settlers broke out in Western Australia in the 1830s as the Swan River Colony expanded from Perth.[125] The Nyungar people forced from traditional hunting grounds and denied access to sacred sites turned to stealing settlers' crops and killing livestock to supplement their food supply. In 1831, a Nyungar was killed taking potatoes and this led to Yagan killing a servant of the household, a response permitted under tribal law.[126] In 1832, Yagan and two others were arrested and sentenced to death but settler Robert Lyon argued that Yagan was defending his land from invasion and for that reason he should be treated as a prisoner of war. This proved successful and the three men were exiled to Carnac Island under the supervision of Lyon and two soldiers but the group later escaped. Yagan and his tribe were again involved in theft and murder and Yagan was eventually shot and killed in July 1833. Like Pemulwuy, his head was cut off but, following an Indigenous Australian campaign, it was returned and buried according to tribal custom in 2010.[127] The location of Pemulwuy's head remains unresolved though it is believed to have been returned to Australia in the 1950s and a skull was identified as Pemulway's in 1998 but this is disputed.

In response to calls from Pinjarra settlers for protection against the increased hostility of local Binjareb Indigenous Australians, Stirling organised a mounted force of police, Bushmen and ex-soldiers. His attack at Pinjarra was intended to punish the Binjareb for their earlier individual attacks and enable Thomas Peel to attract settlers onto his lands at Mandurah. This followed an earlier failure by Peel who had led an expedition to the area with the goal of

---

[124] The details of his death in 1829 are sketchy but some believed he survived his wounds, discharged himself from hospital, returned to his homeland where he died of gangrene. See Suttor, W. H., *Australian Stories Retold and Sketches of Country Life*, (Glyndwr Whalan), 1887, pp. 44-45.

[125] Ibid, Connor, John, *The Australian Frontier Wars 1788-1838*, pp. 68-101, examines events in WA.

[126] See, Hasluck, Alexandra, 'Yagan (? –1833)', *ADB*, Vol. 2, p. 412.

[127] Fforde, Cressida, 'Yagan', in Fforde, Cressida, Hubert, Jane, and Turnbull, Paul, (eds.), *The Dead and Their Possessions: Repatriation in Principle, Policy, and Practice*, (Routledge), 2002, pp. 229-241.

improving security and negotiating peaceful co-existence. Stirling now wanted decisive action that would end the attacks. The Pinjarra massacre on 28 October 1834 resulted when a party of British soldiers and mounted police led by Governor Stirling attacked a campsite on the banks of the Murray River subjecting it to withering fire from 24 guns for over an hour. The number of casualties sustained by the Binjareb has been hotly debated over the years. Stirling indicated that around 15 were killed while another report put the number at 25 to 30. All accounts admit that women and children were amongst the dead. Oral histories handed down amongst the Binjareb give a much higher casualty figure. The consequences of the massacre seem to have deepened the settlers' fears rather than allaying them.[128]

Western Australia's *The Inquirer* in October 1853 commented 'Crime is a great leveller'.

> Policy requires that we should convince the native population that in our Courts of Justice they really are what we profess and tell them they are—the equals of the white man, whatever they may be elsewhere.[129]

John Jones was tried on 5 October before Perth's Quarter Sessions for the murder of Neader, an Indigenous Australian in the colony's southwest. Jones was found guilty of manslaughter and sentenced to transportation for life. Given that Australia's colonies were notable for their failure to bring settlers to trial for violence against Indigenous Australians, it is significant that *The Inquirer*'s editor[130] did not regard Jones' conviction and sentence as a sign that the Courts of Justice were working as they professed to do. The charge was one of wilful murder, and the evidence indicated that 'if ever a foul and deliberate murder was committed, it was on the occasion which led to this trial.' The verdict that Jones was guilty only of manslaughter was indicative of the jury's disregard of the law's impartiality when a white man was on trial for the murder of an Indigenous Australian man. If the law was to make a distinction between white and black, the editor commented: 'let it be declared: but to say there is none, and to act as if there were, is a mockery.'[131]

Fighting continued into the 1840s along the Avon River near York and further European expansion led to frontier conflict with Banuba raiders attacking European settlements during the 1890s until their leader was killed in 1897. About half of the Kimberley Indigenous Australians were killed as reprisals for cattle spearing and revenge killings of European settlers. Sporadic conflict continued in northern WA until the 1920s and a Royal Commission held in 1926

---

[128] Moore, George Fletcher, 'Letters Illustrative of the Early History of the Colony', *The Western Australian*, 3 June 1881, p. 3, prints extracts for Moore's diary of the events leading to the massacre. See also, 'Encounter with the Natives in the Pinjarra District', *Perth Gazette and Western Australian Journal*, 1 November 1834, pp. 382, 383, and 'Editorial', *Hobart Town Courier*, 28 November 1834, p. 2.

[129] 'Quarter Sessions', *The Inquirer*, 12 October 1853, p. 2.

[130] 'Quarter Sessions', *Supplement to The Inquirer*, 12 October 1853, p. 1.

[131] Nettelbeck, Amanda, ''Equals of the White Man': Prosecution of Settlers for Violence against Aboriginal Subjects of the Crown, Colonial Western Australia', *Law and History Review*, Vol. 31, (2), (2013), pp. 355-390.

found that at least eleven Indigenous Australians had been killed in the Forrest River massacre by a police expedition in retaliation for the death of a European. The massacre was the culmination of years of violence by police and pastoralists against Indigenous Australian people in WA and was not an aberration, but part of a culture of decades of violence.[132]

Van Diemen's Land 1804-1836

When Trouwunna–the term used for the island by some of its people–was invaded by British settlers, there was a vibrant, sophisticated and long-established indigenous population of between 6,000 and 10,000 with a clearly defined social organisation based around family, clans and nations. Within 30 years, that society was destroyed by colonial settlement and its people almost wiped out. If the mainland Indigenous Australians were viewed by settlers as barely human, one contemporary maintained that 'the Aboriginals of Tasmania have been usually regarded as exhibiting the human character in its lowest form.'[133] The Reverend Joseph Orton, a Methodist missionary in Australia in the 1830s, summed up the prevailing view:

> It is the universal opinion of all who have seen them that it is impossible to find men and women sunk lower in the scale of human society. With regard to their manners and customs, they are little better than the beasts.[134]

Hostilities between settlers and Indigenous Australians in VDL began within a year of the official settlement of the colony in 1803. On 3 May 1804, a large group of Indigenous Australian, possibly numbering 300 or more attacked the British settlement at Risdon Cove.[135] The conflict apparently arose when Indigenous Australians discovered that some of the settlers had been hunting kangaroos. The official report by Lieutenant William Moore, the commanding officer, referred to an 'attack' by Indigenous Australians armed with spears and indicated that two were killed and an unknown number wounded.[136] Moore reported having fired a shot from a carronade to 'intimidate' and disperse the Indigenous Australians but he reported no deaths from the cannon shot. A second account, also recorded shortly after the events, was contained in a letter written by Jacob Mountgarrett the surgeon, referring to a 'premeditated' attack on

---

[132] On this event see Report of Commissioner G. T. Wood, 'Inquiry into alleged killing and burning of bodies of Aboriginals in East Kimberley and into police methods when effecting arrests', *Western Australia, Votes and Proceedings*, Paper No. 3, 1927, and Green, Neville, *The Forest River massacres*, (Freemantle Art Centre Press), 1995. Moran, Rod, *Massacre myth: an investigation into allegations concerning the mass murder of Aboriginals at Forrest River*, (Access Press), 1999, controversially argued that there had been no massacre.

[133] Dove, T., 'Moral and Social Characteristics of the Aboriginals of Tasmania', *Tasmanian Journal of Natural Science*, Vol. 1, (1842), p. 249. See also Ryan, L., *Tasmanian Aboriginals: A New History*, (Allen & Unwin), 2012.

[134] Orton, Joseph, *Aboriginals of Australia*, (Thoms), 1836, p. 3.

[135] Ryan, L., 'Risdon Cove and the Massacre of 3 May 1804: Their Place in Tasmanian History', *Tasmanian Historical Studies*, Vol. 9, (2004), pp. 107-123.

[136] *HRA*, Series III, Vol. 1, pp. 242-244.

the settlers in which three Indigenous Australians were killed. In addition to the cannon shot, two soldiers fired muskets in protection of a Risdon Cove settler being beaten on his farm by Indigenous Australians carrying clubs. These soldiers killed one Indigenous Australian outright and mortally wounded another who was later found dead in a valley. The last of the three accounts claimed that, 'There were a great many of the Natives slaughtered and wounded.' This was according to Edward White, an Irish convict present on the scene of the events, speaking before a committee of inquiry in 1830, nearly 30 years later, but just how many he did not know. White, apparently the first to see the approaching Indigenous Australians, also testified that, 'the natives did not threaten me; I was not afraid of them; (they) did not attack the soldiers; they would not have molested them; they had no spears with them; only waddies' [clubs].[137] The perpetrators were able to act with impunity because of a court judgement in Sydney which had overturned the legal status of Indigenous Australians from British subjects with legal rights, to 'savages' with none. Judge Advocate Richard Atkins had ruled that 'it was impossible to bring an Indigenous Australian to trial for a crime committed against either a colonist or another Aborigine' justifying sanctions without trial and violent reprisals. Determined to settle the island to ward off any potential French claims, Lieutenant-Governor David Collins implemented a policy of *'distance and fear'* to clear Aboriginals out of the new settlement and adjacent hunting grounds. Whether this was a massacre or a minor skirmish–I have no doubt it was the former--both scenarios put forward in recent years by historians, reflect the contradictory nature of the available evidence and are illustrative of the current controversy over the extent of Indigenous Australian resistance and settler response.[138]

For the next twenty years, there was sporadic hostility between colonists and Indigenous Australians escalating in the 1820s with the spread of pastoralism. The colonial population dramatically increased from 7,185 in 1821 to 24,279 in 1830 exacerbating tensions between the two communities. At least 362 Indigenous Australians were killed by settlers between 1800 and 1835 compared to 183 colonists.[139] In 1826, the *Colonial Times* recognised that relations between Indigenous Australians and settlers had almost reached the stage of open hostility, a result partly of the usurpation of the natives' kangaroo hunting grounds, partly of the cruel treatment and killing of natives by shepherds, stockmen, bushrangers and sealers and partly of the kidnapping of native children.[140] Settlers wanted

---

[137] Testimony of Edward White, in 'Minutes of Evidence Taken Before the Committee for the Affairs of the Aboriginals', *Commons Papers*, Vol. 19, 1831, p. 53.

[138] See for instance, the tendentious interpretation of Windschuttle, Keith, *The Fabrication of Aboriginal History: Volume 1, Van Diemen's Land 1803-1847*, (Macleay Press), 2002, pp. 11-28, and the response by Phillip Tardif in Manne, Robert, (ed.), *Whitewash: On Keith Windschuttle's Fabrication of Aboriginal History*, (Black Inc. Agenda), 2003, pp. 218-224.

[139] *HRA*, Series III: Vol. 8, p. xxxix.

[140] For instance, see 'Government Notice', *Colonial Times and Tasmanian Advertiser*, 22 September 1826, p. 1, 'Government Notice', *Colonial Times and Tasmanian Advertiser*, 8 December 1826, p. 1. Ryan, Lyndall, ''No Right to the Land' The Role of the Wool Industry in the Destruction of Aboriginal Societies in Tasmania (1817-1832) and Victoria

either the extermination of the Indigenous Australians or their removal from lands that the settlers wanted to possess. Attempts by Lieutenant-Governor Arthur to contain the Indigenous Australians in the 'unsettled' Districts and prevent their incursions into the 'settled' Districts after introducing martial law in 1828 had largely failed by early 1829. During 1829, there were over 40 clashes during which 22 settlers were killed and a further 28 deaths the following years. These episodes were counterbalanced by similar atrocities committed by colonists against Indigenous Australians.[141] As in NSW and WA, the Colonial Office in London, while sympathetic to the problems of colonial Governors, sought a humane solution that would prevent the extinction of the native race since, as Sir George Murray, briefly Colonial Secretary, warned Arthur in 1830, this 'could not fail to leave an indelible stain upon the character of the British Government.'

Arthur, who had experience of dealing with natives during his administration in Honduras, was under direct pressure to reduce or, for some settlers eradicate, the Indigenous Australian threat while developing a policy that sought to establish a controlled Christian civilisation and acculturation of the surviving Indigenous Australian community while making efforts to separate the two peoples.[142] In fact, Arthur concluded in 1832 that had there been a treaty with the Indigenous Australian peoples much of the subsequent conflict with settlers could have been avoided. In February 1830, the government offered a bounty of £5.00 per adult and £2.00 per child, for Indigenous Australians captured alive.[143] This was clarified on 20 August 1830, by Governor Arthur's office and it was made clear that the bounty was only for Indigenous Australians caught whilst engaged in aggression in the settled districts and that settlers or convicts who went out and captured 'inoffensive Natives in the remote of the remote and unsettled parts of the territory' would not receive a reward. Instead it was decreed:

> If, after the promulgation of this Notice, any wanton attack or aggression against the Natives becomes known to the Government, the offenders will be immediately brought to justice and punished.[144]

By the time Arthur declared martial law it had dwindled to between 1,000 and 2,000 people. In October 1830, Arthur assembled the Black Line, a human chain of 1,000 armed convicts and 500 British troops reinforced by police and settlers that stretched across the island and was intended to drive the native population southwards towards the Tasman Peninsula. Arthur intended to have the Indigenous Australians live together on the peninsula where they could maintain their culture and language. The government and historians consider the

---

(1835-1851) Compared', in Adhikari, Mohamed, (ed.), *Genocide on Settler Frontiers*, (Berghahn), 2015, pp. 185-209.

[141] *HRA*, Series III: Vol. 8, pp. xxxix-xl.

[142] Forsyth, W. D., *Governor Arthur's Convict System: Van Diemen's Land, 1824-36*, (Sydney University Press), 1970. Shaw, A. G. L., *Sir George Arthur, Bart, 1784-1854*, (Melbourne University Press), 1980, and Shaw, A. G. L., 'Sir George Arthur, (1784-1854)', *ADB*, Vol. 1, pp. 32-38.

[143] *HRA*, Series III: Vol. 9, pp. 200-201.

[144] Ibid, *HRA*, Series III: Vol. 9, pp. 587-595.

Black Line to have been a costly and unsuccessful action largely because it only caught two Indigenous Australians. It may have been a futile but the tribes that managed to avoid capture were shaken by the size of the campaigns against them.[145]

The war on the pastoral frontier in VDL had terrifying consequences for its Indigenous Australians. At the outset, in 1823, an estimated 2,000 Indigenous Australians were in the war zone. By 1831, over a fifth of this population had been killed by the colonists. In VDL, more Indigenous Australians were killed in a shorter period than perhaps in any other part of Australia. Arthur lifted martial law in 1832 and the following year, about 220 Tasmanian Indigenous Australians were persuaded to surrender with assurances that they would be protected and provided for by the government. By August 1834, the Indigenous Australian problem, as the colonists saw it, had been settled since all but about a dozen natives had been removed from the mainland to the Wybalenna Aboriginal Establishment on Flinders Island. Nonetheless, contact with introduced settler diseases continued to reduce their numbers. By 1835, the Indigenous Australian population had shrunk to fewer than 150 natives, of whom about half were the survivors of those sent to Flinders Island. In 1847, the surviving 47 inhabitants of Wybalenna were transferred to Oyster Cove, south of Hobart, on the main island of Tasmania. When the number of detained Indigenous Australians fell below 20 in 1854, there was growing appreciation that they were a unique human group, distinctly different from mainland Australian Aboriginals.

The last full-blooded tribal-born Palawa from the Oyster Cove community was a woman named Truganina, who died in 1876 in Hobart. Born in 1812, she was one of the few Indigenous Australian Tasmanians rooted in pre-contact language and culture, who survived beyond the mid-nineteenth century.[146] When Truganina died, the Tasmanian Government declared the island's indigenous population to be extinct. Its intention was to make everyone understand that the native problem was over, but the government was wrong on both counts. Other Indigenous Australian women born from full-blooded tribal parents outlived her and the mixed-blood Indigenous Australian community on the Furneaux group of islands still constitutes a native community. Albeit Truganini's passing was used to suggest the extinction of Tasmanian Indigenous Australians and it was taught as fact in schools around the world and was accepted for a long time, even in

[145] Lester, Alan, and Dussart, Fae, *Colonization and the Origins of Humanitarian Governance: Protecting Aborigines across the Nineteenth-Century British Empire*, (Cambridge University Press), 2014, pp. 37-76, considers the role of Sir George Arthur.

[146] Truganini is often considered to be the last full-blood speaker of a Tasmanian language but she was not the last surviving Palawa. *The Companion to Tasmanian History* details three full-blood Tasmanian Aboriginal women, Sal, Suke and Betty, who lived on Kangaroo Island in South Australia in the late 1870s and 'all three outlived Truganini'. There were also Tasmanian Aboriginals living on Flinders and Lady Barron Islands. Fanny Cochrane Smith (1834-1905) outlived Truganini by 30 years. In 1854, in recognition of her claim as a Tasmanian Aborigine, the colonial government paid her an annuity of £48, increasing it to £100 in 1876 after the death of Truganini, and granting her 300 acres of land. In 1889 was officially recognised as the last full-blood Tasmanian Aboriginal. She recorded songs in her native language, the only audio recordings that exist of an indigenous Tasmanian language.

Tasmania. The reason that the myth that Truganini was the 'last' Tasmanian Aborigine had any credence was that her remains were desecrated and displayed in the Hobart Museum: it was populist myth-making backed up by 'science'. It was also because Tasmanians wanted to believe that their island's indigenous people were extinct. It has taken a long time for this distortion to be overturned.[147]

The nature of conflict in VDL is controversial. The government inquiry in 1830 suggested that Indigenous Australian violence was not warfare but largely the plundering of settlers' property for sugar, flour, tea and bedding, and 120 Indigenous Australians died violently while 187 colonists were killed.[148] James Calder, writing in the 1870s, argued that, 'the warfare, though pretty continuous, was rather a petty affair with grossly exaggerated details - something like the story of the hundred dead men, reduced, on inquiry, to three dead dogs.'[149] Keith Windschuttle's *The Fabrication of Aboriginal History*, restated the view that there was no genocide in Tasmania and that most natives succumbed to European diseases especially pneumonia and influenza.[150] He also rejected the idea that there was 'frontier warfare' and that recent historians had inflated the level of conflict between Indigenous Australians and settlers. He claimed to have exposed a deliberate fabrication of evidence regarding the extent of violence against Indigenous Australians by left-wing historians seeking to promote Indigenous Australian claims to compensation or redress based on past wrongs.[151] Although *Fabrication* proved popular, especially among the ruling Conservative Party led by John Howard who had said in 1996 that he hoped to make Australians feel

---

[147] Brantlinger, Patrick, *Discourse on the Extinction of Primitive Races, 1800-1930*, (Cornell University Press), 2003, examines the commonly held nineteenth-century view that all 'primitive' or 'savage' races around the world were doomed sooner or later to extinction after contact with white civilization. For Australia see, pp. 117-140

[148] Ibid, *HRA*, Series III: Vol. 9, pp. 202-236, contains the report and the evidence collected.

[149] Calder, James Erskine, *Some account of the wars, extirpation, habits, &c., of the native tribes of Tasmania*, (Henn and Co.), 1875, p. 8.

[150] The Tasmanian Aboriginals' long isolation from mainland Australia made them especially vulnerable to introduced disease. James Bonwick and Henry Roth, both writing in the nineteenth century, also pointed to the significant role of epidemics and infertility without clear attribution of the sources of the diseases as having been introduced through contact with Europeans. Bonwick recorded an Indigenous Australian oral tradition of a devastating epidemic that may be linked to contact with sealers or whalers before formal colonisation in 1803. See Bonwick, James, *Last of the Tasmanians*, (Sampson Low, Son & Marston), 1870, and Roth, Henry Ling, *The Aboriginals of Tasmania*, 2nd ed., (F. King & Sons, Printers and Publishers), 1899.

[151] Even if his conclusions are fundamentally flawed, Windschuttle exposed the somewhat cavalier ways in which some evidence had been used to sustain the case for frontier violence. For instance, he cites a reference in Robson, Lloyd, *A History of Tasmania*, Vol. 1, (Oxford University Press), 1983, p. 50. Robson, he argues, claims the settler James Hobbs in 1815 witnessed Aboriginals killing 300 sheep at Oyster Bay and the following day the 48th Regiment killed 22 Aboriginals in retaliation. Windschuttle then points out that Hobbs was in India in 1815, the first sheep did not arrive at Oyster Bay until 1821 and the 48th Regiment was on garrison duty in Ireland. Perhaps the only beneficial effect of *Fabrication* has been a more critical assessment of evidence by subsequent historians.

'relaxed and comfortable' about their past, numerous errors in the book led to a robust rebuttal of Windschuttle's counter-history of race relations in Australia.[152]

How many?

Many Australians and Indigenous Australians remain far from 'relaxed and comfortable' about their past. The well-regarded *End of Certainty: the Story of the 1980s* maintained that 'the Australian Settlement' endured for eight decades after Federation.[153] Its five principles: White Australia; arbitration; protection; 'state paternalism'; and, 'imperial benevolence' are represented as unique and distinctively Australian. These centred on the ethnic solidarity of the 'white races', oriented against aliens (especially blacks and Asians) and assumed that native peoples would either die out or amalgamate with settler society. The changing character of the global economy and the international community contributed to a critical and incomplete rethinking of Australian national identity that opened up the interconnections between class, race and gender, addressed what was still regarded as the taint of convictism and sought a new, inclusive historiography. The debate over the Indigenous Australian and settler responses to colonial expansion was part of that process but it remains intensely contested and politicised.[154]

Violence was endemic on the Australian frontier, as settlers killed Indigenous Australians, Indigenous Australians killed settlers and Indigenous Australians killed each other in the disruptions of invasion. In Britain, Sir William Molesworth, chairman of the Select Committee on Transportation (1837-1838) fostered the view that settler violence was a pervasive feature of colonial life, a claim he borrowed from the anti-slavery movement and it was a view that remained for much of the remaining century.[155] Although genocide was never the policy of the authorities, Barta argues that it was the *effectual* policy of the state since little was done to restrain the settlers.[156] Exactly how many Indigenous Australians were killed on the frontier will never be known. Statistics

---

152 Ibid, Manne, Robert, (ed.), *Whitewash: On Keith Windschuttle's Fabrication of Aboriginal History*, provides the most comprehensive critique of Windschuttle's work. Reynolds, Henry, *A History of Tasmania*, (Cambridge University Press), 2012, pp. 47-87, discusses colonial policy towards the Tasmanian Aboriginals and makes no reference to Windschuttle at all.

153 Kelly, Paul, *The End of Certainty: The Story of the 1980s,* (Allen & Unwin), 1994, p. 1.

154 Haebich, Anna, 'The battlefields of Aboriginal history', in Lyons, Martyn, and Russell, Penny, (eds.), *Australia's History: themes & debates*, (University of New South Wales Press), 2005, pp. 1-21, is a useful summary of the debates. See also, Evans, Julie, Grimshaw, Patricia, Philips, David and Swain, Shurlee, *Equal Subjects, Unequal Rights: Indigenous People in British settler colonies, 1830s-1910*, (Manchester University Press), 2003, pp. 63-87, 134-156.

155 Meyering, Isobelle Barrett, 'Abolition, settler violence and the case against flogging: A reassessment of Sir William Molesworth's contribution to the transportation debate', *History Australia*, Vol. 7, (1), (2010), pp. 1-18, seeks to reconcile Molesworth as an agent of metropolitan prejudice and as a champion of colonial interests.

156 Barta, T., 'Discourses of genocide in Germany and Australia', *Aboriginal History*, Vol. 25, (2001), p. 42, Dwyer, Philip and Ryan, Lyndall, 'Reflections on genocide and settler-colonial violence', *History Australia*, Vol. 13, (3), (2016), pp. 335-350.

of frontier violence are inaccurate as the historical record is by its nature fragmentary and the records of the frontier and of violence markedly so.[157] The issue of violence led people to be secretive and wary of what they said or recorded. The frontier was beyond rigorous administrative, policing and judicial systems, where many settlers struggled to survive and prosper in psychologically and physically threatening surroundings. Estimates of frontier deaths began on the Hawkesbury where early settlers began to count the cost and send tallies to Governors calling for action against Indigenous Australian attackers. Indigenous Australians soon protested to officials and protectors about the violence practised against them by settlers. However, in the late-nineteenth century, as histories began to be written and the dispossession was rationalised, estimates of frontier deaths became vague or non-existent; the 'Great Australian Silence' ensured that little was said.

From the 1970s, estimates of Indigenous Australian deaths proliferated, some plausible, others less so. The figure of at least 20,000 Indigenous Australian deaths and about 2,000 colonial police, soldiers and settlers as a direct result of frontier violence across Australia provides a credible estimate of the enormity of colonial action.[158] That figure--translating to about 10 Indigenous Australian deaths for each European killed--has been hotly contested by conservative historians who insist that the figure was far lower, but new collaborative research now suggests that the real figure could be at least three times greater and that the ratio of black to white deaths could be 44 to one. Raymond Evans and Robert Ørsted-Jensen, have concluded that in Queensland alone--the epicentre of frontier war in mid-nineteenth century Australia--at least 65,180 Indigenous Australians were killed from the 1820s until the early 1900s.[159] They have scoured the remaining records of the Queensland Native Police Force and studied the prevalence of 'black police' barracks across the colony's frontier from 1859 to 1898 to determine the approximate number of patrols, contacts and killings. Based on a sample of 644 frontier clashes, Ørsted-Jensen found 57 per cent involved Native Police and the remaining 43 per cent settlers. Given there were 3,420 official dispersals across 40 years, the historians argue 'the settlers' 43% must approximate to another 2,580 attacks'. 'Together, our totals for settlers and Native Police amount to no less than 61,680 in 6,000 attacks,' they conclude. Evans and Ørsted-Jensen add an estimated minimum of 3,500 kills associated with Native Police activity and 1,500 European deaths to 'arrive at an aggregate 66,800 killed' between the 1820s and early 1900s.

---

[157] Broome, Richard, 'The Statistics of Frontier Conflict', examines the nature of the statistics at http://www.kooriweb.org/foley/news/story28.html.

[158] The figure of 20,000 derives from Reynolds, Henry, *Frontier*, (Allen and Unwin), 1996, pp. 29-30, 53. For a counter-argument see Windshuttle, Keith, 'The Myths of Frontier Massacres in Australian History. Part II: The Fabrication of the Aboriginal Death Toll', *Quadrant*, Vol. 44, (November 2000), pp. 17-24.

[159] Evans, Raymond, and Ørsted-Jensen, Robert, ''I Cannot Say the Numbers that Were Killed': Assessing Violent Mortality on the Queensland Frontier', 2014. Available at SSRN: http://ssrn.com/abstract=2467836 or http://dx.doi.org/10.2139/ssrn.2467836 Ørsted-Jensen, Robert, *Frontier History Revisited—Colonial Queensland and the 'History War'*, (Lex Mundi Publishing), 2011. See also, Bottoms, Timothy, *Conspiracy of Silence: Queensland's frontier killing times*, (Allen & Unwin), 2013.

A new narrative?

History could also be summoned to destroy what Clark might have described as the 'comforting' myths with which white Europeans had obscured their treatment of the native peoples. Obsolete assumptions about a largely benign colonisation process have now been jettisoned; Indigenous Australians and the frequently violent history of their dispossession is now visible again. 'We committed the murders', Keating bluntly reminded white Australians in his Redfern Park speech, as he stood before a stunned and largely native audience.[160] 'We practiced discrimination and exclusion.' The High Court of Australia's *Mabo* judgement in 1992[161] that recognised native title and the historic connection of Australia's native people to the land would form the basis of 'righting an historic wrong.'[162] Historians had also played a vital role in rethinking the nation's relationship with its native peoples and laying the intellectual framework for the *Mabo* Judgement and the Keating Government's response. Rowley and Stanner's work began the task of revision in both historiography and in wider public discourse.[163] Attwood expressed concern about the role historians should play in redefining national identity in the wake of Mabo; historians had to retain a critical distance from a tendency to 'essentialise' claims about the past, propagating a 'delusion' that the past can be repossessed as 'it really was'. A 'new history' could:

[160] On 10 December 1992, Keating gave a speech, written by Don Watson, on Aboriginal reconciliation addressing issues faced by Indigenous Australians such as their land and children being taken away. This speech became known as 'The Redfern Address' and was given in Redfern Park to a crowd of predominantly native people, and although it was not given a lot of media attention at the time it is now regarded by many to be one the greatest Australian speeches. Keating was the first Australian Prime Minister publicly to acknowledge to Indigenous Australians that European settlers were responsible for the difficulties their communities continued to face: 'We committed the murders. We took the children from their mothers. We practiced discrimination and exclusion. It was our ignorance and our prejudice'. 'Keating's apology wins black praise', *The Canberra Times*, 11 December 1992, pp. 1, 2.

[161] The judgments of the High Court in the *Mabo* case inserted the legal doctrine of native title into Australian law. In recognising the traditional rights of the Meriam people to their islands in the eastern Torres Strait, the Court also held that native title existed for all Native people in Australia prior to Cook's Instructions and the establishment of the British Colony of New South Wales in 1788. The *Mabo* decision thus resolved the problem posed by the Gove Land Rights Case in 1971, which followed the 'legal fiction' of *terra nullius*. In recognising that native people in Australia had a prior title to land taken by the Crown since Cook's declaration of possession in 1770, the Court held that this title exists today in any portion of land where it has not legally been extinguished.

[162] Ryan, Mark, (ed.), *Advancing Australia, The Speeches of Paul Keating, Prime Minister*, (Big Picture Publications), 1995, pp. 227, 232; Watson, Don, *Recollections of a Bleeding Heart, A Portrait of Paul Keating PM,* (Random House Australia), 2002, pp. 288-291.

[163] Rowley, C. D., *The Destruction of Aboriginal Society*, (Australian National University Press), 1970; Stanner, W. E. H., *After the Dreaming: black and white Australians – an anthropologist's view*, (Australian Broadcasting Corporation), 1969.

> ...examine the moments when the ideals and values of both settler Australians and Aboriginals have been upheld such that all peoples have benefited, and so genuine human progress can be said to be achieved.[164]

The moment of optimism about reconciliation between white and black Australia that might be drawn from shaping a new history after Mabo was soon subdued by a revival of conflict and division, a situation exacerbated by the election of John Howard's Conservative government in 1996. The growing importance of revisionism led Howard to say in 1996 that Australian history was being 'rewritten' and taught 'as a basis for obsessive and consuming national guilt and shame'. His government insisted on a celebratory historical perspective that told:

> ...the story of [all] our people ... broadly constituting a scale of heroic and unique achievement against the odds ... The 'black armband' view of our history reflects a belief that most Australian history since 1788 has been little more than a disgraceful story of imperialism, exploitation, racism, sexism and other forms of discrimination.[165]

Not all Australians accepted that the nation owed a debt of land or even an apology to the nation's native peoples and historians played a crucial role in defining a symbolic language of resistance to Labor's proposals and Keating's reshaping of the national story. In 1993, Geoffrey Blainey lamented the predominating influence of a 'black armband' interpretation of Australian historiography that had 'assailed' its previously optimistic tone. Australian historians had once patriotically given 'three cheers' to a story of progress but Manning Clark 'had done much to spread the gloomy view' and the multiculturalism, embraced by the Labor Party, preached that, '... much of Australian history was a disgrace', because of the mistreatment and racialisation of the variety of labour forms used across the colonies: Indigenous Australians, Indian servants, Chinese indentured workers and Pacific Islanders. Blainey revealed himself as a pessimistic conservative, observing Australia's once impressive economic achievements and vibrant democracy threatened by a poor work ethic and a low sense of 'individual responsibility' in a 'rights-mad' society.[166] Blainey's black armband is a phrase that has produced its own literature and entered national political discourse, embraced by Prime Minister John Howard in his conservative reading of Australia's history and his resistance to offering Indigenous Australians a formal apology.[167]

---

[164] Attwood, Bain, 'The past as future: Aboriginals, Australia and the (dis)course of History', in Attwood, Bain, (ed.), *In the Age of Mabo*, (Allen and Unwin), 1996, pp. xxxvii-xxxviii.

[165] His position can be found in Howard, John, 'The Liberal Tradition: The Beliefs and Values which Guide the Federal Government', *Sir Robert Menzies Lecture*, 18 November 1996.

[166] Blainey, Geoffrey, 'Drawing up a Balance Sheet of Our History', *Quadrant*, July-August 1993, p. 10.

[167] Davison, Graeme, *The Use and Abuse of Australian History*, (Allen and Unwin), 2000, pp. 16-17, and Macintyre, Stuart, and Clark, Anna, *The History Wars*, (Melbourne University Press), 2004, pp. 128-132.

Howard's defeat in the 2007 General Election and his replacement by the government of Kevin Rudd and his apology in early 2008 may have marked the end of the dominance of conservative revisionism. However, the decision by Sydney City Council's council to ban the use of 'European arrival' in official documents in favour of 'invasion or illegal colonisation'[168] and calls by some that the celebrations on Australia Day on 26 January should be renamed Invasion Day illustrate that the Australian national narrative remains intensely contested. As Anne Curthoys observed:

> ...in their increased attention to Aboriginal history, however, it seemed that historians paid a high price, losing their earlier ability to provide apparently unifying national narratives. Popular understandings of the place of Aboriginal history in Australian history remain unsettled and deeply divided.[169]

This issue erupted again in March 2016 when the University of New South Wales urged students in its *Indigenous Terminology Guide* to use the term 'invaded' rather than 'settled' or 'discovered' and to avoid the word 'Aboriginals' and use 'indigenous Australian people or 'Aboriginal peoples'. Use of a term such as 'nomadic' was discouraged on the grounds that it implies Indigenous Australians were not permanently settled, supporting the doctrine of *terra nullius* that British settlers used to justify occupying their land.[170] It is time that it is accepted that Australia was not settled peacefully—it was invaded, occupied and then colonised and one consequence of the creation of that settler society was that many Indigenous Australians lost their lives in frontier wars and massacres and from introduced diseases and that their lands were appropriated or stolen without their consent.[171]

Treaty and war in New Zealand 1832-1846

Terra nullius is such a contested feature of Australian history that it is easy to lose sight of how unusual it was in the broader context of British colonisation. The British had been colonising North America for two centuries before they reached Australia, but by the mid-eighteenth century, imperial policy in North America had already turned away from *terra nullius.* There remained advocates of *terra nullius* in Britain and North America and settlers trespassed in large numbers on Indian land.[172] Nevertheless, in the eighteenth century, as a matter of official

---

[168] Barrowclough, Anne, 'Botany Bay convicts were invaders, Sydney admits', *The Times*, 29 June 2011.

[169] Curthoys, Anne, 'Aboriginal History', in Davison, Graeme, (ed.), *The Oxford Companion to Australian History*, 2nd ed., (Oxford University Press), 2001, p. 5.

[170] Daley, Paul, 'It's not 'politically correct' to say Australia was invaded, it's history', *The Guardian,* 20 March 2016, 'Australian university accused of 'rewriting history' over British invasion language', *The Telegraph*, 30 March 2016.

[171] Naimark, Norman M., *Genocide: A World History*, (Oxford University Press), 2015, pp. 48-55, considers settler genocide in Australia. See also, Clendinnen, Inga, *Dancing with Strangers: Europeans and Australians at First Contact*, (Cambridge University Press), 2005.

[172] For a different slant on British land policy in North America, see Seed, Patricia, *American Pentimento: The Invention of Indians and the Pursuit of Riches*, (University of

policy, Native Americans were recognised as possessors of property rights in their land and in practice, settlers and colonial governments often acquired their lands in transactions structured as purchases. The British began colonising NZ a few decades after Australia, but did not treat NZ as *terra nullius* either. Instead, they signed a treaty explicitly though ambiguously recognising as owners of the land.[173] As in North America, the practice of land acquisition in NZ at times looked rather different from the way it was envisioned in London, but there was no formal policy of ignoring Māori property rights.[174]

Until relatively recently NZ was thought to have been settled by Polynesians between 950 and 1130 A.D., arriving in several twin-hulled or outrigger canoes. Most researchers now agree that human arrival and permanent Polynesian settlement occurred between 1250 and 1300.[175] The first Polynesians settled mainly around the coast of NZ, and especially the east coast with its more hospitable and temperate climate. Māori culture was highly evolved but had no metals and no written language. Stone was used for many tools and weapons until the arrival of Europeans. The Polynesians introduced the *kumara* or sweet potato, a quick maturing crop that grew particularly well in the warmer northern region of NZ. The kumara was the staple diet of the Māori and was stored in deep cool pits on sloping hillsides. The Polynesians also introduced the taro, yam and the paper mulberry that was used to make bark cloth. Further south where the climate was cooler and crops less easily cultivated, hunting the moa and the seal provided the main diet. When the moa and other species of flightless birds were eventually hunted to extinction a few centuries later, fish and shellfish become the staple diet of the Māori, supplementing the kumara.

The early settlers lived in small, initially undefended settlements known as *kainga*. These were largely established in sheltered coastal locations, often near to harbours or estuaries. The most famous of these sites is situated at Wairau Bar, in the northern area of the South Island, and appears to have been a centre of stone adze production. Tensions between different tribal groups over rights to areas rich in resources saw the *kainga* increase in size and include some defences. Construction of the larger *pa* began in the sixteenth century. A *pa* is a fortified

---

Minnesota Press), 2001, pp. 12-44, and Armitage, David, *The Ideological Origins of the British Empire*, (Cambridge University Press), 2000, p. 97.

[173] Banner, Stuart, 'Conquest by Contract: Wealth Transfer and Land Market Structure in Colonial New Zealand', *Law and Society Review*, Vol. 34 (2000), pp. 47-96, and 'Two Properties, One Land: Law and Space in Nineteenth-Century New Zealand', *Law and Social Inquiry*, Vol. 24 (1999), pp. 807-852.

[174] The most recent general studies of NZ include, King, M., *The Penguin History of New Zealand*, (Penguin), 2003, Smith, P. Mein, *A Concise History of New Zealand*, (Cambridge University Press), 2005, 2nd ed., 2012, and Byrnes, Giselle, (ed.), *The New Oxford History of New Zealand*, (Oxford University Press), 2009. Belich, James, *Making Peoples: A History of the New Zealanders, from Polynesian Settlement to the End of the Nineteenth Century*, (Allen Lane), 1996, and *Paradise Reforged: A History of New Zealanders from the 1880s to the year 2000*, (Allen Lane), 2001, is a major revisionist study.

[175] Anderson, Atholl, 'Origins, Settlement and Society of Pre-European South Polynesia', in ibid, Byrnes, Giselle, (ed.), *The New Oxford History of New Zealand*, pp. 21-46, is a convenient summary of current thinking.

settlement, including ditches, banks and palisades as protection. The fortified *pa* included a much more complex internal organisation than that of the smaller *kainga* dwelling. While the *kainga* had only one cooking area, the *pa* had several. Pits for storing food were established outside of the perimeter palisades.

Early contacts

New Zealand was discovered by Abel Tasman, the Dutch navigator, in December 1642 but conflict with local Māori left four of his crew dead. Contact between Māori and Europeans was not renewed until 1769, when English and French explorers arrived under James Cook and Jean de Surville. In late 1769 and early 1770, James Cook first mapped 2,400 miles of its coastline.[176] Relations with Māori were more sympathetic and exploration continued, motivated by science, profit and great power rivalry. Cook made two more visits between 1773 and 1777 and there were further French expeditions.

Many Māori welcomed the new experiences that contact with Europeans brought. For instance, in the early 1830s, when Taranaki Māori migrated south to lands they had recently conquered, they were accompanied by about a dozen European men, who had formed partnerships with high-ranked Te Atiawa women. Most were involved with whaling stations in Tory Channel. Māori played a variety of roles. Local chiefs negotiated payment to allow a ship to establish a shore base, and to obtain wood and water; their people were often contracted to build shore bases. Sometimes chiefs provided women (probably slaves), again for a price. Communities across Te Tau Ihu expanded cultivations and supplied fish and pork in return for European food, clothing, cloth and blankets, guns and ammunition, metal tools and equipment, tobacco, and beads. Although most whalers used alcohol regularly, Māori usually rejected it.

Unofficial visits by whaling ships in the north and sealing gangs in the south began in the early 1790s. Deep-sea whaling started during 1791 and 1792, with the arrival of the whaler, *William and Ann* and shortly later, *Britannia* began operating in Dusky Sound (South Island).[177] The success of whaling and sealing owed much to the later encouragement of Philip Gidley King, Governor of NSW between 1800 and 1806.[178] He was a friend of whale fleet owner Samuel Enderby and advised the British government to allow the whalers to carry merchandise to NSW.[179] He encouraged sealers to go to Bass Strait and whaling ships to visit NZ and the Pacific.[180] From 1797, American whalers arrived, and during the 1830s,

---

176 Ibid, Edwards, Philip, (ed.), *James Cook: The Journals*, pp. 68-119.

177 *HRNZ*, Vol. 2, pp. 509-517, 536,

178 On the development of the South Sea whale-fishery, see, minutes of the Board of Trade, 4 December 1801, *HRNSW*, Vol. 4, p. 630. See also, Little, B., 'Sealing and Whaling in Australia Before 1850', *Australian Economic History Review*, Vol. 9, (1969), pp. 109-127. McNab, Robert, *The Old Whaling Days: A History of Southern New Zealand from 1830 to 1840*, (Kiwi Publisher), 1913, and Rickard, L. S., *The Whaling Trade in Old New Zealand*, (Minerva), 1965.

179 Dallas, K. M., 'Enderby, Samuel (1756-1829)', *ADB*, Vol. 1, p. 357.

180 As early as 1792, Sydney Cove was the centre for the profitable whale and seal trade around the southern coasts. Whaling brought profit to NSW since ships came into Sydney to refit. King referred to whaling as the only 'staple' and saw visions of secondary profits.

the French whaling ships turned up in significant numbers. Seals were hunted and their skins taken for the Chinese market. Spars were also cut for the Chinese market and the Royal Navy in India and the flax trade grew. The most numerous visitors were probably American and New England whaling ships favoured the Bay of Islands for rest and recreation; 271 called there between 1833 and 1839.[181] To whalers, 'rest and recreation' meant sex and drink. Their favourite haunt, the little town of Kororareka (now Russell) was known to missionaries as 'the hellhole of the Pacific'. Tensions arose sometimes between ships' crews and local Māoris. The Ngati Tama and Ngati Mutunga tribes allegedly killed the crew of the French whaling ship *Jean Bart* and in retaliation, the French corvette *L'Heroine* burnt a village and reportedly took a captive back to France. Given the number of visits, inter-racial conflict was modest. Europeans needed Māori protection, food and labour and Māori came to need European wares, especially muskets. Whaling stations and mission stations were linked to local Māori groups by intermarriage that helped maintain the peace. Until the late 1830s, Europeans came mainly to exploit the country's natural resources but around the early 1820s, British and American sperm whalers used northern harbours to refit and refresh. By 1830, NZ trade, in terms of both exports and imports, grew rapidly and became increasingly important to the merchants and capitalists of NSW.[182]

Missionaries had arrived in the 1810s, bringing new ideas and concepts drawn from both the Bible and the wider world.[183] They introduced Māori to literacy in the Māori language with the translation of parts of the Bible. Māori visited NSW and England, enlarging their experience of commerce, the role of monarchy, alternative systems of law and government and the treatment of native peoples.[184] By 1840, there were three different missionary societies active in NZ. The Anglicans were represented by the Church Missionary Society, the

---

The American whalers provided a market for foodstuffs, water and timber. By 1800, London was unloading 300 tons of sperm oil fished off the coast of NSW. On 9 May 1803, King wrote, *HRA*, Series I: Vol. 4, p. 249, 'Since I took command 16,000 gallons of oil and 27,800 seal skins have been imported from thence by individuals, 1,063 tuns of spermaceti oil have also been procured by the south whalers, all which I need not point out as a rising nursery for Seamen.' See also *HRNZ*, Vol. 1, pp. 234-236.

[181] *HRNZ*, Vol. 2, pp. 606, 612, 615-619, details American ships in 1840 and 1841.

[182] Wilkes, Annette, *Between People and Things. Understanding Violence and Theft in early New Zealand transactions*, Ph.D., Thesis, University of Canterbury, 2013, an important anthropological study.

[183] Newman, Keith, *Bible & Treaty: Missionaries among the Māoris*, (Penguin), 2010, Fitzgerald, Caroline, (ed.), *Letters from the Bay of Islands: The Story of Marianne Williams*, (Sutton), 2004, Strong, Rowan, *Anglicanism and the British Empire, c.1700-1850*, (Oxford University Press), 2007, pp. 222-282, Ballantyne, Tony, *Entanglements of Empire: Missionaries, Māori and the Question of the Body*, (Duke University Press), 2014, Davidson, Allan K., 'Anglicanism in New Zealand and the South Pacific', in Strong, Rowan, (ed.), *The Oxford History of Anglicanism, Volume III: Partisan Anglicanism and its Global Expansion 1829-c.1914*, (Oxford University Press), 2017, pp. 352-365, Larsen, Timothy, and Ledger-Lomas, Michael, (eds.), *The Oxford History of the Protestant Dissenting Traditions, Volume III: The Nineteenth Century*, (Oxford University Press), 2017.

[184] See for instance, the visit of Tip-a-he to Sydney in 1806 and Māori chief to Parramatta in 1815: *HRNZ*, Vol. 1, pp. 263-268, 403-404.

Wesleyans, and the French Bishop Jean Baptiste François Pompallier set up the first Roman Catholic mission in Hokianga in 1838. Māori proved a fertile ground for conversion and by 1841 over a quarter had become Christians.[185]

Whilst Europe exported items such as pigs and potatoes that benefited Māori, muskets and diseases had the opposite effect. Muskets added a new dimension to traditional Māori conflict and for over two decades led to widespread and devastating inter-tribal warfare. The Ngapuhi tribe, from the north Auckland region, traded with Europeans and was the first tribe to obtain the musket. Other northern tribes also obtained the musket from the many traders in the Bay of Islands and this gave them a major military advantage over tribes further south. The result was the inter-tribal wars in the North between 1818 and 1833 that became known as the 'Musket Wars' and accounted for perhaps 20,000 deaths and considerable population movement.[186] They ended in 1835 with the conquest and settlement of the Chatham Islands by Ngati Mutunga and Ngati Tama. Although sporadic warfare continued until the 1840s, the influence of missionaries and the restoration of a balance of terror when all tribes had access to the coveted muskets led to an uneasy peace among Māori. Māori population was also reduced because of the introduction of disease from Europe, and although it did considerable damage NZ had the natural quarantine of distance. Infected Europeans usually recovered or died during the long voyage, and smallpox, which devastated Native Americans, did not have any impact. Nonetheless, Māori population fell from current estimates of between 85,000 and 110,000 in 1769 to about 70,000 by 1840, a decline of at least 20 per cent.[187]

The impact on internal Māori politics aside the Musket Wars and the unease of British authorities regarding trader participation in them contributed to the colonisation of NZ in 1840. Initially, NZ was a relatively minor issue for the Colonial Office in London but in NSW, its Governors, merchants and investors took a keen interest in events across the Tasman Sea, regarding control of NZ as essential for British command of the South Pacific.[188] By 1830, Sydney was a major and extremely active trading port and its mercantile and commercial community had important interests in the Pacific and NZ. The Governors of NSW sometimes saw NZ as part of their unofficial sphere of influence, were

---

[185] Owens, J. M. R., 'Christianity and the Maoris to 1840', *New Zealand Journal of History*, Vol. 2, (1968), pp. 18-40, Binney, Judith, 'Christianity and the Maoris to 1840: A Comment', *New Zealand Journal of History*, Vol. 3, (1969), pp. 143-165, Lange, Stuart. 'Christian Beginnings in New Zealand: Some Historiographical Issues', *Stimulus*, Vol. 21, (2), (2014), pp. 4-13.

[186] On the impact of weapon technology on Māori society see Crosby, R. D., *The Musket Wars: a history of inter-iwi conflict, 1806-45*, (Reed), 1999, and Ballara, Angela, *Taua: 'Musket Wars', 'Land Wars' or tikanga? Warfare in Maori society in the early nineteenth century*, (Penguin), 2003.

[187] Pool, D. Ian, *The Maori Population of New Zealand 1769-1971*, (Auckland University Press), 1977. There is some debate over the exact size of Māori population in 1840 with some putting it as high as 125,000.

[188] By the 1820s, there was growing concern that France planned to establish a colony in NZ and the effects that this would have on the commerce and fisheries of NSW and VDL: 'Colonel's Robert Torren's Proposal', 4 July 1826, *HRNZ*, Vol. 1, pp. 665-666, Anonymous letter, April 1828, *HRNZ*, Vol. 1, pp. 681-683.

concerned about the activities of British subjects there and tried to regulate the inevitable problems between traders and Māori.[189] The NSW government also supported the efforts of British missionary organisations in NZ especially the Anglican Church Missionary Society that established its first mission station at Rangihoua in 1815. There were legal difficulties about extending the NSW courts to NZ and some British subjects who took part in tribal warfare escaped prosecution in Sydney. The most notorious case was in 1830, involving Captain Stewart of the brig *Elizabeth.* He allowed the Ngati Toa chief Te Rauparaha and his allies to use his ship in an attack on Ngai Tahu, leaving about 300 killed and others enslaved.[190]

Establishing authority

This episode convinced the NSW government that it needed a stronger official presence in NZ.[191] With the agreement of the British government, James Busby was appointed as British Resident in 1832 arriving in NZ in May 1833 to watch over British interests.[192] It was an impossible task, with virtually no budget and no real authority.[193] The British government refused to station a warship in NZ and as a civilian, Busby was not entitled to troops.[194] His appointment to an independent territory precluded his holding magisterial office and he had no powers of arrest and was unable to take sworn testimony. He was expected to apprehend criminals and escaped convicts and return them to NSW but had no police or other resources except for periodic visits from a warship from the Sydney Royal Navy squadron. His role was limited to mediating on matters affecting British subjects alone and as a mediator between Māori and Pākehā (non-Māori New Zealanders), and in inter-tribal disputes. In both areas his

[189] This was evident in a letter from Reverend Samuel Marsden to Reverend J. Pratt, 4 June 1824: *HRNZ*, Vol. 1, pp. 627-629. 'They cannot establish a colony there without penal and civil laws. Crimes will be committed, both by Europeans and the natives, and if these crimes cannot be punished the colony would be soon overturned…'
[190] See, *HRNZ*, Vol. 1, pp. 703-708, *HRA*, Series I: Vol. 15, pp. 702-705, and *HRA*, Series I: Vol. 16, pp. 237-240, for intervention by British ships in Māori politics.
[191] Darling to Goderich, 13 April 1831, *HRA*, Series I: Vol. 16, p. 240. Darling had intended to appoint a Captain Barker who was killed while on an expedition in Australia. Whether this led Darling to have a change of heart is questionable but, in Darling to Goderich, 7 September 1831, *HRA*, Series I: Vol. 16, p. 345, he had decided not to appoint a resident in NZ. Yet, by early 1832, Goderich had decided that an appointment would be beneficial to British interests: Under Secretary Hay to Governor Bourke, 21 January 1832, *HRA*, Series I: Vol. 16, p. 505.
[192] Ramsden, Eric, *Busby of Waitangi: H.M.'s Resident at New Zealand, 1833-40,* (A. H., and A. W. Reed), 1942, and Orange, Claudia, 'Busby, James-Biography', *Dictionary of New Zealand Biography*, *Te Ara-the Encyclopedia of New Zealand*, updated 1 January 2017. See also, Davidson, J. W., 'Busby, James (1801-1871)', *ADB*, Vol. 1, pp. 186-188.
[193] Samuel Marsden commented in August 1837, 'There is a British Resident there, but he has no authority to act. Why he was stationed there without powers I cannot tell…', *HRNZ*, Vol. 1, p. 723.
[194] Goderich to Bourke, 18 March 1832, *HRA*, Series I: Vol. 16, pp. 562-563, details Busby's appointment in London. Goderich to Bourke, 14 June 1832, *HRA*, Series I: Vol. 16, pp. 662-664, lays down Busby's limited powers.

performance was indifferent.[195] NSW's Governor Sir Richard Bourke and his successor Sir George Gipps disliked Busby and had little sympathy for his quandary while their Executive Council resented NZ being a charge upon NSW revenue, treating Busby's requests for money equally unsympathetically.[196] British intervention in NZ at this stage was cautious and frugal.[197]

Māori society had its own systems of authority and regulation but Busby was meant to organise these into a form that would be more recognisable to the British, and encourage chiefs to make and enforce western-style laws. Local *rangatira* (hereditary Māori political leaders of kinship groups) were concerned (and they had been for some time) by the increase in European settlers. Some chiefs had met with King George IV in 1820 and 13 had petitioned King William IV in 1831 for formal protection from other powers. In March 1834, Busby invited northern chiefs to a meeting at Waitangi to select a national flag so that locally registered ships could be clearly identified and trade.[198] He hoped that the flag would bring into existence a Māori federation with 'an established government' capable of orderly judicial and political action. The following year, the Declaration of Independence of NZ created what some people now consider a show of Māori unity. Busby seems to have used de Thierry's plan to come to NZ with French ships, weapons and hundreds of settlers as an opportunity to establish a settled form of government among Māori and saw the Declaration as a means to make the country a dependency of the British Empire in everything but name. The Declaration, affirming Māori sovereignty and land rights, was signed at Waitangi in late October 1835 by 35 Māori chiefs.[199] It seems that Busby and the chiefs had different views of the Declaration. Busby regarded it as a step towards making NZ a British possession. The chiefs saw it as a guarantee of their independence, a strengthening of their relationship with the British, and a promise of protection in this case from the French. In practice, the Declaration had little practical impact since no chief was prepared to subordinate his own authority to that of the United Tribes. It did not create a new system of

---

[195] Bourke to Lord Stanley, 6 December 1834, *HRA*, Series I: Vol. 17, pp. 596-597. Bourke was so disillusioned with Busby's performance that he recommended his withdrawal from NZ, something that he repeated to London at regular intervals.

[196] This was evident from the outset: protest in Executive Council against Busby's proposed £500 per year salary, Bourke to Goderich, 28 October 1832, *HRA*, Series I: Vol. 16, p. 775.

[197] Tapp, E. J., *Early New Zealand: A Dependency of New South Wales, 1788-1841*, (Melbourne University Press), 1958.

[198] The Flag of the Independent Tribes of New Zealand was gazetted in Sydney on 17 August 1835: *New South Wales Government Gazette*, 19 August 1835, p. 580. The flag was approved in Aberdeen to Bourke, 21 December 1834, *HRA*, Series I: Vol. 17, pp. 608-609.

[199] The Declaration is a short-handwritten document of four articles. It states that all sovereign power and authority in the resided with the chiefs 'in their collective capacity', expressed as the United Tribes of New Zealand. It also states that the chiefs would meet annually at Waitangi to make laws. In return for the 'friendship and protection' that Māori were to give British subjects in NZ, the chiefs invited King William IV 'to continue to be the parent of their infant state and its Protector from all attempts upon its independence.' See also Bourke to Glenelg, 10 March 1836, *HRA*, Series I: Vol. 18, pp. 352-355.

government and, although the Declaration was printed and published in 1836 and 1837, it proved to be an obstacle to the annexation of NZ. One purpose of the Treaty of Waitangi in 1840 was to revoke the Declaration thus allowing the transmission of sovereignty to the Crown.

Busby's position was increasingly difficult: John Dunmore Lang who visited the Bay of Islands in 1839, wrote without exaggeration that Busby seemed to have 'no employment ... but that of standing sentinel upon the British Ensign'.[200] He received little support from NSW where Bourke regarded the Declaration as premature and his relationship with missionaries broke down. In 1836-1837, there were outbreaks of tribal fighting in the Bay of Islands, Rotorua and elsewhere and all attempts by Busby to mediate failed. British settlers also petitioned the Crown for protection arguing that the French adventurer Charles de Thierry was threatening to establish a 'sovereign and independent state' in Hokianga to pre-empt any British attempt to claim sovereignty.[201] The British government was increasingly concerned about how land was obtained from Māori and it was evident that action was necessary to protect the interests of Māori from exploitation. Increasing instability, the necessity of policing land transactions and the enhanced threat of French or American intervention resulted in a gradual shift towards annexation.[202] In London and in NSW, politicians and officials decided that they could no longer allow matters to drift.[203]

In view of the deteriorating situation in NZ, Governor Bourke decided to send Captain William Hobson to support Busby.[204] During a two-month stay in May and June 1837, Hobson visited the main European and native settlements and went as far south as Cloudy Bay in the South Island. His mission accomplished, he returned to Sydney where he called for negotiated treaties with Māori chiefs and recommended the adaptation of imperial models from British India as the basis for controlling British activities in NZ. He called for the purchase of two or three delimited areas of land and through a treaty placed under British jurisdiction. These 'factory' enclaves would be overseen by an

---

200 Lang, J. D., *New Zealand in 1839: or, Four letters, to the Right Hon. Earl Durham, Governor of the New Zealand Land Company, on the colonization of that island and on the present condition and prospects of its native inhabitants*, (Smith, Elder & Co.), 1839, p. 11.

201 Letter from Baron de Thierry to the editor of the *Sydney Gazette*, 17 December 1837, HRNZ, Vol. 1, pp. 724-728, outlines his grandiose and unrealistic plans. See also, Raeside, J. D., 'Thierry, Charles Philippe Hippolyte de', *Dictionary of New Zealand Biography, Te Ara-the Encyclopedia of New Zealand*, updated 1 January 2017, see http://www.TeAra.govt.nz/en/biographies/1t93/1

202 French and American whalers used NZ waters and ports. The Americans had appointed James Clendon as consul to NZ in 1839 and a shipload of French colonists was already heading to NZ.

203 Glenelg to Bourke, 28 October 1835, *HRA*, Series I: Vol. 18, pp. 173-174, gave Bourke the authority to remove Busby.

204 Scholefield, *Captain William Hobson, First Governor of New Zealand*, (Oxford University Press), 1934, Moon, Paul, *Hobson: Governor of New Zealand, 1840-1842*, (Auckland University Press), 1998, Tapp, E. J., 'Hobson, William (1793-1842), *ADB*, Vol. 1, pp. 545-546, and Simpson, W. A., 'Hobson, William', *Dictionary of New Zealand Biography, Te Ara-the Encyclopedia of New Zealand*, updated 1 January 2017. See http://www.TeAra.govt.nz/en/biographies/1h29.

appointed head who would also act as consul to the local raNgatira.[205] This, Hobson believed, would provide the foundations for civil government and impose boundaries on British activities in NZ. Busby criticised this proposal pointing out the impossibility of collecting all the 'pig and potato merchants', sawyers, flax gatherers, whalers and farmers into 'factories'. A House of Lords report in 1838 and the dispatches of Governor Sir George Gipps and Busby all argued strongly for greater British responsibility in the islands than Hobson had initially advocated. Concerned by the activities of the New Zealand Company, Hobson quickly abandoned his limited proposal and called for a more interventionist and extensive form of 'protection'.

Until the late 1830s, the British government had supported trade with NZ but not its settlement. This was part of broader British imperial policy to limit military and financial costs. An empire of commerce based on free trade was the aim, not an empire of settlement that could bring expense and trouble. This policy was increasingly untenable and underwent a radical rethink in late 1838 and early 1839. The British government had been impressed by Hobson's report on the country and in December 1838, he was appointed British consul in NZ. The decision to annex at least some of New Zealand dates from 30 May 1839 and was made by Lord Normanby, the Colonial Secretary. In June 1839, Queen Victoria signed Letters Patent that altered the definition of the boundaries of NSW to include 'any territory which is or may be acquired in sovereignty by Her Majesty within that group of islands in the Pacific Ocean commonly called New Zealand'. This meant that when the Crown's sovereignty over Ne was proclaimed in 1840, technically NZ became part of NSW. The drafting of Hobson's instructions took place in mid-1839 and they were formally issued on 11 August. The departure of three New Zealand Company ships to the Cook Strait region in May 1839 led to him being instructed to secure the whole of New Zealand if he thought fit. How much discretion Hobson had is a matter of debate but his instructions strongly suggested that annexing the whole country was desirable and in the best interests of Māori. The British government had concluded that, because of the intrusion of settlers and their claims to have bought vast lands, Māori sovereignty was now 'little more than nominal' and British protection 'would far more than compensate for the sacrifice, by the natives, of a national independence, which they are no longer able to maintain'.[206] Protecting Māori, regulating land transactions, controlling the activities of settlers and dealing with the influx of New Zealand Company migrants all came together in British policy in 1839.

Hobson left England in August 1839 and arrived in Sydney at the end of December to seek assistance from Sir George Gipps, who had replaced Bourke as Governor in late 1837, on whom he was to be temporarily dependent. After proclaiming the extension of the boundaries of NSW to cover any territory that might be acquired in NZ and providing Hobson with appropriate powers,

---

[205] Bourke to Glenelg, 9 September 1837, *HRA*, Series I: Vol. 19, pp. 84-87, details Hobson's proposals and Bourke's and Busby's reactions.

[206] Normanby to Captain Hobson, 14 August 1839, *HRNZ*, Vol. 1, pp. 729-739. See also Lord John Russell to Sir George Gipps, 3 December 1839, *HRA* Series I: Vol. 20, pp. 409-411.

especially over the sale of land, Gipps in January 1840 sent him with a detachment of troops to be Lieutenant-Governor of NZ.[207] Although Busby had achieved little concrete in the previous seven years and was passed over without thanks, he nevertheless acted as a crucial source of intelligence for the British state. His dispatches played a significant part in the fierce debates during the 1830s over NZ's position within the British Empire, and Hobson generously recognised his important role in drafting the Treaty of Waitangi and securing its acceptance.[208]

Treaty of Waitangi 1840

Trade between Māori and Pākehā had been established since the late-eighteenth century and part of their exchanges included transactions for land. There were also small-scale transactions when whalers, timber millers and merchants acquired pieces of land. Some were for commercial purposes, but sometimes traders attained property for their part-Māori families. Missionary organisations made arrangements with chiefs for the land needed for their stations and farms. Some missionaries, against orders from London, reserved tracts of land for tribes to prevent speculative sales. As British intervention became more likely by the end of the 1830s, capitalists in NSW became involved in land speculation claiming to have bought large areas in the hope of converting them to secure titles later. Finally, in 1839-1840, there were the massive and controversial claims of the New Zealand Company to some 20 million acres in central NZ.[209]

In 1825, George Lambton had sent agents to NZ who allegedly bought land in Cloudy Bay, Stewart Island and on the North Island but this first New Zealand Company collapsed because of lack of backing from the British government. The New Zealand Association was formed in early 1837 to colonise NZ. Lord Glenelg, the Colonial Secretary, intimated that the government would consider chartering the Association as an agency of colonisation. The government expected the Association's members to subscribe capital and gain Māori consent to any settlement. The Association rejected these proposals and in June 1838 was unsuccessful in carrying a private member's Bill through Parliament to achieve its original aims. It was then dissolved and the New Zealand Colonisation Company was then founded with nominal capital of £400,000 and is better known as the New Zealand Company.[210] The promoters of the company, led by Edward Gibbon Wakefield, saw emigration as a cure for Britain's social problems.[211]

[207] *New South Wales, Government Gazette*, 18 January 1840.

[208] Moon, Paul, 'The Influence of 'Benthamite'Philosophies on British Colonial Policy in New Zealand in the Era of the Treaty of Waitangi', *Journal of Imperial and Commonwealth History*, Vol. 43, (3), (2015), pp. 367-386.

[209] On the events leading to the Treaty of Waitangi see Moon, Paul, *Te ara ki te Tiriti: the path to the Treaty of Waitangi*, (David Ling), 2002, and Adams, Peter, *Fatal Necessity: British intervention in New Zealand, 1830-1847*, (Auckland University Press), 1977.

[210] Burns, Patricia, *Fatal Success: A History of the New Zealand Company*, (Heinemann Reed), 1989.

[211] On Wakefield see Bloomfield, P., *Edward Gibbon Wakefield*, (Longman), 1961, and the broader study by Temple, Philip, *A Sort of Conscience: The Wakefields*, (Auckland University Press), 2002. Prichard, M. F. Lloyd, (ed.), *The Collected Works of Edward Gibbon Wakefield*, (Collins), 1968, contains his important writings.

Those involved in the company had already established a colony in South Australia in 1834 and now made plans to create British settlements in NZ. The company's programme of 'systematic colonisation' would, in theory, attract the right balance of migrants. Investors in the company were promised 100 acres of farmland and one town acre; the initial 1,000 subscribers signed up in a month. There would be a privileged landowning class and a good supply of carefully selected labourers to work the land. This all depended on buying land cheaply from Māori and selling it at a 'sufficient price' since part of the profits would cover the free passage of 'mechanics, gardeners and agricultural labourers'.[212] To combat negative notions about NZ, the company used books, pamphlets and broadsheets to promote the country as 'a Britain of the South', a fertile land with a benign climate, free of starvation, class war and teeming cities.[213] In late 1839, several hundred company settlers, with no government approval, set sail for Port Nicholson. The first ships arrived in Wellington in January 1840 with settlements established at Wanganui in September 1840, New Plymouth in November 1841 and Nelson in February 1842. Two branches of the company, the Otago Association and the Canterbury Association, brought people to Dunedin in 1848 and Christchurch in 1850.

In London, key figures in the Colonial Office worried about the impact of Wakefield's colonisation plans on Māori. The most prominent was James Stephen, the Permanent Under-Secretary who was strongly influenced by humanitarian Christian ideals. Like many others, he knew that European contact had led to the collapse or near extinction of some native societies and wanted to avoid a similar pattern in NZ.[214] The Aboriginals Protection Society, founded in 1836, aimed to improve the situation of native peoples throughout the British Empire. In 1837, a Select Parliamentary Committee reported the dismal story of Britain's impact on native peoples.[215] Humanitarian groups, rightly sceptical of the Association's plans, believed that 'systematic colonisation' would be destructive of both the rights and traditional way of life of the Māori and likely to hinder or cancel the good work of missionaries. They opposed the formal colonisation and

---

[212] Apart from the Otago Association settlers, who were recruited largely from Edinburgh and Glasgow in Scotland, most were from England. Fewer than 2 per cent came from Ireland. Almost two-thirds came from three areas in the south of England (Kent and Sussex, the far south-west of Cornwall and Devon, and London itself). These were places close to the ports of London and Plymouth from which ships set sail for NZ.

[213] See for instance, *Letters from Settlers & Labouring Emigrants in the New Zealand Company's settlements of Wellington, Nelson, & New Plymouth: from February, 1842, to January, 1843*, (Smith, Elder), 1843.

[214] Knaplund, Paul, *James Stephen & The British Colonial System 1813-1847*, (University of Wisconsin Press), 1953, is an excellent biography but see also Ward, C. J. M., 'The Retirement of a Titan: James Stephen 1847-50', *Journal of Modern History*, Vol. 31, (1959), pp. 189-205, and Foden, Norman Arthur, *James Stephen, architect of empire*, (New Zealand Historical Bulletins), 1, Auckland, 1938.

[215] Parliamentary Papers, *Report of the Parliamentary Select Committee on Aboriginal Tribes, (British settlements)*, (Printed by Order of the House of Commons), 1837, pp. 13-29, examines the degenerating situation in NZ. See also, Heartfield, James, *The Aboriginals' Protection Society: Humanitarian Imperialism in Australia, New Zealand, Fiji, Canada, South Africa and the Congo, 1836-1900*, (C. Hurst & Co.), 2011, pp. 125-158.

settlement of NZ as mapped out by Wakefield, and for some years they blocked his efforts to obtain official support or approval. As with his settlement in South Australia, the New Zealand Company's case was based on a combination of anecdotes and the suppression of other information. The Colonial Office's decision to oppose Wakefield's plans for colonising South Australia--a decision borne out by the initially shambolic nature of that colony--helps explain their opposition to the similar scheme for NZ.

Although Hobson had been given guidance for making a treaty with Māori leaders, he was not provided with a draft document prepared by lawyers or Colonial Office officials.[216] As a result, the treaty was prepared in four days by Hobson with the help of his secretary, James Freeman, and British Resident James Busby, neither of whom were lawyers. A treaty in English would not have been understood, debated or agreed to by Māori and Hobson instructed missionary Henry Williams and his son Edward to translate the document into Māori and this was done overnight on 4 February.[217] Following an extensive debate among the northern Māori chiefs, on 6 February 1840, the treaty was signed at Waitangi in the Bay of Islands by Hobson, several English residents and approximately 45 Māori *rangatira* including Hone Heke. Between February and September, about fifty meetings were held around North Island to discuss and sign the Māori text of the Treaty, but the English text was signed only at Waikato Heads and at Manukau by 39 *rangatira*. By the end of that year, over 500 Māori had signed the Treaty including 13 women.[218]

Both as a constitutional source and as a translation, the Treaty was and remains problematic. It consists of three articles but the English text is not an exact translation of the Māori text. Despite the problems caused by the different versions, both represent an agreement in which Māori gave the Crown rights to govern and to develop British settlement, while the Crown guaranteed Māori full protection of their interests and status and full citizenship rights.[219] The preamble to the English version states that the British intentions were to protect Māori interests from the encroaching British settlement; provide for British settlement; and, establish a government to maintain peace and order. The Māori text has a different emphasis suggesting that the Crown's main promises to Māori were to secure tribal *rangatiratanga* and Māori land ownership.[220]

---

[216] Buick, T. Lindsay, *The Treaty of Waitangi: or How New Zealand became a British Colony*, (S. W. Mackay), 1914, was the first major, almost hagiographical work on the Treaty, but for modern interpretations see Orange, Claudia, *The Treaty of Waitangi*, (Allen & Unwin), 1987, revised edition, 2010.

[217] Moon, Paul, 'Bound into a Fateful Union: Henry Williams' Translation of the Treaty of Waitangi into Māori in February 1840', *Journal of the Polynesian Society*, Vol. 111, (1), (2002), pp. 51-63, suggests that Williams colluded with the Crown by arranging the wording and deliberately using ambiguous words to secure Māori agreement to the Treaty.

[218] Ibid, Orange, Claudia, *The Treaty of Waitangi*, pp. 24-76, considers the treaty and its multiple signings.

[219] In addition to the treaty signed at Waitangi eight further copies were made and circulated around the country to gather additional signatures, the effect of which was to enhance its authority.

[220] Kawharu, Ian, H., (ed.), *Waitangi: Maori and Pākehā perspectives of the Treaty of Waitangi*, (Oxford University Press), 1989, and Belgrave, M., Kawharu, M., and

In the Māori text of article 1, Māori gave the British a right of governance, *kawanatanga*, while in the English text, Māori ceded 'sovereignty'. One of the problems that faced the original translators of the English draft of the Treaty was that 'sovereignty', as the British understood it, had no direct parallel in Māori society. The treaty negotiators failed to clarify the implications of the European concept of a *national* authority as opposed to the iwi-based system to which Māori were accustomed. Chiefs held '*rangatiratanga*', autonomy and authority over their own domains but there was no supreme ruler of the whole country. In the Māori version, the translators used the term 'kawanatanga' that was then in current use. Māori understanding of this word came from familiar use in the New Testament of the Bible and from their knowledge of the role of the 'Kawana' or Governor of NSW, whose jurisdiction then extended to British subjects in NZ. As a result, Māori believed they ceded to the Crown a right of governance in return for the promise of protection, but had retained their authority to manage their own affairs.[221]

The Māori version of article 2 uses the word '*rangatiratanga*' in promising to uphold the authority that tribes had always had over their lands. This choice of wording emphasises status and authority. In the English text, the Crown guaranteed to Māori the undisturbed possession of their properties, including their lands, forests, and fisheries, if they wished to retain them. This text emphasises property and ownership rights. Article 2 provides for land sales to be effected only through the Crown giving it the right of pre-emption in land sales.[222] The Waitangi Tribunal, after reading the instructions for the Treaty provided by Lord Normanby, concluded that the purpose of this provision was not just to regulate settlement but to ensure that each tribe retained sufficient land for its own purposes and needs. In article 3, the Crown promised to Māori the benefits of royal protection and full citizenship emphasising equality between Māori and settler.

As far as British law and practice was concerned, it was not the signing of the Treaty of Waitangi that transferred sovereignty to Great Britain but the formal proclamations of sovereignty later in 1840. Hobson decided that it was urgent to proclaim sovereignty over the whole country largely since New Zealand Company settlers had arrived at Port Nicholson, were laying out town sites, and flying the national flag of independent NZ. On 21 May 1840, he proclaimed British

---

Williams, D. V., (eds.), *Waitangi revisited: perspectives on the Treaty of Waitangi,* 2nd ed., (Oxford University Press), 2005, remain valuable studies of the legal and historical issues surrounding the treaty.

[221] Pocock, J. G. A., 'Law, sovereignty and history in a divided culture: the case of New Zealand and the Treaty of Waitangi', (University of Lancaster: The Irdell Memorial Lecture), 1992, reprinted in *McGill Law Journal*, Vol. 43, (3), (1998), pp. 481-506, and in his *The Discovery of Islands*, (Cambridge University Press), 2005, pp. 226-257.

[222] See Belgrave, M., 'Pre-emption, the Treaty of Waitangi and the Politics of Crown Purchase', *New Zealand Journal of History*, Vol. 31, (1997), pp. 23-37, and Hickford, Mark, '"Vague Native Rights to Land": British Imperial Policy on Native Title and Custom in New Zealand', *Journal of Imperial and Commonwealth History*, Vol. 38, (2), (2010), pp. 175-206, and 'Law and Politics in the Constitutional Delineation of Indigenous Property Rights in 1840s New Zealand', in ibid, Dorsett, Shaunnagh, and Hunter, Ian, (eds.), *Law and Politics in British Colonial Thought*, pp. 249-268.

sovereignty over the North Island by cession and over the South Island by discovery. Some soldiers were sent to Port Nicholson on 25 May; the settlers' Council was disbanded and the offending flags struck. Later, the settlers' leader, William Wakefield, went to the Bay of Islands with an address pledging their allegiance to the Crown and suggesting that Hobson make Port Nicholson the capital. This was declined, but Hobson was reassured by their gesture In June 1840, Major Thomas Bunbury, unaware of Hobson's actions, separately proclaimed British sovereignty over the South Island by cession.[223] The last formal steps were taken later in 1840 when the boundaries of the colony of NSW were formally altered to include NZ. This was a temporary situation and in November 1840, a Royal Charter was signed by Queen Victoria proclaiming NZ as a separate colony. In May 1841, NZ was finally constituted as a separate Crown Colony. The Chatham Islands were inadvertently left out of the official boundaries of NZ until 1842.

Despite the stress laid by some historians on the uniqueness of Waitangi and its centrality to NZ's national narrative, it must also be seen in the long tradition of treaty making within the British Empire.[224] Making treaties was a fundamental feature of British territorial influence in North America, South Asia and elsewhere. The East India Company regularly entered treaties to extend its political and commercial influence between 1765 and 1856 and, during the same period, treaties were integral to extending British influence among Native Americans. By the 1830s, however, it was recognised by many British politicians and reformers that treaties with native peoples enabled the extension of Britain's imperial sovereignty and that they were rarely lasting compacts between equals or the basis for a developing social contract. The Waitangi Tribunal may have concluded that the authority of settler government and Māori chiefs was separate but equal but that was not how the Treaty[225] was perceived by many officials and most settlers in the 1840s. The result was sustained Māori resistance in the 1840s, 1860s and 1870s.[226]

Resistance at Wairau 1843

The 1840s saw substantial settler immigration to NZ. On North Island, Australian, English and Irish settlers founded Auckland in 1840 and the Plymouth Company of settlers from the west of England founded New Plymouth the following year. On South Island, the Otago Association of settlers from central Scotland founded Orago in 1848 and Southland in 1861 while the

---

[223] *New Zealand Advertiser and Bay of Islands Gazette*, 19 June 1840.

[224] Renwick, W., *Sovereignty & Indigenous Rights: The Treaty of Waitangi in international contexts*, (Victoria University Press), 1991.

[225] Hickford, Mark, *Lords of the Land: Indigenous Property Rights and the Jurisprudence of Empire*, (Oxford University Press), 2011, examines how the vocabularies of property rights were mediated between empire and Māori political communities in NZ between 1840 and the 1860s. See also his 'Framing and Reframing the Agon: Contesting Narratives and Counter-Narratives on Māori Property Rights and Political Constitutionalism, 1840-1861', in Belmessous, Saliha, (ed.), *Native Claims: Indigenous Law against Empire, 1500-1920*, (Oxford University Press), 2012, pp. 152-181.

[226] Belich, James, *The New Zealand Wars and the Victorian Interpretation of Racial Conflict*, (Auckland University Press), 1986, is the central modern analysis.

Canterbury Association from the south of England established Canterbury and Lyttelton in 1850. More important and certainly more publicised was Wakefield's New Zealand Company, popular in the Home Counties, that established Wellington and Wanganui on North Island in 1840 and Nelson[227] on South Island two years later.

Whether Waitangi established a system of 'shared' sovereignty is debatable but its recognition of alternative claims to sovereignty in NZ could and would resist the assertion of exclusive British sovereignty. The Treaty became an official and publicly vaunted reference against which British actions could be judged and made it difficult to mute Māori resistance when it appeared to have been breached. For instance, towards the end of 1841 a series of events unfolded that unsettled northern Māori. In November, Hobson issued a proclamation banning the cutting of kauri.[228] Although it was intended to curb the wanton destruction of forests by settlers, it contravened the Treaty's guarantee of Māori possession of their forests and encroached on an important source of revenue. There has been considerable debate about whether land transactions meant the same thing to European 'purchasers' and Māori 'sellers'. Contemporaries certainly recognised that Māori cultural understanding was different from British views of land ownership. In 1843, Dieffenbach noted:

> ...the chief has no authority to give away what he does not himself individually possess; each of its [the tribe's] members is the sovereign possessor of his own plot of ground, and to have the consent of all would have amounted nearly to an impossibility.[229]

George Clarke, with direct experience of Māori land-holdings during the early 1840s in his capacity as Protector of Aboriginals, agreed:

> The private, separate, and exclusive ownership of land was not recognised among them [Māori], though I have seen this denied ... No Chief, however high his rank, could dispose of a single acre without the concurrence of his tribe. Without such a law, no tribe could be sure of its integrity, and any number of wedges might be driven into its territory ... It was fatal to the tribe to allow the individual, on his own mere motion, to admit a stranger to get a foothold on its land.[230]

Many historians and some of the reports of the Waitangi Tribunal considered that Māori saw the transactions more akin to use rights as part of a reciprocal relationship between tribes and the Europeans who traded with and lived among them and did not necessarily see the trade in land as a permanent

---

[227] Fox, William, *Report of the Settlement of Nelson in New Zealand*, (Smith, Elder and Co.), 1849.

[228] Kauri forests—with trees growing to 50 metres tall with trunk girths of 16 metres--once covered 1.2 million hectares from the Far North of Northland to Te Kauri, near Kawhia. Sailors quickly realised the trunks of young kauri were ideal for ships' masts and spars while settlers felled mature trees for sawn timber of unsurpassed quality for building or for arable land. Its gum became essential to the manufacture of varnishes and other resin-based products.

[229] Dieffenbach, E., *Travels in New Zealand*, 2 Vols. (J. Murray), 1843, Vol. 2, p. 142.

[230] Clarke, G., *Notes on Early Life in New Zealand*, (J. Walch), 1903, p. 46.

loss. A key feature of the Treaty of Waitangi was the imposition of Crown pre-emption, making it clear that private settlers could not buy land directly from Māori. Instead, Māori could sell land only to the Crown and not to anyone else if the government did not want to buy it. Land sold to the government was sold on to settlers, usually at a much higher price than that received by the Māori owners. The oral explanation about this aspect of the Treaty was that the government's intention was to protect Māori and it was a way of bringing order to an increasingly confused and disorderly situation.[231]

Recent historiography has moved away from the view that relations between Māori and settlers were fundamentally harmonious to one that reveals the extent of the developing state's reliance on force from the mid-1840s. Despite assurances by the British Government that Māori people owned all New Zealand, not just the lands they occupied, within a few years, pressure from new settlers for land led to the taking of the unoccupied land, described as 'wastelands' by the Crown. Māori had good reason to feel that the pledge made at Waitangi to protect their rights was not being fulfilled. This was particularly the case in the forceful behaviour of the New Zealand Company, whose settlers the government favoured at the expense of Māori rights. On 17 June 1843, 22 Europeans and Māori were killed when an armed party of New Zealand Company settlers and warriors of the Ngati Toa iwi clashed over the purchase of land in the Wairau valley at Tuamarina, six miles north of present-day Blenheim.[232] This was the most significant clash of arms between Māori and British settlers in the years immediately after the signing of the Treaty of Waitangi but symptomatic of conflict within NZ over the next thirty years. In a country where land disputes were the chief cause of conflict between the coloniser and the colonised, surveying could never be a neutral, depoliticised activity and surveyors were figuratively and literally at the cutting edge of colonisation.[233]

The Wairau incident had its origins in the migration of Ngati Toa and their allies from Kawhia to the Kapiti region of the southern North Island. Led by Te Rauparaha and armed with muskets, Ngati Toa had defeated traditionally armed local tribes.[234] After the decisive battle for Kapiti Island in 1824, Ngati Toa extended its sphere of influence into the South Island. Combining brute force with diplomacy, Te Rauparaha developed alliances with other tribes to maintain control of the lands throughout the Cook Strait region and Kapiti became the centre of a lucrative maritime trading empire.[235] Trade with Pākehā was nurtured

---

[231] Hickford, M., '"Vague Native Rights to Land": British Imperial Policy on Native Title and Custom in New Zealand, 1837-53', *Journal of Imperial and Commonwealth History*, Vol. 38, (2), (2010), pp. 175-206.

[232] Andrews, J. L., *The Wairau Massacre: Mindsets of the 1840s*, (J. L. Andrews), 1999.

[233] Byrnes, Giselle, *Boundary Markers: Land Surveying and the Colonisation of New Zealand*, (Bridget Williams Books), 2015. Māori did not hesitate to demonstrate their oposition to the conduct of surveys, something evident at Wairau.

[234] Burns, P., *Te Rauperaha: A New Perspective*, (A. H. & A. W. Reed), 1980, Oliver, Steven, 'Te Rauparaha, (?-1849)', *Dictionary of New Zealand Biography*, *Te Ara-the Encyclopedia of New Zealand*, updated 18 January 2017, http://www.TeAra.govt.nz/en/biographies/1t74/1.

[235] Carbeek, W., *The Kapita Coast: Maori History and Place Names*, (Reed), 1966, pp. 11-32, considers the Ngāti Toa in the area.

and whalers and traders were encouraged to live among Ngati Toa. On 14 May 1840, Te Rauparaha signed a copy of the Treaty of Waitangi, believing that the treaty would guarantee him and his allies the possession of territories gained by conquest over the previous 18 years. On 19 June, he signed another copy of the treaty, when Major Thomas Bunbury insisted that he do so.

It was with these conquering tribes that the New Zealand Company had to negotiate when it arrived in 1839. The Company, through the operations of its chief negotiator Colonel William Wakefield, eventually claimed to have purchased 1.2 million hectares on both sides of Cook Strait.[236] Because of three dubious and soon discredited purchases, the Company set about establishing its main settlement at Port Nicholson (Wellington), where the first settlers arrived in January 1840. Port Nicholson struggled to establish itself but flooding in the Hutt Valley forced the settlers to abandon their original site but when they moved across the harbour to Te Aro and present-day Thorndon, they ran into more problems. Māori occupants of these sites denied the Company's claims to the area. Reliance on Māori for their well-being did not sit well with many Company settlers since they viewed Māori as meddlesome and a hindrance to European settlement. The second of the Company's planned settlements was Nelson. The Company claimed to have purchased land at Port Whakatu (Nelson) from Ngati Toa in 1839. Captain Arthur Wakefield, William's brother, negotiated with the resident Te Tau Ihu chiefs who rejected Ngati Toa's claims to the area. By the end of February 1842, there were 500 settlers in Nelson with a further 1,500 on the way. Nelson Māori initially benefited from supplying the new settlers with food but relations began to sour when both the Company and Crown reneged on certain terms of their purchases. When the Company decided to push ahead with plans to survey the Wairau plains, further tensions were raised between Māori and settlers.[237]

'Manifestly illegal, unjust and unwise'

The fertile plains of the Wairau Valley, south-east of Nelson, were the answer to the Nelson settlement's lack of flat land suitable for agriculture. In January 1843, Captain Arthur Wakefield, who had been dispatched by the New Zealand Company to lead the first group of settlers to Nelson, wrote to his brother, Colonel Edward Gibbon Wakefield, one of the principal officers of the New Zealand Company, that he had located the required amount of land at Wairau,

---

[236] Mitchell, Hilary, and Mitchell, Maui John, *Te Tau Ihu O Te Waka: A History of Maori of Nelson and Marlborough*, 2 Vols. (Huia Publishers), 2004, 2007, Vol. 1, pp. 252-355, examines relations between Māori and The New Zealand Land Company and places Wairau in context.

[237] The Waitangi Tribunal found in 2008 (*Te Tau Ihu: Wai*, p. 785) that, contrary to Treaty principles, the Crown granted lands at Nelson and Golden Bay to the New Zealand Company without first ensuring that all customary owners were fairly dealt with. It then proceeded with its own large-scale Wairau and Waipounamu purchases, making predetermined decisions as to ownership which ignored the rights of Te Tau Ihu Māori or left them with little meaningful choice over the alienation of their lands. For early Crown and New Zealand Company dealings in Nelson and the Wairau incident, see, Waitangi Tribunal, *Te Tau Ihu o te Waka a Maui: Report on Northern South Island Claims*, Vol. 1, (Legislation Direct), 2008, pp. 172-199.

fifteen miles from Nelson. He held a deed to the land, having bought it from the widow of a whaling Captain John Blenkinsop, who in turn had bought the land from Te Rauparaha of the Ngati Toa iwi at Tuamarina but had not taken up the use of the land. As with all land purchases at that time it is probable that the parties saw the 'purchase' in different ways. Blenkinsop thought that he had purchased outright freehold while the Ngati Toa believed they had received *koha* or a gift from the captain to have use of the land, like rental or lease in the modern sense. Chiefs Te Rauparaha and Te Rangihaeata along with their kinsman of Ngati Toa owned the land and had not been paid for it. But similar disputes had been previously settled through negotiation and Te Rauparaha was willing to negotiate on the Wairau land.

It became increasingly clear that the New Zealand Company was unwilling to do this and in early 1843, sent surveyors to the area. Te Rauparaha was adamant that these lands were not part of the Company's 1839 'purchases'. In January 1843, Nohorua, the older brother of Te Rauparaha, led a delegation of chiefs to Nelson to protest about British activity in the Wairau Plains. Two months later, accompanied by his nephew Te Rangihaeata, Te Rauparaha went to Nelson to discuss the matter with Arthur Wakefield.[238] Ngati Toa wanted the matter to be considered as part of Land Commissioner William Spain's investigation into land purchases made prior to Britain's annexation of New Zealand. Arthur Wakefield rejected the request, informing Te Rauparaha that if local Māori interfered with company surveyors, he would lead 300 constables to arrest the Māori chief.[239]

Ngati Toa ordered a halt to the survey but William Wakefield instructed his brother Arthur to continue and a fresh survey party arrived in the Wairau valley in April 1843. The Company planned to put its faith in the notion that 'possession is nine-tenths of the law' hoping that with settlers occupying the land the Crown would have little choice but to recognise their claims retrospectively. Te Rauparaha and Nohorua wrote to Commissioner Spain on 12 May, urgently requesting him to travel to the South Island to settle the Company's claim to Wairau. Spain replied that he would do so when his business in Wellington was complete. A month later, with still no sign of the Commissioner, in early June 1843, Te Rauparaha and Te Rangihaeata had evicted the Company surveyors and burnt their temporary shelters. The surveyors were rounded up and sent back to Nelson unharmed. As these had been built from materials growing on Ngati Toa land Te Rauparaha maintained that he was within his rights to take this action.[240]

---

238 Angela Ballara, Angela, 'Te Rangihaeata, (?-1855)', from the *Dictionary of New Zealand Biography*, *Te Ara-the Encyclopedia of New Zealand*, updated 18 January 2017, see http://www.TeAra.govt.nz/en/biographies/1t63/1

239 Carfeek, W., 'Te Rauparaha: Part III, Wairau, the Porirua Quarrel and Imprisonment', *Te Ao Hou: The New World*, No. 32, (September 1960), pp. 6-9, and ibid, Temple, Philip, *A Sort of Conscience: The Wakefields*, pp. 298-322, provide a detailed account of events.

240 British Parliamentary Papers, *Report from the Select Committee on New Zealand,* 1844, Appendix 4, pp. 107-196, printed correspondence relevant to the Wairau incident including first-hand accounts. 'Narrative of the Waurau Massacre, and Proceedings Connected Therewith', *Nelson Examiner and New Zealand Chronicle*, 23 December 1843, Supplement, pp. 1-10, provides a detailed, if slanted account. See also Stokes, Robert, (of Wellington, New Zealand), *A letter to the ... earl of Devon, on the late massacre at*

The New Zealand Company disagreed. This was clearly an act of arson and there was a general feeling amongst the settler population that Te Rauparaha needed to be put in his place. Some pointed to the fact that Ngati Toa had acquired this land through conquest so it was not theirs to sell. This argument was weak. How Te Rauparaha had acquired the land did not alter the fact that he had not included it in the sale to the Company. The decision was made to arrest Te Rauparaha and Te Rangihaeata on arson charges.[241] Bolstered by an ill-considered report in the Nelson *Examiner* of 'Outrages by the Māori at Wairoo' that was ironically published on the day of the massacre, Wakefield assembled a party of men, including newspaper editor G. R. Richardson and 47 special constables, largely labourers press-ganged into service.[242] An armed group of Europeans, including Nelson Chief Constable Henry Thompson and Arthur Wakefield, arrived near the Tuamarina Stream on 17 June 1843. Te Rauparaha, Te Rangihaeata and approximately 120 Māori had gathered on the opposite bank. There were perhaps 40 women and children present.[243] He allowed Thompson and five other men to approach him, but ordered the rest of the British party to remain on their side of the stream.

Thompson aggressively insisted on arresting Te Rauparaha and attempted to handcuff him. Te Rangihaeata spoke up, insisting that he was on his own land pointing out that Māori did not go to England to take 'Pākehā' land. Thompson quickly lost patience saying that it had nothing to do with land but was a case of arson. He then called out to the men on the far side of the stream, ordering them to fix bayonets and advance, but as they began to cross, a shot was fired though it is unclear which side it came from.[244] Fighting broke out and about eleven settlers and two Māori were killed, including Te Rongo, Te Rangihaeata's wife. The British retreated across the stream, scrambling up the hill under fire from the Ngati Toa. Te Rauparaha ordered the Ngati Toa warriors to cross the stream in pursuit. Those British who had not initially escaped were quickly overtaken. Wakefield called for a ceasefire and surrendered along with Thompson, Richardson and ten others. Two of the British were killed immediately. Te Rauparaha appeared willing to spare the lives of those who had surrendered, but Te Rangihaeata demanded *utu* or revenge for the death of his wife and comrades

---

Wairau [by R. Stokes. With various accounts of the massacre], (Longman, Brown, Green and Longmans), 1844, and Bevan, Thomas, *The Reminiscences of An Old Colonist*, (*Otaki Mail*), 1907, pp. 52-59, for accounts of Wairau.

241 Questions about the legality of this action were raised in 'Editorial', *New Zealand Colonist and Port Nicholson Advertiser*, 4 July 1843, p. 2.

242 'Outrages by the Maories at the Wairoo', *Nelson Examiner and New Zealand Chronicle*, 17 June 1843, p. 266.

243 His account of the Wairau affair was given on 1 July 1843 before Land Claims Commissioner William Spain.

244 'Mr M'Donogh's Statement', *New Zealand Gazette and Wellington Spectator*, 5 August 1843, p. 3, makes clear the attitude of settlers as to who fired first after the '*accidental discharge* of the first musket…followed by an instantaneous volley from the Maories…' while the evidence of Joseph Morgan printed in 'Important Evidence concerning the Wairau Masacre', *New Zealand Gazette and Wellington Spectator*, 13 September 1843, p. 3, suggests the Māori fired first. Māori accounts maintain that it was deliberate.

but also for the accumulated wrongs he felt they had suffered from the Crown and the New Zealand Company. These included the failure to convict the whaler, Dick Cook, for the rape and murder of Te Rangihaeata's close relative, Rangiawa Kuika and her child. Te Rauparaha ceded to his nephew's demand and eleven European prisoners, including Arthur Wakefield and Henry Thompson were killed on the spot.[245]

The news from Wairau shocked settlers throughout the colony, a Public Safety Committee was formed and Church Hill in Nelson was fortified.[246] Reverberations of a reported massacre were felt as far away as England, where the New Zealand Company was practically ruined by the news of 'British citizens being murdered by barbarous natives'. The killing of men who had surrendered was viewed as cold-blooded murder and there were fears that these events signaled the beginning of a widespread Māori insurrection. Tt became obvious the company was being less than honest in its land purchasing tactics and reports on the events in local newspapers were far from accurate. Land sales almost halted as Māori responded with a new firmness in negotiations. Tuhawaiki and Taiaroa, for instance, refused to sell the whole Otago block insisting that village cultivation, burial grounds and reserves should be clearly demarcated and specified in the agreement as remaining in Māori hands. The clash of interests at Wairau left a lasting impression on both Māori and settlers leading to a deep-seated prejudice and suspicion of each other's motives. Māori were determined to resist what they considered acts of aggression or injustice by the settlers especially in relation to the question of the land. The more resolute Māori stance in other atreas such as the Hutt Valley reinforced a growing conviction by settlers that the government should take a firmer line with Māori.

Fitzroy's responds

Robert FitzRoy was appointed Governor of NZ on 7 April 1843 succeeding William Hobson who had died the previous September. His appointment was strongly supported by the Church Missionary Society that had been impressed by

---

[245] Letter by J. W. Barnicoat, a surveyor who escaped from the massacre, dated 23 August 1843 recounting details of the incident, published in 'Massacre at the Wairoo', *Nelson Examiner and New Zealand Chronicle*, 26 August 1843, p. 306. For early accounts of events based largely on the testimony of survivors, see 'Editorial', *New Zealand Colonist and Port Nicholson Advertiser*, 27 June 1843, p. 2, 'Editorial', *New Zealand Colonist and Port Nicholson Advertiser*, 30 June 1843, p. 2, 'Editorial', *New Zealand Colonist and Port Nicholson Advertiser*, 4 July 1843, p. 2, 'Editorial', *New Zealand Gazette and Wellington Spectator*, 28 June 1843, pp. 2-3, 'Massacre at Wairau' *New Zealand Gazette and Wellington Spectator*, 1 July 1843, p. 1, and, 'Nelson', *New Zealand Gazette and Wellington Spectator*, 12 July 1843, p. 3.

[246] Ibid, Temple, Philip, *A Sort of Conscience: The Wakefields*, pp. 351-356, considers the settlers' response to the massacre. Wakefield, Edward Jerningham, *Adventure in New Zealand, From 1839-1844*, 2 Vols. (John Murray), 1845, Vol. 2, pp. 361-401, gives an account my Arthur Wakefield's nephew. See also *New Zealand Colonist and Port Nicholson Advertiser*, 4 July 1843, on calling out the militia, and 'Narrative of the Wairau Massacre…', *Nelson Examiner and New Zealand Chronicle*, Supplement, p. 10, 23 December 1843, 'Wairau Massacre', *Nelson Examiner and New Zealand Chronicle*, 22 June 1844, p. 62.

the evidence he gave to the House of Lords Select Committee in 1838 on conditions in NZ and, ironically given later events, by the directors of the New Zealand Company.[247] When he arrived in the colony on 23 December 1843, one of his immediate tasks was to deal with the aftermath of the Wairau incident. NZ was bankrupt and on the verge of more serious conflict in the Bay of Islands. New Zealand Company settlers formed the bulk of the European population, were politically organised, controlled the most influential newspapers, were determined to acquire further land and had powerful supporters in London.[248] The British government had provided FitzRoy with no funds, troops or a warship and had given him little freedom of action. His options were limited and the settlers expected him to avenge the deaths at Wairau.

The Nelson settlers expected that FitzRoy would take strong action against Te Rauparaha and Te Rangihaeata, but were to be disappointed. FitzRoy acted out of justice and expediency.[249] In late January and early February 1844, a month after taking up his post, he visited Wellington and Nelson in a bid to quell the hostility between Māori and British, particularly in the wake of the Wairau incident. So many conflicting statements had been published that it was impossible for him to decide who had been at fault. Nonetheless, he immediately upbraided New Zealand Company representatives and the editor of a Wellington newspaper, *The New Zealand Gazette*, for their aggressive attitude towards Māori, warning that he would ensure that, 'not an acre, not an inch of land belonging to the natives shall be touched without their consent'. He also demanded the resignations of the magistrates who had issued the arrest warrants for the Māori chiefs. From Nelson, FitzRoy and his officials sailed to Waikanai in the North Island, where he conducted a one-man inquiry into the Wairau incident.[250] On 12 February 1844, he opened proceedings by telling a meeting of 500 Māori:

> When I first heard of the Wairau massacre ... I was exceedingly angry ... My first thought was to revenge the deaths of my friends, and the other Pākehā who had been killed, and for that purpose to bring many ships of war ... with many soldiers; and had I done so, you would have been sacrificed and your pa destroyed. But when I considered, I saw that the Pākehā had in the first instance been very much to blame; and I determined to come down and inquire into all the circumstances and see who was really in the wrong.[251]

---

[247] Moon, Paul, *FitzRoy: Governor in Crisis 1843-1845*, (David Ling Publishing), 2000 and Wards, Ian, 'FitzRoy, Robert', from the *Dictionary of New Zealand Biography*, *Te Ara-the Encyclopedia of New Zealand*, updated 1 September 2016, see http://www.TeAra.govt.nz/en/biographies/1f12/1.

[248] The New Zealand Company was the dominant influence on the press in Wellington but this dominance waned by the mid-1840s, see Day, Patrick A., *The Making of the New Zealand Press: A Study of the Organizational and Political Concerns of New Zealand newspaper controllers, 1840*-1880, (Victoria University Press), 1990, pp. 24-33.

[249] Ibid, Temple, Philip, *A Sort of Conscience: The Wakefields*, pp. 356-372, examines FitzRoy's early experiences in NZ.

[250] This was reported in 'The Investigation at Waikanai', *Nelson Examiner and New Zealand Chronicle*, 2 March 1844, p. 412.

[251] 'His Excellency Captain Fitzroy, R.N.', *New Zealand Gazette*, 17 February 1844, p. 2.

Te Rauparaha, Te Rangihaeata and other Māori present were invited to give their version of events, whilst FitzRoy took notes and interrupted with further questions. There was no evidence that the land had been sold and it would be impossible to protect out-settlers against hostile Māori. The government resisted the calls to bring those responsible to justice. He concluded the meeting by addressing the gathering again, to announce he had made his decision:

> In the first place, the white men were in the wrong. They had no right to survey the land ... they had no right to build the houses on the land. As they were, then, first in the wrong, I will not avenge their deaths.[252]

In effect the Company had brought the tragedy upon itself and there was no evidence that the Nelson settlers had any legitimate claims to land beyond Tasman Bay.

The government's lack of action confirmed the settlers' long-held belief that the government put the needs of Māori above their own.[253] FitzRoy's decision won the approval of the Colonial Office that described the actions of the party led by Wakefield and Thompson as 'manifestly illegal, unjust and unwise' and was unwilling to incur the costs involved in any military action against Ngati Toa. But it earned FitzRoy the permanent hostility of both New Zealand Company officials and settlers and the *Nelson Examiner*. He reinforced settler antagonism by treating land claims as if there were Māori legal rights and making fewer Crown grants for land in Wellington and Nelson than demanded by the Company, and only after the payment of more money. By being awarded a more secure title, although on less land, the Company settlers had greater security but did not recognise that FitzRoy was acting in their best long-term interests. Had he attempted to force the issue with Ngati Toa, he would have made the situation far worse for settlers to establish themselves in a new land. FitzRoy's actions, judicious and firm, sparked off attempts by the New Zealand Company officials to have him replaced.[254]

Despite FitzRoy's measured response to the events at Wairau, the political and economic power of Ngati Toa was under considerable pressure as the government asserted its right to the lands, harbours and coastline of the Cook Strait region. Ngati Toa made every attempt to protect their land as they had done in 1843. But by 1846 their leading chiefs had been removed as part of Governor Grey's strategy for the pacification of the Wellington region. Te Rauparaha was

---

[252] British Parliamentary Papers, *Report from the Select Committee on New Zealand,* 1844, Minutes of Evidence, pp. 197-199. See also 'His Excellency Captain Fitzroy, R.N.', *New Zealand Gazette and Wellington Spectator*, 17 February 1844, p. 2.

[253] See the response in 'Editorial', *Nelson Examiner and New Zealand Chronicle*, 24 February 1844, p. 408.

[254] Domett, A., *Petition to Parliament for the recall of Governor Fitzroy, together with, A narrative of the Wairau massacre*, (New Zealand Company), 1844-1846. See also 'Petition to Parliament', *Nelson Examiner and New Zealand Chronicle*, 15 June 1844, p. 59, 'Meeting to Petition for the Recall of Captain Fitzroy', *Nelson Examiner and New Zealand Chronicle*, 8 February 1845, p. 195, and 'Opinions of the Press on the Parliamentary Report…', *Nelson Examiner and New Zealand Chronicle*, 22 February 1845, p. 203.

imprisoned in Auckland without trial for eighteen months between 1846 and 1848 and Te Rangihaeata forced into exile. While Ngati Toa leaders were effectively held to ransom, the Crown forced the sale of most of the tribe's lands on both sides of Cook Strait.

FitzRoy dismissed

Lack of money proved an insuperable problem.[255] Not only was there no cash to meet the day-to-day costs of administration but there was none either for the purchase of Māori land. For settlers, with little fresh land for selection, the price of available land inevitably remained high. And with no sales there was no revenue. At the domestic level, with no coinage, barter was becoming commonplace. The single bank in NZ provided support but only at 12 to 15 per cent levels of interest. Depression in NSW affected NZ and there was a large drop in revenue from trade and customs levies.[256] Governor Hobson and Acting-Governor Willoughby Shortland had financed land sales by issuing unauthorised promissory notes, the redemption of which became an added burden for FitzRoy. He set out the fiscal problems quite clearly in dispatches, and although they did not provoke actual disapprobation, they elicited no succour. FitzRoy, following the example of other hard-pressed colonial administrators, issued debentures in April 1844. Altogether, by November 1845, he had issued debentures with a total face value of £37,000, a paltry enough sum when backed by the future prosperity of the colony or when compared with the resources given to his successor, George Grey.[257]

To remedy his economic plight and to placate hostile Māori opinion, FitzRoy, on 26 March 1844, waived his government's pre-emption right over Māori land, if a tax of 10 shillings an acre was paid on lands so bought. On 10 October 1844, after representations that government was making more money from the sale of lands than the Māori owners, he reduced the tax to 1d an acre. Customs duties were lifted from Kororareka (Russell) in September 1844 and from the colony in October. This replicated Peel's policy of free trade in Britain and ended nearly five years of relying on simple indirect tax to raise revenue. FitzRoy replaced it with the Property Rate Ordinance based on a direct system of taxation on wealth and income. The value of property and income combined needed to be more than £50 before any liability to pay tax existed. Beyond £50, tax was paid at 1 per cent to a maximum of £10 on incomes greater than £1,000. Widespread opposition saw the Ordinance repealed the following year and the return of customs duties.[258] In August 1844, FitzRoy quashed the award of the land commissioner, William Spain to the New Zealand Company of 60,000 acres

---

[255] McLintock, A. H., *Crown Colony Government in New* Zealand, (R. E. Owen, Government Printer), 1958, pp. 143-192, examines FitzRoy's policies in terms of improvisation and 'moral suasion'. See also Bedford, H. D., 'The Monetary Difficulties of Early Colonisation in New Zealand', *Economic Journal*, Vol. 26, (1916), pp. 257-276.

[256] McKinnon, Malcolm, *Treasury: The New Zealand Treasury, 1840-2000*, (Auckland University Press), 2003, pp. 24-27, examines the early development of the institution.

[257] On this issue see Adams, J, 'Governor FitzRoy's debentures and their role in his recall', *New Zealand Journal of History* Vol. 20, (1), (1986), pp. 44-63.

[258] Heagney, Kevin, *The Politics of Tax, New Zealand 1844-45*, Massey University, School of Economics and Finance, Discussion Paper: 10:13, August 2010.

of Taranaki land, reassuring the Māori chiefs but stiffening the hostility of the company.

Before peace was concluded in the north, hostilities had broken out at Wellington. FitzRoy had upheld Commissioner Spain's revision of the New Zealand Company claim there and his stipulation that *pa* sites and actual cultivations were excluded. The clash at the Wairau had exacerbated the situation. FitzRoy was determined that the settlers would not be permitted to use any of his limited military force to dispossess Māori claimants. After Heke had erupted in the north, FitzRoy came to a carefully considered decision that the north would have priority. He left the Wellington troubles to his successor. For FitzRoy was relieved of his commission as Governor by a dispatch dated 30 April and received on 1 October 1845: the announcement had been made in the Commons on 5 May 1845, and FitzRoy had unofficially heard in September.[259]

The reasons given for FitzRoy's recall were that he had issued debentures against instructions, had not raised a militia and failed to keep the Colonial Office sufficiently informed. Peel's government was embarrassed in the House of Commons by Charles Buller with information supplied by the New Zealand Company about which they knew nothing.[260] FitzRoy's dispatches to the Colonial Office were far from candid about the situation in NZ. One important consequence of FitzRoy's recall was a change in the attitude of the Colonial Office to NZ affairs. FitzRoy had been instructed to pursue a policy that ignored the increasing settlement that was taking place and gave lip service to 'moral suasion'. In effect, this involved a refusal to incur expense or upset military dispositions based on requirements for India. FitzRoy's successor, before his identity was certain, was to be given twice the salary of FitzRoy and more than double the parliamentary grant. He was also instructed to put the interests of the settlers first and imperial military arrangements were altered to give New Zealand an adequate establishment. FitzRoy left NZ in January 1846, having handed over to George Grey on 18 November the previous year. Before leaving, FitzRoy had co-operated generously with Grey and had given him much useful information.[261] In England, he was treated with personal courtesy and for a year or two Grey's dispatches were referred to him for comment but he was unable to concede failure. In a judicious pamphlet he defended his administration and pointed out misapprehensions, if not serious practical errors, in the conduct from London of NZ affairs.[262] The consequence, wrote FitzRoy presciently, was that the British government was faced with a problem the solution of which would require more

---

[259] 'Governor Fitzroy Recalled', *Nelson Examiner and New Zealand Chronicle*, 18 October 1845, p. 130, called the announcement of FitzRoy's recall 'Glorious News', and on 25 October, reported a meeting of the working-classes of Nelson agreeing that his recall should be commemorated by a public dinner and festival.

[260] See Peel and Buller, *Hansard*, House of Commons, Debates, Vol. 78, 11 March 1845, cc644-94, and House of Commons, Debates, Vol. 80, 30 May 1845, cc1088-1094.

[261] Rees, William Lee, and Rees, L., *The Life and Times of Sir George Grey, K.C.B.*, 2 Vols. (Hutchinson & Co.), 1892, Vol. 1, pp. 88-202, and Rutherford, J., *Sir George Grey, K.C.B., 1812-1898: A Study in Colonial Government*, (Cassell), 1961, pp. 73-290, deal with his first governorship of NZ, 1845-1853.

[262] FitzRoy, Robert, *Remarks on New Zealand*, (W. & H. White), 1846, pp. 15-56, deals with his period as Governor.

time, more trouble and more men and money than most people were willing to believe.[263] His views were largely supported by contemporaries such as Bishop G. A. Selwyn and Chief Justice William Martin. FitzRoy probably could never have succeeded within the terms of his appointment, something evident in Grey's changed instructions and conditions.

Conflict in the North

FitzRoy was then called on to deal with New Zealand's first racial war, sparked off by Chief Hone Heke of the Bay of Islands. Its causes were not of FitzRoy's making, arising rather from economic failure and the diminished importance of the Far North after the removal of the government to Auckland. The first overt act of significance was the cutting down of the flagstaff on Maiki Hill above Kororareka on 8 July 1844. Heke took exception to it because he saw it as a sign that NK had passed into Britain's control. The initial incident developed into confrontation between Māori tribes and Btitish troops between Heke and his followers and the government and between Heke and other Nga Puhi, of whom Waka Nene and Patuone were the most important. Some tribes remained neutral largely because they believed Heke acted on his own initiative and that it was his own fight. The military engagements spread over 18 months and were ended by FitzRoy's successor, Grey, on 23 January 1846 in a battle with Heke's main ally Kawiti.[264] FitzRoy, with insufficient funds to pay a militia, and whose first call for troops from NSW was regarded as totally unjustifiable by the Colonial Office, maintained the credibility of his government beyond the New Zealand Company settlements. No leader of importance, except Kawiti in the north and Te Rauparaha and Te Rangihaeata in the Wellington area, acted against him. It was a major achievement, of which his successor was to reap the reward.[265]

Māori frustration with the government had many causes. Fitzroy had shifted the centre of government to Auckland; land sale revenue had fallen; overseas shipping had declined and port charges were now taken by the government; there was falling demand for Māori labour and goods; and, customs duties had pushed up the cost of imported goods. In addition, there was a deepening financial depression across the colony. For many Northern Māori in 1844, there was a stark contrast with their previous wealth and independence for which they held the government responsible. Heke resented the intrusion of British authority and the loss of Māori independence–he wanted British authority to be removed. He regarded the erection of the flagpost at Maiki Hill as a slight to his *mana* and that he had a right to the post since he had originally provided it to fly the flag of the United Tribes of New Zealand, the Confederation of 1835. This claim has never

[263] Ibid, FitzRoy, Robert, *Remarks on New Zealand*, pp. 16-18, 25-27, 55-64.
[264] Wards, Ian, 'The Generalship of Governor Grey 1846-52), in Murtz, Peter, (ed.), *The Feel of Truth: Essays in New Zealand and Pacific History*, (Consolidated Press Holdings Ltd.), 1969, pp. 95-112, especially 96-100.
[265] 'Narrative of Events at the Bay of Islands', *New Zealander*, 7 June 1845, p. 2, 'Narrative of Events at the Bay of Islands', *New Zealander*, 19 November 1845, p. 2. Buick, T. Lindsay, *New Zealand's First War. Or, the Rebellion of Hone Heke*, (Government Printer), 1926, and Moon, Paul, *Hone Heke: Nga Puhi Warrior*, (David Ling Pub.), 2001.

been treated seriously by historians but it may be true: for instance, Te Kemara, a major Waitangi chief recalled his personal loss when the flag was moved to Maiki Hill and other chiefs asked that the New Zealand flag should be flown alongside the Union Jack. Whether fighting with Heke or with the government, Māori wanted to fly their own national flag believing that their *rangatiratanga* was recognised in that flag and the 1835 Declaration. Heke had been mission-educated and was conversant with the history of England and of the American War of Independence and he did gain support from Americans living in the Bay of Islands who had their own agenda in overthrowing British power.

Balancing sovereignty and rangatiratanga

Tensions over the precise meaning of Waitangi and its application in practice grew after 1840. Māori expectation was that joint authority would lead to an increase in trade and for protection of Māori interests in land sales but from the outset there were questions over how far the Crown could honour the Treaty guarantees given to Māori. Some Māori worried that they would share the same fate of Indigenous Australians under British rule. Heke had a greater understanding than other Māori leaders of an abstract nature of sovereignty. The critical question was whether the real intentions of the British government was to seize Māori lands. While most Māori sought reassurances from Fitzroy, Heke took the view that the British flag was a sign that the land already belonged to the British Crown and tghat in chopping it down he was making the clear point that he wanted British authority to be removed. It was a conviction that did not waver until his death in 1850.

Former missionary George Clarke had been appointed in 1840 as Protector of Aboriginals to guard Māori interests, but his position was hardly neutral since before 1842, he was also expected to negotiate purchases of land from Māori. Extending Crown sovereignty beyond the pockets of European settlement initially meant negotiating with and persuading Māori communities. Even Clarke admitted that rights of *rangatiratanga* would ultimately have to give way to Crown authority, despite Māori confidence that Waitangi had confirmed these rights. When war broke out in the Bay of Islands in the mid-1840s and later elsewhere, the Crown needed the support of Māori allies to bring an end to the conflict. But after a series of inter-tribal conflicts in the Bay of Plenty, the Colonial Office ruled in 1843 that British law and the terms of the Treaty applied even to those chiefs and their tribes who had not signed the agreement. Balancing Crown sovereignty and *rangatiratanga* would prove difficult.[266]

The growing number of European migrants needed land, and some grew impatient. They thought that officials such as Hobson and FitzRoy were soft on Māori and did not protect settler interests. The New Zealand Company argued that the recognition of Māori land rights contained in article 2 of the Treaty should be restricted to 'a few patches of potato-ground, and rude dwelling places' and dismissed the Treaty as 'a praiseworthy device for amusing and pacifying

[266] Dorsett, Shaunnagh, 'Sovereignty as Governance in the Early New Zealand Crown Colony Period', in Dorsett, Shaunnagh, and Hunter, Ian, (eds.), *Law and Politics in British Colonial Thought*, pp. 209-228, is a valuable discussion on this issue.

savages for the moment'. This hardening of official policy reflected the seriousness with which the Colonial Office regarded the alternative claim to sovereignty that the Wairau incident represented. It was already clear that Britain intended to pursue an exclusive rather than shared sovereignty. There was some support for this view in London, but missionaries and Crown officials in NZ did not agree. In 1844, a British parliamentary committee declared the Treaty 'injudicious' and proposed a tax on all 'uncultivated' Māori lands with confiscation as the penalty for non-payment. A new constitution and charter for the colony in 1846 reflected such ideas.[267] The Governor was to assume ownership of large areas of Māori land not occupied. Missionaries had pointed out that a specific standard of 'occupation', defined as the cultivation of crops, was being applied to Māori. This constitution was never implemented when Grey realised that policies which, in effect, seized land from Māori could provoke a mass uprising arguing that Māori would willingly sell large areas of land to the Crown. Once given adequate funds, Grey initiated an ambitious programme of land purchasing. Nearly all the South Island and about one-fifth of the North Island had passed into Crown ownership by 1865.

Many Māori prospered economically during the 1840s and 1850s supplying vital goods and labour to the fledgling European settlements. Māori agricultural goods found Australian markets, making a significant contribution to NZ's revenue. Māori communities obtained loans for flour mills, agricultural implements and ships and there was investment in Māori health and education. By the 1850s, coastal tribes owned and operated most of the coastal shipping in the North Island. By 1858, 53 Māori vessels of more than 14 tonnes were registered in Auckland alone. Despite mutual mistrust at first, by the early 1850s the Treaty relationship seemed generally positive. Amalgamation was a key part of that relationship. Māori would share the rights and privileges of British subjects under a common system as indicated in the terms of the Treaty and early colonial laws. The Crown and settlers, not Māori, would set the terms of this process. This would be a process of assimilation or absorption of Māori into the white settler world.[268]

When George Grey became Governor in late 1845, he was suspicious of anyone else who exercised influence over Māori and abolished the Aboriginal Protectorate the following year. Grey enacted the Resident Magistrates Ordinance 1847 that enabled Māori *rangatira* to be appointed to courts as assessors and Māori police to be recruited. Many Māori supported these steps, but, always anxious to promote his reputation in London, Grey exaggerated the progress of amalgamation. He saw no need to declare Native districts, provided for under the New Zealand Constitution Act 1852 that would recognise Māori authority over their own affairs. In his view, trade and mission schools promoted amalgamation

---

[267] See above Rutherford, J., *Sir George Grey, K.C.B., 1812-1898: A Study in Colonial Government*, pp. 142-163, for an analysis of the 1846 constitution.

[268] Ibid, Brantlinger, Patrick, *Discourse on the Extinction of Primitive Races, 1800-1930*, (Cornell University Press), 2003, pp. 141-163 examines the commonly held nineteenth-century view about the extinction all 'primitive' or 'savage' races around the world after contact with white civilization in relation to NZ.

well.[269] This was especially so in the 1860s when, after self-government had been granted in 1852, the Crown no longer meant only British officials but included legislatures elected by settlers. Power had moved from the Governor, the Queen's representative, with whom Māori had signed the Treaty to an often-unsympathetic institution in which Māori interests were excluded or marginalised. The shift revealed the underlying struggle for control between Māori and the settlers leading to Māori resistance in the 1860s and 1870s.[270]

The signing of the Treaty of Waitangi has become a 'central tableau' in New Zealanders' collective memory. The Treaty has been described as the 'Māori Magna Carta' and as 'the great charter of Māori rights'.[271] It had also been referred to as a fraud, sham and, in Chief Justice Prendergast's terms 'a legal nullity'.[272] Until the mid-1980s, references to the Waitangi Treaty were virtually absent in the school curriculum and it was overshadowed by the pioneering settlers' narrative. Since the Court of Appeal handed down its decision in the *New Zealand Māori Council v. Attorney-General* (1987), a veritable flood of publications has examined the place of the Treaty in contemporary NZ society.[273]

For Māori, the Treaty has been and continues to be the binding covenant between Māori and the Crown. Since 1840, Māori have claimed that the Crown has consistently failed to honour its Treaty obligations. Māori disaffection reached a peak in the 1970s and early 1980s when Māori land rights and protest movement appeared to be on a collision course with the political establishment. The Labour Government recognised that Māori needed a forum within which to present their grievances and have their claims heard. As a result, in 1975, it established the Waitangi Tribunal as a Commission of Inquiry to examine claims from Māori that they had been prejudicially affected by an action or omission inconsistent with the principles of the Treaty. Amending legislation in 1985 extended the jurisdiction of the Tribunal to investigate historical claims concerning the action of the Crown from 1840 to the present.[274]

---

[269] Ibid, Rutherford, J., *Sir George Grey, K.C.B., 1812-1898*, pp. 204-233, for native policy under Grey.

[270] Ibid, Boast, Richard, 'Vanished theocracies: Christianity, war and politics in colonial New Zealand 1830-80', in Ford, Lisa, and Rowse, Tim, (eds.), *Between Indigenous and Settler Governance*, pp. 70-82.

[271] McHugh, Paul G., *The Maori Magna Carta: New Zealand Law and the Treaty of Waitangi*, (Oxford University Press), 1991.

[272] In *Wi Parata v Bishop of Wellington* (1877), Prendergast called the Treaty 'a simple nullity' and claimed that it was neither a valid treaty nor binding on the Crown. Although the Treaty's status was not a major part of the case, Prendergast's judgment on its validity was considered definitive for many decades.

[273] This case established the principle that if the Treaty is mentioned in a piece of legislation, it takes precedence over other parts of that legislation should they come into conflict. Hill, Richard S., *Maori and the State: Crown-Maori Relations in New Zealand/Aotearoa, 1950-2000*, (Victoria University Press), 2009, examines the move from the official pursuit of assimilation to bicultural politics.

[274] Byrnes, Giselle, 'Jackals of the Crown? Historians and the Treaty Claims Process', in Dalley, Bronwyn, and Phillips, Jock, (eds.), *Going Public: The Changing Face of New Zealand History*, (Auckland University Press), 2001, pp. 110-122.

Conclusions

In settler colonies, notions of property and sovereignty that had evolved in England during the early-modern period were imposed on native populations who had a very different understanding of land and government. British colonial policy from the outset recognised that native peoples had proprietary rights over their land and sought, through purchase and treaty, to accommodate those rights with the needs of settlers for land but how this developed in practice proved problematic. Were indigenous peoples coerced or did they voluntarily surrender title to their property, or was it some combination of the two? How did native peoples understand the concept of property ownership in comparison to whites? Colonial authorities attempted to superimpose their own land tenure systems on native customary tenure systems in their colonies. English common law did not require that the Crown alone could purchase land from native landowners but where colonial officials chose to implement pre-emption as a matter of policy, it was generally backed by legislation. In doing so, settlers often failed to grasp the principles and inner logic of native land tenure systems and how they had evolved in their own unique socio-political environments. They thus believed that their own land tenure systems were intrinsically superior to those of their colonies. As a result, they treated customary and frequently communal land tenure as an obstacle to land development based on individual entrepreneurship and investment in productive land use. Native title became a key construct for relations between Empire and tribes, but how it acted more broadly as a constitutional frame within which discourses of political authority formed and were contested at the heart of Empire and the colonial peripheries. Native title became another feature of imperial political history in which increasingly fierce and highly polemical debate burst into violence.[275]

Whether in the frontier regions of Virginia or in NZ, this policy generally failed as the practical realities of the seemingly inexhaustible demand of settlers for land came into conflict with native resistance to further settler expansion. Across the Empire there came a point at which native peoples were forced to make a choice between resisting further expropriation of their lands and resignation to their fate as marginal, discriminated peoples. Already weakened by the effects of European diseases against which they had little immunity, native resistance could only temporarily delay the inexorable advance of settler colonialism. Treaties made by colonial officials and the instructions from the Colonial Office in London to limit the alienation of native land were frequently ignored by settlers on the frontiers where accommodation with local natives proved largely ineffective. Throughout Britain's empire, the massive transfer of land from natives to settlers always included elements of law and elements of power and together they allowed settlers to gain the upper hand in terms both of sovereignty over tribal nations and proprietary rights to native lands.[276]

---

[275] Ibid, Brantlinger, Patrick, *Discourse on the Extinction of Primitive Races, 1800-1930*, (Cornell University Press), 2003, examines the commonly held nineteenth century view that all 'primitive' or 'savage' races around the world were doomed sooner or later to extinction after contact with white civilization.

[276] Banner, Stuart, *How Indians Lost Their Land: Law and Power on the Frontier*, (Harvard University Press), 2005, pp. 4-6. See also Banner's *Possessing the Pacific: Land,*

With the establishment of colonial self-government in the 1840s and 1850s in many white settler colonies, control of native policy moved increasing away from the Colonial Office and to the frontiers of empire.[277] Colonial Office directives, which he never been especially effective, were supplanted by the exigencies of meeting the needs of settlers for land. This resulted in tensions between the two contemporary approaches for dealing with native peoples: amalgamation or the gradual union of races leading to assimilation and insulation or the maintenance of separate development by reservation policies. British colonial policy increasingly posed two questions. How consistent was self-government with the reliance of colonies on imperial military force for internal and external security and how should colonists in the name of self-government control and govern natives within their borders? These represented the pragmatic recognition that the cost of empire needed to be reduced and the limited extent to which policy made in London could address the needs of settlers in the newly emancipated colonies. The Colonial Office quickly learned not to interfere and land policies were formulated by locally elected politicians.

Ultimately, the colonial authorities could take native lands because they had greater 'power'. In coastal area, settler control was maintained by using naval power. It was more frequently displayed than used. Following summary trials, there may have been a few hangings from the yardarm of Royal Navy frigates and a few villages might have been shelled and destroyed; spectacles to instil 'fear'. Generally, it was sufficient to anchor a warship just off a native village and ostentatiously run out the guns. In the interior, beyond the reach of naval guns, the military equation was more evenly balanced. From the seventeenth century, settler incursions were accompanied by native leaders talking of war. Settlers feared that a native rebellion could wipe them out in a single day but native chiefs had long recognised that a short-term victory would not keep settlers at bay. Those who counselled war generally did so out of desperation since the balance of physical power on sea and on land overwhelmingly lay with the colonial state.

Physical violence, unsuccessful native resistance and the framework of the colonial state were necessary preconditions for successful settler colonialism. The impetus for such colonialism was associated primarily with the interest of capital and settlers in land. The legitimation of the dispossession of land associated with settler colonialism came from a cultural perception that emphasised the gulf between civilisation and savagery and the different land uses associated with each. Native peoples were unable to contain this juggernaut of power and stop the expropriation of their land but they could slow it down or mitigate its effects and they engaged in a virtually constant politics of resistance. They used a range of resistance strategies from a stream of letters and petitions, often written with missionaries, to officials in colonies and in London, meetings with government ministers and even with monarchs to outright rebellion. This resistance was not without effect and gradually politicians and a growing number of settlers became

---

Settlers and Indigenous People from Australia to Alaska, (Harvard University Press), 2007.

[277] Elbourne, Elizabeth, 'The Sins of the Settler: The 1835-36 Select Committee on Aborgines and Debates over Virtue and Conquest in the Early Nineteenth-Century British White Settler Empire', *Journal of Colonialism and Colonial History*, Vol. 4, (3), (2003).

convinced that native peoples had been poorly used and that, in justice, they deserved some redress. The Australian government's apology to Aboriginals, the Waitangi Tribunal and the claims of natives for legal recognition of their land rights in Canada all suggest that native resistance still thrives.

3 Slave resistance and rebellion

One of the problems with slavery is that it seems to have been boiled down into a potted version: the middle passage, cruel plantation life and the struggle to end it. It could almost have been a morality play with the planters as the villains, Wilberforce as the hero and the slaves as simply a mass of wretched, voiceless victims. The problem with this is that it neglects the historical facts. Slavery was a vast social system that endured for three hundred years. If you were a slave in Jamaica in 1815, it was possible that your ancestors stretching back twelve or more generations had also been slaves in the same place. A whole society had been built up over time according to the distorted rules that slavery imposed.[1]

The timing of the Cape uprising in 1808 was influenced by stories and rumours of uprisings in America, Ireland and the Caribbean, as well as the recent British abolition of the slave trade. News of these events inspired an ethnically mixed band of conspirators: Louis van Mauritius, a slave tailor; two Irishmen, James Hooper and Michael Kelly; three other slaves Jeptha van Batavia, Abraham van de Kaapand Adonis. They were later joined by an Indian slave and two Khoi men. Their plan was to march from the rural districts gathering slaves on the way and then to enter Cape Town, seize the Amsterdam Battery, turn the guns on the Castle and then negotiate a peace that involved establishing a free state and freedom for all slaves.[2]

On the evening of 27 October 1808, on the farm of Gerhardus Louw, Vogelgezang, just north of Malmesbury, Louis arrived on horseback dressed as a visiting Spanish sea captain. Hooper and Kelly rode up by his side, disguised as British officers. They managed to convince the absentee farmer's wife to hand over all their slaves into the hands of the 'military' party. They even charmed the farmer's wife into supplying them with a good meal and a place to rest for the night. The next morning the party proceeded from farm to farm, persuading slaves and Khoi servants to join them. Only in one instance did the march encounter resistance. Given the scale of the revolt, overall there was surprisingly little violence.

A march of some 300 mutinous slaves and servants was difficult to keep secret and news soon reached the Governor of the Cape. He ordered regular troops to lay in wait for the insurgents at Salt River just outside the city and they quickly scattered in the face of superior forces. Dragoons captured 326 of the marchers and 47 were put on trial including the leadership group of Hooper, Kelly, Louis and the two Khoi leaders. Nine, including Louis van Mauritius and James Hooper were found guilty of treason and sentenced to be hanged and a further 11 were sentenced to death for 'active particpation'. Others were given lessor sentences including imprisonment on Robben Island.

The resistance and rebellion of 'free and unfree labour' is the subject of the next three chapters.[3] 'Unfree labour' covers a spectrum of restrictive, enforced

---

[1] Levy, Andrea, 'A lost voice speaks from the age of slavery', *The Times*, 30 January 2010.

[2] Harris, Karen, 'The slave 'rebellion' of 1808', *Kleio*, Vol. 20, (1), (1988), pp. 54-65, Kelly, Adrinda, *The Cape Town Slave Rebellion of 1808 and the Limits of Historicity*, MA, Thesis, New York University, 2009.

[3] Bush, M. L., *Servitude in Modern Times*, (Polity), 2000, offers a comparative analysis of the major systems of global servitude since 1500. See also, Eltis, David, and Engerman,

labour: chattel slavery, serfdom, debt bondage, prisoners of war and convict labour. 'Free labour' refers to the varieties of contractual labour relations, often labour for wages that workers could legally quit without punishment. These terms are not absolute and there was a continuum between 'free' and 'unfree' in the colonial period Historians of labour also talk about slavery in terms of 'open' and 'closed' systems.[4] Closed systems, as in India and North America, meant that slaves were held in the system for life with little possibility of gaining their freedom through manumission and where children born to slaves also became slaves. In this sense, the development of racial thinking to separate and privilege the mainly white labourers from black slaves solidified the institution of slavery even as it opened opportunities for lower-class whites. Open systems, as in some Southeast Asian societies, were characterised by regimes in which upward mobility and manumission were distinct possibilities. The emergence of an international system of slavery tied the Americas and Africa together just as the earlier history of slavery in Muslim countries had drawn some parts of Africa into the Islamic world. In other words, slavery varied over place and time; it was not a static concept.[5]

African resistance to the slave trade has often been overlooked and underestimated. It began in Africa, continued in the middle passage and in the Americas. Slaves ran away, established Maroon communities, used sabotage, conspired, and rose against those who held them in captivity. Freed people petitioned the authorities, led information campaigns and worked actively to abolish the slave trade and slavery. In Europe, black abolitionists launched or participated in political campaigns to end the deportation and enslavement of Africans. Over four centuries, across four continents, using violent and non-violent means, Africans were constantly involved in the fight for freedom.

Out of Africa

Expanding European empires lacked one major resource, a work force. In most cases in the Americas, native peoples had proved unreliable, many dying from diseases brought over from Europe and Europeans were ill-suited to the climate and suffered under tropical diseases. Africans, on the other hand, were regarded as excellent workers, often had experience of farming and keeping cattle, they were used to a tropical climate, resistant to tropical diseases and could be 'worked very hard' on plantations or in mines.[6] The result was a dramatic and

---

Stanley L., 'Dependence, Servility and Coerced Labor in Time and Space', Eltis, David, and Engerman, Stanley L., (eds.), *The Cambridge World History of Slavery*, Vol. 3, (Cambridge University Press), 2011, pp. 1-24.

[4] Watson, James L., 'Slavery as an Institution, Open and Closed Systems', in Watson, James L., (ed.), *Asian and African Systems of Slavery*, (Basil Blackwell), 1980, pp. 1-15.

[5] For the range of slavery see, Bradley, Keith, Cartledge, Paul, Eltis, David, and Engerman, Stanley L., (eds.), *The Cambridge World History of Slavery*, 4 Vols. (Cambridge University Press), 2011-, Rodriguez, Junius P., (ed.), *The Historical Encyclopedia of World Slavery*, 2 Vols. (ABC-CLIO), 1997, and Heuman, Gad, and Burnard, Trevor, (eds.), *The Routledge History of Slavery*, (Routledge), 2010.

[6] Thomas, Hugh, *The Slave Trade: The story of the Atlantic slave trade, 1440-1870*, (Simon & Schuster), 1997, is the most accessible and elegant study of European nations' involvement in the slave trade. See also, Klein, Herbert S., *The Atlantic Slave Trade*, 2nd

systematic expansion of the long-established slave trade in Africa into a forced diaspora of monumental proportions.

For over a thousand years, the African continent was systematically bled of its human resource across the Sahara, through the Red Sea, from the Indian Ocean ports and across the Atlantic. Africans experienced slavery not only in the Americas and Asia but in Africa itself. From the ninth to the nineteenth centuries, slavery was principally for the benefit of the Muslim countries and this combined with more than four centuries of a regular slave trade to build the Americas and its colonies by the Christian states of Europe.[7] Just how many Africans were enslaved during this bloody millennium is impossible to say with any certainty but estimates suggest that four million slaves were exported via the Red Sea, another four million through the Swahili ports of the Indian Ocean, perhaps as many as nine million along the trans-Saharan caravan route and over twelve million across the Atlantic Ocean.[8] Of all these slave routes, the European Atlantic trade has attracted most attention and most debate. In part, this was a consequence of better documentation, but more significantly, whereas the Muslim countries enslaved both black and white, it was directed only at Africans.[9]

In the early-seventeenth century, slaves for the transatlantic slave trade were obtained in Senegambia and the Windward Coast, a region with a long history of providing slaves for the Islamic trans-Saharan trade.[10] Around 1650, the focus shifted to the Kingdom of the Kongo that already had ties with the Portuguese and to neighbouring northern Angola.[11] Kongo and Angola were

---

ed., (Cambridge University Press), 2010, Morgan, K., *Slavery and the British Empire: From Africa to America*, (Oxford Univertsity Press), 2007, Rawley, James A., with Behrendt, Stephen D., *The Transatlantic Slave Trade: A History*, (University of Nebraska Press), 1999, Postma, Johannes M., *The Dutch in the Atlantic Slave Trade, 1600-1815*, (Cambridge University Press), 1992, pp. 149-173, and Emmer, P. C., *The Dutch Slave Trade, 1500-1850*, (Berghahn Books), 2006, pp. 68-99, and Curtin, Philip D., *The Rise and Fall of the Plantation Complex: Essays in Atlantic History,* 2nd ed., (Cambridge University Press), 1998, pp. 29-45, 113-128.

[7] See, Ware, Rudolph T., 'Slavery in Islamic Africa, 1400-1800', in ibid, Eltis, David, and Engerman, Stanley L., (eds.), *The Cambridge World History of Slavery*, Vol. 3, pp. 47-80.

[8] The most extensive database on the Atlantic slave trade suggests a figure of 12,521,336 slaves: http://www.slavevoyages.org/tast/index.faces See also, Eltis, David, and Richardson, David, *Atlas of the Transatlantic Slave Trade*, (Yale University Press), 2010, for a visual application of this data.

[9] Thornton, John, *Africa and Africans in the making of the Atlantic world, 1400-1800*, 2nd ed., (Cambridge University Press), 1998, pp. 72-127, is an examination of the development of the slave trade and the process of enslavement to 1800. See also, Lovejoy, Paul E., *Transformations in Slavery: A History of Slavery in Africa*, (Cambridge University Press), 2011, and Stilwell, Sean, *Slavery and Slaving in African History*, (Cambridge University Press), 2014.

[10] Barry, Boubacar, *Senegambia and the Atlantic Slave Trade*, (Cambridge University Press), 1999, pp. 36-45, 61-80, 107-126, and Searing, James F., *West African slavery and Atlantic commerce: The Senegal river valley, 1700-1860*, (Cambridge University Press), 1993, pp. 27-58, 93-128, analyse the development of the trade between 1500 and 1800.

[11] Hilton, Anne, *The Kingdom of Kongo*, (Oxford University Press), 1985, Thornton, John, *The Kingdom of Kongo: Civil War and Transition 1641-1718*, (University of Wisconsin Press), 1983, and Broadhead, Susan H., 'Beyond Decline: The Kingdom of Kongo in the

substantial exporters of slaves until the nineteenth century while Senegambia continued to provide a steady trickle of slaves, but not on the same scale as the other regions of Africa. From the 1670s, the Slave Coast in the Bight of Benin saw a rapid expansion of trade in slaves that lasted until the end of the slave trade in the nineteenth century.[12] Gold Coast slave exports rose sharply in the eighteenth century, but dropped markedly when Britain abolished the slave trade in 1807 and began anti-slavery patrols along the coast. The Bight of Biafra, centred on the Niger Delta and the Cross River, also became a significant exporter of slaves from the 1740s. With the Bight of Benin, it accounted for two-thirds of the transatlantic slave trade during the first half of the nineteenth century.[13]

Each stage of the transatlantic slave trade could be profitable for colonial merchants. The first involved taking manufactured goods from Europe to Africa: cloth, spirit, tobacco, beads, cowrie shells, metal goods and guns that were exchanged for African slaves. The guns were used to help expand empires and obtain more slaves. The second stage or middle passage involved shipping the slaves to the Americas.[14] Conditions on the slave ships were appalling, but the estimated death rate of around 13 per cent was lower than the mortality rate for seamen, officers and passengers on the same voyages. As a result of the slave trade, five times as many Africans arrived in the Americas as Europeans. Slaves were needed on plantations and for mines and the majority were shipped to Brazil, the Caribbean and the Spanish Empire. Less than 5 per cent travelled to the Northern American colonies and later to the United States. The final stage of the triangular trade involved the return to Europe with the produce from the slave-labour plantations especially cotton, sugar, tobacco, molasses and rum.

The slave trade from the Bight of Biafra gradually declined in the nineteenth century because of a reduction in demand for slaves from America, but also because of local shortages of slaves.[15] To fulfil the demands for slaves, the significant tribes in the region, such as the Luba, Lunda, and Kazanje, turned

---

Eighteenth and Nineteenth Centuries', *International Journal of African Historical Studies*, Vol. 12, (1979), pp. 615-650, provide the context for Kongo's experience of the slave trade.

[12] Mann, Kristin, and Bay, Edna G., (eds.), *Rethinking the African Diaspora: The Making of a Black Atlantic World in the Bight of Benin and Brazil*, (Frank Cass), 2001, pp. 3-22, 42-60, provides valuable insights into the character of the slave trade.

[13] Nwokeji, G. Ugo, *The Slave Trade and Culture in the Bight of Biafra: An African Society in the Atlantic World*, (Cambridge University Press), 2010, considers the impact of the slave trade on the Aro merchant class. See also, Law, Robin, *The Slave Coast of West Africa 1550-1750: The impact of the Atlantic slave trade on an African Society*, (Oxford University Press), 1991, pp. 116-155, and Brown, Carolyn A., and Lovejoy, Paul E., (eds.), *Repercussions of the Atlantic Slave Trade: The Interior of the Bight of the Biafra and the African Diaspora*, (Africa World Press), 2011.

[14] Falola, Toyin and Warnock, Amanda, (eds.), *Encyclopedia of the Middle Passage*, (Greenwood Publishing Group), 2007, is a valuable contribution on the experience of the middle passage. Walvin, James, *Crossings. Africa, the Americas and the Atlantic Slave Trade*, (Reaktion Books), 2013.

[15] Law, Robin, (ed.), *From Slave Trade to 'Legitimate' Commerce: The commercial transition in nineteenth-century West Africa*, (Cambridge University Press), 1995, pp. 32-56, explores the impact of the British abolition of the slave trade in West Africa.

on each other using the Cokwe, hunters from further inland as mercenaries. Slaves were the result of raids. The Cokwe, however, became dependent on this new form of employment and turned on their employers when the coastal slave trade evaporated. The increased activities of British anti-slavery patrols along the West African coast resulted in a brief upturn in trade from west-central and south-east Africa as increasingly desperate slave ships visited ports under Portuguese protection where the authorities were less inclined to intervene. With a general abolition of slavery by the end of the nineteenth century, Africa started to be seen as a difference resource. Instead of slaves, the continent was expropriated for its land and minerals in a scramble for Africa and its people coerced into 'employment' in its mines and plantations.

The focus for much of the historiography of slavery has been on the transatlantic and West Coast traffic in slaves. This neglects the long-term significance of slavery on the East Coast and across the Indian Ocean.[16] In the second half of the eighteenth century and especially after anti-slavery ships made the operation of the slave trade from West Africa more difficult, there was a revival in the long-established slave trade on the East Coast.[17] French merchants bought enslaved Africans from East Africa for the growing sugar and coffee plantations on the French owned islands in the Indian Ocean such as Mauritius and Réunion. After 1800, Brazilian merchants also began to buy from the same area to provide labour for their sugar plantations. By 1830, traders in East Africa were largely Arab or African and sold about 30,000 people into slavery every year. The island of Zanzibar and the port of Kilwa slightly to the south on the mainland became the largest African shipping points for the trade. In search of slaves Arab traders began to penetrate further inland, as far as Uganda and the Congo. Merchants transported the enslaved Africans in dhows, traditional Arab vessels known for their sailing speed. Conditions on the slaving dhows were often worse than those endured by captured Africans during the middle passage although the journeys were frequently shorter.[18] British pressure finally forced Zanzibar's ruler to close his slave markets in 1873 and forbid the export of slaves from his dominions. Enforcement proved difficult until an agreement was made

---

[16] See, Jayasuriya, Shihan de Silva, and Pankhurst, Richard, 'On the African Diaspora in the Indian Ocean', in Jayasuriya, Shihan de Silva, and Pankhurst, Richard, (eds.), *The Africa Diaspora in the Indian Ocean*, (Africa World Press), 2003, pp. 7-18, and Jayasuriya, Shihan de Silva, and Angenot, Jean-Pierre, (eds.), *Uncovering the History of Africans in Asia*, (Brill), 2008. Allen, Richard B., *European Slave Trading in the Indian Ocean, 1500-1850*, (Ohio University Press), 2015.

[17] Beachey, R. W., *The Slave Trade of Eastern Africa*, (Rex Collings), 1976, and Beachey, R. W., (ed.), *A Collection of Documents on the Slave Trade in Eastern Africa*, (Rex Collings), 1976, form the most extensive study. Clarence-Smith, William, (ed.), *The Economics of the Indian Ocean Slave Trade*, (Frank Cass), 1989, is valuable on the East African slave trade. See also, Admiralty, *East African Slave Trade*, (HMSO), 1892, and Mwulia, Moses D. A., *Britain and Slavery in East Africa*, (Lynne Reinner Publishers), 1975.

[18] Alpers, Edward A., 'The Other Middle Passage: The African Slave Trade in the Indian Ocean', in Christopher, Emma, Pybus, Cassandra, and Rediker, Marcus, (eds.), *Many Middle Passages: Force Migration and the Making of the Modern World*, (University of California Press), 2007, pp. 20-38. Allen, Richard B., *European Slave Trading in the Indian Ocean, 1500-1850*, (Ohio University Press), 2015.

by the great powers in 1890 to police the coast effectively.[19] Although the League of Nations agreed a slavery convention in 1926 that was amended in 1953 and a supplementary convention was agreed by the United Nations in 1956, *Anti-Slavery International* reported in mid-2003 that slavery was rampant in Niger and the Sudan, something unconvincingly denied by their respective governments while today trafficking especially of children and women remains an unsolved problem.[20]

Resistance in Africa

Evidence from shippers, merchants, banks and insurance companies provide the most extensive data for the Atlantic slave trade and consequently economic and statistical studies are disproportionately represented in slave trade studies. Most of these studies focus on questions about the volume of the trade, the supply of slaves, the cost of supplying slaves and their profitability, prices paid for slaves and the nature of competition and partnerships. But a substantial number see Africans almost exclusively as trading partners on the one hand and cargo on the other. But there was also resistance.

In Africa, sporadic raids by Europeans soon gave way to regular commerce. African societies were drawn into the slavery system, hoping that, once inside it, they would be able to derive maximum benefit for themselves. For instance, Nzinga Mbemba, ruler of the Kongo Kingdom had converted to Christianity in 1491 and referred to the king of Portugal as his brother. When he came to power in 1506, he protested strongly that the Portuguese, his brother's subjects, felt entitled to rob his possessions and carry off his people into slavery. This made little impact and he gradually became convinced that the slave trade was both useful and necessary. Among the goods offered in exchange for human cargo, muskets were especially prized since states with them could resist attacks from their neighbours and pursue expansionist policies.[21] All the states on the coast or close to slave trading areas had to resolve the tensions between their interests in exploiting available resources and ensuring national security by defending the lives, property and rights of their subjects. In 1670, when the French requested permission to establish a trading post on his territory, King Tezifon of Allada was perceptive in his reply:

> You will make a house in which you will put at first two little pieces of cannon, the next year you will mount four, and in a little time your factory will metamorphosed into a fort that will make you master of my dominions and enable you to give laws to me.[22]

---

[19] Cave, Basil S., 'The End of Slavery in Zanzibar and British East Africa', *Journal of the African Society*, Vol. 9, (1909), pp. 20-33, remains a valuable paper.

[20] See, 'Slavery flourishing despite strong laws', *Toronto Star*, 22 June 2003, and Bales, Kevin, *Disposable People: New Slavery in the Global Economy*, (University of California Press), 1999, and *New Slavery: A Reference Handbook*, (ABC-CLIO), 2004.

[21] On this issue see, Newbury, C. W., *The Western Slave Coast and its Rulers*, (Oxford University Press), 1961.

[22] Cit, Akinjogbin, I. A., *Dahomey and its Neighbours, 1708-1818,* (Cambridge University Press), 1967, p. 26. See also, Manning, Patrick, *Slavery, Colonisation and Economic Growth in Dahomey, 1640-1960*, (Cambridge University Press), 1982, pp. 22-56, for the slave economy.

As well as those who suffered, there were many Africans who benefited and control of the slave supply remained firmly in the hands of African brokers and merchants. European slavers waited at coastal ports to pick up their cargoes that were captured in the hinterland by African dealers and tribal leaders. Richardson notes the terms of trade, the amount of goods given for each slave bought moved heavily in favour of African traders from 1750 onwards. This meant that native commercial and political élite s within West and Central Africa made large and growing profits from slavery increasing both their wealth and political power.[23] The states involved in the slave trade sought to keep it within strict limits and the local societies and states largely succeeded by pursuing ambiguous policies of collaboration, suspicion and control.

Resistance to capture and deportation was an integral part of the Africans' actions, but their strategies against the slave trade did not necessarily translate into acts of resistance. In some states, the trade was manipulated for the protection of oneself or one's group. The exchange of two captives for the freedom of one or the sale of people to acquire weapons were strategies intended to protect specific individuals, groups and states from the slave trade. These strategies appeared to be accommodation rather than resistance but need to be seen in a broader context. Strategic accommodation did not mean that people who had redeemed a relative by giving two slaves in exchange were not at some other point also involved in burning down a factory or that the guns acquired through the sale of captives were not turned directly against the trade.[24]

Violence was an intrinsic though not exclusive part of these strategies, whether on the part of the direct victims or of the larger population. Western slavers were cautious when taking people by force out of Africa. Wherever possible, as in Saint-Louis and Gorée in Senegal, St. James in Gambia and Bance in Sierra Leone, slave factories were located on islands to reduce the threat of escapes and to make attacks difficult. This did not prevent several conspiracies and revolts by captives erupting on Gorée Island[25] and resulted in the death of a Governor and several soldiers. In addition, the crews of several slave ships were killed in the Gambia River and some free people attacked slave ships and burned down factories. Men and women revolted in the barracks or barracoons where they were temporarily confined or aboard the ships that transported them to the Americas, whilst others jumped overboard or starved themselves to death.[26] Alexander Falconbridge recounted resistance by slaves in Gambia in the 1780s:

[23] See, Richardson, David, 'The British Empire and the Atlantic Slave Trade 1660-1807', in *OHBE,* Vol. 2, pp. 462-464.

[24] See, for instance, Diouf, S. A., 'The Last Resort: Redeeming Family and Friends', and Hawthorne, Walter, 'Strategies of the Decentralized: Defending Communities from Slave Raiders in Coastal Guinea-Bissau, 1450-1815', in Diouf, S. A., (ed.), *Fighting the Slave Trade: West African* Strategies, (Ohio University Press), 2005, pp. 81-10, 152-169.

[25] Adanson, M., *A Voyage to Senegal, The Isle of Goree, and the River Gambia*, (J. Nourse), 1759, Wilson, Patricia, and Gamble, David, (eds.), *John Hill's Account of Life on Goree Island, 1807-1808*, (D. P. Gamble), 2005.

[26] Piersen, W. D., 'White Cannibals, Black Martyrs: Fear, Depression and Religious Faith as Causes of Suicide among New Slaves'. *Journal of Negro History*, Vol. 62, (2), (1977), pp. 147-159, explores the native fear that they were going to be eaten by whites.

for instance, fifteen slaves threw themselves overboard into the Bonny River (despite netting rigged to prevent this) and were eaten by sharks; a negro woman starved herself to death; and a young negro girl sent back to shore because she was ill, hanged herself when later told she was returning to the ship.[27] Details of damage to vessels insured by Lloyds of London from its foundation in 1689 throw light on resistance to the slave trade in African coastal societies. For instance, *Lloyd's Lists* for 5 January 1749 noted:

> The Scipio, Stewart, Of Leverpool for America, was blown up on the Coast [of Africa], occasion'd by an Insurrection of the Negroes.

Ten years later, the captain and crew of the *Snow Perfect* were killed and the vessel lost while a sloop commanded by Captain Ingledieu was attacked in the Gambia River and he was so badly wounded that he blew the ship up to prevent it falling into native hands. The *Lists* show that in more than 17 per cent of cases, damage was caused by local rebellion or plundering in Africa.[28]

The slaves who resisted were often assisted by the coastal population. There were two separate interests at work: the interest of states that had allowed their peoples to become incorporated in the slavery system and the interest of free peoples who were under constant threat of enslavement and were moved to act in solidarity with those already reduced to slavery. Violence was particularly evident in Senegambia and Kongo throughout the late-seventeenth and eighteenth centuries, when resistance to slavery became an important feature of African reformist movements. In Senegambia at the end of the seventeenth century, there was an economic shift towards transatlantic trade that led to a decline in trans-Saharan trade and to the emergence of the Islamic Toubenan movement amongst the Berber tribes.[29] Its founder, the Mauritanian cleric Nasir al-Din,[30] proclaimed:

> God does not permit kings to pillage, kill or enslave their peoples. He appointed them, on the contrary, to preserve their subjects and protect them from their enemies. Peoples were not made for kings, but kings for peoples.

It was a puritan, jihadist and reformist movement that opposed the slave trade and denounced the tyranny of Arab rulers who played an active role in the

---

27 Falconbridge, Alexander, *An Account of the Slave Trade on the Coast of Africa*, (J. Phillips), 1788, pp. 30-32.

28 Rathbone, Richard, 'Some thoughts on resistance to enslavement in west Africa', *Slavery and Abolition*, Vol. 6, (1985), pp. 173-184; McGowan, Winston, 'African resistance to the Atlantic Slave trade in west Africa', *Slavery and Abolition*, Vol. 11, (1990), pp. 1-29.

29 Ibid, Barry, Boubacar, *Senegambia and the Atlantic Slave Trade*, pp. 50-54. See also, Glover, John, *Sufism and Jihad in modern Senegal The Murid Order*, (University of Rochester Press), 2007, pp. 38-39, and Ogot, Bethwell A., (ed.), *Africa from the Sixteenth to the Eighteenth Century*, (UNESCO), 1992, pp. 273-278.

30 Diouf, Sylviane A., *Servants of Allah. African Muslims enslaved in the Americas*, (New York University Press), 2013, pp. 39-43. Fage, J. D, Gray, Richard, Oliver, Roland, (eds.), *The Cambridge History of Africa, Volume 4*, (Cambridge University Press), 2003, pp. 199-203.

capture and collection of slaves. The result was a populist reaction to the arbitrary rule of ruling élites in selling their own subjects to buy European commodities and it quickly proved successful in replacing traditional governments with religious leaders. However, after the death of Nasir al-Din in 1674, the movement rapidly declined and was finally defeated in 1677 by a coalition of Muslim dissenters, French traders and local Arab aristocracies. French assistance from Saint-Louis proved central to the demise of the movement and the reestablishment of traditional aristocracies while reprisals against Muslims swelled the slave trade and the profits of French slavers.

Further south, the Kongo peoples invoked Christianity in the same way, both against Portuguese missionaries, who were compromised both by their involvement in the slave trade and intrusion into the internal political affairs of the kingdom and against fractious local powers. In the early-eighteenth century Kimpa Vita, also known as Doña Beatrice, a prophetess in her twenties, turned the slave traders' racist arguments on their head by preaching that 'there are no Blacks or Whites in heaven' and that 'Jesus Christ and other saints are black and come from the Congo'.[31] She created a movement that appealed both to the élite who wanted a return to centralised government and to the people who wanted security and a reduction in the Portuguese slave trade. Though Kimpa Vita failed and was executed for heresy in 1706, her attempts to re-establish élite control over Kongo illustrated native resistance to the increased labour imposed by the introduction of new European crops and attempts by the ruling élite to exact increasingly large numbers of slaves from their communities.

The idea that the slave trade would have stopped if a continental armed movement had been launched persists in contemporary popular culture but Africans did not constitute one population and had divergent interests. Nowhere in the Africans' testimonies is there any indication that they felt betrayed by people 'the colour of their own skin'. They recognised ethnic, political and religious differences but not the modern concepts of a black race or 'Africanness'.[32] African resistance did not stop the slave trade but reduced its effectiveness. Slave traders had to go further inland to look for captives, spend time locating them and raiders suffered more casualties. It also took longer to transport captives to the coast, with greater risks for escape, injury and death and there were additional costs in securing barracoons and slave ships. Resistance held down the numbers entering the trade by raising the costs of carrying on the business.

Resistance shipboard

The horrors of the 'middle passage' were well-known to people by the early-eighteenth century and their telling and re-telling formed an emotive focus for

---

[31] Thornton, John, *The Kongolese Saint Anthony: Dona Beatriz Kimpa Vita and the Antonian Movement, 1684–1706,* (Cambridge University Press), 1998. See also, Hastings, Adrian, *The Church in Adrica, 1450-1950,* (Oxford University Press), 1996, pp. 102-106.

[32] Falola, Toyin, *Nationalism and African Intellectuals*, (University Rochester Press), 2001, and *The Power of African Cultures*, (University Rochester Press), 2008, explore Pan-Africanism.

abolitionists in Britain.[33] Captives were packed into the lower decks 'like books on a shelf', according to a contemporary observer. The overcrowded ships were insanitary and disease was a constant threat for slaves and crew alike.[34] The prevailing assumptions that rebellions on board slave ships were minor, rare, insignificant and occurred only occasionally and had little effect on the abolition of the slave trade was certainly not the view of contemporaries.[35] Alexander Falconbridge, a prominent abolitionist who had once worked as a surgeon aboard slave ships, wrote that slaves:

> ...were always ready to seize every opportunity for committing some act of desperation to free themselves from their miserable state.[36]

Contemporaries did not need to be reminded of the ever-present risk of revolt. John Newton, slave captain turned abolitionist hymn-writer, made this clear:

> One unguarded hour, one minute, is sufficient to give the slaves the opportunity they are always waiting for. An attempt to rise upon the ship's company brings an instantaneous and horrid war: for when they are once in motion they are desperate; and where they do not conquer they are seldom quelled without much mischief and bloodshed on both sides.[37]

Embarkation was regarded by many captains of slave ships as the most dangerous since captives might resist their forced removal from their homeland by refusing to board the canoes and boats that carried them from shore to ship and the most defiant were severely beaten. The early stage of the voyage to the Americas could also be perilous especially if the captives were all from the same tribe. For instance, in 1701, the *Don Carlos* of London left the Congo River with slaves for Jamaica but after a few miles sailing slaves managed to get free, killed one crew member and wounded five others. Twenty-eight slaves were either killed or jumped overboard and drowned before order was restored. There were also occasions when slaves successfully took over ships. In 1729, there was a mutiny on the *Clare* bound for South Carolina when the slaves took control of the ship's firearms and after beaching the ship escaped.[38] On 26 July

---

[33] Ibid, Klein, Herbert S., *The Atlantic Slave Trade*, pp. 132-161, provides a succinct and lucid account of different aspects of the middle passage. See also, Rediker, Marcus, *The Slave Ship: A Human History*, (Viking), 2007, and Christopher, Emma, *Slave Ship Sailors and their Captive Cargo, 1730-1807*, (Cambridge University Press), 2006.

[34] Newton, John, *Thoughts Upon the African Slave Trade*, (Printed for J. Buckland, in Pater-Noster Row; and J. Johnson, in St. Paul's Church-yard), 1788, p. 19.

[35] See, Snelgrave, William, *A New Account of Some Parts of Guinea and the Slave Trade*, (J. J. and P. Knapton), 1734, pp. 162-191, who considers the four slave mutinies that occurred to the vessels in which he was attached. Three were suppressed by the ships' crews and in the fourth the captain was killed along with 80 of the enslaved men and women.

[36] Ibid, Falconbridge, Alexander, *An Account of the Slave Trade on the Coast of Africa*, p. 30.

[37] Ibid, Newton, John, *Thoughts Upon the African Slave Trade*, pp. 15-16.

[38] *Boston News Letter*, 25 September 1729.

1753, the consortium of Liverpool merchants who owned the Gambia-bound ship commanded by Samuel Sacheverall warned him to 'keep a watchful Eye over you[r] Slaves to prevent any insurrections, which has too often been the Case'.[39] This was a well-known and frequently issued instruction from anxious slaving companies to their captains departing for the west coast of Africa. For European merchants, rebellion was a threat to their investments and profits, but for Africans it was perhaps their last chance to regain their freedom, families and homelands.

The Transatlantic Slave Trade Database suggests that nearly 10 per cent of voyages had some form of organised, collective resistance on board these slave ships. Given the stakes involved, the prevalence of rebellions and uprisings by large numbers of enslaved Africans, together with their brutal suppression by mainly European crewmen, was not surprising. Between 1509 and 1865, at least 493 shipboard uprisings took place during transatlantic crossings, almost certainly an under-estimate Taylor suggests since much slave resistance went unrecorded.[40] Ship owners, underwriters and company executives looked unfavourably on ships' captains who could not control their cargoes and consequently did not mention minor revolts where no or few lives were lost or no major damage done to their ships to ensure that they would be rehired for subsequent voyages. It is estimated that about one-third of all crew on board slave ships were there to help manage and control the enslaved in one way or another, driving up costs and making the operation less attractive to potential European slave traders. Richardson concludes that rebelliousness by slaves on ships and the threat of insurrection and the resulting attempts by slave traders to curb such behaviour appear to have significantly reduced the shipment of slaves.[41]

Once a month, on average, a European ship carrying enslaved Africans was violently, aggressively and sometimes successfully taken by the enslaved. Although three out of every four rebellions took place within sight of the coast of Africa, these insurrections affected slave traders and, perhaps most importantly, their profits at every stage: at anchor, along the African coast, during the middle passage and off the coast of the Americas. Most revolts were crushed quickly, but others raged on for hours, days or even weeks. However, despite the overwhelming odds stacked against them, 120 out of the nearly 500 insurrections

---

[39] Cit, Richardson, David, 'Shipboard Revolts, African Authority and the Transatlantic Slave Trade', *William and Mary Quarterly*, Vol. 58, (1), (2001), pp. 69-92, reprinted in ibid, Diouf, S. A., (ed.), *Fighting the Slave Trade: West African Strategies*, pp. 199-218, at p. 205.

[40] Taylor, Eric Robert, *If We Must Die: Shipboard Insurrections in the Era of the Atlantic Slave Trade*, (Louisiana State University Press), 2006, pp. 179-213. See also, Uya, Okon E., 'Slave Revolts of the Middle Passage: A Neglected Theme', *Calabar Historical Journal* 1, (1976), pp. 65-88, and Sheridan, Richard, 'Resistance and rebellion of African captives in the transatlantic slave trade before becoming seasoned labourers in the British Caribbean, 1690-1807', in Shepherd, Verene, (ed.), *Working Slavery, Pricing Freedom: Perspectives from the Caribbean, Africa and the African Diaspora*, (Palgrave Macmillan), 2002, pp. 181-205. Anderson, Clare, Frykman, Niklas, Voss, Lex Heerma van, and Rediker, Marcus, (eds.), *Mutiny and Maritime Radicalism in the Age of Revolution: A Global Survey*, (Cambridge University Press), 2013, is a valuable study.

[41] Ibid, Richardson, David, 'Shipboard Revolts, African Authority and the Transatlantic Slave Trade', p. 217.

Taylor examined led to the freedom of at least one of the Africans aboard these ships.[42] Assaults, attacks and attempted takeovers frequently occurred at night or during scheduled routines such as meals when shipboard defence was at its weakest, were waged with whatever objects and implements could be procured. Women and children sometimes played pivotal roles because of their privileged positions or unusual mobility on board.[43]

Taylor suggests that the wider history of resistance by members of the African diaspora in the Americas derives from formative experiences in rebelling against the shipboard conditions of their own or their ancestors' enslavement. Despite the limitations of this argument, it does point to ways in which stories of rebellion stretching beyond the plantation might be incorporated into the history of resistance. Africans from whatever region did not succumb to a life of enslavement with indifference or submit to the financial imperatives of plantation-driven economics without struggle. 'Revolt', as Taylor points out, 'is the assertion of humanity, and humanity is the antithesis of slavery'.[44]

American colonies

The slave systems of the Caribbean and Latin America were well established by 1680 but in North America, where there were less than 7,000 slaves, it had still to develop. Although the first Africans were brought to Jamestown in 1619, the large-scale introduction of black slaves in the American colonies occurred later in the century because of initial reliance placed by settlers on white indentured labour.[45] The eighteenth century saw increased reliance on slave plantations and by 1790, the number of slaves approached 700,000.[46]

Slavery in the American colonies

---

[42] Ibid, Taylor, Eric Robert, *If We Must Die: Shipboard Insurrections in the Era of the Atlantic Slave Trade*, pp. 119-138

[43] Ibid, Taylor, Eric Robert, *If We Must Die: Shipboard Insurrections in the Era of the Atlantic Slave Trade*, pp. 41-66, 85-118.

[44] Ibid, Taylor, Eric Robert, *If We Must Die: Shipboard Insurrections in the Era of the Atlantic Slave Trade*, p. 176.

[45] On this issue see, Galenson, David W., 'The Rise and Fall of Indentured Servitude in the Americas: An Economic Analysis', *Journal of Economic History*, Vol. 44, (1984), pp. 1-26.

[46] Ibid, Bush, M. L., *Servitude in Modern Times*, pp. 105-116, Littlefield, Daniel C., 'Colonial and Revolutionary United States', in Paquette, Robert L, and Smith, Mark M., (eds.), *The Oxford Handbook of Slavery in the Americas*, (Oxford University Press), 2010, pp. 201-226, and Walsh, Lorena S., 'Slavery in the North American Mainland Colonies', in ibid, Eltis, David, and Engerman, Stanley L., (eds.), *The Cambridge World History of Slavery*, Vol. 3, pp. 407-430, provide succinct accounts of slavery in North America. See also, Kolchin, Peter, *American Slavery, 1619-1877*, (Penguin), 1995, pp. 3-62, Berlin, Ira, *Many Thousands Gone: The First Two Centuries of Slavery in North America*, (Harvard University Press), 1998, Wood, Betty, *Slavery in Colonial America, 1619-1776*, (Rowman & Littlefield), 2005, Morgan, Kenneth, *Slavery and Servitude in North America, 1607-1800*, (Edinburgh University Press), 2000, and Reiss, Oscar, *Blacks in Colonial America*, (McFarland), 2006. Gallay, Alan, (ed.), *Indian Slavery in Colonial America*, (University of Nebraska Press), 2009, a seminal collection of essays.

There were important differences between the American colonies and those in the Caribbean.[47] Sugar played a limited role in the development of the slave system in North America and only in the French colony of Louisiana and in Spanish-controlled Texas were sugar and slaves linked. Initially, it was tobacco production that resulted in the development of the slave system at the end of the seventeenth century in the Chesapeake colonies of Virginia, Maryland and North Carolina.[48] In the early- to mid-eighteenth century, it was extended to rice production in the low country of South Carolina and Georgia.[49] Although cotton production began when the colonies were under British rule, it was not until the 1790s that the slave system moved from the eastern seaboard to cover much of the South. Tobacco, rice and cotton made less exacting demands on field labour than sugar and slaves were not subject to the tropical diseases prevalent in the Caribbean and Latin America. Slaves in North America received rations unlike their Caribbean counterparts who had to grow their own food in their spare time to supplement the often-meagre rations they were given. The result was relatively low mortality levels. The massive growth of the slave population in the American colonies from the early-eighteenth century was based on the fertility of slaves rather than their importation. By 1700, the slave population was self-reproducing as surviving births equalled deaths. By 1730, growth occurred in the tobacco areas and by 1770, this had extended to the rice-producing colonies. As a result, North American slavery relied less on the African slave trade and once that trade was ended in 1808, the new American republic could easily expand its slave population that reached 4 million by the late 1850s.[50]

By 1750, only one in three black adults were African-born.[51] There were, however, differences between colonies. In 1700, the slave populations of the Chesapeake and the low country of South Carolina were equally divided between African- and American-born but by 1750 on the Chesapeake the African-born had fallen to 21 per cent and 9 per cent by 1770 whereas in South Carolina it still comprised 42 per cent in 1750 and 35 per cent by 1770. One important consequence of a self-reproducing slave population was the increased likelihood of sale where planters had a surplus population. This led to the development of

---

[47] Galenson, David W., 'The Settlement and Growth of the Colonies: Population, Labor, and Economic Development', in Engerman, Stanley L., and Gallman, Robert E., (eds.), *The Cambridge Economic History of the United States*, 3 Vols. (Cambridge University Press), 1996, *Volume 1: The Colonial Era*, pp. 135-208, provides the context. See also the papers in, Canny, Nicholas, and Morgan Philip, (eds.), *The Oxford Handbook of The Atlantic World 1450-1850*, (Oxford University Press), 2011.

[48] Ibid, Berlin, Ira, *Many Thousands Gone*, pp. 109-141, ibid, Engerman, Stanley L., and Gallman, Robert E., (eds.), *The Cambridge Economic History of the United States*, pp. 209-248, and Horn, James, 'Tobacco Colonies: The Shaping of English Society in the Seventeenth century Chesapeake', in *OHBE,* Vol. 1, pp. 170-192.

[49] Ibid, Berlin, Ira, *Many Thousands Gone*, pp. 142-176, and ibid, Engerman, Stanley L., and Gallman, Robert E., (eds.), *The Cambridge Economic History of the United States*, pp. 249-296.

[50] Holloway, Joseph, (ed.), *A History of Slave Resistance in the United States*, (New World African Press), 2016.

[51] McCusker, John J., & Menard, Russell, R., *The Economy of British America 1607-1789, With Supplementary Bibliography*, (University of North Carolina Press), 1985, pp. 211-245, examines colonial demographic growth.

an inter-colonial trade that, like the transatlantic slave trade, broke up families and uprooted slaves from their place of birth. The threat of being sold reinforced the control of planters over their slaves and was evident on the Chesapeake from the 1730s. In this region of small planters, there was an increase in slave sales occasioned by the need to maximise plantation profitability. In addition, the settlement of the inland areas of Virginia between 1730 and 1780 resulted in the movement of 60,000 slaves from the coastal plantations.

Unlike in the Caribbean where slaves threw off their bondage by running away and establishing Maroon settlements or by gaining manumission, slaves in the American colonies acquired few rights, either in law or custom, and their acquiescence is evidenced by the small-scale and infrequent nature of most slave rebellions.[52] There are several reasons for this relative compliance such as the significant size of the white settler population, the dispersal of slaves in small groupings under a resident master whose paternalism protected slaves against the excesses of a racist society and the presence of hostile Indian tribes ruling out the establishment of frontier Maroon settlements. These factors led to a broadly conformist attitude by most slaves, something that was strengthened by the fear of sale. It would, however, be misleading to suggest that slaves in the American colonies were totally dependent on their masters' instructions. There were acts of non-cooperation especially slow work, feigning sickness, misplacing goods and equipment and formally complaining to their masters when their rights were breached. Although legislation reserved trading activities for the free, generally poor whites operating as small producers and petty traders, slaves did trade in produce often grown in their small garden plots that was either sold to the master and his family or bartered with other slaves. This allowed slaves to accumulate cash that elsewhere in the Americas could have been used to buy their freedom but in the British colonies there was a policy of banning manumission.[53] Virginia, for instance, only allowed masters to free slaves in 1691 if they took responsibility for transporting them out of the colony and in 1723 masters lost the right to manumit slaves completely. This reflected the settlers' attitudes to free blacks in a society where enslavement was synonymous with colour and cultural values privileged free whites and where it was feared that freed blacks would lead attempts to overthrow the slave system.[54] Virginia criminalised interracial marriages in 1691 and subsequently abolished blacks' rights to vote, hold office or carry arms.[55]

It is important not to neglect, given the nineteenth century polarities between the free North and slave-owning South, the slave system in the northern

---

[52] Peabody, Sue, 'Slavery, Freedom and the Law in the Atlantic World', in ibid, Eltis, David, and Engerman, Stanley L., (eds.), *The Cambridge World History of Slavery*, Vol. 3, pp. 594-630.

[53] On the freedmen see above, Reiss, Oscar, *Blacks in Colonial America*, pp. 123-144.

[54] Competition between free blacks and poor white workers, especially Irish immigrants, led to growing tensions during the nineteenth century culminating in the 1863 Draft riots: see, Brown, Richard, *Famine, Fenians and Freedom 1830-1882*, pp. 274-276.

[55] Taylor, Alan, *American Colonies: The Settling of North America*, (Penguin), 2001, p. 136.

colonial colonies.[56] In 1700, there were 5,206 slaves in the North compared to 23,750 in the South. By 1770, this had increased to nearly 48,000 with 422,000 in the south. In the colony of New York in 1750, slaves accounted for 14 per cent of the total population and 7 per cent in New Jersey and 10 per cent in Rhode Island. Slaves were important where there was large-scale commercial farming and replaced white indentured labour as the work force. Their use was restricted by the small-scale nature of much farming where labour was provided largely by the farmer's family. In the absence of a widespread plantation system, slaves were employed in various roles such as domestic servants, artisans, small traders and porters. Slavery in the northern and southern colonies may have been different but, unlike slavery elsewhere in the Americas, they were both found in what was essentially a white society with blacks, rather than a black society with whites.[57] It is also important to recognise that the debate over the political rights of the North American colonies in the 1760s and 1770s and especially the anxieties and dislocation spurred by the American Revolution led to calls for antislavery and abolition gaining a moral legitimacy in Britain that previously had not been the case.[58]

Resistance in Virginia

The first Africans were brought to Jamestown in 1619. Labour was scarce and they were quickly employed on the same terms as English indentured servants: after seven years of labour, they were free.[59] Masters were buying labour, not people, although the distinction was lost on many. By 1625, there were said to be 23 Africans serving in Virginia; twenty-five years later, there were 300, some 2 per cent of the population. There was also a flourishing trade in Native American slaves especially in Virginia and South Carolina. The native tribes practised a form of slavery though recent research suggests that it was a system for assimilating outside individuals into groups rather than an issue of property or ownership.[60] American Indian slaves were familiar with the environment and proved easier for them to escape making them an unreliable source of forced labour. This and the increasing problem of obtaining white indentured labour,

---

[56] Ibid, Reiss, Oscar, *Blacks in Colonial America*, pp. 65-78.

[57] Ibid, Bush, M. L., *Servitude in Modern Times*, p. 115.

[58] Brown, Christopher Leslie, *Moral Capital: Foundations of British Abolitionism*, University of North Carolina Press), 2006, pp. 105-154, 209-258, Horne, Gerald, *The Counter-Revolution of 1776: Slave Resistance and the Origins of the United States of America*, (New York University Press), 2016.

[59] On indentured labour see, Ballagh, J. C., *White Servitude in the Colony of Virginia*, (John Hopkins Press), 1895, and McCormac, Eugene I., *White Servitude in Maryland, 1643-1820*, (John Hopkins Press), 1904.

[60] See the contrasting views of Gallay, Alan, *The Indian Slave Trade: The Rise of the English Empire in the American South 1670-1717*, (Yale University Press), 2002, and White, Richard, *The Middle Ground: Indians, Empires, and Republics in the Great Lakes Region*, (Cambridge University Press), 1991. See also, Gallay, Alan, 'Indian Slavery', in ibid, Paquette, Robert L, and Smith, Mark M., (eds.), *The Oxford Handbook of Slavery in the Americas*, pp. 312-335, and Donald, Leland, 'Slavery in Indigenous North America', in ibid, Eltis, David, and Engerman, Stanley L., (eds.), *The Cambridge World History of Slavery*, Vol. 3, pp. 217-247.

help to explain why black slaves were increasingly seen as the solution to labour shortages. Slaves were more expensive than indentured labour and initially only wealthy planters had the necessary capital to invest. They began to buy slaves in preference to indentured servants in the 1660s and 1670s and poorer planters adopted this practice after 1700. The Caribbean colonies were a more profitable destination for slave traders and, until the early eighteenth century, it proved difficult and expensive for American colonists to acquire African slaves.[61] As early as 1662, the Virginia House of Burgesses passed legislation which stated that any child born in the colony would follow the status of its mother, bond or free. This overturned the principle in English Common Law that a child's status followed that of the father and enabled white men to abdicate any responsibility to acknowledge, support or emancipate the mixed-race offspring of slave women.

Owners made no secret of the fact that one of the most common reasons why slaves took flight was to be reunited with loved ones from whom they had been forcibly separated. Running away was a major form of rebellion and proved very expensive for slave-owners with the cost of newspaper advertisements, bribing slave informers and the cost of slave catchers.[62] In 89 per cent of cases, the runaway was male and usually between 20 and 35 and seldom more than 50 years of age. Artisans, river workers and African-born slaves were more likely to abscond than field-hands and house servants. In 70 per cent of cases, two slaves were involved but any larger group ran an increased risk of betrayal, detection and capture. Running away was normally a carefully planned decision involving the hiding of money, food and clothing until the opportune moment usually during the spring planting season or during harvesting.[63] Between 1650 and 1700, black slaves sometimes left with white indentured workers reflecting their common interest to act against their masters. Slightly under half were recaptured or killed (though some committed suicide) but among African-born slaves recapture occurred in three-quarters of cases. The process was aided by the introduction of slave patrols in Virginia in response to crises such as slave rebellions but which had a broader role in the daily enforcement of slave laws.[64] Some slaves, especially those recently enslaved may have hoped to return to Africa. In 1774, for instance, a group of African-born slaves made their way down the Savannah River heading for the open sea in a canoe and their owner was convinced they were trying to get back to Africa. There is no record of what happened to them. Other slaves went to ports hoping to persuade a ship's captain that they were free and experienced crew or they went to towns hoping to

---

[61] Morgan, Edmund S., *American Slavery, American Freedom: The Ordeal of Colonial Virginia*, (Norton), 1995, pp. 295-315, examines the shift towards slave labour following Bacon's rebellion. See also, Oast, Jennifer, *Institutional Slavery. Slaveholding Churches, Schools and Business in Virginia, 1680-1860*, (Cambridge University Press), 2016.

[62] Bly, Antonio T., and Haygood, Tamia, *Escaping Servitude. A Documentary History of Runaway Servants in Eighteenth-Century Virginia*, (Lexington Books), 2015.

[63] Windley, Lathan A., *A Profile of Runaway Slaves in Virginia and South Carolina from 1730 through 1787*, (Garland Publishing), 1995, pp. 157-182, provides detailed data on different features of slave runaways.

[64] Hadden, Sally E., *Slave Patrols: Law and Violence in Virginia and the Carolinas*, (Harvard University Press), 2001, pp. 6-40, examines the colonial origins of this race police.

blend into the urban black population. Some simply disappeared into the American wilderness, sometimes living with Native Americans. On occasions, runaways could join a group of Maroons who often inhabited the barely penetrable swamplands.[65] These Maroon communities were generally located in the southern colonies where escapees hid in caves and forests as well as swamps. Few of these communities were long-lasting though the largest, in the Dismal Swamp between Virginia and North Carolina, contained up to 2,000 escaped slaves who often raided neighbouring plantations for food. Such was the threat from the Maroons that Virginia offered rewards for hunting and killing these outlaws as early as 1672 and in the late-seventeenth and eighteenth centuries, colonial militia and, in the case of the larger communities, regular troops were deployed to destroy them.[66]

Criminal activity by slaves, generally regarded as resistance to authority, was viewed by the law as either minor or major.[67] Minor offences included pilfering and striking a white person were generally dealt with by slave owners without legal intervention by whipping though a second case of striking a white person could result in execution. More serious offences such as murder, arson, attempted or actual poisoning, burglary, rape or attempted rape of a white women or stealing cattle as well as rebellion were regarded as capital offences but in many cases the sentence was not carried out because the slave was too valuable. Execution was usually by hanging but burning at the stake was used for particularly heinous crimes.

The fear of slave uprisings was a persistent feature and frequently the fantasy of fearful settlers in colonial Virginia.[68] Indentured workers, landless whites and blacks had fought together during Bacon's rebellion in Virginia in 1676 and the possibility that this might occur again, but on a larger scale, was never completely absent from the minds of plantation owners. Rumours and reports fed the anxieties of a slaveholding society, some of them founded in fact. But there was no organised slave uprising in Virginia until well into the nineteenth century. All the plots were uncovered or betrayed before they could be carried out. There were various reasons for this. Until the early-eighteenth century, there were too few slaves in Virginia to form the critical mass necessary for successful rebellion. Illiteracy and the lack of a common language among Africans scattered across unfamiliar territory hindered communication as did the dispersed nature of plantations.

By the 1660s, the status of African servants had hardened into permanent servitude based on skin colour. Now that there were slaves in Virginia and

---

[65] The term 'Maroon' derived from the Spanish *cimarrones* meaning outlaws or runaways.

[66] Taylor, Alan, *The Internal Enemy: Slavery and War in Virginia, 1772-1832*, (W. W. Norton & Company), 2013.

[67] See, for instance, Schwarz, Philip J., *Twice Condemned: Slaves and the Criminal Laws of Virginia, 1705-1865*, (Louisiana State University Press), 1998, pp. 66-136, for discussion of the nature of slave crime. See also the essays in his *Slave Laws in Virginia*, (University of Georgia Press), 2010.

[68] Parent, Anthony S., *Foul Means: The Formation of a Slave Society in Virginia, 1660-1740*, (University of North Carolina Press), 2003, pp. 135-172, examines black resistance between 1676 and 1740. See also, Mullin, Gerald W., *Flight and Rebellion: Slave Resistance in Eighteenth-Century Virginia*, (Oxford University Press), 1972.

labour-starved tobacco planters wanted more. The plot exposed during this decade was a conspiracy largely of indentured servants in Gloucester County who planned 'to destroy their masters and afterwards to set up for themselves.' According to colonist Robert Beverley, the uprising was led by nine mutinous and rebellious followers of Oliver Cromwell, 'soldiers that were sent thither as servants' when King Charles II was restored to the throne in 1660.[69] It was well-planned and the rebels resolved to depose Governor Berkley in 6 September 1663. As frequently happened, the plot was betrayed by an informant, an indentured servant named Birkenhead, who received a reward of 5,000 pounds of tobacco and his freedom. The conspirators were arrested on 14 September and four leaders were hanged and their bloody heads were spiked as a gruesome warning to others. Charles II was sufficiently concerned by the plot to order the building of a fort at Jamestown but the planters felt that they had dealt with the threat and erected only a battery of a few cannon about the town.[70] By 1670, however, the Council of State had received several petitions concerning the rowdiness of transported felons and, recalling the Gloucester plot, banned the import of further convicts from England.[71]

By 1680, about 3,000 slaves worked alongside 15,000 white indentured servants, about 4 per cent of the population.[72] During this decade, Virginia's first significant slave conspiracies were discovered. When authorities learned that plotting occurred during gatherings for slave funerals, they prohibited slave funerals in 1680 and this was followed by the prohibition of black assemblies seven years later. A widespread conspiracy, which included white indentured servants, in the Northern Neck was crushed in 1687.[73] The following year, the Northern Neck was the site of another attempted uprising. Slaves were rounded up, questioned and punished. Frank, a black slave, was imprisoned in Warwick County for his role in organising slaves in Charles City and New Kent Counties but no further action was taken against him. The focus of attention for the authorities was 'Sam, a Negro Servt to Richard Metcalfe', who was clearly used as an appropriate scapegoat. A repeat offender, he had 'several times endeavoured to promote a Negro Insurrection in this Colony.'[74]

---

[69] Beverley, Robert, *The History and Present State of Virginia*, (B. & S. Tooke), 1705, pp. 55-56. See also, 'Virginia Colonial Records: The Servants' Plot of 1663', *Virginia Magazine of History of Biography*, Vol. 15, (1907-1908), pp. 38-43.

[70] Governor Berkeley to Lord Arlington, 13 July 1666, *Calendar of State Papers, Colonial Papers,* Vol. 5, p. 396, responds to king's command to build a fort by asking for a frigate to defend the harbour.

[71] Ibid, Beverley, Robert, *The History and Present State of Virginia*, pp. 69-70. See also, *Calendar of State Papers, Colonial Papers,* Vol. 7, pp. 64, 175, 178.

[72] Parent, Anthony S., *Foul Means. The Formation of a Slave Society in Virginia, 1660-1740*, (University of North Carolina Press), 2003, especially 105-194, and Goetz, Rebecca Anne, *The Baptism of Early Virginia. How Christianity Created* Race, (John Hopkins University Press), 2012, examine the institutional framework for slavery.

[73] Minutes of the Council of Virginia, 24 October 1687, *Calendar of State Papers, Colonial Papers,* Vol. 12, p. 456.

[74] Cit, 'Punishment for a Negro Rebel', *William and Mary College Quarterly Historical Magazine*, Vol.10, (1901-1902), pp. 177-178.

To deter him & others from the like evil practice for time to come, the court ordered the sheriff of James City County to whip him severely, and return him to the Westmoreland County sheriff to be whipped again. Sam would forever wear 'a strong Iron collar affixed about his neck with four spri[n]ggs.' Should he leave his master's plantation or remove the collar, he would be hanged.[75]

Although the authorities had laid down regulations to stop blacks gathering together, it had considerable difficulty enforcing it. Poorer planters had no interest in policing slaves and slave-owners did not have the resources to police slave movements during on Saturday evening and Sunday when custom allowed slaves a holiday. In 1688 and 1693, the elected burgesses, under pressure from their constituents who were concerned by blacks massing in the countryside, called for further restrictions on black assemblies. To enforce this, they proposed a poll tax on each of the enslaved paid by the wealthier planters. The nominated Council, representing the interests of the planter class, opposed the tax arguing that existing laws were sufficient to deal with the issue. Governor Sir Edmund Andros agreed with the Council about enforcing existing laws but in 1694, he made it clear that planters had been lax in their application of the law and that failure to enforce legislation, especially the acts of 1680 and 1682 for preventing rebellion, would ultimately have serious consequences.[76]

During the early years of the eighteenth century, slave conspiracies became more frequent and ambitious. In 1710, a plot involving enslaved Indians as well as black slaves and at least one free black spread through at least three counties, James City, Surrey and Isle of Wight. The conspiracy demonstrated the ability of the enslaved to organise across ethnic lines. Its aim was to escape, if necessary by force of arms and settle in the Dismal Swamp. A slave named Will, however, betrayed the plan to that authorities gaining his freedom and his owner Robert Ruffin was reimbursed for his value with £40 of public money. Of the four ringleaders, Scipio, Salvadore, Tom Shaw, and Peter, all but Peter were quickly jailed. Scipio and Salvadore were tried by the General Court for high treason, convicted, and in June 1710 were hung, drawn and quartered and their remains displayed across the colony. Peter escaped and remained at large for at least a year since a reward of £10 for his capture alive; £5 if dead was still being offered in 1711. Edmund Jenings, President of the Council, wrote in his report to the Board of Trade:

---

[75] Ibid, Beverley, Robert, *The History and Present State of Virginia*, pp. 75-75. See also, http://www.history.org/Foundation/journal/Winter05-06/conspiracy.cfm, Theobald, Mary Miley, 'Slave Conspiracies in Colonial Virginia', *Colonial Williamsburg Journal*, (2005-2006).

[76] *Calendar of State Papers, Colonial Papers,* Vol. 14, p. 132, expressed Andros' concern about the 'indifferent' nature of the militia. For Andros in Virginia see Lustig, Mary Lou, *The Imperial Executive in America: Sir Edmund Andros, 1637-1714*, (Associated University Presses), 2002, pp. 227-265.

I hope their fate will strike such terror in the other negroes as will keep them from forming such designs for the future, without being obliged to make an example of any more of them.[77]

When Hugh Drysdale arrived in Williamsburg in 1722 to begin his term as Virginia's Lieutenant-Governor, he found the jail full of mutinous slaves awaiting trial. Three of the leaders were convicted of 'Conspiring among themselves and with the said other Slaves to kill murder & destroy very many' of His Majesty's subjects and sentenced to be sold out of the colony. Drysdale made clear that their design:

...was to cutt off their masters, and possess themselves of the country; but as this would have been as impracticable in the attempt as it was foolish in the contrivance, I can foresee no other consequence of this conspiracy than the stirring up the next Assembly to make more severe laws for keeping their slaves in greater subjection etc.[78]

After the 1722 conspiracy, a second, perhaps related to Middlesex and Gloucester counties, occurred. It involved free blacks as well as slaves and mulattos. There was insufficient evidence to convict the free blacks. Seven slaves were sentenced to be sold and transported out of the colony, a decision explained by the high cost to the public purse of reimbursing masters for executed slaves. Drysdale told the General Assembly that the laws were:

...very deficient in the due punishing any intended Insurrection of your Slaves, you have had a Late Experience of the Lameness of them; I am persuaded you are too well acquainted with the Cruel dispositions of those Creatures, when they have it in their power to destroy or distress, to let Slipp this faire opportunity of making more proper Laws against them.[79]

Every slave rebellion or rumour of plotting resulted in legislation increasing the severity of punishment, curtailing slaves' movements and restricting their ability to assemble, attend funerals or religious services or possess weapons. The legislature agreed and in 1723 passed additional regulations, including several aimed squarely at free blacks. Their right to vote was expressly denied, as was their ability to possess firearms. Conspiracy by six or more slaves was also made a capital offence, something easier to prove than the charge of high treason previously used.

By 1730, American Indian slavery had largely ended and the number of white indentured servants was dwindling, but black slaves had risen to about a quarter of Virginia's population. Many of these came from Kongo and a significant number of the captives were already Christians before they arrived in the colony. White Virginians' anxiety increased proportionately. In the autumn

---

[77] Jenings to Lords of Trade, 10 June 1710, *Calendar of State Papers, Colonial Papers,* Vol. 25, pp. 82-83.
[78] Drysdale to Board of Trade, 20 December 1722, *Calendar of State Papers, Colonial Papers,* Vol. 33, p. 392.
[79] Drysdale's speech to the General Assembly, 10 May 1723, printed in *The Virginia Historical Register and Literary Note Book*, Vol. 4, (2), (1851), pp.61-64, at p. 63.

of 1730, Governor William Gooch reported to the Board of Trade that another slave uprising had been scotched.[80] The spark was a false rumour that 'His Majesty had sent Orders for setting of them free as soon as they were Christians, and that these Orders were Suppressed.' Gooch tried to learn the source of this falsehood and called out the militia to take up any slave found off his master's plantation. 'A great many' were made prisoner and were whipped for 'rambling Abroad' and by this method Gooch hoped 'to Convince them that their best way is to rest contented with their Condition.' Despite this, the rebellion threatened in September occurred six weeks later. In Philadelphia, the *Pennsylvania Gazette* reported that the insurrection was:

> Occasioned by a Report at Col. Spottswood's Arrival, that he had Direction from his Majesty to free all baptiz'd Negroes; many Masters and Mistresses having baptized their Slaves in Order to instruct them in the Christian Faith: The Negroes have improve'd this Notion to a great Height: It is said some of the Ringleaders are taken: Five Counties are in Arms pursuing others, with Order to kill them if they do not Submit.[81]

More than 300 rebels escaped to the Dismal Swamp but, with the aid of local Indians, the rebellion was quickly suppressed. Summary justice was meted out to 24 rebels who were hanged in the woods but the five ringleaders were tried and then executed. The insurrection had spread to as many as five other counties, Gooch informed the government in London, though the plot had not advanced as far as it had in Norfolk County.

> Negros, in the Countys of Norfolk & Princess Anne, had the boldness to Assemble on a Sunday while the People were at Church, and to Chuse from amongst themselves Officers to Comand them in their intended Insurrection, which was to have been put in Execution very soon after: But this Meeting being happily discovered and many of them taken up and examined, the whole Plot was detected.[82]

He ordered the militia to patrol two or three times a week to prevent night meetings and had every man bring his guns to church on Sundays so that they would not 'be Seized by the Slaves in their Absence, if the same mutinous Spirit should be Revived amongst them.' Gooch told the Bishop of London that some of the blame for slave unrest fell on cruel masters who 'use their Negroes no better than their Cattle.'[83]

---

[80] Lorenz, Stacy L., 'Policy and Patronage: Governor William Gooch and Anglo-Virginia Politics, 1727-1749', in Rhoden, Nancy Lee, (ed.), *English Atlantics Revisited: Essays honouring Professor Ian K. Steele*, (McGill-Queen's University Press), 2007, pp. 81-103, consider Gooch's tenure as governor though it does not deal with the slave rebellion in 1730.
[81] *Pennsylvania Gazette*, 28 October 1730.
[82] Gooch to the Council of Trade and Plantations, 12 February 1731, *Calendar of State Papers, Colonial Papers,* Vol. 38, pp. 41-42.
[83] Gooch to Bishop of London, 28 May 1731, Lambeth Palace Library, *Fulham Palace Papers*, Vol. 15, SR 650, cit, Morgan, Philip D., *Slave Counterpoint: Black Culture in Eighteenth-Century Chesapeake & Low Country*, (University of South Carolina Press), 1998, p. 263.

The Norfolk conspiracy led to further crackdowns on the slave population and stringent demands on Virginia's militia.[84] The militia was made up of farmers and planters, many of whom did not own slaves. Armed and mounted, the militia's job was to patrol the countryside in search of suspicious gatherings but proved time-consuming and 'has occasioned a good deal of Fatigue to the Militia, and some loss in their Crops, as happening at a time their Labour & Industry were much wanted in their Grounds.'[85] This expensive system of policing brought complaints from the poorer whites without slaves that they were unable to pay fines for failing to perform the required militia duty. They recognised that the system favoured the slave-owning minority who were compensated from public funds for slaves who were executed and who could buy their way out of participating in the patrols.

Between 1730 and 1830, Virginia's enslaved and free blacks whether under colonial rule or under the American republic continued to plot uprisings but like Gabriel Prosser's 1800 rebellion near Richmond and the 'Easter Plot' two years later, all were discovered or abandoned before they could be put into motion.[86] A century after the discovery of the Norfolk conspiracy, the worst fear of Virginia's whites was finally realised. In 1831, in Southampton County, Nat Turner led the first successful slave revolt even though it involved only about 70 slaves.[87] Inspired by the success of a Haitian revolution in 1790 that freed the island's slaves and threw off French rule, Turner aimed for no less. The immediate result was about sixty white farmers killed but Turner and the other slaves' ammunition ran out within a few days. They were caught although Turner evaded capture for more than two months. Eighteen slaves, including Nat Turner, were hanged for their part in the rebellion, and 100 to 200 African Americans were killed by militias and angry mobs in retaliation. As a direct result of the fear the rebellion inspired among slave owners and supporters of the institution of slavery, Southern states passed legislation prohibiting the movement, assembly and education of slaves and reduced the rights of free people of colour.[88]

Virginia's African American population had grown to nearly half a million or 40 per cent of the state's total population. No Africans had been brought to America legally since the end of the slave trade in 1808, so most of Virginia's slaves were 'country born' and communicated easily amongst themselves in English, were familiar with the countryside and with white customs and habits. The leaders of the most elaborate slave insurrections, men such as Gabriel

---

[84] On this issue see, Whisker, James B., *The American Colonial Militia: The colonial militia of the Southern States, 1606-1785,* (Edward Mellen Press), 1997, pp. 5-51, Shea, William, L., *The Virginia Militia in the Seventeenth Century*, (Louisiana State University Press), 1983, and Crozier, William A., *Virginia Colonial Militia, 1651-1776*, (Genealogical Publishing Co.), 1965.

[85] Gooch to Council of Trade and Plantations, 14 September 1730, *Calendar of State Papers, Colonial Papers,* Vol. 37, pp. 276-277.

[86] Egerton, Douglas R., *Gabriel's Rebellion: The Virginia Slave Conspiracies of 1800 and 1802*, (University of North Carolina Press), 1993.

[87] Greenberg, Kenneth S., (ed.), *Nat Turner: A Slave Rebellion in History and Memory*, (Oxford University Press), 2004.

[88] Aptheker, Herbert, *American Negro Slave Revolts*, (Columbia University Press), 1943, remains the classic account for the decades after 1791.

Prosser, Denmark Vesey and Nat Turner were also literate. They were preachers or possessed specific skills such as blacksmithing or carpentry that enabled them to move about with greater freedom than field hands. Ironically, the more valuable certain slaves became in terms of skills and abilities, the more adept they were in resisting slavery. They had acculturated and, having done so, had greater talent for coordinating rebellion.

During the period of colonial rule and after, slaves and indentured servants in Virginia from different ethnic groups were prepared, sometimes in co-operation, to contemplate and plan rebellions against slave-owning planters. It is difficult to estimate what the slaves hoped to achieve other than their freedom, increasingly under threat after the hardening of the legal position of blacks, whether free or enslaved, from the 1660s. Like rebellions elsewhere in the British Empire, they were invariably betrayed and rarely translated into action. The initial response of the authorities was swift and draconian with the execution of a few leaders and punishment, such as imprisonment or whipping, for the remainder. Longer-term, the consequence of rebellions was that black legal rights were further reduced and the security of the enslaved tightened. Despite the pervasive paranoia of slave-owning planters, it was the persistence of lower-level resistance, such as absconding, malingering and working slowly that were far more common and undoubtedly more effective than plotting rebellion. The relationship between masters and slaves was never entirely one of coercion but involved an element of negotiation, albeit an unequal one between free and unfree. Slaves and their masters in Virginia engaged in struggles marked by acceptance and resistance, coercion and consent. This was essential if planters were to protect their economic investment and preserve a modicum of stability. The example of Virginia illustrates that the institution of slavery and experience of the enslaved changed over time and that slavery was far from monolithic in character. The changing nature of resistance and the gradual decay in the legal status of slaves were part of that process.[89]

The Caribbean

Of all the plantation crops of the Atlantic slave trade, the most pernicious, profitable and popular was sugar. Seventy per cent of slaves on plantations in the Americas were involved in sugar production.[90] Sugar cane has always been unusually labour-intensive to grow, harvest and process, requiring lots of water and sun as it grows and to turn the sap into crystalline sugar. Sugar cane is 'inherently perishable' and:

> ...must be cut when it is ripe, and ground as soon as it is cut. These simple facts give a special character to any enterprise dedicated to the production of sugar. [91]

---

[89] Dunn, Richard S., *A Tale of Two Plantations. Slave Life and Labor in Jamaica and Virginia*, (Harvard University Press), 2014, A useful comparative study.

[90] Klein, Herbert D., and Vinson III, Ben, (eds.), *African Slavery in Latin America and the Caribbean*, 2nd ed., (Oxford University Press), 2007, provides a broad overview.

[91] Mintz, Sidney, *Sweetness and Power: The Place of Sugar in Modern History*, (Penguin), 1986, p. 47. See also, Abbott, Elizabeth, *Sugar: A Bittersweet Harvest*, (Overlook Press), 2010, Deerr, Noel, *The History of Sugar*, (Chapman & Hall), 1949-

After the cane was cut, the sap was immediately boiled and eventually crystallised. In 1700, Thomas Tryon described conditions in the infernal boiling houses in Barbados as 'perpetual noise and hurry' where slaves were forced to work throughout the six-month growing season:

> The Climate is so hot, and the labour so constant, that the Servants [slaves] night and day stand in great Boyling Houses, where there are six or seven large Coppers or Furnaces kept perpetually Boyling; and from which heavy Ladles and Scummers they Skim off the excrementious parts of the Canes, till it comes to its perfection and cleanness, while others as Stoakers, Broil as it were, alive, in managing the Fires.[92]

The life of slaves in eighteenth century sugar plantations across the Caribbean was one of unremitting toil combined the floggings and lashings and other ill-treatment from plantation owners. This misery fed the growing appetite of British workers for sugary tea, something that mitigated the misery of their own working lives. British per capita sugar consumption rose from 4lbs in 1700-1709 to 8lb in 1720-1729; 12lbs by 1780-1789 and 18lbs in 1800-1809. In 1788, in his abolitionist poem *The Negro's Complaint*, William Cowper lamented the link between sugar and slavery:

> Why did all-creating Nature
> Make the plant for which we toil?
> Think how many Backs have smarted
> For the sweets your Cane affords.[93]

Slavery in the Caribbean

Critical to the development of slavery in the Caribbean were two developments in the seventeenth century.[94] Certain islands were transferred from Spanish to

---

1950, though his statistics are not always reliable, and Parker, Matthew, *The Sugar Barons: Family, Corruption, Empire and War*, (Hutchinson), 2011.

[92] Tryon, Thomas, *Tryon's Letters, Domestick and Foreign, to Several Persons of Quality: occasionally distributed in subjects, viz. philosophical, theological, and moral*, (Geo. Conyers…and Eliz. Harris), 1700, pp. 200-201.

[93] Cowper, William, *Poems by William Cowper*, 2 Vols. (R. & W. A. Bartow), 1818, Vol. 1, pp. 239-240. See also, the version published in 1826 by Harvey and Darton in 1826 with colourful woodcuts as it was probably intended to be read by children. Members of the Committee for the Abolition of the Slave Trade were keen to encourage the writers and artists of the day to support their cause. This poem came about when John Newton, anti-slavery campaigner and writer of hymns asked his friend William Cowper for some verses. The poem was so popular that it spread all over Britain and was sometimes put to music and sung as a ballad.

[94] For general works on the Caribbean see, Pons, Frank Moya, *History of the Caribbean: Plantations, Trade and War in the Atlantic world*, (Markus Weiner Publications), 2007, Higman, B. W., *A Concise History of the Caribbean*, (Cambridge University Press), 2011, pp. 97-195, and Sheridan, Richard B., *Sugar and Slavery: An economic history of the British West Indies, 1623-1775*, (Canoe Press), 2000. See also the contributions in, Emmer, P. C., and Higman, B. W., (eds.), *General History of the Caribbean, Volume 3: The slave societies of the Caribbean*, (UNESCO), 1997, Knight, Franklin W., and Laurence, K. O., (eds.), *General History of the Caribbean, Volume 4: The long nineteenth*

English and French control. In the early-seventeenth century, Spain lost several islands in the Lesser Antilles: the English seized Barbados, St Kitts, Nevis and Antigua while the French took Guadeloupe and Martinique.[95] Later in the century, Spain also lost control of key islands in the Greater Antilles, notably Jamaica to England in 1655 and the western end of Hispaniola (later known as St. Domingue and then Haiti) to France in 1697.[96] All these islands quickly became sugar plantation colonies while the islands that remained Spanish such as Cuba, Trinidad and Puerto Rico did not acquire substantial sugar production until the nineteenth century.

The Dutch were also active in introducing sugar farming to the Caribbean. Evicted from Brazil in 1654, Dutch exiles brought sugar plants, capital, machinery and expertise to Barbados, Martinique, Guadeloupe and Jamaica, took charge of the slave trade from Africa to the Caribbean and also the sugar export trade from the Caribbean to Europe.[97] In Brazil, the sugar industry remained the domain of small cane farmers, but the Caribbean industry operated a system of large-scale plantations.[98] Protectionist policies initiated by Colbert in France in the 1660s and the English Navigation Acts of 1652, 1660, 1661 and 1673 effectively excluded many Brazilian products from northern European markets significantly weakening Brazilian production. In 1670, the British West Indies produced 48,000 metric tons of sugar compared to 73,000 tons in Brazil but by 1720, 461,000 metric tons were produced in the British West Indies while Brazil's production remained static.[99] Even so Brazil still accounted for a third of the sugar produced in the Americas in 1730 and held 10 per cent of the market in 1776.[100]

The native Caribs, though decimated by European diseases brought by the Spanish, survived in the mid-seventeenth century as a substantial proportion of

---

century, (UNESCO), 2011 and ibid, Engerman, Stanley L., and Gallman, Robert E., (eds.), *The Cambridge Economic History of the United States*, pp. 297-336.

[95] See, Paquette, Robert L., and Engerman, Stanley L., (eds.), *The Lesser Antilles in the Age of European Expansion*, (University Press of Florida), 1996, especially pp. 1-15. 86-127, 182-205.

[96] Beckles, Hilary, 'The 'Hub of Empire': the Caribbean and Britain in the Seventeenth Century', *OHBE,* Vol. 1, pp. 218-240.

[97] Klooster, Wim, *Illicit Riches: Dutch Trade in the Caribbean, 1648-1795*, (KITLV Press), 1998, and ibid, Emmer, P. C., *The Dutch Slave Trade, 1500-1850*, pp. 22-35, 86-99.

[98] Galloway, J. H., *The Sugar Cane Industry: An historical geography of its origins to 1914*, (Cambridge University Press), 1989, pp. 48-83, examines the development of the sugar industry between 1450 and 1680. See also Curtin, Philip D., *The Rise and Fall of the Plantation Complex: Essays in Atlantic history*, 2nd ed., (Cambridge University Press) 1998, pp. 73-112, and Sheridan, Richard B., 'The Formation of Caribbean Plantation Society, 1689-1748' in *OHBE,* Vol. 2, pp. 394-414.

[99] Bulmer-Thomas, Victor, Coatsworth, J. H., and Conde, Roberto Cortes, (eds.), *The Cambridge Economic History of Latin America, Volume 1: The Colonial Era and the Short Nineteenth Century*, (Cambridge University Press), 2006, Table 10.1, p. 368.

[100] For comparisons with the Brazilian sugar industry see, Fausto, Boris, *The Concise History of Brazil*, (Cambridge University Press), 1999, pp. 25-58, and Schwartz, Stuart B., *Sugar Plantations in the Formation of Brazilian Society: Bahia, 1550-1835*, (Cambridge University Press) 1985.

the free population. They were replaced by free white settlers and indentured servants (themselves farmers after their five years' servitude) who produced export crops such as tobacco and cotton. Unlike in the American colonies where capitalist farmers amalgamated smallholding into larger farms and created a white rural wage class, in the Caribbean this did not occur. From the 1650s, the move to sugar production led, in the absence of a large native population to enslave, to the widespread use of imported slave labour largely for field work with white employment confined to artisans or a few managers.[101] Much of the white population left: poorer farmers because land was consolidated into larger plantations and the larger planters, often absentee landlords, remained in England.[102] By 1700, the ratio of blacks to whites in the English sugar colonies was 4:1. The system of large plantations was adopted in Nevis, St Kitts, Antigua and Montserrat between 1687 and 1713 and in Jamaica between 1700 and 1774. It was massively extended when Britain acquired Dominica, Grenada, St. Vincent and Tobago from the French in 1763 and sugar production was extended to the northern side of Jamaica.[103] The key to the profitability of the sugar industry was a ready supply of black slaves exploited by overseers for short-term profits. By 1700, 75 per cent of the Caribbean population were slaves unlike the American colonies where slaves were a small minority. Despite the growth in American slavery during the eighteenth century, the proportion of slaves still remained lower than in the British West Indies. In the Leeward Islands, for instance, slaves made up 95 per cent of the population in 1800, while in Jamaica the figure was only slightly lower at 89 per cent.

British colonies enjoyed a considerable degree of autonomy.[104] Planters ruled because they owned the bulk of the population but also because their control of colonial legislatures was unchecked by meddling from London.[105]

---

[101] Ibid, Bush, M. L., *Servitude in Modern Times*, pp. 90-105, Burnard, Trevor, 'British West Indies and Bermuda', in ibid, Paquette, Robert L, and Smith, Mark M., (eds.), *The Oxford Handbook of Slavery in the Americas*, pp. 134-153, and Morgan Philip D., 'Slavery in the British Caribbean', in ibid, Eltis, David, and Engerman, Stanley L., (eds.), *The Cambridge World History of Slavery*, Vol. 3, pp. 378-409, examine slavery in the Caribbean.

[102] Beckles, Hilary M., *White Servitude and Black Slavery in Barbados, 1627-1715*, (University of Tennessee Press), 1999, examines this transition, while her *History of Barbados: from Amerindian Society to Nation-State*, (Cambridge University Press), 1990, provides a general history. See also two early histories of the island, one published before emancipation, the other after: Poyer, John, *History of Barbados from the First Discovery of the Island in the year 1605 till the Accession of Lord Seaforth, 1801*, (J. G. Barnard), 1808, and Schomburgk, Sir Robert H., *The History of Barbados comprising a Geographical and Statistical Description of the Island*, (Longman, Brown, Green and Longmans), 1848, especially pp. 520-530.

[103] On the technological basis for this expansion see, Satchell, Veront, 'Innovations in sugar-cane mill technology in Jamaica, 1760-1830, in ibid, Shepherd, Verene, (ed.), *Working Slavery, Pricing Freedom: Perspectives from the Caribbean, Africa and the African Diaspora*, pp. 93-111.

[104] Murray, D. J., *The West Indies and the Development of Colonial Government*, (Oxford University Press), 1965, pp. 1-31, 89-108.

[105] Dunn, Richard, S., *Sugar and Slaves: The Rise of the Planter Class in the English West Indies 1634-1713*, (University of North Carolina Press), 1972.

Laws for slave protection were only introduced in the late-eighteenth century as a response to pressure from the abolitionist lobby but these were often difficult to enforce. Equally, slaves ignored the restrictive laws introduced by the legislative assemblies that were then either not enforced or allowed to lapse. Slaves were better able to improve their customary rights through negotiation with plantation managers backed up by threats of non-cooperation than through laws imposed on colonies from London that planters simply ignored. But opportunities for emancipation were limited. Most slaves were field-hands and this gave them little prospect of accumulating the money necessary to buy their freedom.[106] They could escape from plantations to freedom in Maroon communities but this only happened on the larger islands. Barbados, a small island without forests or hills offered slaves little prospect of escape while its mountainous and wooded terrain in Jamaica provided refuge for runaways. Despite this, over time a large number of free blacks emerged in the British colonies and the distinction between slaves and free men ceased to be one between black and white. In Jamaica by 1800, the 10,000 free blacks made up 27 per cent of the free population and 2.9 per cent of all blacks on the island, the largest population of free people of colour in the British colonies, while in the Leeward Islands they made up 83 per cent of the free community. Only on Barbados, was there a significant white population accounting for a fifth of the population.[107]

The dependence of production on slave labour gave Caribbean blacks considerable leverage to develop their own customs and beliefs, something that was continuously reinforced by the links to Africa. Unlike in the American colonies, Caribbean slave populations suffered from very low birth-rates and high mortality making fresh supplies of slaves essential to maintain the work force.[108] Plantation owners blamed slave women for their failure to reproduce, accusing them of practicing birth control and procuring abortions. In some cases, planters accused slave women of committing infanticide.[109] Almost half of the slaves transported to the Americas after 1680 went to the Caribbean but this created a gender-imbalance, since males made the best workers and contributed to low levels of fertility. For plantations to function effectively, overseers were dependent on the co-operation of slave-drivers and drivers on commanding the respect of slave labourers. Planters, who found purchasing food for their workforce costly, were prepared to allow slaves to grow their own food and rear animals in their own time. By 1800, two days were guaranteed by custom and

---

[106] Campbell, John, 'How Free is 'Free'? The Limits of Manumission for Enslaved Africans in Eighteenth-Century Caribbean Sugar Society', in Curry, Dawne Y., Duke, Eric D., Smith, Marshanda A., and Hine, Darlene Clark, (eds.), *Extending the Diaspora: New Histories of Black People*, (University of Illinois Press), 2009, pp. 2-23, is a valuable restatement of the difficulty of achieving manumission.

[107] Heuman, Gad J., *Between Black and White: Race, Politics and Free Coloreds in Jamaica*, (Greenwood Press), 1981, pp. 7-8, examines the free population of Jamaica.

[108] Sheridan, Richard R., *Doctors and Slaves: A Medical and Demographic History of Slavery in the British West Indies, 1680-1834*, (Cambridge University Press), 1984, remains the most detailed analysis of this issue.

[109] Allain, J. M., "Infanticide as Slave Resistance: Evidence from Barbados, Jamaica, and Saint-Domingue." *Inquiries*, Vol. 6, (4), (2014) Retrieved from http://www.inquiriesjournal.com/a?id=893

there was increasing pressure to increase this to three days. The result was an independent slave economy based around Sunday markets where slaves traded their surplus for cash or goods they could not make or grow themselves.[110] The freedoms acquired by custom were given legislative basis by colonial assemblies as a response to the criticism of slavery as a brutal system trumpeted in abolitionist literature.

African influences on Caribbean slavery never disappeared but were substantially modified as a result of the campaign against the slave trade and as abolitionists and enslaved peoples began to agitate for the ending of slavery. As a result, planters adopted ameliorationist policies towards their slaves while imperial officials were finally able to rein in the worst excesses of slavery.[111] Critical to the continuance of the slave system, especially after 1808, was a creolisation of the slave population but only Barbados managed to achieve a natural increase in the slave population and then only in 1810.[112] In the other British colonies, birth rates continued to be less than death rates leading to a slow decay in total slave numbers. Many of the creole slaves became evangelical Christians and could articulate their resistance to the slave system in Christian terms. It is no coincidence that the most serious slave rebellions came towards the end of slavery: in Barbados in 1816, Demerara in Guyana in 1823 and Jamaica in 1831.[113]

The Maroon Wars

The history of Caribbean slavery was not simply one of rampant profit-making but also one of effective slave resistance. Terror of slave rebellion, especially after the bloody rebellion in the French colony of St. Domingue during the 1790s when slaves sought revenge on their masters through pillage, rape, torture, mutilation and death, was endemic among the white ruling minority.[114] The late-eighteenth century French writer Mirabeau once wrote that St. Domingue's white minority 'slept at the foot of Vesuvius'. While Lady Nugent, wife of the

---

[110] Berlin, Ira, and Morgan, Philip D., *The Slaves' Economy: Independent production by slaves in the Americas*, (Routledge), 1995, pp. 31-67, 92-106, examines the slave economy in the Caribbean.

[111] On the process of amelioration before and after emancipation see, Ward, J. R., *British West Indies Slavery 1750-1834: The Process of Amelioration*, (Oxford University Press), 1988, and Green, William A., *British Slave Emancipation: The Sugar Colonies and the Great Experiment 1830-1865*, (Oxford University Press), 1976.

[112] See, Braithwaite, Edward, *The Development of Creole Society in Jamaica, 1770-1820*, (Ian Randle Publishers), 1971, and Price, Richard, 'The Concept of Creolization', in ibid, Eltis, David, and Engerman, Stanley L., (eds.), *The Cambridge World History of Slavery*, Vol. 3, pp. 513-537. See also, Handler, Jerome S., *The Unappropriated People: Freedmen in Politics, and the Free Coloreds in Jamaica, 1792-1865*, (John Hopkins University Press), 1981, and Cox, Edward L., *Free Coloureds in Jamaica, 1792-1865*, (Greenwood Press), 1984.

[113] Costa, Emilia Viotti da, *Crowns of Glory, Tears of Blood: The Demerara Slave Rebellion of 1823*, (Oxford University Press), 1994.

[114] Geggus, David P, (ed.), T*he Impact of the Haitian Revolution in the Atlantic World*, (University of South Carolina Press), 2001, pp. 3-22, provides an overview of the impact of the revolution. See also, Geggus, David P., and Fiering, Norman, (eds.), *The World of the Haitian Revolution*, (Indiana University Press), 2009.

Governor of Jamaica, recorded an example of dumb insolence in her journal in 1802:

> The sea was rather rough this evening, and I took a walk with the little ones, instead of a row. We met a horrid looking blackman, who passed us several times, without making any bow, although I recollect him as one of the boatmen in the canoe we used to go out in....he was then very humble, but tonight he only grinned and gave us a sort of fierce look that struck me with a terror I could not shake off.[115]

Low-level incidences of slave resistance were far more common than slave rebellions.[116] In Barbados, for instance, slave revolts were infrequent and masters adopted a more liberal approach to running their estates with slaves successfully securing better conditions within the system. This was a practical solution in a situation where escape was difficult since Barbados lacked the mountainous areas or forests in which they could hide.[117] By contrast, Jamaican slaves resisted their masters by flight and force because there were few white residents and the geography of the island afforded sanctuaries for runaways. Until 1739, slaves were inclined to establish enclaves of freedom on the island but, following the First Maroon War (1725-1740), those already living in the enclaves agreed to live in peace with the colonial government and to return all future runaways. With successful escape effectively closed, slave rebellions were increasingly characterised by attacks on whites as in 1760, 1766, 1776, 1798 and 1808 culminating in the Baptist War of 1831.[118] Where freedom could not be seized through escape, bought or negotiated, rebellion took on an enhanced significance.

Maroon communities, autonomous societies of runaway slaves, were most developed on islands such as Jamaica, St. Vincent and Grenada with mountains and forests.[119] They were subsistence smallholders, peasant cultivators who lived in inaccessible, fortified villages at the frontier of plantation society, occupying land that was either unsuitable for sugar production or would later be absorbed into the plantation system. Maroon societies had existed in Jamaica in the Blue Mountains and the Cockpit regions since it was acquired by England in 1655 forming the Windward Maroon communities utilising the secluded locations and

---

[115] Wright, Philip, (ed.), *Lady Nugent's Journal of Her Residence in Jamaica from 1801 to 1805*, (University of the West Indies Press), 2000, p. 227.

[116] Craton, Michael, *Testing the Chains: Resistance to Slavery in the British West Indies*, (Cornell University Press), 1982, remains the best general examination of slave rebellions in British colonies. In addition, see his collection of essays, *Empire, Enslavement and Freedom in the Caribbean*, (Ian Randall Publishers), 1997.

[117] Ibid, Craton, Michael, *Testing the Chains: Resistance to Slavery in the British West Indies*, pp. 254-266, examines Bussa's rebellion in Barbados in 1816.

[118] Turner, Mary, *Slaves and Missionaries: The Disintegration of Jamaican Slave Society, 1787-1834*, (University of the West Indies Press), 1982, pp. 148-178, and Ibid, Craton, Michael, *Testing the Chains: Resistance to Slavery in the British West Indies*, pp. 291-32, discuss the Baptist War.

[119] Thompson, Alvin O., *Flight to Freedom: African Runaways and Maroons in the Americas*, (University of West Indies Press), 2006, provides a broader context.

harsh environments to remain autonomous.[120] Maroons built their own unique communities that combined elements of African culture that made them distinct from slaves on plantations or free blacks in urban areas. Early Maroon communities depended on slaves for goods and information but after 1740, many maroons saw them as little more than economic opportunities rather than fellow Africans united in a struggle against the colonial system.

In 1663, the Governor and Council of Jamaica offered each Maroon who surrendered his freedom and 20 acres of land but none accepted the terms. During the following forty years, 44 Acts of Assembly were passed in respect to them and at least £250,000 was spent on periodic skirmishes between the British and the Maroons as well as occasional slave revolts. In 1673, a revolt of 200 slaves in St. Ann's Parish created the separate group of Leeward Maroons. These Maroons joined with a group of Malagasy who had survived the shipwreck of a slave ship and formed their own Maroon community in St. George's parish. Further rebellions considerably strengthened the numbers of the Leeward Maroons; for instance, a revolt of 400 slaves at Sutton's plantation, Clarendon in 1690. The Leeward Maroons inhabited caves or deep ravines that were easily defended, even against troops with superior firepower. Such guerrilla warfare and the use of scouts to warn of approaching British soldiers allowed the Maroons to evade, thwart, frustrate and defeat regular troops and local militias.[121]

The Maroons represented the greatest challenge to white authority on the island until the early 1740s.[122] The presence of these communities in Jamaica and later in the Windward Islands heightened the fears of the white minority that sought protection from metropolitan troops.[123] By the mid-1720s, white planters and the militia became increasingly aggressive towards the Maroons and the clashes became more violent. In September 1728, the British sent more troops to Jamaica, but by the late-1730s, the colonial government in Jamaica recognised that it could not defeat the Maroons and reached an agreement with them in 1739. The Maroons were to remain in their five main towns, Accompong, Trelawny Town, Moore Town, Scots Hall and Nanny Town, with their own rulers but with a British supervisor. In exchange, they agreed not to harbour new

[120] Adjaye, Joseph, 'Jamaican Maroons: Time and Historical Identity, in Adjaye, Joseph, (ed.), *Time and the The Black Experience*, (Greenwood Press), 1994, pp. 55-79, and Debien, Gabriel, 'Le Maroonage aux Antilles Françaises au XVIIIle siecle', *Caribbean Studies*, Vol.6, (1966), pp. 3-44, examine Maroons in British and French colonies.

[121] Patterson, Orlando, 'Slavery and Slave Revolts: A Sociohistorical Analysis of the First Maroon War, 1665-1740', *Social and Economic Studies*, Vol. 19, (1970), pp. 289-325, reprinted in Price, Richard, (ed.), *Maroon Societies: Rebel Slave Communities in the Americas*, (Anchor Books), 1973, pp. 246-292. See also above, Craton, Michael, *Testing the Chains: Resistance to Slavery in the British West Indies*, pp. 61-96, 211-223, and Hart, Richard, *Slaves who Abolished Slavery: Blacks in Rebellion*, (University of the West Indies Press), 2002, pp. 32-59.

[122] Campbell, Mavis C., *The Maroons of Jamaica 1655-1796: A History of Resistance, Collaboration and Betrayal*, (Bergin & Garvey), 1988, remains the most important study.

[123] Dallas, Robert C., *The History of the Maroons*, 2 Vols. (T. N. Longman and O. Rees), 1803, and Edwards, Bryan, (1796) 'Observations on the disposition, character, manners, and habits of life, of the Maroon negroes of the island of Jamaica…', in Edwards, Bryan, *Historical Survey of the Island of Saint Domingo*, (J. Stockdale), 1801, pp. 303-360, provides valuable contemporary coverage.

runaway slaves, but rather to help catch them. In addition, the Maroons agreed to protect the island from invaders a reflection of the British regard for the Maroons as skilled guerrilla fighters. In 1740, under pressure from both white Jamaicans and the Leeward Maroons, the Windward Maroons of Trelawny Town also begrudgingly agreed to sign a treaty.[124]

Although the Maroons were weakened by the peace treaties with Britain in 1739 and 1740, they remained a source of terror for the white population. That Maroon communities existed at all was seen as an affront to planter power by suggesting viable alternatives to the slave-plantation system and exposed the limitations of colonial power. The 1739 peace treaties were unpopular with whites and Maroons, especially those in Trelawny Town. Whites suspected that the Maroons were likely to foment slave rebellion or join an external enemy to topple the government. Justification for this viewpoint was evident in Maroon complicity in a slave rebellion in 1742 though generally they provided support to planters in suppressing rebellion as in 1760, 1761, 1765 and 1766. By 1773, the colonial assembly complained that Maroons had grown 'formidable' in several districts, caused several plantations to be abandoned and were a source of 'great terror' to the white population. Maroons also caused concern among British settlers in the recently acquired Windward Islands. For instance, in Grenada after 1763, a Maroon population of 600-700 escaped French slaves began a guerrilla campaign that lasted until 1771 slowing down the process of colonisation.[125] By 1775, many Maroon groups openly voiced their complaints about a lack of space to the colonial authorities. Expansion of sugar plantations restricted the dwindling amount of Maroon land as the eighteenth century progressed. The increased number of slaves created difficulties in upholding the treaties as more slaves brought frequent disturbances to the island. This change was a direct influence of the increased value of sugar throughout the Atlantic World as Jamaican planters sought to maximise their profits by exploiting all available land for production.

Tension between the Maroons, especially those on the Trelawny frontier and colonial authorities increased in the 1780s and early 1790s. In part, this was the result of planter expansion but also the impact of the slave rebellion in neighbouring St. Domingue that from 1791 sent Jamaica into a panic about the possibility of a Maroon-slave rebellion. Paranoia among officials and planters was endemic and provided further justification for controlling Maroon activities. In 1795, Lord Balcarres, the Governor of Jamaica, decided to deal with some minor breaches of the peace treaty by the Trelawney Town Maroons.[126] The

---

[124] Long, Edward, *The History of Jamaica: or, General Survey of the Antient and Modern State of That Island...*, 3 Vols. (T. Lowndes), 1774, Vol. 2, pp. 338-383, 440-475, provides contemporary comment on the First Maroon War. See also, Wright, Philip, 'War and Peace with the Maroons, 1730-1739', *Caribbean Quarterly*, Vol. 16, (1970), pp. 5-27.

[125] On the significance of the treaty see, Kopytoff, Barbara, 'Colonial Treaty as a Sacred Charter of the Jamaican Maroons, *Ethnohistory*, Vol. 26, (1978), pp. 45-64, and 'Jamaican maroon Political Organizations: The Effects of the Treaties', *Social and Economic Studies*, Vol. 25, (1977), pp. 87-105.

[126] Balcarres, Alexander Lindsay, 6th Earl of, *The Rise, Progress and Termination of the Maroon War*, (C. S. Simms), 1840, contains much of the correspondence of Balcarres during the rebellion and provides one slant on the war. It is also printed in Balcarres,

spark that ignited the war occurred when two Maroons were flogged by a black slave for stealing two pigs. The incident directly challenged the Maroons' ability to maintain autonomous communities outside the realm of punishment intended for free blacks and slaves and reflected the increasing pressure on resources. The plantation owners asked the governor not to take any further action since they felt that an agreement should be reached with the Maroons to maintain the peace of the island. The governor went ahead against this advice, arresting several of the leaders of Trelawney Town when they came to present their grievances.

The Trelawny Town Maroons resumed the guerrilla war but their fellow Maroons refused to join forces with them. Even without this support, the Trelawny Maroons were a formidable force, fighting began in May 1795 and Balcarres proclaimed martial law. 300 Maroons held out against 1,500 troops and 3,000 local militia troops raiding outlying plantations, killing the planters and their families and releasing the slaves. By the end of September, they had inflicted defeats on local forces and the Jamaican legislature sent for large hunting dogs from Cuba to seek out and destroy the blacks in their stronghold.[127] Before the dogs arrived in December, Major General George Walpole succeeded in limiting Maroon supplies of food and water and the Maroons had already offered a truce. The treaty signed in December between Walpole and the Maroon leaders established that the Maroons would beg on their knees for the King's forgiveness, return all runaway slaves and be relocated elsewhere in Jamaica. On 21 December, the remaining Maroons were given ten days to surrender but few did so. Walpole took no further action in January 1796 and 400 surrendered during the months. Balcarres then ordered Walpole to advance against the remaining Maroons holding the dogs in reserve as both men knew their use would be unpopular in England. By March, Walpole had crushed the rebellion. The Jamaican legislature advised Balcarres that those Maroons who had not surrendered within the original ten-day period should be deported.[128]

Alexander Lindsay, 7th Earl of, (ed.), *Lives of the Lindsays: or, A memoir of the houses of Crawford and Balcarres*, 3 Vols. (John Murray), 1849, Vol. 3, pp. 1-146. See also, Bridges, G. W., *The Annals of Jamaica*, 2 Vols. (John Murray), 1828, Vol. 2, pp. 219-240, and Edwards, Bryan, *The History, Civil and Commercial of the British Colonies in the West Indies*, 2 Vols. (James Humphreys), 1805, Vol. 1, pp. 337-394. Ibid, Dallas, Robert C., *The History of the Maroons*, provides a very detailed account. See also, Furness, A. E., 'The Maroon War of 1795', *Jamaican Historical Review*, Vol. 5, (1965), pp. 79-154, and ibid, Hart, Richard, *Slaves who Abolished Slavery: Blacks in Rebellion*, pp.157-206.

[127] The threatened use of 100 bloodhounds managed by 20 Spanish chasseurs brought from Cuba, which may have induced the Maroons to seek terms, resulted in questions in Parliament about whether this was a 'sportsmanlike' and justifiable method of war: see A Society of Literary Gentlemen, *A Complete and Impartial History of the Rise, Progress, & Termination of the Late War, which commenced in the year 1791: To which is prefixed a brief sketch of the French Revolution*, 2 Vols. (Vint & Anderson), 1802, Vol. 2, pp. 34-36. The attacks on the government in 1798 were given added strength since Walpole was now an MP and spoke warmly on the Maroons' behalf largely it appears, because he felt that his honour had been impugned by the actions of Balcarres and the Jamaican legislature.

[128] *The Proceedings of the Governor and Assembly of Jamaica in Regard to the Maroon Negroes: Published by order of the Assembly. To which is prefixed, an introductory account, containing, observations on the disposition, character, manners, and habits of*

Walpole disagreed with this decision since he had accepted surrenders in January 1796 on the secretly given promise that the Maroons would be able to stay on their land, something Balcarres had accepted. Both Walpole and the Maroons felt betrayed by Balcarres and the attitude of the legislature and showed this by refusing the legislature's offer of 500 guineas for the purchase of a sword of honour.

In June 1796, 556 Trelawney Town Maroons were placed on three ships and transported to Halifax, Nova Scotia.[129] In 1800, 550 Maroons, frustrated because the climate precluded them from growing familiar crops and resentful of colonial attempts to use them as cheap labour, took advantage of the opportunity to resettle in the new British settlement of Sierra Leone in West Africa.[130] Other Maroon groups remaining in Jamaica continued to fight for autonomy and land throughout the nineteenth century. Slowly the rights and property they fought many decades to protect vanished. In 1842, the Jamaican government passed the Land Allotment Act officially voiding the treaty agreements signed nearly a century ago. The success of the Maroons in maintaining their freedom when faced with the full weight of the colonial state stands in stark contrast with the failure of other slave rebellions in the British West Indies.

Mauritius

Originally settled by the Dutch[131] between 1638 and 1658 and then from 1664 to 1710, for much of the eighteenth century Mauritius was a French colony, Île de France.[132] Its economic development was increasingly based on the cultivation of sugar as a cash crop based on the labour of slaves imported from the African

---

life, of the maroons, and a detail of the origin, progress and termination of the late war between those people and the white inhabitants, (John Stockdale), 1796.

[129] *Extracts and Copies of Letters from Sir John Wentworth, Lieutenant Governor of Nova Scotia, to his Grace the Duke of Portland: respecting the Settlement of the Maroons in that Province*, London, 1797, provides a sympathetic account of their reception and settlement in Nova Scotia. See also, *Papers relative to the Settling of the Maroons in His Majesty's Province of Nova Scotia*, London, 1798. See also, Campbell, Mavis, *Nova Scotia ad the fighting Maroons: A Documentary History*, (Dept. of Anthropology, College of William and Mary), 1990.

[130] Winks, Robin W., *The Blacks in Canada: A History*, 2nd ed., (McGill-Queen's University Press), 1997, pp. 78-96, Landon, Fred, *Ontario's African-Canadian Heritage: Collected Writings by Fred Landon 1918-1967*, (Dundurn), 2009, Mackey, Frank, *Done with Slavery: The Black Fact in Montreal 1760-1840*, (McGill-Queen's University Press), 2010, and Grant, John N., *The Maroons in Nova Scotia*, (Formac Publishing Co. Ltd.), 2002, deal with this aspect of Maroon history.

[131] Moree, Perry J., *A Concise History of Dutch Mausitius, 1598-1710*, (Kegan Paul), 1998.

[132] Vaughan, Megan, *Creating the Creole Island: Slavery in Eighteenth-Century Mauritius*, (Duke University Press), 2005, especially, pp. 33-90, 229-275. See also, Vaux, Charles Grant de, *The History of Mauritius, or the Isle of France, and the neighbouring islands: From their First Discovery to the Present Time: Composed Principally from the Papers and Memoirs of Baron Grant, who resided 20 years in the island*, (Nicol), 1801.

continent and Madagascar.[133] Estimates suggest that 70 per cent of the slaves imported by the French to Mauritius and Réunion between 1670 and 1769 originated in Madagascar.[134] As the economy of the island became ever more dependent on the labour intensive production of sugar for the prosperity of its settler population, so the employment of slaves became increasingly brutal leading to high levels of slave mortality.[135]

During the Napoleonic Wars, Mauritius was used as a base for raiding British shipping. British forces seized Rodrigues from the French in 1809 and use it as a base to overrun Mauritius in late 1810.[136] Mauritius was ceded to Britain in the Treaty of Paris in 1814 and the island served as a strategic base for the British in the Indian Ocean and was a Crown Colony.[137] Under the terms of the treaty, the colonies retained its French language, culture and laws and also its Catholic faith.[138] Few British settled there, apart from the Governor, a handful of officials and a garrison, and the island retained its French character. Crown Colony government concentrated power in the hands of a Governor, who was closely supervised from London, and, from 1825, assisted by a Legislative Council of Government initially composed of officials.[139] Like most colonial societies, Mauritian society was hierarchically structured in a steep pyramid of power and wealth. At its base was a vast population of black slaves, imported Madagascans, Mozambicans and others from the Indian Ocean basin. There was a class of artisans of heterogeneous decent and white élite of French decent, comprising of landowners, merchants, officials and professionals. By 1830, the estimated population of Mauritius was 96,945: 8.9 per cent were categorised as Europeans, 19.5 per cent were free coloureds and 71.7 per cent slaves.[140]

---

[133] See also, Newitt, Martyn, 'Madagascar and the African Diaspora', in ibid, Jayasuriya, Shihan de Silva, and Pankhurst, Richard, (eds.), *The Africa Diaspora in the Indian Ocean*, pp. 81-98.

[134] Vink, M., ''The World's Oldest Trade': Dutch Slavery and Slave Trade in the Indian Ocean in the Seventeenth Century', *Journal of World History*, (Vol. 14, (2), (2003), pp. 131-177.

[135] For general histories of Mauritius see, Toussaint, A. *History of Mauritius*, (Macmillan), 1971, Selvon, Sydney, *A Comprehensive History of Mauritius: From the Beginning to 2001*, (M. D. S.), 2005. See also, Allen, Richard, *Slaves, Freemen and Indentured Laborers in Colonial Mauritius*, (Cambridge University Press), 1999, pp. 9-33, and North-Coombes, Alfred, *A History of Sugar-Production in Mauritius*, (A. North-Coombes), 1993.

[136] See, Taylor, Stephen. *Storm and Conquest: The Battle for the Indian Ocean, 1809*, (Faber and Faber), 2007.

[137] The Crown Colony of Mauritius included the islands that later became the Seychelles, all its present territory, including Rodrigues and the Chagos archipelago over a thousand miles the north-east. Its strategic importance was especially evident during the Second World War: see, Jackson, Ashley, *War and Empire in Mauritius and the Indian Ocean*, (Palgrave Macmillan), 2001.

[138] Moore, J., 'Exporting European Core Values: British and French Influences on Education in Mauritius', *European Journal of Education*, Vol. 19, (1984), pp. 39-52 at 39-41.

[139] Martin, T. Montgomery, *History of the British Colonies*, 5 Vols. (James Cochrane and Co.), 1835, Vol. 4, pp. 161-212, provides a good contemporary account of the colony.

[140] Christopher, A. J., 'Ethnicity, Community and the Census in Mauritius, 1830-1990', *Geographical Journal*, Vol. 158, (1992), pp. 57-64, at pp. 58-59.

London expected the small British colonial administration to be financially self-sufficient and the Governor was forced to turn to the white élite for support and assistance in governance, safe-guarding their economic interests in return. An uneasy alliance developed between the two in which mutual distaste was tempered by common interests: The British provided the military presence necessary to maintain the oppressive economic and social status quo while the Franco-Mauritians supplied the economic base and revenue flow that was necessary to finance colonial rule.[141]

On becoming a Crown Colony, Mauritius was subject to the Navigations Act, ending Port Louis' status as a free port.[142] It was now subjected to commercial competition from Britain's newly acquired Cape Colony leading to the demise of Port Louis as a commercial entrepôt in the region and to the decline of Mauritius' merchant class. On the other hand, as part of the British Empire, Mauritian sugar planters obtained a huge and lucrative market for their products. Sugar production now increasingly dominated the Mauritian economy, a process accelerated by the abolition of preferential tariffs for West Indian sugar exports to Britain. By 1830, the amount of land under sugar cultivation had increased by almost 113 per cent.[143] The expansion of sugar cultivation stimulated by the development of dependent economic activities including centralisation of mills, marketing, research, banking, and insurance that introduced important economies of scale This reinforced the profitability of sugar compared with other forms of production in Mauritius and sugar production and related activities became the main and then virtually sole economic activity of the Island. All other activities declined and everything else needed, including food, had to be imported.[144]

Slavery in Mauritius

The history of Mauritius is inextricably linked to the slave trade.[145] In a debate in the House of Commons in May 1826, Fowell Buxton, an abolitionist MP commented:

> ...in the Mauritius, where slavery is the very soul of their existence, where universal torpor and poverty must reign without it, so that the islands must become deserts, if the importation of new negroes was denied.[146]

---

[141] See, Ballhatchet, K., 'The Structure of British Official Attitudes: Colonial Mauritius, 1883-1968', *The Historical Journal*, Vol. 38, (4), (1995), pp. 989-1011

[142] Ibid, Toussaint, A. *History of Mauritius*, p. 63.

[143] Ibid, Allen, Richard *Slaves, Freemen and Indentured Laborers in Colonial Mauritius*, p. 12.

[144] Allen, Richard, 'Capital, Illegal Slaves, Indentured Labourers and the Creation of a Sugar Plantation Economy in Mauritius, 1810-60', *Journal of Imperial and Commonwealth History*, Vol. 36, (2008), pp. 151-170.

[145] See, Benedict, Burton, 'Slavery and Indenture in Mauritius and Seychelles', in ibid, Watson, James L., (ed.), *Asian and African Systems of Slavery*, pp. 135-168, and Nwulia, Moses S. E., *The History of Slavery in Mauritius and the Seychelles, 1810-1875*, (Fairleigh Dickenson University Press), 1981, pp. 13-37.

[146] *Hansard*, House of Commons, Debates, 9 May 1826, Vol. 15, cc1031-1032.

The expansion of sugar production, the high mortality and low birth rates amongst slaves[147] and natural disasters such as the cholera epidemic of 1819-1820 created an acute shortage of labour.[148] The slave trade had been outlawed since 1807, but slaves continued to be imported illicitly with local authorities turning a blind eye.[149] Between 1810 and 1820, 20,000 slaves were imported into Mauritius.[150] Robert Farquhar, Governor from 1810 to 1817 and again from 1820 to 1823, took an ambivalent view on slavery. Initially, since the French settlers had been allowed their customs, he permitted them to continue with the slave trade despite the legislation in 1807. He believed in attacking slavery at its source in Madagascar and worked for its elimination there was the way to end the trade to Mauritius. He set up an office for the registration of slaves and tried to improve their conditions in the face of concerted opposition from slave-owners.[151] The colonial government introduced further measures to curtail excesses of maltreatment in 1826 and in 1829 a charter was issued that permitted slaves to own property and to marry and prohibited the breakup of families in transfers of ownership.[152] The granting of full legal rights to free blacks in 1830 and the inexorable progress of the abolitionist movement led to resentment and resistance among the white élite. This forced the government to reinforce the garrison, reform the Council of Government in 1832 to include seven nominated members of 'notables' to represent the wealthy classes and promise slave owners compensation.[153] Since the remaining seven official members were members of the colonial establishment after lengthy residence on the island, the Council was united when the health of the sugar industry and colonial prosperity were threatened.

Slaves changed masters through open bid auctions; males were sold separately, women and their children were sold together. The price of slaves increased dramatically in the 1820s: in 1822, the price was £40-50; by October

[147] Kuczynski, R. R., *Demographic Survey of the British Colonial Empire*, Vol. 2, (Oxford University Press), 1949, p. 869, argued that this was the result of high levels of birth control and abortion among slave women, especially from Madagascar. Under French rule, an edict in 1778 inflicted the death penalty on women who concealed their pregnancies.

[148] Ibid, Moses S. E., *The History of Slavery in Mauritius and the Seychelles,* p. 15. See also, Telfair, Charles, *Some Account of the State of Slavery at Mauritius since the British Occupation in 1810*, (James Ridgway), 1830, pp. 125-127.

[149] At least 30,000 slaves were smuggled into the colony in the 1820s: ibid, Moses S. E., *The History of Slavery in Mauritius and the Seychelles,* p. 15. See also, Scarr, Deryck, *Slaving and Slavery in the Indian Ocean*, (Macmillan), 1998, pp. 87-127. See also, Barker, Anthony J., *Slavery and Anti-Slavery in Mauritius, 1810-33*, (Palgrave Macmillan), 1996, pp. 53-71, on the demographic position of slavery in 1826.

[150] British Parliamentary Papers, Vol. 25, *Report on the Slave Trade*, 1829, pp. 10, 20.

[151] Ibid, Barker, Anthony J., *Slavery and Anti-Slavery in Mauritius, 1810-33*, pp. 24-42, for the Farquhar era.

[152] Fokeer, A. F., 'The Negroes in Mauritius', *Journal of Negro History*, Vol. 7, (2), (1922), pp. 197-205, at p. 204. See also, H. R., 'Progress of Colonial Reform at the Mauritius and Cape of Good Hope, as regards the Treatment of the Slave Population', *The Oriental Herald and Journal of General Literature*, Vol. 21, (1829), pp. 145-155

[153] Ibid, Toussaint, A. *History of Mauritius*, pp. 64-65, 67-68. It was not until 1866 that elected members were introduced.

1827, £80-90; and by July the following year, it had risen to £120.[154] By 1830, prices fell parallel to falling sugar prices because of over-production but prices for slaves rose again in 1833. Between 1825 and 1835, 2,827 slaves were bought and sold at an average price of £100 for male and £80 for female slaves. Between 1785 and 1826, male slaves outnumbered female slaves by about two to one. Slaves were apparently eager to take wives and Grant de Vaux suggested that women were expected to do the cooking and that men gave them whatever possessions they might have.[155] Until 1829, slaves had to have their master's permission to marry but they often simply cohabited. Competition for slave women was widespread and many white men had concubines often freeing these women and their children. Between 1785 and 1834, the number of free coloured women outnumbered males by more than two to one. For female slaves becoming concubines could prove to be a very favourable option.[156]

The Act for the Abolition of Slavery in the British Empire of 1833 became effective in Mauritius on 1 February 1835 and, after six years of apprenticeship for all ex-slaves over age six, they attained their freedom. Planters on Mauritius had fiercely resisted the abolition of slavery and control of the courts meant that ex-slaves had little recourse to the law.[157] Severe vagrancy laws were introduced to force apprentices to remain on estates with draconian punishments including flogging for the slightest breaches of the law. Only a quarter of their time was allowed off to work for wages. One observer of apprenticeship in Mauritius wrote: 'the blacks themselves have ever regarded, and to the last hour of their apprenticeship will regard it as a grievous continuation of slavery.'[158] Such was the severity of apprenticeship in Mauritius that when it was finally abolished on 31 March 1839, there was a mass desertion of ex-slaves from field labour. In 1840, some 20,000 blacks still worked on the sugar plantations but within a decade this was dwindled to practically nil. 'La liberté c'est la promenade' cynically concluded an article in the Mauritius daily *Le Cernéen* about the mass movement of ex-apprentices to the towns or to remote uncultivated areas becoming market gardeners, charcoal burners, artisans and fishermen. Indian slaves had been imported to Mauritius since the eighteenth century though they do not appear to have been used as field labour. Many were artisans and others worked as clerks and messengers in government offices and for commercial firms. Indian convicts were brought to the island after 1815 to work on roads and government buildings though transportation was abolished in 1837. The regular use of indentured Indian labour began in 1835 but expanded

---

[154] Ibid, Benedict, Burton, 'Slavery and Indenture in Mauritius and Seychelles', p. 138.

[155] Ibid, Vaux, Charles Grant de, *The History of Mauritius, or the Isle of France, and the neighbouring islands*, pp. 76-77.

[156] Ibid, Kuczynski, R. R., *Demographic Survey of the British Colonial Empire*, pp. 760, 770-772.

[157] Michel, Didier, and Croucher, Richard, 'Legal at the time?' The case of Mauritian slavery', *Journal of African Law*, Vol. 58, (1), (2014), pp. 89-108.

[158] Baker, Edward, 'Observations on the Apprenticeship System in Mauritius, 1st May, 1836', in *Extracts from the Letters of James Backhous*, (Harvey and Darton), 1839, Sixth Part, p. 73.

dramatically in response to labour shortages from 1839.[159] By 1861, two-thirds of the population of Mauritius was Indian.[160]

Resistance in Mauritius

Settlements were created by runaway slaves in Mauritius in the interior highlands and forests from the mid-seventeenth century. It was the beginnings of sugar production from the 1680s and its need for a continuous supply of slaves that led to an increase in runaways and Maroon communities expanded. This led to conflict first with Dutch colonists, who left the island in 1710 and then with the French.[161] Population expansion in the eighteenth century and encroachment on their forest retreats as well as improved policing and the periodic deployment of Maroon-hunting units made it impossible for Maroons to establish large-scale communities as they did in the Caribbean.[162] Nonetheless, Le Morne Mountain, an isolated massif in the south-western edge of Mauritius, proved a refuge and natural fortress for large numbers of escapees to such an extent that it became known as the 'Maroon Republic'. By the early-nineteenth century when Britain seized the island, the number of Maroons had already significantly declined. Under the British, sugar plantations reached their peak driving Maroon bands further into a few remaining isolated refuges where they survived under constant threat of recapture. By 1835 when slavery was abolished, few Maroon communities remained and surviving Maroons intermingled with the free black population in Port Louis by pretending to be free.

Slaves under British rule were still subject to the draconian slave laws established by the French, the so-called *Code Noir*. But resistance was not confined to slaves and opposition to the amelioration of slave conditions and of the moves towards abolition of slavery during the 1820s led the French planters to threaten civil rebellion in 1831 and 1832. If the 1832 rebellion in Jamaica was the climax of slave resistance, in Mauritius it was the symbol and climax of the planters' attempt to maintain their authority and dominance over their slaves. For French planters opposition to abolition was a matter of preserving the colony's French identity and way of life as well as its economic survival. While abolition in the West Indies may have been in Britain's interests since the soils on its sugar plantations were exhausted after a long period of production, this could not be said of Mauritius where they were still fresh. But it was moral not

[159] Thiara, Ravi, 'Indian indentured workers in Mauritius, Natal and Fiji', in Cohen, Robin, (ed.), *The Cambridge survey of world migration* (Cambridge University Press), 1995, pp. 57-62. See also, North-Coombes, M. D., 'From Slavery to Indenture: Forced Labor in the Political Economy of Mauritius, 1834-1867', in Saunders, Kay, (ed.), *Indentured Labor in the British Empire, 1834-1920*, (Croom Helm), 1984, pp. 78-125. Dhanda, Pravina, *History of Indentured Immigration into Mauritius*, M.Ph., Thesis, University of London, 1970.

[160] Carter, Marina, 'The Transition from Slave to Indentured Labour in Mauritius', in Twaddle, Michael, (ed.), *The Wages of Slavery. From Chattel Slavery to Wage Labour in Africa, the Caribbean and England*, (Frank Cass), 1993, pp. 114-130.

[161] Edouard, Stephano, *The 1706 Slave Conspiracy in Dutch Mauritius: A Case of Collective Resistance*, BA, Thesis, Leiden University, 2014.

[162] Nagapen, Amédés, *Le Marronnage a L'Isle de France-Ile Maurice Réve ou Riposte de l'esclave*, (Nelson Mandela Centre for African Culture), 1999, is the most extensive study.

economic considerations that motivated the abolitionists who increasingly objected to the violence involved in slavery.[163]

Slaves

The existence of group resistance by Mauritian slaves is evident in the 1820s and 1830s from the records in the Mauritius Archives. In 1829, Roger Thomas arrived as the newly appointed Protector of Slaves as part of the British amelioration measures to reform slavery in the colony.[164] Some of the major functions of this new colonial official were to record the complaints lodged by the slaves against their masters and safeguard the interests and rights of the Mauritian slaves. Between March 1829 and September 1831, the reports and complaint books of the Protector of Slaves and his assistants indicate that there were 18 cases where groups of slaves filed complaints against their masters, estate managers and commandeurs.[165] In April 1831, while reviewing some of the cases of group resistance or collective resistance by Mauritian slaves from the first three reports of the Protector of Slaves between March 1829 and June 1830, Viscount Goderich, the Secretary of State for the Colonies observed: 'The Protector indeed has asserted in his Reports that a conspiracy and spirit insubordination existed among some of the rural slaves.'

In September 1831, some of the leading Franco-Mauritian sugar planters and slave owners sent a common letter to Governor Colville in which they stated that there was a proliferation in violent acts of resistance such as arson by large groups of slaves as well as non-violent acts of collective resistance such as work stoppage, go-slows and filing complaints with the Protector of Slaves against their masters and estate managers. Between March 1829 and January 1835, there were a total of 42 cases of collective resistance involving anywhere from 3 to 69 slaves. These cases represent around 4 per cent of the 1,060 cases that were dealt with by Protector and his assistants. Most of these acts were committed by field slaves who worked on the large sugar plantations. The case of the slaves from Wolmar Sugar Estate highlights this fact. In November 1829, 69 slaves belonging to Mr. Brue, the owner of Wolmar Sugar Estate in Black River district, lodged a complaint at the office of Protector Thomas against their master and two estate managers, Mr. Osurghren and Mr. Porte. Since the slaves were in an agitated state, Thomas explained to them, through the intervention of his free coloured translator, that only seven slaves would remain behind to provide details about their complaints while the rest would have to return to their master's estate under police escort. The slaves unanimously chose Egisse and Porphire, the two slave

---

163 'Recent Events at Mauritius', *Guernsey and Jersey Magazine*, Vol. 2, (1836), pp. 154-161, and *Annual Register*, Vol. 78, (1837), pp. 252-258, provide contemporary comment, while Burroughs, Peter, 'The Mauritius Rebellion of 1832 and the Abolition of British Colonial Slavery', *Journal of Imperial and Commonwealth History*, Vol. 4, (3), (1976), pp. 243-265, is a lucid analysis.

164 Spence, Caroline Quarrier, *Ameliorating Empire: Slavery and Protection in the British Colonies, 1783-1865*, Ph.D., Thesis, Harvard University, 2014.

165 *The Anti-Slavery Reporter*, Vol. 2, (1829), pp. 332-340, 373-395, 430, *The Anti-Slavery Reporter*, Vol. 3, (1830), pp. 6-53, 281-297, *The Anti-Slavery Reporter*, Vol. 4, (1831), pp. 385-420

commandeurs of Wolmar Estate, as well as Suzanne, Berenice, Francoeur, Cololas, and Clement. Unfortunately, shortly after cross-examining the slaves and a brief visit to the sugar estate, the Protector of Slaves dismissed the case and the seven slaves who stayed behind to speak on behalf of their comrades were punished. During the last week of December 1829, in his second report as Protector of Slaves, while commenting on five cases of collective resistance by plantation slaves in some of the colony's rural districts, Thomas observed of the Wolmar Sugar Estate: '...the spirit of collective insubordination and conspiracy that existed among the plantation slaves could not be overlooked.'

Between 1829 and 1835, when large groups of rural slaves deserted the sugar estates of their owners to lodge complaints with the Protector of Slaves, especially during the sugar harvest season, sugar production came to a halt for more than two days on those plantations. Through their acts of collective resistance, they temporarily removed themselves from production processes on the sugar estates denying their masters their labour as well as time and money. During the last years of slavery, collective resistance by Mauritian slaves was a direct and open challenge to sugar planters and estate managers.

> Insolence and resistance to work demands became more challenging when several slaves were involved, rather than isolated individuals. The challenges in these cases were not simply to individual owners but to the whole society.[166]

Planters

Slave owners in Mauritius had a proven record of resistance to abolition. In 1796, they had ejected two anti-slavery Commissioners of the French Republic who had come to the colony and the arrival of John Jeremie to be the first non-Creole Procureur-General in 1832 provoked a similar response. By the late 1820s, there was increasing parliamentary criticism of the lax ways in which the colonial administration addressed the illegal importation of slaves and that taking their lead from the Governor Sir Charles Colville, nearly all the officials had evaded the Order in Council expressly forbidding colonial officials from holding any slave property. Jeremie was a known abolitionist who had written *Four Essays on Colonial Slavery* in which he had criticised the Mauritian slave system and charged the colonial legislatures with 'downright contumacy' in evading parliamentary orders.[167] White and non-white slave owners, for once united, mustered a volunteer force and successfully opposed Jeremie's appointment. When Jeremie landed in the colony on 5 June 1832 escorted by regular troops, slave owners threatened open rebellion against his appointment. There were plans to ambush the British garrison and turn Mauritius into an independent Ile de France but much of this was simply talk since there was no will to secede from the British Empire that provided a huge market for their sugar. Whether the action of slave owners was about achieving the maximum indemnity payments for the Emancipation of their slaves is debatable. A public meeting on 17 June unanimously agreed that Jeremie should not remain in Mauritius, something with

166 Ibid, Barker, Anthony J., *Slavery and Anti-Slavery in Mauritius, 1810-33*, p. 115.

167 Jeremie, John, *Four Essays on Colonial Slavery*, (J. Hatchard and Son), 1831, pp. 23-24. 111-113.

which Colville concurred and on 18 June, he left the island. On Colville's resignation and the appointment of Sir William Nicolay as his successor and despite the opposition of merchants in London, Jeremie returned to Mauritius in late April 1833 seeking to assuage 'his wounded pride'.[168] He tried to disarm the volunteers but as they had been armed with sporting rifles, perfectly legal in Mauritius, this proved unsuccessful. He then gathered information about the alleged Grand Rebellion arraigning five gentlemen from Grand Port again unsuccessfully. His behaviour in the court was vindictive, prejudiced against the defendants and ill-tempered and, as a result, the Governor dismissed him. In his defence of his position, published in 1836, he abused virtually everyone involved in the sorry affair including successive Colonial Secretaries.[169]

Slave Emancipation led to a universal decline in sugar production but it was Mauritius that weathered the threat of Emancipation most successfully. Before 1834, Jamaica had produced twice as much sugar but within twenty years Mauritius had become Britain's leading sugar colony. Its production had increased to five times that of Jamaica and twice as much as British Guiana. Mauritian slave owners were adequately compensated for the loss of their slaves and the leading planters did not suffer drastic property losses from Emancipation. When apprenticeship was ended prematurely in May 1839, most former slaves withdrew from employment on the sugar plantations but, unlike in the other sugar colonies Mauritius had already begun the massive importation of indentured Indian labour. The 30,000 apprentices at work on plantations in 1839 were replaced by over 34,000 Indian indentured labourers. This, plus the conversion of large numbers of sugar factories to steam power, ensured Mauritian primacy in the industry.[170]

Morant Bay, 1865

There had been several rebellions by enslaved Africns on Jamaica and a widespread tradition of disruptive daily behaviour. Sixteen uprisings occurred between 1655 and 1813 and there were major uprisings in 1813 and 1823. During the largest rebellion in 1831, 200 Africans and 14 British planters and overseers were killed, over 200 plantations were attacked causing over £1m of damage and 138 rebels were executed in its aftermath. The revolt was important in helping to end British slavery by shocking the British government into recognising that the costs and dangers of keeping slavery in the West Indies were too high.

In 1833, the formal end of slavery in Jamaica removed the most horrendous abuses of slavery for 311,000 enslaved people bringing the possibility of constructing new lives beyond the boundaries of exploitative plantation labour. By 1865, black expectations and initiatives had been largely frustrated by strong

---

[168] Macmillan, Allister, *Mauritius Illustrated: Historical and Descriptive, Commercial and Industrial Facts & Resources*, (W. H. & L. Collingridge), 1914, p. 50.

[169] Jeremie, John, *Recent Events in Mauritius*, (Hanchard and Son), 1836.

[170] The number of sugar mills rose from 167 in 1833 to 203 by 1838 and the number of steam mills rose from 67 to 130 in the same period: North-Coombes, A., *The Evolution of the Sugar Cane Culture in Mauritius*, (General Printing and Stationary Co. Ltd.), 1937, p. 165.

continuities between the period of enslavement and the decades after Emancipation. Whites maintained their near monopoly of the island's economic resources and dominated local political structures. Furthermore, the 'aristocracy' of white skin buttressed their social privileges and the first generation of black adults in freedom was returned to dependence on the plantation and to a standard of living not far removed from their experiences of enslavement. The Morant Bay Rebellion of 1865 represented a clash between a decaying white plantocracy bolstered by the colonial authorities and the black freed people who were asserting and defending their new rights and political and economic aspirations.

Frustration

Britain abolished the slave trade in 1807, required British slave owners to ameliorate the living and working conditions of slaves in 1823, abolished slavery as a legal institution in 1833 and, following a period of apprenticeship, proclaimed complete Emancipation in 1838.[171] Abolitionists had produced a forceful critique of slavery but they were less clear about what equality meant for the newly freed people. It was not to be immediate but deferred until those freed had been transformed into an educated and Christian working-class. This ambivalence was evident in the attitude of Lord Glenelg, the Colonial Secretary between 1835 and 1839.[172] In a circular dispatch to the governors of the various slave colonies in 1837, he strongly advocated slave rights but was also concerned about the need to maintain a reliable labour force:

> The great cardinal principle of the law for the abolition of slavery is, that the apprenticeship of the emancipated slaves is to be immediately succeeded by personal freedom, in that full and unlimited sense of the term in which it is used in reference to the other subjects of the British Crown.[173]

Glenelg was equally adamant that there should be restrictions placed on the ability of freemen to acquire land, an important expression of status and privilege as well as a statement of economic independence from the sugar estates.[174]

Jamaica had the largest slave population and, despite being atypical of sugar colonies, provided the model for British policy and thinking before, during and after Emancipation. Central to this were notions of economic and political

---

[171] Heuman, Gad, 'Riots and Resistance in the Caribbean at the Moment of Freedom', in Temperley, Howard, (ed.), *After Slavery: Emancipation and its Discontents*, (Routledge), 2000, pp. 135-149, demonstrates that in opposing apprenticeship across the Caribbean, blacks were expressing their own vision of freedom that was very different to the planters' perception of the aftermath of slavery. The events in Morant Bay in 1865 were, in many respects, a consequence of those differences.

[172] *Jamaica under the Apprenticeship System. By A Proprietor*, (J. Andrews), 1838, a contemporary critique of the apprenticeship system.

[173] Cit, Holt, T. C., *The Problem of Freedom: Race, Labor and Politics in Jamaica and Britain, 1832-1938*, (JHU Press), 1992, p. 72.

[174] Hall, D. G., 'The Apprenticeship Period in Jamaica, 1834-1838', *Caribbean Quarterly*, Vol. 3, (3), (1953), pp. 142-166.

liberalism that had evolved during the eighteenth century based upon a view of human nature. For British liberals, human nature was defined in terms of bourgeois man and anything that deviated from this premise was regarded as primitive, savage and undeveloped. Planters preferred coercion while policy-makers emphasised voluntary wage labour, but neither accepted the right of the freed people to choose an alternative path. After Emancipation, freed people moved away in large numbers from the centres of sugar production and established new villages and market centres. By the 1850s, this had resulted in the precipitous decline of the Jamaican plantation economy and the rise of an increasingly politically aware black peasantry with an alternative view of freedom that challenged bourgeois assumptions. Growing economic freedom and calls for political Emancipation brought a virulent racist counterattack.[175]

Emancipation upset the social order by releasing the enormous voting potential of a freed population that far exceeded the whites' voting capacity whose interests they challenged. Recollections of the slave rebellion of 1831 were fresh in the memories of planters. With only 14,000 whites on the island and 430,000 blacks, every new expression of colonial resistance across the Empire, especially the Sepoy Mutiny in India in 1857 and 1858, reinforced white fears of black rebellion. With 900 largely black troops on the island, there were fears that they would follow the example of the sepoys and join a rebellion. the violent British reprisals against the Sepoys in India could be used to justify the settlers' own reprisals against rebels and the reassertion of imperial control in Jamaica and could be interpreted as legitimising their own dispossession of blacks. Attempting to withhold or at least restrict political rights was as important a feature of post-Emancipation Jamaica as attempting to control the labour force. Formal politics in Jamaica after 1838 was restricted to the male propertied class of merchants, planters and professionals. The Assembly was divided between two loose blocs called political parties but having neither the ideological nor organisational coherence associated with the modern sense of the term. The Country Party was composed of the white plantocracy while the Town Party included merchants, lawyers and some planters, many from mixed-race backgrounds and who had supported the abolition of slavery. Moderate, reform-oriented politics developed among a section of the coloured middle-class but its influence was limited by the bitterly conservative ruling class. The franchise had expanded after Emancipation but it was far from a system of popular democracy. In the 1864 election, only 1,903 people were eligible to vote out of a population of 436,807 and actual voters numbered only 1,457.[176]

It has been assumed that property qualifications excluded most of the black community from electoral politics and that, even if they had sufficient

---

[175] Ibid, Holt, T. C., *The Problem of Freedom: Race, Labor and Politics in Jamaica and Britain, 1832-1938*, provides a cogent analysis of the emancipation experience. Green, William A., *British Slave Emancipation: The Sugar Colonies and the Great Experiment 1830-1865*, (Oxford University Press), 1976, pp. 129-190, examines the problems posed by emancipation to plantation owners. See also, Heuman, Gad, 'The British West Indies', in *OHBE*, Vol. 3, pp. 495-521.

[176] Cit, Bakan, Abigail, *Ideology and Class Conflict in Jamaica: The Politics of Rebellion*, (McGill-Queen's University Press), 1990, p. 70. Ibid, Green, William A., *British Slave Emancipation*, pp. 353-379, examines constitutional reform and colonial politics.

property to qualify, they were politically apathetic. However, this was not the case with vestry politics in which blacks competed with other social groups for election.[177] Largely excluded from the Assembly, vestries became the medium through which black freemen could assert and protect their new privileges and led to the genesis of a combative political culture reflecting the evolving creole society of nineteenth century Jamaica.[178] By the 1850s, vestries had become the vehicle that allowed black leaders to articulate their political vision for post-slavery society. This alarmed white and coloured élites and increased in the early 1860s when blacks from Kingston began to mobilise small black and coloured freeholders in the adjoining parishes of Port Royal and St. Andrew. Alexander Heslop, the coloured Attorney-General during the Morant Bay rebellion, reflected the attitude of the island's élites when he urged the abolition of vestries because they had become 'training grounds for demagogues'.[179] Although this exaggerated the significance of those blacks elected to various vestries since 1838, it reflected the growing influence of black freeholders in local politics and their threat to the traditional political hegemony of the planter interest. Local élites and the Colonial Office were increased faced by the growing 'politics of numbers' and used the Morant Bay rebellion to suffocate these embryonic signs of black politics.

Between 1855 and 1865, the economic, social and political tensions created, in part, by Emancipation multiplied reaching breaking point at Morant Bay. The decade saw a series of disasters with outbreaks of smallpox and cholera and drought and floods that hit gravely the economic state of Jamaica. Political reforms in 1854, which vested power in a popularly elected Assembly and a nominated Legislative Council with the power of veto, had not stemmed the tide of bankruptcies in the sugar industry and the small farm sector was insufficiently developed to bridge the growing economic void.[180] Between 1861 and 1865, the American Civil War led to a precipitous fall of imported food pushing prices to levels that most Jamaican workers were unable to pay while the Union blockade on Southern ports increased prices of cotton goods and

---

177 Vestries were first established in Jamaica in 1677 and until Emancipation were the traditional bastions of white power. Each Vestry had 12 elected members: 10 vestrymen and 2 churchwardens. The Vestry also included as ex officio members the *custos rotulorum* (Keeper of the Roll of the Justices of the Peace and Chief Magistrate for the parish first mentioned in Jamaica in 1668 and remains an important position today), the magistrates and the parish rector. Until they were abolished in 1866, vestries administered parochial schooling and health provision, maintained roads, regulated markets, licensed retailers, directed the local police and provided for paupers and levied taxes to support these roles.

178 Wilmot, Swithin, 'From Bondage to Political Office: Blacks and Vestry Politics in Two Jamaican Parishes, Kingston and St David, 1831-1865', in Monteith, Kathleen E. A., and Richards, Glen, (eds.), *Jamaica in Slavery and Freedom: History, Heritage and Culture*, (University of the West Indies Press), 2002, pp. 307-323, is a major contribution to this issue.

179 Cit, ibid, Wilmot, Swithin, 'From Bondage to Political Office...', p. 319; representational politics were swept away in 1866 with the establishment of Crown Colony government in the aftermath of the rebellion.

180 Ibid, Holt, T. C., *The Problem of Freedom: Race, Labor and Politics in Jamaica and Britain, 1832-1938*, pp. 233-249, examines attempts to improve government.

clothing. This combined with the unsympathetic attitudes of the British and Jamaican governments to squatting on vacant Crown lands or abandoned plantations, the one opportunity blacks had to raise their own food. The white élite did little positive to address the religious, political and economic grievances expressed by Afro-Jamaicans through petitions, public meetings and demonstrations since those charged with redressing the island's decline were fundamentally hostile to black aspirations. For instance, of the 40 bills passed in 1861-1862, only two were concerned with improving conditions for the Jamaican working-class and many enacted in previous years were designed to restrict the mobility of newly emancipated slaves. Blind to the potential of peasant farming, for the colonial authorities Jamaica's future lay with the large sugar estates that depended on a disciplined, waged labour force. For them, the issue was not ineffective policies but proof of the racial deficiencies of a degraded people.[181]

White missionaries were the only Europeans in close and friendly contact with the emancipated blacks and were particularly concerned in developing education in which the plantocracy was disinterested.[182] Its success is evidenced by the high levels of literacy among the black population: in 1862, about 45 per cent of the 175,000 with elementary education could read and about a third could read and write. Baptist missionaries were aggressive in their efforts relying on their historical legacy as the defenders of the black population before Emancipation.[183] Baptist membership grew from about 10,000 in 1831 to 34,000 by 1845, although after this apart from the Great Revival of 1860-1862, there was a loss in numbers and power. Missionaries were not simply seeking to convert people to Christianity but also to what they saw as a superior, 'civilised' society with an agenda that encompassed moral as well as religious authority. With the emergence of Native Baptist leaders and revival of Afro-Christian religious traditions, direct contact between mission leaders and blacks declined and by 1860 Native Baptists accounted for half the entire churchgoing population. Knowledge of Christian doctrines led many Blacks to interpret their social position highly unfavourably. One black slave had told a missionary in the 1820s: 'Buckra (the white man) left him God in England, and devil in Jamaica stir him to do all this wickedness.'

---

[181] On changing attitudes to race see, Beasley, Edward, *The Victorian Reinvention of Race: New Racisms and the Problem of Grouping in the Human Sciences*, (Routledge), 2010.

[182] Porter, Andrew, *Religion versus Empire? British Protestant missionaries and overseas expansion, 1700-1914*, (Manchester University Press), 2004, pp. 181-183, provides a succinct discussion of missionary activity in the Caribbean. See also, Hunte, Keith, 'Protestantism and Slavery in the British Caribbean', in Lampe, Armando, (ed.), *Christianity in the Caribbean: Essays on Church History*, (University of West Indies Press), 2001, p. 86-125, Edmonds, Ennis B., and Gonzalez, Michelle A., *Caribbean Religious History: An Introduction*, (New York University Press), 2010, pp. 65-92, 121-154 and Stewart, Robert J., *Religion and Society in Post-Emancipation Jamaica*, (University of Tennessee Press), 1992, pp. 110-189.

[183] Hall, Catherine, *Civilising Subjects: Metropole and Colony in the English Imagination 1830-1867*, (Polity), 2002, pp. 84-139, examines the role of Baptist missionaries between 1830 and 1842.

The Colonial Office was fully aware of the grim depths of Jamaican conditions through persistent efforts by Baptist missionaries to secure relief from London. Central to this was Dr Edward B. Underhill, the Secretary of the Baptist Missionary Society in England who had visited Jamaica in 1859-1860.[184] He received a letter from fellow Baptists in Jamaica in 1864 in which they outlined the depression in Jamaica and its social consequences.[185] His response was a length letter of Edward Cardwell, the Colonial Secretary in January 1865 in which he called attention to numerous grievances that he felt demanded immediate and forceful attention.[186] He cited high levels of taxation, issues relating to wages, land tenure, access to markets and labour rights and called for a comprehensive review of Jamaican legislation passed since Emancipation. Cardwell acknowledged and forwarded the letter to Edward Eyre. Eyre circulated Underhill's letter among leading planters, parish custodes, judges and magistrates as well as among clergymen of all denominations requesting information that he could use to rebut the allegations.[187] Eyre's response to the Colonial Office, except for a lengthy report presented by Baptist missionaries, was that there was no real distress on the island and that if there was, its major cause was the traditional 'laziness' of the Negro.[188]

Edward Eyre had come to Jamaica in March 1862 to deputise temporarily for Governor Sir Charles Darling who was on extended leave of absence and who then accepted the governorship of Victoria.[189] Eyre had a reputation as a highly successful, experienced and efficient colonial administrator and despite his unpopularity on the island he confirmed his reputation and in April 1864 Eyre was confirmed as Governor. Traditionally, Jamaican governors had worked with the Town Party to challenge the resistance of most planters to moderate reform but Eyre supported the Country Party, the traditional voice of white planters.

---

[184] Underhill, Edward B., *The Tragedy of Morant Bay: A Narrative of the Disturbances in the Island of Jamaica in 1865*, (Alexander & Shepheard), 1895, gives Underhill's view of events. See also, *Emancipation in the West Indies: Two Addresses by E. B. Underhilll... and the Rev. J. T. Brown, the deputation from the Baptist Missionary Society to the West Indies....*, (British and Foreign Anti-Slavery Society), 1861 and Underhill, Edward B., *The West Indies: Their Social and Religious Condition*, (Jackson, Walford and Hodder), 1862, reflect his response to his experiences in Jamaica in 1859-1860.

[185] Ibid, Underhill, Edward B., *The Tragedy of Morant Bay*, pp. 1-11.

[186] Underhill, Edward B., *Dr Underhill's Letter: A letter addressed to the Rt. Honourable E. Cardwell, with illustrative documents on the conditions of Jamaica and an explanatory statement*, (A. Miall), 1866.

[187] Underhill's letter is described as 'most injudicious' in Hume, Hamilton, *The Life of Edward John Eyre: Late Governor of Jamaica*, (William Clowes and Sons), 1867, pp. 131-132.

[188] Ibid, Underhill, Edward B., *The Tragedy of Morant Bay*, pp. 12-29, 34-44, considers the letter, its reception in Jamaica and Eyre's response.

[189] Evans, Julie, *Edward Eyre, race and colonial governance*, (University of Otago Press), 2005, pp. 83-132, examines his tenure in the Caribbean from 1854 to 1866 on St Vincent and Antigua and then Jamaica. Ibid, Hume, Hamilton, *The Life of Edward John Eyre: Late Governor of Jamaica*, pp. 109-256, is a pro-Eyre hagiography based on a highly selective use of contemporary evidence. Dutton, Geoffrey, *The Hero as Murderer: The Life of Edward John Eyre, Australian Explorer and Governor of Jamaica, 1815-1901*, (Collins), 1967, is also a sympathetic biography of Eyre.

Whether he was ignorant of conditions for peasant farmers or not, he did little to address the problems they faced. The burden of taxation had begun shifting from planters to smallholders in the early 1840s when import duties became increasingly important and by the 1860s, there was a yawning disparity between the tax burden on property and on the people. For instance, between 1840 and 1865, import duties on herrings rose 166 per cent and on imported clothing by 1,150 per cent while duties on plantation stock, horses and mules were reduced by 40 per cent.[190]

Symptomatic of the attitudes of the colonial authorities in Jamaica and London was the response to a memorial sent in April 1865 by the smallholders of St. Ann to Queen Victoria detailing grievances that became familiar in the Underhill meetings later that spring and autumn.[191] The memorial called for an opening up of the land, for which they would pay by instalments, to facilitate the development of a peasant farming economy. The Queen's response, drafted by Henry Taylor, Permanent-Secretary at the Colonial Office, was a lecture in classical political economy stating or rather restating the case for wage labour to sustain the sugar industry.[192] Taylor assumed the petitioners did not want to work and that they wanted something for nothing. In fact, the petitioners wanted to secure the means of production and intended to earn their living. His response saw wage labour as the solution when the sugar estates could not possibly absorb the labour force. For Eyre, who had 'the Queen's Advice' printed, distributed and posted in public places and read aloud in churches and other public meetings, it was a vindication of his policies and the planters' view of the island's problems and was consistent with his view of the causes of Jamaican distress. Both the Colonial Office and the Jamaican administration were deaf to any suggestion that peasant ownership might offer a solution to Jamaica's economic plight.[193]

In late March 1865, Underhill's letter was published in the Jamaican press without Eyre's knowledge and this proved of crucial importance in creating a public debate about the island's conditions. Eyre may have dismissed Underhill's allegations but a series of public meetings were organised across the island largely attended by coloured middle-class reformers and discontented peasants and workers. They had no central organisation but the meetings passed a series of differently worded resolutions endorsing the contents of Underhill's letter and provided an outlet for political expression denied to the bulk of the population through normal channels. Complaints included a series of economic

---

[190] Ibid, Evans, Julie, *Edward Eyre, race and colonial governance*, pp. 121-125, examines the problems Eyre encountered with the growing demands for a peasant economy.

[191] Ibid, Holt, T. C., *The Problem of Freedom: Race, Labor and Politics in Jamaica and Britain, 1832-1938*, pp. 276-278. Eyre and the custos of St. Ann's parish maintained that the petition was linked to the climate of discontent occasioned by Underhill's letter. In fact, it was drafted several days before the letter was published.

[192] Taylor, Henry, *Autobiography*, 2 vols. (Longmans, Green and Co.), 1885, Dowden, Edward (ed.), *The Correspondence of Sir Henry Taylor*, (Longmans, Green and Co.), 1888.

[193] Mandle, Jay R., *Persistent Underdevelopment: Change and Economic Modernization in the West Indies*, (Taylor & Francis), 1996, pp. 19-56, explores the nature of the plantation economy and its erosion.

issues related to wages, land tenure, access to markets and labour rights; political issues related to unfair taxation, no justice in the courts, and élite -biased government policies; and civil issues that included voting rights, and access to healthcare, education and land.[194] Eyre later stated that the meetings were organised or led by Baptist ministers but Underhill stressed that in the twenty-one parishes where Baptist ministers were active, only eleven held meetings and of the thirty-six official Baptist ministers on the island, only eleven took part in proceedings.[195] Although Baptist missionaries had played a major part in the production of the Underhill letter, they did not actually play a leading role in subsequent events.[196] The timing of Underhill's letter and Eyre's dismissive handling of local responses to it contributed to the growing discontent and tensions that finally spilled over at Morant Bay in October 1865.

Eyre's attitudes reflected changing perceptions towards race across Britain's colonies and the persistent deferral of civil and political rights to colonial subjects. While Lord Durham's *Report* of 1839 called for self-government in colonies of white settlement to secure allegiance to the empire, the same process of devolving power and democratising colonial institutions was not extended to colonies where 'natives' formed a majority.[197] The abolitionist expectation that social inequality would be removed by 'civilising' former slaves and native people was replaced by a biologically defined view. Thomas Carlyle's pamphlet, *Occasional Discourse on the Nigger Question,* initially published in 1853 proved influential in giving the idea of the inferiority of black peoples' respectability and in recognising that they could never achieve the level of European civilisation.[198] Discourses of race increasingly determined the attitudes

[194] Robotham, Don, *'The Notorious Riot': The Socio-Economic and Political Bases of Paul Bogle's Revolt*, (Institute of Social and Economic Research, University of the West Indies), 1984, provides a Jamaican nationalist treatment of the causes of the rebellion.

[195] Ibid, Underhill, Edward B., *The Tragedy of Morant Bay*, pp. 22-23.

[196] Ibid, Underhill, Edward B., *The Tragedy of Morant Bay*, pp. 158-184, provides a detailed rebuttal to Eyre's allegations. Eyre laid the weight of the rebellion firmly on Underhill's shoulders and he was forced to defend his position in late 1865 something that was widely reported in the London and provincial press. See, for instance, 'The State of Things in Jamaica', *Preston Chronicle*, 25 November 1865, p. 5, 'The Outbreak in Jamaica', *York Herald*, 25 November 1865, pp. 8, 11, 'The Jamaica Riots', *Kentish Chronicle*, 25 November 1865, p. 2, 'Opinions of the Press', *Kentish Chronicle*, 25 November 1865, p. 3, and 'Jamaica', *Manchester Courier and Lancashire General Advertiser*, 9 December 1865, p. 6.

[197] Lucas, C. P., (ed.), *Lord Durham's Report on the affairs of British North America*, 3 Vols. (Oxford University Press), 1912, is the standard edition of the Report. See, Ajzenstat, Janet, 'Liberalism and assimilation: Lord Durham reconsidered', Brooks, Stephen, (ed.), *Political thought in Canada: contemporary perspectives*, (Toronto University Press), 1984, pp. 239-257, Ajzenstat, Janet, *The Political Thought of Lord Durham*, (McGill-Queen's University Press), 1988, Ducharme, Michel, 'L'État selon Lord Durham: liberté et nationalité dans l'empire britannique', *Cahiers d'Histoire*, Vol. 18, (1998), pp. 39-64, and the discussion in Brown, Richard, *Three Rebellions*, pp. 497-508.

[198] Originally published anonymously in *Fraser's Magazine* Vol. 40, (1849), pp. 670-679, entitled 'Occasional Discourse on the Negro Question', it was republished in *The Latter Day Pamphlets* in 1853 with the significant shift from 'negro' to 'nigger' in its title. For discussion of this pamphlet see, ibid, Hall, Catherine, *Civilising Subjects: Metropole and Colony in the English Imagination 1830-1867*, pp. 348-353.

of the Colonial Office and more generally those of colonial government and justified exploitative colonial economies, buttressed local authority and sustained British imperial sovereignty.[199] For Eyre, race was central to his understanding of the Caribbean: he saw freed people not as a peasant class capable of education and reform but as a race of innately inferior people susceptible to repression.[200]

Rebellion

The rebellion at Morant Bay in 1865 followed the Underhill meetings and the peaceful expression of grievances through petitions.[201] Comparisons have been made between events in 1831 and 1865 but there were significant differences. The rebellion in 1831 was more widespread and organised than in 1865. The resistance at Morant Bay expressed the attachment to private landholding among peasants. Unlike in 1831, where the central demand was for wages paid for labour on the estates, in 1865, the central issue was access to land as a means of resisting the need to work on the estates. Plantation owners were challenged as landlords, not as employers. In that sense, it was less a planned rebellion than a peaceful and legitimate social movement that was rejected by the Governor and finally turned to violence against the representatives of the local government.[202]

The parish of St. Thomas-in-the-East, where Morant Bay is located, was one of the few areas of the island where the Baptist Missionary Society had no representatives. Local magistrates, during slavery and after, successfully prevented the establishment of any missionary activity in the district. At the time of the rebellion, Underhill estimated that 80 per cent of the people in St. Thomas were 'in want of religious instruction'.[203] This had not prevented the development of a Native Baptist tradition in the area. Paul Bogle, the leader of the resistance, was a Native Baptist preacher and peasant landowner and used his chapel as an organising centre. Given the hostility of the political leaders in the parish to formal Christian teaching, participation in Native Baptist activities took

---

[199] Goldberg, David Theo, 'Liberalism's Limits: Carlyle and Mill on the 'Negro Question'', in Ward, Julie K., and Lott, Tommy L., (eds.), *Philosophers on Race: Critical Essays*, (Blackwell Publishing), 2002, pp. 195-204, Groenewegen, Peter, 'Thomas Carlyle, 'The Dismal Science', and Contemporary Political Economy of Slavery', *History of Economics Review*, Vol. 54, (2001), pp. 74-94.

[200] Ibid, Evans, Julie, *Edward Eyre, race and colonial governance*, pp. 95-101.

[201] For contemporary comment on Morant Bay see, 'The Town of Morant Bay, Morant Bay, Jamaica', *Harper's Weekly*, 23 December 1865, 'The Negro Insurrection in Jamaica', *The Illustrated London News*, 25 November 1865, pp. 1, 17, 18. Richard, Rev. Henry, *The Troubles in Jamaica: A Condensed Statement of the Facts*, (Jackson, Walford & Hodder), 1866.

[202] For the rebellion see, Heuman, Gad, *The Killing Time, The Morant Bay Rebellion in Jamaica*, (Macmillan), 1994, Olusoga, David, *Black and British: A Forgotten History*, (Macmillan), 2016, pp. 378-398, ibid, Green, William A., *British Slave Emancipation*, pp. 381-405, Erickson, Arvel B., 'Empire or Anarchy: The Jamaica Rebellion of 1865', *Journal of Negro History*, Vol. 44, (1959), pp. 99-122, ibid, Bakan, Abigail, *Ideology and Class Conflict in Jamaica: The Politics of Rebellion*, pp. 68-93. Morrell, W. P., *British Colonial Policy in the Mid-Victorian Age: South Africa, New Zealand and the West Indies*, (Oxford University Press), 1969, pp. 399-427, provides a general examination of the background and character of the rebellion.

[203] Ibid, Underhill, Edward B., *The Tragedy of Morant Bay*, p. 181.

on a more assertive and political importance. George William Gordon, a coloured member of the Assembly and active lay preacher in the Morant Bay district, was the illegitimate son of a black slave and wealthy white planter who had, by the 1860s, established himself as a successful planter and large landowner in St. Thomas and other parts of the island. In 1861, he adopted the Baptist faith and the following year opened two mission stations near Stony Gut, the centre of the rebellion in 1865. Gordon was a long-standing political opponent of Governor Eyre, who had been instrumental in Gordon's dismissal as a magistrate in St. Thomas in 1862.[204] However, in 1863, with the support of the peasants in St. Thomas, many of whom were influenced by the Native Baptist tradition, Gordon was elected to the Assembly.

Eyre had been expecting a 'Negro uprising' for several months especially as there was widespread unrest in the northern parishes of the island and rumours of preparations for rebellion were widespread although there were no indications of planning in St. Thomas.[205] Eyre wrote to the Colonial Office in July and August 1865 expressing his concerns commenting that it was his 'firm conviction that the day will come when Jamaica will become little better than a second Hayti'.[206] At the end of July 1865, a printed leaflet, unsigned but attributed to Gordon, called on the residents of St. Thomas and those of St. Ann's to attend a public meeting at Morant Bay Courthouse.[207] Held on 12 August, it was one of the last of the Underhill meetings, was chaired by Gordon and passed a series of resolutions on 'the misgovernment of the island'.[208] A delegation that included Bogle was selected to take their grievances to Eyre at Spanish Town but he refused to see them further increasing frustration and resentment.[209] This failure led to political divisions developing among the black population in the district. Bogle moved away from formal political channels and organised independent popular societies to challenge the discredited colonial authorities while Gordon followed a traditional approach and began to campaign for funds to send a delegation directly to the Queen over the Governor's head.

---

[204] See, 'Correspondence in relation to the Removal of Mr G. W. Gordon from the Magistracy in Jamaica...', in *Accounts and papers of the House of Commons*, Vol. 13, pp. 1-44.

[205] See, for instance, 'Rumours of Popular Outbreaks', *Falmouth Post and Jamaica General Advertiser*, 11 August 1865, p. 3. Ibid, Hume, Hamilton, *The Life of Edward John Eyre: Late Governor of Jamaica*, pp. 176-177, suggests that illegal drilling was reported across the island and arms and ammunition were being collected and hidden in many districts. See also, ibid, Evans, Julie, *Edward Eyre, race and colonial governance*, pp. 130-132.

[206] Cit, ibid, Hume, Hamilton, *The Life of Edward John Eyre: Late Governor of Jamaica*, p. 177.

[207] Ibid, Hume, Hamilton, *The Life of Edward John Eyre: Late Governor of Jamaica*, pp. 191-194, prints what Hume regarded as 'this incendiary document'.

[208] See, 'The Claims of Coloured Persons', *Falmouth Post and Jamaica General Advertiser*, 15 August 1865, p. 3.

[209] For contemporary newspaper comment on Bogle see, *Colonial Standard and Jamaica Despatch*, 18, 19, 21, 24, 28 October 1865, *Falmouth Post and Jamaica General Advertiser*, 24 October 1865, and *Gleaner and DeCordova's Advertising Sheet*, 19 October, 16 November 1865.

A black farmer Lewis Miller squatted on a piece of land adjoining Stony Gut belonging to Jonas Hart, an absentee plantation owner and refused to pay rent on the estate. He wrongly argued that the land was the property of the Crown and was therefore rent-free. He was summoned to a magistrates' court presided over by Baron von Ketelhodt, the Custos and owner of five plantations, in the Morant Bay courthouse on Saturday 7 October 1865. Miller happened to be the cousin of Paul Bogle who had assembled a group of some 150-people armed with sticks, guns and cutlasses that accompanied Miller into Morant Bay. Miller was convicted on his own plea of guilty but Bogle came forward from the crowd and urged him to refuse to pay the fine and to appeal his conviction. The appeal was duly registered. Matters deteriorated when James Geoghagan disrupted further proceedings by shouting that a boy convicted of assault against a woman should pay his fine of four shillings but not have to pay costs and was ordered to be brought before the justices.[210] When he did not go quietly, von Ketelhodt ordered his arrest that occurred outside the court. However, his sister Isabella challenged the police and a 'mob' including Bogle and some of his followers from the hamlet of Stony Gut rescued him from the police.

The following Monday, 9 October, warrants were issued for the arrest of Bogle, his brother Moses and some twenty-five others and the following day, six policemen and two constables went up to Stony Gut to arrest those involved. There they encountered between three and five hundred people, armed with sticks and cutlasses, prepared to assist those charges with resisting arrest. The police were captured and beaten, some were detained as prisoners and made to swear an oath to 'join their colour' and 'cleave to the black'. By evening, news had reached Morant that the following day an assembly would again present the Vestry authorities with their grievances. Underhill argued that 'there was no formal intention on the part of the people to rebel', citing a petition sent to the Governor by Bogle and twenty others on 9 October and:

> ...at this supreme moment, kind treatment and an effort to deal impartially with grievances...would have averted the calamity that fell on the magistrates and community of Morant Bay on this Wednesday afternoon.[211]

The issue of *being heard* was important but the unresponsive reactions of the authorities had created an impasse that local officials now exacerbated. At this point, the Custos decided to summon the militia and called on Governor Eyre to provide military assistance. On Wednesday 11 October, the Custos, magistrates and vestrymen met at the courthouse around noon and conducted their ordinary business but made no effort to address Bogle's petition. In the afternoon, a crowd of several hundred-armed people, who had previously raided the police station for weapons, led by Bogle assembled in the open space before the Vestry Hall facing the Volunteers who had been drawn up to protect it. The seizure of weapons suggests that Underhill's view that there was 'no intention to rebel' needs to be questioned. The Custos read the Riot Act and, ostensibly in response to stone throwing, ordered the militia to open fire killing or wounding

---

[210] 'James Geoghegan', *Colonial Standard and Jamaica Despatch*, 28 October 1865.
[211] Ibid, Underhill, Edward B., *The Tragedy of Morant Bay*, pp. 60-61.

some of the crowd that then rushed the courthouse and fired the building.[212] Among those killed during the seizure of the Morant Bay courthouse were Baron von Ketelhodt and Reverend Herschell, curate of Bath who were both disliked and distrusted by blacks.[213] Fifty-one prisoners were released from Morant Bay gaol and unsuccessful attempts were made to take 300 weapons from the magazine. On Thursday 12 October, the rioters travelled to Bath, a town eight miles from Morant Bay attacking several estate houses and continuing along the Plantain Garden River.[214] By this time, the first troops had arrived in the district and the rebellion was quickly crushed.[215]

In total, eighteen people were killed and thirty-one wounded by the rebels on 11 October. Twenty houses were looted and five buildings, including the Morant Bay courthouse were burnt. When the rebels travelled to Bath, damage to estate houses was extensive and several other people were killed including an attorney or agent for Amity Hall Estates. After the bloodbath at Morant Bay, it appears that the rebels were selective in their targets dealing harshly only with those whites who had oppressed blacks while sparing those seen as sympathetic to the black cause. These figures pale in comparison with the repression that followed. Eyre acted quickly after receiving news from Morant Bay, called an emergency meeting of the Privy Council and on 13 October 1865 declared martial law covering the whole of the county of Surrey, which included the parish of St Thomas-in-the-East, but civil law continued to operate in Kingston. Regular troops of West India Regiment, 6th Regiment, marines from the warship *Wolverine*, militia and groups of Maroons were involved into the suppression of the revolt. More troops were sent from Barbados and the Bahamas. Rapid and well coordinated actions of army, Volunteers and Maroons contained rebels in few days and organised resistance ceased on 15 October 1865.

Martial law remained in force for a month.[216] During this time, 439 blacks were killed in fight or executed, 100 men were imprisoned for terms ranging from six to twelve years, more than 600 persons including women and children were flogged, and about thousand dwellings were burned.[217] 85 prisoners were shot without a proper trial. Governor Eyre was convinced that this 'reign of terror' had prevented a 'new Mutiny'. After Thursday 12 October, no one was

[212] The Royal Commission concluded that if stones were thrown, the action was not taken by major participants in the incident but by some women standing by: cit, Underhill, Edward B., *The Tragedy of Morant Bay*, p. 62.

[213] Ibid, Hume, Hamilton, *The Life of Edward John Eyre: Late Governor of Jamaica*, pp. 185-202, gives a deliberately graphic description of the attack on the courthouse designed to inflame opinion against the rebels. For instance, on p. 202: 'The Rev. Mr Hershell's tongue was cut our and the fingers of Baron von Ketelhodt severed from his hands.' See, ibid, Heuman, Gad, *The Killing Time, The Morant Bay Rebellion in Jamaica*, pp. 3-16, for the Morant Bay massacre.

[214] 'From the Plantain Garden River District', *Colonial Standard and Jamaica Despatch*, 16 October 1865.

[215] *Colonial Standard and Jamaica Despatch*, 13, 14, 16, 18 October 1865, reported on riots in St Thomas in the East. See also *Falmouth Post and Jamaica General Advertiser*, 17, 20 October 1865.

[216] 'Martial Law', *Falmouth Post and Jamaica General Advertiser*, 7 November 1865.

[217] 'The Massacres in St. Thomas in the East', *Falmouth Post and Jamaica General Advertiser*, 24 October 1865.

killed or injured at the hands of the rebels and, in no instance, were the soldiers resisted. [218] The imposition of martial law gave free rein to the revenge of the plantocracy and one white resident commented:

> We are living in fear all the day long. Our lives were in danger during the first few days of the rioters' success and were no less so when they were crushed. Martial law is a dreadful thing! A horrible affair! [219]

The Maroons, who Bogle hoped would join the rebels, supported the Jamaican government and played a major role in hunting down rebels, capturing Bogle on 24 October who was then summarily executed, hanged from the arch of the ruined courthouse in Morant Bay.[220] Eyre was convinced that Gordon was the chief instigator of the rebellion. Gordon, then living in Kingston, was arrested and brought to Morant Bay where martial law was in force.[221] He was charged with having conspired to instigate the rebellion at Morant Bay, though evidence suggests that he only found out about the outbreak after it had started.[222] He was then tried by a dubiously constituted and managed court martial, found guilty of high treason and executed on 23 October.[223] This was judicial murder of an individual whom Eyre regarded as a threat to the established order. There was also religious bigotry in Eyre's actions. As a committed Anglican, he hated Dissenters and Baptists and Gordon's execution reflected that prejudice.[224] Baptist missionaries were repeatedly implicated during the period of martial law

---

[218] 'The Influence of the Maroons, and 'The Volunteers'', *Colonial Standard and Jamaica Despatch*, 17 October 1865, deals with the early stages of repression.

[219] *The Freeman*, 3 January 1866, cit, Underhill, Edward B., *The Tragedy of Morant Bay*, p. 51.

[220] 'Report of Colonel Fyfe on their proceedings', *Accounts and papers of the House of Commons*, Vol. 13, pp. 280-281, examines the role of the Maroons. See also, ibid, Heuman, Gad, *The Killing Time, The Morant Bay Rebellion in Jamaica*, pp. 131-145.

[221] 'Arrest in Kingston', *Colonial Standard and Jamaica Despatch*, 20 October 1865, and *Gleaner and DeCordova's Advertising Sheet*, 23 October 1865.

[222] Hume, Hamilton, *The Life of Edward John Eyre: Late Governor of Jamaica*, pp. 184-190, cited a letter dated 12 December 1865, from Lieutenant Edenborough, late of the Confederate States Navy to Edward Cardwell stating that Gordon was actively involved in conspiracy and in obtaining arms and spoke of a 'New West India Republic'. Given Hume's pro-Eyre stance and, as he recognised in a footnote on p. 185, Edenborough's testimony had not been tested by the Royal Commission, this evidence is generally regarded as unreliable. Hume, pp. 257-267, prints the evidence against Gordon from the Royal Commission's Report.

[223] 'Trial of G. W. Gordon', *Colonial Standard and Jamaica Despatch*, 23 October 1865. See also, 'Trial of George William Gordon', *Colonial Standard and Jamaica Despatch*, 6 January 1866, 'George William Gordon', *Falmouth Post and Jamaica General Advertiser*, 31 October 1865, and 'The Traitor George W. Gordon', *Gleaner and DeCordova's Advertising Sheet*, 28 October 1865. See also, Brock, Peggy, Etherington, Norman, Griffiths, Gareth and Van Gent, Jacqueline, *Indigenous Evangelists and Questions of Authority in the British Empire 1750-1940*, (Brill), 2015, pp. 211-238, on George Gordon, Paul Bogle and the Martyred Dead of Morant Bay.

[224] Fletcher, Rev. Duncan, *The Life of the Honourable George W. Gordon, the Martyr of Jamaica*, 2nd ed., (Elliott Stock), 1867, and *Personal Reflections of Honourable George W. Gordon, Late of Jamaica*, (Elliott Stock), 1867, established the hagiography.

although they had no direct involvement in the events at Morant Bay. Eyre named several Baptist ministers whom he considered responsible for the uprising but the later Royal Commission found no grounds for his charges. Baptist ministers were harassed and arrested, their mail was opened and there were some reports of torture.

The Morant Bay rebellion had two main features. There was a general lack of organisation and leadership among those involved in the different events. There was also division within the black community between the rebels who were largely peasants and those who saw themselves as permanently employed estate workers. Both Eyre and Underhill later commented on the lack of organisation among the rebels but even if Bogle never intended to ignite a rebellion on 11 October, there was both prior organisation and premeditation.[225] Henry Theophilus Bogle, nephew of Paul Bogle, and some other persons allegedly testified that about two weeks before the rebellion, secret meetings were held, oaths administered and the leaders of revolt elected. Eyre argued that it was only his decisive and effective suppression of rebellion that prevented it spreading to the rest of Jamaica but this notion was only raised *after* the Morant Bay rebellion had taken place.

Although Eyre insisted that the outbreak at Morant Bay was local, he pointed out that a seditious spirit was general, and that potential for revolt could be found especially in those parishes frequently visited by George William Gordon.[226] Eyre later suggested that Morant Bay was a premature development of a plan of a more general rising like at Saint Domingue during the French Revolution where whites had been massacred and expelled from the island.[227] Former Governors strongly argued that there was abundant testimony with regard to the black people having expressed an intention to exterminate all the whites and brown people: 'An intended slaughter of the whites and colored inhabitants of Jamaica was to have been carried out on Christmas.'[228] This view has some support among historians with Green, for instance, arguing that the implications of the rebellion were 'broad and dangerous' and that without Eyre's prompt action at Morant Bay outbreaks could have occurred across the island.[229] Events in 1865 lacked the organisation and prepared collective action of the slave rebellion in 1831 largely because the idea of mass action, endemic in the slave society in 1831, was no longer present in the conditions of peasant production.

---

[225] 'The Conspirators Plan', *Gleaner and DeCordova's Advertising Sheet*, 26 October 1865, gives a pro-Eyre view. Recently historians have shifted from seeing Morant Bay as a 'local riot' to agree that the events on 11 October constituted a rebellion citing evidence of the planning involved: see, ibid, Heuman, Gad, *The Killing Time, The Morant Bay Rebellion in Jamaica*, pp. xviii-xix, and ibid, Holt, T. C., *The Problem of Freedom: Race, Labor and Politics in Jamaica and Britain, 1832-1938*, pp. 301-302.

[226] Finlason, W. F., *The History of the Jamaica Case: Being an Account, Founded upon Official Documents of the Rebellion of the Negroes in Jamaica: The Causes which led to it, and the Measures Taken for its Suppression; the Agitation Excited on the Subjects, its Causes and its Character; and the Debates in Parliament, and the Criminal Prosecutions, Arising out of it*, (London 1869), p. 130.

[227] Ibid, Finlason, W. F., *The History of the Jamaica Case*..., p. 134.

[228] Ibid, Finlason, W. F., *The History of the Jamaica Case*..., p. 129.

[229] Ibid, Green, William A., *British Slave Emancipation*, p. 390.

What was important for rebels in 1865 was more concrete: their common interest in obtaining great access to land.

Reactions

The tragic events and atrocities committed by both sides in India during 1857 and 1858 influenced widely the British thinking and perception of the racial issue. It seemed that policy of modernisation, philanthropy, education and evangelisation had completely failed. News first reached Britain on 3 November, but in was not until 13November that details of the disturbances and suppression became available and not until 18 November that full accounts, accompanied by exaggerated reports of the atrocities committed by the rebels, appeared in the press.[230] Eyre's report of events, dated 20 October, reached the Colonial Office on 16 November reinforced the sense that he had 'saved the colony' from wholesale destruction.[231] In his letter from 17 November 1865, Edward Cardwell, the Colonial Secretary, expressed his 'high approval of the spirit, energy, and judgement with which you have acted in your measures for repressing and preventing the spread of insurrection.' Later, once the extent of British oppression and Eyre's responsibility for it became known, Cardwell became more circumspect and on 23 November, demanded more information on the measures of suppression mentioning the Gordon case.[232]

Newspapers in the United States were first to report on the atrocities: the Baltimore *Sun* reported on 'the massacre in Jamaica' on 18 November while the *New York Herald*'s sensationalist headline 'Eight Miles of Dead Bodies' was quickly appropriated by Nonconformist groups in England.[233] On 18 November 1865, *The Times* attacked 'agitators from Haiti' and 'the natural barbarity' of Africans. On the other hand, the *Economist*, the *Manchester Guardian*, the *Oxford Chronicle*, or the *Saturday Review* criticised the Eyre's severe actions,

[230] For instance, the rebellion was reported in a supplement to the *London Gazette* and in 'Rebellion in Jamaica', *The Times* on 18 November 1865, p. 8. The provincial press began reporting the rebellion on Monday 13 November with the 'The Black Rebellion in Jamaica', *Birmingham Daily Post,* 13 November 1865, pp. 6, 8, 'A Black Business in Jamaica', *Western Daily Press*, 13 November 1865, p.p. 2, 3, and 'The Negro Insurrection in Jamaica', *Manchester Courier and Lancashire General Advertiser*, 13 November 1865, p. 3, with the *Western Daily Press* commenting: 'we can scarcely help thinking that the negro…is a somewhat disagreeable and intractable customer…'

[231] Price, G. E., *Jamaica and the Colonial Office: Who caused the crisis*? (Low and Marston), 1866, provides a highly critical account of the actions of the Colonial Office; see especially, pp. 118-137.

[232] Kostal, R. W., *A Jurisprudence of Power: Victorian Empire and the Rule of Law*, (Oxford University Press), 2005, provides the most detailed analysis of the Jamaica controversy. See also, Semmel, Bernard, *Jamaican Blood and Victorian Conscience: The Governor Eyre Controversy*, (Houghton Mifflin), 1962, and ibid, Hall, Catherine, *Civilising Subjects: Metropole and Colony in the English Imagination 1830-1867*, pp. 406-433 and her 'Imperial Man: Edward Eyre in Australasia and the West Indies 1833-66', in Schwarz, Bill, (ed.), *The Expansion of England: Race, Ethnicity and Cultural History*, (Routledge), 1996, pp. 130-170.

[233] Evidence of British repression was briefly reported in *Providence Evening Post*, 10 November 1865, *Detroit Free Press*, 15, 17 November 1865 and in the *New York Times*, 17 November 1865.

backed Baptist ministers, and doubted on the justice of the sentence on George William Gordon. For Radical and Progressive jurist and historian Frederic Harrison:

> ...on the one hand stands the cause of personal liberty, the inviolability of law, just procedure, official responsibility, equal justice, and ancient precedent. On the other hand, that of arbitrary rule, military jurisdiction, wild unjustice, martial licence, race prejudice, and strange prerogative. Let us see on which side the English public will be.

In a similar vein, John Stuart Mill wrote:

> There was much more at stake than only justice to the negroes, imperative as was that consideration. The question was, whether the British dependencies, and eventually, perhaps, Great Britain itself, were to be under the government of law or of military license.

The attitude of the provincial press from 23 November reflected changing public opinion. On 26 November, *Reynolds's Newspaper* not only condemned the indiscriminate killing and 'wanton and unnecessary cruelty' by Eyre's forces but maintained that the rebellion had been 'provoked' by the actions of the magistrates at Morant Bay in 'hastily firing upon and killing and wounding the people...'[234] while on 30 November, the *Lincolnshire Chronicle* commented that way that the rebellion 'had been suppressed was a course which does not appear to us to have been dictated either by prudence or justice.'[235] This was not a universal view and the *Birmingham Gazette* on 2 December observed that the way in which the rebellion was suppressed was 'a matter of congratulations rather than regret' and that 'we are disposed to look leniently even on excesses committed in hot blood under of sting of so terrible a provocation and in the face of such an awful peril.'[236]

In the initial phase of the anti-Eyre protest, there were deputations to the Prime Minister and during the first two weeks in December the Colonial Office was besieged by delegations demanding Eyre's immediate removal from office. On Saturday 9 December, over 250 gentlemen from the British and Foreign Anti-Slavery Society presented a memorial to Cardwell, now under growing pressure from the Liberal and Progressive press. Cardwell responded by stating his respect for Eyre and stressing the difficulties of the situation. A few days later Cardwell, this time accompanied by Russell, the Prime Minister, received a delegation from the London Missionary Society. Russell urged the delegation not to underestimate the gravity of the Morant Bay rebellion. The government was disposed to defend Eyre but its resolve was weakened by the vehement campaign in the press and in the country combined with Eyre's unwillingness to provide detailed explanations for his actions. In early December, it relieved Eyre of his

[234] 'The British Atrocities in Jamaica', *Reynolds's Newspaper*, 26 November 1865, p. 1.
[235] 'Suppression of the Jamaican Insurrection', *Lincolnshire Chronicle*, 30 November 1865, p. 7.
[236] 'The Jamaica Insurrection', *Birmingham Gazette*, 2 December 1865, p. 8.

duties in Jamaica and appointed a three-member Royal Commission headed by Sir Henry Storks, Governor of Malta.[237]

The delegations took place against the background of growing extra-parliamentary pressure that polarised public opinion into pro- and anti-Eyre camps.[238] Large protest meetings were held mainly in strongly Nonconformist urban centres such as Bradford, Leeds, Manchester, Newcastle, Plymouth, Reading and York.[239] In late November, the meeting in Brighton was addressed by Henry Fawcett, the blind Liberal MP, who described what had taken place in Jamaica as 'a barbarity which never occurred in the time of the blackest pages of history'. The London press took sides. The radical *Morning Star* stressed the atrocities committed against the blacks by British troops while the weekly *News of the World* reported 'savageries' against the whites. Those arguing against Eyre included John Stuart Mill, Charles Darwin, Charles Lyell, Herbert Spencer, John Bright and Frederick Harrison who believed that martial law had been misused: British subjects were being denied their rights under the rule of law. The behaviour of the governor was an attack on Englishness. But Eyre had his defenders. His sister, Mary, wrote a letter to the *Morning Star*:

> It is not fair, Sir, it is not English, to publish only letters abusing a man and stigmatizing him as 'a wholesale murderer and a Robespierre.

The *Pall Mall Gazette* also sprang to Eyre's defence.[240] *The Times* demanded an impartial investigation, reminding its readers that Eyre had been the protector of the Australian Aboriginals.

In early December 1865, the Jamaica Committee was organised in London calling on the British government to repudiate the actions of the authorities in Jamaica and to secure justice for those who had been repressed.[241] Chairing the committee was Charles Buxton MP, son of Thomas Fowell Buxton who had been a major figure in the abolition movement. P. A. Taylor, a Unitarian and Radical MP for Leicester, became treasurer and Frederick William Chesson, who wrote for the *Morning Star*, became secretary. Other members of the Jamaica Committee included John Bright, Thomas Hughes, J. M. Ludlow and Goldwin Smith. The Committee sent Sir John Gorrie to Jamaica to monitor the work of Royal Commission[242] and retained the barristers Edward James QC and James Fitzjames Stephen to draft a memorandum concerning the legality of the

---

[237] Storks was at the same time appointed acting governor of Jamaica. The other members of the commission were: Russell Gurney, MP and Recorder of the City of London and J. B. Maule, Recorder of Leeds.

[238] See the valuable discussion in, Watson, Tim, *Caribbean Culture and British Fiction in the Atlantic World, 1780-1870*, (Cambridge University Press), 2008, pp. 154-186.

[239] *The Times*, 22, 28 and 29 November, and 2, 4, 12, 13 and 15 December 1865.

[240] For instance, 'Summary of this Morning's Papers', *Pall Mall Gazette*, 29 January 1866, p. 5.

[241] 'Statement of the Committee and Other Documents', *Jamaica Papers,* No. III, (Jamaica Committee), 1866, pp. 3-7.

[242] Gorrie, John, 'Illustrations of Martial Law in Jamaica; compiled from the Report of the Royal Commissioners, and other Blue Books Laid Before Parliament', *Jamaica Papers*, No. VI, (Jamaica Committee), 1867.

use of martial law in Jamaica. In January 1866, the James-Stephen memorandum was published as the first of a series of pamphlets that came to be known as the *Jamaica Papers*. The James-Stephen memorandum argued that while 'the suppression of revolts by military force was undoubtedly legal', the 'subsequent punishment of offenders' by courts martial was not and that Eyre and his field commanders were legally culpable for a long list of serious, in some instances capital, crimes.[243]

The Royal Commission report, the product of three months' intensive investigation in Jamaica–it examined 730 witnesses in 51 days[244]--was published on 18 June 1866[245] and was later described as 'a masterly and notably impartial document'.[246] Neither Eyre's supporters nor detractors took serious exception to its findings. It concluded the disturbances at St. Thomas were a 'planned resistance to lawful authority', though it rejected the notion of a planned conspiracy aimed at subverting the government. It argued that the threat of rebellion had spread quickly and praised Eyre for the vigour with which he dealt with it. However, the commissioners were critical, not of the imposition of martial law but that it had been maintained far longer than was necessary and were damning in their comments about punishment: 'the punishment of death was unnecessarily frequent', 'the floggings were reckless and at Bath positively barbarous', and 'the burning of 1,000 houses was wanton and cruel'.[247] In reviewing the case of G. W. Gordon, the Commission concluded that his conduct had markedly contributed to the poisoning of the political atmosphere in Jamaica but, without taking a position on the procedural irregularities of his court martial and execution, suggested that the evidence was wholly insufficient to justify conviction for high treason.

> On the assumption that, if there was in fact a widespread conspiracy, Mr G. W. Gordon must have been party to is, the conclusion at which we have arrived in his case is decisive as to the non-existence of such a conspiracy.[248]

Russell's government accepted the conclusions of the Royal Commission on 16 June. Eyre was officially recalled and dismissed though the government declined to assign legal responsibility or initiate criminal prosecutions. A week

---

[243] See also, Finlason, W. F., *Commentaries on Martial Law, with special reference to... the Jamaica Case*, (Stevens and Hall), 1868, for a pro-Eyre stance. For discussion of Finlason's work see, ibid, Kostal, R. W., *A Jurisprudence of Power*, pp. 228-245, and more generally, Townshend, Charles, 'Martial Law: Legal and Administrative Problems of Civil Emergency in Britain and the Empire, 1800-1940', *Historical Journal*, Vol. 25, (2009), pp. 167-195.

[244] Jemmott, Jenny M., 'Surviving the Suppression: The Significance of Witnesses' Testimonies before the Jamaica Royal Commission of 1866', *Journal of Caribbean History*, Vol. 50, (1), (2016).

[245] 'Report of the Jamaica Royal Commission', *Parliamentary Papers*, Vol. 30, 1866, pp. 489-531, Vol. 31, pp. 1-1172. Other documents include 'Papers Laid before the Royal Commission of Inquiry by Governor Eyre', ibid, Vol. 30, pp., 1-488, and 'Papers Relating to the Disturbances in Jamaica', ibid, Vol. 51, pp. 145-506.

[246] Ibid, Morrell, W. P., *British Colonial Policy in the Mid-Victorian Age*, p. 418.

[247] Ibid, 'Report of the Jamaica Royal Commission', pp. 530-531.

[248] Ibid, 'Report of the Jamaica Royal Commission', pp. 518-528.

later, it resigned defeated on parliamentary reform and was replaced by Lord Derby's Conservative administration. Although the Jamaica question was debated in Parliament[249] on 31 July 1866, the fight now moved into the narrower confines of the courts while the moral debate was played out on a broader canvas as opposing side sought to gain the support of English public opinion.[250]

Eyre had remained in Jamaica for the hearings of the Royal Commission but finally left the colony on 24 July 1866 and returned to England. Despite the controversy in England about his role in the rebellion and the conclusions of the Royal Commission, he had received numerous addresses from grateful planters and merchants and the Bishop and clergy of Kingston[251] and a local paper wrote that he was the 'ill-used but faithful and true servant of the British Crown, and the heroic and valiant rescuer of the well-disposed and peaceable and loyal inhabitants of poor Jamaica.'[252] In February 1866, Commander Bedford Pym, a prominent defender of Eyre's presented a paper to the newly formed Anthropological Society of London:

> We do not admit equality even among our own race, as is provided by the state of the franchise at this hour in England. The principles on which alien and dissimilar races ought to be governed is not yet understood by our rulers. Jamaica is not the only proof of this: the state of St Vincent, Antigua, New Zealand, the Cape of Good Hope, to say nothing of India, attests that 'how to govern alien races' has yet to be learned. Let us take the negro as we find him, as God designed him, not a white man, nor the equal of a white man. [253]

With Eyre's return to England in August, the dynamic of the controversy changed with his supporters prepared to answer the campaign of the Jamaica Committee with the Eyre Testimonial and Defence Fund Committee that took shape in the late summer of 1866.[254] Spearheading Eyre's defence was Thomas Carlyle, supported by Charles Dickens, John Ruskin and Lord Tennyson.[255] *The Times* published a letter written by Carlyle on 12 September:

---

[249] *Hansard*, House of Commons, Debates, 31 July 1866, Vol. 184, cc1763-1840.

[250] Bleby, Henry, *The Reign of Terror: a Narrative of Facts concerning Ex-Governor Eyre, George William Gordon, and the Jamaica Atrocities*, (William Nichols), 1868, pp. 49-91, provided a graphic account of the brutality of Eyre's repression.

[251] *Jamaica: Addresses to His Excellency Edward John Eyre, Esquire, &c., &c., 1865, 1866*, (M. DeCordova & Co.), 1866, prints thirty-five addresses and Eyre's replies.

[252] *Colonial Standard and Jamaica Despatch*, 25 July 1866. See also, ibid, Hume, Hamilton, *The Life of Edward John Eyre: Late Governor of Jamaica*, Appendix E, pp. 292-304, for a highly selective collection of pro-Eyre reports from Jamaican newspapers.

[253] Pym, Commander Bedford, *The Negro and Jamaica, Read Before the Anthropological Society of London, February 1, 1866, at St. James's Hall, London*, (Trübner and Co.), 1866, p. 50.

[254] Its formation was reported, for instance, in the 'News of the Day', *Birmingham Daily Post*, 1 September 1866, p. 2, 'Condensed Intelligence', *Reading Mercury*, 1 September 1866, p. 4, and 'General News', *Bristol Mercury*, 1 September 1866, p. 6.

[255] Webb, Jack, 'The Morant Bay Rebellion, British Colonial Policy and Travelling Ideas about Haiti', *Journal of Caribbean History*, Vol. 50, (1), (2016), pp. 70-90, argues that Eyre's defence was bolstered by proliferating notions of scientific racism. Scientists, such as members of the Anthropological Society of London, that included many politicians and colonial administrators amongst it ranks, promoted the notion that Haitians and Jamaicans

The clamour raised against Governor Eyre appears to me to be disgraceful to the good sense of England...For my own share, all the light that has yet reached me on Mr Eyre and his history in the world goes steadily to establish the conclusion that he is a just, humane and valiant man...that his late services in Jamaica were of great, perhaps of incalculable value, as certainly they were of perilous and appalling difficulty...and, in short, that penalty and clamour are not the thing the Governor merits from any of us, but honour and thanks and wise imitation (I will farther say), should similar emergencies arise, on the great scale or on the small, in whatever we are governing.[256]

If the existence of the Jamaica Committee induced Carlyle to enter the argument on Eyre's behalf, the publication of his letter confirmed John Stuart Mill's determination to press forward. Failing government action, Mill, MP for Westminster and the Jamaica Committee were prepared to proceed with a private prosecution. Mill had joined the Jamaica Committee in January 1866 and maintained that the rebellion and its suppression raised an issue of fundamental importance. There were divisions within the Jamaica Committee over whether to bring a private criminal prosecution of Edward Eyre for the murder of Gordon and after an acrimonious meeting on 9 July 1866, Buxton resigned the chairmanship and Mill was elected in his place. In Mill's view, if the Jamaica atrocities were not decisively condemned in the High Court, then they represented a perilous threat to British liberty and constitutionalism.

The question was, whether the British Dependencies, and eventually, perhaps, Great Britain itself, were to be under the government of law, or of military licence.[257]

For the next two years, Mill expended the resources of the Jamaica Committee in an ultimately fruitless attempt to prosecute Eyre, Lieutenant Herbert Brand, who had presided over Gordon's court martial and Colonel Alexander Nelson who commanded the troops at Morant Bay.[258]

---

were inherently united through shared racial characteristics. As events at Morant Bay took shape, both Eyre and observers in Britain looked to Haitian history for an analysis of the motives of the protestors

256 The letter and other documents relevant to Carlyle's connection with the Eyre controversy are printed in Workman, Gillian, 'Thomas Carlyle and the Governor Eyre Controversy: An Account with Some New Material', *Victorian Studies*, Vol. 18, (1974), pp. 77-102. See also, C. Hall, C., 'The economy of intellectual prestige: Thomas Carlyle, John Stuart Mill, and the case of Governor Eyre', *Labour/Le Travail*, Vol. 22 (1989), pp. 167-196. Carlyle's longer discussion of 'The Niger Question' was in *Shooting Niagara: and After?* (Chapman and Hall), 1867, reprinted with some additions and corrections from *Macmillan's Magazine*, August 1867.

257 Mill, J. S., *Autobiography*, (Longmans, Green, Reader and Dyer), 1873, p. 281.

258 For a narrative of the prosecutions see, ibid, Semmel, Bernard, *Jamaican Blood and Victorian Conscience: The Governor Eyre Controversy*, pp. 142-170, and ibid, Kostal, R. W., *A Jurisprudence of Power*, pp. 258-369. For contemporary accounts of the Eyre prosecutions, written from a pro-Eyre perspective, see Finlason, W. F., *Justice to a Colonial Governor; or, Some Considerations on the Case of Mr. Eyre: Containing the Substance of All the Documents, Discussions, and Proceedings Relating Thereto*, (Chapman and Hall), 1868, and *A History of the Jamaica Case, Founded upon Official or Authentic Documents and Containing an Account of the Debates in Parliament, and the Criminal Prosecutions, Arising out of the Case*, (Chapman and Hall), 1869.

Between the summers of 1866 and 1867, public opinion swung away from the Jamaica Committee to the supporters of Eyre. This was in part a consequence of what many regarded as its vindictive persistence in pursuing Edward Eyre. Perhaps more important was the political and social unrest in Britain and reports of disturbances elsewhere in the empire. The conservative middle-classes increasingly drew comparisons between events in the colonies and challenges to their domestic status from Fenians, women and the working-class 'rabble'.[259] Despite opposition in influential quarters, majority feeling and official judgements sided with Eyre and the need to enforce state authority. The principal goal Mill had fought for, a decisive court precedent limiting the compass of martial law continued to elude him and in declining to confront the constitutional limitations on executive power, British governments subsequently used methods of repression that were no longer acceptable in Britain. *The Times* summed up the controversy with candid clarity:

> The fact is that great lawyers are almost as much divided as the unlearned public on the conduct of Mr Eyre, and it would not be right, even if it were possible, to disguise this fact.[260]

In 1868 and 1870, further unsuccessful attempts were made to prosecute Eyre for the murder of Gordon. It was clear that the defence of black Jamaican rights was no longer a popular cause. Public opinion had concluded that black people were different from whites and could not expect the same rights. British subjects across the empire were not all the same or could expect to be treated the same. In February 1874, Eyre asked for a pension of the first class--£1,000 a year–under the Colonial Governors Pensions Act of 1865, but this was rejected by Lord Carnarvon at the Colonial Office. Eyre had to accept a 'second class' pension of £750 pounds a year. He spent the rest of his life in seclusion and died at Walreddon Manor, Tavistock, on 30 November 1901.

Morant Bay marked an important watershed in the post-Emancipation history of Jamaica.[261] It showed that the small, white plantocracy was unfit to continue exercising political power over the large black majority and that political change was essential. The Colonial Office, local white élites, many coloureds and even some social aspiring blacks maintained that the ex-slaves and their descendants had hardly advanced as human beings, something amply demonstrated by the 'barbarity' of events at Morant Bay, and it was this that determined the nature of reform not black aspirations. Within months of the rebellion, the Jamaican Assembly was persuaded to transfer its power to the British Crown and on 11 June 1866 Jamaica became a Crown Colony ruled from London. Representative institutions were abolished; elections ceased and, all Jamaicans, white, coloured and black, were disfranchised and all power was

---

[259] This is explored in Brown, Richard, *Famine, Fenians and Freedom, 1840-1882*, (Clio Publishing), 2011, pp. 279-284.

[260] 'Editorial', *The Times*, 11 June 1868, p. 8.

[261] Moore, Brian L., and Johnson, Michele A., *Neither Led nor Driven: Contesting British Cultural Imperialism in Jamaica, 1865-1920*, (University of the West Indies Press), 2004, pp. 1-13.

vested in officials appointed by the Colonial Office under the autocratic authority of the Governor.

The alternative, extending the franchise to the black majority, was inconceivable to officials in London and local whites who both agreed that white leadership was essential for the well-being of Jamaica. Direct rule from London proved to be more efficient than self-government. Governor John Peter Grant established a proper police force, public medical departments, schools financially supported by state, irrigation and public works and reformed land tenure laws. Limited elected representation was reintroduced by the Colonial Office in 1884 on similar qualifications to those that had existed before 1865. Despite, blacks making up a slight majority of the electorate (50.7 per cent in 1885) with coloureds making over a third (34.6 per cent), representation on the new Legislative Council was dominated by spokesmen of the landed and business interests as it had been before 1865 and this remained the case up to the end of the First World War.

Conclusions

Slave resistance covered a broad spectrum. Some resistance was overt, communal and systematic while individual resistance was often regarded as intransigence. Armed rebellion was only one extreme of a continuum that stretched from satire, lying, feigning illness and working slow, through tool-breaking, theft, flight and strikes, to self-mutilation, suicide and infanticide, [262] arson, poisoning and physical assault. 'Day-to-day resistance' was the most common form of resistance and expression of slaves' alienation from their masters. Running away was another form of resistance. Most slaves absconded relatively short distances and were not trying to escape permanently from slavery. Instead, they were temporarily withholding their labour as a form of economic bargaining and negotiation. This has led historians to argue that resistance permeated the culture of slaves.

Slavery also involved a process of negotiation and accommodation as slaves bargained over the pace of work, the amount of free time they enjoyed, monetary rewards, access to land to cultivate food to supplement often meagre rations and the freedom to practice burials, marriages, and religious ceremonies free from white oversight. Enslaved Africans also fought against slavery by keeping their African cultures and traditions alive in words, names, music and beliefs. Slave owners often tried to control this. For instance, except at Christmas, slave drumming was banned by plantation owners on the Caribbean island of St Kitts. Such activity was a threat since owners recognised that if slaves developed a common identity through African culture and traditions, they would be more likely to band together and rebel. Drumming was an important part of many African musical and religious traditions. Slave revolts were most likely when slaves outnumbered whites, when planters were absent, during periods of economic distress and when there was a division within the ruling élite.

---

[262] Allain, J. M., "Infanticide as Slave Resistance: Evidence from Barbados, Jamaica, and Saint-Domingue." *Inquiries*, Vol. 6, (4), (2014)
Retrieved from http://www.inquiriesjournal.com/a?id=893

How far did slave resistance and rebellion lead to the abolition, first of the slave trade and then slavery itself in the British Empire?[263] If this was the case then it would need to be shown that the cost of preventing resistance and rebellion in Africa, during the middle passage and finally on the plantations themselves was at a sufficient level to make the use of slaves uneconomic. There is evidence that the threat of rebellion from enslaved Africans was significant both after their capture in Africa and during their passage to the Americas and that this did lead to increased costs for slave traders. Although this appears to have resulted in increasing costs, these proved insufficient to end the slave trade and the traffic in human cargoes was still profitable.[264] Combined with the continual resistance of the slaves themselves, and the change in opinion in Britain about the slave trade, abolition and Emancipation eventually occurred. Often, the role of the campaigners in Britain is the only reason for the end of the slave trade and slavery.[265] The problems caused by the slaves themselves were a severe threat to the continuation of slavery and the economic viability of the plantation system but, despite the rhetoric and apocalyptic warnings of abolitionists, whether they would alone have been sufficient to end the practice is questionable.[266]

Abolitionists may have won the argument for ending slavery in the British Empire by the 1830s but they lamentably failed to address the question of what happens after slavery was abolished. They made two assumptions, supported by successive governments and Colonial Secretaries that emancipated slaves would want to continue working on plantations as wage-labour and not develop their own economic aspirations and that they could be transformed through education and religion into citizens within the Empire. This was resisted and, as the Morant Bay rebellion illustrates, led to a shift in ideological attitudes to race and cultural inferiority in which freed slaves were denied the same economic, social and political aspirations and rights as whites simply because of the colour of their skins. The stereotyping and discrimination of slavery and the racist treatment of the unfree survived Emancipation and paradoxically became the racism of the free.

---

263 On this issue see, Drescher, Seymour & Emmer, Pieter C., (eds.), *Who Abolished Slavery? Slave Revolts and Abolitionism: A debate with Joao Pedro Marques*, (Berghahn Books), 2010.

264 See, Davis, David Brion, 'Slave Revolts and Abolitionism', in ibid, Drescher, Seymour & Emmer, Pieter C., (eds.), *Who Abolished Slavery?* pp. 163-168.

265 On British abolitionism see, Peterson, Derek R., (ed.), *Abolitionism and Imperialism in Britain, Africa and the Atlantic*, (Ohio University Press), 2010, Drescher, Seymour, *Abolition: A History of Slavery and Antislavery*, (Cambridge University Press), 2009, pp. 205-266, and Powell, Jim, *Greatest Emancipations: How the West Abolished Slavery*, (Palgrave Macmillan), 2009, pp. 67-116.

266 Matthews, Gelien, *Caribbean Slave Revolts and the British Abolitionist Movement*, (Louisiana State University Press), 2006, pp. 135-179.

4 Convict resistance and rebellion

...no happiness nor prosperity without personal security and this could only be secured by 'severe discipline.[1]

For the British Empire to function effectively as an economic unit, it needed a reliable supply of cheap labour to exploit land and mineral resources. Transporting convicts was one solution to this problem. This chapter explores the role played by transportees in imperial development and how they could circumvent the system through different types of resistance and, in extreme cases, through rebellion. As with rebellions by native peoples and slaves, the likelihood of success was slight given the overwhelming military superiority of the colonial authorities but the possibility of 'liberty'--even though 'death' was the almost inevitable outcome--provided a spark of hope transforming resistance into physical action.

Portugal was the first of the major global powers to use transported convict labour in North Africa in 1415 and this lasted until the dissolution of Stalin's gulags in the 1960s.[2] Although it is generally seen as a feature of the criminal justice system, transportation is increasingly seen in the context of global expansion and colonisation and penal colonies as engines of global change.[3] The transportation of convicts to English colonies had its origins in the late-sixteenth century over two hundred years.[4] Parliament gave magistrates the power to exile rogues and vagabonds 'beyond the seas' in 1597 and James I authorised pardons for condemned felons on condition that they went to the New World. From 1654 onwards, some prisoners who received a reprieve from the death sentence were sent to work on the plantations in North America and the West Indies and in 1678, Parliament approved the idea of sending prisoners to serve their sentences in the American colonies of Virginia and Maryland and in the West Indies where they could be used in developing those lands. It was the Transportation Act 1718 that finally adopted foreign exile as a punishment for serious crime.

Between 1719 and 1776, some 50,000 people were transported. As with gaols, transportation was run as a business. For instance, Stephenson and Randolph of Bristol called themselves 'felon-dealers' and arranged for the transport of convicts selling them to the Caribbean plantations for up to £80 each.[5] While some contemporary critics such as Dr Johnson insisted that

---

[1] National Archives, CO280: Sir George Arthur to William Hanley, 4 April 1834.

[2] De Vito, Christian Giuseppe, and Lichtenstein, Alex, 'Writing a Global History of Convict Labour', in De Vito, Christian Giuseppe, and Lichtenstein, Alex, (eds.), *Global Convict Labour*, (Brill), 2015, pp. 1-46.

[3] Anderson, Clare, 'Transnational Histories of Penal Transportation: Punishment, Labour and Governance in the British Imperial World, 1788-1939', *Australian Historical Studies*, Vol. 47, (2016), 381-397.

[4] Innes, Joanna, 'The role of transportation in seventeenth and eighteenth century English penal practice', in Bridge, Carl, (ed.), *New Perspectives in Australian History*, (Sir Robert Menzies Centre for Australian Studies, Institute of Commonwealth Studies, University of London), 1990, pp. 1-24.

[5] Ekirch, A. Roger, *Bound for America: The Transportation of British Convicts to the Colonies, 1718-1775*, (Oxford University Press), 1987, and Morgan, Gwenda, and

transportation was not a true deterrent since, unlike hanging, it was an 'invisible' punishment, Nonetheless Morgan and Rushton insist that 'far from being invisible...transportation stimulated cultural and political exchanges between Britain and its colonies'.[6] Colonial newspapers devoted an extraordinary amount of space to accounts of trials of criminals in London, and to accounts from English newspapers of the crimes of transportees who had secretly returned to England. A handful of dramatic and probably unreliable pamphlets reinforced the narrative of return, providing apparent confirmation that the punishment meant nothing to the determined criminal. Morgan and Rushton found that out of some 2,536 convicts transported between 1745 and 1776 from England's western, north-eastern, and north-western circuits, only 125 were reported in colonial newspapers as having absconded from their masters and of these only two could be positively identified as having returned to England before their sentences expired.

While convict runaways were the major form of resistance, convict rebellion was not unknown. In 1721, there was a conspiracy among a small group of Annapolis convicts to seize the town's arms and magazine but, whether this was intended to launch a full-scale rebellion is unknown since the plot was uncovered by local magistrates before any violence occurred. In 1735, a more substantial group of Irish convicts in Georgia planned an uprising that included setting Savannah on fire and killing scores of fleeing townspeople. This too was quashed as the plotters assembled.[7] These two planned rebellions showed that convicts were prepared to rebel against colonial authorities and that the risk of collective convict resistance was a persistent threat. The prospect of a successful convict rebellion in the colonies was, however, slight. Convicts were often widely dispersed and their social origins were diverse. This prevented convicts from forming cohesive groups with common grievances. For those convicts with skills or sufficient wealth to buy their freedom, there was no advantage to be gained from mixing with field servants. The loyalties convicts possessed were focussed on family, community and religion and expressions of group consciousness were few. Support from the slave labour force had the potential for a large-scale rebellion, but while white and black labour had much in common, by the early-eighteenth century white racialist views meant that this never became a reality. Concern about the impact of convicts on colonial society was evident as early as 1670 when a Virginia enactment of 1670 spoke of 'the great number of felons and other desperate villains sent hither from the several prisons of England' adding 'we are believed to be a place only fit to receive such base and lewd persons.'[8] However, relations between Britain and the colonies in the eighteenth century were dominated more by the French and Indian threat and smuggling and imperial taxes than by conflict over the convict trade and were not of defining importance in colonial relations with Britain.

Rushton, Peter, *Eighteenth-Century Criminal Transportation: The Formation of the Criminal Atlantic,* (Palgrave Macmillan), 2004, provide a detailed account of the operation of the transportation system.

[6] Ibid, Morgan, Gwenda and Rushton, Peter, *Eighteenth-Century Criminal Transportation,* p. 4.

[7] Ibid, Ekirch, A. Roger, *Bound for America*, pp. 191-193.

[8] Cit, *Southern Literary Messenger*, Vol. 25, (1857), p. 127.

Why Australia?

Transportation to the American colonies effectively ended in 1775 with the American War of Independence though there was an abortive attempt to revive it in 1783. By the early 1780s, the numbers of convicts in Britain reached dangerous levels as gaols and hulks—generally regarded as places to hold prisoners prior to transportation—became over-crowded: the prison population doubled between 1782 and 1787. Given that transportation was a major punishment with upwards of 1,000 convicts transported each year between 1750 and 1775, an alternative to the American colonies was a priority for William Pitt's government from 1783. Convicts were used as forced labour on public works and this could have been extended but was unpopular among those living nearby and Englishmen, as Lecky later commented:

> ... [eighteenth century society] allowed the execution of criminals to be treated as a popular amusement but at the same time revolted against the continental emotion of compelling chained prisoners to work in public as utterly inconsistent with English liberty.[9]

Canada refused to take any more convicts owing to poor previous experiences, even though this time the convicts were to be guarded. British Honduras was not an option as the settlers preferred coloured slaves to convicted white slaves. The West Indies were not viable as the influential slave traders did not want their profitable slave market, already in decline, to be further weakened by competition from English gaols. Transportation to Africa began in a small-scale way during the war and subsequently several more ambitious schemes were proposed. In 1782, 350 convicts were transported to settlements on the Gold Coast but only seven were alive three years later. Most had died of disease but others had joined local pirates or absconded to neighbouring settlements of foreign powers. The result was that penal transportation to Africa was also abandoned in 1786.[10]

As Africa and America were unsuitable, the South-West Pacific was considered though New Zealand was disregarded because of the Maori presence. In desperation because no alternative could be found and for a jumble of reasons, the decision was made to send convicts to Australia.[11] Shaw, Mackay and Gillen argue that convicts were unwanted at home and that the remoteness of NSW provided an answer to an intolerable logistical problem.[12] Gillen also

[9] Lecky, William, *A History of England in the Eighteenth Century*, Vol. 6, (D. Appleton and Company), 1887, p. 251.

[10] Christopher, Emma, *A Merciless Place: The Fate of Britain's Convicts after the American Revolution*, (Oxford University Press), 2011, examines the available if abortive alternatives especially in West Africa.

[11] Frost, Alan, *Botany Bay: The Real Story*, (Black Inc), 2011, provides the most recent consideration of the decision.

[12] Shaw, Alan, *Convicts and the colonies: a study of penal transportation from Great Britain and Ireland to Australia and other parts of the British Empire*, (Faber), 1966, and Mackay, D., *A Place of Exile: European Settlement of New South Wales*, (Oxford University Press), 1985.

suggested that NSW had always been a back-up plan since 1786.[13] Traditionalists stand firm to the opinion that Botany Bay was only colonised to 'rid the nation's (Britain) prisons and hulks of convicts'. Atkinson believes that 'Botany Bay was chosen as a convict settlement not because of, but despite the possibility that it might become a trading post.'[14] Blainey argues that there were closer alternatives, such as the uninhabited islands of Bermuda or the West Indies and that the availability of other lands suggests that there were other reasons for the decision.[15] Frost suggests that there were commercial and strategic considerations in Pitt's Cabinet decision especially naval trade, supply of flax and naval timber from Norfolk Island–discovered by Cook in 1775--and the fact that convict labour might serve these purposes.[16] It limited the territorial ambitions of the French and the claims of the Spanish and Dutch to the continent. It helped repair the damage done to British imperial prestige by the disaster in America. A strategic location needed to be secured that could support its empire from French invasion. A safe harbour was also needed for the British fleet in the Pacific and Indian Oceans, from where supplies of food and other materials could be obtained cheaply and at short notice. Botany Bay, with its supposed ability to shelter a fleet of ships, had already been surveyed by Cook in 1770. By colonising NSW, Britain would protect Cook's 'right of possession' over Botany Bay and gave Britain a more secure base to exploit any possible trade.

It helped the whaling industry that needed a sheltered base in the Pacific and secured a route for those who wanted to expand trade with China.[17] Dallas suggested that Britain wanted to establish a trading post to spearhead British penetration of the Pacific and to service an alternative sea route to China.[18] Later

[13] Gillen, Mollie, 'The Botany Bay decision, 1786: convicts not empire', *English Historical Review*, Vol. 97, (1982), pp. 740-766, but see also her *The Search for John Small: First Fleeter*, (Library of Australian History), 1988, and *The Founders of Australia, A Biographical Dictionary of The First Fleet*, (Library of Australian History), 1989

[14] Atkinson, Alan, 'A Counter-Riposte', in Martin, Ged, (ed.), *The Founding of Australia: The Argument about Australia's Origins*, (Hale and Iremonger), 1978, pp. 265-269.

[15] Blainey, G. C., *The Tyranny of Distance: How Distance Shaped Australia's History*, (Macmillan), 1977, pp. 20-39.

[16] Frost, A., *Convicts and Empire: A Naval Question 1776-1811*, (Oxford University Press), 1980, but see also his 'A fit of absence of mind? The Decision to Colonise New South Wales', in *Botany Bay Mirages: Illusions of Australia's Convict Beginning*, (Melbourne University Press), 1994, pp. 98-109.

[17] Dallas, K. M., 'The First Settlement in Australia; considered in relation to sea-power in world politics', *Papers and Proceedings of the Tasmanian Historical Research Association*, number 3, (1952), pp. 1-12, reprinted in ibid, Martin, Ged, (ed.), *The Founding of Australia: The Argument about Australia's Origins*, pp. 39-49. His ideas were extended in Dallas, K. M., *Trading Posts or Penal Colonies*, (Richmond and Son), 1969. See also, Stevens, M., *Trade, Tactics and Territory: Britain in the Pacific 1783-1823*, (Manchester University Press), 1983.

[18] Dallas, K. M., 'The First Settlement in Australia; considered in relation to sea-power in world politics', *Papers and Proceedings of the Tasmanian Historical Research Association*, number 3 (1952), pp. 1-12, reprinted in ibid, Martin, Ged, (ed.), *The Founding of Australia: The Argument about Australia's Origins*, pp. 39-49. His ideas were extended in *Trading Posts or Penal Colonies*, (Richmond and Son), 1969.

he maintained that it was the fur trade of the north Pacific, trade opportunities with China and South America and the development of sealing and whaling in the Pacific that combined to make British settlement of Australia a viable economic project. There was substantial demand for whale and seal oil in Britain and many of the ships from the Second Fleet were converted whalers that were reconverted to their original use after the voyage. Blainey shared Dallas' belief that there was a positive reason for the choice of colony. He emphasised Lord Sydney's announcement that the choice of colony was to be 'reciprocally beneficial'. This is the only reason given in official documents to explain why such a remote land was chosen. An export trade was to be started in flax, hemp and in wood for mainmasts that would strengthen Britain's naval power in the event of a Baltic blockade preventing England getting flax from its usual supply in Russia. Frost's modified theory[19] maintains the British sought supplies for their ships in eastern waters that needed to refit without sailing home to defend British lands in India against the French. Another commercial benefit was that the empty convict ships could carry cargoes of tea back. However, during the debates in the 1960s, the fact that NSW was almost entirely a convict settlement tended to be overlooked. Both the 'flax and timber' theorists and the 'China route' party have had to admit that the early years of NSW did not triumphantly vindicate their arguments.

Stevens[20] and Fry[21] indicated that the British were concerned over the security of trade routes to China and that Pitt's policies in the 1780s were dictated primarily by commercial considerations. Mackay disputes this arguing that the First Fleet was not sufficiently equipped to provide the protection and manpower necessary to defend the strategic position of Botany Bay.[22] Mackay also argued against the strategic position of Botany Bay in relationship to naval trade. Like many, he feels that the establishment of the colony was 'crisis orientated' not a good start if the motives were really for naval trade and timber supply. After viewing many of what seems to be a circle of comments and opinions that formed the Botany Bay debate, he then accused the non-traditionalists of: 'Distorting our records of the past, and sought to create a myth of a better national origin.' Mackay still acknowledges that regardless of the 'shoddy' way in which Botany Bay was set up that 'from such inauspicious beginnings Australia grew to maturity and nationhood'. The strategic argument is perhaps supported by the choice of Captain Phillip as the first governor and Frost points out that both Phillip and Hunter and King, his two successors, were naval officers. Above all, it was economical since convict labour was expected to become self-funding after initial financial help from the Exchequer. For British politicians, colonising Australia

---

[19] Frost, A., 'Botany Bay: An Imperial Venture of the 1780s', *English Historical Review*, Vol. 100, (1985), pp. 309-330.

[20] Stevens, Margaret, *Trade, Tactics and Territory: Britain in the Pacific 1783-1823*, (Manchester University Press), 1983.

[21] Fry, H. T., 'Captain James Cook: the historical perspective', in *The significance of Cook's 'Endeavour' voyage: Three Bicentennial Lectures*, (James Cook University of North Queensland), 1970, pp. 1-23, and ''Cathay And The Way Thither': The Background To Botany Bay', in ibid, Martin, Ged, (ed.), *The Founding of Australia: The Argument about Australia's Origins*, pp. 136-149.

[22] Ibid, Mackay, David, *A Place of Exile: European Settlement of New South Wales*.

with transported convicts satisfied the different interests that were clamouring for action.[23]

From the foundation of NSW in January 1788 until 1867, transportation was an important, though increasingly contentious, feature of colonial life. More than 187,000 convicts were sent to Australia, most after 1815. In 1817, Lord Bathurst, Colonial Secretary expressed concern that Governor Macquarie's policies were undermining the effectiveness of the transportation system as a means of criminal punishment. As a result, John Thomas Bigge was appointed to inquire into the overall value of the system, with sweeping inquisitional powers. His reports sought to restore transportation as 'an object of real terror' by calling for greater severity in the treatment of convicts, an end to free grants of land at the end of their sentences and a continuance of their subordinate status by not admitting them to positions of social responsibility. For Bigge, the future of the colony lay with the free settlers who would farm the land, employ the convicts and produce wool.[24]

Until the 1830s when newly emerging humanitarian and liberal views gained support in Britain, most people accepted that transportation was an efficient and acceptable system for criminal punishment. As the British penal code became less harsh, it was generally only the more dangerous and hardened criminals or 'political prisoners' who were transported. A deepening gulf developed between the newly arrived convicts and the rest of Sydney's population led many colonists to claim that transportation was neither desirable nor necessary. Assigned convicts, it was said, were lazy, unreliable and dangerous. There was now also a readily available supply of free immigrant labour arriving in NSW and VDL. Newspapers wrote of a growing crime wave fed by desperate convicts who threatened the fabric of colonial society. Opposition to transportation grew in NSW during the 1830s especially amongst the urban, immigrant middle- and working-classes although not the wealthy squatters and landowners who were heavily dependent on cheap convict labour. In 1837, the Molesworth Committee recommended that transportation should cease as soon as was practicable and that a punishment of hard labour be substituted for transportation.[25] In 1840, transportation to NSW was discontinued but continued to VDL until 1853 and on Norfolk Island until 1856.

---

[23] Foley, Daniel J., *The British Government Decision to Found a Colony at Botany Bay in New South Wales in 1786*, Ph.D., Thesis, King's College, London, 2004.

[24] Bigge's *Reports* were printed in three volumes. Vol. 1: *The State of the Colony of New South Wales*, The House of Lords, (Papers 119), printed, 5 August 1822, Vol. 2: *The State of Agriculture and Trade in the Colony of New South Wales*, The House of Lords, (Paper 119), printed, 4 July 1823, and Vol. 3: *The Judicial Establishments of New South Wales and Van Diemen's Lands*, The House of Lords, (Paper 118), printed, 4 July 1823. See also Ritchie, J., (ed.), *The Evidence to the Bigge Reports: New South Wales under Governor Macquarie*, 2 Vols. (Heinemann), 1971, and Bennett, J. M., 'Bigge, John Thomas (1780-1843)', *ADB*, Vol. 1, pp. 99-100.

[25] *Report from the Select Committee of the House of Commons on Transportation: Together with a Letter from the Archbishop of Dublin on the Same Subject; and Notes by Sir William Molesworth, Bart., Chairman of the Committee*, (Henry Hooper), 1838, pp. xx-xxii. See also, Whately, R., 'Transportation', c.1833, printed in his *Miscellaneous Lectures and Reviews*, (Parker, Son and Bourn), 1861, pp. 258-259.

In 1849, transportation started to WA. Long-term transportation was retained in the 1853 Penal Servitude Act but was finally abolished four years later and replaced by penal servitude, a term of imprisonment that usually included hard labour and was served in British gaols. Convicts were transported to WA until 1867 but the sentence of transportation was not finally abolished until 1887.

Convict labour in Australia

Thirty years ago, Russel Ward suggested, '...the convict influence on Australian society was very much more important than has usually been supposed.'[26] For him, the unusual and discomfiting origins of Australian society had plagued Australian history and Australians' view of themselves for many years and had led people to ignore their convict heritage, to excuse it or to downplay its significance in the development of Australian identities and institutions.[27]

When sentenced to transportation, prisoners were initially imprisoned and then removed to the hulks prior to transportation but often had to wait up to two years before they were taken to Australia. As soon as a ship arrived, it notified the port if there were male or female convicts on board.[28] The port authorities inspected the ship and the convicts who were then brought up on deck and inspected by the Colonial Secretary or other officials. Convicts were interviewed to ascertain qualifications and previous work history and then usually assigned to free settlers or emancipists as servants, farm labourers and mechanics. The more dangerous prisoners provided labour for public works such as road-making in gangs of up to 300 men guarded by the military.[29]

The convict system operated based on a graduated hierarchy where through good behaviour progressively rewarded convicts with increasing levels of freedom and where poor behaviour led to the removal of these privileges, restrictions on freedom, imprisonment and corporal punishment and in extreme cases capital punishment.[30] Tickets-of-leave were normally granted after four or six years allowing convicts to work for themselves outside the 'assignment' system on condition that they remained in a specified area, reported regularly to authorities and attended divine worship each Sunday. Ticket-of-leave men were also allowed to marry or bring their families from Britain and to acquire property, but they were not permitted to carry firearms or board a ship. Minor

---

[26] Ward, Russel, *The Australian legend*, 2nd ed., (Oxford University Press), 1978, p. 37.

[27] Smith, Babette, *Australia's Birthstain: the startling legacy of the convict era*, (Allen & Unwin), 2008, examines why Australians are still misled by myths about their convict heritage.

[28] Bateson, Charles, *The Convict Ships, 1787-1868*, (Brown), 1959, remains the best study of the sea voyage though some of his statistics have been questioned.

[29] Ibid, Shaw, Alan, *Convicts & the Colonies*, and Robson, L. L., *The Convict Settlers of Australia,* (Melbourne University Press), 1976, examine the process and the participants. Robson, L. L., 'The origins of the women convicts sent to Australia 1787-1852', *Historical Studies of Australia and New Zealand*, Vol. 11, (1963), pp. 43-53, and Robinson, Portia, 'From Colleen to Matilda', in Costello, Con, (ed.), *Ireland and Australia: Bicentenary Essays 1788-1988,* (Gill & Macmillan), 1986, pp. 96-110, look at the role of women.

[30] Byrne, P. J., ''The public good': Competing visions of freedom in early New South Wales', *Labour History*, Vol. 58, (1990), pp. 76-83.

offences could see a ticket revoked by the magistrates and the holder returned to government service. Certificates of freedom were available to convicts who had completed their sentences. Convicts serving a life sentence generally received pardons rather than tickets of leave. Conditional pardons allowed convicts their freedom if they remained in the colony while absolute pardons remitted the entire sentence and convicts were free within and outside the colony and could return to Britain.[31]

The attitude of Australians to their 'convict past' and the perceived ignominy of their nation's origins have changed significantly in the past half century but remains a source of some ambiguity. Unlike the United States that at least could point to the role of 'pilgrims and martyrs' in its national development, until the 1950s the criminality of Australia's founders posed a real problem since the convict past retained its immediacy. There was simply no way of ignoring Australia's origins as a penal colony but it was rationalised in different and contradictory ways. For some, British convicts were 'exiled' for trivial offences and were barely criminals at all while others saw them as thieves pure and simple whose character need not be whitewashed. Convict transportation was part of the country's economic history, a central element in producing the wealth and later 'freedom' of the colonies rather than a matter of social origins. The economic benefits of convictism outweighed moral questions about why individuals ended up on the convict ships. By the 1920s, convicts were seen as victims of misfortune, oppressed and persecuted by those corrupt and culpable élites in Britain for whom the Australian colonies (that 'poisonous prison') epitomised aristocratic tyranny and suffering of displaced 'Village Hampdens'.[32] Convicts may have been redeemed but historians still knew little about who they were or how they lived and worked.

In the 1950s and 1960s, Manning Clark, Alan Shaw and Lloyd Robson challenged the prevailing view of convicts as more sinned against than sinning.[33] Based on an analysis of a one in twenty sample of transported convicts, Robson concluded:

> ...the convicts were neither 'village Hampdens' nor merely 'ne'er-do-wells from the city slums.' But if the Hampdens are placed on one side of a scale and the ne'er-do-wells on the other, the scale must tip toward the ne'er-do-wells.[34]

Robson's work established a view of convict transportation that was firmly entrenched for the next twenty-five years. Convicts were largely work-shy,

---

[31] Durston, Gregory, Magwitch's Forbears: Returning from Transportation in Eighteenth-Century London, *Australian Journal of Legal History*, Vol. 9, (2005), pp. 137-158.

[32] Wood, G. A., 'Convicts', *Royal Australian Historical Society: Journal and Proceedings*, Vol. 8, (4), (1922), pp. 177-208, and Roberts, D. A., ''More sinned against than sinning': George Arnold Wood and the noble convict', in Gare, D., and Ritter, D., (eds.), *Making Australian History: Perspectives on the Past since 1788*, (Cengage Learning Australia), 2007.

[33] Ibid, Shaw, Alan, *Convicts and the colonies*; Clark, C. M. H., 'The origins of the convicts transported to eastern Australia, 1787-1852', *Historical Studies*, Vol. 7, (1956), pp. 121-135, 314-327, and ibid, Robson, L. L., *The convict settlers of Australia.*

[34] Ibid, Robson, L. L., *The Convict Settlers of Australia*, pp. 157-158.

unskilled urban thieves and prostitutes, who probably contributed little to the economy.[35] Even left-wing historians concluded that the bulk of the convict population was unable to combine effectively to challenge the conditions under which they toiled.[36] This tradition of historical writing reached its zenith in Robert Hughes' international bestseller, *The Fatal Shore* depicting Australia as a vast gulag populated by convicts who were largely from the ranks of a professional criminal class and produced crime in the same way that hatters produced hats and miners coal.[37]

The publication of *Convict Workers* in 1988 had a profound impact on the way transportation was viewed.[38] Written by economic historians and based on quantitative analysis of a sample of nearly 20,000 convicts transported to NSW, it challenged the prevailing consensus. Historians had previously focused on qualitative accounts written by middle-class gaolers, chaplains and other moral entrepreneurs but as Sturma had already pointed out, a moral ideology played an important part in controlling convict labour and this was widely reflected in middle-class nineteenth century writing about convicts.[39] The 'reformed' convict was the man or woman who made a profit for a master or mistress, while those who resisted merely confirmed their wickedness.[40] *Convict Workers* found that most convicts were victims of economic conditions, were generally convicted of petty non-violent crimes especially theft and most did not re-offend at the completion of their sentence. Nicholas and Robson agreed that most convicts were single, male and in their twenties, two-thirds were Protestant, one-third Catholic, most came from cities or industrialised towns and possessed skills that were broadly representative of the British and Irish working-classes. Many of the convicts were literate and Nicholas pointed out that three-quarters of convict were literate compared to 58 per cent among the English working-class.[41] More controversially, *Convict Workers* claimed that these skills were effectively deployed by the colonial state in a system that was marked by efficiency and in which the lash was largely silent. Skilled labour was an important commodity in the new colony. Kent and Townsend claim that convicts with agricultural skills

---

[35] Moore, F., *The convicts of Van Diemen's Land, (1840-1853),* (Cat & Fiddle Press), 1976, Alexander, Alison, *Tasmania's Convicts: How Felons Built a Free Society*, (Allen & Unwin), 2010, and Hirst, J. B., *Convict society and its enemies: a history of early New South Wales,* (Allen and Unwin), 1983.

[36] McQueen, H., 'Convicts and rebels', *Labour History,* Vol. 15, (1968), pp. 3-30, and Connell, R. W., and Irving, T. H., *Class Structure in Australian history: documents, narrative and argument,* (Longman Cheshire), 1982, pp. 44-50.

[37] Hughes, R., *The Fatal Shore: a history of the transportation of convicts to Australia, 1787-1868,* (Collins Harvill), 1987, p. 165.

[38] Nicholas, Stephen, (ed.), *Convict workers: reinterpreting Australia's past,* (Cambridge University Press), 1988.

[39] Sturma, M., 'Eye of the beholder: the stereotype of women convicts 1788-1852', *Labour History,* Vol. 34, (1978), pp. 3-10.

[40] Garton, S., 'The Convict Origins Debate: Historians and the Problem of the 'Criminal Class'', *Australian and New Zealand Journal of Criminology*, Vol. 24, (1991), pp. 66-82.

[41] Nicholas, S., and Shergold, P. R., 'Unshackling the Past', in ibid, Nicholas, S., (ed.), *Convict Workers*, pp. 3-12.

were in high demand as supply was scarce and convicts had to be rationed.[42] Rather than restricting the development of the colonial economy, cheap drafts of compliant and often skilled convict labour stimulated colonial growth rates.

Convict Workers moved the spotlight away from 'who were the convicts' and focused instead on the nature of the colonial experience of transportation.[43] This has been evident in research since the millennium.[44] What has been highlighted was the varied nature of convict experience and how individual experience changed with increasing levels of freedom or repression.[45] There has also been a growing awareness of how the practical arrangements for what constituted appropriate treatment changed over the fifty year's operation of the system in NSW and VDL. The publication of Babette Smith's *Australia's Birthstain* in 2008 and Grace Karskens' *The Colony* the following year explored and exploded some of the myths and stereotypes of the convict system and examined the part played by convicts and emancipated convicts in the formation of early Australian society highlighting especially the blurring of class lines that accompanied it.[46] The diversity of convict work and work relations and how both changed over time has also been a fruitful area of research. Robbins has explored how convicts influenced their employment conditions negotiating and resisting the approaches adopted by the colonial state and by employers to control labour and maximise profitability.[47] He dismisses the view that convict labour was not systematically structured rather he argues that convict administration under Macquarie displayed a deliberate attempt to regulate, motivate and direct labour in ways that were designed to increase productivity, something achieved by defining convict work through job descriptions and regulations. There has also been a proliferation of local studies; for instance,

---

[42] Kent, D., and Townsend, N., (eds.), *The Convicts of the Eleanor: Protest in rural England, New Lives in Australia*, (Merlin Press), 2002.

[43] Reid, K., 'Moving on: resolving the convict origins debate', *Australian Studies,* Vol. 12, (1), (1997), pp. 139-155.

[44] Gibbs, M., 'The Convict System of New South Wales: A review of archaeological research since 2001', *Archaeology in Oceania*, Vol. 47, (2012), pp. 78-83, Roberts, D., 'The 'Knotted Hands that Set is High': Labour History and the Study of Convict Australia', *Labour History*, Vol. 100, (2011), pp. 33-50, Tuffin, Richard, 'Australia's industrious convicts: A reappraisal of archaeological approaches to convict labour', *Australian Archaeology*, Vol. 76, (1), (2013), pp. 1-12.

[45] See, for instance, Harman, Kristyn, ''The Art of Cutting Stone': Aboriginal convict labour in nineteenth-century New South Wales and Van Diemen's Land', in Fijn, Natasha, Keen, Ian, Lloyd, Christopher, and Pickering, Michael, (eds.), *Indigenous Participation in Australian Economies II*, (ANU Press), 2012, pp. 119-134.

[46] Woollacott, Angela, *Settler Society in the Australian Colonies: Self-Government and Imperial Culture*, (Oxford University Press), 2015.

[47] Robbins, W., 'The Lumber Yards: a Case Study in the Management of Convict Labour, 1788-1832', *Labour History*, Vol. 79, (2000), pp. 141-161, 'Management and Resistance in Convict Work Gangs, 1788-1830', *Journal of Industrial Relations*, Vol. 45, (3), (2003), pp. 360-377, 'The Supervision of Convict Gangs in New South Wales, 1788-1830', *Australian Economic History Review*, Vol. 44, (1), (2004), pp. 79-100, 'Spacial Escape and the Hyde Park Barracks', *Journal of Australian Colonial History*, Vol. 7, (2005), pp. 81-96, and 'Governor Macquarie's Job Descriptions and the Bureaucratic Control of the Convict Labour Process', *Labour History*, Vol. 96, (2009), pp. 1-18.

Walsh in his studies of the Tocal area has examined aspects of assignment and rural labour.[48] In addition, there have been developments in considering the available archaeological evidence of the convict heritage and the Internet has boosted the growth of genealogical consideration of individuals pre- and post-transportation. The result is that the convict system is now recognised as more variegated in nature and that the five decades in which it operated in NSW and VDL saw significant alterations in the nature of convict experience and how that experience was mediated in relation to both the colonial state and employers.

Evans and Thorpe accept *Convict Workers* broader conclusions on the nature of transportees but were critical of the book's portrayal of the colonial economy as a benign, paternalistic structure where the values of the state ruled supreme. *Convict Workers* claimed, 'The convicts speak not in words, but out of the dry dust of the statistics collected in order to regulate their convict life', but Evans and Thorpe pointed out only five transportees, all male, were named in the entire book.[49] They claimed that along with the horrors of the lash, punishment cells and penal stations, real convict voices had been largely ignored in *Convict Workers*.[50] Subsequent work has examined the way in which convicts articulated their lives, whether through resistance and other acts such as involvement in black market activities or by writing but this has raised more questions than they have answered.[51] Analysis of convict narratives uncovered a plethora of problems in interpreting these texts. Many of them were heavily shaped by middle-class editors to prepare them for wider consumption while others were at odds with archival accounts, leaving issues over their reliability.[52]

For instance, when John Frost, the Chartist leader during the Newport Rebellion in 1839 was finally released in 1856, he embarked upon a speaking tour of Britain. His lectures presented as a sensational exposé of the horrors of transportation and were dominated by a tale of brutal tyranny, arbitrary rule, physical torture, human degradation and destruction faced by convicts that was neither novel nor new. Allegations of cruelty, inhumanity and the prevalence of 'unnatural' sexual acts among convicts had been central to attacks on

[48] Walsh, Brian, 'Assigned convicts at Tocal: 'ne'er-do-wells' or exceptional workers?', *Journal of Australian Colonial History*, Vol. 8, (2006), pp. 67-90, provides a detailed local study.

[49] Ibid, Nicholas, S., (ed.), *Convict Workers*, p. 45.

[50] Evans, R., and Thorpe, W., 'Power, punishment and penal labour: *Convict Workers* and Moreton Bay', *Australian Historical Studies,* Vol. 25, (1992), pp. 90-111, and Nicholas, S., and Shergold, P., 'Convicts as migrants', in ibid, Nicholas, Stephen, (ed.), *Convict workers,* p. 45.

[51] Duffield, I., 'Problematic passages: 'Jack Bushman's' Convict narrative', in Duffield, I., and Bradley, J., (eds.), *Representing convicts: New Perspectives on Convict Forced Labour Migration,* (Leicester University Press), 1997, pp. 20-42, Maxwell-Stewart, Hamish, 'The search for the convict voice', *Tasmanian Historical Studies,* Vol. 6, (1), (1998), pp. 75-89, and, Frost L., and Maxwell-Stewart, Hamish, (eds.), *Chain letters: narrating convict lives,* (Melbourne University Press), 2001. There is a brief discussion of convict literature produced by Canadian transportees in ibid, Brown, Richard, *Three Rebellions: Canada, South Wales and Australia*, pp. 481-485, 494-497.

[52] See, for instance, Boissery, Beverley, *A deep sense of wrong: the treason, trials and transportation to NSW of Lower Canadian rebels after the 1838 rebellion*, (Dundurn Press), 1995.

transportation for decades, transportation to VDL had ended in 1853 and Frost's audiences were undoubtedly aware in the 'horrors' of convict life. His *Horrors* were not a condemnation of the penal colonies *per se* but a radical allegory of a coming British anarchy. His lectures set out a nightmarish vision of the ultimate physical and spiritual degradation that tyranny would bring.[53] Like the convict experiences of the Patriotes from Lower Canada recounted in their memoirs, Frost was using the convict experience to re-establish a political agenda that had already, like transportation, been superseded. Attempts to use the words of convicts to create accurate windows on the past have proved as problematic as earlier endeavours to use middle-class descriptions of convict lives to try and establish who the convicts were.

The development of Australia lay in the creation of self-sustaining settlements involving convict labour that was intended to be retributive and reformative, but also economically productive. Although motivated initially by penal imperatives and imperial ambitions, Australian settlement curtailed laissez-faire ideas replacing them with strict state-controlled economic and social regulation. Until the mid-1830s, convicts dominated the colonial working population and convict labour built the colony's infrastructure and its emerging industries and businesses. Its nature, management and outcomes and its role in penal policy was integral to the ways in which the colony was administered and interpreted between 1788 and 1850.

Protest and violence

Violence accompanied the birth of NSW and was a constant presence during its formative years. Before the colony was two months old, convicts had been flogged and hung for theft. Violence, threat of violence and fear of violence were major features of the system. The convict system, a deterrent system intended to reduce crime, was central to Australian experience during the first two generations of settlement. Until the 1840s, both NSW and VDL were brutalised societies in which protest of whatever form was vigorously resisted and repressed.[54] In late 1830, the Ribbon gang led by Ralph (Ralf) Entwistle, an English convict, terrorised the Bathurst district of NSW. He had been sentenced to transportation for life to NSW for stealing clothing and was sent to work near Bathurst. In November 1829, Entwistle and another convict were given the task of driving a bullock dray to Sydney. On returning to Bathurst, they paused for a dip in Macquarie River. Unfortunately, Governor Darling was in the area to inspect the new settlement of Bathurst. The convicts were they were trying to dress and were arrested by a group of soldiers led by Thomas Evernden,

---

[53] Frost published several versions of his account of convict life: *A Letter to the people of the United States showing the effects of aristocratic rule*, New York, 1855, *The Horrors of Convict Life: two lectures*, (Holyoake), 1856, and a reworked version published in two editions in 1857, *A Letter to the People of Great Britain and Ireland on Transportation showing the effects of Irresponsible Power on the Physical and Moral Conditions of Convicts, by John Frost, late of Van Diemen's Land*, (Holyoake), 1857. Reid, Kirsty, 'The Horrors of Convict Life: British Radical Visions of the Australian Penal Colonies', *Cultural and Social History*, Vol. 5, (4), (2008), pp. 481-495.

[54] Moore, Tony, *Death or Liberty: Rebel Exiles in Australia 1788-1868*, (Murdoch Books), 2010, is a detailed survey of resistance and rebellion.

Bathurst's police magistrate between 1825 and his death in 1839, 'a martinet of extravagant refinery', charged with 'causing an affront' to the Governor and sentenced to a public flogging of 50 lashes. It is generally argued that Entwistle was embittered by this incident and that it led to the first major rebellion of convicts west of the Blue Mountains.[55] However, given the interval before he took any action and the lack of planning involved, this seems a less likely explanation than the actions of a landowner who deprived Entwistle of food and clothing to maximise the profitability of his farm.[56]

On 23 September 1830, Entwistle and at least 4 others absconded from the farm where they were assigned in Fitzgerald's Valley, some twelve miles south-west of Bathurst.[57] The men visited other properties in the following days stealing food, guns, horses and ammunition and persuading or more probably forcing other convicts to join in until the band grew to around 50 men. At one farm owned by Thomas Everden, James Greenwood, a convict overseer was killed for refusing to allow any of his convicts to join the uprising.[58] The convicts there joined the gang, bringing its membership to about 80 though few had any enthusiasm for the cause and deserted at the first opportunity.[59] A press report mentioned the leader of the gang wearing 'a profusion of white streamers in his hat', probably an attempt by Entwistle to dispel the view that he was merely leading a band of thieves. This later led to comparisons being drawn with the Ribbonmen, nationalist rebels in Ireland, though there is no evidence that the Irish members of Entwistle's band had a political agenda.[60]

On 25 September, recognising that he could not rely on most his men, Entwistle dismissed all but the most committed and with no more than a dozen men rode off towards the caves alongside the Abercrombie River.[61] Local landowners reacted quickly to the activities of the band and on 27 September raised a small volunteer cavalry corps of twelve men under William Suttor who, with the assistance of two Aborigine trackers, found the men the following day in

---

55 On the problem of bushrangers in the 1820s and early 1830s, see, Fletcher, B. H., *Ralph Darling A Governor Maligned*, (Oxford University Press), 1984, pp. 180-182.

56 'Justification of the Sydney Monitor by The General', *The Sydney Monitor*, 30 October 1830, p. 2, in an article attacking Governor Darling, suggested that the insurrection at Bathurst 'had taken place on account of bad and insufficient food and clothing'. *The Australian*, 3 December 1830, p. 3, included a long letter on 'The Bathurst Insurgents' by an 'eye witness'.

57 'Editorial', *Sydney Gazette and New South Wales Advertiser*, 7 October 1830, p. 2.

58 'Editorial', *Sydney Gazette and New South Wales Advertiser*, 30 October 1830, p. 2, details the attack on Greenwood, the subsequent trial and executions. *The Australian*, 3 December 1830, p. 3, included a long letter on 'The Bathurst Insurgents' by an 'eye witness'.

59 'Editorial', *Sydney Gazette and New South Wales Advertiser*, 2 October 1830, p. 2, commented that 'the disturbances at Bathurst are, as usual, enormously exaggerated'. See also the report, 'Editorial: Bathurst', *Sydney Gazette and New South Wales Advertiser*, 7 October 1830, p. 3.

60 http://www.entwistlefamily.org.uk/ribbongang.htm states that six of those eventually hanged were from Ireland.

61 Fry, Eric, (ed.), *Rebels and Radicals*, (Allen & Unwin), 1983, and Williams, Stephen, *Ralph Entwistle & the Bathurst Insurgency*, (Popinjay Publications), 1994, provide accounts of the rebellion.

a rocky glen near Captain Cook's Lookout and prepared to attack. The ensuing gun battle, during which an estimated 300 shots were exchanged, lasted for about an hour but with night approaching and short of ammunition, the volunteers withdrew.[62] Suttor's leadership was later criticised as lacking both energy and courage.[63] This setback led Major Donald McPherson, commandant at Bathurst to send a detachment of mounted soldiers of the 39th Regiment and mounted police on 29 September. Led by Lieutenant James Brown and reinforced with a second volunteer force, the troops sighted the rebels on 30 September at Bushrangers' Hill and set off in pursuit. But, having lost two men and five horses in the ensuing fight, Brown fell back and allowed Entwistle and his men to continue westwards.[64]

The band was active along the Lachlan River for the next few days but then disappeared. Entwistle was finally located on 13 October by a detachment of ten mounted police and in a sharp exchange of fire near Borowa Plains lasting twenty minutes, four of the police were wounded and three rebels shot and captured. The rebels were again allowed to escape as the police were low on ammunition but the following day, faced with a fresh detachment of the 39th Regiment force-marched from Sydney under Captain Horatio Walpole and by various parties of volunteers, Entwistle and his six remaining men surrendered without a struggle.[65] Ralph Entwistle and his men were charged with murder, bushranging and horse thieving in Bathurst and tried before a Special Commission consisting of Chief Justice, Sir Francis Forbes and a jury of eight military officers, two of whom had taken part in the campaign against the rebels. The outcome was a foregone conclusion and on 3 November 1830, ten rebels were hanged, the first and largest public hanging in Bathurst.[66] The Bathurst rising was one of many protests by convicts either individually or collectively as they sought to escape the vicious realities of a penal society.[67]

A system of terror

The gallows stood at the apex of the system of terror. There were 260 executions between 1824 and 1836 in VDL and 308 in NSW between 1825 and 1834.

> On Monday, Alexander Pearce, for murder, and yesterday, John Butler, for sheep stealing, John Thompson, Patrick Connolly, James Tierney and George Lacey, for burglary and highway robbery, were executed in this town pursuant to their sentence. Pearce's body was, after it had been suspended the usual time, delivered at the hospital for dissection.

---

[62] Suttor's account, dated 7 October, was printed in 'The Bushrangers at Bathurst', *Sydney Gazette and New South Wales Advertiser*, 21 October 1830, pp. 2-3.

[63] 'Domestic Intelligence', *The Sydney Monitor*, 27 October 1830, p. 3, included a poem 'The Wars of Bathurst' in which Suttor was comprehensively satirised for his failure against the rebels.

[64] Darling to Sir George Murray, 5 October 1830, *HRA*, Series I: Vol. 15, pp. 769-770, provides details of the alarm among settlers and Darling's response.

[65] This was briefly reported in 'Bathurst', *Sydney Gazette and New South Wales Advertiser*, 21 October 1830, p. 2.

[66] Ibid, Hirst, J. B., *Convict Society and its Enemies: A History of Early New South Wales*, pp. 133-150.

[67] See, Atkinson, Alan, 'Four patterns of convict protest', *Labour History*, Vol. 37, (1979), pp. 28-51, for an important study of the nature of convict protest.

> We trust these awful and ignominious results of disobedience to law and humanity will act as a powerful caution; for blood must expiate blood! and the welfare of society imperatively requires, that all whose crimes are so confirmed, and systematic, as not to be redeemed by lenity, shall be pursued in vengeance and extirpated with death.[68]

One in ten convicts spent time in the various penal settlements where discipline was harsh and unremitting. The chain-gangs provided another means of brutal regimentation. At any one time in the 1830s about a thousand convicts worked in the gangs in NSW and around seven hundred in VDL. Being consigned to the gangs was meant to be a severe punishment, 'as severe a one as could be inflicted on man', according to VDL's Sir George Arthur while his NSW counterpart Richard Bourke believed that 'the condition of the convicts in the chain gangs was one of great privation and unhappiness'.[69] For fifty years, the lash was the most widely used form of punishment: quick, cheap and readily available. During the 1830s, 38 per cent of VDL convicts were flogged.[70] Almost any misdemeanour could warrant the lash, 'absconding, insubordination, drunkenness, indecent conduct, neglect or wilful mismanagement of work, neglect of duty, indecent or abusive language, swearing, insolence, or other disorderly conduct'.[71] In NSW between 1830 and 1837, 42,000 floggings were administered with each victim receiving on average over 40 lashes. In just over eight years the 'cat' was laid across convict backs more than 1.6 million times.[72] Flogging deterred some but hardened and brutalised others.

> The floggings are hideously frequent. On flogging mornings I have seen the ground where the men stood at the triangles saturated with blood, as if a bucket of blood had been spilled on it, covering a space three feet in diameter, and running out in various directions, in little streams two or three feet long.... Frere gave him fifty more lashes, and sent him the next day to grind cayenne pepper. This was a punishment more dreaded by the convicts than any other. The pungent dust filled their eyes and lungs, causing them the most excruciating torments. For a man with a raw back the work is one of continued agony. In four days Rufus Dawes, emaciated, blistered, blinded, broke down 'For God's sake, Captain Frere, kill me at once!', he said.[73]

By all accounts the convicts waged sullen, surreptitious resistance against the system. Occasionally resistance flared into open rebellion most seriously at Castle Hill to the west of Sydney in March 1804.

Escaped convicts, or 'bolters' were of more concern to the authorities than armed rebellion. From the earliest years of settlement convicts slipped out of the

---

[68] 'Executions', *Hobart Town Gazette*, 24 July 1824, p. 2.
[69] Cit, Evans, L., and Nicholls, P., *Convicts and Colonial Society, 1788-1853*, (Cassell), 1976, pp. 77-78.
[70] Ibid, Robson, L. L., *The Convict Settlers of Australia*, p. 102.
[71] West, J., *The History of Tasmania*, rev. ed., A. G. L. Shaw, (ed.), (Angus & Robertson), 1971, p. 414. See also, Nichol, W., 'Malingering and convict protest', *Labour History*, Vol. 47, (1984), pp. 18-27.
[72] Ibid, Shaw, Alan, *Convicts and Colonies*, p. 202.
[73] Clarke, Marcus, *For the Term of His Natural Life*, (George Robertson), 1874, pp. 339-340. Although the novel is made up of a series of semi-fictional accounts of actual event, its descriptions of the brutality of the convict system are generally regarded as accurate.

settlements and attempted to survive on the outer fringes of the colonies by armed robbery. As settlers moved into the interior the scope for successful bushranging increased. The extent of bushranging is evident in over 6,800 articles published in newspapers in NSW and VDL between 1820 and 1860. These suggest that there was a dramatic increase in the 1830s (2,353 articles, over double the number printed in the 1820s), that there was a further increase in the 1840s (3,282 articles) and that its incidence did not decline significantly until the 1850s (1,780 article). In VDL between 1810 and 1825, there were as many as 100 'bolters' in the bush at any one time. The more formidable gangs led by men such as Cash and Brady were well armed and mounted and knew enough about the country to elude capture frequently, to travel rapidly from district to district and to retreat when pressed to carefully prepared hide-outs. They had well maintained networks of sympathisers and informers among the convict population. During the early 1820s, 'bolters' were so successful in their raids that settlers abandoned farms in the interior and moved into the larger towns for security. Inevitably perhaps crime was more prevalent in the convict colonies than in Britain although most felons were convicted for crime against property rather than offences against the person. In the mid-1840s, the crime rate in VDL was double that in England with convicts and ex-convicts responsible for more than 90 per cent of serious offences.[74]

Whether the violence of the convict system survived the end of transportation has been a matter of much debate but little resolution. In *Convicts and Colonies,* Shaw argued that socially, transportation did 'no great harm'.[75] By contrast, Lewis believed that 'a tradition of brutality and sadism was established at the centre of Australian life during the convict years' and that it 'has left a lasting if indefinable imprint'.[76] However, the evidence from Tasmania does not support this view. As ex-convicts died or left the colony, its crime rate fell away and by the 1880s was the lowest in Australia. Celebrating the fading of the 'hated stain' of convictism a Tasmanian statistician argued in 1891 that 'crime and pauperism' were 'simply noxious foreign plants' that found 'no congenial soil in Tasmania for their propagation'.[77]

Political consciousness

Although there were many occasions for mass political action and widespread public anger during the nineteenth century, the bloodshed at the Eureka Stockade assumed heightened significance because it was exceptional. Violence was often threatened by orators, but it rarely went further than fiery rhetoric, brawling and minor destruction of property; its nature was symbolic rather than physical. Even in the outback where practically everyone was armed, guns were rarely used to settle political or even personal disputes. The struggle against imperial land policy in the 1840s, against continued transportation in the early 1850s and in favour of radical land legislation later in the decade all produced

[74] Ibid, Shaw, Alan, *Convicts and Colonies*, p. 343.
[75] Ibid, Shaw, Alan, *Convicts and Colonies*, p. 358.
[76] Lewis, G., 'Violence and Nationalism in Australia', *Arena*, Vol. 43, (1976), p. 53
[77] Reynolds, H., ''That Hated Stain': the Aftermath of Transportation in Tasmania', *Historical Studies*, Vol. 14, (1969), pp. 22-23.

mass meetings, torch-lit processions and the implicit threat of violence. Shaw observed:

> Up to the middle of the 19th century...it seems clear enough that Australians had taken over the British tradition of threatening–and if need be of using violence, as a normal means of influencing political processes. Such methods seem to have achieved considerable success, either because the authorities thought it not worth-while to make a serious issue of what to them were somewhat petty concerns, or because they realised that the force at their disposal was relatively weak; because of these easy successes, the protests did not have to be taken so far as to create a revolutionary tradition akin to that which... [existed] in many other countries.[78]

How far convicts were politically conscious is difficult to determine. Some were skilled workers, who later found their way into the early craft unions. Others were primarily Irish or drawn from the British middle-classes. In 1793, the barrister Thomas Muir and the clergyman Thomas Palmer were transported for sedition with three leaders of Scottish corresponding societies. Over the rest of the decade the authorities in Britain enacted repressive legislation against political radicals and strikers and some of those convicted were also transported. After the 1798 Irish rebellion, hundreds of prisoners arrived in Sydney, raising the spectre of an Irish republican revolt in the colony. The authorities, haunted from the earliest days by 'the nightmare vision of a convict republic' were prepared to take harsh measures to prevent trouble. In 1806, the convict Joseph Smallsalts was punished for extolling the revolutionary views of Thomas Paine.

> Joseph Smallsalts, a prisoner for life, was on Tuesday last brought before the Judge Advocate, charged with having uttered expressions of an inflammatory and seditious tendency...the offender was ordered 100 lashes...and sent to public labour at the Coal Mines at Newcastle. He was permitted to travel to Newcastle...with a label on his back, on which Thomas Paine was decyphered in large characters, the culprit having declared that 'he would be worse than Tom Paine if thwarted'.[79]

John Dunmore Lang later joked that in some countries the clergy might 'take the fleece' but NSW was the only place they were 'openly authorised...to take the hide also, or to flay their flock alive.'[80] Religion sometimes restrained the Irish but because of hostility to the Roman Catholic Church, the authorities seldom allowed Catholic priests to hold mass before 1810 when they recognised priests would counsel submission to the system. However even among the Irish, probably only a minority heeded such counsel. Other clergy had very little effect. Many non-Catholic convicts were hostile to religion because, from the 'flogging parson' Samuel Marsden onwards, they were part of a repressive apparatus, often serving as magistrates and ordering the lash.

---

[78] Shaw, Alan, 'Violent Protest in Australian History', *Historical Studies*, Vol. 15, (1973), p. 554.
[79] 'Sydney', *Sydney Gazette and New South Wales Advertiser*, 30 March 1806, p. 2.
[80] Lang, John Dunmore, *An historical and statistical account of New South Wales*, 2 Vols. (Longman, Brown, Green, and Longmans), 1837, Vol. 2, p. 233.

Although the 'nightmare vision' did not materialise, in fact rebellion was reasonably common. The problem was that it was always fragmented, poorly organised and collapsed easily. Actual convict rebellions were betrayed with monotonous regularity and within convict society resistance took many forms short of armed uprising. The most common response of forced labour was passive resistance:

> Early dispatches show governors almost foaming at the mouth over the difficulty of getting the convicts to raise crops. Slow-down is the meaning of the 'neglect of duty' charges that crop up so often in the punishment books. It is the situation behind respectable settlers' endless complaints about the laziness of the convicts.[81]

Such tactics often won substantial informal concessions, first limitations on the hours of work, then the right to work for pay part of the time. In addition, convicts found ways to corrupt their overseers and cheat the system: during King's governorship the convict clerks in the government stores turned to forgery on a considerable scale. These accomplishments do suggest a degree of solidarity among sections of the convicts that made more violent forms of resistance possible from time to time although solidarity was always very fragile. This had much to do with to the uneven and changeable circumstances of convict life:

> ...clerks and tradesmen might get to work at their usual jobs, though they might also be set to labouring; labourers might be set to quarrying stone...or following a flock of five hundred sheep around in the bush. Women would not be sent to heavy outdoor labour, but might indiscriminately find themselves doing housework in central Sydney or deep in the bush. The personal relations in which this work was done varied unpredictably in both public and private sectors...A single convict's career...might lead through all these types of situations in a few years.[82]

Middle-class radicals were effectively bought off. The small number of 'gentlemen' convicts received preferential treatment, comfortable jobs and early tickets-of-leave. Many of the political prisoners transported after the 1798 Irish Rebellion, the 1838 Canadian Rebellions and the upheavals of the Chartist movement were not ideological rebels, while others seem to have tired of strife by the time they reached Australia. The Young Irelanders transported to VDL and Fenians transported to WA for their respective involvement in the abortive 1848 and 1867 Irish Rebellions were the exceptions though they had little lasting. impact on Australian politics. With Irish-American assistance, many of the Young Irelanders escaped to the United States in the early 1850s while the Fenians escaped on the *Catalpa* in 1876.[83] What was clear is that the authorities emphasised the temporal and divine rightness of the punishment of those punished, that those who transgressed recognised the certainty of punishment and that, for those not involved in criminal activity, the wisdom of the authorities.

---

[81] Connell, R. W., and Irving, T. H., *Class Structure in Australian History, Documents, Narrative and Argument*, (Longman Cheshire), 1980, p. 45.
[82] Ibid, Connell, R. W., and Irving, T. H., *Class Structure in Australian History,* p. 47.
[83] See, Brown, Richard, *Famine, Fenians and Freedom, 1830-1882*, pp. 523-530, 559-568.

Bushranging as rebellion

Whether they were what Eric Hobsbawm christened 'social bandits', bushrangers operated in the shadows, often on the fringes of society, in geographically isolated areas.[84] Their lives and actions, like those of other frontier figures, remain shrouded in mystery and legend. Some have been lionised and romanticised in popular fiction. These individuals were admired for flaunting authority and championing the interests of the masses against élite oppression and were often seen by ordinary people as beacons of popular resistance. The *Colonial Times* reported in August 1825 that a poem had been found in the pocket of a bushranger 'written in blood':

> We are the boys that fears no dangers,
> And what you term us is bush-rangers;
> If it is our lives you do demand,
> True to our guns, then we must stand.
> We all are young and in our prime,
> To meet our hardships we incline
> And if our blood you mean to shed,
> Life for life before we yield.
> 'Tis in the bush we are forced to go-
> You settlers prove our overthrow:
> To rob and plunder is against our will.
> But we must have a living still.
> Now to this country we are come,
> Banished from our native home,
> And if we can't go back no more,
> We will rob the rich to feed the poor.[85]

Banditry often involved violent acts by brutal common criminals for whom theft was simply an economic expedient. Contemporary sources tend to focus on individual bushrangers and often projected the urban middle-class views of writers who romanticised often oral traditions for their own literary and political reasons.

Bushranging was the natural consequence of a system that assigned convicts to forced labour in remote locations across a sparsely occupied countryside.[86] It first became extensive in VDL, where hunting rather than

---

[84] The notion of the 'social bandit' originated in Hobsbawm, Eric, *Primitive Rebels: Studies in Archaic Forms of Social Movement in the 19th and 20th Centuries*, (Manchester University Press), 1959, and was fleshed out a decade later in Hobsbawm, Eric, *Bandits*, (Weidenfeld & Nicholson), 1969, revised edition, (Pantheon), 1981.

[85] *Colonial Times*, 25 August 1825, p. 3

[86] Bonwick, James, *The Bushrangers: Illustrating the Early Days of Van Diemen's Land*, (G. Robertson), 1856, White, Charles, *History of Australian Bushranging: Early days to 1862*, (Angus and Robertson), 1900, and Boxall, George, *The story of the Australian bush-rangers*, (Swan Sonnenschein & Co., Ltd.), 1899, still provide the best narrative accounts of early bushrangers. See also, Karskens, Grace, *The Colony: A History of Early Sydney*, (Allen & Unwin), 2009, pp. 300-309.

farming became for a time the basis of the economy.[87] For survival, the colony had to give guns to convicts and send them out to hunt kangaroos. Initially they had to return to Hobart or Port Dalrymple to sell the meat and get more ammunition. But once settlement proceeded beyond the initial beachheads and settlers became dispersed, the hunters had alternative sources of supply and could operate independently as outlaws. Settlers had an interest in protecting them and trading with them, and often they had the sympathy of emancipists and assigned servants. They were colourful figures with 'long ratty hair, thick beards, roughly sewn garments and moccasins of kangaroo hide, a pistol stuck in a rope belt, a stolen musket, a polecat's stench'.[88] By 1814, they were such a problem that Macquarie offered an amnesty to those bushrangers who turned themselves in by 1 December 1814. This foolhardy proclamation seemed to suggest that all crimes except murder could be committed with impunity until that date; it provoked a carnival of robbery and mayhem. Few surrendered and there was panic in Hobart, prompting Lieutenant-Governor Thomas Davey, who lacked a criminal court to try bushrangers or sufficient troops, to declare martial law in 1815.[89] But the problem did not go away.[90]

William was appointed Lieutenant-Governor of VDL in 1817 in the hope that he would be able to restore order and bring direction and organisation into its government.[91] He immediately proceeded to try to reform the abuses prevalent on the Derwent. He found much disorder in the administration, government activities were not co-ordinated and corruption was common.[92] The convicts were under little control and bushranging had almost reached open armed revolt against the colonial authorities. Sorell firmly met the challenge of Michael Howe, the leader of the bushrangers and self-styled 'Governor of the Woods'.[93] Howe already had a gang of 28 by 1814 and had excellent intelligence about troop movements from small farmers and convicts. Well-planned and executed military operations quickly ended Howe's career and sent most of his followers to the gallows. The stern warning was not lost on those runaway convicts who sought to emulate Howe.[94] Sorell knew that large-scale bushranging

[87] Petrow, Stefan, ''Military Police', Bushrangers and the Struggle for Order in Van Diemen's Land 1803-1826', *Law & History*, Vol. 77, (1), (2014), pp. 77-109.

[88] Ibid, Hughes, Robert, *The Fatal Shore*, p. 227.

[89] Eldershaw, P. R., 'Davey, Thomas (1758-1823)', *ADB*, Vol. 1, pp. 288-289.

[90] See, for instance, reports of bushranging in 'Public Notice', *Hobart Town Gazette and Southern Reporter*, 5 October 1816, p. 1, Public Notice', *Hobart Town Gazette and Southern Reporter*, 19 October 1816, p. 1, 2 Public Notice', *Hobart Town Gazette and Southern Reporter*, 3 November 1816, p. 1, Public Notice', *Hobart Town Gazette and Southern Reporter*, 14 December 1816, p. 1.

[91] Reynolds, John, 'Sorell, William (1775-1848)', *ADB*, Vol. 2, pp. 459-462.

[92] See discussion by Curnow, R., 'What's Past is Prologue: Administrative Corruption in Australia', in Tiihonen, Seppo, (ed.), *The history of corruption in central government*, (IOS Press), 2003, pp. 37-64, especially pp. 39-46.

[93] Von Stieglitz, K. R., 'Howe, Michael (1787-1818)', *ADB*, Vol. 1, pp. 560-561. See also, the pamphlet by Thomas Wells, Sorell's secretary, *Michael Howe, the Last and Worst of the Bushrangers*, (Andrew Bent, Hobart), 1818, and ibid, Bonwick, James, *The Bushrangers: Illustrating the Early Days of Van Diemen's Land*, pp. 47-57.

[94] On Proclamation offering 100 guineas for Howe's apprehension was issued in 'Proclamation', *Hobart Town Gazette and Southern Reporter*, 6 September 1817, p. 1.

was only possible where help was given by outwardly law-abiding free colonists and, in less than eighteen months after taking office, he had arrested all known sympathisers of the bushrangers and those who assisted them.[95] Macquarie optimistically but inaccurately ventured the hope that the 'Bush-Ranging System' was now in decline.[96]

In addition to the soldiers sent against the bushrangers, a force of field police was raised composed largely of convict volunteers, motivated by promises of freedom, money, free passages back home or grants of land. Soldiers and police were assisted by male and female Indigenous Australian trackers, such as Musquito, an Indigenous Australian convict from NSW who had helped track and kill Michael Howe in 1818.[97] He was denied his promised reward of being allowed to return home and walked into the bush joining a 'tame gang' that was linked to the Oyster Bay Aborigines. However, the spread of settlement in VDL increasingly threatened their lands and some of his band became progressively more antagonistic towards settlers, attacking several shopkeepers in raids on the east coast in November 1823 and in 1824.[98] Trained by their leader in the use of firearms, they became a formidable force. In August 1824, Musquito was shot and captured by Teague, a Tasmanian Aborigine, but Teague was not given the boat promised as a reward, so he too took to the bush and led a band of Indigenous Australian bushrangers. No action was taken against him when he came in, but Musquito, convicted on dubious evidence as it is unclear whether he committed any of the murders, was hanged in February 1825.[99] In 1830, a Committee into the Military Operations against Aborigines questioned settlers about the origins of Indigenous Australian hostility and it concluded, though it makes only the briefest mention of Musquito that the hanging of the four Aborigines in 1825 and 1826 contributed to the permanent rift between the Aborigines and settler society. There remains some disagreement about the significance of Musquito and whether he was a resistance leader or simply a criminal.[100]

The reward was extended to include a free pardon for any convict following Howe's involvement in the murder of William Drew, 'Government & General Orders', *Hobart Town Gazette and Southern Reporter*, 27 December 1817, p. 1.

[95] 'Hobart Town', *Hobart Town Gazette and Van Diemen's Land Advertiser*, 18 August 1821, p. 2, reported that a melodrama called 'Michael Howe, the Terror of Van Diemen's Land' was performed at the Cobourg Theatre in London.

[96] *HRA*, Series I: Vol. 14, p. 292.

[97] Parry, Naomi, 'Musquito (1780-1825)', *ADB*, Supplementary Volume, p. 299.

[98] Melville, Henry, *The History of the Island of Van Diemen's Land from the year 1824 to 1835*, (Smith and Elder), 1835, pp. 32-35, provides later evidence for Sorell's broken promises initially given in 1817.

[99] 'Executions', *Hobart Town Gazette and Van Diemen's Land Advertiser*, 25 February 1825, p. 2, reported his execution.

[100] West, John, *The History of Tasmania,* 2 Vols. (Henry Dowling), 1852, Vol. 2, pp. 11-16, and Bonwick, James, *The Last of the Tasmanians: or, the Black War of Van Diemen's Land*, (Samson Low), 1870, pp. 93-107, and *The Lost Tasmanian Race*, (Samson Low), 1884, pp. 78-83, discuss Musquito within the view that the destruction of the Tasmanian Aborigines was inevitable. By contrast and often overlooked Calder, James Erskine, *Some Account of the Wars, Extirpation, Habits etc. of the Native Tribes of Tasmania*, (Henn & Co.), 1875, pp. 47-56, took a more sympathetic view of Musquito and did not see the

In 1824, Colonel George Arthur, a strict disciplinarian was appointed Lieutenant-Governor and seeking to make transportation feared by British criminals, he increased convict discipline and ensured that punishment was uniform and assured.[101] The British government responded by increasing the annual average of convicts sent to VDL from about 800 between 1817 and 1827 to about 1,800 between 1828 and 1835; between 1830 and 1836, convicts formed on average 44 per cent of the population.[102] The increase in convicts and free settlers swelled the total population from 5,468 in 1820 to 24,279 by 1830. Arthur imposed severe punishments and floggings on convicts who disobeyed his regulations and many were hung for committing serious crimes, but order was also encouraged by offering inducements, such as a ticket-of-leave and a pardon, to those who behaved correctly and showed signs of reformation.[103] There could be:

> ...no happiness nor prosperity without personal security,' and this could only be secured by 'severe discipline'.[104]

Although Arthur was instructed by the British government to establish 'a stricter surveillance and discipline' over convicts, on his arrival in 1824 Arthur first had to deal with several threats to effective government.[105] Of particular concern was 'a vast amount of crime amongst the Prisoners—Murders, constant Robberies, and other atrocious acts,' perpetrated especially by bushrangers.[106] Given his 'exceedingly limited' military force, and his 'inadequate means of punishing offences,' Arthur was thankful that crime was not more widespread,

---

destruction of the Tasmanian Aborigines as either inevitable or necessary. Attempts by historians in the 1970s to elevate Musquito to the status of a resistance leader were rebuffed by Windschuttle, Keith, *The Fabrication of Aboriginal History: Volume 1, Van Diemen's Land*, (Macleay Press), 2002, pp. 61-82, an inherently flawed study that views him as a bushranger whose criminal behaviour was inimical to resistance.

[101] Shaw, A. G. L., *Sir George Arthur, Bart, 1784-1854*, (Melbourne University Press), 1980, Shaw, A. G. L., 'Sir George Arthur, (1784-1854)', *ADB*, Vol. 1, 1966, pp. 32-38, and Buckner, Phillip, 'Sir George Arthur', *DCB*, Vol. 8, pp. 26-31.

[102] Ibid, Shaw Alan, *Convicts and Colonies*, pp. 365-367, Forsyth, W. D., *Governor Arthur's Convict System: Van Diemen's Land, 1824-36*, (Sydney University Press), 1970, p. 150, ibid, Alexander, Alison, *Tasmania's Convicts: How Felons Built a Free Society*, pp. 34-89, and Hartwell, R. M., *The Economic Development of Van Diemen's Land, 1820-1850*, (Oxford University Press), 1954, p. 68.

[103] Arthur, George, *Defence of Transportation, in Reply to the Remarks of the Archbishop of Dublin in His Second Letter to Earl Grey*, (Gowie), 1835, pp. 48, 96-100, ibid, Shaw Alan, *Convicts and Colonies*, pp. 217-48, and Davis, R. P., *The Tasmanian Gallows: A Study of Capital Punishment*, (Cat and Fiddle Press), 1974, pp. 13-33.

[104] CO 280, Arthur to Hanley, 4 April 1834, emphasis in original.

[105] Arthur to Bathurst, 14 September 1825, Arthur to Huskisson, 21 April 1828, minute by Arthur, 26 February 1828, Arthur to Murray, 25 May 1829, *HRA*, Resumed Series III: Vol. 8, pp. 367-371.

[106] Arthur to Bathurst, 3 July 1825, ibid, Levy, M. C. I., *Governor George Arthur*, pp. 90-96, and Maxwell-Stewart, Hamish, ''I Could Not Blame the Rangers...': Tasmanian Bushranging, Convicts and Convict Management', *Tasmanian Historical Research Association Papers and Proceedings*, Vol. 42, (1995), pp. 109-126.

but it was 'truly distressing' to the settlers on isolated farms.[107] The activities of Matthew Brady and thirteen other convicts who had escaped from Macquarie Harbour in 1824 demonstrate the problem of suppressing bushranging. Arthur's methodical police methods, rewards and spies eventually wore down the Brady gang, and Brady himself was captured in 1826.[108] It now became clear to what extent the bushrangers symbolised popular hostility to the rulers and dozens of petitions arrived at Government seeking clemency but Brady was still hanged.[109] For the remainder of his period in office, Arthur sought to limit bushranger activity by reducing levels of convict escapes but, with growing convict numbers, he had limited success.[110]

Under Arthur's successors, Sir John Franklin[111] and Sir John Eardley-Wilmot,[112] bushranging still posed a major threat. In 1838, Franklin reported 'several daring outrages, attended with personal violence, robbery, and murder' committed by four armed convicts.[113] Reacting to the 'alarm' of settlers, Franklin took 'the most vigorous measures' to catch the bushrangers. He sent all able-bodied constables in pursuit and offered 'extraordinary rewards' for their capture and free pardons to convict servants who defended their masters. Convicts who helped capture bushrangers were liable to be killed for their betrayal and were thus given free passage to England.[114] Franklin encouraged settlers to defend themselves resolutely, to tell the nearest Police Magistrate of the appearance of bushrangers as quickly as they could, and to scour the country for signs of bushrangers.[115] Four bushrangers were captured, but magistrates remained vigilant.[116] Most landholders willingly defended themselves but had farms to work and relied on 'the protecting care of the Government'.[117] This protection was weakened by the withdrawal of regular troops and in November 1840, Franklin reported that he had three companies of infantry less than he had in May 1839. He protested that, as the convict population increased and spread throughout the

[107] Examples of bushranging in VDL are taken from, Petrow, Stefan, 'Policing in a Penal Colony: Governor Arthur's Police System in Van Diemen's Land, 1826-1836', *Law and History Review*, Vol. 18, (2000), pp. 351-395, and 'After Arthur: Policing in Van Diemen's Land 1837-46', in Enders, Mike and Dupont, Benoît, (eds.), *Policing the Lucky Country*, (Hawkins Press), 2002, pp. 176-198.

[108] 'Brady, the Bush-ranger', *Colonial Times and Tasmanian Advertiser*, 17 March 1826, p. 3, 'Editorial', *Hobart Town Gazette*, 6 May 1826, p. 2.

[109] Robson, L. L., 'Brady, Matthew (1799?-1826)', *ADB*, Vol. 1, pp. 147-148.

[110] Plater, David, and Crofts, Penny, *Bushrangers, the Exercise of Mercy and the 'Last Penalty of the Law' in New South Wales and Tasmania 1824-1856*, University of Tasmania, 2013: https://papers.ssrn.com/sol3/papers.cfm?abstract_id=2826903

[111] Fitzpatrick, Kathleen, *Sir John Franklin in Tasmania 1837-1843*, (Melbourne University Press), 1949, and 'Franklin, Sir John (1786-1847), *ADB*, Vol. 1, pp. 412-415.

[112] Roe, Michael, 'Eardley-Wilmot, Sir John Eardley (1783-1847)', *ADB*, Vol. 1, pp. 345-346, Shaw, A. G. L., 'Three Knights: Sir James Stephen, Sir John Franklin, and Sir John Eardley-Wilmot', *Tasmanian Historical Research Association Papers and Proceedings*, Vol. 36, (1989), pp. 141-153.

[113] Franklin to Glenelg, 14 May 1838, Forster to Colonial Secretary, 25 April 1838.

[114] Franklin to Stanley, 21 July 1843.

[115] *Hobart Town Gazette*, 18 May 1838, p. 3.

[116] Forster to Police Magistrates, 6 July 1838.

[117] Memorial from landholders at Swanport, 25 August 1838.

island on public works and roads, absconding would increase unless the military could be located at each probation station.[118]

In 1843, bushranging reached especially dangerous levels. The *Cornwall Chronicle* identified seven gangs of bushrangers comprised of from two to fifteen men operating in the north alone.[119] Three 'very determined' bushrangers, including Martin Cash and Laurence Kavenagh, escaped from Port Arthur, committed various acts of robbery and eluded capture.[120] Cash had experience as a splitter in 'the most intricate and impenetrable districts' and knew where to hide.[121] Kangaroo hunters and shepherds allegedly harboured bushrangers and supplied them with ammunition and provisions.[122] Cash used a telescope to watch from the hills and attacked farms at the most vulnerable times, when men were in the fields or constables were not in the vicinity.[123] Bushrangers laughed at the ineffective efforts of convict constables to find them and their 'overweening confidence' encouraged others to abscond to the bush. According to the *Hobart Town Advertiser,* colonists faced a more numerous, desperate and dangerous breed of convicts than the petty thieves of the past. The most desperate were the 'dark, stern, and determined' Irish prisoners, whose crimes had imperilled the lives of others and risked their own.[124] Convicts who had spent time at Norfolk Island and who were 'anxious for plunder, and, if necessary, bloodshed', were especially feared.[125]

Franklin was sensitive to charges of inefficiency and despite the large numbers of convicts dispersed throughout the colony and a relatively small police force, he pointed out that few convicts absconded and, when they did, committed a 'small amount of crime' and were usually captured quickly.[126] Only Riley Jeffs and John Conway, who shot District Constable Ward at Avoca and the Cash gang retained their freedom for long periods. In July 1844, Burgess reported that, during the first half year of his tenure, the average period of freedom was twenty-four days.[127] The police adopted various measures to recapture bushrangers. In July 1843, each magistrate selected four constables as Field Police, men of 'good conduct' with knowledge of the bush. They were stationed at the headquarters of each district ready for immediate deployment and were trained in the use of firearms by the military stationed in their districts. Between January and March 1844, 90 constables were taken from other stations to pursue absconders.

---

[118] Franklin to Russell, 3 April 1840, Franklin to Russell, 18 November 1840.
[119] 'Bushranging', *Cornwall Chronicle*, 6 May 1843, p. 2.
[120] Franklin to Stanley, 3 June 1843.
[121] Cash, M., *Martin Cash: The Bushranger of Van Diemen's Land in 1843-4*, (Walch and Sons), 1870.
[122] 'The Dog Nuisance', *Launceston Advertiser*, 14 September 1843, p. 3.
[123] *Hobart Town Courier*, 17 February 1843, *Hobart Town Courier*, 24 February 1843, *Hobart Town Courier*, 31 March 1843.
[124] *Hobart Town Advertiser*, 28 March 1843, p. 2; compare this claim with an analysis of offences by Irish convicts in VDL, see Williams, J., *Ordered to the Island: Irish Convicts and Van Diemen's Land*, (Crossing Press), 1994.
[125] 'Hobart Town', *Colonial Times*, 2 April 1844, p. 2.
[126] Franklin to Stanley, 3 June 1843, *Hobart Town Courier*, 12 May 1843.
[127] Burgess to Colonial Secretary, 22 July 1844.

Bushranging was a form of protest and on occasions an organised one. Indeed, there are cases where bushranging was a clear consequence of failed collective protest. The most infamous of these occurred at the Castle Forbes Estate in the Hunter Valley, north of Sydney in 1833.[128] Responding to repeated ill-treatment such as striking men and bringing them before magistrates to be flogged for trivial offences, the convict servants sent a representative to the Governor with a petition. However, as his application was irregular and his absence unauthorised, the man was put in chains and flogged at which point the men rose in revolt, robbed the estate and sought to murder the estate manager. At their trial and speeches on the gallows prior to being hanged, the men implored the Governor to prevent cruelties that had led to their act of desperation. In 1846, a gang of probationer convicts employed at Deloraine went on strike when the superintendent refused to make up for rations stolen by several absconding colleagues. Punished for their refusal to work, the men absconded and raided neighbouring properties until they were apprehended and charged with armed robbery. At the resulting trial 12 of the 21 involved were sentenced to death, but this was commuted and all were sent to Port Arthur.[129] Such cases highlight the risks of overt collective action. In several other cases, groups of convicts in chain gangs attacked their supervisor in response to harsh treatment or poor rations even at the almost certain risk of being executed and there are also cases where the murder of a fellow prisoner was reportedly instigated as an extreme means of escaping conditions that were no longer seen as endurable by those involved.[130]

As a form of convict rebellion bushranging was fragmented with individuals or gangs operating largely independently of each other. Although they posed a threat of public order and were especially feared in the poorly policed frontier areas, their ability to threaten the colonial authorities was limited. They may have been seen by some contemporaries and by later historians as 'banditti' or social bandits, contemporary evidence suggests that many were simply criminals and often very brutal ones. Only in rare cases, such as that of Matthew Brady, and Daniel Priest 'the friendly bushranger', did bushrangers gain significant public sympathy. Priest, for instance, was spared execution by the intercession of several clergymen and a petition signed by many country people.[131] Their

[128] This is fully explored in Brown, Richard, *Famine, Fenians and Freedom 1830-1882*, pp. 484-488.

[129] 'Court of Requests', *Launceston Examiner*, 14 January 1846, p. 3. For a detailed account see Dunning, Tom, and Maxwell-Stewart, Hamish, 'Mutiny at Deloraine: Ganging and Convict Resistance in 1840s Van Diemen's Land', *Labour History*, Vol. 82, (2002), pp. 35-47.

[130] The assaults often involved more than three workers and the role of employment conditions as the underlying cause is not only raised but in many cases widely acknowledged at the subsequent court proceedings. For references to several such cases tried in the Supreme Court of New South Wales, see 'Executions', *Australian*, 21 April 1829, (*R. v. Burgen, Allen, Mathews and Sullivan*); 'Editorial', *Sydney Gazette*, 11 November 1833, (*R. v. Smith and others*); and 'Law Intelligence', *Sydney Herald*, 6 August 1835, p. 2, (*R. v. Cassidy and Bagley*).

[131] A reward for Priest's capture dated 12 April 1843 was reported in 'Gazette', *Courier*, 21 April 1843, p. 4. This was increased to £100 as well as a conditional pardon 19 May 1845, 'Reward', *Courier*, 22 May 1845, p. 2. His arrest followed in September 1845,

support within local communities was based on their ability to terrorise isolated homesteads or small rural communities and they had little impact on larger centres of colonial power though Brady captured the township of Sorell for a night. From the 1820s, better organised military forces and police led to the quicker apprehension of convicts who 'bolted' but convict bushranging remained a persistent problem until transportation ended. From the 1850s, especially with the discovery of gold, the character of bushranging changed from an often-vapid expression of rebellious liberation by brutalised convicts to criminal activity by free men in some cases in search for social justice. The growth of the electric telegraph in the 1860s and the growth of illustrated newspapers in the 1880s made bushrangers a popular subject in British and Australian newspapers and they continued to be a persistent problem for the forces of law and order across Australia for the remainder of the century.

Female convicts and rebellion

Although much has been written about male convict resistance, contemporaries were equally concerned by the activities of female convicts. Governor Hunter described female convicts as a

> ...disgrace to their sex, are far worse than the men, and are generally found at the bottom of every infamous transaction committed in the colony.[132]

Popular attitudes towards women were expressed in the Molesworth Report:

> ...that society had fixed the standard of the average moral excellence required of women much higher than that which it had erected for men...a higher degree of reformation is required in the case of a female, before society will concede to her that she has reformed at all.[133]

Anne Summers, writing during a wave of Australian feminism in the mid-1970s, attempted to explain the common perception of women convicts as almost universally immoral:

> The whore stereotype was devised as a calculated sexist means of social control and then...characterized as being the fault of the women who were damned by it.[134]

In contrast, free settler women were characterised as 'God's police' in Summers' work, as these women, with no criminal past, have been seen by both

---

'Further Particulars of Priest', *Courier*, 27 September 1845, p. 2. His trial took place on 8 October, *Cornwall Chronicle*, 11 October 1845, pp. 235-236, and he was condemned to hang but the Lieutenant-Governor agreed to the petition on 'condition of transportation for life', *Launceston Examiner*, 1 November 1845, p. 4. Priest died in 1883.

[132] Hunter to Portland, 3 July 1799, *HRA*, Series I, Vol. 4, p. 586.

[133] *Report from the Select Committee on Transportation*, (Ordered to be Printed by the House of Commons), 1837.

[134] Summers, Anne, *Damned Whores and God's Police: The Colonization of Women in Australia*, (Penguin), 1975, p. 286.

their contemporaries and historians as more moral and upright than the convict women.

Some 25,000 female convicts were transported to NSW and VDL between 1788 and 1856. The life of female convicts was dominated by two unequal relationships, with the colonial authorities and with men.[135] Women were not subjected to the same levels of physical punishment as male convicts but there was a strong belief in discipline to reform women and the ways in which this operated was of considerable import.[136] Contemporaries tended to view convict women in two contrasting ways, moral dichotomies that pervade current historiography on female convicts.[137] Some observers saw all convict women as 'whores', immoral, degraded and irredeemable. In 1843, for instance, Lucretia Dunkley and her lover Martin Beech were executed for the murder of her husband:

> A wife - the drunken polluter of the rites of Hymen, the violator of every tie by which the scared institution of marriage can unite in holy wedlock, yielding to brutal lust, and with her paramour consummating her guilty passion in the blood of her husband.[138]

Others, however, made a distinction between those women who could be 'reformed' and became ordinary wives and mothers and those of 'bad character' who were 'incorrigible' in their anti-social behaviour and who could or would not be reformed.[139]

> It is sometimes said, that there is no medium with respect the female character, that either they are all that's good and virtuous, or that they are depraved and abandoned in the extreme; how then is it that in a place like this, where the most profligate and wicked of the female sex are to be found how is it, we say, that the proportionate number of females suffering the severe penalty of the law, should be so comparatively small, when compared with the number of male malefactor.[140]

---

[135] For women as convicts, see, Daniels, Kay, *Convict Women*, (Allen & Unwin), 1998, Oxley, Deborah, *Convict Maids: The Forced Migration of Women to Australia*, (Cambridge University Press), 1996, Damousi, Joy, *Depraved and disorderly: female convicts, sexuality and gender in Colonial Australia,* (Cambridge University Press), 1997, Reid, Kirsty, *Gender, Crime and Empire: Convicts, settlers and the state in early colonial Australia*, (Manchester University Press), 2007, and the discussion in Brown, Richard, *Three Rebellions: Canada 1837-1838, South Wales 1839 and Victoria, Australia 1854*, pp. 806-807, 821-822.

[136] Women who challenged male authority were punished severely. Though these punishments involved physical pain, more important was their visibility and humiliating nature. Floggings were used but rarely more than 25 lashes. More common were hard labour, fines and occasionally the stocks. Most hated by women was having their heads shaved.

[137] Ibid, Daniels, Kay, *Convict Women*, pp. 31-48, provides a good summary of the pervading historiography in the late 1990s.

[138] 'Assize Intelligence', *Sydney Morning Herald*, 15 September 1843, p. 3.

[139] Ibid, Reid, Kirsty, *Gender, Crime and Empire: Convicts, settlers and the state in early colonial Australia*, pp. 17-52, examines the relationship between gender and 'visions of order'.

[140] 'Editorial', *Colonial Times*, 23 April 1830, p. 3.

Although the factories at Parramatta and the Cascades in Hobart were the largest and attracted most public attention, there were 13 female factories operating between 1804 and 1856: 8 in NSW–Parramatta (2 factories), Port Macquarie (2 factories), Moreton Bay (2 factories), Newcastle and Bathurst–and 5 in VDL–Hobart Town, the Cascades, Launceston, Ross and Georgetown. Termed 'factories', a variety of work was carried out in them, but employment it appears was the least of their roles.[141] They had a multiple role acting as arrival depots where women were held before assignment or reassignment and as places of refuge for women when ill or pregnant or when conditions outside became intolerable. They were also places of imprisonment where women served out sentences for colonial crimes. They may have been seen by some women as an escape from the dominant male culture of the colonies but most were there because their 'bad behaviour' that was an affront to male authority especially what employers characterised as insolence. The position of convict women in NSW and VDL, whether inside factories or not, resulted in resistance and rebellion. Damousi identified three different types of resistance.[142] Female sexuality and especially promiscuity limited the extent to which the colonial authorities could mould these women in 'respectable' colonists. Overstepping spatial boundaries and moving into uncontrolled space through drunkenness, abusive language, insolence or petty crime challenged colonial authorities. Finally, there were occasions when women took collective action and rebelled. This was frequently represented by observers as a spectacle--and there were elements of 'rough music' in their actions--and as bizarre or absurd.[143] The press characterised their actions as expressions of wild emotions and those involved in suppressing women's rebellions were 'taming' their recalcitrant excesses.

The Female Factory in Parramatta was a frequent centre of rebellion.[144] Its inmates were divided into three classes. The first was women returned from assignment without complaint and eligible for re-assignment; the second for those pregnant or nursing or moved up from the third-class on probation; the third was a criminal division.

---

[141] There was, for instance, widespread public concern and criticism about the mismanagement of the Cascades Factory following the death of child were evident in the Hobart 'The Female Factory', *Colonial Times*, 13 March 1838, p. 5, with calls on 27 March 1838 for Governor Sir John Franklin to 'dismiss the persons under whose carelessness or indolence these shocking occurrences take place' and a damning coroner's court verdict reported on 3 April 1838. Despite this, 'Female Factory—Verdict of the Coroner', *Colonial Times*, 29 May 1838, p. 4, reported a further fatality in the factory nursery.

[142] Ibid, Damousi, Joy, *Depraved and disorderly: female convicts, sexuality and gender in Colonial Australia,* pp. 65-66.

[143] On this issue see, Thompson, E. P., 'Rough Music' in his *Customs in Common*, (Merlin Press), 1991, pp. 467-538, an extended version of 'Rough Music: Le Charivari anglais', *Annales: Économies, Sociétés, Civilisations*, Vol. 27, (1972), pp. 285-315, Hardy, René, *Charivari et justice populaire au Québec*, (Septentrion), 2015.

[144] On female factories and the issue of rebellion, see, ibid, Daniels, Kay, *Convict Women*, pp. 103-156, and Salt, Annette. *These outcast women: the Parramatta Female Factory, 1821-1848*, (Hale & Iremonger), 1984.

> The factory operated as a prison, a maternity home, a marriage bureau, an employment exchange and a hostel or refuge for women in transit between jobs. All its inmates, however, were strictly speaking prisoners...[145]

Originally intended for 300 occupants, by 1830 the factory rarely contained fewer than 500 adults and 100 or so children. There were never enough places to assign female convicts, so a larger proportion of females than males remained in government employment, primarily in wool manufacture. In addition, women returned to the factory over and over because of mistreatment during assignment or were returned there as vagrants because they were unable to find respectable employment. Some committed offences to get back to the factory. Females, unlike males, were chosen for assignment individually by settlers, and were likely to be selected based on physical appearance as their skills or previous work history. Apart from the male settlers' sexual intentions, this highlighted the low value placed on female convict labour. Women convicts were seen as immoral and troublesome and as hampered by children; penal authorities regarded their work as a cost saving rather than a source of income for the Crown. Yet the Parramatta factory did profit from their labour. Between 1838 and 1842, there was a return of over £5,000, probably an underestimate.[146]

Exploitation provoked resistance: the go-slow was as common among women as men. When Governor Gipps visited in 1838 he found the third-class women idle because they had no handles for their hammers; they simply broke the handles as soon as they were provided.[147] The Parramatta factory was also famous for its riots especially over food and comparisons have been drawn with the actions of women in food riots in Britain.[148] In October 1827, the authorities reduced the inmates' ration of bread and sugar, provoking 100 women to break out and march to Parramatta for provisions.[149]

> A numerous party again assailed the gates, with pick axes, axes, iron crows...and the inmates were quickly poured forth, thick as bees from a hive...About one hundred came into town...Constables were seen running in all directions. A captain, a Lieutenant, two serjents; and about forty rank and file...were seen flying in all directions with fixed bayonets...and so violent were the Amazonian banditti, that nothing less was expected but that the soldiers would be obliged to commence firing on them... [the convict women] Went along, carrying with them their aprons loaded with bread and meat. [150]

---

145 Smith, Babette, *A Cargo of Women: Susannah Watson and the Convicts of the Princess Royal*, (New South Wales University Press) 1988, p. 53.

146 Alford, Katrina, *Production or Reproduction? An Economic History of Women in Australia*, (Oxford University Press), 1984, p. 164.

147 'Domestic Intelligence', *Sydney Herald*, 1 March 1838, p. 2, 'Our New Governor', *Sydney Gazette and New South Wales Advertiser*, 8 March 1838, p. 2.

148 Dunn, Judith, *Colonial Ladies, lovely, lively, and lamentably loose: Crime reports from the Sydney Herald relating to the Female Factory, Parramatta, 1831-1835*, (Judith Dunn), 2008, a useful collation of primary material.

149 Kent, D., 'Customary Behaviour Transported: A Note on the Parramatta Female Factory Riot of 1827', *Journal of Australian Studies*, No. 40, (March 1994), pp. 75-79.

150 'Riot at the Female Factory', *Sydney Gazette and New South Wales Advertiser,* 31 October 1827, p. 2.

The press viewed this event with a combination of amazement and whimsy, trivialising what was a potentially dangerous rebellion.[151] In 1831, a crowd of several hundred women broke out, seized a particularly hated overseer and shaved her head, threatening to go to Sydney and shave the head of 'the Governor and his mob' as well. One of their leaders suggested they demolish the press of the *Sydney Monitor* to punish its editor, who had portrayed the female convicts as 'the worst and vilest of their sex'.[152] Soldiers were called in to round the women up on both occasions and all of Parramatta was amused by the sight of the local police and military chasing the women replete with provisions in their aprons. The troops turned out again in 1832 to quell 'extremely unruly' behaviour.[153]

Prisoners bitterly resented having their hair cropped and staged a further riot in 1833 on a day set for hair-cutting.[154] The Reverend Samuel Marsden himself appeared to confront them later lamenting:

> The women had collected large heaps of stones and as soon as we entered the 3rd Class they threw a shower of stones as fast as they possibly could and at the whole of us...It will never do to show them any clemency...I have no doubt but all the officers who saw their riotous conduct will be convinced of the necessity of keeping them under the hand of power.[155]

Yet keeping them under the 'hand of power' seldom proved easy. 1836 saw further problems and in 1852 a visiting writer recorded stories of another riot in 1839 over cropping convicts' hair that apparently achieved a relaxation of the 'depilatory laws':

> ...it is not many years ago that the Amazonian inmates, amounting to seven or eight hundred, and headed by a ferocious giantess...rose upon the guards and turnkeys, and made a desperate attempt to escape by burning the building. The officer commanding... sent a subaltern with a hundred men, half of them armed only with sticks...They laughed at the cane carrying soldiers, refuting their argumentum baculinum by a furious charge upon the gates, in which one man was knocked over by a brickbat...This unladylike ebullition was considered, as I am assured, the most formidable convict that ever occurred in the colony, not even excepting that of Castle Hill, in the year 1804![156]

---

[151] 'The Factory', *Sydney Gazette and New South Wales Advertiser,* 2 November 1827, p. 2.

[152] 'Female Insurrection at the Factory', *Sydney Monitor*, 5 February 1831, p. 3.

[153] 'Police Report', *Sydney Gazette and New South Wales Advertiser*, 3 March 1832, p. 2.

[154] Ibid, Damousi, Joy, *Depraved and disorderly: female convicts, sexuality and gender in Colonial Australia,* pp. 86-87, views head-shaving as a 'process of defeminisation', and as 'a lasting sign of punishment and an outward sign of moral corruption and weak character.' It also denoted 'feminine shame as those so punished were de-sexed and defeminised with their vanity undermined.'

[155] Samuel Marsden to Colonial Secretary, 7 March 1833, cit, ibid, Smith, Babette, *A Cargo of Women: Susannah Watson and the Convicts of the Princess Royal*, pp. 54-55.

[156] Mundy, Godfrey Charles, *Our Antipodes; or, Residence and rambles in the Australian colonies: With a glimpse of the gold fields*, 2 Vols. (R. Bentley), 1852, Vol. 1, p. 137.

Similar events also occurred in VDL.[157] In 1838, on a visit to the Cascades[158] Factory in Hobart, Sir John Franklin, his wife and guests were subjected to a direct action by 300 female inmates who bared their buttocks which they then slapped in front of the governor's party. Though some of the females in the party 'could not control their laughing', expressions of jest or 'play' were punishable offences for convict women. Franklin, by contrast, was horrified by the event and vowed never to visit the institution again. In 1841, a prisoner in the Female Factory at Launceston asked to be released from solitary confinement on grounds of illness and when the Surgeon refused, a group of inmates seized and held the Sub-Matron while releasing the prisoner. Eighty-five women barricaded themselves in a section of the Factory beating off police attacks by arming themselves with parts of their spinning wheels, bricks, knives and bottles. After the authorities refused to make concessions, they 'became very outrageous, breaking the Furniture and windows and attempting to burn the Building'. When the ringleaders were eventually brought to trial they continued to 'exhibit the most outrageous Conducts abusing and threatening the Magistrates to their face.'[159]

Resistance by convict women received less attention by contemporaries and subsequently by historians than convict rebellions by men. The important difference from male convict rebellions lay in the ways in which women's actions were regarded by the press. Rebellion was seen in two contrasting ways: on the one hand, there was the fear engendered by the 'unruly mob'; on the other, rebellions by women were seen as less threatening than those by men, more of a 'frolic' or spectacle. In extreme cases, however, the rioters were de-sexed or masculinised by the press, as their actions overtly crossed the boundary between socially acceptable and unacceptable female behaviour in their challenge to male hegemony.

Rebellion in New South Wales, 1804

From the early 1790s through to the last group of convicts transported to WA in 1868, Australia was frequently the destination for Ireland's political prisoners. The Defenders and United Irishmen were transported to NSW in the 1790s and early 1800s, the rural rebels and defeated members of Young Ireland to VDL between the 1820s and early 1850s and Fenians to WA.[160] These convicts brought the conflicts from Ireland with them and especially their struggle against 'Imperial' Britain. As a result, they were among the most fractious and, from the

---

[157] See Daniels, K., 'The Flash Mob: Rebellion, Rough Culture and Sexuality in the Female Factories of Van Diemen's Land', *Australian Feminist Studies*, Vol. 18, (1993), pp. 133-150, and Reid, Kirsty, ''Contumacious, ungovernable and incorrigible': convict women and workplace resistance, Van Diemen's Land 1820-1839', in Duffield, Ian, and Bradley, James, (eds.), *Representing Convicts: New Perspectives on Convict Forced Labour Migration*, (Leicester University Press), 1997, pp. 88-105.

[158] Alexander, Alison, (ed.), *Repression, Reform & Resilience: A history of the Cascades Female Factory*, (Convict Women's Press), 2016.

[159] Daniels, Kay, and Murnane, Mary, *Uphill All the Way, A Documentary History of Women in Australia*, (University of Queensland Press), 1980, p. 20.

[160] Whitaker, Anne-Maree, 'Swords to ploughshares? The 1798 Irish rebels in New South Wales', *Labour History*, Vol. 75, (1998), pp. 9-32.

perspective of the colonial authorities, the most dangerous and disruptive group in the emerging colonies. Between 1800 and 1807, there were at least three planned rebellions that were thwarted before they could break out and the Castle Hill Rising of 1804 when a convict rebellion was put down with considerable ferocity.

An Irish context

During the eighteenth and nineteenth centuries, the fundamental division in Ireland was religious.[161] To be a full member of Irish civil society, individuals had to be members of the Anglican Church of Ireland. Until 1829, Irish Roman Catholics and Protestant Dissenters were barred from certain professions such as law, the judiciary and the army and had restrictions on inheriting land. Catholics could not bear arms or exercise their religion publicly. With papal recognition of the Hanoverian dynasty in 1766, the threat to the ruling Protestant Ascendancy eased and many Penal Laws were relaxed or lightly enforced. From 1766, Catholics favoured reform and their views were represented by the 'Catholic Committees', a moderate organisation of Catholic gentry and clergy in each county that called for the repeal of the Penal Laws and emphasised their loyalty. Calls for change were also evident among the Irish Protestant élite that had come to see Ireland as their native country. Politically active Irishmen were far from disinterested when arguing about issues such as Irish independence or parliamentary reform.[162] During the American War of Independence, the government in London needed the support of Ireland and as a result, a Parliamentary faction led by Henry Grattan agitated for more favourable political and trading relationships with England.[163] Many of their demands were met in 1782, when Free Trade was granted between Ireland and England and legislative powers devolved to Dublin. Partly as a result of the trade laws being liberalised, Ireland went through an economic boom in the 1780s. Canals extended from Dublin westwards and the Four Courts and Post Office were established. Dublin's granite-lined quays were built and it boasted that it was the 'second city of the Empire'. Corn Laws were introduced in 1784 to give a bounty on flour shipped to Dublin promoting the spread of mills and tillage.

The French Revolution had a dramatic impact on Irish politics.[164] In 1792, Grattan succeeded in carrying an Act conferring the franchise on the Roman

---

[161] Elliott, Marianne, *When God Took Sides: Religion and Identity in Irish History*, (Oxford University Press), 2009, considers this division through to the twenty-first century.

[162] Small, Stephen, *Political Thought in Ireland 1776-1798: Republicanism, Patriotism and Radicalism*, (Oxford University Press), 2002, provides a detailed analysis of the development of Irish Patriotism into radical republicanism.

[163] On Grattan see, Madden, D. O., (ed.), *The speeches of the Right Hon. Henry Grattan: to which is added his letter on the union, with a commentary on his career and character*, 2 Vols. (J. Duffy), 1822, Grattan, Henry, *Memoirs of the life and times of the Rt. Hon. Henry Grattan by his son*, 2 Vols. (H. Colburn), 1839, 1846. See also, Mansergh D., *Grattan's Failure: Parliamentary Opposition and the People in Ireland*, (Irish Academic Press), 2005.

[164] Smyth, Jim, (ed.), *Revolution, counter-revolution, and union: Ireland in the 1790s*, (Cambridge University Press), 2000, especially pp. 1-38.

Catholics; in 1794, he introduced a reform bill that sought to retain legislative power in the hands of men of property. He had a strong conviction that while Ireland could best be governed by Irish hands, democracy in Ireland would inevitably turn to plunder and anarchy. The defeat of Grattan's mild proposals helped to promote more extreme opinions. Conservative loyalists such as John Foster, John Fitzgibbon and John Beresford remained opposed to further concessions to Catholics and argued that the 'Protestant Interest' could only be secured by maintaining the connection with Britain. The French Revolution prompted relentless action against the radical United Irishmen and deprived the Patriot movement of solidarity and unity.

The United Irishmen movement, formed in 1791, was based on an non-sectarian alliance between the Dissenter and Catholic bourgeoisie including Northern manufacturers, merchants and professionals, Belfast and Dublin artisans and Catholic peasants (the Defenders), against an entrenched Protestant Ascendancy that had many features of the French pre-revolutionary 'Ancien regime'. Initially the United Irishmen campaigned for the end to religious discrimination and the widening of the right to vote. With this route effectively blocked by the mid-1790s, the group soon radicalised its aims and sought to overthrow British rule and found a non-sectarian republic.[165] The United Irishmen spread quickly throughout the country. Republicanism was particularly attractive to the largely literate Ulster Presbyterian community, who were also discriminated against for their religion. Many Catholics, particularly the emergent Catholic middle-class, were also attracted to the movement and it claimed over 200,000 members by 1798. Violence and disorder became widespread and in 1795, hardening loyalist attitudes led to the foundation of the Orange Order, an uncompromising Protestant grouping.

The United Irishmen now dedicated to armed revolution, forged links with the Defenders, a militant Catholic society.[166] Wolfe Tone, the United Irish leader, went to France to seek French military support and a French expeditionary force of 15,000 troops arrived off Bantry Bay in December 1796,

---

[165] Elliott, Marianne, *Partners in Revolution: the United Irishmen and France*, (Yale University Press), 1990, Dickson, David Keogh, Dáire and Whelan, Kevin, (eds.), *The United Irishmen: republicanism, radicalism, and rebellion*, (Lilliput Press), 1993, and Curtin, Nancy, *The United Irishmen: popular politics in Ulster and Dublin, 1791-1798*, (Oxford University Press), 1998

[166] From its origins in Armagh in 1784 as the Catholic faction in a local sectarian feud, the Defender movement had gradually spread along lines of religious cleavage or cultural frontiers into County Down, Louth and south Ulster. Stimulated by the news and controversy about the French revolution and encouraged by the Catholic agitation, the Defenders were transformed into a politicised secret society. This process was then reinforced and the Defender organisation expanded from Meath across the north midlands into Connaught, by the continuing economic, political, and law-and-order crisis. By 1795, Defenderism had a presence in at least sixteen counties and in Dublin. They had successfully infiltrated the militia and knit far-flung lodges into a co-ordinated, if not well-disciplined, organisation. Defenderism had evolved a chameleon ideology infinitely adaptable to varying local conditions: on some occasions sectarian, then agrarian, always francophile and anti-ascendancy. With the emergence of a recognisable regional command structure in Ulster and a Catholic leadership aligned to the radical northern wing of the United Irishmen, the stage had been set for the making of a revolutionary coalition.

but failed to land due to a combination of indecisiveness, poor seamanship and storms off the Bantry coast.[167] The government began a campaign of repression against the United Irishmen, including executions, routine use of torture, transportation to penal colonies and house burnings. As the repression began to bite, the United Irishmen decided to go ahead with an insurrection without French help. Their activity culminated in the Irish Rebellion of 1798.[168] The uprising in Dublin failed but the rebellion then spread in an apparently random fashion firstly around Dublin, then briefly in Kildare[169] Meath, Carlow and Wicklow.[170] County Wexford[171] in the southeast saw the most sustained fighting, to be briefly joined by rebels who took to the field in Antrim and Down in the north.[172] A small French force landed in Killala Bay in Mayo leading to a last outbreak of rebellion in counties Mayo, Leitrim and Longford. The rebellion lasted three months before it was suppressed, but claimed up to an estimated 25,000 lives.

Irish Transportation

Most rebels became fiercely republican after having seen the successful creation of the United States and the changes caused by the French Revolution. Republican notions such as natural rights and a popularly elected upper house were a major threat to those whose power rested on established monarchical and oligarchic institutions. Political dissidents were regarded and treated as a threat to British society and Oldfield suggests:

> There is a case for contending that Britain (unlike many other European nations) escaped outright revolution in the nineteenth century by being able to siphon off its radicals (as convicts) and its paupers (as assisted immigrants) to the other side of the world.[173]

The British Government preferred deporting or exiling political prisoners to Botany Bay rather than risk creating martyrs if they were executed, something that was largely confined to leaders.[174] This proved an effective policy for the

---

[167] Elliott, Marianne, *Wolfe Tone: Prophet of Irish Independence*, (Yale University Press), 1991.

[168] Pakenham, T., *The Year of Liberty: the great Irish rebellion of 1798*, (Weidenfeld & Nicholson), 1998, remains an excellent narrative. See also, Bartlett, Thomas, (ed.), *1798: a bicentenary perspective*, (Four Courts), 2003.

[169] Chambers, Liam, *Rebellion in Kildare 1790-1803*, (Four Courts), 1998.

[170] O'Donnell, Ruán, *The rebellion in Wicklow, 1798*, (Irish Academic Press), 2003.

[171] Hay, Edward, *History of the Insurrection of County Wexford*, (J. Stockdale), 1803, Wheeler, H. F. B., & Broadley, A. M., *The war in Wexford: an account of the rebellion in the south of Ireland in 1798, told from original documents*, (J. Lane), 1910, Dickson, Charles, *The Wexford Rising in 1798: its causes and course*, (The Kerryman), 1955, and Keogh, Dáire, and Furlong, Nicholas, (eds.), *The Mighty Wave: the 1798 rebellion in Wexford*, (Four Courts), 1996.

[172] Stewart, A. T. Q., *The Summer Soldiers: the 1798 Rebellion in Antrim and Down*, (Blackstaff Press), 1995.

[173] Oldfield, Audrey, *The Great Republic of the Southern Seas: Republicans in Nineteenth-Century Australia*, (Hale & Iremonger), 1999, p. 212.

[174] Retribution for the rebel leaders in 1798 was swift and largely uncompromising. Bagenal Harvey, Cornelius Grogan, Mathew Keogh, and Anthony Perry, all Wexford

British and the way they dealt with all political dissent in England, Scotland and the British colonies.[175]

The precise number of Defenders and United Irishmen transported to NSW before 1800 cannot be resolved conclusively from the available sources.[176] Whitaker argues that about 400 of the several thousand United Irishmen sentenced to transportation reached NSW; a total 58 less than Shaw's figure but 75 more than Rudé.[177] However, of the 519 male prisoners disembarked in NSW from four ships between 1793 and 1797, between 200 and 300 convicts were probably Defenders and they made up at least half of all Irish political prisoners who arrived in NSW before 1806. While it seems that there were very few political prisoners on the *Queen* in 1791, an unknown number were put on board the *Boddingtons* and *Sugar Cane* in 1793. The 233 men landed in Port Jackson from the *Boddingtons* and *Sugar Cane* had all been sentenced in or before 1793, predating the merger with the United Irishmen.[178] As 60-70 men on the *Boddingtons* were convicted in counties where Defender disturbances had occurred it can be assumed, following Shaw's rule of thumb, that many of them were members of that organisation.[179] The *Sugar Cane* carried fewer prisoners from these districts and a higher proportion of Dubliners, an area not significantly affected by Defenderism at that time.[180]

There were many Defenders among the 286 male convicts transported on the *Marquis Cornwallis* and *Britannia* in 1796-1797.[181] They were, however, described as United Irishmen and although they did not take part in the 1798 Rebellion, there was little to distinguish them from later political

---

commanders and all Protestants were executed; their heads stuck on spikes outside the courthouse in Wexford town. Father John Murphy, the hero of Oulart and Enniscorthy was captured in Tullow, County Carlow. He was stripped, flogged, hanged and beheaded: his corpse was burned in a barrel. With an eye for detail, the local Yeomanry spiked his head on a building directly opposite the local Catholic church. By the end of the rebellion between 10,000 and 25,000 rebels including a high proportion of non-combatants had been killed, most summarily.

[175] Ibid, Moore, Tony, *Death or Liberty*, pp. 67-133, considers Irish rebels in Ireland and Australia.

[176] The discussion of Defenders draws heavily on O'Donnell, Ruán, 'Desperate and Diabolical': Defenders and United Irishmen in early NSW', unpublished paper.

[177] Whitaker, Anne-Maree, *Unfinished Revolution*: *United Irishmen in New South Wales, 1800-1810*, (Crossing Press), 1994, p. 29, Rudé, George, 'Early Irish Rebels in Australia', *Historical Studies*, Vol. 16, (1974-1975), p. 23, and ibid, Shaw, Alan, *Convicts & the Colonies*, p. 170.

[178] Hall, Barbara, *Of Infamous Character: The Convicts of the Boddingtons, Ireland to Botany Bay, 1793*, (B. Hall), 2004, Hall, Barbara, *A Nimble Fingered Tribe: The Convicts of the Sugar Cane, Ireland to Botany Bay, 1793*, (B. Hall), 2002, 2nd ed., 2009.

[179] Shaw, Alan, *Convicts & the Colonies*, p. 171.

[180] There were 53 county and city Dubliners on the *Sugar Cane* as opposed to 36 on the *Boddingtons* and 12 Corconians up from 3. Only one convict on *Sugar Cane* came from Louth and Monaghan and none from Donegal.

[181] Hall, Barbara, *A Desperate Set of Villains: The Convicts of the Marquis Cornwallis, Ireland to Botany Bay, 1796*, (B. Hall), 2000, 3rd ed., 2005, Hall, Barbara, *Death or Liberty: The Convicts of the Britannia, Ireland to Botany Bay, 1797*, (B. Hall), 2006.

prisoners.[182] There is no reason to assume that the political prisoners of the *Marquis Cornwallis* and *Britannia* would have been regarded as anything but comrades by rebels arriving on the *Minerva* and *Friendship* in 1800. Close ideological ties are also likely to have existed between them and the Defenders of the *Boddingtons* and *Sugar Cane*. Information on these two ships is more conclusive and Rudé agreed with Shaw's identification of 'about' 100 Defenders on these Ships.[183] However, a close comparison of disturbed districts with trial locations yields a figure only slightly lower than the total male complement of 163 men on the *Marquis Cornwallis*. Sufficient numbers of Defenders were sentenced in 1793 to fill several ships but relatively few were transported NSW. Of the 25 Louth Defenders sentenced to transportation at Dundalk Assizes in March 1793, only four embarked. Similarly, only two of the twelve sentenced at the Cork City and County Assizes in March 1794 arrived.

In 1795, the *Marquis Cornwallis* was a 'political' ship; contemporary accounts stated it left Cork on 9 August with 'seventy...Defenders' on board.[184] The *Britannia* also embarked substantial numbers of Defender/United Irish convicts given the turmoil in which that year's assizes had taken place. A county breakdown of the most likely Defender prisoners on the *Britannia* gives a figure of 145 men that included some criminals and omitted political prisoners from less disturbed counties. That 60 of the 107 non-Dubliners received life sentences, a marked increase on the 40 per cent rate on the non-political *Queen*, may indicate a high incidence of seditious crimes. *Britannia* was also the first ship to leave Ireland after the passage of the draconian Insurrection Act in 1796 that may explain a Dublin press report of August 1796 stating 'fifty convicts...[were] shipped from the North Wall for Botany Bay' of whom 'three quarters' were Defenders. As the *Britannia* landed only 39 male convicts from Dublin City and County in Port Jackson in May 1797, it too was a 'political' ship.

The intriguing and ill-discipline of the exiled Defenders that concerned Governor Hunter and frightened Governor King was very apparent during the voyages of the ships with Defender convicts.[185] One man was summarily executed for mutiny on the *Sugar Cane* and some details of a plot on the *Boddingtons* reached the colony.[186] While mutiny and escape were common topics of conversation among all convicts, the Defender/United Irishmen of the *Britannia* and *Marquis Cornwallis* planned uprisings that resulted in the deaths of about 26 men and two official enquiries in Port Jackson.[187] The rebellious conduct of the convicts on the *Britannia* and *Marquis Cornwallis* before and after arrival in NSW seems to have prejudiced the colonial administration against later shipments of prisoners who had taken part in the 1798 rebellion. That two

---

182 *Boddingtons* arrived 7 August 1793, *Sugar Cane* 17 September 1793, *Marquis Cornwallis* in February 1796, and *Britannia* on 27 May 1797. See also, *HRA*, Series I: Vol. 1, pp. 446, 454, and Vol. 2, p. 31.

183 See, ibid, Shaw, Alan, *Convicts & the Colonies*, p. 171, and ibid, Rudé, George, 'Early Irish Rebels in Australia', p. 19.

184 *New Cork Evening Post*, 10 August 1795.

185 Ibid, Shaw, Alan, *Convicts & the Colonies*, p. 168.

186 Ibid, Bateson, Charles, *The Convict Ships, 1787-1868*, pp. 129-130.

187 Hunter to Portland, 5 September 1796, *HRA*, Series I: Vol. 1, p. 653, *HRNSW*, Vol. 3, pp. 102-111.

mutinies of a similar nature had been suppressed on successive voyages must have struck Hunter as the probable consequence of transporting Defenders and United Irishmen en masse. Serious problems also occurred on the *Anne, Hercules, Atlas I* and *Minerva* in 1800-1802 but not among the largely criminal cargo on the *Queen* and *Rolla* further highlighting the combustible nature of 'political' ships. The *Minerva* contained amongst the Irish rebels, Joseph Holt and James Harold.[188] Joseph Holt had struck up a friendship with the landowner William Cox on the ship and was given a job managing Cox's Dundas farm in western Sydney. Many of the United Irishmen on the *Minerva* were sent off to Norfolk Island to disperse them. Although Hunter and his successor Governor King expressed considerable opposition to such transports, neither had any real control over the numbers or type of prisoners embarked for NSW.[189] The Governors were also remarkably ill-informed as to the character of Irish prisoners as documents setting down their names and crimes and sentences generally only arrived after the ships had docked if at all.[190] This created an atmosphere of paranoia in the colony that was accentuated by the United Irish plots of 1800 and the Castle Hill uprising in March 1804.[191]

Discussion of rank and file Defenders in the Australian context has hitherto centred on a series of oft quoted comments made by Governor Hunter[192] in 1796 regarding 'those turbulent and worthless characters called Irish Defenders' who had boldly 'threatened resistance to all orders'.[193] As no such opinions were expressed by Hunter's predecessor in relation to the Defenders sent out in 1793, his blanket hostility was a response to the ability of the convicts on the *Britannia* and *Marquis Cornwallis* to destabilise the colony and his

[188] Joseph Holt was born in Ireland in 1756 and became a tenant farmer and as a trusted Protestant loyalist held some minor local positions. About 1797, he joined the United Irishmen in part because of a private feud with the landlord Thomas Hugo. In 1798, the Fermanagh Militia burned his house down on Hugo's orders. Holt fought in the Wexford County rebellion before successfully leading a rebel guerrilla group in Wicklow County. Eventually he concluded that it was in his interests to surrender in order to get the best terms he could for himself and his wife. This led to exile without trial in the colony of NSW. After the 1804 Rebellion, he was exiled again to Norfolk Island and then VDL. He returned to Sydney and was given a land grant in order to farm. Holt was granted a pardon in 1809 before returning to Ireland in 1812. He wrote a personnel account of the rebellions in Wicklow and NSW: Croker, T. C., (ed.), *Memoirs of Joseph Holt: general of the Irish rebels, in 1798*, 2 Vols. (H. Colburn), 1838, Vol. 2, covers his life in Australia. See also, Bolton, G. C., 'Holt, Joseph (1756-1826)', *ADB*, Vol. 1, pp. 550-551.

[189] King to Portland, 21 May 1802, *HRA*, Series I: Vol. 3, p. 489.

[190] Portland to Hunter, 2 March 1797, *HRA*, Series I: Vol. 2, p. 9. King to Castlereagh, 24 July 1798, and Hunter to Portland, 1 November 1798, *HRA*, Series I: Vol. 2, pp. 234-236.

[191] King came to regard virtually all Irish male prisoners sent to New South Wales after 1793 as dangerous as the 'diabolical characters' of the *Anne*: King to Portland, 28 September 1800, *HRA*, Series I: Vol. 2, p. 614. See also King to Portland, 10 March 1801, *HRA*, Series I: Vol. 3, p. 9.

[192] For Hunter, see Hoyle, Arthur, *The Life of John Hunter, Navigator, Governor, Admiral*, (Mulini Press), 2001, Auchmuty, J. J., 'Hunter, John (1737-1821)', *ADB*, Vol. 1, pp 566-572. See also, Wood, G.A., 'Governor Hunter', *Journal and Proceedings* (Royal Australian Historical Society), Vol. 14, (6), (1928), pp. 344-362.

[193] Hunter to Portland, 12 November 1796, *HRA*, Series I: Vol. 1, p. 674.

knowledge of their plotting on the voyages from Ireland. To the Governor's intense annoyance, the Defenders who arrived in 1796-1797 not only disaffected otherwise peaceable English convicts but escaped both frequently and in large numbers. Hunter complained they had 'completely ruined... [those] formerly received from England' and threatened 'that order so highly essential to our well being'.[194] One of the more serious and disruptive breakouts involved a twenty strong 'gang of...Defenders' who were so obstinate when apprehended that Hunter had two executed.[195] Hunter's exasperation with the 'Defenders' moved him to suggest that they should not be sent to NSW but rather to 'Africa, or some other place as fit for them'.[196]

The impact of the 1798 exiles in their destination was profound. In 1800, when the *Minerva* and *Friendship* arrived from Ireland, Sydney Town was a 12-year old settlement with a population of some 2,500, of whom 43 per cent were convicts. The combined population of Parramatta and Toongabbie was slightly under 1,500, of whom over two-thirds were convicts. The Hawkesbury was predominantly a free settlement, with convicts comprising only 13 per cent of its 1,100 residents. The military were mainly concentrated in Sydney, with small garrisons at the other settlements. Within months of the arrival of United Irishmen, a series of interlinked conspiracies were uncovered in Sydney, Toongabbie, Parramatta and Norfolk Island. Severe flogging and re-transportation did nothing to reconcile the imported Irishmen to their new environment.

Uncovering insurrection

Anti-authoritarianism was characteristic of republican subversives and part of a pattern of behaviour established in Ireland. The Irish could scent the vulnerability of their place of exile leading to their rebelliousness continuing.[197] In NSW, it was coupled with the desire to escape, return to their homeland and assist in the anticipated renewal of rebellion. To see their sustained defiance of the colonial government simply as a reaction to the prospects of overdue emancipation greatly underestimates their shared ideology and paramilitary experience that provided a firm grounding for undercover activities. Many urban criminals would also have possessed skills of this type but it was primarily the Irish convicts with political associations who were credited with unsettling the colony. Hunter was right to worry; in 1800 just six months after the arrival of the *Minerva* a rebellion was being planned on the Government Farm at Toongabbie.[198]

---

[194] Hunter to Portland, 10 January 1798, *HRA*, Series I: Vol. 2, p. 118.
[195] Hunter to Portland, 15 February 1798, *HRA*, Series I: Vol. 2, p. 129, *HRNSW*, Vol. 3, pp. 359-360.
[196] Hunter to Portland, 12 November 1796, *HRA*, Series I: Vol. 1, p. 675.
[197] Ibid, Whitaker, Anne-Maree, *Unfinished Revolution*: *United Irishmen in New South Wales, 1800-1810*, pp. 23-88, covers who the Irish rebels were and the threats of rebellion between 1800 and 1803.
[198] Hunter to Officers, 4 September 1800, *HRNSW*, Vol. 4, pp. 119-130, details the enquiry into the insurrection.

The rebellion involved taking Parramatta and killing Samuel Marsden who had earned a reputation as the 'flogging parson'.[199] The rebels would then pike the soldiers in their beds, take their muskets and march on Sydney. Its leaders had planned for pikes to be manufactured and hidden to ensure the rebels were well armed. The plan was betrayed by informants who gave Marsden word of the insurrection. When the leaders of the rebellion learned this they quickly cancelled the uprising. Governor Hunter led an inquiry into the insurrection in which Marsden over-zealously pursued the issue of the hidden pikes. He threatened the Irish Catholic preacher James Harold over of the location of the pikes.[200] Harold prevaricated but under pressure finally revealed the name of a supposed pike maker, Bryan Furey. Furey denied making the pikes but later told Marsden that Harold had contacted him to make some fake ones to get Marsden off Harold's back. Marsden eventually sent Harold to Norfolk Island and Furey to gaol despite the lack of evidence against them.[201]

The failed insurrection of August 1800 and the removal of the suspected Irish leaders to remote parts of the colony did not dampen the convicts' enthusiasm for organised rebellion.[202] In September 1800, another insurrection was planned.[203] The rebels were to assemble at Parramatta on a Sunday morning when the local authorities and hierarchies would be in Church service. There the rebels would overpower the soldiers and then march on Sydney. The leaders used an escaped convict, John Lewis to send messages from farm to farm. Unfortunately, Lewis was captured, gaoled and eventually talked of the rebellion. From the information Lewis gave, Captain John MacArthur of the NSW Corps received a shakily written letter that relayed that a 'Croppie' uprising was about to occur. MacArthur's advice to the Governor was to wait for the convicts to rebel and once they were out in the open deal with them. The rebel leaders learned that their plan had been discovered and halted their operations. Marsden once again zealously set about trying to discover the hidden pikes. Several more informants came forward and one named the still gaoled Bryan Furey as a pike maker. This enabled the NSW Corps to round up the ringleaders; William Silk, Micheal Quintan, Maurice Wood, John Burke and Thomas Brannon. They were flogged and isolated from the general convict population on the hulk *Supply* in Sydney Harbour. The remainder of the rebels were given either two hundred or five hundred lashes.

The authorities seem to have feared that Holt, an experienced rebel leader, would be a centre of disaffection, but nothing was farther from his plans.

---

[199] Yarwood, A. T., 'Marsden, Samuel (1765-1838)', *ADB*, Vol. 2, pp. 207-212.

[200] Perkins, Harold, 'Harold, James (1744-1830)', *ADB*, Vol. 1, pp. 512-513.

[201] Hunter to Officers, 4 September 1800, *HRNSW*, Vol. 4, pp. 119-130, details the inquiry into an Irish plot in 1800 and King to Banks, 8 October 1800, on a threatened rebellion by United Irishmen at Parramatta, *HRNSW*, Vol. 4, p. 229 and pp. 235-238

[202] Most of the Irish rebellions took place during King's term of office. For biographical information, see Shaw, A. G. L., 'King, Philip Gidley (1758-1808)', *ADB*, Vol. 2, pp. 55-61; King, J., and J., *Philip Gidley King: a biography of the third governor of New South Wales*, (Methuen), 1981.

[203] King to Portland, 12 October 1800, *HRNSW*, Vol. 4, pp. 234-238. See also the detailed papers relating to the Irish conspiracy in 1800 in, *HRA*, Series I: Vol. 2, pp. 575-583, 637-651, and King to Banks, 8 October 1800, *HRNSW*, Vol. 4, pp. 235-238.

As a lower middle-class Irish Protestant with firm notions of respectability, Holt wanted to better his position by thrift and hard work and remained divorced from what he saw as impractical insurrection. Despite this, he was implicated as a leader in the rebellion but without substantial proof of his involvement he was spared the lash as was Harold.[204] As a form of punishment for their suspected complicity with the rebels both Holt and Harold, who were still being detained from the previous insurrection, were made to watch the floggings of two convicted offenders, Maurice Fitzgerald and Paddy Galvin on the orders of Judge-Advocate Richard Atkins and Marsden. Holt left a vivid account:

> The place they flogged them their arms pulled around a large tree and their breasts squeezed against the trunk so the men had no power to cringe ... There was two floggers, Richard Rice and John Johnson the Hangman from Sydney. Rice was left-handed man and Johnson was right-handed, so they stood at each side, and I never saw two threchers in a barn move their strokes more handier than those two man-killers did...I [Holt] was to the leeward of the floggers...I was two perches from them. The flesh and skin blew in my face as it shook off the cats. Fitzgerald received his 300 lashes. Doctor Mason - I will never forget him - he used to go feel his pulse, and he smiled, and said: 'This man will tire you before he will fail - Go on.'...During this time [Fitzgerald] was getting his punishment he never gave so much as a word - only one, and that was saying, 'Don't strike me on the neck, flog me fair.' ...Next was tied up Paddy Galvin, a young boy about 20 years of age. He was ordered to get 300 lashes. He got one hundred on the back, and you could see his backbone between his shoulder blades. Then the Doctor ordered him to get another hundred on his bottom. He got it, and then his haunches were in such a jelly that the Doctor ordered him to be flogged on the calves of his legs. He got one hundred there and as much as a whimper he never gave. They asked him if he would tell where the pikes were hid. He said he did not know, and would not tell. 'You may as well hang me now,' he said, 'for you never will get any music from me so.' They put him in the cart and sent him to the Hospital.[205]

No aspect of Marsden's activities did more harm to his reputation than his severity as a magistrate. This action was scarcely defensible, but Marsden was not the only magistrate who ordered the infliction of illegal punishments.

In 1801, the transport ship *Anne* arrived at Sydney with 69 United Irishmen out of the 178 convicts on-board. Governor King was disturbed as the rebel leaders from the previous rebellions had been uncovered and sent to

---

[204] Despite his vigorous protests, Holt was arrested twice more for suspected complicity in plans for an Irish rising. On Christmas Eve 1803 he was hauled before Atkins on a false accusation of plotting his murder, but was again cleared. Three months later, however, he was detained after the Castle Hill rising and transported to Norfolk Island, where he remained until November 1805. Nevertheless, he seems to have held aloof from conspiracies, having a lively fear of informers and contempt for the amateurish tactics of the disaffected Irish Catholics. Returning to his farm, Holt met no further trouble except the confiscation of an illicit still in 1806. Through Major Edward Abbott he secured a free pardon from Lieutenant-Governor William Paterson in 1809, confirmed by Governor Lachlan Macquarie in 1811. Next year, Holt sold his properties for over £1,800 and returned to Ireland often lamenting that he had left NSW.

[205] Ibid, Croker, T. C., (ed.), *Memoirs of Joseph Holt: general of the Irish rebels, in 1798*, Vol. 2, pp. 119-122.

remote parts of the colony.[206] The arrival of the *Anne* promised another group of United Irishmen leaders who could cause problems in the convict population, a view reinforced by the convict mutiny on the ship en route. The *Anne* brought news of Irish Union and King hoped that this would persuade the Irish convicts to accept their fate in Australia. This proved a forlorn hope. The Irish political prisoners had been fighting against English rule for several years and wanted to go home. The main opponent preventing this was the British authorities in Sydney and Parramatta. During the next year four more rebellion plots were uncovered. All were foiled by informants in the convict population. Two of the plots involved escaping by ship, either by seizing a ship or seeking passage on a French ship. The Governor was so concerned that convicts would escape by sea that in 1804 with word of a possible convict uprising, several American ships were sent out of Sydney Harbour because King suspected that they would be sympathetic to the rebelling Irish convicts.[207]

In 1803, there were still outstanding issues for the Irish convicts. The idents stating the term the prisoners were to remain exiled in NSW still had not arrived from England.[208] Until the idents arrived all Irish prisoners were stuck in the penal colony. There continued to be escape attempts by convicts both English and Irish. Inevitably the escapees would raid nearby farms for liquor and firearms. In February 1803, fifteen convicts escaped from a farm at Castle Hill and raided the farm of Verincourt de Clambe for liquor, silverware and firearms.[209] Two of the convicts, Patrick Gannan and Francis Simpson went on to the farmhouse of James Bean and raped his seventeen-year-old daughter but were captured two days later asleep in the bush and hanged.[210] The *Sydney Gazette* commented:

> Justice to the Prisoners at large in the Colony requires that we should here observe, that this banditti is entirely composed of Irish prisoners, brought by the Hercules and Atlas.[211]

The United Irishmen in NSW were divided into loose factions: *Minerva* men Joseph Holt and Thomas Brady headed the largest single county group from Wicklow and plotted, in many instances, with life-long friends and subordinates from the Rebellion of 1798. Their Dublin comrade and shipmate, Martin Short, was an early and enthusiastic conspirator in Sydney. John Neil was respected by

---

[206] King to Portland, 10 March 1801, *HRNSW*, Vol. 4, pp. 325-326.

[207] This was followed up in the Government and General Order, 31 March 1805, *HRNSW*, Vol. 5, pp. 588-589, that laid down penalties for helping convicts to abscond.

[208] King had commented on this problem earlier in, Portland, 21 August 1801, *HRNSW*, Vol. 4, pp. 463-464.

[209] Details of this can be found in George Caley's account of the colony of NSW from 1800 to 1803, *HRNSW*, Vol. 5, p. 300, and in King to Hobart, 9 May 1803, *HRA*, Series I: Vol. 4, pp. 84-85.

[210] Additional soldiers were sent to Castle Hill as a result; see Government and General Order, 16 February 1803, *HRNSW*, Vol. 5, p. 22. See also 'Fugitives', *Sydney Gazette*, 5 March 1803, p. 3, 'Trials of Insurgents', *Sydney Gazette*, 19 March 1803, p. 2. The executions occurred on 23 March, *HRNSW*, Vol. 5, p. 74.

[211] 'Insurgents', *Sydney Gazette*, 5 March 1803, p. 3.

the substantial Wexford contingent in the colony that included Mathew Sutton of Enniscorthy and other important United Irishmen. Phillip Cunningham exerted much influence over the Munster faction in 1804, by which time he worked as the overseer of stonemasons in Castle Hill. Antrim arms raider Samuel Hume, a survivor of the *Hercules* disaster, was then overseer of carpentry at the same location. William Johnson, another Ulster United Irishman with Tyrone connections, had served as a sergeant in the military or militia. The ready cooperation of Johnson, Cunningham and Hume, 'Protestant, Catholic and Dissenter', underlined the essential viability of the republican project after the setback of 1798. The United Irishmen were by no means a spent force in Ireland and this impression was confirmed by belated news of Robert Emmet's July 1803 rising. In November 1803, they learned of the collapse of the Peace of Amiens and the resumption of the war with France. After much discussion, it was decided to rise in early March 1804 using a nucleus of men who worked at the Castle Hill farming settlement, north-east of Sydney. The rising of 1804 had a long and complex gestation.

Rebellion at Castle Hill in 1804

By 1800, the colony at Sydney was not yet self-sufficient in food and was dependent on imported food.[212] To remove this dependency King expanded the Government farm at Castle Hill and by 1804, there was a significant concentration of 474 convicts on the farm.[213] It was rare for so many convicts to live and work together and there is little doubt that this situation aided preparations for insurrection by bringing together seasoned campaigners in rebellion. The previous year, King, influenced by the uneasiness of the Irish convicts, had allowed the Roman Catholic clergyman Father James Dixon to preach Mass to the Irish.[214] The first public mass was celebrated in Sydney on 15 May 1803 and others followed later at Parramatta and the Hawkesbury. In doing so, King gave the Irish the legal means of coming together. King was so pleased at the salutary effect on the Irish Catholics that he decided to pay Dixon a salary of £60. But after praising the experiment in a dispatch of 1 March 1804, he soon ended it determined to enforce the convicts' attendance at Anglican services because he believed that, especially after the rising of Irish convicts, seditious meetings took place when Catholics met to attend Mass.[215]

On 22 January 1804, the *Ferret*, a whaler arrived in Sydney with news of Robert Emmett's uprising in Dublin in 1803. Exactly six weeks later, on Sunday 4 March, the Irish prisoners at Castle Hill staged their rebellion. By 1804, most of the Irish leaders of the previous attempts at rebellion had been imprisoned

---

212 The system of public farming, originally introduced by Hunter, proved remarkably successful under King to such an extent that by 1802 it was producing a surplus of grain: King to Hobart, 9 November 1802, *HRNSW*, Vol. 4, pp. 899-900.
213 King to Major Johnston, 25 February 1803, *HRNSW*, Vol. 5, pp. 51-51, suggests that there were already problems at Castle Hill with only '200 refractory convicts'.
214 Parsons, Vivienne, 'Dixon, James (1758-1840)', *ADB*, Vol. 1, p. 309. For, King's proclamation and regulations governing Roman Catholic congregations, 19 April 1803, see, *HRNSW*, Vol. 5, pp. 97-98, and King to Hobart, 9 May 1803, *HRA*, Series I: Vol. 3, pp. 104-105; King to Hobart, 9 May 1803, *HRNSW*, Vol. 5, p. 116.
215 King to Hobart, 1 March 1804, *HRNSW*, Vol. 5, p. 324.

and moved to outlying areas of the colony such as Norfolk Island. Dispersal had worked well for the authorities but with each new rebellion plan, new Irish leaders rose among the convicts more aware of what not to do next time. The leaders of rebellion were Phillip Cunningham. From his experiences in Ireland and NSW, he understood that secrecy and an effective system of communication were essential to a successful rebellion[216] and this proved so successful that the authorities knew nothing until the day before the rebellion. On the evening of 3 March, one of the Irish convict overseers turned informant. On Sunday 4 March, the day of the rebellion, two more informants came forward and provided names. John Griffen was one of the informants and had been relaying a message to the pike-maker Bryan Furey that the rebellion was on for Sunday night. Since Furey did not get the message the areas of Sydney, Parramatta and Windsor did not rebel. Castle Hill was the only district that rose in rebellion.

Despite this intelligence, the authorities in Parramatta and Sydney did not act immediately and on 4 March 1804, John Cavenah set fire to his hut in Castle Hill at 8.00 pm. This was the signal for the rebellion to begin. With Cunningham leading, 200 rebels broke into the Government Farm's buildings, taking firearms, ammunition and other weapons. Initially there was mayhem as buildings were ransacked to cries of 'Death or Liberty'. Two English convicts dragged the Hills District flogger, Robert Duggan from under his bed and George Harrington an English convict beat him unconscious. A constable was saved from a musket ball in the face when John Brannon's musket misfired. Another constable was saved when Jonathon Place's musket also misfired. Cunningham gathered the rebels and reprimanded them for their lack of disciplined behaviour. The rebels then went from farm to farm on their way to Constitution Hill at Parramatta gathering firearms, supplies and drinking any liquor they found. The looting of farms gave the rebels over 180 swords, muskets and pistols that accounted for a third of the colony's entire armoury.[217]

Within an hour of Cavenah firing his hut, word of the rebellion had reached Parramatta causing considerable panic and by 11.00 pm Governor King in Sydney was aware of the situation. In Parramatta, Samuel Marsden, an obvious target for the rebels, fled the town by boat with his and John MacArthur's family.[218] Governor King immediately set off for Parramatta and

[216] Silver, Lynette Ramsay, *The Battle of Vinegar Hill: Australia's Irish Rebellion*, (Doubleday), 1989, (Watermark Press), 2002 remains the only substantial study. 'Insurrection', *Sydney Gazette*, 11 March 1804, pp. 2, 3, contained a detailed account based on King's despatch. See also, ibid, Karskens, Grace, *The Colony: A History of Early Sydney*, pp. 292-297 and ibid, Whitaker, Anne-Maree, *Unfinished Revolution: United Irishmen in New South Wales, 1800-1810*, pp. 89-120.

[217] W. Pascoe Crook, a missionary provided a detailed account of the early stage of the rebellion, *HRNSW*, Vol. 5, pp. 314-315, while George Suttor to Sir Joseph Banks, 10 March 1804, *HRNSW*, Vol. 5, pp. 350-352, is more detailed on its aftermath.

[218] Surgeon Thomas Arndell had written from the Hawkesbury to 'the Reverend Mr. Marsden, or in his absence, the Officer commanding at Parramatta', 4 March, 1804: 'Revr. Sir, From Strong and confirmed information I have every reason to believe that many of those deluded prisoners that call themselves United Irishmen and others had an Insurrection in project this night, and I beg you will be so kind as to forward some ammunition with the bearer sent on purpose for our Defence here' *HRA* Series I: Vol. 4, p. 567. This warning may account for Marsden's escape.

arrived around 4 am on 5 March where one of his first actions was to declare martial law in the affected districts.[219]

> I do therefore proclaim the Districts of Parramatta, Castle Hill, Toongabbie, Prospect, Seven and Baulkham Hills, Hawkesbury and Nepean to be in a STATE of REBELLION; and to establish Martial Law throughout those Districts...[220]

Lieutenant Colonel William Paterson, the lieutenant governor, called out the guard and 140 marines from the HMS *Calcutta*–in fact the rebellion had been timed to allow the ship to leave Sydney but this had been delayed--as well as the Sydney Loyal Association militia, were deployed in Sydney to contain any disturbances. A New South Wales Corps contingent of 56 officers and men including Lieutenant William Davies and Quartermaster Sergeant Thomas Laycock were dispatched to march through the night to bolster the garrison at Parramatta. Meanwhile, the provost marshal, Thomas Smyth, was sent ahead to contact Major George Johnston at Annandale. The troops from Sydney arrived at 1:30 am, and after a quick inspection an advanced guard was sent to the west of the town. Johnston arrived at Government House in Parramatta about four hours later just before dawn not long after King had declared martial law.[221] He was an experienced officer who had fought at Bunker Hill and understood the necessity of striking aggressively against irregulars at the earliest possible moment.

Cunningham's plan involved burning the MacArthur property of 'Elizabeth Farm' to draw the Parramatta garrison out of the town. Once this was done the rebels in Parramatta would rise and set fire to the town as a signal. The Castle Hill rebels would gather at Constitution Hill and then raid the barracks for more arms and ammunition. From there the rebels would march to Windsor and join up with the rebels in the Hawkesbury before marching on Sydney. At dawn on 5 March, Cunningham was having difficulties coordinating his forces with several groups including one under Samuel Humes of 70 men lost their way at night and rebels were still straggling in to Constitution Hill. On 3 March, Joseph Holt, the famed Wicklow guerrilla fighter had learned that the rebellion's secrecy had been compromised and lost no time in severing his links with the plotters and going to the Brush Farm home of his employer, William Cox. The Parramatta attack he had previously undertaken to lead was in doubt from that moment, although many Wicklowmen ignored Holt's advice to stay at home.

After fruitlessly waiting for a signal of a successful internal takeover of Parramatta and the non-appearance of reinforcements, Cunningham was forced to withdraw from Parramatta to Toongabbie to re-assess his strategy. His messages to the Parramatta and Windsor rebels and to Sydney had not got through and he decided that the rebels would head down the Hawkesbury Road to Windsor to meet up with the rebels from the Hawkesbury. Had Cunningham effected this, King maintained it would have increased his force by a further

---

[219] See, King's proclamation of martial law, 5 March 1804, *HRNSW*, Vol. 5, pp. 345-346. The statement in the 'Proclamation', *Sydney Gazette*, p. 1, is more of a summary.

[220] *HRNSW*, Vol. 5, p. 346.

[221] For Johnston's account of events see his succinct report to Lieutenant-Colonel Paterson, 9 March 1804, *HRNSW*, Vol. 5, pp. 348-349.

hundred rebels.[222] Having already declared his hand, and deprived of both surprise and facing a superior and well disciplined force of regulars and enthusiastic militia, Cunningham had no recourse but to withdraw west towards the Hawkesbury hoping to pick up more recruits and meeting his missing forces on the way to add to his forces.

Shortly after 5:00 am Johnston set out to locate the main rebel force. In addition to the troops he had brought with him, several civilians volunteered along with the 36 armed members of the Parramatta Loyal Association militia were also called out and took over defence of the town. Over 50 enrolled in a reserve militia combined with the NSW Corps to march out and confront the rebels. Johnson decided to divide his troops: Lieutenant William Davies led half north from Parramatta towards Castle Hill while Johnston headed west to the rebel camp at Toongabbie.[223] When he reached the camp, Johnston was told that 400 rebels were on the top of Rouse Hill. He sent an advance guard of five soldiers and six or eight settlers armed with muskets along the Hawkesbury Road to flank the rebels, while he and Quartermaster Sergeant Laycock led the remaining 20 troops and nearly 40 armed volunteers up the hill. They found that the rebels had retreated towards the Hawkesbury. After a forced march through the night, the troops now faced a pursuit on a day which was 'intensely hot'. Johnston and Trooper Thomas Anlezark[224] rode ahead while the main party proceeded on foot. After a chase of 10 miles Johnston finally received word about 10.30 am on Monday 5 March that the rebels were less than two miles ahead.

Johnston sent Father Dixon ahead to convince the rebels to surrender but he also wanted Father Dixon to slow the rebels down so his foot soldiers could make up the few miles' difference. When Father Dixon failed to halt the rebels, Major Johnston and Trooper Anlezark attempted to persuade them to take the Governor's offer of clemency. Johnston and Anlezark galloped after the rebels and asked to speak to their leaders. The estimated rebel force of 250 called to Major Johnston to come among them. He replied that he was within pistol shot so was no threat and that their commanders should come out and speak to him. Eventually after some delay Philip Cunningham and William Johnson advanced from the 233 rebels and Johnston told them he wanted to avoid bloodshed. It was agreed that Major Johnston would bring back Father Dixon to talk with them again. This delay gave sufficient time for the NSW Corps soldiers and militia to catch up to the rebels. When Major Johnston and Trooper Thomas Anlezark returned with Father Dixon they knew that their troops were not far behind. Once again Phillip Cunningham and William Johnston walked out to meet them while the rebels formed ranks. Johnson asked the rebel leaders what they really

---

[222] King to Hobart, 12 March 1804, *HRNSW*, Vol. 5, pp. 355-356.

[223] Sydney and Parramatta also raised militias to defend the towns from the rebels but neither of these forces took part in the Battle of Vinegar Hill. The 'Parramatta Loyalists' militia numbered 36 and remained in Parramatta. The 'Sydney Loyalists' did not march with Major Johnston and remained in Sydney during the rebellion.

[224] Thomas Ainsworth Anlezark (1772-1815) was a regular soldier between 1789 and 1797 but in 1800 was convicted of theft and sentence to death but this was quickly commutted to life imprisonment. Two years later he was transported to NSW and received a Conditional Pardon on June 1803 and, following his role in putting down the rebellion, he received an Absolute Pardon.

wanted and Cunningham replied 'Death or Liberty' adding, according to one account, 'and a ship to take us home'. At that moment, however, Quartermaster Laycock and his force came into view. With the rebels distracted, Major Johnston held a pistol to William Johnston's head and ordered him to move toward the soldiers and militia that had appeared over the rise. Anlezark did the same with Cunningham.

Retiring with their prisoners, Major Johnston without any other preliminaries ordered his men open fire and charge. Over fifty armed civilians, a mounted trooper, and 29 military men, most capable of firing 780 prepared rounds of ammunition in 10 to 15 minutes, were pitted against 233 rebels. Although the odds were technically with the rebels, it was an unequal 'battle' with an imbalance between makeshift pikes and some assorted firearms in the hands of the rebels and the massed, trained firepower of the army. With the precision and economy of movement that came from practice and military training, the soldiers formed ranks and for fifteen minutes directed musket fire at the rebels and then charged. Leaderless, caught completely unawares and totally unprepared, the rebels weakly returned fire before fleeing in all directions leaving fifteen dead that are said to have been left to rot on the ground where they fell. There is no report of any deaths or injuries among the soldiers and their volunteer supporters. After the battle, several prisoners were summarily killed by the soldiers and militia until Major Johnston intervened and threatened his troops with his pistol. During the battle, William Johnston escaped his captor's attention and fled into the bush. Cunningham was not so lucky and was either struck by a cutlass or shot in the back by Quartermaster Thomas Laycock and left for dead as the soldiers rounded up the rebels. Amazingly Cunningham survived the blow and, critically wounded, was picked up by soldiers and dragged to the Hawkesbury. In the official reports that followed the battle neither Major Johnston's actions nor Laycock's were mentioned.[225]

Retribution was swift as King believed that punishing the leaders would pacify the convicts who had followed them. The 1804 Rebellion is referred to as an Irish rebellion or 'Australia's Irish rebellion'. This is misleading as of rebels included convicts and free men of different nationalities such as Charles Hill. Of

[225] Vinegar Hill was not a formal location in 1804. The battle between the rebels and the soldiers became commonly known as the 'Second Battle of Vinegar Hill' after the Irish battle in 1798. Common usage of the name Vinegar Hill began to appear in the 1810s and 1830s in the Rouse Hill area. But Vinegar Hill is not on a map. There have been competing views on the location of Vinegar Hill. Originally thought to be Rouse Hill, George Mackanass challenged this in the 1950s marking the location of Vinegar Hill as the crossroads between Windsor Road and Schofields Road. In the 1980s, several other local historians came to the same conclusion as did the NSW Commissioner for the Department of Planning and the Environment in 1982. Lynette Ramsay Silver points to the letter of Major Johnston which talks of his troops turning at the 'Government Stock Fence' to the second hill from Half Way Pond. By her reckoning the Government Stock Fence is where Old Windsor Road and Windsor Road meet today and Old Ponds Creek is known today as Second Ponds Creek. For Silver, the location of the battle is approximately at the crossroads of Schofields Road and Windsor Road. The area occupied by Castlebrook Lawn Cemetery satisfies the criteria in every respect and in 1988 a sculpture commemorating the battle was dedicated at Castlebrook Lawn Cemetery by former Australian Prime Minister Gough Whitlam.

those hanged, several were English convicts. King's decision meant that most of the rebels were not punished, a pragmatic decision as the captured rebels were still needed to work the Government Farm. Cunningham was summarily hanged from the staircase of the public store at Windsor on 6 March. It has been suggested that he was already dead prior to his 'execution' as all the other leaders faced a court martial four days later. The other explanation is that he was not expected to survive the trip to Parramatta and was executed before he could die of his wounds, a position possibly supported in correspondence between Johnston and King.[226] The rest of the leaders were brought before a court martial. William Johnston who had surrendered to the authorities pleaded guilty. John Neale admitted he was in the rebel group. Jonathon Place denied all charges and the rest claimed they had been forced to join the rebellion. William Johnston and Samuel Humes as leaders in the rebellion were executed in a public place with their bodies to be hung in chains. One was hanged from a tree on the road to Prospect near Parramatta, the other probably near Johnston's Bridge at Toongabbie on the road to Hawkesbury. Six others were executed: Charles Hill and Jonathon Place at Parramatta on 8 March, John Neil and George Harrington at Castle Hill the following day and John Brannan and Timothy Hogan in Sydney on 10 March. The *Sydney Gazette* of 18 March 1804 reported on the background of the 'Principal Offenders':

> Philip Cunningham the Principal Rebel leader, who was executed at Hawkesbury, was one of the Prisoners by the Ann, and was remarkably active in the mutinous transactions on board that vessel which rendered a recourse to rigorous exertions necessary to the safety of the Officers and crew. Some time after his arrival he was sent up to the Settlement at Castle Hill, whence he was appointed overseer of the Government Stone-masons and such was the...indulgence shown him, that in the Course of little more than a twelvemonth he had nearly erected on his own account, a stone building of considerable value.
>
> Samuel Humes officiated as overseer of the Carpenters, and had a convenient house, and received also many indulgences that might have awakened a sentiment of gratitude in his breast which would have prevented his disgrace and untimely exit.
>
> John Place was the only survivor of the three who embarked on the fatal enterprise of crossing the Mountains, under the ludicrous supposition of an unknown Settlement there existing, and was pardoned on account of the pitiable and deplorable plight in which he was found. He was afterwards corporally punished for a second time absconding in order to subsist in the woods, and his restless and relentless disposition at length drew down upon him the provoked vengeance of the Law.
>
> Charles Hill, although several years a free man had lost all sight of character, and was in consequence frequently implicated in theft and misdemeanour. He rented a farm, and might have procured an honest and comfortable livelihood, but the hope of plunder could alone induce him to join the infatuated people, and his atrocious designs obtained their due reward.

The same edition also reported:

[226] Johnson to King, 6 March 1804, *HRNSW*, Vol. 5, p. 345, states that 'C_______, who is one of the rebel chiefs, who was supposed to be dead on the field, was brought in here alive, and I immediately - with the opinion of the officers - ordered him to be hung up.'

Francois Girault, a Frenchman, in obedience to HIS EXCELLENCY'S positive command, quitted the Colony, in His Majesty's ship Calcutta, having been charged on evidence strongly presumptive with secretly abetting and encouraging the late Revolt. This man resided at Parramatta, and had for several months past devoted much of his time to trafficking as a pedlar to and from Castle Hill during which intercourse he too probably obtained an undue influence among the people at the Settlement, and availing himself of an unhappy credulity, disseminated gradually the seeds of dissention and discontent, but ingeniously in the end found means to avoid open detection and to escape condign punishment.[227]

Martial law gave King carte blanche to punish refractory United Irishmen and scores were dispersed to the struggling outposts of the colony. Many of the remaining leaders were flogged with either 200 or 500 lashes and then sent to the new penal settlement at Coal River (Newcastle).[228] Finally, Joseph Holt and Maurice Margarot were arrested on suspicion of involvement. Holt was kept in gaol before sent to Norfolk Island on 19 April, on the instructions of the magistrates who decided that, although there was insufficient evidence to convict him of treason before a criminal court, 'the tranquillity of the colony' required such a measure. Margarot joined Holt in exile at Norfolk Island. Other suspected rebels who had not been openly involved in the rebellion were also sent to Norfolk Island without proof of their involvement.[229] By August 1804, King was sufficiently confident to write to Lord Hobart:

I am happy to inform your Lordship that no late circumstances of that kind have occurred to disturb the tranquillity of the colony, notwithstanding which I rather hope than am confident that anything of the kind may never happen again-nothing so daring I think ever will; yet, altho' every exertion is made to counteract their being misled, I am sorry to say that a few disaffected characters will always be endeavouring to poison the minds of the greater part of those who have been sent here for sedition and rebellion in Ireland, who, notwithstanding the lenity shewn them so lately, have been endeavouring to resume their wild plans, which has rendered it necessary to put the worst of that class under greater restrictions than has hitherto been the case.[230]

However, Johnston took a more sanguine view, if only to support his argument that the NSW Corps should be reinforced:

Should Insurrection again appear, it may not be in the feeble way in which the last broke out; therefore, a stronger hand must be applied to put it down; or should it be found necessary to form other Settlements where a Military Force would be required, or to augment the Detached Posts already out, the King's Service must materially suffer, either

---

[227] The same edition of the *Sydney Gazette* included a report that war between Britain and France had restarted. There is an unproven, but significant implication that Girault was a French agent.
[228] Lieutenant Menzies to King, 15 June 1804, *HRNSW*, Vol. 5, pp. 385-386, gives brief details of a conspiracy at Newcastle. See also, King to Hobart, 14 August 1804, *HRA*, Series I: Vol. 5, pp. 1-2.
[229] King to Under-Secretary Cooke, 20 July 1805, *HRNSW*, Vol. 5, pp. 663-667, detailed how political prisoners and especially Margarot were treated.
[230] King to Hobart, 14 August 1804, *HRA*, Series I: Vol. 5, p. 1.

by weakening Head Quarters so as to render due subordination to the Government unfortified, or deferring that Service till a representation was made Home.[231]

It is uncertain what the rebels intended to do in the event of success, but escape to Batavia (Jakarta) in the Dutch East Indies or to America was feasible if trading vessels could be commandeered. The French may have been tempted to use their Indian Ocean bases in Mauritius and Réunion to supplant the British in Australia, possibly with Irish assistance, but such footholds could not long have withstood the response from the Royal Navy.

A possible insurrection in 1807

Michael Dwyer had been involved in the 1798 rebellion and later contacted Robert Emmett but was reluctant to commit his followers to march to Dublin unless the rebellion showed some initial success. The subsequent failure of Emmett's rising in 1803 led to a period of repression and renewed attempts by the Government to wipe out Dwyer's forces. In December 1803, Dwyer finally capitulated on terms that would allow him safe passage to America but the government reneged on the agreement holding him in Kilmainham Jail until August 1805, when they transported him to NSW as an unsentenced exile.[232]

Dwyer arrived in Sydney on 14 February 1806 in the *Tellicherry* and was given free settler status.[233] He arrived with his wife and two children. He was given a grant of 100 acres of land on Cabramatta Creek in Sydney adjacent to grants to his comrades Hugh 'Vesty' Byrne, John Mernagh, Arthur Devlin and Martin Burke. Michael Dwyer was quoted as saying that all Irish would be free in this new country. This statement had been used against him and he and several others in the group were arrested in February 1807 and imprisoned.[234] Bligh reported to William Windham, on 19 March, 1807:

No arms have been found, or any positive overt act committed, our information leading only to declared plans which were to be put into execution by the Irish convicts, headed by O'Dwyer and some of the Irish state prisoners, as they are here called.

It appears that, in order to avoid detection, they determined to rest their success on seizing the arms of the loyal inhabitants; and to effect this, the Irish servants of the inhabitants were on a certain time fixed to massacre their respective masters, and the principal persons of the colony, and then to possess themselves of their arms.

Of this determination, I continued to have proofs more or less, when I determined on seizing the persons represented as the ring-leaders, and effected my purpose. O'Dwyer I

231 Johnston to King, 24 April 1805, *HRA*, Series I: Vol. 5, p. 448.

232 Ibid, Whitaker, Anne-Maree, *Unfinished Revolution: United Irishmen in New South Wales, 1800-1810*, pp. 141-166, is the best discussion of Dwyer.

233 See, O'Donnell, Ruan, 'Dwyer, Michael (1772?-1825)', *ADB*, Supplementary Vol. p. 110, Dickson, C., *The Life of Michael Dwyer: With some account of his companions*, (Browne and Nolan), 1944, and Lawlor, Chris, *In search of Michael Dwyer*, (Chris Lawlor), 2003.

234 O'Dwyer, B. W., 'Michael Dwyer and the 1807 plan of insurrection', *Journal of the Royal Australian Historical Society*, Vol. 69, (1983), pp. 73-82, remains the only account of the supposed insurrection.

have put on board the Porpoise. Byrn (sic), Burke, and some others are in jail for trial, and will be brought forward as soon as our evidences are all arranged and prepared.[235]

On 11 May 1807, Dwyer was charged with conspiring to mount an Irish insurrection against British rule. An Irish convict stated in court that Michael Dwyer had plans to march on Parramatta. Dwyer did not deny that he had said that all Irish will be free but he did deny the charges of organising an Irish insurrection in Sydney. On 18 May 1807, Dwyer was found not guilty of the charges of organising an Irish insurrection in Sydney. Bligh informed Windham of his actions on 31 October 1807:

> ...they have since been tried, and the fact, in my opinion, proved, yet they were acquitted - except two, who were sentenced to corporeal (sic) punishment. The whole being prisoners for life I immediately divided the gang and sent two of each to the settlements of Norfolk Island, the Derwent, and Port Dalrymple, and kept two here. The two men who informed of this conspiracy gave their evidence so steadily as to induce me to give them free pardons, and they remain here without any apprehension of being molested by the disaffected Irishmen.[236]

Bligh regarded the Irish and many other nationalities with contempt and disregarded the first trial acquittal of Michael Dwyer. Dwyer was stripped of his free settler status and transported to Norfolk Island and later to VDL. On 27 May, 1807, Bligh sent Dwyer and Morris to Norfolk Island with instructions to the Commandant, Captain Piper:

> Michael O'Dwyer and William Morris, two convicts for life, being found to be persons necessary to be removed from this settlement, you are hereby required and directed to receive the two said men, and victual them accordingly, taking care that they are not suffered to quit Norfolk Island unless by authority from under my hand. And the said William Morris, having received five hundred and twenty-five lashes, pursuant to his sentence of one thousand, you are hereby required to direct the remaining part of four hundred and seventy-five lashes to be inflicted according to the warrant sent herein by the Judge-Advocate.[237]

Dwyer, a sociable and affable individual, was popular among some of the officers of the NSW Corps and this act of arbitrary justice became one of the Corps' many grievances against Bligh. After Governor Bligh was deposed in the Rum Rebellion in 1808, the acting Governor of NSW, George Johnston ordered that Dwyer should be freed and his lands restored, a decision later confirmed by Macquarie. He later became Chief of Police in May 1820 at Liverpool, NSW but was dismissed in October 1820 for drunken conduct and mislaying important documents. With a farm of 610 acres, Dwyer had been reintegrated into colonial society but in late 1822 he was sued over his farm prompting Daniel Cooper, a major debtor to demand restitution of £2,000 invested in Dwyer's popular Harrow Inn. Bankrupted, Dwyer was forced to sell off most of his assets but this did not save him from several weeks' imprisonment in the Sydney

[235] Bligh to Windham, 19 March 1807, *HRNSW*, Vol. 6, pp. 259-260.
[236] Bligh to Windham, 31 October 1807, *HRNSW*, Vol. 6, p. 363.
[237] Bligh to Windham, 31 October 1807, *HRNSW*, Vol. 6, p. 354.

debtors' prison in May 1825 where he contracted dysentery from which he died in August 1825.

Conclusion

Unlike the Eureka rebellion in 1854, Australian historians have been slow to see the 1804 convict revolt as a legitimate expression of political resistance. Established in 1788, the fledgling British colony of NSW was small and isolated, but with a significant cadre of political rebels among its convict population. As a result, it had a strong undercurrent of republicanism and a persistent anti-authoritarianism to British rule. To O'Farrell, the Irish were led to rebel by semi-mystical impulses, 'frustrations, sickness of heart, and impulses of affront: in a word pride' and Silver also implies that the rebels were merely homesick romantics.[238] More recently Ann-Maree Whitaker and Ruan O'Donnell have recognised the political imperatives that shaped rebellion. Although it is easy to dismiss rebellions as wild and absurd, they generally involved detailed planning but there was also a wider vision that transcended ethnicity. Those planning rebellions believed that all disaffected men, free and convict, would join them to throw off their shared oppression and that together they would seize a ship and sail to freedom.

Except for Joseph Holt's *Memoirs*, published in 1838 twelve years after his death and decidedly critical of seditious activities, the accounts of planned or actual Irish rebellions in the first decade of the nineteenth century were written by those who sympathised with or supported the actions of the authorities. The rebels themselves have little or no voice and where it is evident it is generally mediated through the voice of the authorities in despatches, reports and accounts. Reliance on 'official' sources poses problems especially since their attitudes towards Irish 'politicals' from the early 1790s was broadly negative. This can be seen David Collins' comments on the fractious character of Irish convicts in 1798 and 1799 and of the need to take firm action against them:

> The Irish prisoners who had arrived in the last ships from that country had about this period become so turbulent and refractory, and so dissatisfied with their situation, that, without the most rigid and severe punishment, it was impossible to derive from them any labour whatever.[239]

> A numerous body of the Irish convicts, many of whom had but lately arrived, insisted that 'their times were out', and could not be persuaded that they were mistaken by any remonstrance or argument. They grew noisy and insolent, and even made use of threats; upon which a few of the most forward and daring were secured, and instantly punished; after which they were ordered to go back to their work. They had also taken up the idea that Ireland had shaken off its connection with England, and they were no longer to be considered as convicts under the British government. This was a most pernicious idea

[238] O'Farrell, Patrick, *The Irish in Australia: 1788 to the Present*, (University of New South Wales Press), 2000, p. 38.
[239] Collins, David, *An account of the English colony in New South Wales from its first settlement in January 1788, to August 1801: with remarks on the dispositions, customs, manners, &c., of the native inhabitants of that country*, 2 Vols. (T. Cadell and W. Davies), 1798, Vol. 2, p. 54.

to be entertained by such a lawless set of people, and requiring the strong arm of government to eradicate it.[240]

More problematic were the political ideas circulating among Irish convicts especially their belief in their ultimate liberation through French intervention. To the authorities, isolated in NSW, this posed a major threat.

A report prevailed at this time among the labouring people, particularly the Irish, who were always foremost in every mischief and discontent, that an old woman had prophesied the arrival of several French frigates, or large ships of war, who were, after destroying the settlement, to liberate and take off the whole of the convicts. The rapidity with which this ridiculous tale was circulated is incredible. The effect was such as might be expected. One refractory fellow, while working...at Toongabbie, threw down his hoe, advancing before the rest, and gave three cheers for liberty. This for a while seemed well received; but, a magistrate fortunately being at hand, the business was put to an end, by securing the advocate for liberty, tying him up in the field, and giving him a severe flogging.[241]

Colonial paranoia increased once evidence of planned rebellion became evident after 1800 but how real was the threat from Irish convicts? The Defenders and United Irishmen transported between 1795 and 1806 provided leadership to those convicts who were prepared to take direct action to overthrow the colonial authorities. Although it was the Irish convicts who were of concern to Hunter, King and Bligh, it is important not to over-exaggerate their significance while underestimating the part played by convicts of other nationalities. The Irish convict leadership had considerable experience in planning and implementing rebellious activities. This explains why successive governors sent leaders or presumed leaders--whether there was concrete evidence of sedition or not--to penal settlements on Norfolk Island and VDL. This had the effect of disrupting planning for insurrection. Finally, the hatred of the British in Ireland was transposed to NSW and Irish leaders had a willing supply of convicts prepared to support their actions. That support came from non-Irish convicts reflects the punitive and arbitrary nature of convict life. Where they were concentrated in one area, as on the Castle Hill farm, Ireland's cause helped bind these men together.

However, there were major problems for those seeking rebellion. Keeping planning secret was a major difficulty and only the Castle Hill revolt in 1804 saw planning converted into action. Convicts were always willing to 'split upon each other' and this allowed the authorities to intervene before matters spiralled out of control. The objectives of rebellion such as the rallying cry of 'Death or Liberty' or demands for a ship home were idealistic and unrealistic dreaming. Although these may have been the aims of rebel leaders, there is little evidence that they were widely held by the rank-and-file, many of whom claimed that they had been

240 Ibid, Collins, David, *An account of the English colony in New South Wales*, Vol. 2, pp. 102-103.

241 Ibid, Collins, David, *An account of the English colony in New South Wales*, Vol. 2, p. 77.

forced into rebellion.[242] As in Ireland during the 1798 Rebellion, when faced with even inferior military force, the rebels could not translate numerical strength into military advantage. Finally, the hoped-for French aid was illusory: it was never part of French strategy and, during the critical years between 1801 and 1804, war in Europe had been suspended.

It was the British government that was constantly afraid of convict rebellion and disorder though this did not stop it sending political prisoners to NSW despite the concerns of successive governors. For the authorities, a colony composed largely of convicts was inevitably turbulent and rebellious, something reflected in Hunter's and King's despatches. In his reports on NSW and VDL in the early 1820s, Bigge considered that the best security against rebellion was the higher standard of living that convicts generally enjoyed in NSW than in Britain and the opportunities and rewards open to those with industry and skill. Some convicts 'bolted' but only a few rebelled.

Norfolk Island

Convict resistance was widespread in NSW and then VDL in the decades following the unsuccessful rebellion in 1804. The major reason why there were no further large-scale rebellions on mainland Australia was that recalcitrant convicts were increasingly isolated in punishment settlements. The discovery of coal in NSW resulted in the development of Newcastle and its example was later following in VDL with the establishment of the prison settlement at Port Arthur. However, the most feared and infamous settlement was on Norfolk Island that lay about a thousand miles from both Australia and NZ and covers an area of just over thirteen square miles and was represented as all that was bad about the convict system. Bathurst's 1824 proclamation stated that the 'worst description' of convicts from NSW and VDL would be sent to the Island.[243] Its isolation and the draconian nature of its administration, especially after 1825, made it one of the most brutal penal settlements of the nineteenth century and it was the location for the other major convict rebellion in 1834.[244] In 1840, Charles Dickens volunteered to write a cheap government-sanctioned narrative of Norfolk Island

---

[242] The major source for the attitudes of ordinary rebels comes from after the rebellion had failed. Faced with possible hanging, it is hardly surprising that many claimed they had been coerced into rebelling. This was evident in other rebellions, for instance, after the Chartist rebellion at Newport in 1839, many of those arrested claimed coercion as a defence.

[243] Bathurst to Brisbane, 22 July 1824, *HRA*, Series I, Vol. 11, p. 322.

[244] See, Hoare, Merval, *Norfolk Island; An outline of its history 1774-1968*, 5th ed., (University of Queensland Press), 1999, Hazzard, Margaret, *Punishment Short of Death: A History of the Penal Settlement at Norfolk Island*, (Hyland House), 1984, Treadgold, M. L., *Bounteous Bestowal: The economic history of Norfolk Island*, (Australian National University), 1988, O'Collins, Maev, *An Uneasy Relationship: Norfolk Island and the Commonwealth of Australia*, (ANU Press), 2002, pp. 1-19, and Macklin, Robert, *Dark Paradise: Norfolk Island—Isolation, Savagery, Mystery and Murder*, (Hachette Australia), 2013. Benton, Laura, *A Search for Sovereignty: Law and Geography in European Empires, 1400-1900*, (Cambridge University Press), 2010, pp. 197-208, examines the uses made of extra-legal disciplinary systems.

to ensure that the lower orders held it in sufficient dread.[245] Such a work was unnecessary since the Island was already a byword for criminality and obstinacy.

Settling Norfolk Island

Sighted and named by Captain Cook in 1774, Norfolk Island was included as an auxiliary settlement in the British government's plan for colonisation of NSW in 1786 and initially settled in March 1788. The decision to settle Norfolk Island, as well as the main settlement at Botany Bay, was based on its natural resources: tall, straight Norfolk Island pines and the NZ flax plant.[246] Cook had taken samples back to Britain and reported on their potential uses for the Royal Navy. Britain was heavily dependent on flax for sails and hemp for ropes largely imported from Russia through the Baltic Sea ports and on timbers for mainmasts from New England. Relying on potentially erratic imports of these supplies posed a threat to Britain's naval supremacy. Norfolk Island offered an alternative source and some historians, notably Geoffrey Blainey, have argued that this was a major reason for the founding of the convict settlement of NSW in 1788. The *Universal Daily Register* revealed the plan for a dual colonisation of Norfolk Island and Botany Bay:

> The ships for Botany Bay are not to leave all the convicts there; some of them are to be taken to Norfolk Island, which is about eight hundred miles East of Botany Bay, and about four hundred miles short of New Zealand.[247]

The advantage of a non-Russian source of flax and hemp for naval supplies was referred to in *Lloyd's Evening Post*:

> It is undoubtedly the interest of Great-Britain to remain neutral in the present contest between the Russians and the Turks...Should England cease to render her services to the Empress of Russia, in a war against the Turks, there can be little of nothing to fear from her ill-will. England will speedily be enabled to draw from her colony of New South Wales, the staple of Russia, hemp and flax.[248]

Governor Arthur Phillip's final instructions, given him in April 1787 less than three weeks before sailing, included the requirement to colonise Norfolk Island to prevent it falling into the hands of France, whose naval leaders were also showing interest in the Pacific.[249]

---

[245] Dickens to Normanby, 3 July 1840, in Storey, Graham, Tillotson, Kathleen, and Easson, Angus, (eds.), *The Letters of Charles Dickens, Volume 7, 1853-1855*, (Oxford University Press), 1993, p. 818. The letter was referred to in the context of *Hard Times*, (Bradbury & Evans), 1854, p. 178, where Norfolk Island is briefly mentioned.

[246] See, Nobbs, R., (ed.), *Norfolk Island and its First Settlement, 1788-1814*, (Library of Australian History), 1988, and Donohoe, J. H., *Norfolk Island, 1788-1813: the people and their families*, (J. H. Donohoe), 1986.

[247] *Universal Daily Register*, 23 December 1786.

[248] *Lloyd's Evening Post*, 5 October 1787.

[249] Dyer, Colin, *The French Explorers and Sydney*, (University of Queensland Press), 2009, draws on French observations of the British convict settlement in NSW.

...as soon as Circumstances may admit of it...to prevent its being occupied by the Subjects of any other European Power.[250]

Phillip had chosen King as second lieutenant on HMS *Sirius* for the expedition to establish a convict settlement in NSW. King had served with Phillip before the First Fleet and was regarded as his protégé. Phillip certainly had a high opinion of King and consciously promoted his interests throughout the late 1780s and 1790s. Despite his lowly rank, soon after the settlement was established at Sydney Cove, King was selected to lead a small party of convicts and guards to set up a settlement at Norfolk Island. On 14 February 1788, he sailed for his new post with a party of twenty-three, including fifteen convicts.[251] On 6 March 1788, King and his party landed with difficulty, owing to the lack of a suitable harbour and set about building huts, clearing the land, planting crops and resisting the ravages of grubs, salt air and hurricanes.[252] More convicts were sent and these proved occasionally troublesome. Early in 1789, King prevented a mutiny when some of the convicts planned to take him and the other officers prisoner and escape on the next boat to arrive.[253] Despite the lack of a safe harbour, of lime and timbered land, there was plenty of fish, the stock flourished and the soil was good. It could maintain 'at least one hundred families', King told Phillip. Impressed by his work, the governor several times recommended his subordinate for naval promotion, but this would have raised difficulties because of King's lack of seniority. To resolve this the Secretary of State announced in December 1789 that King would be appointed Lieutenant-Governor of Norfolk Island at a salary of £250.[254]

Following the wreck of *Sirius* at Norfolk Island in March 1790, King left and returned to England to report on the difficulties facing the settlements in NSW. During his twenty months absence, the island was under the command of Lieutenant-Governor Robert Ross[255] but Ross was not an easy commandant and

---

[250] *HRNSW*, Vol. 1, (2), pp. 84-91, *HRA*, Series I: Vol. 1, pp. 2-9.

[251] Crittenden, Victor, *King of Norfolk Island: The Story of Philip Gidley King as Commandant and Lieutenant-Governor of Norfolk Island*, (Mulini Press), 1993. For King's appointment and instructions see, *HRNSW*, Vol. 1, (2), pp. 136-138. Fidlon, P. G., and Ryan, R. J., (eds.), *The Journal of Philip Gidley King: Lieutenant, R.N., 1787-1790*, (Australian Documents Library), 1980, gives King's view of his governance of Norfolk Island until 1790.

[252] Phillip to Sydney, 28 September 1788, *HRNSW*, Vol. 1, (2), pp. 185-187, provides analysis of the resources of Norfolk Island. See also, Phillip, Arthur, *The voyage of Governor Phillip to Botany Bay: with an account of the establishment of the colonies of Port Jackson & Norfolk Island*, 3rd ed., (Printed for J. Stockdale), 1790. Ross to Phillip, 11 February 1791, gives a detailed discussion of problems encountered, *HRNSW*, Vol. 1, (2), pp. 434-450.

[253] Phillip to Sydney, 12 February 1790, *HRNSW*, Vol. 1, (2), pp. 293-294. Since Phillip had corresponded with Sydney during 1789, it is difficult to explain why he left it a year before informing him of the mutiny.

[254] For King's commission dated 28 January 1790, see, *HRNSW*, Vol. 1, (2), pp. 287-288.

[255] For Ross' instruction dated 2 March 1790, see, *HRNSW*, Vol. 1, (2), pp. 314-316. See also his observations on the island in December 1790, *HRNSW*, Vol. 1, (2), pp. 416-420, and the contrast with King's observations in January 1791 when he was in London,

convicts, settlers, soldiers and officials had become discontented under his rule.[256] King found 'discord and strife on every person's countenance' and was 'pestered with complaints, bitter revilings, back-biting'.[257] Tools and skilled labour were both in short supply. Thefts were common and there was still no criminal court on the island, despite the representations he had made in London on the need for better judicial arrangements.[258] However, King's guidance helped to improve conditions. The regulations he issued in 1792 encouraged the settlers, who were drawn from ex-marines and ex-convicts, and he was willing to listen to their advice on fixing wages and prices and other things. Unfortunately, King had no success with growing the flax that so interested the British government.[259] The pine timber was found to be not durable enough for masts and this industry was also abandoned. By 1794, the island was self-sufficient in grain and had a surplus of swine that it could send to Sydney. Maize, wheat, potatoes, cabbage, timber, flax and fruit of all kinds grew well, the population grew to more than 1,100 and about a quarter of the island was cleared. Suffering from gout, King returned to England in October 1796, and after regaining his health, he resumed his naval career.

Between 1796 and 1800, Norfolk Island was ruled by Captain John Townson and then briefly by Captain Thomas Rowley. Townson spent six years on Norfolk Island between late 1791 and 1799 and received a twenty-acre lease.[260] His administration was capable and he seems to have had a steadying influence on both convicts and settlers. When Townson left prematurely in November 1799, Rowley, as the senior officer, took charge of the settlement. He ordered liquor stills to be demolished to reduce the drunkenness on the island, and this move brought threats of prosecution from their owners.[261] King returned to NSW in early 1800 as Governor.[262] He appointed Major Joseph Foveaux as Lieutenant-Governor of Norfolk Island in June 1800.

HRNSW, Vol. 1, (2), pp. 428-431. See also, Macmillan, David S., 'Ross, Robert (1740?-1794)', *ADB*, Vol. 2, pp. 397-398.

[256] Ross had introduced martial law almost as soon as he arrived at Norfolk Island because of the loss of the *Sirius*; see, Ross to Phillip, 22 March 1790, *HRNSW*, Vol. 1, (2), pp. 319-320, and also the enclosures pp. 321-323, in which Ross laid down the standards that would now operate on the island. Phillip informed Grenville in a letter dated 14 July 1790, *HRNSW*, Vol. 1, (2), pp. 357-358. Food shortages on Norfolk Island led Ross to introduce draconian measures to conserve supplies in proclamations on 7 August 1790, *HRNSW*, Vol. 1, (2), pp. 390-393.

[257] King to Under Secretary Evan Nepean, 23 November 1791, *HRNSW*, Vol. 1, (2), p. 562; see also King to Phillip, 29 December 1791, *HRNSW*, Vol. 1, (2), pp. 572-580.

[258] See Phillip to Dundas, 4 October 1791, *HRNSW*, Vol. 1, (2), p. 655, on the inconveniences of the lack of a criminal court on Norfolk Island. Legislation was finally passed in London establishing a criminal court on Norfolk Island on 9 May 1794, *HRNSW*, Vol. 2, pp. 235-236.

[259] King to Dundas, 19 November 1793, *HRNSW*, Vol. 2, pp. 86-98, details the voyage to NZ to obtain Maori help with flax production. This failed and the natives returned to NZ, *HRNSW*, Vol. 2, p. 174.

[260] Austin, M., 'Townson, John (1759?-1835)', *ADB*, Vol. 2, pp. 536-537.

[261] Fletcher, B. H., 'Rowley, Thomas (1748?-1806)', *ADB*, Vol. 2, p. 403.

[262] King arrived in NSW with the letter (Portland to Hunter, 5 November 1799, *HRNSW*, Vol. 3, pp. 733-738, *HRA*, Series I: Vol. 2, pp. 387-392, recalling Governor John Hunter

Foveaux[263] found the settlement quite run down, little maintenance having been carried out in the previous four years. Its population consisted of 519 men, 165 women and 269 children and had an unusually high ratio of free settlers to convicts: not including children, there were 308 free settlers and 272 convicts. Foveaux was unimpressed with his civil administration regarding the NSW Corps officers generally unfavourably.[264] He set about building up the community, particularly through public works and attempted to improve education. By 1800, Norfolk Island was a regular stop from the increasing number of whaling ships from the United States and Britain. Whale oil was much in demand, not least as a means of street lighting and by 1802 almost a hundred ships were involved in the Southern Ocean fishery. Whalers made lengthy voyages, often lasting two or three years and they found that wood and food were cheaper on Norfolk Island than in Sydney. This gave a welcome boost to the island's economy. Whaling captains were often of assistance to Foveaux, selling tools and other goods needed on the island and carrying despatches to and from England. However, on occasions Foveaux complained that whalers overcharged for taking goods and passengers to Sydney and demanded urgent repairs that interfered with his plans for public works and farming.[265]

Foveaux and rebellion in 1800

There had been attempted convict rebellions in 1789 and 1794 and this situation intensified with the arrival on the island in early November 1800 of a group of United Irish prisoners, several of whom had been implicated in conspiracies in Sydney in September and October. Although Foveaux was aware of the need for surveillance over the convicts, he believed that lenient treatment and the isolation of the island would discourage any attempts at escape. The United Irishmen were allowed free association with each other and with earlier arrivals. Farrell Cuffe, a school teacher and United Irishman from County Offaly struck up or possibly renewed a friendship with Peter McLean, a political prisoner from County Cavan who had arrived with Foveaux in July. The result was preparations for an armed escape. Convicts began making pikes and Cockerton Ross, an expiree, promised to give them 15 muskets. McLean was also in correspondence

---

was received on 16 April 1800, but he did not hand over the government to King until 28 September.

[263] See, King to Portland, 29 April 1800, *HRNSW*, Vol. 4, p. 79, makes clear King's decision and King to Foveaux, 26 June 1800, *HRNSW*, Vol. 4, pp. 96-108, details Foveaux's appointment and instructions. See also, Fletcher, B. H., 'Foveaux, Joseph (1767-1846)', *ADB*, Vol. 1, pp. 407-409, and Whitaker, Ann-Maree, *Joseph Foveaux: power and patronage in early New South Wales*, (University of New South Wales Press), 2000, pp. 55-80, for his years on Norfolk Island.

[264] State of the Settlement in Norfolk Island, 6 November 1800, *HRNSW*, Vol. 4, pp. 252-253.

[265] On the development of the South Sea whale-fishery, see, minutes of the Board of Trade, 4 December 1801, *HRNSW*, Vol. 4, p. 630. See also, Little, B., 'Sealing and Whaling in Australia Before 1850', *Australian Economic History Review*, Vol. 9, (1969), pp. 109-127.

with Thomas Pyshe Palmer in Sydney who promised that a ship would come to take them away once the conspirators had seized the settlement.[266]

The rebellion was originally planned for Christmas Day when McLean and sympathetic soldiers would open the barracks and the rebels would seize weapons and proceed to the guardhouse, magazine and gaol. The fraternisation of several of the soldiers with the Irish convicts had already caused some concern but no action had been taken. However, preparations were so advanced that the plan was brought forward to the night of Saturday 13 December but was deferred for twenty-four hours following a meeting at which the rebels disagreed about whether the officers, their wives and children should be killed or not. In the interim, the conspiracy was betrayed to Foveaux by Henry Grady, a reluctant rebel and Thomas Hodges. Foveaux acted decisively and with his civil and military officers agreed that capital punishment should be used, perhaps angered that his leniency had been abused or by the threat of violence to women and children.[267] McLean and John Houlahan, named as the chief organiser of the pike-making were arrested on the Sunday morning and hanged in the afternoon before the assembled convicts and soldiers. The four soldiers involved were ceremoniously drummed out of the NSW Corps and received 500 lashes each. Although there were some questions about the legality of summary executions, King supported Foveaux's actions and submitted a favourable report to London.[268]

Until severe asthma forced him to return first to Sydney in September 1803 and to London a year later, Foveaux concentrated his efforts on improving conditions on Norfolk Island, paying particular attention to public works, with results that earned high praise from both King and Lord Hobart, the Secretary of State. More questionable, however, was the dubious morality of allowing the sale of female convicts to settlers. Despite these advances, the future of Norfolk Island as a penal settlement, initially questioned by King as early as 1794, had already been decided before Foveaux left. It was too remote, too costly to maintain and the lack of a harbour made it difficult for shipping and, with the establishment of a settlement in VDL in 1803, there was now an alternative location for a penal settlement for difficult convicts. By 1803, Lord Hobart called for the removal of part of the Norfolk Island military establishment, settlers and convicts to VDL, due to its great expense and the difficulties of communication with Sydney.[269] Foveaux made his view clear to the Colonial Office that Norfolk Island should be abandoned in favour of VDL on his leave in England.[270]

John Houston, a naval lieutenant, was sent from Sydney to take over as Lieutenant-Governor and arrived at Norfolk Island on 13 February 1804 with Captain John Piper of the NSW Corps. Foveaux also returned to the island in February and continued with his plans for improvement but in July 1804

---

[266] Earnshaw, John, 'Palmer, Thomas Fyshe (1747-1802)', *ADB*, Vol. 2, pp. 312-313.

[267] *HRNSW*, Vol. 4, pp. 266-267, details the meeting

[268] King to Portland, 10 March 1801, *HRNSW*, Vol. 4, p. 319, 325,

[269] Hobart to King, 24 June 1803, *HRNSW*, Vol. 5, pp. 157-159; this was not received by King until May 1804.

[270] See, Lieutenant-Governor Foveaux's Observations concerning the Removal of the Settlement at Norfolk Island, 25 March 1805, *HRNSW*, Vol. 5, pp. 581-585.

received a despatch from King ordering evacuation of the island.[271] Houston returned to Sydney and Piper became Lieutenant-Governor, a position he held until January 1810.[272] The duty of carrying out the frequently altered instructions fell to Piper and he appears to have exhibited both tact and organising ability. The evacuation was achieved more slowly than anticipated because of the reluctance of settlers to uproot themselves from the land they had struggled to tame and compensation claims for loss of stock. It was also delayed by King who insisted on the importance of the island for the whaling industry and probably his own personal attachment to it.[273] The first group of 159 left in February 1805 and comprised mainly convicts and their families and military personnel, only four settlers departing.[274] Between November 1807 and September 1808, five groups of 554 people left. Only about 200 remained, forming a small settlement until the remnants were removed in 1813. A small party led by a trusted emancipated convict William Hutchinson, which finally left on 15 February 1814, remained to slaughter stock and destroy all buildings so that there would be no incentive for anyone, especially from another European power, to visit or attempt to colonise it.[275]

'Hell in Paradise'

The ways in which Norfolk Island was regarded in the nineteenth century have led to stories to be told that do not correspond to its reality. The Norfolk Island legend has several defining characteristics that include assumptions that the prisoners were universally brutalised and had no hope, that commandants and their subordinates were sadists, sexual violence was widespread, and that 'unnatural crimes'-Victorian shorthand for homosexuality-were rampant.

During Norfolk Island's second settlement between 1825 and 1855, it was indeed the 'Hell of the Pacific', a place dominated by death and despair.[276] In 1824, the Governor of NSW, Sir Thomas Brisbane,[277] received a directive from Lord Bathurst, the Colonial Secretary that Norfolk Island was again to be turned into a penitentiary.[278] Its remoteness, seen previously as a disadvantage, was now viewed as an asset for the detention of those 'twice-convicted', men who had committed further crimes since arriving in NSW and VDL. Brisbane decided

---

271 King to Foveaux, 20 July 1804, *HRNSW*, Vol. 5, pp. 403-406, detailed how the partial evacuation was to be managed.

272 Barnard, Marjorie, 'Piper, John (1773-1851)', *ADB*, Vol. 2, pp. 334-335.

273 King to Sir Joseph Banks, 14 August 1804, *HRNSW*, Vol. 5, pp. 447-448, expressed King's belief in the importance of Norfolk Island and King to Camden, 30 April 1805, *HRNSW*, Vol. 5, pp. 600-601, concerning the whalers.

274 See King to Camden, 30 April 1805, *HRNSW*, Vol. 5, pp. 600-601, on the first tranche of the removal.

275 Le Roy, Paul Edwin, 'Hutchinson, William (1772-1846)', *ADB*, Vol. 1, pp. 574-575.

276 See, Nobbs, R., (ed.), *Norfolk Island and its Second Settlement, 1825-1855*, (Library of Australian History), 1991.

277 Heydon, J. D., 'Brisbane, Sir Thomas Makdougall (1773-1860)', *ADB*, Vol. 1, pp. 151-155, and Brisbane, Sir Thomas Makdougall, *Reminiscences of General Sir Thomas Makdougall Brisbane*, (T. Constable), 1860, pp. 43-60.

278 Bathurst to Brisbane, 22 July 1824, *HRA*, Series I: Vol. 11, pp. 321-322, acknowledged by Brisbane, 21 May 1825.

that it was the best place to send the worst felons 'forever to be excluded from all hope of return'. Norfolk Island would be 'the *nec plus ultra* of Convict degradation'.[279]

His successor, Governor Ralph Darling[280] was even more severe than Brisbane, and made it clear in 1827 that he wished that 'every man should be worked in irons that the example may deter others from the commission of crime'[281] and that 'My object was to hold out [Norfolk Island] as a place of the extremest punishment short of death'.[282] Governor George Arthur, in VDL, also believed that 'when prisoners are sent to Norfolk Island, they should on no account be permitted to return. Transportation thither should be considered as the ultimate limit and a punishment short only of death'. Sir Richard Bourke instructed Major Joseph Anderson, the notorious Commandant of Norfolk Island from 1834 to 1839, to keep prisoners working manually in irons even though it was expensive and inefficient, as the penal settlement was considered a place of punishment. He deliberately warned him against implementing any more efficient methods of production, such as mills that were not 'urged by the labour of convicts'.[283] Despite the reliance on manual labour, prisoners on Norfolk Island were cheaper to keep than chained convicts in NSW and the existence of the place at all was considered by many in Britain to be part of the 'moral cost' of the transportation system. Convicts so feared Norfolk Island that Elliott one of the prisoners declared that he would rather hang than be sent there.[284] The Norfolk Island penal settlement was not primarily for the reformation of convicts.

Conditions for convicts, many of them Irish Catholics, were unrelentingly brutal. A large percentage of the convicts were sentenced to remain in heavy chains for the terms of their natural lives and most convicts were chained during the day. Convicts were used primarily as farm labourers or in building much of what today is Kingston. Stone was quarried for building from Nepean Island, a rock close to shore and coral rubble was rendered with lime and sand. Norfolk Pine was used for joinery and roofs and floors were made from thin stone slabs. Flogging was common, sometimes up to 500 strokes. Dumb-cells were constructed to exclude light and sound in which some lost their sanity. Solitary confinement, increased workloads and decreased rations were also common forms of punishment. Michael Burns, for instance, suffered a total of 2,210 lashes and almost two years in confinement, much of it in solitary with at least six

---

[279] Brisbane to Under-Secretary Horton, 24 March 1825, *HRA*, Series I: Vol. 11, p. 553.
[280] 'Sir Ralph Darling (1772-1858), *ADB*, Vol. 1, 1966, pp. 282-286, and ibid, Fletcher, Brian, *Ralph Darling: A Governor Maligned*, provide biographical material.
[281] Darling to Under-Secretary Hay, 10 February 1827, *HRA*, Series I: Vol. 13, p. 106.
[282] Cit, ibid, Hazzard, Margaret, *Punishment Short of Death*, p. 111.
[283] See, Bourke to Stanley, 15 January 1834, *HRA*, Series I: Vol. 17, pp. 319-320, 327-328.
[284] *R. v. Jones, Giles and Elliot*: report of execution, 'Editorial', *Australian*, 13 September 1833, p. 2. For other declarations of preference for death over transportation to Norfolk Island, see *R v Gough, Watson and Muir*, 1827, Therry, R., *Reminiscences of Thirty Years' Residence in New South Wales and Victoria: with a supplementary chapter on transportation and the ticket-of-leave system,* (Sampson Low, Son, and Co.), 1863, pp. 19, 24, and *R v Pegg*, 1831, who preferred death to 14 years' transportation.

months of those two years on a diet of bread and water. His crimes were insolence, suspected robbery and neglect of work, striking a fellow prisoner, bushranging, singing a song, calling for a doctor, attempted escape and inability to work caused by his punishments.[285] Thomas Bunbury, briefly commandant in 1839 after the brief mutiny by the 80th Regiment on the island,[286] wrote that he could not understand why 'a villain who has been guilty of every enormity, should feel shame at having his back scratched with the cat-o-nine-tails when he felt none for his atrocious crimes' and that 'if a man is too sick to work he is too sick to eat'.[287]

Such was the harshness of both hard labour and punishment that for some death was preferable to continued torment though contemporary evidence for this is limited. When Father William Ullathorne, Vicar general of Sydney, visited Norfolk Island to comfort those due for execution after the 1834 rebellion, he found it 'the most heartrending scene that I ever witnessed'. Having the duty of informing the prisoners as to who was reprieved and who was to die, he was shocked to record as 'a literal fact that each man who heard his reprieve wept bitterly, and that each man who heard of his condemnation to death went down on his knees with dry eyes, and thanked God.'[288] John Frederick Mortlock, who wrote about his own treatment at various settlements around Australia and arrived on Norfolk Island in 1845, explained:

> ...instead of awakening moral responsibility, it [injudicious severity] strengthens the Devil, and makes men more difficult to manage-more likely to be dangerous when restored to society.[289]

There is evidence that some men committed capital offences with 'suicidal intent' so that they would be executed. For instance, William Westwood, one of the leaders of the 1846 riot suggested in a conversation with Stipendiary Magistrate Samuel Barrow that he 'became careless and reckless of life' and that 'the death I am going to suffer could be preferable to Norfolk Island.'[290]

---

[285] Cook, Thomas, *The exile's lamentations or biographical sketch of Thomas Cook who was convicted at the Assizes held at Shrewsbury in March 1831 for 'writing threatening letters' and sentenced 14 yrs transportation and re-convicted for forgery and sentenced to Norfolk Island for life*, 1840, reprinted, (Library of Australian History), 1978, p. 48.

[286] Sargent, Clem, 'The British Garrison in Australia 1788-1841: the mutiny of the 80th Regiment on Norfolk Island', *Sabretache*, Vol. 59, (3), (2005), pp. 5-22, is essential on this neglected rebellion.

[287] Bunbury, Thomas, *Reminiscences of a Veteran: being personal and military adventures in Portugal, Spain, France, Malta, New South Wales, Norfolk Island, New Zealand, Andaman Islands, and India*, 3 Vols. (C. J. Skeet), 1861, reprinted (N & M Press), 2009, cit. ibid, Hazzard, Margaret, *Punishment Short of Death*, p. 152

[288] Cit, Birt, Henry Norbert, *Benedictine Pioneers in Australia*, 2 Vols. (Herbert & Daniel), Vol. 1, 1911, p. 178, and Butler, Edward Cuthbert, *The life & times of Bishop Ullathorne, 1806-1889*, 2 Vols. (Burns, Oates, and Washbourne, Ltd.), 1926, Vol. 1, p. 94.

[289] Mortlock, J. F., *Experiences of a Convict Transported for twenty one years: an autobiographical memoir*, (Richard Barrett, Printers), 1864, p. 67.

[290] Barrow to Comptroller-General of Convicts 2 November 1846, cit, Causer, Tim, 'Norfolk Island's 'suicide lotteries': myth and reality', unpublished paper, p. 5. http://www.academia.edu/1109987/Norfolk_Islands_suicide_lotteries_myth_and_reality

However, an attempted escape from gaol suggests that his claims should be treated with some scepticism. These incidents were embellished into stories of 'suicide lotteries' by some contemporary writers. John West, for instance, argued that men at Macquarie Harbour 'gambled for life'.[291] The Norfolk Island suicide lottery myth relies on an extremely limited number of sources and despite the continued currency of these tales, the suicide rate on the Island was extremely low with only three recorded attempted suicides, a consequence Causer argues 'that convicts were averse to suicide for explicitly religious reasons'.[292]

By the mid-1840s, there was increasing concern among humanitarians and those concerned with managing convicts that the regime on Norfolk Island was too brutal and that it left no room for rehabilitation. In 1846, Robert Pringle Stuart, a magistrate in the VDL Convict Department exposed the scarcity and poor quality of food, inadequacy of housing, horrors of torture and incessant flogging, insubordination of convicts and corruption of overseers.[293] Robert Willson, Catholic bishop of Hobart visited Norfolk Island from VDL on three occasions. Following his first visit in 1846, he reported to the House of Lords who, for the first time, realised the enormity of the cruelty perpetrated under the British flag and attempted to remedy the evils.[294] A number of days before his visit 34 men were flogged; the day after his arrival, another 14; and at the service he held on the island, 218 of the 270 men attending were in chains. He returned three years later and found that many of the reforms had been implemented. However, rumours of resumed brutality brought him back in 1852 and this visit resulted in a damning report, listing atrocities and blaming the system that gave successive commandants absolute power over so many people.[295] He observed:

> ...the state of the yard, from the blood running down men's backs, mingled with the water used in washing them when taken down from the triangle - the degrading scene of a large number of men...waiting their turn to be tortured, and the more humiliating spectacle presented by those who had undergone the scourging...were painful to listen to.[296]

In the thirty years that Norfolk Island was settled for a second time, there were sixteen commandants, most of whom lasted less than a year.[297] Lieutenant-Colonel James Thomas Morisset (1829-1834), Major Joseph Anderson (1834-

---

[291] Ibid, West, John, *The History of Tasmania*, p. 397.

[292] Causer, Tim, 'Norfolk Island's 'suicide lotteries': myth and reality', unpublished paper, pp. 5-6.

[293] Stuart, Robert Pringle, and Naylor, Thomas Beagley, *Norfolk Island, 1846: the accounts of Robert Pringle Stuart and Thomas Beagley Naylor*, (Sullivan's Cove), 1979, pp. 9, 12, 18, 23, 27.

[294] *Hobart Courier*, 29 December 1847, printed the evidence Willson gave to the Select Committee the previous June.

[295] 'Norfolk Island Prisoners', *Colonial Times* (Hobart), 15 October 1852, p. 4.

[296] Robert Willson to Sir William Denison, Governor of VDL, 22 May 1852, Convict Discipline and Transportation, Further Correspondence, *Parliamentary Papers*, Vol. LXXXII, (1852-1853), p. 89.

[297] Britts, M. G., *The Commandants: The Tyrants Who Ruled Norfolk Island*, (Herron Publications), 1980.

1839),[298] Captain Alexander Maconochie (1840-1844) and John Giles Price (1846-1853)[299] lasted significantly longer and of them Morisset and Price were regarded as exceptionally harsh. Only Maconochie concluded that brutality bred defiance and attempted to apply his theories of penal reform, providing incentives as well as punishment.[300] His methods were criticised by many in the settler community as being too lenient and, although he had the support of Sir George Gipps, the NSW Governor who briefly visited the island in 1843, he was recalled by the Colonial Secretary Lord Stanley who stated that 'Norfolk Island would again become a place of the severest punishment'.[301] Apart from Price, all the commandants were military officers, brought up in a system where discipline was severe and they relied on a large number of military guards, civil overseers, ex-convict constables and convict informers to provide them with intelligence and carry out their orders. They ruled a brutalised and brutalising society.

Recent research provides a more nuanced view of the convicts who were transported to Norfolk Island between 1825 and 1855.[302] This has called into question the accuracy of the received interpretation that the convicts were the most incorrigible men transported to NSW and VDL and that they had been re-transported to Norfolk Island as a result of further offences. Causer's database of 6,458 Norfolk Island convicts shows that 3,860 were originally transported to NSW or VDL and also 165 men were either free or native-born, but that 2,403 men were transported directly from England immediately challenging the theory that all the prisoners were doubly convicted.[303] The age, marital status, occupation and literacy of the Norfolk Island convicts broadly corresponded with the conclusions reached in *Convict Workers*: transportees were generally of

---

[298] Barry, John V., 'Anderson, Joseph (1790-1877)', *ADB*, Vol. 1, pp. 13-14. Atkins, Thomas, *Reminiscences of Twelve Years' Residence in Tasmania and New South Wales*, (Printed and published at the *Advertiser* Office, Malvern) 1869, pp. 21-57, gives a very critical account of Anderson's brutality from the viewpoint of the Church of England chaplain on the island from November 1836 to January 1837.

[299] Barry, John V., *The life and death of John Price: a study of the exercise of naked power*, (Melbourne University Press), 1964, and more succinctly 'Price, John Giles (1808-1857)', *ADB*, Vol. 2, pp. 351-352.

[300] Barry, John V., 'Maconochie, Alexander (1787-1860)', *ADB*, Vol. 2, pp. 185-186. See also, Ward, Gerard, 'Captain Alexander Maconochie, R.N., K.H., 1787-1860', *Geographical Journal*, Vol. 126, (4), (1960), pp. 459-468. Maconochie, Alexander, *Norfolk Island*, (J. Hatchard), 1847, gives a brief overview of his experience. Morris, Norval, *Maconochie's gentlemen: the story of Norfolk Island & the roots of modern prison reform*, (Oxford University Press), 2004, pp. 1-160, details Maconochie's period as commandant using a unique combination of fictionalised history and critical commentary.

[301] On Gipps' visit to Norfolk Island, see 'The Governor's Visit to Norfolk Island', *The Australian*, 13 February 1843, p. 2, 'Norfolk Island', *Australasian Chronicle*, 2 March 1843, p. 2.

[302] What follows draws on Causer, Tim, 'The worst types of sub-human beings'? The myth and reality of the convicts of the Norfolk Island penal settlement, 1825-1855', http://www.academia.edu/1109979/The_worst_types_of_subhuman_beings_The_myth_and_reality_of_the_convicts_of_the_Norfolk_Island_penal_settlement_1825-1855

[303] 730 men were transported from England and Ireland in 1840 for Alexander Maconochie's experimental system while 1,703 were transported from England between 1844 and 1846 to undergo a period of probation.

prime working age, most were single and most were functionally literate although Norfolk Island men were slightly less skilled overall largely because of the greater proportion of unskilled rural workers essential for the labour-intensive farming on Norfolk Island.[304]

The strongly expressed views of contemporaries, something reinforced by later historians is that the penal settlement on Norfolk Island was established to detain a particularly dangerous sub-stratum of depraved criminals. In fact, few of them had originally been transported for explicitly violent offences and 70 per cent were convicted of non-violent crimes against property, a conclusion that accords with the sample used in *Convict Workers*. Why did these men eventually end up on Norfolk Island?[305] Of the 3,840 men sent from NSW and VDL to Norfolk Island, only 2,258 men were recorded as being detained under a colonial conviction. The majority (66.5 per cent) were reconvicted of non-violent property offences, mostly burglary, housebreaking, highway robbery and stock theft. Just over a fifth of Norfolk Island convicts were detained for explicitly violent offences, a much lower proportion than might be expected. Beyond those transported to Norfolk Island by order of a colonial court, the fate of the remaining NSW and VDL men exposed the system's arbitrariness. A number were removed from other penal stations to Norfolk Island; for instance, 60 capital respites and lifers were transferred from Port Macquarie in July 1830 and 109 men from Cockatoo Island in two drafts during 1844 and 1848. Nearly 55 per cent of the convicts were sent to Norfolk Island either under their original sentence of transportation or without being subject to a colonial conviction. The 'deviancy' of Norfolk Island's convicts was and is embedded in the public imagination but Causer's research demonstrates that the convicts were not necessarily the most depraved in the colonies. This, however, does not alter the fact that the conditions in which they lived were regarded as unremittingly brutal.

Rebellion in 1834

Convict rebellions were a feature of Norfolk Island almost from its foundation. There was a spate of small-scale risings between 1826 and 1830. In September 1826, an attempt was made by convicts led by 'Black' John Goff to escape from the island by boat, having been told that there was an island within a hundred miles where they could safely hide and never be found. While most of the soldiers were chasing two absconders, about fifty prisoners seized and bound their overseers, robbed the Stores for provisions and weapons and put three boats to sea, killing a soldier and wound others. The commandant, Captain Vance Young Donaldson and soldiers followed them to the nearby small and uninhabited Phillip Island, where they were captured.[306] The ringleaders—Goff,

---

[304] Causer, Tim, 'The worst types of sub-human beings'? The myth and reality of the convicts of the Norfolk Island penal settlement, 1825-1855', pp. 4-17. On the conclusions of *Convict Workers*, see above pp. 276-280.

[305] Causer, Tim, 'The worst types of sub-human beings'? The myth and reality of the convicts of the Norfolk Island penal settlement, 1825-1855', pp. 17-30.

[306] *HRA*, Series I: Vol. 15, pp. 596-597, 'Insurrection at Norfolk Island', *Sydney Gazette and New South Wales Advertiser*, 6 April 1827, p. 2.

William Moore and Edward Watson--were sent to 'Sydney for trial and were sentenced to death in 1827.[307]

On 21 December 1826, the ship *Wellington* was seized by the 66 convicts it was taking to Norfolk Island.[308] 20 of the ship's crew and soldiers were kept prisoners.[309] The *Wellington* then sailed to the Bay of Islands in New Zealand, where they were recaptured by a whaler, *The Sisters* under the command of Captain Duke.[310] Because of their good treatment of the captured ship's guards and crew, only five of the prisoners were executed although 23 were condemned to hang. There was a further uprising in 1827 with an attempt made on the life of new commandant Thomas Wright by Patrick Clynch who was captured and then summarily shot.[311] Wright was later arrested for ordering Clynch's murder and put on trial but was acquited.[312] In 1830 there was a successful escape of convicts from the island on a whaleboat. They went to Phillip Island, where they robbed Mr Cunningham, a visiting botanist. They then took to sea and were never heard of again, presumably they all drowned.[313]

Lieutenant-Colonel James Thomas Morisset was appointed commandant of Norfolk Island in 1829.[314] During his period in office, the convict population grew from about 200 to over 700 by 1832 and there were several attempts at rebellion that were strenuously suppressed. Governor Darling was supportive of Morisset, regarding him 'a very Zealous Officer' whose duties were of 'a most arduous nature' observing that 'the Conduct of the Prisoners has of late been outrageous in the extreme, having repeatedly avowed...to Murder every one employed at the Settlement, and it is only by the utmost vigilance that they have been prevented accomplishing their object.'[315] There was, however, growing criticism of Morisset's rule within the more radical sections of NSW society. In 1832, Edward Hall, editor of the *Sydney Gazette*, wrote that the convicts on Norfolk Island had been:

> ...made the prey of hunger and nakedness at the caprice of monsters in human form...and cut to pieces by the scourge...have no redress or the least enquiry made into their suffering.[316]

---

[307] 'Supreme Court', *Sydney Gazette and New South Wales Advertiser*, 24 September 1827, p. 2.

[308] 'Piratical Seizure of the Brig Wellington', *Sydney Gazette and New South Wales Advertiser*, 19 February 1827, p. 2.

[309] 'Further Particulars of the Piratical Seizure and re-capture of the Brig Wellington', *The Sydney Monitor*, 17 February 1827, p. 5.

[310] 'Piracy by Prisoners and Re-Capture', *The Australian*, 10 February 1827, p. 3.

[311] 'Domestic Intelligence', *The Sydney Monitor*, 8 June 1829, p. 2.

[312] 'Important Trial', *The Sydney Monitor*, 17 October 1829, pp. 1, 2.

[313] 'Norfolk Island', *Sydney Gazette and New South Wales Advertiser*, 30 October 1830, p. 2.

[314] Parsons, Vivienne, 'Morisset, James Thomas (1780-1852)', *ADB*, Vol. 2, pp. 260-261. See, Huskisson to Darling, 19 May 1828, *HRA*, Series I: Vol. 14, pp. 192-193, and Darling to Sir George Murray, 12 February 1829, *HRA*, Series I: Vol. 14, pp. 641-642.

[315] Darling to Goderich, 26 August 1831, *HRA*, Series I: Vol. 16, p. 339

[316] 'Editorial', *Sydney Gazette and New South Wales Advertiser*, 4 December 1832, p. 2.

By the beginning of 1834, there were widespread rumours of rebellion across the island.[317] According to a convict named Laurence Frayne, Morisset was about to flog confessions out of the convicts, as the Reverend Samuel Marsden had done to Irish convicts thirty years earlier. Morisset was increasingly incapacitated by a head wound he had received in 1811 during the Peninsular War and had already decided to sell his commission. In practice, the running of the island was devolved to his second-in-command, Captain Foster Fyans.[318] Fyans was an experienced officer who had served in Portugal and Spain between 1811 and 1814 and in India and Mauritius from 1818 until he arrived in Sydney in 1833. He was firm but fair in his attitude to convicts and later wrote of his experience as commandant of the Moreton Bay penal colony:

> Five hundred convicts on this establishment were well and usefully employed; there was none of that lurking feeling in the men, and I may add that the settlement appeared to me not unlike a free overgrown establishment...I was always of opinion that mitigation to the deserving tended to good, and feel not sorry to acknowledge that I was instrumental to mitigating to a great extent seventy convicts, and well pleased often I have been in meeting some of these men doing well in the world as respectable citizens, and only in one solitary instance I failed in my hope.[319]

However, his view of Norfolk Island was emphatic: 'to the latest hour [it] was a disgrace to England...the true discipline of the penal settlement subverted.'

Fyans was right to be concerned as an anonymous note, left in the soldiers' barracks warned them to 'beware of poison'. He had clear memories of a plot hatched by fifteen convicts two years before on the *Governor Phillip* to poison the ship's company with arsenic in their food on the voyage to Norfolk Island. Fortunately, this attempt was prevented by one of his fellow prisoners turning informer. Fyans was especially concerned by John Knatchbull in whose cabin a pound of arsenic was found though neither he nor the other convicts were charged.[320] Knatchbull came from a privileged landed background, the son of Sir Edward Knatchbull and his second wife. Educated at Winchester School, he had volunteered for the navy in 1804 becoming a lieutenant in 1810 and retiring on full-pay after Napoleon's defeat at Waterloo.[321] The Admiralty stopped his

---

[317] Kercher, Bruce, *Outsiders: tales from the Supreme Court of NSW, 1824-1836*, (Australian Scholarly Publishing), 2006, pp. 109-124 considers violence on Norfolk Island. *R v. Douglas and others*, Supreme Court of NSW, July 1834, printed in *Sydney Gazette and New South Wales Advertiser Supplement*, 13 September 1834, p. 1, *Sydney Gazette and New South Wales Advertiser Supplement*, 20 September 1834, p. 1, *Sydney Gazette and New South Wales Advertiser Supplement*, 27 September, 1834, p. 1, see http://www.law.mq.edu.au/scnsw/Cases1834/html/r_v_douglas_and_others__1834.htm

[318] Brown, P. L., 'Fyans, Foster (1790-1870)', *ADB*, Vol. 1, pp. 422-424. See also, *Memoirs recorded at Geelong, Victoria, Australia by Captain Foster Fyans, 1790-1870: transcribed from his holograph manuscript given by descendants to the State Library, Melbourne 1962*, (Geelong Advertiser), 1986.

[319] Cit, ibid, Brown, P. L., 'Fyans, Foster (1790-1870)', p. 424.

[320] 'Diabolical Conspiracy to Murder…', *Sydney Gazette and New South Wales Advertiser*, 4 December 1832, p. 2, detailed the 'diabolical conspiracy'.

[321] 'Knatchbull, John (1792?-1844)', *ADB*, Vol. 2, pp. 65-66, and Knatchbull, John, *Life of John Knatchbull. Written by Himself, 23rd January-13th February, 1844, in Darlinghurst*

pay in 1818 because of a debt he incurred in the Azores. Convicted of stealing with force and arms in 1824, he was sentenced to transportation for fourteen years and arrived in NSW in April 1825. Initially, he adapted well to the colonial environment and was given his ticket-of-leave in 1829. However, two years later, he was successfully prosecuted for forgery but his death sentence was commuted to transportation for seven years to Norfolk Island where he arrived on the *Governor Phillip* in late 1832.[322] Knatchbull was central to the rebellion as the only way off the island was by ship and claimed that although he was unable to take part, he had offered to command a ship to South America if one could be captured.

On 1 August 1833, Knatchbull, George Farrell and Dominick McCoy agreed on a complex plan. First, it linked the convicts in the lumberyard and sawpits to those at the lime-burners' kiln and the stone quarry and called for a simultaneous rebellion. At the dawn muster in the convict barracks yard, they would rush Fyans and his soldiers and overpower them. If any of the guard managed to barricade themselves in the guardhouse, the prisoners would set fire to it and flush them out. Meanwhile the gaol gang, made up of prisoners under special punishment, would also rush their own guard as they were being mustered for work in the stone quarry. The rebels would then seize the apparatus of colonial rule. The two columns of convicts would then advance on Government House and capture Morisset, seize the 18-pound cannon there and turn it on the military barracks. If the soldiers surrendered they would be spared; if not, they would hang with the hated convict constables, overseers and informers. Finally, the convicts would escape from the island. They would force Morisset to hand over his codebook of signals, so that they could flag false messages to the next ship to anchor off the reef. They would get on board by wearing the overseers' blue jackets and seize the vessel that Knatchbull would pilot to America, for 'if he once got there, the Americans would not allow them to be given up again.' In the months between the formulation of the plan and the rebellion, Redmond Moss successfully carried messages between the different gangs.

Shortly after 5 am on Wednesday 15 January 1834, men in the military barracks heard a ragged volley of musket fire. The rebellion had begun. At the dawn muster in the prisoners' barracks thirty-eight men, an unusually large number, had reported sick and were marched off to hospital by John Higgins, a warder. Once inside the hospital lockup, they overpowered Higgins and locked him in a sickroom. The prisoners struck off each other's irons, burst into the wards and armed themselves with weapons ranging from chair legs to scalpels and a poker. Some even found axes. They massed in the entrance of the hospital in silence, ready to fall on the guard when it came by. A hundred yards away this guard was mustering the gaol gang, about thirty convicts under the eye of a corporal and twelve privates of the 4th King's Own Regiment. The guard

---

Gaol, first pub., Roderick, Colin, (ed.), *John Knatchbull from Quarterdeck to Gallows*, (Angus and Robertson), 1963.

322 See, 'Diabolical Conspiracy to murder the crew and guard of the *Governor Philip* transport on her passage to Norfolk Island', *Sydney Gazette and New South Wales Advertiser*, 4 December 1832, p. 2, and the report in *Hobart Town Courier*, 4 January 1833, p. 2.

corporal ordered the prisoners to march, but they would not budge. They stood there, rattling their chains. The signal was given. At that moment, Frayne looked toward the sawpits and cried, 'Are you ready?' Seconds later, forty convicts from the sawpits attacked the guards from behind, while the hospital gang burst from hiding and attacked their front. Taken completely by surprise, the soldiers could not get their weapons to their shoulders. The convicts 'were within the bayonets of the Guard, before they were aware of them' and for a few moments the convicts and guards locked, grappling for their guns. After a brief melee, military discipline prevailed and the guards now began firing as they backed into the gateway of the gaol, frantically loading and firing while their comrades kept the lunging convicts back at sabre-point. Several convicts, including Henry Drummond, one of the ringleaders went down and, as suddenly as it began, the fracas broke up.

Half a mile away in Quality Row, where the barracks and officers' houses stood, Foster Fyans and his reacted quickly to the situation. They double-timed down the road to intercept the mutineers and when they charged again. Fyans gave the order to fire and, when the black-powder smoke cleared fifteen rebels were stretched on the ground while most of the others had plunged into the sugar cane that grew beside the road. Only the remnants of the gaol gang, hampered by their irons stood dumbly in surrender. Soldiers followed the escapees into the vegetable gardens and sugar cane. Fyans then led a detachment up the hill to deal with the convicts at the agricultural station at Longridge. They had lookouts where they could see the Kingston gaol buildings and signal the start of the mutiny. Convicts crowded exultantly around and Walter Bourke, their leader smashed the lock on the main tool chest and started passing out axes and pitchforks to the men. Crying 'Liberty or Death!' about eighty convicts followed him down the road to Flagstaff Hill. They expected to see a victorious crowd of fellow rebels surging to meet them. Instead they saw two men stumbling up the hill, one of them wounded pursued by redcoats. The soldiers fired a few rounds at the rebels, but the range was too great. Soon, they closed in and beat the rebels back to Longridge, taking twenty-eight prisoners on the way. With difficulty, Fyans kept the soldiers from bayoneting them to death on the spot, but felt later that 'perhaps such lenity is ill bestowed'. Within a couple of hours, all the Longridge rebels were subdued and bound together with rope in a line, the soldiers marched them down the hill to Kingston.

By noon, Fyans had the mutineers confined in the main prison barracks, 'nearly one thousand Ruffians', he wrote later. A few were still missing, among them Robert Douglas, who was found later the other side of the island at Anson's Bay, still carrying a musket with ninety rounds of ammunition wrapped in a palm leaf. A bayonet thrust had destroyed his left eye and infection blinded the other a few days later. Fyans interrogated him daily in the hospital, but Douglas refused to say anything about the rebellion. The final tally of casualties was nine rebels dead and about fifty wounded. No guard was killed until the night of 17 January, when two military search parties met in a cornfield while looking for rebels still at large and, each believing the other to be convicts, opened fire. One fluke shot killed both a civilian constable and Thomas York a young private of the 4th Regiment.

Captain Fyans adopted harsh measures against the rebels. Blacksmiths took nine days to make new irons for the prisoners. Rebels locked in the gaol awaiting trial were kept naked in a yard so crowded that not a third of them could sit at a time. For the next five months, while the reports went back to Sydney and arrangements were being made to send a judge to Norfolk Island, the rebels were kept locked to a chain cable. Mass floggings went on into the evening, until the 'desperate lawless and listless mob' had been scourged into submission. Some convicts, weary of their 'acute and intolerable sufferings', according to Fyans alone, planned to commit group suicide, but never put their plan into action. It took Fyans and his staff five months to interrogate all the witnesses and take their depositions for trial. In this, Fyans was supported from March 1834 by Joseph Anderson, the new commandant of the island. Of those charged with mutiny, half were lifers and another third had sentences of fourteen years. During the rebellion's suppression, Knatchbull turned informer. 162 rebels were charged but the Attorney-General ruled that only 59 should be tried. The trials took place on Norfolk Island in July and twenty-nine rebels were sentenced to death.[323] Thirteen were eventually executed in front of their fellows on 22 and 23 September.

After the trials, Judge Sir William Burton severely reprimanded Fyans:

> Most improperly, Sir, did you act as a magistrate, in accepting a confession from Knatchbull; neither should any deposition have been taken from him. Throughout the trials his name has been connected in every case: he was the chief of the mutineers, the man you should have named first in the Calendar. You have saved his life, or prolonged it. He never can do good.

Fyans blamed himself for saving Knatchbull's neck by accepting his depositions and 'for so gross an act, in setting this monster loose on society.' Burton was proved right. Knatchbull returned from Norfolk Island in May 1839[324] and gained his second ticket-of-leave in July 1842 but was hanged early in 1844 for the murder of Ellen Jamieson, a shopkeeper.[325] There had been little surprise at the outcome of his trial since he had been caught red-handed with £17 taken from the victim and the public called for hime to be hanged. Defended by Robert Lowe, later British Home Secretary, the trial was not

---

[323] The trial of the rebels, *R v. Douglas and others*, Supreme Court of NSW, July 1834, printed in *Sydney Gazette and New South Wales Advertiser*, 13, 20, 27 September, 1834. The *Sydney Herald* and *Australian* gave no formal reports of these trials, although the *Australian* listed them on 22 August 1834. The *Sydney Herald* reported the second to seventh trials on 27 September 1834. Bourke to Spring Rice, 15 January 1835, *HRA*, Series I: Vol. 17, pp. 638-639, provides the only 'official' discussion of the rebellion and trials.

[324] By 1839, fifteen years had elapsed since his initial sentence and Knatchbull assumed that his absolute pardon would follow when he wrote a most eloquent petition informing Governor Gipps after his return from Norfolk Island. His hopes were dashed by the note the Barracks clerk, Thomas Ryan, penned on the back of the document, repeating the unproven claim that Knatchbull had tried to poison the ship's crew on the *Governor Phillip*. Ryan also drew the governor's attention to the regulation that recommended a colonial conviction should not be served concurrently but be added to the original sentence. Rather than being released, Knatchbull was re-transported to Port Macquarie

[325] See, NSW State Archives, Supreme Court: Police report on John Knatchbull, 1844, 9/6329, No. 135.

delayed by Lowe's attempt to get an adjournment to seek medical opinion on Knatchbull's sanity. Since Lowe could not offer a defence questioning what happened, he chose to argue a novel case for moral insanity.[326] This was rejected both by Judge Burton and the jury that found him guilty, a verdict widely supported in the press and by the public.[327] His execution on 13 February 1844 was attended by at least 5,000 people with *The Australian* putting the figure at double that amount.[328]

A final flourish

There were minor disturbances in 1841, 1842 and 1843 but a more violent affair in 1846.[329] Joseph Childs, commandant from 1844 to 1846, proved to be no match for the hardened convicts largely because he had no experience of life in a penal settlement.[330] When Robert Pringle Stuart visited Norfolk Island, he reported that Childs was 'a most amiable benevolent gentleman and honourable officer' but that what was needed to avoid anarchy and insubordination was 'an officer of experience in, or capacity for, government, judgement, energy, decision and firmness'.[331] Childs was recalled but, before he left, a group of convicts revolted in July 1846, murdering four officials.[332]

As was usual with new commandants, Childs had cracked down on discipline and removed some privileges that convicts had become accustomed to. On 1 July 1846, William Westwood, a convicted bushranger also known as 'Jackey Jackey' led a mutiny provoked by Childs' decision the previous day to remove the prisoners' tins and knives and other utensils used for cooking their food and that all food would in future be cooked for them.[333] He attacked and brutally killed two overseers, a guard who called out that he had seen it all and another guard who was asleep. In half an hour, the military restored order at the point of the bayonet and convicts who had joined the riot quickly returned to their cells. Sentenced to death with twelve others, Westwood was hanged on 13 October by Childs' successor, John Price, who considered Childs responsible for

---

[326] 'Supreme Court', *Sydney Morning Herald*, 25 January 1844, p. 2. See also, 'Mental Epidemics', *The Australian*, 1 February 1844, p. 2, and 'Monomania', *Sydney Morning Chronicle*, 3 February 1844. The debate over Lowe's novel defence continued after the execution, see *Sydney Morning Chronicle*, 8 June 1844, p. 3.

[327] On *R v. Knatchbull* and the defence of 'moral insanity', see Woods, Gregory D., *A history of criminal law in New South Wales: the colonial period 1788-1900*, (Federation Press), 2002, pp. 159-162.

[328] The execution was reported in 'Execution of Knatchbull', *Sydney Morning Herald*, 14 February 1844, p. 2, and 'Execution of John Knatchbull', *The Australian*, 15 February 1844, p. 3.

[329] On the attempted escape on the *Governor Phillip*, see Gipps to Lord Stanley, 15 August 1842, *HRA* Series I: Vol. 22, pp. 200-201.

[330] Barry, John V., 'Childs, Joseph (1787-1870)', *ADB*, Vol. 1, pp. 220-221.

[331] Ibid, Stuart, Robert Pringle, and Naylor, Thomas Beagley, *Norfolk Island, 1846: the accounts of Robert Pringle Stuart and Thomas Beagley Naylor*, p. 69.

[332] 'Disturbances at Norfolk Island', *The Australian*, 8 August 1846, provides an account of events.

[333] Rutledge, Martha, 'Westwood, William [Jackey Jackey] (1820-1846)', *ADB*, Supplementary Volume, pp. 404-405.

the state of affairs that led to the revolt.[334] A contemporary report blamed the situation on Childs' 'utter imbecility'.[335] There was one last act of convict defiance when, in March 1853, some convicts seized a government launch and attempted to row to freedom. In July, news was received that the launch had reached the coast of NSW and some of the runaways had been captured.

From the mid-1840s, there was growing pressure to end transportation to VDL, something that was finally achieved in 1853. The cost of maintaining the penal settlement on Norfolk Island was growing and Port Arthur in VDL was a less costly alternative. This combined with increasing criticism by magistrates and clergymen of the nature of penal rule on Norfolk Island led to the decision to abandon the island for a second time.[336] The process began in 1847 and was completed in May 1855 when the last convicts were moved to VDL.[337] There was a further factor that played a part in this decision. With some irony, Earl Grey, the Colonial Secretary, saw Norfolk as a possible home for the inhabitants of Pitcairn Islands, descendants of the mutineers from the *Bounty* and their Tahitian-Polynesian wives.[338]

Convict rebellion beyond Australia

Although it is undoubtedly the best known, the use of convict labour was not confined to the Australian colonies. Convicts transported to South-East Asia in the late-eighteenth and early-nineteenth centuries were part of a global system of forced migration. Together with slaves and bonded and indentured labourers, they helped settle and colonise the overseas European Empires. [339] Along with the convicts sent to Australia from Britain and Ireland, they were:

> ...part of a larger international and intercontinental flow of forced migration including ... French, Spanish and Russian convicts, and 'bonded' Indian and Melanesian contract labour. After 1820 a quarter of a million convicts were shipped across the world's oceans to colonise Australia, New Caledonia, Singapore and French Guiana, and to meet labour demand in Gibraltar, Bermuda, Penang, Malacca and Mauritius....Transportation, like the recruiting of slaves and the contracting of bonded workers, was complementary to

[334] 'Norfolk Island', *The Australian*, 14 November 1846, p. 3.

[335] Rogers, Henry, (ed.), *Essays, Selected from Contributions to the Edinburgh Review*, 2 Vols. (Longman, Brown, Green and Longmans), 1850, Vol. 2, 'Treatment of Criminals', p. 506. The article was originally published in 1847.

[336] 'Norfolk Island and Transportation', *The Australian*, 18 February 1847, p. 2, indicated that the 'island establishment is to be immediately reduced to a very small scale'.

[337] Earl Grey to Sir Charles Fitzroy, 27 February 1847, *HRA*, Series I: Vol. 25, pp. 375-376.

[338] Murray, Thomas Boyles, *Pitcairn, the island, the people, and the pastor: to which is added a short notice of the original settlement and present condition of Norfolk Island*, (Society for Promoting Christian Knowledge), 1857, pp. 363-428, provides a valuable contemporary account of this process. See also, Belcher, Lady, (Diana Joliffe), *The Mutineers of the Bounty and Their Descendants in Pitcairn and Norfolk Islands*, (Harmer & Brothers Publishers), 1871.

[339] Allen, Richard B., *European Slave Trading in the Indian Ocean, 1500-1850*, (Ohio University Press), 2015, and Amrith, Sunil S., *Bay of Bengal: The Furies of Nature and the Fortunes of Migrants*, (Havard University Press), 2013, pp. 101-143.

the international migration of free European peoples before 1914. Convictism was a labour system existing in many countries of the world in the nineteenth century.[340]

Recent writing has designated them as 'convict workers', an emphasis that shifts attention away from their earlier characterisation as 'professional and habitual criminals' to highlight their lived experiences in the penal settlements. Indian 'convict workers' filled a critical need for labour in South-East Asia, playing an especially significant role in carrying out the public works projects that were so essential to the establishment and consolidation of the British Empire in the region. This convict system came to an end in the late-nineteenth century.[341]

Smaller in scale and far less known are the movements of convicts from South Asia to South-East Asia.[342] From 1788, the British government of India began the transportation of convicts. Yang explains that the British Crown had a dual purpose for the forced migration of Indian convicts to South-East Asia: it was a harsh alternative to capital punishment and functioned as a deterrent for Indians and it provided labour to British Imperial projects, especially in South-East Asian colonies.[343] The first convicts were sent to Penang in 1790. 4,000-6,000 convicts sentenced to more than seven years were transported to Bencoolen, Sumatra between 1789 and 1825 and 15,000 to the Straits Settlements between 1790 and 1860.[344] From 1825, Malacca and Singapore also became convict stations. Up to 40 per cent of convicts elected to stay in South-East Asia after they had served their terms and integrated into the local populations.[345] This reciprocal system worked well until the British began dumping Indian mutineers and rebels from the Sepoy Rebellion (1857-1859) into the South-East Asian colonies. At that point, the local administrators refused to accept any more transportees and the system of forced Indian convict migration came to an end.[346] Another 1,000-1,500 were transported from Ceylon to Malacca in the Straits Settlements between 1849 and 1873 and several thousand more were sent to Burma and to areas outside of Southeast Asia,

---

[340] Ibid, Nicholas, S., (ed.), *Convict Workers*, p. 7.

[341] Anderson, Clare, 'Penal Settlement in Southeast Asia', in Ooi, Keat Gin, (ed.), *Southeast Asia: A historical encyclopedia, from Angkor Wat to East to East Timor*, 3 Vols. (ABC-Clio), 2004, Vol. 1, pp. 1046-1047, provides a succinct overview.

[342] See, Yang, Anand A., 'Indian Convict Workers in Southeast Asia in the Late Eighteenth and Early Nineteenth Centuries', *Journal of World History*, Vol. 14, (2), (2003), pp. 179-208.

[343] Ibid, Yang, Anand A., 'Indian Convict Workers in Southeast Asia in the Late Eighteenth and Early Nineteenth Centuries', p. 201.

[344] Bencoolen is now called Bengkulu. From 1824 until the Japanese occupation, it was part of the Dutch East Indies. It is one of the Provinces of Indonesia and is located on the wouthwest coast of Sumatra.

[345] Ibid, Yang, Anand A., 'Indian Convict Workers in Southeast Asia in the Late Eighteenth and Early Nineteenth Centuries', p. 204.

[346] Prasad, G. S. V., and Kanakarathnam, N., 'Colonial India and transportation: Indian convicts in south East Asia and elsewhere', *International Journal of Applied Research*, Vol. 1, (13), (2015), pp. 5-8.

principally Mauritius between 1815 and 1837 and the Andaman Islands after 1857.[347]

Singapore

In 1787, the British began the transportation of English convicts to Australia, the same year that the British government of India began the transportation of convicts to Bencoolen, a penal settlement in Sumatra.[348] The following year, Indian convicts who were sentenced to more than seven years' imprisonment started to be transported to Penang. From 1825, Malacca and Singapore also became convict stations.[349] Singapore received its first batch of convicts--80 men and women from Madras--on 18 April 1825 and a week later, a second group of 122 convicts arrived from Bengal.[350] Singapore quickly became the major convict centre among the Straits Settlements[351] because of the colony's speedy development. Also, because the Indian population in Singapore was smaller than that in Penang where a larger Indian community was already established, it was harder for Indian convicts to escape into the community.[352] Convicts were essential to the economy of the Straits Settlements as a steady supply of cheap labour, and although the European community had no objections to receiving Indian convicts, some maintained that such labour was inefficient, slow and ill-supervised.[353] By 1841, the Straits Settlements had become the 'Sydney convict settlements of British India' and there were between 1,100 and 1,200 of such transported convicts just in Singapore. In 1845, the numbers of 'local and

---

[347] Several convicts were transported to NSW from India most of whom had been tried by military courts.

[348] McNair, J. F. A., *Prisoners their own warders: A record of the convict prison at Singapore in the Straits Settlements, established 1825, discontinued 1873, together with a cursory history of the convict establishments at Bencoolen, Penang and Malacca from the year*, (Hardpress Publishing), 2013, p. 1. Tan, Bonny, 'Convict Labour in Colonial Singapore', *Bibliosia*, October-December 2015, pp. 36-41.

[349] Turnbull, C. M., *The Straits Settlements, 1826-67: Indian Presidency to Crown Colony*, (Athlone Press), 1972, p. 47.

[350] Ibid, McNair, J. F. A., *Prisoners their own warders: A record of the convict prison at Singapore in the Straits Settlements, established 1825, discontinued 1873, together with a cursory history of the convict establishments at Bencoolen, Penang and Malacca from the year*, p. 39.

[351] Makepeace, W., Brooke, G. E., and Braddell, R. St. J., (eds.), *One hundred years of Singapore*, 2 Vols. (Oxford University Press), 1991, Vol. 1, p. 512; Vol. 2, pp. 282-286, and ibid, Turnbull, C. M., *The Straits Settlements, 1826-67: Indian Presidency to Crown Colony*, pp. 46-49, 51, 104-106, 185, 236, 239, provide useful material on the use of convict labour. For a post-colonial perspective see Pieras, Anoma, *Hidden Hands and Divided Landscapes: A penal history of Singapore's plural society*, (University of Hawaii Press), 2009, pp. 62-94.

[352] Ibid, Turnbull, C. M., *The Straits Settlements, 1826-67: Indian Presidency to Crown Colony*, p. 47.

[353] On the development of Indian society in Singapore from the early-nineteenth century, see, Sandhu, Kernial Singh, *Indians in Malaya*, (Cambridge University Press), 1969, pp. 21-74, Sandhu, Kernial Singh, 'Indian immigration and settlement in Singapore', and Mani, A., 'Indians in Singapore Society', in Sandhu, Kernial Singh, and Mani, A., (eds.), *Indian Communities in Southeast Asia*, (Institute of Southeast Asian Studies), 1993, revised, 2006, pp. 774-809.

continental convicts' had risen to 1,500[354] and by 1860 there were 2,275 convicts in Singapore.[355]

Although the colonial authorities were eager to accept Indian convicts, there was fierce opposition to the transportation of Chinese convicts from Hong Kong, who, with the connivance of secret societies, could easily escape and blend into the general community. In January 1848, a boat carrying 93 Chinese convicts sailed into Singapore and within sight of the island, they murdered the Captain, kidnapped three European passengers and forced the crew to set sail for China. The ship then ran aground, and Malays from a nearby island rescued the passengers and crew, killed some of the convicts and the remaining 23 captives were sent back to Singapore. The incident and a sensational trial that followed led to appeals from the press, grand juries and public to stop the transportation of Chinese convicts to Singapore. But it was only in 1856, after several years of agitation, that their transportation to the Straits was abandoned.[356]

Between 1825 and 1872, Indian convicts made the bulk of the labour force for public works in Singapore. Indian convict labour came largely from the Coromandel Coast especially the Madras area, northern India and Calcutta and was from a variety of castes. Some were political prisoners and a few were of high standing but most were thieves and murderers. They were initially brought to a convict centre at Bencoolen and then transported to the Straits Settlements to serve out their sentences. Initially, convicts were housed in temporary wooden attap huts, built in 1821, located near the east bank at the mouth of the Singapore River. From 1833, they moved to a bigger and more centrally located convict gaol built between Bras Basah Road and Stamford Road that was used until the 1880s. Between 1852 and 1854, when labour costs rose 30 per cent, the government came to rely almost entirely on convict labour for the construction of public works.

Unlike in the Australian penal colonies where convicts were treated with little regard, Sir Stamford Raffles laid the foundation of the Singapore system based on humanitarian and economic principles and the management of convicts was both liberal and effective.[357] Convicts were the solution to the scarcity and expense of labour and Raffles initially sought to improve the living conditions for convicts in Bencoolen. In April 1825, when the British vacated Bencoolen following the Anglo-Dutch Treaty of the previous year that had ceded Sumatra to

---

[354] Ibid, Turnbull, C. M., *The Straits Settlements, 1826-67: Indian Presidency to Crown Colony*, p. 42. Cit, Turnbull, C. M., 'Convicts in the Strait Settlements', 1826-1867', *Journal of the Malaysian Branch of the Royal Asiatic Society*, Vol. 43, (1), (1970), p. 87.

[355] *Singapore Free Press*, 22 July 1847.

[356] Ibid, Turnbull, C. M., *The Straits Settlements, 1826-67: Indian Presidency to Crown Colony*, p. 347

[357] Of the many biographies of Raffles, Raffles, Lady Sophia, *Memoir of the Life and Public Services of Sir Thomas Stamford Raffles...*, (John Murray), 1830, Coupland, R., *Raffles 1781-1826*, (Oxford University Press), 1926, and Alatas, Syed Hussein, *Thomas Stamford Raffles, 1781-1826: Schemer or Reformer?* (Angus and Robertson), 1971 are valuable. Raffles has long been a controversial figure, see Wright, Nadia, 'Sir Stamford Raffles: a Manufactured Hero?', paper presented to the 17th Biennial Conference of the Asian Studies Association of Australia in Melbourne, 1-3 July 2008: http://arts.monash.edu.au/mai/asaa/nadiawright.pdf

Holland, 900 convicts were moved to Singapore that Raffles had founded in 1819 where his system continued to be applied. Until the first convict regulations were devised by Raffles in 1824, convict discipline was relatively lax. The Bencoolen Regulations drew on the carrot-and-stick approach already used in NSW and VDL and formed the basis for later convict regulations such as the 1827 Penang Rules and Butterworth Rules of 1860. Convicts were divided into classes based on the length of sentence, time in the settlement and conduct. The system rewarded good behaviour and punished convicts for misdemeanours. The prospect of ticket-of-leave was held out to all convicts. Good behaviour could be rewarded with a gratuity or appointment to the position of a petty official while poor behaviour could lead to convicts being downgraded or punished by flogging or labour in iron.

Deployed as labourers for the public works, Indian convicts contributed much towards the early development of the Settlement.[358] They first worked clearing land, reclaiming and filling in swamps to create Commercial Square (Raffles Place), Thomson Road and Bukit Timah, making the earliest roads and erecting buildings and bridges. It is not surprising that the Engineer responsible for public works was also appointed Overseer of Convicts.[359] Between 1833 and 1855, George D. Coleman and then Captain Henry Mann were Superintendents of Public Works and Convicts. Mann initiated the system of 'industrial training' among these convicts, something carried on and improved by his successor, Colonel Ronald MacPherson. There was even a complaint that Chief Engineer, Captain George Chancellor Collyer, who spearheaded the building of Fort Canning and the reclamation and development of Collyer Quay, had monopolised convict labour since August 1858. Another prominent person in-charge of convicts was Major J. F. A. McNair, who used industrial-trained convicts to build the gothic-styled St. Andrew's Cathedral.[360] When F. J. Mouat, Inspector-General of Prisons in Bengal visited the Straits in 1861, he commented that its penal settlements provided the most successful industrial training of convicts in the world. Despite the freedom granted them, very few Indian convicts absconded. Over the years many Indian convicts, released in the Straits at the end of their term, married local girls and settled down.[361] Many convicts with savings went into business and bought property, some sought employment with the Public Works Department and skilled artisans were made Sub-Assistant Overseers on Public Works. Others worked in trades they had learnt while in gaol such as plumbers, tailors, printers, shoemakers, stone-cutters and quarry blasters.

---

[358] On how ethnic communities were managed in the context of the colonial urban project in Singapore, see Pieris, Anoma, *Hidden hands and divided landscapes: a penal history of Singapore's plural society*, (University of Hawaii Press), 2009, pp. 1-29, 62-94.

[359] Cheong, C., *Framework and foundation: A history of the Public Works Department*, (Times Editions), 1992, pp. 17, 29, 31, 81, on the use of convict labour.

[360] McNair, J. F. A., *Prisoners their own warders: A record of the convict prison at Singapore in the Straits Settlements established 1825, discontinued 1873, together with a cursory history of the convict establishements at Bencoolen, Penang and Malacca from the year 1797*, (Archibald Constable), 1899, is a valuable account of the convict system.

[361] Ibid, Turnbull, C. M., *The Straits Settlements, 1826-67: Indian Presidency to Crown Colony*, p. 49.

The position of the convict in Singapore was a frequent cause for debate largely because the degree of mobility across penal boundaries was kept conveniently ambivalent by an opportunistic colonial government. There were questions about whether the privileges awarded to convicts contradicted their penal status. The Indian colonial authorities may have seen Singapore as a punitive penal settlement but that was far from the reality of convict experience in a community where labour was in demand. Laws that favoured stricter regulation were constantly being revoked by the government using arguments that were in the convicts' favour. The objective of the Singapore model was to create an industrious body of men operating in large gangs that required little control or supervision. Unlike European convicts who retreated into a hidden and coercive environment, the Indian convict in Singapore became a common public figure.

This helps to explain why rebellion tended to occur during the transportation voyage to Singapore rather than in Singapore itself.[362] For Indian convicts the ship was unfamiliar marking the beginning of their cultural, social and geographical dislocation. Normal Indian religious practices regarding the preparation and eating of food and the performance of ablutions could not be respected in the overcrowded context of a transport ship; in fact, the Indian colonial authorities saw this as an important part of the punishment of transportation. This, combined with the lack of any regulation of convict transports until 1838 after convicts attempted to take over the *Catherine* on its voyage to the Strait Settlements, resulted in a potent cocktail for potential mutiny. Cultural transgressions may have been the prime cause of rebellion but it was made it possible by the slack management of the ships. There were also political factors. In February 1858, forty convicted rebels embarked on the *Julia* bound for Singapore and this led to unrest and mutiny on board. As these men were political prisoners, the authorities promptly transferred them to the Andaman Islands and, much to the annoyance of the Singapore authorities, none were tried for mutiny.

As Singapore grew more prosperous, European merchants began to question the need for continued convict transportation. Despite the obvious benefits of convict labour, there was growing sense of resentment among British residents that Singapore was used as a dumping ground for India's convicts. The *Singapore Free Press* declared that the Straits Settlements was:

> ...the common sewer...for all the scum and refuse of the population of nearly the whole British possessions in the East.[363]

---

[362] From the 1830s there were more than a dozen incidents in which convicts rose against their captains and made a bid for freedom. See, Anderson, Clare, ''The Ferringees are flying—the ship is ours!', The convict middle passage in colonial South and Southeast Asia, 1790-1860', *Indian Economic & Social History Review*, Vol. 42, (2), (2005), pp. 143-186, and 'Convict Passages in the Indian Ocean, c.1790-1860', in Christopher, Emma, Pybus, Cassandra, and Rediker, Marcus, (eds.), *Many middle passages: forced migration and the making of the modern world*, (University of California Press), 2007, pp. 129-149.

[363] *Singapore Free Press*, 25 July 1851, cit, ibid, Turnbull, C. M., *The Straits Settlements, 1826-67*, p. 55.

The end of the transportation was motivated largely by the potential threat from the large population of Indian convicts that increasingly alarmed many inhabitants. This sense of impending rebellion escalated in the 1850s when European immigrants feared that social unrest in China and India would spill over into Singapore. These concerns were heightened by civil war in China and the mutiny in India in 1857. It was apparent from the scare of 1853 when lightning struck St. Andrew's Church and parishioners had to carry out their services in the courthouse. This change of locale prompted a swirl of rumours, especially in the Chinese community that the authorities had sent convicts to gather human heads to placate the evil spirits that had taken up residence in the church. Also in 1853, about a hundred Sikh prisoners, forwarded from Calcutta's Alipur jail, attempted to break out of the Singapore Convict Gaol. This further fuelled the concern of many in city about the presence of dangerous criminals in their midst. Moreover, there was also vocal opposition to plans to add European convicts to Singapore's Indian and Chinese convict population. Governor E. A. Blundell, who took the lead on this issue, spoke out in 1856 against any further importation of Chinese convicts who had been coming in from Hong Kong since the late 1840s. The periodic riots by Chinese and Indians in the 1850s, especially the disturbance by Indian convicts during the Muslim festival of Mohurrum in 1856, did little to allay fears about the growing ethnic mix of the city.[364]

On Wednesday 10 September 1856, the night of the Mohorrum festival in Singapore, a few hundred Indian convicts forced their way out of their lines and lighting their way by torches carried their taboot in procession through the public streets to the house of the Resident Councillor and to the Government offices. This public rioting was their collective response to a government order that prevented them from carrying their taboot through the streets as in former years. They vented their displeasure by noisy cries and excited gestures protesting the curtailment of their freedom. In former years we are told 'they were allowed to indulge in their Saturnalia without restraint, their taboot was the gayest and their processions the noisiest to be seen on public streets'. Once they had vented their grievances, they were persuaded to return quietly to the prison. A year later in August 1857, because of the previous year's protests the local government decided to repeal this order and allow the convicts the liberty of parading the streets during this same festival. The Governor stated that permission was granted under the conviction that 'to refuse it would have the effect of needlessly exasperating the convict body, and of driving them to acts of desperation more dangerous to the peace and good order of the town than those that occurred the previous year'. The convicts, however, are said to have refused to avail themselves of the permission given them.[365]

---

364 Buckley, C. B., *An Anecdotal History of Old Times in Singapore*, (Fraser & Neave, Limited), 1902, reprinted, (Oxford University Press), 1984, pp. 575-631.
365 Ibid, Buckley, C. B., *An Anecdotal History of Old Times in Singapore*, p. 531.

The rising tide of opinion against any further Indian convicts peaked during the Indian Rebellion of 1857-1858.[366] News of the rebellion first filtered through to Singapore in May 1857 and rumours soon circulated that the 3,000 Indian convicts in the colony were planning an imminent rebellion. The resultant panic was compounded when the colonial government in India, faced with having to dispense with huge numbers of mutineers and rebels, suggested transportation to Singapore. One solution considered in Calcutta was to transport them to the Settlements or to send criminals who were already in prison to open up space in the jails for the newest offenders. Singapore authorities were especially angered by the public declaration by the Lieutenant-Governor of Bengal calling for the right to banish to the Straits:

> ...all prisoners sentenced to more than three years imprisonment, whose retention...may, from political reasons, or from the insecurity of their jails, be deemed unadvisable.

Neither suggestion was acceptable in Singapore—or in Burma--where the response from the Governor down was swift and emphatic. Concerns were expressed about the loyalty of its Indian garrison and that British troops should be sent as soon as possible. The justifiable fear was that a new wave of Indian convicts drawn from the ranks of rebels would destabilise the delicate balance within the colony. Nor were the colonial authorities willing to mix these newcomers in with those who were beginning to make their way into these settlements as indentured labourers.[367] Calls for an end to transportation intensified in the 1860s and led to the closing of Singapore as a penal settlement. In 1867, control of the Straits Settlements government administration was transferred from Calcutta to the Colonial Office in London. By 1873, when the system of convict labour ended in Singapore, the convicts were either sent to the Andaman Islands,[368] given freedom to settle in Singapore or repatriated. Instead of returning to India, many who had savings went into business and bought landed property, while some sought employment with the Public Works Department. The skilled artisans were made as sub-assistant overseers for public works.[369]

Because of the conflicting interests of Indian and South-East Asian colonial authorities, transportation never developed as the severe punishment it was intended to be for heinous crimes committed against the 'law and order' regime of the emerging colonial state in India. For the local authorities in Southeast

---

[366] Anderson, Clare, *The Indian Uprising of 1857-8: prisons, prisoners, and rebellion*, (Anthem Press), 2007, pp. 95-126, provides a detailed analysis of the 'panic of 1857' in Singapore.

[367] See, Anderson, Clare, *Convicts in the Indian Ocean: Transportation from South Asia to Mauritius, 1815-53*, (Palgrave), 2000.

[368] Ibid, McNair, J. F. A., *Prisoners their own warders: A record of the convict prison at Singapore in the Straits Settlements, established 1825, discontinued 1873, together with a cursory history of the convict establishments at Bencoolen, Penang and Malacca from the year*, pp. 41, 143–146.

[369] Pieris, A., *Hidden hands and divided landscapes: A penal history of Singapore's plural society*, (University of Hawaii Press), 2009, p. 192.

Asia, Indian convicts were a source of labour, men and a few women who were recruited to form the workforce needed to build the infrastructure of rule in the settlements of Bencoolen, Penang, and Singapore. Colonial labour imperatives defined and shaped convict experiences, as did convict initiatives in fashioning their own community within the larger local society made up of different occupational and ethnic groups.[370]

Andaman Islands

Lying on important East India Company trading routes in the Bay of Bengal, the British first colonised the Andamans in 1793--eight hundred miles off the east coast of India--when they transported three hundred convicts from Bengal to establish a settlement on the Islands. This proved short-lived and in 1796 with outbreaks of disease devastating the settlement, the British abandoned the Islands sending survivors to the neighbouring penal settlement of Prince of Wales Island (Penang). Their strategic position and the need to provide protection for ships wrecked on the islands and prospectors from the attacks of the native population in the 1840s led to plans to to establish a penal settlement on the Andaman Islands[371] that had already been discussed before the Indian rebellion erupted in May 1857.[372] This was, in part, a solution of the growing number of convicts in Indian gaol—something exacerbated in the Sepoy rebellion as rebels destroyed dozens of gaols--because of the increasing reluctance of the Strait Settlements and especially Singapore to accepted further transportees, a situation exacerbated by the aftermath of the rebellion.

Captain Henry Mann had formally annexed the islands on 22 January 1858 when he raised the Union Flag at the harbour at what became Port Blair. Two hundred convicts under Superintendent Dr James Walker followed in early March 1858. The number of convicts increased from 773 in June to 1,330 by late September. Walker was unsympathetic to both convicts and the native population and just two months after the colony was established, he ordered a mass hanging of 81 convicts who had attempted to escape. This led to an attempt by Punjabi inmates to kill him on 1 April 1859 and an unsuccessful rebellion by the natives that was defeated in May. Under Walker's successors, the number of convicts continued to rise reaching almost 7,000 by 1868. The most unexpected

[370] Chanderbali, David, *Indian Indenture in the Straits Settlemens, 1872-1910*, (Peepal Tree), 2008.

[371] Ibid, Anderson, Clare, *The Indian Uprising of 1857-8: prisons, prisoners, and rebellion*, pp. 127-176, Sen, Satadru, *Disciplining Punishment: Colonialism and Convict Society in the Andaman Islands*, (Oxford University Press), 2000, Vaidik, Aparna, *Imperial Andamans: A Spatial History of Britain's Indian Ocean Colony, 1858-1921*, (Palgrave Macmillan), 2010, Murthy, R. V. R., *Andaman and Nicobar Islands: A Saga of Freedom Struggle*, (Kalpaz Publications), 2013, pp. 45-130, and Anderson, Clare, Mazumdar, Madhumita, and Pandya, Vishvajit, (eds.), *New Histories of the Andaman Islands: Landscape, Place and Identity in the Bay of Bengal, 1790-1920*, (Cambridge University Press), 2015, consider the Andaman penal colony.

[372] There had been a previous unsuccessful attempt to colonise the islands in the 1790s. See, Venkateswar, Sita, *Development and ethnocide: colonial practices in the Andaman Islands*, (IWGIA), 2004, pp. 89-92, and more generally on how the native peoples were treated.

act of rebellion was the assassination of the Viceroy of India, the Earl of Mayo, during an official visit to the Andamans in 1872. He had climbed Mount Harriet to enjoy the sunset, and after descending to Hope Town, convict Shere Ali stabbed him in the back. A subsequent investigation amongst convicts living in the town revealed that Ali had received letters describing mainland Wahabi agitation and had thrown a feast the night before the well-planned attack.

It was not until Henry Mann, now a General, returned as Superintendent in 1868 and Chief Commissioner after 1872 that the Singapore system was introduced though it was not formalised until the Andaman and Nicobar regulations were framed eight years later. To create an impression of order in this settlement that grew to 12,000 rebels, murderers, thieves, members of so-called 'criminal tribes' and thousands of native Andamanese, colonial administrators devised a complex system of punishment and reward, control and patronage, utilising systems of labour, segregation, surveillance, medical supervision, and family-based rehabilitation. As these systems emerged, the prisoners themselves became partially and inconsistently self-policing, trying to access the advantages of cooperation with the colonial regime, even as they resisted or remained indifferent towards British authority.[373]

During the early years of the British permanent settlement of the Andamans, the convicts were organised in section gangs (*challan*) under convict gangsmen and were used as forced labour on various development projects. Once they had cleared their initial base on Chatham Island, they cut down jungle, cleared swamps and built the basic infrastructure. Ross Island, with its grand colonial residences, swimming baths, tennis courts and bazaar, became the Islands' headquarters. Over time, the settlement expanded, and as the construction of barracks, stores and roads was completed, there were various experiments in agriculture, including in the cultivation of coffee, cotton and tea. It was always intended that the Islands would become self-sufficient, though this goal was never achieved. In many penal colonies, there were constant tensions between enforcing punishment and extracting labour. As the Andamans penal colony evolved over time, however, and as its basic needs were met, convict occupations further diversified, with convicts employed as servants, boatmen, cooks, ayahs, tailors and clerks.

In the nineteenth century, criminality was generally defined as the reluctance to work.[374] In general, punishment in Victorian Britain and its colonies was geared towards putting the idle to work, within and without the prison. The labour regime in the Andaman Islands was divided very broadly into two phases. In the first phase, which lasted up to ten years, convicts were involved in closely supervised forced labour. This underlined the political supremacy of the colonial state over the individual criminal. It was followed by a period of rehabilitative labour, when convicts worked under conditions of greater autonomy and were given a tangible share in the fruits of their exertions. Offenders could be

---

[373] What follows draws on Sen, Satadru, 'Contexts, Representation and the Colonized Convict: Maulana Thanesari in the Andaman Islands', *Crime, History and Society*, Vol. 8, (2), (2004), pp. 117-139.

[374] Wiener, M., *Reconstructing the criminal: culture, law and policy in England, 1830-1914*, (Cambridge University Press), 1990, p. 47.

rewarded for their obedience and integrated into the legitimate structures and hierarchies of the penal colony. Nine out of ten prisoners were men, including a substantial minority of people from Burma. Female convicts worked in the 'Female Factory,' at domestic work including sewing, and could not leave until they found employment as servants or got married. There were sporadic efforts to introduce women including through family emigration schemes but none proved very successful.

At least some convicts could bypass the initial stage of punitive labour largely because of the colonial state's perpetual search for reliable prison employees. British prison administrators in India in the second half of the nineteenth century preferred convict workers over free employees when it came to appointing guards, overseers, and clerks. Free workers were almost uniformly seen as corrupt, sullen, lazy and disorderly and as agents of disorder among the convict population. Convict employees, on the other hand, tended to be the 'better sort' of prisoners, who had acquired their positions of responsibility by demonstrating their obedience. In the Andaman Islands, free employees were almost completely avoided by the British authorities. There was a ready supply of long-term convicts who could be trained to carry out hierarchically organised tasks.[375] Colonial administrators saw the Andaman Islands not simply a prison, but a colony where people were brought here not simply to be punished, but to be redeemed and re-socialised through the discipline of labour.

The Andamans penal colony bore some resemblance to the early Australian colonies and to the French penal colony of New Caledonia. The Islands did not have an alternative working population or labour supply, other than Indigenous hunter-gatherer peoples who were hostile to colonial invasion. The regime's reliance on convict labour gave prisoners the power to bargain for status, comfort and, ironically, freedom from labour. The settlement's need for qualified clerical staff created an instant élite among literate convicts. The privileged status of clerical workers was part of the folk knowledge of the penal colony. Those identified as potential clerks escaped the humiliating interrogations, the classificatory procedures, the close confinement, the bar fetters (a prime cause of gangrene and death) and the chain gangs that lay ahead for most newly arrived convicts. They also escaped convict uniforms and meagre rations. When Maulana Thanesari arrived in the colony, he was appointed Deputy Chief Clerk at the court of the superintendent of the penal colony. He moved into a comfortable house, and not the barracks in which convicts usually lived in the initial phase of their stay in the Andamans. He was given complete freedom within the confines of the penal colony and was assigned a servant, whose wages were paid by the authorities. For a twenty-seven year-old who had been convicted of sedition and almost hanged, this was a remarkable recovery that would not have been possible on the Indian mainland. However, the frontier conditions and the agenda of rehabilitation combined to create such opportunities in the Andamans.

Not long after his arrival in the islands, Thanesari began to write letters to old acquaintances in Punjab, filled with exaggerated descriptions of his comfortable life and his government job. However, they came to the attention of

---

[375] Ibid, Sen, Satadru, *Disciplining Punishment*, pp. 175-182.

John Lawrence, the Governor of Punjab, who demanded that Thanesari be subjected to hard labour for the duration of his sentence and that Henry Mann, the Superintendent of the settlement, should explain why Thanesari was living an apparently painless life. In spite of this embarrassment, Mann's administration did not retaliate against Thanesari and his house, job and servant were not touched. Tensions between administrators in Calcutta who wanted predictable punishment and administrators in Port Blair who wanted to maximise their own flexibility, was a persistent feature in the history of the penal settlement.[376]

The most persistent cause of resistance and rebellion in the Andamans was less between the colonial authorities and the convicts than between Muslims and Hindus convicts. Employment in the prison administration and the maintenance of the political status of communities defined in terms of religion and race, were closely connected in the Andamans. This connection was by no means universal in nineteenth-century penal colonies. Anderson's study of Mauritius in the first half of the nineteenth century does not reveal any persistent Hindu-Muslim rivalry.[377] In the Andamans, race and religion were both officially recognised as principles of social organisation. European and Eurasian convicts lived separately from other prisoners and were subject to different codes of discipline and punishment. Muslims and Hindus were classified, transported, and fed separately, as were 'up-country men' and those from the south and the east of India. There were regulations in place that recognised and regulated the boundaries of caste.[378] In the twentieth century, the British routinely used subaltern Muslim convicts as overseers with authority over élite Hindu political prisoners and this double deployment of religion and class was resented by at least some of the Hindus and relished by the overseers.

These tensions were particularly evident over cattle-slaughter in the colony. John McLane has dated the modern cow-protection movement on the Indian mainland to Kuka revivalism in Punjab in 1870 and located it within a larger context of Islamic revivalism as well as the mobilisation of Hindu nationalism.[379] It appears that convicts in the Andamans anticipated the Kukas by a year. The specifics of bovine politics in the islands reinforce Freitag's contention that cattle riots in British India functioned to create new public spaces, agendas and organisations in partial autonomy from the state, but they also show how political affiliations could be asserted, negotiated, qualified and represented within such semi-autonomous forums.[380] In April 1869, Muslim convicts in the settlement decided to sacrifice a bull during the Id festival. Hindu prisoners objected vehemently, but the bull was killed anyway. Police intervention prevented a wider riot but the cow-protection battle moved into the local courts and into the domain of convict clerks. When the court disappointed the defenders of the

---

[376] Ibid, Sen, Satadru, *Disciplining Punishment*, p. 96.

[377] Ibid, Anderson, Clare, *Convicts in the Indian Ocean: Transportation from South Asia to Mauritius, 1815-53*, pp. 91-94.

[378] Ibid, Sen, Satadru, *Disciplining Punishment*, pp. 105-106, 221-223.

[379] McLane, J., *Indian nationalism and the early Congress*, (Princeton University Press, 1977), pp. 271-331.

[380] Freitag, S., 'Contesting in Public: Colonial Legacies and Contemporary Communalism', in Ludden, D., (ed.), *Contesting the nation: religion, community, and the politics of democracy in India*, (University of Pennsylvania Press), 1996, pp. 211-223.

local cattle, the enraged Hindus apparently retaliated against Thanesari by framing him unsuccessfully on charges of embezzlement. Convicts recognised that the court in Port Blair was not simply the voice of British administrators, but also the voice of the convict intermediaries who influenced colonial opinion.

The Andaman Islands remained a penal colony until the 1940s and during its existence there were changes in the ways in which political prisoners were dealt with. A distinction can be made between Mutiny-era political prisoners like Thanesari and the thousand political prisoners imprisoned because of nationalist agitation in the twentieth century. The earlier generation of rebels were seen by the British as relatively amenable to reincorporation into the political order of the colonial state, provided they could be attached to the 'right' leadership.[381] Some sought to escape: in March 1868, 238 prisoners absconded but they were all caught within a month; one committed suicide and of the remainder, 87 were hanged. The twentieth century political prisoners were ideologically distinct from the 'common' convicts and not intended for any kind of rehabilitation since the reason for their imprisonment on the islands was their removal from political agitation on the mainland.[382]

Although the nature of penal settlement remained almost the same throughout nineteenth century, meaningful protest was not witnessed before 1912. Political prisoners were isolated from the mas of convicts in the Cellular Jail for all their sentence and were subjected to non-productive forms of labour such as picking oakum. These were punishments that aimed to humiliate and degrade, something vividly described in memoirs written after their release. The nature of resistance and rebellion for these nationalist political prisoners took on a new form. Hunger strikes by the political convicts in the mainland prisons and in the Cellular Jail on the Andamans were an extension of the resistance movement against British colonialism. At the cost of three lives the forty-five day hunger strike of 1933 kept the spirit of anti-colonial struggle alive during the lull created after Gandhi's Civil Disobedience Movement of 1930 and exposed the mistreatment of political prisoners and the degrading and dangerous nature of forced feeding.[383] The colonial bureaucracy was determinate that the use of hunger strike as a technique of insubordination should be discouraged by not making any concessions, yet it was forced to accept a humiliating compromise. On 24 July 1937, 187 political prisoners of Cellular Jail undertook the fourth and last hunger strike that led to all political prisoners being send back to India.

It had been government policy to end transportation since 1921 following the recommendation of the Indian Jails Committee of 1919-1920 and in 1921 the government of India started the process of repatriating Andaman convicts to mainland jails. This led to prison overcrowding across India and early in 1922, transportation of non-political prisoners was renewed. Transportation of political prisoners was restarted ten years later. In practice, it was only stopped during Second World War when Japanese forces captured the Andamans on 23 March

[381] Ibid, Sen, Satadru, *Disciplining Punishment*, pp. 61-75.

[382] Singh, U. K., *Political Prisoners in India*, (Oxford University Press), 1998, pp. 23-69.

[383] Srivastava, Pramod Kumar, 'Resistance and repression in India: the hunger strike at the Andaman cellular jail in 1933', *Crime, History & Societies*, Vol. 7, (2), (2003), pp. 81-102.

1942. The victory of the Allies leading to the surrender of Japan on 15 August 1945 paved the way for the reoccupation of these Islands by the British forces in October 1945. Meanwhile the Home Department of the Government of India had recommended the closure of the penal settlement. The colonial policy of maintaining a penal settlement at Andaman Islands ended shortly before the transfer of power from London to New Delhi in 1947.

Conclusions

During the nineteenth century, there were conflicting approaches to colonial prison administration. The first was grounded in the Benthamite prescription that justice must be consistent and precise, and as such, neither vicious nor merciful and led to attempts to standardise colonial penal practices. However, a second and older tradition, evident in eighteenth-century English criminal justice, made provision for discretion in the enforcement of the law allowing judges, police officers and administrators to be unpredictably merciful.[384] Mercy as an instrument of authority was imprecise, irrational and pre-modern, but it was well-suited to a political environment that privileged personalised ties of deference, gratitude, loyalty and obedience. In England and in Australia's penal colonies the transition between these two ideological positions was complete by mid-nineteenth century while both were still evident in colonial South-East Asia.

This helps to explain why there were significant differences in the ways that convicts were treated in Australia and the approaches used in Singapore and the Andamans. The British sought to standardise penal practices in mainland India and in NSW and VDL while the British in the Andamans and Singapore operated on the understanding that their control over the convict population depended upon the power to intervene personally and randomly in local society. This meant not only the power to be unpredictably punitive, but also the power to be unexpectedly lenient. The combination of draconian force and rehabilitative clemency was an unpredictable combination and led to different forms of resistance and rebellion than in the antipodes where, although there were changes in colonial policy towards convicts, these changes were always directed at ensuring a standardised, non-discretionary structure. Colonial authorities could remit sentences, governors could use their prerogative of mercy and there was widespread use of prison settlements such as Norfolk Island and Port Macquarie for persistent and intransigent offenders but there was far less flexibility in these practices than in Singapore and the Andamans where convicts, once they had earned a degree of trust, were given greater personal autonomy in their activities.

---

[384] Hay, D., Linebaugh, P., and Thompson, E. P., (eds.), *Albion's Fatal Tree: Crime and Society in 18th-century England*, (Penguin), 1975, pp. 39-41.

5 Migration and white settler resistance

...every man is a magistrate on his own estate, you know, and therefore as long as the man is working for you, you have a right to do what you like with him, that is, short of killing.[1]

The movement of individuals, groups or peoples for economic reasons has been and remains an important and controversial feature in people's lives. Whether in search of better hunting grounds, new natural resources to exploit or opportunities for a 'better life', economic migrants have played the most significant role in global settlement. The obverse of this has been resistance from native peoples and later from existing settlers to this process. What may be an opportunity for an economic migrant may be perceived as a threat by those who already occupy the territory. For native peoples, economic migrants represent a danger to their ways of life and to their control over the environment and its resources. For colonists, while economic migrants brought benefits in terms of reducing production costs to landowners and capitalists, they represented competition to existing labour largely because of their lower wages or should white and immigrant labour recognise that they had a common interest as workers, a class threat to the ruling settler élite. Economic migrants have also been seen as a danger to what peoples regarded as their racial purity through the potential for its dilution resulting in the emergence of racial policies to control, limit or even stop further immigration. This chapter explores these attitudes through the question of indentured labour, how colonial labour resisted exploitation and how settlers sought to resist migration.[2]

Indentured labour

Servitude was not confined to slaves or convicts and, from the seventeenth century through to the early-twentieth century, indentured, bonded or contract labour was also widely used.[3] An indentured servant was a labourer under contract to an employer for a fixed period, generally from three to seven years, in exchange for their transportation, food, clothing, lodging and other necessities. Unlike slaves, indentured servants were required to work only for a limited term specified in a signed contract. Like slaves, servants could be bought and sold, could not marry without the permission of their owner, were subject to physical punishment and their obligation to labour was enforceable in the courts. But unlike slaves, if they survived their period of labour, servants would become free members of society. The early tobacco plantations in Virginia were, from the 1620s, worked by indentured servants, most of them young and male recruited in the ports of Bristol and London. About 70 per cent of migrants from England who came to the American colonies between 1630 and 1660 were indentured

[1] Knighton, William, *Forest life in Ceylon*, 2 Vols. (Hurst and Blackett), 1854, Vol. 1, p. 281.

[2] Madhwi, 'Recruiting Indentured Labour for Overseas Colonies, circa 1834-1910', *Social Scientist*, Vol. 43, (2015), pp. 53-68.

[3] Saunders, Kay, (ed.), *Indentured labour in the British Empire, 1834-1920*, (Croom Helm), 1984, and Northrup, David, *Indentured labor in an age of imperialism, 1834-1922*, (Cambridge University Press), 1994. See also, Amrith, Sunil, *Migration and Diaspora in Modern Asia*, (Cambridge University Press), 2011.

servants. Although the trade peaked about 1680 when indentured labourers were increasing replaced by African slaves, it persisted until the 1770s.[4] For instance, on 31 October 1730, Thomas Pitcher, a tailor aged 20 from the parish of St. Peter's, Norwich was indentured to serve William Burge of London, chapman for four years in Virginia 'at £8 per annum courant money of Virginia, £50 penalty...cloths only excepted and provided he is a workman and understands his trade of tailor.'

Migrating labour

Although the focus of this section is on migration to Caribbean colonies, especially British Guiana and to South Africa by Indian and Chinese labour, the use of indentured labour was a global phenomenon.[5] For instance, 90,000 individuals from the south-west Pacific basin were recruited to the British colonies of Queensland and Fiji and approximately 16,000 Pacific islanders went to German Samoa, French Polynesia and New Caledonia. The abolition of the trans-Atlantic slave trade and slavery in Britain's colonies in 1807 and 1833 resulted in the adoption of a system of indentured and other low wage labour. However, this solution to labour shortages had several important implications. Many planters faced with a loss of their slaves and offered the possibility of acquiring labour from Asia or Africa saw their new workers as a different kind of slave. The mechanics of slavery were deep seated and difficult to dismantle. Indentured workers were often housed in empty slave quarters on plantations and were always under scrutiny. Just as the African slaves, they were often restricted to their plantations and severely punished for leaving without permission. Wages and food rations could also be withheld for uncompleted tasks, illness or absence for any reason. In 1871, fifteen estates in British Guiana withheld wages for three months or more. Bonded workers had little recourse to the law if victimised, as many officials sympathised more with the planter than the 'coolie'. In many cases, the seclusion and autonomy of the plantations was such that harsher penalties were common.

Planters in the Caribbean islands were required to maintain a hospital for workers who were ill but many evaded the law and the buildings were hardly hygienic. In 1871, the British Guiana Commission noted that one estate took three years to build a hospital that was then occupied by the manager as his residence.[6] The building was only converted to its proper purpose when the supply of workers to the plantation was withheld, but even then it had no beds.

---

[4] See, Tomlins, Christopher L., 'Indentured servitude in perspective: European migration into North America and the composition of the early American labor force, 1600-1775', in Matson, Cathy D., (ed.), *The economy of early America: historical perspectives & new directions*, (Pennsylvania State University Press), 2006, pp. 146-182, and Tomlins, Christopher L., 'Reconsidering Indentured Servitude: European Migration and the Early American Labor Force, 1600-1775', *Labor History*, Vol. 42, (2001), pp. 5-43.

[5] Northrup, David, 'Migration from Africa, Asia and the South Pacific', *OHBE*, Vol. 3, pp. 88-100.

[6] See, Ithell, W. D., *Report of the commissioners Commission of Inquiry into the Treatment of Immigrants in British Guiana*, 4 Vols. (L. M'Dermott), 1871, and Jenkins, Edward, *The coolie, his rights and wrongs: Notes of a journey to British Guiana, with a review of the system and of the recent commission of inquiry*, (Strahan), 1871.

Some planters, rather than deal with the expense of ill workers, simply threw them off the plantations. Indentured workers often took the place of freed slaves and prevailing racist attitudes affected how these migrant groups were perceived and they were almost inevitably placed on the lowest rung of the social ladder.

Indian labour

In the nineteenth and early-twentieth centuries, the largest number of indentured workers, approximately 1.5 million people, migrated from India.[7] Changing conditions within India, as in many other Asian countries, made migration increasingly a necessity rather than a choice. Altered economic circumstances, political upheaval and ecological disasters such as droughts, floods, and famines led to increased internal migration as rural peasants sought work in the cities or as seasonal labourers, a process facilitated by the construction of the railway network. During the nineteenth century, India's population rose from 185 million to 285 million increasing pressure on rural resources and exacerbating poverty. Famines resulting from crop failure produced large refugee populations and emigration peaked during years of want. Although many Indian communities were close-knit and, in some cases, migration overseas violated certain caste restrictions, many people often felt compelled to abandon their homes and families and seek work in other areas of India or across the ocean to improve their situations. However, only a small portion of this total migratory population was funnelled into indentured labour.[8]

Initial support and opposition to emigration

Two contrasting areas where Indian indentured labour was widely used were in the Caribbean and in South Africa. A growing demand for tea and sugar was instrumental in the growth of sugar plantation in the Caribbean and Indian Ocean. The situation in India was ripe for exploitation by British planters in the former slave-owning colonies, who wished to adopt the indenture system used by South American planters to obtain Chinese labour from the Portuguese settlement of Macao. Under this system labour was recruited for the planters by their agents to work usually five years, during which the employer was legally obliged to provide fixed wages, medical attention and other amenities for the labourers. Once their contracts had elapsed labourers could either renew their term of employment or return to their native land. To the landless unemployed of India emigration offered economic opportunities and since the early

---

[7] Cohen, Robin, *Global Diasporas: An Introduction*, 2nd ed., (Routledge), 2008, pp. 61-82, provides a good overview of the Indian diaspora. See also, Tinker, H., *A New System of Slavery: The Export of Indian Labour Overseas: 1830–1920*, (Oxford University Press), 1974, and Thiara, Ravi, 'Indian indentured workers in Mauritius, Natal and Fiji', and, Sen, Sunanda, 'Indentured Labour from India in the Age of Empire', *Social Scientist, New Dehli*, Vol. 44, (2016), pp. 35-74, Vertovec, Steven, 'Indian indentured migration to the Caribbean', in Cohen, Robin, (ed.), *The Cambridge Survey of World Migration* (Cambridge University Press), 1995, pp. 57-62, 63-68.

[8] Carter, Marina, 'Indian Indentured Migration and the Forced Labour Debate', *Itinerario*, Vol. 21, (1), (1997), pp. 52-61.

eighteenth century many from the over-populated east coast of the country had crossed to Burma.[9]

Indian emigration to Mauritius began as early as 1830, but the labourers selected were described as 'people taken from the refuse of the population of Madras'[10] and they were dismissed from the island. Yet on 9 September 1834, 36 men of the Dhangar or hill caste voluntarily attached their marks to an agreement in the Calcutta Police Office to work for five years on a sugar estate in Mauritius in return for a salary of 5 rupees per month, with six months' pay in advance and the payment of their outward and return passages. As the men accepted voluntarily to go to Mauritius the Bengal Government raised no objections.[11] From 1 August 1834 to the end of 1835, fourteen ships landed 'coolie' labourers from Calcutta in Mauritius and the West Indian colonies were to follow in the recruitment of free Indian labour. The recruits came mainly from the Tamil areas of Madras in Southern India, from the United Provinces and from Bihar in the north. But to many of the recruits' new employers there was little difference between their new charges and their former slaves.

The British government was initially cautious about sending Indian indentured labour to its Caribbean colonies, fearing that the practice would become a new system of slavery.[12] Following the emancipation of slaves in 1833 and the period of apprenticeship that followed, many liberated Africans left their former masters. For the owners of sugar-cane plantations, who required a low-waged labour force, this posed major economic problems.[13] Britain was forced to look elsewhere for cheap labour and turned its attention briefly to China and then to India. In 1836, the first Indians arrived in British Guiana.[14] Under a scheme ordered by Lord Stanley, Colonial Secretary, a civil contract between Britain and Indian workers was drawn up for an initial period of five years.[15] In the early phase, Indians were treated as inhumanely as the enslaved Africans had

---

[9] Brennan, Lance, et al, 'The Geographic and Social Origins of Indian Indentured Labourers in Mauritius, Natal, Fiji, Guyana and Jamaica', *South Asia*, Vol. 21, (1998), pp. 39-71.

[10] *Parliamentary Papers*, 1840, Vol. 37, no. 331, pp. 194-197.

[11] Secretary, Government of Bengal to Chief Magistrate Calcutta, 22 September 1834, cit, Cumpston, I. M., *Indians Overseas in British Territories 1834-1854*, (Oxford University Press), 1969, p.12.

[12] This issue was raised, for instance, by Thomas Wakley in 1842 when he said that 'the emigration of Hill Coolies would lead to a sort of legalised slave-trade', *Hansard*, House of Commons, Debates, 1 March 1842, Vol. 60, cc 1321-1355. See also, Cullen, Rose, 'Empire, Indian Indentured Labour and the Colony: The Debate over 'coolie' Labour in New South Wales, 1836-1838', *History Australia*, Vol. 9, (1), (2012), pp. 84-109.

[13] Green, William A., *British Slave Emancipation: The Sugar Colonies and the Great Experiment 1830-1865*, (Oxford University Press), 1976, examines the problems posed by emancipation to plantation owners.

[14] Laurence, K. O., *A Question of Labour: Indentured Immigration into Trinidad and British Guiana 1875-1917*, (St. Martin's Press), 1994, provides a good overview of the last decades of indentured labour. See also, Roopnarine, Lomarsh, *Indo-Caribbean Indenture: Resistance and Accommodation*, (University of West Indies Press), 2006.

[15] On Stanley at the Colonial Office 1833-1834, see Hawkins, Angus, *The Forgotten Prime Minister, The 14th Earl of Derby*, 2 Vols. (Oxford University Press), 2007, 2008, Vol. 1, pp. 127-143.

been. They were confined to their estates living in flimsy living quarters still known as 'nigger yards' and only paid a shilling per day. Any breach of contract brought automatic criminal penalties of two months' imprisonment or a fine of £5. In 1838, a special magistrate, Charles Anderson, wrote to the Colonial Secretary declaring that 'with few exceptions they [the Indians] are treated with great and unjust severity, by overwork and by personal chastisement'.[16] If labourers did not work, they were not paid or fed and simply starved. Plantation owners enforced the regulations so harshly that 'the decaying remains of immigrants were frequently discovered in cane fields...'[17] Importing contract labour from India was suspended in 1840.[18]

The Colonial Office felt there was no need for an Order in Council for the admission of the labourers into the colony, and the scheme itself was thought 'novel'.[19] But the Government of India banned all Indian labour to the colonies until 1838 because of the abuses within the system. The Court of Directors of the East India Company also discussed the question of total prohibition of emigration from India and, in 1838, after a meeting called at the Calcutta Town Hall by Thomas Boaz, a minister of the United Chapel there, a petition was presented of the Governor-General in Council protesting against the export of Indian labour and begging the Council to stop the traffic until it could be proved as beneficial to the Indian labourer as to the exporter and the employer.[20] Through such protests, mainly by Evangelicals in Britain and India, a proposal was introduced that each Presidency should establish committees to enquire into malpractices in the system, and that the labour-importing colonies should also appoint Committees of Investigation to report on conditions in their areas. It also led to the 'Natives of India Protection Bill' that was debated in the House of Commons on 20 July 1838. *The Times* called the delivery of coolies to the West Indies at £25 a head 'a novel abomination'.[21] The result was banning indentured

[16] Anderson to Glenelg, 18 November 1838, cit, Barrow, John H., (ed.), *The Mirror of Parliament: Session of 1840*, Vol. 4, (Longman, Orme, Brown, Green & Longmans), 1840, p. 3564.

[17] Sundararajan, Saroja, *From bondage to deliverance: indentured labour in Mauritius and British Guiana*, (Allied Publishers), 2006, p. 98. See also, *Hill Coolies: A Brief Exposure of the Deplorable Condition of the Hill Coolies in British Guiana and Mauritius*, (Harvey and Darton), 1840, ibid, Green, William A., *British Slave Emancipation: The Sugar Colonies and the Great Experiment 1830-1865*, pp. 276-288, Mangru, B., *Benevolent Neutrality, Indian Government Policy and labour migration to British Guiana, 1854-1884*, (Hansib Publishing Ltd.), 1987, and Hollett, Dave, *Passage from India to El Dorado: Guyana and the great migration*, (Fairleigh Dickinson University Press), 1999.

[18] The debates on whether hill coolies should or should not be allowed to migrate to Mauritius occurred during June 1840: see, for instance, the debate on the third reading of the Colonial Passengers Bill, *Hansard*, House of Commons, Debates, 22 June 1840, Vol. 54, cc1386-1409.

[19] National Archives: CO 111/61, Minute of James Stephen, 10 March 1837, cit, ibid, Cumpston, I. M., *Indians Overseas in British Territories 1834-1854*, p.17.

[20] *Parliamentary Papers* 1841, Vol. 16, no.45, Appendix p.14

[21] *The Times*, 21 July 1838. See also House of Commons debate on the Natives of India Protection Bill, *Hansard*, House of Commons, Debates, 20 July 1838, Vol. 44, cc 382-383.

emigration from India in May 1839 though this was lifted in the India Act XXI in 1843.

After the supply of Indian contract labour was cut off, 105 European men landed in St Lucia in 1843 to resolve the labour shortage but proved inadequate for the task. At this point, the disgruntled plantation owners, deprived of their enslaved workforce, pleaded with the colonial government to find a fresh supply of labour. Lord Stanley experimented with schemes for bringing in Chinese people from British settlements in Malacca, and Africans from Sierra Leone. These yielded few results and, as a result, he had little option but to reinstate immigration from India.[22] Legislation was passed to protect the well-being of the Indian immigrants and provision was made for basic housing, food rations, clothing and wages. The colonial government, with authority from London, engaged agents, described as 'generally people of bad character', to recruit indentured labourers and who fully utilised the harsh economic and social conditions in India to lure the dispossessed into their trap.

Emigration in practice in British Guiana

The recruiters selected so-called 'hill coolies', who were generally employed as labourers on indigo plantations and during the low season came into the towns to seek work. From 1844, certain towns in the Northern provinces, Delhi, Bihar, Oudh and Bengawere were recognised as centres for potential recruits. East Indian workers had a wide variety of skills. A report investigating conditions in the colonies listed arrivals as agricultural labourers, weavers, cooks, dancers, musicians, priests and scribes. Some were Indian landowners forced off their land when wealthy colonists began to buy up smallholdings for nominal rates and in desperation, high-caste Brahmans, who rarely worked the land, also enlisted as emigrants to the colonies. Recruitment to the islands of the West Indies began in earnest in 1844 despite sustained opposition from anti-slavery societies.[23] Hindu and, to a lesser extent Muslim men were among the emigrants and in time the numbers of female indentured labourers rose. Despite the safeguards put in place by Parliament to prevent indentured workers suffering a new form of enslavement, plantation owners continued to abuse their Indian workers.[24]

The planters were also at this period agitating for state-aided immigration even though this was opposed by the influential Anti-Slavery Society in England.[25] But in British Guiana,[26] the planters, with their majority on the

[22] Ibid, Hawkins, Angus, *The Forgotten Prime Minister, The 14th Earl of Derby*, Vol. 1, pp. 238-239. See also debate on the Colonial Passengers Bill, *Hansard,* House of Commons, Debates, 26 July 1842, Vol. 65, cc 644-666

[23] Lord Stanley in *Hansard*, House of Commons, Debates, 15 July 1844, Vol. 76, cc 829-830.

[24] Hangloo, Rattan Lal, (ed.), *Indian Diaspora in the Caribbean: History, Culture and Identity*, (Primus Books), 2012.

[25] Debate on the 'importation of Hindoos into Guinea', *Hansard*, House of Lords, Debates, 6 March 1838, Vol. 41, cc416-476.

[26] The area was originally settled by the Dutch early in the seventeenth century as the colonies of Essequibo, Demerara, and Berbice. The three colonies were captured by the British in 1796 and returned to the (Dutch) Batavian Republic in 1802. However, they were recaptured by British forces a year later, officially ceded to the United Kingdom in

Combined Court of Policy, decided to pressurise the British Government to agree to help fund immigration from India.[27] Their chance came in 1840 when the Combined Court of Policy was presented with a proposed tax ordinance to approve funds totalling £206,000 to pay civil servants in the colony. The planters refused to approve it unless immigration from India and elsewhere was permitted. The British Government then sent the Governor of Trinidad, Sir Henry McLeod, to negotiate with the planters who eventually won their demand. After the British Government agreed to re-open immigration, the Combined Court of Policy passed the tax ordinance.[28]

The end of slavery led to important changes in British Guiana. Many former slaves rapidly left the plantations with some who felt that field labour was degrading and inconsistent with freedom moving to towns and villages. Others pooled their resources to purchase the abandoned estates of their former masters and created village communities. Establishing small settlements provided the new Afro-Guyanese communities with opportunities to grow and sell food, extending a practice under which slaves had been allowed to keep the money that came from the sale of any surplus produce. The emergence of an independent-minded Afro-Guyanese peasant class, however, threatened the planters' political power since they no longer had a monopoly on the colony's economic activity. The departure of the Afro-Guyanese from the sugar plantations soon led to labour shortages. The sugar planters tried to resolve their labour shortage by bringing indentured Portuguese workers from the Atlantic island of Madeira. When the Portuguese completed their labour contracts, some moved from the plantations

---

1814 and consolidated into a single colony of British Guiana in 1831. The colony's capital was at Georgetown (known as Stabroek prior to 1812). British Guiana became independent on 26 May 1966 as Guyana. For the history of Guyana see, Dalton, Henry G., *The History of British Guiana*, 2 Vols. (Longman, Brown, Green, and Longmans), 1855, Bronkhurst, H. V. P., *The Colony of British Guyana and its Labouring Population*, (T. Woolmer), 1883, Rodway, James, *History of British Guiana from 1668*, 3 Vols. (J. Thomson), 1891-1894, Netscher, P. M., *History of the Colonies: Essequebo, Demerary, and Berbice: From the Dutch Establishment to the year 1888*, trans. by W. E. Roth, (Daily Chronicle, Georgetown), 1931, and Daly, Vere T., *The Making of Guyana*, (Macmillan), 1974. Marshall, Woodville, and Brereton, Bridget, 'Historiography of Barbados, the Windward Islands, Trinidad and Tobago and Guyana', in Highman, W. B., (ed.), *General History of the Caribbean, Vol. VI, Methodology and Historiography of the Caribbean*, (UNESCO Publishing/Macmillan), 1999, pp. 590-603, provides a detailed critique of historiography.

[27] Planter political power in British Guiana was based in the Court of Policy and the two courts of justice, established under Dutch rule. The Court of Policy, with both legislative and administrative functions, was composed of the Governor, three colonial officials, and four colonists, with the Governor presiding. The courts of justice resolved judicial matters, such as licensing and civil service appointments that were brought before them by petition. The colonists who sat on the Court of Policy and the courts of justice were appointed by the Governor from a list of nominees submitted by two electoral colleges. The seven members of each College of Electors were elected for life by those planters with 25 or more slaves. Raising and spending revenue was the responsibility of the Combined Court that included members of the Court of Policy and six additional financial representatives appointed by the College of Electors.

[28] Adamson, Alan H., *Sugar Without Slaves: The Political Economy of British Guiana, 1838-1904*, (Yale University Press), 1972.

to the towns and into other parts of the economy, especially retail business. By 1851, 173 out of the 296 shops in Georgetown belonged to Portuguese. In New Amsterdam, they owned 28 of the 52 registered shops while in the villages they had 283 of the 432 shops.

With the implementation of the Government of India Act in 1844, the subsequent approval of £500,000 loan by the British Government for future investment in immigration and a further worsening of the labour situation in the colony, East Indian immigration to British Guiana resumed in 1845. In that year, two ships transported 593 Indians from Calcutta while one ship brought 233 from Madras. A steady flow continued in 1846 when 4,019 arrived from Calcutta and Madras. In 1847, 3,461 arrived and 3,545 came the following year. Many of the immigrants who came from 1845 to 1848 were unsuitable for field work since they were generally poor city dwellers. On arrival in British Guiana, some of them abandoned their tasks on the plantations and resorted to a life of wandering, begging and doing menial jobs.[29] Much of the labour undertaken by the emigrants was as arduous as that of the former slaves and remnants of slavery remained, such as the coolie accommodation or 'lines' in British Guiana still bearing the title of the 'Nigger Yard'.

In addition to the labour shortages caused by the abolition of slavery, the Sugar Duties Act 1846 caused a second crisis for the West Indian sugar industry by reducing preferential tariffs so that, by 1874, all sugar entered Britain free of duty.[30] The result was a period of economic dislocation in which the number of sugar-producing estates in British Guiana declined: they fell from 404 in 1838 to 135 in 1870.[31] The establishment of large estates and sugar factories brought more acreage under cultivation and altered the nature of the plantation system leading to a more commercial approach to production. With the introduction of steam power combined with improved capital and technological innovation and the introduction of indentured labour, British Guiana emerged as the prime sugar-producing colony in the British West Indies.

During the second half of the nineteenth century, Indian indentured labour posed three major problems for the colonial authorities. When this new batch of Indians first began to arrive in 1845, they refused to sign any written agreements with the plantation owners. As a result, they had the option of working for not more than four weeks. In 1846, this increased to six months, but the planters felt that even this period was insufficient. Two years later, the hiring period was extended to one year; later in 1848, the British government extended it to three years just before another ban was placed by the Indian Government on emigration from India. This ban was introduced because of the high death

---

[29] Ibid, Dalton, Henry G., *The History of British Guiana*, Vol. 1, pp. 471-479, provides vivid descriptions of the flaws in Indian indentured labour. See also, Brumell, John, *British Guiana: Demerara after fifteen years of freedom*, (T. Bosworth), 1853, pp. 51-59.

[30] See, *Hansard*, House of Commons, Debates, 20 July 1846, House of Lords, Debates, 27 July 1846. The debilitating impact of the legislation on British Guiana was debated in 1850: *Hansard*, House of Commons, Debates, 31 May 1850, cc528-593 and in the petition sent from British Guiana, *Hansard*, House of Commons, Debates, 10 May 1852, cc430-432.

[31] Lobell, Richard, 'Patterns of Investment and Sources of Credit in the British West Indian Sugar Industry, 1838-1897', *Journal of Caribbean History*, Vol. 4, (1972), p. 32.

rate among Indians in British Guiana. When Indian immigration to British Guiana resumed in 1851, indentured labourers were required to agree to a five-year contract though this was reduced to three years in 1853.[32] The 1860s also saw a resolution of the problem of financing Indian immigration.[33] Indian immigration continued to be financed by the government into the 1860s raised through loans obtained in Great Britain, by advances from the British government and from the general revenue of the colony. However, this system created financial problems and in 1864 a decision was taken by the British Guiana government to create an Immigration Fund to finance the cost of immigration. This Fund was draw from general revenue, duties levied on estates' supplies, indenture and re-indenture fees paid by planters, fees paid for renewal of certificates of exemption from labour and fees for the registration of Indian marriages. The amount paid into this Fund grew significantly with each succeeding year.[34]

Finally, there was the problem of what should happen to migrant labour once indentures had been completed. Individuals had two choices: return to India or remain in the colony. By 1869, about 30,000 Indians were eligible for return passages at an estimated cost of over £150,000, an expense the Government could not easily bear. Repatriation to India depleted plantations of their labour force while the Government was losing money by paying for the return trip. To prevent the reduction of this work force, the Government promoted the idea of granting land to the Indians instead of the return passage.[35] This idea was originally proposed by the Immigration-General, James Crosby, but it was not until 1877 that Indians began to seek permission from the Government to purchase abandoned estates. In 1880, the Government bought Huist Dieren, an abandoned estate in Essequibo and divided it into lots that were offered to some Indian families in exchange for the return passages to India. In 1882, the new Governor, Sir Henry Irving, halted this process because of its cost replacing it with a scheme to sell Crown land cheaply to Indians though they did not surrender their right to return passages. Many Indians liked Irving's policy and very soon Indian settlements were formed at Cotton Tree (West Berbice),

---

[32] Ramsarran, Parbattie, 'The Indentured contract and its Impact on Labor Relationship and Community Reconstruction in British Guiana', *International Journal of Criminology and Sociological Theory*, Vol. 1, (2), (2008), pp. 177-188.

[33] Carter, Marina, and Bates, Crispin, 'Empire and locality: a global dimension to the 1857 Indian Uprising', *Journal of Global History*, Vol. 5, (1), (2010), pp. 51-73, suggests that many individuals who participated in the insurgency in India did indeed make their way overseas especially to the sugar colonies, quietly ignored and only mentioned in subsequent decades when 'scares' about mutinous sepoys in their midst were raised in the colonial press as explanation for strikes and labour agitations on colonial sugar estates.

[34] Mangru, Basdeo, *Benevolent Neutrality: Indian Government Policy and Labour Migration to British Guiana, 1854-1888*, (Hansib Publishing Lrd.), 1988, examines the changing nature of public policy.

[35] Greenidge, Carl B., *Empowering a peasantry in a Caribbean context: the case of land settlement schemes in Guyana 1865-1985*, (University of the West Indies Press), 2001, pp. 24-48, considers developments to 1905. See also, Rose, James G., 'The Repatriation Controversy and the Beginning of an East Indian Village System', *Guyana Historical Journal*, Vol. 1, (1989), pp. 51-67.

Brighton (Corentyne) and Maria's Lodge (Essequibo).[36] But Irving's plan did not receive full support from planters and after he left British Guiana in 1894, the original plan of giving land to Indians in exchange for the return passages was reintroduced. Under this arrangement, the Indians were to be selected by the government for lands in some settlements to be created.[37] It was as a result of this change that Helena (East Demerara), Bush Lot (West Berbice) and Whim (Corentyne) were purchased by the Government and house lots and farm plots were given to selected Indian families in 1897.[38] In 1905, the government abandoned the scheme to settle Indians in exchange for their return passages and agreed instead to assist them in purchasing land.

From around 1912, members of the Indian legislature, the Imperial Council of India increased their demands for an end to Indian emigration. As a result of this agitation, the Council, after consulting with the British government, sent two of its members, to British Guiana to examine the working and living conditions of Indians. Their report, made in 1915, described these conditions as favourable. This encouraged A. P. Sherlock, a member of the Court of Policy to suggest the establishment of a committee to examine how the immigration of Indians to British Guiana could be expanded. This committee was formally established, but before it could begin its work, the British Government announced that emigration from India would end in September 1917. The conditions in Guiana were relatively better for many compared to repatriation because those returning suffered severe socio-religious ostracising in India. For the next ten years, there were a series of largely unsuccessful attempts to revive Indian immigration to British Guiana and it was not until 1928 that emigration finally ceased.[39]

In 1924 an enquiry into the working conditions of Indians revealed that wages were not in line with the rise in the cost of living. The position of Indian labourers further deteriorated in 1932 when the post of Agent-General was abolished. Between 1933 and 1936 there were serious labour troubles, and in 1934 11,000 Indians emigrated, which was taken as proof that wages had declined on the sugar estates, and that their interests were not being properly protected. The West India Royal Commission of 1938 exposed considerable unemployment among Indians on sugar estates, and the use of child labour to reduce the employers' wage bills. In July of that year a standard wage system was introduced, but the shortage of work remained acute. The Labour Disturbances Committee of 1937 recommended the establishment of an authority for the protection of both employees' and employers' interests, and the Labour

---

[36] See, Rauf, Mohammad Abdur, *Indian village in Guyana: a study of cultural change and ethnic identity*, (Brill), 1974, and Silverman, Marilyn, *Rich people and rice: factional politics in rural Guyana*, (Brill), 1980, have some useful historical analysis on the village movement.

[37] Jain, Prakash C., 'Exploitation and reproduction of migrant Indian labour in colonial Guyana and Malaysia', *Journal of Contemporary Asia*, Vol. 18, (2), (1988), pp. 189-206.

[38] Bisnauth, D. A., *The settlement of Indians in Guyana, 1890-1930*, (Peepul Tree), 2000.

[39] See, for instance, Delegation to British Guiana on Scheme for Indian Emigration: Kesava Pillai, P., Venkatesh Narayan Tivary, Gerald Francis Keatinge, *Reports on the Scheme for Indian Immigration to British Guiana*, (Superintendent Government Monotype Press), 1924.

Ordinance of 1942 introduced an Advisory Committee which investigated conditions of employment and recommended minimum wage rates.

South Africa

South Africa, and especially Natal, was also an important destination for Indian indentured labour in the nineteenth and early-twentieth century.[40] In the aftermath of emancipation in 1833, freed African slaves could be indentured for five years after being freed and slave children and destitute children without custodians could also be indentured until they reach the age of 25.[41] The aim of indenturing slaves was to ease the transition from slave labour to free labour. However, for many Boer settlers it was a substitute for slave labour and they introduced this system, known as *inboekeling* into the interior and Natal. For settlers, indentured labour wholly beneficial to Africans, especially children who were left destitute after tribal war, because they gained employment and could sustain their lives. For the Cape Colony and missionaries and philanthropists, the inboekeling system was slavery. In 1843, the Cape Colony annexed Natal under the pretext that it was acting against slavery. This action and the subsequent migration of British settlers into Natal compounded the problem of labour shortages.[42]

In 1855, Natal, following the successful introduction of sugar farming, sugar farmers began to lobby the government of Natal to introduce indentured Indian labourers to work on their sugar plantations.[43] Indians were regarded as suitable workers since they were already worked on sugar plantations in

---

[40] Ross, Robert, *A Concise History of South Africa*, (Cambridge University Press), 1999, pp. 21-83, and Worden, Nigel, *The making of modern South Africa: conquest, segregation, and apartheid*, 3rd ed., (Wiley-Blackwell), 2000, pp. 6-73, provide a succinct overview of nineteenth century developments. Hamilton, Carolyn, Mbenga, Bernard, and Ross, Robert, (eds.), *The Cambridge History of South Africa, Vol. 1: From Early Times to 1885*, (Cambridge University Press), 2010, pp. 253-381, provides a more detailed analysis of much of the nineteenth century. On the development of Natal see, Hattersley, Alan E., *The British Settlement of Natal: A Study of Imperial Migration*, (Cambridge University Press), 1950, 2009.

[41] Boeyens, C. A., ''Black Ivory': The Indenture System and Slavery in Zoutpansberg', in Eldredge, E., and Morton, F., (eds.), *Slavery in South Africa: Captive Labour on the Dutch Frontier*, (University of Natal Press), 1994.

[42] On the development and problems facing the industry, see Richardson, P., 'The Natal Sugar Industry, 1849-1905: An Interpretative Essay, *Journal of African History*, Vol. 23, (1982), pp. 515-527.

[43] Huttenback, Robert A., *Gandhi in South Africa: British imperialism and the Indian question, 1860-1914*, (Cornell University Press), 1971, pp. 1-44, provides the context for Indian immigration while Palmer, Mabel, *The History of the Indians in Natal*, (Oxford University Press), 1957, and Henning, C. G., *The Indentured Indian in Natal: 1860-1917*, (Promila and Co.), 1993 focus on the specifics of indentured labour. See also, Bhana, Surendra, *Essays on indentured Indians in Natal*, (Peepal Tree Press), 1990, Meer, Y. S., *Documents of indentured labour: Natal 1851-1917*, (Institute of Black Research), 1980, and Harris, Karen, 'Sugar and Gold: Indentured Indian and Chinese Labour in South Africa', *Journal of Social Sciences*, Vol. 25, (2010), pp. 147-158.

Mauritius and Madagascar.[44] Following the abolition of slavery, there was a shortage of labour throughout South Africa.[45] African labour was scarce because the socio-economic system in southern African societies remained economically productive and was able to compete in European markets. Also, employment in other areas such as mining and railway construction was open to them resulting in little incentive for Africans to work for the sugar farmers either permanently or on a long-term basis.[46] Although there may have been sound economic reasons for using African labour, the Native Administrator of Natal, Theophilus Shepstone sought to avoid them settling for long periods in the colony. His policy was to restrict Natal Africans to Zululand and the Eastern Cape while Natal retained only those essential for labour purposes. In addition, since sugar was not significant for the economy of Natal, Shepstone was not prepared to interfere to secure the labour needs of sugar farmers. For those Africans already in Natal, their taxes were an essential contribution to the coffers of the Natal administration and £17,925 from natives taxes were used to subsidise the cost of Indian indentured labour.

In 1855, sugar planters petitioned the government to introduce indentured Indians in Natal. The Indian colonial government was not satisfied with conditions, especially legal conditions of indentured labourers in Natal and the first request was not successful. As a result, provisions were improved to secure the release of indentured labourers to Natal in Law 14 including the appointment of the Protector of Immigrants to oversee labour conditions and treatment of Indians. This initiative to protect indentured labourers built on the experience of the Slave Protector's office that existed during years of slavery in the Cape. The contract for labour was primarily between the Indian colony and colony of Natal. Individuals were requested to swear an oath of allegiance to their unknown prospective employer, who at the time of the swearing of an oath was in Natal. Indentured workers were not consulted and no provision was made to ensure they understood the laws and conditions of employment. Once in Natal, they did not choose their employers and were divided among sugar planters.

The first wave of indentured labourers from India was from Calcutta. The *SS Truro* sailed from Calcutta in 4 October 1860 reaching Natal on 16 November 1860. On 12 October 1860, Indians from Madras boarded their ship and sailed to South Africa. Within six months, the number of Indians in South

---

[44] On Indian indentured labour in Madagascar see, Campbell, Gwyn, *An Economic History of Imperial Madagascar, 1750-1895: The Rise and Fall of an Island Empire*, (Cambridge University Press), 2005, pp. 215-217, 229-235. On Mauritius see, Allen, Richard Blair, 'Capital, Illegal Slaves, Indentured Labourers and the Creation of a Sugar Plantation Economy in Mauritius, 1810-60', *Journal of Imperial and Commonwealth History*, Vol. 36, (2), (2008), pp. 151-170, and *Slaves, freedmen, and indentured laborers in colonial Mauritius*, (Cambridge University Press), 1999, pp. 55-77, 136-171, Bissoondoyal, U., *Indians overseas, the Mauritian experience*, (Mahatma Gandhi Institute), 1984, and Miège, Jean Louis, *Indentured labour in the Indian Ocean and the particular case of Mauritius*, (Centre for the History of European Expansion, University of Leiden), 1986.

[45] Doling, Wayne, *Slavery, Emancipation and Colonial Rule in South Africa*, University of Kwa-Zulu-Natal Press), 2007, pp. 112-158, considers the problems of negotiating emancipation after 1833.

[46] Van der Horst, Sheila T., *Native labour in South Africa*, (Cass), 1971, pp. 51.

Africa totalled 1,029.[47] In addition to indentured labour, there was an increasing flow of 'Passenger Indians' mainly from Bombay and other parts of the west coast of India who formed an independent, privileged group setting up a variety of businesses among the new immigrants.[48] Immigration was temporarily stopped in 1871 to deal with complaints about the treatment if Indians in Natal and then resumed in 1874 and the community in Natal rose from 10,626 in 1876 to 20,536 in 1880. The stream of Indian emigrants to Natal was small but steady and in 1895 the British opened up East Africa, using indentured labour to build the railway.

Many Indians established themselves as traders in East Africa especially in the settlements that sprang up alongside the railway. Lord Lugard saw golden opportunities in emigration and settlement for the expanding Indian population in the territory. Recruits for the Uganda Railway came mainly from Karachi, but it was not until 1901 that a Protector of Emigrants was appointed there. Over half the coolies returned to India at the end of their indentured term while others returned home as invalids. About 7 per cent died and the remainder became traders or bought small tracts of land to work for their own purposes. The life of the railway coolie was very like that of the plantation labourer; the indenture period was only three years with payment of 15 rupees a month, plus rations. There were no restrictions on off-duty hours and workers made their own living arrangements. By 1911, a total of 152,184 indentured migrants had arrived in Natal from India and an estimated 30,000 Passenger Indians.[49] At the same time, the tonnage of sugar produced in Natal doubled. With the introduction of steamboats or paddleboats, conditions on board improved and because of these improvements and strict medical observation of emigrants on board, there are no reports of pandemics or introduction of new diseases in Natal. Between 1860 and 1911, of the 152,184 Indians who arrived in Natal only 34,001 returned to India. This was a low figure compared with other colonies such as Réunion where 88,000 of 118,000 immigrants returned to India.

Initially, historians believed that indentured labourers were from the lower Hindu caste. However, Ebr-Vally has shown that Indians who arrived in Natal were from a mixture of social backgrounds and that indentured labour was not an importation of the caste system.[50] Those individuals who accepted indenture often faced pressure from agents within India to migrate but also from local Indian officials to stay. Known as an *arkatia,* recruiters received financial incentives to procure as many workers as possible. False promises were often

---

[47] Ibid, Palmer, Mabel, *The History of the Indians in Natal*, pp. 9-29, considers immigration in the 1860s, and Metcalf, Thomas R., *Imperial Connections: Indian in the Indian Ocean Area, 1860-1920*, (University of California Press), 2008, pp. 136-164, and more generally, Bhana, S., and Brain, J., (eds.), *Putting Down Roots: Indians Migrants to South Africa, 1860-1911*, (Witwatersrand University Press), 1990, and Banerjee, Sukanya, *Becoming Imperial Citizens: Indians in the Late-Victorian Empire*, (Duke University Press), 2010, pp. 75-115.

[48] Padayachee, V., and Morrell, R., 'Indian merchants and dukawallahs in the Natal economy, c1875-1914', *Journal of Southern African Studies*, (1991), Vol. 17, pp. 71-102, examines the impact of Passenger Indians.

[49] Ibid, Bhana, S., and Brain, J., (eds.), *Putting Down Roots*, pp. 15, 36.

[50] Ebr-Vally, Rehana, *Kala Pani: Caste and Colour in South Africa*, (Kwela Books), 2001.

made to prospective emigrants about the nature of work they are being recruited for and many did not even know where they were going. At the same time, local Indian officials attempted to prevent Indians from emigrating by telling them that they would be forced to eat pork. Hindus, the largest group to immigrate to Natal, were often told that once outside India they would be made to eat beef. Moreover, local officials, such as the village landowner or tapu, were concerned that large-scale emigration would deplete their labour force. By 1877, economic conditions in India were improving, as a result of railway constructions, public works and irrigation projects to improve agricultural productivity and consequently emigration to Natal declined.[51]

By the 1870s, the India trade, unlike the African or Chinese systems ensured the consent of its participants and fraudulent behaviour diminished as the trade developed. The government of India also responded to reports of abuse involving their treatment in overseas estates. For instance, accounts of the harsh conditions suffered by Indians sailing to the Danish colony of Saint Croix were such that the government subsequently refused the colony further labourers after only a single shipment of workers. Although the indentured labour system officially ended by 1917, Indian labour continued to be employed overseas in large numbers until the 1930s, responding to labour demands in Ceylon, Burma and Malaya on the tea, rice and rubber plantations. During the Depression and post-Depression eras, more Indians returned home than left and indentured emigration had largely ceased by 1938.

Chinese labour

China provided the second largest population of indentured workers, although the reasons for migration were often different from those of India.[52] Like India, China was also faced with a nineteenth century boom in population that had risen from approximately 150 million in 1700 to 430 million in 1850 causing economic and social conditions to deteriorate. As well, there were further disruptions caused as a result of internal conflicts and wars against foreigners, such as the Taiping Rebellion from 1850 to 1864. Because of these disruptions, as well as natural disasters such as droughts and floods, many Chinese migrated internally, either to the northern regions of Manchuria or to the coastal cities, which became ports for further migrations across the ocean. The most obvious difference lies in the fact that China was not under direct foreign control and the European recruiters for Chinese labour were obliged to restrict their activities to a few coastal regions.[53] Britain, however, had control of Hong Kong and had opened five other Chinese port cities as a result of China's defeat in the First Opium War and the 1842 Treaty of Nanking. As well, the lack of an effective system of regulation because of the division of political authority between the

---

[51] Swan, M., 'Indentured Indians: Accommodation and Resistance, 1980-1913', in ibid, Bhana, S., and Brain, J., (eds.), *Putting Down Roots*, pp. 117-136.

[52] Lai, Walton Look, *The Chinese in the West Indies, 1806-1995: A documentary history*, (University of the West Indies Press), 1998, pp. 98-189. See also, McKeown, 'Chinese emigration in global context, 1850-1940, *Journal of Global History*, Vol. 5, (1) (2010), pp. 95-124.

[53] Meagher, Arnold J., *The Coolie Trade*, (Xlibris Corporation), 2008, focuses on Latin America but has much to say about the trade elsewhere.

Chinese and British governments, as well as the presence of other Europeans who had been granted special trading concessions, meant that both Western and Chinese recruiters greater freedom to deceive and coerce potential recruits into signing indenture contracts. From 1847 to 1874, 1.5 million Chinese emigrated of whom over 17,000 went to the British Caribbean.[54]

Unlike India, where indentured labour was state-sponsored, emigration was technically illegal under Chinese law and recruitment was largely a private enterprise. Despite this, the first transport of Chinese workers occurred in 1843, when 582 individuals were indentured in Mauritius. The experiment was a success and between 1847 and 1852 the trade grew rapidly, largely under two British firms. Because of the illegality of the trade in China, recruiters, or 'crimps' often resorted to deception to gain recruits, obtain debtors or prisoners of clan wars and would even resort to kidnapping. European shippers, for their part, had extremely uneven screening procedures and minimal health requirements. In debates about the Passengers Act Amendment Bill in 1853, Sir Frederick Peel commented:

> The West India Colonies and Guiana desired to have labour imported from China. Not only had there been great mortality in vessels which had gone from Amoy to British Guiana and other Colonies, but speculators had employed Chinese crimps, who had practised every species of deception on their fellow-countrymen.[55]

The abuses of the system were so bad that they sometimes led to mutinies on board the ships.[56] Reforms were implemented to stop the most flagrant abuses of the system, although scandals continued to surface. Although efforts to regulate the trade continued, international publicity of abuses aided efforts to stop the trade altogether. In Britain and the United States there was growing anti-coolie sentiment and their governments feared that anger directed at indentured labour could lead to anti-foreigner attitudes within the Qing Empire. Aware of growing western concerns, in 1873-1874, the Qing government renewed anti-coolie measures in several provinces and local Qing authorities used all available means to punish coolie brokers and to cut off the supply of coolies.[57] However, Chinese labourers continued to enter contracts of indenture and would migrate to the Americas in search of employment without signing such contracts. As well, the use of indentured labour from China was once again allowed by both Europeans and the imperial court in China in 1893, although this time the trade was strictly regulated on both ends to prevent abuses. Chinese labour was not only required in the Americas, but was sought in other European

---

[54] Yap, Melanie, and Man, Dianne Leong, *Colour, confusion and concessions: the history of the Chinese in South Africa*, (Hong Kong University Press), 1996

[55] *Hansard*, House of Commons, Debates, 13 August 1853, cc1705-1706.

[56] Sing-Wu, Wang, *The Organization of Chinese Emigration 1848-1888*, (Chinese Material Centre), 1978, pp. 47-64, 165-208, considers the organisation of indentured labour and its arbitrary nature. See also, Campbell, P. C., *Chinese Coolie Emigration within the British Empire*, (P. S. King & Son Ltd.), 1923, pp. 86-160.

[57] Irick, Robert, *Ch'ing Policy towards the Coolie Trade 1847-1878*, (Chinese Material Center), 1982, provides the best analysis of the ambiguous attitude of the Qing regime to indentured labour.

colonies. For instance, from 1904-1907, over 60,000 Chinese labourers were hired to work the gold mines in South Africa.[58] In the last years of World War One, at least 140,000 Chinese contract labourers were employed in Europe mainly in support roles such as burying the dead[59] and until 1914 in Malaya a minority of rubber planers relied on Chinese indentured labour.[60]

Planters in British Guiana had expressed interest in introducing Chinese labourers since Emancipation but they were not initially recruited since it was cheaper to transport Indians: £13 to transport an Indian labourer from Calcutta or Madras compared to £15 for a Chinese immigrant from any of the Chinese ports. But because of the growing need for labourers for the sugar estates, some planters decided to recruit Chinese workers especially between 1848 and 1851 when Indian immigration was suspended. In August 1851, the British Guiana government agreed to pay planters a bounty of £50 for each Chinese landed in the colony. Between 1852 and 1884, 50 coolie ships brought nearly 18,000 Chinese labourers to the British West Indies, of whom 13,541 went to British Guiana.[61] The first Chinese labourers, on five year contracts, arrived in British Guiana in January 1853 and were assigned to estates in West Demerara.[62] The British Guiana government expressed concerns about the physical quality of those recruited and also about the large number of boys who were apparently passed off as adults and on 1 August 1853 withdrew the bounty payment to the recruiting planters. However, the British government had decided to support a government-sponsored recruitment programme, but by May 1854, the British Guiana government decided to halt immigration from China due to increasing transportation costs and also because of the failure to recruit women.

---

[58] See, Richardson, Peter, *Chinese mine labour in the Transvaal*, (Macmillan), 1982, Harris, Karen, 'Sugar and Gold: Indentured Indian and Chinese Labour in South Africa', *Journal of Social Sciences,* Vol. 25, (2010), pp. 147-158, and the more general study, Yap, Melanie, and Man, Dianne Leong, *Colour, Confusion and Concessions: The history of the Chinese in South Africa*, (Hong Kong University Press), 1996, pp. 41-166.

[59] See, Summerskill, Michael, *China on the Western Front: Britain's Chinese Work Force in the First World War*, (M. Summerskill), 1982, Fawcett, B., 'The Chinese Labour Force in France, 1917-1918', *Journal of the Hong Kong Branch of the Royal Asiatic Society*, Vol. 40, (2000), pp. 33-111, and Bailey, Paul, 'From Shandong to the Somme: Chinese Indentured Labour in France during World War I', in Kashen, Anne J., (ed.), *Language, Labour and Migration*, (Ashgate), 2000, pp. 179-196.

[60] Beeman, M. A., *The migrant labor system: the case of Malaysian rubber workers*, (University of Illinois at Urbana-Champaign), 1985, pp. 110-126.

[61] Clementi, Cecil, *The Chinese in British Guiana*, (Argosy Co.), 1915, and Sue-a-Quan, Trev, *Cane Ripples: The Chinese in Guyana*, (Cane Press), 1999, provide general histories. Wilson, Andrew R., (ed.), *The Chinese in the Caribbean*, (Markus Wiener Publishers), 2004, is an excellent collection of essays but see especially, pp. 3-40. See also, ibid, Green, William A., *British Slave Emancipation: The Sugar Colonies and the Great Experiment 1830-1865*, pp. 289-290 and Lai, Wally Look, 'Chinese Indentured Labour: Migrations to the British West Indies in the Nineteenth Century', *Amerasia*, Vol. 15, (2), (1989), pp. 117-138.

[62] In 1859, contracts were amended to permit labourers to buy themselves out of indenture after three years' service. In 1860, the period of indenture was reduced to a year but two years later, the five-year contract was restored.

The Chinese proved to be good workers and planters persuaded Governor Philip Wodehouse to appeal to the British government on their behalf to allow the transport of Chinese to British Guiana through private enterprise. Initially, this was not supported by the British government, but eventually in 1857 permission was granted for recruitment for a one-year period.[63] Towards the end of 1858, two ships overloaded with 761 passengers left Hong Kong for Georgetown arriving in March and May 1859 respectively. In 1858, the authorities in the Chinese provinces of Kwangtung and Kwangsi began to encourage people to migrate and this enabled recruiting agents to contract females who were part of entire families. On 24 December 1859, the *Whirlwind* sailed from Hong Kong with 304 men, 56 women, 7 boys and 4 girls. During 1859 and 1860, five more ships left Hong Kong and Canton for British Guiana landing 1,549 men, 298 women, 53 boys, 26 girls and 18 infants. For the next eighteen years, ships continued to sail from Hong Kong, Canton, Amoy, Swatow, and Whampoa with Chinese immigrants who included a disproportionate number of women. The *Dartmouth* made the final voyage from Hong Kong on 24 December 1878. As with Indian indentured workers, Chinese labourers were indentured for five years and assigned such specific tasks as weeding, hoeing, planting and cutting. At the termination of their contract, they, like Indian workers, were offered a bounty of £25 to re-indenture for another five years. While some Chinese accepted the re-indenture bounty, which was equivalent to a year's pay, many became tailors, butchers, cooks, carpenters and tinsmiths. A few turned to shop-keeping, providing rural workers and others with various items of foodstuff. In Georgetown and New Amsterdam, the two main towns, Chinatown districts emerged with trading stores, small restaurants and laundry and jewellery establishments. The Chinese used their savings to purchase land from African landowners. They were also astute businessmen and, by the 1880s, had established grocery stores in the rural villages and in Georgetown and New Amsterdam.

Generally, Chinese immigrants, unlike Indians, did not meet the planters' expectations. Planters and others viewed Chinese emigration as an expensive undertaking without an adequate return. Not only were many Chinese labourers non-agriculturists, many were considered 'turbulent and refractory'. The flow of labour from China was irregular, but also there was a paucity of Chinese women willing to emigrate.[64] When the emigration system began, women were obtained largely through purchase. Women whose husbands had died during inter-clan feuds were brought from rural to urban areas to be sold as concubines, domestic servants and labourers. Through a tempting monetary offer from recruiting agents, intending male emigrants purchased wives from these groups and emigrated with them. However, with the end of inter-clan feuds, colonial emigration agents found it impossible to obtain the requisite number of 33 women to every 100 men. This difficulty produced widespread kidnapping in the

---

[63] *Hansard*, House of Commons, Debates, 3 July 1857, cc 885-893.

[64] Lai, Walton Look, *Indentured labor, Caribbean sugar: Chinese and Indian migrants to the British West Indies, 1838-1918*, (John Hopkins University Press), 1993, Wang, L. Ling-chi, and Wang, Gungwu, (eds.), *The Chinese diaspora: selected essays*, (Times Academic Press), 1998, pp. 103-108.

streets of Canton. It was estimated that only about 15 per cent of Chinese emigrants were women and this shortage was a significant reason for this short-lived emigration scheme. By 1900, the Chinese population in British Guiana had dwindled to 2,919 with many moving to other colonies, particularly French Guiana, Surinam and Trinidad.

Resistance and rebellion

Plantations were large-scale agricultural enterprises in tropical and sub-tropical areas of the British Empire. They were generally engaged in monoculture or dual cropping, export oriented, under foreign ownership and management and dependent on a large, compliant, low-paid labour force. What limited the potential of plantations was not the availability of land or capital but labour.[65] It was generally difficult to obtain, often expensive, not always dependable and constantly in need of replenishment.[66] The solution was the use of indentured labour but the extent to which its use was successful depended largely on how that labour was managed. Some plantations adopted a coercive approach to worker control using the police and the courts as well as more direct forms of discipline.[67] Others used a more paternalist approach seeking an accommodating workforce that was managed by subtler but nonetheless effective means such as introducing a system of rewards and bonuses or improving workers' housing, medical care and recreational facilities. In both approaches, control lay firmly in the hands of the planters. This was symbolised by the location of planters' houses that were generally placed on elevated ground looking down on the labourers' quarters in the same way that overseers rode horses, not simply for mobility and safety, but to reinforce their sitting in judgement over their workers.

Indentured workers were not, however, powerless victims of the plantation system.[68] It is possible to identify three main types of resistance.[69] There was passive resistance such as absenteeism, malingering, shirking or feigning ignorance.[70] There was also inner-directed aggression such as suicide, self-maiming and attacks on other workers, a tension that may have been a

[65] See, Denoon, Donald, 'The Political Economy of Labour Migration to Settler Societies: Australasia, southern Africa and southern South America', in Marks, S., and Richardson, P., (eds.), *International Labour Migration: Historical Perspectives*, (Institute of Commonwealth Studies), 1984, pp. 186-205. See also, Denoon, Donald, *Settler capitalism: the dynamics of dependent development in the southern hemisphere*, (Oxford University Press), 1983.

[66] On this issue see, Lal, Brij V., Munro, Doug, and Beechert, Edward D., (eds.), *Plantation Workers: Resistance and Accommodation*, (University of Hawaii Press), 1993, pp. 1-4, 10-13.

[67] See, for instance, Moroney, S., 'The Development of the Compound as a Mechanism of Worker Control: 1900-1912', *South African Labour Bulletin*, Vol. 4, 1978, pp. 29-49.

[68] See, Haraksingh, Kusha, 'Control and Resistance among Overseas Indian Workers: A study of labour on the sugar plantations of Trinidad, 1875-1917', *Journal of Caribbean History*, Vol. 14, (1980), pp. 1-17.

[69] On this see, Saunders, Kay, *Bondage: The origins and bases of unfree labour in Queensland, 1824-1916*, (University of Queensland Press), 1982.

[70] Lal, Brij V. ''Nonresistance' on Fiji Plantations: The Fiji Indian Experience, 1879-1920', in ibid, Lal, Brij V., Munro, Doug, and Beechert, Edward D., (eds.), *Plantation Workers: Resistance and Accommodation*, pp. 187-216.

consequence of planters' preference for a multi-ethnic workforce to hinder the development of conspiracy and worker solidarity. For instance, suicide was the highest for any group in Natal, second only to Fiji among the sugar colonies that used indentured labour. In Natal, suicides among Indian indentured workers were recorded from 1880 and in the two decades after 1886, they represented about 5 per cent of deaths and were evident among recently arrived young men.[71] In Fiji, suicides among Indian indentured labour reached 831 per million or one in every 900 in 1910.[72] The final category was resistance directed at planters whether through overt disobedience, desertion, industrial action, destruction or property or physical intimidation. Resistance occurred at three points of the system of indenture. There was resistance before individuals signed their contracts of indenture. Once the conditions of their employment were explained to them, individuals could either refuse to sign their contracts or simply return home. However, the great demand for labour resulted in abuses in the system and often led recruiters to mislead recruits leading them to sign contracts of labour without being fully aware of their legal implications. It is difficult to estimate the extent of this practice but misleading potential workers who were frequently illiterate and unable to read their contracts or who were seduced by what had been told them about the work and their destination were undoubtedly not unusual.

Shipboard revolts were also not uncommon.[73] The Chinese word for coolie ships translates into 'floating hells' and poor conditions often prompted violent response. Mortality on board ships was high, up to 18 per cent, including a significant number of suicides. Although the ships carrying indentured migrants had a generally good safety record, that safety could be compromised because of on-board rebellion. In October 1858, for instance, a mutiny of 850 Chinese passengers on the *Flora Temple* caused the ship to run onto a reef and all the Chinese workers who had been locked below deck to quell the uprising were drowned. Ships in the first decades of the indentured trade to China were commonly fitted out like slave ships with iron gratings over hatchways, walls between crew and coolie quarters, armed guards and cannons trained on hatchways. One historian catalogued 68 uprisings out of 736 voyages from China.[74] Instances of rebellion fell significantly as the trade became better regulated, shipboard conditions improved and the abuses that caused workers to be deceived or kidnapped lessened. Voyages from India were more uniformly

[71] Parle, Judith, ''This Painful Subject': Racial Politics and Suicide in Colonial Natal and Zululand', in Weaver, John, and Wright, David, (eds.), *Histories of Suicide: International perspectives on self-destruction in the modern world*, (University of Toronto Press), 2009, pp. 156-177.
[72] Lal, Brij, V., 'Veil of Dishonour: Sexual Jealousy and Suicide on Fiji Plantations', *Journal of Pacific History*, Vol. 20, (1985), pp. 135-155, examines the causes of suicide.
[73] Christopher, Emma, Pybus, Cassandra, and Rediker, Marcus, (eds.), *Many Middle Passages: Forced Migration and the Making of the Modern World*, (University of California Press), 2007, provides a cogent analysis of the nature of the 'middle passage'.
[74] See the comments on mutinies in, Hu-DeHart, Evelyn, 'La Trata Amirilla: The 'Yellow Trade' and the Middle Passage, 1847-1884', in ibid, Christopher, Emma, Pybus, Cassandra, and Rediker, Marcus, (eds.), *Many Middle Passages: Forced Migration and the Making of the Modern World*, pp. 176-179.

governed as Britain was only one carrier. Indian protests on board ship were generally isolated and not very ominous, possibly because these individuals were generally better informed and more prepared to accept their conditions.

Finally, once arrived at their destinations and set to work, resistance to the abuses of the system of indenture occurred despite repression by planters and overseers. Many Asian workers accepted certain conditions of indenture, such as the loss of status and the acceptance of lower pay. However, the wages that they did receive were fiercely protected, as money was often the only reason they had agreed to a term of overseas employment. Although commonly-held stereotypes such as the Indians docility and capacity to endure suffering were prevalent amongst European planters, violence was not uncommon. Acts of revenge against employers or their tools or animals were widespread types of resistance, but sabotage could erupt into larger-scale resistance. Unlike slave rebellions that involved large numbers of slaves and several plantations, rebellions by indentured workers were slightly different. Generally, they were short-lived, usually small in scale and did not spread to other plantations. This revealed the effectiveness of isolation, harsh plantation discipline and hierarchical structures. What may also have prevented the large-scale rebellions experienced during the era of slavery was that indentured workers had willingly signed contracts of labour and perhaps felt that they lacked the leverage or justification for complaint. Any protest, regardless of the underlying reason, was put down severely by plantation owners. Even if the workers were granted some of their demands, which was the case only through the intervention of the Immigration Department, the ringleaders would still be singled out for punishment. One of the problems preventing more effective protests was the fact that many of the labour leaders or 'drivers' were older individuals who often had a personal stake in the advantages offered them by the plantation system.

Analysis of indentured labour has generated a dichotomous model in which the actions of workers are seen either in terms of accommodation or resistance. Labour endured oppressive and harsh conditions and had no alternative short of rebellion but to submit to the uncompromising system of plantation discipline with its battery of legal and extra-legal supports. The problem with this model is that it restricts discussion of indentured labour whereas worker attitudes lay on a continuum between resistance at one extreme and accommodation at the other. Given the authoritarian hegemony of the planters and the means of enforcement at their disposal, it is surprising that there was so much resistance but it is evident that workers used ingenious ways to fight back against the plantation system even if they lacked the tactical power to do more than win the occasional skirmish. This was clearly the case in British Guiana in the late-nineteenth and early-twentieth centuries.

Resistance in British Guiana, 1872-1917

The decades after the final emancipation of slaves in 1838 saw a demographic transformation of British Guiana. In 1838, the population in the plantation areas was about 95,000; about 97 per cent were black or of mixed race but did not include the indigenous native population who lived in the hinterland outside the plantation economic sphere. By 1900, this essentially bi-racial society had been significantly altered. The total population increased by 183 per cent between 1841 and 1891 largely due to immigration of indentured labour and by 1900 immigrants and their descendants exceeded the native population. One reason for the dramatic increase in economic migrants to British Guiana was the success of its sugar production. In 1850, the Caribbean plantation system looked vulnerable to pressure from labour costs and the impact of moves towards free trade by Britain that threatened to deprive planters of their guaranteed markets.[75]

> ...the great mass of Planters are men of oppressed fortunes, consigned by debt to unremitting drudgery in the Colonies, with a hope, which eternally mocks their grasp, of happier days, and a release from their embarrassments.[76]

British Guiana with Trinidad, however, could respond better than their neighbours to changing conditions since they had less debt and still had room for expansion provided an assured and reliable source of labour could be found. As a result, planters were able to increase pre-emancipation levels of sugar production with exports reaching a peak of 116,550 tons in 1891, 80 per cent higher than during the 1830s.[77]

The dominant white minority in British Guiana placed great emphasis on political control and military coercion to maintain social stability spending between 14 and 25 per cent of annual revenue on the police and judiciary compared to around 7½ per cent on education. This did not include expenditure on the militia or maintaining imperial troops in the colony. For planters, the reality of everyday life demanded unequivocal or even brutal treatment to deal with the mass of potentially hostile natives and immigrants. Although building a consensus within society was not ignored by the colonial élite, it was accorded a low priority.[78] Ethnic tensions were encouraged by competition over scarce resources leading to a society that tended to be segregated residentially, culturally and economically.[79] By the 1870s, this hegemony began to break down as occupational specialisation by ethnicity lessened and education increased opportunities for Creoles in white collar employment in public and private sectors and in the professions. Portuguese

---

75 See, Curtin, Philip D., 'The British Sugar Duties and West Indian Prosperity', *Journal of Economic History*, Vol. 14, (1954), pp. 157-164.

76 Martin, Robert Montgomery, *The sugar question in relation to free trade and protection*, (J. B. Nichols), 1848, p. 12. See also, Higgins, Matthew James, *Is cheap sugar the triumph of free trade?: a second letter to the Rt. Hon. Lord John Russell*, (J. Ridgway), 1848.

77 Engerman, Stanley L., 'Contract Labor, Sugar and Technology in the Nineteenth Century', *Journal of Economic History*, Vol. 43, (1983), pp. 635-659.

78 Heuman, Gad, *Contesting freedom: control and resistance in the post-emancipation Caribbean*, (Macmillan Caribbean), 2005, Birbalsingh, Frank, *Indo-Caribbean resistance*, (Ontario Society for Studies in Indo-Caribbean Culture), 1993, Moore, Brian L., *Cultural power, resistance, and pluralism: colonial Guyana, 1838-1900*, (McGill-Queen's University Press), 1995, and Mangru, Basdeo, *A history of East Indian resistance on the Guyana sugar estates, 1869-1948*, (Edwin Mellen Press), 1996. See also, Rodney, Walter, *Guyanese sugar plantations in the late nineteenth century: a contemporary description from the 'Argosy'*, (Release Publishers), 1979.

79 Moore, Brian L., 'Ethnicity and economic behaviour in nineteenth-century Guyana', in Shepherd, Verene, (ed.), *Working Slavery, Pricing Freedom: Perspectives from the Caribbean, Africa and the African Diaspora*, (Palgrave Macmillan), 2002, pp. 377-395.

immigrants diversified their commercial activities into forestry and gold mining. Indian and Chinese immigrants freed from indenture acquired land and became small farmers and, in the case of the Chinese increasingly competed with the Portuguese in commerce and business. The result was increasing pressure on the dominant white planter élite, whose monopoly on political power was finally breached in the 1890s. By the early 1920s, the legislature (the Combined Court) comprised elected members who were primarily non-White (African, Indian, Portuguese and Mixed) and there was only one member drawn from sugar plantation owners.[80]

1872-1897

Resistance by indentured workers was largely caused by dissatisfaction over tasks allocated to them, poor wages and long working hours and complaints about unfair deductions from their wages and ill-treatment and abuse experienced at the hands of overseers. Periodically they expressed their grievances to planters who did little to alleviate these problems. During the 1860s, for instance, over 85,000 indentured workers were convicted for breaches of their labour contracts.[81] The first major disturbance and strike took place at Plantation Leonora, West Coast Demerara in 1869 and this was followed by violence on Plantations Hague, Uitvlugt, Mon Repos, Non-Pareil, Zeelugt and Vergenoegen during the next two years. In September 1872, matters came to a head among Indian indentured labourers on sugar plantations on the Essequibo coast.[82] So marked had the agitation become that there was a motion before the Court of Policy recommending the appointment of a Commission of Inquiry to settle serious disputes. The motion was approved, but for several reasons, the Commission was not appointed.

Initially the workers used the legitimate avenues at their disposal.[83] On Tuesday, 24 September 1872, field labourers at Devonshire Castle Plantation complained to the acting Sub-Immigration Agent in the district that they were being underpaid for their work and, at the same time, Parag, a factory worker accused the plantation owners of forcing him to work all night in the factory. The official showed little concern over this accusation, saying that workers could not be ordered to work more than ten hours in the factory. The next day, Parag

[80] St. Pierre, Maurice, 'The Nature and Development of Social Conflict in Guyana', in Grant, Cedric H., (ed.), *Governance, conflict analysis and conflict resolution*, (Ian Randle Publishers), 2007, pp. 177-193, provides an overview.

[81] Cummings, Leroy, 'Labour rebellion and labour relations in Guyana 1763-1939', *Sunday Stabroek*, 25 November 1996.

[82] Mangar, Tota C., 'The Devonshire Castle strike and the riots of 1872 revisited', *Stabroek News*, 7 October 2005, provides an overview.

[83] Ibid, Bronkhurst, H. V. P., *The Colony of British Guyana and its Labouring Population*, pp. 127-163, and Kirke, Henry, *Twenty-five Years in British Guiana*, (Sampson Low, Marston & Co.), 1898, pp. 75-77, provides the context of Indian discontent. Hollett, Dave, *Passage from India to El Dorado: Guyana and the great migration*, (Associated Universities Press), 1999, pp. 155-162 gives a detailed account. See also, Glasgow, Roy Arthur, *Guyana: race and politics among Africans and East Indians*, (M. Nijhoff), 1970, pp. 92-93, and Gibson, Kean, *The cycle of racial oppression in Guyana*, (University Press of America), 2003, pp. 20-21.

encouraged his colleagues to stop working after they had laboured for ten hours. This brought him into conflict with the estate manager who ordered his arrest but his fellow workers prevented such action and, as a result they were accused of threatening the manager's life.

Recognising that their problems would not be resolved by the local officials or the estate managers, the labourers of Devonshire Castle, accompanied by those of Anna Regina who were experiencing similar problems, planned to go, but in fact never went to Georgetown to seek a resolution of their grievances from either the Immigration Agent-General or the Governor. However, the workers at Anna Regina met with the Acting-Inspector of Police and Mr Trotter, the Sub-Immigration Agent from whom they received promises that their grievances would be investigated. On 28 September 1872, the Devonshire Castle workers went to the local magistrate and voiced their dissatisfaction with the rates of wages they were receiving. The magistrate, who was empowered to deal with labour disputes, also promised to examine their complaints and to ensure that they obtained justice. However, the workers did not feel confident with his response and on their return to the estate some attempted to attack an overseer but were restrained by others. Having exhausted lawful protest, the following day the labourers decided to strike. Despite this, the plantation management made little effort to listen to their complaints. However, later that morning, they were asked by officials to appear at an inquiry four miles away at Danielstown Village but refused since they felt that their complaints would again be dismissed. Increasingly frustrated by the attitude of the authorities, a large crowd armed with sticks swarmed towards the overseers' compound from which the overseers and their families were forced to flee.

The police were notified of situation on the plantation and 24 armed policemen under a police inspector arrived to face a riotous crowd of striking workers. With the police was a local magistrate who unsuccessfully ordered the crowd to disperse and then read the Riot Act. He gave the workers an hour in which to return to their homes, specifically appealing to women and children to leave the area and warned that if they refused stern actions would be taken. The crowd ignored these orders and the magistrate advised the police inspector to position his men so that they could not be surrounded. As the crowd became unrulier, the inspector ordered his armed men to break up the mob but the incensed crowd also advanced and attacked them with sticks. The police then opened fire and five workers were killed and seven others seriously injured. The authorities later claimed that the inspector gave no order to fire, but that the shooting occurred after a policeman's rifle went off accidentally after a striker's stick hit the barrel and this caused the other policemen to assume that the order to shoot was given. Fifteen labourers were subsequently arrested for unlawful assembly and rioting, but they were later freed by the Supreme Court of Criminal Justice.[84]

The Devonshire Castle protest was the first major incident in which Indian indentured labourers were killed by the colonial police. Soon after, an inquest

---

[84] 'British Guiana: Correspondence Respecting a Disturbance among the Indian Emigrants Employed on the Devonshire Castle Estate', *Parliamentary Papers*, 1873, C. 879, Vol. 49, provides the official account.

was held but found no fault with the action of the police. The coroner declared that 'the riot...would, but for the fortunate explosion of these rifles, have become a widespread rebellion, most disastrous in its consequences'.[85] One local newspaper, *The Colonist*, commented: 'the leaden argument has brought submission quicker than all honeyed words that could have been used'. This reflected the view of the colonial authorities and the local business community that showed no sympathy for the problems experienced by the Indian plantation labourers. Neither did the pro-black newspapers which, having conveniently forgotten the anti-Portuguese riots in 1856 when blacks ransacked Portuguese shops along the coast, contrasted the peace loving blacks who used legitimate means of secure justice and the mutinous, disloyal East Indians.[86] The *Working Man* asserted in the autumn of 1872 that Indians were known to be buying guns to re-enact the Indian Mutiny.[87] Its editor may have been uneasy about the police killing of Indian rioters but he also expressed the hope that it meant the end of Indian immigration.

The agitation between 1869 and 1872 marked the beginnings of collective action by Indian workers. An important victory was achieved by indentured workers in 1882 when they won the right to time off to meet the Colonial Agent-General to bring problems about working conditions to his attention. During July and August 1873, there were fourteen strikes, some of which involved assaults on overseers and managers and a further eighty-two strikes between 1874 and 1882. In 1884, the international market for sugar was glutted, the result of stronger economic challenges in sugar from Cuba and Brazil and the rise of European beet sugar. This led to estates closures, amalgamation and economies of scale and between 1886 and 1889, there were at least a hundred strikes, with forty-two alone in 1888 initiated by Indian workers on plantations and in 1894, there were major disturbances at Leguan, Farm Success, Skeldon and La Bonne Mere estates.[88] However, the most serious disturbances occurred between 1906 and 1917 with widespread industrial dissatisfaction, disputes, discontent and protests over terms and conditions of work on the waterfront, in the commercial sector, mainly in the capital city, Georgetown and in the rural areas, mainly among sugar workers. Urban and rural workers found common cause against the labour exploitation by the merchants and the sugar planters. The workers'

[85] In subsequent inquests, coroners were less sympathetic to the authorities. In 1903, for instance, after six Indians were killed at disturbances at Plantation Friends, a flourishing plantation on the east bank of the Berbice River, the coroner sharply criticised the Immigration Agent for not visiting Plantation Friends before the tragic event even though he knew of the existing labour problem. The coroner noted that the Agent's presence at the plantation on 7 May could have prevented the arrest of the six men and averted the disturbances that led to the shootings.

[86] On the 'Angel Gabriel' riots see, Chan, V. O., 'The Riots of 1856 in British Guiana', *Caribbean Journal*, Vol. 16, (1970), pp. 39-50.

[87] *Working Man*, 29 September 1872.

[88] Seecharan, Clem, (ed.), *Joseph Ruhomon's India: the progress of her people at home and abroad, and how those in British Guiana may improve themselves*, (University of the West Indies), 2001, pp. 23-26. The pamphlet was originally published in 1894.

protest actions and confrontation with the merchant class and the planters pitted them against the colonial police.[89]

1905-1910

By the early-twentieth century, the results of the economic changes and monetary dislocations and social protest came to a head. With a slump in worldwide sugar production and the challenge from sugar beet, a report noted in the late 1890s that British Guiana was in a 'perilous position' because of its dependence on a single agricultural industry. Between 1894 and 1897, there were significant wage reductions of 20-25 per cent, possible because of the increasing use of new machinery. By 1905, female cane-cutters were earning as little as 7-8 cents a day with the men earning only 12-17 cents.[90] Poor wages were the most incendiary cause of conflict in 1905. This situation was exacerbated by the high direct and indirect taxations imposed on the poorest classes in the society. Commodities needed by the planters attracted low or no duties and taxes while basic consumer goods used by the poorer groups in the society, such as flour, oatmeal, corn, dried fish and rice attracted high taxes.The poor were also faced by the inflexibility of planters in the face of change. There were no organisations to negotiate with employers on behalf of workers and the colonial authorities defended the interests of planters and the business community and were prepared to use its military power to quell worker unrest. The franchise may have been liberalised in 1891 but it still excluded most workers from participating in the Legislature. Planters used their dominance in the Legislature to introduce regulations to advance sugar interests and retard the development of any other activity that competed for labour, capital and land. By 1905, some diversification in the economy of British Guiana was apparent, with East Indians branching out into rice production and forestry and Africans in the gold fields and with jobs in the urban centres.

Unable to seek redress through constitutional means, in 1905 workers took direct action. The literature on what happened is small in quantity and varied in terms of treatment. Webber betrays his anti-working-class credentials while Walter Rodney is more detailed in his explanation of the social movement and of some of those involved. Ashton Chase provides a basic interpretation of the events of November-December 1905 but is cautious with his descriptions referring positively to the formal strike, of which he approved but is more disapprovingly about what he terms the riot. Rodney, by contrast, places the disturbances squarely in the context of an explosion of indignant working people and unemployed, together with its effect on the colonial authorities.[91]

---

[89] See Chase, Ashton, *A History of Trade Unionism in Guyana, 1900-1961*, (New Guyana Co.), 1966, pp. 1-24, and Alexander, Robert J., and Parker, Eldon M., *A history of organized labor in the English-speaking West Indies*, (Greenwood Publishing Group), 2004, pp. 327-363, for discussion of these events in the context of emerging trade unionism.

[90] (Drakes, Francis), Nehusi, Kimani S. K., 'The Causes of the Protest of 1905', *History Gazette*, No. 22, (University of Guyana), September 1991, p. 7.

[91] Ibid, Chase, Ashton, *A History of Trade Unionism in Guyana,* Rodney, Walter, *A History of the Guyanese Working People, 1881-1905*, (John Hopkins University Press), 1981 and Webber, A.R.F., *Centenary History of British Guiana*, Georgetown, 1931.

The immediate cause of the protest was the poor compensation and working conditions at Sandbach Parker & Company[92] that led dockers striking to demand higher wages between 28 November and 5 December 1905 demanding 16 cents per hour in place of the exiting rates of 48 cents per day for 'boys' and 64 cents per day for men.[93] Led by Hubert Nathaniel Critchlow, striking workers' demands were met with strong resistance from the shipping companies and the conflict eventually turned violent that led to involvement by British troops.[94] The first two days of the strike witnessed its slow spread across sectors, as street activity in support picked up. By 30 November, Chase reported that 'hoodlums and gangs of work shirkers took matters...out of the hands of the strikers, and by their frequent acts of violence at various wharves on the third afternoon it was plain that the strike had turned into a riot.'[95] In particular, women, whose wages and working conditions were even lower than their male counterparts played an active part. The biggest day of the riot was on 1 December when, one newspaper report claimed 'three-fourths of the populace of Georgetown seemed to have gone stark staring mad.'[96] Rodney placed the centre of the strike in the Ruimveldt factory where the grinding of cane began. Although the factory had operated from 4 am, work came to a stop by 5 am after cane-cutters joined the factory hands to confront the manager, who not only rejected their wage demands, but sent for the police, alleging that he had been assaulted and that the workers were rioting. At 7:55 am, the police and a detachment of artillery were in position on Ruimveldt Bridge, over which the east Bank workers were about to cross to link up with Georgetown, the Riot Act was read and, on the orders of Inspector-General Lushington and Major de Rinzy the police opened fire when the crowd failed to disperse.[97] Because of the shootings, thousands came out on to the streets. The *London Morning Post* described the rioters as 'largely composed of half-civilized Amazons and idle ruffians.'[98]

The hostile crowd invaded public buildings, forcing the Governor to take refuge behind the locked doors in the Court of Policy Hall. The rioters stopped horse-drawn carriages carrying persons of European descent, whom rioters saw as associated with the owners of the wharves and other businesses. Whenever

[92] James McInroy came to Demerara in 1782, and planted or acquired a sugar plantation soon after his arrival. By 1790, he was joined by Samuel Sandbach, Charles Stewart Parker and George Robertson, and the company, McInroy Sandbach & Co. was founded. At first the head office was in Glasgow under the name McInroy Parker & Co., and in 1804 a branch was founded in Liverpool, which later became the company headquarters. In 1813, Philip Tinne was taken into the partnership and the company became known as Sandbach, Tinne & Co in Liverpool, and McInroy Sandbach & Co in Demerara and in 1861 changed to Sandbach Parker & Co. They were importers and exporters, shipping and estate agents, mainly concerned with sugar, coffee, molasses and rum.

[93] Ibid, Chase, Ashton, *A History of Trade Unionism in Guyana, 1900-1961*, pp. 20-21.

[94] Alert, Carlton Vincent, *Life and Work of Hubert Nathaniel Critchlow: A Sketch*, (Georgetown: Daily Chronicle Ltd.), 1949, and Harry, Carlyle, *Hubert Nathaniel Critchlow: His Main Tasks and Achievements*, (Guyana National Service Pub. Centre), 1977, provide brief biographical details.

[95] Ibid, Chase, Ashton, *A History of Trade Unionism in Guyana*, p. 21.

[96] Cit, Chase, Ashton, *A History of Trade Unionism in Guyana*, ibid, p. 22.

[97] Ibid, Rodney, Walter, *A History of the Guyanese Working People*, p. 192.

[98] Cit, ibid, Rodney, Walter, *A History of the Guyanese Working People*, p. 207.

encountered, they were assaulted and robbed by gangs of workers who also threw stones and bottles at carriages that refused to stop. Other, including three magistrates and the Attorney-General, Sir T. C. Rainer were also chased and beaten by the people. Later in the afternoon, the rioters moved along Main and High Streets and attacked and looted the homes of Europeans. The police, in an effort to disperse the rebelling crowd, opened fire resulting in several further deaths. Chase reported that according to official reports by dusk on 1 December, eight persons had been killed and over 30 wounded.[99] However, the following day people again returned to the streets. The Governor, Sir Frederic Hodgson took what Chase called 'an unprecedented step of addressing the workers.'[100] Although he promised an inquiry, he was unwilling to compromise over low wage rates or public order but the people refused his call to disperse continuing to mingle and discuss the strike in groups.[101] The momentum of the rebellion was, however, spent and the police now hundreds of arrests. Identified protesters, mostly male, were whipped and the hair of some rebel women was cut off. Order was finally restored with the arrival of the *Diamond* and the *Sappho* on 5 December and the docking of fresh troops.[102] Although the strike failed to achieve its objectives, it demonstrated clearly that to advance their interests workers needed to organise themselves more effectively through trade union activity. In 1906, the possibility of forming a trade union was discussed at a meeting in Georgetown but it was not until January 1919 that the British Guiana Labour Union was finally formed.[103]

Despite repression by the authorities after the rebellion in 1905, further disturbances occurred the following year.[104] On 25 September 1906, workers employed at the Bookers and Sandbach Parker wharves in Georgetown went on strike to demand increases ranging from 48 cents to 72 cents a day.[105] Unlike 1905 when protests spilled into the streets, workers decided to stay at home and this limited its effect since both Bookers and Sandbach Parker employed black-leg labour to do the jobs of the striking workers. The strike had collapsed by 28 September, but many of the workers on returning to work found that they had been dismissed. As in 1905, there were simultaneous protests on the sugar

---

[99] Ibid, Chase, Ashton, *A History of Trade Unionism in Guyana*, p. 22. See also, *The Riots of 1905: Details of the Outbreak, Its Causes and the Measures Taken for its Suppression; Inquest on the Victims and Punishment of the Rioters*, (Georgetown Chronicle) 1906.

[100] Ibid, Chase, Ashton, *A History of Trade Unionism in Guyana*, p. 23.

[101] For the official response to the disturbances in 1905, see 'Correspondence relation to Disturbances in British Guiana', and 'Further Correspondence relation to Disturbances in British Guiana', *Parliamentary Papers*, Vol. 77, 1906.

[102] Ibid, Rodney, Walter, *A History of the Guyanese Working People*, p. 194. The *HMS Sappho* was a cruiser of 3,400 tons and had 272 men on board and *HMS Diamond* held 300. Troops from these vessels were used to arrest the leaders of the strike.

[103] The riots were widely reported in the British national and provincial press from 2 December: for instance, 'Riotous Scenes', *Western Times*, 2 December 1905, p. 4, 'The Georgetown Riots Official Telegrams', *Western Daily Press*, 5 December 1905, p. 10.

[104] *Pittsburgh Press*, 28 January 1906, details the repression after the rebellion including the creation of a militia of 250 English and Portuguese residents.

[105] De Barros, Juanita, *Order and place in a colonial city: patterns of struggle and resistance in Georgetown, British Guiana, 1889-1924*, (McGill-Queen's University Press), 2003, pp. 94-115, 138-166, considers public protest in an urban context.

estates. East Indian workers at Providence, East Bank Demerara stopped work in protest against low wages.[106] Armed with forks and other agricultural tools, they marched to Georgetown to voice their grievances to the Immigration Agent. Further confrontation was averted when the police persuaded them to lay down their tools and the Immigration Agent listened to them and promised to investigate the issue. In December 1908, workers at Plantation Friends, East Bank Berbice took strike action, armed with their tools, marched to New Amsterdam where they met the Immigration Agent who promised to look into their complaint. This resulted in the manager of the plantation agreeing to a small increase in payment to the workers. Similar strikes occurred at Plantation Wales, La Bonne Intention, Marionville (Leguan), Leonora and Peter's Hall between 1908 and 1910. In most cases, the Immigration Agent, after investigating, sided with the management of the plantations and pay increases were refused.[107]

1912-1917

On 18 September 1912, many Indian indentured workers in the shovel gang went on strike at Lusignan Estate, East Coast Demerara.[108] They were protesting at the low wages paid for digging trenches and argued the rising cost of food products had not led to higher wages. Other workers on the estate were encouraged to join them and soon a large noisy crowd of workers gathered near the public road but the police quickly arrived on the scene to prevent any disturbance. The workers moved to the estate office to meet Brassington, the manager but with his deputy McKenzie were riding their horses to return to the office when a worker told them that the men were on strike. Brassington sent a message that he would meet with the strikers to examine their problems. But before he and McKenzie could get back to the estate office, a large group of angry strikers approached them in an aggressive manner. The strikers rushed at them, but they raced their horses away from the area and headed to Brassington's home. The strikers chased behind them, surrounded the home and cut telephone wires leading to it. Brassington, meantime, had collected all the ammunition he could find and gathered nineteen African factory workers whom he provided with guns and placed as guards by the windows.[109]

Some of the strikers attempted to cross a bridge leading to the house. They were warned that they would be fired on unless they retired. However, this was not heeded and as some rushed into the yard, Brassington and McKenzie fired, first above their heads and then at them after they continued to press forward. One worker, Nankoo was fatally wounded and this forced a general

[106] Nehusi, Kimani S. K., 'The Causes of the Protest of 1905', *History Gazette*, No. 22, (University of Guyana), September 1991, reprinted in McGowan, W. F., Rose, J. G., and Granger, D. A., (eds.), *Themes in African-Guyanese History*, (Free Press), 1998, 2nd ed., (Hansib Publications), 2009.

[107] For the problems faced by employers, see *Report of the Commission upon the Labour Supply of British Guiana,* (Court of Policy), 1911.

[108] 'News from British Guiana', *Belfast News-Latter*, 6 September 1912, p. 8, 'Manslaughter Case in British Guiana', *The Scotsman*, 15 October 1912, p. 5, 'Manager's House is Besieged', *Dundee Courier*, 17 October 1912, p 6.

[109] See http://www.guyana.org/features/guyanastory/chapter1.html for what follows.

retreat. The striking workers then decided to take their protest to the Governor and about 300 men, armed with shovels, marched the 12 miles to Georgetown. They were prevented by the police from entering Government House and while they grouped on the roadside, the Immigration Agent-General, A. H. Hill, arrived to talk with them. Eventually, a small delegation met with the Governor, Sir Walter Egerton and explained their grievances to him. In a subsequent statement to the police, Brassington insisted that he feared for his life and for those in the house and that he had ordered the shooting in self-defence. At an inquest, some workers accused Brassington of shooting Nankoo but it concluded that the worker died after being shot by 'a person or persons unknown, to prevent serious outrage.' Despite the finding of the inquest, Brassington was arrested and charged for murder though he was subsequently acquitted at his trial. Twenty-four workers were also charged for riotous behaviour, but after two trials where the jury disagreed, the case was dismissed. However, as a form of punishment, sixteen men were transferred to other estates.[110]

At Plantation Rose Hall, it was customary to grant two to four days' holiday at the end of the grinding season. Because the men had done satisfactory work throughout 1912, with some of them even working on Sundays, the manager, Smith, promised them four days of holiday. On 27 January 1913, one week after the grinding season, the holidays were granted by the manager but with the condition that the labourers used the time to clean up the area in which they lived. However, the workers were dissatisfied with this requirement and this increased when the manager cancelled the holidays the following day, claiming that planting had to be done. He promised to grant the remaining part of the holidays later in the year. But the workers refused to obey this order and even those who wanted to return to work were prevented by others from doing so. On 29 January, all the indentured labourers turned up for work, but at the end of the week Smith took legal action against seven men whom he felt had influenced others from not resuming work the previous day. When asked him to withdraw the summons, Smith refused and a large group of the indentured labourers marched to New Amsterdam to complain to the Immigration Agent. After hearing their case, the Agent managed to persuade Smith to agree to his original promise of four days of holiday. The manager also agreed to withdraw the summons against the seven men providing they paid the legal costs. However, when the men made a plea for the costs to be paid in instalments, Smith angrily refused this request and re-instituted the summons against them.

During the trial in mid-February 1913, about 300 indentured labourers from Rose Hall gathered in the New Amsterdam court compound threatening retaliation if their colleagues were convicted. In the trial, Joseph Eleazer, their defence counsel advised the seven men to plead guilty and the magistrate fined them three shillings each and ordered them keep the peace for six months. This did not satisfy Smith and on 17 February, he asked the Immigration-Agent General for permission to transfer Jangi Khan with his wife and four other indentured labourers to other estates claiming that they had instigated the latest protests. However, the five workers were not immediately informed of this and the police, who had received orders to carry out the transfers, did not take

[110] *Hansard,* House of Commons, Debates, 11 June 1913, Vol. 53, cc1628-1630.

immediate action. What had begun as a protest about holidays now deteriorated into a more serious confrontation. On 4 March, some indentured labourers were charged for bad work and wilful deception and for the next nine days, the labourers refused to work and periodically issued threats to their supervisors. They called for the dismissal of the deputy manager and insisted that the five workers should not be transferred. They also prevented other drivers and overseers from entering their workplaces and tried to stop non-indentured Indians from going to work. As tension, rose, there was some lawlessness, including damage to estate property.

On 13 March, the day of the trial of those who were charged, the other workers refused to work and instead went to the court to hear the cases. By this time, the number of men at the police station at Reliance, Canje had been increased on the request of the assistant manager of Plantation Rose Hall since Smith was away on leave. However, with remarkably bad timing, the Inspector-General of Police (equivalent to Commissioner) and the Immigration Agent decided that since police motor-cars were present at the court house, the transfers of the five labourers could be done then. Jangi Khan, who was among those in the court compound, was held by the police and was being placed in a car to be taken away, but some of his colleagues, armed with sticks pulled him away and prevented him from entering the vehicle. The news of the planned transfers of the five persons spread very quickly and this incensed other workers. The authorities, recognising the strong opposition from the crowd, decided not to proceed with the transfers hoping to carry them out later.

Later that day, a large force of policemen headed by the Inspector-General of Police and a Police Inspector went to Rose Hall to prevent intimidation and acts of vandalism and to arrest five indentured labourers for threatening violence. The crowd apparently felt that the policemen were about to seize the five to be transferred, since many were unaware that arrest warrants were issued for another five who had threatened violence. The police called on the workers to disperse and the Riot Act was read but was immediately attacked by the crowd with sticks and broken bottles. The police then opened fire killing fourteen men in the crowd. A Commissioner, appointed by the Governor to investigate the circumstances of the killings at Rose Hall, found that police did not inform the labourers very clearly whom they were about to arrest and that if they had been told more clearly that the men who were to be transferred would not be removed by force, the tragic event would not have taken place. Despite these findings, no blame was attached to the police for the killings.[111]

With the outbreak of war in Europe in 1914, the price of imported food supplies rapidly increased. Many merchants in British Guiana were involved in black-marketing and this caused prices of foodstuffs to rise even more. However, increases in prices were not accompanied by a comparable increase in wages. Workers were very dissatisfied, and throughout 1915 and 1916 there were short strikes in Georgetown and on the sugar estates. By the beginning of 1917, the economic situation had further deteriorated. Food items had doubled in price since the war started but between January and October 1917 there were further

[111] National Archives, CO 111/594, 12 June 1914, states that the Rose Hall riot was caused by 'injudicious action on the part of the management.'

increases of between 50 and 100 per cent. Wharf workers went on a ten-day strike from 4 January 1917 demanding increased pay and a shorter working day. Hubert Critchlow, the leader of the wharf workers, led a three-man team to meet with the Chamber of Commerce to discuss the issues affecting the workers. Three days after the strike started, the employers agreed to a nine-hour day and a 25 per cent increase in wages, though the workers did not agree to the latter. The strike therefore continued but on 13 January, the employers were forced to agree to the workers' demand: a nine-hour work day, increased wages and overtime payment for any work after 5 pm.

As had occurred on previous occasions, from 9 January 1917 the wharf strike spread to other industries. Rubbish collectors went on strike, but their demands were quickly met and workers at some saw mills stopped working but they too returned to work after their employers agreed to their demand for increased wages. Workers of the Demerara Railway Company, the Ice Factory and the Match Factory also stopped work demanding increases in wages. The strikes at the Ice Factory and the Match Factory were also settled quickly with workers receiving increases but the price of soft drinks, was immediately raised to offset the increased costs of labour. The railway strike lasted for one week seriously affecting movement of people and goods from Georgetown to the rural areas. Eventually it ended after all categories of railways workers were granted a 7 per cent increase. Non-indentured Indian workers on the sugar estates in Demerara between March and May also agitated for higher wages. This demand was taken up by 'free' Indians employed at Plantation Golden Fleece on the Essequibo Coast in September. The intervention of the Immigration Agent-General was necessary to bring about a solution in all these cases. This strike fever gained momentum because all workers were concerned over the rising cost of living and they felt that they had a justifiable case for better wages. The Government was obviously concerned about these stoppages and examined and sought to resolve Government workers' issues as soon as they arose. Towards the end of the year when the Post Office and the Public Hospital workers protested for higher wages without striking, the Government immediately set up a committee to work out a satisfactory arrangement.

Between 1872 and 1917, resistance by indentured labour evolved from direct, if often ineffective action into the more effective use of collective bargaining to achieve its aims. This was, however, far from an even process and it took the outbreak of war in 1914 to move the authorities away from the use of the police and the courts to contain protest to a less confrontational approach to labour relations. Despite this, the issues that led indentured labour to act changed little. They remained heavily focussed on low wages and poor and frequently arbitrary working conditions. Though there may have been some reduction in the draconian use of coercive force, the use of armed police and the courts in support of the management of plantations remained common and were, in general supported by the colonial authorities.

Ending indentures

Although voices had been raised against the use of indentured labour since its inception in the 1830s, opposition did not become sufficiently powerful to end the system until the early-twentieth century.[112] The 1885 Commission was appointed to examine the question of Indian immigration to Natal after European businessmen complained of being swamped by Indians. Its report, published two years later, favoured a ban on the entry of free Indians into the colony and a restriction on imported indentured labour arguing that employers should use Africans instead. Joseph Chamberlain sympathised with the white settlers overseas and 'Alien Immigration' was discussed at the 1897 Imperial Conference. Chamberlain supported the determination of the colonies to prohibit influxes of Asiatics, with their alien religion and customs. But he had to qualify his support by stating that no distinction or favours should be made against or to any person on the grounds of race or colour. Yet his speech made it clear that in any struggle over equality in the colonies the white settlers would have the upper hand

The push to end indentured servitude was linked closely to anti-slavery campaigns to abolish global forced labour practices that stressed both the inhumanity of the system as well as the fact that free labour would be more efficient and economical for employers.[113] In 1875, Edward Stanley described, in critical terms, the use of indentured labour in the late-nineteenth century Mauritius:

> The whole system of coolie immigration is bad from the beginning...no tinkering will mend it...and the government should learn that it has a higher duty than that of producing 100,000 tons of sugar a year - the welfare of two thousand Indians, who have been brought thither by false promises, whose whole social system, based on the ancestral community, on the restraints of caste and custom, has been broken up and thrown to the winds, while no elevating influence or higher code of education and morals has been substituted for the ancient standards...Commerce has done much for the civilisation of the world, but commerce when the rights of inferior races clash with the developments of industry, is very ruthless.[114]

The attack on indentured servitude was also affected by changing judgements on the definition of free and unfree labour. The earliest shift in attitude occurred in the United States where, as early as the 1850s, especially the non-slave states in the north, indentured servitude or peonage was increasingly seen as equivalent to slavery. The Anti-Peonage Act of 1867 banned 'voluntary or involuntary servitude' to the United States and was extended to Hawaii when the islands were annexed in 1900. The Indian government refused to allow further shipments of indentured Indians to some French plantation colonies in the 1880s because colonial authorities did not protect immigrants' rights or ensure their repatriation. The Cadbury Chocolate Company of England drew

---

112 Miles, Robert, *Capitalism and unfree labour: anomaly or necessity?* (Taylor & Francis), 1987, contains valuable case studies of the Caribbean, Australia and South Africa.

113 Walvin, James, *Questioning Slavery*, (Routledge), 1996, pp. 172-182, considers anti-slavery after 1834. See also, Grant, Kevin, *A civilised savagery: Britain and the new slaveries in Africa 1884-1926*, (Routledge), 2005, pp. 11-38.

114 Stanley, Edward Lyulph, 'Treatment of Indian immigrants in Mauritius', *Fortnightly Review*, Vol. 23, 1 June 1875, p. 819.

attention to the abuses of indenture when it boycotted cocoa produced by African labour from the Portuguese-held colony of Angola to São Tomé, and further importation of contract labour to the island was halted in 1909.[115] Highlighting indentured labour in its worst light, much as the anti-slavery movement had done from the 1790s, enabled reformers to raise questions about its justification under even good conditions.

Although the anti-slavery rhetoric played a central role in raising awareness of the repressive nature of indentured labour, the ending of the practice was linked to ideologies grounded in race and exclusion. Once workers had fulfilled their indenture, they could return to their homes or remain in the colonies that often led to competition with white labourers and businessmen, competition that increased with the rising numbers of emigrants from Europe. From the 1880s, there were increasing demands in settler economies to introduce policies that restricting further Asian immigration. An 1892 manifesto, for instance, maintained that one of the reasons that indentured labour should not be used was that the:

> ...permanent existence of a large servile population amongst us, not admitted to the franchise, is not compatible with the continuance of our free [Australian] political institutions.[116]

Asians also began to be excluded from certain occupations to prevent their further immigration. For instance, Pacific Islanders were banned from gaining employment in the any occupation but the sugar industry in 1880 and by 1884 were excluded from all skilled positions in Queensland, following the example of exclusionist policies in Natal. In the 1890s, Europeans in Natal imposed a £3 head tax on un-indentured labourers and barred Indians from legal equality to maintain their subservient position.[117] The advent of the federated Australian nation in 1901 coincided with the abolition of indentured labour in the sugar industry, formalised in the Pacific Islanders Act of 1901. In addition, the Immigration Restriction Act of 1901, commonly referred to as the White Australia policy, was intended to restrict 'coloured' labour from being introduced into Australia. Another factor that encouraged the phasing out of indentured labour was the concern that governments would have to cover the expenses for indentured labourers wishing to return to their homelands after their term had

---

115 Clarence-Smith, W. G., 'Cocoa Plantations and Coerced Labor in the Gulf of Guinea, 1870-1914', in Klein, Martin, A., (ed.), *Breaking the Chains: Slavery, Bondage and Emancipation in Modern Africa and Asia*, (University of Wisconsin Press), 1993, pp. 150-170. See also, ibid, Grant, Kevin, *A civilised savagery: Britain and the new slaveries in Africa 1884-1926*, pp. 109-134 on Cadbury's, Clarence-Smith, W. G., *Cocoa and Chocolate 1765-1914*, (Routledge), 2000, pp. 140-161, Satre, Lowell Joseph, *Chocolate on trial: slavery, politics, and the ethics of business*, (Ohio University Press), 2005, and Off, Carol, *Bitter Chocolate: Investigating the Dark Side of the World's Most Seductive Sweet*, (Vintage Canada), 2007, for a more general approach.

116 *The Living Age*, Vol. 198, (1893), p. 54, cit, *Parliamentary debates: Senate and House of Representatives*, Vol. 5, (Commonwealth Govt. Printer), 1902, p. 5948.

117 Keegan, Timothy J., *Colonial South Africa and the origins of the racial order*, (Continuum International Publishing Group), 1996.

expired because of the increasing instability of certain colonial economies, such as Jamaica, whose sugar economy was faltering.[118]

Critical to the ending of indentured labour was the position in India where the momentum behind its abolition was found among Indian politicians particularly from the Indian National Congress rather than opposition from indentured labourers themselves. Between 1900 and 1914, public opinion in India, Britain and elsewhere grew against the indenture of Indian labourers.[119] Like Gandhi in South Africa, Manilal Maganlal Doctor, who arrived in Mauritius in 1907 to practise at the Bar, was soon involved with the struggle for Indian rights. The native population in the Caribbean colonies were opposed to indentured Indian labour and black working men's associations began to be formed to protect their livelihoods. In 1910, the Sanderson Committee caused the system to be further modified. For although it had found that indentured labour was a system of free labour and was beneficial, even given the many drawbacks in the system, the general effect of their recommendations was a rapid decrease in importation of Indians. Indenture to Mauritius and Malaya was ended in 1910 and to Natal the following year. In the same year, the Indian Legislative Council passed the Indian Emigration (Amendment) Act that permitted emigration to be banned and made unlawful in any designated country. Questions were asked in the Indian Legislative Council after the shooting of Indians by police at the riot on the Rose Hill estate in British Guiana in 1913.

In 1912, the Colonial Office proposed that recruiting labour should only take place in certain ports of India. Nationalist and anti-indenture sentiments were most popular with the Indian bourgeoisie and itinerant politicians brought opposition to indenture to local levels. The response from India was clear and efforts by British politicians to mitigate the abolition of the trade by suggesting other possibilities were refused. For Indian politicians, these alternatives were simply indentured labour shorn of its penal clauses. Gandhi introduced the Abolition of Indenture Bill in 1916 that was carried unanimously in the Indian National Congress. Indentured labour was stopped by regulation in India in 1917 though it was five years before this proved effective.

Ironically, the system of indentured emigration was already in decline as protests in India became louder. Because of the war recruiting had already stopped and all that was left for the British government to do was abolish the system officially. On 21 September, 1917, a dispatch from the British government stated that 'indentured emigration, temporarily prohibited because of urgent military needs, cannot be resumed.' Although certain colonies were reluctant to end indenture, such as in Fiji, other colonies, such as British Guiana, moved much more quickly. They ended all outstanding indentures in December 1919, while trying to clear up the entire system in Fiji was much more problematic and anyone in authority over Indians in Fiji was regarded with

---

118 Miers, Suzanne, *Slavery in the Twentieth Century: The evolution of a global pattern*, (AltaMira Press), 2003, pp. 47-66, considers the ending of indentured labour and the creation of international constraints on slavery through the League of Nations.

119 On rising levels of opposition in South Africa led by Gandhi, see Swan, Maureen, 'The 1913 Natal Indian Strike', *Journal of Southern African Studies*, Vol. 10, (1984), pp. 239-258.

animosity in India.[120] Although the Fijian government had abolished indenture by January 1920, problems with repatriation of labourers led to strikes in the Fijian sugar industry and other economic problems that made free repatriation difficult for the government.[121] In Trinidad and the other Caribbean colonies, the trade was never resumed after its wartime stoppage and the last indentured Indians in Trinidad were freed in April 1922. In the same year, the government of India passed Indian Act VII banning the emigration of unskilled workers expect where approved by both chambers of the Indian legislature and authorised by the Governor-General in Council.

With the end of the indenture system, Indians were now faced with the problem of deciding whether to return to India or to settle in their homes in the colonies and new Dominions. Many Indians had seen the 1918 Imperial War Conference as an important step on the road of equality with the new Dominions, and felt therefore that some reality should be given to the concept of equality under the British Crown. The Indian National Congress in 1920 demanded that Indians be given equal status in the Dominions at the same time India was seeking Dominion status as a stepping-stone to achieving home rule. The reality was very different with increasing demands to strengthen white supremacy in settler colonies. The result was the imposition of restrictions on what Indians could and could not do. For instance, in Kenya, the best residential and commercial areas in Nairobi and the best farming districts in the White Highlands were reserved for whites. The planning of the town of Kampala in Uganda was also based on a similar segregation system. Few Indians wanted a revival of full-scale emigration, but neither did they want restrictions on their movements within the Empire and felt a loss of honour over the racial nature of the Dominion immigration restrictions, and the denial by the Dominions of full rights of citizenship to Indian residents. As well as hostility from the white communities in the colonies, Indians also began to bear the brunt of native hostility. From 1830 to 1950 the history of both India and Indians abroad was one of struggles for equal rights and against discrimination. In 1949 India called for the equality of Commonwealth citizens and pledged that when a republic she would remain within the Commonwealth, with her membership full and equal.

There is a well-established view suggesting that the indenture system did not survive past the first two decades of the twentieth century. David Northrup's and Kay Saunders' studies of indentured labour in the British Empire both end in the early 1920s. Indentures were only gradually phased out over a period of several decades. By the 1930s, the International Labor Organisation had expressed its determination to abolish all forms of unfree labour and by 1940 it appeared that indenture was at an end. However, some countries continued the practice. In British Malaya, for instance, indentured labour was abolished for Indians in 1910 and for Chinese in 1914, but Javanese labourers were still subject to penal sanctions in the 1920s. The labour trade in New Caledonia began in 1865 and lasted well into the 1930s. In fact, Javanese men and women

---

[120] Gillion, Kenneth L., *Fiji's Indian migrants: a history to the end of indenture in 1920*, (Oxford University Press), 1962.

[121] On the ending of indentured labour see, ibid, Northrup, David, *Indentured labor in an age of imperialism, 1834-1922*, pp. 141-147.

were brought to New Caledonia as late as 1949 and in 1955 the French negotiated a new contract agreement with the independent Indonesian government. The indenture system remained in place in Australia's colonial administration of Papua New Guinea until 1950. Peter Fitzpatrick argues that even the 'agreement system' that replaced indenture, was essentially the same system by a different name.[122] The only significant change was that the penal provisions were repealed, but these were replaced with alternative sanctions whereby absence from work could result in court action to terminate the contract and have damages paid to the employer out of the worker's deferred pay. In 1963, restrictions on entering employment outside the agreement system were abolished, but the system survived into the 1970s. It is not possible to set a single date for the abolition of indenture because the indenture system was dismantled in a piecemeal fashion.

Resisting migration

Myra Willard's highly contradictory account of the development of the White Australia policy argued that preserving the 'British' character of the new Australian nation was the most vital preoccupation of the first Federal legislators.[123] While Willard lauded Australia as a highly democratic country with government policy clearly expressing 'the will of the people', she defended Federal parliamentarians for championing nationalistic reasons for the adoption of immigration restriction.[124] She argued that the racism inherent in the exclusionary legislation was regrettable, but future generations would appreciate the benefits that such restrictions would bequeath especially the preservation of Australia's British character and the promotion of racial unity and as a result national unity. She was clearly in sympathy with anti-slavery reformer, Sir William Molesworth, who, in 1838, argued that Australia would be spared from disruptions to social cohesion if a proposal to allow Indian immigration was avoided, as this would only create:

> ...a class separated by race and habits from the rest of the labouring population...Indian immigration would only curse Australia with the social and political difficulties of a racial problem.[125]

Despite its inconsistencies, Willard's argument regarding working-class support for a racially discriminatory immigration policy achieved such dominance that it was handed down from generation to generation without

---

[122] Fitzpatrick, Peter, ''Really Rather Like Slavery': Law and Labour in the Colonial Economy in Papua New Guinea,' *Contemporary Crises*, Vol. 4, (1980), pp. 77-95, reprinted in Wheelwright, E. L., and Buckley, Ken, (eds.), *Essays in the Political Economy of Australian Capitalism,* Vol. 3, (Australia and New Zealand Book Co.), 1978, see especially pp. 109-112.

[123] See, Willard, M., *History of the White Australia Policy to 1920*, (Melbourne University Press), 1923. See also, Evans, Julie, Grimshaw, Patricia, Philips, David, and Swain, Shurlee, *Equal Subjects, Unequal Rights: Indigenous People in British settler colonies, 1830s-1910*, (Manchester University Press), 2003, pp. 134-156.

[124] Ibid, Willard, M., *History of the White Australia Policy to 1920*, pp. xi, 88-89.

[125] Ibid, Willard, M., *History of the White Australia Policy to 1920*, pp. 6-7.

serious challenge. What is striking about the historiography on racism is the degree to which many of the authors share Willard's obvious sympathy for the 'higher ideals' that prompted the first Federal legislators to institute immigration restriction. In Australia, for instance, there was a distinctly ruling class agitation for the White Australia policy in the 1870s and 1880s that led to demands for restrictions on non-British immigration being actively pursued by newspaper editors, large urban and pastoralist employers and colonial parliaments. An exploration of the events in Clunes in 1873 and Vancouver in 1907 allows us to ask whether racism was the result of demands by the working-class for restrictions on immigration to protect their jobs. Also, whether this led to working people being 'natural' supporters of racist exclusion or whether it was the result of the ruling élite, concerned at attempts by white and immigrant labour to make common cause, to portray it as a 'racial' as opposed to a 'class' struggle or whether it was a combination of the two.

Clunes, 1873

During the 1840s and 1850s, the discovery of major gold reserves in northern California, Victoria and later British Columbia and NZ transformed the European settler societies of the Pacific Rim.[126] The full extent of the Chinese role in the emergent central Victorian goldfields society has only recently been recognised. Although best known for their role in the gold mining industry, they were involved in other activities on the goldfields working as herbalists, merchants and restaurateurs.[127] There was growing racial tensions on the diggings where there were 3,000 Chinese out of about 18,000 men and the proportion of Chinese to European was steadily increasing. As a cultural group, they stood out because most retained their identity and customs and the 'Chinese question' began to vie with the other major populist issue of the day, the 'unlocking' of

---

[126] General discussion can be found in 'The Chinese', in Jupp, James, (ed.), *The Australian people: An encyclopedia of the nation, its people and their origins*, (Cambridge University Press), 2001, pp. 197-204, Curthoys, Ann, 'Men of All Nations, except Chinamen': Europeans and Chinese on the Goldfields of New South Wales', in McCalman, Iain, Cook, Alexander, and Reeves, Andrew, (eds.), *Gold: Forgotten histories and lost objects of Australia*, (Cambridge University Press), 2001, pp. 100-123, and Lake, Marilyn, and Reynolds, Henry, *Drawing the Global Colour Line: White Men's Countries and the International Challenge of Racial Equality*, (Cambridge University Press), 2008, pp. 15-47. The experience of Chinese immigrants in Victoria during the 1850s and after can be explored in, Daley, C., 'The Chinese in Victoria', *Victorian Historical Magazine*, Vol. 14, (1931-1932), pp. 23-35, Price, C., *The Great White Walls are Built: Restrictive Immigration to North America and Australasia 1836-1888*, (Australian National University Press), 1974, Markus, A., *Fear and Hatred: Purifying Australia and California 1850-1901*, (Hale & Iremonger), 1979, Gittins, J., *The Diggers from China: The Story of the Chinese on the Goldfields*, (Quartet Books), 1981, Cronin, K., *Colonial Casualties: Chinese in Early Australia,* (Melbourne University Press), 1982, and Fitzgerald, John, *Big White Lie: Chinese Australians in White Australia*, (University of South Wales Press), 2007, pp. 57-80. McLaren, Ian F., *The Chinese in Victoria: Official Reports and Documents*, (Red Rooster Press), 1985, is an invaluable study including critical sources from the 1850s.

[127] Lovejoy, Valerie, 'Depending upon Diligence: Chinese at work in Bendigo 1861-1881', *Journal of Historical and European Studies*, Vol. 1, (2007), pp. 23-37, provides a valuable case study.

Crown Lands. European miners were angered by their increasing presence in the fields and in 1854, an irritated group of European and American miners met in Bendigo and declared that a 'general and unanimous rising should take place to drive the Chinese off the goldfield'. Prompt action by local constables prevented any further vigilante action but the movement was only the beginning of greater anti-Chinese tensions.[128] Racism functioned as an outlet or 'safety valve' for tensions produced by the colonial style of administration that were otherwise not permitted expression.

In December 1873, a major disturbance against Chinese miners occurred in the Victorian gold mining town of Clunes, some twenty miles north of Ballarat.[129] The first such riot occurred in March 1851 at Ipswich in Queensland when twelve unarmed Chinese were savagely beaten by a European mob. The scale of the incident at Clunes and the level of violence were only slightly less than occurred in the riots at Buckland River in 1857 and Lambing Flat in 1860 and 1861.[130] Despite this, the incident at Clunes has not been accorded the same significance and the incident is mentioned in passing or used to moralise about colonial Australia's hostility towards Asian peoples but contemporary colonial newspapers cast doubt on the traditional ethnic explanation.

Once occupied by the Wemba-Wemba people, the first European settler was Donald Cameron, an overlander from Sydney who took up a pastoral run in

---

[128] Debney, Ben, 'The Yellow Peril: The Chinese Scapegoat on the Goldfields as Ideological Safety Valve', paper presented at Australian History Association annual conference, June 2016: https://www.academia.edu/26818721/The_Yellow_Peril_The_Chinese_Scapegoat_on_the_Goldfields_as_Ideological_Safety_Valve

[129] The most recent historiographical discussion can be found in Heathcote, Christopher, 'Clunes 1873: The Uprising that Wasn't', *Quadrant*, Vol. LIII, (12), (2008), pp. 72-82. See also, Baker, David, 'Barricades and batons: A historical perspective of the policing of major industrial disorder in Australia', in Enders, Mike, and Dupont, Benoît, (eds.), *Policing the Lucky Country*, (The Federation Press), 2001, pp. 199-222, especially pp. 202-204, Small, Jerome, 'Reconsidering White Australia: Class and anti-Chinese racism in the 1873 Clunes riot', BA (Hons), Thesis, La Trobe University, 1997, and Griffiths, P.G. 'The making of White Australia: Ruling class agendas, 1876-1888', Ph.D., Thesis, Australian National University, 2006, pp. 97-136, 349-458.

[130] Reeves, Keir, and Wong Hoy, Kevin, 'Beyond a European protest: reappraising Chinese agency on the Victorian goldfields', in Mayne, Alan, (ed.), *Eureka: Reappraising an Australian Legend*, (Network), 2006, pp. 153-174, is a crucial revisionist contribution to discussions of the Chinese in Victoria in the 1850s. There is a growing literature on Lambing Flat: Carrington, D. L., 'Riots at Lambing Flat 1860-1861', *Journal of the Royal Australian Historical Society*, Vol. 46, (1960), pp. 223-243, Walker, R. B., 'Another Look at the Lambing Flat Riots 1860-1861', *Journal of the Royal Australian Historical Society*, Vol. 56, (1970), pp. 193-205, Selth, P., 'The Burrangong (Lambing Flat) Riots 1860-61: A Closer Look', *Journal of the Royal Australian Historical Society*, Vol. 60, (1974), pp. 48-69, Connolly, C. N., 'Miners' Rights: Explaining the 'Lambing Flat' Riots of 1860-61', in Curthoys, A., and Markus, A., (eds.), *Who are Our Enemies? Racism and the Australian Working class*, (Neutral Bay), 1978, pp. 35-47, and Messner, Andrew, 'Popular Constitutionalism and Chinese Protest on the Victoria Goldfields', *Journal of Australian Colonial History*, Vol. 2, (2), (2000), pp. 63-78.

1839, naming it Clunes after his birthplace in Scotland.[131] Gold traces were first found on this property in March 1850, although news of the find was concealed. James Esmond was later shown the site of the find.[132] Like Edward Hargreaves, who was involved in NSW's first gold strike, he was one of the few men in Australia who had some experience of gold-bearing quartz reefs as he, like Hargreaves, had been on the Californian goldfields. Esmond's tests verified the existence of the reefs and his findings were announced in the *Geelong Advertiser* on 7 July 1851 resulting in Victoria's first gold rush.[133] Individual prospectors found the reefs too deep and major production was only possible by large companies using the latest equipment and skilled miners. By 1873, gold mining at Clunes was in the hands of several businesses; the most prominent were the Port Phillip, New North Clunes, South Clunes, Criterion and United mining companies.

Dispute and strike

In late 1873, there were acrimonious industrial disputes over working conditions at both the South Clunes mine and the Lothair mine.[134] For reasons that are unclear, each company proposed to increase miners' individual working hours from eleven to twelve shifts per fortnight.[135] The significance of the Clunes riot in the protracted war between workers and employers over hours worked and the relationship of those hours to wages has been largely unacknowledged. The commentaries in contemporary newspapers are clear that there was more a determination to defend the rights of working people and to save the Eight-Hour system than to target the Chinese racially. In early September, management at the South Clunes mine told their workers that new contracts would not be accepted unless they agreed to work a Saturday afternoon shift. On Monday 15 September, the management at the neighbouring Lothair mine announced that the contract system was to be abolished and two extra shifts (Sunday night and Saturday afternoon) introduced. The intended changes were considerable. Most mines in the region stopped work at 1 pm on Saturdays (a few in Clunes ran until 3 pm) and did not start up again until 7 am on Mondays, but the two companies wanted shifts to run until 11 pm on Saturday and from 10 pm on Sunday. For this extra work, South Clunes offered its employees a small wage increase, while

---

[131] Bradford, William, *The Clunes Goldfield*, (Government Printer), 1903, is a valuable geographical survey.

[132] Cranfield, Louis R., 'James William Esmond (1822-1890)', *ADB*, Vol. 4, p. 142, is a brief, biography.

[133] 'Gold in the Pyrenees', *Geelong Advertiser*, 7 July 1851, p. 2.

[134] The industrial tension at Clunes was heightened by the type of mining employed on the Clunes goldfields, the foul air and very hot conditions. Health was affected because it was argued that 'quartz reefing affects the lungs to a greater extent than alluvial mining'. 'Editorial', *Ballarat Courier*, 9 September 1873, p. 2.

[135] The decision may have been motivated by the volatile movements in share prices in 1873 and the increasing cost of digging shafts: see, 'Mining News. Mining Share Market', *Maitland Mercury & Hunter River General Advertiser*, 1 July 1873, p. 2, 'The state of the Share market on Thursday was a near approach of absolute stagnation…', 'Commercial Intelligence', *Argus*, 2 July, p. 4, 'Commercial Intelligence', *Argus*, 1 September 1873, p. 4.

Lothair proposed to put its miners on contract and pay only for work performed. The miners offered to extend working hours until 3 pm on Saturdays and wanted new wages to be negotiated but management would not budge.

On Friday 5 September, a section of the miners of the South Clunes mine went out on strike.[136] 110 miners at the Lothair mine downed tools on Monday 15 September bringing the total number of strikers to 150. The outraged response of the miners and their families to management's violation of Clunes custom that included the Saturday afternoon off, was summed up by 'A Miner's Wife, One of the Union', who wrote to the *Ballarat Courier.* She could name more than a dozen miners who had fallen victim to 'the foul air of the Clunes mines'. Some impoverished wife and children:

> ...have been obliged to leave the district...with bleeding hearts at being torn from the remains of the beloved one who had made this earth their paradise...Directors, not satisfied with the old process of slowly poisoning our husbands, seem determined of making it both wholesale and rapid.[137]

The dispute seems to have been compounded by work conditions in the Lothair mine that was poorly ventilated. Some miners wanted it fixed. An Old Miner wrote that he had, 'through foul air' in the Clunes mines, been 'laid aside, and many are in their graves'. The Lothair mine, he wrote:

> ...has only one shaft, no means of ventilation, and in case of water breaking in...they have no means of escape...allow me to urge my brother miners not to allow anything to induce them to resume work till some means are set on foot for the preservation of their lives.

The immediate outcome of the strike was the formation of the Clunes Miners' Association and the town's mayor, William Blanchard, a former miner, was elected the association's president and charged with handling negotiations.[138] The South Clunes mine backed down after several weeks, but the directors of the Lothair Gold Mining Company did not waver.[139] The company tried to break the strike by obtaining European miners from Ballarat. An appeal by the Clunes Miners' Association for Ballarat miners to refuse work was published prominently in the *Ballarat Courier.* The Ballarat miners did not come either through persuasion or intimidation.

In late October, the directors threatened to employ a team of Chinese who were amenable to working all week and at a reduced wage. The threat of Chinese strike-breakers had previously been used to discipline European miners in Creswick in 1872, when discontent flared over the extension of the Saturday night shift by two and a half hours. On 25 October, a deputation from the

---

[136] 'Editorial', *Ballarat Courier*, 5 September 1873, p. 2, reported that only the alluvial miners of the South Clunes Mine had gone in strike over new contracts.

[137] 'Editorial', *Ballarat Courier*, 16 September 1873, p. 2.

[138] 'Miners' Strike at Clunes', *Argus*, 22 September 1873, p. 5, reported a meeting of striking miners two days earlier to negotiate with the companies.

[139] 'Editorial', *Argus*, 26 September 1873, stated that work resumed in the South Clunes mine on 25 September, reporting news in the *Ballarat Courier*.

Miners' Association travelled to Ballarat where, assisted by a government interpreter and the Rev. Young, a social worker from the Chinese Christian Mission, they spoke with the Chinese community and explained the situation.[140] Contrary to many accounts, the Ballarat Chinese heeded the Clunes miners' call and did not break their strike. The miners' union had some influence in the Golden Point camp but did not seem to have similar influence the source of the strike-breakers in the Creswick Chinese camp that was more segregated from the town. The following day the directors of the Lothair mine who included James Francis,[141] the Premier of Victoria and the wealthy businessman Peter Lalor[142] met and agreed to hire blackleg labour if needed. Matters simmered for another four weeks. By the end of November[143], the Lothair directors had accepted that the shift on Sunday night would not be worked, but refused to give ground on Saturday afternoon. After the failure of negotiations, they convened a meeting of shareholders, who decided to 'employ Chinese labor at once, in consequence of the refusal of the European miners to work the mine'.[144]

Miners' resistance

In early December, Chinese labourers were hired by the company's agent making their way from Ballarat to Creswick over the weekend of 6 and 7 December. News of their imminent departure from Creswick for Clunes was telegraphed and almost immediately circulated around the Clunes district. Unsurprisingly there were rumours that inflated the number of strike-breakers from 50 to 90 and then 150 individuals. The townspeople of Clunes considered this intolerable. They were not just hostile because miners' livelihoods were endangered, they were angry that a local business would operate on Sundays and feared that others would follow.[145] The *Creswick Advertiser*, although it refrained from taking sides in the dispute, commented that many people in the region were angered that the sanctity of the Sabbath was to be broken.[146]

Tensions rose further on Monday 8 December. Telegraphs received at Clunes warned that coaches had been hired in Ballarat to transport the strike-

---

140 Chan, Adrian, 'Young Wai, John (1847?-1930)', *ADB*, Vol. 12, pp. 602-603.
141 Bartlett, Geoffrey, 'Francis, James Goodall (1819-1884)', *ADB*, Vol. 4, pp. 211-213.
142 Turner, Ian, 'Lalor, Peter (1827-1889)', *ADB*, Vol. 5, pp. 50-54.
143 Between 26 November and 31 December 1873, Victoria's Parliament was prorogued. Whether this was the reason why the Lothair directors, having procrastinated for several months, decided to take direct action may or may not have been a coincidence. 'Propogation of the Parliament of Victoria', *Sydney Morning Herald*, 1 December 1873, p. 3.
144 Initially there was some confusion about where the Chinese were coming from. Newspaper reports quoted telegrams to the Clunes Miners Association saying that there were 80 Chinese coming from Ballarat 'by way of Creswick', or that 150 Chinese were coming from Creswick. The people who knew about where the Chinese were brought from were those who organised the strike-breaking operation: Lothair management and the police and both parties repeatedly stated that the Chinese came from Creswick.
145 'Latest Intelligece. Telegraphic Despatches. Demonstration of Miners at Clunes', *Ballarat Star*, 8 December 1873, p. 2., 'Riots at Clunes. Attack on the Police by Crowds of Miners and their Wives', *Ballarat Star*, 10 December 1873, p. 2.
146 *Creswick Advertiser*, 8 December 1873, p. 3.

breakers and were expected at Creswick later in the day.[147] From there, the Chinese would proceed directly to Clunes with an escort of armed police to begin work. William Blanchard, as town mayor and local Miners' Association president, sent a bell man around the streets to call the town's 5,000 inhabitants to a public meeting and all other activity including mining ceased in Clunes for the day. In the afternoon, '500 men, members of the Miners Association marched around the town, headed by the Clunes Brass Band, and armed with pick-handles, battens, and waddies...' They stopped before the town hall, several hotels and apparently, churches, where speeches were delivered by civic and religious leaders: those who dared labour on the Sabbath would not enter Clunes. According to the *Courier*, 'nearly the whole male population, and a good many women--to say nothing of the boys...' were in the streets.[148] The major speakers at the meeting that generated a lot of anti-Chinese rhetoric were Blanchard, a municipal rates collector and a Member of the Legislative Assembly. No striking miners spoke although they have been painted as most opposed to Chinese workers and Chinese people. Ralph Coundon, a director of the Lothair mine, put the company's position to the assembly before the Royal Hotel and John Pascoe, another director also tried to speak, but he was shouted down.[149]

In the interim, the mayor of Creswick, who had spent the morning in Clunes, returned to his own town, where he found that five Cobb coaches had arrived and were preparing to leave with 45 Chinese passengers, along with Samuels, a company director and an escort of twelve troopers from Ballarat led by Sergeant Larner, who was responsible for supervising the Chinese encampment in Ballarat. The mayor and Sergeant Cooper, the Creswick District policeman, spoke with Sergeant Larner, McPhee of Cobb & Co and Samuels of the Lothair mine, advising them that it was unwise to proceed that afternoon owing to public unrest at their destination. A telegram also arrived from Superintendent Hill, who had gone ahead to Clunes and who ordered the coaches to delay. It was, he believed, better to leave at first light and get into town as people were getting up.

Back in Clunes, the townspeople prepared as night fell.[150] Meetings of the miners resolved to discontinue work in all mines and to order some men working at Lothair in defiance of the Miners' Association to stop work. The town fire bell was rung, and 200 miners marched to the Lothair claim. Cages were lowered to the bottom level, the lift engine disabled, planks bolted across the shafts, ladders removed from the site, gates padlocked and a picket line established. A shed that had been erected to house the blacklegs was pulled down. Lookouts and mounted scouts were also sent along the main road, and all tracks, running to Creswick and Ballarat. A team of men went out to the toll gate on the Creswick Road, which they took over and locked. Expecting a confrontation, most men armed themselves with sticks, while the town's youth

147 'Editorial', *Argus*, 9 December 1872, p. 4.
148 'Editorial', *Ballarat Courier*, 9 December 1873, p. 2, 'Serious Disturbances at Clunes, *The Age*, 10 December 1873, p. 3.
149 'Local Intelligence', *Argus*, 9 December 1873, p. 6.
150 'Disturbances at Clunes', *Ballarat Courier*, 10 December 1873, p. 2, spoke of the 'ugly temper' of the miners.

filled their pockets with stones. It was an expectant night. The town's two fire bells were rung in false alarm after garbled reports were received that the coaches were nearby (in fact, the regular mail coach) and, from midnight onwards, a large body of townsmen roamed from one hill to another, scrambling about in the dark.

The coach party left the Chinese encampment at Creswick at 5 am. It was soon met by four mounted troopers who warned that the toll road was blocked. With Sergeant Larner sitting beside him in the box, McPhee turned the lead coach into the Tourella Road and took the party over to the Ballarat Road, from where it could drive straight into Clunes without obstruction. News came through at dawn that the coaches and a mounted escort had been sighted and would soon be along the Ballarat Road. The fire bells were again rung and an estimated thousand people rushed *en masse* up the hill then out along the Ballarat Road, stopping at the intersection with Coghill's Creek Road, adjacent to Short's Farm on the edge of town. Farmers nearby called on the leaders to take their drays, ploughs, harrows, assorted agricultural equipment and some loose lumber to build a barricade, which they hastily did.[151]

They were still piling on rocks when, at around 7 am, the Cobb coaches and police escort drew into sight. McPhee, who was leading with a full team of horses, cracked his whip and bore down upon the miners. The *Creswick Advertiser* explained:

> Some primitive barricades of drays and earthwork had been erected...but the great and real barricade was the living acting mass before them. There was a little parley, but it was to no avail. An attempt was made by the police to break through, but the attempt was easily frustrated...[152]

The five coaches were met by 'a fast and furious storm of stones' and the occupants huddled behind their belongings as more missiles were flung their way. Sergeant Larner was knocked off one of the coaches by a large stone. Meanwhile one enterprising miner darted forward and determinedly tried to unbuckle the bridle of the lead horse in McPhee's team. Constable Durack and Sergeant Larner sprang on to the top of the barricade their weapons drawn ordering the townspeople to stop throwing stones at them and the coaches. But their bold gesture was undermined by an unidentified trooper at the rear, who shouted to the miners that none of the squad had loaded weapons. Despite these heroics, crowds 'rushed over the barricades and, surrounding the coaches, struck at them with sticks, threw stones through them at the Chinamen, and drove them far away... and assisted by, who dismounted his horse, clambering onto the barricade. According to the *Star*, the women played a prominent role in smashing the windows of the coaches, 'and pelted the unfortunate Chinamen'

---

[151] 'Riots at Clunes', *Ballarat Star*, 10 December 1873, p. 2 estimated 2,000; the *Daylesford Mercury and Express*, 11 December 1873, p. 2, stated that 1,000 men assembled on the Ballarat Road. In many subsequent mining and dock confrontations, women assisted the males in their battles with employers and authorities.

[152] 'Chinese Labout at Clunes', *Argus*, 10 December 1873, p. 5, called it a 'formidable structure'.

and Mr Bryant, the manager of Lothair, 'received a blow with a stone'.[153] The newspapers tend to corroborate each other, but on what happened next at the barricade they differ. In the *Clunes Guardian* and *Ballarat Star*, the crowd threw stones at the coaches and police without break while the *Creswick Advertiser* and *Ballarat Courier* stated that the volley eventually halted and the police, the coachmen, Bryant the mine manager, Pascoe, a company directors present and the Chinese were harangued for threatening the livelihoods of decent family men. In the meantime, the crowd swelled by hundreds as more residents and their families flocked to the barricade.

Around forty minutes after it began, the confrontation was over. The *Argus* commented that 'The battle, for nothing else can it be designated, was fought with determined energy and bravery on both sides.'[154] Under sustained attack, one of the mounted troopers, Senior Constable Carden, announced that the coaches would withdraw. An intimidated McPhee ordered his drivers to turn back for Ballarat, with the crowd giving three hearty cheers as the party disappeared. Meanwhile, Pascoe, the unpopular company director, who had been jostled, pelted with sods of earth and threatened at the barricade, was escorted back to his hotel by a policeman. By 8.30 am the barricade had been dismantled and led by the Clunes Brass Band, the demonstrators were parading back to the Town Hotel. The miners:

> ...accompanied by troops of women and children proceeded to the residences of several miners who had rendered themselves obnoxious...by continuing work...Warnings were given those offending men to leave the town...[155]

They then marched to Mr Bryant's home to demand his resignation as mine manager. However, some of the men claimed consideration for Bryant's family' and Bryant assured them that 'he had all along been opposed to bringing Chinamen' and could stay.

An outdoor meeting was held in the evening attended by 800 and 1,000 people. William Blanchard declared that justice had been served. Then a resolution to be sent to the government that expressed their 'utter abhorrence at the conduct of those persons, with whom the heavy responsibility rests, in having attempted to subject our prosperous and hitherto irreproachable town to the moral pollution and attendant horrors of a Chinese encampment', affirming the town's opposition to the introduction of Chinese labour and criticising the police for their role. This was endorsed by the meeting. Philipps, the local Member of the Legislative Assembly congratulated the miners for driving off the strike-breakers, praised the townspeople for their restraint, thanked other mines for supporting the action and criticised the authorities for intervening in a labour dispute. Bryant, the manager of the Lothair mine, again declared that he was never in favour of the company's use of Chinese labour and offered to donate £50 to the Clunes hospital. The day ended with the 800 members of the new Miners' Association marching five abreast through the town behind the brass

153 'Riots at Clunes', *Ballarat Star*, 10 December 1873, p. 2.
154 'Chinese Labour at Clunes', *Argus*, 10 December 1873, p. 5.
155 'Chinese Labour ay Clunes', *Argus*, 10 December 1873, p. 5.

band, and triumphantly singing 'God Save the Queen'. A further meeting, held on Saturday 13 December reiterated opposition to the Chinese labourers and the actions of the police.[156] Like the English bread riots described by E. P. Thompson, the Clunes riot was not the work of a lawless, aimless mob.[157] There was obviously a high level of organisation: mounted scouts on the roads and meetings to decide the course of action. More particularly, there was a high level of civic organisation, for instance the use of the town fire bell as an alarm. Respect for property, consideration of Bryant's family, the singing of 'God Save the Queen' marked the event as a patriotic gathering of Britons doing no more than upholding their constitutional rights.[158]

Aftermath

It was not the end of the affair. On 10 December, a squad of fifteen armed constables arrived from Ballarat, setting up a guard-post at the mine and re-establishing public order in the town.[159] The Victorian government distanced itself from the affair and decided not to prosecute anyone. It was left to the police to prosecute five of the rowdier protesters who were each fined £5 by the district magistrate later in the month.[160] This outcome reflected local feelings and considering the charge was obstructing the police, the penalties imposed on the guilty were light. No major crime against the state was alleged; no crime of conspiracy, no crime of provoking a riot.[161] The Victorian Solicitor-General wrote to Blanchard on 19 December asking him to account for his actions and querying whether he had abused his mayoral office on the day of the incident.[162] There was the question of which government authority had despatched the troopers. The *Maryborough & Dunolly Advertiser* did not carry a report on the trouble at nearby Clunes, but ran an editorial on the immorality of policemen the following Friday. A fortnight later the *Clunes Guardian* reported that an official investigation by the Governor of Victoria had failed to determine who authorised the escort of armed police though many in the district suspected James Francis, the Premier of protecting his business interests. The Miners' Association at Sandhurst requested a government inquiry but this did not occur.[163] The failure of government to hold the police accountable for alleged violence while

156 'The Clunes Riots' *Argus*, 15 December 1873, p. 8.
157 Thompson, E. P., 'The Moral Economy of the Crowd in the Eighteenth Century', *Past and Present*, Vol. 50, (1971), pp. 76-136, reprinted in his *Customs in Common*, (Merlin Press), 1991, pp. 185-259, with 'The Moral Economy Reviewed', pp. 259-351.
158 A meeting also heard several references of properly constituted arbitration 'bringing strikes in the old country to amicable settlement', 'The Clunes Riots', *Ballarat Star*, 15 December 1873, p. 2.
159 'Local Intelligence', *Argus*, 11, December 1873, p. 5, 'Mining Meeting', *Argus*, 12 December 1873, p. 5.
160 Summons were issued on 22 December, 'Editorial', *Argus*, 22 December 1873, pp. 4, 5, and the five men were tried on 23 December, 'The Clunes Riots', *Argus*, 24 December 1873, p. 5.
161 'News of the Day', *Age*, 19 December 1873, p. 2.
162 For the letter and Blanchard's response, see 'The Clunes Disturbance', *Argus*, 21 January 1874, p. 6.
163 'News of the Day', *Age*, 15 December 1873, p. 2.

controlling industrial disputes was a common feature of Australia's industrial history.[164]

Staunch supporters of authority condemned the Clunes rioters 'for their deliberate contempt for constituted authority.' The *Daylesford Mercury* ironically lauded the coercive baton as a sign of British justice: 'It is a just subject for pride among the British race that they respect the constable's baton as the symbol of law and order.'[165] By contrast, the *Herald* saw the police as 'violent partisans' in league with the Melbourne establishment, especially the government and the directors of the Lothair Company.[166] The *Herald* alone of colonial newspapers attacked the police involvement on legal and constitutional grounds appealing to English policing precedent and tradition in relation to industrial disputes: 'They are enjoined under no circumstances whatever to appear as partisans in strikes, but are told not to interfere on one side or the other until a breach of the peace is committed.'[167] The Clunes riot raised the fundamental issue of whether or not police facing industrial confrontation should wait for the law to be broken before becoming involved or whether they should act beforehand if they believe in the likelihood of a breach of the peace.[168]

There was also considerable, generally unsubstantiated, gossip. 'We are glad to report,' the *Creswick Advertiser* assured its readers the day after, 'that with the exception of the damage to the coaches, the injuries were small and unimportant.'[169] Nevertheless, the same piece expressed concern that 'rumours of all kinds, and of the most alarming nature, were meanwhile circulating', among them claims that the troopers had been escorting 150 Chinese labourers, that the mayor had refused to read the Riot Act to the protesters, that up to thirty police had been mobbed by the protesters and were gravely wounded and that led by Mrs Bailey, a pillar of respectability and wife of a mine manager, the leading matrons of the town were responsible for hurling yonnies.[170] One miner, whose identity kept changing, had heroically stood his ground when Sergeant Larner put a pistol against his chest and threatened to shoot.[171] Only hours after the confrontation, the *Ballarat Evening Post* reported:

> ...a party of Chinese were proceeding to Clunes by coach when they were met by a number of the wives and children of the disaffected miners, who stuck up the coach, upset it, and chased the Chinamen from the field.[172]

---

[164] Ibid, Baker, David, 'Barricades and batons: A historical perspective of the policing of major industrial disorder in Australia'.

[165] *Daylesford Mercury*, 18 December 1873.

[166] *Daylesford Mercury and Express*, 11 December 1873. Similar sentiments were expressed in, *Creswick Advertiser*, 12 December 1873. See also, 'This Week', *Melbourne Leader*, 20 December 1873, p. 16.

[167] 'Evening News' *Sydney Morning Herald*, 20 December 1873, p. 3.

[168] For the politics of criminalising collective behaviour, see Cuneen, C., and Findlay, M., 'The Functions of Criminal Law in Riot Control', in Lucas, R., and Tomasic, R., (eds.), *Power, Regulation and Resistance*, (Canberra College of Advanced Education), 1986, pp. 137-149.

[169] *Creswick Advertiser*, 10 December 1873.

[170] This is Australian slang for casually throwing small rocks or stones.

[171] *Creswick Advertiser*, 15 December 1873.

[172] *Ballarat Evening Post*, 8 December 1873.

However, the *Argus* by mid-December took a more critical stance towards the disturbances calling them 'disgraceful' on 20 December. Accounts were soon carried in newspapers across Australia and the myth of a large-scale race riot rapidly spread.[173] For instance, the *Brisbane Courier Mail* carried news on consecutive mornings:

> Melbourne. December 10. A great riot took place today at Clunes. Two thousand (2000) diggers attacked one hundred and fifty (150) Chinamen who had been engaged by the Lothian Company and were under police escort. The diggers drove them back, and wounded the sergeant of police.[174]

> Melbourne. December 11. An increased force of the police has been sent to Clunes, but the Chinese refuse to return to their claims.[175]

By Saturday, the popular Sydney weekly the *Town & Country Journal*, with a considerable circulation through rural NSW, was also reporting that there had been a violent clash between miners and a 'gang' of 150 Chinese labourers at Clunes. The *Argus* printed a letter from the Clunes miners on 19 January 1874 in which they outlined their reasons for the dispute with the Lothair Company concluding with:

> Upon the Clunes outrage, as it is called, most miners acknowledge that the officers of the law must be respected and that it is especially necessary to their interests that the laws should be impartially administered...[176]

However, it added an editorial postscript:

> We insert this letter on the principle of hearing both sides, but it really does not touch the point at issue. That point is not whether the Clunes miners or the Lothair directors were right as to the ground of quarrel, but whether the quarrel is to be fought out by lawful means or by violence and intimidation.

The dispute at the Lothair mine was finally settled through discussions between the directors of the company and the Miners' Association and the miners returned to work on 4 February 1874.[177]

---

[173] News of what occurred in Clunes spread very quickly aided by the telegraph system. As a result, the disturbances were reported in Sydney the following day: 'Melbourne', *Sydney Morning Herald*, 10 December 1873, p. 7, 'Melbourne', *Empire*, 10 December 1873, p. 2, and in Queensland and Tasmania briefly on 10 December and in greater detail the following day.

[174] 'Melbourne', *Brisbane Courier*, 11 December 1873, p. 2.

[175] 'Melbourne', *Brisbane Courier*, 12 December 1873.

[176] 'The Clunes Miners', *Argus*, 19 January 1874, p. 5.

[177] 'Mining Meeting', *Argus*, 6 February 1874, p. 7.

Alternative explanations

There appears to be two different explanations for what happened at Clunes in December 1873 in both the contemporary record and among later historians. The first maintains that the attack on Chinese labour was simply part of industrial action and that race played no part in the disturbances.[178] Attacks on blackleg labour were not uncommon in Australia or in other parts of Britain's Empire. In this explanation, the race of the blackleg labourers was irrelevant. The *Age*, during its successful attempt to push the Lothair dispute to arbitration in January 1874, argued that the miners were keen to prevent 'any body of men, be they moon-faced opium eating celestials, or sturdy British diggers' working the strike-bound mine. The *Argus* also thought the 'hypocritical and canting' motion passed after the riot was a cover: 'The 'moral pollution' business was only put forward because [the rioters] felt ashamed of having broken the Queen's peace in the pursuit of sordid gain.'[179]

The second explanation sees the events at Clunes as motivated by race.[180] One Clunes resident who wrote to the *Age* recounted the response of some rioters to appeals to stop:

> We will keep the peace if possible, but we must stop the Chinamen. If the company can get Europeans to fill our places we will submit, but we cannot compete with these Chinamen...

This represented a further expression of anti-Asian prejudice that can be traced back to the 1840s when squatters first began agitating for the systematic introduction of Asian labour.[181] During a deep depression this was hardly a welcome proposal. The *Sun* blamed the pastoralists for igniting the issue at a time when 'hundreds of free mechanics were wandering about the streets of Sydney seeking employment of any kind in vain'.[182] Some of the agitation was undeniably racist: a mass petition warned of the 'vices particular to the Natives of India' that would hinder 'the growth of virtue and morality amongst us'.[183] These early attempts by the pastoral interest failed, but in 1844, with increased numbers in the NSW Legislative Council, they felt sufficiently confident to re-visit the

---

[178] See, Rolls, Eric, *Sojourners: The Epic Story of China's Centuries-Old Relationship with Australia*, (University of Queensland Press), 1992, pp. 181-182, Ross, Edgar, *A History of the Miner's Federation of Australia*, (Australasian Coal and Shale Employees' Federation), 1970, p. 49, and Blainey, G., *The Rush that Never Ended: A History of Australian Mining, A History of Australian Mining*, (Melbourne University Press), 2nd ed., 1969, p. 89, and Blainey, G., *A History of Victoria*, 3rd ed., (Cambridge University Press), 2007, p. 50.

[179] 'Telegraphic Despatches', *Argus*, 15 December 1873, p. 7.

[180] See, for instance, Clark, C. M. H., *A History of Australia*, Vol. 4, The earth abideth for ever 1851-1888, (Melbourne University Press), 1978, p. 350, and ibid, Markus, A., *Fear and Hatred: Purifying Australia and California 1850-1901*, pp. 76-77.

[181] The question had already been raised the previous year: see *Free Press and Commercial Journal*, 27 February, 1841.

[182] 'The Cruelty and Injustice of Coolie Advocacy Exposed', *Sun*, 28 January 1843, p. 3.

[183] Burgmann, Verity, 'Capital and Labour', in ibid, Curthoys, Ann, and Markus, Andrew, (eds.), *Who Are Our Enemies? Racism and the Working Class in Australia*, p. 25.

proposal. The *Guardian* reported that a committee on immigration had been set up and was about to recommend the import of Indian labour, the result of which would invariably be the 'depreciation of labor' and the 'distress of the working-classes'.[184] Public opinion was again mobilised and the squatters' second attempt to introduce indentured labour was dropped and 'free-born Englishmen, Scotsmen, and Irishmen' no longer faced the prospect of having to compete in the labour market with 'heathen slaves'.[185] Towards the end of the 1840s, the source for potential cheap labour turned towards China and marked the beginnings of a shift away from anti-immigration rhetoric framed in simple class terms to a more sophisticated racist discourse in which radical newspaper editors played a significant role. It was an attitude that was exacerbated by the unparalleled immigration from Asia, and China following the discovery of gold in the 1850s. This represented the beginnings of a long tradition in the Australian labour movement of antagonism toward the use of Asian indentured labour and marked the beginnings of what fifty years later would become the 'White Australia' policy.

The problem is that the evidence is ambiguous on whether the protest would have occurred anyway in Clunes or whether negative views of the Chinese motivated the protesters to act. The active involvement of women in the protest might be taken as evidence of opposition to the 'morally polluting' Chinese given the emphasis in contemporary public culture on women as protectors of moral virtue. Certainly, the involvement of women in the march around Clunes the afternoon before the riot was a departure from the norm. A union march earlier in the strike, before the issue of Chinese labour was raised, was composed solely of men, the custom on such ceremonial occasions. Women's involvement in the Broken Hill strikes of the 1880s shows the same pattern as at Clunes and at Broken Hill, Chinese labour was not an issue. Women at Broken Hill, like those in Clunes generally did not take part in the miners' union marches and mass meetings. However, they were often prominent when it came to picketing including physical violence to would-be strike-breakers and on rare occasions, around high points of a struggle such as mass pickets, would also participate in the union marches. Women acted largely in defence of their maternal responsibilities that they believed was threatened by attacks on the 'moral economy' and in support of their menfolk.

There was one interesting difference between the attitude of the press to Broken Hill and Clunes. Conservative newspapers savaged the women at Broken Hill. 'they hardly deserve to be called women' for their participation in the picketing. However, of the newspapers that commented on the Clunes riot, only one expressed any regrets that 'women, lovely women, should so readily engage in aggressive warfare.'[186] By contrast, women were cast in heroic terms and the *Bendigo Advertiser* noted:

---

[184] 'The Mutual Protection Assoction', *Guardian*, 30 March 1844, p. 1.
[185] 'The Labour Market', *Sun*, 25 February 1843, p. 1.
[186] 'Disturbances at Clunes', *Age*, 11 December 1873, p. 3.

> ...the wives of the miners took a prominent part in the unfortunate affair...When women are led to take up arms, we may be sure that the cause is one in which it would be utter folly for the adverse party to persist.[187]

In the absence of compelling evidence, it is impossible to tell if the response at Clunes would have been the same to Chinese as to other strike-breakers. However, the involvement of Chinese gave newspapers and other 'respectable' opinion the option of cultivating working-class support, despite the townspeople's involvement in action that they would normally have condemned. The *Age* unequivocally condemned the violence:

> A greater disgrace could not have befallen the working men of Victoria, whose grievances have hitherto been adjusted without appeal...to physical force...[188]

Having condemned 'opposition to constituted authority', the *Age* made its views clear on the Chinese:

> ...this community would suffer severely were the mining leases...to be worked by an inferior and barely tolerated race...If it be not advisable as a matter of public policy for the capitalist to have resort to a semi-barbarous race when unable to bend his fellow-countrymen to his will, then the police...were wrongfully employed in furnishing aid to the one set of disputants against the other.[189]

The argument put forward in the more liberal newspaper leaders had four dimensions. Workers were condemned for taking action against strike-breakers into their own hands, rather than leaving matters to their 'warm friends and assiduous advocates'. But there was clear hostility to the Chinese and the provocative decision by the company to employ Chinese labour as strike-breakers was attacked. Finally, the police were criticised for favouring one party. In some goldfields newspapers, the issue was not seen to be the use of strike breakers, but the 'insult to our race' by 'the introduction of Chinese labour' in any form. The conservative press ran only the first two arguments with a heavy emphasis on the first. The *Argus* warned:

> For the first time in our history, rioting has been resorted to...to enforce the demands of labour...employers have as much right to employ Chinese labour...as the miners have to strike...[190]

Legitimating racism

The *Argus* did not oppose anti-Chinese racism arguing that 'Englishmen should give their own countrymen the refusal of employment before applying to aliens.' The condemnation was limited to 'the exorbitant demands of grasping unionists, enforced by violence.'[191] In Bendigo, Stawell, and Maryborough, local Miners'

---

[187] 'The Clunes Riots', *Bendigo Advertiser*, 11 December 1873, p. 2.
[188] 'Disturbances at Clunes', *Age*, 11 December 1873, p. 3.
[189] 'Disturbances at Clunes', *Age*, 12 December 1873, p. 3.
[190] 'Disturbances at Clunes', *Argus*, 11 December 1873, p. 3.
[191] 'The Clunes Riots', *Argus*, 15 December 1873, p. 8.

Associations organised well-attended meetings in the wake of the riot.[192] Newspaper reports of the Maryborough and Stawell meetings are vague, but both approved motions supporting the rioters' action at Clunes. The most detailed reports covered the large meeting of the Bendigo Miners' Association. Association where its president Robert Clark defended the action of the miners while regretting the law breaking. Noting the 'well-known fact that Chinamen as a class were very objectionable to a large portion of the population', Clark read negative comments on the Chinese from the *Age* before introducing the speakers.[193] One of these Mr Hattam argued that the issue of the strike and riot was entirely subsumed under the 'Chinese question'. Though starting with the usual disclaimer that he 'did not intend to incite feelings of hostility or that the law should be broken', by the end of his speech Hattam was referring to Chinese as 'savages' and 'barbarians'. The response showed that he was speaking to a largely sympathetic meeting. He stated:

> ...he would not object to Chinese labor if it was found prudent to employ it...but he objected to the manner in which it had been attempted to be introduced. (Hear, hear.) What right had the Government to try to force Chinese labor upon them...the people of Clunes objected strongly to it. (Applause) It was not long ago since a poll tax on Chinamen was in operation. This showed that they...would not suit to mix with Europeans... (Cheers.). ...Why should these Mongolians...enjoy the advantages of this colony, which were only intended for Europeans. (Loud applause.)

Opposition to the torrent of racism was slight and met a hostile reception from some of the crowd. The *Bendigo Advertiser* reported on the fate of a speaker during another virulently anti-Chinese speech:

> ...nothing could be heard but cries of 'He's a capitalist,'...'Put him out,'...it seemed for a moment as if a general fight was about to take place... Mr Matthew Barker came on to the platform...bleeding profusely... [he] stated that the only remark he had made was, 'Wasn't a Chinaman a man and a brother.[194]

Opposition to anti-Chinese discourse[195] was also in the minority six months later, in June 1874, when delegates from ten miners' associations met in Bendigo to form the Amalgamated Miners' Association (AMA).[196] Along with the adoption of motions on the eight hours' system, ventilation of mines, and draft

---

[192] 'Editorial', *Argus*, 16 December 1873, p. 6.
[193] 'The Clunes Riots', *Argus*, 18 December 1873, p. 5, printed a letter from 'Quartz-Miner' that took issue with Clark's and Hattam's stance: 'As a resident in Bendigo for over 20 years, will you let me assure the Victorian public that the people of Bendigo generally do not entertain the principles advocated by the two magistrates who took part in the demonstration here on Saturday night last...We in Bendigo have been accustomed to use Chinese labour for years. Chinese have lived here for years, and we have two or three encampments, and until now we never heard a word against them or against any other aliens, such as the Germans, Swiss, Italians, &c, of whom large numbers live here.'
[194] *Bendigo Advertiser*, 18 December 1873.
[195] Griffiths, Philip, *The making of White Australia: Ruling class agendas, 1876-1888,* Ph.D., Thesis, Australian National University, 2006
[196] 'Sandhurst', *Argus*, 25 June 1874, p. 7.

bills relating to mining, there was a 'lengthy discussion' of the 'Chinese Question'. A Clunes delegate, Mr W. Taylor, moved to insert a clause in the rules 'prohibiting any member thereof working in any mine where Chinese are employed.' He argued that 'European labour could not compete with Chinese... [who] morally speaking, were a pest...'[197] Blanchard agreed with his fellow delegate, as did others, who suggested reimposing the residence tax initially imposed in the 1850s on Chinese residents. It seems that the motion in favour of a poll tax was defeated and that some delegates had reservations about Taylor's motion:

> Some of the members thought that the subject was too difficult...and others believed that the majority of miners would think the terms of the resolution were very arbitrary...

Probably to placate these sentiments, the motion was modified so as not to affect existing claims. Reservations were also expressed by Robert Burrowes, Member of the Legislative Assembly for Sandhurst at the public meeting following the conference attended by some hundreds of miners. Burrowes declared that he was 'strongly opposed' to the AMA decision:

> ...that Chinese labour should not be admitted to mines...It was unjust oppression of foreigners...He thought that, no matter what the man was, he ought to have fair play.

Although some had reservations, there was clearly a strong sentiment for shutting out the Chinese. Markus points out:

> ...even the diluted motion meant that the Association became the first major union to adopt a clause debarring its members from working with Chinese and by implication, debarring Chinese from membership.[198]

This represented the beginning of a long tradition in the Australian labour movement. Gold miners with experience in the AMA such as W. G. Spence went on to form the Australian Shearers Union in 1886, later to become the giant Australian Workers Union. The ASU and AWU continued the policy of the AMA, effectively barring Chinese from joining. In 1878 Queensland passed legislation banning the employment of Asians in the gold mines, later extended to the sugar and banana industries. In histories of 'White Australia', the Clunes riot of 1873 is usually seen as the start of a second wave of agitation that led to new restrictions on Chinese immigration passed in 1881 and eventually to the systematic exclusion of Chinese and other non-whites. Though the agitation following the riot only continued for a few months, Markus argues that it helped to pressure a key, conservative section of the ruling class into supporting the 1881 restrictions. The Clunes riot, like the 1878 seamen's strike against Chinese labour, highlighted the role of organised labour as the greatest single influence in

---

[197] See, Amalgamated Miners' Association of Victoria, *General rules of the Amalgamated Miners' Association of Victoria, as compiled the 27th June, 1874, and revised the 16th September, 1880*, (F. N. Martin and Grose), 1884.
[198] Ibid, Markus, A., *Fear and Hatred: Purifying Australia and California 1850-1901*, p. 77.

this phase of the anti-Chinese movement. To restrict the entry of Asians the Australian government officially abolished the indenture system and in 1897 adopted a non-discriminatory literacy test in the English language. In 1901 the Immigration Act defined a prohibited immigrant to include any person who failed to pass the dictation test in any European language. From this date policy was aimed towards a white Australia, though in 1949 it was suggested that Asians should be admitted on a quota plan.

In 1994, the Sydney *Daily Mirror* headlined an historical feature on the Clunes riot of 1873: 'White Australia Policy sprang from workers' uprising'.[199] The mythology of White Australia was based on the fear of large-scale Chinese immigration during the gold rushes and that this had alerted working-class people to see Chinese people as a danger and all classes increasingly agreed that the white-working class had to be protected from Asian immigration. The Government, the police, the press, colonial politicians, capitalists and small town shopkeepers fostered division between European and Chinese miners. Demands for anti-Chinese laws came from ruling class politicians and rich newspaper proprietors. In the move towards an Australian nationalism, the White Australia idea was a neat ideological construct that helped preserve Empire links and structures against the rising tide of class warfare that would link workers from different ethnic backgrounds. In the labourist version of this myth, White Australia was the product of a class struggle between pastoralists and sugar planters, who wanted to exploit 'cheap coloured labour' and the working people who fought to stop them. It is the working-class that imposed the policy against exploitative employers.

There is little direct evidence in newspaper reports immediately after the disturbance at Clunes that the protesters attacked the Chinese labour on racial grounds. Of more immediate importance was the impact that the successful employment of Chinese labour could have had on the living standards of miners. However, it was a short step from seeing Chinese labour as an attempt to dilute the position of European workers to a discourse in which the language of racism played a central role. What was significant about the incident at Clunes was not the 'incident' itself but the ways in which Australia 'experienced' the event through the press. Newspapers were not simply reporting the news, they were making it. After the event, a struggle between employer and employees became part of an anti-Chinese crusade and what occurred in Clunes developed from an 'incident' into a 'ferocious uprising'.

Vancouver, 1907

It may be an exaggeration to describe Clunes as a 'ferocious uprising', but the same cannot be said of events in Vancouver in 1907. Immigration from Asia became a major feature of the economic, social and political development of the west coast of North America from the mid-nineteenth century.[200] In the

---

[199] *Daily Mirror* (Sydney), 30 September 1994.

[200] Cummings, Bruce, *Dominion from Sea to Sea: Pacific Ascendancy and American Power*, (Yale University Press), 2009, pp. 197-217, considers this issue from an American perspective. Roy, Patricia E., *A White Man's Province: British Columbia Politicians and Chinese and Japanese Immigrants, 1858-1914*, (University of British Columbia Press),

American states of California, Oregon and Washington and in British Columbia, the result was growing calls for immigration control or exclusion of those seen both as economic migrants who threatened white workers because they were paid less and as a racial threat to established predominantly white communities. In 1907, tensions between the different communities spilled over into violent riots in San Francisco, Bellingham and in Vancouver.[201]

Riots in Bellingham

By 1907, there were no more than 2,000 Asian Indians to be found along the United States Pacific Coast.[202] Thousands more had migrated to Vancouver, British Columbia and 'migrated south, seeking work in lumber camps and on railroads, or in other jobs.'[203] Several hundred of these migrants found work as contract labourers in the lumber mills of the newly-incorporated city of Bellingham. The Great Northern Railway had recently connected Bellingham to the outside economy and helped quickly turn it into a prosperous community built primarily on timber and fishing. Bellingham had been one of the centres of the Pacific Northwest anti-Chinese campaigns of the late 1880s and there was a strong local tradition of not letting Chinese live in town except during the salmon season. The influx of Sikhs was unwelcome. Bellingham had an eight-hundred strong chapter of the Japanese-Korean Exclusion League, a national labour organisation with the avowed mission 'to guard the gateway of Occidental Civilization [West Coast] against Oriental invasion.'[204] Members of the League demanded that no South Asians be employed in the lumber mills or anywhere in Bellingham after Labor Day, 2 September 1907 when over a thousand union

---

1989, Anderson, Kay J., *Vancouver's Chinatown: Racial Discourse in Canada, 1875-1980*, (McGill-Queen's University Press), 1991, and Ward, W. Peter, *White Canada forever: popular attitudes and public policy toward Orientals in British Columbia*, (McGill-Queen's University Press), 3rd ed., 2002, examines issues from a British Columbian's stance.

[201] Lee, Erika, 'Hemispheric Orientalism and the 1907 Pacific Coast Race Riots', *Amerasia Journal*, Vol. 33, (2), (2007), pp. 19-48, argues that the riots in San Francisco, Bellingham and Vancouver in 1907 were not isolated events. Rather, they were the most public, violent and extreme expression of an interconnected anti-Asian racism gripping the Pacific coast in the early-twentieth century. See also, Allerfeldt, Kristofer, 'Race and Restriction: Anti-Asian Immigration Pressures in the Pacific North-west of America during the Progressive Era, 1885–1924', *History*, Vol. 88, (2003), pp. 53-73, and Chang, Kornel, 'Enforcing Transnational White Solidarity: Asian Migration and the Formation of the U.S.-Canadian Boundary', *American Quarterly*, Vol. 60, (3), (2008), pp. 671-696, and 'Circulating Race and Empire: Transnational Labor Activism and the Politics of Anti-Asian Agitation in the Anglo-Pacific World, 1880-1910', *Journal of American History*, Vol. 96, (2009), pp. 678-701.

[202] Cahn, David, 'The 1907 Bellingham Riots in Historical Context', 2008, at http://depts.washington.edu/civilr/bham_history.htm

[203] Wunder, John R., 'South Asians, Civil Rights, and the Pacific Northwest: The 1907 Bellingham Anti-Indian Riot and Subsequent Citizenship and Deportation Struggles', *Western Legal History*, Vol. 4, (1991), pp. 59-68, at p. 60.

[204] Hallberg, Gerald N., 'Bellingham, Washington's Anti-Hindu Riot', in Halseth, James A., and Glasrud, Bruce A., (eds.), *Northwest Mosaics: minority conflicts in Pacific Northwest history*, (J. A. Pruett Pub.), 1977, pp. 140-155, at p. 147.

members paraded through town to show their organised strength. However, Sikh workers continued to work the following day.

On 4 September 1907, five-hundred white working men in Bellingham in Washington gathered to attack a community of South Asian migrant workers with the intention of 'scar[ing] them so badly that they will not crowd white labor out of the mills'.[205] For five hours, the mob destroyed property, indiscriminately attacking people and dragging men from their workplaces and homes. The few police officers could do nothing to prevent this. The mob eventually rounded up around 200 South Asian immigrant workers in the basement of City Hall where they stayed for the night. While the City authorities considered what actions to take, local newspapers commented on what had happened. The *Bellingham Herald* condemned the violence but was sympathetic to the rioters' objective in its editorial:

> The Hindu is not a good citizen...It would require centuries to assimilate him, and this country need not take the trouble. Our racial burdens are already heavy enough to bear.[206]

The *Reveille* commented:

> While any good citizen must be opposed to the means employed, the result of the crusade against the Hindus cannot but cause a general and intense satisfaction, and the departure of the Hindus will leave no regrets.[207]

The *Seattle Morning Times* insisted that the matter was:

> ...not a question of race, but of wages; not a question of men, but modes of life; not a matter of nations, but of habits of life...When men who require meat to eat and real beds to sleep in are ousted from their employment to make room for vegetarians who can find the bliss of sleep in some filthy corner, it is rather difficult to say at what limit indignation ceases to be righteous.[208]

This view was not, however, accepted by all local newspapers with the *Polk County News* commenting:

> Racial feeling has played no small part in affairs here. Every day whites have been replaced in the mills by Asiatics...General uneasiness of the whites is given as a reason for the outbreak.[209]

By 12 September, rumours were spread through Bellingham that Chinese and Japanese workers were also being warned to leave though the general manager of the Pacific-American fisheries said that should this occur 'the salmon

---

[205] *Bellingham Reveille*, 5 September 1907.
[206] Cit, ibid, Wunder, John R., 'South Asians, Civil Rights, and the Pacific Northwest: The 1907 Bellingham Anti-Indian Riot and Subsequent Citizenship and Deportation Struggles', p. 63.
[207] *Bellingham Reveille*, 5 September 1907.
[208] *Seattle Morning Times*, 5 September 1907.
[209] *Polk County News,* 12 September 1907.

canning industry is doomed'.[210] Shortly after the riot, hundreds of white working-class men and leaders of the Japanese-Korean Exclusion League, soon affiliated to the Asiatic Exclusion League, convened in Bellingham to hold a mass meeting and demonstration in favour of further 'Oriental exclusion laws'.[211] The *Bellingham Herald* reported:

> ...the league is not working to incite the laboring men to the shirt-sleeve method of expelling foreigners, but desires to have laws passed by the national congress restricting immigration of what it considers a menace to American labor.[212]

Within ten days the entire South Asian population had left the town.[213] Despite promises of protections from city officials, the South Asian workers well understood that there was no protection for them in Bellingham and migrated up and down the Pacific coast looking for safer working and living conditions.[214] The Bellingham riots triggered similar riots and 'expulsions' throughout the Pacific Northwest and East Indians faced organised movements to force them out of Washington in Everett, Aberdeen and Danville, in Oregon at St. John and Boring and communities in California and Alaska.[215] Three days after the riots in Bellingham, a huge anti-Asian rally took place in Vancouver.

Asian immigration to British Columbia

Chinese and Japanese immigrants to Canada had a troubled relationship with the federal government throughout the late-nineteenth and early-twentieth centuries largely because of institutionalised racism and a prevailing notion that they were a burden on white society.[216] Immigration to Canada from China stretched back to 1788 but did not become significant until the 1850s. The discovery of gold in the Fraser valley of British Columbia in the late 1850s resulted in Chinese migrants arriving from the goldfields of California attracted by the new

---

[210] *Lewiston Evening News*, 12 September 1907

[211] The Asiatic Exclusion League was formed on 14 May 1905 in San Francisco by 67 labour unions. It aimed to spread anti-Asian propaganda and influence legislation restricting Asian immigration especially by Japanese, Chinese and Koreans. By 1908, the Asiatic Exclusion League reported 231 organisations affiliated, 195 of them labour unions.

[212] 'Hundreds Will Attend Mass Meeting', *Bellingham Herald*, 14 September 1907. See also, 'Industrial War is Waged', *Bellingham Herald*, 16 September 1907.

[213] *Dawson Daily News*, 9 September 1907, spoke of 750 Sikhs somewhere between Bellingham and Vancouver.

[214] The British Ambassador in Washington D.C. protested to the State Department over the riots suggesting that those affected might seek civil damages from the Bellingham authorities: *New York Times*, 6 September 1907.

[215] Some of the Indians who were driven from Bellingham went to Everett, another town in Washington state sixty miles south of Bellingham. On 5 November 1907, in Everett, Washington over five-hundred armed men attacked and beat the Indians and robbed and destroyed their belongings. The result was the same as in Bellingham.

[216] Ibid, Roy, Patricia, *A White Man's Province: British Columbia politicians and Chinese and Japanese immigrants, 1858-1914*, pp. 64-152, examines economic restrictions on Chinese and Japanese immigrants from 1886-1902.

opportunities further north. During 1860s and 1870s, many Chinese came as independent miners and workers while others were recruited as contract or indentured labourers. The first wave of settlement from Japan to Canada occurred between 1877 and 1928, when mostly young, literate men came to work as fishermen or lumbermen along the Pacific coast of British Columbia. They also settled in British Columbia's Fraser Valley and in parts of Alberta. Large-scale immigration of Chinese coincided with the construction of the western section of the Canadian Pacific Railway. Over 11,000 Chinese arrived in Victoria by ship in 1881 and 1882 alone. Although some workers eventually returned to the homeland, this wave of immigration substantially increased the number of Chinese in Canada that more than doubled in the official census records from 4,383 in 1881 to 9,126 ten years later. By 1901, the figure had reached 17,314. Apart from a few merchants, most of the newcomers were from lower levels of Chinese society.

While Chinese immigration was acceptable during the construction of the Canadian Pacific Railway when the federal government needed a cheap source of labour, this was not the case by 1885 when work on the railway was nearing completion. Among trade union workers and some politicians, there were growing calls for exclusion since many white workers feared that the Chinese would take their jobs and reduce their standard of living.[217] The problem was whether federal or provincial government should act and, for the next twenty years what had been described as a 'constitutional tango' took place between Ottawa and British Columbia. From 1884, British Columbia passed nine immigration acts restricting Asian immigration but, under the authority of the British North America Act, the federal government disallowed eight, while the Lieutenant-Governor reserved one in 1907. In the face of mounting public dissatisfaction, a Royal Commission was held by the federal government in 1885 to consider the effects of Chinese immigration.[218] As a result, the federal government passed the Chinese Immigration Act in 1885 placing a $50 head tax on Chinese immigrants and stipulated that vessels docking in Canadian ports could carry no more than one Chinese for every fifty tons of cargo. This legislation was amended in 1887 and 1892 and a further statute passed in 1901. The head tax was increased several times and by 1903 reached $500 per person, roughly two years' wages for a Chinese labourer living in Canada at the time. In addition to limiting levels of immigration, restrictions were also placed on Chinese immigrants once they were in Canada. For instance, in 1884, a bill prevented them from acquiring Crown lands and diverting water from natural channels, the Coal Mines Regulation Amendment Act in 1890 prohibited them from working underground and an amendment in 1903 from performing skilled jobs in coal mines. In the twenty years before 1904, twenty-two provincial acts had been passed in British Columbia restricting Chinese activity.

---

[217] Gouter, David, 'Construction the 'Great Menace': Canadian Labour's Opposition to Asian Immigration, 1880-1914' *Canadian Historical Review*, Vol. 88, (4), (2007), pp. 549-576, provides a detailed analysis of the development of trade union and labour opposition.

[218] Chapleau, J. A., and Gray, John Hamilton, *Report of the Royal Commission on Chinese immigration: report and evidence*, (Printed by order of the Commission), 1885.

Japanese immigrants were also subject to rigid controls.[219] By 1891, provincial legislators were complaining that they were 'just as injurious' as the long-despised Chinese and in 1897 unanimously asked the federal government to 'prevent unrestricted immigration of Japanese.' As a result, the Japanese consul in Vancouver persuaded the Japanese Foreign Office to halt emigration from 30 July 1900. The provincial legislature believed that this was only a temporary gesture and passed legislation 'to Regulate Immigration into British Columbia'. This required any immigrant, on request, to fill out an application for entry in a European language and applied only to the Japanese since Chinese immigration was regulated by a head tax. The consul immediately protested that this was a violation of the Anglo-Japanese Commercial Treaty of 1894 that guaranteed Japanese the 'full liberty to enter, travel, and reside in any part of the Dominion of Canada' and the federal government disallowed this provincial law. To mollify British Columbians, upset by the repeated disallowance of the province's immigration laws, in 1902 the federal government appointed a further Royal Commission on Chinese and Japanese Immigration. The commission agreed with white witnesses that the Japanese impeded the permanent settlement of the country and that, since they had 'more energy, push and independence', they were more dangerous competitors to working men than the Chinese. However, it recommended that Canada legislate against them only if Japan lifted its prohibition on the emigration of labourers. Although this prohibition operated effectively until 1905, increasing numbers of Japanese immigrants arrived in British Columbia. By the spring of 1907, the trickle of immigrants had become a flood. Employment agencies and Japanese emigration companies, eager to increase their profits, had found a loophole in Japanese regulations. Emigrants secured passports for Hawaii and, once they were beyond Japan's control proceeded to Canada, sometimes en route to the continental United States. Between January and June 1907, 3,247 Japanese entered Canada, in July another 2,324 arrived and more were anticipated.

Many people in British Columbia believed that the measures taken by the federal government in Ottawa had not stopped the immigration of cheap labour and the unfair competition it caused in the labour market. In 1907, Vancouver's population was 60,000 and unexpected arrival of over 10,000 Japanese, Chinese and East Asian immigrants increased its population by 20 per cent and acted as the catalyst for the riots. This was investigated by Mackenzie King, Deputy Minister of Labour who was sent to Vancouver in the aftermath of the riots to determine levels of compensation to be paid to those whose property had been damaged.[220] Most of the immigrants arrived before the riot and Mackenzie King concluded that this had 'naturally caused great alarm and, if anything more were

---

219 Adachi, Ken, *The Enemy That Never Was: a history of the Japanese Canadians*, (McClelland and Stewart), 2nd ed., 1991, remains the standard text.

220 *Report by W. L. Mackenzie King, C.M.G., Deputy Minister of Labour, commissioner appointed to investigate into the losses sustained by the Chinese population of Vancouver, B.C. on the occasion of the riots in that city in September, 1907*, (S. E. Dawson), 1908, and *Report by W. L. Mackenzie King, C.M.G., Deputy Minister of Labour, commissioner appointed to investigate into the losses sustained by the Japanese population of Vancouver, B.C., on the occasion of the riots in that city in September, 1907*, (S. E. Dawson), 1908.

needed to occasion unrest, it was found in the simultaneous arrival from the Orient of Hindus by the hundreds and Chinese in larger numbers than in preceding years.'[221]

Riots in Vancouver

Violence was not a novel experience for the Chinese especially after the influx of Chinese workers in 1880 and 1881 when construction of the Canadian Pacific Railway began in British Columbia. White construction workers attacked a Chinese camp near Lytton in May 1883 because they believed the Chinese were stealing white jobs and in the melee one Chinese was killed and eight seriously injured. In 1887, there was a major riot in Vancouver when hundreds of whites converged on the Chinese district, chased the people out of town and looted and burned their houses. The allegation was also that the Chinese were taking jobs that rightfully belonged to whites.[222] In 1892, 300 whites attacked Calgarry's Chinese blaming them for a recent smallpox epidemic. There were also scattered outbursts of vigilante activity directed at forcing the Chinese out of communities in Slocan Valley, Atlin, Samlo and Penticton in British Columbia and Whitehorse in Yukon between 1989 and 1906 and mobs demolished Chinese restaurants in Lethbridge in 1907.

In August 1907, the Vancouver Trades and Labour Council invited elected officials and anyone who believed in keeping Canada 'a white man's country' and this led to the formation of a branch of the Asiatic Exclusion League on 12 August. To recruit members, the League sponsored a parade and rally at Vancouver City Hall on Saturday 7 September. Thousands of people, many carrying signs with slogans reading 'Stand for a White Canada' and 'No cheap Asiatic labor' flooded the streets. Several American visitors, J. B Wilson from NZ, two local clergymen and prominent Liberals and Conservatives spoke inside the hall and repeated some of their fiery speeches to the overflow crowd outside. Eilson was reportedly the 'best received' speaker explaining how the problem of Asian migration had been dealt with in other British colonies.[223] A. E. Fowler, a leader of the Asian exclusionary movement in Seattle, perching on a telegraph pole told the crowd about how Bellingham residents had just driven out East Indians. Fowler specifically used Bellingham as an example of what could be done and then proposed to march through Chinatown. Soon, the crowd turned into a mob of some nine-thousand people throwing bricks and stones through shop windows. In neighbouring 'Little Tokyo', where residents already knew about the riot, they armed themselves with knives and clubs and repelled the rioters but many windows were broken. The riot in Vancouver was more extensive than in Bellingham with a reported $40,000 in damage and several injuries.[224] The anti-Asian hostility and political agitation outlasted the riots and

[221] Cit, Morton, James W., *In the Sea of Sterile Mountains: the Chinese in British Columbia*, (J. J. Douglas), 1974, p. 210.
[222] Roy, Patricia, 'The Preservation of the Peace in Vancouver: The Aftermath of the Anti-Chinese Riot of 1887,' *BC Studies*, Vol. 31, (1976), pp. 44-59.
[223] *Daily News Advertiser*, 8 September 1907.
[224] Ibid, Roy, Patricia E., *A White Man's Province: British Columbia Politicians and Chinese and Japanese Immigrants, 1858-1914*, pp. 185-228, ibid, Ward, W. Peter, *White Canada forever: popular attitudes and public policy toward Orientals in British*

in January 1908, there was another anti-Japanese disturbance but on a far smaller scale. However, the League, though it established branches in several coastal cities, had trouble maintaining its members' interest and in little more than a year it had disappeared. This did not, however, mean that the racism it propounded disappeared.[225]

Contemporary newspapers gave conflicting accounts of the level of violence.[226] Local English language newspapers tended to down play the extent it was used during the riots and this perspective dominated later historical thinking on the subject. Robert Wynne concluded from reading local papers:

> There was considerable damage to property held by Chinese and Japanese, but there were no deaths.[227]

Most English and American media blamed the riots on Americans belonging to the Asiatic Exclusion League. They neglected the long hostility against Asian migrants in British Columbia and gave the impression that local British Columbian social organisations such as local churches and labour unions and politicians had little to do with the riot. *The Times*, for instance, emphasised that Americans were blame for the riots:

> The leaders of the demonstration were not Canadians, but citizens of the United States. They were Frank Cotterill, president of the Federation of Labour of the State of Washington, A.E. Fowler, secretary of the Anti-Japanese and Korean League of the same State, and George P. Listman, a prominent Labour leader of Seattle...The actual acts of violence seem to have been committed for the most part by Canadians, but that the violence was due to the agitation of the Americans there appears to be not a shadow of doubt.[228]

Chinese and Japanese language newspapers described the riots in far more violent terms and placed them within the context of anti-Asian immigration attitudes. For instance, an article published in Taiwan in both Japanese and Chinese, roughly two weeks after the riot, reported that there had been multiple deaths and significant damage to property:

> The Japanese stores in Vancouver on the evening of September 8th were damaged by a thousand rioters; The Japanese fought with them and killed four white men...The eighteen stores ran by the Japanese, including nine hotels, two public bathing places, two

---

Columbia, pp. 53-78, and Sugimoto, Howard Hiroshi, *Japanese immigration, the Vancouver riots, and Canadian diplomacy*, (Arno Press), 1978.

225 Gilmour, Julie F., *Trouble on Main Street. Mackenzie King, Reason, Race, and the 1907 Vancouver Riots*, (Allen Lane), 2014.

226 See the website www.instrcc.ubc.ca/1907_riot/index_1.html by Woan-Jen Wang on *Perspectives on the 1907 Riots in Selected Asian Languages and International Newspapers*.

227 Wynne, Robert E., 'American Labor Leaders and the Vancouver Anti-Oriental Riot', *Pacific Northwest Quarterly*, Vol. 57, (4), (1966), pp. 172-179.

228 'The Vancouver Outrages', *The Times*, 11 September 1907, p. 7.

shoes stores, five barber shop, a bank, a press, a Japanese food restaurant, and a glass store, were all damaged.[229]

The Japanese authorities responded to the riots with Mr Ishii, the special envoy of the Japanese government requesting $25,000 compensation first from the authorities in Vancouver and, on their refusal, from the Canadian government. The riots became an international issue affecting the previously close links between Britain and Japan.[230] Local English newspapers were quick to express the sympathy of federal and British officials for the victims of the riot and this proved deeply embarrassing for Sir Wilfred Laurier's government. As a result, it sent W. L. Mackenzie King to investigate damage claims and Labour Minister Rodolphe Lemieux to Tokyo to negotiate a gentlemen's agreement whereby Japan limited emigration to Canada.[231]

Japan was interested in controlling its emigration levels and the Hayashi-Lemieux Agreement of 1908 limited the number of Japanese immigrants entering Canada to 450 a year, though in practice the number was much less. One of the major results of King's investigation was the passing of Continuous Journey Act in 1908 requiring Japanese labourers to come directly from Japan. This was a response to the inflow of 4,000 Japanese labourers who had come from Hawaii in 1907 without the permission of the Japanese government. This illegal emigration, the scheming of the Canadian Nippon Supply Company that brought additional labourers and the 1907 riot that resulted from this illegal activity were major embarrassments to Japan and it quickly agreed to the continuous passage law. The federal government ended the only direct shipping line between India[232] and Vancouver effectively ensuring that Indian immigration would be curtailed. The 1910 Immigration Act stipulated that Indians should possess the sum of $200 when landing in Canada, although for other Asians it was only $25. In 1913 an Order-in-Council banned Indians who were artisans, skilled or unskilled workers from landing in any port in British Columbia. To challenge the regulation, the chartered ship ***Komagata Maru*** left Hong Kong and travelled to Vancouver in 1914 with more than 350 passengers from Punjab, most of them Sikhs. The ship was forced to leave after sitting in Burrard Inlet for two months; two months later, in India, some of the passengers ended up being shot and killed by British colonial soldiers.[233] There was another recession in Canada from 1918 to the mid-1920s. In 1923, the federal government passed the

[229] 'The Detailed Report of the Vancouver Riot', *Taiwan Daily News*, 22 September 1907.
[230] See, Sugimoto, Howard H., 'The Vancouver Riot and Its International Significance', *Pacific Northwest Quarterly & Washington Historical Quarterly*, Vol. 64, (4), (1973), pp. 163-174.
[231] In his final report on the matter, Mackenzie King agreed to award about $26,000 to Chinese businesses and $9,000 to the Japanese community in damages.
[232] Sheffauer, Herman, 'The Tide of Turbans', *The Forum*, 1910.
[233] On this incident see, ibid, Ward, W. Peter, *White Canada forever: popular attitudes and public policy toward Orientals in British Columbia*, pp. 79-95, and Srikanth, Rajini, 'The *Komagata Maru*: Memory and Mobility among the South Asian Diaspora in North America', in Lee, Josephine D., Lim, Imogene L., and Matsukawa, Yuko, (eds.), *Recollecting early Asian America: essays in cultural history*, (Temple University Press), 2002, pp. 78-93.

Chinese Exclusion Act preventing any immigration from China. Only 15 Chinese immigrants were allowed into Canada between 1923 and 1947 when this law was finally revoked after a Supreme Court ruling.[234] In 1947, Chinese and Indians were finally granted the rights of domicile and citizenship.

The resistance to economic migrants evident in Clunes in 1873 and Vancouver almost four decades later were expressions of a growing white supremacist discourse of the British world. In both communities, the anti-Asian arguments deployed were the same. Migrant labour was a threat to the employment of white labour because it was cheaper. Economic migrants were carriers of disease and their values were inimical to white society threatening to dilute its racial purity and potency. Direct action against economic migrants was justifiable to persuade politicians that they needed to act to limit the number of economic migrants or exclude them altogether. These arguments were expressed widely in the colonial press and, with the ready availability of the telegraph easily transmitted from colony to colony. The result of a widely-accepted discourse and its easy dissemination was the emergence of similar racist policies across the British Empire.[235]

Conclusions

The view that there was a common global experience for indentured labour based upon exploitation and abuse contains sufficient truth to have been widely accepted by contemporaries. In practice, the experiences of indentured workers and other economic migrants varied across time and place. Clare Anderson argues that it is important to shift the frame of analysis within which discussions of indentured migration occur.[236] She maintains that colonial discourses and practices of indenture are best understood in the context of colonial innovations in incarceration and confinement rather than whether it was 'a new system of slavery',

Although there were parallels between the subjugation and exploitation of indentured labour and the experiences of slaves and convicts, there was one important difference: indentured labourers were, at least nominally, free. However, colonial narratives of migration masked the underlying exploitation of immigrants by projecting the plantation system as a colonial space ideal for civilising the colonised subject.In relation to British Guiana, Clementi constructed an idealised indentured labourer who thrived in the plantation system while Kirke revealed uncertainty about Chinese immigrants who, he argued, should always be carefully watched and policed.[237] For Kirke, the

---

234 Roy, Patricia, *The Oriental question: consolidating a white man's province, 1914-1941*, (University of British Columbia Press), 2003, shows how British Columbians consolidated a 'white man's province' from 1914 to 1941 by securing a virtual end to Asian immigration and placing stringent legal restrictions on Asian competition in the major industries of lumber and fishing.

235 On this issue see, ibid, Lake, Marilyn, and Reynolds, Henry, *Drawing the Global Colour Line: White Men's Countries and the International Challenge of Racial Equality*.

236 Anderson, Clare, 'Convicts and Coolies: Rethinking Indentured Labour in the Nineteenth Century', *Slavery & Abolition*, Vol. 30, (1), (2009), pp. 93-109.

237 Kirke, Henry, *Twenty-five Years in British Guiana*, (Sampson Low, Marston & Co.), 1898.

Chinese were 'exotic', a colonial discourse that included body, food and language.[238] They were poor agricultural labourers, resisted planter control and for Kirke, their high rate of desertion reflected their lack of moral character.[239] Their group cohesion was built, not as Clementi argued on the Anglican faith, but on their joint defiance of the plantation regime meaning that Chinese immigrants might be beyond the control of colonial authorities. For Kirke, the idea that a non-white could adopt British notions of respectability was ridiculous.[240] Despite his critique, for Kirke the Chinese labourer is far more accepting of colonial rule, manners and social conventions than Indian indentured labour. Clementi, by contrast, viewed the Chinese as a 'model community' with successful labourers industriously working on successful sugar plantations. To make the most of their opportunities, they both accepted and adopted British culture and mannerisms as part of their personal belief system.[241] Clementi is more circumspect that Kirke in his approach excluding information about the Chinese community that contradicted or challenged imperial hegemony but even he is forced to admit in his conclusions that, though Chinese immigration may have been a success for planers, it must 'from the point of view of colonization be pronounced to have failed.'[242] Despite, their differences of emphasis and levels of disclosure, Kirke and Clementi both used colonial discourse as an instrument of colonial power and it is against this discourse that both the use of indentured labour and the later development of an exclusionist, racist ideology among settlers must be judged.

[238] Ibid, Kirke, Henry, *Twenty-five Years in British Guiana*, p. 216.
[239] Ibid, Kirke, Henry, *Twenty-five Years in British Guiana*, p. 207.
[240] Ibid, Kirke, Henry, *Twenty-five Years in British Guiana*, pp. 216-218.
[241] Ibid, Clementi, Cecil, *The Chinese in British Guiana*, p. 24.
[242] Ibid, Clementi, Cecil, *The Chinese in British Guiana*, p. 357.

6 Tax rebellion

A Poll Tax on free men is either altogether arbitrary or altogether unequal, and in most cases is the one and the other.[1]

Gandhi broke the law to oppose the salt tax. The early Americans railed against the tax on tea. In late 1789, Benjamin Franklin wrote:

> Our new Constitution is now established, and has an appearance that promises permanency; but in this world nothing can be said to be certain, except death and taxes.[2]

From when taxes were first levied, people have found ways to evade paying for reasons that have been honourable, ideological, greedy and selfish. People have evaded taxes illegally, some have resisted paying taxes and others have simply refused. As Gandhi wrote in 1922:

> Withholding payment of taxes is one of the quickest methods of overthrowing a government [but] that we have not evolved that degree of strength and discipline which are necessary for conducting a successful campaign of non-payment of taxes...[3]

Taxation is almost by definition unfair. It is imposed on people by government generally without consultation and is frequently used to pay for things of which people do not approve or do not need. Getting the level of taxation in society right, or at least politically acceptable, has always been a problem for government. If the level of taxation is set too low then it may have insufficient funds to rule effectively with the likelihood of the same consequences as setting taxes too high; anger, discontent and even resistance. Resistance can be caused by the perceived unfairness of the tax or the tax itself or, in the case of the decade leading to the American Revolution that the paying of taxes should be linked to some form of political representation. This may lead to refusal to pay the tax or, in extreme cases, rebellion.

Resistance to taxation is generally symptomatic of a broader malaise in society and, because it is imposed on individuals, it may act as a catalyst for direct action. In 1837, for instance, following the rejection of the 92 Resolutions calling for greater self-government for Lower Canada, Louis-Joseph Papineau called for a boycott of goods imported from Britain on which duty was paid to increase

[1] Smith, Adam, *An Inquiry into the Nature and Causes of the Wealth of Nations: with A Life of the Author*, 3 Vols. (Creech), 1806, Vol. 3, p. 309.

[2] Benjamin Franklin to Jean-Baptiste Leroy, 13 November 1789, Sparks, Jared, *The Works of Benjamin Franklin, with Notes and a Life of the Author*, 10 Vols. (Hilliard, Gray and Company), 1836-1840, Vol. 10, pp. 409-410. Daniel Defoe was the first author to use words to this effect in *The Political History of the Devil*, (T. Warner), 1726, p. 246, 'Things as certain as death and taxes, can be more firmly believed.'

[3] Gandhi, Mahatma, *Satyagraha: non-violent resistance*, (Navajivan Pub. House), 1951, p. 140, reprinted in *The Collected Works of Mahatma Gandhi*, Vol. 22, (Publications Division, Ministry of Information and Broadcasting, Govt. of India), 1984, p. 225.

pressure on the British government to make constitutional concessions.[4] Some members of the Women's Freedom League, a group formed after some Suffragettes were expelled from the movement in 1907, refused to pay taxes because they were denied the vote as part of their campaign for women's emancipation.[5] The Women's Tax Resistance League was formed in 1909 and those who followed its principles and whose actions extended to refusing to pay for certain types of licences such as Inhabited House Duty, dog licenses and servant's licences were liable to have goods seized or could be imprisoned.[6] House clearances by bailiffs were used as an opportunity to hold open-air suffrage meetings and the group was also involved in resistance to the census in 1911:

> Tax resistance proved to be the longest-lived form of militancy, and the most difficult to prosecute. More than 220 women, mostly middle-class, participated in tax resistance between 1906 and 1918, some continuing to resist through the First World War, despite a general suspension of militancy.[7]

It spread to the United States where tax resistance had a long pedigree invoking the principles of the American Revolution:

> ...I believe that the spirit of 'no taxation without representation' that resulted in the Revolutionary War is inherent and just as actual in the women of the country as it was then in the men of the country.[8]

The Community Charge, quickly dubbed the Poll Tax because of its similarity to the tax that precipitated the Peasants' Revolt in 1381, led to widespread protest, riots and non-payment largely because it was yet another unfair feature of Margaret Thatcher's policies in the late 1980s. With the fall of Thatcher in late 1990, her flagship policy was quickly ditched, something that may have contributed to the Conservatives' fourth electoral victory in 1992.[9]

---

[4] This demand was initially contained in the Declaration of St-Ours, the first of the Patriote assemblies, a demand repeated in seven of the other fourteen meetings see, Bernard, Jean-Paul, *Assemblées publiques, résolutions et déclarations de 1837-1838*, (VLB), 1987, p. 27.

[5] Eustance, Claire, 'Meanings of militancy: the ideas and practice of the Women's Freedom League, 1907-14', in Joannou, Maroula and Purvis, June, (eds.), *The Women's Suffrage Movement: New feminist perspectives*, (Manchester University Press), 1998, pp. 51-64, Francis, Hilary, 'Dare to be free!: the Women's Freedom League and its legacy', in Purvis, June and Holton, Sandra Stanley, (eds.), *Votes for Women*, (Routledge), 2000, pp. 181-202, and Liddington, Jill, *Vanishing for the Vote: Suffrage, Citizenship and the Battle for the Census*, (Manchester Univertsity Press), 2014, are the most recent studies.

[6] Frances, Hilary, ''Pay the piper, call the tune!': the Women's Tax Resistance League', in ibid, Joannou, Maroula and Purvis, June (eds.), *The women's suffrage movement: new feminist perspectives*, pp. 65-76.

[7] Nym Mayhall, Laura E., *The Militant Suffrage Movement: Citizenship and Resistance in Britain, 1860-1930*, (Oxford University Press), 2003, p. 60.

[8] 'Women's Tax Fight Will Be Passive', *New York Times*, 30 December 1913.

[9] Burns, Danny, *Poll Tax Rebellion*, (AK Press), 1992 remains a sound, if partisan account. See also, Lavalette, Michael and Mooney, Gerry, ''No poll tax here': the Tories,

Local taxation based on property was retained since, as one Conservative wit put it, 'people may move but houses don't!' What Adam Smith had written two hundred years before had been borne out by events:

> A Poll Tax on free men is either altogether arbitrary or altogether unequal, and in most cases is the one and the other.[10]

In 2008, opposition led the Labour Prime Minister Gordon Brown to placate public opinion for his decision to abolish the 10p tax rate.[11] On 21 March 2007, he had used his final budget as chancellor to announce a surprise cut in the basic rate to 20p from 22p and the abolition of the 10p starting rate. The new tax rates came into force on 1 April but, while Downing Street initially dismissed calls for a rethink over abolition or concessions to its critics, growing opposition within the Labour Party led to a rapid U-turn. By 23 April, the number of Labour rebels had grown to forty-five and the Chancellor Alistair Darling defused the crisis by sending a letter to the chairman of the Commons Treasury committee, promising to provide backdated compensation for poor households who had lost out, using the minimum wage, tax credits and winter-fuel payments to do so, a package later extended to all tax-payers. Unlike with Margaret Thatcher and the poll tax where characteristically she was prepared to fight to keep the tax despite its unpopularity, Gordon Brown was in a much weaker position and decided that the fight to retain the 10p reduction without compensation would be politically too damaging.

The potential of what was regarded as unfair taxation in the past to cause and still cause resistance and protest within Britain was magnified in her colonies where people were generally denied the liberties available to British citizens and where exploitative taxes, however justified, were viewed as symbols of colonial oppression. The result was not simply resistance but rebellion. In 1848, for instance, there was a rebellion against the British authorities in Ceylon that illustrates the causes, nature and response to resistance.[12] The growth of the plantation economy, facilitated by favourable government policies, negatively affected peasant cultivators: slash and burn agriculture (*chena*) was in decline; new roads cut across their land that was also flooded by silt from the plantations; and, wandering cattle were impounded or shot.[13] Other economic grievances that affected both native peasants and Europeans fuelled disaffection. After the

---

social policy and the great poll tax rebellion, 1987-91', in Lavalette, Michael and Mooney, Gerry, (eds.), *Class struggle and social welfare*, (Routledge), 2000, pp. 199-227.

[10] Smith, Adam, *An Inquiry into the Nature And Causes of the Wealth of Nations*, 1776, (Printed by N. Kelly for P. Wogan), 1801, Vol. 2, p. 385.

[11] Summers, Deborah, and Owen, Paul, 'Timeline: the 10p tax rebellion', guardian.co.uk, 23 April 2008.

[12] For narratives of the revolt see: Mills, Lennox A., *Ceylon Under British Rule, 1795-1932*, (Oxford University Press), 1933, pp. 168-202, and de Silva, K. M., 'The 'Rebellion' of 1848 in Ceylon', *Ceylon Journal of Historical Social Studies*, Vol. 7, (2), (1964), pp. 144-170.

[13] Meyer, Eric, 'Forests, Chena Cultivation, Plantations and the Colonial State in Ceylon 1840-1940,' in Grove, Richard H., Damodara, Vinita, and Sangwan, Satpal, (eds.), *Nature & the Orient*, (Oxford University Press), 1998, pp. 793-827.

collapse of the coffee industry in the late 1840s, the government was operating on a heavy deficit budget, and Earl Grey, the Whig Colonial Secretary ordered the imposition of additional taxes. A gun tax, a dog tax, a tax on verandas, the Road Ordinance that required each inhabitant of Ceylon to either pay a road tax or work six days annually on the repair and construction of roads and rumours about the imminence of thirty new taxes further aggravated the situation. The rebellion of 1848 was peasant-led and had sympathisers in the European community, who brought the revolt and its brutal suppression to the attention of MPs in London. The authorities responded by declaring martial law,[14] executing eighteen insurgents, including a Buddhist priest and imprisoning or transporting others. The severity of the repression split public opinion in Ceylon and in Britain.[15] Taxation focused political anger like no other political issue.

America, 1775

British taxation caused the American Revolution, but more importantly, it acted as a unifying force around which the disorganised and squabbling colonies could rally.[16] Resistance to taxation was deeply rooted in the Thirteen Colonies in British North America. Although the American Revolution occurred because colonists objected to paying taxes without representation, attitudes did not change after the war. In 1765, colonists were tarring and feathering British tax agents while three decades later they were doing the same thing to American tax agents.[17]

The revenue potential of the fledgling American colonies was initially largely ignored by English government.[18] The Restoration of Charles II in 1660

---

[14] Joseph Hume was highly critical of the government's position on martial law in an extensive Commons debate: *Hansard*, House of Commons, Debates, 28 March 1849, Vol. 103, cc1442-1443.

[15] The Parliamentary Committee Inquiry's reports were published in *Parliamentary Papers*, 1851, Vol. XXII, pp. 1-238. Also, see de Silva, K. M., 'The 1848 'Rebellion' in Ceylon: the British Parliamentary Post-Mortem; Part I', *Modern Ceylon Studies*, Vol. 5, (1), (1974), pp. 40-76.

[16] The literature on the causes of the American Revolution is immense, but three contrasting studies are Black, Jeremy, *Crisis of Empire: Britain and America in the Eighteenth Century*, (Continuum), 2008, Middlekauff, *The Glorious Cause: The American Revolution, 1763-1789*, 2nd ed., (Oxford University Press), 2007, and Greene, Jack P., and Pole, J. R., *Companion to the American Revolution*, 2nd ed., (Wiley-Blackwell), 2003. Marshall, P. J., *The Making and Unmaking of Empires: Britain, India, and America c.1750-1783*, (Oxford University Press), 2005, places events in America in the broader context of Britain's imperial ambitions.

[17] Adams, Charles, *Those Dirty Rotten Taxes: The Tax Revolts that built America*, (Free Press), 1998, pp. 5-73, and *Good and Evil: The Impact of Taxes on the Course of Civilization*, 2nd ed., (Madison Books), 2001, pp. 297-344, provides an overview of the key issues in the American colonies and the early American republic. For a detailed examination see Rabushka, Alvin, *Taxation in Colonial America*, (Princeton University Press), 2008, a monumental study.

[18] On the development of colonial America see, Taylor, Alan, *American Colonies: The Settlement of North America to 1800*, (Penguin), 2003, Middleton, Richard, *Colonial America: A History 1565-1776*, 3rd ed., (Blackwell Publishing), 2002, and Vickers, Daniel, (ed.), *A Companion to Colonial America*, (Blackwell Publishing), 2003.

saw a shift in attitude as he was determined to incorporate the colonies more fully into a mercantilist trading system resulting in a variety of measures to tighten control over colonial trade practices and governance. A series of Navigations Acts between 1651 and 1750 established a framework for imperial regulation of colonial trade along mercantilist lines.[19] As the institutions of colonial self-government developed and civic upheaval transformed political discourse in England, concerns about the relationship between representation and taxation grew more relevant. By 1681, royally appointed customs collectors resided in every colony, supervised by a resident surveyor. A Surveyor-General oversaw this colonial customs bureaucracy, reporting violations of the Navigations Acts to his London superiors. Although the Acts established a policy for imperial regulation of colonial trade, in practice colonial merchants often resisted or evaded royal authority. Local inhabitants physically accosted customs officials, while colonial juries in New England and the Chesapeake tended to acquit merchants accused of illegal trade practices.[20]

In 1691, William III granted Massachusetts a new charter establishing it as a royal colony.[21] The charter affirmed the Crown's authority to appoint the governor and naval officers to supervise ports, while guaranteeing that delegates to the colonial assembly were to be popularly elected by property-owning males. This division of authority between colony and Crown, governor and elected assembly gradually became the norm in the North American colonies.[22] It tended to increase political autonomy for property-owning colonists whilst extending royal authority over military affairs and trade. From the early-eighteenth century, the colonies of North America flourished, as they were

---

McFarlane, Anthony, *The British in the Americas 1480-1815*, (Longman), 1992, takes a broader geographical stance.

[19] Traditional mercantilism advocated the expansion of national wealth through a favourable balance of trade. By encouraging exports and restricting imports, nations built up a favourable trading surplus. Colonies represented potential new export markets but by channelling colonial trade with the rest of the world through English ports, the monarch could expect a surplus of customs duties to supplement royal finances. For instance, imperial duties levied on colonial tobacco brought in £100,000 annually by the mid-1670s. See, Harper, Lawrence A., *The English Navigation Laws: A Seventeenth Century Experiment in Social Engineering*, (Columbia University Press), 1939.

[20] Labaree, Leonard W., *Royal Government in America: A Study of the British Colonial System before 1783*, (Yale University Press), 1930, remains unmatched as a dissection of royal government in America while Barrow, Thomas, *Trade and Empire: The British Customs Service in Colonial America, 1660-1775*, (Cambridge University Press), 1975, provides detailed discussion of how revenue was collected. See also, Mason, Keith, 'Britain and the Administration of the American Colonies', in Dickinson, H. T., (ed.), *Britain and the American Revolution*, (Longman), 1998, pp. 21-43.

[21] On the context for the parallel redefinition of royal power and the development of colonial groups concerned to advance their own local interests see, Lovejoy, David, *The Glorious Revolution in America*, (Harper and Row), 1972, and Bliss, Robert, *Revolution and Empire: English Politics and the American Colonies in the Seventeenth Century*, (Manchester University Press), 1990.

[22] The monarch appointed governors in all other colonies except the proprietary colonies of Pennsylvania and Maryland, where the Penn and Calvert families, respectively, exercised that power.

drawn more integrally into a rapidly expanding Atlantic trading system.[23] This prosperity fostered ever-increasing exposure to British manufactured goods and culture, prompting colonial society to grow more Anglicised. Colonists on the edge of the American wilderness increasingly saw themselves as British subjects abroad, heirs to the motherland's constitution and institutions and beneficiaries of its rights and privileges. In the decade before the outbreak of the American Revolution, thousands of colonists flocked to Georgian London in its first big wave of American visitors. At the very point of political rupture, mother country and colonies were socially and culturally closer than ever before.[24] As colonial societies expanded and matured, colonists expected Britain's home government to uphold, or at least not interfere with, the prosperity and autonomy they enjoyed. When changes in British external affairs and the instability of internal politics in the 1760s inspired a fundamental reorientation of imperial policies, the colonies resisted changes they viewed as damaging to their interests and challenging their fundamental liberties. The mid-eighteenth century may have witnessed a greater attachment to English ways of life and government for many colonists but this did not extend to unconditional allegiance to the Crown.

As colonial societies became more pluralist, politics tended to become more factional within and between colonies, a reflection of the emergence of influential transatlantic interest groups as well as colonial agents.[25] These groups lobbied London to prevent the passage of unpalatable trading regulations, connived with their evasion or helped in gaining exemptions and also sought to influence the political ambitions of colonial assemblies. Control of colonial taxation by the assemblies served as a means to procure greater constitutional parity with royal or proprietary governors and also served to block the implementation of unpopular imperial policy. Assemblies voted for taxes that paid the governor's salary, an important bargaining chip in negotiations over the control of patronage and the budget. Royal bureaucrats and absentee proprietors disliked this tendency, but legislative autonomy became part of political life in the colonies. Royal governors continued to exert their influence through control of patronage and land grants, but political authority gradually reverted to parochial leaders who controlled the assemblies and marshalled local support to resist unwarranted intrusions by royal officials.[26]

---

[23] Egnal, Marc, *New World Economies: The Growth of the Thirteen Colonies and Early Canada*, (Oxford University Press), 1998, pp. 25-120, examines the eighteenth-century growth of the colonies. See also, Gould, Eliga H. And Onuf, Peter S., (eds.), *Empire and Nation: The American Revolution in the Atlantic World*, (John Hopkins University Press), 2005.

[24] This is examined in, Flavell, Julie, *When London was Capital of America*, (Yale University Press), 2010.

[25] Olson, A. D., *Making the Empire Work: London and American Interest Groups 1690-1790*, (Harvard University Press), 1992, pp. 126-173.

[26] There is some disagreement about the balance of power between royal government and the expanding influence of colonial assemblies. Stephen Saunders, for instance, argues for the existence of 'garrison government' in the American colonies from the late-seventeenth century and that English rule from the outset was militant and imperial: see his *The Governors-General: The English Army and the Definition of the Empire, 1519-1681*, (University of North Carolina Press), 1979, and *1676: The End of American Independence*, (Alfred A. Knopf), 1984.

One of the major problems that arose from the growing prosperity of the colonies was that it produced a surplus of goods which, contrary to England's trading policies, was shipped directly to French colonies. This enabled French sugar growers to gain control of the competitive European sugar market and led to 1733 the Molasses Act that imposed a high tariff on molasses imported into colonies from non-British possessions.[27] New England merchants, who often imported molasses from the French West Indies and New England distillers, who needed it to produce rum cheaply, stood to suffer financially. This protective tariff favoured British agricultural producers over colonial merchants and distillers promoting the integrity of the imperial Atlantic trade over the profitability of colonial commerce. New England merchants were largely able to ignore the Molasses Act, however, bribing customs officials and smuggling French contraband while British sugar merchants complained bitterly:

> The American derived his right of cheating the Revenue, and of perjuring himself, from the example of his fathers and the rights of nature... [to]complain and smuggle, and smuggle and complain, till all Restraints are removed, and till he can both buy and sell, whenever, and wheresoever, he pleases. Anything short of this, is still a Grievance, a Badge of Slavery.[28]

Despite the Board of Trade's efforts to oversee colonial customs officers, the flow of goods through American ports largely evaded imperial control. Further legislation such as the 1732 Hat Act and the 1750 Iron Act sought to discourage colonial manufacturing in competition with Britain but there was widespread colonial evasion. Prosperity did not guarantee unanimity among colonies, however. When various colonial representatives convened in Albany in 1754 to discuss war plans against the French and certain Native American tribes, Benjamin Franklin suggested a Plan of Union. The plan collapsed in part because individual colonial assemblies had no intention of surrendering their autonomy.[29]

Increasingly, taxation policy became a central area of disagreement between Britain and her colonies largely because it threatened the prosperity and rights of colonial society.[30] The Seven Years' War (1756-1763) reinforced

---

[27] For the context for the legislation see, Langford, Paul, *The Excise Crisis: Society and Politics in the Age of Walpole*, (Oxford University Press), 1975, pp. 28-29.

[28] Cit, ibid, Adams, Charles, *Good and Evil: The Impact of Taxes on the Course of Civilization*, p. 295.

[29] Labaree, Leonard, (ed.), *Papers of Benjamin Franklin*, Vol. 5, (Yale University Press), 1962, pp. 387-392. Newbold, Robert C., *The Albany Congress and the Plan of Union of 1754*, (Vantage Press), 1955, and Shannon, Timothy J., *Indians and Colonists at the Crossroads of Empire: The Albany Congress of 1754*, (Cornell University Press), 2000.

[30] The question of taxation and its constitutional implications has formed an important part of the researches of Jack P. Greene: see especially his *Peripheries and Center: Constitutional Development in the Extended Politics of the British Empire and the United States*, (University of Georgia Press), 1986, and *The Constitutional Origins of the American Revolution*, (Cambridge University Press), 2011. See also, the fundamental work of John Phillip Reid summarised in his *Constitutional History of the American Revolution: Abridged Edition*, (University of Wisconsin Press), 1995, *Rule of Law: The Jurisprudence of Liberty in the Seventeenth and Eighteenth Centuries* (Northern Illinois

Britain's control over North America following the conquest of French Canada in 1760.[31] It also highlighted two issues that led to colonial opposition. Britain's involvement in the colonial struggle in North America had been costly and both ministers and members of Parliament determined that the colonies should share the costs of imperial security. The war had also exposed weaknesses in Britain's administrative control in the colonies and resulted in a more aggressive stance by royal officials collecting revenue. During the late 1750s, the Board of Trade cited the war as justification for cracking down on smugglers and other abuses of the Navigations Acts. Parliament passed the Revenue Act of 1762 to halt bribery routinely practiced by colonists to circumvent the Molasses Act and the British government also encouraged the Royal navy to apprehend and detain smugglers. Customs officials became more aggressive in using search warrants, called 'writs of assistance' to track down smuggled goods. By the mid-1760s, however, the custom service collected more than £30,000 a year in duties, a substantial increase on the £2,000 annually in the 1730s.

'Rather a dangerous liberty than a peaceful servitude'

> From the fullest conviction, I disclaim every idea both of policy and the right internally to tax America. I disavow the whole system. It is commenced in iniquity; it is pursued with resentment; and it can terminate in nothing but blood.[32]

The American Revolution should not have occurred over taxation. The taxes imposed by the British government in the 1760s were neither unfair nor oppressive and the money was to be spent entirely in the colonies for their benefit and protection. Colonists were the beneficiaries of recent military victories that removed the threat of French imperialism and Indian wars and opened up the western frontier. Did they not have a moral obligation to pay for some of the costs incurred in securing these benefits? If this was the case, why did these taxes elicit such a violent response from colonists and why was the British government unable to resolve the problem in ways that satisfied both London and the colonies? The root of the problem lay in the constitutional attitudes that early settlers brought to the New World in the seventeenth century and which had been developed by them almost from the beginnings of colonisation. In their escape from what they saw as monarchical tyranny, they gave primacy to the notion of 'all the rights, privileges, and immunities of Englishmen', something later guaranteed in their colonial charters by Parliament. This meant that they would have the right to trial by jury, would be governed by the Common Law, could not be arbitrarily imprisoned and could not be taxed without their consent.

Although colonists were given substantial legislative autonomy through assemblies, they were not represented in the British Parliament. In practice, it

---

University Press), 2005, and *The Ancient Constitution and the Origins of Anglo-American Liberty*, (Northern Illinois University Press), 2005.

[31] Anderson, F., *Crucible of War: The Seven Years' War and the Fate of Empire in British North America, 1754-1766*, (Vintage), 2001, pp. 572-734, examines the aftermath of the war. See also, Baugh, D. A., *The Global Seven Years War 1754-1763: Britain and France in a Great Power Contest*, (Longman), 2011.

[32] Marquis of Granby, Speech in House of Commons, 5 April 1775.

was not possible for them to 'consent' to statute laws and parliamentary taxation. Their rights as Englishmen were conditional and they found that their ways of life were increasingly compromised by the attitudes of often arrogant officials sent out from England and local assemblies could be overruled by the Crown. Local courts supported colonial aspirations, jury trials were provided and the 'rule of law' was expressed through the Common Law but there were no constitutional or practical structures through which they could debate or consent to parliamentary taxation. The issue was not simply one of a contrast between two competing views of the British constitution, an older view that emphasised customary restraints on political institutions and a newer Blackstonian view stressing the omnipotence of the Crown in Parliament, but a failure to recognise the existence of and ultimately tensions between three constitutional positions that drew on the same legal principles, the metropolitan British constitution, an emerging imperial constitution and the colonial constitutions. It may be that the real cause of the American Revolution was this lack of political machinery to protect the colonists' rights. The basic problem in eighteenth century North America was that British colonial practices were increasingly incompatible with the 'rights of Englishmen' and the American Revolution was an expression of that incompatibility.[33]

From the 1650s, customs officers had been authorised to search for smuggled goods in Britain by a Writ of Assistance issued by the Exchequer Court.[34] To obtain this writ, the customs officer would swear under oath before a judge that smuggled property was in a particular place and if probable cause was shown, the writ would be signed and the customs officer would conduct the search with the assistance of a local peace officer. This writ was introduced into the American colonies in 1755 in a novel form that attracted no attention at first. However, in 1761, in Boston, James Otis resigned as Advocate-General of the Admiralty Court to represent the merchants of Boston in a law suit to prevent the renewal of the writ. George II had died the previous year and a new authorisation was required by the courts.[35] Otis argued that the writ was directly contrary to English liberties:

> ...was the worst instrument of arbitrary power, the most destructive of English Liberty and the fundamental principles of law that ever was found in an English law-book...Not more than one instance can be found of it in all our law-books and that was in the zenith of arbitrary power, namely, the reign of Charles I, when the Star Chamber powers were pushed to extremity.[36]

---

[33] Ibid, Adams, Charles, *Good and Evil: The Impact of Taxes on the Course of Civilization*, p. 299.

[34] Parliament had passed legislation in 1662 granting the English Court of Exchequer the power to issue the writ in Great Britain and passed a second law in 1696 enabling customs officials to apply for the writ in America.

[35] Frese, Joseph, 'James Otis and the Writs of Assistance', *New England Quarterly*, Vol. 30, (1957), pp. 496-508, Purcell, Jeffrey W., 'James Otis, 'Flame of Fire' Revolutionary Opposing the Writs of Assistance and Loyal British Subject?', *Massachusetts Legal History*, Vol. 5, (1999), pp. 147-178, and Smith, M. H., *The Writs of Assistance Case*, (University of California Press), 1978.

[36] Adams, John, and Adams, Charles F., *The Works of John Adams, Second President of the United States*, Vol. 2, (Little, Brown), 1850, p. 525.

Though England did not have a written constitution, Otis referred to the accumulation of practices and attitudes throughout English history that set limits on the power of government. In his view, there were traditional limits beyond which the Parliament or the monarch could not legitimately go and that even Parliament could not infringe certain basic rights that stood at the core of the Constitution, often termed 'the rights of Englishmen'. The writs exceeded these bounds and were therefore invalid:

> Not even Parliament could authorize such a monstrosity...An act against the Constitution is void.[37]

The case presented the first formidable challenge to general search warrants in the colonies. Otis thought that more restrictions should be placed on the government's authority to intrude upon places ordinarily kept private by homeowners and business proprietors. In America, Otis argued, the law should require that all searches be conducted pursuant to a lawful warrant that is obtained by an official who is placed under oath before a neutral third party and compelled to disclose the precise nature of any incriminating evidence. Any warrant that might be issued should fully describe the person or premises to be searched. The judges of the court ruled against Otis and issued the writ to the customs officers in Boston. Contrary to popular belief the colonists were never oppressed by the use of the writ of assistance and because of the actions of judges and lawyers, most writs gathered dust waiting to be signed in the chambers of colonial judges.

Crisis and resolution

Success in the Seven Years' War had shown the strength of British state but coping with its consequences soon reveals the limitations of its imperial power. The war had been expensive and post-war British governments faced with an expanding national debt, looked to the colonies for a large contribution to the costs of empire. Within Britain, where ministries legitimated their fiscal demands through parliamentary legislation, significant increases in taxation could generally be achieved without provoking major political instability. In the American colonies, where taxes were customarily low and colonial assemblies demanded the right to consent to taxation, there was strong resistance as colonists challenged the right of Parliament to tax them directly without their consent.[38]

After the Peace of Paris in 1763, the Britain began to organise the new lands it had acquired in America. France ceded all her North American

---

[37] Ibid, Adams, John, and Adams, Charles F., *The Works of John Adams, Second President of the United States*, Vol. 2, p. 522.

[38] One of the major problems in the 1760s under George III was the ministerial instability of British government. There were six Prime Ministers during the decade: Newcastle, Bute, Grenville, Rockingham, Chatham and Grafton. See, Thomas, Peter D. G., *George II: King and Politicians, 1760-1770*, (Manchester University Press), 2002, Ditchfield, G. M., *George III: An Essay in Monarchy*, (Palgrave Macmillan), 2002, pp. 49-76, and Black, Jeremy, *George III: America's Last King*, (Yale University Press), 2006, pp. 43-96.

possessions to Britain, apart from Louisiana west of the Mississippi.[39] The result was 'a belated, clumsy and tragic attempt to systematise and standardise her North American Empire.'[40] The Royal Proclamation of 7 October 1763 established boundaries, government, law and regulation for land that stretched from the West Indies and Florida to Canada. Pontiac's Indian rising in the spring of 1763 demonstrated the extent to which colonists were hated by many of the tribes of the interior.[41] British officials were determined to establish a temporary Indian reserve in which they would seek a peaceful solution to their Indian problems. These areas were under British protection, in which no lands beyond the 'Proclamation Line' were in future to be settled until officially purchased by the Crown. The intention was to ensure an orderly method of 'clearing' native titles to land through official negotiations before any white occupation took place. This proved unpopular with colonials since it obstructed the westward expansionist ambitions of settlers and land speculators. They were also angered by having to pay for the costs of maintaining garrisons along the Proclamation line.

Raising additional imperial revenue in Britain was difficult and there was strong parliamentary opposition to any further increases. The British were already among the most highly taxed people in Europe and, fear of the political consequence meant that the British government was wary of imposing new taxes at home. Americans paid little in taxes largely because the cost of provincial government was low and colonial assemblies voted only for small sums for government services. By the early 1760s, provincial taxation represented about 1.5 per cent of per capita income compared to between 5 and 7 per cent in Britain. After Pontiac's Rising and the Proclamation Act, George Grenville the new Prime Minister felt justified in asking the colonies to contribute to the costs of their own defence.[42]

Initially, Grenville decided that the colonies should pay more duties on their trade and on the import of some foreign goods. Parliament responded in 1764 with the Sugar Act, the Crown's first and only successful tax law in the colonies.[43] It was an extension of previous legislation to regulate trade and was seen as an 'external tax', but what was novel was that it collected revenue directly from colonists for a specific purpose. To make the British sugar industry competitive without completely wrecking the mainland export trade or distilling industry, it amended the Molasses Act of 1733, halving the import duty on foreign molasses to 3 pence. Decades later, President John Adams said the Sugar Act imposed 'enormous taxes, burdensome taxes, oppressive, ruinous,

---

[39] Galloway, Colin G., *The Scratch of a Pen: 1763 and the Transformation of North America*, (Oxford University Press), 2006, illuminates this neglected subject.
[40] Creighton, Donald G., *The Story of Canada*, (Macmillan of Canada), 1959, p. 79.
[41] Middleton, Richard, *Pontiac's War: its causes, course and consequences*, (Routledge), 2007, provides the most recent discussion.
[42] Johnson, Allen S., *A Prologue to Revolution: The Political Career of George Grenville (1712-1770)*, (University Press of America), 1997, pp. 129-178, considers the events leading to the passage of the Sugar Act. See also Lawson, Philip, *George Grenville: A Political Life*, (Oxford University Press), 1984.
[43] On the impact of the legislation see, Blankenship, B. C., *The Sugar Act in the Colonial South, 1764-1767*, (Louisiana State University), 1981.

intolerable taxes.'[44] He exaggerated but there was protest in Massachusetts, New York and Pennsylvania, where distillers and merchants were hardest hit emphasising their financial hardship but also significantly that taxation of the colonies without colonial assent was a violation of their rights. Yankee traders in New England protested vehemently because their trade was affected by new customs regulations included in the Act, but the rest of the colonies showed little interest in their plight. Colonists generally understood such regulatory powers as a legitimate authority of Parliament. Taxes under the Sugar Act covered a wide range of non-British goods and rates were quite modest. More contentious was the Currency Act 1764 prohibiting the issue of colonial paper money that, for the colonies meant Parliament could annul legislation passed by colonial assemblies. This caused discontent in the colonies since it threatened to hinder trade when the substantial cash injections made by Britain during the war had dried up and led to a short-term recession.

Revenue from the Sugar Act did not bring much relief to taxpayers and in 1765 there were serious riots in Britain.[45] After excise tax collectors were mobbed, cider excises were repealed. In the search for new revenue, George Grenville, asked Parliament if any members questioned the right of the Crown to tax the colonists. There were no dissenters. He then asked if the colonies would refuse 'to contribute their mite to relieve us from the heavy burdens which we lie under?' Approximately 10,000 British troops were stationed in America for its defence costing £200,000 and Grenville suggested that the colonies contributed £60,000. Stamp taxes were popular throughout Europe at this time and had been a very successful method of taxation within Britain generating over £100,000 in tax revenue at very little cost. By requiring an official stamp on most legal documents, the system was almost self-regulating since a document without the required stamp would be null and void under British law. Imposition of such a tax on the colonies had been considered twice before the Seven Years' War and once again in 1761. Grenville had been presented with draft legislation in September and October 1763 and during the passage of the Sugar Act in April 1764 and had made it clear that the right to tax the colonies was not in question.

Grenville always maintained that he wanted to raise the money 'by means the most easy and least objectionable to the Colonies' and had told colonial agents that he was not opposed to the Americans suggesting an alternative way of raising the money. This would have entailed each colony determining how to raise their share. The problem was that this had not worked before and there was no political mechanism that would have ensured the success of such cooperation.[46] On 2 February 1765, Grenville met with Benjamin Franklin, Jared

---

[44] John Adams to William Tudor, 9 June 1818, in ibid, Adams, John, and Adams, Charles F., *The Works of John Adams, Second President of the United States*, Vol. 10, General correspondence, 1811-1825, p. 319.

[45] Randall, Adrian, *Riotous Assemblies: Popular Protest in Hanoverian England*, (Oxford University Press), 2006, pp. 91-118, provides a valuable context for food riots before 1790 while Shelton, Walter J., *English Hunger and Industrial Disorders: A study of social conflict during the first decade of George III's reign*, (Macmillan), 1973, is more focussed.

[46] Gould, Eliga H., *The Persistence of Empire: British Political Culture in the Age of the American Revolution*, (University of North Carolina Press), 2000, pp. 106-147.

Ingersoll from Philadelphia and Richard Jackson the agent for Connecticut and Charles Garth the agent for South Carolina, who were also MPs to discuss the tax. But they had no alternative to present simply suggesting that the decision be left to the colonies. Unlike the Molasses or Sugar Acts, in the Stamp Act Parliament levied a direct 'internal' tax on the colonies designed to raise revenue rather than to regulate trade. While colonists tolerated indirect taxation on trade goods, they considered direct taxation unconstitutional. Colonial legislatures had exercised exclusive authority to levy direct revenue taxes in North America, their sovereignty derived directly from the people they represented. During the debate on the legislation, Benjamin Franklin informed British officials that the colonies would need to be represented in Parliament if such taxes were to be imposed. In doing so he was restating the principle of 'no taxation without representation' and questioning whether parliamentary sovereignty included the direct taxation of the colonies.[47]

The question of representation lay at the heart of the subsequent debates. The colonists' position was that direct taxation was unconstitutional unless the colonists had given consent through their representatives. The British position relied on the theory of virtual representation and Thomas Whately who developed the theory recognised that there could be no taxation without consent.[48] Nevertheless, he argued that most adult males in Britain did not have the vote but since MPs were bound to represent the interests of all British subjects, colonists were virtually represented in Parliament. There was an important difference between those unrepresented in Britain and the colonists: the colonists enjoyed representation in their colonial assemblies. The issue was whether these legislatures rather than Parliament provided the constitutional justification for the colonists' consent to taxation.

The 1765 Stamp Act followed the established practice of taxing newspapers, legal documents, business licenses, diplomas and a few other items. The funds from these taxes were to be used exclusively to pay for British troops stationed in North America. The Crown may have regarded the existence of a standing army in the colonies as necessary for colonial defence but colonists increasingly saw it as a potential threat to their liberties. To make the tax more tolerable, local citizens were granted the exclusive right to sell or issue the stamps. No bureaucrats would be sent out from the mother country, as had been the case with customs. However, following the principle established by the Sugar Act, the legislation gave the Vice Admiralty Court established in Halifax in 1764 the jurisdiction for trying offenders. This proved unpopular in two respects:

---

[47] Bullion, J. L., *A Great and Necessary Measure: George Grenville and the Genesis of the Stamp Act, 1763-1765*, (University of Missouri Press), 1982, Morgan, Edmund S., and Morgan, Helen M., *The Stamp Act Crisis: Prologue to Revolution*, (University of North Carolina Press), 1953, Thomas, Peter G. T., *British Politics and the Stamp Act Crisis: The First Phase of the American Revolution 1763-1767*, (Oxford University Press), 1975. See also, ibid, Johnson, Allen S., *A Prologue to Revolution: The Political Career of George Grenville (1712-1770)*, pp. 179-238.

[48] Whately, Thomas, *The Controversy between Great Britain and Her Colonies Reviewed...*, (J. Almon), 1769, and *Considerations on the Trade and Finances of this Kingdom: and on the Measures of Administration, with respect to those Great National Objects since the Conclusion of the Peace*, (J. Wilkie), 1766.

those accused had to post bond for the cost of the trial and travel at their own expense to Halifax whether they were guilty or not and the Vice Admiralty Court with decisions made by a single judge did not use jury trials, something colonists regarded as a fundamental right. Admiralty courts had traditionally been limited to cases involved with the high seas and while the Sugar Act seemed to fall within this precedent, the Stamp Act did not. Colonists saw this as a further attempt to replace their local courts with courts controlled by England.

By late December 1764, pamphlets and petitions protesting both the Sugar Act and the proposed stamp tax from the colonies provided early warning of serious colonial opposition. The Stamp Act galvanised colonial society and engendered widespread resistance and also served as a unifying force among the individual colonies. For the first time since 1754, colonial delegates convened an inter-colonial body, the Stamp Act Congress in October 1765 that petitioned Parliament for repeal, arguing that taxes were internal and required the consent of the colonists. Parliament could not speak for them, as it lacked a natural bond to the colonists. The Congress issued the Stamp Act Resolves, declaring: colonists owed allegiance to the Crown like any other British subject; taxes could be imposed only by the elected officials of the colonies; the distance between Britain and North America precluded colonial representation in Parliament, virtual or otherwise; and the compromise of jury trials represented an abrogation of traditional 'rights and liberties'.[49] This represented an important step towards colonial unity.

The Stamp Act Congress took place against a background of rising levels of popular resistance and violence.[50] Mob violence erupted; property was destroyed. Governors wrote home to Britain advising the government that the rebellion could not be curbed. Widespread mob uprisings in colonial seaport towns served to harass British stamp agents and tax collectors. For instance, in Boston, on 14 August 1765 Andrew Oliver, distributor of stamps for Massachusetts, was hung in effigy 'from a giant elm tree at the crossing of Essex and Orange Streets in the city's South End.' The sheriff, Stephen Greenleaf, was ordered by Lieutenant-Governor Thomas Hutchinson to take the effigy down, but was opposed by a large crowd. All day the crowd detoured merchants on Orange Street to have their goods symbolically stamped under the elm that later became known as the 'Liberty Tree'. At night, a crowd, led by Ebenezer MacIntosh, a Seven Years' War veteran and shoemaker, cut down the mock Oliver and took it in a funeral procession to the Town House where the legislature met. From there they went to Oliver's office, tore it down, symbolically stamped the timbers and took the effigy to Oliver's home at the foot of Fort Hill where they beheaded and burned the effigy and Oliver's stable house and coach and chaise. Greenleaf and Hutchinson were stoned when they tried to stop the mob that then looted and destroyed the contents of Oliver's house. Oliver asked to be relieved of his duties the next day. This was not enough and

[49] Weslager, C. A., *The Stamp Act Congress*, (University of Delaware Press), 1976.

[50] Maier, Pauline, *From Resistance to Revolution: Colonial radicals and the Development of American Opposition to Britain, 1765-1776*, (Alfred A. Knopf), 1972, (W. W. Norton), 1991, pp. 51-113, remains essential. See also, Jensen, Merrill, *The Founding of a Nation: A History of the American Revolution, 1763-1776*, (Hackett Publishing), 2004, pp. 36-182, on the Stamp Act crisis.

he was ultimately forced by MacIntosh to be paraded through the streets and publicly resign under the Liberty Tree.[51]

Boston's waterfront community, New York's taverns and Newport's congregations provided fertile ground for the development of political consciousness, political persuasion, and political action. Merchants began meeting to discuss the repercussions of new laws, printers published provocative pamphlets and protesters took to the streets. Indeed, the cities became the flashpoints for legislative protests, committee meetings, massive outdoor gatherings, newspaper harangues, boycotts, customs evasion, violence and riots.[52] Largely unsuccessful attempts were made by respectable public leaders such as James Otis and Samuel Adams to control these populist and increasingly radical activities but protest spread from Massachusetts to Rhode Island and New York. Gary Nash noted:

> Both loyal supporters of English authority and well-established colonial protest leaders underestimated the self-activating capacity of ordinary colonists. By the end of 1765...people in the streets had astounded, dismayed, and frightened their social superiors.[53]

Such mob activity was not simply anarchistic rioting. It constituted an accepted, semi-choreographed form of political activity, an expression of the will of the people. The sudden emergence of an inter-colonial organisation such as the Boston Sons of Liberty led primarily by colonial artisans reflected the particularly intense urban resistance to the Stamp Act. Originating in Boston, it soon spread to other colonies: New York, Connecticut, New Hampshire, Rhode Island, and south to Maryland, Virginia and North Carolina. The Sons of Liberty maintained its loyalty to the Crown because they believed that Parliament would do the right thing and repeal the Stamp Act. Recent British policies embodied in the Sugar Act, Currency Act, and Stamp Act targeted city-based products, industry, trade, and financial activity. Middling artisans and wealthy merchants alike had experienced economic dislocations that stemmed from recession and an influx of cheap British goods and foreign labour. The combination of British governmental regulation and business competition had begun to undermine loyalty to empire.[54]

Grenville was replaced as Prime Minister on 10 July 1765, by Lord Rockingham, a less confrontational Whig politician with strong links with

---

[51] Nash, Gary B., *The Unknown American Revolution: The Unruly Birth of Democracy and the Struggle to Create America*, (Viking), 2005, pp. 55-57.

[52] For discussion of the urban dimension to pre-war politics see, Carp, Benjamin L., *Rebels Rising: Cities and the American Revolution*, (Oxford University Press), 2007.

[53] Ibid, Nash, Gary B., *The Unknown American Revolution: The Unruly Birth of Democracy and the Struggle to Create America*, p. 59

[54] The impact of the Stamp Act was felt beyond the American colonies: O'Shaughnessy, Andrew, J., 'The Stamp Act Crisis in the British Caribbean', *William and Mary Quarterly*, third series, Vol. 51, (1994), pp. 203-226, Kerr, W. B., 'The Stamp Act in Quebec', *English Historical Review*, Vol.48, (1932), pp. 648-651, and Kerr, W. B., 'The Stamp Act in Nova Scotia', *New England Quarterly*, Vol. 6, (1933), pp. 552-566.

merchants aggravated by resistance in the colonies.[55] News of the mob violence began to reach England in October. At the same time that resistance in America was building and accelerating, conflicting attitudes were taking hold in Britain. Some wanted to enforce the Stamp Act despite colonial resistance, concerned that a precedent would be set by backing down. Calls for a colonial boycott of British manufactured goods to protest the Stamp Act's implementation appealed to a wide audience. The so-called Non-Importation Agreement represented a form of economic coercion against London merchants and their representatives in Parliament, but it was also an appealing economic gesture. Colonists throughout the colonies subscribed enthusiastically to the plan, reducing British imports to a trickle. This strategy had its desired effect and Lord Rockingham encouraged hard-pressed merchants from London, Liverpool, Bristol, and Glasgow to petition Parliament to repeal the Stamp Act. In December, Grenville called on Parliament to condemn colonial resistance to the legislation but in January 1787 Rockingham's administration proposed to repeal the Act and this was easily carried on 21 February.

Repeal was followed by further concessions to the colonies. The Sugar Act was modified and in 1766 the Free Port Act was passed to encourage an inflow of specie to the American colonies through the West Indies. Rockingham may have repealed the Stamp Act, but in March 1766 he also secured a Declaratory Act reaffirming that Parliament:

> ...had, hath, and of right ought to have, full power and authority to make laws and statutes of sufficient force and vitality to bind the colonies and people of America...in all cases whatsoever.

In effect, colonists could not take exception to any Parliamentary law that many British politicians assumed included those authorising taxation. However, the subtleties and intentional ambiguity of the Act were largely ignored by colonists busy celebrating their political victory. At the time, Franklin said this provision would not have any adverse consequences as long as Parliament did not try to assert it. Later, on the eve of the revolution, Franklin felt otherwise, saying with bitter derision:

> But remember to make your arbitrary tax more grievous to your provinces, by public declarations importing that your power of taxing them without their consent has no limits; so that when you take from them without their consent one shilling in a pound, you have a clear right to the other nineteen.[56]

The end of the Stamp Act crisis may have eased tensions but it had not eliminated their cause.

---

[55] Langford, Paul, *The First Rockingham Administration, 1765-1766*, (Oxford University Press), 1973, remains the best study of this short government. See also, Gutteridge, G. H., *English Whiggism and the American Revolution*, (University of California Press), 1942, pp. 58-102.

[56] Franklin, Benjamin, 'Rules for Reducing a Great Empire to a Small One', 1773, in Bigelow, John, (ed.), *The Complete Works of Benjamin Franklin*, Vol. 5, (Putnam), 1887, p. 227.

Crisis and conflict

The debates and protest over the Stamp Act had laid bare the fundamental differences between the British and colonial positions on colonial taxation. The colonists may have seen the hated legislation repealed but Parliament had restated its absolute authority to pass legislation on colonial matters. Further conflict might have been avoided had Britain's government remained in the hands of politicians who were prepared to avoid further confrontation over colonial taxation and sustain the appearance of consensus. Whether this could have been maintained was never tested since, with the fall of Rockingham's government in July 1766, a new ministry headed by William Pitt, Earl of Chatham but effectively led by Charles Townshend, Chancellor of the Exchequer adopted policies that again set Britain and the colonies on a collision course.[57] The result was the 'Townshend Acts', a series of five pieces of legislation: the Revenue Act of 1767, the Indemnity Act, the Commissioners of Customs Act, the Vice Admiralty Court Act and the New York Restraining Act. [58]

When the uproar over the Stamp Act subsided, Parliament followed Franklin's suggestion and adopted a number of new customs duties on goods imported from Britain. Since the Americans believed there was a difference between external and internal taxation, the Crown was willing to give them the kind of taxation they asked for, however absurd and ridiculous their thinking might be. These new duties, said a member of the British Cabinet, were 'perfectly consistent with Doctor Franklin's own arguments, while he was soliciting the repeal of the Stamp Act.' These new customs ran into some opposition in the Commons when Edmund Burke argued that the Townshend duties did not differ from the Stamp Act predicting that the Americans would soon see the folly of their own thinking. The Crown would not receive a shilling from the Americans, regardless of whether the taxes were internal or external.

Under the Revenue Act, customs were charged on a few items imported from Britain, paper, dyes, glass, and tea. Townshend originally earmarked anticipated revenue to help pay for the cost of maintaining British troops in North America but eventually decided to use the money raised to fund the salaries of governors and other colonial administrators. Previously this had been paid by colonial assemblies and represented a conscious effort to shift the balance of power in colonial government by making royal officials from their financially independent of American legislatures. The Revenue Act was passed in conjunction with the Indemnity Act of 1767 that intended to make the tea of the British East India Company more competitive with smuggled Dutch tea. The Indemnity Act repealed taxes on tea imported to England allowing it to be re-exported more cheaply to the colonies. This tax cut in England was partially offset by the new Revenue Act taxes on tea in the colonies. The Revenue Act

---

[57] Namier, L. B., and Brooke, John, *Charles Townshend*, (Macmillan), 1964, provides the best biography.

[58] Brooke, John, *The Chatham Administration, 1766-1768,* (Macmillan), 1956 provides the British political context. Thomas, Peter D. G., *The Townshend Duties Crisis: The Second Phase of the American Revolution, 1767-1773*, (Oxford University Press), 1987, is a detailed study but see also, ibid, Jensen, Merrill, *The Founding of a Nation: A History of the American Revolution, 1763-1776*, pp. 215-287.

also reaffirmed the legality of writs of assistance or general search warrants giving broad powers to customs officials to search houses and businesses for smuggled goods. Townshend expected that the legislation would raise the relatively low sum of £40,000 a year but, more importantly, having established the precedent for taxing the colonists, he intended to increase taxes gradually until the colonies paid for themselves. His aims were political more than financial.

Townshend also introduced legislation to improve the collection and enforcement of taxes. The Commissioners of Customs Act of 1767 established an American Board of Customs Commissioners of five commissioners based in Boston modelled on the British Board of Customs. It was created to resolve the problems faced by the British Board in enforcing trade regulations in the colonies. The enforcement of trade laws was the main reason for the Vice Admiralty Courts Act of 1768.[59] The Vice Admiralty court in Halifax was too remote to serve all the colonies and the legislation created four district courts, which were located at Halifax, Boston, Philadelphia and Charleston. The purpose of the Vice Admiralty courts was to help customs officials prosecute smugglers, since colonial juries were reluctant to convict persons for violating unpopular trade regulations.

The Quartering Act passed in 1765 provided that Great Britain would house its soldiers in American barracks and public houses, but if its soldiers outnumbered the housing available, would quarter them 'in inns, livery stables, ale houses, victualing houses, and the houses of sellers of wine and houses of persons selling of rum...' or in 'uninhabited houses, outhouses, barns, or other buildings.' Colonial authorities were required to pay the cost of housing and feeding these troops. When 1,500 British troops arrived at New York City in 1766 the New York Provincial Assembly refused to comply with the Quartering Act because its members regarded it as an unconstitutional tax and the troops had to remain on their ships. The New York Restraining Act suspended the power of the Assembly until it complied with the provisions of the Quartering Act. This act took effect on October 1, 1767. A new assembly was elected and also dissolved when it would not comply either. A third assembly was elected in 1769, but its compliance was considered betrayal by radical colonists.

Townshend knew that this legislation would be controversial but died suddenly in September 1767 and did not witness the colonial reaction. Unlike the immediate opposition to the Stamp Act, opposition to the Townshend duties developed more gradually. He mistakenly believed that Americans regarded internal taxes as unconstitutional and external taxes as constitutional. This distinction collapsed once the colonists realised that Townshend's 'external' taxes on imports, rather than regulating commerce, sought to raise revenue much like the 'internal' Stamp Act. The colonists' objection to internal taxes did not mean that they would accept external taxes and their position was that any tax laid by Parliament for the purpose of raising revenue was unconstitutional. The fact that the duties imposed were moderate did not mollify the critics. Their supposedly

---

59 Ubbelohde, Carl, *The Vice-Admiralty Courts and the American Revolution*, (University of North Carolina Press), 1960, but see also, Lovejoy, David S., 'Rights Imply Equality: The Case Against Admiralty Jurisdiction in America, 1764-1776', *William and Mary Quarterly*, third series, Vol. 16, (1959), pp. 459-484.

innocuous nature, argued John Dickinson in *Letters from a Farmer in Pennsylvania* that began appearing in December 1767 masked the true perniciousness of the taxes:

> Nothing is wanted at home but a PRECEDENT, the force of which shall be established by the tacit submission of the colonies...IF Parliament succeeds in this attempt, other statutes will impose sums of money as they choose to take, without any other LIMITATION than their PLEASURE.[60]

The Massachusetts House of Representatives began a campaign against the Townshend Acts by first sending a petition to George III asking for the repeal of the Revenue Act and then sending a letter to the other colonial assemblies, asking them to join the resistance movement. Upon receipt of the Massachusetts Circular Letter, other colonies also sent petitions to the king and Virginia and Pennsylvania also sent petitions to Parliament. The Sons of Liberty and other colonial leaders again resorted to a non-importation strategy to coerce Parliament into repealing the Revenue Act. Although it was embraced less rapidly and was less effective than in 1765 as many merchants did not participate, the boycott took hold throughout the colonies and by 1769, colonial exports exceeded imports by over £800,000.[61]

The effect of the Revenue Act was felt most keenly in Boston, the location of the newly created American Customs Board.[62] It proved so unpopular that the Customs Board requested naval and military assistance and on 1 October 1768 the first of four regiments began disembarking in Boston. This focused colonial assumptions that they were being treated differently and reflected what they saw as the increasingly tyrannical nature of British rule. The *Journal of Occurrences*, an anonymously written series of newspaper articles, chronicled clashes between civilians and soldiers during the military occupation of Boston. Drawing upon the traditional Anglo-American distrust of standing armies garrisoned among civilians, the *Journal*, with considerable exaggeration presented a Boston besieged by unruly British soldiers, who assaulted men and raped women with impunity. Tensions rose after Christopher Seider, a Boston teenager was killed by a customs employee on 22 February 1770. Although British soldiers were not involved in that incident, resentment against the occupation escalated in the days that followed, resulting in the killing of five civilians in the so-called Boston Massacre of 5 March 1770.[63]

---

[60] Dickinson, John, *Letters from a Farmer in Pennsylvania, to the Inhabitants of the British Colonies*, (Mein and Fleeming), 1768, p. 111.

[61] Ibid, Maier, Pauline, *From Resistance to Revolution: Colonial radicals and the Development of American Opposition to Britain, 1765-1776*, pp. 113-160.

[62] Archer, Richard, *As If an Enemy's Country: The British Occupation of Boston and the Origins of Revolution*, (Oxford University Press), 2010. See also, Dickerson, Oliver M., *The Navigation Acts and the American Revolution*, (Octagon Books), 1951, and Dickerson, Oliver M., 'The Commissioners of Customs and the 'Boston Massacre', *New England Quarterly*, Vol. 27, (1954), pp. 307-325

[63] Zobel, Hiller B., *The Boston Massacre*, (W. W. Norton), 1970. See also, ibid, Archer, Richard, *As If an Enemy's Country: The British Occupation of Boston and the Origins of Revolution*, pp. 166-206.

Whether it was the result of deliberately provocative and planned actions by colonists as the British asserted or was evidence of British military tyranny as colonists maintained, the 'massacre' reinforced each sides' perceptions of the other. Ironically, on the same day, Lord North called for the partial repeal of the Revenue Act. Although some MPs wanted complete repeal, Lord North argued that keeping the tea duty asserted the right of Parliament to tax the colonies. The compromise temporarily eased tensions but the root causes of discontent remained. The American Board of Customs and the principle of making governors and magistrates independent were retained. Military occupation and bloodshed cannot be forgotten easily. Although imports had largely been resumed, the problems of customs officers continued. The situation remained tense for the next three years.

Following the retention of the three pence Townshend duty on tea in 1770, colonists had generally boycotted British brands, turning instead to contraband Dutch teas. An estimated 90 per cent of all tea consumed in the colonies was smuggled. The East India Company was on the brink of financial collapse by the early 1770s. In 1773, in an attempt to prop up the company, Parliament passed the Tea Act granting it a virtual monopoly over the British tea market and allowing direct sales access to the colonies effectively cutting out colonial merchants. The tax on tea was maintained, but the company was able to sell its tea for a price that was lower than before and, as a consequence, East India Company tea cost the least of any available tea, foreign or domestic. The colonists, Lord North hoped, would be happy to receive cheaper tea and willing to pay the tax. This would have the dual result of saving the tea company and securing compliance from Americans on the tax issue. Lord North miscalculated the unity and magnitude of the colonial response. The colonists saw through this thinly veiled plan to encourage tax payment by establishing an effective monopoly and again there were calls for a boycott. Many went further. British ships carrying the controversial cargo were met with threats of violence in virtually all colonial ports. This was usually sufficient to convince the ships to turn around. In Annapolis, citizens burned a ship and the tea it carried while in Charleston tea was unloaded and left on the dock to rot.[64]

The protest movement culminated with the Boston Tea Party. For three weeks in late November-early December 1773, the radicals in Boston called on the ships to leave without paying the tea duty while Governor Hutchinson refused to allow them to leave the port. On the night of December 16, Massachusetts Patriots disguised as Indians illegally boarded the *Dartmouth*, a cargo ship bearing 342 chests of East India Tea valued at about £10,000. In defiance of Governor Thomas Hutchinson and British tax authority in general, the intruders dumped the entire shipment into Boston Harbor.[65] The Boston Tea Party, as it was later called, is a sobering event that raises difficult legal and moral issues and is anything but the cause célèbre contemporaries and later

---

[64] Thomas, Peter D. G., *Tea Party to Independence: The Third Phase of the American Revolution, 1773-1776*, (Oxford University Press), 1991.

[65] Labaree, Benjamin W., *The Boston Tea Party*, (Oxford University Press), 1964, remains the most detailed study. See also, ibid, Archer, Richard, *As If an Enemy's Country: The British Occupation of Boston and the Origins of Revolution*, pp. 207-225.

American historians have made of it. This wanton destruction of property was not well received in the colonies. Franklin was shocked and acknowledged that full restitution should be paid at once to the owners of the tea.

In Britain, even those politicians considered friends of the colonies were appalled and this act united all parties there against the colonies.[66] In 1774, Parliament passed a series of Coercive Acts, dubbed Intolerable Acts by the Colonists to re-establish British dominion over the insubordinate colonies. The Massachusetts Government Act annulled the colonial charter of 1691 and strengthened the power of the Royal Governor, restricting the power of the House of Representatives and banning most local town assemblies. A Port Bill closed Boston Harbor to all shipping until restitution was made to the East India Company. None was forthcoming. While Lord North attempted to focus retribution on Massachusetts, his coercive laws encouraged the other colonies to unite in sympathy. Colonists saw a threat to one colony as a threat to them all: Boston's cause was their cause. In late August 1774, a Continental Congress was convened in Philadelphia to devise a common policy for confronting the British government. The meeting of the First Continental Congress is important for four reasons: it forced the colonists to clarify and define their grievances with Britain, it helped to form ties between the colonies; it served as a training ground for young colonial politicians and in some British eyes, it symbolised a step towards rebellion. Ultimately, although its delegates represented a range of opinions, the voices of the political radicals in the Congress were the loudest. In October 1774, the Continental Congress passed both the radical Suffolk Resolves and the Declaration and Resolves that laid out the colonists' grievances with Parliament. The Congress also sent a petition to the King warning him that the British Parliament was stripping the American colonists of their rights as English citizens. British and American citizens were operating under different assumptions about how the conflict between them could be resolved. The American colonists began to organise themselves to protect what they saw as their British constitutional liberties against an aggressive British state supported by a standing army and the arbitrary power of Parliament while the British assumed that the rebels were a minority group, and if they could suppress this radical minority through an impressive display of force, the rest of the colonists would again submit to their governance.

Given such radical measures, by early 1775, many American colonists were choosing sides in the growing conflict, and many chose to be Loyalists. Attempts at conciliation failed largely because of lack of confidence in the British Parliament. In February 1775, Britain passed the Conciliatory Resolution ending taxation for any colony that satisfactorily provided for the imperial defence and the upkeep of imperial officers. In a last attempt at reconciliation, the Second Continental Congress sent George III the Olive Branch Petition but he ignored their pleas and declared the colonies to be in rebellion. The Tea Act was repealed with the Taxation of Colonies Act 1778 that finally conceded that Parliament would only impose such duties as expedient to regulate commerce and the net income from these duties would be given to the colonies. But, by

---

[66] Donoughue, Bernard, *British Politics and the American Revolution: The Path to War 1773-75*, (Macmillan), 1964, analyses Britain's policies in the two years before war.

1778, it was too late. The colonies had already declared their independence, war had broken out and the dispute was no longer specifically about taxation.

A taxing Republic

The right to tax remained a contentious issue in the early years of the new Republic. In June 1776, a month before the signing of the Declaration of Independence, the Continental Congress appointed a committee to draft Articles of Confederation for the colonies. Since the revolution was against taxation by an external political agency, the right to raise taxes was restricted to the thirteen states while the federal government had wide powers other than the right to to levy 'any Taxes or Duties.' The final draft of Articles was ratified by the states in 1781. The national government, called the 'United States in Congress assembled,' was limited. Many of its powers required a three-fourths vote, especially on matters of finance and war. The Congress could not tax and but when money was needed, a requisition was made upon the states based on the value of privately owned real property. The requisition system of finance did not work. Most of the new states were in desperate financial shape and simply did not have the money required of them by the Congress. Within two years the Congress was debating the tax issue again. As much as everyone disliked the idea, resort to import taxation by the federal government appeared essential. An amendment to the Articles required unanimous consent and a Massachusetts veto was a certainty. For the next four years the Congress accomplished absolutely nothing. Robert Morris, its chief financial officer summed up the situation in these words: 'The Congress had the privilege of asking for everything,' but the states were given 'the prerogative of granting nothing.'[67]

Shays's Rebellion was the first of three tax revolts that plagued the new nation in the first fifteen years of its existence.[68] The rebels were overburdened with state taxes and debts from the war and demanded a constitutional amendment to curb the spending and taxing powers of Massachusetts.[69] Old war veterans formed several regiments and there was talk of rebellion. When one of these regiments tried to seize a federal arsenal, two volleys of cannon were fired, the rebels dispersed and the rebellion was over. Like the Stamp Act of 1765, Shays' Rebellion brought the squabbling states together again, this time to form 'a more perfect Union.' By 1787, everyone agreed the federal government must be able to tax, but what limitations should there be on that power? The Framers of the Constitution decided to define and control the taxing powers of the Congress. Controls were needed besides the 'consent' of the taxpayers through

[67] Pollack, Sheldon D., *War, Revenue and State Building: Financing the Development of the American State*, (Cornell University Press), 2009, pp. 100-164.

[68] Danver, S. L., (ed.), *Revolts, Protests, Demonstrations and Rebellions in American History: An Encyclopedia*, 3 Vols. (ABC-CLIO), 2011, Vol. 1, pp. 207-250.

[69] Richards, Leonard L., *Shays's Rebellion: The American Revolution's Final Battle*, (University of Pennsylvania Press), 2002, and Szarmary, David P., *Shays's Rebellion: The Making of an Agrarian Insurrection*, (University of Massachusetts Press), 1980, provide a narrative. Gross, Robert A., (ed.), *In Debt to Shays: The Bicentennial of an agrarian rebellion*, (University Press of Virginia), 1993, contains valuable papers. Hull, Mary E., *Shays' Rebellion and the Constitution in American History*, (Enslow Publishers), 2000, places the rebellion within America's constitutional development.

their representatives. It would be easy for one class of citizen to gain control of the tax-making machinery and adopt taxes that oppressed some minority group. Whatever taxes were adopted, they should fall equally upon the majority and the minority and the delegates at the Constitutional Convention were not blind to the evils inherent in democratic tax-making without constitutional standards to prevent injustices.[70] The result in Section 8 of the Constitution was

> The Congress shall have Power to lay and collect Taxes, Duties, Imposts and Excises, to pay the Debts and provide for the common Defence and general Welfare of the United States; but all Duties, Imposts and Excises shall be uniform throughout the United States.

The authority to initiate money and tax bills, however, resided exclusively with the House of Representatives, although the Senate did reserve the right to revise such bills. Since the people would vote for House legislators directly, the federal government, in theory, derived its authority to tax from the sovereignty of the people, not the states.[71]

Alexander Hamilton became Washington's Secretary of the Treasury. In 1792, Hamilton, following Adam Smith's *Wealth of Nations*, persuaded Congress to adopt an excise tax on whiskey to supplement revenues from customs that were insufficient to pay the war debts of the states. The whiskey tax was, in Hamilton's words, a luxury tax. Furthermore, the nation drank too much of it, so the tax would be a health measure as well. Also, there had been taxes on whiskey before the war, and those experiences had not been bad. Congress eventually followed Hamilton's request and placed a tax on whiskey, some luxury items, auction sales, and negotiable instruments. To many in America, Hamilton's excise was a betrayal of the revolution. The whiskey excise ran into trouble immediately.[72] On the western frontier, whiskey was not a luxury item, but rather the basic medium of exchange. The 25 per cent excise in hard cash was outrageous; it was in reality a tax on money. In 1792, when the tax was adopted, the frontier region initially protested peacefully. There were speeches, meetings, and petitions. When the government did not take any steps to repeal the tax, reasoned arguments soon turned into demands for secession. Liberty polls were erected as they had been in Boston to protest the Stamp Act.[73]

---

[70] Maier, Pauline, *Ratification: The People Debate the Constitution 1878-1788*, (Simon & Schuster), 2010, provides a dramatic account of the ratification of the Constitution. See also, Beeman, Richard R., *Plain, Honest Men: The Making of the American Constitution*, (Random House), 2009, and Holton, Woody, *Unruly Americans and the Origins of the Constitution*, (Farrar, Straus and Giroux), 2008.

[71] Wood, Gordon S., *Empire of Liberty: A History of the Early Republic, 1789-1815*, (Oxford University Press), 2009, provides detailed analysis of the 1790s.

[72] Slaughter, Thomas P., *The Whiskey Rebellion: Frontier epilogue to the American Revolution*, (Oxford University Press), 1988, Hogeland, William, *The Whiskey Rebellion: George Washington, Alexander Hamilton, and the Frontier Rebels Who Challenged America's Newfound Sovereignty*, (Simon & Schuster), 2006.

[73] Cornell, S., 'Mobs, Militias and Magistrates: Popular Constitutionalism and the Whiskey Rebellion', *Chicago-Kent Law Review*, Vol. 81, (2006), pp. 883-903.

By 1794, the entire region was in open revolt. Excisemen were tarred and feathered, their houses were burned and it was fortunate they were not lynched. When civil order collapsed by 1794, a judge of the Supreme Court certified the existence of a state of insurrection in Western Pennsylvania. Hamilton persuaded Congress to authorise President Washington to call out the militia from four adjacent states to make a show of force and lead the troops. By November, prominent members of the rebellion in Pennsylvania were arrested, and the militia occupied the area until the following spring. Organised opposition to the tax evaporated. Ultimately, Washington's administration demonstrated leniency; few of the rebels were ultimately convicted and the president soon pardoned those who were. The final outcome of the rebellion favoured the rebels. Thomas Jefferson repealed the entire excise tax law in 1800 that these farmers considered unconstitutional. The excise was not uniform. Southern planters paid no excise on their basic farm production; the produce of New England farmers was not taxed; other farmers, merchants and artisans throughout the nation were not taxed. In order for taxation to be uniform to all, under varying circumstances, should not these other people have borne a similar burden? This argument was never answered.

Soon after the Whiskey Rebellion was crushed, another tax revolt erupted on the eastern seaboard, this one by German settlers. In 1798, Congress levied its first direct tax of $2,000,000 on land, houses and slaves and allocated among the states as the Constitution required. With few slaves, Pennsylvania's quota was $237,000 that fell largely on land and houses. Houses presented a valuation problem. Assessments were determined by the number and size of windows on each dwelling.[74] When assessors arrived to count and measure windows, the German settlers thought the government was about to levy the hated European hearth tax. John Fries, an auctioneer who had served during the Revolutionary War, organised meetings from February 1799 to discuss a collective response to the tax. Many advocated tax resistance and particularly in Milford Township, assessors were unsuccessful in completing their tax assessments due to intimidation. In 1799 and 1800, organised into small armed bands, they scoured the countryside for assessors, who were then seized, assaulted, and driven from these counties. When some of the rebels were arrested, Fries marched on the courthouse to free them. President John Adams called out the militia, Fries was arrested, tried, convicted of treason and sentenced to death but pardoned by Adams, against the advice of his entire cabinet.

The Constitution gave federal authority the right to levy federal taxes but many Americans bitterly resented such internal taxes especially when levied by a far-removed central government. Customs duties were acceptable as indirect taxes paid on imported goods and most consumers were unaware that they were paying these taxes since they were blended into the price of the goods. Direct taxes were different and, especially in the case of excise taxes, people were well aware of the burdens they imposed. Excise taxes were regarded as the 'most

---

[74] Newman, Paul D., *Fries's Rebellion: The Enduring Struggle for the American Revolution*, (University of Pennsylvania Press), 2004, and Smith, Nicholas E., *Fries' Rebellion Reconsidered: Pennsylvania's House Tax Resistance*, (Eastern Washington University), 2001.

odious of taxes' by the Continental Congress in 1775 and twenty-five years later the attitude of Americans was unchanged. In achieving their independence, many Americans felt that they had replaced one remote tax-grabbing authority with another.

Sierra Leone, 1898

Portuguese navigators landed on the Sierra Leone Peninsula in 1460, naming it Serra Lyoa (Lion Mountains) after the mountains located there. The Temne were already living along the northern coastal region but from the mid-sixteenth century, Mande-speaking people migrated into Sierra Leone from present-day Liberia establishing the states of Bullom, Loko, Boure and Sherbro. In the early eighteenth century, Fulani and Mande-speakers from present-day Guinea converted numerous Temne in northern Sierra Leone to Islam. From 1500, European traders were exchanging cloth and metal goods for ivory, timber and small numbers of slaves and by 1630 British traders became increasingly active along the Sierra Leone coast.[75]

Following the American War of Independence, attempts were made to resettle freed slaves who had sided with Great Britain in Africa.[76] In 1787, 400 arrived at the Sierra Leone Peninsula, bought land from local Temne leaders and established the Province of Freedom near present-day Freetown. The settlement proved unsuccessful and most of the inhabitants died of disease in the first year. A renewed attempt at settlement was made in 1792, when about 1,100 freed former American slaves (known as Creoles or today Krios) under the leadership of the abolitionist Thomas Clarkson landed on the peninsula and founded Freetown. They were joined by about 500 free blacks from Jamaica in

[75] For general studies of Sierra Leone, see, Allie, Joe, A. D., *A new history of Sierra Leone*, (St Martin's Press), 1990, Fyfe, Christopher, *The History of Sierra Leone*, (Oxford University Press), 1981, Kup, A. Peter, *Sierra Leone: A Concise History*, (David & Charles), 1975, Utting, F. A. J., *The Story of Sierra Leone*, (Longman, Green), 1931, reprinted (Ayer Publishing), 1971, and Peterson, John, *Province of Freedom: A History of Sierra Leone, 1787-1870*, (Northwestern University Press), 1969. See also, Bangura, Joseph, 'Understanding Sierra Leone in Colonial West Africa: A Synoptic Socio-Political History', *History Compass*, Vol. 7, (3), (2009), pp. 583-603. Ojukutu-Macauley, Sylvia and Rashid, Ismail, (eds.) *Paradoxes of History and Memory in Post-Colonial Sierra Leone*, (Lexington Books), 2013, is a useful post-colonial anthology.

[76] Fyfe, Christopher, 'Freed Slave Colonies in West Africa', in Fage, J. D., Flint, J. D., John E., and Oliver, Roland A., (eds.), *The Cambridge History of Africa: From c. 1790 to c. 1870*, (Cambridge University Press), 1986, pp. 170-199, provides a valuable overview. See also, Sanneh, Lamin O., *Abolitionists abroad: American blacks and the making of modern West Africa*, (Harvard University Press), 1999, Braidwood, Stephen J., *Black poor and white philanthropists: London's blacks and the foundation of the Sierra Leone settlement, 1786-1791*, (Liverpool University Press), 1993, Walker, James W. St. G., *The black loyalists: the search for a promised land in Nova Scotia and Sierra Leone, 1783-1870*, (University of Toronto Press), 1993, and Pybus, Cassandra, ''A Less Favourable Specimen': The Abolitionist Response to Self-Emancipated Slaves in Sierra Leone, 1793-1808', in Farrell, Stephen, Unwin, Melanie, and Walvin, James, (eds.), *The British slave trade: abolition, parliament and people: including the illustrated catalogue of the parliamentary exhibition in Westminster Hall, 23 May - 23 September 2007*, (Edinburgh University Press for the Parliamentary History Yearbook Trust), 2007, pp. 97-112.

1800. The new colony was controlled by the Sierra Leone Company[77] that forcefully held off the Temne while the settlers supported themselves by farming. In 1807, Great Britain outlawed the slave trade and in early 1808 the British government took over Freetown as a Crown Colony from the financially troubled company, using it as a naval base for anti-slavery patrols.[78] Between 1808 and 1864, approximately 120,000 liberated slaves settled at Freetown. Protestant missionaries were active there and most of the freedmen and their descendants were Christians. They became active as missionaries, traders and civil servants along the Sierra Leone coast as well as in other regions of coastal West Africa, especially among the Yoruba of present-day Nigeria. When slavery was abolished in the British Empire in 1833, slavery was also abolished in Sierra Leone. However, slavery outside the borders of the Crown Colony was not affected. Even when the Protectorate was established in 1896, slavery was still legal and remained the case in the Protectorate until 1 January 1928[79]

Establishing boundaries

During the nineteenth century the area around the coastal settlements was drawn increasingly into the British economic sphere.[80] There was a market in Britain for shipbuilding timber and most of the accessible forest in the coastal region was felled. There was also a European market for vegetable oils and unprocessed palm produce and peanuts were supplied in return for imported manufactures. The colonial government made treaties of friendship with neighbouring rulers and gradually acquired jurisdiction over the coastline. Between 1821-1827, 1843-1850 and 1866-1874, British holdings on the Gold Coast (present-day Ghana) were placed under the governor of Sierra Leone. In 1863, an advisory legislative council was established but the British were reluctant to assume further responsibility by increasing the size of the colony beyond the coastal region.[81]

---

[77] Schwarz, Suzanne, 'Commerce, civilization and Christianity: the development of the Sierra Leone Company', in Richardson, David, Tibbles, Anthony, and Schwarz, Suzanne, (eds.), *Liverpool and transatlantic slavery*, (Liverpool University Press), 2007, pp. 252-276.

[78] Rees, Siân, *Sweet Water and Bitter: The ships that stopped the slave trade*, (Chatto and Windus), 2009, Howard, Allen M., 'Nineteenth-Century Coastal Slave Trading and the British Abolition Campaign in Sierra Leone', *Slavery & Abolition*, Vol. 27, (1), (2006), pp. 23-49.

[79] Arkley, Alfred, '1926 Slave Revolt in Sierra Leone', *Journal of Sierra Leone Studies,* Vol. 5, (2), (2016), pp. 5-22, provides a good summary fo slavery beyond the Crown Colony and under the Protectorate.

[80] On 1 January 1808, Sierra Leone (including the coastal area) became a Crown Colony and the Sierra Leone Company rule ended. Between 1821 and 1850, Sierra Leone was part of the British West African Territories with Gambia and the Gold Coast. On 13 January 1850, the British West African Territories was dissolved and Sierra Leone again became a separate Crown Colony. From 1866 to 1888, Sierra Leone part of the British West African Settlements (renamed British West Africa Settlements in 1874). It again became a separate Crown Colony. On 24 August 1895, hinterland of Sierra Leone became a British protectorate and the Crown Colony was renamed Sierra Leone Colony and Protectorate.

[81] Wylie, Kenneth C., *Political Kingdoms of the Temne: Temne Government in Sierra Leone 1825-1910*, (Africana Publishing Company), 1977, and Abraham, Arthur, *Mende*

In January 1895, a boundary agreement was signed in Paris, roughly fixing the line between French Guinea and Sierra Leone. The exact frontier was to be determined by surveyors later. However, in August 1896, the interior became a British Protectorate, mainly to forestall French ambitions in the region, though the original Crown Colony retained its status. The Protectorate was divided into five districts and was ruled 'indirectly' rather than by creating an entirely new administrative structure. Although no hierarchical order might previously have existed, the title of 'King' was abolished and the leaders of more important groups were styled paramount chiefs; in each area less important groups were headed by chiefs and sub-chiefs administratively subordinate to the paramount chief.[82] A British district commissioner acted as overseer of the paramount chiefs in his district and as judge in serious crimes. Minor crimes and most civil matters were left to traditional systems. In the colony many Creoles, known locally as Krios had previously held senior official posts and looked forward ultimately to governing themselves. After the Protectorate was proclaimed on 31 August 1896, they were gradually removed from office and the Colony and the Protectorate were governed by British administrators.[83] Although they had treaties of friendship with the colonial authorities and were sovereign powers not subordinates, some of the traditional rulers were not consulted and did not favour the reduction in their powers, the slave clause in the proclamation or the imposition of a hut tax to raise revenue to pay for administration of the Protectorate.[84]

A hut tax

The governor, Sir Frederick Cardew, had decreed that the inhabitants of the new Protectorate should be taxed on the size of their huts: the owner of a four-roomed hut would pay ten shillings a year while those with smaller huts would pay five shillings. The result in 1898 was rebellion.[85] Cardew was not an administrator, but a professional soldier who had spent years in India and South Africa. First imposed on January 1, 1898, the tax was often more than the value of the dwelling and in many instances the dwellings were unoccupied. Cardew

---

Government and Politics under Colonial Rule: Historical Study of Sierra Leone, 1890-1937, (Oxford University Press), 1978, examine governance in the main tribal groupings and tensions with the colonial authorities.

[82] On chieftancy see, Acemoglu, Daron, Reed, Tristan, and Robinson, James A., *Chiefs: Economic Development and Élite Control of Civil Society in Sierra* Leone, (International Growth Centre: Working paper), 2015, pp. 6-9.

[83] Wyse, Akintola J. G., *The Krio of Sierra Leone: an interpretive history*, (C. Hurst & Co. Publishers), 1989, pp. 26-29, considers the impact of the Protectorate. See also, Spitzer, Leo, *The Creoles of Sierra Leone: Responses to Colonialism 1870-1945*, (University of Wisconsin Press), 1974,

[84] Cardew was an aggressive abolitionist and more than preceding governors encouraged slaves to escape from the hinterland to Freetown causing further tensions with tribal leaders. See, Rashid, Ismail, ''Do Dady nor Lef me Make dem Carry me': Slave Resistance and Emancipation in Sierra Leone, 1894-1928', Miers, Suzanne and Klein, Martin A., (eds.), *Slavery and colonial rule in Africa*, (Routledge), 1999, pp. 208-231.

[85] Hargreaves, John D., 'The establishment of the Sierra Leone protectorate and the insurrection of 1898', *Cambridge Historical Journal*, Vol. 12, (1956), pp. 56-80.

also demanded that the chiefs and inhabitants maintain the roads, taking labour needed for subsistence farming. Initially, the chiefs of the Temne pursued peaceful protest, petitioning the colonial authorities and sending a deputation to Freetown but their concerns went unheeded. This sparked two rebellions in three of the five districts of the Protectorate, one by the Temne, led by Bai Bureh, the other by the Mende.[86]

The hut tax[87] may have been the pretext for rebellion, but it was secondary to the threatened loss of sovereignty. The Creoles were increasingly resented by the inland tribes because they took advantage of their privileged position to monopolise trade in the interior. They played a central role in missionary activity clashing with the Muslim tribes, controlled education and excluded native peoples from its benefits while openly condemning their traditional practices and beliefs. In addition, Creoles made up most of the Frontier Police Force established in 1890 and were characterised by repressive and violent behaviour. Resentment against them was almost universal despite Creole opposition to the tax from its inception. The native peoples also resented what they saw as the usurpation of their ancestral lands and sovereignty when the Protectorate was established without their participation or consent. Chiefs were now appointed who had no traditional claim to chieftaincy and, is they showed any 'disrespect' for the British could be summarily tried and imprisoned. The Frontier Police Force not only took the law into their own hands but was seen as agents of terror. The new administration was riddled with inefficiency and corruption and some members of the hated Frontier Police Force were given administrative powers because of a shortage of suitable personnel. A new land policy also caused great resentment. In 1896, an ordinance was passed that all mineral rights would belong to the Crown and that waste or uninhabited lands would be allocated to settlers. The policy failed to recognise that native peoples used a shifting system of agricultural cultivation and that their 'waste' land would be alienated as a result causing considerable economic problems. This policy was seen as another assault on traditional ways of life. The rebellion was an attempt by local chiefs to maintain their independence in the face of growing British control and the hut

---

[86] Short discussion of the rebellion can be found in Gueye, M'Baye and Boahen, A. Adu, 'The Hut Tax Rebellion', in Boahen, A. du, (ed.), *Unesco General History of Africa Volume VII: Africa under Colonial Domination 1880-1935*, (University of California Press), 1900, pp. 68-69, and Chalmers, David, 'Mende Rising against British Tax Administration in Sierra Leone, 1898', in Cartey, W. and Kilson, M., (eds.), *The Africa Reader: Colonial Africa*, (Vintage), 1970, pp. 62-69. For more detailed discussion, see, Denzer, Laray and Crowder, Michael, 'Bai Bureh and the Sierra Leone Hut Tax War of 1898', in Rotberg, Robert I., and Mazrui, Ali A., (eds.), *Protest and Power in Black Africa*, (Oxford University Press), 1970, pp. 169-212, Ijagbemi, E. Adeleye, 'Fula Mansa Gbanka and the Hut Tax Rising of 1898', *Odù [Ife-Ife, Nigeria]*, Vol. 15, (1977), pp. 104-114, and Abraham, Arthur, 'Bai Bureh, the British, and the Hut Tax War', *International Journal of African Historical Studies*, Vol. 7, (1), (1974), pp. 99-106.

[87] Opposition in Sierra Leone to excessive forms of taxation dated back to the 1800 settler rebellion and disputes between the Nova Scotian settlers and the Sierra Leone Company over the imposition of a quit rent. See Cox-George, N. A., *Finance and Development in West Africa: The Sierra Leone Experience*, (D. Dobson), 1961, pp. 40-44 and more generally, Gardner, Leigh A., *Taxing Colonial Africa: The Political Economy of British Imperialism*, (Oxford University Press), 2012.

tax–which the Chalmer's Commission concluded the people could pay--was viewed as a symbol of their loss of sovereignty. It was simply a means for the colonial authorities to get the local rulers to acknowledge British suzerainty and the rulers dug their heels in and resisted. The rebellions were the first serious uprising in opposition to taxation in British West Africa and caused the British to be cautious about implementing direct taxation or infringing on the rights of traditional rulers to control their land in other territories such as Nigeria and the Gold Coast. Furthermore, unlike some other conflicts in West Africa, the uprising was a complex series of events that placed a Westernised Creole élite as middlemen between the expansionist aims of the British colonisers and the struggle for autonomy by indigenous African kingdoms.

Rebellion

Bai Bureh was born in 1840 and during the 1860s and 1870s gained a reputation as a formidable warrior in the Northern Province. He successfully fought and won wars against other villages and tribal leaders who were against his plan to establish correct Islamic and native practices throughout Northern Sierra Leone. In 1882, Bureh fought against the Susu people from French Guinea who invaded Kambia, a town in northern Sierra Leone pushing them back into French Guinea and returned the land to the local Kambia people. After winning several major wars, his popularity spread and in 1886, he was crowned as the chief of Northern Sierra Leone. As a ruler, Bureh never wanted to co-operate with the British who were living in the capital city of Freetown.

Bai Bureh refused to recognise the hut tax the British had imposed, believed that the Sierra Leonean people had a duty not to pay taxes to foreigners and wanted the British to leave and allow the Sierra Leoneans solve their own problems. After refusing to pay his taxes on several occasions, the British issued a warrant for his arrest. Sir Frederic Cardew offered £100 pounds as a reward for his capture, but Bai Bureh reciprocated by offering £500 for the capture of the Governor. Most of Bureh's fighters came from several Temne villages under his command, as well as fighters from Limba, Loco, Kissi and Kuranko villages who were sent to his aid. Bai Bureh had the advantage over the vastly more powerful British for several months of the war. By 19 February 1898, his men had severed the British line of communication between Freetown and Port Loko and had blocked the road and the river from Freetown.[88] Despite their arrest warrant, the British forces initially failed to defeat Bureh and his rebels.[89] By May,[90] they were making important advances against the rebels but the rainy season interrupted hostilities until October.

The tactics employed by Bai Bureh during the rebellion were the forerunner of tactics employed by guerrilla armies worldwide. His forces surprised the British troops time and again, subjecting them to punishing fire

[88] 'Rising in the Sierra Leone Hinterland', *St James' Gazette*, 25 February 1898, pp. 8, 9, 'The Revolution in Sierra Leone', *Sheffield Daily Telegraph*, 7 March 1898, p. 7, 'Disturbances in Sierra Leone', *Glasgow Herald*, 30 March 1898, p. 9.
[89] For the military dimensions of the rebellion see, Hernon, Ian, *Britain's Forgotten Wars: Colonial Campaigns in the 19th century*, (Sutton Publishing), 2003, pp. 707-733.
[90] 'The Sierra Leone Rising', *London Evening Standard*, 7 May 1898, p. 5.

from behind concealed war fences, before slipping away unseen into the bush. At the time these tactics were revolutionary and he 'succeeded' because he had expert knowledge of the terrain across which the rebellion took place. This involved 'some of the most stubborn fighting that has been seen in West Africa', wrote Colonel Marshal, the British commander. 'No such continuity of opposition had at any previous time been experienced on this part of the coast.'[91] The British campaigned for ten months, burning 97 villages but gradually the rebels were worn down and their leaders arrested. Bai Bureh was finally tracked down and was either captured by or surrendered to a small patrolling party of the newly organised West African Regiment on 11 November 1898 in Port Loko and taken under guard to Freetown.[92] Some officials wanted to try him for treason but he never faced trial because the Colonial Office decided that as he owed no allegiance to the British monarchy, his actions could not therefore be deemed treasonous. He was, however, too dangerous to release and was deported to Gambia on 30 July 1899, with two other chiefs. His companions died in exile but Bai Bureh returned to Sierra Leone in 1905, three years before his death, and was reinstated as the chief of Kasseh.

The rebellion by the Mende in the south was a mass uprising that broke out on 27 April 1898, was more destructive and was a form of anti-colonial nationalism that powerfully conflicted with the pro-British stance of the Creoles. Unlike Bai Bureh who restricted himself to fighting British forces and with one notable exception did not kill missionaries or traders, the rebels attacked all people they considered enemies: white settlers, Creoles and even the Mende who had adopted European culture were slaughtered. Some 1,000 Creoles of the Sierra Leone peninsula were killed. Without a leader of Bai Bureh's calibre, the Mende were neither organised nor united and their resistance in most areas was broken in two months. Some Mende rebels in the centre of the country were not beaten until November, however; Mende king Nyagua's son Maghi, in alliance with some Kissi, fought on in the East of the Protectorate until August 1899. Several hundred leaders were tried and ninety-six hanged.

The rebellion had important consequences for Sierra Leone.[93] The defeat of the Temne and Mende rebellions reinforced their loss of ancestral sovereignty and independence. There was also a considerable loss of life among the tribes and the Creoles, who were mistrusted by both British officials and native peoples alike. At the time, it was the Creoles who were blamed for inciting the rebellion though Wyse noted that more recent historiography had placed them as victims.[94] However, he did not explore the rationale of indigenous peoples in their slaughter of the Creoles and like previous historians attributed it to the notion that the Creoles represented the 'onslaught of western culture and

---

[91] *Report by Her Majesty's Commissioner and correspondence on the subject of the insurrection in the Sierra Leone Protectorate, 1898*, (Darling & Son), 1899, p. 618.

[92] 'Sierra Leone Campaign', *Diss Express*, 4 November 1898, p. 3, 'Sierra Leone Revolt', *Dundee Courier*, 16 November 1898, p. 5.

[93] See, Okoth, Assa, *A History of Africa: African societies and the establishment of colonial rule, 1800-1915*, (East African Publishers), 2006, pp. 184-185.

[94] Wyse, Akintola J. G., *H. C. Bankole-Bright and Politics in Colonial Sierra Leone, 1919-1958*, (Cambridge University Press), 1990, p. 29.

colonialism.'[95] Following the rebellions, the economic and political power of the Creoles declined dramatically and British colonial policy toward the Creoles shifted considering the events of the uprisings. Furthermore, the political advancement of the Creoles was significantly undermined and the British no longer viewed them as their political protégés and they were gradually replaced by British officials in the interior. The rebellions also played a significant role in undermining relations between the Creole population and indigenous tribes; a theme that would become representative of Colony-Protectorate relations decolonisation.

The Colonial Office sent Sir David Chalmers to investigate the causes of the war and to determine whether the hut tax should continue or not and he concluded that the tax and the brutal ways it was enforced was the cause of the war. It was considered oppressive and unjust and was higher than most people could afford. He recommended that the hut tax should be dropped as unworkable and that British administrators should concentrate on rebuilding the damaged countryside and the confidence of the native peoples. However, Governor Cardew produced a counter-report in which he insisted that the tax should remain suggesting that the creation of the Protectorate had caused considerable disruption to the slave trade and that this was the primary cause of discontent and rebellion. He argued that without the tax there would be no money to develop the Protectorate as neither London nor the Colony government was prepared to fund it. He also maintained that abolishing the tax would damage British prestige as it might be seen as a victory by the Temne and Mende and their supporters. Chalmers did not live to see the British government accept Cardew's assertion that the commissioner had over-stated the grievances of the natives; he died in August 1899 a month after he had presented his damning report. Finally, the division between the Colony and the Protectorate meant that people in Sierra Leone were all subject to colonial control based in Freetown but were governed under different administrations. In the Colony, people were British subjects with British culture imposed on their African culture while in the Protectorate where there was indirect rule, tribal Africans lived under their chiefs, governed by traditional laws and institutions reinforced by Protectorate Ordinances.[96]

Further unrest

Although the hut tax was reintroduced into Sierra Leone in 1900 at a slightly lower minimum rate of three shillings, it remained a persistent problem for the colonial authorities and played a role in the Bububya rebellion in 1931.[97] Haidara Kontorfilli was a charismatic Islamic religious reformer and an anti-colonialist who entered Sierra Leone from the French colony of Guinea in May

[95] Birchall, John, (ed.), *Journal of Sierra Leone Studies*, Vol. 3, (2014), is the most recent detailed discussion of Creoles and the rebellions.

[96] Sibanda, M. J. M., 'Dependency and Underdevelopment in north-western Sierra Leone, 1896-1939', *African Affairs*, Vol. 71, (1979), pp. 481-492, is useful on this issue.

[97] See, Rashid, Ismail, 'Messianism and anti-colonialism in Sierra Leone: the Bububya Rebellion revisited', in Falola, Toyin, (ed.), *Ghana in Africa and the World: Essays in honor of Adu Boahen*, (Africa World Press), 2003, pp. 269-294.

1930. He settled in Bubuya in the Kambia District, from where he disseminated his religious teachings. His influence spread quickly and widely and he attracted a considerable following mainly to the rural poor. The colonial administration increasingly saw Haidara as a threat to the stability of the government and on 9 February 1931, served him with an expulsion order, charging him with sedition. Haidara ignored the order and, in reply, wrote an open letter to the people of Kambia in which he told them not to fear the Europeans and not to pay the hated hut tax, a proposal popular with the peasant masses hard pressed by deteriorating economic and social conditions.[98] This was an open challenge to the colonial regime and the Royal West African Frontier Force stationed in Kambia was ordered to arrest Haidara at Bubuya. Haidara was determined not to submit to the humiliation of an arrest and organised and armed his followers with machetes, swords and guns in readiness for the inevitable encounter. The confrontation that took place on 16 February 1931 was brief. Haidara succeeded in killing the commanding British officer but with four of his men he was killed almost immediately and the other protesters were dispersed.[99]

The Hut Tax rebellion in 1898 was the last substantial military resistance to colonialism in Sierra Leone but protest and dissent continued. Vocal political dissent came mainly from the Creoles, who continued to press for political rights and operated a variety of newspapers that successive governors considered taxing and demagogic. African resistance was not confined to political discussion. Sierra Leone developed an active trade union movement whose strikes were often accompanied by sympathetic rioting among the general population. For instance, the Railway Workers' Union was on strike from 13 January to 26 February 1926 with Creole support. Rioting erupted in Freetown and according to Wyse this is the first time that workers and intelligentsia acted in harmony. The strike was viewed as a threat to stability by the government and suppressed by troops and police.[100]

South Africa, 1906

Nelson Mandela delivered a speech in Durban shortly after his release from prison about apartheid in Natal in which he referred to the Bhambatha Rebellion, a protest against a poll tax in 1906:

> The Zulu people, led by Chief Bhambatha [kaMancinza], refused to bow their proud heads and a powerful spirit of resistance developed, which, like the battle of Isandlwana, inspired generations of South Africans.[101]

President Thabo Mbeki referred to the Bhambatha Rebellion and how it inspired the people to fight colonialism and then apartheid that followed at the tenth anniversary celebration of the adoption of the South African Constitution

[98] Ibid, Wyse, Akintola J. G., *H. C. Bankole-Bright and Politics in Colonial Sierra Leone, 1919-1958*, pp. 109-110.
[99] 'Mad Mullah in West Africa', *Western Monring News*, 21 February 1931, p. 7, 'Officer Killed in Ambush', *Yorkshire Post and Leeds Intelligencer*, 21 February 1931, p. 11.
[100] Ibid, Wyse, Akintola J. G., *H. C. Bankole-Bright*, pp. 69-76.
[101] Mandela, Nelson, 'Address to Rally in Durban', 25 February 1990, http://www.anc.org.za/ancdocs/history/mandela/1990/sp900225-1.html

in Cape Town on 8 May 2006.[102] Reference to the Bhambatha Rebellion raised powerful images of the long struggle against oppression in South Africa and many claim that it was the first resistance to apartheid in South Africa.[103]

By the early 1870s, the Zulu nation was already ruled in two different ways. South of the Thukela River in Natal, Zulu 'client' chiefdoms were under British influence and responded loyally to the defence of Natal at the outbreak of the Zulu war in 1879, while to the north of the river the Zulu warrior kingdom retained an uneasy independence under the long rule of Mpande and his son Cetshwayo. Overconfidence in his ability to manage the Zulu led Theophilus Shepstone, Secretary of Native Affairs in Natal to resolve Natal's labour problems by urging war on Zulu north of the Thukela in 1879. The eventual defeat of Cetshwayo and his temporary exile led to Zululand's partition into a 'settlement' that surrounded the core kingdom with the territories of thirteen 'appointed' chiefs. By 1883, when Cetshwayo returned to his capital in the partitioned Zululand, much of his authority, lands and cattle had been seized by the British client chiefs altering the power balance within the Zulu nation and saw his defeat and death in 1884. With the removal of a strong, centralising authority and caught between the demands for land and labour exerted by both the British colony of Natal and the Boer South African Republic, Zululand was destroyed by civil war and external pressures. The Zulu military state was dismembered rather than being incorporated politically into growing hegemony of the British colonial state.[104]

Incorporation into the colonial state

In 1897, Zululand was finally incorporated into the colony of Natal but despite its loss of political independence, superficially little appeared to have changed in Zulu society. However, the realities of colonial rule led to increasing tensions between generations within Zulu society. In 1898, 345 young men left Ndwandwe to seek work elsewhere to meet their payment of the hut tax and there were complaints from their elders about their 'lack of respect' and unwillingness to return home.[105] By 1904, 17,000 Zulu were working outside the Province of Zululand and had become migrant workers on white farms and in the growing towns and cities.[106] Traditional customs, kinship relations and regard

---

[102] Mbeki, Thabo, 'Address of the President of South Africa' at a Joint Sitting of the Houses of Parliament on the 10th Anniversary of the Adoption of the Constitution of the Republic of South Africa, Cape Town, 8 May 2006, http://www.dfa.gov.za/docs/speeches/2006/mbek0508.htm

[103] See, Mathieson, Susan, and Attwell, David, 'Between Ethnicity and Nationhood: Shaka Day and the struggle over Zuluness in post-apartheid South Africa', in Bennett, David, (ed.), *Multicultural States: Rethinking Difference and Identity*, (Routledge), 1998, pp. 111-124.

[104] For the background to this see, Laband, John, *The Rise and Fall of the Zulu Nation*, (Arms and Armour Press), 1997, and Guy, Jeff, *The Destruction of the Zulu Kingdom: The Civil War, 1879-1884*, (Longman), 1979, 3rd ed., (University of Natal Press), 1994.

[105] See, Carton, Benedict, *Blood from your children: the colonial origins of generational conflict in South Africa*, (University of Virginia Press), 2000.

[106] Dhupelia, Uma, 'African Labour in Natal: Attempts at Coercion and Control 1893-1903', *Journal of Natal and Zulu History*, Vol. 5, (1982), pp. 36-48.

for the authorities of elders and chiefs were in the process of redefinition, a process accelerated by a series of natural disasters. In 1895-1896, 1898, 1903-1904 and 1906 crops were decimated by immense swarms of red locusts. Between 1895 and 1907, there were six years of serious drought that devastated the pastures the Zulu relied on for their cattle. This was compounded by the rinderpest epidemic that broke out in 1897 and led to the destruction of the Zululand cattle herds and, before the herds had time to recover, they were struck by an epidemic of East Coast fever. Cattle remained the basis of Zulu economic and social life and their chief source of wealth and the sudden obliteration of their cattle shook Zulu society to its core.

The loss of their wealth in cattle was accompanied by the loss of their lands. No white settlement had been allowed in the British Colony of Zululand but the British government had conceded in 1897 when it was incorporated into Natal that the new Province of Zululand would eventually be thrown open to white farmers. This was subject to the proviso that this should not occur for five years. On 1 August 1902, the Zululand Lands Delimitation Commission was established to identify 'sufficient land' for 'native locations' with the remainder being set aside for grants to whites.[107] Critical in its deliberations was to need to distinguish between land that was suitable for commercial farming and white settlement and those areas suitable for the Zulu. The result was a decision in the Commission's final report, published in October 1904 to allocated 1.057 million hectares of Zululand, 40.2 per cent of its total area for white purchase and occupation leaving the remaining 1.57 million hectares for black reserves. Those Zulu who found themselves on land allocated to white settlers either became workers on the new farms or were reduced to the status of squatters on land their ancestors had held for a century. This situation was given legitimacy in the Native Land Act of 1913.

Africans had to pay a hut tax and a dog tax[108] and were also subjected to a system of forced labour called *isibalo* that caused widespread hardship and resentment.[109] White farmers occupied more and more land, establishing farms and sugar plantations but after the South African War ended in 1902 there was a shortage of agricultural labour.[110] Rather than work for the white farmers, the black workforce was increasingly attracted to the gold mines of the Witwatersrand, where wages were higher. In May 1905, Charles Smythe formed a coalition government in Natal and one of his main priorities was to increase revenue. The result was the imposition of a £1 poll tax on all men over the age

[107] *Zululand Lands Delimitation Commission: 1902-1904*, (P. Davis), 1905.

[108] Ramdhani, Narissa, 'Taxation without Representation: The Hut Tax system in Colonial Natal 1849-1878', *Journal of Natal and Zulu History*, Vol. 9, (1986), pp. 56-69, considers the early development of this tax.

[109] The isibalo system in Natal obliged chiefs to call out 15 per cent of adult males among their people for work on public works programmes, usually local road-building. The labour was, in effect, forced and the wages uncompetitive.

[110] Bundy, Colin, *The rise and fall of the South African peasantry*, (Heinemann), 1979, 2nd ed., (James Currey Publishers), 1988, pp. 174-196, considers developments in farming in Natal from the 1870s to 1913.

of 18.[111] Those already paying hut tax were exempted but Zulus strongly objected to the tax because of the significant difference between their own wages and those of white workers:

> In order to increase the Negro's wants or to teach him the value of labour a hut tax has been imposed on him. If these imposts were not levied, this race of agriculturists living on their farms would not enter mines hundreds of feet deep in order to extract gold or diamonds, and if their labour were not available for the mines, gold as well as diamonds would remain in the bowels of the earth. Like, the Europeans would find it difficult to get any servants, if no such tax was imposed.[112]

The date for the introduction of the tax was set for 20 January 1906, although native were given until 31 May to pay before action would be taken against them for non-compliance.[113] On 22 November 1905, instructions were issued to all magistrates to assemble the chiefs in their areas, to explain the new law, and the reasons for its introduction. Chiefs and their subjects were required to report to the offices of their respective resident magistrates to pay the poll tax on 1 January 1906. However, while some chiefs ordered their subjects to pay, many people opted for passive resistance and simply refused to pay.[114]

Rebellions

The rebellions occurred in three uncoordinated phases. Initially, there was an attack on the police near Richmond in February, with implications of a wider outbreak in the south of the Colony that was prevented by the expedition of a colonial field force in the area in March.[115] There were then attacks in the Umvoti Division in April, similarly checked, but the leader, Bhambatha

---

[111] King, R. J. H., *The premiership of C. J. Smythe, 1905-1906, and the Bambatha rebellion*, (University of Natal), 1979, and 'The Smythe Administration and the Zulu Rebellion of 1906,' *New Contree*, Vol. 42, (1997), pp. 91-109.
[112] Ibid, Gandhi, Mahatma, *Satyagraha: non-violent resistance*, p. 12.
[113] Redding, Sean, 'A Blood-Stained Tax: Poll Tax and the Bambatha Rebellion in Soh Africa', *African Studies Review*, Vol. 43, (2), (2000), pp. 29-54.
[114] On rebellion in 1906, see, *The Natal native rebellion as told in official despatches, from January 1st to June 23rd, 1906*, (P. Davis & Sons), 1906, also published in *The Natal Government Gazette*, No. 3568A, 2 October 1906, Colenbrander, Benjamin, *An account of the Bambata Rebellion*, 1906, an unofficial account by the Resident Magistrate of the Nklandhla District, Bosman, Walter, *The Natal rebellion of 1906*, (Longman, Green), 1907, and Stuart, James, *A history of the Zulu Rebellion 1906: and of Dinuzulu's arrest, trial, and expatriation*, (Macmillan), 1913, provide contemporary accounts. Marks, Shula, *Reluctant rebellion: the 1906-8 disturbances in Natal*, (Clarendon Press), 1970, Guy, Jeff, *The Maphumulo Uprising: war, law and ritual in the Zulu Rebellion*, (University of KwaZulu-Natal Press), 2005, Guy, Jeff, *Remembering the rebellion: the Zulu Uprising of 1906*, (University of KwaZulu-Natal Press), 2006, Redding, Sean, *Sorcery and sovereignty: taxation, power, and rebellion in South Africa, 1880-1963*, (Ohio University Press), 2006, pp. 89-122, Mahoney, Michael S., *The Other Zulus. The Spread of Zulu Ethnicity in Colonial South Africa*, (Duke University Press), 2012, pp. 182-216, and Thompson, Paul S., *An Historical Atlas of the Zulu Rebellion of 1906*, (P. S. Thompson), 2001, provide more recent analysis.
[115] 'Native Troubles in Natal', *Aberdeen Press and Journal*, 17 March 1906, p. 5.

transferred activity to the Nkandhla Division in Zululand,[116] where the rebellion became a war and was suppressed with great effort and difficulty by the colonial government in June.[117] Finally, a futile insurrection in the Mapumulo Division was put down quickly in June and July.[118] A minority of the African people, who made up 82 per cent of the colony's population, participated in the rebellion. However, there was the potential for a mass uprising that inspired a degree of paranoia among the European settlers who made up just 8.3 per cent of the population and prompted the colony's responsible government to take quick and vigorous action to crush the rebellion before it could spread.

Initial resistance against payment of the tax occurred when A. W. Leslie, a magistrate went to collect taxes from the Hlongwa and Cele clans in the Silverstream district. The Hlongwa refused to pay and were taken to the Kranskop Court, where they were each sentenced to a term of imprisonment and 25 lashes. On 17 January 1906, a white farmer from Camperdown was murdered after he took his labourers to Pietermaritzburg to pay their taxes. Another incident occurred on 7 February in the Mgeni district, where a small group of protesters known as Ibandla Lika Musi resisted Chief Mveli's efforts to take members of the Fungi clan to the magistrate's office to pay taxes. Mveli reported the matter to the magistrate and police were dispatched to investigate and the following day, two police officers were killed in the Richmond District trying to arrest Mlongo, the leader of the resisters. There were other instances of protest and resistance and white settlers demanded that the colonial government take firm action to deal with it. In February, martial law was introduced in Natal and the militia mobilised under Colonel Duncan Mackenzie to restore order.[119] Troops were sent to the Mgeni district brutally crushing resistance, burning down homesteads and seizing livestock. Twenty-four tribesmen were arrested, also tried by court martial and twelve were sentenced to death. When news of their imminent execution reached England, there was uproar and the Secretary of State for the Colonies, Lord Elgin, cabled Sir Henry MacCallum, Governor of Natal with an order to suspend the executions pending further investigation. As a result, Smythe and his entire Cabinet resigned. But, after a great deal of communication between Elgin and MacCallum, the former gave authority for the executions to go ahead and the Natal government decided to stay on. On 2 April, the sentence was carried out in a valley on the outskirts of Richmond.[120] After this incident the Natal government demobilised its forces, mistakenly believing that it had beaten the Zulu population into submission.[121]

---

[116] Thompson, Paul S., 'Crossroads of War: The People of the Nkandlka in the Zulu Rebellion of 1906', *Scientia Militaria, South African Journal of Military Studies*, Vol. 35, (2), (2007), pp. 95-127.
[117] 'The Natal Native Revolt', *Aberdeen Press and Journal*, 19 April 1906, p. 5.
[118] 'Victory in Natal', *London Daily News*, 9 July 1906, p. 7.
[119] Thompson, Paul, ''Loyalty's Fair Reward': The Natal Native Horse in the Zulu Rebellion of 1906', *South African Historical Journal*, Vol. 66, (4), (2014), pp. 656-676.
[120] 'The Natal Crisis', *Derry Journal*, 2 April 1906, p. 3.
[121] Thompson, Paul S., 'Colonial Military Intelligence in the Zulu Rebellion, 1906', *Scientia Militaria, South African Journal of Military Studies*, Vol. 42, (1), (2014), pp. 18-43.

The second phase of the rebellion occurred when Chief Bhambatha kaMancinza, leader of the Zondi clan who was initially willing to pay the tax, was held back when he discovered that his subjects were refusing to pay. The Natal government suspected that he had joined other Chiefs in the region who had voiced their discontent and rejection of the tax. J. W. Cross, the magistrate summoned Bhambatha to Greytown. Fearing arrest, he excused himself, saying that he was ill sending his elders on 22 February to meet with Cross on his behalf and promising to report to the magistrate at a later date. However, his headman Nhlonhlo openly rebelled against the tax and vowed to fight if the government attempted to collect the tax by force. Bhambatha's attempt to dissuade his subjects from open rebellion had failed. On 9 March, when Bhambatha did not appear, the magistrate sent Major W. J. Clark of the Natal Police with 170 policemen to arrest him. To avoid arrest on 11 March, Bhambatha fled the Mpanza Valley with his family and sought refuge with King Dinizulu kaCetshwayo in Zululand. If Dinuzulu had put himself at the head of the rebels, there probably would have been a large-scale uprising; but he did not although he provided tacit support by harbouring Bhambatha and his family.[122] On his return from Zululand on 31 March, Bhambatha found that the colonial government had deposed him from his chieftaincy replacing him with Magwababa, his uncle.

On the night of 4 April, Bambatha gathered together his warriors and attacked a police patrol, killing four white men. After ousting Magwababa, the outraged Bhambatha and a group of his supporters retreated to the Nkandla Forest. They were given refuge by 96-year-old Sigananda Shezi of the Ncube, a clan of iron-workers and assegai-makers. Sigananda was loyal to the Zulu royal house and asked Dinuzulu if he should join the rebels. Dinuzulu was evasive but instead of handing Bhambatha over to the authorities as he was instructed, Sigananda decided to join Bhambatha and the two leaders combined their forces to launch a series of guerrilla attacks. They were later joined by other chiefs and hundreds of young warriors. As the revolt gained momentum, the government stepped up its repressive measures, but these proved counter-productive as more and more clans joined the rebellion. A force was put together under the command of Colonel Duncan McKenzie and in late April they headed south from Eshowe into steep sided valleys of the Cube district. The rebels, each identified by wearing the *uboshkobezi*--a stiff piece of cowhide or cow-tail worn upright in a headdress--made the Nkandla forest, where King Cetshwayo was buried, their rallying point. Apart from a few out-dated guns, they were armed with traditional short spear and shield.[123] On 5 May, over a thousand of Bhambatha's warriors attacked the colonial forces as they were descending a

---

[122] Thompson, Paul S., 'The Zulu Rebellion of 1906: The Collusion of Bambatha and Dinuzulu', *International Journal of African Historical Studies*, Vol. 36, (3), (2003), pp. 533-557, Thompson, P. S., 'Dinizulu and Bhambatha, 1906: An invasion of Natal and an uprising in Zululand that almost took place', *Historia*, Vol. 58, (2), (2013), pp. 40-69.

[123] 'Advance in Natal', *Exeter and Plymouth Gazette*, 11 May 1906, p. 16, and 'The Outbreak in Natal', *Yorkshire Post and Leeds Intelligencer*, 11 May 1906, p. 7, each gave over a thousand words to the subject. See also, 'Government and Natal', *Belfast Weekly News*, 17 May 1906, p. 2, and 'The position in Natal', *Sheffield Independent*, 21 May 1906, p. 10.

steep ridge. Mackenzie tracked the rebels to the Mome Gorge, where he was able to encircle Bhambatha and his army and defeat them. Bhambatha's men were armed mainly with traditional short spears and shields, while Mackenzie's men had firearms. Bhambatha was captured and killed during the battle at Mome Gorge[124] on 10 June, while Sigananda and his men surrendered.[125] Bhambatha was decapitated and his head displayed as a trophy by the colonial troops.[126]

The Bhambatha Rebellion claimed the lives of 3-4,000 Zulu and 30 white people and cost the colonial government £740,000. Some of the Zulu died fighting on the side of the Natal government.[127] More than 7,000 people were imprisoned and 4,000 were flogged. Chiefs who had supported the rebels were arrested and charged with high treason. Initially sentenced to death, their sentences were later commuted to life imprisonment on the island of St. Helena. In 1910, they were granted amnesty and resumed their roles as chiefs. King Dinizulu was arrested near Nongoma. His trial took place in Greytown. Although he was defended by William Philip Schreiner, a top lawyer from the Cape Colony, Dinizulu was convicted of treason and sentenced to four years' imprisonment. Upon his release, he was banished to Rustenburg in the Transvaal, where he later died.[128]

The authorities believed that this marked an end to the rebellion, but a third and superficially unconnected rising occurred.[129] In June 1906, the protest against the poll tax turned violent with the killing and mutilations of Adolph Sangereid, Albert Powell and Oliver Veal. Two influential groups living the Maphumulo district of Natal inland from the town of Stanger attacked a local store and ambushed a column of militia wagons on the march. Troops, including those fresh from suppressing the rebellion in Zululand, were hurried into the area and began to sweep through the valleys and bush, breaking up rebel

---

[124] 'The Natal Trouble', *Nottingham Evening Post*, 13 June 1906, p. 6, 'The Natal Rising', *Nottingham Evening Post*, 28 June 1906, p. 3, 'The Natal Native Rising', *Army and Navy Gazette*, 16 June 1906, p. 7.

[125] Gillings, K. G., The Bambata rebellion of 1906: Nkandla operations and the Battle of Mome Gorge, 10 June 1906, *Military History Journal*, Vol. 8, (1), (1989), at http://samilitaryhistory.org/vol081kg.html. See also, Sly, Jeremy, 'The Zulu rebellion of 1906', *Journal of the Society for Army Historical Research*, Vol. 66, (1988), pp. 112-118.

[126] Some of Bhambatha's supporters claimed that he escaped to Mozambique and lived in hiding there until he died in the 1920s. However, the Natal forces asserted he was killed in Nkandla Forest and that it was his head displayed to the public. However, DNA testing on a lock of hair found in one of the Natal officers' belonging failed to conclusively prove whether the hair belonged to Bhambatha. See, Thompson, Paul S., 'Bambatha after Mome: Dead or Alive?' *Historia*, Vol. 50, (1), (2005), pp. 23-48.

[127] Colonial Office, *Natal: Correspondence and Further correspondence relating to native disturbances in Natal*, (Darling & Son Ltd.), 1908, provides an official stance.

[128] *Further correspondence relating to the trial of Dinuzulu and other natives in Natal: (in continuation of Cd. 4404 November, 1908)*, (Darling & Son, Ltd.), 1909. See also, *The trial of Dinuzulu on charges of high treason, at Greytown, Natal, 1908-09: before His Honour Sir William Smith, President of the Special Court, the Honourable Mr. Justice H.G. Boshoff and the Honourable Mr. Justice H.C. Shepstone*, (Times), 1910.

[129] Ibid, Guy, Jeff, *The Maphumulo Uprising: war, law and ritual in the Zulu Rebellion*, details this phase of the rebellion.

concentrations. Into this military conflict rode Oliver Veal, a young white civilian, a clerk in the Works Department. Veal was a keen cyclist and had bet a friend that he could cycle from Pietermaritzburg to Kranskop, visit a friend in the militia posted there and then return to Durban before the weekend was over. He made the first part of his journey safely enough, though he missed his friend at Kranskop but his return route took him through Maphumulo. Here he was warned by an officer he met on the road to stick to the main route that was patrolled by militia but was running late and decided to take a short-cut, following a track that took him into the territory of the Qwabe inkosi Meseni kaMusi, a fatal mistake. Meseni had just joined the rising and his young men guarded the track against militia patrols. Veal was captured by warriors and taken to Meseni's principle homestead where, after a brief debate about what to do with him, he was killed and his body mutilated. His organs were removed to provide powerful medicine to prepare Meseni's warriors in their struggle against the militia.[130]

Meseni's men were destroyed by the militia with a thoroughness that disconcerted many at the time and some 1,500 people were killed. Winston Churchill, then an Under-Secretary in the Colonial Office was scathing about the colonial reaction and when consulted about a campaign medal to be awarded to the troops, he suggested that it should be struck in bronze at the colony's expense and depict not the head of King Edward VII but the severed head of a rebel leader. The militia was spoiling for a fight and burned homes, looted, and shot Africans under arms or not with impunity. Both Meseni and Ndlovu kaThimuni, the other Maphumulo inkosi who had joined the rebellion, fled to Zululand fearing that they would be shot if they tried to surrender to local troops. There they were arrested, returned to Stanger and tried for treason. The government focused its attention on the two *inkosi* accused of leading the rebellion and Meseni and Ndlovi were accused of armed insurrection with the intention of overthrowing the government and of murder. In all, the government accused twenty-one men of murder. All were found guilty and sentenced to death. However, the government commuted all but five of the death sentences to prison sentences. Both Meseni and Ndlovi were sent to St. Helena rather than to the gallows, but eventually were released and exiled.

Explaining rebellion

The Zulu rebellion was undoubtedly precipitated by the announcement of a poll tax levied on all men who did not pay the hut tax. The tax directly challenged the traditional patriarchal authority of Zulus after the British conquest of Zululand in the late-nineteenth century. By directly taxing unmarried young men, the British colonial authorities:

> ...hastened the breaking up of the patriarchal rural homestead, the rupture of kinship links, and the further fragmentation of African communal life... [disrupting] the

---

[130] 'The Natal Rising', *Wells Journal*, 21 June 1906, p. 6, 'The Natal Outbreak', *Dublin Daily Express*, 30 June 1906, p. 5, 'The Native Question in Natal', *Edinburgh Evening News*, 19 July 1906, p. 2, 'The Natal Rebellion', *Edinburgh Evening News*, 25 July 1906, p. 4.

spiritual forces that linked sons to their fathers and their fathers' fathers whose shades watched over the homestead.[131]

The Zulu Rebellion was as much a spiritual action as it was a physical response to British imperial authority. Many saw the imposition of the poll tax as a direct challenge to their ancestors' power. Redding sees the rebellion against the poll tax as 'placating the ancestors' suggesting that their 'ancestors strongly supported their resistance and would allow them to prevail.'[132] By 1906, the African peoples of Natal had come to look upon the lost independence of the neighbouring Zulu kingdom with nostalgia and some regretted this seeing in the old Zulu way of life a vanished age of African power, glory and economic vitality. The rebels drew on the power of that mythic image; Bhambatha adopted the war-cry of the Zulu Royal House, 'uSuthu!' and used King Cetshwayo's grave as his rallying point. In Maphumulo, the groups who resisted were historically linked to the Zulu. Meseni's Qwabe had once been one of the most powerful chiefdoms in Zululand. The chiefdom of inkosi Ndlovu, the Nodunga had split away from Zululand to escape the repression of the Zulu king Mpande. Yet life in Natal soon turned sour for the Nodunga, who had placed their trust in Theophilus Shepstone's assurances that they would grow prosperous under colonial rule. However, after decades of taxation, forced labour and the erosion of traditional ways, the Nodunga believed that they had been deceived by Shepstone. Ndlovi found himself in an impossible position since the colonial authorities' use of the chiefs as agents of their administration conflicted with their responsibilities to their own people.

Guy regards the rebellion as a response to colonial attempts to replace patriarchal rule with a modern capitalistic system by separating native South Africans from their homelands and forcing them into the wage-labour system. Bhambatha, Ndlovu and Meseni felt driven to rebellion in 1906. They recognised the grievances of their people but had no meaningful influence on the increasingly self-confident colonial administration. They were also aware what had happened to the Zulu in 1879 and that the numerical and technological disparity between their followers and the militia was overwhelming. Out-gunned, they turned to traditional methods of warfare rooted in war medicine and native religion. It was to to call upon spiritual forces to offset the inescapable military advantages held by the militia that Oliver Veal was killed.

An alternative explanation for the rebellion has been put forward by Benedict Carton.[133] Carton takes the view that the rebellion was not primarily aimed at colonial rule but represented conflict between was between young native South Africans and the older generation. Both young men and women

---

[131] Ibid, Guy, Jeff, *The Maphumulo Uprising: war, law and ritual in the Zulu Rebellion*, pp. 21-22.

[132] Ibid, Redding, Sean, 'A Blood-Stained Tax: Poll Tax and the Bambatha Rebellion in South Africa', p. 29. See also, Marks, Shula, 'Class, ideology and the Bambatha rebellion, in Crummey, Donald, (ed.), *Banditry, Rebellion and Protest in Africa*, (James Currey Publishers), 1986, pp. 351-372.

[133] Ibid, Carton, Benedict, *Blood from your children: the colonial origins of generational conflict in South Africa*, pp. 114-137, discussed the rebellion in the context of generational rivalry.

were rebelling against the patriarchal system that existed among the native South Africans in Natal and Zululand. Facing a series of ecological disasters that crippled agriculture in the 1890s, African youths in colonial Natal and Zululand perceived their fathers' struggle to meet increased colonial demands as an act of betrayal. Young people engaged more frequently in premarital sex, while young men sparked widespread gang fights and young women rejected traditional filial and marital obligations.[134] By 1906, after the imposition of an onerous poll tax on young men, this domestic turmoil exploded into an armed rebellion. The young men sought revenge by attacking both the African patriarchs whose apparent accommodation they considered traitorous and the colonial troops dispatched to quell the violence. After the Natal forces crushed the insurrection, some captured rebels faced trial for treason under martial law and often their fathers testified against them.

The Zulu Rebellion was the last armed resistance against white rule before the formation of the Union of South Africa in 1910. The Zulu population of Natal were pushed deeper into poverty and became a source of cheap labour for the new capitalist state and in particular for the mining and agricultural sectors. However, the failure of the rebellion and the political exclusion of Africans, Coloured and Indians from the new Union constitution, forced the new urban European educated and traditional African leadership to establish the first national political formation the South African Native Congress, from which to challenge white rule. Bhambatha became a source of pride and inspiration to both nationalists and socialist anti-apartheid activists and movements over the years.

Conclusions

The events leading up to the outbreak of the American Revolution in 1775 show just how potent taxation was as a cause of imperial unrest and how easily it could be mishandled by the British government in London or by colonial governors. In white settler colonies where the notion of British liberties had been transposed, the need for constitutional sensitivity was essential and, when lacking, caused tensions that if unresolved led to direct resistance. In the case of the American colonies, the issue was not whether Parliament could pass laws imposing indirect taxes on colonists through trade regulations but whether direct taxes, however modest, could legitimately be imposed without representation. In Sierra Leone, although the colonial administration had the authority to impose taxes on natives, whether those taxes were proportionate and fair were the key questions. In both cases, there were also grievances about the perceived draconian manner of tax collection by officials that reinforced principled opposition to taxation. It was the failure of Parliament and colonial officials to recognise the depth of opposition and attempts to coerce individuals into paying that precipitated protest and ultimately rebellion.

---

134 La Hausse, Paul. ''The cows of Nongoloza': youth, crime and amalaita gangs in Durban, 1900-1936', *Journal of Southern African Studies*, Vol. 16, (1), (1990), pp. 79-111, considers the emergence of youth organisation and culture among African migrants in towns in the wake of the massive social dislocation experienced by African societies in Natal and Zululand in the late nineteenth century.

Once lawful avenues of protest such as petitions, meetings and demonstrations had been exhausted, pressure was put in government through more confrontational approaches such as boycotting imported goods or tax strikes and only if these failed was there recourse to rebellion and even then rebellions tended to be couched in terms of defending individual rights. Rebels hoped that their willingness to fight for their rights would persuade the authorities to reform the grievances that were the cause of the rebellion. Calls for independence were initially the preserve of a minority though, as in the case of the American colonists, this was the ultimate outcome of their tax rebellion and became a precedent that dominated subsequent British imperial thinking. What happened in the American colonies served as a warning to the colonial authorities that they needed to buttress feelings of imperial cohesion. Edmund Burke had emphasised that ties within the Empire should be 'light as air but strong as iron' but, as the experience of America and Victoria illustrates government without constitutional and political sensitivity could prove fatally damaging to those ties.

Although the context for rebellion in Sierra Leone and Zululand was different, there are parallels with the experience of the white settler colonies. All four societies were to some extent in a state of flux that put pressure on existing systems of government. In each case, rebellions only occurred when established channels of communication had been exhausted and the colonial authorities had demonstrated failure to grasp the depth of grievances. The major difference is that Sierra Leone and Zululand were largely native societies in which there was a small colonial military and administrative presence to maintain what had largely been achieved by conquest. Taxation became an issue because it was perceived by natives as unfair but it also represented the unacceptable face of administrations that were coercive and unwilling to accept the nature of existing societies. It was not, as in the American colonies, a constitutional issue but one of the survival of native social values and tribal organisation. The rebellions were a last-ditch attempt to maintain traditional native societies faced with the military dominance and modernising values of the colonial authorities. Initial success was followed by inevitable military defeat, further colonial integration and growing racial inferiority and discrimination. Yet, the rebellions retained their power to inspire later generations seeking independence or in its aftermath.

Thomas Jefferson said that it was good medicine for government to have a rebellion every twenty years or so. During his lifetime, there had been almost a dozen rebellions he was acutely aware of. Six were in the United States, starting with the Stamp Act Rebellion and ending with the Fries Rebellion. All these rebellions, including the American Revolution, were tax revolts of varying degrees of intensity. For a nation that believes in checks and balances in government, no doubt the most effective check on a bad tax system is what Jefferson had in mind. Unlike Britain's colonial and imperial administrators, Jefferson tolerated civic disorder and rebellion since 'rather a dangerous liberty than a peaceful servitude'.

7 Millenarian rebellion

Then shall the world be united in one amiable society. All nations, in all parts of the world, on every side of the globe, shall then be knit together in sweet harmony. All parts of God's church shall assist and promote the spiritual good of one another. [1]

The threat from Dutch settlers in the Cape Colony to the independence of a local Khoikhoi community set in motion the millenarian movement. During the latter half of 1788, Jan Paerl, Khoikhoi[2] announced that he was a prophet, Onsen Liewen Heer, literally 'Our Dear Lord'.[3] Claiming to be endowed with magical powers, he predicted that the world would end on 25 October 1788, urging his followers to slaughter their white cattle, build new straw huts with two doors and burn their European clothes. At an appointed time, they were to flee to the mountains and wait for the specific day when, with divine intervention, they would kill all the whites and have their land and cattle restored to them before the 'new world' would be ushered in. It is unclear why he ordered the killing of cattle. Was it a sign of their utter dependence and trust in God on the eve of such an apocalyptic moment? Was it to show that the things of 'this world' would and should not be part of the 'new world'? Or was it meant to be a sacrifice to secure the success of the venture? Within weeks, mainly through word of mouth and the efforts of zealous disciples, the millenarian movement secured a substantial following demonstrating the power of his ideas both to his own people and to worried settlers.

On 23 October 1788, Khoikhoi adherents assembled in the mountains overlooking the Swellendam drostdy.[4] Farmers petitioned Constant van Nult Onkruijdt, the Landdrost, for assistance and he sanctioned an attack on Khoikhoi kraals seizing large quantities of weapons. He commented that he had 'never seen so many livestock slaughtered' suggesting that Khoikhoi followers had already slaughtered their livestock in line with Paerl's millenarian utterances. The attack on the kraals and the loss of weapons effectively neutralised the Khoikhoi uprising. The millenarian movement was symptomatic of the breakdown and destruction of Khoikhoi society, including the incorporation of Christianity into native beliefs indicated by Paerl's Dutch title 'Onsen Liewen Heer'. Divisions also existed within the colonial administration with the central authorities theoretically trying to uphold native rights but unable to make local officials and settlers enforce decrees against their will

---

[1] Edwards, Jonathan, 'Christ's Resurrection to the End of the World', *The Works of President Edwards, in Four Volumes*, (Isaac Sturtevant, Printer), 1808, Vol. 1, pp. 423-317, at p. 493.

[2] The Khoikhoi ('people people' or 'real people') practised pastoral farming in the Cape and were known to the settlers as Hottentots, derived from a Dutch word for 'stutterer', a probable allusion to the distinctive 'clicking' sounds that are an essential feature of their language.

[3] Viljoen, Russel, *Jean Paerl, a Khoikhoi in Cape Colonial Society, 1761-1851*, (Brill), 2006. See also, Dooling Wayne, *Slavery, Emancipation and Colonial Rule in South Africa*, (University of KwaZulu-Natal Press), 2007, pp. 16-57.

[4] Under Dutch rule, the Cape Colony was divided into districts under the control of a Landdrost, whose seat of government and area of jurisdiction was called a drostdy.

The millenarian movement disintegrated shortly after and Paerl fled in the direction of Stellenbosch, a colonial village founded in the 1680s. He remained a fugitive for nearly a year but was eventually arrested and imprisoned towards the end of 1789.[5] The Court of Justice sat in April 1790 and concluded that the uprising was not an act of sedition and offered no significant threat to Company rule at the Cape. They claimed that the upheaval was inspired by an 'aboriginal superstition', orchestrated by a lunatic who called himself Onsen Liewen Heer. Paerl was not executed or banished to Robben Island but placed under house arrest in Stellenbosch. In 1796, Paerl trekked to Genadendal and soon converted to the Christian faith as preached by the Moravian church. Throughout his life, Paerl enjoyed excellent health, but during the late 1840s, this deteriorated rapidly and he found solace in meditating outside his cottage staring into the sky 'looking for Him, who will fetch [his] soul', dying aged 90 in April 1851.

All resistance and rebellion has a millenarian element. People resist or rebel because they are angered, exploited, frustrated or oppressed by the existing situation and want to change it into something better, fairer or freer. They want a society different, often in an ill-defined way, from what currently exists. An alternative or utopian society is a practical and visible solution to what has become intolerable.[6] In some instances, however, resistance had a religious or spiritual dimension, a prophetic, charismatic, invisible imperative that lifted resistance and rebellion to a different level.[7] Many of the early 'pilgrims' who emigrated to the English colonies in New England in the seventeenth century were motivated by establishing 'plantations of religion'. They enthusiastically supported their leaders' efforts of create 'a city upon a hill', a phase taken straight out of the *Book of Revelations* or a 'holy experiment' whose success would prove that God's plan for his churches could be successfully accomplished in the American wilderness.[8] Millenarianism provides a concrete version of the universal eschatological belief that at the 'end of time' God will judge the living and the resurrected dead.[9] This belief in ultimate divine justice has provided the solution to the problem of theodicy for believers in all religions suffering hardship and oppression and historically this has had immense populist appeal.[10] There is

---

[5] For Paerl's brief years as a colonial prophet, see, ibid, Viljoen, Russel, *Jean Paerl, a Khoikhoi in Cape Colonial Society, 1761-1851*, pp. 23-92.

[6] For the development of the discourse of Utopian societies, see Claeys, Gregory, *Searching for Utopia: The History of an Idea*, (Thames & Hudson), 2011, and Claeys, Gregory, (ed.), *The Cambridge Companion to Utopian Literature*, (Cambridge University Press), 2010, especially pp. 3-27, 79-106.

[7] Baumgartner, Frederic J., *Longing for the End: A History of Millennialism in Western Civilization*, (Palgrave), 1999, and Wessinger, Catherine, (ed.), *The Oxford Handbook of Millennialism*, (Oxford University Press), 2011, provide excellent summaries of the development of millenarian ideas.

[8] Weir, David A., *Early New England: A Convenanted Society*, (Wm. B. Eerdmans Publishing Co.), 2005,

[9] Thompson, Damian, *The End of Time: Faith and Fear in the Shadow of the Millennium*, (Sinclair Stevenson), 1996.

[10] Cohn, Norman, *The Pursuit of the Millennium*, (Oxford University Press), 1961, and *Cosmos, Chaos and the World to Come: The Ancient Roots of Apocalyptic Faith*, (Yale University Press), 1993, are rightly regarded as seminal studies. Landes, Richard, *Heaven on Earth: The Varieties of Millennial Experience*, (Oxford University Press), 2011,

an apocalyptic curve in millenarianism from enthusiastic launch through disappointment and restoration of 'normal times'.

The key issue in terms of millenarianism's impact on society is the question of timing. If the day of redemption is yet to come, millenarian hopes provide solace for the suffering, inspire patience and political quietism and can have a profoundly conservative influence. But driven by an apocalyptic sense of imminence, believers may become unruly, even engaging in revolutionary efforts to overthrow an unjust socio-political order in an attempt to bring about the kingdom of 'peace' for the meek and the defenceless.[11] For instance, the rapid spread of modern capitalism into peasant societies in the nineteenth and twentieth centuries where land was enclosed and customary rights taken away frequently created the context for millenarian movements.[12] Apocalyptic millenarianism creates a potent and volatile mixture and even if apocalyptic efforts to establish God's kingdom on earth have led to disastrous results, apocalyptic expectations repeatedly revive. It offers immense rewards for believers who find themselves at the centre of the ultimate universal drama where every act, however small, has cosmic significance. They can almost taste the fulfilment of their burning desire to see justice done with the good lavishly rewarded and the evil savagely punished. The approach of the end of time and the promise of a new world also liberates believers from all earthly inhibitions. Their fear of future punishment by those who now hold power vanishes and a wide range of often repressed feelings explode. Such a combination proves irresistible to many: millenarian hope possesses believers.

Millenarian views were not the domain solely of Christians but played a significant role in the development of other world religions and in the belief systems of native peoples. In fact, they were often at their more apocalyptic when there was a degree of fusion between native religious views and those of a world religion linked to a prophetic individual.[13] Islam, as a 'religion of revelation', began as an apocalyptic movement anticipating the 'Day of Judgment' and retains its populist, apocalyptic and millennial elements especially in Shi'ite theology.[14] In particular, the Mujaddid tradition foresees a 'renewer' at the turn of each century and constitutes a form of apocalyptic messianic expectation in the coming of the

---

provides an important revisionist study of the historical significance of millenarianism. See also, St. Clair, Michael J., *Millenarian Movements in Historical Context*, (Garland), 1992.

[11] Fritzie P., *Utopian Thought in the Western World*, (Harvard University Press), 1979.

[12] Hobsbawm, E. J., *Primitive Rebels: Studies in Archaic Forms of Social Movement in the 19th and 20th Centuries*, (Manchester University Press), 1959, pp. 57-107. See also, Crummey, Donald, (ed.), *Banditry, Rebellion and Protest in Africa*, (James Currey Publishers), 1986.

[13] Amanat, Abbas, and Bernhardsson, (eds.), *Imagining the End: Visions of Apocalypse from the Ancient Middle East to Modern America*, (I. B. Tauris), 2002, is a valuable and wide-ranging collection of essays.

[14] See, for instance, Cole, Juan Ricardo, *Sacred Space and Holy War: The Politics, Culture and History of Shi'ite Islam*, (I. B. Tauris), 2002, pp. 123-171, Crone, Patricia, and Cook, Michael, *Hagarism: The Making of the Islamic World*, (Cambridge University Press), 1977, and Ali, Shaukat, *Millenarian and Messianic Tendencies in Islamic History*, (Publishers United Ltd.), 1993, pp. 13-44.

hidden Mahdi.[15] Many often anti-imperialist, native movements were millennial in character.[16] This was evident, for instance, in the Gaiwiio of Handsome Lake c. 1800 and the Ghost Dance of the prophet Wovoka in the 1890s.[17] In the Pacific southwest, Cargo Cults emerged in the late-nineteenth century in which cult members believed that manufactured goods of the non-native culture had been created by spiritual means, such as through their deities and ancestors and were intended for the local native people, but that the foreigners had unfairly gained control of these objects through malice or mistake. By conducting rituals, they believe that their deities and ancestors will recognise their own people and send the cargo to them instead.[18]

The most powerful non-western millenarianism is found in Buddhism. The tradition is found in the Pure Land traditions and the expectation of the Maitreya Buddha, a kind of messianic final incarnation of the Buddha and was especially strong in China, but also in Korea, Japan, Vietnam, and Burma.[19] The millenarian strains of Buddhism gave birth to secret societies such as White Lotus and some powerful popular movements.[20] One toppled the Mongol dynasty in the fourteenth century while the Taiping, a mixture of native Buddhist and imported Christian millenarianism, almost toppled the Qing dynasty in the mid-nineteenth century.[21] The core of the Taiping faith was inspired by a Protestant

---

[15] Furnish, Timothy R. *Holiest Wars: Islamic Mahdis, Their Jihads and Osama bin Laden*, (Greenwood Publishing), 2005, pp. 1-71, and Darmesteter, *Le Mahdi: depuis les origines de l'Islam jusqu'a nos jours*, (Ernest Leroux), 1885, pp. 9-28 See also, Bashear, Suliman, 'Muslim Apocalypses and the Hour: A Case-Study in Traditional Reinterpretation', *Israel Oriental Studies*, Vol. 13, (1993), pp. 75-99, and Cook, David, 'Moral Apocalyptic in Islam', *Studia Islamica*, Vol. 86, (1997), pp. 37-69.

[16] Adas, Michael, *Prophets of Rebellion: Millenarian Protest Movements against the European Colonial Order*, (Cambridge University Press), 1979, is an important comparative study.

[17] La Barre, Weston, *The Ghost Dance: The Origins of Religion*, (Doubleday), 1970, presents a worldwide survey of religious movements from a psychological and anthropological perspective.

[18] Burridge, Kenelm, *New Heaven, New Earth: A Study of Millenarian Activities*, (Schocken Books, 1969, and Trompf, G. W., (ed.), *Cargo Cults and Millenarian Movements: Transoceanic Comparisons of New Religious Movements*, (Walter de Gruyter), 1990, pp. 1-95. See also, Jebens, Holger, (ed.), *Cargo, Cult*, and *Culture Critique*, (University of Hawaii Press), 2004.

[19] Sponberg, Alan, and Hardacre, Helen, (eds.), *Maitreya, The Future Buddha*, (Cambridge University Press), 1988, and Foard, J. H., Solomon, M., and Payne, R. K., (eds.), *The Pure Land Tradition: History and Development*, (Regents of the University of California), 1996.

[20] For instance, see Naquin, Susan, *Millenarian Rebellion in China: The Eight Trigrams Uprising of 1813*, (Yale University Press), 1976, and Kim, Sun Joo, *Marginality and Subversion in Korea: The Hong Kyongnae Rebellion of 1812*, (University of Washington Press), 2007.

[21] Spence, Jonathan, *God's Chinese Son: The Taiping Heavenly Kingdom of Hong Xiuquan*, (W. W. Norton and Co.), 1996, Reilly, Thomas H., *The Taiping Heavenly Kingdom: Rebellion and the Blasphemy of Empire*, (University of Washington Press), 2004, pp. 150-171, Rhee, Hong Beom, *Asian Millenarianism: An Interdisciplinary Study of the Taiping and Tonghak Rebellions in a Global Context*, (Cambria Press), 2007, pp. 59-80, and Hunt, Stephen, 'The Revolutionary Dimension of Millenarianism: The Case of

missionary tract and focused on the belief that Shangdi, the high God of classical China had chosen the Taiping leader, Hong Xiuquan, to establish his Heavenly Kingdom on Earth. Previous rebellions had declared their contemporary dynasties corrupt and in need of revival; the Taiping, by contrast, branded the entire imperial order blasphemous and in need of replacement. By the time, Taiping had been suppressed, some 20-35 million people were dead. The Boxer rebellion[22] of the late-nineteenth century demonstrated the power of millenarian beliefs, especially the belief, shared by the Ghost Dancers of North America and the Kartélite Cults of Africa that certain incantations made the believer invulnerable to bullets.[23]

Xhosa Cattle-Killing Movement, 1856-1857

The development of Cape Colony first under the Dutch and after 1795 the British was achieved at the expense of the Xhosa people who inhabited the Eastern Cape.[24] It was to be a war of attrition that lasted a century in which Xhosa lands were gradually seized to accommodate the economic needs of a growing number of white settlers. No event was more disastrous to the demographic and economic prosperity of the Xhosa than the cattle-killing movement in the mid-1850s.[25]

Settlers, the Xhosa and Cape government, 1760-1855

From the 1760s, white farmers trekked into the Eastern Cape in search of new lands. This brought them into initially peaceful contact with the Xhosa. The Xhosa state was a large decentralised kingdom of perhaps 70,000 people. The power of the king was in practice severely limited and effective political power lay with the various chiefs. Chiefs ruled their districts but without a permanent army or bureaucracy depended on the cooperation of their councillors, generally men

---

the T'aiping Rebellion', in Stephen Hunt, (ed.), *Christian Millenarianism: From the Early Church to Waco*, (C. Hurst and Co.), 2001.

[22] Esherick, Joseph, *The Origins of the Boxer Rising*, (University of California Press), 1987, pp. 206-240.

[23] Lanternari, Vittorio, *Religions of the Oppressed: A Study of Modern Messianic Cults*, (Alfred A. Knopf), 1963, pp. 19-55, ibid, La Barre, Weston, *The Ghost Dance: The Origins of Religion*, and Smoak, Gregory E., *Ghost Dances and Identity: Prophetic Religion and American Indian Ethnogenesis in the Nineteenth Century*, (University of California Press), 2006, pp. 132-190.

[24] Britain seized the Cape in 1795 to prevent it falling into French hands. It was briefly handed back to the Dutch in 1803 but retaken in 1806. British sovereignty of the area was finally recognised at the Congress of Vienna in 1815.

[25] Valuable general studies of the development of nineteenth century South Africa include, Worden, Nigel, *The Making of Modern South Africa: Conquest, Segregation and Apartheid*, 4th ed., (Blackwell Publishing), 2007, Ross, Robert, *A Concise History of South Africa*, 2nd ed., (Cambridge University Press), 2008, Welsh, Frank, *South Africa: A Narrative History*, (Kodansha International), 1999, and Hamilton, Carolyn, Mbenga, Bernard K., and Ross, Robert, (eds.), *The Cambridge History of South Africa: Volume 1, From Early Times to 1885*, (Cambridge University Press), 2010. Theal, George McCall, *History of South Africa*, 5 Vols. (Cambridge University Press), 1908-1910, reprinted 2010, remains a valuable study; see also his *Records of Cape Colony*, 36 Vols. (William Clowes and Sons), 1897-1905, for sources from 1795 to 1831.

of wealth. Eastern Cape farmers began to employ Xhosa workers, paid one cow or its equivalent in smaller stock a year, in the late 1770s and their incorporation into the settler economy as subordinate labourers accelerated as colonial military forces seized Xhosa lands and legislation provided for the employment of these 'native foreigners' as contractual workers.[26] Relations between the two people deteriorated with growing pressure on and competition for land, cattle and good grazing.[27] The result, in 1779, was the first of nine Frontier Wars between settlers and the Xhosa that lasted intermittently for the next century.[28] The three wars in the 1780s and 1790s were small-scale affairs consisting largely of Xhosa cattle raids and settler retaliation. Both Xhosa and settlers were reliant on farming and the conflicts were limited by the demands of seasonal farming and the need for labour during the harvest. The possession of guns initially gave the settlers a tactical advantage but this was soon cancelled as the Xhosa acquired guns as well. As pressures grew, the settlers organised into local militia but could not leave their homes and families undefended and vulnerable to attack for long and this limited the extent to which they could pursue Xhosa raiding parties. Even so, the settlers could extend the border of their territory: in 1781, it was established between the Great Fish and Sundays Rivers; eight years later, the boundary was moved west to the Sunday's River, something confirmed after the third war in 1803.[29]

Cape Colony was annexed by the British in 1806 and the new rulers introduced a professional army and based it at Cape Town. This altered the balance of power between whites and the Xhosa. British regular soldiers were better trained and armed than the settler militia and their actions were not constrained by families and farms. They could pursue Xhosa raiding parties across the border with single-mindedness the militia lacked. The fourth Cape-Xhosa War (1811-1812), the first involving British troops, pushed the Xhosa back to the east of the Great Fish River. When overcrowding among the Xhosa east of the Fish River led to civil war, the British intervened triggering the fifth war in 1818-1819. The Xhosa prophet-chief Maqana Nxele or Makana saw the world as a battleground between the Gods of the blacks and of the whites and promised 'to

---

[26] Mason, John E., *Social Death and Transformation: Slavery and Emancipation in South Africa*, (University of Virginia Press), 2003, pp. 139-140.

[27] Peires, Jeffrey B., *The House of Phalo: A History of the Xhosa People in the Days of their Independence*, (University of California Press), 1981, is the best study of the Xhosa to 1850. See also, Anderson, Elisabeth, *A History of the Xhosa of the Northern Cape, 1795-1879*, (University of Cape Town Press), 1987, and Price, Richard, *Making Empire: Colonial Encounters and the Creation of Imperial Rule in Nineteenth-Century South Africa*, (Cambridge University Press), 2008.

[28] Smithers, A. J., *The Kaffir Wars, 1779-1877*, (Leo Cooper), 1973, Mostert, Noel, *Frontiers: The Epic of South Africa's Creation and the Tragedy of the Xhosa People*, (Alfred A. Knopf), 1992, and Stapleton, Timothy J., *Maqoma: Xhosa Resistance to Colonial Advance, 1798-1873*, (Jonathan Bell), 1994, provides detailed analysis of the Cape-Xhosa wars.

[29] Alberti, Ludwig, *Account of the Tribal Life and Customs of the Xhosa in 1807*, translated by William Fehr, (Balkema), 1968, provides a contemporary account. The account was first published in Dutch in 1810. See also, Stocker, I., 'Report on Kaffraria, March 1820', in ibid, *Records of Cape Colony*, Vol. 13, pp. 32-81.

turn bullets into water' but his troops were repulsed.[30] The British forced the Xhosa even further east, beyond the Keiskama River and tried to settle the buffer zone with loyal Africans.[31]

Until the early 1820s, the Xhosa had lived according to their age-old customs and beliefs and saw no reason to change their ways because of the arrival of white settlers.[32] Consequently, hostile chiefs forced the earliest missionaries to abandon their attempts to evangelise them.[33] But, the situation changed after 1820, when John Brownlee founded a mission on the Tyhume River and William Shaw established a chain of Methodist stations throughout the Transkei. Other denominations followed suit. Education and medical work were to become major contributions of the missions, but the Xhosa people largely proved intellectually and culturally impermeable to missionary attempts of conversion. Furthermore, by 1828, continued pressure from expanding colonial society, population increase and limited availability of land threatened the Xhosa way of life. As white rule encroached on the resilient Xhosa communities, the culture of imperial rule evolved. From the beginning, missionary efforts floundered: many recruits were poorly educated and poorly training. The religious mission imploded and this resulted in increasing intervention by the state. Cultural interaction by missionaries gave ways to a settler culture and to the state's indirect rule. Missionaries adopted a new discourse in which the Xhosa were now perceived as a degenerate race unable to survive and destined for extinction. By the mid-1830s, a new knowledge system about the Xhosa was established. It perceived them as cunning, deceitful, and inveterate thieves and irredeemably savage; their chiefs, who were the major link with the imperial administration, as conspiring manipulators and agents of tyranny. Great Xhosa chiefs, such as Maqoma, Ngqika, Mhala, and Xhoxho, for long reputed for their wisdom, intellect and political vocation, were seen as obstacles to the spread of British civilization and progress. The Xhosa peoples, who refused to cease to be Xhosa, became the enemies of the empire and characters in the imperial literature of stereotypes. No

---

[30] Mabona, Mongameili, *Diviners and Prophets among the Xhosa (1853-1856): A study in Xhosa cultural History*, (Lit Verlag Munster), 2004, pp. 300-303.

[31] Duly, L. C., *British Land Policy at the Cape, 1795-1844: A Study of Administrative Procedures in the Empire*, (Duke University Press), 1968, remains a valuable study of the issue of land alienation.

[32] Peires, J. B., 'Nxele, Ntsikana and the Origins of the Xhosa Religious Reaction', *Journal of African Studies*, Vol. 20, (1979), pp. 51-61, shows how Nxele and Ntsikana responded to the crisis caused by the expulsion of the Xhosa across the Fish River in 1811-1812. By incorporating selected Christian concepts with the Xhosa world-view, Nxele and Ntsikana could provide the Xhosa with acceptable explanations of past events and prescriptions for future action. Nxele urged resistance and Ntsikana preached submission. See also, Hodgson, Janet, *Ntsinka, History and Symbol: Studies in the Process of Religious Change among Xhosa-speaking People*, Ph.D. Thesis, (University of Cape Town), 1986, and ibid, Mabona, Mongameli, *Diviners and Prophets among the Xhosa (1593-1856)*, pp. 303-305.

[33] Ibid, Peires, Jeffrey B., *The House of Phalo*, pp. 64-78, examines AmaXhosa religion and the impact of missionaries.

options were left but coercion, humiliation and violence against the Xhosa. The frontier wars continued.[34]

Sir Benjamin D'Urban was appointed Governor of the Cape Colony in January 1834 and he introduced a more peace-making policy on the frontier.[35] It was based on treaties with Xhosa chiefs and the appointment of white resident magistrates. But Xhosa grievances were still great and in late 1834, the Xhosa, under the paramount chief Hintsa chief of the Gcaleka, invaded the Cape Colony. The main reasons for the outbreak of the sixth Cape-Xhosa war was the confiscation of some of their lands and the killing of a high-ranking chief by a government commando party on 11 December 1834.[36] Later in the month, 12,000 Xhosa raiders destroyed the homes of many white settlers in the Eastern Cape districts, killing the men, but sparing the women and children and driving off their cattle. Colonel Harry Smith led the counter attack against the Xhosa. Hintsa, trusting in British assurances of his safety entered their camp, was kept a prisoner and later was shot trying to escape.[37]

Smith successfully repelled the Xhosa and in 1835, D'Urban annexed the area between the Keiskamma and the Kei Rivers. He ordered the defeated chiefs and their followers to move across the Kei River and planned to establish military posts with white resident magistrates so that all the Xhosa would lose their independence. In 1836, the task of putting these plans into practice was given to Harry Smith. While the Xhosa chiefs were laying plans to attack King William's Town, missionaries were protesting about the attacks by whites on Xhosa homesteads.[38] This led to the appointment of the Aboriginals Committee to investigate matters on the Eastern Cape frontier.[39] D'Urban's and Smith's aggressive policies did not find favour in London and the Colonial Secretary, Lord Glenelg informed D'Urban that the Xhosa 'had ample justification' for invading the colony.[40] Glenelg reversed D'Urban's frontier policy and this prevented a further Xhosa uprising. Andries Stockenström was appointed Lieutenant-Governor of the Eastern Districts and he concluded new treaties with the Xhosa chiefs. The chiefs regarded him as their protector, but Stockenström was unpopular among the colonists, who wanted Xhosa lands. Sir Peregrine Maitland was appointed Governor in 1844 and thought the Xhosa could be

---

[34] Ross, Robert, 'The Possession and Dispossession of the Kat River Settlement', in Laidlaw, Zoe., and Lester, Alan, (eds.), *Indigenous Communities and Settler Colonialism*, (Palgrave Macmillan), 2015, pp. 86-101.

[35] Lancaster, J. C. S., *The Governorship of Sir Benjamin D'Urban at the Cape of Good Hope, 1834-1838*, (Government Printer), 1991, provides a valuable analysis of his years as governor.

[36] Theal, George McCall, *Documents relating to the Kaffir War of 1835: arranged and seen through the press*, (Government of the Union of South Africa), 1912, contains the major official sources.

[37] *Report of the Parliamentary Committee on Aboriginal Tribes, (British Settlement)*, (William Ball), 1837, pp. 114-115, provides an account of his death.

[38] 'Justus', *The Wrongs of the Caffre Nation: A Narrative*, (James Duncan), 1837. See also, Boyce, William Binnington, *Notes on South-African Affairs*, (J. Mason), 1839.

[39] Ibid, *Report of the Parliamentary Committee on Aboriginal Tribes, (British Settlement)*, pp. 29-59, 83-102, 107-116.

[40] Glenelg to D'Urban, 17 February 1836, printed in ibid, *The Wrongs of the Caffre Nation: A Narrative*, pp. 328-331.

harassed into obedience. To their dismay, he substituted new treaties for those negotiated by Stockenström. Forts were built, missions and Christians were placed above Xhosa law and white farmers were again allowed to follow up stolen cattle or claim compensation.

Sarhili became paramount chief of all the Xhosa and chief of the Gcaleka after the death of his father Hintsa in 1835. His reign lasted until the ninth Cape-Xhosa War when he was finally defeated in 1878. Settler demand for Xhosa land and African labour continued to grow, a situation exacerbated by a series of droughts in the 1840s. The seventh Cape-Xhosa War or the War of the Axe broke out in 1846 with both the British government and humanitarians in South Africa convinced that it was caused by Xhosa actions although on no better grounds than a decade earlier. The Xhosa gathered in the Amathole Mountains, captured British supply wagons and after forcing the British to retreat, invaded the colony. By January 1847, Colonel Henry Somerset's troops were engaged in a disastrous campaign against Phato, Chief of the Gqunukwebe, a people who were largely Khoikhoi by descent. Rain, dysentery and cumbersome equipment impeded Somerset's progress and his men never engaged the enemy. Sir Harry Smith returned to the Cape in December 1847 as Governor and High Commissioner and defeated a large force of Xhosa warriors on the banks of the Gwangqa River. They sued for peace because they needed to sow their lands, but Smith tightened his grip on the exhausted territory. Chiefly rule was based on the ownership and distribution of cattle and 40,000 had been seized as reparations. The disaster of the war and the droughts, which returned in the 1850s, convinced the Xhosa that evil was abroad in their lands but chiefs were now forbidden by the colonial authorities from rooting out the witches who they believed caused their misfortunes.

Convinced that he would resolve the frontier problems, Smith ordered a return to the D'Urban system that he had administered during the brief existence of the province of Queen Adelaide. He concluded a treaty with the Gcaleka, the Ciskei Xhosa, acknowledging Paramount Chief Hintsa's son, Sarhili, whose authority was not yet well established, as an independent chief. He also annexed the land between the Fish and the Keiskamma Rivers as the district of Victoria. In 1847, about half of the Xhosa territory was annexed to the British Empire under the name of British Kaffraria and it was surveyed and lands were allotted to whites who had lost their possessions during Xhosa attacks. Smith, as High Commissioner, directly administered British Kaffraria on behalf of Britain. The creation of British Kaffraria effectively divided the Xhosa kingdom between Sarhili's Gcaleka and the Rharhabe led by Sandile.[41]

Deprived of their lands and bitter at their recent defeat in the War of the Axe, the Xhosa found hope in a new prophet Mlangeni, who, like Makana, promised supernatural aid to assist in the overthrow of the white oppressors.[42] Mlanjeni's promises did not materialise but resulted in the longest and most costly

---

[41] See, *Report from the Select Committee on the Kafir Tribes: Together with the Proceedings of the Committee, Minutes of Evidence, Appendix, and Index*, (Ordered by the House of Commons, to be Printed), 1851.

[42] Ibid, Mabona, Mongameli, *Diviners and Prophets among the Xhosa (1593-1856)*, pp. 205-307.

war of Xhosa resistance. Believing that the chiefs were responsible for the unrest caused by Mlanjeni's preaching, Smith travelled to British Kaffraria to meet with the prominent chiefs. When Sandile refused to attend a meeting outside Fort Cox, Governor Smith deposed him, declared him a fugitive and appointed Charles Brownlee, a white commissioner, in his place. An expedition sent to arrest Sandile was attacked and British Kaffraria erupted in a massive uprising in December 1850. The eighth Cape-Xhosa War lasted for three years, was brutally put down and 16,000 Xhosa were killed or died of starvation.[43] Governor Sir George Cathcart and the Xhosa chiefs agreed that the chiefs would be allowed to govern their own people according to their own laws. The Xhosa surrendered territory in the Amathole Mountains and along the Kei and Tyhume Rivers that were then resettled by the military, by white settlers and by Mfengu groups who had been loyal to the British during the war. However, when Sir George Grey came to the Cape from the governorship of New Zealand in 1854, he rescinded the agreement with Cathcart and installed magistrates to 'assist' the chiefs and their councillors in deciding legal cases and introduced further white settlement interspersed with the Xhosa population in British Kaffraria.[44] He hoped that, with considerably increased opportunities for education, the Xhosa would learn the values of Western civilisation, develop improved agricultural methods or be drawn into the labour market as wage earners. His schemes were in their infancy when the cattle-killing erupted but they thoroughly alarmed the Xhosa who saw their ancestral values and cultural beliefs threatened. This gave Nongqawuse's prophecy considerable popular appeal.

Vision of Doom or Deliverance?

The Xhosa cattle-killing movement of 1856-1857 was a millenarian reflection of the collapse of Xhosa society following the Cape-Xhosa wars.[45] Further disaster

---

[43] Stapleton, Tim, 'Valuable, Gallant and Faithful Assistants': The Fingo (or Mfengu) as Colonial Allies during the Cape-Xhosa Wars 1835-1881', in Miller, Stephen M., (ed.) *Soldiers and Settlers in Africa, 1850-1918*, (Brill), 2000, pp. 15-49, at pp. 16-36, and Galbraith, John S., *Reluctant Empire: British Policy on the South African Frontier, 1834-54*, (University of California Press), 1963, are valuable on the sixth, seventh and eighth Cape-Xhosa wars. For comparative analysis see, Gump, James, 'A Spirit of Resistance: Sioux, Xhosa, and Māori Responses to Western Dominance, 1840-1920', *Pacific Historical Review*, Vol. 66, (1997), pp. 21-52.

[44] For Sir George Grey in South Africa see, Rees, William Lee, and Rees, L., *The Life and Times of Sir George Grey, K.C.B.*, 2 Vols. (Hutchinson & Co.), 1892, Vol. 1, pp. 203-289, and Rutherford, J., *Sir George Grey, K.C.B., 1812-1898: A Study in Colonial Government*, (Cassell), 1961, pp. 291-442, Gump, James, 'The Imperialism of Cultural Assimilation: Sir George Grey's Encounter with the Māori and the Xhosa, 1845-1868', *Journal of World History*, Vol. 9, (1998), pp. 89-106. Ibid, Price, Richard, *Making Empire: Colonial Encounters and the Creation of Imperial Rule in Nineteenth-Century South Africa*, pp. 266-295, examines the development of the Grey system of imperial rule.

[45] Peires, J. B., *The Dead Will Arise: Nongqawuse and the Great Xhosa Cattle-Killing Movement of 1856-7*, (James Currey), 1989, is a contested deconstruction of the event. See also, Wenzel, Jennifer, *Bulletproof: Afterlives of Anticolonial Prophecy in South Africa and Beyond*, (University of Chicago Press), 2009, pp. 32-68, 195-234, and ibid, Landes, Richard, *Heaven on Earth: The Varieties of Millennial Experience*, pp. 91-122. In addition of the articles written by Peires see, Steyn, Christine, 'Millenarian Tragedies in

struck the Xhosa in 1855 with an epidemic of bovine pleuro-pneumonia or lung-sickness that arrived at the Cape in 1853. Lung-sickness is highly infectious and spreads rapidly and could only be halted by culling all infected animals. The policies the Xhosa applied for the containment of lung-sickness were far more stringent and successful than those of the colonial government and they managed to keep their herds free from the disease for almost a whole year after it had broken out on the colonial side of the frontier.[46] In the Xhosa worldview, good health was the normal state and disease must be caused either by failure of their duty towards the ancestors or malevolent forces. As many as 150,000 cattle died or were culled and the herds of the cattle-rich chiefs were decimated lending credence to Nongqawuse's contention that Xhosa land was polluted and drastic measures were necessary to restore it to health.[47]

In April or May 1856, Nongqawuse, an orphaned fifteen year old, and her friend Nombanda went to fetch water from a pool near the mouth of the Gxarha River.[48] When she returned, Nongqawuse told her uncle (though in some versions of the story her father) and guardian Mhlakaza, a Xhosa diviner, a chief's councillor and owner of large herds and, according to Grey, 'partially deranged' that she had met the spirits of her ancestors coming from the sea.[49] Her

---

Southern Africa: The Xhosa Cattle-Killing Movement and the Bulhock Massacre', in Wessinger, Catherine, (ed.), *Millennialism, Persecution and Violence: Historical Cases*, (Syracuse University Press), 2000, pp. 205-219, ibid, Mabona, Mongameli, *Diviners and Prophets among the Xhosa (1593-1856)*, pp. 307-313, Stapleton, Timothy J., 'Reluctant Slaughter: Rethinking Maqoma's Role in the Xhosa Cattle-Killing (1853-1857)', *International Journal of African Historical Studies*, Vol. 26, (1993), pp. 345-369, Stapleton, Timothy J., ''They No Longer Care for Their Chiefs': Another Look at the Xhosa Cattle-Killing of 1856-1857', *The International Journal of African Historical Studies*, Vol. 24, (1991), pp. 383-392, and Zarwan, John, 'The Xhosa Cattle Killings, 1856-57, *Cahiers d'Études Africaines*, Vol. 16, (1976), pp. 519-539. For a feminist perspective see, Bradford, Helen, 'Not a Nongqawuse story: An anti-heroine in historical perspective', in Gasa, Nomboniso, (ed.), *Women in South African History*, (HSRC Press), 2007, pp. 43-90, and more generally in 'Women, Gender and Colonialism: Rethinking the History of the British Cape Colony and its Frontier Zones c. 1806-70', *Journal of African History*, Vol. 37, (1996), pp. 351-370.

[46] See, Andries, Chris, 'The Spread and Impact of the Lungsickness Epizootic of 1853-57 in the Cape Colony and the Xhosa Chiefdoms', *South African Historical Journal*, Vol. 53, (2005), pp. 50-72.

[47] Wenzel, Jennifer, 'Literacy and Futurity: Millennial Dreaming on the Nineteenth-Century South African Frontier', in Gordin, Michael D., Tilley, Helen, and Prakash, Gyan, (eds.), *Utopia/Dystopia: Conditions of Historical Possibility*, (Princeton University Press), 2010, pp. 45-72, especially, pp. 45-51.

[48] Jordan, A. C., *Towards an African Literature: The emergence of literary form in Xhosa*, (University of California Press), 1973, pp. 69-76, offers a dialectical approach while, Bailey, Brett, *The Plays of Miracle & Wonder: Bewitching Visions and Primal High-Jinx from the South African stage*, (Jut and Company Ltd.), 2003, pp. 149-197, provides a dramatic depiction of the Nongqawuse story. Ibid, Wessinger, Catherine, *The Oxford Handbook of Millennialism*, pp. 387-389, gives a succinct account.

[49] Ibid, Peires, J. B., *The Dead Will Arise*, p. 35, maintains that in April 1850, Mhlakaza had become the first Xhosa to be confirmed as an Anglican and hoped to return to his people to evangelise but this had been prevented by the archdeacon of Grahamstown and

millenarian prophecy had three parts: the spirits had told her that the Xhosa people should destroy their crops and stored food and kill their cattle, the source of their wealth as well as food; in return the spirits would sweep the British settlers into the sea; and finally, the Xhosa were to prepared new corn pits, strengthen their houses, refrain from witchcraft and sexual impropriety and await the return of the ancestors who would bring new herds of cattle and large amounts of grain. The idea of the resurrection of the dead was first introduced by Christian missionaries but fitted well with Xhosa beliefs regarding the life in death of ancestors, the creation of the world and the cyclical regeneration of the seasons. These corresponded to sacrifice, deliverance from colonial rule and resurrection, each of which appealed to a society under pressure. During 1855, well before Nongqawuse's vision, news of the outbreak of the Crimean War had reached South Africa. The Xhosa hoped that the British would be beaten and that the Russians would come and force the whites to leave Africa as well. The idea soon took root that Nongqawuse's strangers had been Russians, black men in military coats. To the Xhosa, the Russians were the ghosts of past Xhosa warriors and therefore must be black.[50] To a people desperate for deliverance, this made perfect sense. Everything they owned was bewitched and unclean and had to be destroyed.

The slaughter of their cattle by the Xhosa was an enormous act of faith, a ritual suicide though no one suggests that the Xhosa nation intended to destroy itself. [51] By the summer of 1856, Mhlakaza's message had spread across the independent Xhosa lands but soon spread to the Xhosa in British Kaffraria and some cattle were dying at the hands of their owners although until July 1856 the fate of the cattle-killing movement was uncertain. Historians estimate that the Gcaleka eventually killed between 300,000 and 400,000 head of cattle. British officials were horrified at the developments, but were helpless to stop them. Charles Brownlee, brought up among the Xhosa and fluent in their language, was prominent in visiting kraals to try to offset Mhlakaza's influence, but most would not listen to his warnings. The Xhosa were profoundly divided over the prophecy between 'believers' and 'unbelievers'. This was not a unified millenarian vision: some Xhosa hoped for the restoration of the old world, while others eagerly grasped at the new. The choice involved more than whether to kill cattle or not. The unbelievers' embrace of innovation as opposed to the believers' hopes for renovation was informed by, though not identical with the hopes of missionaries and colonial officials to make the Xhosa a new people shaped by European values. But once Sarhili admitted that he believed Mhlakaza's message, most followed their paramount chief. John Maclean, the British representative at Port

---

when he returned to Xhosaland he began preaching a gospel of his own. However, there seems little evidence for this.

[50] Grey to Henry Labouchere, 16 August 1856, Parliamentary Papers, *Accounts and Papers,* Vol. 40, Colonies, 1857-58, (Eyre and Spottiswoode), 1858, pp. 4-6, outlines the beginnings of the cattle-killing movement. He makes it clear throughout that he regarded it as a 'delusion'.

[51] On this issue see, Peires, J. 'Suicide or genocide?: Xhosa perceptions of the Nongqawuse catastrophe', *Radical History Review*, Vol. 46-47, (1990), pp. 48-57, reprinted in Brown, Joshua, (ed.), *History from South Africa: Alternative Visions and Practices,* (Temple University Press), 1991, pp. 29-38.

Elizabeth reported on events though he probably failed to grasp the enormity of the situation sensing a plot against British authority in Cape Colony and Natal.[52] Sir George Grey was also alerted about the supposed plot and he and Maclean prepared to intervene militarily. Nongqawuse's prophecy promised a radical renewal in which the ancestors would return as 'new people' while the colonial vision imagined a world in which people would be radically transformed.

The part played by Sarhili in the cattle-killing movement proved crucial though initially he threatened to fine anyone who killed their cattle.[53] He held tenaciously to the old Xhosa traditions and this was a sign of his strength but also the source of his greatest weakness. He had recently lost his sons, was helpless in the face of lung-sickness and easily convinced by the stories he had heard of the miracles at the Gxarha. On 10 July 1856, Sarhili went with the prophet to the Gxarha riverbank where the strangers had first appeared to Nongqawuse. Sarhili was impressed and when Mhlakaza told him that all his cattle and goats must immediately die, he readily agreed and issued formal commands to the Xhosa nation ordering them to obey Mhlakaza's instructions. Mhlakaza warned everyone present that the Russians would not come nor would any of the other predictions take place until all the cattle had been killed and all the grain destroyed. He then named the places within the Xhosa lands where the Russians would appear and where the dead would return to life. Sarhili at once returned to his kraal and began to kill his cattle, as did all the other 'believers'. Sarhili had wanted the story of his meeting with the strangers to be kept secret, but soon pilgrims from throughout his lands were hurrying towards the River Gxarha in the hope of witnessing a miracle. Visitors to the riverbank were not allowed to get close enough to speak to the distant shapes or hear what they said. They seemed to speak only to Nongqawuse or through her to Mhlakaza.

Although Nongqawuse's demonstrations may have convinced those who had already been converted, they failed to convince sceptics but few Xhosa had the courage or authority to confront Nongqawuse openly. Many of the leading believers including Sarhili and Sandile had played a leading role in the previous Xhosa-Cape war while the Mfengu and most Xhosa chiefs who were unbelievers were allies or clients of the colonial government. There were exceptions to this: for instance, Chief Anta had been deprived of his ancestral lands because of the war but was strong unbeliever while Phatho had supported the government was an important believer in Nongqawuse.[54] Nongqawuse and Mhlakaza were circumspect about when the great day of resurrection would occur but many Xhosa expected it to occur as early as the full moon in June 1856 and for the following year, the full moon was awaited with anticipation. When this day passed, many believers were seriously disturbed and Sarhili called a meeting at his Great Place. The prophets were severely criticised but Mhlakaza attempted to evade calls to produce the new people and new cattle by saying that the new people, unimpressed with the numbers of cattle that had been killed, had moved to 'a

---

[52] John Maclean to Grey, 7 August 1856, Parliamentary Papers, *Accounts and Papers,* Vol. 40, Colonies, 1857-58, pp. 10-11.

[53] Charles Brownlee to John Maclean, 30 July 1856, ibid, p. 7.

[54] Peires, J. B., ''Soft' Believers and 'Hard' Unbelievers in the Xhosa Cattle-Killing', *Journal of African History*, Vol. 27, (1986), pp. 445-451.

stronghold' to wait the day but was finally forced to name the next full moon on 16 August as the 'moon of wonder and danger'. On the great day, Mhlakaza said that two suns would rise in the heavens and collide and all the whites would march into the sea, which would divide revealing a road down which they would march to Uhlanga, the place of creation. There Satan would take his revenge on both the whites and on those Xhosa who had disobeyed the call to kill their cattle. Then the world would be plunged into darkness until a new sun would rise and herald the new world.

In the aftermath of 16 August, there was bitter disappointment and disillusion among many believers. Sarhili sent orders to all Xhosa chiefs to stop the cattle-killing laying the blame not on Mhlakaza, who had denied ever uttering prophecies but entirely on Nongqawuse. Chief Namba commented:

> We did hear all about the Prophets but did not believe. "How could we?" We who had been so lately deceived by a Prophet. We attached so little weight to the words we heard. We thought them only the words of a little child...We did not wish our people to be tainted with things of this nature. We wished to prove our loyalty by deeds not by words... My people did not follow the advice of the Prophets, they had my orders not to do so. We all will sow our land, we are only waiting the rain.[55]

Had the movement collapsed in August 1856, relatively little damage would have been done since most Xhosa had slaughtered only a small number of cattle. In fact, it was the survival of so many cattle that made the continuation of the movement possible especially after Mhlakaza said that the new people would not appear unless the Xhosa obeyed Nongqawuse's words to the letter. In early September 1856, Sarhili again visited Mhlakaza at the riverbank to speak to the strangers. He was told by Mhlakaza to look at the ground and, under no circumstances, to look up. He would then see the shadows of the New People passing across the ground in front of him. Sarhili was taken in by this deception and was convinced when the shadows had passed by him. But reports of this meeting were so embroidered that eventually it was claimed Sarhili had seen boatloads of new people arrive at the mouth of the river, informing him they had come to establish the freedom of the black people. Just when cattle-killing had lost its momentum, Sarhili drove it forward. Further disappointments followed in November 1856, and January, February and finally May 1857.

The complex political geography of the Xhosa lands constrained the colonial response. Sir George Grey threatened Sarhili and other chiefs with dire consequences if he encouraged his people to kill any more cattle.[56] Although the Ngqika and Ndlambe Xhosa clans lived in British Kaffraria and could be influenced by colonial orders, they all recognised the authority of Sarhili, chief of the Gcaleka Xhosa who lived beyond British rule north of the Kei River. Grey saw that famine in the land of the Xhosa was now unavoidable, but he could do nothing to prevent it and did not understand why they were blind to their own danger. 40,000 cattle had already been slaughtered and at least 10,000 Xhosa had

---

[55] 'Statement of Namba', H. Lucas to John Mclean, 27 August 1856, Cape Archives: BK140.

[56] This occurred in letters dated 27 September 1856, *Accounts and Papers,* Vol. 40, Colonies, 1857-58, pp. 29-30.

already died of starvation between the Fish and Kei Rivers. Sarhili, meanwhile, retained his blind faith in the word of Mhlakaza who had a new explanation for why nothing had happened at successive new moons. With the situation deteriorating rapidly, on or about 3 January 1857, Sarhili held a great assembly of more than 6,000 Xhosa met near the town of Butterworth. Nongqawuse and Mhlakaza had vanished but left a message saying that, disgusted by the attitude of unbelieving chiefs, the new people had left. Sarhili was so upset that he had tried to kill himself and his servants were forced to remove all knives and sharp objects from near him. With hysteria mounting and cattle-killing increasing, Nongqawuse predicted that the ancestors' promise would be fulfilled on 18 February 1857, when the sun would turn red but the prophecy was not realised.[57] An English settler, Robert Mullins, was with a group of Xhosa when the great moment came. 'The sun rose...the sun set, as usual', Mullins recorded in his diary with clinical accuracy. 'In between, nothing much happened, except a lot of waiting and hoping on the part of the Xhosa.' Frances Brownlee, wife of Charles Brownlee Ngqika Commissioner to Sandile, a more sensitive witness, noted:

> One of the saddest sights was that of an old woman wizened with age, and doubly wrinkled by starvation, decked out with brass rings jingling on her withered arms and legs. They had kept on their ornaments hoping against hope, till too weak to remove them. As the sun set there was a silence across the land as of death. No children laughed and played, no cattle lowed, no sheep bleated, and no happy herdsmen laughed and joked with his friends at the end of a day's work.[58]

The dead ancestors did not appear and yet they did if the aftermath is a reversal of the prophecy. What Mrs Brownlee and others described were 'living skeletons' with the appearance of the 'living dead'. Initially after the Great Disappointment, Nongqawuse's followers blamed those unbelievers who had not obeyed her instructions and who suffered attacks, but they later turned against her. But she was not to blame. Sarhili had succumbed to the fantasies of Mhlakaza but the tragedy was that so too did most of the Xhosa people. This did not prevent cattle-killing continuing into the middle of 1857. In late May, Charles Brownlee informed Maclean that Sandile had destroyed his last remaining cattle and:

> The Kafirs are now everywhere preparing to receive the cattle which are to rise, their corn floors and pits are cleared to receive the grains & in consequence of their expectation, no people can be obtained at present in this neighbourhood willing to take service in the colony, and large group who had come out with the families to take service in the colony after staying here a night, returned to Kafirland to be at their kraals at the accomplishment of the promises.[59]

---

[57] Grey to Labouhere, 6 March 1857, ibid, pp. 67-68.

[58] Brownlee, Frances Thomson, 'The Cattle-Killing Delusion', in Brownlee, Charles, Pacalt, *Reminiscences of Kafir Life and History, and Other Papers*, (Lovedale Mission Press), 1896, pp. 125- 170, at p. 135.

[59] Brownlee to John Maclean, 28 May 1857, Cape Archives: BK71.

The strength of the prophecy retained its hold over the Xhosa and in late 1858, Brownlee reported that a new prophet had emerged and cattle-killing had resumed among the Xhosa though to a considerably lesser extent that the previous year.[60]

The human cost was overwhelming: about 40,000 people (including Mhlakaza) died of starvation and a further 50,000 left to become labourers in the Cape Colony.[61] Those who remained were forced into villages as the British seized more than 600,000 acres of land. In the aftermath of the crisis, the population of British Kaffraria dropped from 105,000 to fewer than 27,000 due to the resulting famine. In some places, people had climbed into their grain pits to see if they had been miraculously filled in their absence. But, too weak to climb out again, they had died there. Emaciated women with children clinging to their flattened breasts raked the hard ground for roots and those who reached the soup kitchens provided by the British were no more than walking skeletons. Nongqawuse was arrested by the British authorities and imprisoned on Robben Island. After her release, she lived on a farm in the Alexandria district of the Eastern Cape and died in 1898.

Both Sarhili and Sir George Grey have been accused of engineering the crisis through Nongqawuse. Those who blame Sarhili claim he intended to manipulate the famine-struck Xhosa into attacking British settlers. Grey's accusers--most Xhosa people today--believe he used Nongqawuse deliberately to weaken the Xhosa people or may even have initiated it.[62] Grey's project for the Xhosa predated the cattle-killing and he aimed to transform the chiefs in British Kaffraria into paid agents of the colonial administration and replace the Xhosa pastoral economy with wage-labour in European farms. For him, the 'new men' were not the prophesised ancestors but British settlers whose influence would transform the Xhosa by capturing their labour.[63] He instigated a massive programme of labour 'recruitment' which led to thousands of Xhosa being transported across the border into Cape Colony. Magistrates were instructed only to give food and relief to those who were willing to be contracted for labour in the colony. Those who agreed were obliged to sign a term of agreement whereby they expressed their willingness to work anywhere in Cape Colony for any wage that was offered Grey certainly exploited the situation to his advantage, dispossessing Sarhili and his people and giving the land to white settlers and the Mfengu people. He brought charges of treason and cattle theft against some of the Xhosa chiefs and imprisoned them on Robben Island.[64] He sent military forces into

---

[60] Brownlee to John Maclean, 12 October 1858, Cape Archives: BK2.

[61] For the state of Kaffraria, see Grey to Labouchere, 18 October 1856, Parliamentary Papers, *Accounts and Papers,* Vol. 40, Colonies, 1857-58, pp. 36-45.

[62] Ibid, Wenzel, Jennifer, *Bulletproof,* pp. 19-20, cites a 1975 narration in which a young girl is paid by white people to tell the Xhosa that she had been sent by the Creator who wanted them to destroy their food and livestock and await the resurrection of the land.

[63] See, Bundy, Colin, *The Rise and Fall of the South African Peasantry*, (University of California Press), 1979, pp. 44-64.

[64] Sophia Fisher to Elizabeth Constable, 14 March 1857, Cape Archives, BK377: 'There is some talk of the Caffir War but Sir George Grey seems very determined & has transported some Caffirs for 14 years in a most summary manner, which it is hoped will check their ravages…'

independent Xhosa land and drove its starving people into exile. Grey's policies tied famine relief to labour contracts that drew the Xhosa away from their lands and introduced 'passes' that allowed some Africans but not others to enter Cape Colony based on ethnicity. As Grey told the Cape parliament:

> If we leave the natives beyond our border ignorant barbarians, they must always remain a race of troublesome marauders.[65]

For Grey and the settlers, the motives behind the movement especially the 'golden era of liberty' and the catastrophic fates awaiting whites foretold in the prophecy threatened Britain's control of southern Africa.[66] Cattle-killing was, at least in part, anti-colonial directed at the destruction of whites and colonial rule. Grey's official correspondence emphasised that cattle-killing was part of a plot by Xhosa chiefs to drive their desperate people into war though he recognised that a starving people was hardly able to mount aggressive war.[67] Charles Brownlee commented in early August 1856:

> ...they [the Xhosa] may have an object in view if in their right mind and the only one which I can arrive at is, that if the Kaffirs will not make war by choice, they must do so of necessity, famine being the cause...[68]

The chiefs' plot dominated colonial historiography until the late-twentieth century and although recent historians have rejected it, they disagree about the extent to which the movement was an anti-colonial movement directed not merely against the effects of colonial presence but against the colonists themselves. Grey remarked in March 1857:

> However much Her Majesty's Government may deplore the sufferings which necessarily attend the crisis through which this country is passing, they may rest assured that ultimately the most beneficial consequences will follow from what is now taking place. All that is necessary is, that every exertion should be made to improve, to the utmost, the present occasion.[69]

Peires said the Nongqawuse saga followed the British army's defeat in one of the wars being fought in the Nkonkobe area and another war that ended in stalemate. He said there were other incidents before Xhosas slaughtered their cattle that included the British bringing in cattle with lung-sickess to infect Xhosa

---

[65] Cit. ibid, Wenzel, Jennifer, 'Literacy and Futurity: Millennial Dreaming on the Nineteenth-Century South African Frontier', p. 48.
[66] These included being metamorphosed into frogs, mice and ants, by the sky falling and crushing them and most spectacularly being driven into the sea (together with Xhosa unbelievers) by a mighty wind or the massed armies of the resurrected Xhosa ancestors.
[67] For discussion of the 'chiefs' plot', see ibid, Peires, J. B., *The Dead Will Arise*, pp. 218-240.
[68] Parliamentary Papers, *Accounts and Papers,* Vol. 40, Colonies, 1857-58, p. 13.
[69] Grey to Henry Labouchere, 27 March 1857, Parliamentary Papers, 'Further Papers relative to the Kaffir Tribes', *Accounts and Papers,* Vol. 40, Colonies, 1857-58, pp. 84-85.

cattle herds. Prophetic delusion and providential suffering were followed by Christian relief; then colonial expansion and the subjugation of the Xhosa.

Retrospectives

The cattle-killing was the climax of nearly a decade of millenarian prophecies among the Xhosa and half a century of concerted colonial pressure on their lands. But this occurred in a global imperial context and should not be seen simply as a localised response to colonial expansion. Cattle-killing took place just after the Crimean War and just before the Sepoy Mutiny in India in 1857-1858. Grey had to send troops to India and worried about leaving the Xhosa frontier exposed. From 1856 to 1860, Britain fought the Arrow War in China to break resistance to the opium trade and its imperialism was challenged during the 1860s by wars in NZ and the Morant Bay rebellion in 1865. There are parallels between the colonial response to famine among the Xhosa and Grey's exploitation of relief in other colonial settings. Mike Davies points out that 'colonial expansion uncannily syncopated the rhythms of natural disasters and epidemic disease'.[70] It is clear that the Xhosa saw themselves, however tentatively, as part of a global anti-colonial movement. The belief that the ancestors were Russian and were battling the British in the Crimea, where Cathcart the former governor had been killed illustrates this. News of rebellion in India renewed hope among Xhosa that another 'black race' would deliver them and some Xhosa recognised the war in China as a war of black peoples against British imperial aggression. This transnationalism would resonate in the liberation movement in South Africa in the second half of the twentieth century.[71]

Seen as responsible for destroying a patriarchal pre-colonial society, Nongqawuse attracted much negative comment among the Xhosa and within the white colonial state. The dominant explanation of how Nongqawuse became one of the most destructive women in history begins with a golden age among the Xhosa when rains fell, crops flourished and everyone ate beef. Then a maiden entered this Eden saying that men who had died and were now resurrected had arrived and had asked her to pass on their message. Kill your cattle, stop growing crops and then an even better world would be born. The resurrected men would become visible, eliminate their white oppressors and a Paradise would emerge in which the Xhosa would be immortal. The Xhosa swallowed her lies and destroyed their Eden but no new Eden was born and whites ruthlessly dispossessed the famine-stricken survivors. Hers was a sophisticated and highly detailed vision. There is a strong place in traditional African religion of vision and prophecy, especially by girls and women. It was therefore not difficult for the Xhosa to believe in Nongqawuse and her prophecies.

Nongqawuse was one of perhaps twenty visionaries operating in southern Africa between 1850 and 1857. She appears to have worked alongside a dozen other people near her kraal. She was a visionary but other seers had different functions. Her uncle, Mhlakaza, was skilled in oratory and it was he who would

[70] Davies, Mike, *Late Victorian Holocausts: El Niño Famines and the Making of the Third World*, (Verso), 2001, p. 12.
[71] See, Ashforth, Adam, 'The Xhosa Cattle Killing and the Politics of Memory', *Sociological Forum*, Vol. 6, (1991), pp. 581-592.

carry to message to Sarhili, the paramount chief. Yet it is Nongqawuse who was remembered as other influential participants faded from memory and is remembered for having given birth in monstrous ways, indicative of the importance of female fertility in the patriarchal society of the Xhosa and for the strength of her challenge to patriarchal power. Chief Anta commented in early 1857 that 'I thought it was very childish destroying so much valuable property at the orders of a girl'.[72] The view that Nongqawuse was a foolish young girl who was incited into suicidal action remains a congenial explanation for many in modern South Africa. Women's marriages were accompanied by cattle, the main masculine resource that could be reclaimed if they produced no offspring. Nongqawuse was well aware of the turmoil within Xhosa families because of colonial wars and predation. In particular, the carrying off the herds from the defeated Xhosa prevented the completion of marriage through bride-wealth payments. Men who killed their cattle, without gaining the world reborn, had good reason to attach a insult to Nongqawuse's monstrous birth.[73] The problem with Nongqawuse is that she has been invented and reinvented by successive generations.

In the 1970s, for instance, it was widely accepted amongst the Xhosa that she had been manipulated by Sir George Grey the British Governor to such an extent that some commentators maintained that he was in the reeds whispering the words of the prophecy.[74] This raised important questions about the culpability of the British authorities for the cattle-killing. By the millennium, Nongqawuse had lost her sexuality becoming younger and slipped into the ranks of pre-pubertal girls. The shift over time has been from fertility to sexuality to childishness based not on new sources being found but on broader social transformations in South Africa.[75] How could an adolescent girl with little social power as female galvanise popular belief in divine deliverance?

There are severe limitations to the conventional story of Nongqawuse.[76] Her active participation in events lasted nine months and the deep-rooted crises in Xhosa society and preceding visionaries were of little interest or relevance. Yet it is only by placing her in a long line of Xhosa seers that she makes any real

---

[72] Minutes of a conversation between Captain R. E. Robertson and Chief Anta, 8 January 1857, Parliamentary Papers, *Accounts and Papers,* Vol. 40, Colonies, 1857-58, p. 65.

[73] Ibid, Bradford, Helen, 'Not a Nongqawuse story: An anti-heroine in historical perspective', pp. 45-47.

[74] Ibid, Peires, J. B., *The Dead Will Arise*, pp. 316-317, states that 'I have looked very closely into all the surviving documents, including the private correspondence between Grey and his chief subordinate Maclean, and must state unequivocally that there is no documentary evidence whatsoever to support this view.' The critical words here are 'documentary evidence' but even Peires admits that Grey's secretive and deceptive character means that 'we shall never know exactly what happened down there at the Gxarha'. Xhosa oral evidence provides a different perspective.

[75] Oddenburger, Andrew, 'The Xhosa Cattle-Killing Movement in History and Literature'. *History Compass*, Vol. 7, (2009), pp. 1428-1443, examines the historiography. See also, Davies, Sheila, *History in the Literary Imagination: The Telling of Nongqawuse and the Xhosa Cattle-Kinning in South African Literature and Culture (1891-1937)*, Pd. D., Thesis, University of Cambridge, 2010.

[76] Ibid, Bradford, Helen, 'Not a Nongqawuse story: An anti-heroine in historical perspective', pp. 49-51.

sense.[77] Nongqawuse was regarded as a prophet because of her message of national salvation. Her prophecies drew on the traditions established by Nxele in the 1810s who claimed he was a messianic son of the creator god Uhlanga as well as the brother of Christ, for whose murder Europeans were to be punished. His insistence that his followers kill some of their cattle and give up witchcraft, in anticipation of the emergence of ancestors and new cattle was a precursor of the events in the mid-1850s. There is no evidence that Nongqawuse herself had direct contact with missionaries but this was possibly not the case for Mhlakaza.[78]

A second limitation is the focus on the at best fanciful, at worst delusional female visions and the consequent cattle-killing while excluding the role played by the masculine colonial state that was actively involved in war against the Xhosa. Warning against planting crops, which soldiers would then destroy and urging self-consumption of resources that they could steal, gave Nongqawuse's visions a contemporary resonance. By proclaiming the arrival of an invisible male black army, far from luring a nation to its death, Nongqawuse provided an antidote to the policies being prepared by male colonial forces. The third problem is that historians have paid less attention to vernacular sources than they deserve. Various interpretations provide what one would call hysteria or the Nongqawuse syndrome that legitimise a theory of national suicide. The sources of this these interpretations generally fail to acknowledge the authority of 'traditional' or 'cultural', oral texts. Contemporary Xhosa orality, especially praise poems rather than literacy was both more substantial and significant as a means of telling the story and explaining Nongqawuse. The Xhosa Cattle-Killing has been imagined and re-imagined many times over the years. Its manifestations chart not only the shifting 'truth' of the event but also the ways in which it has been made relevant and useable for different communities at various points in South Africa's history.

The Xhosa Cattle-Killing was a very early example of a mass movement. The self-sacrifice involved in destroying the resources controlled by the ruling classes, but needed by the nation can perhaps be connected to elements in twentieth century nationalist activity, such as bus or shop boycotts, civil disobedience or mass arrests. Although not an anti-European movement, the Xhosa Cattle-Killing can be seen as an assertion of black identity and whites were simply ignored in the prophecies of Mhalakaza and Nongqawuse and had no part to play in the New World of the Xhosa. This suggest that the Cattle-Killing could be viewed as a prelude to later resistance ideologies of Africanism and Black Consciousness and as an early form of black consciousness and resistance.

Pai Marire, New Zealand, 1864-1866

The propensity of charismatic individuals to lead social as well as ethnic resistance is well known and Māori prophets, as historic guardians of the land, were no exception. Between 1840 and 1900, when the Māori were dispossessed of their lands, prophets flourished on the North Island. Inspired by the search for freedom from bondage by the Israélites in the Old Testament, Māori religious

[77] Ibid, Mabona, Mongameli, *Diviners and Prophets among the Xhosa (1593-1856)*, pp. 291-314.

[78] For discussion of Xhosa prophecy and Christian theology see, ibid, Peires, J. B., *The Dead Will Arise*, pp. 134-138.

leaders concluded that they too were a chosen people and had a covenant with God.[79] During his first tenure as Governor of NZ, Sir George Grey adopted an ambiguous policy towards the Māori and their lands using the Treaty of Waitangi to protect Māori land rights but he also launched major purchases of Māori land.[80] Sorrenson argued that the Māori did not present a long-term threat to colonisation largely because tribal fighting and geographical dispersal precluded a united approach to countering the rapid growth of settlement.[81] Amalgamation rather than pacification or extermination may have been a plausible goal but both Pākehā settlers and the Māori adopted a robust attitude to land and this led to the Land Wars of the 1840s, 1860s and 1870s.

Land Wars

There is some debate over what the Māori-settler conflicts that occurred between 1843 and 1872 should be called.[82] Initially, they were called the Māori Wars after the nineteenth century British practice of naming wars after their enemies but by the 1970s this lost favour. Historians argued that the term was divisive and suggested Māori responsibility for the conflicts while neglecting the inter-tribal dimensions of the conflict. The New Zealand Wars, the Colonial New Zealand Wars, the Anglo-Māori Wars and the New Zealand Civil War have also been suggested as possible titles with varying degrees of success. For instance, the idea of the conflict as a civil war lacked credibility since historians argued, Māori society was too fragmented, did not represent a single polity and that small autonomous and divided tribes waged war against the singular Crown. However, although the Māori may not have been united, they did see themselves as having a common interest in defending the land and *rangatiratanga* against the Crown. Despite today's overwhelming popularity for New Zealand Wars, it is Land Wars that has the greatest resonance especially as colonial conflict over land was a major cause of war. Just what the Land Wars were is also a matter of disagreement. Conflicts between 1843 and 1872 have sufficient in common to be

---

[79] Ibid, Boast, Richard, 'Vanished theocracies: Christianity, war and politics in colonial New Zealand 1830-80', in Ford, Lisa, and Rowse, Tim, (eds.), *Between Indigenous and Settler Governance*, pp. 70-82.

[80] For Grey's religious attitudes see, Grant, Susannah, 'God and the Governor: George Grey in New Zealand', in Stenhouse John, (ed.), *Christianity, Modernity and Culture: New Perspectives on New Zealand History*, (Australian Theological Forum Press), 2005, pp. 240-268.

[81] Sorrenson, M. P. K., 'How to Civilize Savages: Some 'Answers' from Nineteenth-Century New Zealand', *New Zealand Journal of History*, Vol. 9, (1975), p. 103, and 'Land Purchase Methods and Their Effect on Maori Population, 1865-1901', *Journal of the Polynesian Society*, Vol. 65, (1956), pp. 183-199.

[82] See, for instance, Cowan, James, *The New Zealand Wars and the Pioneering Period*, 2 Vols. (Government Printer), 1922, Sinclair, James, *Origins of the Māori Wars*, (Auckland University Press), 1957, Belich, James, *The New Zealand Wars and the Victorian interpretation of racial conflict*, (Auckland University Press), 1986, Ryan, Tim, *The Colonial New Zealand Wars*, (Grantham House), 1986, Matthew, *Two Peoples, One Land: The New Zealand* Wright *Wars,* (Reed), 2006, and Keenan, Danny, *Wars Without End. The Land Wars in Nineteenth Century New Zealand*, (Penguin Books), 2009.

regarded as a 'war' but were sufficiently distinct to justify the plural 'wars'.[83] For others, the Land Wars were a series of discrete conflicts that were only tenuously linked with causes that focused closely on local issues and tensions.

The events at Wairau between settlers and Māori on South Island in 1843 marked the beginning of the Land Wars. It was not, however, until the outbreak of the Northern or 'Flagstaff' War around of Bay of Islands in 1845 and 1846 that British troops became involved. It was a complex affair that largely revolved around the issue of sovereignty with Hone Heke leading one faction of the Nga Puhi against the Crown allied to a second faction headed by Tamati Waka Nen. Continued tensions over disputed lands in the Hutt Valley led to war between Ngati Toa, settlers and the British army in 1846. The Māori were not beaten and appear to have had the better of the skirmishes. They simply withdrew and chose no longer to resist European settlement into some areas. The final war concerned disputed land sales around Wanganui in 1847 and 1848.[84] In these three wars, the Māori proved to be resourceful opponents, but they had no wish to defeat the British settlers or to drive them from NZ. The issues were land and *rangatiratanga* and a tentative understanding was reached that English law prevailed in the townships and settlements with Māori law and customs elsewhere. Between 1848 and 1860, there was a period of relative peace and economic cooperation but tensions remained and there were serious threats to Pākehā such as the threatened attack on Auckland at Mechanics Bay by 250-300 Ngati Paoa in 1851.

Initially Māori land purchases were discussed in open meetings, but by the late 1840s secret agreements with individual Māori or groups, who did not represent all the owners, and the government dragged Māori into disputes with each other. In 1854, meetings held in Taranaki and Waikato resolved to retain intact all Māori land within certain boundaries. When Māori living at Manukau attempted to sell their claims on the lower Waikato river banks, they were confronted by a large armed party that had travelled down the river to set up boundary marks beyond which no sales were permitted. In August 1854, Rawiri Waiaua and four others were killed near New Plymouth for attempting to sell land. In response, British troops were stationed in New Plymouth to protect European settlers.[85] The critical question was could the Māori protect their lands against government incursions? In 1852, Tamihana Te Rauparaha, son of the powerful Ngati Toa chief, met Queen Victoria in England and concluded that establishing a monarchy for the Māori provided a solution. Although this was not a new idea, he believed that the Māori would be more secure if they could achieve unity beyond that of the tribe since as individual tribes they were more susceptible to the threats posed by colonisation. The result was the Kingitanga or

[83] When the 'wars' ended is difficult to determine. The last British troops were withdrawn from NZ in 1870 and military action was replaced by actions by the Armed Constabulary such as the Parihaka invasion of 1881, the 'Dog Tax War' of 1898 and the police invasion of Maugapohatu in 1916.

[84] Tim Ryan, Tim, and Parham, Bill, *The Colonial New Zealand Wars,* (Grantham House), 1986, pp. 15-37.

[85] Sinclair, Keith, 'Te Tikanga Pakeke: The Maori Anti-Land-Selling Movement in Taranaki, 1849-59', in Munz, Peter, (ed.), *The Feel of Truth. Essays in New Zealand and Pacific History,* (Reed), 1969), pp. 77-92.

Māori King Movement that in 1858 led to Potatau Te Wherowhero being crowned.[86] His aim was not to oppose the Crown but to provide complementary authority in the lands placed under his authority. A number of tribes supported the movement, but it became centred on the Waikato region and people. The desire to retain land was a central concern of the movement and Kingitanga was an effective land league in which all chiefs who owed allegiance to the King accepted his veto over their sale of land.[87] To Māori, the Kingitanga was a development for the Māori, not against Europeans although this is not how it was received:

> It was not a declaration of Māori independence - this already existed - and it added no new territory to the Māori sphere. It sought merely to unite pre-existing polities. But in other ways the Movement was an important change. Together with the rise in anti-land-selling generally, it raised the profile of Māori independence from a level which the British disliked but tolerated, to a level which many found entirely unacceptable.[88]

During the 1850s, European settlement accelerated and by 1859, the number of Pākehā equaled the number of Māori, at around 60,000 each. Settlers were keen to obtain land and some Māori were willing to sell but were prevented by Kingitanga Māori wishing to exert their authority. Settlers and the government tried to avoid involvement in these largely inter-Māori disputes until settlers were harmed. War broke out in North Taranaki in March 1860. The cause of the war was a block of land, called the Pekapeka Block, now largely corresponding to the township of Waitara. In 1859, Te Teira a local Te Atiawa chief offered to sell the Pekapeka Block to the Crown, an offer he had made on several earlier occasions. Many Māori objected to the sale led by Wiremu Kingi, regarded by Te Atiawa as their paramount chief and who spoke for all Te Atiawa, especially for the 2,000 Māori living on the block itself. His customary right to oppose the sale far outweighed the right of Te Teira to force a sale through. The Governor, Thomas Gore Browne, had just announced a new Government policy that the Government would accept any offer of land from any individual Māori who wished to sell and that no Māori of rank or customary status could obstruct this policy. Māori must not be permitted to usurp the authority of the Crown and the sale would go through provided Te Teira's title to the land could be confirmed.

For Gore Browne, it was a matter of whether the Governor-General or the paramount Māori had the ultimate authority. This decision angered Te Atiawa

---

[86] Jones, Pei Te Hurinui, *King Potatair: An Account of the Life of Potatau Te Wherowhero the First Māori King,* (Polynesian Society), 1959.

[87] Buddle, Thomas, *The Maori King Movement in New Zealand: With a Full Report of the Native Meetings held at Waikato, April and May, 1860*, (Published at the 'New-Zealander' Office), 1860, Gorst, Sir John Eldon, *The Maori King*, (Paul's Book Arcade), 1864. Sorrenson, M. P. K., 'The Maori King Movement, 1858-1885', in Chapman, R. M., and Sinclair, K., (eds.), *Studies in a Small Democracy: Essays in honour of Willis Airey*, (Blackwood and Jean Paul Ltd.), 1965, pp. 48-55.

[88] Ibid, Belich, James, *The New Zealand Wars and the Victorian Interpretation of Racial Conflict,* p. 78.

that was not prepared to allow the Crown to occupy the disputed Block. Wiremu Kingi warned the Governor that he did not desire war against the Pākehā but would not allow the sale to proceed. When an attempt was later made to survey the Block, Te Atiawa obstructed the surveyors and removed them from the area. The Governor saw this obstruction as tantamount to treason and the Māori were instructed to apologise, and to remove themselves from the Block. Te Atiawa refused and hastily built a defensive pa at Te Kohia, symbolically sited just inside the south-eastern corner of the Block. Browne declared martial law in Taranaki on 22 February 1860 and on 17 March 17, the British Army marched out from New Plymouth and opened fire on the pa beginning what is generally called the 'First Taranaki War'. The opening battle then was fought at Te Kohia and further important engagements were fought at Puketekauere, Mahoetahi, No 3 Redoubt and Te Arei. During this war, the British Army suffered some setbacks but ultimately prevailed over the Māori. A truce was signed at Te Arei Pa in 1861.[89]

The NZ Government was not prepared to tolerate the rebel Māori Kingitanga controlling and ruling most of the central North Island. War broke out again in 1863 with the ambush and killing of British soldiers. The massive invasion of 14,000 men in July 1863 of the Māori King's avowed home area, the Waikato is often regarded as the defining event of the Land Wars.[90] Skirmishing at Koheroa and Meremere followed by a major engagement at Rangiriri. With Rangiriri taken, the British army pushed south, ultimately defeating Waikato and its allies at Orakau in 1864. Māori King Tawhiao fled west and took refuge amongst Ngati Maniapoto in dense bush country later known as the 'King Country'. Events at Tauranga in 1864 are sometimes seen as a part of the Waikato war, which strictly speaking it is not. The war focussed on Ngai Te Rangi defence of land against the British army and settlers.[91]

South Taranaki remained on an uneasy war-footing after 1860 and elements of Ngati Ruanui travelled north to support their related tribes of North Taranaki in 1860. Ngati Ruanui returned south after the war and later attacked Tataraimaka in 1863. British troops, especially under the command of Major General Trevor Chute, were sent into the area to 'repress the Māori' which it did with some ruthlessness. Increasingly, the Armed Constabulary was taking over the war, with the reduction in the number of British troops. War was made more complex by the rise of Hau Hau in 1864 especially when it spread beyond Taranaki. A short period of peace was sharply broken by the 'Second Taranika War' was fought in South Taranaki in 1868 and 1869 by Titokowaru against Armed Constabulary and settler Volunteer units.[92]

---

[89] Ibid, Belich, James, *The New Zealand Wars and the Victorian Interpretation of Racial Conflict,* pp. 73-116, Finlay, Neil, *Sacred Soil: Images and Stories of the New Zealand Wars,* (Auckland University Press), 1998, pp. 29-44, and ibid, Ryan, Tim, and Parham, Bill, *The Colonial New Zealand Wars,* pp. 37-46. See also, ibid, Sole, Tony, *Ngati Ruanui: A History*, pp. 229-242

[90] Ibid, Belich, James, *The New Zealand Wars and the Victorian Interpretation of Racial Conflict,* pp. 73-176.

[91] Ibid, Belich, James, *The New Zealand Wars and the Victorian Interpretation of Racial Conflict,* pp. 177-202.

[92] Ibid, Belich, James, *The New Zealand Wars and the Victorian Interpretation of Racial Conflict,* pp. 235-274.

Following the earlier war in North Taranaki of 1860-1861, the lands of Māori 'deemed to have been in armed rebellion against the Crown' were confiscated. On 19 June 1867, during a short skirmish, two surveyors and a military settler were killed by Māori at Ketemarae, a large bush clearing near Normanby. The Māori involved fled to Te Ngutu O Te Manu, the bush stronghold of Titokowaru who refused to hand them over to the authorities. War was the result. Titokowaru's fighting force mainly came from Ngati Ruanui and Nga Ruahine, two southern Taranaki tribes. On 12 July 1868, the Redoubt at Turuturumokai was attacked by a *taua* (war party) from Titokowaru's base camp. On 21 August 1868, the first Armed Constabulary retaliatory attack was launched on Titokowaru followed by a second unsuccessful attack on Te Ngutu O Te Manu on 7 September. Two months later, Armed Constabulary attacked Moturoa pa, near present day Waverley but were once again beaten back. On 2 February 1869, Titokowaru abandoned his pa and fled inland into the Ngati Maru country behind Waitara.

The final war took place on the east coast of North Island between 1868 and 1872. Te Kooti of Rongowhakaata escaped from imprisonment on the Chatham Islands and with adherents was pursued across the breadth of the North Island. A very long and complex guerrilla war involving alliances of Crown, settlers and Māori pitted against Te Kooti's people in flight.[93] Te Kooti finally accepted an offer of refuge from Tawhiao and retired into the King Country in 1872.

Māori and prophecy

Whether prophetic leaders existing among the Māori before colonisation is not known with any certainly. Oral histories of tribes describe seers and those who were spiritually gifted but the emergence of prophecy appears to have coincided with European settlement, the introduction of literacy and, in the wake of loss of land, warfare and conversion, a merging of Christianity with their own beliefs.[94] Papahurihia and Āperahama Taonui are the earliest recorded prophets in the heavily missionised northern areas of North Island.[95] Both prophets questioned the honesty of missionaries, not surprising as they were associated with negotiating land purchases with Taonui especially recognising the importance of land:

---

[93] Ibid, Belich, James, *The New Zealand Wars and the Victorian Interpretation of Racial Conflict*, pp. 275-290.

[94] Elsmore, Bronwyn, *Like Them That Dream: The Māori and the Old Testament*, 2nd ed., (Reed), 2000, pp. 12-26, and *Mana from Heaven: A Century of Māori Prophets in New Zealand*, 2nd ed., (Reed), 1999. Valuable articles include, Owens, J. M. R., 'Christianity and the Māoris to 1840', *New Zealand Journal of History*, Vol. 2, (1968), pp. 18-40, Binney, Judith, 'Christianity and the Māoris in 1840: A Comment', *New Zealand Journal of History*, Vol. 3, (1969), pp. 143-165, and 'Ancestral Voices: Māori Prophet Leaders', in Sinclair, Keith, (ed.), *The Oxford Illustrated History of New Zealand*, (Oxford University Press), 1990, pp. 153-184.

[95] Binney, Judith, 'Papahurihia, Pukerenga, Te Atua Wera and Te Nakahi: How Many Prophets?', *Journal of the Polynesian Society*, Vol. 116, (2007), pp. 309-320, and Wilson, Ormond, 'Papahurihia, First Māori Prophet', *Journal of the Polynesian Society*, Vol. 74, (1965), pp. 473-483.

> It is from the earth we obtain all things. The land is our father; the land is our chieftainship; we will not give it up.[96]

They combined introduced beliefs and old convictions and attracted followers that ought to have warned missionaries and settlers of Māori disaffection.

It was, however, Te Ua Haumene, a Christian convert from Taraniki, who made a durable impression on NZ society. The angel Gabriel inspired Te Ua with a solution to the problems facing Māori revealing a new religion, Pai Marire, 'Good and Peaceful' to replace the teachings of missionaries especially those that privileged Pākehā. Te Ua's cosmology incorporated not only Jehovah but also Rura and Rika, Māori sky deities and Ripe, a bird that carried divine messages from heaven to earth. Pai Marire expressed anti-mission sentiments by changing the day of the Sabbath, concentrating on Jehovah rather than Jesus, an emphasis on the Old Testament that distanced it from the New Testament of the missionaries, and depicting a future in which Māori priests would supplant Pākehā clergy. As a result of the spread of this new religion, there would be no more Pākehā although Māori would have appropriated their achievements. With the exile of the Pākehā, justice would be achieved in Aotearoa and once it belonged to Māori, the angels would instruct them in the languages and sciences of the white man. The Māori were selective in their rejection of European ideas and culture readily adopting any that aided resistance. However, Te Ua's influence lay largely on the west coast of North Island highlighting the limits of Māori tribalism that prevented the organisation of effective military resistance.

On the east coast, Te Kooti, the founder of the Ringatū church, took up the spirit of prophecy.[97] Well-schooled in Christianity and Pākehā learning, he laid the foundation of his movement while exiled to the Chatham Islands by recovering from an advanced case of tuberculosis.[98] He announced that a spirit had appeared to him and proclaimed: 'Rise and come forth. You are spared to be made well to be the founder of a new church and religion of the Faithful Māori people, and to release them from Bondage.' Colonial authorities were warned about his prophetic impact in the Chatham Islands but dismissed the threat. Te Koori prophesised than an ark would come and deliver them from captivity, seized a ship and escaped with 298 people and established a community at Puketapu.[99] Captivity and exile were central themes in the ideology of Ringatū and Passover was the most distinctive festival of its calendar. Te Koori revived elements of the pre-missionary Māori religion calling its priests 'tohunga', reviving

---

[96] Caselberg, John, (ed.), *Maori is My Name*, (Otago University Press), 1975, p. 48. See also, Ballara, Angela, 'The Pursuit of Mana? A Re-evaluation of the Process of Land Alienation by Māoris, 1840-1890', *Journal of the Polynesian Society*, Vol. 91, 1982, pp. 519-541.

[97] Binney, Judith, *Redemption Songs: A Life of Te Kooti Arikirangi Te Turuki*, (Auckland University Press), 1995, is the best biography.

[98] Ibid, Binney, Judith, *Redemption Songs*, pp. 63-86.

[99] Ibid, Binney, Judith, *Redemption Songs*, pp. 87-118.

faith-healing and using sorcery to explain ill-fortune.[100] These assured a receptive audience that ancestral sources of power and authority were still important.[101]

As European settlement expanded, two further prophets attempted to establish self-sufficient communities that had little trade with the Europeans: Rua Kēnana in the Urewera Mountains in the east and Te Whiti's pacifist community in the west.[102] They too adopted Old Testament ideology and identified with Biblical Jews combining it with Māori virtues of cooperation and community life. Ancestral ways were regarded as powerful but these were increased when augmented by Christianity. To defeat Pākehā and survive in an environment in the process of dramatic change, Māori prophets did not find it contradictory to return to more traditional explanations and values while recognising that Pākehā society had its attractions.[103] The problem was that there was a chasm between Māori prophets and their ideas of peace and good living and the Pākehā rule that was generally not characterised by non-violent means.[104] Te Ua adopted a more militant, direct approach to the Supreme Being in their crusade against the encroaching Europeans. Te Kooti created a new moral order for his disciplines blending Biblical and older teachings while the separatist communities of Te Whiti and Rua gave their followers dignity and identity. For Māori society, land and people were intimately linked from birth to death and it was this sense of 'belonging', the Promised Land of the Old Testament, which the prophets exploited.

Establishing Pai Marire

The Pai Marire movement was founded by Te Ua Haumene in Taranaki and flourished in the decade after 1863.[105] Te Ua Haumene was born in Taranaki in

[100] Salmond, Anne, *Hui: A Study of Maori Ceremonial Gatherings*, (Taylor & Francis), 1975, pp. 197-202. See also, Roxburgh, Irvine, *The Ringatu Movement: A Phenomenological Essay on Culture Shock in New Zealand/Aotearoa*, (Cadsonbury), 1998.

[101] On the Ringatu movement after 1900, see Garrett, John, *Footsteps in the Sea; Christianity in Oceania to World War II*, Institute of Pacific Studies, (University of the South Pacific), 1992, pp. 125-129.

[102] Binney, Judith, Chaplin, G., and Wallace, C., (eds.), *Mihaia: The Prophet Rua Kenana and his Community at Maungapohatu*, (Auckland University Press), 1996, and Ward, John P., *Wanderings with the Māori prophets, Te Whiti & Tohu: Being Reminiscences of a Twelve Months' Companionship with them, from their arrival in Christchurch in April, 1882, until their return to Parihaka in March, 1883*, (Bond, Finney & Co.), 1883.

[103] Beattie, James, and Stenhouse, John, 'God and the Natural World in Nineteenth-century New Zealand', in ibid, Stenhouse, John, (ed.), *Christianity, Modernity and Culture*, pp. 180-205, is valuable on the impact of natural theology issues.

[104] Within Māori society, there was evident scepticism of the prophets. For instance, Te Whiti invited the Ngati Ruanui at Oeo to come to Parihaka but evidently most refused because they were tired of 'prophets inspired by false gods and possessed by madness': Sole, Tony, *Ngati Ruanui: A History*, (Huia Publishers), 2005, p. 348.

[105] For general discussion of Pai Mārire see, King, M., *The Penguin History of New Zealand*, (Penguin), 2003, Smith, P. Mein, *A Concise History of New Zealand*, (Cambridge University Press), 2005, and Byrnes, Giselle, (ed.), *The New Oxford History of New Zealand*, (Oxford University Press), 2009. Belich, James, *Making Peoples: A History of the New Zealanders, from Polynesian Settlement to the End of the Nineteenth*

the early 1820s but he and his mother were captured and enslaved by a rival tribe in 1826. He learned to read and write in Māori while in captivity and began studying the New Testament and was baptised by the Rev John Whiteley in the Wesleyan mission at Kawhia in 1843. He later returned to Taranaki. During the 1850s, he became a supporter of the King Movement and fought against colonial forces in the First Taranaki War and Waikato War, in which he also acted as a chaplain to the Māori soldiers. By the early 1860s, Te Ua was part of a *runanga* (local board of management) that administered local government and ensured that boundaries of land covered by the authority of the Māori King were undisturbed.

By 1860, the foundations of Te Ua's religious teaching were already established incorporating elements of Biblical and Māori spiritual traditions.[106] Every address Te Ua gave began and ended with the words 'Pai Marire', an injunction to 'live peaceably' but it was only when he unfolded his revelation that he found a wide audience. The elevation of Te Ua to the role of prophet followed an incident in September 1862 when *Lord Worsley*, a British steamer was wrecked off the Taranaki coast and local Māori debated what action should be taken with the cargo and crew.[107] Te Ua argued that goods salvaged from the vessel should be sent to New Plymouth untouched, but was ignored and the cargo was instead plundered. Distressed by what had taken place, he claimed to have experienced a vision in which the Archangel Gabriel announced to him that the last days were at hand and that God had chosen him as a prophet who would cast out the Pākehā and restore Israel (Māori) to their birthright in the land of Aotearoa/New Zealand (Canaan). There was contemporary disagreement over Te Ua, who changed his name to Zerubbabel, responded to the vision. He is claimed to have killed his child, explaining in a letter circulated to tribes that it was as a redemption for his people, 'forgetful, desolate and in doubt', while there are

---

Century, (Allen Lane), 1996, is a major revisionist study. More specific studies are, Babbage, S. B., *Hauhauism: An Episode in the Māori Wars 1863-1866*, (A. H. & A. W. Reed), 1937, though weak on Māori prophetic context, Clark, P., *Hauhau: The Pai Marire Search for Māori Identity*, (Auckland University Press), 1975, ibid, Adas, Michael, *Prophets of Rebellion: Millenarian Protest Movements against the European Colonial Order*, and Rosenfeld, Jean E., 'Pai Mārire: Peace and Violence in a New Zealand Millenarian Tradition', in Barkun, Michael, (ed.), *Millennialism and Violence*, (Routledge), 1996, pp. 83-108. See also, Wessinger, Catherine, (ed.), *The Oxford Handbook of Millenialism*, pp. 89-100.

[106] Parr, C. J., 'Before the Pai Marire', *Journal of the Polynesian Society*, Vol. 76, (1967), pp. 35-46, Winks, R. W., 'The Doctrine of Hau-Hauism', *Journal of the Polynesian Society*, Vol. 62, (1953), pp. 199-236, and Head, L. F., 'The Gospel of Te Ua Haumene', *Journal of the Polynesian Society*, Vol. 101, (1992), pp. 7-44. Ibid, Babbage, S. B., *Hauhauism*, p. 85, dismissed some contemporary comments on the religious basis of Pai Mārire as 'of little real historical value…rhetorical rather than scientific' with some justification; Lusk, H. H., 'Maori Mahommedanism', *Fortnightly Review*, Vol. 2, (1865), p. 731, is representative of the rhetorical approach while P. C. B., 'A Chapter on Pai Marire, the new religion of the Māori, by an Army Chaplain', *Fraser's Magazine*, Vol. 72, (1865), pp. 423-438, is more analytical.

[107] 'Wreck of the Lord Worsley', *Taranaki Herald*, 6 September 1862, p. 1, 'Wreck of the Lord Worsley', *Colonist*, 9 September 1862, p. 1, reported the wreck.

also claims he broke the child's leg and healed it miraculously.[108] These discrepancies did not damage Te Ua's standing and he quickly gained a reputation for having other miraculous powers. The view among settlers was less sympathetic: Bishop William Williams claimed Te Ua showed strong signs of insanity [109] while T. W. Gudgeon, a colonial soldier and historian, concluded that he had been thus far regarded as a 'harmless lunatic' of 'weak intellect, but of peaceful disposition'.[110] To help him disseminate the religion, Te Ua chose three men, Tahutaki, Hepenaia and Wi Parara.

In promising his followers deliverance from Pākehā domination, it provided a religious dimension to the issue of Māori independence that had previously been a purely political movement. It also signalled a Māori rejection of Christianity and a distrust of missionaries over their involvement in land purchases. Te Ua began to formulate his new religion, complete with a holy book, *Ua Rongo Pai* (Gospel according to Ua) that combined elements of Old Testament morality, Christian doctrine and traditional Māori religion. Its goal was to create a peaceful society in which righteousness and justice prevailed. Te Ua believed the Māori were a second Chosen People and that, with divine aid, they would regain control of their hereditary land when the Creator, Jehovah, fought for them and drove the Pākehā into the sea. When the last of the enemy had perished, every Māori who had died since the beginning of the world would be resurrected and men would be sent from heaven to teach Māori all the arts and sciences known by Europeans. Their first great day of deliverance would be on 26 December 1864. He urged men and women to abandon monogamy and live together communally to produce as many children as possible. Even when the prediction failed, Pai Marire was still adopted by many and the millenarian element remained strong.

Services were held at a sacred or miracle pole (niu) with yard-arms from which ropes were hung and by the end of 1865, there was a niu in almost every large village from Taranaki to the Bay of Plenty and from the north of the Wellington district to the Waikato frontier.[111] The tohunga priests, who had been schooled in Māori ancient religion, were the first to accept Pai Marire though whether from conviction or from a desire to retain their spiritual influence is questionable. Members of the congregation circled the niu several times a day, chanting and touching a decapitated head mounted on a pole while priests conducted prayer services. The 'angels of the wind' were said to be present during the service climbing up and down the ropes dangling from the mast's yard-arm. Most the chants used appear to have been unintelligible even to Māori adherents: 'A jumble of Christian and ancient concepts, of soldier and sailor terms, of English and Māori language with the barking watchword [Hau, Hau] of

---

[108] Ibid, Babbage, S. B., *Hauhauism*, pp. 24-25.
[109] Williams, Rt. Rev. William, *Christianity Among the New Zealanders*, (Seely, Jackson & Halliday), 1867, pp. 366-367.
[110] Gudgeon, T. W., *Reminiscences of the War in New Zealand*, (Samson Low), 1879, p. 24.
[111] Ibid, P. C. B., 'A Chapter on Pai Marire, the new religion of the Maori, by an Army Chaplain', pp. 428-431, provides a lucid contemporary account of Pai Mārire rituals.

the cult interspersed.'[112] The congregation worked itself up into a frenzied state during the ritual. Also, central to Pai Marire was the belief in divine protection from Pākehā bullets and the faithful marched into battle chanting their hymns and holding their right hands level with their faces with the palms towards the enemy. The tasting of human blood was one of the most solemn Pai Marire rites and the preserved heads of murdered soldiers were carried for divination. Although founded with peaceful motives, Pai Marire became better-known for its extremist and politicised form popularly known as Hauhau, though there is evidence the most violent activities were led by subordinate prophets acting against the wishes of Te Ua and the basic precepts of the religion. The millenarianism of Te Ua and the fanaticism induced among believers provided the movement with a potent, anti-colonial message and a powerful instrument for Māori nationalist propaganda that was exploited to arouse support by rebel leaders to considerable effect in 1864 and 1865.[113]

Militant fanaticism

The rise and spread of the violent expression of Pai Marire was largely a response to the NZ Government's military operations against North Island Māori that were aimed at exerting European sovereignty and gaining more land for white settlement. Pai Marire spread rapidly through the North Island from 1864, welding tribes in a bond of passionate hatred of Pākehā and helping to inspire fierce military resistance to colonial forces, particularly during the Second Taranaki War.[114]

Among white settlers, the existence of the new religion was brought into dramatic focus with a series of attacks in April and May 1864.[115] There is no indication in the available sources on which of Te Ua's lieutenants turned his teachings to bellicose ends but it suddenly transformed the movement in ways he had never envisaged. On 6 April 1864, a force led by Tahutaki and Hepenaia but including Te Au mounted an expedition to Te Ahuahu village, set amid dense bush south of Oakura, near New Plymouth, believing some Pākehā would be delivered into their hands. The group surprised a combined force of 57th Regiment and the newly-formed Taranaki Military Settlers, a total of 101 men, as they rested during a mission to destroy native crops. Captain T. W. J. Lloyd was new to Māori warfare and had not taken ordinary military precautions to guard against a common Māori method of guerilla attack. Most of the soldiers escaped but Māori force killed seven including Lloyd and wounded twelve. The bodies of the seven dead were stripped naked and decapitated and several of the heads

[112] Keesing, J. M., *The Changing Maori*, (T. Avery & Sons Ltd.), 1928, p. 50.
[113] Meade, H. A., *Ride Through the Disturbed Districts of New Zealand*, (John Murray), 1870, p. 32.
[114] Ibid, Cowan, James, *The New Zealand Wars and the Pioneering Period*, Vol. 2, pp. 1-83, provides a detailed account of events in 1864 and 1865. Cowan entitled this volume, *The Hauhau Wars, 1864-1872* and Hauhau prophets were involved in military operations after 1866, but the millenarian importance of Pai Mārire effectively ended with the death of Te Ua in 1866 although its political influence remained important until 1872.
[115] See comments in 'Pai Marire', *Taranaki Herald*, 8 April 1865, p. 1.

were preserved.[116] Te Ua was then commanded by the Archangel Gabriel to send the Pākehā officer's head from tribe to tribe through the North Island. When all the tribes had been visited, and converted to Pai Marire, Māori people would be endowed with such power and wisdom that they would be able to conquer the white race and restore New Zealand to its original owners.[117]

The attack on Captain Lloyd's party was a consequence of the usurpation of authority in the Pai Marire movement by leaders who were committed the violent anti-colonial resistance. How this transfer of power occurred is not known but Te Ua certainly chose the leaders who later led the movement and it marked an end to his effective control of the Pai Marire. The easy victory of the Māori over a far stronger British-led force gave a powerful impetus to the Pai Marire movement and confirmed in the minds of many Māori the protection of the Archangel Gabriel, of whom Te Ua was now regarded as a prophet. The number of adherents swelled and Pai Marire rites continued to develop, some incorporating the decapitated heads of the slain soldiers through which Te Ua claimed to communicate with Jehovah. Initial success also bred over-confidence that has disastrous consequences three weeks later.

On 30 April 1864, 200 picked warriors led by Hepanaia demonstrated their faith in divine protection when they marched on the Sentry Hill redoubt, five miles north-west of New Plymouth.[118] The redoubt had been constructed in late 1863 and Atiawa Māori regarded the outpost on their land as a challenge and formed a war party of the best fighting men from west coast iwi. The redoubt, on the crown of a hill, was defended by 75 imperial soldiers under Captain Shortt with two Coehorn mortars. When they came under fire at close range, they shielded themselves from the fusillade only by holding their right hands up and chanting. About 34 Māori and one imperial soldier were killed. Among those shot dead, at almost point-blank range, were Hepanaia and Hare Te Kokai, who had advocated the frontal attack on the redoubt.[119] The slaughter temporarily weakened confidence in Pai Marire, but Te Ua explained that those who fell were to blame because they did not have absolute faith in the karakia or incantation.

Two weeks later, on 14 May 1864, a Pai Marire war party led by the prophet Mantene from the upper Whanganui River advanced on the settlement of Wanganui, intent on raiding it.[120] A message was sent to the Ngati Hau iwi at Hiruharama asking them to join in the attack on the whites but this was refused

---

[116] Ibid, Babbage, S. B., *Hauhauism*, pp. 27-28, and ibid, Cowan, James, *The New Zealand Wars and the Pioneering Period*, Vol. 2, pp. 16-18, detail the skirmish.

[117] The decapitation of soldiers at Te Ahuahu was the first instance of this mutilation of enemies' bodies during the 1860s. To decapitation, the West Coast Hauhaus added cannibalism in 1868-1869 when Tamaikowha of Ngai-Tama and Urewera revived the practice of eating the hearts of his enemies. The last instance in NZ of the beheading an enemy occurred in 1873.

[118] See, ibid, Babbage, S. B., *Hauhauism*, pp. 41-43, and ibid, Cowan, James, *The New Zealand Wars and the Pioneering Period*, Vol. 2, pp. 21-29.

[119] Ibid, Cowan, pp. 22-26, contains a dramatic narrative of the battle obtained from Te Kahu-pukoro of Otakeho just before his death in 1920. At the age of twelve, he had taken part in the debacle in which his father and uncle were killed: 'It was a one-sided fight, a miserable fight…'

[120] Ibid, Cowan, pp. 30-36.

and Ngati Hau summoned the down-river tribes to their assistance against the Pai Marire. For Ngati Hau the actions of the Pai Marire, even if they sympathised with their aims, was an attack on their authority over the river. In what became known as the Battle of Moutoa, the war party was defeated, leaving fifty dead including Matene. There was desultory fighting between the Upper and Lower Wanganui tribes following Moutoa that lasted until early in 1865. The reverses at Sentry Hill and Moutoa Island far from reducing support reinforced Māori belief in Te Ua's movement with the conviction that the defeats had been caused by disobedience to the leader by the prophets Hepanaia and Matene. More iwi joined Te Ua and in early 1865, emissaries in two parties carrying smoke-dried decapitated heads were sent from Taranaki to Poverty Bay via Wanganui and Taupo.

Political power among Māori was highly localised and it was essential to win over local leaders. The result, in early 1865, was a concerted effort to build support by sending two parties across the North Island. The first party went to Whakatane, Opotiki, and East Cape, after which it proceeded to Poverty Bay by way of the coast while the other party went through the centre of the island by Ruatahuna and Wairoa and eventually to Poverty Bay. But on 23 February 1865, the group clashed with Māori loyal to the NZ government at Pipiriki near Wanganui and after this defeat its leaders, the prophets Kereopa and Patara, proceeded with the intention of murdering any missionaries they encountered and began to pillage and murder. As a result of the deteriorating situation on the Wanganui River, a military force of settler volunteers was sent to Pipiriki at the end of April 1865 to establish a military post on the frontier between those tribes that supported Pai Marire and those loyal to the Crown.[121] With the support of the loyalists, the troops were able to beat off a concerted Pai Marire attack and siege in July though it was not finally relievd until August 1865. The consequence of the dispersal of the Pai Marire was that the movement fragmented into localised rebellions led by tribal chiefs in the southern and eastern areas of the North Island.

Denouement

There was growing concern among European settlers uneasy at the spreading influence of Pai Marire especially along the Wanganui River. The Native Minister, the Resident Magistrate for Central Wanganui warned: 'The Hauhau fanaticism is spreading very rapidly in the Province, and I fear will be the cause of great mischief. It is now the mainstay of the King movement.' The Pai Marire continued their journey up the Wanganui River until they reached Taupo where they ransacked the house of the Reverend T. S. Grace, the local missionary who had already fled.[122] At Taupo, the Pai Marire group divided as previously planned

---

[121] Ibid, Cowan, pp. 37-45.

[122] Brittan, S. J., Grace, G. F., Grace, C. W., and Grace, A. V., (eds.), *A Pioneer Missionary among the Maoris 1850-1879: Being Letters and Journals of Thomas Samuel Grace*, (Bennett and Co.), 1928, pp. 110-143, provides Grace's account of events in March 1865.

with one group reaching Opotiki on 1 March 1865 while the other reached Turanga on 16 March.[123]

Existing grievances among the Opotiki were exploited by the Pai Marire group. The people of Opotiki had been sympathetic to the Waikato War and some had taken part. Their minister was Reverend Carl Volkner, a native of Cassell in Germany who had come to NZ in 1847, who they suspected of being in secret correspondence with the government. It was thought he sent Governor George Grey a plan of a pa near Te Awamutu where British troops burned women and children alive in a building that had been converted to a church. The wife and two daughters of Kereopa where among the victims. Their suspicions were aggravated by his several visits to Auckland though, in reality, these were concerned with improving their living conditions not informing the authorities about disaffection. On 2 March 1865, Volkner–who had been warned to stay away from the town–and Grace arrived at Opotiki on board *HMS Eclipse* but when they went ashore they were seized on the orders of Kereopa, the Pai Marire prophet and held in the Roman Catholic Chapel. In the evening, a meeting of the chiefs decided to hang Volkner but to keep Grace as a prisoner, a decision supported by most of the people of Opotiki though they probably had little choice. The following morning, Volkner was led to a willow tree that was used as the gallows and hanged. It was alleged that his head was then taken to the local church, where his eyes were removed and eaten by Kereopa. The brutality of the killing was claimed to be in part revenge for Volkner's suspected spying activities for the government but may also have been motivated by Kereopa's wish to bring government retaliation on local Te Whakatōhea Māori in revenge for an earlier intertribal battle with his Te Arawa iwi.[124]

After the killing, Kereopa left Opotiki and refused to return when called upon to account for his actions by Patara and continued his journey towards Poverty Bay. On 5 March, Grace was put on trial by the Pai Marire party but a decision was made to seek to exchange him for Tauranga chief Hori Tupaea. In the event, on 16 March Grace was rescued from captivity by the British man-of-war, *HMS Eclipse*. One leader of the Pai Marire party repudiated the murder as contrary to the teachings of the new faith, as did Te Ua himself. William Williams, upon receiving news of the arrival of the Pai Marire party at Opotiki, also recorded rumours that Te Ua had ordered 'that all the Pākehā shall be killed whether they are clergymen or laymen'. Williams received a copy of Te Ua's instructions a few weeks later, after he had first heard of the killing of Volkner, and noted that these rumours were unfounded. There was, he wrote, 'no sanction...to murder' contained within the instructions. Nevertheless, further murders took place in late July. Horomona, a Pai Marire prophet from Taranaki arrived at Whakatane and called a meeting of the Patutatahi tribe. On 22 July 1865, the cutter *Kate* had arrived at Whakatane, with Mr. Fulloon, of mixed-race who was a Government Interpreter and three men, including the captain. The

[123] Mackay, J. A., *Historic Poverty Bay and the East Coast, N. I., N. Z.,* (J. A. Mackay), 1949, pp. 215-227, provides details of the Volkner murder and Pai Mārire activities around Poverty Bay in 1865.

[124] This was certainly the view of Patara, the other prophet, who had returned in Opotiki later that day: ibid, Babbage, S. B., *Hauhauism*, pp. 52-53.

cutter anchored off the bar to await high tide. Horomona demanded that the crew and passengers should be killed and the chief Te Hura agreed. Twenty men manned two whale boats and boarded the cutter. Kirimangu, one of the leaders, went down into the cabin and found Fulloon and shot him dead, followed by the master and two of his crew.[125]

The spread of Pai Marire and the killing of Volkner terrorised the European population, polarised Māori tribes with the Māori king denouncing Te Ua and alarmed the government that responded in an unequivocal fashion. Donald McLean, the Superintendent of the Hawke's Bay Province, was appointed General Agent for the Government in March 1865 to co-ordinate its response. On 29 April 1865, Governor George Grey issued a proclamation condemning 'revolting acts...repugnant to all humanity' carried out by Pai Marire followers and warned the government would 'resist and suppress by force of arms if necessary and by every means in my power, fanatical doctrines, rites, and practices of the aforesaid character'.[126] The Crown's capacity to enforce this proclamation was limited and Grey called on all 'well-disposed' persons to assist in its enforcement. McLean was instructed to capture the Pai Marire leaders if this was practical.

Pai Marire emissaries carried the religion to the East Coast north of Tūranga in June 1865.[127] Chiefs favourably disposed towards the Crown resolved to make war upon the Pai Marire emissaries, despite the efforts of the leader of the Pai Marire party Patara Rakatauri to leave the district to avoid such an outcome. The 'loyalist' party were quickly provided with arms, ammunition and other logistical support from the Crown and was supported by colonial troops. Fighting took place between Pai Marire adherents and other East Coast Māori between June and October 1865. The Pai Marire adherents were defeated. Horomona and Kirimangu were hanged in May 1866 for their killings on *Kate* although it was not until January 1872[128] that Kereopa–after a brief hearing that was a show trial rather than a quest for justice and regarded by his iwi as a miscarriage of justice--suffered the same fate for Volkner's murder.[129] In March 1866, Te Ua was captured near Opunake in Taranaki and was immediately abandoned by all those in his village, who swore an oath of allegiance to the Crown and was set free and it was reported that loyal Māori urged his immediate

---

[125] 'The Whakatane Massacre. The trial of Fulloon's Murderers', *Daily Southern Cross*, 29 December 1865, p. 3, *Daily Southern Cross*, 29 December 1865, p. 3, 'The Whakatane Massacre: Examination of the Accused', *Daily Southern Cross*, 13 February 1866, p. 4, 'The Whakatane Murders: Examination of the Accused', *Daily Southern Cross*, 14 February 1866, p. 5, 'The Whakatane Murders: Examination on the Charge of Being Accessories', *Daily Southern Cross*, 17 February 1866, p. 4, 'The Whakatane Affair', *Daily Southern Cross*, 24 February 1866, p. 4.

[126] *New Zealand Government Gazette*, 29 April 1865.

[127] Ibid, Cowan, pp. 117-128, examines the East Coast operations against the Pai Mārire.

[128] For details of the executions see, 'Execution of Five Maoris for the Murders of Fulloon and Volkner', *Daily Southern Cross*, 18 May 1866, p. 2, and 'The Execution of Kereopa', *Taranaki Herald*, 6 January 1872, p. 1. The coverage of Kereopa's execution was given far less column space than those in 1866.

[129] A rare statutory pardon for Kereopa Te Rau was included in a Treaty of Waitangi settlement with a Rotorua iwi in June 2014.

execution. Te Ua was taken to Wanganui, writing en route to his North Island supporters, urging: 'Let evil be brought to an end ... in order that the General may cease operations against you.'[130] Te Ua and Patara were freed in Auckland and most other leaders were pardoned, but Grey transported 400 East Coast followers, including Te Kooti, to the Chatham Islands.- Elements of Pai Marire were later incorporated into the Ringatu religion founded by Te Kooti. Te Ua died at Oeo in Taranaki in October 1866.

The critical problem with Pai Marire is whether it was simply a bloodthirsty and millenarian belief that gave new savagery to Māori resistance. This was certainly the view of contemporaries and, until recently, remained the view of most historians. Central to this argument was the murders of Volkner and the crew of the *Kate* but both incidents involved subordinate prophets acting against Te Ua's instructions and against the basic ideas of Pai Marire. Although it may have been a peace-oriented movement, Pai Marire was strongly opposed to the alienation of Māori land and keen to strengthen Māori identity and it proved disastrously easy for some of Te Ua's more secular subordinates to interpret this in a less peaceful way. The crude Māori tactics in the frontal attack on Sentry Hill and in the battle at Moutoa in 1864 reflected the millenarian fanaticism of the movement but in 1865 Māori adherents reverted to more traditional methods of warfare though these proved equally unsuccessful. Although Māori in arms after 1865 were almost invariably termed Hauhaus, Pai Marire had virtually died out by Te Ua's capture and what was subsequently attributed to its influence was a series of distinct, if broadly similar movements arising from similar causes. As a religion, Pai Marire was quickly superseded by the creeds propounded by Tawhio the Māori King and Te Kooti, the Māori guerrilla leader. Although short-lived, the militantly apocalyptic nature of Pai Marire caused it to overshadow later religious movements. Yet as Babbage commented:

> Its end left the Māori in a curiously unsettled state, his faith in Pākehā justice and truth undermined, his belief in Christianity shaken, his land still in danger, and his confidence in himself weakened. Though Hauhauism itself was dead, the discontents that had given rise to it were not allayed and further trouble lay ahead.[131]

Canada, 1885

The question of whether millenarian prophets were mentally disturbed or simply insane was evident in the Xhosa cattle-killing and in Pai Marire. Did the colonial authorities believe Nongqawuse and Te Ua were mentally ill or did they use the pretext of 'madness' to curb their activism? For the authorities, the actions of the Xhosa in following Nongqawuse's instructions and the destruction they wrought could only be explained in terms of delusion in that no sane people would destroy their means of subsistence. Te Ua was also regarded as a delusional figure by opponents within the settler and Māori communities. Despite provoking widespread anti-colonial resistance and rebellion, neither was severely punished for their actions unlike some of their supporters.

---

[130] Ibid, Babbage, S. B., *Hauhauism*, p. 64.
[131] Ibid, Babbage, S. B., *Hauhauism*, p. 72.

Whether the prophets ware sane or not, there is no question that they led millenarian anti-colonial movements but in the case of Louis Riel and the North-West rebellion in Canada in 1885 there is considerable disagreement about whether he was the leader of a millenarian movement and whether he was sane. George Stanley portrays him as the Métis madman who led frontier resistance to the westward advance of white settlement and political control.[132] He rejected the notion that the rebellions were part of traditional hostilities between French Catholic Quebec and British Protestant Ontario but rather a clash between primitive and civilised peoples. By contrast, Thomas Flanagan sees Riel as a legitimate religious figure and the founder and leader in 1885 of what was 'as much a religious movement as a political uprising' against the Canadian state.[133] He does not accept that Riel's religion was a symptom of a deranged mind even though he accepts that he 'might be insane from a psychiatric point of view'. Rather, he compares Riel's 'new religion' and Métis responses to conditions in the North West with millenarian movements examined in Norman Cohn's *The Pursuit of the Millennium* and Vittorio Lanternari's *Religions of the Oppressed* to garner support for the claim that Riel's behaviour in 1885 was 'typical of millenarian leaders'.[134]

The Métis: a 'New Nation'

In the eighteenth and nineteenth centuries, many British and French-Canadian fur traders married First Nations and Inuit women, mainly First Nations Cree, Ojibwa or Saulteaux. Their children, the Métis,[135] were exposed to both the Catholic and indigenous belief systems creating a new distinct aboriginal people in North America that bridged the frontier[136] between Canada and the later United States.[137] The Métis distinguished themselves from both Indians and whites and

---

[132] Stanley, George F. G., *Louis Riel: Patriot or Rebel,* (Canadian Historical Association), 1954, and *The Birth of Western Canada: A history of the Riel Rebellions*, (Longman, Green and Co.), 1936.

[133] Flanagan, Thomas, *Louis 'David' Riel: Prophet of the New World*, (University of Toronto Press), 1979, and 'Louis Riel: Was he really crazy?', in Barron, F. Laurie, and Waldram, James B., (eds.), *1885 and After: Native Society in Transition*, (University of Regina Press), 1986, pp. 105-120.

[134] Brown, Richard, *Rebellion in Canada, 1837-1885, Volume 2: The Irish, the Fenians and the Metis*, (Authoring History), 2012, pp. 246-352, provides a more detailed discussion of the rebellions in 1869-1870 and 1885.

[135] Following the increasingly common practice of the Métis themselves, 'Métis' without an accent is used except when quoting texts or titles where the accent is found. When it is necessary to differentiate between mixed-blood communities, the adjectives 'French' and 'English' are used to qualify 'Métis'.

[136] Hogue, Michel, *Metis and the Medicine Line. Creating a Border and Dividing a People*, (University of North Carolina Press), 2015, pp. 100-182.

[137] On the Métis, see, Giraud, Marcel, *Le Métis Canadien: son Rŏle dans l'Histoire des Provinces de l'Est*, (Institut d'Ethnologie), 1945, translated by George Woodcock as *The Métis in the Canadian West*, 2 Vols. (University of Alberta Press), 1986, remains a valuable if controversial study. More recent studies include, Peterson, Jacqueline, and Brown, Jennifer S.H., (eds.), *The New Peoples: Being and Becoming Métis in North America*, (University of Manitoba Press), 1985, Purich, Donald J., *The Métis*, (Lorimer), 1988, Ens, Gerhard J., and Sawchuk, Joe, *From New Peoples to New Nations: Aspects of*

the Manitoba Act in 1870 recognised a new civil status of 'half-breeds'. First Nations women provided a link between cultures and were able to translate the language and more generally were involved in resolving any cultural issues that arose and the fur traders benefited greatly from their First Nations wives' knowledge of the land and its resources. The Métis played a central role in the success of the western fur trade.[138] Not only were they skilled hunters, but they were also raised to appreciate both Aboriginal and European cultures. Métis understanding of both societies and customs helped bridge cultural gaps, resulting in better trading relationships.[139]

The fur trade was dominated by two competing companies: the Hudson's Bay Company formed in London in 1670 and the North-West Company formed a century later in Montreal. The NWC dominated the plains and forests from Upper Canada, even though the lands stretching eastward from the Rockies legally formed part of Rupert's Land owned by the HBC. Confrontation between the fur trade's blend of Amerindian and European ways and the European attitudes of incoming agricultural settlers exacerbated rivalry between the NWC and the HBC. Matters came to a head after 1809 when Lord Selkirk bought financial control of the HBC, in order to found a new colony within its territory of Rupert's Land.[140] He obtained an 116,000 square mile grant for a nominal sum of ten shillings, known as the District Assiniboia or the Red River Colony on fertile prairie accessible by lake and river from Hudson Bay. In 1812, the first Scottish settlers arrived in Red River, but were too few to challenge the dominance of the Métis and were also dependent upon them for subsistence during the settlement's first difficult years.[141] The allocation of Red River land initially caused conflict with those already living in the area as well as with the NWC, whose trade routes had been cut in half.

The War of 1812 and the hard winters of 1812-1813 and 1813-1814 led to restrictions on the export of pemmican and on running buffalo, a practice seen as

---

Metis History and Identity from the Eighteenth to Twenty-first Centuries, (University of Toronto Press), 2016, pp. 71-132, and Friesen, Gerald, *The Canadian Prairies: A History*, (University of Toronto Press), 1987, pp. 66-128.

[138] Innis, Harold, *The Fur Trade in Canada: An Introduction to Canadian Economic History*, revised edition, (University of Toronto Press), 1956, and Rich, E. E., *The Fur Trade and the Northwest to 1857*, (McClelland & Stewart), 1967, provide the best introduction to this subject. Beinart, William, and Hughes, Lotte, *Environment and Empire*, (Oxford University Press), 2007, pp. 40-57, provides an interesting slant on the trade.

[139] Bumsted, John M., *Trials and Tribulations: The Emergence of Manitoba 1821-1870*, (Great Plains Publications), 2003, set the context for events in the late 1860s. See also, Morton, W. L., *Manitoba: A History*, (University of Toronto Press), 1957, 2nd ed., (University of Toronto Press), 1967.

[140] Gray, J. M., *Lord Selkirk of Red River*, (Macmillan), 1964, remains useful but has been largely superseded by Bumsted, J. M., *Lord Selkirk: A Life*, (University of Manitoba Press), 2008; see especially pp. 181-218, on the establishment of Red River.

[141] Ibid, Bumsted, J. M., *Lord Selkirk*, pp. 219-302. See also, Ross, Alexander, *The Red River Settlement: Its Rise, Progress and Present State*, (Smith, Elder and Co.), 1856, pp. 20-42.

driving herds out of the reach of the settlers.[142] To the Métis, these were direct attacks on their way of life. In 1816, asserting what they saw as their rights, a group of Métis buffalo hunters led by Cuthbert Grant, of Scots and Cree descent, were involved in a prairie skirmish at Seven Oaks, where twenty settlers, their new governor, Robert Semple and one Métis were killed.[143] The killings appear not to have been planned but it was to the advantage of the settlers and other Canadians to call Seven Oaks a 'massacre'. By doing this, they justified the subjugation of the Métis and confirmed the image of the Métis as a barbaric and savage people. This view of the Métis as less than civilised people was then reinforced by generations of historians that allowed the rebellions in 1869 and 1885 to be viewed as inevitable clashes between civilised and primitive societies. Selkirk quickly re-established control over the area and before his death in 1820 ensured that the Red River Colony was given permanence as a pioneer agricultural community on the plains.[144] The fur trade war between the two companies, whose resources had been sapped by rising costs and falling profits, had reached an impasse and in 1821 they amalgamated as a renewed HBC that was to dominate the development of the western areas of British North America until Confederation in 1867.[145]

Instead of overwhelming the Métis, the settlers acted as a catalyst that sharpened awareness of their own distinctive culture and way of life. The concept of a 'New Nation', evident at Seven Oaks, would be reinforced by another victory against a much larger body of Sioux in 1851 in the Battle of Grand Coteau. Central to the emergence of the New Nation was Cuthbert Grant whose exclusion from service in the new HBC increased his prestige among the Métis who had suffered as a result of the merger and were an especially unstable feature of the Red River region. In July 1828, recognising his value, the HBC appointed Grant as 'warden of the plains of Red River' to prevent the illicit trade in furs though he retained sufficient respect among the Métis to be elected captain of the annual buffalo hunt. By the 1840s, his influence among the Métis had waned. A new generation of younger and more rebellious men had appeared and a French element led by men such as the elder Louis Riel began to take leadership away from the Scots Métis such as Grant. The crucial issue was freedom of trade; in defiance of the HBC monopoly, the Métis were beginning to trade furs with Americans at Pembina, North Dakota and St. Paul, Minnesota.[146] When Pierre-

---

[142] Pemmican, a high-energy food, was made from buffalo, elk or deer meat that was dried, pounded and mixed with melted fat and sometimes fruit such as cranberries and by the 1840s, the Métis were its main producers for the northern fur trade.

[143] Ibid, Bumsted, J. M., *Lord Selkirk*, pp. 303-316. See also, Bakewell, Lawrence J., *The Battle of Seven Oaks: A Métis Perspective*, (Louis Riel Institute), 2010. On Grant see, Woodcock, George, 'Cuthbert Grant', *DCB*, Vol. 8, pp. 341-344.

[144] The HBC dominated the Red River Colony and in 1850, almost every adult male in the colony had some tie to the company: selling the company his labour or selling some semi-finished commodity generated from local resources.

[145] For the continuing role of the HBC in the Red River settlement see, Martin, A., *The Hudson's Bay Company's Land Tenures and the Occupation of Assiniboia*, (W. Clowes & Sons), 1898.

[146] St-Onge, Nicole, 'Variations in Red River: The Traders and Free Métis of Saint-Laurent, Manitoba', *Canadian Ethnic Studies*, Vol. 24, (2), (1992), pp. 1-21, and in greater detail in her *Saint-Laurent Manitoba: Evolving Métis Identities, 1850-1914*, (Canadian Plains Research Centre), 2004.

Guillaume Sayer was tried for illicit trading in 1849, Grant was one of the magistrates. With a large body of armed Métis vociferously supporting Sayer in the court-room, he was found guilty of trading furs but went unpunished. The verdict was regarded in the colony as the end of the HBC monopoly.[147] A division now appeared between the militant Métis of the Red River settlements and the people of White Horse Plain, who remained under Grant's conservative influence until his death in 1854. His followers, such as his son-in-law Pascal Breland became leaders of the moderate Métis who held aloof from Louis Riel in 1870 and were opposed to Gabriel Dumont's activism.

If the HBC was increasingly incapable of prevent Métis operating as free traders, especially after the freeing of Sayer, this was offset by diminishing prospects within the company's hierarchy. The Métis were the principal source of manpower in the fur trade and by the mid-1840s, accounted for two-thirds of the HBC's rank and file and one-third of its officers. By the 1880s, Métis made up 72 per cent of the company's workforce but this expansion was largely in the lower ranks and the limits on promotion became steadily more restrictive as the century progressed. In the Red River Settlement, Ens argues that the Métis participated with growing confidence in two worlds: one Indian and pre-capitalist, the other European and capitalist.[148] He maintains that Métis identity was defined less by biology or blood but by the economic and social niche they carved out for themselves within the fur trade. Far from being overwhelmed, the Métis adapted quickly to the changed economic conditions of the 1840s and influenced the nature of change by helping to open new markets especially in the buffalo robe trade. The greatest degree of adaptation was found in the Assiniboia area while those who resisted changed drifted into the farther North-West. Nonetheless, pressures on the Métis way of life were increasing and rising industrial demand for buffalo hides resulted in overhunting.[149] Also native belief that the free gifts of nature were to be shared was being challenged by an increasing number of settlers, whose agricultural and industrial way of life was based on a more restricted access to the land and its resources. The Métis claim to special status by right of their native blood was dismissed because they had no more rights than those enjoyed by British subjects. In the 1871 census, 9,800 Métis were counted, of whom 5,720 were French speaking compared with about 4,000 English speakers and less than 1,000 Canadian settlers.[150] Despite their numerical dominance, Métis unease about their position in relation to Britain had been growing ever since the 1820s and reached a crisis in the late 1860s.

---

147 Ibid, Friesen, Gerald, *The Canadian Prairies*, pp. 99-101, provides a succinct explanation of the Sayer case.
148 Ens, Gerhard J., *Homeland to Hinterland: The Changing Worlds of the Red River Métis in the Nineteenth Century*, (University of Toronto Press), 1996, provides an overview of change for the Red River Métis.
149 Foster, John, 'The Metis and the End of the Plains Buffalo in Alberta', in Foster, John, Harrison, Dick, and MacLaren, I. S., (eds.), *Buffalo*, (University of Alberta Press), 1992, pp. 61-78.
150 *Census of Canada, 1870-71*, (I. B. Taylor), 1876, Vol. 4, pp.380-387.

Red River resistance, 1869-1870

What became a crisis for the Métis began in the 1850s with a fundamental shift in how the western interior of Canada was perceived. [151] It was no longer seen as a wilderness but as a potential location for settler expansion. Rising land prices in Ontario and the explosion in railway construction that eventually led to the building of Canadian Pacific Railway (CPR) created visions of commercial, continental wealth that could only be accomplished by western expansion. [152] Two expeditions in the late 1850s, one British the other Canadian, established its physical geography and recognised the agricultural potential of the fertile belt stretching from the Red River settlement northwest to the Saskatchewan River and the Rockies. This reinforced the views of travellers who had begun to think of the western interior in terms of agricultural production rather than the fur trade and the buffalo herds. The Canadian desire for a new farming frontier in the 1850s and 1860s was stimulated by prosperity as much as by the fear of containment. For Canadian propagandists, the western interior was the keystone in the arch of the Canadian empire:[153]

> The NOW of this country finds a territory of immense extent occupied by about 14,000 civilized people; the THEN of ten years shall see a population of 500,000...Now the eye wanders, without a resting place over our unoccupied plains, then it shall be arrested by the happy homes of thousands which dot the horizon.[154]

Between 1862 and 1868, the Métis were afflicted by a series of environmental disasters that challenged their way of life: drought, prairie fires, grasshoppers and crop failures. The buffalo hunt gradually declined as competition for the diminishing herds increased and the lake fisheries were poor. There were also profound changes in the ways the Métis were regarded by an increasing number of settlers, a consequence of the widespread acceptance of the biological inferiority of some 'races' and, especially relevant to the Métis, theories of racial miscegenation that suggested marriage between 'races' diluted the blood stock of the superior race. The *Nor'Wester* commented in 1860 that after annexation, 'the indolent and the careless like the native tribes of the country will fall back before the march of superior intelligence.'[155] During the late 1860s, the Red River Settlement was also changing rapidly. Its population had been largely composed mainly of Francophone Métis, with a minority of English-speaking, mixed-race, 'country born' or Anglo-Métis and a small number of Presbyterian

[151] Owram, Doug, *Promise of Eden: The Canadian Expansionist Movement and the Idea of the West, 1856-1900*, (Toronto University Press), 1980, pp. 38-78, explores the expansionist campaign 'new worlds to conquer' between 1856 and 1869.
[152] Warner, Donald F., *The Idea of Continental Union: Agitation for the Annexation of Canada to the United States 1849-1893*, (University of Kentucky Press), 1960, pp. 99-127, considers the annexationist issues in relation to the Red River settlement.
[153] Sprague, Douglas N., *Canada and the Métis, 1869-1885*, (Wilfrid Laurier University Press), 1988, pp. 19-30.
[154] *Nor'Wester*, 21 September 1869. It was Red River's first newspaper, pro-annexationist in attitude.
[155] *Nor'Wester*, 14 January 1860.

Scottish settlers. From the early-1860s, increasing numbers of Anglophone Protestants settlers arrived from Ontario, generally insensitive to Métis culture, hostile to Roman Catholicism and many were advocates of Canadian expansionism. At the same time, many Americans migrated there, some of whom favoured annexation of the territory by the United States. These perceptions of race, class and religion reinforced social divisions in Red River even within the Métis. The English-speaking Métis saw themselves as part of a 'European or agricultural party' and closer to civilisation than the French-speaking Métis who continued to hunt or take part in trading expeditions and who seemed to be veering towards 'the native or aboriginal party'.[156] The problem was that the Canadian image of the Métis was distorted and incomplete.

Against this backdrop of religious, nationalist and racial tensions, political uncertainty was high and was now handled with monumental ineptness.[157] For the previous two centuries, the British government had been content to leave the fate of the western interior in the hands of the HBC. This view changed in the 1850s and especially the 1860s as its image of the land was influences by its responsibility for administering a North American empire within its world-wide possessions. To prevent United States' expansionism, the British and Canadian governments had been for some time negotiating the transfer of Rupert's Land from the HBC to Canada.[158] The Rupert's Land Act 1868 authorised the transfer and on 1 December 1869, Canada purchased the territory.[159] By treating the transfer of sovereignty from Britain to Canada simply as a land transaction, there had been no consideration of the residents on the land, no guarantee of native rights, of land title or participation in government by Canada, Britain or the HBC. In fact, the little contact that Ottawa had with the Red River settlers were numerous petitions beginning in 1857 from the small number of expansionists calling for development of the region. The government quickly jumped to the erroneous conclusion that the settlers of Red River wanted annexation and that no consultation was necessary.[160] This proved to be a costly blunder.[161]

---

156 Ibid, Friesen, Gerald, *The Canadian Prairies: A History*, pp. 92-97.

157 It is important not to overemphasise the divided and unstable nature of Red River. It exaggerates the weakness of the community while neglecting the extent to which Red River was integrated into the wider world in the 1850s and 1860s.

158 Before Confederation had been proclaimed on 1 July 1867, arrangements were already under way for the transfer of Rupert's Land to Canada. Paragraph 146 of the British North America Act laid the basis for that eventuality.

159 Creighton, D. G., *John A. Macdonald: Volume 2, The Old Chieftain*, (Macmillan), 1955, pp. 33-69, and Gwyn, Richard, *Nation Maker, Sir John A. Macdonald: His Life, Our Times, Volume 2: 1867-1891*, (Random House), 2011, pp. 86-140, examine how the Canadian government addressed the problem of the north-west to the Manitoba Act 1870.

160 Ibid, Owram, Doug, *Promise of Eden*, pp. 79-84, examines the development of expansionist rhetoric in the east and especially the role of the *Nor'Wester* in this process.

161 For the imperial view of event at Red River see, *Correspondence Relative to the Recent Disturbances in the Red River Settlement*, (William Clowes), 1870, and *Report on the Red River Expedition of 1870*, (William Clowes), 1871. See also, *The Red River Insurrection: Three Letters and a Narrative of Events*, (Aboriginals Protection Society), 1870, and Corbett, G. O., *The Red River Rebellion: The Cause of It in a Series of Letters to the British Government*, (Cassell, Peter & Galpin), 1870, for a Canadian nationalist perspective.

The terms of political authority were unresolved in the 1868 legislation and a political and legal vacuum existed in the territory.[162] If, in retrospect, Métis resistance was understandable, it should have been foreseen and there were warnings. French-Catholic Métis were unenthusiastic about Confederation and, fearing floods of agricultural settlers whose presence would make their hunting life untenable, would have preferred maintenance of HBC rule. Anglo-Métis, by contrast, were less dependent on the hunt, increasingly identified themselves with immigrants from Ontario, were religiously hostile to the French-Catholics and consequently were less eager to block the Canadian takeover. Their growing mistrust of the French Métis meant that they would only accept a British-Canadian Protestant view of the world and this explains why many opposed Riel's resistance in 1869 and 1870 though whether this constituted a 'civil war' between different Métis groups is debatable.[163] The critical issue was land. [164] The HBC had created a system of clear titles in British law along the Red and part of the Assiniboine Rivers but elsewhere there was no land law. In practice, the native concept of common property resources had given way to a system of open access and now to property ownership.

With unstable government and uncertain land rights, political tensions rose. Until the resistance, neither the Canadian government nor the expansionists had paid much attention to the Métis. It was assumed that their attitudes were the same as other segments of Red River society and consequently, they were ignored. Both Catholic and Anglican bishops and the HBC governor of Assiniboia warned the government that any land survey would precipitate unrest. The Métis took the survey to be a harbinger of increased Canadian migration to the territory. Many did not possess clear title to their lands that had been laid out in long, narrow ribbons assuring each landholder access to the river rather than the square lots preferred by the British. The survey party arrived at Fort Garry on 20 August 1869 without consultation or notice.[165] The result was a confrontation in which Louis Riel denounced the survey party in a speech delivered from the steps of Saint-Boniface Cathedral informing them that they had no right to be doing such work without the permission of the people. Riel's position was that the HBC's trade monopoly did not include rights over the land and the people and that before any transfer could be negotiated it would be necessary to deal with Amerindian and Métis rights. Recently returned from studying law in Montreal, Riel now took over the reins of Métis leadership.[166] For Riel, the issue was not simply one of owning the land they now farmed but a defence of Métis rights as full citizens in the new Confederation including the right to sit in government, to

[162] For Métis attitudes to Confederation see, Silver, A. I., *The French-Canadian Idea of Confederation, 1864-1900*, (University of Toronto Press), 1887, pp. 12-14, 74-87, 92-110,

[163] On religious tensions see, Pannekoek, F., 'The Rev. Griffiths Owen Corbett and the Red River Civil War of 1869-70', *CHR*, Vol. 57, (1976), pp. 133-149.

[164] Ibid, Sprague, Douglas N., *Canada and the Métis, 1869-1885*, pp. 19-66.

[165] Ibid, Sprague, Douglas N., *Canada and the Métis, 1869-1885*, pp. 35-40, deals with the survey party and Métis refusal to allow McDougall to enter Assiniboia.

[166] For Riel see, Stanley, George F., *Louis Riel*, (McGraw-Hill Ryerson), 1972, Siggins, Maggie, *Riel: A Life of* Revolution, (HarperCollins), 1994, Boyden, Joseph, *Louis Riel & Gabriel Dumont*, (Penguin), 2010, and Thomas, Lewis H., 'Louis Riel', *DCB*, Vol. 11, pp. 736-752.

hold jobs in the civil service and in the business, that would spring up. In addition to recognition of individual rights, the Métis also expressed vaguer and more complex collective cultural rights concerning language, faith, kinship and schools. By treating the western interior simply as property, the Canadian government exacerbated an already fragile situation. The appointment of the Francophobe William McDougall as the Lieutenant-Governor of the Northwest Territories-designate on 28 September 1869, in anticipation of a formal transfer of power to the Canadian government at the beginning of December reinforced Métis fears.[167]

Eastern newspapers saw this as a conspiracy rather than a desire for national recognition by the Métis.[168] Expansionists pointed to the role of Americans who had their own expansionist agenda reinforcing long-held concerns about American pretensions in the north-west. Although their influence rapidly declined the inclusion of some annexationists in Riel's provisional government in December 1869 and January 1870 gave some credence to their claims. The attitude of the HBC also came in for criticism and was seen by some as deliberately block Canadian annexation of the north-west. It is true that some HBC officials were sympathetic to the Métis but they were a small minority and at no time did the Canadian government accept that the HBC was involved in inciting and supporting the Métis resistance. Expansionists also saw the representatives of the Roman Catholic Church in Red River as aiding the Métis in their resistance.[169] This reflected the innate suspicion of Ontarians for Roman Catholics, a position reinforced by the active involvement of some clergy in the provisional government and the unwillingness of Alexandre Taché, bishop of St.-

[167] For the resistance that followed see, Canadian House of Commons, Select Committee on the Causes of the Difficulties in the North-West Territory in 1869-1870, *Report*, (Ottawa), 1874, MacBeth, Roderick George, *The Making of the Canadian West, being the Reminiscences of an Eyewitness*, (W. Briggs), 1898, Dugas, Georges, *Histoire véridique des faits qui ont preparé le mouvement des Métis à la Rivière-Rouge en 1869*, (Montreal), 1905, Morton, W. L., (ed.), *Alexander Begg's Red River journal; and other papers relative to the Red River resistance of 1869-1970*, (Champlain Society), 1956, and Bumsted, J. M., (ed.), *Reporting the Resistance: Alexander Begg and Joseph Hargrave on the Red River Resistance*, (University of Manitoba Press), 2003, McArthur, Alexander, *The Causes of the Rising in the Red River Settlement, 1869-1870*, (Manitoba Historical and Scientific Society), 1882, for contemporary comment. Bumsted, J. M., *The Red River Rebellion*, (Watson & Dwyer), 1996, is the most detailed modern study. See also, ibid, Owram, Doug, *Promise of Eden*, pp. 79-100, ibid, Sprague, Douglas N., *Canada and the Métis, 1869-1885*, pp. 33-66.

[168] See, for instance, the *Nor'Wester*, 29 November 1869, maintained the Métis had been led into rebellion while the *Globe*, 13 November 1869, pointed to the role of certain individuals' hostile to Confederation in stirring up discontent 'among the most foolish and ignorant of the population'.

[169] Lalonde, Andre N., 'The Attitude of the Roman Catholic Clergy towards the Rebellions in 1870 and 1885', *Native Studies Review*, Vol. 1, (1984), pp. 79-81, contrasts the tacit endorsement of Riel in 1869-1870 with its outright condemnation in 1884-1885. Dorge, Lionel, 'Bishop Taché and the Confederation of Manitoba, 1869-1870', Manitoba Historical Society, *Transactions*, 3rd series, Vol. 26, (1969-1970), pp. 93-109.

Boniface[170] to speak out against the rebellion: difficult since he was at the Vatican Council in Rome for much of the resistance.[171]

On 11 October, Riel and other Métis disrupted the survey's work and a week later this group organised as the 'National Committee' to represent Métis interest with John Bruce as president, Riel as secretary and two representatives were elected from each parish.[172] Because the Council of Assiniboia still had authority over the area, its representatives summoned Riel on 25 October to explain his actions. Riel declared that any attempt by McDougall to enter would be blocked unless the Canadians first negotiated terms with the Métis and with the general population of the settlement and on 2 November, the Métis turned back McDougall's party near the United States border and forced it to retreat to Pembina. The number of Riel's followers had grown rapidly. The same day Riel led about 400 Métis in seizing Upper Fort Garry without bloodshed. This was a very able tactical decision since in addition to seizing arms and sufficient pemmican to feed an army for the winter, it enabled Riel to negotiate from a position of military strength. Riel was accused of rebellion which he denied insisting throughout the resistance that the Métis were loyal subjects of the Crown. The Métis resistance did not involve all the French-speaking community and it won and lost supporters during its ten-month life. Riel was opposed by Canadian annexationists associated with Dr. John Christian Schultz, who had been at Red River for nearly a decade and recent Ontario settlers west of Winnipeg on the Assiniboine River as well as by the Indians in the 'Lower Settlement' where British patriotism was strong. Riel's support came from largely Roman Catholic clergy, American settlers and many French-speaking Métis though their enthusiasm for the resistance was erratic. There was also a volatile group of French and Anglo-Métis and many English-speaking settlers who were prepared to support either side depending on the issue or circumstances.[173]

---

[170] Benoit, D. P., *Vie de Monseigneur Taché, Archevêque de Saint-Boniface,* 2 Vols. (Librarie Beauchemin), 1904, remains the most detailed study. Taché, Alexandre, *Vingt Annees de Missions Dans Le Nord-Ouest de L'Amerique*, (Eusèbe Senécal), 1866, is a narrative account, written in the form of yearly journals, of Oblate missionary work in the West 1845-1866.

[171] *Globe*, 11 December 1869, was especially critical of clergy who 'worked on the ignorance and fears of the French speaking portion of the people to such an extent as to lead them to armed resistance.'

[172] One of the problems with understanding Riel during the resistance is the paucity of contemporary material from Riel or other French writers. Riel's own writings on events in 1869 and 1870, especially *L'Amnestie: Mémoire sur les causes des troubles du Nord-Ouest* published in 1874, Louis Schmidt's *Memoirs*, published in *Le Patriot de l'Ouest* in 1912 and articles by Joseph Dubuc in *La Minerve* in late 1870 were written after the event and are explanatory and defensive.

[173] Whether the events at Red River were a rebellion is a moot point. There is no doubt that there was resistance to the imposition of change by the Canadian government and that that resistance included the use of arms but for there to be a rebellion, it needs to be directed against a legally constituted authority. The critical issue therefore is what was the legally constituted authority in Red River between November 1869 and May 1870? Was it the HBC or the Canadian government in Ottawa or both? Or was Riel caught in a constitutional vacuum between the end of one legal authority and the beginning of another? What was the legal status of the provisional government? Although Canadian

This was evident in the problems Riel faced with the residents of the Red River Settlement because they disagreed over how to negotiate with Canada. In a conciliatory gesture and because he wanted to create common cause with all groups in the settlement, on 6 November Riel asked the English-speaking inhabitants to elect delegates to attend a convention with the Métis representatives but this proved largely unsuccessful. Ten days later, the Council of Assiniboia made a final unsuccessful attempt to assert its authority calling on the Métis to lay down their arms. Instead, on 23 November, Riel proposed the formation of a provisional government to enter into direct negotiations with Canada but without the support of the English-speakers. On 1 December, McDougall proclaimed that the HBC was no longer in control of Rupert's Land, but this was to later prove problematic, as it effectively ended the authority of the Council, while failing to establish Canadian authority since unbeknown to McDougall, the transfer had been postponed once news of the unrest reached Ottawa.[174] Canadian loyalists saw this as justification for putting down those in arms against constituted authority and the Red River community moved to the brink of armed conflict. A loosely organised, pro-Canadian minority led by John Schultz and Charles Mair supported by militia major Charles Boulton now proposed to attack Upper Fort Carry and arrest Riel but Riel acted quickly and arrested them on 7 December.[175] He established a provisional government the following day.[176] Riel presented the convention with a moderate list of fourteen rights to be demanded as a condition of union included representation in Parliament, a bilingual legislature and chief justice and recognition of certain land claims. While the convention did not adopt a second modified list until early February 1870, most English-speakers accepted the bulk of the demands as reasonable.[177]

---

expansionists and the Ontario press certainly saw events as part of a rebellion, Riel took a more sanguine view seeing resistance as part of a negotiating strategy to achieve defined Métis rights.

[174] MacDougall, W. M., *The Red River Rebellion: Eight Letters to Hon. Joseph Howe in reply to an official pamphlet*, (Hunter, Rose & Co.), 1870, gives MacDougall's view of events in which he was highly critical of the government's reactions. See also, *Red River Insurrection: Hon. Wm. McDougall's Conduct Reviewed,* (John Lovell), 1870, for official views.

[175] See, Latham, David, 'Charles Mair', *DCB*, Vol. 15, online, Clark, Lovell, 'Sir John Christian Schultz', *DCB*, Vol. 12, pp. 949-954. See also, Bumsted, J. M., with the assistance of Wendy Owen, 'John Christian Schultz and the Founding of Manitoba', in his *Thomas Scott's Body and Other Essays on Early Manitoba History*, (University of Manitoba Press), 2000, pp. 163-178.

[176] Flanagan, Thomas, 'Political Theory of the Red River Resistance: The Declaration of December 8, 1869', *Canadian Journal of Political Science,* Vol. 11, (1978), pp. 153-164.

[177] The provisional government produced a further list of rights in March 1870 and these formed the basis of negotiations with the Canadian government in Ottawa. They included: establishing a province that was not liable for any portion of the public debt of the dominion; that it have control of the public lands; that treaties with Indians accord with the wishes of the province; that the English and French languages be used in the provincial legislature and courts and in all public documents and acts; that the lieutenant-governor and the judge of the superior court should be familiar with both the English and the French languages; that an amnesty be extended to all members of the provisional government and its servants; and that no further customs duties be imposed until there was uninterrupted

Prime Minister Sir John A. Macdonald sought to defuse the situation.[178] He concluded, rightly that expansionist arrogance and Métis suspicions lay behind the resistance and that what was needed was a patient and conciliatory approach. Since he saw the movement as a search for political guarantees under Confederation, then he needed to find a political solution. In Ottawa, the Governor General Lord Lisgar had, at Macdonald's behest, proclaimed an amnesty on 6 December for all in Red River who would lay down their arms. He dispatched two commissioners, Abbé Jean-Baptiste Thibault and Charles-René d'Irumberry de Salaberry on a mission of reconciliation, but failed to give them authority to negotiate on behalf of the Government. He also appointed Donald Alexander Smith, chief factor in charge of HBC affairs in North America, as a special commissioner with greater authority to negotiate. Nonetheless, Macdonald prepared for a military expedition in the summer of 1870. On 27 December, John Bruce resigned as president of the provisional government and Riel was elected president. On the same day Donald Smith arrived in the settlement, followed shortly by de Salaberry, joining Thibault, who had arrived on Christmas Day. They met with Riel on January 5 1870, but reached no conclusions. Smith's goal was to negotiate the transfer with the people of Red River while Riel wanted Canada to deal only with the provisional government. The result was a series of public meetings beginning on 19 January and, with the settlement firmly behind him, Riel proposed the formation of a new convention of forty representatives, split evenly between French- and English-speaking settlers, to consider the Canadian government's intention to grant representation and its willingness to extend concessions with respect to land claims. By 10 February, when the meetings ended, Riel had won his way.[179]

It now appeared that a united front had been achieved in the settlement. The pro-American element that was intriguing in favour of annexation to the United States and promoting it through the *New Nation* begun in Winnipeg on 7 January saw its limited influence on events diminishing. On the other hand, Schultz and Mair were determined to eliminate Métis power but misjudged the willingness of the country-born and Scottish settlers to oppose the Métis. Having either escaped from the prison at Fort Garry or being paroled, Schultz, Mair and , variously described as a surveyor or a labourer sought to overthrow the provisional government.[180] They failed and Schultz and Mair fled to Ontario but

---

railway communication between Winnipeg and St Paul. Before the delegates left, a provision was added for separate schools according to the system existing in the province of Quebec, and outlined the structure for a provincial government.

[178] Creighton, D. G., *John A. Macdonald: Volume 2, The Old Chieftain*, (Macmillan), 1955, pp. 33-69, and Gwyn, Richard, *Nation Maker, Sir John A. Macdonald: His Life, Our Times, Volume 2: 1867-1891*, (Random House), 2011, pp. 86-140, examine how the Canadian government addressed the problem of the North-West.

[179] Ibid, Sprague, Douglas N., *Canada and the Métis, 1869-1885*, pp. 46-50, deals with Smith's diplomatic mission. For Smith's own view of events see, Willson, H. B., *Lord Strathcona, The Story of his Life*, (George N. Morang), 1902, Appendix A: 'Hon. Donald A. Smith's own narrative of events during the Red River Rebellion, 1869-1870', pp. 252-279, and Redford, Alexander, 'Donald A. Smith, 1st Baron Strathcona and Mount Royal', *DCB*, Vol. 14, pp. 939-947.

[180] Rea, J. E., 'Thomas Scott', *DCB*, Vol. 9, pp. 707-709.

Boulton and Scott were arrested.[181] Although both were sentenced to death, Boulton was pardoned but Scott, an inconsequential figure whose contempt for his Métis guards probably sealed his fate, was executed by a firing squad on 4 March.[182] Although the Ontario press soon established his Orange Order credentials, it appears that his execution was not caused by either his membership of the Order since there is no evidence that anyone in Red River knew before or immediately after his death that he was a member of the Orange Order. Indeed, Bumsted suggests that had his affiliations been known they might well have saved his life. Why Riel allowed the execution to take place has divided historians especially as they, like Riel himself, consider it his one great political blunder because he had created a 'political martyr'.[183] His own justification was that he felt it necessary to demonstrate to the Canadians that the Métis must be taken seriously: 'We must make Canada respect us'.[184]

To French Canada, Riel and the Provisional government would come to stand as a geographically and culturally distant 'provisional' ally and instrument in fulfilling French Canadian priorities. During the early months of the Provisional government, there was little support for the Métis from Quebec or serious criticism of the federal government. This changed with the execution of Thomas Scott when the rage of English Canada toward the Métis and Riel provoked French Canada to come to their defence. *Le Journal des Trois-Rivières*, for instance, asserted that 'the inhabitants of Ontario want to see a policy adopted that will undermine French influence in the North-West...on that point the Province of Québec will have only one answer: to protect and assist our brothers out there.'[185] French Canada had quickly developed a fraternal identification with

---

[181] For Major Charles Boulton's view of events and his visceral hatred of Riel see, Robertson Heather, (ed.), *I Fought Riel: A Military Memoir*, (Lorimer & Company), 1985, pp. 3-69.

[182] Ibid, Sprague, Douglas N., *Canada and the Métis, 1869-1885*, pp. 50-51, suggested that it was to be a 'mock' execution and that the firing squad is said to have loaded their guns only with 'powder and wad'. Although this story appeared in the American press within a few days, it never appeared in the Ontario newspapers for whom Scott had been murdered by a 'half breed papal rabble'. Riel never attempted to shift responsibility to O'Donoghue, though just after the execution he did say it had been 'mismanaged' without specifying how. See, Spry, Irene, (ed.), 'The Memories of George William Sanderson', *Canadian Ethnic Studies*, Vol. 17, (1985), pp. 115-134, and Stanley, George F. G., 'William Bernard O'Donoghue', *DCB*, Vol. 10, pp. 556-557.

[183] Ibid, Siggins, Maggie, *Riel: A Life of Revolution*, pp. 161-165, is one of the few historians who gives some credence to the notion that the execution, whether one agreed with it or not, was the legitimate act of a sovereign government. Many historians, whether generally sympathetic or not to Riel and the Rebellion, view the execution as a rash mistake or, at worse, cold blooded murder.

[184] Bumsted, J. M., 'Thomas Scott's Body', and 'Why Shoot Thomas Scott? A Study in Historical Evidence', in ibid, *Thomas Scott's Body and Other Essays on Early Manitoba History*, pp. 3-10, 197-210, seek to provide an explanation from the mass of contradictory evidence. He concluded that Scott may have still been alive after being shot by the firing squad and by an officer who shot him in the head to complete the botched execution but this did not prove fatal and he was dispatched later in the day, according to one report, by Riel himself.

[185] *Le Journal des Trois-Rivières*, 18 April 1870.

the Métis people and the cause of the Provisional government. For the English, the Métis resistance was an indigenous rebellion against settler sovereignty, but for French-Canadians, Métis claims reflected their own concerns about the future of English-French relations. In many respects, the resolution of the Red River resistance was the result of English and French Canada seeking to resolve their own particular tensions within Confederation. The English wanted to crush the resistance and the French wanted a province west of Ontario constitutionally supportive of French Canadian language culture: 'to please Québec they negotiated with the Red River delegates; to placate Ontario they dispatched the military force.'[186]

The focus now moved to Ontario.[187] Mair and Schultz arrived in Toronto and immediately set about inflaming anti-Métis and anti-Catholic sentiment over the execution of Scott in the editorial pages of the Ontario press. Nevertheless, Macdonald had decided before the provisional government was established that Canada must negotiate with the Métis. Although the delegates were arrested following their arrival in Ottawa on April 11 on charges of abetting Scott's murder, they were quickly released and soon entered into direct talks with the government. An agreement enshrining many of the demands in the list of rights was soon reached and formed the basis for the Manitoba Act of 12 May that admitted Manitoba into the Canadian Confederation on 15 July 1870. It contained most of the rights demanded by the Métis including responsible government and provincial status, bilingual institutions, denominational schools, guarantees of land title and federal respect for Indian title. The legislation provided for substantial grants of land to Métis inhabitants of the new province: 1.4 million acres to be distributed to the 'children of the half-breed heads of families', confirmation of title to the river lots that the old settlers, most of whom were Métis, had already occupied; and, grants of land to commute the 'rights of hay and common' that settlers had enjoyed under the HBC regime. Macdonald, a skillful negotiator, had not created a province of the North-West but a small self-governing province of Manitoba, one hundred miles square, and the North-West Territories, a vast area governed from Ottawa.

For Riel it was an acceptable deal although demands for amnesty for those involved in the resistance were not granted in writing even if some verbal reassurances were given. Anger over Scott's execution had hardened in Ontario and a guarantee of amnesty was not politically expedient. Whether Macdonald promised an amnesty remains a contentious issue at the time. Certainly he and his Minister of Militia and Defence, George-Étienne Cartier allowed Riel's emissaries to believe that a general amnesty from Britain would be forthcoming but whether one was actually promised is another matter.[188] Although militarily

[186] Ibid, Stanley, George F., *The Birth of Western Canada*, p. 145.

[187] Ibid, Sprague, Douglas N., *Canada and the Métis, 1869-1885*, pp. 55-66, considers the negotiations in Ottawa.

[188] The problem with amnesty was that Macdonald thought of it as exclusive of those charged with Scott's murder while Riel's emissaries always included them. The *Globe* was normally highly critical of Macdonald, but concluded in 1874 that Macdonald had fallen 'short of pledging the government to grant an amnesty'. See ibid, Gwyn, Richard, *Nation Maker, Sir John A. Macdonald: His Life, Our Times, Volume 2: 1867-1891*, pp. 150-152.

unnecessary, but important as a means of exercising Canadian authority in the settlement, dissuading the Minnesota expansionists and as a sop to Ontarian nationalists fuming over Scott's death, a military expedition of 800 militia from Ontario and Quebec and 400 British regulars under a British officer Colonel Garnet Wolseley, was dispatched to the Red River on what the Canadian government described as an 'errand of peace'. It raised religious and racial issues that had been muted during the resistance to the fore. French-Canadian opposition was regarded in Ontario as a sign of disloyalty and the focus of the conspiratorial analysis of the rebellion shifted with greater emphasis on the role played by priests.[189] Riel and the Métis were increasingly identified with the case of French-Canadian rights. In the absence of civil government until 2 September when Adams George Archibald, the new Lieutenant-Governor, [190] arrived and learning that some of the Canadian militia in the expedition had threatened to lynch him, Riel fled as the expedition approached the Red River on 24 August and Wolseley's arrival marked the effective end of resistance.[191]

The Pembina raid in October 1871 represented an epilogue to the Red River resistance.[192] According to William O'Donoghue, the Métis were ready to rise up and join the Fenians. The notion of a joint attack by Métis and Fenians may appear unlikely but, despite different ethnic backgrounds, the Pembina Métis and Irish-Americans had things in common. They were both Roman Catholics and shared a less than positive experience of British rule. O'Donoghue hoped that by mobilising the Métis to join the United States he could hurt Great Britain and help the cause of Irish independence. Although he had been closely associated with Riel's Provisional Government in 1869-1870, Riel did not endorse

---

[189] *Globe*, 14 April 1870, addressed criticism of Ontarian militancy in the Quebec press: 'If anyone is fanatical in this matter, it is certainly not the people of Upper Canada [Ontario] who desire merely to seek law and order restored in the Territory...the fanatics are the French Canadians who are striving to obtain for themselves peculiar and exclusive privileges.'

[190] Pryke, K. G., 'Sir Adams George Archibald', *DCB*, Vol. 12, pp. 30-36. See also, Bowles, R. S., 'Adams George Archibald, first lieutenant-governor of Manitoba', Manitoba Historical Society, *Transactions*, 3rd series, no. 25, (1968-1969), pp. 75-88.

[191] Wolseley, Garnet, Joseph, 1st Viscount, *The Story of a Soldier's Life*, 2 Vols. (Constable & Co.), 1903, Vol. 2, pp. 145-225, describes his involvement in the Red River campaign while Huyshe, George L., *The Red River Expedition*, (Macmillan and Co.), 1871, provides a description of the expedition by one of Wolseley's staff. See also, Sulte, Benjamin, *L'expédition militaire du Manitoba, 1870,* (E. Senécal), 1871, and Smith, James Patterson, 'The Riel Rebellion of 1869: New Light on British Liberals and the Use of Force on the Canadian Frontier', *Journal of Canadian Studies,* Vol. 30, (2), (1995), pp. 58-73.

[192] For reports on the raid see, *Ottawa Free Press*, 13, 14 October 1871, *New York Times*, 13 October 1871, *Hartford Weekly Times*, 14 October 1871. Stanley, George F. G., *Toil & trouble: military expeditions to Red River*, (Dundurn Press), 1989, pp. 202-286, provides important context while Brown, Richard, *Famine, Fenians and Freedom, 1830-1882*, pp. 494-500, examines the raid as the third Fenian incursion into Canada. See also Tremaudan, A. H. de, 'Louis Riel and the Fenian Raid of 1871', *Canadian Historical Review*, Vol. 4, (1923), pp. 132-144, Stanley, Georges F. G., 'L'invasion Fenienne au Manitoba. Un journal contemporain', *Revue d'histoire de l'Amérique française*, Vol. 17, (2) (1963), pp. 260-268, and Swann, Ruth, and Jerome, Edward A., 'Unequal justice: The Métis in O'Donoghue's Raid of 1871', *Manitoba History*, Vol. 39, (2000), pp. 24-38.

O'Donoghue's attempts to annexe the North West to the United States, believing that he 'was more concerned with striking a blow at Great Britain than with relieving the plight of the Métis.'[193] The raid, on 5 October 1871, was a comical affair. The small band of rebels seized the HBC post just north of the border but the raid was fated from the start. In fact, there was no invasion of Canada at all. Revisions to the international border had placed the HBC post in American territory and two Métis subsequently captured O'Donoghue and turned him over to the American Government. Although the Métis in the Red River Valley had good reasons for assisting the Fenians, the majority under Riel's leadership decided to support the new Canadian regime and Riel offered a force of Métis cavalry to Lieutenant-Governor Archibald, but some were sufficiently disillusioned to support the Fenians. Unlike the Fenians who escaped to Minnesota and beyond, the Pembina Métis were arrested and brought to Winnipeg for trial. Canadian officials were aware of O'Donoghue's involvement and, given the strong feelings against the Métis in Ontario it is probable that they were trying to implicate Riel in the Fenian raid to arrest him.[194]

Most recent historians have dismissed the raid as marginal to the mainstream of Canadian history but this was not the view of the Canadian authorities:

> We have passed through a frightful crisis and have escaped by the skin of our teeth...The danger was not from without, but within...But if 200 French Halfbreeds had joined them on the frontier, we should have had a rough time of it.[195]

The combination of Irish-American soldiers aided by Minnesota and Pembina speculators wanting new territory combined with dissident Métis was a genuine threat. Their fear was that, if dissatisfied Métis supported American annexationists Manitoba would withdraw from Confederation and join the United States.

The Red River rebellion was essentially non-violent resistance directed against government policy. It was non-violent largely because the physical remoteness of the Red River settlement made an immediate governmental resort to coercion impossible. In fact, the federal government showed considerable restraint in resisting strong Ontarian pressure to avenge Scott's death and succeeded in not provoking the Metis into prolonging their resistance or resisting the advance of the Wolseley expedition. Riel was also able to impose and largely maintain discipline on the armed Metis and sought to secure co-operation with the diverse elements on Red River. The violence that did occur was the consequence of breakdowns in discipline and unity on both sides: for Riel and the Metis, the challenge posed by the Canadian party and the exemplary execution of Scott; for the federal government, McDougall's unauthorised attempt to seize power and possibly some members of the Ontarian militia taking the law into their own hands. There was no official violence between the two sides. In fact,

---

[193] Ibid, Stanley, George F. G., 'William Bernard O'Donoghue', p. 557.

[194] Ibid, Swann, Ruth, and Jerome, Edward A., 'Unequal justice: The Métis in O'Donoghue's Raid of 1871', especially pp. 30-38.

[195] Archibald to Macdonald, 13 October 1871, cit, ibid, Swan, Ruth, and Jerome, Edward A., 'Unequal justice: The Métis in O'Donoghue's Raid of 1871', p. 24.

both Riel and the federal government showed a degree of political acumen recognising an awareness of what was possible and what was necessary.[196]

For the emerging Canadian state, the events between 1869 and 1871 had resulted in the transfer of the north-west to Canada rather than the United States and had established Canada as a continent-wide nation. Riel had given the Métis a political voice, won a temporary victory on land tenure, a political and institutional structure through which they would assert their rights and, with the creation of Manitoba, a buffer against Canadian expansion that was increasingly grounded in Canadian Protestantism. But, he had been forced into exile and the victories achieved for the Métis through their resistance could easily be overturned. Riel's vision for the Métis, yet not millenarian in nature, was to develop during the 1870s and early 1880s as the victories achieved in 1869 and 1870 were gradually eroded. The resistance had achieved its major objectives, a distinct province with land and cultural rights guaranteed but it proved a hollow victory for the Métis.

Transition

Without an amnesty, Riel had fled to the safety of the St. Joseph's mission across the border in the Dakota Territory but did not return to Manitoba until May 1871 largely because stress and financial troubles precipitated a serious illness, perhaps a precursor of his future mental problems. During the exaggerated threat of Fenian invasion, on 4 October Archibald issued a general call to arms. Companies of armed horsemen were raised, including one led by Riel and when he reviewed the troops in St. Boniface on 8 October, he made the significant gesture of publicly shaking Riel's hand, knowing that this would cause problems. When this news reached Ontario, Mair and members of the Canada First movement manufactured a resurgence of anti-Riel and anti-Archibald sentiment. On 25 November, Archibald sent in his resignation in order, he said, to give the government a free hand in dealing with the controversy that had developed over his actions. He also privately informed Macdonald that the Prime Minister's rejection of his conduct reflected a complete lack of understanding of the situation in Manitoba arguing that his policies were approved by most residents in the province and according to the principles of self-government their views should be his sole guide. It was not until October 1872 that he finally left the province.

The major problem facing Archibald was the geographical isolation of Manitoba that made direct communications with Ottawa almost impossible until a telegraph line through the United States was completed in November 1871.[197] He also had to deal with the factional bitterness that survived the resistance especially as a minority of Canadian loyalists led by Schultz was prepared to use violence in exacting retribution from Métis leaders and many Métis were sullen and suspicious of Archibald. There was also a lack of political experience in the province largely because the political organisation of Assiniboia had needed only

---

[196] Torrance, Judy M., *Public Violence in Canada, 1867-1982*, (McGill-Queen's University Press), 1986, pp. 17-19.

[197] Milligan, F. A., 'The Establishment of Manitoba's First Provincial Government', Manitoba Historical and Scientific Society, *Transactions*, 3rd series, no. 5, (1968-1949), pp. 5-18.

to be simple to meet the simple needs of the colony. Until elections for the Manitoba legislature were held on 30 December 1870, Archibald ruled by proclamation. During the election campaign, in which Archibald took a personal interest in trying to return a moderate body representing all interests and ethnic groups, a clear division emerged between three groups: a Government party that sought to forget past problems and heal factional divisions; a solid Métis bloc that was allied with but separate from the Government party whose support came largely from French-speakers; and a loyalist opposition led by Schultz that demanded punishment of the leaders of the resistance. In the elections, the Government party won an overwhelming victory. Only five loyalist candidates were returned and one of these was subsequently unseated in favour of a Government supporter. None of the settlers from Ontario including Schultz was elected. Archibald formed his government in January 1871, appointed his Legislative Council on 10 March and opened the first session of the Provincial Legislature on 15 March.[198] Its bicameral system was modelled on that of Quebec rather than the unicameral system of Ontario.[199]

Despite his considerable success in establishing an effective machinery of central and local government during 1871, something recognised in Ottawa as well as in Manitoba, there was much over which Archibald had little control such as the continuing sense of grievance among the Métis over amnesty.[200] Nor did he have the authority to distribute the 1,400,000 acres promised the Métis in the Manitoba Act.[201] However, he decided to intervene in July 1871 when a group of Métis complained that while they had been on the plains, settlers from Ontario had staked out claims by the Rivière aux Îlets-de-Bois that they renamed the Boyne River. This posed a direct challenge to the Métis system of common lands while the new name emphasised the religious and ethnic nature of the confrontation. Sensitive to the seriousness of the provocation, Archibald attempted to make the Métis aware of the folly of offering any resistance to the

---

[198] Although Henry Clarke was the Government leader in the Legislature and is sometimes regarded as the first premier, in practice the functions of premier were performed by Archibald himself. He argued that, in addition to his executive powers as Lieutenant-Governor, he needed to direct the legislative programme necessary to complete the constitution of the Province.

[199] In 1874, when a delegation of Manitobans went to Ottawa to demand additional financial support from the federal government, it was suggested that the province should curtail its expenditure by abolishing its Legislative Council, something the Council refused to accept. See, Stevenson, Gareth, *Ex Uno Plures: Federal-Provincial Relations in Canada, 1867-1896*, (McGill-Queen's University Press), 1997, pp. 146-147.

[200] Taché, Alexandre A., *L'Amnistie,* (Impr. par le journal 'Le nouveau monde'), 1874 and *The Amnesty Again, or, Charges Refuted,* (Printed at 'The Standard' Office), 1875, examine the corrosive impact of this issue. See also, Jonasson, Jonas A., 'The Red River Amnesty Question', *Pacific Historical Review,* Vol. 6, (1937), pp. 58-66, and Huel, Raymond J. A., *Archbishop A.-A. Taché of St. Boniface: The 'Good Fight' and the Illusive Vision*, (University of Alberta Press), 2003, pp. 103-142.

[201] Kemp, H. Douglas, 'Land Grants under the Manitoba Act', Manitoba Historical Society, *Transactions*, third series, no. 9, (1952-1953), pp. 33-52, Friesen, J., 'Expansion of Settlement in Manitoba, 1870-1890', Manitoba Historical Society, *Transactions*, third series, no. 20, (1963-1964), pp. 35-48, and Ens, Gerhard, 'Métis Lands in Manitoba 1870-1887', *Manitoba History,* Vol. 5, (1983), pp. 2-11.

settlers while advising them to file claims to consolidate their existing communities. He was convinced that they would soon sell off their land scrip to settlers who would be better able to exploit the land. His strategy was designed to appease the Métis in the short term without interfering with the long-term strategies of the federal government. Unfortunately, his actions contradicted recent federal policy that allowed Ontario settlers to stake claims on unsurveyed lands. He was curtly rebuked by Joseph Howe, Secretary of State for the Provinces and Macdonald was unwilling to consider Archibald's opinion. Macdonald may well have been influenced by fears about the potential electoral impact of the Orange vote in Ontario. At the same time, he gave little indication of any understanding of or sympathy for the Métis. The incident of the Rivière aux Îlets-de-Bois weakened Archibald's position in Ottawa, aggravated the federal government's grievance against the Métis and fed the deeply held conviction of some Métis that they had been betrayed by Ottawa.[202]

Riel wanted land transferred to the Métis en bloc to ensure the cultural and political integrity of what he saw as the Métis Nation. The tragedy for the Métis was that he was physically absent in the crucial period of land distribution and, in the absence of a leader with Riel's political acumen and vision the Métis nation disintegrated between 1870 and 1885. This is reflected in Riel's failure to marshal the level of support on the Saskatchewan River in 1885 as he had at Red River fifteen years earlier. Until the 1970s, most historians viewed the intentions, if not the consequences, of federal government in relation to land grants favourably.[203] The rapid alienation of Métis land was blamed on the overwhelming numbers of Ontario settlers arriving in Manitoba after 1870, the 'thriftless' and 'improvident' character of the Métis and land speculators who took advantage of the unwitting Métis. This view came under attack in the 1970s and 1980s when historians re-examined the alienation of Métis land grants. They concluded that the Métis were not improvident and nomadic people but 'persistent settlers' strongly attached to their land and that the rapid alienation of their land was the result, not of Ontarian settlers or speculators, but of dispossession as a result of the federal government not allowing the bulk of land grants to pass into Métis hands. Although there is disagreement over the extent of government dishonesty and its complicity with speculators, the Métis acquired only a fraction of the land to which they were entitled and because of this alienation, many Red River Métis left Manitoba.[204]

More recent studies suggest that the Métis had little difficulty receiving title to the lands promised them in the Manitoba Act, that they behaved rationally in the land market of the 1870s and 1880s, and that they received, on the whole, substantial monetary benefits when they sold these lands and that there is no evidence that difficulty in getting title to land drove the Métis to leave Manitoba.[205]

---

[202] See also, Milne, Brad, 'The Historiography of Métis Land Dispersal, 1870-1890', *Manitoba History,* Vol. 30, (1995), pp. 30-41.

[203] See, for instance, ibid, Creighton, D. G., *John A. Macdonald: The Old Chieftain*, pp. 386-387, and ibid, Morton, W. L., *Manitoba: A History*, pp. 147-155.

[204] Ibid, Sprague, D. N., *Canada and the Métis, 1869-1885*, and ibid, Friesen, G., *The Canadian Prairies: A History*, pp. 197-199.

[205] Flanagan, Thomas and Ens, Gerhard, 'Métis Land Grants in Manitoba, A Statistical Study, *Histoire sociale/Social History*, Vol. 27, (1994), pp. 65-87.

Métis communities had already been established in the interior of Western Canada before 1869. In 1821, the union of the NWC and the HBC had thrown hundreds of mixed-blood employees out of work. Rather than go to Red River, many Métis chose to remain in the interior settling on transportation routes with reliable food supplies. Nascent settlements of scattered cabins occurred at Cold Lake, Lesser Slave Lake, Lac La Biche, Beaver River, Hay Lake, Egg Lake, and at various locations on the Saskatchewan plains, particularly where trails crossed the major rivers. In the 1860s, some of these settlements attracted missionaries and experienced increased stability and growth. In 1865, Lac St. Anne was founded and in 1866, St. Albert. Initially, none of these settlements had ties with Red River but, after the exodus following the resistance in 1869-1870 almost all of them attracted refugees from Red River. It is now believed that the increase in the number of Métis wintering settlements in the 1870s was due to the economics of the buffalo robe trade, not to migrations from Red River. While some of these communities were temporary, others became the home for missionaries and for Métis merchants, who initially profited from the trade. When the robe trade collapsed in the late 1870s, some larger settlements became more permanent. There was a strong interior Métis tradition distinct from that of the Red River Métis and that it was the buffalo robe trade, not the economics and politics of Red River that shaped the Métis communities of the interior.[206]

If the revisionist argument is correct, then the Métis diaspora, the migration and dispersal of the Métis after the 1869 resistance in Manitoba and the Riel Rebellion of 1885 in the North-West Territories cannot be explained simply in terms of the aggressive economics and innate racism and religious bigotry of Ontarian immigrants. Stanley, for instance, maintained that the Métis could not cope with the changing economic environment and this pushed them further into the interior and that 1885 marked the end of the Métis nation, its last stand. The reasons for the Métis diaspora to the Saskatchewan country and to the United States were far more complex. The grasshopper plagues of the 1860s, for instance, drove some Red River Métis to St. Laurent on Lake Manitoba, to the White Mud River valley and to the mouth of the Winnipeg River. While admitting that there were economic hardships and racism after 1870, historians now point to the increasing division within Métis society between a merchant class and a buffalo-hunting class that worked almost exclusively on producing buffalo hides for the Eastern markets. In this interpretation, the Métis had adapted well to their new economic realities and had become successful farmers, merchants and professionals and that, far from being pushed out of Red River, they were attracted by economic opportunities in the Western interior. This reinforces the view that, in addition to being part of a mobile community, the Métis were also persistent settlers.

During the 1870s and early 1880s, Ontario and Quebec seemed to be battling over the future of the North-West. With Federal elections in 1872, Macdonald could ill-afford further deterioration in relations between Quebec and Ontario. In Ontario, however, Riel was widely denounced as Thomas Scott's 'murderer' and a reward of $5,000 was offered by Edward Blake, the Premier of

[206] Ens, G., *Homeland to Hinterland: The Changing Worlds of the Red River Métis in the Nineteenth Century*, (University of Toronto Press), 1996.

Ontario for his arrest. In Quebec he was regarded as a hero, a defender of the Roman Catholic faith and French culture in Manitoba. Anxious to avoid a political confrontation between Ontario and Quebec, Sir John A. Macdonald tried to persuade Riel to remain in voluntary exile in the United States, even providing him with funds. Riel accepted, arriving in St. Paul on 2 March 1872, but encouraged by his friends and back in Manitoba by June, Riel entered federal politics. Successful in a by-election in 1873, he stood aside so that George-Etienne Cartier, who had been defeated in his home riding in Quebec and was on record of being in favour of amnesty for Riel, might secure a seat.[207] However, Riel's hopes for a swift resolution to the amnesty question were dashed following Cartier's death on 20 May 1873. In the ensuing by-election in October 1873, Riel ran unopposed as an Independent, although, after a warrant was issued for his arrest in September he had again fled. He later made his way to Montreal and, fearing arrest or assassination, vacillated as to whether he should attempt to take up his seat in the House of Commons and he was the only Member of Parliament who was not present for the great Pacific Scandal debate of 1873 that led to the resignation of the Macdonald government in November.[208] Liberal leader Alexander Mackenzie became the interim prime minister and a general election was held in January 1874. In the general election of 1874, Riel went to Ottawa and but was expelled from the House on a motion introduced by the Ontario Orange leader Mackenzie Bowell. Although re-elected, Riel did not attempt to take his seat again. Meanwhile, Ambroise Lépine, a member of Riel's provisional government who presided over Thomas Scott's trial, was arrested, tried and in October 1874 sentenced to death for his 'murder'.[209] This sparked outrage in the sympathetic Quebec press and calls for amnesty for both Lépine and Riel were renewed. This presented a severe political difficulty for Mackenzie, who was hopelessly caught between the demands of Quebec and Ontario, until acting on his own initiative the Governor-General Lord Dufferin commuted Lépine's sentence in January 1875 to two years' imprisonment and loss of political rights.[210] In February 1875, this allowed Mackenzie to secure

---

[207] Young, Brian, *George-Etienne Cartier, Montreal Bourgeois*, (McGill-Queen's University Press), 1981, pp. 119-126, and Boyd, John, *Sir George Etienne Cartier, bart.: His Life and Times,* (Ayer Publishing), 1914, pp. 310-346, examine his role in Canadian politics from 1870 until his death.

[208] Ibid, Creighton, D. G., *John A. Macdonald: Volume 2, The Old Chieftain*, pp. 129-179, examines the Pacific Scandal. See also, *Royal Commission on the Canadian Pacific Railway*, (Canada, House of Commons Journal, appendix 1), 1873, and *Correspondence relative to the Canadian Pacific Railway*, (William Clowes), 1874.

[209] *Preliminary Investigation and Trial of Ambroise D. Lepine for the Murder of Thomas Scott,* (Burland-Desbarats), 1874, provides valuable detail on the issue. See also, Ens, Gerhard J., 'Ambroise-Dydime Lépine', *DCB*, Vol. 15, online, Bumsted, J. M., 'The trial of Ambroise Lépine', *Beaver,* Vol. 77, (2), (1997-1998), pp. 9-19, and especially Knafla, Louis A., 'Treasonous Murder: The Trial of Ambroise Lépine, 1874', in Wright, Barry, and Binnie, Susan, (eds.), *Canadian State Trials, Volume III: Political Trials and Security Measures, 1840-1914*, (University of Toronto Press), 2009, pp. 297-352.

[210] Buckingham, William, and Ross, Sir George William, *The Hon. Alexander Mackenzie: His Life and Times*, (Rose Publishing Co.), 1892, pp. 386-402, considers the 1875 parliamentary session. See also, Thomson, Dale C., *Alexander Mackenzie: Clear Grit*, (Macmillan), 1960, pp. 221-222, 227, 297, Stewart, George, *Canada under the*

parliamentary approval for an amnesty for Riel and Lépine, conditional on five years' banishment from 'Her Majesty's dominions'.[211]

Riel in exile, 1875-1884

Exile is strangely compelling to think about but terrible to experience. It is the unhealable rift between a human being and a native place, between the self and its true home: its essential sadness can never be surmounted.[212]

If Said is right, this may explain why, during the first three years of his exile, Riel experienced a mental breakdown that led to him being institutionalised between 1876 and 1878. This was followed by six years spent in the Montana territory, a period described--at least on the surface--as remarkably 'uneventful' by one critic.[213] Flanagan sees these years as dark, negative and frustrating and finds no link between Montana and the events in 1884-1885.[214] Important in understanding how Riel coped with his long exile are his writings and these reflected his desire to give new meaning to his life and to establish new relationships.

Questions about Riel's mental health dominated the first three years of his exile.[215] Intensely religious and initially bound for the priesthood but with an unbreakable faith in the power of Providence to comfort the afflicted and punish the transgressor, his mental problems and irrationality appeared when events challenged his confidence in Providence. This was first evident after the death of his father in early 1864 leading to a personal crisis that lasted into 1865.[216] Doctor Daniel Clark, who examined Riel for the defence in 1885 and concluded that he was insane, regarded this episode as the first of several occasions when Riel became deranged.[217] His conclusion, based on evidence already two decades old, is questionable and it appears more likely that Riel underwent a period of intense religious piety consequent on his father's death. He experienced two bouts of

---

Administration of the Earl of Dufferin, (Rose-Belford Publishing Company), 1979, pp. 381-416, and De Kiewiet, Cornelius William, (ed.), *Dufferin-Carnarvon Correspondence, 1874-1878*, (Greenwood Press), 1969, pp. 98-120, on the amnesty issue.

[211] Lépine, refused the offer, served out his sentence and was released in late October 1876. He remained active in Métis politics until 1879 when the interests of Riel and the Roman Catholic Church began to diverge and he disagreed with Riel who sought to unite the Métis and Indians in the north-west into a confederacy. He had, he said, risked his life once for the Métis cause and was not willing to do so again.

[212] Said, Edward, *Reflections on Exile and Other Literary and Cultural Essays*, (Granta Books), 2001, p. 173.

[213] Braz, Albert, *The False Traitor: Louis Riel in Canadian Culture*, (University of Toronto Press), 2003, p. 31.

[214] Ibid, Flanagan, Thomas, *Louis 'David Riel'*, pp. 105-132, considers Riel's sojourn in Montana.

[215] Betts, Gregory, 'Non Compos Mentis: A Meta-Historical Survey of the Historiographic Narratives of Louis Riel's 'Insanity'', *International Journal of Canadian Studies*, Vol. 38, (2008), pp. 15-40, provides a valuable and recent overview of Riel's mental issues.

[216] Ibid, Betts, Gregory, 'Non Compos Mentis…', pp. 12-17.

[217] Clark, Daniel, 'A Psycho-medical history of Louis Riel', *American Journal of Insanity*, Vol. 44, (1887-1888), pp. 33-51. See also, Gilson, E., 'Etude sur l'état mental de Louis Riel'. *L'Encéphale: journal des maladies mentales et nerveuses*, Vol. 6, (1886), pp. 51-60.

serious illness at the beginning of 1871 and in the winter of 1872-1873. These were physical rather than mental illnesses but the enforced rest resulted in him resolving the dilemma he faced between withdrawing to the religious sphere and remaining in the physical world. The major crisis in Riel's mental health occurred in late 1875 when he experienced a powerful religious experience accompanied by visions.[218] Whether a reaction to the isolation of exile, it led to a complete mental collapse and Riel was taken to Montreal where he was in the care of his uncle John Lee for a few months. When his condition deteriorated, he was initially committed to the asylum in Longue Pointe on 6 March 1876 under the assumed name 'Louis R. David'.[219] Fearing discovery, his doctors soon transferred him to the Beauport Asylum near Quebec City under the name 'Louis La Rochelle' where he remained until January 1878.[220] It is difficult to identify with any clarity what Riel experienced from during these years.[221] Seen by some as delusional, by others as madness, his irrationality between 1875 and 1877 led to a redefinition of his sense of mission and to the belief that he was a divinely chosen leader of the Métis. It turned him from a politician into a prophet.

From 1874 to his death, Riel's religious cosmology and his place within it does change, but only by a small degree. Until his death, he retained the sense of himself as 'Prophet of the New World', devoted to healing the Protestant-Catholic rift in the Christian Church and to his belief in the Métis as a chosen people. Always introspective and strongly religious, Riel became obsessed with the idea that his was a religious mission to establish a new American Catholicism with Bishop Bourget of Montreal as Pope of the New World. While he suffered from sporadic irrational outbursts, he continued his religious writing, composing theological tracts that mixed Christian and Judaic ideas and included a return to Mosaic Law, endorsement of polygamy and a belief in the Hebraic descent of North American indigenous peoples. He began calling himself Louis 'David' Riel, Prophet of the New World, and would pray standing for hours, having servants help him to hold his arms in the shape of a cross. For Mossmann:

> Louis Riel in 1885 was primarily a millenarian leader, not a political one...These movements see the rise of a prophetic leader, who through his charisma strikes a supernatural chord in his mainly peasant or semi-nomadic followers and through his exceptional personality is able to inspire his followers with a desperately needed hope for [his] god-like powers.[222]

---

[218] Moran, James, *Committed to the State Asylum: Insanity and Society in Nineteenth-Century Quebec and Ontario,* (McGill-Queen's University Press), 2000, provides the context.

[219] Howard, Henry, 'Medical History of Louis David Riel during his Detention in Longue Pointe Asylum', *Canada Medical & Surgical Journal,* Vol. 14, (1886), pp. 641-649. See also, Flanagan, Thomas, *Louis 'David Riel'*, pp. 63-72.

[220] Ibid, Flanagan, Thomas, *Louis 'David Riel'*, pp. 72-78.

[221] Desjardins, Édouard, and Charles Dumas, 'Le complexe médical de Louis Riel', *L'Union Médicale du Canada*, Vol. 99, (1970), pp. 1870-1878, diagnosed 'a delirious and hallucinatory syndrome of a mystico-religious type', while Littman, S. K., 'A Pathology of Louis Riel', *Canadian Psychiatric Association Journal,* Vol. 23, (1978), pp. 449-462, regards him as a 'paranoid schizophrenic'

[222] Mossmann, Manfred, 'The Charismatic Pattern: Canada's Riel Rebellion of 1885 as a Millenarian Protest Movement', in Bowsfield, Harwell, (ed.), *Louis Riel: Selected*

For Flanagan, Riel can only be understood if he is seen as a 'spiritual figure, a would-be founder and millenarian prophet'.[223] His religion provided the promise of ultimate escape from colonial domination and was an exaggeration of French-Canadian Catholic theology combining Catholic ultramontanism with its recognition of the authority of the Pope over the state and French-Canadian nationalism. It maintained a providential theory of history in which French Canada had the responsibility for extending the Kingdom of God in North America. Central to Riel's thinking was his reading of the Book of Daniel with its prediction of the rise and fall of four earthly empires, the last for Riel was the British colonial empire, before the emergence of the Kingdom of God. Riel's was an inclusive millenarian vision in which native peoples, the Métis and French-Canadians and European immigrants would ethnically merge and become a 'new race' and with the disappearance of the border between Canada and the United States, a 'new nation'. He had an unfailing certainly about the truth of this transcendental relationship and in his belief that God would ultimately ensure Métis victory in their anti-colonial battles. For instance, at Batoche in 1885, Riel prayed continuously and believed throughout the battle, as did his soldiers, that a miracle would occur.

Released from the asylum on 12 January 1878 with instructions to lead a quiet life, Riel spent some time in Keeseville, New York. Here, he became involved in a passionate romance with Evelina Martin *dit* Barnabé, sister of his friend, the oblate father Fabien Barnabé. But with insufficient means to propose marriage, Riel set out for the Upper Missouri region of Montana territory where he remained until the spring of 1884, hoping that she might follow. However, she decided that she would be unsuited to prairie life and their correspondence soon ended.[224] Riel firmly believed in the superiority of the United States compared to Canada as the Americans had separated from the influence of the mother country, abolished slavery and supported the cause of the Métis in 1869-1870 in the hope of later annexing the territory. In a letter to his mother written in October 1879, Riel wrote, '...I was delighted to see the prairies. It gives me strength, the prairie is medicinal.' For the first time in his life, he took part in the hunt and the trading that followed and this provided him with the opportunity to affirm his Métis identity. But, as in Canada, the Montana Métis were under increasing pressure from the ranchers and homesteaders who were flooding the territory. In addition, the American authorities were faced with Native Americans, such as the Blackfoot, Cree and Assiniboine who crossed the border from Canada in search of the dwindling herds of buffalo.[225] They went so far as

---

Readings, (Copp Clark), 1988, pp. 227-245, at p. 241. This view was also expressed in Martel, Gilles, *Le Messianisme de Louis Riel*, (Wilfrid Laurier University Press), 1984.

[223] Ibid, Flanagan, Thomas, *Louis 'David Riel'*, pp. xi, 45-47, 197-198; see also the contrasting discussion in, Reid, Jennifer I. M., 'Faire Place à une Race Métisse': Colonial Crisis and the Vision of Louis Riel', in Reid, Jennifer I. M., (ed.), *Religion and Global Culture: New Terrains in the Study of Religion and the work of Charles H. Long*, (Lexington Books), 2003, pp. 51-66.

[224] Montana became a United States territory in 1864 and the forty-first state in 1889.

[225] Harroun, Foster, Martha, 'The Spring Creek (Lewistown) Métis: Métis Identity in Montana', in Barkwell, L., *et al.* (eds.), *Métis Legacy*, (Pemmican Publications Inc.), 2001, pp. 99-104, and Sudenberry, Verne, 'Waiting for a Day That Never Comes: The

accusing the Métis of hunting illegally and a number were escorted back across the border including some Métis born in the United States. The Métis remaining in the Territory were concerned about their future and, in 1879, turned to Riel to act as their spokesman to negotiate hunting rights with the First Nations and the American government [226]

Although he waited until May 1880 after the terms of his banishment expired, Riel concluded that becoming an American citizen was the best way he could help the Métis.[227] The Canadian Naturalisation Act of 1881 for the first time allowed emigrants to renounce their British allegiance and this could have been at issue in Riel's trial in 1885 since his legal status was no different from that of any foreigner and to charge a foreigner with treason was unusual and could have been controversial. In 1882, he married a Métis woman, Marguerite Monet, dit Bellehumeur.[228] Observing rampant alcoholism and its detrimental impact on Native American and Métis peoples, he adopted the same tactical approach he had used in Manitoba especially letters and petitions engaging in an unsuccessful attempt to curtail the whisky trade. The Canadian and American governments had established a certain number of measures to control the sale of alcohol but, as Riel noted, these policies had varying degrees of success. During the 1870s, the North West Mounted Police has rid the Canadian West of the American whisky traders but on the American side of the border, enforcement of the law was lax. Local juries refused to convict their neighbours who were involved in one of the most lucrative private undertakings in Montana. The rights of white citizens took precedence over those of the Natives or the Métis while no one worried about alcohol's destructive toll on the Indian reserves. As Riel saw it, alcohol prevented a hunter from setting himself up on a piece of land.[229] The problem was that the Americans, much as their Canadian counterparts, were unwilling to recognise the Métis as a distinct people. This became evident to Riel in 1880 when he attempted to negotiate with the American authorities to set aside land for the Métis than would isolate them from the Americans. He had two possible sites in mind, one to the south of Yellowstone on the Crow River and the other between the Yellowstone and Musselshell Rivers. However, the Crows had no intention of sharing their territory and the Indian Agent on the Crow Reserve made it clear that since the Métis were British, they had no rights to this land.

Riel rebelled against the lamentable conditions in which the First Nations in the United States and Canada lived and condemned the nomadic existence the

---

Dispossessed Métis of Montana', in ibid, Peterson, J., and Brown, J. S. H., (eds.), *The New People: Being and Becoming Métis in North America*, pp. 119-136.

[226] Kermoal, Nathalie, 'Les années américaines de Louis Riel: l'exil au Montana', *Études Canadiennes/Canadian Studies*, Vol. 43, (1997), pp. 31-42, and Anctil, Pierre, 'L'exil américain de Louis Riel, 1874-1884', *Recherches Amérindiennes au Québec*, Vol. 11, (3), (1981), pp. 239-249.

[227] Riel applied for United States citizenship and was naturalised on 16 March 1883.

[228] He married Marguerite Monet *dit* Bellehumeur (1861-1886) a young Métis, 'in the fashion of the country' on 28 April 1881, an arrangement that was solemnised on 9 March 1882. They had three children: Jean-Louis (1882-1908), Marie-Angélique (1883-1897) and a boy who was born and died on 21 October 1885, less than one month before Riel was hanged.

[229] See Riel's letter to *Helena Independent*, 29 May 1882.

American government imposed on the Métis. This was not an inactive exile and his involvement was such that in 1882 he was accused of having influenced the Métis to vote Republican when they were not actually American citizens. His exile in Montana intensified his sense of identity as a Métis and he began to put forward the millenarian idea of a Métis independence movement to establish a republic in the provinces of Assiniboia and Saskatchewan for all Métis from Canada and the United States. This was to be a new political and religious utopia, a multinational confederation. Faced with the indifference of the American authorities to the plight of the Métis, when he had to decide whether to re-join his people at Batoche, Saskatchewan, he hesitated if only briefly.

Crisis in the North-West

In the decade after 1875, the North-West became a seething mass of discontent with the Canadian government. Under John A. Macdonald, the interests of Canada in the North-West lay in agricultural settlement as an outlet for excess eastern population and as a stimulus to transcontinental nation-building. The problem was it lacked sufficient finances to develop the province as quickly as settlers wanted. By the early 1880s, the three main groups living in the North-West Territories had grievances against the government of Canada. European and Canadian settlers accused the Canadian government of operating the Territory solely for the benefit of Eastern Canadian business to the detriment of local interests. The life of the First Nations changed irrevocably during the 1870s with the extinguishing of the buffalo herds that made them increasingly dependent upon the treaties signed with the federal government. The Métis, who had moved from Manitoba and settled in the Saskatchewan Territories, saw their traditional lifestyle threatened by settler immigration. Nevertheless, when they migrated to the South Saskatchewan district, some Métis commercial traders and farmers were keenly aware of the economic opportunities available. Others were less adaptable but for both groups, by the early 1880s, there were growing concerns about their status in the evolving North-West Territories. By the middle of the decade all parties in the west were holding meetings, sending petitions and discussing political tactics for redress of their grievances against a government that appeared as uninterested as it was remote. In was in this context that Riel was persuaded to come to Batoche in 1884.

The late 1870s saw the development of the National Policy, a combination of settlement, railways and tariffs that, with the police, was imposed on the western interior.[230] The West became a new investment frontier in which its settlement and economic exploitation would enrich Ontario, Quebec and Maritime Canada and, in the absence of imperial preference and of continental economic integration, would lead to an integrated Canadian economy. It would also thwart the ambitions of American annexationists. Important, though perhaps not as pivotal as some earlier historians believed, was the building of the Canadian

[230] See, Brown, Robert Craig, *Canada's National Policy, 1883-1900: A Study in Canadian-American Relations*, (Princeton University Press), 1964, and a broader analysis in, Fowke, Vernon C., 'National Policy and Western Development in North America', *Journal of Economic History*, Vol. 16, (1956), pp. 461-479.

Pacific Railway that was completed in 1885.[231] The building of the CPR would assure the sovereignty of Canada over the territory and eastern industry would have access to the resources and the customers of the West. The criticism of the CPR from settlers in the North-West was its high cost of carrying freight and attempts by the Manitoban government to create competition by establishing provincial lines were disallowed by the federal government as not being in the interests of Canada. Such was the anger in Manitoba that there was a vociferous agitation for its secession from the Confederation and the federal government was sufficiently concerned to ask the Colonial Office in London if imperial troops would be available if national policies led to armed confrontation between federal authorities and western farmers.[232] The North-West Mounted Police, founded in 1873, was another instrument of federal control chasing America traders out of south Alberta, policing the First Nations and Métis and providing the stability and order that white settlers wanted.[233]

This situation was exacerbated by the end of the land boom in the North-West in 1883 with the collapse of land prices and a consequent decline in crop prices, commercial transactions and a significant decline in the rate of settlement. At the height of the boom in 1882, over 2.5 million acres of land were alienated but within two years this had fallen to 1.1 million and, in the troubled year of 1885, 481,000 acres. This marked the beginning of a widespread depression that did not lift until the mid-1890s.[234] Federal commentators, almost inevitably from Ontario, blamed settlers for not applying themselves to their farming, something farmers angrily rejected. Individuals such as Charles Mair, who had previously dismissed the concerns of Red River Métis as sectional, found it necessary in the 1880s to assert western rights in the face of eastern indifference.[235] Several prominent farmers and political leaders in the North-West supported joint protest with the Métis but few were prepared to follow Riel in another attempt to defy the Canadian government. Despite this, they remained sympathetic to the aspirations of the Métis even if they did not approve of their methods. An anonymous correspondent to *The Week* wrote from Calgary in April 1885: 'It is a mistake to

---

[231] Murray, Tom, *Canadian Pacific Railway*, (Voyageur Press), 2006, pp. 10-35, examines its development to 1885. See also, Innis, Harold A., *A History of the Canadian Pacific Railway*, (P. S. King & Son), 1923, and Hedges, James B., *Building the Canadian West: The Land and Colonization Policies of the Canadian Pacific Railway*, (Russell & Russell), 1939.

[232] The intensity of feeling can be seen, for instance, in December 1883, when a Manitoba and North-West farmers' union was organised in Winnipeg. A motion calling for the repeal of the 1867 British North America Act and the formation of a new confederacy of the North-West Provinces and British Columbia was only narrowly defeated.

[233] Atkin, R., *Maintain the right: The early history of the North West Mounted Police, 1873-1900*, (John Day Co.), 1973, Turner, John P., *The North-West Mounted Police, 1873-1893*, 2 Vols. (E. Cloutier), 1950, an official history, and Macleod, R. C., *The NWMP and Law Enforcement, 1873-1905*, (University of Toronto Press), 1976, provide details on its role in the early years.

[234] Breen, D., *The Canadian Prairie West and the Ranching Frontier, 1874-1924*, (University of Toronto Press), 1983.

[235] Ibid, Owram, Doug, *Promise of Eden*, pp. 168-178.

suppose the rising is factious and sudden...It is the growth of years...the whole country sympathizes with the rebels'.[236]

The Indians and the Métis also suffered from the results of depression in the 1880s leading to the growth of their own complaints.[237] In the early 1880s, this discontent was increasingly expressed in vocal protests and isolated outbreaks of defiance to federal authority. This made little impact on Ottawa where politicians continued to ignore their protests resulting in the attitudes of both Indians and Métis becoming increasingly extreme. The Métis resistance in 1869 and 1870 and the resulting Manitoba Act underlined the Canadian government's prudence in negotiating with First Nations living in the North-West Territory rather than attempting to push into the area.[238] There were 25,000-30,000 Indians in the western interior in 1870 and another 10,000 Métis but fewer than 2,000 European or Canadian settlers and this reinforced the government's concern. The federal government could not afford adequately to protect settlers in the west or to force its way into the area. In 1870, the annual Canadian federal budget was about $19 million in comparison to the £20 million the American government was spending on Indian wars in its mid-west. Between 1866 and 1895, the United States Army fought 943 military engagements with native peoples; Canadian troops fought seven, all but one of them in 1885. Weakened by epidemics, especially smallpox, endemic warfare between the Blackfoot and Cree that culminated in a devastating Cree defeat in 1870 and by the illegal whisky trade, the Saulteaux, Assiniboine, Cree and Blackfoot were prepared to negotiate.[239] They recognised that war would be both self-defeating and not prevent an influx of settlers, especially as the buffalo, the main resource on which the Plains culture was built, was rapidly declining. As a result, between 1871 and 1877, seven numbered treaties were negotiated covering a vast territory from north-western Ontario to the Rocky Mountains. In return for unhindered access to this enormous area, Canada gave initial payments and annuities to each aboriginal person, promised reserves on which native peoples could learn alternative ways of supporting themselves if that became necessary, and provided a variety of other forms of help such as farming assistance, and, in Treaty 6 aid in the event of 'famine' or 'pestilence' in the North-West Territories. The government had achieved title to the soil according to its view of the law and the Indians had achieved recognition of their needs and some measure of protection against the influx of Canadian settlers. The Indians had won more than the

---

[236] Cit, ibid, Owram, Doug, *Promise of Eden*, p. 174.

[237] Daschuk, James, *Cearing the Plains. Disease, Politics of Starvation and the Loss of Aboriginal Life*, (University of Regina Press), 2013, pp. 79-158, is a damning indictment of the politics of ethnocide.

[238] Ibid, Friesen, Gerald, *The Canadian Prairies*, pp. 129-161, provides a succinct discussion of the end of the autonomy of the Plains Indians between 1840 and 1900. See also, Miller, J. R., *Skyscrapers Hide the Heavens: A History of Indian-White Relations in Canada*, 3rd ed., (University of Toronto Press), 2000, pp. 148-253.

[239] Dempsey, Hugh, *Firewater: The impact of the whisky trade on the Blackfoot nation*, (Fifth House Publishers), 2002, examines the impact of the trade in the 1870s.

government had planned but lost out on the crucial issue of sovereignty over the land.[240]

The federal Indian policy aimed to assimilate First Nations while many of the native groups expected the reserves to operate as refuges in which they could adapt to Euro-Canadian economic ways while maintaining traditional hunting and gathering practices. The catastrophic collapse of the buffalo economy between 1875 and 1885 left the Plains Indians destitute and this meant that the transition to more sedentary agriculture on the reserves occurred far more rapidly than either Indians or the federal government expected.[241] From 1882, as frustration was increasing among the Métis, Big Bear chief of the Plains Cree sought to renegotiate the treaties and found an ally in Crowfoot, leading chief of the Blackfoot.[242] He called an assembly of the Plains chiefs in June 1884 and the Duck Lake people drafted a petition detailing government violations of their treaty accusing federal commissioners of misleading them in the treaty negotiations. Big Bear had managed to unite the plains Cree and even interested the Blackfoot in a council planned for 1885.[243] A Cree revolt, political not military, was brewing. The authorities were prepared for problems by the end of 1884 but did not expect violence.[244]

Although Big Bear had proved an astute political leader, his authority was increasingly challenged by militants led by Little Poplar who rejected his leader's diplomatic campaign of Indian solidarity. He called for violence as a means of restoring Cree independence and found a sympathetic audience among the disillusioned youths in the Fort Pitt-Frog Lake area. When news of a fight between the Métis and Mounted Police at Duck Lake reached their camp, some two hundred miles to the east, open warfare followed. They seized the HBC

---

[240] For the context and nature of the numbered treaties see, Miller, J. R., *Compact, Contract, Covenant: Aboriginal Treaty-Making in Canada*, (University of Toronto Press), 2009, pp. 123-186, and St. Germain, Jill, *Broken Treaties: United States and Canadian Relations with the Lakota and the Plains Cree, 1868-1885*, (University of Nebraska Press), 2009, pp. 101-133. *The Administration of Indian Affairs in the North-West*, (s.n.), 1886, is a short, blistering attack on Macdonald's Indian policies. For a defence of the character of government officials see, Department of Indian Affairs, *The Facts respecting Indian Administration in the North-West*, (s.n.), 1887, pp. 9-18.

[241] For discussion of the relationship between the grasslands, buffalo and native peoples see, Binnema, T., *Common and Contested Ground: A Human and Environmental History of the Northwestern Plains*, (University of Oklahoma Press), 2001, pp. 17-54. See also, Ens, Gerhard, 'The Border, the Buffalo and the Metis of Montana', in Evans, Sterling, (ed.), *The Borderlands of the American and Canadian Wests: Essays on Regional History of the Forty-Ninth Parallel*, (University of Nebraska Press), 2006, pp. 139-154.

[242] Dempsey, Hugh, *Crowfoot: Chief of the Blackfeet*, (University of Oklahoms Press), 1972, pp. 154-193, examines his role in the events leading to the Indian uprising in 1885. See also, pp. St. Germain, Jill, *Broken Treaties*, pp. 311-343, examines events in 1884 and 1885.

[243] Dempsey, Hugh, *Big Bear: The End of Freedom*, (University of Nebraska Press), 1984, details his diplomatic initiatives.

[244] Waiser, Bill, and Stonechild, Blair, *Loyal Till Death: Indians and the North-West Rebellion*, (Fifth House Publishers), 1997, 2010, explodes the myth of a grand Métis-Indian alliance. See also, Tobias, John L., 'Canada's Subjugation of the Plains Cree', *Canadian Historical Review*, Vol. 64, (1983), pp. 519-548.

store at Frog Lake on 2 April 1885 killing nine men and creating an atmosphere of terror among the white settlers.[245] Although the 'massacre' and the later Cree action at Frog Lake was the result of desperate and starving people and was unconnected to the Métis rebellion, as Indian Affairs Commissioner and Lieutenant-Governor of the North-West Territories Edgar Dewdney quietly signalled to Ottawa, he publicly claimed that the Cree and the Métis had joined forces. Inevitably, the 1885 rebellion has been described as a Métis and Indian uprising and the coincidence of the two movements was certainly used by Dewdney to further his political goals, but, in reality, the Indian uprising was the action of a few young warriors, acting without the approval of their chiefs and without widespread support. Some sixty Cree and Dakota were present at Batoche suggests some Indian complicity with the Métis but it is likely that they acted without the authority of their chiefs. The leading chiefs remained aloof from the Métis battles in 1885 with Little Bear moving his band into the bush country of the North Saskatchewan so it would be far from the action. Beardy, another chief, and his followers refused Riel's invitation to join the Métis and the Blackfoot remained peaceful largely due to the efforts of their chiefs to prevent it and the timely arrival of added rations from white officials anxious to placate them. Despite their actions, the uprising provided the opportunity for the government to end the Cree diplomatic campaign for native unity and treaty revision. After the rebellion, twenty-eight reserves were officially identified as disloyal, more than fifty Indians, including Poundmaker and Big Bear were convicted of rebellion-related crimes and there was a mass execution of eight Indian warriors at Fort Battleford in November 1885.[246]

During the 1870s and 1880s, the West was Canadianised, a process that generated resistance. The government of Manitoba challenged the CPR's monopoly and sought better financial terms. Farmers in Manitoba and on the Saskatchewan River agitated for lower tariffs and the transportation system that met their needs not those of eastern businessmen. Territorial politicians crusaded for representation in Parliament and responsible government for the North-West Territories. Chiefs of the First Nations sought to renegotiate the federal treaties but it was only a minority of Métis who supported Riel in 1885. Like states' rights in the United States, provincial rights in Canada became a long-standing source of constitutional, political and cultural tension.

Rebellion, 1885

By the beginning of 1884, many among the Métis in the North-West Territories were under pressure.[247] The buffalo had gone and the agrarian economy was in

[245] Stanley, George, 'An Account of the Frog Lake Massacre', *Alberta Historical Review*, Vol. 4, (1), (1956), pp. 23-27, an account by George Stanley, a member of the Frog Lake Cree who, aged seventeen, witnessed the killing of nine residents on 2 April 1885. He gave his account in an interview in 1931.

[246] Waiser, Bill, 'The White Man Governs: The 1885 Indian Trials', in ibid, Wright, Barry, and Binnie, Susan, (eds.), *Canadian State Trials, Volume III*, pp. 451-480. See also, McCoy, Ted, 'Legal Ideology in the Aftermath of Rebellion: The Convicted First Nations Participants, 1885', *Histoire sociale/Social History*, Vol. 42, (2009), pp. 175-201.

[247] For the North-West Rebellion and the military campaign see, Boulton, C. A., *Reminiscences of the North-West Rebellion*, (Grip Printing and Publishing Co.), 1886,

depression. The arrival of government surveyors sparked the same level of unease and suspicion along the Saskatchewan River as had been the case on the Red River a decade earlier. The same question arose: would the river-lot holdings of the Métis be allowed to survive in a square-survey system? Part of the uncertainly was that the surveying was not occurring fast enough, equally a complaint among white settlers, and the Métis did not know whether they would be exempt from it. The main problem, however, was a lack of political leadership and it was for this reason that a delegation from the Saskatchewan country, which had the support of all ethnic communities, visited Riel in Montana on 4 June 1884.[248]

Within a month, Riel and his family were in Batoche where he organised a peaceful campaign of protest against Canadian policies organising a series of meetings to unite all settlers in the region behind a petition of grievances. By December 1884, Riel and William Jackson, Secretary of the North-West Settlers' Union had drafted a long petition that was sent to Ottawa on 16 December. It concluded by requesting that the petitioners should be allowed, as had been the case in 1870, to send delegates to Ottawa to discuss the North-West Territories becoming part of the confederation with the constitution of a free province. Ottawa acknowledged receipt of the petition but made no other response. It did, however, attempt to address Métis concerns about land and in 28 January 1885 said that a commission would be appointed to enumerate the Métis and they were invited to register their river lot claims at the Dominion Lands Office in Prince Albert.

Riel was mistaken in thinking that the approach he has used in 1869 and 1870 would be equally successful in 1885. John A. Macdonald was again Prime Minister but was not going to be drawn into negotiations to resolve the problems of the North-West, most of which, unlike in 1870, he did not recognise.[249] Neither was he prepared to pay Riel to leave Canada as he had in 1872. The federal government was in a far stronger position than in 1870 and that may explain why Macdonald was unwilling to negotiate with Riel.[250] The building of

---

ibid, Robertson Heather, (ed.), *I Fought Riel: A Military Memoir*, pp. 71-219, provides a short account by Boulton, and Mulvany, Charles, *The History of the North-West Rebellion of 1885*, (A. H. Hovey & Co.), 1886, provide contemporary accounts For a government slant see, *Epitome of Parliamentary Documents in Connection with the North-West Rebellion 1885*, (Maclean, Roger & Company), 1886. Morton, Desmond, *The Last War Drum: The North-West Campaign of 1885*, (Hakkert), 1972, and Beal, Bob, and Macleod, R. C., *Prairie Fire: The 1885 North-West Rebellion*, (Hurtig), 1984, are the best modern accounts.

[248] *Sun River Sun*, 12 June 1884, gives an account of the four Métis, James Isbister, Gabriel Dumont, Moise Ouellette and Michel Dumas who were sent to Montana to find Riel to invite him to lead the Métis in winning their rights.

[249] For Macdonald and the problems posed by the 1885 rebellion see, ibid, Gwyn, Richard, *Nation Maker, Sir John A. Macdonald: His Life, Our Times, Volume 2: 1867-1891*, pp. 391-474, and Gibson, Sarah, & Milnes, Arthur, (eds.), *The Speeches of Sir John A. MacDonald*, (McClelland & Stewart), 2014, pp. 324-345.

[250] McLean, Don, *1885: Métis Rebellion or Government Conspiracy*, (Pemmican Publications), 1985, suggests based on tenuous evidence that either the Canadian government duped Riel into rebellion or deliberately provoked it. Flanagan, Thomas *Riel*

the PCR, though sections were still under construction north of Lake Superior, made it far easier and quicker to move troops to the area: two weeks in contrast to over sixty days in 1870. The North-West Mounted Police provided local paramilitary support for law and order. In addition, the Catholic Church, stung by Riel's belief that he had a millenarian mission and was God's prophet, did not support his campaign for Métis rights and actively worked with Crowfoot and his Blackfoot warriors to prevent their participation in any rebellion. Riel's position was further weakened by his mistaken belief that he had widespread support across the different communities in the region. Once armed confrontation started, the European settlers and Anglo-Métis, with a handful of exceptions, quickly disassociated themselves from his movement and the First Nations who were at most lukewarm in their support quickly moved in their own directions.

By early March 1885, it was clear to Riel that his initial strategy was unsuccessful and that the federal government was not prepared to negotiate with him.[251] Deeply disappointed, he led his followers to regard the proposed land commission as a provocative denial of their rights. On 5 March, Riel and a group of prominent Métis hold a secret meeting signing an oath to 'save our country from a wicked government by taking up arms if necessary.' At St. Laurent on 8 March 1885, a meeting passed a 10-point 'Revolutionary Bill of Rights' that asserted Métis rights of possession to their farms and made other demands. His rhetoric became increasingly inflammatory until the Métis committed themselves to an armed rebellion on 18 March 1885 seizing control of St. Anthony's Church, taking hostages and cutting the telegraph lines at Clarke's Crossing. On 18 and 19 March, the Métis formed a provisional government and an armed force at Batoche, with Riel president and Gabriel Dumont military commander.[252] The religious dimension was evident from the outset of the rebellion. Riel announced to his followers that 'Rome has fallen!' when he seized the church at Batoche; he arrested missionaries and presided over his own religious ceremonies. The Exovedate, the name Riel gave to the provisional government, was dominated by him although he was not a member and, in addition to giving him the title 'prophet', it voted to break with Rome and adopt the Saturday Sabbath.

How much support Riel had is difficult to estimate. The Métis fortified Batoche and sent messengers to other Métis communities and tribes of the First Nations urging them to make common cause. Although some Indians rose in arms, there was never a joint strategy and their actions were largely independent of Métis control. Most Métis communities stayed out of the fighting and on 22 March, Anglo-Métis of St. Catherine's and the Ridge around Prince Albert voted to remain neutral in the event of armed conflict. It was largely the communities along the South Saskatchewan River at Batoche that provided the bulk of Dumont's troops numbering less than three hundred men. Despite this numerical

---

and the Rebellion: 1885 Reconsidered, (Western Producer Prairie Books), 1983, 2nd ed., (University of Toronto Press), 2000, was also savaged by some reviewers.

[251] Read, Geoff, and Webb, Todd, ''The Catholic Mahdi of the North West': Louis Piel and the Metis Resistance in Transatlantic and Imperial Context', *CHR*,Vol. 93, (2), (2012), pp. 171-195.

[252] Woodcock, George, *Gabriel Dumont: The Métis Chief and his Lost World*, (Hurtig), 1975, Miller, J. R., (ed.), (University of Toronto Press), 2003, pp. 167-225, examines his role in the provisional government and during the military campaign.

weakness, the Métis had several advantages over their largely inexperienced opponents in the militia: they knew the terrain and how to exploit it to maximum military effect; they were well trained and armed, though lack of ammunition posed a major problem in the defence of Batoche; and, formed a cohesive force. Since Riel was convinced that theirs was 'God's fight' and that their victory was ultimately assured, he refused to allow Dumont to use guerrilla tactics that may have delayed a federal victory sufficiently to force it to negotiate. Riel may have been an effective political and even religious leader but he was a fatally-flawed military commander.

Prisoners were taken in the Batoche area and, in anticipation of a police advance on 25 March Métis forces occupied the community of Duck Lake, midway between Batoche and Fort Carlton.[253] NWMP Superintendent Lief Crozier had received warnings that Riel and Dumont were going to make such a move and sent a small force to secure provisions in Duck Lake but retreated to Fort Carlton when confronted by the rebels' superior numbers. On 26 March, Crozier led a combined group of a hundred NWMP and Prince Albert Volunteers towards Duck Lake. A large Métis force met them on the Carlton Trail a mile from the village. It appears that both Crozier and Riel wanted to resolve the situation without bloodshed but the parlay ended in confusion and the Métis envoys, among them Dumont's brother, were killed. The police and Volunteers fired at their enemy hidden in a large hollow north of the road and in a cabin to the south. The Volunteers elected to charge the enemy cabin but they waded into deep snow and, under heavy fire from Métis snipers, the attack foundered, Crozier sounded the retreat and the police and volunteers retreating to Fort Carlton. Dumont was wounded when a bullet grazed his head but, despite his call to finish off the retreating Canadian column, Riel persuaded the rebel soldiers not to pursue the force and the Métis returned to Batoche. Nine volunteers and three police were killed and five Métis and one Indian died. The police evacuated Fort Carlton the following day accidentally burning it as they left and retired to Prince Albert.

The Ottawa government swiftly decided to put down the rebellion by force and Major-General Frederick Middleton, the British officer in charge of the Canadian Militia, was authorised to lead an expeditionary force to the North-West.[254] The constitutional difficulties Macdonald had faced over Red River in 1870 no longer existed and Canada possessed an internationally recognised title to the North-West. There were only a few hundred full-time soldiers in Canada but militia mobilisation in Quebec and Ontario began on 25 March, the day before the Duck Lake battle. The CPR gave the government an immediate

[253] On the battle of Duck Lake see, ibid, Woodcock, George, *Gabriel Dumont*, pp. 179-189, and ibid, Beal, Bob, and Macleod, R. C., *Prairie Fire: The 1885 North-West Rebellion*, pp. 151-167.

[254] Needler, G. H., (ed.), Middleton, Sir Frederick, *Suppression of the Rebellion in the North West Territories of Canada, 1885*, (University of Toronto Press), 1948, an account written eight years after the event and based on his military despatches that was originally published in the *United Service Magazine* between February 1894 and November 1898. Ibid, Beal, Bob, and Macleod, R. C., *Prairie Fire: The 1885 North-West Rebellion*, pp. 168-178, examines mobilisation.

capacity to project military power into the area.[255] CPR manager William Van Horne quickly arranged for Canadian troops to be transported across the gaps on carts and sleighs, enabling them to reach Qu'Appelle by 10 April. In less than a month, almost 3,000 troops had been transported west; most were Ontario militia units but the force included two Quebec battalions and one from Nova Scotia. From the West came about 1,700 of the eventual total of just over 5,000 that Middleton commanded.

The rebel victory at Duck Lake encouraged a party of Cree under the leadership of Poundmaker to move on Battleford from reserves to the west to lobby the Indian agent, Rae for better supplies since many members of the band were starving and to discuss the situation. The precise nature of Cree action has been subject to disagreement among historians. Douglas Hill saw the Cree party as a 'war party...ready to take revenge for a winter of incalculable suffering' while George F. Stanley took the view that the Cree actions were more haphazard 'prowling around the neighbourhood' but without any intention of attacking the town. John Tobias, by contrast, argued that the Cree, by including women and children in their party, demonstrated their peaceful intent, were concerned simply with obtaining food and withdrew to avoid conflict with the NWMP.[256] The people of Battleford and some of the settlers in the surrounding area, hearing reports of large numbers of Cree and Assiniboine leaving reserves and making their way to Battleford, feared for their safety and on 30 March, began abandoning the town and seeking shelter in the NWMP Fort Battleford. Some looting took place by the Indians although one observer alleged that whites were responsible.[257] The following day, Poundmaker led his band west away from the settlement and while the terrified settlers huddled in Fort Battleford for almost a month, the Cree and Assiniboine organised a huge war camp to the west at Cut Knife Creek. On 30 March, a small group of Assiniboine south of Battleford killed a farmer, who had mistreated them in the past, and their Indian agent who had assaulted a teenage girl. They then went north to Battleford to meet up with Poundmaker. The small police force at Battleford was now responsible for nearly five hundred civilians and called on Middleton to send reinforcements.

On the night of 1 April, ignoring Big Bear's opposition, warriors from his band took several whites and Métis at Frog Lake hostage and took control of the village. Shortly after mass on Sunday, 2 April, the Cree ordered the hostages to move to the Cree camp two miles away but Sub-Indian Agent Thomas Quinn steadfastly refused to leave the village and war chief Wandering Spirit shot and killed him. Chief Big Bear tried to stop the violence but the warriors took their own initiative from their war chief and killed two priests, the government farming instructor, an independent trader, a miller and three other men. Several people

---

[255] In 1885, the CPR was close to bankruptcy and was saved by the rebellion, a coincidence that led conspiracy theorists to suggest that Macdonald precipitated the rebellion to bail out his friends in the CPR.

[256] Hill, Douglas, *The Opening of the Canadian West*, (Heinemann), 1967, p. 196, ibid, Stanley, George F., *Louis Riel: Patriot or Rebel*, p. 21, and ibid, Tobias, John L., Canada's Subjugation of the Plains Cree'.

[257] Jefferson, Robert, *Fifty Years on the Saskatchewan: being a history of the Cree Indian domestic life and the difficulties which led to serious agitation and conflict of 1885 in the Battleford locality*, (Canadian North-west Historical Society), 1929, p. 127.

were spared, including the widows of two of the dead men and about seventy others from the village were taken captive. On 13 April, two hundred Frog Lake Cree reached Fort Pitt, on the North Saskatchewan River just east of the modern Alberta-Saskatchewan border and demanded the surrender of the fort. NWMP Inspector Francis Dickens, son of the novelist Charles Dickens, refused and two days of negotiation followed until a scouting party of three policemen stumbled across the Cree camp.[258] In the ensuing gun fight, one constable was killed, a second, wounded and the third captured. On 17 April, surrounded and outnumbered ten to one, the civilians in the fort decided to surrender to Big Bear because Fort Pitt was difficult to defend and lacked an internal water supply. Dickens then decided to abandon the post and retreat down river to Battleford reaching it six days later.[259]

General Middleton's original plan was simple. He intended to march all his troops north from the railhead at Qu'Appelle to Batoche. But the killings at Frog Lake and the 'siege' of Battleford forced him to send a column under Lieutenant-Colonel William Otter north from a second railhead at Swift Current to relieve Battleford.[260] Cree raiding parties pillaged the towns of Saddle Lake, Beaver Lake, Beaverhill Lake, Bear Hills and Lac St. Anne in neighbouring Alberta. This led to the mobilisation of an Alberta field force under Major-General Thomas Bland Strange at Calgary.[261] Middleton set off from Qu'Appelle to Batoche on 10 April and was advancing upstream from Clarke's Crossing on the South Saskatchewan River when he fell into a hastily-organised ambush on 24 April. He had divided his 900 men, including two artillery batteries, into two columns, one for each bank of the river. The Métis were determined to fight but differed about where to make a stand. Riel wanted to concentrate all efforts on defending Batoche while Dumont favoured guerrilla tactics. Dumont won the argument and with about 200 Métis, prepared an ambush at Tourond's Coulee or Fish Creek, twelve miles south of Batoche on the east side of the South Saskatchewan.[262]

As Middleton's scouts approached Fish Creek early on 24 April, the rebels opened fire. The Métis pounded Middleton's men with one devastating fusillade before withdrawing into cover and restricting themselves to sniper fire in order to conserve ammunition. With half his troops on the opposite bank, Middleton was

---

[258] Opinion about Dickens' competence is divided. Carter, David, 'Francis J. Dickens: An Ordinary Officer', *Beaver*, Vol. 78, (1998), questions whether charges of drunkenness, laziness and recklessness were justifiable while Macleod, R. C., 'Francis Jeffrey Dickens', *DCB*, Vol. 11, pp. 261-262, suggests that he was partially responsible for deteriorating relations between the Blackfoot and the NWMP in the early 1880s.

[259] Ibid, Beal, Bob, and Macleod, R. C., *Prairie Fire: The 1885 North-West Rebellion*, pp. 179-204, considers events at Battleford and Frog Lake.

[260] Melgund [Viscount Melgund, later Earl of Minto], 'The Recent Rebellion in North-West Canada', *Nineteenth Century*, Vol. 18, (102), (August 1885), pp. 312-327, provides a detailed account of the campaign from his viewpoint as Middleton's chief of staff.

[261] Jamieson, F. C., *The Alberta Field Force of 1885*, (Canadian North-West Historical Society), 1931, examines the part played by the Alberta field force in defending Edmonton but also pursuing Big Bear. For a more detailed account see, Dunn, Jack F., *The Alberta Field Force of 1885*, (J. Dunn), 1994.

[262] For details on the battle at Fish Creek, see ibid, Woodcock, George, *Gabriel Dumont*, pp. 200-210, and ibid, Beal, Bob, and Macleod, R. C., *Prairie Fire: The 1885 North-West Rebellion*, pp. 220-235.

unable to bring his numerical superiority to bear. His artillery was brought into action although it had little effect on the Métis positions but did succeed in driving off Dumont's Cree allies before their weight could be added to the battle. Until mid-afternoon, Middleton's soldiers tried unsuccessfully to drive Dumont's men from the ravine and suffered heavy casualties, ten killed and forty-five wounded. The rebels had only four killed. It took most of the day for Middleton to get the troops from the west bank across the river on a makeshift ferry and they arrived too late to take part in the fighting. At the end of the day, both commanders decided to pull back. The Métis had held their ground and Middleton's advance was stopped.

Otter's column consisted of 763 men from the Queen's Own Rifles of Canada, a battery from the Regiment of Canadian Artillery, a company of the Infantry School Corps, a party of sharpshooters and a small number of NWMP. From Swift Current, the column marched to Battleford between 13 and 24 April and relieved the fort. The civilians in the fort wanted action taken against Poundmaker's band and, despite orders from Middleton to remain at Battleford he wired the Lieutenant-Governor of the North-West Territories for permission to 'punish Poundmaker'. In the afternoon of 1 May, Colonel Otter led a flying column of 392 men west from Battleford: his force included 75 NWMP, several small units of Canadian regular troops and militia with two antiquated field guns and a Gatling gun.[263] Learning of the relief of Fort Battleford, the Cree decided to protect themselves and, following their custom, the war chief Fine Day replaced Poundmaker until the fighting was over. He decided to move the encampment, now swelled to about 1,500 men, women and children from nine bands of Cree and three Assiniboine, to the western bank of Knife Cut Creek. This meant that Otter's troops would have to wade the creek and through marsh before they reached the encampment.[264]

After on overnight march in freezing weather, the militia stopped for breakfast on a hill bounded by rolling terrain on each side and a ravine beneath. Otter had blundered into a poor tactical position since Poundmaker's camp lay just over the hill on the other side of the ravine. Once Otter's men detected the Cree camp, they set up his artillery and Gatling gun and directed cannon fire at it. Otter ordered the attack on the camp but once his troops had crossed the creek and negotiated the marsh, they found themselves under sustained attack from warriors, generally in small groups who used two wooded ravines to conceal their numbers. Otter could not attack because he did not know either the location of the enemy or their numbers. Otter's force was on an inclined, triangular plain bounded by the two ravines and the marsh and in danger of being flanked. After about six hours of fighting, he decided to retire. Casualties would have been far higher as the militia re-crossed the creek had not Poundmaker persuaded the Indians not to pursue the soldiers. Eight of Otter's force was killed and fourteen wounded; five Indians were killed and three wounded. This proved the greatest

---

[263] Morton, Desmond, *The Canadian General: Sir William Otter*, (A. M. Hakkert Ltd.), 1974, provides a biographical focus on his career. See also, Morton, Desmond, 'Sir William Dillon Otter', *DCB*, Vol. 15, online

[264] For the battle at Knife Cut Creek, see Fryer, Mary Beacock, *More Battlefields of Canada*, (Dundurn Press), 1993, pp. 114-124, and Beal, Bob, and Macleod, R. C., *Prairie Fire: The 1885 North-West Rebellion*, pp. 236-255.

reverse in the North-West campaign but within weeks, the starving Cree went to Fort Battleford to make peace with Middleton. Poundmaker was arrested and jailed while Fine Day fled across the border to the United States.[265] Otter rationalised his adventure as a 'reconnaissance in force': the Indians had been hurt or they would have pursued. Middleton was not deceived, and Otter's subordinates denounced him as an inept martinet. Others, however, eager for a Canadian-born hero, turned the battle into a triumph; the Montreal *Daily Witness* urged 'Otterism' as a synonym for merciless repression while Charles-Eugène Panet, saw Cut Knife Hill as proof that 'Canadians can fight their own battles without foreign help'.[266] However, the attack on Poundmaker's camp pushed him further in the direction of the Métis and he decided to lead his band to the Métis stronghold at Batoche but took a circuitous route during which he learned of the Métis defeat.

Conscious of the setbacks suffered by government forces, Middleton approached Batoche cautiously reaching Gabriel's Crossing on 7 May and advancing to within eight miles of the town the following day.[267] On 9 May, he planned to encircle the town: his main force would advance against the carefully constructed Métis defences at the southern end of the Batoche settlement, while the steamboat *Northcote*, carrying about fifty soldiers, would steam passed the defenders and disembark the troops at the rear of the town.[268] However, Middleton's caution meant that his main force lagged behind schedule and when the *Northcote* attempted to land its troops, the Métis lowered the ferry cable, incapacitating the boat that drifted harmlessly down the South Saskatchewan River and out of the battle. Middleton was unaware of the fate of the *Northcote* and occupied Mission Ridge and this allowed him to shell the town. Dumont led a counter-attack that almost succeeded in the guns being lost. A Métis attempt to surround the Canadian lines failed when the brushfires meant to screen the sortie failed to spread. At the end of the day, both sides held their positions at Mission Ridge.[269]

---

265 Comparisons have been drawn between Knife Cut Creek and the Battle of the Little Big Horn nine years earlier. Both Otter and Custer had disobeyed orders; both misjudged the terrain; and both were surrounded. The difference was that Custer kept fighting while Otter had the sense to retreat or was allowed to do so.

266 'Cut Knife Creek! A well fought battle', *Montreal Daily Witness*, 8 May 1885.

267 The capture of Clarke's Crossing is explained in the *Evening Globe*, 18 May 1885.

268 Tolton, Gordon E., *Prairie Warships: River Navigation in the Northwest Rebellion*, (Heritage House), 2007, pp. 169-193.

269 For the battle of Batoche, see Fryer, Mary Beacock, *Battlefields of Canada*, (Dundurn Press), 1986, pp. 227-241, ibid, Woodcock, George, *Gabriel Dumont*, pp. 211-225, and ibid, Beal, Bob, and Macleod, R. C., *Prairie Fire: The 1885 North-West Rebellion*, pp. 256-276. See also, Barkwell, Lawrence J., *Batoche 1885: The Militia of the Métis Liberation Movement*, (Manitoba Métis Federation), 2005, and Hildebrandt, Walter, *The Battle of Batoche: British Small Warfare and Entrenched Métis*, (National Historic Parks and Sites), 1989. Contemporary comment can be found in, Wrighton, William, 'The Campaign of 1885: A Contemporary Account', *Saskatchewan History*, Vol. 13, (1960), pp. 100-107, contains three letters written by Wrighton, a colour sergeant in the Midland Battalion who took part in the battle, and Allen, Robert K., 'A Rebellion Diary', *Alberta Historical Review*, Vol. 12, (1964), pp. 15-25, prints extracts from his diary including accounts of the battles at Fish Creek and Batoche.

The next two days, 10-11 May, saw a series of probing attacks to gauge the strength of the defenders and the continued shelling of the town. This revealed the weakness of the Métis position and on 12 May, Middleton tried a co-ordinated action from the east and south but the southern group failed to hear a signal gun and did not attack. In the afternoon, apparently without specific orders, two impetuous colonels led several militia units in a charge. The rebels, weary and short of ammunition, were overrun. Eight of Middleton's force died during the Battle of Batoche. The general later reported that 51 rebels were killed, but that number seems high and more recent estimates suggest that 51 rebels were killed, wounded or captured. Riel surrendered on 15 May while Dumont fled to Montana planning a rescue attempt for Riel that never happened.[270]

During the Battle of Batoche, General Strange was resting his Alberta Field Force at Edmonton after a hard march from Calgary. The column left Edmonton on 14 May and on 28 May they caught up to the Frog Lake Indians, dug in at the top of a steep hill near a prominent landmark known as Frenchman Butte, eleven miles north-west of Fort Pitt that they had already burned. The Cree divided into two groups: the war chief Wandering Spirit led two hundred warriors to positions in trenches and rifle pits while Little Poplar remained with a second group protecting the camp. Direct advance against the entrenched Indians would have been very difficult and Strange's scouts found no practical way around the Cree positions. They fired at each other from long range for several hours before Strange withdrew to Fort Pitt. The Cree slipped away later in the day. The battle was a tactical victory for the Cree buying them time to escape but their position was hopeless. Big Bear's band disintegrated as it retreated north and by early July their rebellion was over. The last shots of the rebellion were fired on 3 June at Loon Lake, twenty-five miles north of Frenchman Butte, where a force of NWMP under Major Sam Steele caught up and skirmished with the retreating Frog Lake Cree.[271] None of Steele's men was killed, although seven were wounded, but between five and twelve Indians died. Chief Poundmaker and the Battleford area Indians had already surrendered to General Middleton on 26 May at Battleford. At the end of May, Big Bear was the only important rebel still at large. The Frog Lake Indians released their prisoners on 21 June and Big Bear surrendered to the Mounted Police on 2 July at Fort Pitt.[272]

The rebellion was not a concerted effort by all groups in the North-West and may best be approached as two largely separate uprisings. While the Métis were concerned with defending their provisional government, the First Nations were more concerned with relieving their hunger. The Plains Cree of Big Bear's band had participated, but the neighbouring Woods Cree had not. The Blackfoot had remained neutral and the Blood refusing to abandon their traditional animosity towards the Cree. Almost every white settler had rallied to the

---

[270] Ibid, Woodcock, George, *Gabriel Dumont: The Métis Chief and his Lost World*, pp. 232-235.

[271] Brown, Wayne F., *Steele's Scouts: Samuel Benfield Steele and the North-West Rebellion*, (Heritage House Publishing Co.), 2001, pp. 105-146, deals with Frenchman's Butte and Loon Lake. See also, ibid, Beal, Bob, and Macleod, R. C., *Prairie Fire: The 1885 North-West Rebellion*, pp. 277-291.

[272] The conflict between Strange's column and Big Bear's band is described in *The Graphic; an Illustrated Newspaper*, 18 July 1885.

government cause, even though their vocal agitation before the conflict began had helped to create the environment that had made the rebellion possible.

Riel could have fled to the United States of which he was a citizen but he chose instead to surrender.[273] Woodcock suggests that Riel was not disappointed by the Métis defeat and that his objective had always been to publicise his cause rather than defeat the federal authorities.[274] Riel hoped to have a trial for treason before the Supreme Court of Canada where he could explain his actions to the world. But he was not provided with his platform and was send to the NWMP jail in Regina to be held for trial before a stipendiary magistrate.[275] Riel demanded a political trial and perversely that is what he got. As an opposition Quebec newspaper stated after the sentence was pronounced:

> Riel did not really have a trial. It was a sort of inquisition set up by the government, not for the purpose of enquiring into the guilt or innocence of the prisoner, but only on order to deliver up his head to the fanatics under the cover of a sham trial.[276]

His lawyers failed in their attempt to convince the jury of six British Protestants that Riel's religious and political delusions made him unaware of the nature of his acts, largely because Riel was so eloquent in his address to the jury on 31 July.[277]

The law provided no alternative to the death penalty and on 1 August, Riel was sentenced to be hanged. His execution was postponed three times: twice to allow appeals to the Manitoba Court of Queen's Bench on 9 September and the Judicial Court of the Privy Council that ruled against Riel on 22 October, then for a fuller medical examination of his alleged insanity. The medical commission report was divided on the question of Riel's sanity leaving the final decision to the government; questioning and then dismissing Riel's state of mind was politically expedient. It could have commuted the death sentence but Macdonald showed no mercy. The decision to 'let the law take its course' was in part political: hanging Riel would lose the Conservatives votes in Quebec, but sparing him would have cost them even more in Ontario. Riel was hanged at Regina on 16 November 1885. If Riel's nemesis was Scott's execution, Macdonald's was Riel's.

---

[273] Mumford, J. R., 'Why was Louis Riel, a United States Citizen, Hanged as a Canadian Traitor in 1885?', *Canadian Historical Review*, Vol. 88, (2007), pp. 237-262, examines why the United States did not chose to raise Riel's American citizenship as an issue in 1885.

[274] Ibid, Woodcock, George, *Gabriel Dumont: The Métis Chief and his Lost World*, pp. 186-187.

[275] *The Queen v. Louis Riel*, (University of Toronto Press), 1974, with an introduction by Desmond Morton, reprints the proceedings of Riel's trial from 20 July to 1 August. See also, ibid, Flanagan, Thomas, *Riel and the Rebellion: 1885 Reconsidered*, pp. 131-168, and Bumsted, J. M., 'Another Look at the Riel Trial for Treason', in ibid, Wright, Barry, and Binnie, Susan, (eds.), *Canadian State Trials, Volume III: Political Trials and Security Measures, 1840-1914*, (University of Toronto Press), 2009, pp. 411-450.

[276] *L'Electeur*, 4 August 1885.

[277] The literature on the trial concentrated on the question of Riel's sanity. The major problem with much of this is that it focuses on clinical insanity (for which there is a strong case) and not the narrower definition of legal insanity under the McNaghten Rules that was rejected by three courts: the trial court and the two appeal courts.

His execution has divided opinion in Canada since 1885.[278] French Canadians supported the campaign to suppress the rebellion, but there was widespread outrage in Québec over Riel's execution that did not abate over time leading to the disastrous Conservative defeat in the elections in 1891.[279] Wilfrid Laurier's passionate denunciation of the government's action on 1886 was a major step forward in his career. For many French-Canadians, Riel's execution seemed to symbolise the weakness of Quebec's politicians in federal government and, in part, contributed to a revival in French-Canadian nationalism from the late 1880s.[280]

The debate over whether Riel's execution was justifiable or, as Winnipeg Centre MP Pat Martin maintains, he was only executed because he was a 'nuisance', continues.[281] Riel was not, Martin argues, leading a rebellion against Canada but defending the Métis against an impending attack by Canadian forces.[282] The critical issue is whether Riel should simply be pardoned or whether his conviction should be overturned and the government acknowledge that he was not guilty. While many support his exoneration, many Métis are uncomfortable with a pardon because it implies guilt, mercy and forgiveness. To these people, Riel was not guilty of treason and they do not want him pardoned for something he did not do.[283]

The government initially arrested more than two hundred Métis, whites and Indians on the lesser charge of treason-felony although the government proceeded with only 84 cases.[284] On 24 July and in marked contrast to Riel, William Jackson, his English personal secretary, was found not guilty by reason of insanity and sent to an asylum in Manitoba from where he had no difficulty in escaping to the United States. Most of the provisional government council pleaded guilty and received sentences ranging from conditional discharges to

---

278 For instance, Guillet, Edwin C., *Death for High Treason: A Study of the Evidence in The Queen versus Louis Riel, 1885*, 1944, and Thompson, John S. D., *Discours sur la question Riel: prononcé le 22 mars, 1886 à la Chambre des communes par l'honorable S. D. Thompson*, 1886, are unsympathetic to Riel and suggest that he was fairly tried, convicted and executed while Thomas, Lew, 'A Judicial Murder: The Trial of Louis Riel', in Palmer, Howard, (ed.), *The Settlement of the West*, (University of Calgary Press), 1977, pp. 37-59, views the legal proceedings as biased and that it was a political trial to assuage the 'paranoic fears and passions of Ontario voters'.

279 Pennington, Christopher, *The Destiny of Canada: Macdonald, Laurier and the Election of 1891*, (Allen Lane), 2011, pp. 12-14, 103-112.

280 Ibid, Silver, A. I., *The French-Canadian Idea of Confederation, 1864-1900*, pp. 150-179, examines the transition among French-Canadians from support for the expeditionary force to criticism of the partiality of Riel's trial and opposition to his execution.

281 *Winnipeg Free Press*, 31 March 2011.

282 *Counterweighs*, 17 November 2010.

283 Detailed discussion of the question of exoneration is found in, ibid, Flanagan, Thomas, *Riel and the Rebellion: 1885 Reconsidered*, pp. 169-189. See also, Teillet, Jean, 'Exoneration for Louis Riel: Mercy, Justice or Political Expediency?', *Saskatchewan Law Review*, Vol. 67, (2004), pp. 359-392.

284 Beal, Bob, and Wright, Barry, 'Summary and Incompetent Justice: Legal Responses to the 1885 Crisis', in ibid, Wright, Barry, and Binnie, Susan, (eds.), *Canadian State Trials, Volume III*, pp. 353-410, examines the trials of the lesser offenders. See also, *Trials in connection with the North-west rebellion, 1885*, (Maclean, Rogers & Co.), 1886.

seven years in penitentiary. Chiefs Poundmaker and Big Bear were tried and each sentenced to three years in jail. Several other Indians from Batoche, Frog Lake and Battleford were sentenced to various terms after treason-felony convictions. Eleven Indians were convicted of murder as a result of the Frog Lake 'massacre' and other killings carried out during the rebellion. On 27 November, six Cree and two Assiniboine warriors, including Frog Lake war chief Wandering Spirit, were hanged at Battleford. Three other convicted murderers had their sentences commuted. All the rebels sentenced to jail were released early. In 1888, Gabriel Dumont eventually returned from the United States under the terms of a general amnesty granted two years earlier but it was not until 1893 that he settled in Batoche.

That Riel was a messianic leader is clear but there are problems when relating his ideas to the sense of dislocation and marginalisation that caused disaffection among the Métis at Red River and in Saskatchewan. There are also questions about whether the Métis in Saskatchewan were experiencing the trauma that seemed necessary to prepare for rebellion and a significant number of Métis did not support Riel. He believed he was a prophet of God sent to prepare the chosen Métis people for their future religious inheritance and that Christ would return to meet his Church in Manitoba and establish his kingdom. There is little evidence to suggest that those who did follow Riel in 1885 understood the messianic ideas to which he subscribed and, as a consequence, whether Riel's actions can best be understood as millenarian is open to question. Riel did not share what Flanagan calls his 'secret doctrine' with the people of the North West before 1885. They, not he, initiated the overtures that led to his return to Canada in 1884, and there is no evidence to suggest that millenarian enthusiasm prompted their decision to approach Riel or to follow him later into open revolt. Arguably, Riel's millenarianism was a constraint on Métis action since it alienated the Roman Catholic Church and, at least initially, French-Canadian opinion. That the Métis took the decision to recall Riel to Canada in 1884 is testament to his power of a charismatic leader who was able to inspire his followers with desperately needed hope for the future and that, combined with his belief that with the help of God, resistance would lead to peace, justice and universal harmony for the Métis. It was Riel's hope that by repeating the strategies he had used in 1869 and 1870, the federal government would accede to his demands. His view was that it was Ottawa that was 'insane and irresponsible':

> I have acted reasonably and in self-defence, while the Government, my accuser, being irresponsible, and consequently insane, cannot but have acted wrong, and if high treason there is it must be on its side and not on my part.[285]

Riel remains an elusive figure: prophet and madman; brilliant and unstable; mystic and visionary; religious and political leader; maverick and pan-Canadian patriot. Yet his millenarian vision continues to inspire.

---

[285] Ibid, *The Queen v. Louis Riel*, p. 324.

Conclusions

Millenarian anti-colonial movements develop when people band together and act upon a belief of an imminent and total transformation of society either into something completely new or into a revived and purified society of the past. Riel believed that a 'new nation' would be created in Canada that would be ecumenical and multi-racial in character while for Te Ua saw a world in which Māori would be restored to their divinely ordained place in the world. In some instances, such as the Xhosa experience in the 1850s, individual and groups believe that the power of evil is so great that to eliminate it, the world or existing order had to be destroyed and created afresh by God, his prophets or by a superhuman power. In the colonial context, millenarian movements are associated with periods of change and social upheaval, claims to esoteric knowledge linked to charismatic and messianic leadership and leads to a blanket condemnation of existing social and political authority. They physically and figuratively inhabit the borderland where the religious and the political fuse and provide an emotional framework within which resistance can develop and flourish. Those involved in rebellion recognise that they had to act to realise their own liberation, saw themselves as protected by God and unaccountable to existing human laws. The limitation of millenarian movements lies in the continued reliance on a supernatural force to guarantee this. As long as this faith remained, millenarians tended to place themselves into militarily and politically untenable positions, creating small utopian settlements that they defended with courage and ferocity, but that often ended up being their graveyards.

For the colonial authorities, millenarian movements were generally regarded as no different from any other form of anti-colonial resistance. It was relatively easy to portray the prophets as deluded or mad but it proved less easy to combat the zeal and passion their movements generated except through military force against opponents who believed themselves immune to colonial bullets. The Xhosa resistance was contained largely by its own self-immolating logic but in NZ and the North-West Territories, military intervention was necessary to defeat the Pai Marire and Riel's movement. By demonising the movements, the actions of the authorities seemed justifiable to the public with frequently tragic consequences. Colonial government was swift to exploit these tragedies for social and political gain. After the Xhosa resistance, Sir George Grey could obtain all the cheap labour Cape Colony needed and all the farmland demanded by white settlers, a situation he largely replicated in NZ. In the North-West Territories, the federal government was able to intensify the immigration of settlers to farm the rich grain soils and fertile grasslands of the plains. For the Xhosa, Māori and Métis, the consequence of their resistance was the antithesis of the millenarian prophecies and apocalyptic visions of their leaders. Not only had they been abandoned by the colonial authorities to settler exploitation and their lands expropriated but their belief in a God-given future had been extinguished. The failure of millenarian resistance is perhaps the harshest form of colonial repression because it is accompanied by a loss of hope.

8 Nationalist rebellion

Patriotism is when love of your own people comes first; nationalism, when hate for people other than your own comes first.[1]

Nationalism is a cryptic concept that has produced a diverse array of definitions.[2] Gellner defines nationalism as 'primarily a political principle, which holds that the political and the national unit should be congruent'.[3] The dominant nation within a specified geographical boundary should also wield the political power and run the machinery of government. Hobsbawm appends the characteristic of 'political duty' to Gellner's definition in order to distinguish nationalism from 'other and less demanding forms of national or group identification'.[4] This duty not only comprises notions of loyalty and patriotism, but also 'overrides all other public obligations' to the point that nationalists may be called upon to engage in combat with another national group or even the state in which they currently reside in.[5] However it is defined, any discussion of nationalism is intrinsically based on the concept of the nation.

Anti-colonial nationalism is based on reactions to threats to a nation's survival from an external power and this forces the nation to solidify its heritage through a variety of means. The responsive nature of anti-colonial nationalism developed through three stages: conflict, creation and confrontation. Conflict begins when there is a direct threat from the process of colonisation to the cultural, political, economic or social authority of the colonised and particularly unwillingness by colonial authorities to recognise the validity of national demands. This generally takes the form of a growing sense of grievance over issues such as political disfranchisement, cultural or economic deprivation and threats to religious identity. The creation stage occurs when non-colonial élites resurrect, construct or reconstruct a nationalist sentiment or myth, often grounded in the notion of self-determination. This is used to mobilise the masses into a sense of group identity and to provide some form of opposition to the state's policies in seeking some form of constitutional solution involving self-government and eventually independence. This is particularly problematic in multi-ethnic societies where the colonial state has failed to sustain any sense of solidarity across ethnic lines or where colonial authorities played one ethnic group off against another. Finally, confrontation takes place when nationalist movements have lost the ability to operate through traditional political channels and feel alienated by perceived or actual state repression. This can escalate into militant opposition with secessionist aims that employs protest and ultimately violent forms of political action.

Although anti-colonial nationalist rebellions are seen largely as liberation movements in the context of decolonisation of Britain's empire in the decades after 1945, from the late-eighteenth century nationalist rebellions occurred against

---

[1] General Charles de Gaulle, cit, Gary, Romain, 'To mon Géneral: Farewell with Love and Anger', *Life*, Vol. 66, (18), 9 May 1969, pp. 24-29.
[2] Anderson, Benedict, *Imagined Communities*, (Verso), 1992, pp. 3-4.
[3] Gellner, Ernest, *Nations and Nationalism*, (Cornell University Press), 1983, p. 1.
[4] Hobsbawm, Eric J., *Nations and Nationalism since 1789: Programme, Myth, Reality*, 2nd ed., (Cambridge University Press), 1990, p. 9.
[5] Ibid, Hobsbawm, Eric J., *Nations and Nationalism since 1789*, p. 9.

the British Crown. This was particularly evident in Ireland in the substantial rebellion in 1798 and the shambolic rebellions in 1848 and 1867 and the Easter Rising in 1916 in which separatist, republican nationalism played a pivotal role. The rebellions in Lower Canada in 1837 and 1838 were driven by French Canadian nationalism that, especially in 1838 called for independence from British rule. The Indian Mutiny in 1857, which some historians see as India's 'First War of Independence', undoubtedly had important nationalist elements but, two months after events unfolded, Benjamin Disraeli questioned whether:

> Is this a military mutiny, or is it a national revolt? Is the conduct of the troops the consequence of a sudden impulse or is it the result of an organised conspiracy?[6]

In addition to the problem of defining anti-colonial rebellion as nationalist, there is also the issue of its part in the achievement of constitutional change. The rebellions in Ireland had little military effect on the ultimate achievement of partition and independence in 1922. In Lower Canada, the rebellions resulted in a detailed analysis of the 'problem of Canada' leading to the Durham *Report* and within a decade the granting of responsible or self-government. In India, the Mutiny led to the British government taking responsibility for governing the sub-continent from the East India Company but it was a further ninety years before independence was finally conceded. The liberation movements after 1945, while they placed pressure on the colonial system, state repression played little role in the achievement of independence. In Kenya, for instance, the Mau Mau rebellion was largely contained by 1956 and independence did not occur until 1963 while in Cyprus, the EOKA emergency was over before the independence of the island in 1960. Rebellion may have provided a context within which moves towards independence took place, but independence was largely achieved by political agreement. There is a stronger case for rebellions forcing the colonial authorities to the negotiating table not because of their military success but because of the burgeoning cost of maintaining a heightened colonial military presence. The lesson of the American Revolution--the most successful of all rebellions against the British Crown--is that colonial authorities ultimately could not compel colonies to remain in the Empire and that it was better to grant them self-government and ultimately independence than seek to retain them by force. J. A. Roebuck argued in 1849, 'Every colony ought by us to be looked upon as a country destined, at some period of its existence, to govern itself',[7] a point echoed in 1856 by Arthur Mills, an influential colonial commentator, who suggested:

> ...to ripen those communities to the earliest possible maturity - social, political, and commercial - to qualify them, by all the appliances within the reach of a parent State, for present self-government, and eventual independence, is now the universally admitted object and aim of our Colonial policy.[8]

---

[6] *Hansard*, House of Commons, Debates, 27 July 1857, Vol. 147, cc442-443.

[7] Roebuck, J. A., *The Colonies of England*, (John W. Parker), 1849, p. 170

[8] Mills, Arthur, *Colonial Constitutions: An Outline of the Constitutional History and Existing Government of the British Dependencies*, (John Murray), 1856, p. lxix.

A century later, Michael Bundell, Minister for Agriculture in Kenya in the 1950s and leader of a moderate white settler party, put in more bluntly:

> It boiled down to whether the British Government could or would shoot Africans to maintain the status quo for Europeans.[9]

Earlier empire builders would have done so with little conjunction but that was no longer the case. The critical question about decolonisation was always not if, but when.

Kenya

African nationalism was a struggle *against* European rule and hegemony and a struggle *for* African autonomy and reconstruction. It was ignited by the grievances of different peoples, genders and generations against colonial oppression and exploitation and drew its ideological inspiration from diverse sources, local and transnational, traditional and contemporary. It could entail the expansive visions of Pan-African liberation and integration, territorial nation-building or the appeal of ethnic identities. Secular and religious visions also competed for ascendancy. If the nationalist movement constituted the primary institutional vehicle for nationalist expression and struggle, its immediate objective was decolonisation. The development of nationalism varied from colony to colony, even in colonies under the same imperial power, depending on the way the colony had been acquired and was administered, the presence or absence of settlers, traditions of resistance, the social composition of the nationalist movement and its type of leadership. The nationalist movements encompassed political parties and civic organisations, trade unions, peasant movements, women's movements, religious and cultural movements and youth movements that waged its struggles using methods and tactics that were both separate and interconnected. It is this plurality of the nationalist movements that often sowed the seeds of postcolonial discord as independence removed the sense of unity for the disparate elements struggling for *uhuru.*

Establishing Protectorates, 1885-1914

Colonial involvement In East Africa did not begin until the 1880s. Before then, the area formed the economic hinterland of the commercial centre of Zanzibar. The region included much of what are now Tanzania, Kenya and Uganda and was crossed by trade routes that converged on the Swahili urban concentrations on the east coast. By 1905, Britain and Germany had achieved overall command in military and strategic terms but their control over the African population was uneven and the new colonial economies had only partially superseded older systems of production and exchange.[10] British, American, German and French commercial interests were evident in East Africa by the 1860s. The export of

---

[9] Blundell, Michael, *A Love Affair with the Sun: A Memoir of Seventy Years in Kenya*, (East African Publishers), 1994, p. 97.

[10] Wright, Marcia, 'East Africa, 1870-1905', in Fage, J. D., Oliver, Roland, et al, (eds.), *The Cambridge History of Africa, Volume 6, c.1870-c.1905*, (Cambridge University Press), 1985, pp. 539-591.

slaves was a major feature of the sultan of Zanzibar's revenue and the marketing of slaves was an institutionalised economic activity throughout East Africa. Treaties between Britain and Zanzibar in 1873 and 1876 did much to restrict the slave trade but did little to strike at the institution of slavery within the area. African and Arab traders moved their commercial activities from exporting slaves to legitimate products such as rubber and spices produced on plantations sustained by slave labour. In addition to growing western commercial involvement in East Africa, Christian missionaries became a growing feature of the spread of Western ideologies and cultural values. From 1879, the White Fathers joined the Church Missionary Society in Buganda and spread around Lake Malawi and Lake Tanganyika. The London Missionary Society evangelised south of Lake Tanganyika. From the early 1880s, permanent Christian missions were established and exerted growing social control over native behaviour.

British interest in East Africa was further stimulated by colonial competition with Germany. On 7 August 1885, five German warships steamed into the lagoon of Zanzibar demanding that the Sultan cede his mainland territories to the German Emperor. In the age of the telegram, gunboat diplomacy was no longer a local matter and the crisis immediately raised concerns in London. Britain, eager not to offend Germany, suggests a compromise whereby the two nations agreed spheres of interest over the territory stretching inland to the Great Lakes. This plan was accepted by the end of August and the British consul was ordered to persuade the sultan to sign an agreement ceding the bulk of his mainland territory. A joint Anglo-German boundary commission started work in the interior and by November 1886, it had completed its work and its result had been agreed with the other main colonial power, France. The sultan was left a strip ten miles wide along the coast. Behind that a line was drawn to Mount Kilimanjaro and on to Lake Victoria at latitude 1° S. The British sphere of influence was to the north, the German to the south and the line remains the border between Kenya and Tanzania and was ratified in the Anglo-German Treaty of 1890.

The transition from spheres of influence to colonial states had been accomplished by 1900. Initially colonial ambitions were pursued indirectly through economically feeble chartered companies but between 1888 and 1900, sporadic but sustained military action led to the active conquest of East Africa. This was accompanied by the collapse of the slave-based African commercial system and by ecological crisis caused by drought, cholera and smallpox and by cattle diseases such as rinderpest after 1887 that decimated herds and dispersed populations. Cattle were central to the cultural identity of the Maasai who had arrived in East Africa from the north over a century earlier. The impoverishment of the Maasai in the 1890s resulted in them becoming vital allies in the initial colonial occupation of British East Africa and a ready source of military recruitment in campaigns against the Kikuyu, the largest tribe in the area. [11] This produced an enduring enmity between the two peoples that persisted into the twentieth century.

As with the areas being colonised by Cecil Rhodes in southern Africa, the British government is initially reluctant to take active responsibility for its regional

[11] Waller, Richard, 'The Maasai and the British 1895-1905: the Origins of an Alliance'. *Journal of African History*, Vol. 17, (1976), pp. 529-553.

sphere of influence. In 1888, it assigned the right to administer and develop the territory to the Imperial British East Africa Company, a year before Rhodes established the British South Africa Company. The development of this region depended on the construction of a railway from the coast to Lake Victoria, but this proved to be beyond the abilities of the East Africa Company. The problem lay with the kingdom of Buganda. As it was beyond Lake Victoria, Germany argued that this region was not covered by its territorial agreement with Britain and in 1890, Karl Peters arrived at Kampala hoping to persuade the Kabaka, the king of Buganda to sign a treaty accepting a German protectorate over his kingdom. Confrontation between Britain and Germany was averted when the Prime Minister, Lord Salisbury offered the island of Heligoland, in British possession since 1814, in return for German recognition of British protectorates in Zanzibar, Uganda and Equatoria, the southern province of Sudan.[12]

Meanwhile the East Africa Company faced further problems in Buganda, where there were tensions between Christian and Muslim parties and where in 1890 conflict broke out between factions led by British Protestant missionaries and their French Catholic rivals.[13] The four groups involved in Buganda, the Kabaka, French Catholics, Protestants and the Company could not resolve their disputes amicably and in January 1892, civil war broke out between Protestant and Catholic converts. The Catholics quickly gained the upper hand until Frederick Lugard, the only combatant with the advantage of a Maxim machine gun, intervened. He earned a fruitless victory when the Kabaka signed a treaty giving Buganda the status of protectorate under the authority of the East Africa Company.[14] The East Africa Company was already struggling to finance its operations and funding Lugard's activities had almost bankrupted it. It became increasingly clear that the Company was incapable of fulfilling its duties. In 1894, the British government declared a protectorate over Buganda and two years later, British control was extended over the western kingdoms of Ankole, Toro and Bunyoro, forming with Buganda, the Uganda Protectorate.

The much larger region of Kenya had been relatively calm, but the East Africa Company has achieved little of value there.[15] In taking responsibility for

---

[12] On development in Uganda to 1920 see, Adyanga, Onek C., *Moder of British Imperial Control in Africa: A Case Study of Uganda, c.1890-1990*, (Cambridge Scholar Publishing), 2011, pp. 40-54, and Low, D. A., *Fabrication of Empire: The British and the Uganda Kingdoms, 1890-1902*, (Cambridge University Press), 2009.

[13] Low, D. A., *Buganda in Modern History*, (University of California Press), 1971, pp. 20-54, considers the problems posed by conversion to Christianity and Islam and the conflict that resulted.

[14] Perham, Margery, (ed.), *The Diaries of Lord Lugard: East Africa 1889-1892*, 3 Vols. (Northwestern University Press), 1959. See also, Perham, Margery, *Lugard, Volume 1, The Years of Adventure, 1858-1898*', (Collins), 1956.

[15] For general studies of the development of Kenya see, Berman, Bruce, and Lonsdale, John, *Unhappy Valley: Conflict in Kenya and Africa*, (James Currey), 1992, pp. 13-44, 225-468, Ochieng W. R., and Maxon, R. M., (eds.), *An Economic History of Kenya*, (East African Educational Publishers Ltd.), 1992, Ochieng W. R., (ed.), *A Modern History of Kenya, 1895-1980*, (Evans Brothers), 1989, Mosley, Paul, *The Settler Economies: Studies in the Economic History of Kenya and Southern Rhodesia 1900-1963*, (Cambridge University Press), 1983, and Lonsdale, John, 'Kenya: Home Country and African

Uganda, the British government needed to ensure the new Protectorate's access to the sea. So, in 1895 the company's charter is revoked with compensation of £250,000. Kenya becomes another new responsibility of the British government as the East Africa Protectorate. The early years of the protectorate include several developments of significance in Kenya's subsequent history. The intention was to provide revenue for the railway driven northwest from Mombasa to reach Kisumu on Lake Victoria in 1901. The colonial authorities encouraged the growth of cash crops to help pay for the railway's operating costs and in 1902, the eastern section of the Uganda Protectorate was transferred to the East African Protectorate to keep the entire railway line under one local colonial administration. Over 32,000 indentured workers from Britain's Indian empire was used to construct the railway and many stayed, as did most Indian traders and small businessmen who provided important commercial links from the coast into the interior. By the 1920s, there is a sizable Indian population to demand a share in the developing political life of Kenya.[16]

Building the railway had been expensive and it had experienced cost overruns and the British decided to encourage large-scale settlement by farmers of European origin in Kenya's prosperous temperate highlands that subsequently becomes known as the White Highlands. Most of the early settlers came from South Africa rather than Britain. Short of labour on their new farms where they engaged in large-scale coffee production, they make strenuous efforts to introduce the forced African' largely Kikuyu labour common in many other European colonies. Not until the 1920s were such methods outlawed in Kenya. The resentment of the indigenous population against the settlers is accentuated from 1904, when a policy is introduced of settling Africans on reserves. The Maasai were restricted to the southern Loieta plains in 1913 while the Kikuyu claimed some of the land reserved for Europeans. The railway also opened the interior to systematic colonial legislation that addressed the issues of slavery and witchcraft and sought to reduce disease and famine. For instance, from 1909, the colonial administration passed legislation that made the practice of witchcraft illegal and provided the local population with legal, non-violent ways to stem the activities of witches.[17]

Frontier', in Bicker, Robert, (ed.), *Settlers and Expatriates: Britons over the Seas*, (Oxford University Press), 2010, pp. 74-111.

[16] For the early development of colonial Kenya see, Lonsdale, J. M., 'The Politics of Conquest: The British in Western Kenya, 1894-1908', *Historical Journal*, Vol. 20, (1977), pp. 841-870, and Lonsdale, John, and Berman, Bruce, 'Coping With the Contradictions: The Development of the Colonial State in Kenya, 1895-1914', *Journal of African History*, Vol. 20, (1979), pp. 487-505, reprinted in ibid, Berman, Bruce, and Lonsdale, John, *Unhappy Valley*, pp. 45-100.

[17] Waller, Richard D., 'Witchcraft and Colonial Law in Kenya', *Past & Present*, Vol. 180, (2003), pp. 241-275, and Luongo, Katherine, *Witchcraft and Colonial Rule In Kenya, 1900-1955*, (Cambridge University Press), 2011. The colonial regime had limited success in banning traditional behaviour; for instance, Anderson, David, and Carrier, Neil, 'Khat in Colonial Kenya: A History of Prohibition and Control', *Journal of African History*, Vol. 50, (2009), pp. 377-397, demonstrates the impact of the failure of colonial policy to take account of African opinion on *khat* (its leaves were chewed as a stimulant and recreational drug) and the failure of the policy in the 1940s.

Developing African politics, 1914-1950

The outbreak of war in Europe in 1914 resulted in a truce between the governors of British and German East Africa in an abortive attempt to keep the colonies out of direct hostilities. Despite the orders from Berlin and the colony's governor who insisted on neutrality for German East Africa, Paul Emil von Lettow-Vorbeck, commander of the small garrison was determined to tie down as many British resources as possible and from November 1914 to 1918, he conducted a guerrilla campaign and remained undefeated.[18] The East Africa Protectorate was transformed into a British Crown Colony in 1920.[19] The interwar period was characterised by the consolidation of the colonial order and increasing challenges against it by the landless squatters, impoverished workers and restless indigenous élites. These were reinforced by the disasters of the Great Depression and the Second World War that respectively undermined the promises of colonial capitalism and the supremacy of the colonial powers.[20]

The establishment of the colony of Kenya led to growing racial hostility. New legislation on land tenure shamelessly favoured the settlers. In many areas, Africans were formally dispossessed of their land and confined in reservations, while the 'White Highlands' policy restricted the ownership of the best farming land to Europeans. By the 1930s, 30,000 white settlers lived in the area and to protect their interests they banned natives from growing coffee, introduced a hut tax and reduced the amount of land granted to the landless in return for their labour. These and other tensions were reflected in the developing political scene. From 1907, white settlers were either elected or nominated as members of the Legislative Council and at the end of the war called for 'responsible government'. The other two communities of the colony demanded similar representation. The Indians, enjoying a greater economic strength, were the more adamant. In 1920, they turned down the offer of two seats on the Legislative Council, arguing that this did not reflect the size of their community.[21] Tension remains high until 1927, when the Indians won the right to five seats on the Council, compared to eleven reserved for the Europeans. The government appointed a European to represent African interests on the Council and in 1923, the Colonial Office declared in the 'Devonshire Declaration' that the interests of Africans, who made up 95 per cent of the population, must be paramount, a goal that took four decades to achieve. In 1944, the Legislative Council in Nairobi became the first

---

[18] Paice, Edward, *Tip and Run: The untold tragedy of the Great War in Africa*, (Weidenfeld & Nicolson), 2007, is the best study of the East African campaigns.

[19] The 'Colony of Kenya' referred to the interior lands while the ten-mile coastal strip (technically on lease from the Sultan of Zanzibar) was the 'Protectorate of Kenya' but both were dealt with as a single administrative unit.

[20] On the development of settler colonialism see, Berman, Bruce, *Control and Crisis in Colonial Kenya: The Dialectic of Domination*, (Currey), 1990, Munro, J. Forbes, *Colonial Rule and the Kamba: Social Change in the Kenya Highlands 1889-1939*, (Oxford University Press), 1975, Tignor, Robert L., *The Colonial Transformation of Kenya. The Kamba, Kikuyu and Maasai From 1900 to 1935*, (Princeton University Press), 1975, and Wolff, Richard D., *The Economics of Colonialism: Britain and Kenya, 1870-1930*, (Yale University Press), 1974

[21] In 1921, the estimated population of the Colony and Protectorate of Kenya was 2.376 million including 22,822 Indians, 10,102 Arabs and only 9.651 European.

in any east African colony to include an African member. This doubled to two in 1946, to four in 1948 and to eight in 1951. But these are token politicians, appointed by the colonial governor from local lists.

The war had a significant effect in politically mobilising the African community, then still largely tribal in nature. To provide military support in the campaigns against German forces in East Africa, the colonial administration formed the Carrier Corps that recruited or conscripted over 400,000 African men as porters and for other support roles. This helped to raise African political awareness as well as highlighting the weakness of the European presence in Africa. In addition, Sir Edward Northey, a general during the East African campaign, was appointed Governor in January 1919 and he immediately showed a strong bias in favour of settler demands and against the claims of Asians and Africans. He also implemented the Soldier-Settler Scheme that brought many more Europeans to Kenya by providing land on easy terms.[22] He also continued the trend begun during the war of increasing the taxes paid by Africans while he supported settlers in their opposition to the introduction of an income tax. The result was considerable and widespread nationalist political activity in the 1920s and 1930s.[23] Initially, nationalist politics was diffuse in nature when leaders were unsure exactly what they wanted. The emphasis was then placed more on local than national issues and finally, nationalist leaders emerged out of local into national politics.

The grievances initially spawned two organisations. The Kikuyu Association formed by the privileged minority, chiefs and headmen to attempt to regain expropriated land and in 1921, Harry Thuku established the Young Kikuyu Association largely as an opposition to the elitist politics of the Kikuyu Association.[24] The Young Kikuyu Association protested against the *kipande* (identity papers to be carried by all African males), land policy and rising levels of taxation. Thuku's politics was weakened by not knowing where best to place political pressure and by seeking to do too many things at the same time. He called on Africans to act, such as dumping the kipande and not working for Europeans and also, through his East African Association called for the independence of East Africa from colonial rule. The colonial authorities interpreted some of his actions as civil disobedience and he was arrested on 14 March 1922 and this was followed by two days of demonstrations. The first demonstration on 15 March was peaceful but the following morning when a crowd of around 7,000 supporters gathered round the Nairobi police station demanding his release, the police opened fire killing at least twenty-five demonstrators.[25] White civilians also joined in the shootings and some demonstrators may have been shot in the back. Thuku was exiled without charge or trial to the Northern Frontier Province where he remained until 1930. Thuku

---

[22] On this issue see, Duder, C. J., 'Men of the Officer Class': The Participants in the 1919 Soldier Settlement Scheme in Kenya', *African Affairs*, Vol. 92, (1993), pp. 69-87.

[23] Okoth, Assa, *A History of Africa, Volume 2: 1915-1995*, (East African Publishers), 2006, pp. 70-76, considers Kenyan anti-colonial radicalism in the 1920s and 1930s.

[24] Thuku, Harry, *Harry Thuku: An Autobiography,* (Oxford University Press), 1970, pp. 11-35, deals with the foundation of the Young Kikuyu Association.

[25] Muoria, Henry, *I, the Gikuyu, and the White* Fury, (East African Publishers), 1994, pp. 7-8, provides an account of the demonstrations.

achieved little tangible in the early 1920s helped his successors to recognise the need to develop effective and sustained pressure on the authorities.

Thuku influenced the development of the Young Kavirondo Association in 1921 that was dominated by the Luo and Abaluyia. It was initially very radical in its demands drawing up a memorandum for the colonial authorities calling for the establishment of a paramount chief. Its meetings and resolutions led to the administration making some concessions that included lowering the poll tax, easing labour recruitment and establishing meetings with Luo chiefs. The administration also put pressure on mission societies to control the political activities of its adherents. The Archdeacon of Nyanza from 1918 to 1944, W. Owen worked closely with the Young Kavirondo Association and deliberately diverted it away from radical politics. In 1923, it was renamed the Kavirondo Taxpayers and Welfare Association devoting much of its energies to welfare politics such as tree planting and sanitary improvements and seeking to promote close cooperation with the colonial administration by demanding more government services at local level.

Thuku's activities demonstrated that there was a division within the Kikuyu between the younger and older generations and throughout the 1920s and 1930s there was a struggle for leadership.[26] The younger generation was disenchanted by the lack of machinery for local government and, in response to the disturbing effects of the Nairobi disturbances the British government established a system of Local Native Councils designed to bring young men into moderate politics. In 1924, some educated Kikuyu formed the Kikuyu Central Association that dominated nationalist politics until it was banned in May 1940. The following year, when the governor Sir Edward Grigg visited the Kikuyu districts, the Association made their concerns known. They complained about the loss of land and land rights, criticised the chiefs' abuse of power, called for Thuku's release and called for the right for Africans to grow cash crops such as coffee. Like the Young Kavirondo Association, they called for a paramount chief, arguing that this would put them in a stronger position to negotiate with the British government in defence of their lands. However, the administration was less sympathetic to the Kikuyu Central Association. The organisation continued to gain support among mission-educated young people and in 1928, the Church of Scotland-educated Johnson Kamau, later known as Jomo Kenyatta became Secretary-General of the Kikuyu Central Association and editor of the organisation's newspaper, *Muigwithania* (The Unifier).[27] From 1928, the Kikuyu Central Association began to campaign on issues of cultural nationalism championing traditional Kikuyu values against attacks from European missionaries. The most contentious question was that of female circumcision, an important traditional practice that marked the transition of a girl into womanhood. The different Protestant missions led by the Church of Scotland sought to end the practice partly on health grounds

---

[26] Clough, Marshall S., *Fighting Two Side: Kenyan Chiefs and Politicians, 1918-1940*, (University Press of Colorado), 1990, considers the tensions between the loyalist chiefs and the more radical younger generation.

[27] For Kenyatta see, Murray-Brown, Jeremy, *Kenyatta*, (Allen & Unwin), 1979, Aseka, Eric M., *Jomo Kenyatta: A Biography*, (East African Educational Publishers), 1992, and Assensoh, A. B., *African Political Leadership: Jomo Kenyatta, Kwame Nkrumah and Julius K. Nyerere*, (Krieger Publishing Co.), 1998.

and, despite government advice to proceed carefully, pressed their converts to disassociate themselves from the practice or give up their Church membership. With the support of the Kikuyu Central Association, many Christians left the mission churches and the controversy resulted in the development of independent churches and schools in the 1930s.[28]

In the 1930s, the Kikuyu Central Association became increasingly disillusioned with local politics. It had not replaced the privileged leadership that had been strengthened in 1931 with the formation of the Kikuyu Loyal Patriots with its members support for central government and its focus solely on land for the tribe. It had also proved politically ineffective in addressing the question not of how to defend the land but how to get it back. To achieve political change, it had to attack the actions of the Legislative Council and to do this it needed to broaden its support in other Kenyan communities. It was suspected of being involved in the formation of the North Kavirondo Central Association in 1934 as a result of the government alienation of Luyialand for gold mining and in 1938 the Kikuyu Central Association intervened in Ukambani in support of the Akamba in their quarrel with the government. In the Ukambani reserve, there was a problem of soil erosion and overgrazing that needed immediate action and in 1937, the authorities introduced a compulsory reduction in stock that resulted in Akamba farmers being forced to sell their livestock for slaughter. In 1938, the Ukamba Members' Association was formed and received considerable support from the Kikuyu Central Association. In late July 1938, the movement organised a march in Nairobi to present their grievances to the Governor. Although initially unsympathetic, he accepted calls for the end of forced sale in favour of voluntary transactions and the destocking policy was ended. This kind of rural radicalism would be repeated after the Second World War.

In the mid-1930s, the Kenya government sought to encourage African production, particularly among the Kikuyu and Abaluhya, in order to bolster the fiscal base of the colonial state and to subsidise the survival of the settler farming community. Promotion of African agrarian production brought conflict with the settler farming sector and generated a crisis in the political economy of Kenya. These antagonisms sharpened during the war, when, after the Japanese advance in South-east Asia, the Allied war effort demanded greater production from Kenya's settler farmers.[29] Historians have under-estimated the extent to which African producers capitalised on the economic boom caused by the war since high guaranteed prices meant that both settler and African production could expand during the war. Easily able to by-pass official marketing channels, African peasants produced for the black market and during the mid-war drought and maize crisis of 1942-1943, African producers could obtain very favourable prices. Peasant households among the Kikuyu and Abaluhya were economically

---

[28] The two main separatist churches were the Kikuyu Orthodox Church and the Kikuyu Independent Pentecostal Church that were linked respectively with the Kikuyu Karinga Schools Association and the Kikuyu Independent Schools Association.

[29] Anderson, David, and Throup, David, 'Africans and Agricultural Production in Colonial Kenya: The Myth of the War as a Watershed', *Journal of African History*, Vol. 26, (1985), pp. 327-345. See also, Lonsdale, John, 'The Depression and the Second World War in the Transformation of Kenya', in Killingray, David, and Rathbone, Richard, (eds.), *The Second World War and Africa*, (Macmillan), 1986, pp. 97-142.

strengthened by the war, as was the settler farming sector. From these disruptions emerged a changed colonial order in which the settlers who had expanded their production and power were increasingly pitted against the swelling armies of squatters desperate for land, peasants clamoring for greater access to lucrative cash crops and marketing opportunities.

Immediately after the war, European settlers demanded self-government on the Rhodesian pattern and remained the dominant political force in the country. They resented interference with their exclusive social and political position and assumed that self-government would be based on minority European dominance. However, an expanded African labour force became stronger increasingly militant with the growth of trade unionism and élite protest found political momentum in mass nationalism. The problem was that neither racial domination nor tribal discipline had delivered the peace or progress needed for colonial improvement. The key was to modify the legal structures of the state to promote markets and production without upsetting either. The colonial authorities were conscious of prevailing African attitudes and sought to initiate greater African involvement in the political system. In 1944, one African member was appointed to the Legislative Council to bring Africans into the national political system and so channel emerging African nationalism towards support of the colonial administration. The Kenya African Study Union was established, on the advice of Governor Philip Mitchell, as a colony-wide African organisation that the lone African member could consult. Harry Thuku was elected its President but his anti-imperialism of the 1920s had lost its vibrancy and he was soon replaced by James Gichuru and the organisation dropped the 'Study' part of its name, becoming the Kenya African Union.[30] Until the declaration of the state of emergency in 1952, the Kenya African Union was the militant representative of Kenyan nationalism. Its aims were: independence as soon as possible, the return of all African land taken by settlers and the right to own land in the 'White Highlands', direct elections and immediate increase in the number of Africans on the Legislative Council, free education for Africans, not just Asians and Europeans and better treatment of African workers. But the activities of African nationalists were divided with radicals critical of leaders who were prepared to compromise with the authorities, moderates who believed in effecting change by constitutional means and militant trade unionists calling for increased wages and better working conditions.

The return of Jomo Kenyatta in September 1946 after fifteen years' absence in Britain gave the nationalist movement the charismatic leader it had previously lacked and in June the following year, he was elected President of the Kenya African Union when James Gichuru stepped down to make way for him. Kenyatta quickly built the Union into an orderly united political party and campaigned vigorously for unity, hard work and orderly progress. His major problem was the bitter divisions between radical and moderate nationalists within the party and conservative loyalists largely outside it and this reduced the focus of the party in campaigning for constitutional change. The antagonism between the followers of Thuku and the government-appointed chiefs, a relic of the 1920s,

---

[30] Spencer, John, *KAU: The Kenya African Union*, (Routledge), 1985, pp. 115-249, examine the development of the movement to 1952.

remained and the female circumcision controversy of the 1930s still caused tensions. He also had to address the strong appeal of Mitchell's doctrine of multi-racial progress to moderates who had raised themselves above tribal society through western education and to young radicals who challenged the older generation's traditional position of 'working within the system', had no faith in reform and constitutionalism and whose rhetoric was confrontational.[31] This proved difficult since the radical element in the party, most of whom were Agikuyu, was growing rapidly in strength. The conflict between moderates and radicals reached its climax in 1951 when Kenyatta frustrated the plans of the radicals, insisted that the party must appeal across the country and not turn into a Kikuyu union and was unanimously re-elected president. The radicals were unimpressed by this and remained unconvinced by the emphasis Kenyatta and the party placed on constitutionalism and gradualism. Some radicals had already joined an underground movement that had its roots in the 1930s and by the late 1940s, was already binding its members by oath against the British. In January 1952, a Central Committee was established to control the activities of this anti-colonial movement and to organise oath-taking on a larger scale. [32] This represented the beginnings of the Mau Mau movement. The origins of the term 'Mau Mau' is unclear and most members of the organisation preferred the military title Kenya Land and Freedom Army. The British used the term as a name for the Kikuyu community without assigning is a specific meaning and may also have used it instead of KLFA to deny the Mau Mau rebellion international legitimacy.

Rebellion and repression

By the early 1950s, however, things had begun to change. Both in number and determination, the white plantocracy was stronger, enriched by sustained demand for cereals since the fall of Singapore in 1942 put the agricultural wealth of South-East Asia in enemy hands. One thing it did not want was for the anti-colonialism that was spreading elsewhere in the empire to take root in Kenya. At the same time, a new generation of Kenyan Africans, 75,000 of whom had fought alongside the British against fascism wanted a fairer future, and a more equable division of land and other resources. The British were not prepared to listen and the usually peaceable Kikuyu turned to force, first against their colonial masters and then later, and in far greater number against their loyalist tribal brethren. Despite years cultivating 'the paramountcy of native interests', the British government opposed Kikuyu militancy with force committing the full state apparatus, men, arms and the courts to defending the political and economic status quo. By the early 1950s,

[31] Multiracialism was a convenient policy for not deciding how and when racial and communal distinctions could be reduced. White supremacy may have been dented in the legislative arena but it remained firmly entrenched elsewhere while state intervention to improve African rural and urban life had, by 1952, made little substantive progress.

[32] Corfield, F. D., *Historical Survey of the Origins and Growth of Mau Mau*, (HMSO), 1960, pp. 163-170, examined the development of oath-taking from 'its simple beginning as a comparatively innocuous oath of allegiance to a society or association, to its devastating transformation...[by] the militant members of Mau Mau...'. He suggested that the first recorded use of an oath for political purposes occurred in 1920 and that the Mau Mau oath was already in existence when Kenyatta returned from England in 1946.

Britain had lost India, Palestine and Malaya and now regarded Kenya as its most important colony. The common view was that the rebellion or 'minor civil disturbance' as it was referred to in London, would take just three months to defeat provided that it was dealt with swiftly and firmly.[33]

Concentrated in Central Kenya where the oppressive and exploitative effects of settler colonialism were most concentrated, the Mau Mau struggle was dominated by disposed squatters and poor peasants, found support among radical urban trade unionists and attracted the active participation of many women and youths.[34] Mitchell's plans for the advancement of educated Africans within a framework of multiracialism had made little headway by 1952 and few Africans had any influence in either government or the economy. This, combined with the contemptuous attitude of settlers to education Africans alienated the one group that might have been able to prevent the descent into violence. Land shortages, the result of the policy of forcing Kikuyu squatters off the land that had begun in the 1930s, led to widespread movement to the cities in search of work creating an impoverished and discontented and increasingly radicalised urban African underclass. There was strong resistance to colonial attempts to enforce land use and soil conservation rules and this, combined with lack of access to coffee growing by Kikuyu farmers produced widespread rural unrest. Although there were deep social and economic problems in Kenya, it is possible that the colonial administration could have managed them but it also had to deal with the disillusionment of army veterans who had served abroad during the war and returned to find few economic and political opportunities. In 1945, almost 100,000 ex-servicemen, forming nearly 20 per cent of Kenya's adult male population, were demobilised. Few obtained worked and where they did they found that wages were considerably lower than those they had received in the army. The government failed to address their economic aspirations but also sought to stifle their political development by banning veteran organisations. It was this combination of circumstances that enabled militants to outflank the moderate and Westernised politicians of the Kenya African Union. When the British government refused to see representatives from the Kenya African Union to discuss the land question, this reinforced the position of militants who now saw armed rebellion as the only option left.

On May 15 1952, the mutilated bodies of a village headman and a police informer were found floating in a river. The rebellion had begun. In late August, the Kenyan government imposed a curfew in three districts on the outskirts of Nairobi where gangs of arsonists, believed to be members of Mau Mau, were burning homes of Africans who refused to take the oath. By September 1952, four hundred people were in prisons for having taken or administered the so-called Mau Mau oath but matters came to a head with the assassination of Chief

---

[33] Ibid, Corfield, F. D., *Historical Survey of the Origins and Growth of Mau Mau*, provides the official history. Ibid, Berman, Bruce, and Lonsdale, John, *Unhappy Valley*, pp. 225-466, is particularly useful on the ideology of Mau Mau.

[34] For explanations for the origins the Mau Mau rebellion see, Lonsdale, J., 'Explanations of the Mau Mau Revolt', in Lodge, T., (ed.), *Resistance and Ideology in Settler Societies*, (Ravan Press), 1986, pp. 399-434, Throup, David, *Economic and Social Origins of Mau Mau, 1945-53*, (James Currey), 1987, and Kanogo, Tabitha, *Squatters and the Roots of Mau Mau*, (East African Publishers), 1987.

Kungu Warihiu, the leading spokesman of the government among the Kikuyu on 7 October. In view of the deteriorating situation, the British governed announced that it was to send troops to Kenya to fight against the Mau Mau. With the imminent arrival of British troops, on 20 October 1952 Sir Evelyn Baring, the new governor declared a State of Emergency. During the night, police and army units arrested 180 alleged Mau Mau leaders including key leaders of the Kenya African Union, six of whom including Kenyatta were charged with managing or helping to manage Mau Mau, a proscribed society and causing disaffection.[35] The Kenya African Union continued to protest against emergency measures until it too was banned in June 1953. After the arrests, many men took to the forest and began a guerrilla war to end colonial rule and drive the settlers from Kenya.

The arrests did not weaken the movement as the authorities hoped and the campaign against Mau Mau was marked by considerably brutality on all sides and was as much a civil war among the Kikuyu between loyalists and rebels as conflict between settlers and the state apparatus of coercion and Africans.[36] At Lari, on the night of 25-26 March 1953, Mau Mau forces (seventy-one were later executed for murder, some having openly declared their involvement) herded 120 Christian Kikuyu into huts and set fire to them, hacking to death anyone who tried to escape.[37] Kikuyu loyalists were also tortured, mutilated and murdered by Mau Mau in large numbers. Thirty-two British settlers, 200 British soldiers and policemen and at least 1,800 African civilians were also murdered by Mau Mau militants. The Kenyan authorities were also guilty of atrocities in retaliation raids and in their callous treatment of suspects in custody. They armed the local enemies of the rebels and encouraged them to kill, rape and loot at will. When accounts of British atrocities leaked out, officials in Nairobi and London lied to deny them. The official figure of terrorist casualties is 11,503 but Anderson states that the true figure is likely to be more than 20,000 and Elkins claims it was 70,000 and could have been as high as 300,000.[38] The image of the Mau Mau

---

[35] The Kapenguria trial was notorious in its denial of justice. Kapenguria was a remote village in the Rift Valley without a law library or telephone. Despite the lack of any concrete evidence and Kenyatta's denial that he had was Mau Mau's purported leader and had denounced the organisation at a meeting attended by up to 50,000 people, on 8 April 1953, he was sentenced to seven years' imprisonment with hard labour and was not freed until 1961. See, Christenson, Ron, (ed.), *Political Trials in History: From Antiquity to the Present*, (Transaction Publishers), 1991, pp. 235-239, Slater, Montagu, *The Trial of Jomo Kenyatta*, (Heinemann), 1975, and Macharia, Rawson, *The Truth about the Trial of Jomo Kenyatta*, (Longman Kenya), 1991.

[36] Branch, Daniel, *Defeating Mau Mau, Creating Kenya: Counterinsurgency, Civil War, and Decolonization*, (Cambridge University Press), 2009, Alam, S. M. Shamsul, *Rethinking the Mau Mau in Colonial Kenya*, (Palgrave MacMillan), 2007, Lovatt Smith, David, *Kenya, the Kikuyu and Mau Mau*, (Mawenzi Books), 2005, and Majdalany, Fred, *State of Emergency: The Full Story of Mau Mau*, (Houghton Mifflin), 1963, provide details on different aspects of the rebellion.

[37] Anderson, David, *Histories of the Hanged: The Dirty War in Kenya and the End of Empire*, (Weidenfeld & Nicolson), 2005, pp. 119-180, details the massacre.

[38] Ibid, Corfield, F. D., *Historical Survey of the Origins and Growth of Mau Mau*, p. 316, ibid, Anderson, David, *Histories of the Hanged*, p. 4, and Elkins, Caroline, *Imperial Reckoning: The Untold Story of Britain's Gulag in Kenya*, (Henry Holt and Co.), 2005, pp. xv-xvi. Blacker, John, 'The demography of Mau Mau: fertility and mortality in

fighters skilfully crafted by British propaganda and reinforced in the graphic details of death and mutilation published in British and Kenyan newspapers produced a negative stereotype of dirty, sullen and intransigent fighters from their months on the run in Kenya's equatorial forests. Not since the Black Hole of Calcutta in 1757 did a single phrase instantly conjure up the forces of evil that Britain's civilising mission abroad was doing its best to overcome. Mau Mau was cast as a throwback from a dark and primitive past, with its blood oaths, mutilating and disembowelling as Elspeth Huxley, the white settlers' literary spokesman, wrote in 1956, a 'yell from the swamp'.[39]

The state of emergency enabled Britain to circumvent all the new international conventions on labour and human rights.[40] In Kenya, Britain resorted to more and much more swiftly to imprisonment, flogging and capital punishment than it did in Palestine, Cyprus or Malaya. It was a policy of deliberate terror where settlements suspected of harbouring rebels were torched and Mau Mau suspects tortured. In late 1953 the British opened Operation Anvil, a campaign to cut off the supply network to the KLFA. Its first target was Nairobi that was seen as the centre of their organisation and on 24 April 1954, the police rounded up all the African inhabitants in the city, around 100,000 people. The 70,000 Kikuyu were separated and screened and up to 30,000 men were taken to holding camps. The families of the arrested men were pushed into the already overcrowded native reserves. Thousands of Africans were arrested and detained without trial in a series of squalid camps across the country and thousands more were barricaded inside 'protected villages' where the authorities attempted to win over the hearts and minds of villagers. The authorities devised an elaborate ritual of oaths intended to disinfect detainees from Mau Mau contamination before their release. The system was slow and even those who repented early on spent years being channelled through what was officially known as the 'Pipeline' before being released into the barbed-wire villages on the reserves, to starve the rebellion of food and military supplies. Those who proved intractable after this regime, an estimated 40,000 men were sent to the camps that specialised in 'dilution'. To ensure their repentance, detainees were beaten, electrocuted, dragged behind moving vehicles, burnt with cigarettes and tortured both sexually and psychologically by British and loyalist African warders. 1,090 Kikuyu were hanged, 346 for murder, by the authorities between 1953 and 1958. Nowhere in the history of British imperialism had state execution been used on such a scale.[41]

Kenya in the 1950s: a demographer's viewpoint', *African Affairs*, Vol. 106, (2007), pp. 205-227, dismisses Elkin's allegation that up to 300,000 Kikuyu and others died as a result of the Emergency as over-estimates and concludes that the total number of Africa deaths was 50,000.

[39] Huxley, Elspeth, and Perham, Margery, *Race and Politics in Kenya: A Correspondence between Elspeth Huxley and Margery Perham*, (Faber and Faber), 1956, p. 259.

[40] Two complementary studies are valuable on colonial repression: ibid, Anderson, David, *Histories of the Hanged*, and Elkins, Caroline, *Imperial Reckoning: The Untold Story of Britain's Gulag in Kenya*, (Henry Holt and Co.), 2005. Elkins has been subject to some strenuous criticism of her methodology and use of evidence.

[41] This should be seen in the commonplace use made of hanging in Kenya: 247 non-Mau Mau murderers were executed in the same period.

Kenya's state of emergency was maintained for four years after the fighting ended, while a sustained effort in London and Nairobi covered up the reality on the ground. Violence was enshrined as official policy. Governor Baring was aware of the extreme brutality employed in the camps but chose to do nothing despite the urging of people such as Arthur Young, Commissioner of Police for Kenya who resigned in late 1954 in protest at the horror of some of the camps. Efforts were made by Fenner Brockway, a socialist campaigner, and Barbara Castle, a Labour MP described by a Kenyan attorney-general as 'that castellated bitch', to force the Conservative government to admit to the maltreatment and murder of detainees. It was the Hola massacre in March 1959 that led to the closing of the camps and even the young Enoch Powell, from the far right of the Tory party, declared that if Britain behaved like this it did not deserve an empire.[42] But against the background of the Cold War and without any leverage over the Colonial Office, these critics were routinely painted as liberal rumour-mongering and calls for independent investigations were resisted. No British official, military or civilian, has ever been investigated or prosecuted for what happened in the suppression of Mau Mau. Iain Macleod, the Colonial Secretary, declared as it ended that a veil be drawn over the whole business. It was assumed that on the eve of Britain's withdrawal from Kenya, much of the documentation that related to how Mau Mau was dealt with was destroyed. However, in early 2011, documents 'missing' for fifty years documenting the suppression of the rebellion were uncovered reaffirming the extent of colonial atrocities.[43]

Whether Mau Mau was a nationalist movement or a tribal rebellion and whether it was responsible for Kenya achieving its independence in 1963 has been a matter of considerable debate. The emergency was declared to preserve colonialism in Kenya, but, ironically, the settlers, the custodians of that very regime, were the first to be sacrificed. Soon, the Mau Mau fighters also found themselves side-lined and the loyalists, who shared the same values, not only won the war but were also the more effective nationalists. The emergency generated new social and political processes that destroyed the basis of settler power, restructured the class and institutional bases of the colonial state and altered the balance of class forces, so that both the settlers and the armed freedom fighters, the protagonists in the political crisis of 1952, were marginalised by the time of Kenya's independence in 1963. Robert Buijtenbuijs argues that tribal and nationalist were not mutually exclusive in the case of Mau Mau:

> Mau Mau was a tribal movement, but as a tribal movement it was not hostile to other ethnic groups in Kenya. It was, rather, a case of tribalism serving the nation.[44]

---

[42] On 3 March 1959, 85 prisoners from Hola Camp were marched to a work site but refused to work. They were then systematically beaten by guards for nearly four afters after which 11 men lay dead and 60 were seriously injured. When news reached London, there was a political uproar and within weeks the camps were quietly closed and the detainees released.

[43] *The Times*, 5 April 2011, pp. 1, 2, 6-7.

[44] Buijtenbuijs, Robert, *Mau Mau Twenty Years After*, (Mouton), 1973, p. 84.

Maina wa Kinyatti, a Kenyan historian agrees. He suggests that Mau Mau did not involve simply the Kikuyu but that the fighers were recruited from among the Akamba, Maasai, Luo and Ameru.[45] Benjamin Kipkorir maintains that the Mau Mau factor accelerated Kenya's road to independence and was 'certainly responsible for the precise timing of the conclusion of British rule in Kenya.'[46] His view, however, is weakened by the fact that Kenya was the last of the East African territories to attain independence and that, by 1960, the process was already well underway.

In the immediate aftermath of independence, Mau Mau was largely absent from public discussion in Kenya largely because of the post-colonial dominance of loyalists in government, business and other élite areas of Kenyan society. After 50 years of independence, Kenya still wrestles with the legacy of the Mau Mau revolt of the 1950s. Were its fighters the sole heroes of the anti-colonial struggle, only some of the heroes, or just gangsters, as Kenyatta, once implied and what part should it play in the continuing construction of Kenyan national identity?

Failing to find a solution

At the height of the war, it became clear to the British government, which deployed more than 50,000 troops, that reform was imperative. By requesting British troops and then declaring a State of Emergency in 1952, Governor Baring was admitting that the white settler government could not rule Kenya alone and that the option of devolving power to the colonial government and settlers was no longer viable. Britain's broader colonial aim was to transfer power to 'moderate' local leaders, which in Kenya meant defeating Mau Mau, an objective achieved, for the most part, by 1956. This change would be made within the framework of multi-racialism and Africans would move towards parity of political representation rather than towards majority rule.[47]

This process began in 1954 that not only saw draconian repression, but also the birth of several programmes that in their various ways embodied new state policies that reflected, and further shaped, the underlying structural changes in Kenya's political economy that would set its postcolonial path. The Swynerton Plan, for instance, provided the funding for a programme of capitalist land reform and removed the remaining restrictions against African production of lucrative cash crops. The beneficiaries were the 'loyalists' who became targets of the Mau Mau fighters. The long-term effect was to entrench capitalist agriculture, intensify rural differentiation and increase landlessness among the poor peasants. A new constitution was introduced following a visit by the Colonial Secretary, Oliver Lyttleton that began towards greater African political representation. The Lyttleton Constitution introduced a Council of Ministers, which would help the Governor run the country to replace the advisory Executive Council. The Council

---

[45] See, Kinyatti, Maina wa, *History of Resistance in Kenya*, (Mau Mau Research Centre), 2008, and *Mau Mau: A Revolution Betrayed*, (Mau Mau Research Centre), 1991.

[46] Kipkorir, Benjamin, 'Mau Mau and the Politics of the Transfer of Power in Kenya, 1957-1960', *Kenya Historical Review*, Vol. 5, (2), (1977), pp. 313-328.

[47] Kyle, Keith, *The Politics of the Independence of Kenya*, (St. Martin's Press), 1999, provides a detailed account of the transition from violent rebellion to peaceful independence

would also be multi-racial consisting of three Europeans, two Africans and one Asian. Appolo Ohanga became the first African minister and was responsible for community development and African affairs. The constitution also stated that unofficial members of the Legislative Council would be elected from 1957.

These constitutional developments marked an important move towards African rule but satisfied neither Africans nor settlers. Europeans retained more representation on the Council of Ministers and the Legislative Council and most settlers opposed any extension of African political rights. The changes did not allow Africans to form any political organisations though in mid-1955 political parties were permitted but only at district level. However, political leadership and activity, though forbidden at national level, was provided through the Kenya Federation of Labour established in 1953 and its leader, Tom Mboya emerged as a national spokesman for African political aspirations. With an increase in the number of unofficial African members of the Legislative Council from six to eight members in 1956, conducting elections in African areas was necessary. These occurred in March 1957 under a limited franchise where voters had to meet educational and property qualifications and where only loyalists could vote in the Central Province.[48] The election was a significant step since the newly elected members acquired the legitimacy that they lacked before the elections as well as a public platform to voice their grievances.[49] After the elections, the African elected members formed the African Elected Members Organisation (AEMO) that was quick to express their dissatisfaction over the Lyttleton Constitution: it favoured the white minority, restricted the Africa vote to those with education and wealth and grossly underrepresented Africans on the Legislative Council. AEMO rejected the constitution calling for the franchise for all Kenyans over 21, a single electoral roll rather than the existing separate rolls for Africans, Asians and Europeans, an increase of fifteen African seats on the Legislative Council to give them a majority and the end of the State of Emergency.

Alan Lennox-Boyd was Colonial Secretary between 1954 and 1959 and, following his visit to Kenya in 1957, he proposed what became known as the Lennox-Boyd Constitution.[50] It proposed an increase in African representation on the Legislative Council from 8 to 14 members but there would also be 14 Europeans, 6 Asians and 2 Arabs. The Council would also have 12 special seats elected by its members acting as an electoral college: four each for Africans, Asians and Europeans. The specially elected members would be independent, free to vote for or against the government. AEMO rejected these proposals but despite this, elections were held in 1958 to elect six additional African members. Both the Lyttleton and Lennox-Boyd constitutions were unworkable primarily because neither gave Africans equal political rights. During 1959, pressure grew for a constitutional conference to clarify Kenya's political direction. This process was aided by two developments. The settlers were now divided between the majority United Party that called for white supremacy and segregation in all areas

[48] After these elections, the Legislative Council had 59 members of whom 29 were elected: 8 African, 14 European, 3 Hindu Asians and one Arab.

[49] Branch, Daniel, 'Loyalists, Mau Mau and Elections in Kenya: The First Triumph of the System, 1957-1958', *Africa Today*, Vol. 53, (2006), pp. 27-50, examines the nature and significance of these elections.

[50] Murphy, Philip, *Alan Lennox-Boyd: A Biography*, (I. B. Tauris), 1999

and opposed the conference and the minority New Kenya Party led by Michael Blundell, the Minister for Agriculture that was more moderate and supported a conference.[51] Iain Macleod also became Colonial Secretary in 1959 and was convinced, especially after the Hola Camp massacre that rapid changes were essential in Kenya.[52] The result, in January 1960, was invitations of African, Asian and European leaders to discuss the future of Kenya at Lancaster House, the headquarters of the British Colonial Office, in London.

Independence

The constitutional conference was held in the spirit of Harold Macmillan's 'winds of change' speech and meant that Kenyan nationalism had achieved its goal and a process of decolonisation would begin. The Macleod Constitution accepted by most of the African leaders attending the conference represented a major step towards independence since, for the first time, the British government accepted majority rule ending attempts to bolster white rule through multi-racialism. Africans would have a majority on both the Legislative Council and Council of Ministers. The voting system was also changed: all Kenyans over 40 and any person over 21 who was literate in any language or had a yearly income of £75 would get the vote. Although Blundell's group accepted the new proposals, Macleod was compelled to impose the settlement on other settlers. With the ending of the ban on African national parties, the question was whether responsibility would be handed to the Kenyan African National Union (KANU) or the Kenya African Democratic Union (KADU).

KANU was established in March 1960 and represented the two largest ethnic groups, the Kikuyu and the Luo as well as the Akamba and Agausii. James Gichuru was chosen as its President since Kenyatta was still in prison as a security risk after the completion of his sentence. In May, KANU was formed largely to protect the interests of the smaller tribes, the coastal tribes, the Kalenjin in the Rift Valley and the Abauyia of Western Province and was led by Ronald Ngala as President and Daniel Arap Moi as Chairman. Both agreed on self-government and independence but on different terms and this reflected the tensions between the different peoples of Kenya. KANU wanted a strong unitary state with strong central government while KADU wanted a looser federal state that gave greater power to the regions (majimboism).[53] In the March 1961 elections, the two parties fought for the African seats while Blundell's New Kenya Party and the more reactionary Kenya Coalition, which opposed the direction Kenya was going and

[51] Murphy, Philip, *Party Politics and Decolonization: The Conservative Party and British colonial policy in tropical Africa, 1951-1964*, (Oxford University Press), 1995, pp. 58-73, examines settler pressure on the British government.

[52] See, Shepherd, Robert, *Iain Macleod*, (Hutchinson), 1994, pp. 170-185, and Goldworthy, F. D., *Tom Mboya: The Man Kenya Wanted to Forget*, (Heinemann), 1982, pp. 131-136, are valuable on the Lancaster House conference. See the Cabinet papers printed in Hyam, Ronald and Roger Louis, Wm, *The Conservative Government and the End of Empire 1957-1964*, Part 1, (HMSO), 2000, pp. 506-513.

[53] Anderson, David M., ''Yours in Struggle for Majimbo': Nationalism and the Party Politics of Decolonization in Kenya, 1955-64', *Journal of Contemporary History*, Vol. 40, (2005), pp. 547-564, examines the development of regionalism within the broader nationalist project.

called for the British government to buy out settler farmers, fought the European seats.[54] For Africans, the elections were dominated by calls for Kenyatta's release on which both parties agreed. KANU took nineteen seats and KADU eleven but KANU refused to form any government until Kenyatta was released.[55] KADU agreed to form a government under Ngala and in doing so lost some popular support. In August 1961, Kenyatta was released and after an unsuccessful attempt to get the two parties to united under his leadership, he became President of KANU and in January 1962 was elected unopposed to the Legislative Council. He proved to be the colonial regime's most useful African ally during the transitional period. Far from being a radical or socialist and not the satanic force behind Mau Mau, his detention spared him from having to take sides during the rebellion and established his credentials as a national hero.

A second Lancaster House conference was held in 1962 chaired by Reginald Maudling, the new Secretary of State and Kenyatta led the KANU delegation.[56] The critical issue was the choice between the unitary vision of KANU and the federal alternative of KADU. A complicated Independence Constitution was negotiated in which seven regions with entrenched local powers and regional governments were to be established with a bicameral legislature of House of Representatives and Senate at the centre. A coalition government was formed led jointly by Kenyatta and Ngala and although ZANU accepted the federal system reluctantly it hoped to change the constitution immediately after it won pre-independence elections. In elections in May 1963, KANU won most the seats: 83 seats as opposed to ZADU's 41.[57] Kenyatta was invited to form a government to lead Kenya to self-government and independence on 1 June 1963 and 12 December 1963 respectively and in 1964, Kenyatta was elected as Kenya's first president. Known as *Muigwathania*, 'the Reconciler', he chose to associate his leadership with the West. Declaring that all Kenyans had fought for independence, he passed over the former guerrillas and detainees in favour of influential ex-chiefs and loyalists in forming his new government. He called Mau Mau 'a disease which has been eradicated and must never be remembered'.[58]

The revolution would not take place: Kenyatta stood for continuity not change. There would be no radical redistribution of land or wealth and he committed Kenya to a programme of capitalist development, economic continuity and respect for private property. More importantly for settlers, he agreed to buy at above-market rates the land of any settler who wanted to leave and welcomed

---

[54] The British government in July 1962 agreed to buy out the white settlers and they mostly left Kenya. The Indian minority dominated retail business in the cities and most towns, but was deeply distrusted by the Africans. As a result, 120,000 of the 176,000 Indians kept their old British passports rather than become citizens of an independent Kenya; large numbers left Kenya and most headed to Britain.

[55] Bennett, George, and Rosberg, Carl, *The Kenyatta Election: Kenya 1960-1961*, (Oxford University Press), 1961, remains a central study.

[56] Maudling, Reginald, *Memoirs*, (Sidgwick & Jackson), 1978, pp. 217-220. See the Cabinet papers printed in Hyam, Ronald and Roger Louis, Wm, *The Conservative Government and the End of Empire 1957-1964*, Part 1, (HMSO), 2000, pp. 522-538.

[57] Sanger, C., and Nottingham, J., 'The Kenya General Election of 1963', *Journal of Modern African Studies*, Vol. 2, (1964), pp. 1-40.

[58] Speech by Kenyatta, April 1963.

those who wanted to stay. For many of his supporters who regarded Kenyatta as the champion of the poor and landless, this was immensely disappointing. Kenyatta sought a one-party state and could 'persuade' opposition members to cross the floor by offering them cabinet positions or threatening imprisonment or detention.[59] As a result, KADU announced its dissolution on 10 November 1964 and Kenya became a de-facto one party state.[60] The following month, a constitutional amendment declared Kenya a Sovereign Republic though it took a further four years to legislate the regional system out of the Constitution.[61]

Cyprus

The anti-colonial EOKA campaign in Cyprus between 1955 and 1959 had its origins in the anomalous historical and geographical nature of the island.[62] Its two peoples represent very different cultures: Greek Cypriots who first populated the island over three thousand years ago; and Muslim Turks who arrived after the Ottoman Empire conquered the island in 1571. Greek Cypriot culture has been preserved largely because of the special status accorded to Cypriot Christianity. Evangelised during the early years of the development of the faith, St. Barnabas and St. Paul had established Christianity in Cyprus and in 488 the Byzantine emperor granted the Cypriot Church self-government and temporal power. This political status was especially important during the centuries of Ottoman rule in preventing the erosion of the Orthodox faith.

Although Cyprus' culture largely originated in Greece, the unique position of the Cypriot Orthodox Church, major linguistic differences between Cypriot and mainland Greek and the island's isolation from the mainland meant that, until the 1820s, links tended to be cultural rather than political. The Greeks revolted against Ottoman rule in 1821. Many Cypriots supported Greek independence leading to severe reprisals by the Ottoman authorities: for instance, almost five hundred Greek Cypriots were executed in early July 1821 for conspiring with the rebellion Greeks and in October Turkish mobs hanged most of the Greek Cypriots in Larnaca and other towns. The Greek rebellion was ultimately successful leading to the creation of an independent Greek kingdom

---

[59] Widner, Jerrifer A., *The Rise of a Party-State in Kenya: From 'Harambee' to 'Nyayo'*, (University of California Press), 1992, pp. 4-38, considers the Kenyan case for a one-party state while Throup, David, and Hornsby, Charles, *Multi-party Politics in Kenya: The Kenyatta & Moi States & the Triumph of the System in the 1992 Election*, (James Currey Publishers), 1998, pp. 7-25, examines the Kenyatta state.
[60] See Okoth-Ogendo, H. W. O., 'The Politics of Constitutional Change in Kenya since Independence, 1963-69', *African Affairs*, Vol. 71, (1972), pp. 9-34.
[61] Ahluwalia, D. Pal S., *Post-colonialism and the Politics of Kenya*, (Nova Publishers), 1996, pp. 33-38, examines the demise of regionalism.
[62] Hill, Sir George, *A History of Cyprus*, 4 Vols. (Cambridge University Press), 1940-1952, republished 2010, remains the most accessible, if dated, general study of Cyprus. See also, Morgan, Tabitha, *Sweet and Bitter Island: A History of the British in Cyprus*, (I. B. Tauris), 2010, Richter, Heinz A., *A Concise History of Modern Cyprus, 1878-2009*, (Otto Harrassowitz), 2010, and Holland, Robert, and Markides, Diana, *The British and the Hellenes: Struggles for Mastery of the Eastern Mediterranean 1850-1960*, (Oxford University Press), 2006, pp. 162-240.

eleven years later and that gradually exerted influence over the broader Greek world.[63]

The opening of the Suez Canal in 1869 transformed Cyprus' strategic importance in the Mediterranean and fuelled Britain's interest in the island since the British government was eager to protect the new route to India. This led to a shift in Britain's diplomatic thinking to supporting the declining Ottoman Empire as a bulwark against Russia's aggressive aspirations in the Balkans and more generally in the Mediterranean. The Cyprus Convention of 4 June 1878, a secret agreement reached between the United Kingdom and the Ottoman Empire, granted Britain the right to occupy and administer Cyprus as a military base in exchange for their support of the Ottomans during the Congress of Berlin.[64] Britain also took over Cyprus' annual debt and the financial arrangements with the Sultan that whatever remained of the colony's revenue after expenses for administration had been deducted, meant that the island was a continuing drain on the British Treasury.[65] Cyprus became a protectorate of the British Empire, a status held until the Ottoman Empire declared war against the Entente powers that included Britain in November 1914 when it was unilaterally annexed to the British Empire.[66] It finally became a Crown Colony in 1925.

British rule, 1878-1914

Despite initial military and political reservations about the new colony, its commercial potential was quickly recognised. The first English-language newspaper was established within a month and businesses to cater for the garrison swiftly followed. There were schemes for reopening the island's abandoned

---

[63] Clogg, Richard, *A Concise History of Greece*, 2nd ed., (Cambridge University Press), 2002, pp. 7-45, provides the background while Brewer, David, *The Greek War of Independence: The Struggle for Freedom from Ottoman Oppression and the Birth of the Modern Greek Nation*, (Overlook Press), 2003, and Koumoulides, John, *Cyprus and the Greek War of Independence, 1821-1829*, (Zeno Publishers), 1974, are good modern studies

[64] Kovic, Milos, *Disraeli and the Eastern Question*, (Oxford University Press), 2011, and Perry, Jonathan P., *The Politics of Patriotism: English Liberalism, National Identity and Europe, 1830-1866*, (Cambridge University Press), 2006, pp. 323-386, provide valuable insights into the developing importance of the Eastern Question in British politics. For the initial establishment of British control, see Lee, Dwight, E., 'A memorandum concerning Cyprus, 1878', *Journal of Modern History*, Vol. 3, (1931), pp. 235-241, and *Great Britain and the Cyprus Convention policy of 1878*, (Harvard University Press), 1934, Medlicott, W. N., 'The Gladstone government and the Cyprus convention, 1880-85', *Journal of Modern History*, Vol. 12, (1940), pp. 186-208, and Temperley, H., 'Disraeli and Cyprus', *English Historical Review*, Vol. 46, (1931), pp. 274-279.

[65] What became known as the Tribute was based on previous Ottoman expenditure on the island and once calculated it remained unchanged until abolished in 1927. Ottoman policy was to tax the people heavily and spend as little as possible on development: between 1873 and 1878, Turkish occupation cost £30,000 while the island's income was £130,000. From 1878, it was clear that the economic development of Cyprus would not be self-sustaining and that additional support from the Treasury would prove necessary.

[66] Annexation was ratified in the Treaty of Sèvres, August 1920, articles 115-117, and the Lausanne Convention, July 1923, articles 20-21; printed in Hakki, M. M., *The Cyprus Issue: A Documentary History, 1878-2007*, (I. B. Tauris), 2007, pp. 6-8.

copper mines and more seriously to develop viticulture and no fewer than 63 different Cyprus wines were submitted to the Bordeaux wine exhibition in 1882, nine of which were awarded medals. The British administration invested in new wine-producing technology, a reflection of how it viewed its future role in the island's prosperity. The island's potential as a tourist destination was also recognised by the early 1880s. Commercial speculation was accompanied by the belief that Britain's presence in Cyprus would have a civilising impact of the population that had laboured long under despotic Ottoman rule. In imperial thinking, capitalism and enlightened rule were not only compatible but essential partners in modernising what officials saw as a backward and degraded colony. Most the population was already Christian and were of the 'Greek race' and this immediately elevated them above native in tropical colonies but, many early colonists saw Eastern Christianity as alien and incompatible with the muscular Protestantism of empire, one of the ideological justifications for imperial expansion. The empire may not have brought salvation but it did bring engineering and within ten years a network of roads, the restoration of the irrigation system, improvements to hygiene especially with the draining of low-lying marshes, a haven for mosquitos, and the building of iron piers at Larnaca and Limassol. It was soon apparent that the island would not deliver either the commercial or the geopolitical value expected of it. Cyprus did not live up to its strategic and economic expectations but also disappointed the cultural imperial imaginations of the conservative proponents of its acquisition in 1878. Britain failed to make the intended use of its 'European' possession in the decades that followed. Cyprus was never fortified nor made a naval base unlike the other three British Mediterranean possessions Egypt, Malta and Gibraltar even though Cyprus remained of strategic importance in negative terms: Britain had at least denied possession to other major powers who might have made better military use of it than Britain. The obligation to pay the Tribute meant that many construction projects were scaled down to maintain tight budgets and colonial administration was under almost continuous pressure to economise. These constraints meant that Cyprus could not afford the best colonial administrators, whose salaries differed across the empire, and technical and scientific appointments often remained unfilled for several years because rewards were better in other colonies.[67]

Cyprus remained under Ottoman suzerainty but British officials, many of whom were admirers of classical Greece, regarded the island's majority not as Cypriots but as Greeks. Despite suggestions from Christian Greeks that Greek should be made the official language, English was accorded this position in 1879 with Turkish and Greek translations of all government business, while all three languages were to be used in the small, nominated Legislative Council. The

[67] For the development of the British colony in Cyprus through to the outbreak of war in 1914 see, Varnava, Andrekos, *British Imperial in Cyprus, 1878-1915: the Inconsequential Possession*, (Manchester University Press), 2009, Katsiaounis, Rolandos, *Labour, Society and Politics in Cyprus during the Second Half of the Nineteenth Century*, (Cyprus Research Centre), 1996, Bryant, Rebecca, *Imagining the Modern: The Cultures of Nationalism in Cyprus*, (I. B. Tauris), 2004, and Peristianis, Nicos, and Faustmann, Hubert, (eds.), *Britain in Cyprus: Colonialism and Post-Colonialism, 1878-2006*, (Bibliopolis), 2006

representatives of the Greek community almost immediately began to complain about the operations of the judiciary and discriminatory treatment over official appointments, many of which went to Armenians. Of greater concern to the colonial administration was the attitude of the Orthodox Church that from the outset, made clear its aspiration for union with 'Mother Greece'. The British also brought with them ideas of a strict separation of church and state, problematic given that the Archbishop of Cyprus was both the civil and religious leader of the Orthodox community. Although the colonial administration and the Church quickly found an accommodation based on their mutual interest in preserving social stability in the fractured island, their relations were always uneasy.[68]

In November 1882, a new liberal constitution was introduced. The Legislative Council was expanded to eighteen members: six British officials appointed by the High Commissioner, nine Greeks and three Turks, all elected by their own communities. This bolstered the island's growing ethnic divisions because the allocation of elected places in the chamber recognised that there were important differences between the Greek majority and Muslim minority. Both communities detested the Tribute that they considered a drain of money from the island, but for different reasons. For Greeks, it recognised the continued Turkish stake in the island that they considered obsolete while Turks disliked that money was being taken from their titular sovereign and given to Europeans. If the elected representatives were concerned with securing relief from the Treasury's frugality, relations between the two communities were not compromised but increasingly the Greek élite challenged the principle of the Tribute and this brought their conflicting loyalties into sharp focus. It reinforced Greek desire for *Enosis*, union with Greece. By 1900, Enosis was sweeping through the Greek Cypriot community dividing them from the Turkish-originating communities. Enosis was especially important during a vicious nine-year campaign for the archbishopric between 1900 and 1909 between two candidates, one originally a teacher from Greece, in which both used Enosis as a powerful and emotive political tool. By April 1912, British rule was openly challenged by the Greek nationalists, who demanded a Greek majority in parliament in exchange for postponing their demands for union with Greece. Moreover, within a month, the first Cypriots were killed in bloody inter-communal clashes between Greeks and Muslims. The problem was clearly stated by Joseph Chamberlain in 1902: the only way Britain could disengage from the 1878 Convention was to hand the island back to Turkish control. Enosis was not an option before 1914.

Growing tensions, 1914-1950

With the final disintegration of the Ottoman Empire during and after the First World War, Greek expansionism resulted in the invasion of Greek-inhabited areas of Turkey leading to ethnic cleansing as 1.5 million Turks and Greeks were forced to leave their ancestral homes. Having helped to create the sense of Enosis in Cyprus, Britain then began to oppose it. Although Enosis was a possible outcome of the treaty negotiations in 1919 and 1920, the Colonial Office and the

---

[68] Englezakis, Benedict, *Studies on the History of the Church of Cyprus, 4th-20th centuries*, (Variorum), 1995, pp. 237-256, 421-452. See also, Emilianides, A., *Religion and Law in Cyprus*, (Kluwer Law International), 2011, pp. 41-48,

Admiralty made it clear that retaining Cyprus was essential for effective naval policy in the eastern Mediterranean. After decades of animosity between Greece and Turkey, the war and subsequent peace treaties ended without any account being taken of Cypriot Enosis. This contributed to growing ethnic particularism in Cyprus.

With the Lausanne treaty in 1922, Turkey renounced all its claims over the island.[69] There were specific provisions for Turkish Cypriots who opted for Turkish nationality to immigrate to Turkey. Following the Lausanne agreement, Turkey redefined its policy toward Cyprus, supporting British rule of the island as the best guarantee that the position of the Turkish Cypriots would be secure from the threat of Enosis. Turkey sought to accommodate the British and at the same time intervene in the internal affairs of the island by assisting the Turkish Cypriot community in areas such as health and education. Greece was also keen on maintaining good relations with the British. The official policy of both Britain and Greece was that the matter of ceding Cyprus to Greece, as proposed in 1915 by the British to lure the Greek government to take sides with the Allies but eventually rejected by Athens, was no longer open to discussion. The Greek strategy was to keep Cyprus alive as a diplomatic issue without antagonising the British. When Cyprus became a Crown Colony in 1925, Greek Cypriot leaders protested that this contravened 'the desires of the island's population'. There was an increase in the membership of the Legislative Council but the ratio of Greeks, Turks and British nominees remained unchanged. The result was a splintering of the Greek Cypriot community: some called for increasing levels of self-government that would eventually lead to Enosis while others were uncompromising in their support for Enosis. Both were unpalatable options for the colonial authorities especially as they believed that any measure of self-government would inevitably make the island ungovernable.

The appointment of Sir Ronald Storrs as governor in 1926 was designed to reduce tensions. Storrs was sympathetic to the Greek position and had considerable experience of dealing with Greek bishops in Alexandria and Jerusalem. He sought to develop a distinctive Cypriot patriotism to divert Greek identity away from Enosis. His critics saw this as a deliberate attempt to 'dehellenise' the island and led to the Greek Cypriot political class uniting in a fresh campaign against British colonial autocracy. They used their position in the legislature to attack the annual estimates of government spending as public revenues began to fall consequent on commercial depression. Storrs also faced a younger generation of Turks strongly influenced by the secular modernism and republicanism of Ataturk's Turkey that was less likely to support British nominees in the legislature and even flirted with the Greeks. In November 1926, for instance, the Greek and Turkish Cypriot members of the Legislative Council unanimously rejected the 1927 budget estimates. Matters deteriorated further the following year when Greek Cypriots decided not to take part in the celebrations of the fiftieth anniversary of British occupation while celebrating the anniversary

---

[69] McHenry, James A., *The Uneasy Partnership on Cyprus, 1919-1939: The Political and Diplomatic Interaction between Great Britain, Turkey, and the Turkish Cypriot Community*, (Garland Publishing), 1987.

of the Greek Revolution of 1821 by proclaiming the will of the Greek Cypriots for union with Greece.

The agitation for Enosis was revitalised by the emergence of the Orthodox Church as the 'real leader' of the movement in the person of Nicodemus Mylonas, Metropolitan of Kition. He played a central role in the meeting of Greek deputies and senior clerics on 12 September 1931 near Limassol to discuss the increase in customs taxes. The result was the unveiling of what the colonial authorities regarded as a revolutionary manifesto. Storrs then planned to go to London for emergency talks, something that Greek Cypriots resented, objecting that their future was being determined without their involvement. On 17 October, the bishop of Kition announced his resignation from the Legislative Council, protested against 'arbitrary acts of foreign dynasts' and called on Greek Cypriots to join a campaign to unite Cyprus with Greece. Other Greek deputies followed his lead and resigned from the legislature. News of the speech reached Nicosia the following day and the newly formed National Radicalist Union, an organisation of young Greek Cypriots eager for union with Greece called a meeting on the afternoon of 21 October.

The crowd of around three thousand people heard a series of emotional speeches from Greek Cypriot Legislative Councillors and then decided to march on Government House to confront Storrs. With only few policemen to protect the building and the failure of the Councillors to maintain any control over the crowd, it looted and burned the Governor's House though not before Storrs had made a hasty retreat through the rear. Storrs recorded that six Greek Cypriots were killed and thirty more wounded when the police took more aggressive action. Further disturbances took place in Famagusta, Larnaca and Limassol and, although there was no island-wide, coordinated action as the colonial authorities believed, they were severely threatened. Storrs proclaimed martial law and suspended *habeas corpus* and, with only a reduced garrison of 126 officers and men on the island, telegraphed Malta and Egypt for urgent assistance. By the end of the month, order had been restored across the island and ten men, including the bishops of Kition and Kyrenia and five Greek Cypriot politicians had been arrested and deported and, in the weeks following 2,000 people were imprisoned. This represented the point at which the unstable accommodation between the colonial authorities and the Orthodox Church snapped.[70]

The intensity of the uprising was as much of a shock to the Greek Cypriot political and religious leadership as it was to the colonial authorities. It had been unprepared for mass mobilisation on such a massive scale and its response was disorganised and un-coordinated. Significantly, it was unable to translate the militancy into a political initiative. The riots provided the pretext to seize back

[70] Storrs, Ronald, *Disturbances in Cyprus in October 1931*, (His Majesty's Stationary Office), 1932, provides the 'official' view while Storrs, Ronald, *The Memoirs of Sir Ronald Storrs*, (G. P. Putnam's Sons), 1937, pp. 480-547, give his later views. See also, Georghallides, George S., *Cyprus and the governorship of Sir Ronald Storrs: The causes of the 1931 crisis*, (Cyprus Research Centre), 1985, and Loizos, P., 'Cyprus and the Governorship of Sir Ronald Storrs: The Causes of the 1931 Crisis, *International History Review*, Vol. 10, (1988), pp. 496-499, and Markides, Diana, and Georghallides, G. S., 'British Attitudes to Constitution-Making in Post-1931 Cyprus', *Journal of Modern Greek Studies*, Vol. 13, (1995), pp. 63-81.

the initiative that had been slipping away from British hands for many years. Rapidly recovering from the initial shock, British authorities seized the opportunity to suspend the 1882 constitution, long considered an impediment to the sound administration of the island and impose limitations on freedom of expression and suspended the constitution. A collective fine of £35,000 was imposed on all Greek Cypriots, except civil servants, to finance the rebuilding of Government House. Political parties were proscribed, municipal elections banned and the press censored. Symbols of Hellenism were outlawed: it became illegal to fly the Greek flag or play the Greek national anthem and meetings of more than five people in one place were prohibited. The suspension of the constitution was intended to be temporary measure but soon hardened into something more permanent. The Colonial Office considered re-establishing representative institutions in mid-1933 but this was abandoned when Sir Reginald Stubbs, governor after Storrs was moved to the backwater of Northern Rhodesia, advised that Cypriots respected strong government but were always prepared to take advantage of a weak one. With the demise of the Legislative Council and the traditional influence of the Greek Cypriot right, Cyprus was now ruled by gubernatorial decree, a situation that persisted until 1960.[71]

The broader aim of British rule in the 1930s was to reshape Cyprus as an ideal polity by promoting Cypriot nationalism, an identity designed to transcend Greek and Turkish nationalism.[72] Storrs may have failed to create political stability in Cyprus or to resolve Greek demands for Enosis but his period as governor saw increasing cooperation between Greek and Turkish Cypriots in the Legislative Council that might have laid the foundations for Cypriot nationalism. For instance, in February 1931, the Greek Cypriot newspaper *Eleftheria* criticised the colonial government for attacking the autonomy of the Turkish Cypriot education recognising that oppressive measures could also be used against Greek Cypriots. The Turkish Cypriot newspaper *Soz* responded positively arguing: 'Both our communities are under similar threats and we ask for closer cooperation between the Turkish Cypriots and the Greek Cypriots', a call welcomed in *Eleftheria* on 25 February 1931. The six years of authoritarian rule under General Sir Richmond Palmer between 1933 and 1939 saw a continuation of cooperation between Greek and Turkish Cypriots. Turkish Cypriots had taken no part in the uprising but were as affected by the restrictions as their Greek counterparts and this created common grievances. In 1936, both communities were involved in the miners' strike. This tentative cooperation occurred in the context of continuing colonial repression. Palmer introduced further authoritarian measures including limitations on the administration and functioning of Greek schools, banning the teaching of Greek history and prohibiting trade unions and associations of any kind. Even the ringing of church bells was subject to regulation and, after the death of Kyrillos III in November 1933 the election of a new archbishop was delayed until 1947. This heightened the need to preserve Greek cultural heritage and the Church strongly objected to British attempts to control

[71] Hatzivassiliou, Evanthis, *The Cyprus Question, 1878-1960: The Constitutional Aspect*, (University of Minnesota Press), 2002, pp. 38-42

[72] Rappas, Alexis, 'The Elusive Polity: Imagining and Contesting Colonial Authority in Cyprus during the 1930s', *Journal of Modern Greek Studies*, Vol. 26, (2008), pp. 363-397.

the school curriculum and take control of teacher appointments. Enosis appeared to be in retreat.

There were intermittent protests against the regime led by the Cyprus Communist Party that organised strikes among poorer urban workers but the repressive measures were not lifted until the beginning of the Second World War, during which more than thirty thousand Cypriots joined the British armed forces.[73] Fighting a war for democracy made it difficult for the colonial regime to deny outlets for political activities. In 1941, communists and other left-wing activists formed the Progressive Party for the Working People (AKEL), one of the few organisations in which both Greek and Turkish Cypriots were members. Municipal elections were held in 1943 with AKEL mayors winning in two major towns. However, the authorities were reluctant to ease political restrictions further and their suspicion of the Church remained unchanged. The Greek Cypriot right had been eclipsed with the suspension of electoral institutions but the colonial authorities were concerned by the political dynamism of the left, something that increased as the war entered its final stages. The British authorities had several options available: they could link up with the clerical right in a common hostility to the progressive left or ally with the left and crush the clerical right but chose to do neither, sustained by the belief that they were in control of the island. What proved critical was the need to face down the communist threat in Greece especially after 1945 when the country was riven by a brutal civil war and the need to contain the spread of Soviet imperialism. It was against this background that attempts to resolve the constitutional impasse in Cyprus developed after 1945.[74]

After 1945, Greek Cypriots called for Enosis as a reward for loyally supporting Britain. The Labour government had given India its independence but then became increasingly resistant to any further challenges to the status quo. [75] In 1946, Reginald Fletcher, Lord Winster was appointed Cyprus' governor and as a trade unionist, unlike his predecessors, did not come from the narrow cadre of colonial officials. To improve relations with Greek Cypriots, he authorised the election for Archbishop, a sign that the government in London was prepared to move beyond government by decree. Leontios was elevated to the position but his death shortly after led to the election of Archbishop Makarios II, who as bishop of Kyrenia had been exiled in 1931 and was unequivocal in his support for Enosis. He was also bitterly anti-communist and committed to opposing the emergence of electoral politics in which AKEL, with its mass social bases across

---

[73] Yiangou, Anastania, *Cyprus in World War II: Politics and Conflict in the Eastern Mediterranean*, (I. B. Tauris), 2010, examines the impact of the war on Cyprus and how its wartime experiences laid the foundations for the contemporary situation on the island.

[74] Stefanidis, Ioannis D., *Isle of Discord: Nationalism, Imperialism and the Making of the Cyprus Problem*, (C. Hurst & Co.), 1999, focuses on developments in the decade after the end of the war. See also, Crouzet, François, *Le conflit de Chypre, 1946-1959*, 2 Vols. (E. Bruylant), 1973.

[75] Ibid, Stefanidis, Ioannis D., *Isle of Discord*, pp. 108-174, examines the development of British policy. See also, Holland, Robert, 'Never, Never Land: British Colonial Policy and the Roots of Violence in Cyprus, 1950-1954', *Journal of Imperial and Commonwealth History*, Vol. 21, (1993), pp. 148-176, and Kelling, G. H., *Countdown to Rebellion, British Policy in Cyprus, 1939-1955*, (Greenwood Press), 1990,

both communities, was the likely beneficiary. This was especially significant as the Colonial Secretary had suggested in October 1946 that a local Consultative Assembly should be convened to discuss constitutional developments on the island. While church discipline ensured that most were not involved, ten Greek Cypriots with AKEL connections were present when the Assembly convened under Sir Edward Jackson, Chief Justice of Cyprus on 1 November 1947. That Malta, also an island of strategic importance that had seen disturbances in 1928 leading to its constitution being suspended, had been given a new constitution in 1947 providing for significant self-government was regarded as a measure against which to judge British commitment to self-government by many Cypriots. For left and right, the litmus test for a workable constitution was the control of elected representatives over ministerial departments in Cyprus. The problem was that there were divisions in London between the Colonial Office that wanted a gradual transition to self-government, the Foreign Office that favoured only restricted Cypriot involvement in governing the island and Attlee who favoured immediate self-government. In January 1948, the Cabinet accepted the Colonial Office's limited proposal for an embryonic ministerial system to obtain cooperation from Greek Cypriots. The British government's formal office was given to the Consultative Assembly on 7 May 1948 but it was rejected by the Church and soon after by AKEL ending any possibility of establishing a progressive secular politics. Winster resigned the following October suggesting that violence in Cyprus was not out of the question.

The problem with the 1948 proposals was that, by specifically banning discussion of Enosis in the chamber of the proposed representative legislature, it ensured their rejection by the Church and the Greek Cypriot right.[76] For AKEL, they were not sufficiently robust in moving towards a secular self-governing colony leading, in October 1949, to the party declaring a willingness to join a 'national embassy' to the United Nations to raise the question of Enosis. The Turkish Cypriot representatives on the Consultative Assembly had accepted the May 1948 proposals and had affirmed their opposition to self-government as a precursor of Enosis. Increasing Turkish Cypriots thought in terms of partition as the only way to retain their status and this was reinforced in January 1950, when the Orthodox Church of Cyprus held a referendum by open, not secret ballot in which 96.5 per cent of the Greek Cypriot population voted for union. The United Nations accepted the petition and Enosis became an international issue but the Labour government ignored its results and the local colonial administration dismissed it as 'meaningless' suggesting that it demonstrated that Cypriots were not ready for self-government and called for additional repressive powers. But in Michael Mouskos, who had marshalled support for the referendum, the colonial authorities now faced an opponent with considerable rhetorical and tactical gifts. Five months later, he was elected head of the church, at the age of 37, as Archbishop Makarios III.[77] The referendum had clearly demonstrated the general will and over the

[76] On the politics of Greek Cypriot Irredentism see, ibid, Stefanidis, Ioannis D., *Isle of Discord*, pp. 229-253.

[77] Mayes, Stanley, *Cyprus and Makarios*, (Putnam), 1960, is a valuable thematic study of different aspects of Makarios' attitudes, for instance with EOKA, pp. 25-65. But see also, Mayes, Stanley, *Makarios: A Biography*, (Macmillan), 1981.

next four years, Makarios set about organising it. Conservative peasant associations, right-wing trade unions and a popular youth group were built into a powerful mass base for the national struggle, directly under the auspices of the Church. Mobilisation at home was accompanied by pressure abroad, in the first place on Athens to take up the issue of self-determination in Cyprus at the UN, but also, departing from the traditions of the Church, rallying support from Arab countries in the region.

The intensification of calls for Enosis among Greek Cypriots coincided with pressing strategic arguments for retaining full colonial sovereignty over the island.[78] With Britain's eviction from Palestine in June 1948 and increasing pressure on their Suez base from Egyptian terrorists, Cyprus was a Mediterranean stronghold it had no intention of relinquishing. Indeed, upgrading its strategic role as soon as British garrisons in the Canal Zone were judged insufficiently secure, the High Command in the Middle East was transferred to the island in 1954. A year later, the Conservative Colonial Secretary informed the Commons that possessions like Cyprus could never expect self-determination. Nor was London prepared to revive representative institutions in which the four-fifths of the population in favour of Enosis would enjoy a majority. In September 1953, Sir Anthony Eden, then Foreign Secretary, had declared to the Greek government that Cyprus was a 'closed question' adding with undiplomatic aplomb that there was a large Greek Cypriot population in New York and he did not suppose that the Greek government was demanding Enosis for them.[79] In 1956 during a visit to Norwich, Eden now Prime Minister, provided a succinct, resolute public justification:

> No Cyprus, no certain facilities to protect our supply of oil. No oil, unemployment and hunger in Britain. It is as simple as that.[80]

From 1953, Britain's relations with Greece deteriorated and on 23 February 1954, its government announced that it would take the Cyprus problem to the United Nations unless an acceptable solution was quickly found.[81] The consequence of Greece's action was growing intransigence from Britain and on 28 July, a government minister used the word 'never' when discussion self-determination for Cyprus. With an open assertion of indefinite colonial rule and the decision by the UN General Assembly in December 1954 'not to consider the problem further for the time being, because it does not appear appropriate to adopt a resolution on the question of Cyprus', those supporting Enosis were driven to rebellion. After four years of trying to arouse international opinion to

---

[78] Hatzivassiliou, Evanthis, 'Cold War Pressures, Regional Strategies and Relative Decline: British Military Strategic Planning for Cyprus, 1950-1960', *Journal of Military History*, Vol. 73, (2009), pp. 1143-1166.

[79] Record of conversation between Eden and Field-Marshall Papagos, 22 September 1953, cit, ibid, Holland, Robert, and Markides, Diana, *The British and the Hellenes*, p. 224.

[80] *The Times*, 2 June 1956.

[81] The development of Greek and Turkish policies on Cyprus is explored in ibid, Stefanidis, Ioannis D., *Isle of Discord*, pp. 207-228, 254-293. See also, Xydis, Stephen G., 'The UN General Assembly as an Instrument of Greek Policy: Cyprus, 1954-1958', *Journal of Conflict Resolution*, Vol. 12, (1968), pp. 141-158

bring pressure to bear on Britain, in early 1954, Makarios met secretly with George Grivas, a retired colonel of the Greek army to plan a guerrilla campaign to liberate the island.[82] The problem, evident from the outset was that Makarios was concerned by Grivas' extremism from their first meeting and Grivas resented having to share leadership with the archbishop. Even by the standards of the Greek right, Grivas was on the extreme wing of counter-revolution and was committed to Panhellenism in its most blinkered versions. A veteran of the disastrous Greek thrust into Anatolia after the First World War, he had sat out the German occupation during the Second World War, and then, with assistance from the departing Wehrmacht, organised death squads against the left before the British landed. Informally, he was in contact with the Greek General Staff but the Papagos government, newly admitted to NATO, though careful not to give him official support, looked the other way as he acquired weapons and logistics for a landing on Cyprus, where he arrived late in 1954.[83]

The Emergency

With Britain unwilling to grant Enosis, militant Greek Cypriots formed the National Organisation of Cypriot Fighters (EOKA), a right-wing, anti-British guerrilla movement. Although the authorities had been expected a spontaneous political demonstration like that in 1931, they had not expected the emergence of the targeted use of force like the Zionist campaign in Palestine in the late 1940s.[84] On 1 April 1955, Grivas began his campaign of terror on the island with a well-coordinated series of attacks on police, military and other government buildings in Nicosia, where the radio station was blown up, Famagusta, Larnaca and Limassol. In June, EOKA began to target members of the Cypriot police. Grivas made it clear that EOKA's initial targets were not in the Turkish Cypriot community that he instructed to stand aside while the future of the island was determined. Under EOKA pressure, the number of Greek Cypriots in the police force rapidly dwindled. To replace them, Harding recruited Turks and added a paramilitary Police Mobile Reserve recruited in the Turkish community, which acted with sectarian savagery when the occasion required. By the late 1950s, the British security machine came to depend on Turkish auxiliaries and this created a gulf between the two communities that had not existed before. This widened further when Ankara, increasingly in control of the minority set up its own armed right-wing organisation on the island the TNT and was soon killing Turkish Cypriot members of AKEL, to which the British turned a blind eye. Over the

---

[82] For Grivas' own view of Cyprus and guerrilla war see, Grivas, G., *General Grivas on Guerrilla Warfare*, (Praeger), 1965, and Foley, Charles, (ed.), *The Memoirs of General Grivas*, (Longman), 1964. Alastos, Doros, *Cyprus guerrilla: Grivas, Makarios and the British*, (Heinemann), 1960, Barker, Dudley R., *Grivas: Portrait of a terrorist*, (Cresset Press), 1959, and Byford-Jones, W., *Grivas and the story of EOKA*, (Hale), 1959, provide contemporary comment.

[83] Chatzevasileiou, Euanthes, *Greece and the Cold War: Frontline State, 1952-1967*, (Routledge), 2006, pp. 24-49, considers Greece in NATO between 1952 and 1955.

[84] Holland, Robert F., *Britain and the Revolt in Cyprus, 1954-1959*, (Oxford University Press), 1998, remains the best study but see also, Van Der Bijl, Nick, *The Cyprus Emergency: The Divided Island, 1955-1974*, (Pen & Sword), 2010, and Xydis, Stephen G., *Cyprus: conflict and conciliation, 1954-1958*, (Ohio State University Press), 1967.

next four years, EOKA waged a guerrilla war of lethal efficacy that the British never succeeded in neutralising. With a force of not much more than two hundred men and despite his limited abilities as a commander, Grivas succeeded in pinning down some 28,000 British troops but could not have done so without the widespread support the national cause enjoyed among the population. Between 1955 and 1959, 105 British troops were killed.[85] As a military operation, the EOKA campaign was perhaps the most successful of all anti-colonial resistances in the post-war period. Politically, its impact was more ambiguous and it is debatable whether EOKA had any significant impact on independence in 1960 and certainly played no part in any of the negotiations.

Grivas was virulently anti-Communism and this left no room for AKEL in the armed struggle. AKEL was the only mass organisation with roots in both Greek and Turkish communities, integrating activists across ethnic lines. It was attacked on two fronts: EOKA repeatedly shot down its militants, while the British proscribed the party and put its leaders into detention camps. Driven underground, AKEL was forced to the margins of the anti-colonial struggle. The main force of the Cypriot left, which in normal circumstances would have been a central component of the national liberation movement, was effectively deleted from it. Grivas was, however, mistaken in his assumption that Turkish Cypriots and Turkey as their 'motherland' could be largely ignored. Turkey had left the United Nations debate on Enosis to Britain and Grivas wrongly assumed that the British government could always impose its views on Ankara. He saw his campaign in anti-colonial terms rather than as a communal conflict between Greeks and Turks. Faced with a difficult summer of terrorist attacks and military responses, Britain convened a tripartite conference in London in August 1955 where representatives of the Greek and Turkish governments met the British authorities to discuss Cyprus. This represented a radical departure in traditional British policy since it had previously considered colonial domestic issues as matters not to be discussed with foreigners. Meetings lasted into September but achieved nothing. Both sides were dissatisfied: the Greeks because Cypriot self-determination, in effect Enosis, was not offered and the Turks because it had not been rejected. A bombing incident at the Turkish consulate in Salonika, Greece, on the day before the meeting ended led to widespread rioting in Istanbul that became sufficiently serious for the Turkish premier to call out the army and declare martial law. In fact, the bombing was carried out by Turkish intelligence and the riots had been prearranged to put pressure on the Greeks and show the world that Turkey was keenly interested in Cyprus. As a result, relations between

[85] Van Der Bijl, Nick, *The Cyprus Emergency: The Divided Island, 1955-1974*, pp.212-215, argues that since 1945, successive British governments have played down casualties by 'selectively excluding non-battle casualties'. The 'official' figures during the Cyprus Emergency are 105 Service personnel killed and 603 wounded while the British Cyprus Memorial Trust lists 371 Service personnel killed including non-battle fatalities. There were also significant fatalities among the different police units: the Cyprus Police lost 37 officers (22 Turkish and 15 Greek Cypriots), the Colonial Police Service lost seven officers and the UK Police Unit lost eleven men. In terms of civilian deaths: 26 British and 328 Cypriots civilians were killed. Estimated EOKA casualties were 102.

Greece and Turkey, both now members of NATO, were further strained. From being a little 'local difficulty' Cyprus had become an international question.[86]

To bring the island under control, London dispatched the chief of the Imperial General Staff, Field Marshal Sir John Harding as Governor.[87] Although he immediately held talks with Makarios on his arrival in October 1955, Harding informed the cabinet with brutal candour that if self-determination was ruled out, 'a regime of military government must be established and the country ruled indefinitely as a police state.' He was as good as his word and in November declared a state of emergency. The standard repertoire of repression was applied. Demonstrations were banned, schools closed, trade-unions outlawed and strikes banned. Communists were locked up and EOKA suspects caught carrying a weapon hanged. Curfews, raids, beatings, brutal and extra-legal interrogations and executions were carried out and detention camps filled up. British troops were placed on a wartime footing and about 300 British policemen were brought to the island to replace EOKA sympathisers purged from the local force. Further talks were held with Makarios in January and February 1955 but they broke down with both sides accusing the other of intransigence. A few days later, Makarios was charged with complicity in violence and, with the bishop of Kyrenia and two other priests, exiled to the Seychelles. This removed Makarios' moderating influence over EOKA and left more militant forces in control. Grivas gained political leadership in Makarios' absence, levels of violence in Cyprus increased and a general strike was called.[88]

In June 1956, the British government appointed Lord Radcliffe to the post of commissioner for constitutional affairs. His proposals, submitted in December, contained provisions for a balanced legislature, as in former schemes but also included the option of self-determination, although without a specific time-scale, and safeguards for the Turkish Cypriot minority.[89] Turkey accepted the plan but the Greeks rejected it outright and Makarios refused even to consider it while he was in exile. In January 1957, after the Suez debacle, Harold Macmillan succeeded Eden as Prime Minister. He regarded Cyprus as an albatross around his neck, a conclusion based on his brief period as Foreign Secretary two years before. Good relations with a strong Turkey as a NATO ally was essential and Turkey was vehemently opposed to Enosis while London began

---

[86] Mallinson, William, *Cyprus: A Modern History*, (I. B. Tauris), 2005, revised edition, 2008, *Cyprus: Diplomatic History and the Clash of Theory in International Relations*, (I. B. Tauris), 2010 and *Britain and Cyprus: Key Themes and Documents since World War II*, (I. B. Tauris), 2011, are central to any discussion of the attempted diplomatic resolutions of the 'Cyprus problem'.

[87] Carver, Michael, *Harding of Petherton, Field Marshall*, (Weidenfeld & Nicolson), 1987.

[88] The extent of Makarios' responsibility for the violence is a difficult question. Grivas' diary suggests that Makarios played a central role: he had inspired the Greek government to conspire with EOKA and had sought to indoctrinate children. The oath of the youth organisation of EOKA was administered by priests and monks and the Church was used as a cover. Colonial officials certainly believed that Makarios encouraged violence in support of his own political ambitions.

[89] Radcliffe's report on constitutional proposals is printed in Madden, A. F., (ed.), *The End of Empire: Select Documents on the Constitutional History of the British Empire and Commonwealth*, (Greenwood Publishing Group), 2000, Vol. 1, pp. 439-447.

to hint that the partition might be a solution. Menderes, the Turkish premier, who had already been promised that Turkey could station troops on the island if Britain were ever forced to concede self-determination, was unsurprisingly keen. Harding disliked the idea, regarding it as underhand while United States officials condemned it as a 'forcible vivisection' of the island. If the objective in London was to keep control of Cyprus by splitting it in two under British suzerainty, the Americans feared that this would arouse widespread protest in Greece that risked toppling a loyal regime and handing power to the subversive forces still lurking in the country. In Britain, such concerns were less prevalent although the experience of partition in Ireland showed how complex and bloody it could be. Turkey took the initiative and in June 1958, repeating the operation in Salonika its intelligence agents set off an explosion in the Turkish Information Office in Nicosia that was the signal for orchestrated mob violence against Greek Cypriots. Security forces stood by as houses were set on fire and people killed, in the first major communal clashes since the Emergency was declared. The result, probably planned, was populist partition: the eviction of Greeks from Turkish areas in Nicosia and other cities and the seizure of municipal facilities to create self-contained Turkish enclaves. Its organisers could be sure of British complaisance and Sir Hugh Foot, Harding's flexible replacement as governor Sir Hugh Foot assured its leaders the day before the riots that the Turkish community would enjoy 'a specially favoured and specially protected state' under future British arrangements. A few months later, the colonial secretary was publicly referring to Cyprus as 'an offshore Turkish island'.[90]

Makarios feared that Greece would buckle under British pressure and confronted the Greek premier, Constantine Karamanlis, in Athens. Implementation of the Anglo-Turkish plan for Cyprus, he pointed out, could be blocked simply by Greece threatening to withdraw from NATO if it went ahead. Karamanlis refused to consider the idea. Hellenism was essentially for public consumption, to keep domestic opinion quiet but for the regime, it was anti-Communism that mattered. It was clear to Makarios that if the Greek government had to choose between the two it would, without hesitation, ditch Enosis. Three days later, without informing the Greek regime, he came out publicly for the independence of Cyprus. For the British, this had always been the worst possible solution, 'even worse than enosis' according to the minutes of a meeting two years earlier. Makarios was anathema to London and handing the island over to him would be the ultimate defeat. For Americans, worried at the impact of the partition of Cyprus on a Greek politics where popular feelings on the issue ran high, independence was regarded as a way out of a potentially dangerous conflict between allies. When the United Nations met to debate Cyprus three months later, the United States ensured that a Greek resolution calling for self-determination of the island was once again rejected and that direct talks would be held between Turkey and Greece, to negotiate a deal, something that Karamanlis and Menderes quickly reached in Zurich in February 1959. The outcome was entirely predictable. Turkey was the bigger military power, on closer terms with Britain and was largely immune to diplomatic pressure. By contrast, the post-war

---

[90] Foot, Hugh, *A start in freedom*, (Hodder & Stoughton), 1964, is a valuable memoir of his experience in Cyprus.

Greek state was initially a British protectorate and was then an American dependency and this prevented it taking a stance independent of Britain and the United States. Menderes had no difficulty imposing terms on his Greek counterpart.[91]

To avoid Enosis, Cyprus would be given a neutered independence, with a constitution stationing troops from Ankara and Athens on its soil and a foreign head of the Supreme Court. The new constitution contained important protections for the Turkish minority: it had 30 per cent of the parliamentary seats and a vice-president with powers of veto, 30 per cent of the civil service and 40 per cent of any armed force composed of Turks, plus a requirement that all taxes be approved by a vote of Turks as well as Greeks despite that they only accounted for 18 per cent of the population. The Greeks agreed not to press for Enosis and the Turks not to pursue their preferred outcome of partition. A secret annexe, committed the future Republic of Cyprus to join NATO and to ban AKEL. Finally, and importantly, a Treaty of Guarantee between Britain, Turkey and Greece would allow any of these powers to intervene in the island, if it held there had been a breach of the Zurich agreement. Britain had played no part in the negotiations in Zurich but its agreement was necessary if the agreement was to be implemented. Its price was sovereign military enclaves on Cyprus, little 'Gibraltars', as Macmillan put it. When the final treaties establishing the new state and its constitution were signed, more pages were devoted to British bases in Cyprus than to all its other provisions combined. Makarios, presented with an agreement that was not negotiable, reluctantly accepted the inevitable and took office in 1960 as president of the new republic. Independence had been granted, but as Holland writes: 'In Cyprus 'freedom' as most people understood it had not been won; self-determination, however partisanly defined, was not applied.' [92] The constitution of July 1960 satisfied diplomatic imperatives rather than practical needs but was not exactly a popular solution and rapidly proved unworkable. Decolonisation in Cyprus proved a messy affair that was handled less effectively than elsewhere.

No solution?

Although this compromise suited Britain, Greece and Turkey, it did not address the aspirations of either community in Cyprus and within three years, civil war had broken out. Makarios had accepted their arrangements under duress but never regarding them as permanent, and in November 1963 moved to revise the constitution to establish a more conventional democracy in Cyprus with a unified administration and majority rule. Turkish Cypriots objected and Greek Cypriot militia attacked Turkish villages. All Turkish representatives in the state withdrew from their posts and Turkish Cypriots increasingly retreated into a series of enclaves where they remained virtually under siege. By March 1964, a United Nations force had arrived to secure each community from further violence.[93]

---

[91] Uslu, Nasuh, *The Cyprus Question as an Issue of Turkish Foreign Policy and Turkish-American Relations, 1959-2003*, (Nova Science Publishers), 2003, pp. 11-35, considers the establishment and collapse of the Republic of Cyprus.
[92] Ibid, Holland, Robert F., *Britain and the Revolt in Cyprus, 1954-1959*, p. 336.
[93] Ker-Lindsay, James, *Britain and the Cyprus Crisis, 1963-1964*, (Bibliopolis), 2004.

The imponderable question was Makarios' attitude to the future of Cyprus. He had two options open to him after the Zurich agreement: he could continue to pursue Enosis, the overwhelming view of Greek Cypriots or he could build a truly independent state in Cyprus. Once he became president, he left both options open. Enosis might be deferred, but it was not renounced. Makarios was a charismatic leader of often spellbinding eloquence but he could not ignore the aspirations of his supporters, who saw no reason why they should give them up on foreign instructions. In moving to revise the mock constitution, he was acting as they wanted him to. The Greek military coup in April 1967 resolved the ambiguity of Makarios' political identity. Merging Cyprus into Greece under the junta was unthinkable. Enosis was tacitly dropped though a powerful minority of Greek Cypriots denounced Makarios and received backing from the junta in Athens. Makarios was now regarded as a traitor to Hellenism, resulted in several attempts on his life, in the secret return of Grivas to the island in 1971 and the formation of EOKA-B that he led until his death in January 1974 and the persistent threat of the return to civil war.

On 15 July 1974, after Makarios had denounced the regime in Athens as a dictatorship that was fomenting civil war in Cyprus, tanks from the Greek-led National Guard attacked the presidential palace.[94] Makarios escaped and was airlifted out of the country to Malta. Resistance to the coup was crushed in a few days and a right-wing government established. The coup was an undoubted breach of the Treaty of Guarantee but it quickly became clear that Britain was unwilling to join Turkey in resolving the issue. Britain had sufficient troops and airpower on the island to deal with the situation and had warships off the coast sufficient to deter any unilateral Turkish invasion but it did nothing. On 20 July, Turkey invaded and within seventy-two hours had seized two-fifths of the island. She was acting well within her rights when she acted to prevent Enosis in 1974. Whether Turkey's eventual division of the island into Turkish and Greek sectors had the same justification is more questionable. The political dismembering of the island was achieved with American agreement and British inaction. In 1975-1976, a Select Committee on Cyprus concluded:

> Britain had a legal right to intervene, she had a moral obligation to intervene, she had the military capacity to intervene. She did not intervene for reasons which the government refuses to give.[95]

After three weeks, there was a ceasefire along what is known as the 'Attila Line' running from Morphou Bay to Famagusta dividing the island between the Turkish north and Greek South. With occupation came ethnic cleansing: some 180,000 Greek Cypriots were forced south and 50,000 Turkish Cypriots went north. The Turkish-occupied north, making up 36 per cent of the island, became the Turkish Republic of North Cyprus in 1983, unrecognised except by Turkey. In the south, the Republic of Cyprus was run entirely by Greek Cypriots, is recognised internationally as having rightful sovereignty over the whole island

---

[94] Asmussen, Jan, *Cyprus at War: Diplomacy and Conflict during the 1974 Crisis*, (I. B. Tauris), 2008, provides a detailed analysis of the coup and the Turkish invasion.
[95] Cit, James Spicer MP, House of Commons, Debate, 4 December 1987, Vol. 123, c1225.

even though the bi-communal constitution under which it was founded no longer exists and joined the European Union on 1 May 2004. Negotiations between the two sides continue to make little progress. As in Ireland, the legacy of British colonial rule is partition.

Southern Rhodesia

'Rhodesia' took its name from Cecil Rhodes, the British empire-builder who was the leading force in British expansion north of the Limpopo River into south-central Africa. Rhodes pushed British influence into the region by obtaining mineral rights from local chiefs under questionable circumstances. After making a vast fortune in mining in South Africa, it was his ambition to extend the British Empire north, if possible as far as Cairo. Rhodes' decision to occupy Mashonaland had three main considerations. He wished to build a new British community in the interior that would cut the Transvaal off from its hinterland and hold the balance of power against the Afrikaner republics in a future South African Federation. He also believed that there were gold deposits beneath the northern veld and hoped that they would finance his colonising ventures. Finally, he wanted to spread British middle-class civilisation and to do away with the independent native politics of the interior, either by peaceful settlement or by force, convinced, like Christian missionaries that only the natives' absorption in a Western market economy would solve the problems of Africa.[96]

Private fiefdom and self-government, 1889-1939

In 1889, the British government agreed that Rhodes' British South Africa Company (BSAC) would administer the territory stretching from the Limpopo to Lake Tanganyika under charter as a protectorate.[97] A year later, Rhodes used this charter to justify sending the Pioneer Column, a group of 180 white settlers led by Frank Johnson protected by well-armed 500 British South Africa Company's Police through Matabeleland and into Shona territory establishing Fort Salisbury (now Harare) on 12 September 1890.[98] The early settlers formed an armed aristocracy among the indigenous people, making a scanty livelihood from prospecting, transport riding and share-pushing and the Company, always intent on economy, thought that the colonists could look after themselves in local

[96] For the history of Rhodesia see, Blake, Robert, *A History of Rhodesia*, (Eyre Methuen), 1978, and Raftopoulos, Brian and Mlambo, Alois, (eds.), *Becoming Zimbabwe: A History from the Pre-colonial era to 2008*, (Weaver Press), 2009.

[97] Galbraith, John S., *Crown and Charter: The Early Years of the British South Africa Company*, (University of California Press), 1974, and Keppel-Jones, Arthur, *Rhodes and Rhodesia: The White Conquest of Zimbabwe, 1884-1902*, (McGill-Queen's University Press), 1983, provide a detailed analysis of the Company between the late 1880s and the early twentieth century. See also, Hensman, Howard, *A History of Rhodesia, Compiled from Official Sources*, (William Blackwood and Sons), 1900, and Hole, Hugh Marshall, *The Making of Rhodesia*, (Macmillan), 1926, for the early historiography. For settler society see, Lowry, Donal, 'Rhodesia 1890-1980: 'The Lost Dominion', in ibid, Bickers, Robert, (ed.), *Settlers and Expatriates*, pp. 112-149.

[98] On the Pioneer Column and the early development of the colony see, Johnson, Sir F., *Great Days*, (G. Bell and Sons), 1940, ibid, Galbraith, John S., *Crown and Charter*, pp. 128-153, and ibid, Keppel-Jones, Arthur, *Rhodes and Rhodesia*, pp. 103-188.

clashes with Africans. The directors resented expenditure on the police, an efficient military body well adapted to irregular mounted warfare and in 1892 the police were cut to the bone and defence of the country largely being left to the colonists.[99] These were organised into a volunteer force, known as the Mashonaland Horse, supported by a small troop of artillery stationed at Salisbury.[100]

The BSAC did not want the expense of war and hoped to erode the Ndebele social system gradually by getting the Ndebele to serve for wages, but the Ndebele tried to maintain their warrior state and persisted in raiding Mashonaland. The local settlers, especially those in the Fort Victoria region, determined that the raids must end since they interfered with their native labour and reduced levels of economic activity. Dr Leander Starr Jameson, the Company's senior administrative official eventually came to the same conclusion and during 1893 and 1894, the First Anglo-Ndebele War occurred. Wedded to a military doctrine that attack must invariably prevail over defence that had proved so effective in the past, the Ndebele proved no match for mounted burghers with superior fire-power and mobility.[101] The Europeans mustered just over 1,100 men, including 225 Bechuanaland Border Police: there were also some 2,000 poorly armed and trained auxiliaries from Chief Khama and 400 Shona auxiliaries. They employed Maxim guns to devastating effect and their tactical use of wagons as mobile pivots gave them an additional advantage. After a few fierce and bloody battles, the Ndebele 'spear kingdom' rapidly collapsed, much to the surprise of more orthodox military thinkers who thought that greater numbers of white troops would be required.[102]

The settlers conquered the country, but they lacked the means to consolidate their position. The economy was weak failing to deliver expected profits and administration was inefficient. In December 1895, the disastrous Jameson Raid into the Transvaal Republic involved most of the Mashonaland Mounted Police and this left the settlers open to native attack. In March 1896, the Second Anglo-Ndebele War began and involved rebellion in both Ndebele and some Shona communities.[103] The rebels murdered many isolated settlers, avoided pitched battles and stuck to guerrilla tactics and initially the colonists were under intense pressure. They lost about one-tenth of their number, a very high proportion when compared to the losses suffered by Europeans in the Mau Mau campaign. The rebels enjoyed an enormous numerical superiority over their

---

[99] For the training and organisation of the Police see, British South Africa Company, *Regulations for the BSA Company's Forces*, (The Company), 1890.

[100] British South Africa Company, *Report on the Company's proceedings and the conditions of the Territories within the sphere of its operations 1889-1892*, (The Company), 1892, p. 5. See also, ibid, Galbraith, John S., *Crown and Charter*, pp. 255-286, and ibid, Keppel-Jones, Arthur, *Rhodes and Rhodesia*, pp. 225-289.

[101] Summers R. F. H., 'The military doctrine of the Matabele', *Southern Rhodesia Native Affairs Department Annual*, Vol. 32, (1955), pp.7-15.

[102] For an account of the fighting in the First War see Wills, W. A., and Collingridge, L. T., *The Downfall of Lobengula: the course, history and effect of the Matabeli War*, (The African Review Offices), 1894.

[103] Tsomondo, M., 'Shona reaction and resistance to European colonisation of Zimbabwe', *Journal of Southern African Affairs*, Vol. 2, (1977), pp. 11-31.

opponents but the whites enjoyed superior mobility through their use of mounted troops. Soon the Europeans managed to seize the initiative; rebel groups were broken up and kept on the move; the whites seized crops and cattle, imposing a kind of economic blockade against their opponents who never managed to develop a concerted strategy. The Ndebele, who still possessed the remnants of a centralised state organisation, negotiated as a body and concluded peace with Rhodes. The rebel Shona communities with no common political leadership held out longer, but eventually their resistance collapsed and by 1897 the country was at peace.[104]

The outcome of the war was the creation of a well organised, semi-military body for internal defence initially known as the Rhodesia Mounted Police but renamed the British South Africa Police in late 1896. The Colonial Office and the local settlers also insisted on improved administration.[105] The designation 'Southern' was used from 1901 when the BSAC united Mashonaland and Matabeleland as Southern Rhodesia.[106] In 1899, a Legislative Council was created with five members nominated by the BSAC and four members elected by registered voters, through which the BSAC had to pass government measures.[107] The electorate was almost exclusively white settlers and the proportion of elected seats increased steadily over time. In 1903, the Council was expanded to fourteen members, seven to be directly elected and seven nominated by the BSAC. In 1907, the number of nominated members was reduced from seven to five. In 1913, the Legislative Council decided that it should have twelve elected members with six nominated by the BSAC. Elections to the Legislative Council were contested by individuals standing on their own records. By 1914, although no political parties had been created, the candidates were broadly divided into those who were supporters of the renewal of the Charter from the BSAC and those who favoured moves towards full self-government within the Empire.

---

104 The literature on the Second Anglo-Ndebele War is extensive. Two good contemporary accounts are, Selous, F. C., *Sunshine and Storm in Rhodesia*, (Rowland Ward and Co.), 1896, and Alderson, E. A. H., *With the Mounted Infantry and the Mashonaland Field Force*, (Methuen and Co.), 1898. Ranger, Terence, *Revolt in Southern Rhodesia, 1896-7: A study In African resistance*, (Heinemann), 1967, is the most extensive and controversial study. See also, ibid, Galbraith, John S., *Crown and Charter*, pp. 287-309, and ibid, Keppel-Jones, Arthur, *Rhodes and Rhodesia*, pp. 425-520.

105 Alexander, Jocelyn, *The Unsettled Land: State-making & the Politics of Land in Zimbabwe 1893-2003*, (James Currey Publisher), 2006, pp. 17-43, examines the development of the settler state

106 British South Africa Company, *Reports on the administration of Rhodesia 1900-1902*, (The Company), 1902, p. 25.

107 In 1912, the franchise arrangements were altered for the first time since the Legislative Council was established. To be eligible for registration as an elector, a voter had to be a British subject by birth or naturalisation, male, over the age of 21 and to have lived in Southern Rhodesia for six months continuously, as before. Where previously a voter had to be able to sign their name and write their address and occupation, they were now required to complete the registration form in their own handwriting if required and to write from dictation fifty words in the English language. The means qualifications were doubled. Voters had to have either occupied immovable property worth £150 within the electoral district or have received salary or wages of £100 per annum.

Prior to about 1918, the opinion among the electorate supported continued BSAC rule but opinion changed because of the development of the country and increased settlement. In addition, a decision in the British courts that land not in private ownership belonged to the British Crown rather than the BSAC gave great impetus to the campaign for self-government.[108] In 1917, the settlers, led by Charles Coghlan, formed the Responsible Government Association.[109] The Legislative Council election in 1920 returned a large majority of candidates of the Responsible Government Association that voted in favour of self-government and it became clear that BSAC rule was no longer practical. Opinion in Britain and South Africa still favoured incorporating Southern Rhodesia in the Union of South Africa, but Winston Churchill, the Colonial Secretary appointed the Buxton Commission to examine the question. In 1921, it reported that the colony was ready for responsible government and recommended a referendum that was held in 1922 to confirm this.[110] With an electorate of 18,810, the total number of votes cast was 14,763, a turnout of 78.5 per cent. All but one of the electoral districts supported responsible government and rejected union with South Africa by 59.4 per cent to 40.6 per cent.[111] Self-government began in October 1923 and the Responsible Government Association organised itself into the Rhodesia Party winning 26 of the 30 Legislative Assembly seats in the elections the following year. Charles Coghlan was the first Premier of Southern Rhodesia and upon his death in 1927, he was succeeded by Howard Unwin Moffat. Although the Rhodesia Party won the 1928 elections with a slightly reduced majority of 22 seats, in addition to Independent members there were now three other political parties: the Progressive Party formed in June 1927 and was opposed to monopolies and advocated more development for Matabeleland, the Country Party, also formed in 11927 by dissident farmers in the Rhodesian Agricultural Union (it merged with the Progressive Party in 1929 to form the Reform Party) and the Rhodesia Labour Party.[112]

In the 1933 election, the Reform Party won a narrow majority of two seats in the Legislative Assembly but its victory was short-lived. Less than a year later, in August 1934, most of the Reform Party merged with the Rhodesia Party to form the United Party under the leadership of Godfrey Huggins.[113] The United Party had a clear majority at every election between 1934 and 1958 except 1946,

---

[108] Lee, M. E., 'The Origins of the Responsible Government Movement', *Rhodesia History*, Vol. 6, (1975), pp. 33-52.

[109] Wallis, J. P. R., *One Man's Hand: The Story of Sir Charles Coghlan and the Liberation of Southern Rhodesia*, (Longman, Green and Co.), 1950

[110] Hodder-Williams, R., and Whitely, P., 'The Rhodesian Referendum of October 1922', *Zimbabwean History*, Vol. 11, (1980), pp. 56-74.

[111] For this, and subsequent references to election results, see, Willson, F. M. G., (ed.), *Source Book of Parliamentary Elections and Referenda in Southern Rhodesia 1898-1962*, (Department of Government, University College of Rhodesia and Nyasaland), 1963.

[112] Some of the divisions in the white community are described in Hancock, I., *White Liberals, Moderates and Radicals in Rhodesia*, (Croom Helm), 1984.

[113] Vambe, Lawrence, *From Rhodesia to Zimbabwe*, (University of Pittsburgh Press), 1976, is valuable on Huggins. See also, Gelfand, M., and Gann, H., *Huggins of Rhodesia*, (Allen and Unwin), 1974, and Gann, L. H., 'Lord Malvern (Sir Godfrey Huggins): a Reappraisal', *Journal of Modern African Studies*, Vol. 23, (1985), pp. 723-728.

when Huggins still managed to remain as Prime Minister. Huggins' philosophical roots were grounded in Social Darwinism with its inherent racial inequality. He developed the 'two-pyramids' system, the theory that each race in Rhodesia should develop separately in its own area.[114] In the black areas, Africans could have administrative roles except for those at the very top but in the white areas, Africans merely assisted and did not compete with whites. This system was brought into operation by four pieces of legislation. The Land Apportionment Act of 1931 formalised the division of land between white freehold farms and 'communal' reserves for Africans, said that Africans could no longer get permanent rights in European areas and were to live on a new type of land, the Native Purchase Area. There were now 8.5 million hectares of Reserves and 3 million hectares of Native Purchase areas while European land made up 20 million hectares. The Industrial Conciliation Act of 1934 copied similar legislation in South Africa and introduced the registration of white trade unions with an Industrial Conciliation Board to settle disputes. This legislation did not apply to Africans who were outside the collective bargaining system and had no means of taking industrial action. This position was reaffirmed in amendment to the legislation in 1945 and it was not until 1959 that Africans could form trade unions or compete for jobs in white areas. The Native Councils Act of 1937 reduced the power of chiefs but allowed Africans to establish Councils where they wanted to. In 1943, these councils could raise and spend funds. Finally, the Native Courts Act of 1937 established courts consisting of a chief or headman plus two councillors to settle disputes only between Africans according to traditional law. By August 1938, there were 45 such courts. In passing this discriminatory legislation, the minority whites aimed at protecting their land, work and social and political privileges from the challenge of the majority Africans.

Emerging African politics, 1920-1950

Africans were largely denied the franchise in the aftermath of the First World War. The Nyamanda movement, which called for Matabele Home Rule, placed its emphasis on appeals and petitions to influence the British government but its lack of success led some Africans to look for alternative approaches. Abraham Twala, a South African resident in Rhodesia, and his supporters decided to organise the African voters in Rhodesia and offered their support to the Responsible Government Party in exchange for promises of justice for Africans after they came to power. On 20 January 1923, the Rhodesian Bantu Voters Association (RBVA) was formed but the numbers of African voters were too small and there was no willingness among whites to accept educated African allies for it to have any real influence. The problem was that the new white settler government had no desire to encourage the African élite to act as spokesman of the masses while the RBVA was itself an elitist organisation whose interest lay

[114] Gray, Richard, *The Two Nations: Aspects of the Development of Race Relations in the Rhodesias and Nyasaland*, (Greenwood Press), 1974, considers the issue in a broader context.

primarily in winning concessions only for the emerging African middle-class.[115] Although the RBVA won no concessions from white settlers, it was the first association to focus politics at the centre and some of its leaders attempted to reach a mass audience. For instance, Martha Ngano dominated its activities in the 1920s attacking the leadership of illiterate chiefs and appealing to her audiences by centring on destocking and land shortage as well as the need for higher education for Africans. The RBVA ensured that African opinion was heard when the land issue was reopened. White settlers also wanted the question discussed because they hoped to achieve a system of segregation. Critical in this process was the appointment of the Carter Commission in 1925 in which African evidence varied but there were certain common themes. Africans wanted more land and were prepared to accept segregation to get it leaving the remaining land for the white. For some Africans, this meant a form of black Home Rule but others were opposed to segregation pointing out that all the towns would be in the white area. The Commission report recommended segregation but there was no significant increase in native land: the Reserves were only increased slightly and the new African area, the so-called Native Purchase area was reserved for Africans who could afford freehold plots. In addition, the Native Purchase areas were in remote areas, often arid and unsurveyed and, by 1939 only 893 farmers had settled in the area. The policies of parallel development had proved a chimera: the white settlers achieved segregation but neither tribal Africans nor the progressive leaders of African associations gained real access to the land. In July 1929, bitter and disillusioned, various African associations held a combined meeting and on issue after issue voted against the 'Home Rule trick'. The 'Congress' of associations voted to reject the Land Apportionment Bill but it became law anyway in 1931.

The 1920s also saw the first attempts to organise African workers in Salisbury, Bulawayo and other urban centres.[116] Influenced by the success of the Industrial and Commercial Workers Union in South Africa, its leader Clemens Kadalie sent Robert Sambo to Rhodesia in 1927 to start ICU activity. He compiled information about poor conditions of work and the poor wages on Rhodesian farms as well as attempting to stimulate urban trade unionism. This alarmed the authorities in Salisbury who deported Sambo and sought to destroy the infant ICU organisation. They failed and the ICU held meetings every Saturday and Sunday in Bulawayo and Salisbury but in practice the ICU was weak. It never achieved the same level of mass support as in South Africa and disavowed any intention of using strike action even though this had proved effective in South Africa. Although the Industrial Conciliation Act of 1934 did not end African trade union activity, it was not until after the Second World War that it became a significant feature of urban politics.

Southern Rhodesia developed an economy that was narrowly based on the production of a small number of primary products, notably, chrome and

[115] West, Michael O., *The Rise of an African Middle Class: Colonial Zimbabwe, 1898-1965*, (Indiana University Press), 2002, pp. 12-35, 121-176, considers the emergence of identity and political consciousness.

[116] For the development of the labour movement in Zimbabwe see, Raftopoulos, Brian, and Phimister, Ian, (eds.), *Keep on Knocking: A History of the Labour Movement in Zimbabwe, 1900-97*, (Baobab Books), 1997.

tobacco.[117] It therefore became very vulnerable to the economic cycle. The deep recession of the 1930s gave way to economic growth during the war that continued into a post-war boom. The industrial areas of Bulawayo and Salisbury and of the towns on the routes between them grew and parallel to this there was growth in the number of African workers and African townships. This concentrated the discontent of the African urban population. The boom also prompted the immigration of about 200,000 white settlers, many of British working-class origin, between 1945 and 1970, taking the white population up to 270,000 though Neil Wilson, editor of the *New Rhodesia* warned in 1949 that immigration was too slow to secure white Rhodesians' long-term political future. Unfortunately, white settlers had an infinite capacity for self-deception believing that, even as a minority, they could hold on to power indefinitely. These new white farmers began to develop land in the 'white' areas of Rhodesia creating rural discontent. Africans living on land that was technically 'white' but which had not been developed were obliged to move to the already over-populated Reserves. Land-hunger was felt most acutely in Mashonaland in the 1950s. The Rhodesian government dealt with the problems posed in the Reserves by trying to extend destocking and in 1951, began a revolutionary attempt to change the whole method of tenure and farming in African areas. The Land Husbandry Act gave land rights to individuals and broke away from the old communal ownership of land. For many Africans living in the towns this meant a loss of their land rights but they also had no security in towns which were 'white' and no status as workers. Only white labour was defined as 'workers' under the 1934 legislation. Rural and urban grievances by the early 1950s were clearly part of the same problem. The conditions were right for the creation of a mass nationalist movement.

In the five years after the war, the linking of urban and rural mass discontent with élite African leadership result in vibrant, if ultimately unsuccessful, opposition to white rule. In 1945, African railway workers in Bulawayo staged a successful strike resulting in a wage increase and some official recognition of workers' movements. In Salisbury, the Reformed Industrial and Commercial Workers Union was established while in Bulawayo, Benjamin Burumbo founded the African Voice Association linking the increasingly confident urban protest with grievances in rural areas. This revival of urban and rural protest reached its climax in a general strike in 1948 when workers, ignoring the advice of their leaders to negotiate, took the initiative. The strike achieved lower wage increases than expected and Burumbo's use of legal loopholes in the Land Husbandry Act were soon removed.[118] This led to growing disillusion and growing apathy in rural areas. The flowering of African protest after 1945

---

[117] Bond, Patrick, *Uneven Zimbabwe: A Study of Finance, Development and Underdevelopment*, (Africa World Press), 1998, pp. 85-116, examines the effects of African under-development.

[118] Ibid, Alexander, Jocelyn, *The Unsettled Land*, pp. 44-62, examines the Native Land Husbandry Act. See also, Phimister, I., 'Rethinking the reserves: Southern Rhodesia's Land Husbandry Act revisited', *Journal of Southern African Studies*, Vol. 19, (1993), pp. 225-239, and Machingaidze, V. E. M., 'Agrarian change from above: The Southern Rhodesia Land Husbandry Act and African responses', *International Journal of African Historical Studies*, Vol. 24, (1991), pp. 557-588.

appeared to have emphasised the powerlessness of the nationalist movement. This may also explain why, with the coming of Federation, most African leaders turned to cooperation rather than to oppositional politics.[119]

Decolonisation and decolonisation rejected, 1950-1965

In 1953, with calls for independence mounting in many of its African possessions the United Kingdom created the Federation of Rhodesia and Nyasaland or the Central African Federation consisting of Southern Rhodesia and the protectorates of Northern Rhodesia and Nyasaland. The idea was to try and steer a middle road between the newly independent African independent states and the white-dominated governments of South Africa, Angola and Mozambique. The CAF sought to emulate the experience of Australia, Canada and South Africa where groups of colonies had become federations to establish viable independent nations. Originally designed to be 'an indissoluble federation', the CAF quickly unravelled suffering the fate of similar ventures such as the West Indies Federation undertaken in the closing days of Empire.[120]

Demographically Southern Rhodesia dominated the CAF largely because of the significant growth of its settler population since 1945.[121] By the early 1950s, its white population had reached 135,000 compared to less than 10,000 in the two protectorates. Godfrey Huggins, Southern Rhodesia's long-serving Prime Minister favoured amalgamation of the three colonies rather than federation but for the Rhodesian establishment the critical motive behind federation was access to the substantial copper deposits in Northern Rhodesia. Britain favoured federation as a means of curtailing Southern Rhodesia's dominant position. This reflected the different emphases of the Colonial Office with direct authority over the two protectorates and the Commonwealth Relations Office (CRO) with its formal but indirect authority over Southern Rhodesia. The Colonial Office, more sympathetic to African rights that the CRO, opposed Southern Rhodesian hegemony while the CRO promoted it as a means of protecting the interests of Southern, and to a lesser extent, Northern Rhodesian settlers. From the initial negotiations in late 1950, it took three years to establish the Federation. Its constitutional framework was elaborate with five branches of government: a federal structure under a Prime Minister, three territorial structures and the British colonial framework causing a degree of constitutional confusion and rivalries between the different jurisdictions.[122]

---

[119] Scarnecchia, Timothy, *The Urban Roots of Democracy and Political Violence in Zimbabwe*, (University of Rochester Press), 2008, pp. 12-48, examines immediate post-war African urban protests.

[120] Franklin, Henry, *Unholy Wedlock: The failure of the Central African Federation*, (Allen & Unwin), 1963, Hyam, R., 'The Geopolitical Origins of the Central African Federation: Britain, Rhodesia and South Africa', *Historical Journal*, Vol. 40, (1987), pp. 145-172.

[121] See, Creighton, T. R. M., *Southern Rhodesia and the Central African Federation: The anatomy of partnership*, (Greenwood Press), 1976, and Young, Kenneth, *Rhodesia and Independence: A study of British Colonial Policy*, (Heinemann), 1967, (Dent), 1969.

[122] Murphy, Philip, *Central Africa: Crisis and Dissolution, 1959-1965*, (HMSO), 2005, pp. 24-95, examines the origins of the CAF through relevant sources.

Huggins was Federal Prime Minister from 1953 to 1956 and was succeeded by Sir Roy Welensky who led the Federation until its dissolution in 1963.[123] In Southern Rhodesia, most United Rhodesia Party cabinet members joined Huggins in federal government believing that territorial government had become less important. Africans in Southern Rhodesian were more willing to cooperate with the Federation than those in the northern territories where it acted as a decisive stimulus to nationalist politics. The new Prime Minister of Southern Rhodesia, Sir Garfield Todd, wanted to develop greater 'partnership' between Africans and the white settler community.[124] He aimed to amend the Industrial Conciliation Act so that Africans could be called 'workers' and to expand African education and build up rural and urban middle-class harmony with the whites, Africans were welcomed as members of the ruling white party and delegates from African townships appeared at United Rhodesia Party congresses. Many Africans were attracted by the notion of 'partnership' and this blunted their opposition to white rule. These reformed were regarded by most whites as dangerously liberal and Todd was forced out of power when all his ministers resigned in late 1957 and three months later he was replaced as party leader and premier by Edgar Whitehead.

The focus for African dissent within the CAF during the late 1950s lay in the Northern Territories. In July 1958, Dr. Hastings Banda, the leader of African National Congress (ANC) of Nyasaland returned to Nyasaland, while in October the militant Kenneth Kaunda became the leader of the Zambian African National Congress (ZANC), a faction from the Northern Rhodesian ANC. The increasingly nervous CAF authorities banned ZANC in March 1959 and in June imprisoned Kaunda for nine months. While Kaunda was in jail, his loyal lieutenant Mainza Chona worked with other African nationalists to create the United National Independence Party, a successor to ZANC. In early 1959, unrest broke out in Nyasaland and the CAF government declared a state of emergency. Banda and the rest of Nyasaland's ANC leadership were arrested and their party outlawed and Southern Rhodesian troops were deployed to bring order. The growing unrest called the whole concept of the Federation into question.[125]

In Britain, Harold Macmillan accepted that the CAF had been an economic success but increasingly questioned its political future and established a Royal Commission under Walter Monckton to advise him on its future. There were, however, divisions between Sir Alec Douglas-Home, the Commonwealth Secretary who supported the continuance of the CAF and Ian Macleod, the Colonial Secretary who favoured African rights and its dissolution. Macmillan

---

[123] On Welensky see, Welensky, Roy, *Welensky's 4000 days: the life and death of the Federation of Rhodesia and Nyasaland*, (Collins), 1964, Wood, J. R. T., (ed.), *The Welensky papers: a history of the federation of Rhodesia and Nyasaland*, (Graham Pub.), 1983, and Allighan, Garry, *The Welensky story*, (Macdonald), 1962.

[124] Mungazi, Dickson A., *The Last British Liberals in Africa: Michael Blundell and Garfield Todd*, (Praeger Publishers), 1999, pp. 105-134, 161-190, Weiss, Ruth, *Sir Garfield Todd and the making of Zimbabwe*, (British Academic Press), 1999.

[125] Ibid, Murphy, Philip, *Central Africa: Crisis and Dissolution, 1959-1965*, pp. 168-204, and Baker, Colin, *State of Emergency: Crisis in Central Africa, Nyasaland 1959-1960*, (I. B. Tauris), 1997, examine the emergency in Nyasaland and questions over the Federation's future.

initially supported Douglas-Home but he recognised the 'winds of change' that were buffeting the continent. By 1960, French African colonies had already become independent and the hasty departure of Belgium from the Congo led to brutal civil war with many European refugees fleeing into Southern Rhodesia. The crisis in the Congo reinforced African suspicions of CAF Prime Minister Sir Roy Welensky as an arch-reactionary, a situation reinforced by his support for Katangan separatism in the Congo. A new constitution for the CAF was agreed in 1961 significantly reducing Britain's powers and the following year, the British and CAF cabinets agreed to allow Nyasaland to secede from the Federation and Northern Rhodesia followed suit.[126] Attempts to save the CAF at a conference at the Victoria Falls in June 1963[127] proved fruitless, the Federation of Rhodesia and Nyasaland was dissolved on 1 January 1964 and replaced by the independent African states of Zambia and Malawi.[128]

The gradual but inexorable dismantling of the CAF resulted in a hardening of racial opinion in Southern Rhodesia. Edgar Whitehead had been central in getting agreement for the 1961 Constitution, had managed to carry the changes in a referendum in July 1961 by a 2:1 majority and had relaxed racial discrimination laws. These policies caused alarm among whites but also failed to meet African aspirations. Opponents of the Federation had formed the Dominion Party but the party suffered division before the General Election when in February 1962, Dominion Party leader William Harper resigned stating that he intended this to be the catalyst towards the creation of a united opposition. The Rhodesia Reform Party had been formed by Ian Smith early in 1962 as a more moderate group and by mid-March, the Dominion Party and the Rhodesia Reform Party had put together a broad plan for the new Rhodesian Front (RF) with Winston Field of the Dominion Party as its leader.[129] All those involved in the campaign leading to the ballot on 14 December 1962 recognised that this was a pivotal election. The RF sought to reassure voters that it supported continued links with Northern Rhodesia and called for tougher law enforcement and security. Both the RF and the United Federal Party supported moves for independence but the RF appeared more committed stating that independence could be within the Commonwealth or not. The key difference between the two parties was race relations. Whitehead's liberalising policies were condemned as reckless and endangering white Rhodesian society by the RF while the 1961 Constitution was regarded as leading inevitably to African domination over Europeans. Although Whitehead was expected to win, the RF won 35 of the 50 white seats gaining 56.4

[126] Wood, J. R. T., *So Far and No Further! Rhodesia's Bid for Independence During the Retreat from Empire 1959-1965*, (Trafford Publishing), 2005, pp. 74-123, on the making of the 1961 Constitution.

[127] Ibid, pp. 159-167, looks at the Victoria Falls conference

[128] Sills, H. D., 'The Break-Up of the Central African Federation', *African Affairs*, Vol. 73, (1974), pp. 50-62. See also, ibid, Murphy, Philip, *Central Africa: Crisis and Dissolution, 1959-1965*, 265-401.

[129] Mungazi, Dickson A., *The Last Defenders of the Laager: Ian D. Smith and F. W. de Klerk*, (Praeger Publishing), 1998, pp. 53-78, 107-134, examines Smith's rise to political leadership in the early 1960s. Smith, Ian, *Bitter Harvest: The Great Betrayal*, (Blake), 2001, provides an autobiographical focus.

per cent of the popular vote. Of the 15 District seats included in the 1961 Constitution for blacks, the UFP won 14.[130]

Field provided the RF government with an air of respectability, though his Cabinet was derided by one newspaper as 'by no means an inspiring list'.[131] At the time of Field's election, it was assumed that Britain would delay the process of independence for Rhodesia until an African majority assumed power in Salisbury. Many in the RF felt that Field did not fight hard enough for independence and that the British had deceived him on visits to London in June 1963 and January 1964 over promises of independence. His relatively short time in office saw the dissolution of the CAF though he did win most of the Federation's military and other assets as the British Government did not wish to see them fall into the hands of the nationalist leaders and Southern Rhodesia had borne the majority of the costs of running the Federation. On 2 April 1964, the caucus of the RF asked for Field's resignation but a formal demand was only made a few days later at a Cabinet meeting. Field was replaced as leader of the RF and as Prime Minister by Ian Smith on 14 April 1964.[132] In the May 1965 election, the RF campaigned on the promise of independence and won all fifty of the European-elected seats. The British government adopted a policy of *no independence before majority rule*, dictating that colonies with a minority of white settlers would not receive independence except under conditions of majority rule. The RF government, led by Ian Smith, staunchly opposed the policy and received overwhelming support in a referendum on independence in November 1964.[133]

During 1965, negotiations between Britain and Rhodesia took place but by November they had reached an impasse.[134] As a result, Smith's government declared the country independent from British rule on 11 November 1965 in what became known as Unilateral Declaration of Independence (UDI).[135] Under instructions from Harold Wilson's government, the Governor of Southern Rhodesia, Sir Humphrey Gibbs, formally dismissed Smith and his cabinet for what was deemed 'an act of treason against the United Kingdom'. Smith's government ignored the dismissal, stating that as Rhodesia was no longer a colony and governed under a new constitution that made Gibbs' office obsolete and that, in their view, the dismissal no longer had any legality. Gibbs remained in Government House for the next four years, resigning his office only after the

[130] Ibid, Wood, J. R. T., *So Far and No Further!* pp. 95-121, reviews Whitehead's defeat.
[131] *Daily News*, 18 December 1962.
[132] Ibid, Wood, J. R. T., *So Far and No Further!* pp. 190-224, examines Smith's coup against Field.
[133] Ibid, pp. 241-250, examines at the 1964 referendum.
[134] Windrich, Elaine, *Britain and the Politics of Rhodesian Independence*, (Croom Helm), 1978, looks at the intricacies of negotiations between the Labour government and Ian Smith in the 1960s. Wood, J. R. T., *A Matter of weeks rather than months: The Impasse between Harold Wilson and Ian Smith: Sanctions, Aborted Settlements and War, 1965-1969*, Vol. 1, (Trafford), 2008, provides the most detailed account. See also, ibid, Murphy, Philip, *Central Africa: Crisis and Dissolution, 1959-1965*, pp. 402-443, and Ashton, Stephen, and Louis, William Roger, *East of Suez and the Commonwealth 1964-1971, Part II: Europe, Rhodesia, Commonwealth*, (HMSO), 2004, pp. 192-243, prints important Cabinet papers.
[135] Ibid, Wood, J. R. T., *So Far and No Further!*, pp. 443-474, on UDI.

republic referendum passed in late 1969.[136] Soon, quiet efforts to reach a compromise began. Smith's problem was how to legitimise his rebellion to secure crucial investment capital, markets, trade and more. His antagonist, the British Prime Minister, Harold Wilson, was determined not to transfer sovereignty until Rhodesia accepted African majority rule in common with the rest of Africa. He could only impose sanctions but hoped they would defeat Smith 'in a matter weeks rather than months'.[137] The Rhodesians, however, evaded sanctions so successfully that they forced Wilson to negotiate a settlement. Initially, there were informal exploratory talks, followed by a fruitless meeting in late 1966, between Smith and Wilson aboard HMS *Tiger* in the Mediterranean. The British position was that Smith's government should resign allowing the British Governor to appoint a 'broad-based' government with a RF majority, but with five non-RF members of whom two would be black. The existing 1961 constitution would be modified to accelerate the expansion of black representation leading to majority rule in the near term. This offer was dismissed by Smith, who regarded it as terms for surrender. Despite several attempts during 1967 and 1968 to restart talks, relations between London and Salisbury deteriorated but despite this attempts to find a political solution continued. Between 10 and 13 October 1968, the two leaders tried again on HMS *Fearless*, off Gibraltar. The terms offered on HMS *Tiger* were diluted by dropping the need for an interim return to British rule. However, the requirement for the installation of a broad-based government and an accelerated move to majority rule remained. Smith dismissed this offer as well. There was no bridging the basic disagreement over Rhodesia's refusal to abandon UDI and its existing constitution, pending a settlement acceptable to the black majority.

The international community condemned UDI. The day after UDI the United Nations Security Council adopted Resolution 216 condemning it as a declaration of independence 'made by a racist minority.'[138] The United Nations Security Council authorised the use of sanctions, targeting Rhodesia at the behest of Britain, beginning in 1965 and lasting until the restoration of British rule in December 1979. The terms of these sanctions forbade most forms of trade or financial exchange with Rhodesia. However, not all members of the international

---

[136] Megahey, Alan J., *Humphrey Gibbs, beleaguered Governor: Southern Rhodesia, 1929-69*, (St Martin's Press), 1998.

[137] The Labour government decided against armed intervention largely because of British feelings for their Rhodesian kith and kin and Rhodesia's landlocked position British feelings for their Rhodesian kith and kin and Rhodesia's landlocked position. Wilson commented in his *The Labour Government, 1964-1970: a personal record*, (Weidenfeld & Nicolson), 1971, p. 181, that had the government have decided to intervene, Edward Heath would have 'led a united party, and almost certain won majority support in the country.' Watts, C., 'Killing kith and kin: The viability of British Military Intervention in Rhodesia 1964-5', *Twentieth Century British History*, Vol. 16, (2005), pp. 382-425, by contrast, argues that the military and political obstacles to intervention were grossly exaggerated and that Wilson could have used force to prevent or end UDI. See also, Coggins, R., 'Wilson and Rhodesia: UDI and British Policy towards Africa', *Contemporary British History*, Vol. 20, (2006), pp. 363-381

[138] Mezerik, Avrahm G., *Rhodesia and the United Nations*, (International Service Review), 1966, and Kapunga, Leonard T., *The United Nations and Economic Sanctions against Rhodesia*, (Lexington Books), 1973, examine the issue of sanctions.

community adhered to the Resolution and South Africa, Portugal, Israel, Iran and some Arab nations helped Rhodesia in various ways and Rhodesia's shared border with South Africa made the measures ultimately unenforceable. Britain used economic sanctions that included ending the link between sterling and the Rhodesian currency, seizing assets and banning the import of Rhodesian tobacco. Smith's government retaliated by defaulting on its British-guaranteed debts, leaving the British liable while at the same time balancing its budget. The 1971 Byrd Amendment forbade any prohibition on the importation into the United States of any strategic and critical material from any non-communist country so long as the importation of such material from communist countries was not prohibited. Between 1972 and 1977, the United States imported $212 million worth of Rhodesian ferrochrome, chrome ore, and nickel, as well as asbestos, copper, and other ores and alloys in contravention of United Nations sanctions.[139] Editorials in the *Rhodesian Herald* called the move 'a wonderful boost for Rhodesian morale' and optimistically forecast 'the accelerated erosion of sanctions'. One editorial concluded: 'the American move is at the least a signal to the world that sanctions are not important enough to warrant serious sacrifices; and at the most that their usefulness has lost its credibility in American eyes'.[140] Sanctions have generally been written off as a dismal failure but that was not the view of prominent businessmen interviewed in Zimbabwe in 1986 who maintained that they were the main factor in forcing the Smith regime to negotiate a transition to majority rule in the late 1970s.[141]

The Rhodesian government struggled to obtain international recognition and the lifting of sanctions. No significant state ever granted recognition to Rhodesia and in 1970 the United States government categorically stated that 'under no circumstances' would it recognise Rhodesian independence.[142] Initially, the state maintained its loyalty to Queen Elizabeth II as 'Queen of Rhodesia', a title to which she never consented but not to her representative, Governor Sir Humphrey Gibbs, whose constitutional duties were exercised by Clifford Dupont as 'Officer Administering the Government'. On 20 June 1969, a referendum on the future status of Rhodesia decided by 55,000 votes to 21,000 in favour of severing links with the British Crown and becoming a republic. On 2 March 1970, Rhodesia's government formally declared Rhodesia a republic with

[139] Senator Henry Byrd of Virginia was a long-term opponent of American policy to Rhodesia and made no secret that his amendment was specifically intended to allow the importation of Rhodesian minerals. The most extensive study of the Byrd Amendment controversy to 1976 is, Lake, Anthony, *The 'Tar Baby' Option: American policy toward Southern Rhodesia*, (Columbia University Press), 1976.

[140] *Rhodesian Herald*, 27 January 1972.

[141] Minter, William, and Schmidt, Elizabeth, 'When Sanctions Worked: The Case of Rhodesia Reexamined', *African Affairs*, Vol. 87, (1988), pp. 207-237.

[142] Hubbard, James P., *The United States and the End of British Colonial Rule in Africa, 1941-1968*, (McFarland & Company Inc.), 2010, pp. 321-363, considers American attitudes to the end of the CAF and the Rhodesian problem. See also, DeRoche, Andrew, *Black, White and Chrome: The United States and Zimbabwe, 1953-1998*, (Africa World Press), 2001, Noer, Thomas J., *Cold War and Black Liberation: The United States and White Rule in Africa, 1948-1968*, (University of Missouri Press), 1985, and Watts, Carl P., 'The United States, Britain and the Problem of Rhodesian Independence, 1964-1965', *Diplomatic History*, Vol. 30, (2006), pp. 439-470.

Dupont as President. The Rhodesians vainly hoped that this would end any ambiguity about the country's status, gain diplomatic recognition and bring economic sanctions to an end.

Armed Struggle, 1965-1979

Between 1965 and 1979, Southern Rhodesia was the location for two nationalist rebellions. The white minority was in rebellion against the decolonising policies of the British government while the black majority was in rebellion against the Smith regime. African nationalists waged their rebellion through guerrilla conflict, the white minority sought a diplomatic solution with Britain that was acceptable to white and black Rhodesians. The attack on the traditional African way of life inherent in the 1951 Land Husbandry Act, with its aim of changing the Reserves from communal areas to areas of individual plots and the forced resignation of Garfield Todd in 1958 because of his liberal policies convinced many Africans that their participation in Rhodesian society and politics could not succeed. Young Africans were particularly challenged by these developments: they had most to lose from the 1951 legislation, were not largely involved in trade union politics because they did not see themselves as a permanent working-class and were not part of the educated participant African élite. The result was the rise of radical nationalist parties that, before and after UDI, challenged white hegemony.[143]

In 1957, members of the City Youth League, founded in Salisbury two years earlier, combined with the Bulawayo branch of the old African National Congress to form a revive Southern Rhodesian African National Congress with Joshua Nkomo, a respected trade unionist, as its president.[144] From its urban base, Congress was spread into the rural areas by landless young men who returned home from the cities to call for more vigorous peasant mobilisation. The resultant rural discontent resulted in the Rhodesian government introducing a state of emergency in February 1959, Congress was banned and many of its leaders were arrested, though Nkomo was out of the country and repressive legislation including detaining people without trial indefinitely was passed. The vigour and rapidity of the government's response led to a significant reduction in radical activity and in was not until January 1960 that it revived with the formation of the National Democratic Party by Nkomo, who became its leader in October 1960, and Robert Mugabe, Herbert Chitepo and Ndabaningi Sithole.[145] It drew on continuities from the old Congress, on traditions of deep-seated resentments of rural areas and on Shona expectations of radical change.

The NDP and its successor, the Zimbabwe African People's Union (ZAPU) had a broad populist appeal attracting many of the African intellectual élite as well as landless young men, trade unionists, peasants and rural traders. It

---

[143] Ibid, Scarnecchia, Timothy, *The Urban Roots of Democracy and Political Violence in Zimbabwe*, pp. 69-113, considers the development of Youth League politics and the protests of the early 1960s.

[144] Nkomo, Joshua with Harman, Nicholas, *Nkomo: The Story of my Life*, (Methuen), 1984.

[145] Sithole, Ndabaningi, *Roots of a Revolution: Scenes from Zimbabwe's Struggle*, (Oxford University Press), 1977, and *Letters from Salisbury Prison*, (Transafrica Publishers), 1976, are valuable on Sithole's thinking in the 1970s.

sought overseas support, criticised constitutional proposals and organised urban strikes and encouraged rural resistance to the Land Husbandry legislation. An NDP delegation headed by Nkomo attended the constitutional conference in January 1961. Nkomo initially supported the constitution but reversed his position after other NDP leaders disagreed. The government banned the NDP in December 1961 and arrested NDP leaders, excluding Nkomo who, again, was out of the country. Nkomo formed ZAPU on 17 December 1961 but it too was banned in May 1962 because of its militarism.[146] In July 1963, Nkomo suspended Sithole, Mugabe, Leopold Takawira, and Washington Malianga for their opposition to his support for militant tactics.[147] In August, they announced the establishment of the Zimbabwe African National Union (ZANU).[148] Both parties vied for domination but in 1964 both were banned and their leaders were all arrested and Nkomo, Sithole and Mugabe spent the next ten years in prison. Both parties reorganised outside Rhodesian borders. ZAPU based itself in the West and Zambia where it organised ZIPRA (the Zimbabwe People's Revolutionary Army), allied with the Soviet Union and organised a vanguard of highly trained soldiers. ZANU, however, moved into Tanzania and then to Mozambique and set up ZANLA (Zimbabwe African National Liberation Army) that concentrated more on mobilising the masses in the countryside in a method pioneered by the Chinese.[149] The division between ZAPU and ZANU, reinforced by Sino-Soviet conflict, introduced a new element since, for the first time, blacks fought each other squandering much energy that benefited the white regime. 'It is possible that the two parties fought against each other more than they did against the white supremacist government.'[150] In 1976, ZAPU and ZANU formed a 'Patriotic Front' and at least nominally combined their military forces.[151]

Both ZAPU and ZANU began sustained campaigns of guerrilla warfare in 1966. The conflict was seen by the nationalist groups as a war of national and

---

[146] Sibanda, Eliakim M., *The Zimbabwe African People's Union 1961-1987: A Political History of Insurgency in Southern Rhodesia*, (Africa World Press), 2005, pp. 71-79, details the founding of the organisation and its activities in 1962.

[147] Ibid, pp. 90-93.

[148] On the formation of ZANU see, Norman, Andrew, *Robert Mugabe and the Betrayal of Zimbabwe*, (McFarland & Company Ltd.), 2004, pp. 47-58.

[149] The role played by peasants during the war and their relationship with the guerrillas is an area of debate. Ranger, T. O. *Peasant Consciousness and Guerrilla War in Zimbabwe: A Comparative Study*, (James Currey), 1985, concluded that guerrilla ideology was effective in mobilising peasants and that they voluntarily aided the guerrillas while other nationalist historians take a 'celebratory' view of the war in which peasants willingly cooperated risking their lives in the process. Other studies argue that there was violent coercion to gain the material support and sexual services of peasants and that, as the guerrillas failed to establish 'liberated zone', the use of force was inevitable in recruitment. See, Raftopoulos, B., 'Problematising nationalism in Zimbabwe: A historiographical review', *Zambezia*, Vol. 26, (1999), pp. 115-134.

[150] Ibid, Norman, Andrew, *Robert Mugabe and the Betrayal of Zimbabwe*, pp. 94-95.

[151] Sithole, Masipula, 'Ethnicity and factionalism in Zimbabwean nationalist politics, 1957-79', *Ethnic and Racial Studies*, Vol. 3, (1980), pp. 17-39, 'Class and Factionalism in the Zimbabwe Nationalist Movement', *African Studies Review*, Vol. 27, (1984), pp. 117-125, and *Zimbabwe: Struggles within the Struggle, 1957-1980*, 2nd ed., (Rujeko Publishers), 1999.

racial liberation. The Rhodesian government, by contrast, regarded it as a fight between whites on behalf of the whole population, including the black majority and several externally financed parties made up of predominantly black radicals and communists. The Smith administration maintained that the traditional chiefs were the legitimate voice of the Shona and Ndebele population. It believed that it was defending Western values, Christianity, the rule of law and democracy by fighting Communists and was unwilling to compromise on most political, economic and social inequalities. Ian Smith's view that the Rhodesian regime was battling Communism was evident in the support the nationalist parties received from the Soviet Union and China. In June 1979, the governments of Cuba and Mozambique offered direct military assistance to the Patriotic Front, but Mugabe and Nkomo declined. Other foreign nations also contributed to the conflict, for instance North Korean military officials taught Zimbabwean militants how to use explosives and arms in a camp near Pyongyang. By April 1979, 12,000 ZANLA troops were training in Tanzania, Ethiopia, and Libya.[152] On the other side of the conflict, South Africa clandestinely provided both material and military support to the Rhodesian government. Although Washington officially voiced concerns over human rights violations, an attitude of tolerance generally marked United States relations with the Rhodesian government. Especially under President Lyndon B. Johnson between 1963 and 1968, there were fears that racial conflict abroad could inflame racial hatred at home. Sanctions were imposed but not strictly enforced and American mercenaries joined white Rhodesia's side.

Between 1960 and 1963, a wave of urban and rural unrest swept across Southern Rhodesia and although ZAPU disassociated itself from violent activities carried out mostly by its youth supporters, it had already developed an ideology of violent resistance and armed struggle that was a major cause of the division of the party in 1963.[153] What turned largely uncoordinated violence into armed struggle was the breakdown of the constitutional talks in 1963 and especially UDI in 1965. From 1966 to 1979, the guerrilla war against the Smith regime was continuous and expanding. Until the early 1970s, the guerrilla offensive was largely contained since the Rhodesian government could deploy an overwhelming superiority in manpower, firepower and mobility.[154] By 1971, often regarded as marking the peak of white fortunes in Rhodesia, the most prominent nationalist leaders and trade unionists were either in detention or exile. The Rhodesian army consisted of 3,400 men and 4,000 European reservists reinforced by the British South Africa police of 2,000 Europeans and 5,000 Africans.[155] It was later strengthened by the air force and by the recruitment of mercenaries mainly from South Africa but also from Europe and the United States and direct military assistance from South Africa. Military defeats increased tension and feuding within and between

[152] See, Taylor, Ian, *China and Africa: Engagement and Compromise*, (Routledge), 2006, pp. 106-126, Kempton, Daniel R., *Soviet strategy towards southern Africa: The national liberation movement*, (Praeger), 1989, and Shubin, Vladimir, *The Hot 'Cold War': The USSR in Southern Africa*, (Pluto Press), 2008.
[153] Ibid, Taylor, Ian, *China and Africa: Engagement and Compromise*, 95-96.
[154] Moorcraft, Paul L., and McLaughlin, Peter, *The Rhodesian War: A Military History*, (Pen & Sword Books Ltd.), 2008, pp. 29-36, examines the early phase of the war.
[155] Cilliers, J., *Counter-insurgency in Rhodesia*, (Routledge), 1985, and Ellert, H., *The Rhodesian Front War: Counter-insurgency and guerrilla War,* (Mambo Press), 1989.

the guerrilla movement and ultimately led to new strategies being developed. Although both ZANU and ZAPU received communist support and Marxist sentiments became steadily stronger, especially among the guerrillas in ZANLA, these did not gain widespread backing among the political leadership. The Zimbabwean war never became a revolutionary socialist war and remained primarily a nationalist struggle that aimed to wrest political power from Europeans.

Critical for the early success of the Smith regime was the continued division between ZANU and ZUPA. Attempts were made in 1971-1972 to unite the nationalists. Some members of both organisations announced their merger into the Front for the Liberation of Zimbabwe in October 1971 and in January 1972, ZANU and ZAPU issued a declaration of intent to unite largely because the Organisation of African Unity said it would only give aid to a united front. In practice, nationalist unity failed because of ethnic, ideological and personality disputes and by June 1973 the Front for the Liberation of Zimbabwe had largely collapsed. The situation changed suddenly with the release of Nkomo, Mugabe, Sithole and other nationalist leaders from prison in late 1974 to take part in 'unity' talks in Lusaka and the end of Portuguese colonial rule in Mozambique in 1975. Sithole had been deposed as President of ZANU by his fellow detainees in favour of Mugabe but the Front-line states insisted that he was reinstated. This proved temporary and gradually Mugabe emerged as ZANU's recognised leader though his dominance was not assured until 1977. The new Mozambican government threw its weight behind ZANLA and Rhodesia's border with Mozambique became a front line across which guerrillas began to operate freely. Zambia became another front that was opened when the Zambian government also gave sanctuary to the guerrillas. In October 1976, the two nationalist parties formed a Patriotic Front, an alliance that proved largely ineffective on the battlefield where the military wings continued to operate largely independently. Rhodesia now found itself almost surrounded by hostile states and even South Africa, its only real ally, was pressing for a settlement.[156]

The guerrilla war became increasingly militant after 1971 and it became increasingly clear that an indefinite postponement of majority rule, the cornerstone of the Smith's strategy since UDI, was no longer viable. Late in 1976, Smith accepted the basic elements of the compromise proposals made by United States Secretary of State, Henry Kissinger to introduce majority rule within two years. The Smith Government then sought to negotiate an acceptable settlement with moderate black leaders, while retaining strong white influence in key areas. The Rhodesian army no longer faced the disorganised guerrillas of the 1960s. They were now well-equipped with modern weapons and although many were still untrained, an increasing number had received training in Communist bloc

[156] Ibid, Moorcraft, Paul L., and McLaughlin, Peter, *The Rhodesian War*, pp. 37-46, 147-170, considers the development of the war from 1972 to 1979. See also, Godwin, P. and Hancock, I., *'Rhodesians Never Die': The Impact of War and Political Change on White Rhodesia, c.1970-1980*, (Baobab Books), 1995, and Martin, D. and Johnson, P., *The Struggle for Zimbabwe*, (Zimbabwe Publishing House), 1981

and other sympathetic countries.[157] The Rhodesian military sought to erode the increasing nationalist military strength to 'buy time' for an acceptable political settlement to be reached mounting a major offensive destroying a camp at Nyadzonya in Mozambique containing many hundreds of trainees reporting more than 1,000 insurgents killed while the nationalists claimed the site was a refugee camp. The military also operated into Zambia after Nkomo's nationalists shot down two unarmed Vickers Viscount civilian airliners with Soviet supplied missiles. By 1977, the war had spread throughout Rhodesia. ZANLA continued to operate from Mozambique, remained dominant among the Shona peoples in eastern and central Rhodesia while ZIPRA was active in the north and west, using bases in Zambia and Botswana and were mainly supported by the Ndebele. General Peter Walls told the media the Rhodesian forces were changing tactics from contain and hold to search and destroy, 'adopting hot pursuit when necessary.'

By early 1978, militant victories put the Rhodesian armed forces on the defensive. The government abandoned its strategy of trying to defend the borders in favour of trying to defend key economic areas and lines of communication with South Africa, while the rest of the countryside became a patchwork of 'no-go areas.' Rhodesia's front-line forces never contained more than 25,000 troops but could still launch raids on enemy bases, but Rhodesia faced diplomatic isolation, economic collapse and military defeat. In December 1978, a ZANLA unit attacked the main oil storage depot on the outskirts of Salisbury, the most heavily defended economic asset in the country. Half a million barrels of petroleum product, comprising Rhodesia's strategic oil reserve were lost. At a stroke, the country's annual budget deficit was increased by 20 per cent. In 1980, the post-independence government of Zimbabwe inherited a US$500m national debt. The Rhodesian army continued its 'mobile counter-offensive' strategy of holding key positions while carrying out raids into the no-go areas and into neighbouring countries. These raids became increasingly costly and unproductive. The larger problem was that by 1979, combined ZIRPA and ZANLA strength inside Rhodesia totalled at least 12,500 guerrillas and it was evident that insurgents were entering the country at a rate greater than the Rhodesian forces could kill or capture. In addition, 22,000 ZIPRA and 16,000 ZANLA fighters remained uncommitted outside the country. What was clear was that the insurgency was growing in strength daily and the ability of the security forces to continue to control the entire country was coming under serious challenge.

From White Rule to Independence, 1970-1980

The RF held power from 1962 until 1979, forming the majority in a parliament, in which most seats were reserved for the white minority of the country.[158] It was a

[157] For American attitudes to Smith's regime and its Cold War interests in Rhodesia, see Horne, Gerald, *From the Barrel of a Gun: The United States and the War against Zimbabwe, 1965-1980*, (UNC Press Books), 2001.

[158] Elections in Rhodesia from 1965 to 1979 used two electoral rolls. An 'A' roll was largely white in 1965 and after the constitutional changes in 1969 wholly white. The 'B' roll was largely black in 1965 and wholly so after 1969. Although the number of white seats remained constant at 50, the number of black seats fluctuated slightly: in 1965, there

broadly populist party with support mainly from the working-class and recent immigrants. Economically, at least, the government's policies were quite liberal advocating less government interference in the economy and free trade and many state benefits were provided to the white minority. In 1969, the constitution was modified. The most significant change was the formal separation of two electoral rolls by race. The A roll was reserved for Europeans and the B roll for non-Europeans. The Assembly constituencies were reformed so that there were 50 A roll and 8 B roll seats. In addition, the tribal chiefs could elect another 8 members. Effectively, the result was that 270,000 whites had 50 seats and 6 million Africans had 16 seats in the Assembly. These reforms served only to reinforce black rejection of the system. In April 1970, the first general election since UDI was held. Ian Smith portrayed his government as not being racialist and could do so because more radical and more racist parties stood in the election. The Centre Party, a non-racial party that had been formed in 1968 and was strongest in urban centres, supported the advancement of Africans on merit and the gradual abolition of racial discrimination. The Conservative Alliance was formed in June 1969 and campaigned for the preservation of European civilisation in Rhodesia. It attacked the RF's 'multiracial, integrationist policies' and was subsequently renamed the Republican Alliance. African voters also began to form political parties especially the National People's Union that aimed to unit Africans against white supremacy without violence. The RF won all the white seats while the Centre Party's appeal to non-racial politics proved effective among African voters who gave them seven of the eight seats.

Although negotiations in 1966 and 1968 between Britain and Rhodesia had failed to find a constitutional solution to the question of UDI, in early 1971 secret discussions were held between British and Rhodesian officials that became public in September. Foreign Secretary Alec Douglas-Home held talks with Ian Smith in Salisbury leading to the 'Anglo-Rhodesian Settlement Proposals' signed on 24 November.[159] It called for an immediate increase in African representation in Parliament as more Africans met voting qualifications until it equalled the Europeans' 50 seats. Britain held firm on the principle that the proposals should undergo a 'test of acceptability' by all the people of Rhodesia before they would be implemented. The African National Council, led by Bishop Abel Muzorewa and the Reverend Canaan Banana spearheaded largely non-violent but vigorous opposition to the proposals. The Pearce Commission was established to investigate the acceptability of the proposed changes and completed its work by early March 1972 presenting its formal report in late May.[160] It reported widespread support among European settlers, mixed reactions from Asians and 97 per cent negative response from the more than 100,000 Africans polled and concluded that the proposals were unacceptable as a basis of independence by the

---

were 15 roll seats but after 1969, this was decreased to 8 African roll seats with the addition of 8 tribal seats returned by tribal electoral colleges made up of tribal chiefs.

[159] *Anglo-Rhodesian relations; Proposals for a Settlement: Presented to Parliament by the Prime Minister on 25th November, 1971*, (HMSO), 1971.

[160] For the Pearce Commission, see *Rhodesia: Report of the Commission on Rhodesian Opinion under the Chairmanship of the Right Honourable Lord Pearce*, (HMSO), 1972, and Todd, Judith, *The Right to Say No*, (Sidgwick and Jackson), 1977, and Muzorewa, A. T., *Rise Up and Walk: An Autobiography*, (Evans Brothers), 1979.

people of Rhodesia. For ZAPU and ZANU, this outcome confirmed the correctness of their decision to take up arms in 1966.

Muzorewa and Ian Smith continued to hold secret negotiations that were acknowledged in 1973 but in June 1974, the African National Council rejected proposals that had come out of discussions between itself and the Rhodesian government. In July 1975, a General Election confirmed the dominance of the RF that again won all the seats elected by white voters with 77 per cent of the white vote demonstrating their continued strong opposition to black majority rule. The RF did face white opposition from the Rhodesia Party, a moderate group that advocated more moves towards including the African population in internal politics and which it attacked for holding secret negotiations with the African National Council with the intention of undermining the Rhodesian government. Ian Smith may have held sway inside Rhodesia but events beyond its borders fatally weakened his capacity to maintain white minority rule or make a gradual transition to African majority rule. South Africa no longer regarded Rhodesia as a buffer state that could easily be defended and the South African Prime Minister P. J. Vorster now regarded Smith's regime as unstable and white Rhodesia as expendable[161] South African foreign policy increasingly called for diplomatic relations and expanding commercial links with black Africa to improve its standing in the international community. In late 1974, he made a joint diplomatic move with President Kenneth Kaunda of Zambia to bring Smith and the nationalist leaders to the conference table.[162] Kaunda had strong economic reasons for his stance: he needed urgent imports of South Africa maize and needed secure routes to export its copper through Rhodesia to the ports of Mozambique and South Africa.[163]

Further talks were held between Rhodesian government officials and African nationalist leaders in Lusaka in December 1974. With Kenneth Kaunda's Zambian support the nationalist parties were convinced to come together under the umbrella of Abel Muzorewa's United African National Council. The problem was that neither ZANU nor ZAPU recognised Muzorewa, who they regarded as nothing more than a figurehead. There was supposed to be a ceasefire followed by negotiations between the nationalists and Smith but ZANLA refused to observe it and Mugabe joined the guerrillas and soon emerged as overall leader of ZANU. In February 1975, Smith met with Nkomo, Muzorewa and Sithole to set up a formal constitutional conference. The result was the Victoria Falls meeting of 25-26 August 1975. The conference broke down after two days when Smith refused to consider allowing nationalists who were wanted by the Rhodesian police for 'terrorist' activities to participate freely in politics in Rhodesia. Despite this, between December 1975 and March 1976, Smith held talks with Nkomo, now head of the ANC-Zimbabwe, the internal wing of ZANU but these failed

---

[161] For Vorster's evolving policy towards African states see, Pfister, Roger, *Apartheid South Africa and African States: From pariah to middle power, 1961-1994*, (I. B. Tauris), 2005, pp. 39-103.

[162] Chan, Stephen, *Kaunda and Southern Africa: Image and Reality in Foreign Policy*, (British Academic Press), 1992, pp. 33-62.

[163] Schwartz, Richard, *Coming to Terms: Zimbabwe in the International Arena*, (I. B. Tauris), 2001, pp. 17-34.

because Nkomo wanted a two-year transition to majority rule while Smith wanted fifteen years.

In early 1976, 800 ZANLA guerrillas entered Rhodesia from Mozambique, followed by further groups in May, October and December. In March 1976, Mozambique finally closed its ports to Rhodesia that was now forced to use South Africa's more expensive facilities. The deteriorating military and economic situation forced Smith to further negotiations. In September, he met with Henry Kissinger, the American Secretary of State in Pretoria and, when it became apparent that he could no longer rely on South African support, announced his willingness to bring about African majority rule within two years.[164] Kissinger and Vorster then allowed Britain to take over the decolonisation process and in October, Smith and the nationalists met at a British-chaired conference in Geneva, Switzerland. The talks broke down in January 1977 over the terms of independence and the schedule leading up to it but it did lead to ZANU and ZAPU forming a Patriotic Front to conduct the negotiations and preserved it when they returned to war. New Anglo-American proposals were made in September 1977 that were enforced by the Frontline states and, as pressure for a constitutional settlement mounted, Smith announced on 24 November, conditional acceptance of the principle of 'one man, one vote' for Rhodesia. On 2 December, Smith opened a new round of internal negotiations with Muzorewa and Sithole while in January 1978, the British and American governments met secretly with the leaders of the Patriotic Front in Malta but Smith and the moderate African leaders inside Rhodesia rejected their proposals.

Abandoned by South Africa and denied victory against the guerrilla forces, Smith sought an 'internal settlement' with moderate African politicians hoping that it would be acceptable to both his domestic and international critics. Under the Salisbury Agreement of 3 March 1978, the country was to be known as Zimbabwe-Rhodesia and established a transitional government run by an executive council consisting of Smith, Muzorewa, Sithole and Chief Jeremiah Chirau. This marked the end of exclusive white rule in Rhodesia. The task of the transitional government was to arrange a ceasefire, remove racial discrimination, draft a new constitution and hold elections towards the end of the year before handing over to a black government by 31 December. Smith managed to achieve important and entrenched constitutional safeguards for whites and the agreement and subsequent constitution, finalised in February 1979, were regarded by most Zimbabweans as a victory for Smith and white supremacy. Following the general election on 24 April 1979 Bishop Abel Muzorewa became the country's first black Prime Minister. It proved a failure. Nkomo and Mugabe denounced the new government as a puppet of white Rhodesians and fighting continued. The United Nations Security Council passed several resolutions against the 'illegal' election, including Resolutions 445 and 448, which maintained that the election was not representative of the Zimbabwean people and was designed to entrench white minority rule. Even though the United States Senate

[164] For Kissinger's view of events, see Kissinger, Henry, *Years of Renewal*, (Weidenfeld & Nicolson), 1999, pp. 937-998, and more generally, Hanhimaki, Jussi M., *The Flawed Architect: Henry Kissinger and American Foreign Policy*, (Oxford University Press), 2004.

voted to lift sanctions against Zimbabwe-Rhodesia, the Carter administration also refused to recognise the internal settlement.[165]

Elected in May 1979, Margaret Thatcher sympathised with the internal settlement and saw the ZANLA and ZIPRA leaders as 'terrorists' but Lord Carrington, her Foreign Secretary recognised the need for a wider settlement.[166] Britain was reluctant to recognise the internal settlement for fear of fracturing the unity of the Commonwealth and at the Commonwealth Leaders' Conference in Lusaka in August 1979 pressure from African leaders especially Kenneth Kaunda led Britain to accept a plan to settle the problem of Zimbabwean independence. Lord Carrington persuaded the Prime Minister not to recognise Zimbabwe-Rhodesia because of Commonwealth opposition as well as a desire to protect British trade and investment in black Africa. Between September and December 1979, all-party talks were held in London that led to the Lancaster House Agreement.[167] During the conference, the Zimbabwe-Rhodesian Government accepted a watering down of the 1978 internal settlement while Mugabe and Nkomo agreed to end the war in exchange for new elections in which they could participate. On 12 December, illegal rule was ended when Zimbabwe-Rhodesia renounced independence and reverted to its previous colonial status. Economic sanctions were lifted in late 1979, on 21 December 1979, a cease-fire was announced and British rule resumed under a transitional arrangement leading to full independence.

The elections of 1980 resulted in a victory for Robert Mugabe, who assumed the post of Prime Minister after ZANU-PF received 63 per cent of the vote.[168] This was predictable. Mugabe had never compromised on majority rule while Muzorewa, who had been in power for less than two years and whose UANC only managed to get three seats, had failed to end the war or improve conditions for Africans.[169] There were accusations of voter intimidation by Mugabe's guerrillas, sections of which were accused of not having assembled in the designated guerrilla assembly points as required under the Lancaster House Agreement. Even in this context, widespread support for Mugabe from large sections of the black population from his own Shona tribal group that made up the overwhelming majority of the country's population, his victory was not

---

[165] See, Chung, Fay, and Kaarsholm, Preben, *Re-living the Second Chimurenga: memories from the liberation struggle in Zimbabwe*, (Stylus Publishing), 2006, pp. 229-241, for the intensification of the armed struggle after the 'internal settlement'.

[166] Carrington, Peter, *Reflect on Things Past: The Memoirs of Peter Lord Carrington*, (Collins), 1988, pp. 214-307, considers his views on the Rhodesian settlement.

[167] Kriger, Norma J., *Guerrilla Veterans in Post-war Zimbabwe: Symbolic and Violent Politics, 1980-1987*, (Cambridge University Press), 2003, pp. 36-45, examines the conference and agreement. See also, Chikuhwa, Jacob Wilson, *A Crisis of Governance: Zimbabwe*, (Algora Publishing), 2004, pp. 27-49.

[168] For a nuanced analysis of the 1980 election, see Sithole, Masipula, 'The general elections, 1979-1985', in Mandaza, Ibbo, (ed.), *Zimbabwe: The Political Economy of Transition, 1980-1986*, (CODESRIA), 1986, pp. 75-98, at 81-85.

[169] On Mugabe after 1980, see Meredith, Martin, *Mugabe: Power, Plunder and the Struggle for Zimbabwe*, revised edition, (Public Affairs), 2007, Compagnon, David, *A Predictable Tragedy: Robert Mugabe and the Collapse of Zimbabwe*, (University of Pennsylvania Press), 2011, and Godwin, Peter, *The Fear: The Last Days of Robert Mugabe*, (Pan Macmillan), 2010.

seriously disputed. The result was that on 18 April 1980, Zimbabwe gained its independence and international recognition. Zimbabwean crowds cheered their new Prime Minister with little idea of the misery he would bring them. Instead of leading his people to the 'promised land', Mugabe has amassed a fortune for himself, his family and followers and presided over the murder, torture and starvation of those who oppose him. Zimbabwe is once again subject to international sanctions and its economy has slid from self-sufficiency to poverty to astronomical inflation.[170]

Conclusions

Anti-colonial nationalism and resistance was led by an increasingly education non-colonial élite. Initially, it was based on demands for reforms to the colonial system but especially after 1945 it led to called for independence from colonial rule. Anti-colonial nationalism, especially in Africa, aimed to united all sections of society in a colony irrespective of ethnic origins against colonial authority. Nationalist organisations were formed throughout the continent. The African National Congress was founded in South Africa in 1912. In West Africa, the political and commercial élite of all four British colonies came together in the National Congress of British West Africa in 1920. In East Africa, in the early 1920s, Harry Thuku's East African Association not only united Africans of many nationalities. Colonial rule provoked widespread economic protests that assumed an anticolonial character, especially from the 1930s. Farmers in the Gold Coast, with general popular support, organised two cocoa 'holdups' and in 1937 kept most of the crop off the market, until the major European trading companies agreed to raise the price paid to the producers and the government was forced to intervene to reform the monopolistic practices of the trading companies. After 1945, anti-colonial nationalism entered the era of mass support for nationalist movements and demands for independence. This demand, the need to mobilise the masses in the anti-colonial struggle and the threatened use of force if necessary were evident in the resolutions of the delegates at the Manchester Pan-African Congress held in 1945.

Even if the masses mobilised into a liberation movement and were prepared to fight for their liberation, it is questionable whether conflict led directly to independence. In Cyprus, the EOKA campaign and in Kenya, Mau Mau had largely been contained and defeated by the time independence was achieved and its participants played little or no part in making the tradition from colonial to independent state. Only in Southern Rhodesia, and then only latterly, did guerrilla warfare make independence a military as well as a political imperative. Many observers believed that during the wars of decolonisation in the two decades after 1945, the British had discovered how western liberal notions of right and wrong could be made compatible with the imperatives of waging war amongst the people, that force could be used effectively but with care and that a more just and prosperous society could emerge from these struggles. By using the

---

[170] For the early years of development after independence, see Dashwood, Helena Smith, *Zimbabwe: The Political Economy of Transformation*, (University of Toronto Press), 2000, pp. 3-56, and Herbst, Jeffrey I., *State Politics in Zimbabwe*, (University of Californian Press), 1990.

minimum necessary force, and doing so with the utmost discrimination, the British were able to win by securing the 'hearts and minds' of the people. This is a serious distortion of actual British practice on the ground.[171] Britain was successful in hiding its use of naked force behind a carefully constructed veneer of legality. Colonial warfare involved wholesale coercion, including cordon and search operations, mass detention without trial, forcible population resettlement and the creation of free-fire zones to intimidate and contain civilian populations. The British waged their counter-insurgency campaigns by being nasty, not nice, to the people.

In many respects, one wonders why Britain expended resources and men to maintain an empire in which most of the British political élite had lost interest in after Indian independence in 1947. The gradual winding up of empire was not seriously contested in the upper echelons of government; it was never an electoral issue; and no government lost office for detaching Britain from its imperial responsibilities. Despite anti-colonial resistance and rebellion, decolonisation was achieved with relative ease largely because British public opinion was more concerned with domestic and local issues than with external politics while the political élite, of whatever political hue, presented a remarkably united front and accepted the desirability of continuity of policy. Business interests were largely disinterested in decolonisation if they could still trade with the newly independent states. Across Whitehall, in Parliament and in the key sectors of the economy, the desire to dispense with empire proved far stronger than the desire to hang on to it. This was not the case for white colonial settlers whose position in a decolonising British world was ambiguous. How did they relate to the decolonialised states? If they stayed, did they accept citizenship in these new states or retain their British citizenship as ex-pats? Did they integrate into the new non-white dominated societies or did they try to retain a separate identity? They could 'come home' to Britain but was Britain, in fact, any longer 'home' and if not where was 'home' now? It is not surprising that many 'colonials' felt that they had been betrayed by Whitehall and that they had become the 'orphans of empire'.

Geopolitical considerations had been central to the expansion of Britain's empire and they were decisive in withdrawal from empire. Great power rivalry led Britain to obtain colonies such as Cyprus and into the scramble for Africa, and it was great power rivalry in the form of the Cold War and competition for international respectability and support that induced Britain's post-war scramble to reduce their imperial commitments. In both cases, it was reacting pragmatically to circumstances. Britain had to satisfy the nationalists and hope that colonies could be handed over to moderate politicians. With American support, it sought to encourage the emergence of pro-Western nationalist states and there was a widespread belief that maintaining colonial control would aid the spread of communism. It was, as Iain Macleod the Colonial Secretary from 1959 to 1961 made clear better to grant independence too soon than leave it too late. This was clearly evident in Cyprus, where Greece and Turkey were members of NATO and in Kenya where Jomo Kenyatta adopted a pro-Western stance after

[171] See, French, David, *The British Way in Counter-Insurgency, 1945-1967*, (Oxford University Press), 2011.

independence. The far that African opinion might turn to communism and plunge Africa into chaos was evident in Rhodesia but its impact was lessened by the conflict between Soviet and Chinese aspirations within an ideologically divided liberation movement. This approach was not without its risks. The ethnic divisions in Cyprus proved unbridgeable and the consequence was partition of the island and several of Britain's former colonies in Africa became one-party states in which opposition was brutally repressed by liberation leaders unwilling to hand power to their democraticised post-colonial societies.

Liberation movements and anti-colonial resistance have achieved a certain mythic status that belies their generally limited impact on the achievement of independence. Their military achievements were limited; their mobilisation of the masses was often achieved largely through coercion; and their post-colonial influence constrained by their former leaders. Their achievements retain a rhetorical significance and at ceremonial occasions veterans are frequently feted but who they were and what they did rather than what they achieved is what matters in the post-colonial world.

9 A Very British Coup: A 'Rum' Rebellion

His Excellency the Governor laments at finding, by his late visits through the colony, that the most calamitous evils have been produced by persons bartering or paying in spirits for grain of all kinds...[1]

Just before sunset on 26 January 1808--the twentieth anniversary of the arrival of the First Fleet in Australia--over 300 soldiers of the New South Wales Corps, the 102nd Regiment of the British army expressly created to protect the new colony, gathered on the parade ground in front of their barracks in what is now Wynyard Square. The officers of the Corps who had held a rare full dress dinner at the barracks two nights earlier, had decided the following day, to arrest and depose William Bligh, fourth Governor of the colony.[2] The soldiers were led in formation from the parade ground by their commander, Major George Johnston, with drawn sword in one hand and the other arm in a sling, an injury caused when he fell out of his carriage drunk on the way home after the regimental dinner.[3] Guns loaded, bayonets fixed, sweltering in their scarlet woollen coats, with banners flying and the regimental band playing *The British Grenadiers,* the column marched down High Street, across the new stone bridge spanning the Tank Stream and up Bridge Street to Government House, a show of force designed to impress and more importantly intimidate the general populace. There was no possibility of resistance. Bligh's personal guard had already been suborned and the two naval vessels under his command were out of port. Bligh was taken by surprise and kept under house arrest for a year and it was a further year before Governor Lachlan Macquarie arrived with his own 73rd Regiment to enforce the removal of the NSW Corps. The events were unusual as they occurred within the colonial élite. This was the so-called 'Rum Rebellion'.

Successive Governors were the supreme authority in the colony with autocratic and personal powers though, almost from the outset these were challenged and defined in the courts. The founders of the colony in NSW thought in terms of the Lockean model for the formation of government. Locke maintained that individual liberties were paramount but that in the progression from a state of nature to civil society some of these liberties would be sacrificed in return for the protection that government could give especially in relation to life, liberty and property. Under what circumstances is resistance to established authority permissible? If government acted in a despotic way, the governed could reclaim their original rights through resistance and rebellion. What happened in Sydney at the beginning of 1808 is replete with contrasting personalities and vested interests in open conflict but it is sometimes difficult to avoid a sense of people squabbling over very little, an impression that the British

---

[1] *HRNSW*, Vol. 6, p. 253-254.

[2] Mackaness, G., *The Life of Vice-Admiral William Bligh*, 2 Vols. (Farrar & Rinehart), 1937, Vol. 2, pp. 95-334, covers his rule in NSW, the rebellion and its aftermath. See also, Shaw, A. G. L., 'Bligh, William (1754-1817)', *ADB*, Vol. 1, pp. 118-122.

[3] Lemcke, Geoffrey, *Reluctant Rebel: Lt. Col. George Johnston, 1764-1823*, (Willoughby), 1998, and Yarwood, A. T., 'Johnston, George (1764-1823)', *ADB*, Vol. 2, pp 20-22.

government in London appears to have had. However, for those involved, the disagreements were not about issues of little importance but went to the heart of how they believed a colony should be governed.[4] The 'Rebellion' or rather the coup d'état set the parameters of debate about the constitutional limits required in British colonies governed under extensive prerogative powers.[5]

Bligh as Governor

Settled in 1788, NSW was Britain's first and only convict colony and this made it a site of constitutional exceptionalism. Governors' commissions and instructions placed ultimate judicial, military and administrative power in the hand of a governor without the guidance of an Executive Council and, until 1824, without a legislature. NSW may have been an autocratic place but its governors did not rule untrammelled and Bligh and his predecessors found that there was a considerable difference between how the Crown thought the penal colony should be run and how that worked out in practice. The result was persistent tensions between governors and the governed.

In the early years of the settlement, particularly during the three years between the first Governor Arthur Phillip's retirement in December 1792 and the arrival of John Hunter his successor in mid-1795, when Major Francis Grose and then Captain William Paterson administered the colony, alcohol (generically referred to as 'rum') was readily tradable in the barter-based economy operating beyond the bureaucratic, requisition system at the government store. Rum became a substitute for currency. The shortage of currency in the colony was aggravated by the fact that William Bassett Chinnery,[6] the agent appointed by the British Government to operate the colony's accounts from London was in the process of embezzling some £80,000.[7] The NSW Corps officers' early trading success was based on the fact that they were paid in London and could draw bills there that would be honoured. They alone had access to sterling for trade and a trading cabal that operated as an extension of the officers' mess was able to

---

[4] Karskens, Grace, and Waterhouse, Richard, ''Too Sacred to Be Taken Away': Property, Liberty and the 'Rum' Rebellion', *Journal of Australian Colonial History*, Vol. 12, (2010), pp. 1-22, re-assesses the Rum Rebellion. It is suggested that the rebellion resulted from a notion of Bligh's alleged tyrannical move to take away the property and liberty of NSW citizens, fuelled by the lack of a representative form of government in NSW.

[5] Benton, Lauren, 'Just Despots: The Cultural Construction of Imperial Constitutionalism', *Law, Culture and the Humanities*, Vol. 9, (2), (2013), pp. 213-226.

[6] William Bassett Chinnery, who was appointed Agent for New South Wales on 1 May 1787, was enabled to embezzle more than £80,000 of Treasury funds prior to his dismissal on 17 March 1812. For Chinnery's private life and his love of music, see, Yim, Denise, *Viotti and the Chinnerys: a relationship charted through letters*, (Ashgate), 2004. Chinnery avoided detection for a long time because the accounting and control systems used at the British Treasury and the function and operation of the Audit Office established in 1785 were inadequate.

[7] See Scorgie, Michel E., Wilkinson David J., and Rowe, Julie D., 'The Rise and Fall of a Treasury Clerk: William Bassett Chinnery', paper presented to the Conference of the British Accounting Association, April 1998; compare with Scorgie, Michel E., 'The rise and fall of William Bassett Chinnery', *Abacus*, Vol. 43, (2007), pp. 76-93. See also ibid, Whitaker, Anne-Maree, *Joseph Foveaux: Power and Patronage in Early New South Wales*, pp.155-156.

exploit its monopoly position profitably in rum and other goods. They vigorously defended this position under both Hunter and King. This was no longer the case in 1808 as competition now ensured that monopoly profits were substantially reduced, although high prices were retained by the penumbra of illegality that surrounded the trade.

The relationship between the civil and military establishments had been difficult since 1788 and the decision by Major Francis Grose, acting-Governor between late 1792 and late 1794, to grant land to the NSW Corps and their monopolistic attitude to the spirit trade made existing tensions even more difficult when John Hunter took over as Governor in September 1795.[8]

> Every day convinces me more and more that many of those people, if they cannot be prevail'd on to make their public office their first consideration, shou'd be remov'd. Their private concerns occupy all their time, and £50 per annum seems to be no object when £300, £400, or £500 is to be gained by trade.[9]

The activities of the NSW Corps were not unknown in other British colonies. John Macarthur's profits as regimental paymaster were far less than those often accumulated by similar officers in India.[10] The difference between the commercial activities of Macarthur and his fellow officers in NSW and equivalent operations elsewhere was that in NSW they almost achieved a monopoly, whereas in other colonies this was rarely possible. The result was growing tensions between Hunter and the military with Hunter quickly informing Portland, his superior in London that 'scarcely nothing short of the full power of the Governor' would satisfy him.[11] It also became obvious that the soldiers of the NSW Corps resented the authority of the civil power.

> Continually thwarted and worthless characters encourag'd almost into a state of resistance by those whose schemes might have been in some degree effected by the changes I was about to make, and which in few words may be said to be *order and regularity for confusion and licentiousness.*[12]

---

[8] Hoyle, Arthur, *The Life of John Hunter, Navigator, Governor, Admiral*, (Mulini Press), 2001, Auchmuty, J. J., 'Hunter, John (1737-1821)', *ADB*, Vol. 1, pp. 566-572. See also, Wood, G.A., 'Governor Hunter', *Journal and Proceedings of the Royal Australian Historical Society*, Vol. 14, (6), (1928), pp. 344-362.

[9] Hunter to Portland, 20 June 1797, *HRA*, Series I, Vol. 2, p. 22. The problem of spirits concerned Hunter from the outset. His general order of 23 January 1796 prohibited the making of spirits in the colony: *HRNSW*, Vol. 3, p. 10; general order 11 July 1796 took action over the unlimited sale of spirits, *HRNSW,* Vol. 3, pp. 58-59; general order 12 December 1796, *HRNSW*, Vol. 3, pp. 185-186 on the link between crime and spirits.

[10] Steven, Margaret. 'Macarthur, John (1767-1834)', *ADB*, Vol. 2, pp. 153-159, Ellis, M. H., *John Macarthur*, (Angus & Robertson), 1978.

[11] Hunter to Portland, 14 September 1795, *HRA*, Series I, Vol. 1, pp. 661-663.

[12] Hunter to Portland, 12 November 1796, *HRA*, Series I, Vol. 1, p. 670. See also Hunter to Portland, 25 July 1798, *HRA*, Series I, Vol. 2, pp. 160-171 for further criticism of Macarthur.

Hunter's replacement as Governor in 1800, Philip Gidley King was equally ineffective in controlling the activities of the NSW Corps. [13] He badly needed capable law officers and a change in the personnel of the NSW Corps, but the British government ignored his requests. He was faced with frequent disobedience and insolence that early in 1803, immediately after he had refused to allow a cargo of spirits to be landed from the *Atlas,* culminated in the circulation of libellous 'pipes' against him and his officials.[14] The investigations and courts martial that followed revealed the animosity that existed between the governor and the Corps. The need to rein in the military establishment and especially its officer élite led to a division within the ruling élite as Hunter and then King sought to assert their gubernatorial authority. Faced by a military élite with sympathetic access to the decision-making process in London and the problem of retaining support from successive secretaries of state whose policies were rarely consistent, neither Hunter, who was recalled or King, who 'resigned' made any permanent inroads into the power of the Corps.

Asserting authority

William Bligh was selected by the British Government as Governor in part because of his reputation as a strict but fair disciplinarian. The critical figure in his appointment was Sir Joseph Banks who had accompanied Captain James Cook on his first voyage and was the government's unofficial adviser on matters relating to Australia. Banks had formed an intense dislike of John Macarthur in 1801 when the latter, already one of the wealthiest men in the colony, applied for permission to export some of the king's merino sheep to NSW and for an enormous land grant to help establish a wool industry. Banks did not favour a large land grant to one person but thought the wool industry should be developed by an English company. He also knew that Macarthur, due to a thrusting desire for personal enrichment, was a disruptive force in the colony. When Macarthur's requests for sheep and land were granted, Banks was upset and recommended Bligh for the job of governor because he thought he could manage Macarthur. On 15 March 1805, he wrote to Bligh requesting he consider the post commenting that King's successor must have the following qualities:

> ...one who had integrity unimpeached, a mind capable of providing its own resources in difficulties without leening on others for advice, firm in discipline, civil in deportment and not subject to whimper and whine when severity of discipline is wanted to meet emergencies.[15]

---

[13] For biographical information, see Shaw, A. G. L., 'King, Philip Gidley (1758-1808)', *ADB*, Vol. 2, pp. 55-61; King, J. and J., *Philip Gidley King: a biography of the third governor of New South Wales*, (Methuen), 1981.

[14] The deteriorating relationship between King and the military in early 1803 is detailed in *HRNSW*, Vol. 5, pp. 22-37. Some of these libels are printed in *HRNSW*, Vol. 5, pp. 123-127; see also, King to Hobart, 9 May 1803, *HRA*, Series I, Vol. 4, pp. 159-160, 167-173.

[15] This crucial letter was first quoted, in full, in the *HRNSW,* Vol. 6, pp. xxxv–xxxvi. The editor gave no specific location for this letter, but stated that he had had access to manuscripts in the possession of W. R. Bligh of Sydney, William Bligh's grandson. Bligh presented some of these to the Public (now State) Library of New South Wales in 1902

Banks proceeded to offer several inducements to persuade Bligh to accept. The Governor's salary would be doubled from £1,000 to £2,000 and, in addition, Banks believed Bligh need spend less than half of this because he would have 'the whole of the Government power and stores' at his disposal. His seniority and pension rights would continue. Banks even added that there would be better marriage prospects for his six daughters in NSW. He was not simply using his influence to help Bligh; he was exerting pressure on Bligh to accept the Governorship. He was not ignorant of Bligh's reputation as a disciplinarian: he chose him for that reason. Bligh stood a good chance of standing up to and reining in the maverick NSW Corps, something his predecessors had been unable to do. Earl Camden, Secretary of State for War and the Colonies, who wrote to Banks that he was recommending Bligh for appointment because of Bligh's 'merit & ability & of the character he bears, for firmness & Integrity'.[16] Bligh was persuaded and left for Sydney with his daughter, Mary Putland, and her husband who died on 4 January 1808 of tuberculosis. Bligh's wife remained in England.[17]

Even before his arrival, Bligh's style of governance led to problems with his subordinates. Blight took offence easily and allowed trivial matters to escalate into major confrontations.The Admiralty gave command of the *Porpoise* and the convoy to the lower ranked Captain Joseph Short and Bligh took command of a transport ship.[18] This led to quarrels that eventually resulted in Captain Short firing across Bligh's bow to force Bligh to obey his signals. When this failed, Short tried to give an order to Lieutenant Putland, Bligh's son-in-law to stand by to fire on Bligh's ship. Bligh boarded the *Porpoise* and seized control of the convoy. When it arrived in Sydney, Bligh, backed up by statements from two of Short's officers,[19] had Short stripped of the captaincy of the *Porpoise* that he gave to his son-in-law.[20] He also cancelled the land grant Short had been promised as payment for the voyage[21] and shipped him back to England for court martial, at which he was acquitted.[22] The president of the court, Sir Isaac Coffin, wrote to the Admiralty and made several serious accusations against Bligh, including that he had influenced the officers to testify against Short. Bligh's wife obtained a statement from one of the officers denying this and Banks and other supporters

---

and they were transferred to the Mitchell Library (ML) in 1910. This letter was not amongst the collection and its present location is unknown.

[16] Camden to Bligh, 18 April 1805, ML Banks Papers, Series 59.01.

[17] Bligh's commission, instructions and additional instructions are in *HRA*, Series I, Vol. 6, pp. 1-19.

[18] Short to Secretary Marsden, 12 March 1806, *HRNSW*, Vol. 6, pp. 31-34, Bligh to Secretary Marsden, 30 May 1806, *HRNSW*, Vol. 6, pp. 81-84 and Bligh to Castlereagh, 1 April 1806, *HRNSW*, Vol. 6, pp. 55-57, provide the protagonists' stances. Short to Bligh, 15 May 1806, *HRNSW*, Vol. 6, pp. 74-75 explains Short's position and his offer of an apology.

[19] Lieutenant Tetley to Bligh, 15 November 1806, *HRA*, Series I, Vol. 6, p. 40, and Daniel Lye to Bligh, 22 November 1806, 9 December 1806, *HRA*, Series I, Vol. 6, pp. 41-42.

[20] Bligh to Secretary Marsden, 12 December 1806, *HRNSW*, Vol. 6, pp. 208-221, details the enquiry.

[21] Bligh to Windham, 5 November 1806, *HRA*, Series I, Vol. 6, p. 30.

[22] Rear-Admiral Isaac Coffin to W. W. Pole, 13 December 1807, *HRNSW*, Vol. 6, p. 388.

of Bligh lobbied successfully against his recall. The Secretary of State thought the dispute arose from 'very trivial causes' and:

> ...proceeded to a length to which it could not possibly have advanced had you both been impressed with a just sense...of the propriety...of preserving a good understanding with each other.[23]

Soon after his arrival at Sydney on 13 August 1806, Bligh was given an address of welcome signed by Major Johnston for the military, by Richard Atkins for the civilian officers and by John Macarthur for the free settlers.[24] However, not long after, he also received addresses from the free and freed settlers of Sydney and the Hawkesbury River region, with a total of 369 signatures, many made only with a cross, complaining that Macarthur did not represent them.[25]

> ...We beg to observe that had we deputed anyone, John Macarthur would not have been chosen by us, we considering him an unfit person to step forward upon such an occasion, as we may chiefly attribute the rise in the price of mutton to his withholding the large flock of wethers he now has to make such price as he may choose to demand.[26]

This only confirmed what Bligh would have been told by Banks about Macarthur.

One of Bligh's first actions[27] was to use the colony's stores and herds to provide relief to farmers who had been severely affected by flooding on the Hawkesbury River, a situation that had disrupted the barter economy in the colony.[28] Supplies were divided with priority for those most in need and provisions were made for loans to be drawn from the store based on capacity to repay. Bligh offered to take wheat from the next crop into the Government stores at 15s per bushel.[29] This delighted the settlers, resulting in strong loyalty to Bligh even after the events of 1808 but it earned the enmity of traders in the Corps who had been profiting greatly from the situation.[30] This was evident in an address to Bligh on 17 February 1809:

---

[23] Windham to Bligh, 31 October 1807, *HRA*, Series I, Vol. 6, p. 80.

[24] Address to Governor Bligh, 14 August 1806, *HRNSW*, Vol. 6, pp. 165-166.

[25] Sydney Settlers' Address to Governor Bligh, 22 September 1806, *HRNSW*, Vol. 6, pp. 189-189; see also, Hawkesbury Settlers' Address, undated, 1806, *HRNSW*, Vol. 6, pp. 190-192.

[26] *HRNSW*, Vol. 6, p. 189.

[27] See, Government and General Order, 23 August, 30 August 1806, *HRNSW*, Vol. 6, pp. 173-174, 176.

[28] Samuel Marsden to King, 28 March 1806, *HRNSW*, Vol. 6, pp. 53-54, provides valuable details about the flood while King to Camden, 7 April 1806, *HRNSW*, Vol. 6, pp. 59-61, considers its effects. See also, *HRNSW*, Vol. 6, pp. 176, 186, 237, 823-831. Newspaper coverage of the floods can be found in, *Sydney Gazette and New South Wales Advertiser*, 30 March and 6 April 1806.

[29] *Sydney Gazette and New South Wales Advertiser*, 21 December 1806.

[30] See, Fletcher, Brian H., 'The Hawkesbury settlers and the Rum Rebellion', *Journal of the Royal Australian Historical Society*, Vol. 54, (3), (1968), pp. 217-237, for a detailed discussion of the relationship between Bligh and the Hawkesbury settlers.

That your memorialists had no hand, act, or part in the rebellion that now exists in this colony. That they do abhor and detest the said act, its aiders, and abettors, and were every way fully satisfied and content under His Excellency's administration. His Excellency was doing all that public virtue or private worth could accomplish to correct abuses, re-establish discipline, protect and encourage sobriety and industry. That your memorialists believe the following causes principally led to the rebellion; - That the officers had been (and still continue) merchants, traders, and dealers, which was carried on by employing convicts as their agents in different parts of the colony, by which means a great number of the inhabitants are in debt to them or their agents, which gave them a dangerous influence...The officers were interested in impeding agriculture: the more settlers were ruined the cheaper they could purchase estates; the less grain grown by the settlers, the better prices they had for their own....[31]

Bligh was under instructions from the Colonial Office to normalise trading conditions in the colony by prohibiting the use of spirits as payment for commodities. Bligh was determined to stamp out the barter of spirits for goods or labour, commenting on 7 February 1807:

It is absolutely necessary to be done to bring labour to a true value and support the farming interest... In addition to the reasons already given to prohibit the barter of spirits, is the strong temptation it holds out to the settlers and other inhabitants to erect private stills, which tend to destroy not only the grain but the industry and morals of the people.[32]

This was followed on 14 February 1807 by a further proclamation:

His Excellency the Governor laments at finding, by his late visits through the colony, that the most calamitous evils have been produced by persons bartering or paying in spirits for grain of all kinds...In order to remedy these grievous complaints, and to relieve the inhabitants who have suffered by this traffic, he feels it his duty to put a total stop to this barter in future, and to prohibit the exchange of spirits or other liquors as payment for grain, animal food, labour, wearing apparel, or any other commodity whatever, to all descriptions of persons in the colony and its dependencies. [33]

Between October 1806 and February 1807, he introduced further measures to carry out his instructions. On 4 October 1806, Bligh banned departing ships from leaving crew members behind[34] and issued new port regulations securing government control of ships and boat building and on 28 February 1807 declared that all goods shipped to NSW should only be unloaded at Port Jackson.[35] On 1 November, he issued general orders [36] On 3 January 1807, he proclaimed all promissory notes should be payable only in sterling, not kind[37] and the following month he outlawed the importation of stills for alcohol

[31] Hawkesbury Settlers' Address to Bligh, 17 March 1809, *HRNSW*, Vol. 7, pp. 78-80.

[32] Bligh to Marsden, 7 February 1807, *HRNSW*, Vol. 6, pp. 246-252.

[33] Government and General Order, 14 February 1807, *HRNSW*, Vol. 6, pp. 253-254.

[34] Regulations respecting Vessels: Foreign and English, 4 October 1806, *HRNSW*, Vol. 6, pp. 193-197.

[35] Government and General Order, 28 February 1807, *HRNSW*, Vol. 6, p. 258.

[36] Government and General Order, 1 November 1806, *HRNSW*, Vol. 6, p. 198.

[37] Proclamation, 3 January 1807, *HRNSW*, Vol. 6, p. 236.

production and bartering with spirits.[38] Bligh communicated his policy to the Colonial Office in 1807, advising that it would be met with resistance. Castlereagh, Secretary of State for War and the Colonies wrote back to Bligh, giving instructions to stop the barter of spirits that were received on 31 December 1807 and H. V. Evatt later commented:

> ...Bligh was authorised to prevent free importation, to preserve the trade under his entire control, to enforce all penalties against illegal import, and to establish regulations at his discretion for the sale of spirits.[39]

Bligh had come to administer a penal settlement not facilitate private enterprise.[40] This immediately placed him at odds with marines, soldiers, free settlers and the growing number of emancipated convicts who wanted to make money through commerce. Evatt argues that the enmity of the monopolists within the colony stemmed from this and other policies that attacked the power of the rich and promoted the welfare of the poor settlers. Free settlers such as John and Gregory Blaxland claimed that Bligh had no interest in supporting their enterprises and did not give them the assistance that the British Government had promised.[41] People came to NSW to make money and Bligh seemed oblivious to this. He ceased the practice of handing out large land grants to the powerful in the colony and during his term granted just over 2,180 acres of land, half of it to his daughter and himself. One thousand acres were at the Hawkesbury that he farmed as a 'model farm' for private gain. He allocated himself publicly victualed convicts and animals from the public herds and erected buildings at government expense. This was, to say the least, insensitive, but Bligh was never known for his tact. He was 'making hay while the sun shines as fast as he can', as Surgeon John Harris wrote.[42]

Bligh also upset some people by allowing a group of Irish convicts to be tried for revolt by a court that included their accusers and then when six out of the eight were acquitted, he kept them in custody. Soon after his arrival he replaced most of the officials, many of them from the military, with his own appointments. This did not play well in a small community and did not endear him to the Corps.[43] He dismissed D'Arcy Wentworth[44] from his position of

---

[38] Government and General Order, 14 February 1807, *HRNSW*, Vol. 6, pp. 253-254.

[39] Evatt, H. V., *Rum Rebellion: A Study of the Overthrow of Governor Bligh by John Macarthur and the New South Wales Corps*, (Angus & Robertson), 1938, p. 72.

[40] Karskens, Grace, & Waterhouse, Richard, ''Property is too sacred to be taken away...merely at the will of a Governor': Property, Liberty, Tyranny and the Rum Rebellion', *Journal of Australian Colonial History*, Vol. 12, (2010), pp. 1-22.

[41] This is evident in Gregory Blaxland to Under-Secretary Chapman, 15 October 1807, and John Blaxland to ?, 16 October 1807, *HRNSW*, Vol. 6, pp. 301-304, 308-313. See also, Castlereagh to King, 13 July 1805, *HRA*, Series I, Vol. 5, pp. 490-491, on what the Blaxlands were promised.

[42] Harris to Anna Josepha King, 25 October 1807, *HRNSW*, Vol. 6, p. 347. Bligh has earlier dismissed Harris from the magistracy: Government and General Order, 2 May 1807, *HRNSW*, Vol. 6, p. 266.

[43] On Bligh's early appointments, see Government and General Orders, 15, 16 August 1806, *HRNSW*, Vol. 6, pp. 167-169.

Assistant Surgeon to the Colony and sentenced three merchants to a month's imprisonment and a fine for writing a letter that he considered offensive. Bligh also dismissed Thomas Jamison[45] from the magistracy, describing him in 1807 as being 'inimical' to good government.[46] Jamison the highly capable, if devious Surgeon-General of NSW had accumulated significant personal wealth as a maritime trader and was also a friend and business partner of Macarthur. Jamison, who never forgave Bligh for sacking him as a magistrate and interfering with his private business activities, supported his later deposition.

When Bligh arrived in NSW, 4,000 of the colony's 7,500 residents lived in Sydney. Soldiers and those providing services built houses close to the governor's mansion; shopkeepers and traders congregated around the harbour; and convicts established a thriving township on a rocky outcrop they unimaginatively called 'The Rocks'. Governor Phillip, the first Governor of NSW had intended to reserve the land between, roughly, Hunter Street and the water for public purposes. Cutting into this reserved area, during Phillip's time, was a track formed by the passage of traffic behind the row of tents that the officers of the First Fleet had pitched on arrival, soon replaced by rudimentary huts, on the western bank of the Tank Stream that flowed into Sydney Cove, now Circular Quay.[47]That track became George Street and this, rather than Phillip's conception, proved to be the model for the grand Sydney tradition of urban planning. Phillip's successors gradually abandoned his plan. Although Phillip granted a small number of fourteen-year leases, most houses were built based on 'the Governor's word' or 'letters of occupation' overlaid with dubious contracts of sale.

Governor King attempted to regularise the haphazard 'system' of tenures and to establish clearly defined property rights by creating a register of dealings, quadrupling the rent and granting many leases for periods of fourteen years.[48] Bligh, wanted to return to critical aspects of Phillip's original plan by clearing grand spaces around Government House and the church, but King's leases stood in the way. Bligh used his wide discretionary powers to achieve his objective refusing to issue further leases, announcing that he would not approve building on existing leases, ordering residents to surrender possession of homes and demolishing structures built without approval. Intending to revoke the leases, but

---

[44] Bligh to Windham, 31 October 1807, *HRA*, Series I, Vol. 6, pp. 188-190, stated the Bligh suspended Wentworth on 25 July for 'extreme misconduct': 'it has been a practice to allow them [sick men] to remain victualed as Hospital Patients requiring care, applying their use to private advantage.' D'Arcy Wentworth to Castlereagh, 17 October 1807, *HRNSW*, Vol. 6, pp. 313-328, gives Wentworth's response.

[45] Parsons, Vivienne, 'Jamison, Thomas (1753?-1811)', *ADB*, Vol. 2, pp. 12-13.

[46] Bligh to Windham, 31 October 1807, *HRNSW*, Vol. 6, p. 355; see also, Nicholas Bayly to Jamison, 12 February 1808, *HRNSW*, Vol. 6, pp. 518-519, indicates the cause of his dismissal.

[47] Ibid, Atkinson, Alan, *The Europeans in Australia, A History,* Vol. 1, (Oxford University Press), 1997, p. 273; see also pp. 370-408 on Sydney's rebellion. Bligh to Windham, 31 October 1807, *HRA*, Series I, Vol. 6, pp. 155-156, lists the leases under question.

[48] See generally Atkinson, Alan, 'Taking Possession: Sydney's First Householders', in Aplin, Graeme, (ed.), *A Difficult Infant: Sydney before Macquarie,* (University of NSW Press), 1988, especially pp. 76, 79-82, 83-84.

unsure of his power to do so, he sought instructions from London.[49] The wife of a commercially successful emancipist wrote complaining:

> From some he took good houses and gave them bad ones. From others he took their houses and turned them into the street and made them no recompense whatever. Some he stopped building. Others he made make improvements against their inclinations and on the whole endeavoured to crush every person as much as possible.[50]

When one occupant of a leasehold residence in the environs of Government House objected to Bligh's order to remove it, asserting that he could not be forced to do so by the laws of England, Bligh allegedly exploded:

> Damn your laws of England! Don't talk to me of your laws of England. I will make laws for this colony, and every wretch of you, son of a bitch, shall be governed by them. Or there (pointing over to the gaol) is your habitation![51]

Bligh had quickly made enemies of some of the most influential people in the colony and antagonised some of the less wealthy who had leases on government land within Sydney. Many colonists had loathed Governors Hunter and King but Bligh threatened to evict them from their homes and businesses. Even if these measures affected relatively few, they represented an assault on private property and reinforced Bligh's reputation for tyranny.

The New South Wales Corps

The NSW Corps was a powerful Sydney institution. In 1808, its members made up ten per cent of the white population of 4,000 that included their families and a large number of former soldiers. The Corps owned a considerable amount of property and ran many businesses in Sydney, including one-third of the town's pubs. The numbers of Corps and ex-Corps members, therefore, formed a substantial and influential group, exhibiting what Governor King had called 'the jealousy but too often attendant on professional *esprit de corps*'.[52] The rank-and-file members of the Corps were not recruited from the dregs of society as has often been claimed. Over a third were skilled men.[53] Their life in NSW was a

---

[49] Ibid, Atkinson, Alan, 'Taking Possession: Sydney's First Householders', pp. 84-87; *HRA*, Series I, Vol. 6, pp. 155-156,714-715. See also, Government and General Order, 23 July 1807, *HRNSW*, Vol. 6, pp. 275-276.

[50] Ibid, Atkinson, Alan, *The Europeans in Australia,* Vol. 1, p. 273.

[51] Ritchie, John, *A Charge of Mutiny: The Court Martial of Lieutenant Colonel George Johnston for Deposing Governor William Bligh in the Rebellion of 26 January 1808*, (National Library of Australia), 1988, p. 365.

[52] King to Under-Secretary Cooke, 18 June 1808, *HRNSW*, Vol. 6, p. 656.

[53] McAskill, Tracey, 'An asset to the Colony: The social and economic contribution of Corpsmen to early New South Wales', *Journal of the Royal Australian Historical Society*, Vol. 82, (1), 1996, pp. 40-59 Montague, R. H., 'The Men of the New South Wales Corps: a Comparison?', *Journal of the Royal Australian Historical Society*, Vol. 62, (4), (1977), pp. 217-233, and Stratham, P., 'A new look at the New South Wales Corps, 1790-1810', *Australian Economic History Review*, Vol. 24, (1), 1984, pp. 20-33. Information on the NSW Corps and the trading conducted by its officers, is available in, Statham, Pamela,

vast improvement on what they would have had in Britain and they would fight to retain it. They were used to power and influence but Bligh did not treat them with respect. In October 1807, Major George Johnston wrote a formal letter of complaint to the Commander-in-Chief of the British Army, stating that Bligh was abusive and interfered with the troops of the NSW Corps. Before the rebellion, this was the only official complaint sent to London. However, the burden of his letter was that Bligh did not treat the Corps with the dignity it deserved. He spoke roughly to it, criticised and insulted it: 'his abusing and confining the soldiers without the smallest provocation', 'his casting the most undeserved and opprobrious censure on the Corps'.[54]

Some officers had built up financial capital during the 1790s and early 1800s when profits were high and through their preferential access to land grants, cheap labour by assignment of convicts and supply of provisions, livestock and equipment delivered for government purposes at the cost of the British taxpayer. In 1808, many officers retained an interest in trade, which had become more diverse and much more competitive, but their principal economic interest now lay in agricultural grants and in urban leaseholds in Sydney, where one sub-divided block, for instance, changed hands for £900 just before Bligh's arrival. Although those adversely affected by Bligh's policies included many with no association with the NSW Corps, no coup could have occurred without the united resolve of its officers. Bligh had stirred the acute anxieties of these men by challenging their individual and collective reputation and status. This was a serious affront under the code of honour that they regarded as the most important social bond of their lives.[55] He also offended members of this caste by his conduct and bearing and perhaps most of all, by his language. Devoid of tact, quick tempered, infuriated by insubordination or incompetence, incapable of compromise, prone to indulge in mockery and abuse, he failed to respect the boundary between criticism and derision.[56] Manning Clark described him in the following terms:

> If anyone dared to object or remonstrate with him, he lost his senses and his speech, his features became distorted, he foamed at the mouth, stamped on the ground, shook his fist in the face of the person so presuming, and uttered a torrent of abuse in language disgraceful to him as a governor, an officer and a man.[57]

(ed.), *A Colonial Regiment: New Sources relating to the New South Wales Corps, 1789-1810*, (Australian National University), 1992.

[54] Johnston to Sir James Gordon, military secretary to the Duke of York, 8 October 1807, *HRNSW*, Vol. 6, p. 652.

[55] The emphasis on the code of honour as a critical factor in the coup was first put forward by Parsons, George, 'The Commercialisation of Honour: Early Australian Capitalism 1788-1809', in ibid, Aplin, Graeme, (ed.), *A Difficult Infant: Sydney Before Macquarie,* pp. 18-41. The theme was developed by ibid, Duffy, Michael, *Man of Honour: John Macarthur, Duellist, Rebel, Founding Father,* (Macmillan), 2003.

[56] See, Denning, Greg, *Mr Bligh's Bad Language: Passion, Power and Theatre on the Bounty*, (Cambridge University Press), 1992.

[57] Clark, C. M. H., *A History of Australia,* Vol. 1, (Melbourne University Press), 1962, p. 216.

The officers of the NSW Corps, as well as most free settlers, were attracted to the colony precisely because their social origins did not allow them to live as gentleman in the land of their birth. It was commonplace to buy commissions in the army and for those not able to afford one in the more fashionable and prestigious regiments, the NSW Corps proved a good alternative. The economic and, therefore, the social status of the officers were never secure. Bligh not only attacked their commercial and agricultural interests, he challenged the core of their personal identity.

Whatever his formal powers may have been, Bligh undermined what the local élite regarded as property rights, especially with their urban leases. This was fundamentally inconsistent with contemporary understanding of the rights of free Englishmen. Bligh, of course, relied on his formal authority and had the personal strength to exercise prerogative powers on which Hunter and King, had compromised by permitting private men to grow wealthy at the expense of the Crown. He was determined to reassert the public interest as he saw it and to act strictly in accordance with his instructions. In most respects, his approach to governing was disciplined and purposeful. However, in a small settlement like Sydney, effective and purposive government required an understanding of communal expectations and an element of consent. Bligh proved as oblivious to the fears and aspirations of the Sydney élite as he had earlier been to the delights that the crew of *The Bounty* had experienced in Tahiti. The scene was set for a conflict of institutional cultures between that of the navy, where authority was typically exercised in the confined autocracy of a ship and that of the army, where the exercise of authority often involved interaction with a broader community.

Although Bligh had returned to England a hero in 1790 after the mutiny on the *Bounty* and honourably acquitted by court martial for losing command, he was on his second breadfruit voyage on *HMS Providence* between 1791 and 1793, when ten of the mutineers captured at Tahiti were placed on trial in September 1792 and could not defend himself. Overall the incident ended in his embarrassment. Of the mutineers on trial, four were acquitted, three pardoned and only three hanged. Because of the campaigns launched by Fletcher Christian's brother and others to justify the actions of the mutineers, the view took hold that it was Bligh's tyranny and 'bad language' that had caused the mutiny. Talk of despotism, it seems, almost excused the mutiny in the Admiralty's court martial. This reputation and his unlikable personality made Bligh politically vulnerable in NSW and according to Surgeon Edward Luttrell before:

> Governor Bligh [came] into the colony a clamour [had] been raised against him, and an opposition formed to counteract his government.[58]

The old rhetoric about monarchical tyranny could be revived and intensified against Bligh. The accusations were long on rhetoric but short on evidence. For instance, when Elizabeth Macarthur wrote to a female friend in England in January 1807 she described Bligh in such a fashion:

---

[58] Surgeon Luttrell to Under-Secretary Sullivan, 8 October 1807, *HRNSW*, Vol. 6, p. 296.

The Governor has already shewn the inhabitants of Sydney that he is violent – rash – tyrannical. No very pleasing prospect at the beginning of his reign.[59]

Lieutenant William Minchin commented:

...a deluge worse than that of the Hawkesbury has since swept off every path to...industry and happiness...if a Military Officer might be allowed to use the words Tyranny and oppression, I would inform you that until now I never experienced their weight.[60]

John Harris, the NSW Corps' surgeon, who had been dismissed from his positions as naval officer and magistrate, reported:

...it is completely the reign of Robertspere, or that of Terror...I have heard much said of Bounty Bligh before I saw him, but no person could conceive that he could be such a fellow...Caligula himself never reigned with more despotic sway than he does.[61]

In October 1807, a verse with direct reference to the *Bounty* mutiny was circulating in Sydney:

Oh tempora! Oh Mores! Is there no Christian in New South Wales to put a stop to the Tyranny of the Governor.[62]

Macarthur and Bligh

John Macarthur, attributed as the progenitor of the Australian wool industry--although his wife Elizabeth arguably deserves the title more--precipitated the crisis. Macarthur had arrived with the NSW Corps in 1790 as a lieutenant and by 1805 had substantial farming and commercial interests in the colony.[63] He had quarrelled with governors Hunter and King, and fought two duels. Michael Duffy regards his acute sense of honour as the key to his character and actions. He challenged Bligh to what was, in effect, a political duel in defence of both his honour and his money. Macarthur was as offensive, domineering, short-fused and arrogant as Bligh, but had an unscrupulous shrewdness, indeed subtlety that Bligh both lacked and could not discern in others. Clearly, from the beginning of Bligh's rule, Macarthur saw him as a powerful obstacle to the realisation of his ambitions and their interests clashed in a number of ways.

Macarthur's wealth was regarded by Bligh as the most offensive example of private profit at public expense and determined to reduce it. On one occasion, he refused to make a major land grant that Macarthur believed had been negotiated in London. Bligh's tone was dismissive: 'Are you to have such flocks of sheep and such herds of cattle as no man ever heard before. No

---

[59] See, Elizabeth Macarthur to Miss Kingdon, 29 January 1807, ML, A2908, Vol. 2.
[60] William Minchin to Philip Gidley King, 20 October 1807, ML MSS 681/2, pp. 397-399.
[61] John Harris to Anna Josepha King, 25 October 1807, ML A1980, pp. 237-248.
[62] John Harris to Philip Gidley King, 25 October 1807, ML MSS 681/2, pp. 401-408.
[63] Craig, R. J., and Jenkins, S. A., 'The Cox and Greenwood ledger of the New South Wales Corps 1801-1805: the account of Captain John Macarthur', *Journal of the Royal Australian Historical Society*, Vol. 82, (2), (1996), pp. 138-152.

sir!'[64] Macarthur was right to stress the shortage of herdsmen. Convict labour was scarce. No prisoners had arrived in 1805 and only about 550 males in 1806 and 1807, fewer than those freed by passage of time; but the shortage never affected the farm that Bligh had bought on the Hawkesbury. Bligh stopped Macarthur from cheaply distributing large quantities of wine to the Corps and halted his allegedly illegal importation of brewing stills. In March 1807, a still for Macarthur arrived in Sydney, sent unannounced by his London agent. Bligh impounded it as illegal. Macarthur successfully argued to have the copper body, with goods inside, sent to his private store.[65] In October 1807, Naval Officer Robert Campbell sent his nephew to retrieve the still from Macarthur's store for return to England under Bligh's order. However, his nephew had no official status and Macarthur successfully sued for wrongful seizure.

Macarthur's interest in an area of land granted to him by Governor King conflicted with Bligh's town-planning interests. In December 1807, Bligh challenged Macarthur's lease on Church Hill, given by Governor King despite Phillip's order of no private leases in Sydney town and on 20 January 1808 ordered the demolition of the fence on the lease Macarthur had begun six days earlier.[66] Macarthur and Bligh were also engaged in other disagreements, including a conflict over landing regulations. In June 1807, John Hoare a convict had stowed away and escaped to the Pacific Islands on the *Parramatta*, one of Macarthur's vessels.[67] In December 1807, when that vessel returned to Sydney, the £900 bond to the NSW government for assisting escape was deemed to be forfeited. The ship was consequently impounded. Macarthur now refused to pay or victual the crew, forcing them on 14 December to come ashore illegally breaching the landing regulations. In effect, he abandoned a ship worth £10,000 rather than pay a fine of £900.

Bligh instructed the Judge-Advocate, Richard Atkins to issue an order for John Macarthur to appear on the matter of the bond on the 15 December 1807.[68] Outraged, Macarthur sent an angry reply declaring his contempt for Atkins and the government. The following day, Atkins issued warrant for Macarthur's arrest. Macarthur demanded to be brought before bench of magistrates that granted him bail on condition he appeared again the following day where magistrates, including George Johnston, commit Macarthur to criminal trial and he was bailed to appear for trial at the next sitting of the Sydney Criminal Court on 25 January 1808. However, the Court did not define the

---

[64] Ibid, Duffy, Michael, *Man of Honour: John Macarthur-Duellist, Rebel, Founding Father*, p. 255, n 10.

[65] Bligh to Windham, 31 October 1807, *HRA*, Series I, Vol. 6, pp. 160, 164-178 details the question of Macarthur's still.

[66] Surveyor-General Grimes to Macarthur, 13 January 1808, *HRNSW*, Vol. 6, pp. 413-414, ordered Macarthur not to build on the lease on Church Hill with Macarthur's response reluctantly resigning the land to please Bligh if Bligh allocated him as alternative lease. The matter escalated the following day with correspondence between Grimes and Macarthur in which Grimes made it clear that Macarthur's proposal was unacceptable and that he was unwilling to receive further correspondence on the issue: *HRNSW*, Vol. 6, pp. 416-417.

[67] Macarthur's ship and the runaway, 27 June 1807, *HRNSW*, Vol. 6, p. 270.

[68] Bennett, J. M., 'Atkins, Richard (1745-1820)', *ADB*, Vol. 1, pp. 38-40.

charges.[69] The court was constituted of Atkins and six officers of the NSW Corps: Anthony Fenn Kemp, John Brabyn, William Moore, Thomas Laycock, William Minchin and William Lawson. Macarthur objected to Atkins sitting in judgement of him because he was his debtor[70] and inveterate enemy and read from a lengthy document declaiming in Lockean terms towards the conclusion:

> You will now decide, gentlemen, whether law and justice shall finally prevail...You have the eyes of an anxious public upon you, trembling for the safety of their property, their liberty, and their lives. To you has fallen the lot of deciding a point which perhaps involves the happiness or misery of millions yet unborn. I conjure you in the name of Almighty God, in whose presence you stand, to consider the inestimable value of the precious deposit with which you are entrusted.[71]

This was grossly exaggerated but then gave the Corps its rallying call:

> It is to the Officers of the New South Wales Corps that the administration of Justice is committed; and who that is just has anything to dread? [72]

Macarthur's ranting about the defence of liberty and property that were never in danger, gave Johnston excuse to claim that 'insurrection and massacre' were imminent because Bligh was planning 'to subvert the laws of the country' and 'to terrify and influence the Courts of Justice'.[73]

Atkins rejected this, but Macarthur's protest had the support of the other six Corps members of the court. Atkins threatened to gaol Macarthur. Kemp retaliated by threatening to gaol Atkins who left for Government House, declaring that there was no court without him. A similar manoeuvre had been tried in 1803. Kemp was defendant in a court case and this time Johnston, the acting commanding officer of the Corps, demanded that the Governor, King, replace the Judge-Advocate, John Harris. King buckled and replaced Harris. Bligh, however, stood firm. During the day, messages went back and forth between the court and Government House over Atkins' position. Around 12.30 pm, Bligh made it clear that he had no power to remove Atkins and without Atkins there was no validly constituted court. The officers nevertheless refused to serve with Atkins. Three hours later Macarthur sought military protection due to unspecified threats and at 5.30 pm, Bligh wrote to Johnston with the request that he attend Government House.[74] It is noteworthy that Bligh wrote to Johnston to attempt to resolve this impasse rather than immediately resorting to

---

[69] See Macarthur to Atkins, 20 January 1808, *HRNSW*, Vol. 6, p. 418, and subsequent correspondence on the imprecise nature of the charge, *HRNSW*, Vol. 6, pp. 418-420.

[70] During January 1808, Macarthur had tried to recall debt he held against Atkins but Bligh refused Macarthur's requests to assist his recovery of debt. See Macarthur to Bligh, 29 December 1807, *HRNSW*, Vol. 6, pp. 395-396, and Macarthur to Bligh, 1, 12 January 1808, *HRNSW*, vol 6, pp. 411-412, 413. On Macarthur's 'trial', see the succinct discussion in ibid, Woods, Gregory D., *A history of criminal law in New South Wales: the colonial period 1788-1900*, pp. 33-34.

[71] Johnston to Castlereagh, 11 April 1808, *HRA*, Series I, Vol. 6, p. 227.

[72] Johnston to Castlereagh, 11 April 1808, *HRA*, Series I, Vol. 6, p. 227.

[73] For Macarthur's trial on 25-26 January 1808 see, *HRNSW*, Vol. 6, pp. 422-433, and Johnston to Castlereagh, 11 April 1808, *HRA*, Series I, Vol. 6, pp. 221-234.

[74] Secretary Griffin to Johnston, 25 January 1808, *HRA*, Series I, Vol. 6, p. 234.

action. Johnston sent a message to say he was indisposed, as he had wrecked his 'chaise' on the evening of the 24 January on his way back home to Annandale after dining with officers of the Corps. It was increasingly clear that stalemate had been reached.

Overthrowing Bligh

Events escalated on the morning of 26 January 1808. First, Bligh ordered Provost-Marshall William Gore to arrest Macarthur and again called for the return of the court papers that were now in the hands of officers of the Corps.[75] Then, at 10 am, the officers requested the appointment of a new Judge-Advocate and the release of Macarthur on bail. They had received no reply by 3.00 pm and adjourned the court. After this, Bligh sent a note to the officers summoning them to Government House at 9 am the following morning, indicating that Atkins had charged them with certain crimes, but not revealing what these were.[76] Finally, an hour later, Bligh informed Johnston of his action and additionally told him that the actions of his officers were considered treasonable.[77] As the officers were to appear before Bligh and all the magistrates, this would be a charge under criminal not military law and the charge, if proven, was a capital offence.[78] To make this threat against officers was an intemperate and extreme move. There could be no greater slur on their honour.

Bligh's threat of the charge of treason may have been the turning point. This is certainly the view of McMahon and of Fitzgerald and Hearn who stated that Johnston was motivated because of 'potential danger to his officers (and ... [the] Corps)'.[79] Johnston appears to have felt his relationship with Bligh had broken down so much that there was no point in talking to him. It was unlikely that Bligh would have executed the officers; but very likely they might be sent to gaol pending further advice. If this action had been taken it would have left only two remaining officers in Sydney, aside from Johnston and one of these, Cadwallader Draffin, was deemed mentally unstable.[80] Johnston later maintained that if the officers had been gaoled, the soldiers would have rioted and perhaps killed Bligh as well as prejudicing internal security in the colony. He arrested Bligh for his own protection. Johnston was not particularly close to Macarthur and had in fact been one of the magistrates who ordered the latter be arrested over the incident leading to the court case. He was an experienced officer, had been in the Colony since 1788 and was apparently highly regarded by his men. What Macarthur had started, Johnston would finish in a way perhaps Macarthur never imagined, though Macarthur certainly supported it.

Later that afternoon at 5.00 pm, Johnston went to the barracks and ordered Macarthur's release and assumed, with no vested legal authority, the title

---

[75] King, Hazel, 'Gore, William (1765-1845)', *ADB*, Vol. 1, pp. 459-460.
[76] *HRNSW*, Vol. 6, p. 433.
[77] *HRNSW*, Vol. 6, p. 433, *HRA*, Series I, Vol. 6, p. 236.
[78] McMahon, John, 'Not a Rum Rebellion but a military insurrection', *Journal of the Royal Australian Historical Society*, Vol. 92, (2006), p. 135.
[79] Fitzgerald, Ross and Hearne, Mark, *Bligh, Macarthur and the Rum Rebellion*, (Kangaroo Press), 1988, p. 120.
[80] Duffy, Michael, *Man of honour: John Macarthur, duellist, rebel, founding father*, (Macmillan), 2003, p. 295.

of Lieutenant-Governor.[81] After discussion with fellow officers, several wealthy civilians and the newly-released Macarthur, the decision was taken to depose Bligh. Macarthur duly drafted a petition for Bligh's arrest as a tyrant, and for powers to pass to Johnston.[82] According to Evatt, those who signed the petition probably only agreed to this action once reassured that Bligh was safely under house arrest.[83] An order was duly issued stating that Bligh was charged: 'by the respectable inhabitants of crimes that render you unfit to exercise the supreme authority another moment in this colony; and in that charge all officers under my command have joined'. Johnston went on to call for Bligh's resignation and submission to arrest.[84]

Bligh's loss of NSW was hardly less humiliating than his loss of the *Bounty*. At 6.00 pm the Corps, with full band and colours, marched to Government House to arrest Bligh.[85] They were hindered by Bligh's recently widowed daughter and her parasol at the gates but Captain Thomas Laycock finally found Bligh after an extensive search, in full dress uniform, behind his bed where he claimed he was hiding papers. Bligh was painted as a coward for this but Duffy argues that if Bligh was hiding it would have been to escape and thwart the coup.[86] Stephen Dando-Collins suggests that Bligh was attempting to travel to the garrison at Hawkesbury from where he could lead the fight against Johnston.[87] Bligh said later at Johnston's court martial that he hid:

> ...to defeat their object, and to deliberate on means to be adopted for the restoration of my authority, which in such a critical situation could only be accomplished by my getting into the interior of the country adjacent to the Hawkesbury, where I knew the whole body of the people would flock to my standard.[88]

It is apparent from this statement that Bligh was contemplating a form of civil conflict by raising a militia to oppose the military. While Fletcher casts doubt the level of support Bligh may have had from settlers in the Hawkesbury, he nevertheless concludes 'a balance of probability...seems weighted in

---

[81] *HRNSW*, Vol. 6, p. 433.

[82] *HRNSW*, Vol. 6, p. 434, *HRA*, Series I, Vol. 6, p. 240. Apart from Macarthur and the Blaxland brothers, the petition was signed by James Mileham, James Badgery, Nicholas Bayly and by S. (Simeon) Lord.

[83] For discussion of petitions on 26 and 27 January to Johnston, see Donohoe, J., *Captain Bligh's Petticoat Mutiny*, (J. S. Shaw North Publishing), 2011

[84] Johnston proclaimed martial law, *HRNSW*, Vol. 6, p. 434, *HRA*, Series I, Vol. 6, pp. 240-241, and sent Bligh a letter calling on him to resign, *HRNSW*, Vol. 6, p. 434, *HRA*, Series I, Vol. 6, p. 241.

[85] Ibid, Whitaker, Anne-Maree, *Unfinished Revolution*: *United Irishmen in New South Wales, 1800-1810*, pp. 167-186.

[86] Ibid, Duffy, Michael, *Man of honour: John Macarthur, duellist, rebel, founding father*, pp. 297-298.

[87] Dando-Collins, Stephen, *Captain Bligh's Other Mutiny: the true story of the military coup that turned Australia into a two-year rebel republic*, (Random House), 2007.

[88] Ibid, Ritchie, John, *A Charge of Mutiny: The Court Martial of Lieutenant Colonel George Johnston for Deposing Governor William Bligh in the Rebellion of 26 January 1808*, p. 9

favour...that there was strong support for Bligh at the Hawkesbury'.[89] An alternative scenario suggests that Bligh, as naval commodore with command of the *Porpoise* that had just returned to Sydney, could have sailed to VDL, where he might have sought support from either Lieutenant-Governor Collins at Hobart or from Lieutenant-Colonel Paterson at Port Dalrymple. This would certainly have given encouragement to his supporters in Sydney. It is not surprising that Johnston had been greatly concerned that the soldiers under his command had initially failed to arrest Bligh.

On 27 February, with Bligh confined at Government House, Johnston revoked martial law and dismissed officers of Bligh's government including Atkins and Provost-Marshall Gore. There were all-night celebrations across Sydney that included drinking and dancing around bonfires, burning of effigies, satirical posters, oil-lamp transparencies in windows and 'Bligh under the bed' cartoon displayed in soldiers' homes. Throughout 1808, Bligh was confined to Government House refusing to leave for England until lawfully relieved of his duty.[90] Johnston had no prospect of material advancement from dismissing Bligh; in fact, he was putting his future income as an army officer at grave risk. Bligh's evidence to the court martial in 1811 suggests that Johnston was hesitant in his actions and showed his lack of self-confidence by marching the whole NSW Corps against the undefended Government House. Johnston was in no way Macarthur's tool. This has been obscured by the enthusiasm of both Macarthur's supporters and his detractors to place him more fully in the centre of the rebellion than his actions deserve. He was a competent and independent official, whose motive in removing Bligh was to resolve a crisis in the colony's administration and preserve public order.[91] This was not a rebellion in the sense of people grabbing power and possessions for themselves. A mutiny is much more restricted with the aim of removing a bad leader. There was a strongly held belief in the early-nineteenth century that gentlemen had the right to overthrow leaders who abused their power. In this context, George Johnston's action becomes much more principled and this was acknowledged during his court martial in 1811 when the leniency of his sentence was justified by reference to Bligh's 'impropriety and oppression'. In the days following the 1808 insurrection Daniel McKay, a publican who had once been employed as a gaoler but dismissed by Bligh as too brutal, took relish in erecting a sign outside his establishment. On one side, it depicted a Highland officer thrusting his sword through a snake, whilst the female figure of Liberty presents him with a cap. On the other side emblazoned in large type was the dedication: 'The Ever Memorable 26th January 1808'.[92]

There is some debate over the nature of the 'rebellion' and the degree to which it was planned. Some historians argue that had Johnston been in sufficiently good health to meet Bligh on 25 January 1808, the rebellion would

---

[89] Ibid, Fletcher, B. H., 'The Hawkesbury Settlers and the Rum Rebellion', p. 234.

[90] Atkinson, Alan, 'The British Whigs and the Rum Rebellion', *Journal of the Royal Australian Historical Society*, Vol. 66, (2), (1980), pp. 73-90.

[91] Johnston to Castlereagh, 11 April 1808, *HRA*, Series I, Vol. 6, pp. 208-221, provides Johnston's justification for rebellion.

[92] For Bligh's account of the rebellion, 30 June 1808, *HRNSW*, Vol. 6, p. 670. See also, Bligh to Castlereagh, 30 April 1808, *HRA*, Series I, Vol. 6, pp. 420-440.

perhaps not have occurred. Or had he already decided that Bligh would have to be removed and calculated that ill-health was a good tactic to escalate matters? Johnston consistently represented himself as an agent of the popular will claiming to have found the townsfolk of Sydney on his arrival from Annandale on 26 January 1808 in a state of tumult and apprehension, with no man's life or property safe against a tyrannical governor. The same question could be asked of Macarthur's actions on his trial. The problem is that, while both Johnston and Macarthur had grave doubts about Bligh's method of ruling, there is no evidence to suggest that they colluded in precipitating rebellion, something that would anyway have proved difficult as Macarthur was under arrest for much of 25 and 26 January. The meeting between Johnston, Macarthur and the group of wealthy citizens on 26 January has been mooted as indicative of conspiracy, but arguably its significance lies rather more in giving civilian legitimacy to military action. In fact, the rebellion did not require a great deal of planning and the NSW Corps was willing to support Johnston's order to arrest Bligh. For the rebellion to succeed all that was necessary was to apprehend Bligh.[93]

An interregnum

Removing Bligh has been achieved with relative ease but he legally remained Governor and the *de facto* administration that had been established lacked any constitutional legality.[94] Although there was no breakdown of law and order, there was a division among the colonists and especially within the governing élite between those who supported the rebel administration and those who remained loyal to Bligh. Until a superior officer to Johnston arrived six months after the coup, John Macarthur was effectively in control of civil administration and was not constrained by the operation of the rule of law. During that period the rudimentary legal system was abused, where not suspended and the courts used as a tool of political revenge[95] Magistrates loyal to Bligh were dismissed.[96] Other loyalists were subject to a parody of justice. Gore and George Crossley, the dubious convict attorney–transported for falsifying the wil of a dead client--who had some role in advising Bligh on the rebellion were convicted on bogus charges and transported to the coal mines at Newcastle for seven years.[97] In March 1809, John Palmer, Bligh's Commissary who was charged with sedition for distributing Bligh's Proclamation that the Corps was in a state of mutiny, denied the competency of the court and refused to plead but was unlawfully

---

[93] Gore to Castlereagh, 26 April 1808, *HRNSW*, Vol. 6, pp. 602-606, gives an account of Bligh's arrest by a supporter. Bligh to Castlereagh, 30 April 1808, *HRNSW*, Vol. 6, pp. 607-629, gives his first account of the rebellion.

[94] Johnston did not inform Castlereagh of Bligh's arrest until 11 April 1808, *HRNSW*, Vol. 6, pp. 575-589. For correspondence between Bligh and the rebels see, Johnston to Castlereagh, 11 April 1808, *HRA*, Series I, Vol. 6, pp. 242-271, and Johnston's General Orders, *HRA*, Series I, Vol. 6, pp. 271-276.

[95] *HRNSW*, Vol. 6, pp. 435-453, Johnston to Castlereagh, 11 April 1808, *HRA*, Series I, Vol. 6, pp. 276-291, print the Colonial Secretary's Papers of the examination of officers after Bligh's arrest.

[96] Government and General Order, 27 January 1808, *HRNSW*, Vol. 6, p. 453.

[97] Allars, K. G., 'Crossley, George (1749-1823)', *ADB*, Vol. 1, pp. 262-263.

gaoled for three months and fined £50.[98] The civil court processes were also abused.[99] However, with the exception of politically motivated cases, the legal system continued to operate more or less as before. Commerce was adversely affected as it was uncertain whether the negotiable bills payable in sterling that had traditionally been used for transactions with the government, would be honoured in London.[100] No one who lived through these months was in little doubt that the rule of law was severely compromised.

Atkins was replaced[101] and Johnston initially appointed the Surveyor-General Charles Grimes as Judge-Advocate and ordered that Macarthur and the six officers be tried.[102] On 2 February, they were found not guilty.[103] By contrast, Bligh supporters were sentenced harshly with Provost-Marshall Gore receiving seven years for causing the arrest of Macarthur.[104] On 3 April, Grimes resigned

---

[98] Steven, Margaret, 'Palmer, John (1760-1833)', *ADB*, Vol. 2, pp. 309-311. See also, Palmer to Bligh, 2 March 1808, *HRNSW*, Vol. 6, pp. 530-531, in which he reaffirmed his support for Bligh. Palmer was reinstated by Governor Lachlan Macquarie but failed to receive any official compensation for deprivations suffered in the rebellion. Though the secretary of state instructed Macquarie to examine the commissariat accounts and see that the office was placed on a proper footing, he observed that as the complaints against Palmer 'have been chiefly brought forward since the arrest of Governor Bligh, it is probable they are exaggerated'. Palmer's examiners at the Comptroller's Office in London held that the charges 'seemed to have arisen as much from private pique as from zeal for the public service' and were too vague to justify a formal inquiry. However, they thought it inexpedient to restore Palmer because of his long tenure in office (since 1791) and recommended the appointment of another commissary. On 25 July 1811, Palmer was demoted to assistant commissary and placed on half-pay and next year the entire commissariat system was reorganised.

[99] Kercher, B., *Debt, Seduction and Other Disasters: The Birth of Civil Law in Convict New South Wales*, (Federation Press), 1996, pp. 41-42.

[100] Curry, J. E. B., *Reflections on the Colony of New South Wales: George Caley*, (Lansdowne), 1966, p. 157.

[101] He was, however, reinstated as Judge-Advocate on 13 December 1808. Aitken's conversion to the rebel cause was motivated largely by financial considerations, the capacity of the Corps to pander to his alcoholic tastes and a free grant of 500 acres in the Minto District.

[102] Dowd, Bernard T., 'Grimes, Charles (1772-1858)', *ADB*, Vol. 1, pp. 487-488, and 'Charles Grimes: The Second Surveyor-General of New South Wales', *Journal of the Royal Australian Historical Society*, Vol. 22, (4), (1936), pp. 247-288.

[103] *HRNSW*, Vol. 6, pp. 465-510 and *HRA*, Series I, Vol. 6, pp. 291-352, detail the trial. Johnston then appointed Anthony Fenn Kemp to the post. Aitkens and especially Kemp and Grimes were incompetent but more importantly made judicial decisions unfavourable to Macarthur. Foveaux had little choice but to reinstate Aitkens: Foveaux to Castlereagh, 20 February 1809, *HRA*, Series I, Vol. 7, p. 2, 'I had no choice left but to restore Mr Atkins, or expose the public to the serious inconveniences which must inevitably have followed from leaving so indispensable a department vacated.' See also, *The Trial of John McArthur, Esq. before a court of criminal judicature, assembled at Sydney, in New South Wales, on February the 2d, 1808, and four following days*, (Wood & Innes), 1808.

[104] Gore denied the authority of the rebel court that would not give bail and refused to plead; he was kept in gaol without trial for more than two months, and in a letter to Bligh unfavourably compared his treatment by the NSW rebels with that by the Irish rebels ten years before. On 30 May, Gore was again brought before a rebel court and again refused to plead. He was sentenced to transportation for seven years and was sent to Coal River

after George Johnston, in his role as Acting-Governor, criticised some 'extraordinary' proceedings in his court. Although Grimes' comments were partly due to his ignorance of the law or, as Johnston said, 'errors of judgment more than of design', Grimes was regarded as one of the opponents of his administration. Macarthur was then appointed as the so-called 'Secretary' and ran the business affairs of the colony.[105] Another prominent opponent of Bligh, Macarthur's ally Thomas Jamison, was made the colony's Naval Officer, the equivalent of Collector of Customs and Excise and was also reinstated as a magistrate, which enabled him and his fellow legal officers to scrutinise Bligh's personal papers for evidence of wrong-doing. In June 1809, Jamison sailed to London to bolster his business interests and give evidence against Bligh in any legal prosecutions that might be brought against the mutineers. He never had the opportunity to testify at Johnston's court martial dying in London at the beginning of 1811. Within a few months of Bligh's arrest, divisions emerged within the rebel leadership.[106] Johnston and Macarthur fell out with Blaxland[107] and Macarthur even managed to alienate the NSW Corps, previously his staunchest supporters.[108]

Foveaux, Patterson and Macquarie

Following Bligh's overthrow Johnston had notified his superior officer, Colonel William Patterson who was in Tasmania establishing a settlement at Port Dalrymple (now Launceston) of events.[109] Paterson was reluctant to get involved until clear orders arrived from England.[110] When he learned that Lieutenant-Colonel Joseph Foveaux was returning to Sydney with orders to become acting Lieutenant-Governor, Paterson left Foveaux to deal with the situation.[111] Foveaux arrived on 28 July and immediately took over the colony but left Bligh under house arrest. He felt that Bligh's behaviour had been insufferable but, personal feelings apart, restoring the deposed governor was impractical since the NSW

(Newcastle) where he laboured with ordinary convicts. See, *HRA*, Series I, Vol. 6, pp. 555-563, for a statement of Gore's refusal to recognise the court, his defence and correspondence with Bligh.

105 Government and General Order, 12 February 1808, *HRNSW*, Vol. 6, p. 519.

106 Macarthur to Captain Piper, 24 May 1808, *HRNSW*, Vol. 6, pp. 643-644, indicated that unity was short-lived: '...some of our old acquaintances have behaved most scurvily...'

107 Johnston to Castlereagh, 30 April 1808, *HRA*, Series I, Vol. 6, pp. 453-516, provides details for the reasons behind the rift between the Blaxlands and Johnston and Macarthur.

108 Johnston to Castlereagh, 30 April 1808, *HRA*, Series I, Vol. 6, pp. 518-520.

109 Macmillan, David S., 'Paterson, William (1755-1810)', *ADB*, Vol. 2, pp. 317-319. Johnston's letter is lost but Paterson's reply on 12 March 1808 is printed in, *HRNSW*, Vol. 6, pp. 536-538.

110 Paterson to Castlereagh, 12 March 1808, *HRNSW*, Vol. 6, pp. 538-539. Bligh to Paterson, 8 August 1808, *HRA*, Series I, Vol. 6, pp. 601-601, was the first direct contact between Bligh and Paterson since the coup in which Bligh asked Paterson 'to use your utmost endeavours to suppress this Mutiny of the Corps under your command, that I may proceed in the Government of the Colony according to the powers delegated to me by our Gracious Sovereign.'

111 Ibid, Whitaker, Anne-Maree, *Joseph Foveaux: Power and Patronage in Early New South Wales*, pp. 103-116, deals with his months in charge. See also, Fletcher, B. H., 'Foveaux, Joseph (1767-1846)', *ADB*, Vol. 1, pp. 407-409.

Corps would certainly have opposed such a move.[112] He at once took secure hold of the reins of government, dispensing with the services of John Macarthur who as 'Secretary' had been the power behind Johnston. The broad outlines of his policy were influenced by the same desire for cheap and efficient government that had guided his work on Norfolk Island and he sought to make his administration acceptable to London by pursuing objectives it had long favoured. He attacked the liquor trade and tried to reduce expenditure, reform the administration of the commissariat and improve public works turning his attention to improving the colony's roads, bridges and public buildings. Efforts were made to encourage the raising of beef and mutton, while he tried to persuade smallholders to breed additional swine, so providing an outlet for their surplus maize. His land policy was moderate and he made few grants, though he did alienate some town land that was properly available only for lease.

Little exception can be taken to these aspects of Foveaux's rule. However, his treatment of the pro-Bligh faction was severe and sometimes unfair. The troublesome Bligh refused to depart and was bitterly criticised in Foveaux's dispatches.[113] George Suttor and a group of his associates were imprisoned for challenging his authority for refusing to attend a muster.[114] He disallowed Robert Campbell's contract with David Collins to import cattle to the Derwent, criticised Campbell's assistance to Bligh and accused Campbell and John Palmer of benefiting greatly from the liquor trade.[115] It has been argued that advice from

---

112 Bligh appealed to Foveaux to be reinstated: Bligh to Foveaux, 29 July 1808, *HRNSW*, Vol. 6, p. 713, but Foveaux refused to interfere. His justification can be found in Foveaux to Castlereagh, 4 September 1808, *HRNSW*, Vol. 6, pp. 728-735, and *HRA*, Series I, Vol. 6, pp. 623-631.

113 This was particularly evident in a private letter from Foveaux to Under-Secretary Chapman (?), 10 September 1808, *HRNSW*, Vol. 6, pp. 749-754, and in Foveaux to Under-Secretary Cooke, 21 October 1808, pp. 783-784, where he suggested that Bligh was conspiring with settlers to support his restoration.

114 Parsons, Vivienne, 'Suttor, George (1774-1859)', *ADB*, Vol. 2, pp. 498-500. Suttor was a firm supporter of Bligh and a leader among the settlers. In May 1808, he was instrumental in drawing up an address of welcome to Paterson, anticipating his arrival in Sydney and asking him to take action against the rebels; but as Paterson did not come it was not presented. In November, Suttor drew up another petition to be sent to the Colonial Office and with Martin Mason was chosen for a mission to London to explain the abuses in the colony and ask for the reinstatement of Bligh: Settlers' Petition to Castlereagh, 4 November 1808, *HRNSW*, Vol. 6, pp. 802-804. In the meantime, however, Suttor was imprisoned for six months for failing to attend Foveaux's general muster and for impugning his authority. In 1810, Bligh took Suttor with him in the *Hindostan* as a witness against Colonel George Johnston.

115 Steven, Margaret, 'Campbell, Robert (1769-1846)', *ADB*, Vol. 1, pp. 202-206, and *Robert Campbell and the Bligh rebellion, 1808*, (Canbara & District Historical Society), 1962. During the events that culminated in the deposition of Bligh, Campbell publicly and privately supported the governor's attempts at reform, convinced that it was his liberalising economic measures that had goaded his opponents into open rebellion. In Campbell's opinion Bligh 'wished to administer justice to all ranks of people'. This exposed him to the hostility of the rebels and had such adverse effects on his business interests that he claimed he was never fully able to repair. When Bligh was deposed, Campbell was put under military arrest and subsequently was dismissed as treasurer, Naval Officer and collector of taxes. Because he was suspected of trying to establish a

officers who were jealous of Campbell's trading position underlay these moves and that Foveaux, acting as their tool, sought to destroy the merchant. If true, it was a serious flaw in what was quite an enterprising administration.

When there was still no word from England, he summoned Paterson to Sydney on 9 January 1809 to sort out matters.[116] Paterson sent Johnston and Macarthur to England for trial[117] and confined Bligh to the barracks until he signed a contract agreeing to return to England.[118] His opinion of Bligh was not high and he certainly regarded Bligh as culpable in causing the rebellion:

> He bore the most rancorous ill-will to every Officer and Inhabitant who he conceived could possibly in the remotest manner interfere with a matured plan of exercising the high command with which he was honoured in the purposes of gratifying his insatiably tyrannic Disposition and advancing his pecuniary interest.[119]

Paterson, whose health was failing, then retired to Government House at Parramatta and left Foveaux to run the colony. In January 1809, Bligh was given the control of HMS *Porpoise* on condition that he returned to England.[120] However, he sailed to Hobart in late March seeking the support of the Tasmanian Lieutenant-Governor David Collins to retake control of the colony.[121]

---

trading monopoly in collusion with Bligh, the rebel faction supervised the activities of Campbell & Co., supporting without investigation any damaging allegations concerning irregularities in its trade. In June 1809, Campbell was tried for disobedience in refusing to officiate as coroner. He argued that as he had been charged officially with certain offences he deemed himself incompetent to hold any civil position until such charges had been disproved; but the court, whose authority Campbell refused to acknowledge, found him guilty and fined him £50. Although his business partner and his brother-in-law, Commissary John Palmer, were both gaoled by the rebels, Campbell openly remained a supporter of their victims and a focus for Bligh's allies. In January 1810, he was one of the first of those reinstated in their former offices by Macquarie. On 12 May, Campbell, with his family, sailed unwillingly for England in the *Hindostan* to appear as a witness for Bligh at Lieutenant-Colonel George Johnston's trial.

[116] In poor health and drinking heavily, Paterson was a weak ruler. He spent most of the year at Parramatta as an invalid and the clique that had overthrown Bligh had the real control of affairs. Macquarie reported later, Paterson was 'such an easy, good-natured, thoughtless man, that he latterly granted Lands to almost every person who asked them, without regard to their Merits or pretensions'. Foveaux to Castlereagh, 20 February 1809, *HRA*, Series I, Vol. 7, p. 3.

[117] On 29 March 1809, Macarthur, Johnston and others sailed for England to participate in Johnston's court-martial for mutiny arriving on 9 October.

[118] Like Foveaux, Paterson refused to intervene in the Bligh affair, Paterson to Bligh, 21 January 1809, *HRNSW*, Vol. 7, pp. 8-9.

[119] Paterson to Castlereagh, 12 March 1809, *HRA*, Series I, Vol. 7, p. 18.

[120] Agreement between Bligh and Paterson, 4 February 1809, *HRNSW*, Vol. 7, pp. 17-18, *HRA*, Series I, Vol. 7, pp. 45-46.

[121] Bligh's Proclamation of his authority at the Derwent, 29 April 1809, *HRNSW*, Vol. 7, pp. 108-110, *HRA*, Series I, Vol. 7, pp. 96-99.

Collins did not support him[122] and on Paterson's orders Bligh remained cut off on board the *Porpoise* and moored in Hobart until January 1810.[123]

It was two years before the rebellion was finally quenched. The threat of Napoleon was more important and there was also growing tension between Britain and the United States that eventually led to war in 1812. After considerable delay, the Colonial Office decided that sending further naval governors to rule the colony was untenable. Instead the NSW Corps, now known as the 102nd Regiment of Foot, was to be recalled to England and replaced with the 73rd Regiment of Foot, whose commanding officer would take over as Governor.[124] Bligh was to be reinstated for twenty-four hours and then recalled to England. Johnston was to be sent to England for court martial and Macarthur tried in Sydney though both were already on their way to London. Major-General Lachlan Macquarie[125] was put in charge of the mission after Major-General Miles Nightingall fell ill before departure.[126] He took over as Governor with an elaborate ceremony on 1 January 1810.[127]

Macquarie reinstated all the officials who had been sacked by Johnston and Macarthur and cancelled all land and stock grants that had been made since Bligh's deposition, though to calm things down he then restored grants that he thought appropriate and prevented any settling of scores.[128] When Bligh received the news of Macquarie's arrival, he sailed from Hobart to Sydney, arriving on 17 January 1810 to collect evidence for the forthcoming court martial of Major George Johnston.[129] He departed for the trial in England on 12 May aboard the *Hindostan*, with recalled NSW Corps soldiers and witnesses including Atkins and Paterson, who died en route, for the trial against Johnston arriving on 25 October 1810. Mary Putland, recently married to Lieutenant-Colonel Maurice O'Connell remained in Sydney. Macquarie investigated the mutiny and reported finding no evidence that the insurrection resulted from any direct fault on Bligh's part. Nor did he attribute the blame to any incident in the prolonged power struggle between the naval 'Captain-General and Governor-in-Chief' and the

---

[122] Collins to Bligh, 4 May 1809, *HRNSW*, Vol. 7, p. 125 with Bligh's response, 7 May 1809, *HRNSW*, Vol. 7, pp. 125-126.

[123] See Paterson's Proclamation against Bligh, 19 March 1809, *HRNSW*, Vol. 7, p. 81.

[124] Duke of York to Castlereagh, 30 October 1808, *HRNSW*, Vol. 6, pp. 782-783. Although tainted by mutiny, the 102nd, after a period in England and Guernsey, served creditably in Bermuda and on active service in the war against the United States, returning from Canada in 1817, before being disbanded on 12 March 1818.

[125] McLachlan, N.D., 'Macquarie, Lachlan (1762-1824), *ADB*, Vol. 2, pp. 187-195, Ellis, M.H., *Lachlan Macquarie: His Life, Adventures and Times*, (Dymock's Book Arcade) 1947, 2nd ed., (Angus & Robertson), 1952 and Ritchie, John, *Lachlan Macquarie: a biography*, (Melbourne University Press), 1986 are useful biographies.

[126] Nightingall to Castlereagh, 6 December 1808, *HRNSW*, Vol. 6, pp. 810-811; he accepted the commission. Nightingall to Castlereagh (?), 20 March 1809, *HRNSW*, Vol. 7, p. 64, on the onset of the illness that prevented him from taking up his commission.

[127] Macquarie's Commission, 8 May 1809, *HRNSW*, Vol. 7, pp. 126-133 and his Instructions, 9, 14 May 1809, *HRNSW*, Vol. 7, pp. 122-140, 143-147.

[128] Proclamation, 4 January 1810, *HRNSW*, Vol. 7, pp. 255-257, *HRA*, Series I, Vol. 7, pp. 227-231.

[129] Bligh to Castlereagh, 9 March 1810, *HRNSW*, Vol. 7, pp. 309-312.

military force under his orders. In May 1810, Macquarie wrote to the Secretary of State in London that it was:

> ...extremely difficult to form a just Judgement on this delicate and mysterious subject... in justice to Governor Bligh...I have not been able to discover any Act of his which could in any degree form an excuse for, or in any way warrant, the violence and Mutinous Proceeding pursued against him.[130]

Given that he did not respect Bligh and regarded him as a 'most unsatisfactory Man to transact business with', Macquarie's statement appears unbiased.[131] However, he refrained from negative comment possibly deliberately as he had served with George Johnston in North America in 1777, on who, or what set of circumstances was responsible for the mutiny.

The ambiguity in this investigation was perpetuated in the subsequent court martial in England. On 3 April 1811, the newly appointed Prince Regent ordered the court martial of Johnston and on 7 May 1811, fifteen high-ranking officers and Judge Advocate General convened a court martial. The trial lasted thirteen days, with twenty-two witnesses plus Bligh for Crown and eighteen witnesses for Johnston. Having informally heard arguments from both sides, the government authorities in England were not impressed by either Macarthur's or Johnston's accusations against Bligh or by Bligh's ill-tempered letters accusing key figures in the colony of unacceptable conduct. Against the patent fact of mutiny was set nothing more substantial than the governor's temper and unproven and irrelevant allegations of cowardice at the time of the arrest.[132] On 6 June, Johnston was found guilty and cashiered from the military 'for suffering to be led by Macarthur', the lowest penalty possible.[133] His barrister, John Adolphus who held the view that Johnston was a misled man, wrote after the trial:

> I always considered and indeed understood that the parties who led you into your present most unpleasant and unfortunate situation, would, at least, have taken off your shoulders the expense of the present prosecution, but as you refer in your letter to the smallness of your means, I beg you will consider me as entirely satisfied.[134]

A similar note was struck by Johnston himself when he wrote in June 1820:

---

[130] Macquarie to Castlereagh, 10 May 1810, *HRNSW*, Vol. 7, p. 378.

[131] *HRA*, Series I, Vol. 7, p. 331.

[132] Ibid, Yarwood, A. T., 'Johnston, George (1764-1823)', p. 21.

[133] Ibid, Ritchie, John, *A Charge of Mutiny: The Court Martial of Lieutenant Colonel George Johnston for Deposing Governor William Bligh in the Rebellion of 26 January 1808*, is the most detailed account. On 12 November 1811, Bligh published his account of the court martial: *Account of the rebellion of the New South Wales Corps: communicated to the Rt. Hon. Lord Castlereagh and Sir Joseph Banks, Bart*, (Banks Society Publications), 2003.

[134] Cit, ibid, Yarwood, A. T., 'Johnston, George (1764-1823)', *ADB*, Vol. 2, p. 21.

> Every person that promised [at the time of the deposition of Bligh to support me with their lives and fortunes] has risen upon my ruin. I alone am the sufferer, having lost my commission, and upwards of 6000 pounds for conceding to their requests.[135]

He was then able to return as a free citizen to Annandale his estate in Sydney.

Legal opinion was that none of the civilians involved could be tried for treason in England. Macquarie received instructions from Lord Castlereagh that:

> ...as Gov'r Bligh has represented that Mr McArthur has been the leading Promoter and Instigator of the mutinous Measures...you will, if Examinations be sworn against him...have him arrested thereupon and brought to Trial before the Criminal Court of the Settlement.

Macarthur's obvious course was to remain in England and exert every influence to have this obstacle removed. Because of the uncertainty of his position, he toyed with the idea of taking 'a small Farm of about a Hundred a Year' to help to balance his living expenses. At the same time he tried to resolve the problem of returning to NSW at personal risk and the alternative of withdrawing his family from 'plenty and affluence' in the colony to a life of 'pinching penury' in England. He became increasingly convinced that unless their colonial property would yield the £1,600 a year necessary to support the family and educate and establish his sons, he would have to return. Initially, none of Macarthur's efforts in England clarified his position and it was not until early in 1817 that he received permission to return to NSW on condition that he should not become involved in public affairs. Exile itself was some sort of punishment.

Bligh's promotion to Rear Admiral was delayed until the end of Johnston's trial. Afterward it was backdated to 31 July 1810 and Bligh took up a position that had been kept for him. He continued his naval career in the Admiralty in unspectacular fashion and died in 1817. Macquarie had been impressed with Foveaux's administration. He put Foveaux's name forward to succeed Collins as Lieutenant-Governor of VDL because he could think of no one more fitting and considered that he could not have acted otherwise with regard to Bligh.[136] However, when Foveaux returned to England in 1810, he narrowly escaped court-martial for assenting to Bligh being deposed and imprisoned and Macquarie's recommendation was ignored.[137] Foveaux was taken back into active service and given command of a light regiment in 1811 and pursued an uneventful military career after that, rising to the rank of Lieutenant-General.[138]

---

[135] Cit, ibid, Yarwood, A. T., 'Johnston, George (1764-1823)', p. 22.

[136] Foveaux to Earl Liverpool, 6 July 1811, *HRNSW*, Vol. 7, pp. 553-554, wishes to succeed Collins in VDL but in Liverpool's response, 11 July 1811, *HRNSW*, Vol. 7, p. 555, his application was refused. On 18 July, Foveaux then asked Liverpool that arrears in pay owing him should be paid, *HRNSW*, Vol. 7, pp. 556-557.

[137] Martin Mason to Earl Liverpool, 26 January 1811, *HRNSW*, Vol. 7, pp. 490-491, recounted charges against Foveaux,

[138] Ibid, Whitaker, Anne-Maree, *Joseph Foveaux: Power and Patronage in Early New South Wales*, pp. 162-194, considers his career after 1812.

Conclusion

The 'Rum' Rebellion had nothing to do with rum. Almost no one at the time of the rebellion thought it was about rum. Bligh briefly tried to give it that interpretation to smear his opponents, but there was no evidence for it and he quickly abandoned it. The label was conferred some fifty years after the event by William Howitt,[139] a writer with teetotal sympathies and popularised by H. V. Evatt as the title of the series of lectures he delivered at the University of Queensland for its 150th anniversary.[140] Officers of the NSW Corps had monopolised the rum trade in the 1790s, but this ended years before the rebellion, with the arrival on the commercial scene of successful former convicts such as Simeon Lord and free traders like Robert Campbell. The name seems to have persisted partly due to the power of alliteration and partly because it allowed left-leaning writers to blame the event on Australia's proto-capitalists. Neither was it really a 'rebellion'. Contemporaries thought of it as a mutiny or military insurrection though it might more accurately be described as a *coup d'etat* in that, once the NSW Corps had seized power by arresting Bligh, it was its leaders who ruled the colony and, in the case of Paterson and Foveaux refused to reinstate Bligh, until replaced by Macquarie.

With Macquarie's inconclusive investigation in 1810 and the ambivalence of the court martial findings on the basic cause of the mutiny, there has been a diversity of theories as to why it occurred and these have polarised into two distinct and divergent perspectives. At one extreme, historians argue that the rebels had been granted large tracts of land that they successfully exploited in their own interests and that Bligh's policies threatened their wealth. John Macarthur is cast as a conniving puppet master and Bligh's personal defects are played down. This interpretation appeals to those who have faith in government enterprise and an egalitarian inclination to support, as Bligh did, the small farmers of the settlement on the Hawkesbury flood plain.

At the other extreme, the primary focus is on the part played by the officers of the NSW Corps in providing much of the entrepreneurial drive in trade and agriculture that was necessary to enable the colony to succeed. Bligh's policies threatened that success. His was a static vision of a government-dominated society serviced by yeoman farmers that contrasted with dynamic Sydney-based commerce. Adherents to this approach emphasise the defects in Bligh's character and policy and play down the greed and cunning of the rebels. Certainly those involved in the coup were quick to put their interpretation

---

[139] Howitt, William, *Land, labour, and gold: or, Two years in Victoria: with visits to Sydney and Van Diemen's Land*, 2 Vols. 1st ed., (Longman, Brown, Green, and Longmans), 1855, p. 118, 2nd ed., (Longman, Brown, Green, Longmans, and Roberts), 1858, Vol. 2, p. 78.

[140] Ibid, Evatt, H. V., *Rum Rebellion: A Study of the Overthrow of Governor Bligh by John Macarthur and the New South Wales Corps*, remains useful because, although partisan in favour of Governor Bligh, it was written by an eminent Australian lawyer. Ellis, M. H., *John Macarthur,* (Angus & Robertson), 1955, is partisan in the opposite direction. A more balanced account is ibid, Fitzgerald, Ross, and Hearne, Mark, *Bligh, Macarthur and the Rum Rebellion,* though it does contain errors in military detail. Davis, Russell Earls, *Bligh in Australia: A New Appraisal of William Bligh and the Rum Rebellion*, (Woodslane Pty Limited), 2010, is the most recent narrative.

on events. A picture of Bligh being pulled from beneath the bed where he had hidden for two hours was possibly produced and put on display within hours of the event. It was part of a campaign to brand Bligh a coward and reduce support for him in the colony and in Britain. This seems to have been at least partly successful. Following the rebellion, the NSW Corps was withdrawn, Johnston was cashiered and Macarthur had to stay out of the colony for many years for fear of prosecution had he returned. Yet the outcome could have been far worse for the rebels, but for the antipathy that existed towards Bligh in England at the time of Johnston's trial in 1811. The perspective appears also to have been the judgement of the only systematic contemporary investigation of the events, the court martial that simply cashiered Johnson, a punishment universally regarded as exceptionally lenient.

Both perspectives are plausible because the available contemporary evidence consists largely of assertions by those with a vested interest in the outcome, perhaps inevitable with an event that polarised a small community.[141] Three issues are important when assessing this event. Any explanation of why the coup occurred can look like justification or condemnation. However, it is important not to project today's values backwards to judge the corruption of the officers. Early-nineteenth century British politics and public administration was, by today's standards, profoundly corrupt and the early Sydney colony was no different. Finally, this was an age in which conduct was defined by the code of honour to which all gentlemen had to subscribe. This code is expressed through the tradition of duelling that was already evident in colonial NSW and that provides part of the explanation for the military coup of 1808.

Evatt turned Bligh into a proto-democrat overturned by the corrupt capitalists of the NSW Corps, Ellis claimed the capitalist Macarthur as heroic in his establishment of viable wool and other farming in the colony while Fitzgerald and Hearns explain that both men were on the make, desperate to set themselves up during their time in Australia. The coup was the result of a range of factors including various aspects of commercial self-interest. The traffic in rum was of little if any significance, except to some of the non-commissioned officers. Much more important, amongst multiple causes, was the conflict between real estate developers and the public interest over the exploitation of prime urban land near the water. The tension over urban leases was one of a number of conflicts in which Bligh sought to reverse practices permitted by his less resolute predecessors. He made only three land grants--2,000 acres compared to King's 73,000--in eighteen months; he only pardoned two convicts; he cracked down on profiteering and enforced import restrictions. His policies undermined the wealth and the prospects of that part of the local élite with access to capital. On a number of occasions he deployed his authority over the rudimentary judicial system to attack those he opposed and intervened directly in court cases to achieve his ends.

---

141 This is particularly evident in the correspondence in *HRA*, Series I, Vol. 6, where Bligh, Johnston, Foveaux and Paterson and pro- and anti-Bligh factions placed their positions on the record.

This kind of untrammelled executive power was unacceptable to 'free-born Englishmen'. Government by whim in the exercise of an absolute discretion was tyranny, typical of Continental nations and anathema to the English. Jeremy Bentham maintained that military rule breached the Enlightenment tenet of liberty since there was no separation of powers to prevent the executive becoming excessively powerful and that the colonies reflected the spirit of French absolutism rather than British constitutionalism.[142] The colony was therefore improperly constituted under a strange amalgam of delegated prerogative powers and acts of Parliament. Broad discretionary powers may have been necessary for NSW governors to deal with convicts, but when applied to free settlers and emancipists, they challenged the dominant Lockean ideology of eighteenth century Britain and the principles of the rule of law that provided the civic discourse of early Sydney.[143] Britons in NSW—apart from convicts and serving members of the military bound by martial law--he thought, should have received the benefits of British law. Bligh's conduct may have been acceptable on a ship where a culture of authority created an expectation of unquestioning and immediate execution of orders. However, such conduct was unacceptable when applied to free subjects. Indeed, there were serious doubts, privately expressed by Bentham but known to some settlers, about whether, in the absence of express parliamentary authority, the Governor could lawfully exercise such authority over free men and women at all.[144] The issue for the rebels was not regicide but security of property and a more independent judiciary. Even the Crown, itself involved in a global war to counter the French Revolution, could not ignore accusations of depotism something that goes far in explaining the rebels' escape from hanging and the leniency of their 'sentences'.

The sense of personal security of citizens, indeed the existence of social order, is determined in large measure by the extent to which people can arrange their personal affairs and their relationships with associates, friends, family and neighbours on the assumption that basic standards of propriety are met and reasonable expectations are satisfied. All forms of social relationships, including economic interaction, are impeded by the degree to which personal and property rights are subject to unpredictable and arbitrary incursion and petty despotism, so that people live in fear or act based on suspicion, rather than on the basis that

---

[142] Ibid, Benton, Lauren, *A Search for Sovereignty: Law and Geography in European Empires, 1400-1900*, pp. 191-197, examines the development of Bentham's view of the illegality of governance in NSW.

[143] See Neal, David, *The Rule of Law in a Penal Colony: Law and Power in Early New South Wales*, (Cambridge University Press), 1991, pp. 92-94, 97-98; Braithwaite John, 'Crime in a Convict Republic', *Modern Law Review*, Vol. 64, (2001), p. 11; Gascoigne, John, *The Enlightenment and the Origins of European Australia*, (Cambridge University Press), 2002, pp. 39-44; Krygier, Martin, 'Subjects, Objects and the Colonial Rule of Law', in Krygier, Martin, *Civil Passions: Selected Writings*, (Black Inc), 2005, pp. 56-91; Thompson, E. P., *Whigs and Hunters: The Origin of the Black Act*, (Pantheon), 1975, pp. 265-266; Hay, Douglas, 'Property, Authority and the Criminal Law', in ibid, Hay, Douglas et al, (eds.), *Albion's Fatal Tree: Crime and Society in Eighteenth Century England*, pp. 17-63; Cole, D. H., ''An Unqualified Human Good': E. P. Thompson and the Rule of Law', *Law and Society Review*, Vol. 28, (2001), p. 117.

[144] Atkinson, Alan, 'Jeremy Bentham and the Rum Rebellion', *Journal of the Royal Australian Historical Society*, Vol. 64, (1), (1978), pp. 1-13, at p. 1.

others will act in a predictable way. The rule of law provided the central legitimising discourse of eighteenth century England. It was firmly established in Australia by the experience of the coup itself and, perhaps more significantly, by the experience of government under a military regime. Bligh had united a number of disparate interests. His removal took away that unity.

The absence of a clearly legitimate authority enabled those with a grievance to seek vengeance and anyone with access to power to abuse it. Immediately after the coup, the sense of personal security was largely lost and the rule of law compromised and, on occasions, set aside. This was short-lived and later the courts operated more normally and fairly. However, throughout the two years between the deposition of Bligh and the arrival of Macquarie, the colony was controlled by an illegal government. Every appointment, including to judicial office and every legal and governmental decision was invalid. Personal and property rights were institutionally insecure and the residents of NSW welcomed the restoration of legitimate authority under Lachlan Macquarie. In accordance with his instructions, he invalidated the appointments and the decisions of the rebel administration, including appointments to and decisions by the courts. Completed court orders were not reopened on the basis of necessity, perhaps most poignantly applied in the case of the invalid death sentences that had been carried into effect. Nevertheless, some redress was available for the past illegal exercise of governmental power. One of those banished to the coal mines sued successfully for false imprisonment.[145] The rule of law was emphatically restored.

---

[145] Ibid, Kercher, B., *Debt, Seduction and Other Disasters: The Birth of Civil Law in Convict New South Wales*, p. 40.

10 Empire, Resistance and Rebellion

The only way to deal with an unfree world is to become so absolutely free that your very existence is an act of rebellion.[1]

In 1898, Roger Casement--a controversial Irishman who served the British Crown with loyalty, was knighted in 1911, then hanged for treason five years later--wrote an epic poem 'The Dream of the Celt' that his biographer Angus Mitchell says:

> ...framed by powerful imagery of the sea, it returns to the theme of his youthful efforts: English misrule in Ireland under the Tudors and Stuarts.[2]

Mitchell concludes that underlying the verse was Casement's emerging vision for a new Ireland. When Casement was writing 'The Dream of the Celt' in 1898, the British Consular Service that employed him had little idea of his nationalist views on Ireland. They did not know that Casement, who became an expert in leading a double life, was already nurturing the deepest contempt for the British Empire, while working diligently for his employers.[3]

Casement's reputation was based on investigations into the abuses by Leopold II of Belgium's agents in the Congo and the London-listed Peruvian Amazon Company in Amazonian Peru, where natives who did not tap enough rubber were burnt alive or mutilated depending on the offence, were reflections of the way evil can take over in places where there were no limits to the power of those in charge. In *Heart of Darkness*, Joseph Conrad took an opposite view to Casement. He thought Africa made Europeans become evil, whereas Casement showed in the *Congo Report* that it was Europeans who introduced evil to Africa. Casement believed that Europeans were more evil than any native could ever be. It is not that he had any illusions about the 'noble savage' recognising that natives could be cruel, but he believed that this did not justify the agents of Leopold II and the Peruvian Amazon Company brutally exploiting them.[4] They claimed that the 'savages' were not human and that they could do what they liked to them.

---

[1] Camus, Albert, *The Rebel*, (Penguin), 1951, originally published as *L' Homme Révolté*, (Gallimard), 1951, cited in Bauman, Zygmunt, *44 Letters from the Liquid Modern World*, (Polity), 2010, p. 184.

[2] Mitchell, Angus, Casement, (Haus Publishing), 2003, p. 39.

[3] Burroughs, Robert, 'Imperial Eyes or 'The Eyes of Another Race?': Roger Casement's Travels in West Africa', *Journal of Imperial and Commonwealth History*, Vol. 37, (2009), pp. 383-397, and his *Travel Writing and Atrocities: Eyewitness Accounts of Colonialism in the Congo, Angola and the Putumayo*, (Routledge), 2010, pp. 49-71, 122-143.

[4] Casement's 'official' view of native exploitation in the Congo and Amazon are contained in 'Correspondence and Report from His Majesty's Consul at Boma Respecting the Administration of the Independent State of the Congo', *British Parliamentary Papers*, (Cd 1933), Vol. 62, 1904, pp. 357-396, and in *Correspondence Respecting the Treatment of British Colonial Subjects and Native Indians Employed in the Collection of Rubber in the Putumayo District*, (HMSO), 1912. See also, Cookey, S. J. S., *Britain and the Congo Question, 1885-1913*, (Humanities Press), 1968, and Ewans, Martin, *European Atrocity, African Catastrophe: Leopold II, the Congo Free State and its Aftermath*, (Routledge), 2002, pp. 175-201.

Casement's gradual disillusionment with colonialism came from his growing belief that the destruction of the African, and later Amazonian, way of life by the colonial occupiers, was analogous to what happened when the English occupied Ireland. The only difference, he argued, is that the British in Ireland are more decorous in the ways they despoiled the natives of their heritage. His Irish patriotism developed in the heart of Africa and later in the Peruvian jungle. Contemplating the power of the Peruvian Amazon Company, he concluded that the only way the Putumayo Indians could overcome the miserable conditions into which they have been reduced was by rising up in arms. From this he concluded that the same was true for Ireland: it could never be independent without violence.

Although the treatment of natives in the Congo and in the Peruvian forest may have been extreme, it represented in all its brutality a colonial attitude that was far from uncommon. Imperial power was built upon exploitation of natural resources using, at different times, slaves, convicts, indentured labour and economic migrants or free labour. This cheap labour produced goods for trade with other countries or to satisfy the insatiable desire of Britain's population for cheap food, cheap raw materials and goods that often began as luxuries and then acquired a broader constituency as their cost fell. Whether it was tobacco, sugar, cotton, tea, coffee, rubber or precious metals and minerals, the ways they were produced or extracted were accompanied by working conditions that people in Britain would not have tolerated. They may have been shocked by the exposés of the anti-slavery movement but they still wanted their cheap sugar or cheap tobacco and this often meant they did not think abour or question how they were produced.[5] This attitude remains an important characteristic of British society: we may deplore the exploitation of child labour in Asia or Africa or the often starvation wages paid to economic migrants but we still want the goods or services that they provide as cheaply as possible and are prepared to ignore the realities of how things are produced in our quest for consumer satisfaction. In that respect, the tentacles created by empire persist.

For Britain, the aim of empire was to enhance its power, wealth and status within a geopolitical context though its empire was far from being a centrally organised hegemony. The Royal Navy played a pivotal role as an aggressive and deterrent force that was enhanced by Britain's shipbuilding capacity and by steam technology in the nineteenth century creating a formidable mercantile marine.[6] What marked British rule was the extraordinary range of its constitutional, political, economic and cultural relationships. Rule could be formal or informal and colonies organised in a variety of constitutional forms such as protectorates, crown colonies, dominions or mandates and there were 'dependencies' and the informal empire of influence rather than direct rule. This seemingly chaotic configuration belies any suggestion of a systematic empire built according to a master plan and reflects the pragmatic and serendipitous manner of British

[5] Thompson, Andrew, *The Empire Strikes Back? The Impact of Imperialism on Britain from the Mid-Nineteenth Century*, (Longman), 2005, pp. 4-8, 124-154.
[6] For discussion of this in the nineteenth century, see Matzke, Rebecca Berens, *Deterrence through Strength: British Naval Power and Foreign Policy under the Pax Britannica*, (University of Nebraska Press), 2011.

imperial expansion. Relationships between the centre and the colonial periphery were fluid, contested and unstable. The British Empire paradoxically combined hegemony and diversity. Predictably, to its architects colonialism was not depicted as the violent seizure of lands and peoples but was justified in the more noble names of civilisation and pacification and later, when such patently racist discourses were discarded after the barbarities of Nazism, in seductive terms of development and modernisation. This view of empire was generally apolitical in character, espoused largely uncritically by successive Colonial Secretaries. Before 1964, Hyam argues:

> ...little adjustment to new parties was required. Temperamental differences between ministers of whatever political colour were more important, as garrulous character succeeded taciturn, slave-driver replaced indulgent, intellectual followed near-illiterate, or lazy amateur succeeded dedicated professional.[7]

Yet, before the advent of reliable telegraphy and wireless and the spread of air power, the tyranny of distance meant that there was a looseness of control from the centre and most decisions about imperial direction were made at the peripheries of empire by local colonial officials.[8] Consultation with politicians often thousands of miles away in London was impractical until the advent of reliable telegraphy when local conditions required prompt action. As long as they did not involve the Colonial Office in additional spending, colonial instability or military intervention, they were generally approved by Colonial Secretaries and by Parliament even if they were later subject to review and modification. This was particularly the case with colonial resistance and rebellion where restoring order and preventing further disturbances were an immediate issue that called for speedy local solutions.

The colonial state was the midwife of colonial capitalism. It was a conquest state, established through physical force and maintained through political repression. Created as an adjunct to the imperial state, its hegemony was excessively coercive and consequently, its legitimacy even within the more self-consciously 'British' white-settler colonies was questioned. Its territoriality was often ambiguous and frequently contested, its sovereignty disputed, its institutions of governance, legal order and ideological structures were all grounded in metropolitan practices and traditions that were often inappropriate or impractical as a means of effective government and led to a 'net of processes' that changed over time and in different colonial contexts. The rule of law became a site of struggles between local assemblies, colonial and metropolitan politicians, Crown judges and the Colonial Office. Its revenue base was limited, a critical weakness when metropolitan government expected colonies to be self-funding. Charged with the onerous tasks of creating or promoting colonial capitalism, linking the colony to the metropole and consolidating colonial rule, it is not surprising that the colonial state was both very interventionist and inherently

[7] Hyam, Ronald, *Understanding the British* Empire, (Cambridge University Press), 200, p. 215.

[8] For the developing historiography of metropole and periphery and the impact of 'gentlemanly capitalism', see Webster, Anthony, *The Debate on the Rise of the British Empire*, (Manchester University Press), 2006, pp. 68-92, 114-166.

fragile and overtly authoritarian and structurally weak exercising dominion without hegemony. Colonial states were also critically vulnerable to shifting imperial interests. Colonial rule gave rise to the racialisation and ethnicisation of colonial societies creating divisions between the colonisers and colonised and among the colonised. The colonised were denied the rights of citizenship because of race and subjected to traditions of so-called 'tribal' custom often invented by colonialism itself. Colonial despotism sought to create ethnic identities or to give fluid social structures an ethnic purity that previously did not exist as instruments of divide and rule. As Mamdani has noted the colonial state ordained and enforced so-called customary traditions that had little historical depth and that this reflected the monarchical, authoritarian, racist and patriarchal nature of Britain's society.[9]

Institutional explanations

Resistance and rebellion occurred within and against colonial institutions. But some colonies made the transition from imperial rule to independence through legitimate constitutional means in which resistance to colonial rule never deteriorated into armed struggle, while in others armed struggle was a prologue to independence. Was there an endemic weakness in colonial structures that precipitated resistance and rebellion or were they a consequence of the specific circumstances in a particular colony?

The ways in which colonies were governed varied geographically and across time but there were certain common features that can be illustrated by the example of the Gambia in West Africa.[10] Most of Britain's established colonies had initially been under direct rule from London through their colonial administration but by the time Gambia became a distinct colony in 1888-1889, they had already achieved self-government or, in the case of the United States, independence. The Gambia, like many of the colonies acquired in the nineteenth century combined direct rule (the Colony) with a system of indirect rule through existing native tribal structures (the Protectorate). In Gambia, as elsewhere in the empire, the head of the colonial administration was the Governor who represented and was directly responsible to the British Government and was not accountable to the people of the colony.[11] He was vested with a number of powers including the power of veto, could make laws by proclamation and was the president of both the Executive and Legislative Councils. The courts, the Civil Service and other institutions of the government

---

[9] Mamdani, Mahmood, *Citizen and Subject: Contemporary Africa and the Legacy of Late Colonialism*, (Princeton University Press), 1996.

[10] For the history of Gambia, see Gailey, Harry A., *A History of The Gambia*, (Praeger), 1965, and Gray, John M., *A History of The Gambia*, (Barnes & Noble), 1940. Hughes, Arnold, and Perfect, David, *A Political History of The Gambia, 1816-1994*, (University of Rochester Press), 2008, provides a detailed political history. Wright, Donald R., *The World and a Very Small Place in Africa: A History of Globalization in Niumi, the Gambia*, (M. E. Sharpe), 2004, pp. 113-184, is a valuable study that relates the experience of one community to its global context.

[11] Williams, Stephanie, *Running the Show: Governors of the British Empire: 1857-1912*, (Viking), 2011, is a valuable study of the global characteristics of governors and governorship in the second half of the nineteenth century.

were under his control. Especially in tropical Africa where disease meant that appointments could often prove fatal, governors had to be omnicompetent: they negotiated with tribal leaders, drafted law, collected taxes, planned towns, built roads and railways, improved sanitation and irrigation and founded schools and hospitals.[12]

Yet the task of overseeing the nation's empire was not highly rated in Britain or even by some who did the job. There was little recognition from London when things went well and often immediate recall or dismissal if they did not. Governors regularly died before they were able to clear themselves of charges of incompetence: for instance, Lord Berkeley after the Bacon Rebellion, Sir James Craig in 1812 following a confrontational five years in Lower Canada and his successor Sir George Prevost accused of mishandling of the War of 1812 against the United States.[13] Paradoxically, the more prominent the post, the less power it conferred. Lords Tennyson and Lorne, respectively Governors-General of Australia and Canada were little more than constitutional ornaments. Some governors acted dictatorially such as Sir Bartle Frere, High Commissioner of South Africa in the 1870s who dismissed the Boers as primitives and the 'kaffirs' as animals and, contrary to instructions from the Colonial Office, precipitated war against the Zulus in 1879.[14] Others stood between the native population and the interests of the small white population in their quest for land. For instance, Sir Arthur Gordon, the first Governor of Fiji, ensured that it never became a settler colony by passing an ordinance in 1880 that native land should be inalienable and in the Caribbean William Des Voeux abolished forced labour when he was Governor of St Lucia in the 1870s.[15] The nature of gubernatorial rule played a significant role in the ways in which colonial resistance and rebellion developed and a poor governor might inflame existing grievances while a more responsive governor could calm or even resolve them if they were allowed to do so by the Colonial Office.

Governors were assisted by advisory and legislative bodies that were nominated and, in the older colonies legislative assemblies were elected albeit on an often-restricted franchise.[16] The function of the Executive Council was to

---

[12] Burton, Richard, *Wanderings in West Africa from Liverpool to Fernando Po: by a F. R. G. S.*, 2 Vols. (Tinsley Brothers), 1863, Vol. 2, p. 213, in late 1861, described the typical governor's resident in equatorial Africa as 'a corrugated iron coffin or plank-lined morgue, containing a dead consul once a year.'

[13] See, Christie, Robert, *Memoirs of the administration of the colonial government of Lower-Canada, by Sir James Henry Craig, and Sir George Prevost; from the year 1807 until the year 1815*, (n. p. Quebec), 1818, and Brenton, E. B., *Some accounts of the public life of the late Lieutenant-General Sir George Prevost, Bart., particularly of his services in the Canadas*, (T. Cadell and T. Egerton), 1823.

[14] Martineau, John, *The Life and Correspondence of Sir Bartle Frere*, 2 Vols. (John Murray), 1895.

[15] Chapman, J. K., *The Career of Arthur Hamilton Gordon, first Lord Stanmore, 1829-1912*, (University of Toronto Press), 1964, and Newbury, C. W., *Patronage and Politics in the Victorian Empire: The Personal Governance of Sir Arthur Hamilton Gordon (Lord Stanmore)*, (Cambria Press), 2010.

[16] Morton, W. L., 'The Local Executive in the British Empire, 1763-1828', *English Historical Review*, Vol. 78, (1963), pp. 436-457, considers the development of executive power in the transition period of empire. Bertram, Anton, *The Colonial Service*,

advise the Governor in matters of administration and its members were appointed by the Governor. These included the Colonial Secretary, Director of Medical Services, Collector of Customs Duties and other officials. The Executive Council provided the framework for the day-to-day administration of colonies as well as acting as a forum for developing local colonial policy within the overall constraints of imperial policy. The functions of the Legislative Council were to discuss the affairs of the colony and to make laws for the colony but these required the assent of the Governor who could veto them. [17] This reflected the Colonial Office's concern for a strong executive. However, this observation on the Legislative Council is too restrictive since the presence of unofficial members reflected the view that a central purpose of establishing a legislative body had always been to give the inhabitants of colonies a degree of representation in the decision-making process. In the Gold Coast, for instance, the Legislative Council included the members of the Executive Council and unofficial members initially chosen from British commercial interests. After 1900, three chiefs and three other Africans were added to the Council chosen from the Europeanised communities of Accra, Cape Coast and Sekondi. The inclusion of Africans from Asante and the Northern Territories did not take place until after 1925. Gambia did not have the elected Legislative Assembly that was a feature of direct colonial rule in the seventeenth and eighteenth centuries and was retained under colonial self-government in the nineteenth century. One important characteristic of the bi-cameral system of Legislative Assembly and Council was that, as the system evolved, tensions arose between the two bodies and with the Executive Council over the relationship between representative and nominated institutions. It was tensions between the Legislature and Executive and the support of Britain for the latter that contributed to rebellion in Canada in 1837.

The British policy of indirect rule served as the basis of local government administration in all her West African colonies. The policy was first popularised by Lord Lugard who served as Governor-General of Nigeria between 1914 and 1919:

> The British Empire...has only one mission for liberty and self-development on no standardised lines, so that all may feel that their interests and religion are safe under the British flag. Such liberty and self-development can be best secured to the native population by leaving them free to manage their own affairs through their own rulers, proportionately to their degree of advancement, under the guidance of the British staff, and subject to the laws and policy of the administration.[18]

The theory of indirect rule was aimed at governing colonised peoples through their chiefs and local institutions. A major difficulty the British had in

---

(Cambridge University Press), 1930, remains an important contemporary account of how the empire was administered written by an insider, while Kirk-Greene, Anthony, *On Crown Service: A History of HM Colonial and Overseas Civil Services, 1837-1997*, (I. B. Tauris), 1999, pp. 153-266, contains a valuable collection of sources.

[17] Wight, Martin, *The Development of the Legislative Council, 1606-1945*, (Faber & Faber), 1946, pp. 66-99, examines the development of the Council.

[18] Lugard, Frederick, *The Dual Mandate in British Tropical Africa*, (Blackwood), 1922, p. 94.

administering her colonies in West Africa was that there were simply insufficient individuals prepared to serve as colonial administrators in that part of the empire. Indirect rule had the advantage of being cheap since traditional rulers were less expensive than British officials. For this reason, Lugard, and other British Governors in West Africa, adopted the system for the administration of local government in the region.

The policy was introduced in Gambia by Governor Robert Llewelyn of the Bathurst colony in 1893 when he appointed J. H. Ozane and F. Sitwell as travelling Commissioners for the North and South Banks of the river. Their function was to move from village to village to inform the chiefs about the system of indirect rule that was to be introduced by the colonial government. They were also required to assert their position so that the chiefs and people knew that they represented the authority of the Governor in Bathurst. The Gambia Protectorate Ordinance 1894 divided the Protectorate into administrative districts under the control of chiefs, some from the traditional royal ruling classes but most were appointed by the colonial government. Native courts were also created to exercise civil and criminal jurisdiction in issues where all parties are natives. The head chief of a district was president of the local court and had civil jurisdiction in areas of petty conflict resolution and adjudication and criminal jurisdiction over offences that did not exceed fines of £5 or imprisonment of over three weeks. They were also empowered to detain and send to the commissioner or the courts in Bathurst those accused of major crimes 'such as murder, robbery or slave dealing'. The following year, the colonial government enacted an ordinance for raising and collecting revenue in the Gambia Protectorate. It became known as the 'Yard Tax' ordinance as its purpose was establish a yard tax for the Protectorate since it was the Colonial Government's view that the people of Gambia should share in the cost of the administration. Although this did not lead to resistance in Gambia, in other parts of the empire such as the neighbouring Sierra Leone and South Africa, taxes imposed on areas of indirect rule did. Taxation could also be a source of resistance in colonies of direct rule as the case of the American colonies graphically showed.

The early years of Gambian indirect rule depended to a considerable extent on the personalities or competence of the travelling Commissioners. Even though a Protectorate system had been proclaimed, conditions in the country were still unsettled and there were certain areas where the Travelling Commissioners would not venture without an escort. Indeed, the killings of Sitwell and Silva in 1900 marked a turning point. British and French military forces restored order convincing lesser chiefs of colonial determination to impose their rule over the Protectorate. The 1902 ordinance increased the powers of Travelling Commissioners who were made chief executives in their districts thereby reducing the influence of local élites in the policy of indirect rule. It was not until 1944 that the colonial authorities established an annual chiefs' conference to provide a forum for them to make suggestions and criticise programmes initiated by the central government or the Commissioners. The main aim of British rule was to create and maintain peace in the area with the minimum of expense. The work of the chiefs and Commissioners was to generate revenue to run the administration rather than provide social services. For these reasons, the system of indirect rule in Gambia contributed to the social and political stagnation that prevailed in the rural areas up to the time of independence from Britain.

The system of government largely excluded educated Gambians from taking an active part in the government and this situation, as elsewhere in the empire led to calls for self-government. The question of representation had long been an issue of contention within Britain's empire. Brought to prominence by the American colonies in the 1760s and 1770s, there was a persistent tension between the desire of imperial and colonial authorities to delay calls for independence and calls for greater involvement by settlers and the indigenous population in the governance of their countries. The conundrum posed by the loss of the American economy was how could Britain peacefully ensure transition from direct rule to independence and how long could it be delayed. Imperial government increasingly accepted that some form of responsive, representative and eventually responsible colonial self-government was necessary at least in the settler colonies. The alternative was the possibility of American type 'revolutions' where colonies broke away from Britain. In the Canadas, it was the failure of the reform agenda that precipitated rebellion in 1837. In Australia as it expanded from its founding colony to a multi-colony state, the smouldering instability of the 1820s and 1830s erupted in demands for greater responsibility for colonial government in the 1840s. As a result, the pace towards democratic institutions and the creation of a democratic electorate was accelerated in settler colonies such as Canada, Australia and New Zealand. Self-government may have been an acceptable solution for established settler colonies but for colonies in which there was direct rule the move towards representative institutions was often painfully slow and this generated growing resistance and in some instances armed rebellion.

The experience of the Gambia illustrates the emergence of types of legitimate resistance that were common across Britain's empire in the twentieth century. The pioneer of the move from a colonial to independent Gambia was Edward Francis Small, an Aku, born in Bathurst in 1891.[19] Educated in the Methodist High School in Freetown, he worked first in the Post Office, became a teacher in 1915 and later a clergyman with the Methodist Mission.[20] His early experience of missionary education following by employment within the colonial state was paralleled by other educated people within the empire. It was what became known as the Ballanghar Incident that resulted in him becoming a critic of empire and calling for self-government in 1920. As a Methodist clergyman in Sukutu, he had given instructions that the church bell should be rung to call the faithful to church on New Year's Eve but this annoyed James Walker, a British merchant living in the village. The result was a heated argument that degenerated into a fight between the two men. This and criticism he made of another English clergyman led to him losing his position in the church and caused Small to

---

[19] The Aku form a minority ethnic group in Gambia with roots among the Sierra Leone Creole. In Sierra Leone, Muslim Creoles are known as Akus, while in the Gambia the term Aku refers to the entire Creole population.

[20] Grey-Johnson, Nana, *Edward Francis Small: Watchdog of The Gambia*, (BPMRU), 2002, is the only available biography. See also, Perfect, D., 'The Political Career of Edward Francis Small', in Hughes, A., (ed.), *The Gambia: Studies in Society and Politics*, (University of Birmingham), 1991, pp. 64-79.

question the nature and effects of the colonial system. In 1920, he attended a conference organised by the National Congress of British West Africa (NCBWA) at Accra in the Gold Coast where he gave a speech about the right of West Africans to independent self-rule. He then returned to Bathurst where he set up a branch of the NCBWA. The establishment of branches of pan-African organisations was an important feature in the development of resistance in Africa; for instance, in Southern Rhodesia, establishing a branch of the African National Congress played an important role in the development of liberation ideologies in the 1950s and 1960s.

In the following decade, Small developed different strategies that evolved from campaigning on specific local issues, building and mobilising support for trade unions, to calling for local representative bodies and finally in obtaining representation on the Legislative Council. He was branded as an agitator with communist leanings by British colonial officials but, although Small accepted invitations to communist front organisation conferences in Europe he was, like many African nationalists ambivalent towards Marxism. Initially he campaigned on issues of importance to the citizens of Bathurst as editor and publisher of *The Gambia Outlook and Senegambian Reporter*. In 1928, the country's first trades union was established called the Bathurst Trade Unions (renamed Gambia Labour Union in 1929) and Small organised Gambia's first labour strike Small recognised that effective organisation and motivation were essential in campaigning for African representation and in 1930, the first representative institution, the Bathurst Urban District Council and Board of Health was established. Small was elected to the Legislative Council in 1942 representing the Bathurst municipal council in the legislature between 1942 and 1947 and continued his involvement in political life until his death in early 1958. Like many campaigners for greater representation, Small recognised that success depended on building a strong local base from which to attack national institutional structures.

In the 1950s, political parties emerged among the educated élite and in the Gambia as elsewhere, these gave expression to the different aspirations of different peoples within the colony and began a process of colonial democratisation.[21] The Democratic Party under Reverend J. C. Faye was formed in 1951 followed, a year later, by the Muslim Congress under the leadership of I. M. Garba Jahumpa and the United Party (UP) under P.S. Njie that led the poll in elections to the Legislative Council in 1954. In 1959, the People's Progressive Party (PPP) was formed with a genuine grassroots programme and was led by Dawda Kairaba Jawara, a former veterinary officer. It coincided with the constitution of 1960 that extended voting rights to the people of the colony. At the elections held in 1960 the two main contenders were the UP and the PPP both of which won 8 seats. Due to the lack of provision of a Chief Minister to oversee the various new government departments the Governor, Edward Windley, decided to appoint P. S. Njie in 1961 when most chiefs showed their support for him. This led to the resignation of Jawara as the Minister of Education and precipitated a political crisis. To find a way out of the political

[21] Nyang, S. S., *The Role of Gambian Political Parties in National Integration*, (University of Virginia), 1974.

impasse, the colonial government held constitutional conferences in Bathurst and London during 1961. The outcome of the talks was the 1962 constitution that heralded the way for internal self-rule. In the resultant general election in May 1962, the PPP beat the UP winning 17 of the 25 Protectorate and 1 of the Colony seats giving Jawara and absolute majority in Parliament. Independence followed in 1965 when The Gambia was admitted to the Commonwealth as an independent constitutional monarchy with Queen Elizabeth II as the nominal Head of State. Shortly after, the government held a referendum proposing than an elected president replace the Queen as head of state but this failed to get the two-thirds majority required to amend the constitution. Following on a second successful referendum, Gambia became a republic on 24 April 1970.

The experience of Gambia exemplifies the ways in which independence was achieved through legitimate resistance and constitutional means. One important explanation for this was the lack of ethnic or religious conflict within the colony. The main ethnic groups in Gambia, the Mandinka, Fula, Wolof, Jola and Serahule preserved their own languages and customs. But despite this ethnic and cultural diversity, relations between the different ethnic groups are generally harmonious unlike other colonies where instability and civil strike, often fuelled by nationalist politicians, was a defining feature of colonial resistance.[22] About 90 per cent of the population was Muslim and the remainder Christian, both the consequence of the efforts of Muslim and Christian missionaries before and during British rule and one of the main legacies of colonial rule was a climate of religious pluralism and tolerance. Gambian politics was dominated by educated Africans living in and around the colonial capital and because most people in the Protectorate were poor, largely uneducated and under the tutelage of their conservative chiefs until the mid-twentieth century, rural peasants did not get involved in political activity and were only dragged into political participation after independence became a reality. The emergence of political parties helped to crystallise thinking about the future constitutional direction of the colony as well as providing a framework within which different political strategies could be explored. With elections to national bodies, the next development was the development of constitutional conferences to establish the route-map towards self-government and independence.

This was not the experience of all colonies and for some reform, self-government or independence was only achieved and in some cases not achieved after a period of armed struggle where those disillusioned with or never part of institutional politics sought to impose their solution on an unwilling colonial authority. For instance, Mau Mau had its origins, not in some spasm of anti-colonial violence but in a circumscribed conflict involving a set of four legally committed political actors: Kenyan colonial authorities, British officials, Kenya's white settler community and disillusioned African nationalists. The response of colonial and imperial institutions proved crucial in explaining this situation. If local grievances were carefully handled, it was possible to prevent the situation degenerating into resistance and rebellion. It depended what the grievances were and how far they challenged the hegemony of the colonial state. Questions of

[22] On this issue see, Mwakikagile, Godfrey, *The Gambia and its People: Ethnic Identities and Cultural Integration in Africa*, (New Africa Press), 2011, pp. 1-8.

land, taxation, convict resistance and rebellion, slave rebellion and guerrilla activity were areas where colonial governments were rarely prepared to make accommodations with those who were protesting because they challenged both the authority and legitimacy of the state and the ability of the state to expand economically. The approach may have differed colony to colony, as for instance in the aggressive approach towards Aboriginals compared to the initially more consensual approach adopted towards Māori but the outcome was the same, the coercive expropriation of native lands. In the case of armed struggle, there was no colonial equivocation. The exception was the Rum Rebellion in 1808 that began and essentially remained within institutional politics. The establishment in NSW decided to rid itself of an inconvenient and, from their perspective, tyrannical governor and this enabled them to manipulate Bligh's successors until constitutional norms were restored with the arrival of Lachlan Macquarie as Governor in 1811

When examining the move from resistance to rebellion, four connected institutional processes are evident. Initially, there was mobilisation of support often evident in demonstrations such as those in Cyprus in 1931; these could be spontaneous and largely unplanned or a deliberate part of the process of raising grievances with the colonial authorities. This tended to be followed by a hardening of political identity through growing consciousness of grievances and commitment to remedying them. This helped to broaden support for reform and heightened divisions within colonial and non-colonial political élite s. The emergence of Patriots and Loyalists within settler society in the years before the American War of Independence significantly weakened the colonial authorities and brought about a situation of divided sovereignty or an alternative view of what sovereignty was. The next stage involves the formation of coalitions of support in which weak social and political groups combine to face powerful, entrenched opponents. The attempt by slaves to seek support from Maroon groups is an example of this but, as the case of ZANU and ZAPU demonstrated in Zimbabwe this often proved difficult especially where the groups involve claimed parity of support. Finally, resistance became polarised when the political and social space between protagonists widened, individuals and groups vacated the moderate centre ground and the authorities adopted a repressive approach to protest. Under these circumstances a move from resistance, whether legitimate or not, into open rebellion can occur.[23]

Contesting identities

Central to the tendentious relationship between colonists and colonised is identity. Both individual and group identities have multiple layers, the significance of which varies between cultures and within the experience of individual cultures. Identity was fundamental to the colonial relationship since it determined how different parties within a colony viewed each other and played a major role in how different peoples within a colony reacted to each other. For instance, in colonies in which slavery was fundamental to the economy, the

[23] See, Tarrow, Sidney, and Tilly, Charles, 'Contentious Politics and Social Movements', in Boix, Carles, and Stokes, Susan C., (eds.), *The Oxford Handbook of Comparative Politics*, (Oxford University Press), 2007, pp. 435-460.

relationship between free whites and unfree blacks was defined by clear views of how the other will respond in certain situations establishing clear social parameters in which behaviour was judged and actions taken. There was an expectation that certain types of behaviour would lead to certain, established responses. Escaped slaves expected to be punished severely if they were recaptured but this did not prevent them from planning to escape. In societies where religious belief was central to determining identity, behaviour was based on the view that there was a transcendental world that was superior to or more important than the actual world. This impacted on colonial relationships especially where the non-colonial world was threatened with change by the colonial authorities and the religiosity of identity challenged. Resistance in this context, and this was illustrated in the Xhosa cattle killing, Pai Marire and Riel's rebellion in 1885, was a defence of traditional values against the pervasive modernisation of colonialism. Non-colonial identity institutionalised alienation from the colonial state where individual and group expectations were consistently lowered and where resistance and rebellion were a reassertion of their identity against colonial authority.

Colonial identity developed within framework of the global imperial state and the localised colonial state. Colonists drew on the social and cultural structures of Britain renaming territory after familiar places or individuals such as Sydney, New York, Melbourne and Kingston. Their language was that of the homeland and every aspect of settler society was modelled on this distant and, to some degree, controlling metropole. Both imperial and colonial states were buttressed by claiming to have a monopoly of the legitimate use of force. Unlike non-colonial identity, colonial identity experienced a growing tension between the over-arching but vague notion of 'Britishness' and the evolving localised colonial identity. Individuals could see themselves as British and Scottish and Australian without any sense of contradiction though over time the latter took primacy over the former and links with Britain became diluted. It was as a result of this division within colonial identity that tensions boiled over into resistance and rebellion where colonists regarded the colonial state as having exceeded its constitutional authority and failing to take account of colonists' aspirations. The Upper Canadian rebellion in 1837 and the Southern Rhodesia's UDI in 1965 exemplify this collision between unresponsive colonial and imperial states and colonial ambitions. The move towards self-government in the mid-nineteenth century in white-settler colonies was the imperial state's response to containing calls for colonial independence and cementing the economic ties essential for Britain's continued economic development and global hegemony.

There was an ideological paradox at the heart of Britain's empire. When the British moved overseas, they expected to take their passionate devotion to liberty with them. In fact, one of the reasons why some early settlers established colonies in North America was because they believed that those liberties were being strangled at home. Extending liberty to conquered native peoples and to economic migrants was another matter. White settlers may have been deeply attached to freedom for themselves but they opposed freedom for others. The result was that to be free, individuals needed to be of British origins. However, these colonial freedoms were not freely given to settlers who had to extract recognition of their rights by persuasion, resistance and even rebellion from metropolitan and colonial authorities that wished to maintain centralised control over colonial activities.[24] For instance, in VDL, a struggle emerged over the imposition of quit rents, a symbol of imperial control over land.[25] Pressed by the Colonial Office to generate more revenue, the colonial administration faced strong resistance to the payment of quit rents and were defeated by a powerful combination of landed self-interest, growing support for democratic principles and the political use of juries to vent landowners' grievances.[26] The ideology and practice of the rule of law were exported to Britain's colonies.[27] The English jurist William Blackstone, writing in 1765, maintained:

> ...if an uninhabited country be discovered and planted by English subjects, all the English laws are immediately there in force. For the law is the birthright of every subject, so wherever they go they can carry their laws with them.[28]

In the penal colony of NSW, for instance, until 1823, governors with their autocratic and extensive discretionary powers and the British government agreed that transported criminals needed to be kept under close surveillance and punished firmly and quickly if they broke the rules.[29] This was evident in the case of John Grant. Governor Philip Gidley King reacted sourly to being criticised for abusing the rule of law by John Grant, in 1805.[30] Grant had been transported in 1803 after being sentenced to death for the attempted murder of a solicitor. He had arrived in the colony with 50 hogsheads of brandy purchased in Rio and expected, given his high social status, to be put on the government pay roll. Governor King, distracted by the aftermath of the Castle Hill Rebellion of

---

[24] McLaren, John, 'The Uses of the Rule of Law in British Colonial Societies in the Nineteenth Century', in Dorsett, Shaunnagh, and Hunter, Ian, (eds.), *Law and Politics in British Colonial Thought: Transpositions of Empire*, (Palgrave Macmillan), 2010, pp. 71-90.

[25] Quit rents were effectively though not formally a tax or land tax imposed on freehold and leased land usually by government. Originally, quit rents freed tenants from the obligation to perform services that were mandatory under feudal tenure. Quit rents were frequently used by colonial administrations in the British Empire and were usually attached to land grants as a form of land tax.

[26] On this issue, see Petrow, Stefan, 'Discontent and habits of evasion', *Australian Historical Studies*, Vol. 32, (2001), pp. 240-256.

[27] For Neal, the rule of law had at least three elements: 'general rules laid down in advance, rational argument from those principles to particular cases, and, at least in a developed form, a legal system independent of the executive for adjudication of disputes involving the general rules.' These elements must be applied in the everyday working of the legal system and not be used by the governing classes for rhetorical effect or only when convenient to their interests. See, Neal, David, *The Rule of Law in a Penal Colony: Law and Power in Early New South Wales*, (Cambridge University Press), 1991, p. 67.

[28] Blackstone, William, *Commentaries on the Laws of England*, (University of Chicago Press), 1979, Vol. 1, pp. 104-105.

[29] For the debate on the kind of convicts sent to Australia, see Garton, Stephen, 'The Convict Origins Debate: Historians and the Problem of the 'Criminal Class,'' *Australian and New Zealand Journal of Criminology*, Vol. 24, (1991), pp. 24-82, and Dyster, Barrie, 'Convicts', *Labour History*, Vol. 67, (1994), pp. 74-83.

[30] On this see Cramer, Yvonne, (ed.), *This Beauteous and Wicked Place: Letter and Journals of John Grant, Gentleman Convict,* (National Library of Australia), 2000, pp. 89-153, and Lynravn, N. S., 'Grant, John (1776 -)', *ADB*, Vol. 1, pp. 469-470.

Irish convicts in 1804, was unresponsive to Grant's pleas to be allowed to land his brandy and to be granted a job. The gentleman convict reacted inadvisably when King granted him a conditional pardon in 1805, which he found to his dismay did not allow him to return to England until the close of his sentence. In high dudgeon, he wrote to the Governor and after quoting Blackstone on the rights of English subjects in 'uninhabited' lands and with a brief reference to Magna Carta, he protested:

> Now Sir! I ask you as an Independent Englishman, witnessing with astonishment the miserable state to which Thousands of Unfortunate Men are reduced in this country, by what Authority do those in power at home, by what Right do *you, make Slaves of Britons* in this distant corner of the Globe? ... [A]t your Door lies all the blood spilt in the struggle of half-starved Men for Personal Liberty in this Country.[31]

Even though Grant and several other gentlemen and political prisoners were re-transported for their temerity in accusing the Governor of despotism, they can be said to have kept the discourse and rhetoric of the rule of law alive in the colony, at least in providing a yardstick by which governmental performance should be judged. Moreover, the fact that Grant who had also directed similar sentiments to Judge-Advocate Richard Atkins[32] was called before the judge on the direction of King, convicted of sedition and sentenced to five years hard labour on Norfolk Island and VDL suggests that those in the executive recognised the potential power, and, for them, the subversive quality of this rhetoric.[33]

This repressive approach may have been justifiable for convicts, but colonists whether free settlers or ex-convicts thought they were too closely watched and demanded that the rule of law be recognised as protection against the arbitrary rule of the governor. While the colonists waged their campaign for civil and legal rights, the courts became 'a sort of broking house of power.'[34] Colonists expressed their opposition to the actions of governors, while governors sought to have their actions and authority legitimised by judicial process. They claimed 'no more than their rights as free-born Britons, rights guaranteed by the Magna Carta, Habeas Corpus, the Bill of Rights, [and] the Act of Settlement.' Seeking 'to forge a new social and political order out of the penal colony', they demanded an independent judiciary, trial by civilian, not military, jury, and representative government.[35]

Until representative institutions were introduced in NSW in 1823 and, arguably until those institutions included an element of election in the 1840s and given the highly personal nature of the gubernatorial power, the judiciary was the only body that could effectively question the authority and actions of governors.

---

[31] Ibid, Cramer, Yvonne, (ed.), *This Beauteous and Wicked Place,* p. 105; Grant to King, 1 May 1805, *HRA*, Series I, Vol. 5, p. 537.
[32] Bennett, J. M., 'Atkins, Richard (1745-1820)', *ADB*, Vol. 1, pp. 38-40.
[33] Ibid, Cramer, Yvonne, (ed.), *This Beauteous and Wicked Place,* p. 116.
[34] Ibid, Neal, David, *The Rule of Law in a Penal Colony: Law and Power in Early New South Wales*, p. 190.
[35] See, Blakeney, Michael, 'The reception of Magna Carta in NSW', *Journal of the Royal Australian Historical Society*, Vol. 65, (2), 1979, pp. 124-142.

Tensions between the judiciary and the colonial authorities emerged from the early 1810s and intensified in the 1820s and early 1830s.[36] Successive Colonial Secretaries found themselves having either to support their governor or their judges reflecting the potential conflict between their political and legal roles. The Colonial Office could and did refer the decisions of the colonial judiciary to English law officers and appeal courts but it was also prepared to recall judges whose actions it found unacceptable. This did not prevent their subsequent reappointment in other parts of the empire though the causes of the initial dismissal often reappeared. For instance, Justice John Walpole Willis was dismissed from his position in Upper Canada because he was considered too sympathetic to reformist sentiment in the colony and was prepared to make the administration accountable for its actions.[37] Willis appeared in Victoria in the early 1840s with similar consequences.[38] Similarly, Jeffrey Bent was dismissed as a judge in NSW, largely because of his awkward attitude but reappeared and caused problems in the West Indies first in Grenada then Trinidad and St Lucia and finally British Guiana.[39]

Tensions between Governor Ralph Darling and Chief Justice Sir Francis Forbes reached a peak in the late 1820s.[40] Forbes, a liberal in political and legal terms, was born not in England but in Bermuda.[41] Before going to Sydney, he had been Chief Justice of Newfoundland where he had developed a reputation as a liberal; for Governor Sir Charles Hamilton he was too liberal, because of the judge's belief that law should to some extent reflect and respond to local conditions.[42] Forbes served less than five years on the bench in Newfoundland and his judgments checked the abuse of power by officials, established Newfoundlanders' rights to own property in the island. A major area of conflict between Darling and Forbes was over freedom of the press and the Governor's petulance towards radicalism in the colony, inspired by William Charles Wentworth, who was vocal in his campaign for trial by jury and representative legislative organs to give colonists a voice in the administration of justice and their

---

[36] Ford, L., and Roberts, D. A., ''Mr Peel's Amendments' in New South Wales: Imperial Criminal Reform in a Distant Penal Colony', *The Journal of Legal History*, Vol. 37, (2016), pp. 198-214.

[37] Wilson, Alan, 'John Walpole Willis', *DCB*, Vol. 10, pp. 704-707.

[38] Behan, H. F., *Mr. Justice J. W. Willis: with particular reference to his period as first resident judge in Port Phillip 1841-1843*, (Glen Iris), 1979.

[39] The commentary in *HRA* stated that Bent was not considered 'blameworthy' by the British government that chose to employ him elsewhere: *HRA*, Series I, Vol. 9, p, 864. See also, Currey, C. H., 'Bent, Ellis (1783-1815)' and 'Bent, Jeffrey (1781-1852)', *ADB*, Vol. 1, pp. 87-92.

[40] Bennett, J. M., *Sir Francis Forbes: First Chief Justice on New South Wales 1824-1837*, (Federation Press), 2001, pp. 16-37. See also, Currey, C. H., 'Forbes, Sir Francis (1784-1841)', *ADB*, Vol. 1, pp. 392-399, and Holloway, Ian, 'Sir Francis Forbes and the Earliest Australian Public Law Cases', *Law and History Review*, Vol. 22, (2004), pp. 209-242.

[41] On Forbes, see Castles, Alex C., *An Australian Legal History*, (Law Book Co.), 1982, pp. 182-184.

[42] On his period in Newfoundland, see O'Flaherty, Patrick, 'Sir Francis Forbes', *DCB*, Vol. 7, pp. 301-304.

own governance. Wentworth and fellow journalist Edward Smith Hall[43] labelled Darling as a tyrant.[44] The Attorney-General, Saxe Bannister unsuccessfully and ineptly sought to prosecute them for seditious libel, an offence open to repressive use even in England.[45] Darling then sought to muzzle the press using suggestions from Lieutenant-Governor Sir George Arthur in VDL: a licence revocable at the governor's will had already been submitted to Brisbane who on Forbes' advice declined to sanction it.[46] Initially Darling did not follow Arthur's example until, angered by the criticisms of the *Monitor* and the *Australian*, he submitted legislation to Forbes for his certificate as prescribed in the 1823 Act. Using a broad interpretation of existing constitutional doctrine and a political construction to the rule of law, Forbes refused certificate six clauses as he believed them inconsistent with English law, a view later upheld by the law officers of the Crown.[47] However, he did certify the other clauses and they became law as the Newspaper Regulating Act. Forbes found no objection in law to a newspaper stamp tax and gave his certificate, expecting that, once the level of the tax was determined, the bill would be returned to him for further certification. This was not done and Forbes maintained that these actions contravened the 1823 Act and that the 4d tax was too high intimating that, if the Act were challenged before the Supreme Court, he would declare it invalid, an opinion the authorities in London later upheld.[48] Forbes was not prepared to allow the colony to continue with a form of government that allowed repressive action and in which the governor was not subject to any local authority other than his own.[49]

In Upper Canada, by contrast, judges adopted a different attitude towards the rule of law. There was a close association between the judiciary and the colonial executive and a blurring of the political and judicial roles of the judges emerged after the War of 1812, coming to a head in the 1820s. The members of the 'Family Compact' and especially lawyer later judge, John Beverley Robinson, were unalterably wedded to the imperial connection, believed passionately in the need to replicate the values of the late-eighteenth century British constitution and were arch-conservative in political and social ideology. They were strong supporters of a limited, formal definition of the rule of law and were opposed to constitutional change in the colony, especially if it would rob

[43] See, Kenny, M. J. B., 'Hall, Edward Smith (1786-1860)', *ADB*, Vol. 1, pp. 500-502, and Ferguson, J. A., 'Edward Smith Hall and the "Monitor"', *Journal of the Royal Australian Historical Society*, Vol. 17, (3), (1931), pp. 163-200.

[44] On this see Darling's comments in a letter to Under Secretary Horton, 15 December 1826, *HRA*, Series I, Vol. 12, pp. 761-762.

[45] Currey, C. H., 'Bannister, Saxe (1790-1877)', *ADB*, Vol. 1, pp. 55-56.

[46] Darling to Under Secretary Hay, 4 December 1826, *HRA*, Series I, Vol. 12, pp. 725-729.

[47] *HRA*, Series I, Vol. 13, pp. 285-287, covers the disallowed clauses; see also pp. 289-297, for Forbes' reasons.

[48] Darling to Bathurst 29 May 1827, *HRA*, Series I, Vol. 13, pp. 374-379; Darling to Bathurst 30 May 1827, pp. 380-387.

[49] Waterhouse, Richard, '...a bastard offspring of tyranny under the guise of liberty: Liberty and Representative Government in Australia, 1788-1901', in Greene, Jack, P., (ed.), *Exclusionary Empire: English Liberties Overseas 1600-1900*, (Cambridge University Press), 2009, pp. 220-247.

them of power and influence and afford unnecessary legal protection to radicals and other political dissidents.[50] This group was hostile to the United States and to any expression of republican and even democratic sentiments. Operating variously as law officers of the Crown, judges and members of executive and legislative councils and assemblies they were prepared to manipulate the administration of justice to secure their own interests.[51] In Upper Canada the threat to the rule of law until after the 1837 Rebellion, even in a narrow sense, was from the political and legal conservative élite who normally had the ear of the Lieutenant-Governor. Opposition was based on more liberal and democratic notions of constitutionalism and the rule of law and was located both within the legal profession and the Legislative Assembly.

Resistance to autocratic rule came from legislative bodies and from the courts. The contrasting approaches to rights in NSW and Upper Canada were broadly resolved with the introduction of values of English law to the colonies and responsible government. Constitutional argument and the protection of rights shifted more clearly into the legislative sphere in Australia as it already had in Canada. The definition of rights became increasingly a feature of legislation while the adjudication of the rule of law became more clearly a court-based and legal doctrine within the framework of judicial independence and political neutrality. However, disputes between upper and lower legislatures in several Australian colonies periodically produced legislative stalemate and helped preserve a more overtly political role for the courts in Australia than, at the time, was true in Canada.[52]

Resistance to autocracy did not prevent settlers from attempting to imitate the class structures of Britain. From the outset, there was a tension in Australia between those who wished to construct a replica of the hierarchical society that existed in Britain and the liberties of the 'free-born Englishman'.[53] In the United States, a rapidly moving frontier encouraged relatively small, prosperous independent farmers who were the bedrock of democratic republicanism whereas in the equally expansive Australia poorly-watered land did not benefit smallholders, and conditions favoured the hierarchical societies of South America. Grazing sheep, the most profitable form of farming favoured large landowners, linked land to political power and consequently resulted in the formation of a landowning oligarchy. Leading pastoralists, especially the Macarthurs urged the colonial authorities to develop a political and social structure based on a landed hierarchy as a safeguard against democratic ideas that took early root in the colony. The growth of the wool industry transformed the economies of NSW and VDL and was accompanied by consolidation of the power of the landed classes, a tentative colonial aristocracy of Australian

---

[50] On the influence of John Beverley Robinson, see Brode, Patrick, *Sir John Beverley Robinson: Bone and Sinew of the Compact,* (University of Toronto Press), 1984.

[51] See Romney, Paul, *Mr. Attorney: The Attorney General for Ontario in Court, Cabinet and Legislature 1791-1899,* (University of Toronto Press), 1986, pp. 62-157.

[52] See, Davidson, Alaistair, *The Invisible State: The Formation of the Australian State 1788-1901*, (Cambridge University Press), 1991.

[53] Atkinson, Alan, 'The Free-Born Englishman Transported: Convict Rights as a Measure of Eighteenth-Century Empire', *Past & Present*, Vol. 144, (1994), pp. 88-115, considers the problematic nature of rights and transportation.

'shepherd kings' who dominated Australian society into the 1860s.[54] Yet the systematic sale of land from 1831 resulted in increasing numbers of free settlers and the nature of colonial society began to change. A growing free urban bourgeois population confronted the political dominance of the pastoralists over control of the Legislative Council and this led to calls for properly representative government in the colony. Attacked by conservatives as incompatible with the British Constitution, supporters of a more democratic system appealed for political reform by restating their commitment to 'the inherent birthright of Englishmen'.

Increasingly people concluded that Australian colonial government was out of step with British colonial rule. Critical in this process was William Charles Wentworth whose *A Statistical, Historical and Political Description of the Colony of New South Wales*, was published in 1819.[55] Wentworth voiced disgust with the 'aristocratic body' in NSW 'which would monopolise all situations of power, dignity and emolument, and put themselves in a posture to domineer alike over the governor and the people'.[56] Such people aimed at converting 'the great body of the people into an hereditary deformity'.[57] Wentworth outlined a series of positive reforms that echoed American colonial demands and grievances of the 1770s: an elected assembly of small property holders and a nominated legislative council; equal rights for emancipists; trial by jury and a satisfactory process of appeal; an end to press censorship; and, no taxation without representation.[58] Links between assaults on liberties in both the Old and the New World were made, especially in the third and significantly amended edition of his work, published in 1824 where Wentworth clarified his position. He explained that some colonists might be prepared to follow the example of American independence if their pleas were ignored. If Britain showed it had learned nothing from the American Revolution, Australians would be forced to discard their 'intolerable yoke' and place themselves 'under the government of more just and considerate rulers'.[59] His rationale found wide acceptance amongst his more radical native colleagues throughout the 1820s as they gradually realised the power and influence of a strident colonial press. *Statistical Description* established the effectiveness of America's example as a device to put pressure on

---

[54] Atkinson, Alan, 'Time, Place and Paternalism: Early Conservative Thinking in New South Wales', *Australian Historical Studies*, Vol. 23, (1988), pp. 1-18, surveys this development.

[55] Melbourne, A. C. V., *William Charles Wentworth*, (Biggs & Company), 1932, and Tink, Andrew, *William Charles Wentworth: Australia's greatest native son*, (Allen & Unwin), 2009, provides contrasting biographical studies. See also, Persse, Michael, 'Wentworth, William Charles (1790-1872)', *ADB*, Vol. 2, pp. 582-589.

[56] Wentworth, W. C., *A Statistical, Historical and Political Description of the Colony of New South Wales*, (G. & W.B. Whittaker), 1819, p. 346.

[57] Ibid, Wentworth, W. C., *A Statistical, Historical and Political Description of the Colony of New South Wales*, p. 348.

[58] Ibid, Wentworth, W. C., *A Statistical, Historical and Political Description of the Colony of New South Wales*, pp. 336-380.

[59] Ibid, Wentworth, W. C., *A Statistical, Historical and Political Description of the Colony of New South Wales*, pp. 241-242.

the colonial authorities, and was for many years the decisive source for those colonials who envisaged an independent future.

Despite his rhetoric, Wentworth was no revolutionary. He was fundamentally a Whig and believed in obtaining political concessions within the framework of a British constitution that was rooted in tradition and buttressed by a landed élite.[60] *Statistical Description* was no treatise for an independent Australian republic. Democracy had no place in Wentworth's plans. Landed property, he maintained, constituted 'the only standard by which the right either of electing, or being elected, can in any country be properly regulated'.[61] During the 1830s, he became the increasingly reactionary spokesperson of the claims of property and education for the moulding of a suitable governing class defending the emergent squattocracy against the claims of free settlers agitating for more land. Though he referred as late as 1833 to government chosen by the 'people', he meant government in the hands of his own class.[62] He wanted an educated ruling minority, one constitutionally validated and rich enough to resist the perils of democracy. With Australia Day, 1842, only a week away, the *Australian* pronounced:

> Mr Wentworth is one of those persons who was an influential man. His day is gone by. His opinion is worth nothing He stands alone and is altogether disregarded. Certainly he first taught the natives of this colony what liberty was, but he has betrayed them since and they have withdrawn their confidence in him.[63]

Wentworth's influence did not decline. In fact, for at least the next decade he was as powerful as any single man, other than the governor, in the colony. But his doctrines gained energetic support only from his social equals.

By the 1850s, democracy had become 'the great beast' and Wentworth sought to justify why it had to be tamed. In turning to Alexis de Tocqueville for endorsement, he was only repeating a pattern that had been established in Britain over the previous two decades. British writers such as Adam Hodgson in his *Letters from North America* (1824), William Hazlitt in the later 1820s and Thomas Hamilton in *Men and Manners*, had already singled out several dangerous features of American democracy but it was undoubtedly Tocqueville's *Democracy in America* that exerted the most profound impact on the British public and on its readership of the British colonies as well.[64] Extensive references to *Democracy in America* allowed Wentworth in his speech during the second reading of the Constitution Bill in August 1853 to confirm the effect, as he puts it, of 'this system of democracies on the social condition of the people of

---

[60] Buck, A. R., '"This remnant of feudalism": Primogeniture and political culture in Colonial New South Wales, with some Canadian comparisons', in McLaren, John, and Buck, A. R., and Wright, Nancy E., (ed.), *Despotic dominion: property rights in British settler societies*, (University of British Columbia Press), 2005, pp. 169-189.

[61] Ibid, Wentworth, W. C., *A Statistical, Historical and Political Description of the Colony of New South Wales*, p. 338.

[62] 'Saturday's Public Meeting!'*Australian*, 1 February 1833, p. 3.

[63] 'Editorial', *Australian*, 18 January 1842, p. 2.

[64] Crook, D. P., *American Democracy in English Politics 1815-1850*, (Oxford University Press), 1965, pp. 166-198.

America'.[65] Wentworth developed his case to damn democracy around selective argument for two reasons: Tocqueville's prestige as a commentator on democracy and the fact that, according to Wentworth, Tocqueville, 'so deeply...imbued with democratic prejudices', could nonetheless judge the American example as resulting in a 'degrading tyranny'. Wentworth applied Tocqueville to the Australian situation in the same way that Sir Robert Peel used him in Britain to lay 'the foundations of the great party of conservative resistance, after the popular movement of 1832'.[66] Peel viewed *Democracy in America* as a Tory book, quoting extensively from it in 1835 during the Commons debate on election bribery and again in 1837. Wentworth did not get his hereditary peerage in 1853 but in the debates, he had expressed the arguments for a traditional polity based largely in a fear of democracy.

An Australian aristocracy had no foundation in tradition and lacked an ideological base in a polity that increasingly looked to an Enlightenment-based conception of rights. The attempt to link political rights to property slowed the process of change but was ultimately eroded by the fluid nature of wealth in the colonies that obliged the nascent social élite to mix with a rapidly changing monied élite. Its defeat represented the failure of the aspiring Australian gentry to justify maintaining a hierarchical ordering of society in Australian conditions that were being transformed by the discovery of gold and the influx of gold-seekers in the 1850s. Wentworth's attempt to establish an Australian version of Edmund Burke's defence of a hierarchical society as a bulwark against despotism and a defence of civilised virtues was resisted and crumbled in a political culture sufficiently confident in its institutions to be unconvinced of the need for checks on democratic change. Australia, with its large pastoral holdings may not have been a natural seedbed for democracy but the development of a shared language of rights that inhibited the transfer of hierarchical society provided the social basis for what eventually emerged as a democracy.[67]

Legislative and administrative repression was regularly used to control all aspects of colonial society. White people, especially if they were middle-class, were not simply protected by the police, they were the police. The tensions that existed in Britain between police and public were replicated in the colonies.[68] In broad terms, the colonies adopted the 'English' model for urban policing and the

---

[65] Sylvester, Edward Kennedy, (ed.), *New South Wales Constitution Bill: The Speeches in the Legislative Council of New South Wales on the Second Reading of the Bill for Framing a New Constitution for the Colony*, (Thomas Daniel), 1853, pp. 41, 45, 47-48, 56, 61.

[66] Ibid, Sylvester, Edward Kennedy, (ed.), *New South Wales Constitution Bill...*, p. 169.

[67] Jones, Benjamin Thomas,' Colonial Republicanism: Re-examining the Impact of Civic Republican Ideology in Pre-Constitution New South Wales', *Journal of Australian Colonial History*, Vol. 11, (2009), pp. 129-147.

[68] Jeffries, Sir Charles, *The Colonial Police*, (Max Parrish), 1952, is despite its limitations, the only general history. For more revisionist studies, see, Brogden, Michael, 'An Act to Colonise the Internal Lands of the Island: Empire and the Origins of the Professional Police', *International Journal of the Sociology of Law*, Vol. 15, (1987), pp. 179-208, Anderson, D. M., and Killingray, David, (eds.), *Policing and the Empire: Government, Authority, and Control, 1830-1940*, (Manchester University Press), 1991, and Emsley, Clive, *The Great British Bobby: A history of British policing from the 18th century to the present*, (Quercus), 2009, pp. 104-111.

'Irish' model for rural policing although the sharpness of this distinction has justifiably been questioned.[69] The realities of colonial policing were far less neat and more pragmatic. Colonies, especially rural areas, were not heavily policed with a single European officer, supported by locally recruited and untrained constables, responsible for a large tract of territory. Forces in colonial Africa adopted structures of command and organisation from the 'Irish' model but not for training, method or development while in India policing both models were used. The realities of colonial policing meant that models of policing played a less significant role in establishing colonial control than the rhetoric suggests.[70] Both the New Zealand Police and the Canadian North-West Mounted Police were initially largely paramilitary forces tasked with pacifying the frontier ahead of settlers before being transformed into a civil police force. The apartheid South African Police were authoritarian in their approach to the black Africa population but liberal in its approach to the white population. How a colonial society was policed depended on who was being policed. When it was citizens with civil and political rights, the approach was cautious and arguably consensual but when dealing with non-citizens, the police was free to exercise naked coercive power. The police were often the symbols and instruments of colonial rule and the imposition of policing was an integral part of 'empire building'.

Relations with settlers were based on a calculated pragmatism in which it was acknowledged that attempts to impose unpopular laws rigidly would ultimately meet with resistance resulting in 'damage to the rule of law'.[71] Police administrators and the constables on their beats were required to tread carefully between the demands and expectations of 'respectable' society and the practical need for good relations with the working-class.[72] The police were, for varying reasons and at certain times, unpopular that stemmed from public:

> ...suspicion of the police as an alien force outside the control of the community; resentment at police interference in attempting to regulate traditionally sanctioned behaviour; [and] objections to expense.[73]

In the early decades of NSW, the police system was decentralised. Lay magistrates in rural areas controlled the police and had discretion to decide 'what would and would not be policed' using their powers to protect their class interests and relying upon flogging to enforce order.[74] The assistance of the

---

[69] See, the editorial introduction of ibid, Anderson, D. M., and Killingray, David, (eds.), *Policing and the Empire*, pp. 3-6.

[70] Williams, C., and Sinclair, G., ''Home and Away'; the Cross Fertilisation between 'Colonial' and 'British' Policing, 1921-1985', *Journal of Imperial and Commonwealth History*, Vol. 35, (2007), pp. 221-238, considers later developments.

[71] Inwood, S., 'Policing London's Morals: The Metropolitan Police and Popular Culture, 1829-1850', *London Journal*, Vol. 15, (2), (1990), p. 134.

[72] Ibid, Inwood, S., 'Policing London's Morals…', p. 131.

[73] Weinberger, B., 'The Police and the Public in Mid-nineteenth-century Warwickshire', in Bailey, V., (ed.), *Policing and Punishment in Nineteenth Century Britain*, (Croom Helm), 1981, p. 65.

[74] Ibid, Neal, David, *The Rule of Law in a Penal Colony: Law and Power in Early New South Wales*, p. 163.

military was necessary to quell large-scale disorder, but they were not used for ordinary policing duties. Reflecting the characteristics of the population, most policemen were convicts. In 1823, J. T. Bigge, charged with making transportation more of a deterrent for English criminals, reported to the Colonial Office that police organisation was defective and recommended centralised control rather than retaining local control by unpaid magistrates.[75]

Because magistrates were unwilling to relinquish control of the police, a number of changes were made to weaken their power in 1825, creating a system of divided control. The mounted police, composed mainly of soldiers, was formed to deal with bushrangers and Indigenous Australians. Captain F. N. Rossi became the head of the Sydney police, whose existence was made official by the Sydney Police Act of 1833, a statute based on the London Metropolitan Police Act of 1829. In the absence of local government, the Sydney police were required to assume a range of urban functions. In the 1820s and 1830s, police reform in NSW was a compromise between the English and the more militaristic Irish models, modified to meet the exigencies of a large convict population, the activities of bushrangers, the resistance of the Aboriginals and a growing urban population.[76] In addition to the police, overseers, masters, and private informers ensured that the colonists enjoyed 'a level of surveillance more akin to a penal colony than the society they knew in England.'[77]

Bigge's report influenced thinking about police arrangements in VDL, the second Australian penal colony, far more than in NSW.[78] Governor George Arthur created a more highly centralised policing system and controlled the police, mainly comprised of convicts, through paid magistrates, responsible directly to him.[79] He saw himself as the servant of empire, answerable only to the British government and not local colonists and became the foremost supporter of the benefits of transportation.[80] Feeling that a penal colony was 'an unnatural condition' because 'virtue' was subordinate to 'crime', Arthur believed he had no

---

[75] Ibid, Neal, David, *The Rule of Law in a Penal Colony: Law and Power in Early New South Wales*, pp. 148-149.

[76] King, Hazel, 'Some Aspects of Police Administration in New South Wales, 1825-1851', *Royal Australian Historical Society*, Vol. 42, (4), (1956), pp. 205-230, Sturma, Michael, 'Policing the Criminal Frontier in Mid-Century Australia, Britain, and America', in Finnane, Mark, (ed.), *Policing in Australia: Historical Perspectives*, (University of New South Wales Press), 1987, pp. 15-34, and Finnane, Mark, *Police and Government: Histories of Policing in Australia*, (Oxford University Press), 1994, chapter 1.

[77] Ibid, Neal, David, *The Rule of Law in a Penal Colony: Law and Power in Early New South Wales*, p. 54.

[78] Petrow, Stefan, 'Policing in a Penal Colony: Governor Arthur's Police System in Van Diemen's Land, 1826-1836', *Law and History Review*, Vol. 18, (2000), pp. 351-395, and 'After Arthur: Policing in Van Diemen's Land 1837-46', in Enders, Mike and Dupont, Benoît, (eds.), *Policing the lucky country*, (Hawkins Press), 2002, pp. 176-198.

[79] Arthur, George, *Observations Upon Secondary Punishments*, (James Ross), 1833, and *Defence of Transportation, in Reply to the Remarks of the Archbishop of Dublin in His Second Letter to Earl Grey*, (Gowie), 1835.

[80] *Report from the Select Committee on Transportation, Together with the Minutes of Evidence, Appendix, and Index*, (Irish University Press), 1968, Vol. 2, Appendix, p. 2, Arthur to Howick, 18 February 1832; Chapman, Peter, 'The Island Panopticon', *Historical Records of Australia: A Documentary Periodical*, number 1, (1990), pp. 6-10.

choice but to rule the colony as a jail. His police reforms and their operation made VDL a more intensively policed society than NSW.

Making order his aim, Arthur expected colonists to forgo their rights and liberties in the interests of making transportation a feared punishment and in exchange for the security of person and property that he provided.[81] The majority of colonists, especially those in the interior, resigned themselves to this policy and followed his commands for two reasons.[82] They appreciated the security that Arthur provided after years of anarchy, funded not by local taxes but by the Crown. Given the shortage of free labourers, they feared losing the cheap convict labour that Arthur could withdraw whenever he liked. But those colonists who did not rely on convict servants for their wealth or who had fallen out with Arthur, mainly the residents of the colony's capital Hobart Town, felt that the benefits of transportation were purchased at too high a price and became hostile to attacks on their liberty.[83] They echoed their NSW counterparts by demanding a greater say in determining the colony's future and the rights of freeborn Englishmen railing against what they saw as arbitrary and unjust government interference. Newspapers published in Hobart Town and Launceston were watchdogs of arbitrary government and outspoken proponents of the rights of the people. In 1826, the *Colonial Times,* which regularly referred to 'free-born British subjects,' wrote:

> It must be recollected that we are in these Colonies, as far as our rights go, in England. By the privileges of our birth, the British Law is the only one to which we are subjected. Every immunity possessed by our brethren in England is also equally possessed by us *de jure,* notwithstanding many of them are withheld *de facto.* But when they are withheld, it is by the effect of the Law, specially enacted for that purpose.[84]

For Englishmen, there was:

> ...a natural feeling imbibed with our birth, cherished with our youth, and matured in our riper years which forbids our ever sinking to that abject state of being governed by absolute power or of becoming the slaves of despotism.[85]

As its central aim was to strengthen the authority of the governor and the rule of law as a protection of free citizens was compromised at all levels of the legal system in VDL. Under Arthur's autocratic rule, the nominated Legislative Council, judges of the Supreme Court, paid magistrates and the police generally placed the orderly management of the convict system ahead of rights and

---

[81] Giblin, R. W., *The Early History of Tasmania*, (Melbourne University Press), 1939, Vol. 2, p. 629.

[82] Forsyth, W. D., *Governor Arthur's Convict System: Van Diemen's Land, 1824-36*, (Sydney University Press), 1970, pp. 109, 126-129.

[83] *Report from the Select Committee on Transportation; together with Minutes of Evidence, Appendix, and Index*, (Irish University Press), 1968, pp. 117, 225, West, John, *The History of Tasmania*, (Angus and Robertson), 1971, p. 122, and ibid, Giblin R. W., *The Early History of Tasmania*, Vol. 2, pp. 420-421, 605.

[84] 'Editorial', *Colonial Times,* 28 April 1826, p. 2, 'Editorial', *Colonial Times,* 26 May 1826, p. 2.

[85] 'Editorial', *Colonial Times,* 16 February 1827, pp. 2, 3.

liberties. In the courts, colonists contested arbitrary uses of police power and employed the language of the rule of law when arguing for their rights or defending their liberties. But they realised that the paid magistrates gave prime consideration to convict order and discipline and supported police action unless the evidence clearly demonstrated they had acted illegally or arbitrarily. Police work had an important bearing on whether in practice the rule of law could curb arbitrary power. Not only did the police threaten liberty by treating colonists unequally and unjustly, they also enforced the law, made 'its orders meaningful' and constituted its 'coercive function'.[86]

Centralisation was adopted in all the mainland Australian colonies by 1863 (Tasmania had introduced a decentralised system in 1858 and retained in until 1898) and by New Zealand in stages in 1867 and 1877.[87] The existence of a large convict and ex-convict population, a recalcitrant native population, the problems caused by the discovery of gold and the persistent problem of bushrangers led to the formation of powerful centralised forces that were key agents of the colonial state in establishing social order. This centralised system of policing proved less popular in Canada where policing had a strong local emphasis. Canadian municipal policing was modelled primarily on the London Metropolitan Police, whereas the North-West Mounted Police used the more militaristic Royal Irish Constabulary.[88] Even in Quebec, where the French influence was of importance, public police were organised on the British model. By 1900, there were separate municipal, provincial and federal police forces. The development of intense control over local populations paralleled developments in Britain and Australia. For instance, in York (later Toronto) in 1823, there was one constable to every 75 inhabitants although this had been reduced to one constable for every 291 inhabitants by 1830. The high number of constables was not a consequence of a particularly high crime rate but by their various civic functions such as enforcement of produce and meat market regulations, livestock and animal control, tavern licensing, regulation of carters, health and fire safety and responsibilities for the surrounding area. The police not only suppressed riots but within the various nineteenth-century municipal police forces, Irish immigrants and former Royal Irish Constabulary officers played a large role. This did not always lead to impartial policing. In Toronto, for instance, the largely Orange police force developed a case of collective amnesia after an Orange crowd attacked a St. Patrick's Day dinner at the National Hotel in 1858; the magistrate who investigated the case, himself an Orangeman, publicly condemned those officers who put their fraternal loyalties above the law. Tory politicians routinely used the police to suppress meetings of opposition Reform

---

[86] Ibid, Neal, David, *The Rule of Law in a Penal Colony: Law and Power in Early New South Wales*, p. 143.

[87] On policing the NZ, see the work of Hill, R. S., *Policing the Colonial Frontier: The Theory and Practice of Coercive Social and Racial Control in New Zealand, 1767-1867*, (Historical Branch, Dept. of Internal Affairs), 1986, *The Colonial Frontier Tamed: New Zealand Policing in Transition, 1867-1886*, (Historical Branch, Dept. of Internal Affairs), 1989, and *The Iron Hand in the Velvet Glove: The Modernisation of Policing in New Zealand, 1886-1917*, (Historical Branch, Dept. of Internal Affairs), 1995.

[88] Marquis, G., 'The Irish Model and Nineteenth-Century Canadian Policing', *Journal of Imperial and Commonwealth History*, Vol. 25, (1997), pp. 193-218.

candidates from the 1830s. The regulatory supervision of the working-class life in Toronto increased from the late 1860s where the police were an efficient means to curb immoral behaviour, more unruly aspects of popular culture and arresting drunks and prostitutes. The Toronto Police began as a small parish watch that until 1860 was inadequate and corrupt and tightly controlled by local municipal patronage. By the end of the century, it was a complex institution serving two functions: to fight rebellion by force in the city streets and later to systematically regulate potentially rebellious classes of inhabitants. Fighting rebellion, overall, was the operative function, not preventing crime and apprehending criminals.

Political policing was also evident across the British Empire while Britain itself was slow to develop a system of state security even in the face of Fenian bombs after 1867. The profound suspicion so widespread in Victorian England of spies, spying, and secrecy found little resonance in Canada.[89] The suspension of habeas corpus, political arrests without charges, mail seizure, secret agents, perhaps even the use of agent provocateur were all present in these formatives years of the new nation-state and all went unopposed. After 1867, the federal government was suspected 'seditionists', especially Irish nationalists, who dedicated considerable intellectual and financial resources to raising people's consciousness, articulating a vision of national independence, forging links between those in exile and those at home, and taking action. In Victorian, Australia, police harassment of socialists and militant workers became widespread in the 1880s as class organisation, action, and militancy increased amongst workers.[90] Victoria's first socialist organisation, the Australian Socialist League was established in early 1889 but police forbade property owners to allow the group to use their premises to hold public meetings, arrested or threatened to arrest members selling the group's newspaper, constantly interrupted and threatened to arrest socialist speakers addressing gatherings and hired thugs to beat them up.

In the early days of colonial policing there was little distinction between police and military forces. Britain's military presence across the Empire was important in maintaining order, advancing imperial ambitions and deterring other imperial powers. The role of armed native units that were deployed against local resistance to colonisation was central to this process. India was conquered and held with the assistance of locally recruited Sepoy armies while mercenaries were used in Ceylon. In the Caribbean, former slaves were recruited for the West India Regiment and served as garrison forces there and in West Africa. The Morant Bay rebellion in 1865 was suppressed by black troops of the First West India Regiment and groups of Maroon irregulars. Native soldiers fought in the South African frontier wars until the unit was disbanded in 1870. By deploying technology such as the telegraph and wireless and air power and the ubiquitous Maxim gun, the military was generally able to defeat native forces

[89] See, for instance, Parnaby, Andrew, and Kealey, Gregory S., 'The Origins of Political Policing in Canada: Class, Law and the Burden of Empire', *Osgoode Law Journal*, Vol. 41, (2003), pp. 211-239.

[90] Victoria Police, *Police in Victoria 1836-1980*, (Victoria Police), 1980 and Haldane, R., *The People's Force: A history of the Victoria Police*, (Melbourne University Press), 1986.

although disasters such as the defeat in Afghanistan in 1842, the Zulu victory at Isandlwana in 1879 and the Boer victory at Majuba Hill two years later showed that imperial victory was not inevitable. Native Police units, less police than irregular military forces, were established in Australia specifically to suppress Indigenous Australian resistance to colonisation. Establishing the Native Police, like other military use of native recruits, took advantage of the fact that native peoples had no loyalties to other native groups and were generally posted well away from their tribal areas to prevent partiality or mutiny and reflected the importance of divide and rule in maintaining imperial control. The degree to which the empire expanded and was protected against resistance and rebellion as a consequence of cooperation and collaboration with native peoples has been underestimated.[91]

There was also a close intersection in settler societies of race and class, in which as Frantz Fanon stated, 'the cause is the consequence; you're rich because you're white, you're white because you're rich'.[92] The great divide was between white settlers and the colonised population and the maintenance of that division provided the settler state with much of its cohesion. In most settler societies, the violence of the conquest state and the divisions of colonial society were particularly acute leading to widespread resistance. In such societies, the colonised people faced onerous exclusions from economic and social opportunities including cash crop agriculture, stabilised wage labour, access to education and political representation. Consequently, they were forced to wage protracted liberation wars and after independence they faced the challenges of how to democratise the state and particularly customary power, deracialise civil society, promote native accumulation and restructure unequal external relations of dependency.

Settler colonialism was characterised by several features.[93] There was an increasing monopoly of settler control over key economic resources including land, allocation of infrastructure, banking and marketing at the expense of the indigenous people. The colonial state apparatus was superimposed on civil society not rooted in it even where under indirect rule traditional native élite s exercised administrative duties in the countryside. Settler society became increasingly white and racialist in its attitudes, a consequence of an intellectual shift from liberalism of the late-eighteenth century to notions of cultural and biological superiority in the mid-nineteenth century. Adam Smith, Edmund Burke and Jeremy Bentham were critical of European imperial expansion for the

---

[91] See, for instance, Richards, Jonathan, *The Secret War: A true history of the Queensland Native Police*, (University of Queensland Press), 2008, Fels, Marie Hansen, *Good men and true: the Aboriginal police of the Port Phillip District, 1837-1853*, (Melbourne University Press), 1988, and Bridges, B., 'The Native Police Corps, Port Phillip District and Victoria, 1837-1853', *Journal of the Royal Australian Historical Society*, Vol. 57, (1971), pp. 113-142.

[92] Fanon, Frantz, *The Damned*, (Presence africaine), 1963, p. 32.

[93] On the nature of settler colonialism, see Veracini, Lorenzo, *Settler Colonialism: A Theoretical Overview*, (Palgrave Macmillan), 2010, and Bateman, Fiona, and Pilkington, Lionel, (eds.), *Studies in Settler Colonialism: Politics, Identity and Culture*, (Palgrave Macmillan), 2011.

misery it wreaked on its conquered subjects.[94] This liberal assessment was anchored in a positive view of the capacities of non-Europeans and a 'moral respect' for cultural difference, autonomy and self-determination.[95] Smith argued that European progress was hardly an index of moral superiority justifying Britain's pejorative assessment of 'backward' societies. Edmund Burke's critique of colonies, despite his élitism and authoritarianism in domestic affairs, came not from a conservative instinct to protect traditional societies, but from a liberal commitment to the moral equality of all human beings and a rejection of the 'arbitrary and unaccountable power' colonisers had over their subjects. [96] Both Smith and Burke believed that British commercial society was beneficial, but did not believe that this made European civilisation morally superior and both had:

> ...a sense of wonder at the complexity of societies and at the unintended consequences of human action...and thus respected a multiplicity of values as rational and moral.[97]

By the 1830s, this gave way to a more imperialist variant of liberalism that was driven by a profound sense of national self-confidence and European cultural superiority, exemplified in the thought of John Stuart Mill and Alexis de Tocqueville. British theories of progress became more confident, less nuanced and less tolerant of cultural difference and British liberals became more convinced of Britain's own fitness to spread civilisation. The result was a shift from calls for emancipation to Mill's legitimising of colonial despotism. Both James Mill and his son spent much of their lives working for the East India Company and both favoured a paternalistic despotism designed for the improvement of the indigenous population of India. The pluralist theories of progress in the thought of earlier British liberals such as Smith and Burke was replaced by cultural self-confidence and an increasingly exclusive conception of national community and political capacity. For all his radicalism with regard to domestic politics, Mill was convinced that people in the 'civilised world' occupied a morally privileged position and had a legitimate right to decide the fate of people in 'backward' societies. Catherine Hall suggests:

> ...the period from the mid-1840s to the mid-1860s saw...an increasing turn to the language of race to explain and justify the inequalities and persistent differences between peoples.[98]

In late-nineteenth and early-twentieth century Canada, settler thinking was grounded in race and racial and national purity. Ideal Canadian citizens were

---

[94] This is explored in Pitts, Jennifer, *A Turn to Empire: The Rise of Imperial Liberalism in Britain and France*, (Princeton University Press), 2005, pp. 25-122.
[95] Mehta, Uday Singh, *Liberalism and Empire: a study in nineteenth-century British liberal thought*, (University of Chicago Press), 1999, by contrast, takes the view that imperialism was essential to the liberal project.
[96] Ibid, Pitts, Jennifer, *A Turn to Empire*, p. 63.
[97] Ibid, Pitts, Jennifer, *A Turn to Empire*, p. 245.
[98] Hall, Catherine, *Civilising Subjects: Metropole and Colony in the English Imagination 1830-1867*, (Polity), 2002, p. 338.

those who were born into the British race who spoke English, proclaimed a Protestant faith, were middle-class and had white skin. They lived in specific ways characterised by 'self-control, self-discipline, self-determination...self-mastery'.[99] They embraced 'property ownership, rootedness and an orderly family life'.[100] They were 'well-to-do; Church-going; English speaking'.[101] Languages spoken, faiths professed and the daily ways of living of some groups of people were targeted for replacement by British, Protestant and middle-class ways of living marked by temperance, sexual restraint and other forms of self-control. Nineteenth century colonials and the policies, laws and institutions they produced, were inherently white, patriarchal and bourgeois in nature. It appears that in Canada, this sense of moral responsibility justified efforts within the colonial institutional structure that included education, the penal system, the health and mental health system, the immigration system and Christian churches to produce Canada as a nation to protect Canadian citizens from the threat of degeneracy said to be posed by other racial groups.

For most of the nineteenth century, according to Richard White, there was no strong evidence of a distinctively Australian identity: 'Australians saw themselves, and were seen by others, as part of a group of new, transplanted, predominantly Anglo-Saxon emigrant societies'. It is significant that a sense of national distinctiveness only grew stronger towards the end of the century and that this was accompanied by 'a more explicitly racial element', based on being Anglo-Saxon or, as confidence in the new society grew, 'on being the most vigorous branch of Anglo-Saxondom'.[102] In 1844, an essay celebrated the civilising of Australia, the development of art, commerce, literature and a legislature asking:

> ...may not an Englishman point to it with pride and exultation as a proof of what English energy has accomplished, and what English industry can do? ...Australia may be considered as that part of the British Empire which the prophetic eye regards as the future seat of English power...The sun of English power may set in its present northern sphere, to rise again in the East, in another region, not less English because a mighty ocean divides it from the maternal soil.[103]

This formed the basis for a belief in the emergence of an Australian 'national type' that was given not only physical and racial characteristics, but also a moral, social and psychological identity.[104] The Australian type was believed to be a new product of the multiplying British stock, the 'race' which, in the heyday of British imperialism and legitimated by the then immensely influential ideology of Social Darwinism, saw itself as superior to all other 'races' and therefore

---

[99] Stoler, A. L., *Race and the education of desire: Foucault's history of sexuality and the colonial order of things*, (Duke University Press), 1995, p. 8.

[100] Ibid, Stoler, A. L., *Race and the education of desire*, p. 128.

[101] Anderson, J. T. M., *The education of the new-Canadian: A treatise on Canada's greatest educational problem*, (J. M. Dent & Sons), 1918, p. 27.

[102] White, Richard, *Inventing Australia*, (Allen & Unwin), 1985, p. 47.

[103] 'The March of Civilisation, or News from Australia!', *The Illuminated Magazine*, Vol. II, (January 1844), p. 1.

[104] Ibid, 'The March of Civilisation, or News from Australia!', p. 64.

possessing the duty and destiny to populate and 'civilise' the rest of the world. It is this racialist concern with a distinctively Australian type that led to the so-called White Australia Policy, sanctioned in the Immigration Restriction Bill in 1901 that unambiguously sought to preserve the 'British character' of Australian society.[105] This bill prohibited the immigration into Australia by 'non-Europeans' or 'the coloured races'. The fact that this bill was the first major legislative issue dealt with by the parliament of the newly-created Commonwealth of Australia, suggests the importance of 'racial purity' as the symbolic cement for the imagined community of the fledgling nation.[106] The emerging 'empire of race' represented the colonial-indigenous relationship in polarities such as man and nature, reason and passion, and civilised and savage, and in this process of 'othering', settlers strengthened their own identity. Indigenous culture, language, religious beliefs and law and customs were denigrated and attempts made to destroy them.

Settler colonies were quick to seek political autonomy in order to deal with the 'natives' in their own way and acquire the land they wanted. As long as colonisers in Canada made their living from trading or trapping, tensions between them and the First Nations were limited, however growing demands for agricultural land brought competition between settlers and the First Nations for scarce resources. In NSW, land was an issue for settlers from the beginnings of settlement and this resulted in almost immediate conflict with Aboriginals. Where treaties were made with native peoples such in Virginia in the 1670s, at Waitangi in 1840 and the Canadian Plains Indians in the 1870s, they were almost immediately broken by the flood of settlers or by colonial administrators eager to expand the empire. There was widespread collaboration with the colonial authorities: in Kenya, for instance, during the Mau Mau emergency, loyal Africans were deployed against the terrorists and during the 1837 and 1838 rebellions in Canada, the Iroquois worked with the authorities to contain rebel activity. But this did not prevent the inexorable spread of settler power. Settlers feared the threat of native economic competition and believed that their culture might be swamped by 'native' culture and this heightened their sense of group solidarity and cohesion and their aggressive response to native resistance. This resulted in a collision between the imperial philosophy of a non-racial empire, already in decline by the 1820s and the settlers' determination to create a 'White Man's Country'. Whether benevolent, aggressive or racist, imperialism was met with resistance.

Motive and opportunity

Given the recognised military and policing capacity of the imperial state, what incited communities to intensify their claims to political freedom from inactivity to legitimate protest to resistance and finally rebellion? There appear to be three broad explanations for resistance and rebellion. The first suggests that challenged to existing cultural, linguistic, of geographical structures provide the identity

---

[105] Willard, M., *History of the White Australia Policy to 1920*, (Melbourne University Press), 1923.

[106] Jupp James, *From White Australia to Woomera: The Story of Australian Immigration*, (Cambridge University Press), 2007, pp. 6-18, provides a succinct account of White Australia policy.

necessary to mobilise and activate support for resistance. It was colonial attacks on the basis of Māori society in the 1850s that enabled the mobilisation of tribal support for war. A second approach argues that relative deprivation in the political, cultural or economic field results in a polarisation of discontent and grievance. For instance, the perceived assault on Métis culture in the late 1870s and early 1880s played a major role in the transition from political protest to rebellion between 1882 and 1885. Finally, there is an emphasis on how political and institutional structures, especially repression, impacted on community patterns of resistance and provided opportunities for colonial conflict. The introduction of what natives regarded as repressive taxation in Sierra Leone in the late 1890s led to the 'Hut Tax War'. Existing conditions led to the development of grievances caused by relative deprivation precipitating political mobilisation that in turn resulted in resistance to colonial power. There is no necessary discontinuity between institutional and non-institutional politics and, depending on the situation, resistance and rebellion were simply a further strategic choice by communities. This depended on the means at the disposal of those in dispute with the authorities and the opportunities provided by the circumstances.[107]

Take, for instance, the tribal population of rural India where each community maintained its own social, religious and cultural life and economic and political organisations.[108] British policies disrupted these traditional tribal systems based upon communal ownership of land and the absence of landlords and between 1778 and 1947 there were more than seventy tribal revolts that were, to varying degrees, anti-colonial in character and from the late-nineteenth century were linked to and merged with the Indian National movement.[109] The British changed the land system of the tribals turning the traditional system into tenancy systems that were transferred to a previously unknown class of zamindars or landlord, generally Brahmins and Rajputs brought into the tribal areas to perform military or religious services. As landlords, they introduced land rents and market economy replacing the tribal payment of their chiefs in kind and labour. The British also introduced contractors (*Thekedars*), money lenders from whom tribals borrowed to pay their rents and government officials. Considered by the tribals as dikus or outsiders, they collaborated with the colonial administration to exploit and oppress the tribals extracting exorbitant rents and interest on loans, evicting tribals from their land and using beggar or forcible labour. Tribals retained their customary rights in the forest until 1884 when these were curtailed because the colonial authorities needed to use forest produce. Although some tribals were compensated for losses caused by deforestation, the amounts were small and overall British forest policies were

---

[107] Selbin, Eric, *Revolution, Rebellion, Resistance, The Power of Story*, (Zed Books Ltd.), 2010, examines why revolutions occur looking beyond economic, political and cultural explanations to consider the thoughts and feelings of those involved.

[108] Desai, A. R., (ed.), *Peasant Struggles in India*, (Oxford University Press), 1979, Jagannath, Pathy, *Tribal Peasantry: Dynamics of Development*, (Inter-India), 1984, and Guha, Panajit, *Elementary Aspects of Peasant Insurgency in Colonial India*, (Oxford University Press), 1983.

[109] Patel, Mahendra Lal, *Agrarian Transformation of Tribal India*, (M. D. Publications Pvt Ltd.), 1998.

detrimental to tribal interests.[110] For the tribals, their land was not only a source of food but a spiritual source given to them by their ancestors but increasingly the rights of outsiders were recognised over their land. Growing deprivation, made worse by the effects of famine, resulted in the increasing polarisation of protest. The focus of protest by the tribals was against the dikus who they considered their enemies. Landlords, money-lenders, thekedars, missionaries and officials were all targets for attack and protest frequently led to the murder of their oppressors and the burning of their houses. These attacks often had social and religious overtones but their root cause lay in the perceived attacks on their rights and ways of life.

There was widespread protest among the Santhals that evolved through three phases. Initially, protest was marked by economic clashes between landlords and tribal tenants largely over levels of rent and eviction from land combined with the inability to gaining redress through the courts. These were largely spontaneous and individual in character. Political strategies were adopted to try to achieve reform through constitutional means and only when these failed did widespread violence occur. This was followed by a millenarian phase when the population mobilised behind a charismatic leader in the hope that a past Golden Age could be restored and was accompanied by attacks on all those suspected of collaborating with landlords as part of the purification process. By 1855, the movement against landlordism had evolved from a largely agrarian protest to political protest against the unjust oppression of landlords and was also directed against village money-lenders and officials.[111] Two brothers, Sidhu and Kanhu held a meeting at Bhagnadih where they announced that their oppression could be ended by taking back their land from their oppressors. Following the meeting, thirty thousand Santhals marched armed with their traditional weapons towards Calcutta to present a petition before the Governor. This was prevented by troops and several thousand Santhals were killed in the resultant violence. The protest movement only lasted sixty days but forced the government to change its policy towards them. An area of around 5,000 square miles was established as a 'Non-Regulation' district that came to be known as 'Santhal Parganas' and an administrative head was appointed to recover the alienated land. It was fifteen years before the Santhals launched a further protest movement. The Kherwar protest movement from 1872-1882 was motivated by the desire to return to an idealised past of tribal independence and was started under the charismatic millenarian leadership of Bhagirath Majhi. He announced that the world would be restored to the Golden Age of Santhals, if they returned to the worship of God and cleared themselves from their sins. He vowed to liberate them from the oppression of officials, landlords and money-lenders and called on them to worship the Hindu God Ram, identifying him with Santhal 'Caudo'. He banned

---

[110] Sivaramakrishnan, K., *Modern Forests: Statemaking and Environmental Change in Colonial Eastern India*, (Stanford University Press), 1999, pp. 83-90, examines the importance of forests for the Santhals. See also, Cederlof, Gunnel, and Sivaramakrishnan, K., (eds.), *Ecological Nationalisms: Nature, Livelihoods and Identities in South Asia*, (University of Washington Press), 2006, especially pp. 115-150.

[111] Rycroft, Daniel J., *Representing Rebellion: Visual Aspects of Counter-Insurgency in Colonial India*, (Oxford University Press), 2006, considers resistance among the Santhals between 1845 and 1856.

pigs and fowls assuring the Santhals that their land would be recovered and given back to them. He explained their oppression as a divine punishment for not worshipping God and for turning to veneration of minor and evil spirits imposing rules and behaviour that reflected the Hindu notion of purity and pollution. The shift from economic to political protest was evident in later protest especially the Birsa Munda Revolt between 1895 and 1901 in Bihar and the Devi movement in Gujarat in 1922 and 1923 though this was linked to the non-cooperation movement of Indian nationalists.[112]

Whether in India, the Caribbean, Africa or the Americas, there was a relationship between colonisers and colonised that was based upon varying degrees of coercion and in which the imposition of colonial values and authority was resisted because it irrevocably changed the character of established societies. Where the colonised could not obtain redress for what they saw as justifiable grievances through established constitutional channels and where their rights were trampled by assertive settler economic expansion especially on the frontiers of imperialism, legitimate resistance could easily transpose into increasingly less legitimate forms of resistance and ultimately to direct action and armed struggle. Maintaining colonial control was essential if the economic benefits of empire were to be garnered and rebellion was suppressed with severity from the beginnings of empire in the Caribbean, India and America through to the process of decolonisation in the 1950s and 1960s. Violence was an inherent feature of British imperial expansion and colonial administration and it is hardly surprising that the response of those colonised was equally violent.

Borderlands

Contemporaries used the term 'borderlands' in their discussions of insanity and social degeneration during the late nineteenth and early twentieth centuries. Henry Maudsley wrote that it was impossible to:

> ...draw a hard and fast line, and to declare that all persons who were on one side of it must be sane and all persons who were the other side must be insane.[113]

Rather there needed to be recognition of the borderland between sanity and insanity. The concept was widely used in discussions of 'proper' gender relationships.[114] Contemporary psychiatrists saw the borderland as a deeply

[112] Singh, Kr. Suresh, *Birsa Munda and His Movement, 1874-1901: A Study of Millenarian Movement in Chotanagpur*, (Oxford University Press), 1983

[113] Maudsley, Henry, *Responsibility in Mental Disease*, 2nd ed., (D. Appleton), 1874, pp. 38-40. See also, Showalter, E., *The Female Malady: Women, Madness and English Culture 1830-1980,* (Virago), 1987, pp. 101-120, Scull, Andrew, MacKenzie, Charlotte, and Hervey, Nicholas, *Masters of Bedlam: The Transformation of the Mad-Doctoring Trade*, (Princeton University Press), 1996, pp. 226-267, consider Maudsley while Scull, Andrew, *The Most Solitary of Afflictions: Madness and Society in Britain, 1700-1900*, (Yale University Press), 1993, takes a broader perspective.

[114] For instance, Digby, Anne, 'Victorian Values and Women in Private and Public', in Smout, C., (ed.), *Victorian Values*, (British Academy), 1992, pp. 195-215, and Billington, Rosamund, 'The dominant values of Victorian feminism' in Sigsworth, Eric M., (ed.), *In Search of Victorian Values*, (Manchester University Press), 1990, pp. 116-130.

problematic area into which women ventured at their peril. Yet it could also be a positive place for women to colonise. There were risks for women in establishing frontier posts within this social borderland and these varied according to the behaviour of the colonists. Those who, in demeanour as well as activities, flouted traditional gender conventions might find themselves as occupying not only a social borderland but a psychiatric one as well.[115] This Victorian and Edwardian social borderland related to different networks and organisations in political and economic life and in societies changing at an unprecedented pace, it allowed flexibility. To that extent the borderland accommodated class differences within female experience. Significantly, it allowed 'official' Victorian values to be silently broken but without formal recognition having to be taken that the public-private dichotomy was being infringed.

What is important about this concept is that it can equally be applied to colonial and anti-colonial relationships and especially the boundaries between them. One of the critical functions of the borderlands was to defuse tensions, ambiguities and antagonisms. It allowed boundaries to be infringed but in ways that were largely uncontested, even though they may have subverted official values. As long as certain activities in the borderlands were invisible or extended existing conceptions of the imperial role, there was little overt opposition. But what made certain activities politically visible to the extent of having to be opposed? Colonists and non-colonists became politically visible when their actions were seen as an overt challenge to fundamental imperial strongholds such as economic, political and constitutional structures or direct threats against colonial institutions. Reformers and radicals aroused deep-seated anxieties and antagonisms in metropolitan-dominated societies by moving so openly into spheres of imperial power. The same applied when non-colonial groups such as slaves, convicts and natives sought changes in their relationship to the colonial state or freedom from those constraints. As these studies of resistance and rebellion clearly demonstrated, crossing borders too obviously or prematurely had social, political and human costs.

[115] Ibid, *The Female Malady*, pp. 1-22.

Bibliography

The bibliography provides a general guide to relevant books. More detailed references can be found in the footnotes. Many of the references to primary sources are available on Google Books or Internet Archive either to be read or downloaded.

Bibliographies

Bibliographies for individual colonies are invaluable. See, for instance, Ferguson, John Alexander, *Bibliography of Australia*, 7 Vols., and *Addenda*, facsimile edition, (National Library of Australia), 1975-1986, Taylor, M. Brook, (ed.), *Canadian History: A Reader's Guide, Volume 1: Beginnings to Confederation*, (Toronto University Press), 1994, and Owram, Doug, (ed.), *Canadian History: A Reader's Guide: Volume 2: Confederation to the Present*, (Toronto University Press), 1994, and Brown, L. M., and Christie, I. R., *Bibliography of British History 1789-1851*, (Oxford University Press), 1977, and Hanham, H. J., *Bibliography of British History 1851-1914*, (Oxford University Press), 1976.

Porter, Andrew, (ed.), *Bibliography of Imperial, Colonial and Commonwealth History since 1600*, (Oxford University Press), 2002, is the standard bibliography. See also, *Bibliography of British and Irish History* (BBIH) available on subscription: http://apps.brepolis.net/BrepolisPortal/default.aspx

Biographies

Australian Dictionary of Biography, 17 Vols., an *Index Volume* for Vols. 1-12, (plus consolidated corrigenda), (Melbourne University Press), 1966-, and the *Supplement* that also includes a name index to all published volumes.
Available on: http://www.adb.online.anu.edu.au/adbonline.htm

Dictionary of Canadian Biography, 22 Vols. (University of Toronto and Université Laval), 1966-; an *Index* for Vols. 1-12.
Available on: http://www.biographi.ca/02_e.html

The Dictionary of National Biography (DNB), though old, is still worth consulting and is on CD. *The Oxford Dictionary of National Biography*, 60 Vols. (Oxford University Press), 2004, replaces and extends the original *DNB*.
Available on subscription: http://www.oxforddnb.com/

General works

Rose, J. Holland, (ed.), *Cambridge History of the British Empire*, 8 Vols. (Cambridge University Press), 1929-1959, retain their narrative value even if their interpretations have long been superseded. Louis, Wm. Roger, (general ed.), *Oxford History of the British Empire*, 5 Vols. (Oxford University Press), 1998-1999, and Marshall, P. J., (ed.), *Cambridge Illustrated History of the British Empire*, (Cambridge University Press), 1996, provide modern alternatives. See also, Darwin, John, *After Tamberlane: The Global History of Empire*, (Allen Lane), 2007, and Darwin, John, *The Empire Project: The Rise and Fall of the British World-System, 1830-1970*, (Cambridge University Press), 2009, Magee, Gary B., and Thompson, Andrew S., *Empire and Globalisation: Networks of*

People, Goods and Capital in the British World c.1850-1914, (Cambridge University Press), 2010, and Gott, Richard, *Britain's Empire: Resistance, Repression and Revolt,* (Verso), 2011.

Among the most useful multi-author studies are Buckner, Phillip, and Francis, R. Douglas, (eds.), *Rediscovering the British World,* (University of Calgary Press), 2005, Stockwell, Sarah, (ed.), *The British Empire: Themes and perspectives,* (Blackwell Publishing), 2008, and Harper, Marjorie, and Constantine, Stephen, *Migration and Empire,* (Oxford University Press), 2010; see also, Johnson, Robert, *British Imperialism,* (Palgrave), 2003. Webster, Anthony, *The Debate on the Rise of the British Empire,* (Manchester University Press), 2006, provides a historiographical overview.

The most valuable collections of printed sources are Madden, Frederick, Fieldhouse, David, and Darwin, John, (eds.), *Select Documents on the Constitutional History of the British Empire and Commonwealth,* 8 Vols. (Greenwood Press), 1985-2000, *Calendar of State Papers, Colonial series* 45 Vols. (HMSO), 1860-1994, covering American and West Indian colonies 1574-1739 with documents largely from the National Archives series CO 1 and CO 5, and *British Documents on the End of Empire,* 33 Vols. (HMSO), 1992-2006.

Index

About the Author

Richard Brown was, until he retired, Head of History and Citizenship at Manshead School in Dunstable, and has published 52 print and Kindle books and 50 articles and papers on nineteenth century history. He is the author of a successful blog, The History Zone, which has a wide audience among pupils, students and researchers. He is also a Fellow of both the Royal Historical Society and the Historical Association.

Recent publications

Roger of Sicily: Portrait of a Ruler, (Authoring History), 2016.

Robert Guiscard: Portrait of a Warlord, (Authoring History), 2016.

Suger: The Life of Louis VI 'the Fat', (Authoring History), 2016.

The Chartists, Regions and Economies, (Authoring History), 2016. Also available in a Kindle version.

Chartism: Localities, Spaces and Places, The North, Scotland, Wales and Ireland, (Authoring History), 2015. Also available in a Kindle version.

Chartism: Localities, Spaces and Places, The Midlands and the South, (Authoring History), 2015. Also available in a Kindle version.

Sex, Work and Politics: Women in Britain, 1780-1945, (Authoring History), 2014.

Chartism: Rise and Demise, (*Reconsidering Chartism*, Authoring History), 2014. Also available in a Kindle version.

Before Chartism: Exclusion and Resistance, (*Reconsidering Chartism*, Authoring History), 2014. Also available in a Kindle version.

'A Peaceable Kingdom': Essays on Nineteenth Century Canada, (Authoring History), 2013. Also available in a Kindle version.

Settler Australia, 1780-1880, Vol. 1: Settlement, Protest and Control, Vol. 2: Eureka and Democracy, (Authoring History), 2013. Also available in a Kindle version.

Rebellion in Canada, 1837-1885, Vol. 1: Autocracy, Rebellion and Liberty, Vol. 2: The Irish, the Fenians and the Métis, (Authoring History), 2012. Also available in a Kindle version.

Three Rebellions. Canada 1837-1838, South Wales 1839 and Victoria, Australia 1854, (*Rebellion Trilogy*, Clio Publishing), 2010. Also available in a Kindle version.

68181125R00335

Made in the USA
Charleston, SC
05 March 2017